LEGAL SYSTEMS
OF THE WORLD

LEGAL SYSTEMS OF THE WORLD

A POLITICAL, SOCIAL, AND CULTURAL ENCYCLOPEDIA

Volume I: A–D

Edited by Herbert M. Kritzer

A B C ● C L I O

SANTA BARBARA, CALIFORNIA · DENVER, COLORADO · OXFORD, ENGLAND

Library of Congress Cataloging-in-Publication Data

Legal systems of the world : a political, social, and cultural
encyclopedia / edited by Herbert M. Kritzer.
    p. cm.
Includes index.
    ISBN 1-57607-231-2 (hardcover : alk. paper); 1-57607-758-6 (e-book)
    1. Law—Encyclopedias. I. Kritzer, Herbert M., 1947–
K48 .L44 2002
340'.03—dc21
                    2002002659

"Cape Verde" originally published in the *Journal of African Law* 44, no. 1 (2000): 86–95.

Material in "Comoros" and "Djibouti" used with the kind permission of Kluwer Law International.

Material in "European Court of Justice" from Kenney, Sally J. "The European Court of Justice: Integrating Europe through Law." 81 Judicature 250–255 (1998). Reprinted in *Crime and Justice International,* November.

06 05 04 03   10 9 8 7 6 5 4 3

This book is also available on the World Wide Web as an e-book. Visit abc-clio.com for details.

ABC-CLIO, Inc.
130 Cremona Drive, P.O. Box 1911
Santa Barbara, California 93116–1911

This book is printed on acid-free paper ∞.
Manufactured in the United States of America

CONTENTS

Volume II: E–L

Volume III: M–R

PREFACE

My own interest in comparative analyses of legal system phenomena dates back to the early 1980s, when I undertook a small study in Toronto. From that experience I was impressed by the leverage I obtained in understanding legal phenomena by the simple crossing of a nearby border. Subsequently, my own research has included comparative work involving Canada, England, and Australia (see, for example, Jacob, Blankenburg, Kritzer, Provine, and Sanders 1996). In addition, over the last decade I have worked with students conducting research on legal phenomena in Canada, England, Germany, Israel, India, and South Africa. With this background, it was with much excitement that I agreed to undertake the role of general editor of *Legal Systems of the World*.

While the comparative or cross-national study of law and legal institutions is by no means a new endeavor, it has taken on heightened importance in the last two decades as waves of democratization have swept across Latin America, Africa, and Eastern Europe. Closely associated with democratization has been constitutionalism and the creation of political systems attempting to implement a rule of law , as well as reforms of existing legal systems to improve their operation within a democratic context (Biebesheimer and Meja 2000; Hammergren 1998; Rosenn 1998). While Americans like to think of the U.S. system of a "government of law" as the archetype, there are in fact many different models that a democratizing country can draw from, and around the world one finds a lot of mixing and matching. Thus, while the common law system and the civil law system are two widely used models, there are many countries that employ hybrid systems that incorporate aspects of both of these two common systems. In other countries, one finds systems based on Islamic law, often coexisting with civil law or common law structures. Furthermore, at least in terms of procedure, the common law adversarial approach and the civil law inquisitorial/investigatory approach have in recent years been converging in many respects, as leaders in each system look to the other to try to find ways of reducing costs and speeding legal processes.

In addition to the growth of constitutionalism, the role of courts and judicial processes has been evolving, even in countries with long-standing democratic political structures. Some have described this as an increase in judicial power. Others have described the development in terms of the judicialization of political processes or the rise of adversarialism. In some countries, treaty obligations have thrust courts into new and important roles. Transnational judicial bodies are increasingly becoming key players in the global (or at least regional) community. Simply put, courts have become vastly more important in the last half-century.

One of the challenges of preparing this work was dealing with foreign terms. Where possible, we tried to adopt a standardized spelling for terms that might be rendered as transliterations in different ways from different languages (one example was *sharia,* which appeared in at least four different forms in the various entries. Similarly, we sought to avoid spellings that involved complicated diacritics wherever possible. We did retain diacritics when it was clear that they were part of an accepted, standard form, or where they reflected an important local usage. Our goal was to minimize confusion that might arise as readers moved from one entry to another.

A second challenge that we, and a number of contributors, faced was that legal and political systems are subject to significant change. The result is that we are, in a number of cases, trying to provide information on systems that can only be described as moving targets. One good example was the collapse of the Taliban regime in Afghanistan brought about by the United States–led response to the terrorist attacks of September 11, 2001. The version that appears here was prepared before those events, and the production process was advanced to the stage that it was not possible to fully revise the entry. Undoubtedly, other changes will have transpired there by the time this appears in the summer of 2002.

Given my own experience and interests, I was intrigued when Todd Hallman, then an acquisitions editor at ABC-CLIO, approached me in 1998 about the possibility of serving as general editor for *Legal Systems of the World.* I had never undertaken an editorial project of this type, but it seemed to me to be just the right kind of thing to do. Not only did I believe that the resulting product would be a valuable resource, but I knew that I would learn a tremendous amount about other legal systems as a by-product of my work on the project. It was over a year before my other commitments allowed me to begin significant work on the project. As expected, I have found the work very rewarding. I have a much deeper appreciation for the variety of legal structures, and a clear understanding of the simple fact that there is no one right way to structure a legal or judicial system.

This endeavor would not have been possible without the assistance of many people. At ABC-CLIO, the commitment of Patience Melnik to the never-ending task of managing the flow of manuscripts and paper, and staying on top of the status of various entries, has been absolutely essential. She carried on work that had been started by Karna Hughes. At ABC-CLIO the production process has been overseen by Anna Kaltenbach.

The challenge of finding contributors was one of the major parts of assembling *Legal Systems of the World*. In addition to the editorial advisory board, I have drawn on the assistance of many people in identifying potential authors for contributions. I would particularly like to thank Lynn Khadiagala, Kathryn Hendley, and Ibrahima Kane, plus the many contributors who themselves responded to my requests for suggestions regarding potential contributors. Also very important in this task were the resources of four different law libraries: the University of Wisconsin Law Library, the William Mitchell College of Law Library, the University of Minnesota Law Library, and the library at the Institute for Advanced Legal Studies of the University of London.

Finally, I would like to dedicate this set of volumes to the law and society community at the University of Wisconsin, where I have been happily situated for the last twenty-four years. The intellectual stimulation provided by my current and past colleagues in Political Science, Sociology, History, Psychology, and, of course the University of Wisconsin Law School, has been the single most important part of my professional life for nearly a quarter of a century.

—*Herbert M. Kritzer*
Madison, Wisconsin
December 15, 2001

References and further reading
Becker, Theodore L. 1970. *Comparative Judicial Politics: The Political Functionings of Courts.* Chicago: Rand McNally.
Bedford, Sybille. 1961. *The Faces of Justice: A Traveller's Report.* New York: Simon & Schuster.
Biebesheimer, Christina, and Francisco Meja, eds. 2000. *Justice beyond Our Borders: Judicial Reforms for Latin America and the Caribbean.* Washington, DC: Inter-American Development Bank.
Damaska, Mirjan R. 1986. *The Faces of Justice and State Authority.* New Haven, CT: Yale University Press.
Epp, Charles E. 1998. *The Rights Revolution: Lawyers, Activists, and Supreme Courts in Comparative Perspective.* Chicago: University of Chicago Press.
Hammergren, Linn A. 1998. *The Politics of Justice and Justice Reform in Latin America.* Boulder, CO: Westview Press.
Jackson, Donald W. 1997. *The United Kingdom Confronts the European Convention on Human Rights.* Gainesville: University of Florida Press.
Jacob, Herbert, Erhard Blankenburg, Herbert M. Kritzer, Doris Marie Provine, and Joseph Sanders. 1996. *Courts, Law and Politics in Comparative Perspective.* New Haven, CT: Yale University Press.
Kagan, Robert A. 2001. *Adversarial Legalism: The American Way of Law.* Cambridge: Harvard University Press.
Kommers, Donald P. 1975. *Judicial Politics in West Germany: A Study of the Federal Constitutional Courts.* Beverly Hills, CA: Sage.
Merryman, John Henry. 1969. *The Civil Law Tradition: An Introduction to the Legal Systems of Western Europe and Latin America.* Stanford, CA: Stanford University Press.
Morrison, Fred. 1974. *Courts and the Political Process in England.* Beverly Hills, CA: Sage.
Nader, Laura, ed. 1969. *Law in Culture and Society.* Chicago: Aldine.
Rosenn, Keith S. 1998. "Judicial Reform in Brazil." *NAFTA: Law and Business Review of the Americas* 4: 19–37.
Schubert, Glendon A., and David J. Danelski, eds. 1969. *Comparative Judicial Behavior: Cross-Cultural Studies of Political Decision-Making in the East and West.* New York: Oxford University Press.
Schwartz, Herman. 2000. *The Struggle for Constitutional Justice in Post-Communist Europe.* Chicago: University of Chicago Press.
Shapiro, Martin. 1986 (1981). *Courts.* Chicago: Chicago University Press.
Slaughter, A-M., Alec Stone Sweet, and J. Weiler, eds. 1998. *The European Courts and the National Courts: Legal Change in Its Social, Political, and Economic Context.* Oxford: Hart.
Stone Sweet, Alec. 2000. *Governing with Judges: Constitutional Politics in Europe.* Oxford: Oxford University Press.
Tate, C. Neal, and Torbjörn Vallinder. 1995. "The Global Expansion of Judicial Power: The Judicialization of Politics." In *The Global Expansion of Judicial Power: The Judicialization of Politics.* Edited by C. N. T. Vallinder. New York: New York University Press.
Zuckerman, Adrian. 2000. "Reforming Civil Justice Systems: Trends in Industrial Countries." Washington, DC: World Bank (http://www1.worldbank.org/publicsector/PREMnote46.pdf).

LEGAL SYSTEMS OF THE WORLD

Volume I

LEGAL SYSTEMS
OF THE WORLD

A

ADMINISTRATIVE LAW

Administrative law is a body of law derived from a mixture of constitutional law, statutory law, the judicial review of agency decisions, and the practices of agencies themselves. Administrative law is also based on domestic legislation establishing general procedures for government decision making through administration. In the United States, for example, the Administrative Procedure Act (APA) of 1946 serves as a residual body of procedural rules that come into play when agency rules are insufficient (Shapiro 1986). Since administrative procedures existed prior to these general administrative statues, we think of administrative law as a hybrid of various legal practices and principles.

The substance of all that administrative law covers is broad. Its five functions, or responsibilities, include: (1) regulating the private and public sectors, along with nongovernmental organizations, through licensing, investigating, making rules of conduct, and adjudicating controversy over those rules based on legislative or executive policy goals; (2) securing government resources, such as taxation, military conscription, and eminent domain; (3) distributing money and other benefits, such as Social Security, and subsidies to capital, both direct and indirect; (4) providing direct services and goods, such as postal, police, and fire services and highways; and (5) imposing sanctions for violations of regulatory rules, such as the confiscation and destruction of adulterated food, fines and imprisonment for evading taxes, and deportation (Carter and Harrington 2000).

The responsibilities of agencies are set forth by legislatures in the originating statutes and subsequent amendments to them. Agencies and reviewing courts interpret statutes within the framework of more general constitutional and statutory principles. When courts apply principles of procedural fairness to administration, they take into account the history and reputation of an agency, the legislative mission, and characteristics of the parties that are regulated (for example, single industry versus cross-sector regulation). Thus, the substantive mission of an agency or commission is a factor governing administrative law.

Deference to administration by reviewing courts, legislature, and the executive is more the norm than the ex-ception. This norm is expressed, in part, when broad authority is delegated to agencies. In the United States, for example, the broad delegation model became a statutory blueprint for administrative activity after the 1930s, yet debate over its virtues and vices continues. Louis Jaffe (1973) questioned those who would restrict statutory delegation and cautioned that we must keep in mind the political factors surrounding administration and avoid adherence to simple models. Theodore Lowi (1979) stressed the importance of representative democracy over interest-group liberalism; he argued against interest-group liberalism and proposed judicial democracy, which combines a call to strengthen the rule of law in administrative processes (versus the pressure of interest groups) with more direct congressional input and oversight of administrative decision making.

The administrative accountability of experts and private sector actors to elected official is another serious concern in administrative law. The erosion of administrative boundaries between government and corporate actors is particularly evident in regional administrative tribunals, such as the European Union (EU). The EU's law-making council delegates authority to make regulatory provisions to expert committees, whose members continue to work for corporations and have strong ties to trade associations (Shapiro 2001). Although many countries have domestic legislation against delegation of legislative power to private parties, new administrative frameworks are produced by global processes that do not prohibit indirect private law-making activities.

Determining what is regulated by administrative law and how administrative law regulates tells us much about the trends and developments in the field. In terms of what is regulated, the collapse of the basic assumption underlying the nineteenth-century market economy paralleled the collapse of a strict private law model and led to the rise of the modern, twentieth-century legal consciousness, which embraced stronger notions about public rights that should be protected by administrative law (see Horwitz 1977; Klare 1978). If the collapse of legal formalism and the rise of modern legal consciousness are symptomatic of a more general relationship between economic philosophy and administrative regulation, then today we are witnessing a return to the private law model in many countries and at the regional and global levels (Aman 1992).

For example, in the United States, regulation has been successfully challenged as a "takings" in violation of the Fifth Amendment of the U.S. Constitution: "nor shall private property be taken for public use, without just compensation." In 1987, five members of the U.S. Supreme Court (William Rehnquist, Antonin Scalia, Anthony Kennedy, Sandra Day O'Connor, and Clarence Thomas) held that regulation to protect the California coast lacked a "sufficient nexus" between the "legitimate state interest" (that is, protection of the coastal environment) and the regulatory mechanisms for furthering that interest. They then concluded that the regulatory mechanisms the Coastal Commission used violated the takings clause of the Constitution (*Nollan v. California Coastal Commission,* 483 US 825 [1987]). This case was the beginning of a judicial process in the United States for dismantling welfare-state constitutional jurisprudence on regulation. The Court became part of, if not a leader in, a major ideological shift—one that cut across all governing institutions and is extending globally with the political and economic advancement of neoliberalism, or what was called "free-market economics" at the beginning of the twentieth century. Proponents of this shift in the legal academy and on the federal bench assert that there should be no distinction between government and private property in the constitutional jurisprudence of regulation (Epstein 1985). The public law or public right doctrine is a central target of this conservative movement. Government regulation affecting property (directly and indirectly) is juridically suspect once again, much as it was in the pre–New Deal era.

Notable trends are also evident in terms of how administrative law regulates—in other words, in regard to the procedural question. Prior to 1970, the traditional model of administrative law did not afford redress to private individuals when administrators withheld or terminated benefits not protected by the common law (Stewart 1975). Individuals might seek to recover benefits but only after those benefits had been withheld or terminated. The traditional model was a focal point of citizen mobilization and law reform in the mid-1960s. Recipients of government programs (for example, Social Security, Aid to Families with Dependent Children (AFDC), public schools, state-run hospitals, and prisons), armed with a new breed of government lawyers employed by the Office of Economic Opportunity Legal Services Programs to represent poor people as well as public interest lawyers working at not-for-profit firms, worked in coalitions to successfully overturn the traditional model of administrative law in *Goldberg v. Kelly* (397 US 254 [1970]). In that case, Justice William Brennan held that

a "balancing" logic in the due process clause determined when constitutional protections could be invoked and applied to the withdrawal of public assistance. He found that Kelly, a welfare recipient, had a significant interest in a pretermination hearing because he had no resources to live on while waiting for the posttermination hearing. Further, Justice Brennan held that there are important governmental interests at stake in upholding a pretermination hearing, such as the government's interest in "fostering the dignity and well-being of all persons within its borders." However, Justice Brennan held that the form of the protection need not be a judicial or quasi-judicial trial. Rather, "rudimentary due process" only required that a recipient be given timely and adequate notice, detailing the reasons for a proposed termination, and an effective opportunity to defend by confronting any adverse witness and presenting his or her own arguments and evidence orally.

The *Goldberg* case initiated dramatic changes in administrative law. The Court's decision symbolized a political change in the character of the relationship between the government and its citizens. *Goldberg* articulated a positive role for government in the administration of the welfare state, and it suggested new legal grounds for recipients to protect their government benefits. However, the balancing test Justice Brennan put forth in *Goldberg* did give weight to a public interest in reducing administrative burdens, thereby leaving open the possibility for administrative rationality to outweigh due process protections for beneficiaries.

Only six years later, that is exactly what happened in *Mathews v. Eldridge* (424 US 319, [1976]). Chief Justice Warren Burger held that a Social Security disability recipient, Eldridge, did not deserve an oral pretermination hearing because, unlike Kelly, Eldridge could get other forms of public assistance while awaiting a posttermination hearing. The majority of the Court, believing that this case did not factually resemble *Goldberg,* avoided overturning the earlier ruling but narrowed, if not rebuked, the legal theory on which Justice Brennan based his *Goldberg* decision. Chief Justice Burger argued that in "striking the appropriate due process balance the final factor to be assessed is the public interest. This includes the administrative burden and other societal costs that would be associated with requiring, as a matter of constitutional right, an evidentiary hearing upon demand in all cases prior to the termination of disability benefits." He went on to argue that the "ultimate balance involves a determination as to when, under our constitutional system, judicial-type procedures must be imposed upon administrative action to assure fairness." As to who should make this determination, the majority asserted that "substantial weight must be given to the good-faith judgments of the individuals charged by Congress with the administration of social welfare programs." Justices Brennan and Thurgood Marshall responded by noting in their dissent that "the very legislative determination to provide disability benefits, without any prerequisite determination of need in fact, presumes a need by the recipient which is not the Court's function to denigrate."

Goldberg and *Mathews* are but two in a series of entitlement cases in which the Court pulled back from the extension of rudimentary constitutional due process to beneficiaries of government entitlements. That a resurgent conservative political movement was afoot in the United States by 1975 and had targeted the Supreme Court as an institution to capture is central to any explanation of the developments of administrative procedure.

The Court's preference after 1976 to reduce "administrative burdens" on the state and limit the scope of constitutional due process protections is an early procedural indicator of what was to come—a politically conservative turn in the political economy of regulation itself. The procedural dismantling of some portion of the welfare state, therefore, preceded substantive policy reform, which reallocated tax revenues to the private sector. Only after President Jimmy Carter announced the first U.S. act of deregulation (the Civil Aeronautics Board Deregulation Act) in 1978 and after two decades of both Republican and Democratic privatization policies was a new constitutional theory of regulation *and* administrative procedure in place. The Court's increased deference toward *how* agencies make decisions, along with its embrace of the takings clause jurisprudence regarding *what* agencies can regulate, establishes a significantly new legal approach to administration and regulation. This shift is not limited to the United States alone but has been observed in other countries as well. Similar trends are also evident in several areas within administrative law, such as (1) statutory interpretation, (2) administrative search and seizure, (3) judicial review of agency action, and (4) administrative liability (Carter and Harrington 2000).

Christine B. Harrington

See also Administrative Tribunals

References and further reading
Aman, Alfred C. 1992. *Administrative Law in a Global Era.* Ithaca, NY: Cornell University Press.
Carter, Lief, and Christine B. Harrington. 2000. *Administrative Law and Politics.* 3d ed. New York: Addison, Wesley, Longman Publishers.
Epstein, Richard. 1985. *Takings, Private Property and the Power of Eminent Domain.* Cambridge, MA: Harvard University Press.
Goldberg v. Kelly, 397 US 254 (1970).
Horwitz, Morton. 1977. *The Transformation of American Law, 1780–1860.* Cambridge, MA: Harvard University Press.
Jaffe, Louis L. 1973. "The Illusion of the Ideal Administration." *Harvard Law Review* 86: 1183.
Klare, Karl. 1978. "Judicial Deradicalization of the Wagner Act and the Origins of Modern Legal Consciousness, 1937–1941." *Minnesota Law Review* 62: 280.
Lowi, Theodore J. 1979. *The End of Liberalism.* 2d ed. New York: Norton.
Mathews v. Eldridge, 424 US 319 (1976).
Nollan v. California Coastal Commission, 483 US 825 (1987).
Shapiro, Martin. 1986. "The Supreme Court's 'Return' to Economic Regulation." *Studies in American Political Development* 1: 102.
———. 1988. *Who Guards the Guardians?: Judicial Control of Administration.* Athens: University of Georgia Press.
———. 2001. "Administrative Law Unbounded: Reflection on Government and Governance." *Indiana Journal of Global Legal Studies* 8: 369.
Stewart, Richard. 1975. "The Reformation of American Administrative Law." *Harvard Law Review* 88: 1669.

ADMINISTRATIVE TRIBUNALS

States have established administrative tribunals to make hard decisions concerning who deserves what under statutes. Tribunals are specialized courts, usually associated with appeals of decisions by bureaucracies. Most states have a dizzying array, from trade courts to tax courts, industrial tribunals to immigration appeals tribunals, hearing officers deciding appeals of decisions against those who claimed disability benefits to government committees deciding exclusions from schools or adoption panels choosing which adults to match with which children. Tribunals are often constituted in ways specific to the task at hand, making few general characterizations possible, except that states have established them to address appeals in particular cases within bureaucratic policy.

Sometimes tribunals have been established to escape what seemed to be the hostility to government policy the general jurisdiction courts evinced. In the United States, for example, the National Labor Relations Board (NLRB) was created in 1935 in part because the general jurisdiction courts had proven hostile to any labor organizing, granting injunctions against pickets and insisting that freedom of contract required courts to invalidate prounion legislation. The Wagner Act creating the NLRB gave that body the responsibility of prohibiting "unfair labor practices." The NLRB consists of lawyers appointed by the president for a fixed number of years, though there is no requirement that members be lawyers. Presidents usually appoint experienced labor lawyers who are likely to interpret the law in a way favorable to the current administration. The last thing the Roosevelt administration, which instituted the NLRB, wanted was the general jurisdiction courts determining what "unfair labor practices" were. Similarly, in the United Kingdom, the central government did not want courts deciding, for example, whether doctors had prescribed medicine excessively when the courts were hostile to the entire notion of such regulation (Sterett 1997). In 1927, Germany created a labor court that included one professional judge, a trade unionist, and an employers' representative, also with an eye toward creating industrial democracy (Blankenburg, 1996: 261).

How "courtlike" administrative tribunals are varies. Some were designed to be like courts, but others specifically were not. What makes something a court or not is difficult to assess (Shapiro 1980). A court usually consists of a state-employed decision maker trained in the local culture of legal reasoning, which usually includes adherence to rules from an authoritative body such as a legislature or officials deciding under a legislature. Courts are to apply those rules, which might systematically favor one group or class over another, but they are to apply them without favoritism toward either of the parties before them. Judges in general jurisdiction courts are employees of the state, though in the Anglo-American tradition they are often seen as something other than that (Shapiro 1980). Decision makers in tribunals are also employees of the state, but they usually specialize by subject matter, whereas general judges do not. They also are often employees of the bureaucracy in charge of the policy area, such as immigration, health, or local government. Oftentimes they are bound closely by rules and previous decisions, as courts are, though not always. Some tribunals consist of a committee of decision makers, and some have only one, who might look more like a judge by virtue of legal training or independence from supervision. Tribunals can vary along all these dimensions: specialization, employer, use of rules and precedent, and training of decision makers.

In Britain, for example, industrial tribunals are made up of one legally trained chair and two lay judges, one appointed in consultation with industry and one appointed in consultation with labor. Germany has an array of specialized courts designed to hear complaints concerning administration after appeals internal to the bureaucracy have been exhausted. The first level of what the Germans call courts but what for the purposes of this book are administrative tribunals include a professional judge and two lay members (Blankenburg 1996, 259–266). Since in Germany, as in all civil law countries, all judges are explicitly part of the civil service, appointment to a job within the state bureaucracy distinguishes a court from a tribunal less noticeably than it does in common law jurisdictions. In France, many civil disputes are handled in specialized tribunals, including issues of labor, rent, and national health (Provine 1996, 188). Also as in Britain and Germany, those staffing tribunals often have expertise in the particular policy field, not in law. In Britain, some administrative appeals, such as those concerning a denial of placement in a school of one's choice, are handled by the local government one is appealing against or by a committee of that local government. In these appeals committees, it may be that legal training is simply extraneous. Japan also does not resolve disputes with lawyers and indeed relies on conciliation rather than enforceable legal rights in labor disputes, both those relating to union management and those involving gender discrimination (Sanders 1996, 377–384).

Appearing courtlike in common law countries seems more fair; judges seem to be less like government employees than bureaucrats do. In the United States, that has been a grounds for complaint on the part of administrative hearing officers who decided appeals against denials of disability benefits. The bureaucracy tried to monitor the rates at which hearing officers overturned lower officials' decisions to try to ensure some consistency across officers and to control costs. Hearing officers sued, claiming such a practice violated their judicial independence. A general jurisdiction court held that the officers were bureaucratic employees and therefore superiors could monitor them (*Califano v. Yamasaki* 1979).

States institute tribunals to take decisions out of the ordinary judicial process. Justifications include that specialized courts staffed by administrators or those trained in the policy they are administering will operate more according to the purpose of the statute and the administration than will ordinary courts. Immigration officials will try to keep people out if necessary, with less of a sense of whether the standards they use fit with the ordinary claims to what are proper evidentiary standards. Tribunals to decide whether one was discriminated against at work or otherwise unfairly dismissed are to take into account the purpose of ensuring that people are not unfairly dismissed. Taking into account purpose, of course, could also mean that one stands before some decision makers with interests opposed to one's own (saving the bureaucracy money, preventing transracial adoptions), without procedural protection afforded in general jurisdiction courts, no lawyer, and tribunal members who do not know (and are not expected to know) the law (Abel 1982a,b).

Another justification for tribunals is that they can be cheaper. Without standard evidentiary requirements or staffing by judges, claimants do not need to hire a lawyer to ensure they had some kind of fair representation. Too, tribunals can be inexpensive for the state to administer and can work more quickly than the standard courts do or can. However, because tribunals are not staffed by lawyers, they do not necessarily attend to all the niceties of legal requirements.

If the lack of procedural protections made tribunals easier to use for claimants, it might be of no concern. However, in many tribunals, designed for their informality and ease in use, institutional actors—in industrial tribunals, businesses; in housing tribunals, landlords—might well have representation, while a claimant does not. Without a representative, claimants can be at a substantial disadvantage, though it varies depending on the jurisdiction of the tribunal and the type of representation (Genn and Genn 1989). Claimants often do not find processes easy to use, and processes are easier to use when one has used them before.

From the point of view of Labour governments in Britain, which instituted many administrative tribunals and thought about how to justify them, tribunals seemed to be very friendly to claimants. However, when officials from the bureaucracy staff the tribunal and instruct whatever lay members might be on the tribunal, it is difficult to see how they might be favorable to claimants (Genn and Genn, 1989). Even a Labour government believes that some people ought to receive supplementary benefits or compensation for unemployment, and others should not.

Some administrative tribunals in Britain are constituted as something more approximating ordinary courts than others. In Britain, one way to signal that is to give supervisory jurisdiction not to the department immediately responsible for the area of law but to the Lord Chancellor's Department, which is in charge of the courts. Too, claimants can appeal decisions of some tribunals directly to the Court of Appeal, as though the tribunal had been a lower court, rather than to the High Court, the general jurisdiction court of first instance. The Immigration Appeals Tribunal and the Employment Appeals Tribunal are the two primary examples, and practitioners before both talk of appearing before court, not before a tribunal, a significant distinction in Anglo-American legal thinking.

When not instructed in the law or not told that they should be adhering closely to the law, it is easy for specialized courts administering the law to rely upon ordinary assumptions concerning how the world works and how it should work. For example, in sex discrimination law in Britain, industrial tribunals have applied the legal standard from unfair dismissal cases, which constitutes a substantial portion of its caseload, rather than the legal sex discrimination standard, which is more protective of claimants. The standard they informally apply, that of reasonableness, allows them to make broad judgments the statute does not invite concerning whether people meant well (Kenney 1992, 105–107).

In France, an administrative court, the Conseil d'Etat, resolves disputes concerning administrative actions. Those who staff the court are graduates of a school of public administration and have spent their careers, usually, working in administration. It, too, resolves disputes inexpensively and informally, with an eye to the purpose of the policy in dispute. The Conseil d'Etat could not rely on one level of appeal to address all the complaints

against state bureaucrats that emerged, so it became internally differentiated and specialized, with levels of appeal. Specialized lower divisions deal with tax and employment disputes (Provine, 1996: 185–190). British officials struggling with administrative accountability admired it for its seeming ability to resolve the unresolvable: it addressed complaints that individuals had against the bureaucracy, but it somehow did so with an eye to the purpose of the policy. In addition, it was not bound strictly by the law and could address problems of "maladministration," or simple bad dealing by administrators. Finally, it could take signals from the appeals it sees and distribute memorandums to lower level administrators concerning how they should change their practices (Sterett 1997).

Appeals within bureaucracies, which is what appeals to tribunals usually are, serve two purposes. They may provide a way to vindicate rights, largely serving the interests of those complaining. On that interpretation, statutes confer rights; they are not simply directions within the bureaucracy. Alternatively (or additionally), appeals are useful for the bureaucracy: they provide a way of monitoring what lower-level officials are doing (Shapiro 1980). The French practice of using appeals as reasons for memorandums to those below clearly illustrates that perspective. Appeals provide only one kind of information: that indicating where the subjects of administration are unhappy. Appeals, then, might be just one part of an effort to monitor what bureaucrats do, but that proves unlikely when there are thousands of cases, there is no central means of collecting decisions, and decisions seem so tied to the particular facts that it is difficult to discern what a general problem in decision making might be.

A very different type of tribunal has also been constituted internationally to adjudicate specific complaints concerning the horrific acts people commit against each other. War crimes tribunals decide not the routine complaints concerning whether one has gained unemployment insurance but the extraordinary international disputes between states that have been politically charged enough to seem to require specific, courtlike resolution. The Nuremberg trials of Germans after World War II provide the most notorious example, but the war in the former Yugoslavia also invoked a war crimes tribunal. The problems of bureaucratic tribunals, though, reappear in even more dramatic fashion here: In what sense are these tribunals applying law? In what sense are they a purposely built way of condemning acts politically in legal form?

As long as states distribute rights and goods through bureaucracies, clients will want some form of appeal against unfavorable decisions. States will have a reason to provide appeal, both to ensure that the rules were followed or purpose adhered to and to assure claimants that state administrators concern themselves with fairness. States often prefer specialized tribunals because they are cheaper than relying upon general jurisdiction courts. That moving away from rights enforceable in law toward a more accessible system will provide inexpensive justice favoring a claimant is only a hope. Waiving rights via informality can make a system more difficult to use, particularly if that system is implemented by people not trained in law.

Susan M. Sterett

See also Judicial Independence; War Crimes Tribunals
References and further reading
Abel, Richard L., ed. 1982a. *The Politics of Informal Justice. Volume 1: The American Experience.* New York: Academic Press.
———. 1982b. *The Politics of Informal Justice. Volume 2: Comparative Studies.* New York: Academic Press.
Blankenburg, Erhard. 1996. "Changes in Political Regimes and Continuity of the Rule of Law in Germany." In *Courts, Law and Politics in Comparative Perspective.* Edited by Herbert Jacob, Erhard Blankenburg, Herbert M. Kritzer, Doris Marie Provine, and Joseph Sanders. New Haven, CT: Yale University Press.
Califano v. Yamasaki, 442 U.S. 682 (1979).
Genn, Hazel, and Yvette Genn. 1989. *The Effectiveness of Representation at Tribunals.* London: Lord Chancellor's Department.
Jacob, Herbert, Erhard Blankenburg, Herbert M. Kritzer, Doris Marie Provine, and Joseph Sanders. 1996. *Courts, Law and Politics in Comparative Perspective.* New Haven, CT: Yale University Press.
Kenney, Sally J. 1992. *For Her Own Protection.* Ann Arbor: University of Michigan Press.
Provine, Doris Marie. 1996. "Courts and the Political Process in France." In *Courts, Law and Politics in Comparative Perspective.* Edited by Herbert Jacob, Erhard Blankenburg, Herbert M. Kritzer, Doris Marie Provine, and Joseph Sanders. New Haven, CT: Yale University Press.
Sanders, Joseph. 1996. "Courts and Law in Japan." In *Courts, Law and Politics in Comparative Perspective.* Edited by Herbert Jacob, Erhard Blankenburg, Herbert M. Kritzer, Doris Marie Provine, and Joseph Sanders. New Haven, CT: Yale University Press.
Shapiro, Martin. 1980. *Courts.* Chicago: University of Chicago Press.
Sterett, Susan. 1997. *Creating Constitutionalism? The Politics of Administrative Expertise in England and Wales.* Ann Arbor: University of Michigan Press.

ADVERSARIAL SYSTEMS

Most legal systems are either inquisitorial (sometimes called civilian or civil) or adversarial. Adversarial systems are derived from the model of English courts, whose judges interpret common law, as well as equity, ecclesiastical, statutory, natural, and customary law. Judges are neutral arbiters between plaintiff and defendant in civil

trials, or between the state and the defendant in criminal ones. Cases can be settled at any time before or during a trial. In adversarial systems, the search for the facts in dispute and the applicable law results from adjudication or litigation in which the judge intervenes less often than in inquisitorial systems.

The main reason for judges to intervene is to assure that the presentation of evidence and legal arguments from opposing sides follows mandatory legal procedures. Occasionally, judges will suppress overly emotional attorneys or public observers. The lawyers and the witnesses do most of the talking, while their clients, the protagonists, are largely silent unless called on to testify (which they must do, except to prevent self-incrimination without prejudice). The judge can issue judgments of law at various points, especially involving the admission of evidence during a trial and especially at the end on matters of law. Judges generally do not comment on the facts; an exception is the practice of summing up by judges in England presiding over jury trials. New interpretations of law are rarely applied, although the view that they never occur is a useful fiction. In the absence of a jury, the judge issues a judgment on the facts as well. Appellate courts entertain only legal claims, where some judges directly question lawyers on legal interpretations.

In adversarial systems the opposing sides try to prove their version of the facts and the law, whereas in inquisitorial systems a judge and a prosecutor work together to investigate the matter before the court and to determine the facts on their own. In adversarial processes allegations put forward in an indictment or pretrial motions are not presumed to be established facts. Inquisitorial systems, by constrast, tend to presume the allegations to be facts in a criminal case, and some defendants assume that the allegations are irrefutable; they therefore try to introduce mitigating factors in the hope of persuading the judge to reduce the punishment or damages awarded.

THE CONCENTRATED TRIAL

Because of the relative autonomy of lawyers in the pretrial processes, there is wide variation among adversarial systems in the conduct of litigation of similar cases. Delays can be obtained for nefarious purposes. In countries like Pakistan and the Philippines the elite are rarely prosecuted, except when they become political adversaries of those in power. In the United States and most nations with adversarial systems, judges take charge only after a trial.

Most adversarial systems ask for the basic evidence pertaining to a case, the legal arguments, and the lists of witnesses and other evidentiary plans in advance of the trial. This preparation allows the trial itself to proceed more or less without pause once it has begun. In criminal trials, the defendant does not assist the prosecution and can remain silent. In civil trials, defendants generally do not assist plaintiffs. However, many adversarial and civilian systems may require each side to reveal evidence and planned testimony to the opposing party. Civilian systems, which are civil law or inquisitorial systems, have a more discontinuous procedure. Once the trial begins, the evidence and witnesses are examined under oath. Witnesses can be compelled to testify under a subpoena properly issued (except to avoid self-incrimination) and can be cited and punished for contempt of court if they refuse. The prosecution in a criminal trial and the plaintiff in a civil trial call witnesses first, and each witness is subject to cross-examination by the defense. After the prosecution or plaintiff has rested his or her case, it is the defendant's turn to call witnesses. Any statement that is not challenged by the other side's lawyers is likely to be accepted as fact.

In response to both arbitrary and intentional repression of the politically weak over the eight centuries that the English adversarial system has existed, the rights have emerged in the common law and from statute in order to protect defendants from such abuses. For example, the prosecution must disclose to the defense all material evidence, and especially any exculpatory evidence, to the defense, as the FBI failure to reveal all the government files delayed Timothy McVeigh's execution in 2001. Still, the prosecution, acting on behalf of the state and the people, usually has at its disposal more resources on which to build and proof a case than does the defense. Although defendants can subpoena witnesses to testify, most criminal defendants lack the financial means and organizational support (as the prosecutor has in the police) to discover who could exonerate them. The United States enjoys the most extensive protections of defendants' rights, especially since the Supreme Court ruled in the *Miranda* case (1966) that, "prior to any questioning, the person must be warned that he has a right to remain silent, that any statements he does make may be used as evidence against him, and that he has a right to the presence of an attorney, either retained or appointed." As a result, most US police forces read these rights immediately after arrest. Even England allows officials to admonish defendants that remaining silent might be held prejudicial against them in an eventual trial. In 1988, the United Kingdom eliminated the right to remain silent in terrorism cases in 1988, but the European Court of Human Rights has struck down such repressive British laws.

England and some of its former colonies, such as Pakistan, have criminal practices that favor the prosecution more than procedures do in the United States, where the defendant is said to be favored if a case comes to trial. In England, unlike in the United States, the defendant sits alone in the dock and so cannot communicate with his or her lawyers while court is in session. Other practices that conduce to the prosecution include the wearing of wigs and robes by the judges and prosecuting barristers (attorneys who are full-time litigators) and the usually less adversarial tenor of defense barristers, who generally must be available for either side if so ordered by the bar. The wearing of wigs by judges is said to give a psychological advantage to the prosecution because defense attorneys in England are more deferential to judges than in the United States, where they are more aggressive, in part for this reason. A second factor is that in England, barristers (litigators) serve for either the prosecution or the defense, or for the plaintiff or for the defense; this also makes defense attorneys less aggressive because they do not seek clients based on their reputation for defense histrionics alone. The British courts do not permit re-cross-examination (a second set of cross examinations) of witnesses; the judge is free to comment on the defendant's credibility during the summation of the case at the end; and the defense is burdened with substantial restrictions on challenging the credibility of prosecution witnesses.

Defendants in most adversarial systems plead guilty, though not to the extent found in the United States procedure, where formal plea bargaining contributes to guilty pleas in about 90 percent of criminal cases. In return for a guilty plea, frequently the prosecution promises to press fewer charges or to ask the judge for leniency in sentencing. Although in the vast majority of such cases the defendant who pleads guilty did in fact commit the crime as charged, the innocent are also occasionally convicted because of this imbalance. There is a common misconception that this practice is widespread only in the United States, but in reality it is prevalent in some other countries as well. In the United States and England, more than 90 percent of cases are either dismissed by a judge or, more commonly, settled by attorneys before going to trial. The latter is the only option in England, where the merits of a case are not considered until the trial phase.

Monetary bail, where someone charged with a crime is released from jail prior to trial in return for posting a bond which is forfeited if the defendant does not show up at appointed court dates, is characteristic of adversarial systems. Civil systems occasionally have monetary bail but tend to detain or release the accused on the basis of the expected danger to society the result is lengthy detentions during the pretrial investigation period. Adversarial systems make exceptions for the poor to be released without bail, but the ordinary practice is to rely on the financial incentive not to skip bail and illicitly avoid trial. Sometimes, for serious crimes such as murder, defendants are not permitted bail.

The United States has the most use of juries, although the jury system was developed by England, beginning with King John's concession in Magna Charta to allow trials by juries of one's peers. England, however, has juries in only about 5 percent of trials, and almost exclusively in criminal cases. Most criminal trials in the United States have juries, who must issue a unanimous verdict of either guilty or not guilty in order to avert a mistrial. England allows nonunanimous jury decisions in criminal cases. The United States permits the voir dire process, whereby both sides select jurors and may by peremptory challenge require the dismissal of a finite number of prospective jurors in the interview pool. In England, the selection of juries is out of the attorneys' control, except when a prosecutor asks prospective jurors to "stand aside," which is similar to the preemptory challenge in the U.S. system. There are rarely jury trials in India, Pakistan, or most African common law systems. Some utilize the inquisitorial system's approach of having lay assessors assist judges in their decisions. A few civilian systems, like Spain's, have used juries intermittently over the past two centuries.

HISTORICAL BASIS OF ADVERSARIAL SYSTEMS

Several dozen countries have adversarial legal systems, most often a legacy of British colonialism. Federal systems, such as Australia's, have many more decentralized jurisdictions under stipulated rules where the national rules are mandatory. Canada has ten provinces and two territories, each with its own realm of jurisdiction. Many adversarial systems adopt the English distinction between barristers, who conduct litigation before courts on behalf of clients with whom they usually have little contact, and solicitors, who refer litigation to barristers and who conduct all nonlitigious business, except in the lowest courts. There is no such formal distinction in the United States, although many lawyers specialize in certain types of litigation.

The adversarial system grew out of Anglo-Saxon customs. Common law courts issued legal rules in specific disputes. Equity (chancery) courts offered more discretionary justice, less constrained by precedents, providing injunctions and other nonmonetary relief as part of the broader adversarial system. The rules governing equity remedies, however, were not completely open to discretionary judicial interpretation. A separate system until the twentieth century, equity courts also checked the power of common law courts. Both types of adversarial courts were supposed to rule on the basis of custom, justice, and principles, although only the common law courts were constrained by case precedents.

COST OF LITIGATION

It is sometimes asserted that British courts spare no expense to discover the truth. Civilian systems, such as in Germany, place limits on litigation and thus on the resources to investigate. However, lacking the possibility of settlement and routine de novo appeals, civilian systems generally have a higher percentage of litigation costs associated with trial processes. The English approach generally has two conflicting effects: it increases the accuracy of the information available to both sides in a trial, and it increases the time and cost necessary to complete a trial, thereby sometimes denying justice by the delay or the disincentive to undertake a costly trial. The cost of litigation in England and the United States can be so high as to exceed the imputed benefits to one or both sides. Lawyers generally are paid an hourly fee (except in tort cases), and the rates for litigation can range as high as $1,000 an hour. The ability of wealthy defendants to obtain much more thorough defenses than what poorer ones can afford, or what is available to them through legal aid, also suggests a double standard in practice.

The cost of litigation has a positive incentive because of the option in adversarial systems to settle a case at any stage of litigation. Undoubtedly, however, some defendants choose to settle their cases early to avoid the costs of protracted litigation, even where they are not guilty of the crimes with which they are charged. In this sense, the inquisitorial systems may have greater judicial access. It should be noted that many civilian systems, like France, Italy, Portugal, also suffer from increasing caseloads and litigation costs. Most cases in adversarial systems do not go to trial, and most trials are not completed but end in a settlement between the prosecution or plaintiff and the defendant, contingent on the settlement's acceptance by the judge. Since the 1970s, in criminal cases in the United States and to a large extent for serious crimes in England, the defendant is provided an attorney at the state's expense. Australia, however, has reduced legal aid budgets for criminal defendants as the increase in the volume and complexity of litigation has expanded. In civil litigation in the United States, contingent fees have increased the access of less wealthy plaintiffs, especially in tort cases. The huge settlements paid by defendants (or their insurance companies) have been fueled by punitive or treble damages meted out to punish and deter, not just to compensate the plaintiff for his or her losses. Some punitive damages have been authorized in the United States for civil rights and environmental violations, although most treble damages were established as common law doctrines.

Because adversarial systems generally are more open to the influence of attorneys than inquisitorial systems are, and because civil disputes often have enormous amounts of money at stake, they are prone to more litigation, more lawyers, and more attempts to use the law and the courts in conflict resolution. Other features vary more within than between systems. The United States, unlike England, requires qualified lawyers in court as both attorneys and judges. Judicial review is present in the

United States but not in the United Kingdom. Politics also enter into U.S. litigation more than they do in British litigation because more issues in the United States are resolved by the courts, whereas in England, they are reserved to the legislature or executive branches. This is also related to the proliferation of public interest litigation fostered by "treble," or compensatory, damages, which allows the plaintiff's attorneys to win a "contingent fee" amounting to a percentage of the damages if victorious. The entry of the courts into politics was recently epitomized by the U.S. Supreme Court's decision in *Bush v. Gore,* which effectively chose the winner of the 2000 presidential election. The Supreme Court resolved the dispute on the basis of constitutional interpretation rather than letting the executive branch determine it.

Henry F. Carey

See also Appellate Courts; Barristers; Civil Procedure; Common Law; Customary Law; Federalism; Juries; Federal System; Writ of Habeas Corpus

References and further reading

Brace, Paul, and Melinda Gann Hall. 1995. "Studying Courts Comparatively: The View from the American States," *Political Research Quarterly* 48: 5–29.

David, Rene, and John E. C. Brierley. 1985. *Major Legal Systems in the World Today: An Introduction to the Comparative Study of Law.* London: Stevens and Sons.

Fairchild, Erika. 1993. *Comparative Criminal Justice Systems.* Belmont, CA: Wadsworth.

Glendon, Mary Ann, Michael Wallace Gordon, and Christopher Osakwe. 1985. *Comparative Legal Traditions.* Saint Paul, MN: West, chap. 13.

Jacob, Herbert, et al. 1996. *Courts, Law and Politics in Comparative Perspective.* New Haven: Yale University Press.

Joseph R. Crowley Program. 1999. "Tenth Annual Philip D. Reed Memorial Issue Special Report: One Country, Two Legal Systems?" *Fordham International Law Journal* 23, November. Also available on Lexis-Nexis Academic Universe.

Zuckerman, Adrian A. S., ed., 1999. *Civil Justice in Crisis: Comparative Perspectives on Civil Procedure.* Oxford: Oxford University Press.

ADVOCATES—CIVIL LAW SYSTEMS

See Legal Professionals—Civil Law Traditions

AFGHANISTAN

COUNTRY INFORMATION

Afghanistan is a landlocked country in the central Asian region, bordered by China, Iran, Pakistan, Tajikistan, Turkmenistan, and Uzbekistan. Its geostrategic position has largely shaped its political fate and ethnic form. With a surface area of 652,000 square kilometers (making it almost the size of Texas), Afghanistan can be divided into three regions. The northern plains are mostly cultivable. The central highlands, covered by the Hindu Kush mountain chain (rising some 24,000 feet), form two-thirds of the country and stretch from the northeast, through the center, and to the west. The southwestern lowlands are, for the most part, desert areas. The country's climate is arid to semiarid, with extreme variations in temperature. Afghanistan's estimated population of 25,838,797, based on July 2000 statistics (CIA 2001), has a varied ethnic texture. Two major ethnic groups predominate: Indo-Iranians and Turko-Mongols (Shahrani 1996). The first group constitutes around 90 percent of the nation's inhabitants, and members of this group speak Persian (Dari) and Pashtun dialects. Pashtuns are the major ethnic group, forming 38 percent of the entire population. The Turko-Mongol group is composed of Kazakh, Kirghiz, and Turkmen peoples, who speak Turkic dialects. Islam is the religion of 99 percent of all Afghans, with 84 percent of these individuals being Sunni Muslims and 15 percent Shia Muslims. Religious friction between these groups, added to long-standing tribal and ethnic divisions, is the most important source of the ongoing civil war. One percent of the population consists of Christians, Hindus, Jews, and Sikhs who mostly fled the country for fear of civil war. The course of Afghanistan's history has been determined, in part, by its status as a crossroad since the prehistory of its region, as tribes and peoples arrived from the steppes of central Asia and from China, Persia, Europe, India, and Arabia.

Afghanistan's economy is one of the most underdeveloped in the world, and official statistics have been practically nonexistent since 1992. A constant state of war (beginning in 1979) has put most of the agricultural lands in disuse and especially damaged industrial sectors (Economist Intelligence Unit 1999–2000). In 1999, Afghanistan was by far the largest producer of opium poppies, and drug trafficking is the country's major source of revenue (CIA 2001). Thus far, the wars have left 1 million dead and created 5 million refugees in neighboring countries (Economist Intelligence Unit 1999–2000). Most schools have been shut down, and hospitals have been ruined or closed; those that have survived are poorly equipped. The remaining fragile economic sector is controlled by the Taliban government or by its military opposition in the north. Meanwhile, the private sector economy is mostly an underground operation, and internal civil strife and the Taliban's lack of legitimacy have forestalled foreign investment. The country's rich natural resources (such as natural gas, petroleum, coal, and copper), have been, for the most part, abandoned. As of 1999 (CIA 2001), the total gross domestic product (GDP) was $20 billion and the per capita income was $800. The value of exports for 1996 was $150 million (excluding opium); the value of im-

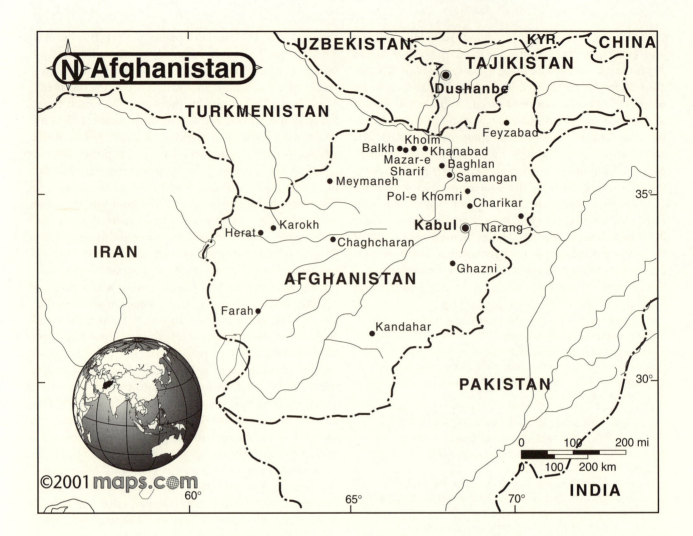

©2001 maps.com

ports was $150 million. Total external debts for 1996 were $5.5 billion (CIA 2001).

HISTORY

Afghanistan has often been a battleground between external powers or opposing internal ethnic and political groups. The country's modern political history can be divided into three periods: monarchy, Marxist state, and Islamic regime.

The modern state of Afghanistan was created in 1747 by Ahmad Shah Durrani. After the decline of Durrani's empire at the beginning of the nineteenth century, the country played the role of a buffer state between Great Britain and Russia from 1800 to 1880. Although the six-year Afghan resistance war against British rule was severely repressed, Great Britain finally granted Afghanistan its independence in 1919. Amir Abdur Rahaman, King Amanullah, and King Nadir Shah, respectively, reigned until 1933, and for forty years thereafter, King Zaher Shah ruled the nation. The last decade of his rule, from 1963 to 1973, witnessed various democratization and modernization reforms that, like the reforms enacted

by some previous kings, ultimately failed. Nonetheless, King Zaher Shah's reign is called "the constitutional period" by some experts (Dupree 1978), for on September 19, 1964, the first important modern Afghan constitution was approved by the Loya Jirga—the highest national assembly (representing all ethnic, religious, and political forces) convened by the king for important national matters. Previous kings had promulgated certain charters of laws (as done, for example, by King Amanullah in October 1923 and King Nadir Shah in October 1931), but the aims announced in these documents were, for the most part, unrealized. The 1964 Constitution can be considered an important step toward both the institutionalization of law (via division of power and individual rights) and the secularization of law (by recognizing the supremacy of king's law over God's law) in order to reduce the influence of traditional forces. This constitution founded a type of moderate absolute monarchy and granted some important powers to the executive and the houses of parliament. However, the king retained supreme powers.

The existing literature on the constitutional and judicial developments in Afghanistan turns around the concept of Islamic law. Before the 1964 Constitution was promulgated, the judiciary system was half secular and half religious (Adamec 1991). The judicial system was judge-based, and the judges, most of whom had graduated from religious schools (*madrasa*), were vested with the power of life and death. After 1964, Zaher Shah's government adopted a number of reforms at different levels of judges' training, administrative reforms designed to modernize the judiciary system and prevent "corruption, nepotism and favoritism" (Dupree 1978, 582). An autonomous judiciary power was created, headed by the Supreme Court, followed in 1967 with the creation of the public prosecutor's office. In penal and civil codes and in criminal procedures, supremacy was given to state law (*qanun*) rather than Islamic law (customary law) (Adamec 1991). Though Islam was declared the official religion of the state in the 1964 Constitution, its legislative role was reduced to a secondary rank. According to Article 69, the two houses of parliament had the exclusive power to make laws; where laws did not exist, Islamic laws based on Hanafi Sunni tenets (Hanafi was one of the four Sunni schools of law) could be considered. Along the same line, Article 64 stated that Islamic law had to be regarded as the last resort and that state law had to be the basic modus operandi of the jurisdiction. Faced with harsh conservative reactions to such directives, liberals referred to the ambiguous second paragraph of Article 64, which read, "There shall be no law repugnant to the basic principles of the sacred religion of Islam" (Dupree 1978). The major opposition emerged in this period, composed of Islamist movements and the Communist Party (Shahrani 1996). Islamist conservatives were not satisfied with their decreasing influence in terms of institutional roles, and Marxist groups, supported by the Soviet Union (with which Afghanistan shared more than 2,000 kilometers of border), opposed the pro-Western tendency of King Zaher Shah.

July 1973 witnessed the end of monarchy and the establishment of a republic in Afghanistan through a coup d'état led by Mohammad Daud with the backing of the Soviet Union. During his absolutist regime, Daud centralized legal institutions, and the Revolutionary Council (RC) and Revolutionary Courts took charge of the jurisdiction and implementation of the law. As a result of these policies as well as Daud's socialist ideology, the gap between Islamic law and state law widened. However, despite the general trend toward secularizing the law in Daud's time, courts continued to function on the basis of traditional norms in some small towns. After five years as the first president of Afghanistan, Daud was killed in the Saur Revolt of April 27, 1978, by his own Communist comrades. The Communist ideology of the new democratic republic of President Nur Muhammad Taraki led to a large popular rebellion in spring 1979. The arrival of Hafizullah Amin, the new president of Afghanistan, together with the Soviet Union's invasion of the country around Christmas 1979, was a turning point in Afghan history.

During the Marxist era, the secularization process was constitutionally strengthened. Beginning in 1978, the role of Islam in the constitution was weakened in unprecedented ways. On April 21, 1980, during the Taraki regime, a provisional constitution was adopted, and the Democratic Republic of Afghanistan emerged. Under the new constitution, all powers were concentrated in the Revolutionary Council. Martial law was declared, and the election of the government was to be done by the RC. The affairs of state were administered by "popular councils." The High Judicial Council replaced the Supreme Court, and the Revolutionary Military Court replaced the civil courts. The verdicts of these bodies were based on the RC's decrees, which were considered the supreme laws of the country.

In this period, Islamic law had to retreat in the face of revolutionary leftist decrees. The decrees announced various reforms in the civil code and penal laws, and judicial authority was finally invested in the president of the Revolutionary Council, who was also in charge of interpreting the laws. However, in cases in which the constitution, laws, and decrees were inexplicit, a judge was directed to refer to the *sharia* (God's law) and "democratic legality" (Spriggs 2001).

With the increasing importance of Islamist forces, on the one hand, and popular dissatisfaction with Marxist rule, on the other, two significant changes were made. First, Islam was again accorded major status; as the Constitution of May 1990 stated, "Islam is the Religion of Afghanistan and no law shall run counter to the principles of Islam" (Law Library of Congress 2001). Second, the historical institution known as the Loya Jirga was once again constitutionally recognized, and that body acquired important powers that earlier were held by the RC. Furthermore, a presidential republic was declared, and the two houses of parliament were reinstated. In addition, some substantial civil and political liberties were recognized.

These constitutional changes as well as the moderate policies of Najibullah Ahmadzai who followed Babrak Karmal, were not enough to overcome the intransigence of the seven-part alliance of *Mujahedin*-Islamic fighters (the Islamic Unity of Afghan mujahideen). The mujahideen (armed and financed by the U.S. government) showed fierce resistance and called for a jihad (Islamic holy war), with the goal of completely liberating the country from Soviet Communist occupation. Afghan resistance forced 120,000 Soviet soldiers to withdraw in February 1989 on the basis of a new UN accord. Weakened by the decreasing Soviet support for his government, Najibullah Ahmad zai was ousted from power on April 16, 1992.

During the Islamist era that started in 1992 and continues to the present, there has been no nationally approved constitution and the country has struggled through a constant civil war between two camps of Islamists. The Afghan legal system has, for the first time swung completely toward God's law, and king's law and Marxist law have been completely abolished. Armed clergy (mullahs) have gained key roles in the political system. The current theocratic nature of the government was apparent from the early charters of Islamist organizations in Afghanistan. The charter of the Islamic Alliance for Afghanistan Freedom Fighters (IAAF), which was adopted in 1982 and envisaged as a provisional constitution, was explicit in declaring, in an unprecedented manner, that Islam was the only source of legislation. The stated objectives of that document were to establish an Islamic government and to apply Islamic laws (Spriggs 2001). On June 28, 1992, after the complete withdrawal of the Soviet army, Burhanuddin Rabbani (one of the *Mujahedin* leaders and supported by Iran) took power and called for general elections. The opposing factions, led by Gulbuddin Hekmatyar, heavily rocketed Kabul, the capital city. In December 1992, Rabbani was finally elected by the *shura* (assembly) as interim president for two years. He promised a new constitution based on the Islamic sharia, but that promise was never realized due to differences of opinion between rival factions in the government (Economist Intelligence Unit 1999–2000) and continuing strife. Rabbani's power was disputed by five members of the nine-party alliance. The mujahideen's inability to reach an agreement and declining foreign support for them prepared the ground for the emergence of a new actor.

The principal event that increased the Islamization of the legal system was the emergence of the Taliban in late 1994, supported by Pakistan and Saudi Arabia. The Taliban, mainly of Pashtun origin, were students in the religious colleges in the Baluchestan region and the northwest frontier. They attacked mujahideen positions and finally seized Kabul in September 1996. Before the 2001 U.S.-led operations in the country, the Taliban controlled around nine-tenths of Afghanistan.

From the outset, the Taliban applied extremely harsh legal practices wherever they ruled. They set up a six-member supreme council, led by second-in-command Mullah Muhammad Rabbani, to govern Kabul on the basis of the strict observance of Islamic principles. They closed girls' schools, prohibited women's employment, and forced men to grow beards and women to wear veils. Severe punishments for infractions of Taliban rules were meted out, such as cutting off a thief's hand or stoning a person convicted of adultery (Economist Intelligence Unit 1999–2000).

LEGAL CONCEPTS

Islam has always played a central role in Afghan public and private life. As noted earlier, the legal system historically has been divided between king's law and God's law—in other words, between state legislation and customary law (Islamic law). The support of the mullahs (that is, the Islamic scholars and clergy) has always been deemed essential for the legitimacy of the kingdom, and mullahs have always taken part in the Loya Jirga (Spriggs 2001). From a political sociology point of view, as M. Nazif Shahrani (1995) observed, Afghan people have always measured the legitimacy of their government first and foremost on the basis of its commitment to Islam. In the periods of monarchy (until 1973) and the republics (from 1973 to 1992), Islamic law was constitutionally less important than secular laws. However, after 1992, the situation changed, and the legal system became the exclusive realm of sharia.

Both the dominant Taliban and their military opposition, the Northern Alliance, led by the nominal president Burhanuddin Rabbani, called for an Islamic government and for the application of Islamic law. However, the Taliban, adopting Hanafi law, implemented an ultraconservative interpretation of Islamic law, and by doing so, they instituted a system similar to the *wahhabi* legal system in Saudi Arabia (wahhabi is a Sunni school of law based on a strict interpretation of the Koran).

In the Taliban's interpretation of Islam, the source of sovereignty is Allah and the only legitimate source of law is the Koran or its interpretations by Hanafi scholars in the early centuries of Islam. Political institutions such as government and parliament are considered no more than executive apparatuses for the application of Koranic laws. There is no separation between church and politics, and the *khalifa* or *amir* (Muslim ruler) is the chief executive in charge of both sacred and profane institutions. The supreme powers are vested in the *amir-ul-muminin* (the commander of the faithful), the leader of the Muslim community. In this conception, democracy and secular laws are rejected as Western products. What made the Taliban's legal practice so harsh was their strict implementation of sharia in accordance with the practice of the prophet Mohammad and the four khalifs following him in the first century of Islam (around 1,400 years ago). This strict application extended to all fields of law, from inheritance, family relationships, and religious endowments to fiscal, commercial, criminal, and constitutional laws. Any modification in the letter of sacred law was considered *bed 'a* (innovation) and therefore forbidden (for causing heresy). The possibility of *ijtihad* (Islamic independent legal reasoning) was excluded. In sum, the combination of an extreme legal interpretation and traditional tribal practices gave rise to one of the harshest systems of law in the world.

Structure of Afghanistan under the Taliban

Structure of the judicial practice in Afghanistan

Inner *Shura* (Council) based in Kandahar
Functioning as the highest political authority
and Supreme Court

Its head is Mulla Muhammad Omar, who is the spiritual
leader commanding all local councils

Ministry for the Promotion of Virtue and
Supression of Vice
Based in Kabul (capital)

Local Islamic Courts as part of the
Taliban's Local Councils

Religious police as law enforcement organ of Inner and
Local Councils

Faith and sex were the basic criteria for the definition of political and constitutional rights. Afghan society is divided into Muslim and non-Muslim parts, and discrimination on the basis of faith is the norm. Women are considered as second-class citizens and have fewer rights than men do. Non-Muslim minorities also have limited rights. Even heretic Muslims (such as Shia or other nonrecognized Muslim minorities) face pressures and persecutions.

Two important points should be mentioned in describing Afghanistan's legal structure during the Taliban period, which ended in late 2001. The first is that there was no functioning central government and that several regions kept changing hands between the Taliban and their military opposition (Law Library of Congress 2001). Formal legal codes and modern administrative institutions of justice did not exist. Afghanistan had, in fact, two states. One—the Islamic State of Afghanistan—was de jure and based abroad. It was recognized by the United Nations on September 31, 1998, and its president since June 6, 1992, was Burhanuddin Rabbani. Most of the Afghan foreign embassies were controlled by Rabbani's officials, and it was his state that retained Afghanistan's seat in the United Nations. The other state had de facto control of the country and was in the hands of the self-proclaimed government of the Taliban, who renamed their regime in 1997 as the Islamic Emirate of Afghanistan. There are thirty provinces. The second important point to consider is that data on the nation and its functioning during this time were sorely missing: Afghanistan was closed to most foreign journalists and international organizations, and those that did manage to enter the country faced a variety of constraints in their work.

JUDICIAL STRUCTURE DURING THE TALIBAN PERIOD

There was neither a constitution recognized across the country nor an independent judiciary power in Afghanistan. Moreover, both the Taliban and their opposition are said to have committed human rights violations.

The following section will focus on the Taliban's legal practices in particular.

Various reports on human rights and development issues in Afghanistan, compiled by international agencies, stress the country's poor human rights record and the tragic situation of Afghani women. Any peaceful change of the political system was blocked under Taliban rule. Commands and rules were implemented by three organs: the Islamic courts, the religious police, and the Ministry for the Promotion of Virtue and Suppression of Vice (PVSV). Arrests were arbitrary, and summary courts and executions were the rule. Some executions, such as those for adultery, were conducted in public.

Discrimination on the basis of sex, ethnicity, and faith was common. The situation of Afghani women was especially bad; as second-rank citizens, they were deprived of many political, civil, and work rights, except in certain public health agencies. They were forced to observe an extreme Islamic code of dress (wearing robes called the *hijab*, which leaves the face uncovered, and the *burqa*, which covers the face) and had to be covered from head to toe. Homosexuals were executed. Amnesty International has reported numerous cases in which individuals were detained on the basis of their ethnic roots (Law Library of Congress 2001). The right to privacy and the sanctity of the home were regularly violated by Islamic police. Non-Muslim residents mostly fled and took refuge in foreign countries. Those who remained were allowed to practice their faith but could not conduct missionary activities. The Shia minorities in the city of Hazara were under constant repression; they could no longer use their mosques, which were given to Sunni Muslims.

There was no effective labor law and cases of forced labor and child labor were frequent. Prisoners were compelled to work in tragic conditions, and the state of the prisons was deplorable. Satellite dishes, music, and movies were prohibited in society and the only official radio was called "the Voice of Shariat," which broadcasted the Taliban's decrees and Islamic programs.

At the level of political rights, the formation of independent political parties was forbidden. A limited number of journals were published sporadically and were affiliated with the warring factions. Independent political meetings and associations were severely repressed (Law Library of Congress 2001). Furthermore, there was no national army, and the elements of the different sectors of the former army were fractionalized among warrior groups (CIA 2001).

The legislative and judiciary systems were essentially nonfunctioning during Taliban rule. Regions and cities were ruled by shuras of mullahs, who had life-and-death power in their realms. Mullah Mohammad Omar, a former member of *mujahideen* and religious student, was based in the southern city of Kandahar and was the spiritual leader and the head of the Taliban state, possessing supreme powers. He issued his decrees as the amir-ul-muminin and ran the inner shura located in Kandahar; local councils operated under his command. As an Amnesty International report (Law Library of Congress 2001) stressed, "Some provisional administrations maintain limited functions, but civil institutions are rudimentary."

IMPACT OF TALIBAN RULE

The Taliban's effort to establish an Islamic government posed serious challenges to the viability of Islam as a political philosophy as well as the application of sharia as a model in the Muslim world. It also brought into question the shortsighted U.S. foreign policy of supporting certain extremist forces in the past. The fierce civil strife and the semianarchic situation that ensued under Taliban rule damaged the economy, affecting both the agricultural and industrial sectors. The Taliban state was internationally isolated, and it was not recognized by the United Nations. The child mortality rate is reported to be 250 out of 1,000, and 5 millions Afghan people have taken refuge in neighboring countries. The harsh legal system and discriminatory policies based on ethnicity, faith, and sex exacerbated social divisions and created serious obstacles in terms of building a nation-state. At the same time, the government's lack of legitimacy favored its military opposition, and due to inefficiency, corruption, and a long and costly war, the Taliban came to face serious problems in military recruitment among Pashtun tribes, their main social base. This government's political extremism and its support for international terrorism led to the easily approved UN sanctions (supported by the United States) against the Taliban beginning in October 1999.

Editor's Note: In December 2001, the Taliban regime collapsed under the pressure of attacks that came in the wake of terrorist incidents in the United States. As this goes to press, an interim government has been established in Kabul, but many areas of the country remain in an unstable, and even lawless, situation. The exact structure and efficacy of Afghanistan's future legal system is unclear, although it is likely to involve some combination of secular and Islamic law and courts.

Ali G. Dizboni

See also Islamic Law; Saudi Arabia

References and further reading
Adamec, Ludwig W. 1991. *Historical Dictionary of Afghanistan*. London: Scarecrow Press, pp. 119–121, 200–201.
CIA, "The World Factbook," http://www.odci.gov/cia/publications/factbook/geos/af.html (cited September 6, 2001).
Dupree, Louis. 1978. *Afghanistan*. Princeton, NJ: Princeton University Press, pp. 559–590.
Dyba, Martha, and John W. Poulos. 1982. "Afghanistan." In *Constitutions of Dependencies and Special Sovereignties*. Edited by Albert P. Blaustein and Eric B. Blaustein. New York: Oceana Publications.
Gregorian, Vartan. 1969. *The Emergence of Modern Afghanistan*. Stanford, CA: Stanford University Press.
Kamali, Mohammad Hashim. 1985. "Law in Afghanistan." In *Social, Economic and Political Studies of the Middle East*. Vol. 36. Leiden, Netherlands: E. J. Brill.
Law Library of Congress. "Afghanistan," http://www.loc.gov/law/guide/afghanis.html (cited September 6, 2001).
Maley, W., ed. 1998. *Fundamentalism Reborn: Afghanistan and the Taliban*. London: Hurst and Company.
Paulson, Elisabeth. 2000. "Afghanistan." Pp. 46–49 in *Economist Intelligence Unit: Country Profile—Pakistan and Afghanistan*. London: Economist Intelligence Unit Limited.
Rashid, A. 2000. *Taliban*. London: Tauris.
Shahrani, M. Nazif. 1995. "Afghanistan." Pp. 27–32 in *The Oxford Encyclopedia of the Modern Islamic World*. Edited by John L. Esposito. New York: Oxford University Press.
———. 1996. "Afghanistan." Pp. 43–47 in *Encyclopedia of the Modern Middle East*. Edited by Reeva S. Simon., Philip Mattar, and Richard W. Bulliet. New York: Macmillan Reference USA and Simon and Schuster Macmillan.
Spriggs, Karyl Terese. 2001. "The Legal System of Afghanistan." Pp. 3–25 in *Modern Legal Systems Cyclopedia*, vol. 9. Edited by Kenneth Robert Redden and Linda L. Schlueter. New York: William S. Hein Publisher.

AFRICAN COURT/ COMMISSION ON HUMAN AND PEOPLES' RIGHTS

MISSION

For the continent of Africa, a regional system standing between the national and international levels promotes and protects human rights. The African Commission and the African Court on Human and Peoples' Rights (see figure) operate within the Organization of African Unity (OAU), deriving their authority from the African Charter on Human and Peoples' Rights (entered into force on 21 October 1986) and its protocol on the establishment of an African Court on Human and Peoples' Rights (adopted December 1997 at a special OAU session of

Legal Structure of the African Court/ Commission on Human and People's Rights

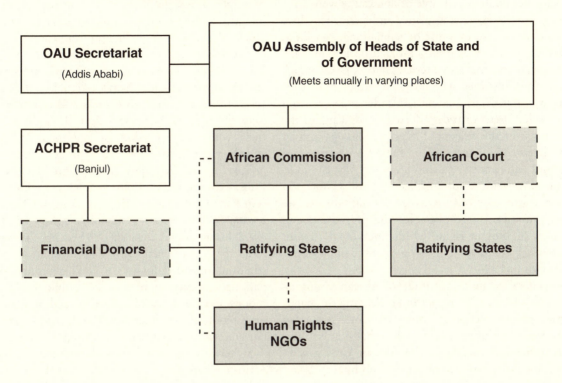

ministers of justice or law; still awaiting the requisite number of ratifications to enter into force).

The operations of both the commission and the court (when established) must be distinguished on the one hand from the legal systems of individual African states and on the other hand from the system of UN treaty bodies supervising agreements such as the International Covenants on Economic, Social, and Cultural Rights and on Civil and Political Rights, the Convention on the Elimination of All Forms of Racial Discrimination, or the Convention on the Rights of the Child. The African Commission and the African Court resemble the European and inter-American human rights systems in their methods of operation, though not in their breadth of rights, historical depth, or legal effects. The commission's powers have been largely promotional in nature, and the court's responsibilities will be primarily protective.

In common with the other treaty-based systems of human rights, the basic powers of legal enforcement rest in the ratifying states, not in the supervising bodies. The African Commission's main duties involve receiving and discussing reports submitted by the states parties, considering communications alleging violations, and expounding the African Charter. Governments that ratify the charter are obligated to bring their constitutions, laws, and national policies into conformity with it. Reports are to be submitted every two years. The African Court,

when functioning, will be able to issue both binding and advisory judgments directed at the states parties to the protocol.

HISTORY

The African Commission and Court of Human Rights are creations of the OAU, which was established in 1963. All the member states of the OAU have ratified or acceded to the African Charter on Human and Peoples' Rights, thus making it the most widely accepted regional human rights agreement. The OAU's current membership of fifty-four states (as of early 2001) excludes only one of the countries on the continent and surrounding islands (Morocco) and includes one entity not recognized as sovereign by other intergovernmental organizations (Sahrawi Arab Democratic Republic). The OAU has suffered from chronic financial problems, and as a result the African Commission has been underfunded for its entire history and has turned increasingly to international donors. (Its average annual budget in its first ten years was under $500,000.)

The fundamental principles of the OAU, its style of operation, and (above all) the authoritarian way in which African presidents have run their countries have affected the OAU's impact on human rights practices within individual states and help explain the systemic weaknesses of the African Commission relative to its European and inter-American counterparts. In common with other interstate groupings, the OAU is based on the equality of member states and the principle of domestic sovereignty. Most African states, having gained independence since 1960 and fearing secessionist or subnational rebellion, emphasized political centralization, authoritarian rule, and distrust of external and internal political pressures for much of their histories. The most important right they sought was self-determination, or independence from colonial rule. These attitudes affected the drafting of the African Charter, the weakest of the three regional human rights agreements in terms of its formal provisions and ambiguous enforcement capabilities of the African Commission. However, the spread since 1990 of democratic, transparent processes of governance has started to create a more propitious atmosphere for the promotion and protection of human rights within individual African states, and the commission itself has become more active, especially since 1994.

The generally cautious attitude of African Commission has also limited its impact in challenging or changing governments' actions. Unlike the Inter-American Commission on Human Rights, which has boldly interpreted ambiguous mandates, the African Commission has been more deliberate in its actions and interpretation of powers. In its early years, it gave cursory attention to reports from states parties, averaging forty-five minutes each for discussion (Gaer 1992); did not widely utilize nonofficial sources of information; dealt slowly with communications; failed to press governments for follow-up actions; and kept crucial documents confidential (Welch 1995: 155–162). Weaknesses in the small secretariat, the result of both funding problems and staff shortcomings, compounded the problems. However, the African Commission has gradually improved its secretariat, reduced the deference it gives to states parties, drawn more extensively on comments and documents from nongovernmental organizations (NGOs) in commenting on the reports submitted by governments, and lifted some of the veil of secrecy that had surrounded communications sent to it. The African Commission thus is becoming, within its limited resources, an influence on how states parties interpret national law and implement legal decisions domestically.

LEGAL PRINCIPLES

In most respects, the African Charter follows the general pattern of organization developed earlier in the European and inter-American systems and in the international covenants and conventions functioning within the United Nations. The African Charter is unique among regional human rights agreements, however, both in incorporating all three "generations" of rights and in setting forth duties for both governments and individuals.

Most space in the African Charter is given to civil and political rights: Articles 3–13 enumerate such familiar principles as equality before the law; respect for life and integrity of the person; prohibition of slavery, torture, and cruel, inhuman, or degrading punishment; no deprivation of freedom except for conditions previously laid down by law; the right to have one's cause heard; freedom of conscience; profession and practice of religion; the right to receive information and to express and disseminate opinions; the right to free association; the right to assemble freely with others; freedom of movement and residence; and the right to participate freely in government. Several political rights are subject, however, to "clawback" provisions, being limited by phrases such as "within the law" (Gittleman 1984, 157–159). The African Charter is thus textually more restrictive than other regional and international human rights treaties, which utilize the general formula that a particular right shall be subject only to restrictions provided for by law and necessary to protect national security, public order, public health, or the morals and freedoms of others. In addition, there is no prohibition of forced labor in the African Charter or any requirement of secret balloting in public elections.

In terms of economic, social, and cultural rights, the African Charter devotes Articles 14–18 to several: the right to property; the right to work under equitable and satisfactory conditions; the right to the "best attainable" state of physical and mental health; the right to obtain an education and to participate freely in cultural life; protection of the family ("the natural unit and basis of society") by the state; elimination of discrimination against women; and the right to special measures of protection for the aged and disabled. The state is to assist the family, "which is the custodian of morals and traditional values recognized by the community."

So-called third generation rights appear in Articles 19–24. These are directed to "all peoples" and concern the "unquestionable and inalienable right to self-determination"; to free disposition of wealth and natural resources; to economic, social, and cultural development; to national and international peace and security; and to a "generally satisfactory environment favourable to their development." No other regional document, whether prepared by governments or NGOs, has as lengthy a list of collective rights.

Finally, in terms of unusual features of the African Charter, Articles 25–29 set forth duties. These include, for states, obligations to "promote and ensure respect for" (not, it will be noted, to "guarantee") the rights and freedoms contained in the charter, as well as to guarantee the independence of the courts and national institutions. In terms of duties of individuals, a wide-ranging list includes such items as to respect parents, not to compromise state security, to preserve and strengthen national independence and territorial integrity, to pay taxes, and to preserve and strengthen positive African cultural values.

Decisions made by the African Commission have primarily involved communications sent to it (more than 200 were received in its first decade, for which 119 decisions were rendered). The commission has been cautious in treating communications, seeing "positive dialogue resulting in an amicable resolution" as its primary objective. Since 1994, it has publicized its decisions on the merits and admissibility of communications (which must conform with strict requirements to be considered). Observers see a gradual strengthening within the commission of its procedures and their impact.

MEMBERSHIP AND PARTICIPATION

The African Commission is constituted of eleven members chosen for renewable six-year terms by the Assembly of Heads of State and of Government, the highest authority in the OAU. Members are to be selected "amongst African personalities of the highest reputation, known for their high morality, integrity, impartiality and competence in matters of human and peoples' rights." The first woman was elected in 1993. A high proportion of commission members concurrently hold or held governmental positions (such as judge, assistant to the president, attorney general, or minister of the interior), often without recusing themselves in consideration of their own countries. Meetings (approximately two weeks in length) are held every six months.

The African Court, when established, will also be composed of eleven members serving in their private capacity (not as official representatives of their own states), elected by the OAU Assembly for six-year terms, renewable once. Judges must recuse themselves when cases involving their own countries are considered.

PROCEDURE

The African Commission has gradually if cautiously established its procedures and extended its impact on states parties. It has become increasingly active both in examining the reports of states parties and communications alleging human rights violations sent to it and in utilizing nonofficial sources of information about governments' actions. It has concentrated far more on promotion than on protection of human rights. As a leading expert has written, "neither the Charter nor the Commission provides for enforceable remedies or a mechanism for encouraging and tracking state compliance with decisions" (Mutua 1999, 349).

Governments submit their reports, according to the African Charter and the commission's Rules of Procedure, every two years, following an initial report setting forth the constitutional framework and relevant demographic information. Most countries have been slow in

meeting their obligations. Especially in the first eight to ten years of the commission's existence, the reports (if submitted at all) were cursory and tended to gloss over serious human rights issues. Their quality is improving. Members of the commission have (after a period of initial uncertainty) increasingly utilized information provided by NGOs to supplement—and even contradict—the official reports. Public discussion varies from three to six hours. Communications sent to the commission are discussed in private sessions.

When the African Court is established, it will automatically adjudicate cases referred to it by the African Commission, states parties, and African intergovernmental organizations. It may also accept cases, on a discretionary basis, from individuals or NGOs , but *only* if the state involved has accepted the court's jurisdiction in such cases. In addition, the court may give advisory opinions on the request of any OAU member state, the OAU or any of its branches, or an African NGO recognized by the OAU.

STAFFING

The eleven commission members are selected by vote of the OAU Assembly of Heads of State and Government, in accordance with principles of representing different types of legal systems, geographic regions, national languages, and the like. They serve on a part-time basis. The office in Banjul, Gambia, which houses the small number of full-time staff, is funded through the OAU, based on the other side of the continent in Addis Ababa, Ethiopia. Supporters and critics of the African Commission concur that greater autonomy for the secretariat would be useful, and greater funding would allow the system as a whole to become more effective. External donations, particularly from Scandinavian governments or NGOs, have palliated the commission's periodic financial crises, but its underfunding is a chronic problem.

In the case of the African Court, the eleven judges will be selected by the OAU Assembly from among "jurists of high moral character and of recognized practical, judicial or academic competence and experience in the field of human and peoples' rights." All save the president of the court will serve on a part-time basis. How the registrar and other court officers will be selected remains to be decided.

CASELOAD

The responsibilities of the African Commission center on the reports of states parties and communications. With respect to individuals, it can act on communications, including sending a mission of inquiry, but implementation of remedies is the responsibility of governments. The African Court, when established, will theoretically have significantly greater enforcement powers than the commission, but its decisions also must be implemented by individual governments.

IMPACT

As is true for all international treaties, a distinction among ratifying states exists between automatic and optional incorporation into national law. Constitutions of some African states provide that international treaty obligations automatically supersede or override locally enacted legislation in cases of conflict. Other countries require explicit government action to modify existing legislation or judicial procedures to conform with the particular treaty. Only a limited number of OAU states with optional incorporation have thoroughly reviewed their constitutions and statutes and brought them in line with the African Charter (or, for that matter, with other human rights treaties the governments may have ratified).

Even with automatic incorporation, no guarantee exists that the African Charter will affect legal decisions. Frans Viljoen (1999), in his survey of sixteen African countries, found that the African Charter has been mentioned in African courts or used to amend laws on only a few occasions. However, some judicial decisions have cited obligations on states imposed by the ratification of the African Charter beyond existing domestic laws.

Awareness of the potential importance of the African Charter is growing among African lawyers and judges, and governments are taking greater notice. For example, the citizenship act of Botswana was modified to ensure gender equality, and Nigerian courts, during a period of military dictatorship, affirmed that the African Charter was superior to ordinary legislation. The trend toward democratization makes it more likely that human rights obligations resulting from the African Charter will receive attention. Accordingly, although the African Court remains to be established and the African Commission has had less than fifteen years' experience, a start has been made within the relatively weak African Charter on Human and Peoples' Rights.

Claude E. Welch

The author wishes to thank Julia Harrington, Makau Mutua, and Olatokunbo Ige for their comments on an earlier draft of this entry.

See also Botswana; European Court and Commission on Human Rights; Human Rights Law; Inter-American Commission and Court on Human Rights; Morocco; Nigeria

References and further reading
Ankumah, Evelyn A. 1996. *The African Commission on Human and Peoples Rights: Practice and Procedures.* The Hague: Nijhoff.
Gaer, Felice. 1992. "First Fruits: Reporting by States under the African Charter of Human and Peoples' Rights." *Netherlands Quarterly of Human Rights* 10: 29–42.
Gittleman, Richard. 1984. "The Banjul Charter on Human and Peoples' Rights: A Legal Analysis." Pp. 152–176 in *Human Rights and Development in Africa.* Edited by Claude E. Welch, Jr., and Ronald I. Meltzer. Philadelphia: University of Pennsylvania Press.
Mohamed, Abdelsalam A. 1999. "Individual and NGO Participation in Human Rights Litigation before the African Court of Human and Peoples' Rights: Lessons from the European and Inter-American Courts of Human Rights." *Journal of African Law* 43: 201–213.
Mutua, Makau. 1999. "The African Court of Human Rights: A Two-Legged Stool?" *Human Rights Quarterly* 21: 342–363.
Naldi, Gino J., and Konstantinos Magliveras. 1998. "Reinforcing the African System of Human Rights." *Netherlands Quarterly of Human Rights* 16: 431–456.
Odinkalu, Chidi Anselm. 1998. "The Individual Complaints Procedures of the African Commission on Human and Peoples' Rights: A Preliminary Assessment." *Transnational Law and Contemporary Problems* 8: 359–405.
Viljoen, Frans. 1999. "Application of the African Charter on Human and Peoples' Rights by Domestic Courts in Africa." *Journal of African Law* 43: 1–17.
Welch, Claude E., Jr. 1992. "The African Commission on Human and Peoples' Rights: A Five-Year Report and Assessment." *Human Rights Quarterly* 14: 43–61.
———. 1995. *Protecting Human Rights in Africa: Roles and Strategies of Non-Governmental Organizations.* Philadelphia: University of Pennsylvania Press.

ALABAMA

GENERAL INFORMATION

Alabama lies to the south of Tennessee and shares borders with Mississippi to the west, Georgia and Florida to the east, and Florida and the Gulf of Mexico to the south. Entry into the Union occurred on December 14, 1819. Alabama ranks twenty-eighth among the states in land area and twenty-second in population. Agriculture (especially timber) is the leading industry, along with some manufacturing in the north, the Port of Mobile to the south, and a variety of military installations dotting the state landscape. Montgomery was the capital of the Confederacy and now is the state capital. The largest city in Alabama is Birmingham. The state flower is the Camellia, and the state bird is the yellowhammer. Alabama's motto is "We Dare Defend Our Rights," and "Heart of Dixie" is its nickname. In fact, much of Alabama's modern history revolves around the issues of secession and civil rights.

EVOLUTION AND HISTORY

Alabama's first constitution was adopted August 3, 1819, establishing the judiciary as one of the three branches of its government. The constitution provided only for a supreme court and circuit courts, and they were not distinct institutional entities. The state's twenty-nine counties were organized into five judicial circuits and, meeting collectively, the circuit judges composed the supreme court. The judges were appointed "for life during good behavior" by the General Assembly, but they could not serve after reaching seventy years of age.

There have been five other constitutions since 1819, the intent of each overhaul closely tracking the political climate of the state at the time. The 1861 version was similar in design to the original document, the major exception being that it engendered secession from the Union. The 1865 constitution was essentially a postwar transitional document that was superseded three years later by a Reconstruction constitution imposed by Northern radicals. The 1868 model was the first submitted to the people for ratification; it provided for the popular election of all judges. The Bourbon constitution of 1875 represented an attempt by white conservatives to undo some of the previous changes, and above all else to institutionalize white supremacy.

The current constitution dates to 1901. It was a loosely veiled effort to disenfranchise black voters, which effectively it did until the changes wrought in the 1960s by the civil rights movement, the Voting Rights Act of 1965, and a host of U.S. Supreme Court decisions. Included in the 1901 constitution were a number of restrictive voting qualifications that were biased against potential black voters: lengthy residence requirements, tests for literacy and "good character," poll taxes, as well as racial gerrymanders. Over time, all were eliminated.

Alabama's constitution is the longest constitution of any state government in the nation. While the U.S. Constitution contains approximately 5,600 words, Alabama's exceeds 310,000. The disparity is attributable primarily to the inordinate number of amendments—more than six hundred. Until the adoption of amendment 425 in 1982, if a city or county wanted a change in, say, jurisdiction or governance, the change had to be submitted to a statewide vote. If passed, it became part of the state constitution. Additionally, owing to historical distrust of government and politicians generally, many matters that in other states are disposed of by conventional legislative statute are, in Alabama, put to the voters in the form of proposed amendments to the state's constitution. All of this culminates in extraordinary inflexibility and complexity of interpretation, often accompanied by contentious legislative interpretation or expensive litigation. In fact, a recent study by the prestigious publication *Governing* ranked Alabama's constitution last among the states in its capacity to govern. The banner of constitutional overhaul is waved continually in the halls of the General Assembly and throughout the state, but thus far the anxieties among various groups over how revision might affect their interests have paralyzed serious reform efforts.

Perhaps the watershed for the Alabama judiciary was wholesale revision of the judicial article (VI) of the state constitution by popular approval in 1973. The Judicial Article Implementation Act of 1975 (Act 1205) modern-ized the judicial system by, among other things: reorganizing more than four hundred trial courts of various types into a unified two-tiered court system; requiring that all judges (except probate) be lawyers; authorizing the Supreme Court to issue uniform rules pertaining to administration, practice, and procedure; adopting a canon of judicial ethics; and establishing Judicial Compensation and Judicial Inquiry Commissions.

CURRENT STRUCTURE

Appellate Courts

The Supreme Court of Alabama is the court of last resort. It is composed of a chief and eight associate justices. Its major responsibility is to review the decisions of lower state courts; the chief justice also serves as the administrative officer of the entire judicial system. The court has exclusive jurisdiction in—that is to say, only the Supreme Court can review—civil cases in which the amount in controversy exceeds $50,000; appeals from decisions by the Alabama Public Service Commission involving utility rates; appeals from disciplinary actions of the Alabama State Bar; and petitions seeking extraordinary relief. The court has discretionary authority to review all decisions of the Court of Civil Appeals and the Court of Criminal Appeals. At its discretion, the court may also respond to questions from federal courts about state law, and render advisory opinions on questions submitted by the governor or either house of the General Assembly.

Unlike the U.S. Supreme Court, the Alabama high court usually works as two panels of four associate justices, with the chief justice sitting on both panels. If all five justices on the panel agree, the case is disposed of: a unanimous panel is effectively a majority of the court. However the court must sit en banc (all nine justices) if a panel does not produce unanimity, as well as in all cases in which a state law has been declared unconstitutional, for review of certiorari petitions in capital cases for which the death penalty was imposed, in advisory opinions to the legislature or governor, in utility rate cases, and in cases that overrule a previous Supreme Court decision.

The Court of Civil Appeals has five judges, with the most senior serving as presiding judge. It is the court of first appeal in all civil cases in which the amount in question does not exceed $50,000; decisions by state administrative agencies (except the Public Service Commission); worker compensation cases; and domestic relations cases.

The Court of Criminal Appeals also has a membership of five, although in this case the presiding judge is elected by the court. The court has exclusive appellate jurisdiction in all appeals in felony and misdemeanor cases, including violations of city ordinances. Jurisdiction also extends to all postconviction matters, and the authority to issue remedial writs to the trial courts to ensure unifor-

Structure of Alabama Courts

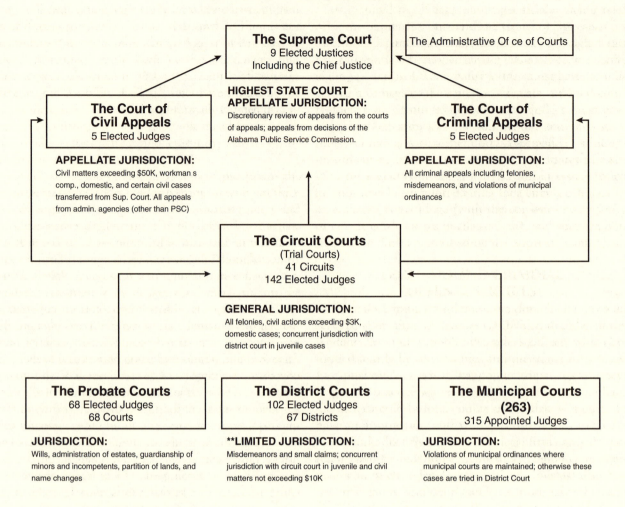

The Supreme Court
9 Elected Justices
Including the Chief Justice

The Administrative Of ce of Courts

HIGHEST STATE COURT
APPELLATE JURISDICTION:
Discretionary review of appeals from the courts of appeals; appeals from decisions of the Alabama Public Service Commission.

The Court of Civil Appeals
5 Elected Judges

APPELLATE JURISDICTION:
Civil matters exceeding $50K, workman s comp., domestic, and certain civil cases transferred from Sup. Court. All appeals from admin. agencies (other than PSC)

The Court of Criminal Appeals
5 Elected Judges

APPELLATE JURISDICTION:
All criminal appeals including felonies, misdemeanors, and violations of municipal ordinances

The Circuit Courts
(Trial Courts)
41 Circuits
142 Elected Judges

GENERAL JURISDICTION:
All felonies, civil actions exceeding $3K, domestic cases; concurrent jurisdiction with district court in juvenile cases

The Probate Courts
68 Elected Judges
68 Courts

JURISDICTION:
Wills, administration of estates, guardianship of minors and incompetents, partition of lands, and name changes

The District Courts
102 Elected Judges
67 Districts

**LIMITED JURISDICTION:
Misdemeanors and small claims; concurrent jurisdiction with circuit court in juvenile and civil matters not exceeding $10K

The Municipal Courts (263)
315 Appointed Judges

JURISDICTION:
Violations of municipal ordinances where municipal courts are maintained; otherwise these cases are tried in District Court

*Under the Administrative Authority of the Chief Justice
** Appeals from courts of limited jurisdiction go to Circuit Court for trial de novo (a new trial).
Source: Alabama Administrative Office of Courts. Used by permission.

mity in criminal proceedings. Cases are heard by panels of three judges, all of whom must agree on the outcome or it is referred to the court sitting en banc.

Trial Courts of General Jurisdiction

Alabama's sixty-seven counties are organized into forty judicial circuits containing anywhere from one to five counties. The *circuit courts* have general jurisdiction in that they hear both civil and criminal cases. Court is held in each county within the circuit. The number of judge-ships authorized for each circuit is determined by case-load volume, ranging from 1 to 24 judges, with a total of 131 on the circuit bench. These courts decide (either by jury or a judge) all civil controversies in which the amount in question exceeds $10,000, and all criminal cases involving alleged felonies. The decisions of district and municipal courts can be appealed to the circuits,

where they are tried again de novo. Circuit courts also exercise supervisory authority over the courts of limited jurisdiction within their geographical spheres.

Courts of Limited Jurisdiction

Municipal courts can be established by any city that wants one, and about three hundred municipalities have such courts. Alternatively, a city can transfer jurisdiction to the district court of the county in which it resides. These courts try alleged infractions of municipal ordinances, and can also try violations of state law if the state law has been incorporated into the municipal ordinance.

Although constitutionally part of the state court system, *Probate courts* are funded by the respective counties. Their jurisdiction is limited to the probate of wills; controversies over intestate estates (that is, estates without wills); name changes; and guardianship over the infirm, the insane, and orphans (unless referred to a juvenile court). A major responsibility of these courts involves property: the recording of all land partitions and sales, deeds, mortgages, and titles.

Each of Alabama's counties has a *district court* that serves the unincorporated areas of the county and those cities that opt not to have their own courts. They have original jurisdiction over criminal misdemeanors, they conduct preliminary hearings in felony cases, and they can accept guilty pleas in felony cases not subject to the death penalty. District courts exercise concurrent jurisdiction with circuit courts in civil matters in which the amount in question is $10,000 or less, and in juvenile cases. Each district court has a small-claims division for controversies involving sums less than $3,000. In such proceedings, litigants do not require lawyers.

Juvenile court jurisdiction is exercised either by the district or circuit court, with the senior circuit judge generally making the assignment. Juvenile court is for children under eighteen years of age who are charged with being delinquent or in need of supervision. Persons sixteen and older can be tried as adults for serious offenses. Juvenile courts can also hear cases involving adults when the charges involve contributing to the delinquency of a minor, questions of paternity, child desertion or nonsupport, and the determination of whether a child is mentally ill and should be committed. Juvenile court proceedings are confidential and tried without juries. It is within the discretion of the juvenile-court judge to transfer cases involving serious crimes to regular court.

STAFFING

The Legal Community
All practicing attorneys must pass the Alabama State Bar exam. Alabama has two law schools accredited by the American Bar Association: the University of Alabama (public) and Cumberland Law School of Samford University (private). In the 1999 ranking of law schools nationwide, *U.S. News & World Report* placed the University of Alabama forty-sixth and relegated Samford to the "fourth tier." A third school, Jones University, does not have ABA certification, so its graduates who pass the bar exam are limited to practicing in Alabama. In the year 2000 there were 12,807 attorneys in Alabama. The state bar association handles disciplinary matters outside of legal violations; appeals of its decisions can be made to the Supreme Court.

Judicial Selection and Removal
With the exception of probate, all judges must be licensed attorneys. Save for municipal court judges, who are appointed by the city's governing body and serve four-year terms (two-year terms if part-time), judges are se-

lected in partisan elections for six-year terms. Elections to the Supreme Court, courts of civil and criminal appeals, and the circuit courts are held statewide. Candidates for circuit or district judge must be residents of that circuit or county for one year prior to the election and must maintain residence during their terms. Vacancies in state judgeships are filled by gubernatorial appointment, and in municipal judgeships by city governing bodies. All judges (except those of the municipal court) are legally prohibited from the private practice of law while in office. Jurists are bound by the canons of judicial ethics.

The Judicial Inquiry Commission is constitutionally charged with investigating allegations of professional misconduct or incapacity to discharge duties on the bench. Upon receipt of a formal complaint, the *Court of the Judiciary* holds a public hearing on the charges and can remove a judge from office, suspend without pay, or censure if the charges are sustained. In cases of incapacity, the court can suspend, either with or without pay, or retire the judge. This nine-member tribunal is composed of one appellate judge, two circuit judges, one district judge, two members of the state bar, two nonlawyers appointed by the governor, and one person appointed by the lieutenant governor with senate confirmation. This process replaced conventional impeachment proceedings. Decisions can be appealed to the Supreme Court.

Judicial Administration
The chief justice of the Supreme Court is the principal administrative officer for the judiciary, and is authorized to appoint an administrative director of courts and other personnel necessary to ensure efficient judicature. The *Administrative Office of Courts,* headed by the administrative director of courts, provides centralized support for constituent courts, collects and disseminates information, and develops administrative procedures to ensure statewide uniformity in court operations. The *Judicial Study Commission,* created by law in 1971, is a thirty-two member body drawn from all three branches, whose ongoing responsibility is to study the administration of justice in Alabama and make recommendations as it sees fit.

THE DETERIORATING EFFECTS OF JUDICIAL ELECTIONS
Alabama is perhaps emblematic of what some consider to be a rather disturbing trend in several states that select their judges via the ballot box: increasingly bitter and costly judicial elections. The pattern is more acute in states whose judicial elections are partisan. In the 2000 Republican primary for chief justice of the Supreme Court, Associate Justice Harold F. See, Jr., opposed Roy S. Moore, a lower-court state judge whose career was propelled by his refusal to remove a copy of the Ten Commandments from his courtroom. A number of states re-

cently established ad hoc commissions to monitor the verity of statements made in judicial campaigns, and for that purpose Alabama uses the extant Judicial Inquiry Commission. It found that Justice See's political ads falsely accused Justice Moore of leniency toward drug dealers. See lost the primary and subsequently faced the possibility of disqualification from his position as associate justice.

As a consequence of this increased contentiousness, the cost of judicial campaigns has soared, and with it the need to seek political contributions from well-heeled individuals and groups. Many who wish to reform the system fear that these developments undermine the perception that judicial decisions are fair, impartial, and the product of the law rather than political ideology.

Gerard Gryski
Gary Zuk

See also Federalism; Judicial Selection, Methods of; United States—Federal System; United States—State Systems

References and further reading
Alabama Administrative Office of Courts, "A Guide to Alabama Court Procedures," http://www.alacourt.org/Publications/alacourt.htm (cited June 15, 2000).
Alabama Supreme Court and State Law Library, "Supreme Court of Alabama," http://www.alalinc.net/appellate.cfm (cited November 4, 1998).
Barrett, Katherine, and Richard Greene. 1999. "Grading the States: A Management Report Card." *Governing* (February): 17–90.
Freyer, Tony, and Timothy Dixon. 1995. *Democracy and Judicial Independence: A History of the Federal Courts of Alabama, 1820–1994*. Brooklyn: Carlson Publishing.
Martin, David L. 1985. *Alabama's State and Local Governments*. 2d ed. University: University of Alabama Press.
Permaloff, Anne, and Carl Grafton. 1995. *Political Power in Alabama*. Athens, GA: University of Georgia Press.

ALASKA

GENERAL INFORMATION

Alaska, the northernmost state, is part of the continental United States but is separated from the "lower" forty-eight states by Canada to the south and east. The forty-ninth state in order of admission to the union, Alaska is also the largest, containing 586,412 square miles or the equivalent of one-fifth of the forty-eight contiguous states. At the same time, Alaska remains one of the least populated states, with a population of 626,932 in 2000. More than 40 percent of Alaskans (260,283) live in the state's principal city, Anchorage. The capitol city, Juneau, is third in population (30,711). The second-largest city is Fairbanks (82,840). About 15 percent of Alaska's population are members of one of 226 recognized native tribes.

At the turn of the twenty-first century, Alaska is still considered a frontier state, owing in no small part to its geography and scale. Largely mountainous, Alaska has seventeen of the twenty tallest peaks in the United States, including Mount McKinley, the highest peak in North America. Alaska has more than 3,000 rivers and 3 million lakes. In addition, Alaska has 6,640 miles of coastline and is home to more active glaciers and ice fields than any other populated area of the world. Alaska remains geologically active, having more than seventy potentially active volcanoes and experiencing approximately 5,000 earthquakes a year.

The geography of the state makes it highly dependent on air and water transportation. Juneau, for example, is accessible only by boat or plane. Alaska's industries, largely based on its natural resources, include oil development, fishing, game hunting, mining, some agriculture, and, most recently, tourism.

Alaska is often delineated into six geographic areas. The area closest to the Pacific Northwest region of the contiguous states is known as Southeast Alaska, a long strip of mainland and offshore islands bordering on the Canadian province of British Columbia. Juneau is located in this region. To the north and west is Southcentral Alaska, where Anchorage is located. North of Mount McKinley begins Interior Alaska, which includes Fairbanks. The northernmost area, which is bounded by the Arctic Ocean, is known as the North Slope. Western Alaska is the coastal area south of the North Slope and west of Fairbanks. The Aleutian Islands are often defined as their own geographic area and sometimes are considered together with the Alaska Peninsula as forming Southwest Alaska.

EVOLUTION AND HISTORY

The United States purchased Alaska from Russia in October 1867. The purchase, arranged for $7.2 million dollars by Secretary of State William H. Seward, became widely known as "Seward's Folly." From 1867 until gold was discovered there thirty years later, the federal government largely ignored Alaska. In 1884, Congress designated Alaska as a government civil and judicial district in 1884 and provided that the laws of the state of Oregon would be in force there. It was not until 1900 that a legal code was adopted and a court system established. Alaska gained the status of territory in 1912. The following year the first territorial legislature met, and three years later the first bill petitioning for statehood for Alaska was introduced in Congress.

As a result of the U.S. declaration of war against Japan in 1941, Alaska gained military strategic importance. At the time that Japan invaded the Aleutian Islands in 1943, there were more than 140,000 troops stationed in Alaska. In 1955, Alaska held a constitutional convention. That same year, the territorial legislature passed the Integrated

Legal Structure of Alaska Courts

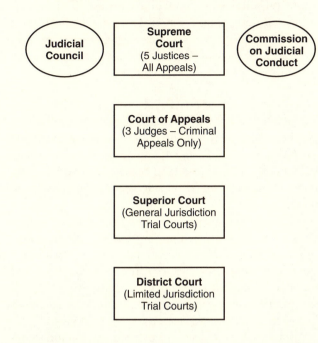

Bar Act, formally establishing the Alaska Bar Association. The following year voters adopted the Alaska constitution, and two years later Congress passed a resolution granting statehood for Alaska. On January 3, 1959, Alaska became the forty-ninth state to enter the union. The first three justices appointed to the Alaska Supreme Court promulgated rules of civil and criminal procedure that became the structure for the state court system.

In its first years, the court system consisted of a general jurisdiction trial court (Superior Court) and an appellate court (Supreme Court). Subsequent legislation has expanded the number of justices serving on the Alaska Supreme Court from three to five and has added a limited jurisdiction appellate court for criminal appeals (Court of Appeals), and a limited jurisdiction trial court (District Court).

Drafters of the Alaska constitution adopted various legal reforms in formulating the state government. They created a unified court system, providing for an appointed judiciary through a judicial nominating agency (the Alaska Judicial Council), and institutionalizing research for improvement of the administration of justice through the Alaska Judicial Council.

CURRENT STRUCTURE

Alaska elects its governor and lieutenant governor to four-year terms. The governor appoints the head of each of the executive agencies of government, including the attorney general, who is responsible for the Department of Law. Alaska's legislature consists of a Senate and a House of Representatives. There are forty representatives, who serve two-year terms, and twenty senators, who serve four-year terms. It is a part-time legislature, meeting annually from January through May with periodic special sessions.

Local government in Alaska is fairly unique compared to the forms typically found in other states. There are no local political subdivisions equivalent to county government. Some local governments are organized into boroughs, but sparsely populated areas of the state remain unorganized. There are two classes of boroughs, and both are governed by elected assemblies and school boards. The boroughs may assess and collect a variety of local taxes. There are also incorporated cities, which also consist of two classes. Taxing authority for first-class cities is broader than that of second-class cities. There are no local courts. The state court system hears both city and borough cases, in addition to all state cases. Moreover, there are 226 federally recognized tribal governments in Alaska. Although many of these have executive agencies and tribal courts as well as governing councils, the extent of their authority remains unclear.

Alaska's state courts are divided into four judicial districts for administrative purposes. An area court administrator and a Superior Court judge, who serves as the presiding judge for the judicial district, administratively govern each of the districts. The highest level of state court is the Alaska Supreme Court. It hears appeals from both the Court of Appeals and the trial courts and also administers the state court system. Under the Alaska constitution, while the state Supreme Court may establish rules for the administration of all courts, the state legislature may change any of those rules by a two-thirds vote of both houses. Alaska's Court of Appeals is a three-judge court created by the legislature in 1980. The Court of Appeals hears only criminal matters and can review appeals directly from the District Court or Superior Court. The Superior Court is the general jurisdiction trial court that has the authority to hear all cases. District Court is the limited jurisdiction trial court and has the power to hear misdemeanors and violations of ordinances, issue warrants, hold preliminary hearings in felony cases, hear civil cases valued up to $50,000, and handle domestic violence and emergency children's cases. Magistrates hear some District Court matters in those areas of the state that are sparsely populated and assist to alleviate the District Court caseload in more populated areas. Magistrates are not required to be lawyers and have more restricted authority than District Court judges.

There are no departments or substantive divisions within the court system, although there has been some experimentation with therapeutic courts for substance abusers and those with chronic mental illnesses or disabilities. Even with these special courts, however, court administration is handled centrally and uniform court rules apply.

NOTABLE FEATURES OF LEGAL SYSTEM

The Alaska Bar Association is responsible for lawyer discipline as well as continuing legal education and ongoing professional development for lawyers. Membership in the association is mandatory for those wishing to practice law in Alaska. The Alaska Bar Association participates in the appointment of representative members to the Alaska Judicial Council and the Alaska Commission on Judicial Conduct, both independent agencies in the judicial branch created by the state constitution. The Judicial Council is a unique agency that functions as both the state judicial nominating commission and the research agency tasked with addressing issues that will improve the administration of justice in the state. The council also, by statute, makes and publicizes evaluations of the performance of judges when they stand for retention election.

In the area of civil law, Alaska is the only state that routinely awards substantial attorneys' fees based on the underlying merits of the civil case. While this practice, known as the English Rule, is a common part of European legal systems, it is contrary to the practice of most other state systems, which do not consider attorneys' fees as recoverable costs in civil litigation except under special circumstances. The Alaska rule has undergone some revisions, the major effect of which has been to allow the trial judge to consider the extent to which a fee award may deter similarly situated litigants from seeking relief in the courts.

In criminal law, Alaska has adopted some unique approaches. From 1975 to 1993, for example, the attorneys general of the state voluntarily enforced a ban on plea bargaining. They were able to do so because the Alaska attorney general hires all prosecutors, with the exception of a handful who work for municipalities and prosecute only misdemeanors. Although the scope and definition of the ban altered with the interpretation given to it by each successive attorney general who administered it, generally they all subscribed to the concept that changing a criminal charge would not be permitted if done solely to obtain a guilty plea, and that prosecutors would not specify sentence length as part of a bargain. The ban was rescinded in 1993 by the attorney general at that time.

Criminal sentencing in Alaska also took an unusual course when in 1980 the Alaska legislature adopted a detailed presumptive sentencing scheme for many felonies. Alaska's criminal code divides crimes into felonies, misdemeanors, and violations. The law further defines six types of felonies and two types of misdemeanors. Felonies include murder, unclassified felonies, unclassified sexual offenses, and class A, B, and C felonies. Misdemeanors are divided into class A and class B misdemeanors. The presumptive sentencing scheme sets presumptive ranges of time to serve, maximum sentences, and maximum fines for most felonies, particularly when committed by repeat and serious offenders. In addition, both the legislation and subsequent developing case law set out aggravating and mitigating factors and a procedure for using a special three-judge panel for reviewing those cases that require, in the view of the sentencing judge, an allowable exception to the presumptive sentence.

STAFFING

The Alaska Bar Association reported having 3,285 members in 1996. Of those, 2,611 were actively practicing law, 628 were inactive, and 45 were retired. Alaska has no law school within the state and therefore must rely on drawing lawyers trained outside the state to come and practice in Alaska.

Alaska's judges are required to be lawyers, but magistrates are not. In 1999, there were five Supreme Court justices, three Court of Appeals judges, thirty-two Superior Court judges, seventeen District Court judges, and sixty magistrates who served a total of fifty-nine court locations. The court system reported 156,212 case filings during fiscal year 1999.

All state judges, but not magistrates, must stand for retention in an election at the end of their terms. The same agency that nominates to the governor the most qualified applicants for judgeships, the Alaska Judicial Council, also evaluates judges at the time of the retention vote and recommends to the voters whether they should be retained. Magistrates are employees of the court system and serve at the pleasure of the presiding judge for their judicial district.

RELATIONSHIP TO NATIONAL SYSTEM

Alaska's origins are in federal law. As a consequence, the federal government has a strong presence in the state through its management of federal lands and, most recently, subsistence hunting and fishing rights for Alaska natives peoples. This presence has created a legal tension between the jurisdiction of the state and the federal legal systems in its management of resources and continues in pending litigation in the federal courts.

In contrast, Alaska's federal district court judges have chosen to work with the state judges to ensure consistent court rules where possible and a cooperative effort on common administrative and professional concerns. There have been several successful joint federal-state task forces, including one addressing issues of gender equality in the courts.

Appeals from the U.S. District Court of Alaska go to the Ninth Circuit Court of Appeals.

Marla N. Greenstein

See also Merit Selection; United States—Federal System; United States—State Systems

References and further reading
Alaska Court System 1999 Annual Report.

Brown, Frederic E. 1973. "The Sources of the Alaska and Oregon Codes. Part II: The Codes and Alaska, 1867–1901," 2 *UCLA-AK L. Rev.* 87.

Carns, Teresa W., and John Kruse. 1991. *A Re-evaluation of Alaska's Ban on Plea-Bargaining.* Alaska Judicial Council.

Di Pietro, Susanne, Teresa W. Carns, and Pamela Kelley. 1995. *Alaska's English Rule: Attorney's Fee Shifting in Civil Cases.* Alaska Judicial Council.

ALBANIA

GENERAL INFORMATION

Albania is in the western part of the Balkan Peninsula. It borders Greece to the southwest, the Federal Republic of Yugoslavia (FRY) to the northeast and northwest, and the Former Yugoslav Republic of Macedonia (FYROM) to the east. Albania shares a sea border with Italy to the west, and Greece to southwest. Two seas wash the Albanian coast: the Adriatic Sea and the Ionian Sea. Within Albania's 28,750 square kilometers are relatively high mountains situated in the north, northeastern, and southeastern part of the country, and small plains situated mainly in the western part of the country along the coast. The country's estimated 3.5 million citizens are descendants of ancient Illyrian tribes. Ethnic groups in the country are Albanian (95 percent); Greek (3–4 percent); other (1–2 percent). Education based on school attendance is 96.6 percent in urban areas, and 41.1 percent in rural areas. The literacy rate is 82 percent. The official language is Albanian.

Tirana, the capital city, is home to more than 550,000 inhabitants. Other principal cities are Durres, Elbasan, Shkoder, Vlore, and Gjirokaster. The main religious denominations are Muslim (60 percent), Orthodox (30 percent), and Catholic (10 percent). Albania is a parliamentary democracy. Gross domestic product (GDP) is estimated at $2.88 billion, with a growth rate of about 10 percent a year. Albania is rich in natural resources such as oil, gas, coal, chromium, copper, iron, and nickel. Agriculture accounts for about 55 percent of GDP, its main output being wheat, corn, potatoes, sugar beets, cotton, and tobacco. Industry accounts for 16 percent of GDP, producing mainly textiles, timber, construction materials, fuels, and semiprocessed minerals. Trade is responsible for about 29 percent of GDP, being focused on annual exports of $343 million. The country's legal system is based on the European civil law tradition. The climate is temperate, with wet winters, colder in the interior of the country, and hot, dry summers.

HISTORY

The name Albania is derived from an ancient Illyrian tribe: the Albanoi. The Albanian name for the country is Shqiperia. Illyria is the ancient region of the Balkan Peninsula. In prehistoric times a group of tribes speaking dialects of an Indo-European language swept down to the northern and eastern shores of the Adriatic and established themselves there.

The mines of the region, located inland, attracted the Greeks, but the terrain was too difficult. Greek cities were established on the coast in the sixth century B.C.E. An Illyrian kingdom was set up in the third century B.C.E., with the capital at Scutari (present-day Shkodër, Albania). The Romans conducted two wars against Scutari (229–228 and 219 B.C.E.). The Romans conquered Genthius, King of Scutari, and established (168–167 B.C.E.) one of the earliest Roman colonies as Illyricum. The southern Illyrians were finally conquered (35–34 B.C.E.) by Augustus—a conquest confirmed by the campaigns of 29–27 B.C.E. The name Illyricum was later given to one of the great prefectures of the late Roman Empire, which included a large part of the Balkan Peninsula.

Owing partly to the weakness of the Byzantine Empire, beginning in the ninth century Albania came under the domination, in whole or in part, of a succession of foreign powers: Bulgarians, Norman crusaders, the Angevins of southern Italy, Serbs, and Venetians. The final occupation of the country in 1347, by the Serbs led by Stefan Dusan, caused massive migrations of Albanians abroad, especially to Greece and the Aegean Islands. By the mid-fourteenth century, Byzantine rule had come to an end in Albania, after nearly one thousand years. A few decades later the country was confronted with a new threat, the Turks, who at this juncture were expanding their power in the Balkans.

The Turks invaded Albania in 1388 and completed the occupation of the country about four decades later. But after 1443 an Albanian of military genius—Gjergj Kastrioti (1405–1468), known as Skenderbeg—rallied the Albanian princes and succeeded in driving out the occupiers. For the next twenty-five years, Skenderbeg frustrated every attempt by the Turks to regain Albania, which they had envisioned as a springboard for the invasion of Italy and western Europe. His unequal fight against the mightiest power of the time won the esteem of Europe. After he died, Albanian resistance gradually collapsed, enabling the Turks to reoccupy the country by 1506. Although the Turks ruled Albania for more than four centuries, they were unable to extend their authority throughout the country. In the highland regions, Turkish authorities exercised only a formal sovereignty, as the highlanders never recognized the authority of Constantinople. Albanians rose in rebellion time and again against Ottoman occupation. To bring Albania spiritually closer to Turkey, the Ottomans initiated a systematic drive toward the end of the sixteenth century to Islamize the population. To overcome religious divisions and foster national unity, the leaders of the Albanian nationalist

movement in the nineteenth century used the rallying cry "The religion of Albanians is Albanianism."

The basis of Ottoman rule in Albania was a feudal-military system of landed estates, which were awarded to military lords for loyalty and service to the empire. As Ottoman power began to decline in the eighteenth century, the central authority of the empire in Albania gave way to the local authority of autonomy-minded lords. The most successful of these lords were three generations of pashas of the Bushati family, which dominated most of northern Albania from 1757 to 1831, and Ali Pasha Tepelena of Janina (now Ioannina, Greece), who ruled in southern Albania and northern Greece from 1788 to 1822. These pashas created separate states within the Turkish state until they were overthrown by the sultan. In the wake of the empire's collapse, economic and social power passed from the feudal lords to private landowning beys and, in the northern highlands, to tribal chieftains called *bajraktars,* who presided over their territories with rigid, patriarchal societies that were often torn by blood feuds. Peasants, who were formerly serfs, now worked on the estates of the beys as tenant farmers. Because of the

oppressive nature of Ottoman rule in Albania, many Albanians went abroad in search of careers and advancement within the empire, and an unusually large number of them rose to positions of prominence as government and military leaders. More than two dozen grand viziers (similar to prime ministers) of Turkey were of Albanian origin.

Shortly after the defeat of Turkey by the Balkan allies, a conference of ambassadors of the Great Powers (Britain, Germany, Russia, Austria-Hungary, France, and Italy) convened in London in December 1912 to settle the outstanding issues raised by the conflict. With Austria-Hungary and Italy supporting the Albanians, the conference agreed to create an independent state of Albania.

In drawing the borders of the new state, however, demographic realities were ignored, and vast regions in which Albanians had lived for centuries were given to neighboring countries. Many observers doubted whether the new state would be viable with about half of its population left outside the borders, and especially inasmuch as those regions were very productive in food grains and livestock.

The Great Powers also appointed a German prince, Wilhelm zu Wied, as ruler of Albania; he was forced to leave Albania shortly after his arrival because of unfamiliarity with Albania as well as complications arising from the outbreak of World War I. The war plunged the country into a new crisis, as the armies of Austria-Hungary, France, Italy, Greece, Montenegro, and Serbia invaded and occupied Albania. Left without any political leadership or authority, the country was in chaos, and its very fate hung in the balance. At the Paris Peace Conference after World War I, the extinction of Albania was averted largely through the efforts of U.S. president Woodrow Wilson, who vetoed a plan by Britain, France, and Italy to partition Albania among its neighbors. A national congress, held in Lushnje in January 1920, laid the foundations of a new government. In December of that year, Albania, this time with the help of Britain, gained admission to the League of Nations, thereby winning for the first time international recognition as a sovereign nation and state.

At the start of the 1920s, Albanian society was divided by two apparently irreconcilable forces. One, made up mainly of deeply conservative landowning beys and tribal leaders, was led by Ahmed Zog. The other, made up of liberal intellectuals, democratic politicians, and progressive merchants who wanted to modernize and Westernize Albania, was led by Bishop Fan S. Noli.

In the unusually open and free political, social, and cultural climate that prevailed in Albania between 1920 and 1924, the liberal forces gathered strength, and, by mid-1924, they seized power through a popular revolt. In June 1924, Bishop Noli was appointed prime minister of the new government and set out to build a Western-style democracy in Albania. He announced a radical program of land reform and modernization. The slow implementation of his program, coupled with failure to obtain international recognition for his revolutionary, left-of-center government, quickly alienated most of Noli's supporters. Six months later he was overthrown by an armed assault and replaced by Ahmed Zog.

Zog began his fourteen-year reign in Albania—first as president (1925–1928), then as King Zog I (1928–1939)—in a country rife with political and social instability. Greatly in need of foreign aid and credit in order to stabilize the country, Zog signed a number of accords with Italy, which viewed Albania primarily as a bridge for military expansion into the Balkans. An efficient police force and Italian money brought King Zog a large degree of stability in Albania. He extended the authority of the government to the highlands, laid the foundations of a modern educational system, and took a few steps to Westernize Albanian social life. On balance, however, his achievements were outweighed by his failures. Although formally a constitutional monarch, Albania under Zog's rule experienced the fragile stability of a dictatorship.

Zog failed to resolve Albania's fundamental problem, that of land reform, and denied democratic freedoms to Albanians. He thus created conditions that spawned periodic revolts against his regime, alienated most of the educated class, fomented labor unrest, and led to the formation of the first communist groups in the country.

On April 7, 1939, Italy invaded Albania. Using Albania as a military base, in October 1940, Italian forces invaded Greece but were quickly thrown back into Albania. Following Italy's surrender in 1943, Nazi Germany replaced the Italian occupation forces until November 1944, which marks the liberation of Albania and the Albanian Communist Party's seizure of control of the country.

Enver Hoxha, who had led the resistance struggle of communist forces, became the leader of Albania by virtue of his post as secretary general of the Communist Party. Albania, which before the war had been under the personal dictatorship of King Zog, now fell under the collective dictatorship of the Albanian Communist Party. The country became officially the People's Republic of Albania in 1946. The new rulers inherited an Albania plagued by a host of ills: pervasive poverty, overwhelming illiteracy, blood feuds, and disease epidemics. In order to eradicate these ills, the communists drafted a radical modernization program intended to bring social and economic liberation to Albania, thus completing the political liberation won in 1912. The government's first major act to "build socialism" was swift, uncompromising agrarian reform, distributing the land of large estates to landless peasants. This destroyed the powerful beys. The government also moved to nationalize industry, banks, and all commercial and foreign properties. Shortly after the agrarian reform, the Albanian government started to collectivize agriculture, completing the job in 1967. As a result, peasants lost title to their land.

The social status of women changed radically as they gained legal equality with men and became active participants in all areas of society. In order to obtain the economic aid needed for modernization, as well as the political and military support to enhance its security, Albania turned to the communist world: Yugoslavia (1944–1948), the Soviet Union (1948–1961), and China (1961–1978). Economically, Albania benefited greatly from these alliances: with hundreds of millions of dollars in aid and credits, Albania was able to build the foundations of a modern industry and to introduce mechanization into agriculture. As a result, for the first time in modern history, the Albanian people began to emerge from age-old backwardness and, for a while, enjoyed a higher standard of living.

To eliminate dissent, the government periodically resorted to purges, in which opponents were subjected to public criticism, dismissed from their jobs, imprisoned in forced-labor camps, or executed. Travel abroad was forbidden to all but those on official business. In 1967 the religious establishment, which party leaders and other atheistic Albanians viewed as a backward, medieval institution that hampered national unity and progress, was officially banned, and all Christian and Muslim houses of worship were closed.

After the break with China in 1978, the leadership imposed the so-called doctrine of absolute self-reliance in domestic resources. It only contributed to a worsening of the economy and standards of living. During 1989 the communist leadership embarked on a number of economic reforms, which, although insufficient, were designed to somehow free the economy from certain rigid rules—that is, they allowed peasants to keep a portion of their agricultural products for domestic use, instead of having to deliver it all in state collection depots. The timing of such measures coincided with the political changes that were quickly advancing throughout eastern Europe. Political pluralism and free market economies were a virtual reality.

Albania began the transition to a democratic, open-market society later than most states in the region. Its communist regime from 1945 to 1991 was isolationist and authoritarian, making the liberalization process difficult. The country made progress, however, between 1992 and 1996, although widespread civil disorder led to the collapse of the government and an Italian-led military/civil intervention in early 1997. Since late 1998, Albania's political economy has stabilized. The Albanian people demonstrated resilience to hardships imposed by the influx of Kosovar refugees.

The source of civil disorders in 1997 was the collapse of a number of fraudulent pyramid savings companies in which many Albanians had deposited their life savings, which were ultimately lost. Widespread civil unrest followed and resulted in the fall of the government. In the spring and summer of 1999, 465,000 Kosovar refugees sought shelter in Albania during the war in Kosovo. Hosting this large refugee community placed a considerable burden on Albania's already weak infrastructure and social institutions.

LEGAL CONCEPTS

The re-establishment of the justice system in Albania started in 1989–1990 with the creation of the Ministry of Justice and the reinstitution of the private legal profession. Communist Albania had tended to minimize the role of the law within a society. The law, according to Marxist-Leninist ideology of the dictatorship of the proletariat, had to be "an expression of the class struggle." As a result, systematic violations of fundamental human rights were permitted, and many civil law categories were simply abandoned or were not given adequate importance. Thus legal

reform was one of the key elements in this reform, and the enactment of a new constitution, new laws, and several important codes was seen as movement in the right direction.

In April 1991 the first postcommunist pluralist Parliament approved the Main Constitutional Provisions, which was an interim constitution, approved by consensus by all political parties. In 1993 the bill of Rights was incorporated into the text of the interim constitution. It solemnly affirmed Albania as "a parliamentary republic," a "secular" and "democratic state, based on the rule of law." Its foundations were "Man's dignity, his rights and freedoms, free development of his personality as well as the constitutional order, equality before the law, social justice, social protection." Separation of powers was a fundamental principle of state organization. The Interim Constitution also affirmed political pluralism as a fundamental principle of democracy in Albania, and diversity of ownership as a basis for economic development, with all its forms enjoying equal protection by law.

The Constitution of Albania was approved on November 28, 1998. The new constitution was adopted on Albanian Independence Day. An ad hoc parliamentary committee had drafted it through an open and participatory process. It was then approved by the Parliament and voted on by the people in a national referendum. Many prominent experts who contributed to the new constitution have stated that it fully complies with democratic standards. The preamble of the constitution reflects the human, moral, ethical, and national aspects of Albanian society. The unity and common good, and the preservation of human values, are contemplated at the very outset of the preamble: "*We, the People of Albania.*" It also indicates that it is a product of aspiration for freedom, prosperity, and progress after prolonged oppression and frequent violation of human dignity.

At the very outset the constitution guarantees a republican form of government, and reaffirms the principle of national sovereignty, separation of powers, and political pluralism. The bill of rights is incorporated in the constitution. It guarantees personal rights and freedoms. Under the constitution, human rights are indivisible, inalienable, and inviolable, and stand at the center of the entire juridical order. The constitution guarantees the freedoms of expression, press, and religion. As a member state of the Council of Europe, Albania also undertakes all rights and obligations deriving from the European Convention of Human Rights. The principle of nondiscrimination and equality before the law is significantly important in a country that has suffered from the violation of those principles. It also provides for the rule of law and fair trial, an opportunity to be heard, and the principle of presumption of innocence.

Economic, social, and cultural rights and freedoms have been dealt with extensively in the Albanian Constitution. The constitution entitles everyone to the right to earn a living by lawful work. Employees have the right to social protection of work, and to unite freely in labor organizations for the defense of their work interests.

The Albanian parliament (Kuvendi) is unicameral. It consists of 140 members, who are elected directly in single-member electoral zones. Forty deputies are elected from the multiname lists of parties or party coalitions according to their respective order. The Albanian election system is a mix between a majority (direct election) and a proportional (general percentage of votes won) system. Parties that receive less than 2.5 percent, and party coalitions that receive less than 4 percent of the valid votes on the national scale in the first round of elections do not benefit from their respective multiname lists. The parliament approves the laws in the country, but the president promulgates them.

The president of Albania is the head of state and represents the unity of the people. Only an Albanian citizen by birth who has been a resident in Albania for not less than ten consecutive years before election and who has reached the age of forty may be elected president. The president may not hold any other public duty, may not be a member of a party or carry out other private activity. The parliament elects the president for a term of five years with the right of re-election only once. The duties of the president vary from the exercise of the right of pardon according to the law to appointments and withdrawals of plenipotentiary representatives of the Republic of Albania to other states and international organizations; from acceptance of letters of credential and the withdrawal of diplomatic representatives of other states and international organizations accredited to the Republic of Albania to the signing of international agreements according to the law. The president of the republic, in the exercise of his powers, issues decrees.

The Council of Ministers is composed of the prime minister, the deputy prime minister, and ministers. The Council of Ministers exercises every state function that is not given to other organs of state power or to local government. The real executive power is exercised by the prime minister, who is formally appointed by the president to form the government. The prime minister ensures the implementation of policies approved by the Council of Ministers, and coordinates and supervises the work of the members of the Council of Ministers and other institutions of the central administration. Public employees apply the law and are in the service of the people. Employees in the public administration are selected through examinations.

THE HIGH COUNCIL OF JUSTICE (HCJ)
The HCJ is the state authority in charge of appointing, dismissing, transferring, and instituting disciplinary proceedings against judges of primary and secondary instance in the Republic of Albania.

The HCJ consists of the president of the republic, the chief judge of the High Court, the minister of justice, three members elected by the parliament, and nine judges of all levels who are elected by the National Judicial Conference. Elected members stay in office for five years. The president of the republic is the chairman of the HCJ. Upon proposal of the president, the HCJ elects a vice chairman from its ranks. Traditionally, the role of the HCJ has been viewed as limited to its disciplinary competencies. On the other hand, the HCJ does exercise quasi-regulatory powers, which consist of establishing the territorial jurisdiction for the courts of primary instance and those of appeals.

Whereas the question of hierarchy of norms is clear (the constitutional text is to prevail), the situation is complicated by Article 178 of the constitution itself, which stipulates that "statutes or any other normative acts which have came into effect before the adoption of the present Constitution shall be applicable as long as they have not been repealed." The Law on Organization of the Judiciary in Albania was adopted by the assembly after the adoption of the constitution and empowers HCJ to make the nominations. Under the constitution, the president of the republic is empowered to make nominations upon proposal by the HCJ.

To avoid a collision of norms, the Law on the Organization of the Judiciary in Albania was to have been repealed. However, as the law is quite new and crucial for the normal functioning of the judiciary, such a move was spared thanks to the intervention of the Constitutional Court. In one of its rulings, the court took a pragmatic approach to this issue, holding that if the constitutionality of a statute is challenged, the Constitutional Court will try to establish whether the contested statute is found incompatible with the constitution in its entirety, in which case it will have to repeal the law, or only with respect to particular articles.

The functioning of the HCJ inspectorate is provided for in the HCJ internal by-laws. However, adoption of a special law for the functioning of the HCJ has been recommended for a long time, inasmuch as the effects of the HCJ's work are potentially huge.

CURRENT COURT SYSTEM STRUCTURE
Under the Albanian Constitution the judicial power is exercised by the High Court, as well as the courts of appeal and courts of first instance, which are established by special law. Parliament has the right to pass special laws by which other courts are contemplated. The members of the High Court are appointed by the president of the republic with the consent of the parliament. The chief judge and members of the High Court hold the office for nine years without the right of reappointment. The other judges in the courts of appeal and first instance courts are

Legal Structure of Albania Courts

High Court
Has original and review jurisdiction.

Organized in colleges, which are: civil, criminal, administrative, and commercial.

6 Courts of Appeal
Review on appeal decisions of Courts of First Instance.

1 Military Court of Appeal
Reviews on appeal decisions of Military Courts of First Instance. Has jurisdiction throughout the territory of the Republic of Albania.

29 Courts of First Instance
With jurisdiction over civil and criminal cases. Administrative, commercial, and family sections operate within the Courts of First Instance.

5 Military Courts of First Instance
Their territorial jurisdiction is established with a presidential decree. They are part of the Courts of First Instance structure.

Constitutional Court
Reviews constitutionality of laws and decisions approved by the Parliament and government. Has original and review jurisdiction over constitutionality matters.

Makes interpretation of the constitution through judicial review.

appointed by the president of the republic upon the proposal of the High Council of Justice. Judges of the High Court enjoy the same guarantees against prosecution as the president.

The Albanian system of justice consists of district courts, courts of appeal, and the High Court. Each level deals with civil, criminal, commercial, and administrative cases. The military system of justice is included in the criminal justice system. The Albanian system of justice has 346 judges and 226 assistant judges divided into twenty-nine district courts, six appellate courts, one military appellate court, and the High Court. Judges are independent and subject only to the constitution and the laws. A law that comes into conflict with the constitution is not applied; judges will suspend the proceedings and send the issue to the Constitutional Court. Decisions of the Constitutional Court are obligatory for all courts.

The time a judge stays on duty cannot be limited; judges' pay and other benefits cannot be lowered.

Courts of First Instance

Also called district courts, these are the basic element of the judiciary system. There are 302 judges, 226 assistant judges, and 341 judicial secretaries working in these courts. The district courts have general jurisdiction. As a consequence they have a considerable workload. Criminal cases are adjudicated in a panel of three judges when they deal with crimes and one judge and two assistant judges when they deal with misdemeanors. This system is due to change soon, as the position of assistant judge is being eliminated as part of the overall reform of Albania's legal system, a World Bank long-term project that is expected to last between five and eight years. A single judge will adjudicate crimes the sentence for which is up to five years' imprisonment. A panel of three judges will adjudicate more serious crimes. The criminal code requires special judges for juvenile cases; however, that has not been implemented at present (as of 2001). The criminal courts have jurisdiction over all criminal cases, with the exception of those that fall under the jurisdiction of the military courts.

Civil cases (including administrative and commercial cases) are reviewed by a panel composed of one judge and two assistant judges (following the approaching reform, civil cases will be adjudicated by a single judge). All civil conflicts fall under their jurisdiction. Special sections on administrative, commercial, and family cases are created within the first instance court.

Although the law provides for the establishment of military courts of first instance, these courts function as specially developed "colleges" within the district courts. There are five military courts that have territorial jurisdiction, as defined in a decree of the president of the republic. These courts deal with military crimes, prisoners of war, and other individuals as provided by law. The military courts administer justice in panels of three judges in cases of felonies and with one judge and two assistant judges in misdemeanor cases.

Courts of Appeal

Albania has six courts of appeal and one military court of appeal, the latter with jurisdiction throughout the territory of the republic. The appellate courts have forty-seven judges and ninety-seven support staff. The courts of appeal review appeals against the decisions of the first instance courts. They deliver their decisions in panels of three judges.

High Court

The High Court has original and review jurisdiction. The organization of the High Court has undergone continuous changes. The procedural competencies of the High Court are provided for in the Codes of Criminal and Civil Procedure. Competencies of a substantive nature are provided for by the Law on the Organization and Functioning of the High Court and the Administration of Judicial Services. High Court judges are organized in "colleges" (civil, criminal, administrative, and commercial). As many as fourteen legal advisors assist the judges with research work. A High Court judge's tenure in office ends when the judge: (a) is convicted of a crime with a final judicial decision; (b) does not appear for duty without reason for more than six months; (c) reaches the age of sixty-five; or (d) resigns. Judicial decisions must be reasoned. The High Court publishes its decisions as well as the minority opinions.

Constitutional Court and Judicial Review

The Albanian Constitution establishes the Constitutional Court, which guarantees respect for the constitution and makes final interpretations of it. Unlike some countries with constitutional courts where only a certain category of persons—that is, public officials—can challenge the constitutionality of a law through judicial review, the Albanian Constitution allows individuals as well to petition the Constitutional Court for judicial review.

STAFFING

These is no limitation on the number of practicing attorneys, although membership in the bar association is required. Albania has two law schools, each belonging to a different university: the University of Tirana, and the University of Shkoder. The more renowned and the larger is that of the University of Tirana. The majority of judges, prosecutors, and practicing attorneys have graduated from the University of Tirana School of Law. Law graduates aspiring to become judges, upon graduation from law school, must attend another three years of specialized education to become a judge at the Magistrates School in Tirana.

IMPACT OF LAW

The efficient operation of the Albanian justice system is of fundamental importance. The collapse of fraudulent pyramid schemes showed that the road toward consolidation of the legal system is long and not an easy one. Along with it, a strong legal culture is being built, first through a massive program of civic and legal education in schools and in the media. The process of selection, nomination, appointment, and education of judges and magistrates must be fair, nonpartisan, and based on merit only. Secondly, legislative drafting must bear in consideration the evolution of Albanian society and its expectations. Adoption of the new constitution as the supreme law has paved the way for other laws as well, which will in turn contribute to the improvement of the administration of justice, and in the long run will be a solid support for the country's future development.

Richard T. Oakes
Agri Verrija

See also Civil Law; Customary Law; Constitutional Law; European Court and Commission of Human Rights; Human Rights Law; Islamic Law; Judicial Independence; Judicial Review; Marxist Jurisprudence
References and further reading
Elezi, Dr. Prof. Ismet. 1999. *Mendimi Juridik Shqiptar.* Albin Tirane.
European Convention of Human Rights.
USAID. 1999. *Albania: Country Profile.* http://www.usaid.gov/ countries/al/alb.htm (cited December 5, 2001).

ALBERTA

Alberta is the fourth-largest of ten provinces in the Canadian federal system; it is also the "average" province, with roughly 10 percent of the national population. As in the other provinces, the population is largely urban. However, Alberta's people are divided between two major cities (Edmonton and Calgary) located 200 miles apart, rather than in a single large urban center, as is the usual Canadian pattern. This demographic fact has had an impact on the structure and the organization of the provincial court system, as will be explained.

JURISDICTION

With regard to the criminal law, the Canadian constitution in practice is a little complicated. The criminal law (most of which is found in the Criminal Code of Canada) is reserved to the exclusive jurisdiction of the Parliament of Canada. As the courts have defined it, criminal law is a prohibition plus a penalty directed to an appropriate public purpose; and the federal power has been treated as "free-standing," which means that by making certain activities criminal the national government can regulate matters which are otherwise within provincial jurisdiction. However, the provincial government can also create prohibitions-plus-penalties (technically "offenses" rather than "crimes"), although these must be clearly ancillary to the province's substantive heads of power and they cannot infringe on federal powers. These offenses often overlap with, or even duplicate, federal criminal laws, but the Supreme Court's very relaxed approach to paramountcy (which is triggered only by explicit contradiction between national and provincial laws) has prevented this from being a problem in practice. Both federal "crimes" and provincial "offenses" are handled by the same courts; the Canadian system is a single rather than a double pyramid. Civil law is largely a matter of provincial legislative jurisdiction—involving contracts, personal property, landlord-tenant disputes, labor relations, and so on—although the federal Parliament enjoys jurisdiction over many labor and commercial issues relating to the essential elements of railway or airplane transportation and radio (and, more recently, telephone) communication.

Most of the judicial pyramid is under provincial jurisdiction. The provincial legislature establishes and maintains the provincial courts and sets the procedure for civil matters, although the federal Parliament has authority over criminal procedure. The question of the prosecution power is curiously clouded; until the 1970s, provincial Crown prosecutors exercised prosecutorial discretion under federal criminal law statutes, but a string of decisions issued by the Supreme Court of Canada cast this in doubt before settling on a de facto concurrent power—*most* such prosecutions are conducted by provincial employees, but *some* are carried out by federal Crown prosecutors. The policing power is almost exclusively in the hands of the provinces (sometimes delegated to cities or municipalities), although this matter is complicated by the fact that eight provinces have contracted with the federal police force (the Royal Canadian Mounted Police) to act as a provincial police force; only Ontario and Quebec operate their own provincial police.

THE LEGAL PROFESSION

The legal profession in Canada is defined on a provincial basis, and provincial law societies are the self-governing bodies that control access to the profession and police its practices. The Law Society of Alberta derives its authority from the Legal Profession Act of Alberta. Its central body is composed of the twenty benchers who are elected at large every two years by the profession, with each of the three districts (north, south, and central) outside of Calgary and Edmonton being entitled to at least one member regardless of the outcome of the vote.

To be admitted to the practice of law, one must have a law degree from a recognized university. In practice, over 90 percent of all Alberta lawyers are graduates of one of the two Alberta law schools (the University of Alberta and the University of Calgary). Lawyers must then serve two years of articles (a practical apprenticeship under the supervision of a qualified lawyer) and pass a bar exam set by the Alberta Law Society. Only members of the society may practice law in the province, and the society has the power to suspend or disbar members who are found to have violated the rules of the profession. There are currently about 5,000 active members of the Alberta bar.

THE COURTS

The Canadian court system in general, of which the Alberta court system is a fairly standard example, has two curious features. The first is that there is a single hierarchy of trial and appeal courts dealing with both federal and provincial laws, rather than two separate hierarchies. The second is that the judges in some provincial courts are appointed by the federal government, a uniquely Canadian device that has historically caused far fewer practical problems than one might have anticipated.

Legal Structure of Alberta Courts

Court of Appeal

Court of Queen's Bench

Provincial Court	
Civil Division	Criminal Division
Family Division	Youth Division

At the lowest formal level of the provincial court system is the Provincial Court of Alberta. This "purely provincial" court was established in 1971, replacing the Magistrates' Court but differing from it in several significant ways. First, although a number of lay magistrates have been "grandfathered" in, only lawyers in good standing with at least five years of experience can become provincial judges. Second, unlike the Magistrates' Court, the Provincial Court is a court of record, meaning that appeals are judged on the record and not tried de novo. Third, again unlike the Magistrates' Court, the Provincial Court has a chief judge, who has general administrative and governmental liaison responsibilities. Fourth, the Judicial Council for Provincial Judges has been established, including judicial members from all three levels of the Provincial Court, a bencher from the law society, and several lay members; this council both screens applications for judicial appointments and sits as a discipline committee without whose recommendation a provincial judge cannot be removed from office.

Judges of the Provincial Court are appointed and paid by the provincial government (after screening by the nonpartisan Judicial Council), and they retire at age seventy. They serve "on good behavior" (the corresponding term for magistrates was "at pleasure") and can only be removed for cause after a formal inquiry process dominated by judicial members. As of 2001, there were 117 provincial judges, including a chief judge and 9 assistant chief judges—1 for the 7-judge Civil Division, 2 for the 18 judges of the Family and Youth Division, and 6 regional assistant chief judges for the 92-judge Criminal Division. As the relative size of these divisions indicates, the bulk of workload of the Provincial Court is in the area of criminal law.

The jurisdiction of the Provincial Court includes:
- Offenses under provincial legislation
- Summary conviction ("misdemeanor") offenses under federal legislation, defined as offenses for which the maximum penalty is six months in prison and/or a fine of Can$2,000
- Preliminary hearings for indictable offenses ("felonies") under federal legislation

- Trials for indictable offenses in which the accused has chosen trial by provincial judge
- Trials for young offenders accused of any federal or provincial offense (unless successful application has been made to move the matter to adult court)
- Family matters, except for divorce and child custody
- Civil matters below an arbitrary dollar limit (currently Can$7,500)

Provincial judges sit alone and without a jury. The fact that the accused can (and often does) elect trial by provincial judge for serious indictable offenses means that it is incorrect to think of provincial judges as dealing only with minor matters; in fact, such an assumption is less true in Canada's judicial system than in any other court system in the world.

On the next level of the court system in Alberta is the Court of Queen's Bench. This is one of the "provincial superior courts" described in Section 96 of the Constitution Act of 1867. It is unusual because it is a provincial court (and therefore established and maintained by the provincial legislature under the authority of Section 92.14) but its judges are appointed and paid by the government of Canada, retiring at age seventy. Each province has a Section 96 trial court; the terminology varies, but "Queen's Bench" is the most common name for such a court.

As a general rule, "purely provincial" lower court judges are rarely elevated to the provincial superior court. The major explanation for this fact is political, for the appointments are made by two different levels of government. A structural element may be involved as well: It is sometimes suggested that the distinction between the two sets of courts is best described in terms of specialization (with criminal and family matters being heard by the "purely provincial" court and mainly civil matters being heard by the provincial superior court). Some observers still maintain that the distinction relates instead to merit: The better lawyers wait for—and would not settle for less than—appointment to the higher court.

Like most of the other provinces, Alberta has consolidated its provincial superior trial courts, which formerly comprised two different levels—the District Court and the Supreme Court, Trial Division. In 1979, the two trial courts were consolidated into the new Court of Queen's Bench, and the numbers of judges significantly expanded. As of 2001, there were 79 Queen's Bench justices, 60 men and 19 women. Of these, 37 (including the chief justice) reside in Edmonton, 34 (including the associate chief justice) reside in Calgary, and 8 reside in smaller cities (3 in Lethbridge in the south, 4 in Red Deer in the central part of the province, and 1 in Grande Prairie in the north). All judges spend a part of the year (theoretically, one-third) on circuit to other parts of the province, the principle being that the Alberta Court of Queen's Bench is a single multijudge court serving the entire province.

The provincial superior trial courts are courts of general jurisdiction, with extensive responsibilities covering both civil and criminal cases. On criminal matters, they hear indictable offenses (that is, felonies) in which the accused has not elected trial by the lower "purely provincial" court; this can include jury trials, which are more common than they were twenty or thirty years ago. On civil matters, which constitute a majority of the caseload, they deal with major lawsuits (those over the small claims limit). The provincial superior courts are the longest-standing courts in Canada, the core around which the other courts have been constructed. The case law still acknowledges the provincial superior court as the court with the power to rule on the constitutionality of statutes and bylaws, the legality of administrative tribunals, and the determination of violation and remedy under the Canadian Charter of Rights and Freedoms. The provincial superior court is also the court of appeal for decisions rendered by a provincial court (except for indictable offenses, for which appeal lies directly to the Alberta Court of Appeal). Since the establishment of the provincial court in 1971, the appeals handled by the provincial superior court are judged "on the record," rather than by trial de novo, and they constitute only a small part of the Queen's Bench caseload. Unlike the lower court, the Court of Queen's Bench is a generalist bench, and the typical judge will, over any reasonable period of time, preside over trials involving all types of cases.

At one time, one would have explained the central position of the provincial superior trial courts by citing the fact that they were the only courts to enjoy a constitutionally entrenched judicial independence: Section 99 of the Constitution Act of 1867 stipulates that their judges hold office "on good behavior" and are removable only by the actions of both the Senate and the House of Commons (something that has happened only once in Canadian history). However, judicial independence now enjoys a firmer constitutional status. For one thing, a guarantee of an "independent and impartial tribunal" is part of the Canadian Charter of Rights and Freedoms; for another, recent Supreme Court decisions have suggested judicial independence as a "constitutive constitutional principle" that is exemplified rather than constituted by Section 99 and the charter. In either case, it is now less accurate than before (and therefore less significant in terms of relative status) to suggest that any one set of courts enjoys a more firmly established degree of judicial independence than the others.

At the highest level of the province's court system is the Court of Appeal of Alberta. In constitutional terms, this court is also a provincial superior court, which means that it is established and maintained by the province, but its judges are appointed and paid by the government of Canada. Over any period of time, it would appear that about half the judges of the Alberta Court of Appeal are elevated from the provincial superior trial courts, and a roughly comparable number are appointed directly to the Court of Appeal as their first judicial appointments.

The Court of Appeal in 2001 consisted of fourteen judges, one of whom is the chief justice of Alberta. Alberta is the first province to have had a woman chief justice (Catherine Fraser) and is also the first province in which women judges have constituted a majority of the Court of Appeal (currently eight of fourteen). The Alberta court is unusual for the fact that not all of its judges reside in the same urban center—seven of the fourteen (including the chief justice) live in Edmonton, and seven live in Calgary. There is an informal convention of alternating the chief justiceship between the two centers. The court generally functions as if it was a single entity—it sits in alternate months in each of the two cities, with the judges relocating to hear oral arguments. There is also a strong attempt to arrange the panel rotations so as to avoid panels consisting only of judges from a single city.

The appellate caseload in Canada varies in a rather haphazard way from province to province. Although Alberta is the fourth-largest province, its Court of Appeal has consistently had the second-largest caseload in the country (the largest belongs to Ontario, which has more than triple the population). This situation is partly the product of different counting procedures—an "appeal from conviction and sentence" in Alberta is normally split into its two elements, both of which are resolved and counted separately—but the observation survives recalculation on a more standardized basis. Alberta is also one of the provinces in which the appellate caseload is predominantly criminal, something that is not true of, for example, the neighboring Province of British Columbia.

Like the other provincial courts of appeal, the Alberta Court of Appeal is required by its governing legislation to receive "reference questions" from the provincial government—that is, it issues "advisory opinions" in response to hypothetical questions framed by the provincial government that do not arise out of concrete cases in the normal appeal process. These questions are often narrowly technical, but they can be politically loaded. For instance, the Alberta court dealt with one reference on the national government's goods and services tax (GST) and another on the more recent federal gun control legislation. These examples demonstrate the blending of federal and provincial responsibilities: The provincial government asked the federally appointed judges of a provincial court about the constitutionality of a piece of federal legislation.

Like the other Canadian courts of appeal, the Alberta court has chosen to deal with the growing caseload by sitting in panels (normally made up of three judges, excep-

tionally consisting of five). The advantage of the panel procedure is that it maximizes the caseload capacity of the court while containing the workload of individual judges; the disadvantage is that it can lead to fragmentation. The Alberta Court of Appeal has sought to contain this danger in several ways. First, panels are rotated frequently. Second, the court is small enough to benefit from a considerable amount of informal exchange at mealtimes or in the coffee room. Third, draft judgments on reserved cases are circulated to all members of the court, not just to members of the immediate panel. If it should turn out that the panel is seriously out of step with from the rest of the court, procedures allow reargument before an expanded panel, a device that is seldom used. Like the provincial superior trial court, the Court of Appeal is a generalist court that works without specialized panels.

The Alberta Court of Appeal uses judges from the provincial superior trial court on an ad hoc basis—a product of the fact that Section 96 courts consist of federally appointed judges on provincially established courts, which means that Alberta can include legislative provisions that have no parallel in other jurisdictions. Many criminal appeal panels include a single provincial superior trial judge sitting with two appeal court judges, and *most* of the sentence appeal panels consist of two provincial superior trial judge sitting with a single appeal court judge. The practice is defended on three grounds. First, it expands the caseload capacity of the court. Second, it prevents the appeal court from losing touch with the working realities of the trial bench (and vice versa). Third, it both permits the identification of potential talent and reduces the transition from trial to appeal for subsequently elevated judges.

Based on such criteria as Supreme Court reversal rates or citation frequencies, the Alberta Court of Appeal ranked second in reputation only to the Ontario Court of Appeal among the English-speaking Canadian provinces before 1945. More recently, however, it has yielded this distinction to the British Columbia Court of Appeal. Although the Alberta court has recently generated a few unusually heated exchanges with the Supreme Court of Canada (SCC) (most particularly between Alberta's John W. McClung and the SCC's Claire L'Heureux-Dubé, which rippled from a Supreme Court decision into the *Toronto Globe and Mail* letters to the editor and finally came before the Canadian Judicial Council), it is not reversed particularly often, and those reversals that do occur do not generally have any persisting ideological or philosophical patterns.

Although it is the pinnacle of the Alberta court system, the Court of Appeal is an intermediate appeal court within the Canadian system, and its decisions are subject to appeal to the Supreme Court of Canada. It is worth noting that this is true of *all* court of appeal decisions:

Under the Canadian Constitution, the Supreme Court is a "General Court of Appeal for Canada," and there is, therefore, no Canadian counterpart to the U.S. principle that state supreme courts are the final courts of appeal on matters of purely state law. The convention of Supreme Court appointments in Canada is that most Supreme Court judges are elevated from provincial courts of appeal, with a "prairie provinces" seat that rotates between Alberta, Saskatchewan, and Manitoba. In 2001, the holder of that seat was John C. Major, who served on the Alberta Court of Appeal for sixteen months in 1991 and 1992.

Peter McCormick

See also British Columbia; Canada; Northern Territories of Canada; Saskatchewan

References and further reading

"Alberta Courts." http://www.albertacourts.ab.ca/index.htm (cited November 29, 2001).

Gall, Gerald. 1995. *The Canadian Legal System.* Toronto: Carswell.

"The Law Society of Alberta." http://www.lawsocietyalberta.com (cited November 29, 2001).

McCormick, Peter. 1994. *Canada's Courts.* Toronto: James Lorimer.

McCormick, Peter, and Ian Greene. 1990. *Judges and Judging: Inside the Canadian Judicial System.* Toronto: James Lorimer.

Russell, Peter. 1987. *The Judiciary in Canada: The Third Branch of Government.* Toronto: McGraw Hill-Ryerson.

ALGERIA

COUNTRY INFORMATION

The Democratic and Popular Republic of Algeria, the second-largest country in Africa, covers an area of 2,381,741 square kilometers (about one-third the size of the continental United States) and shares borders with Morocco and the disputed Western Sahara to the west; Mauritania, Mali, and Niger to the south; and Libya and Tunisia to the east. The country also has a Mediterranean coastline of about 1,500 kilometers. Despite Algeria's huge size, fully 80 percent of the country is desert wasteland, and only 12 percent is suitable for agricultural purposes, almost entirely in the relatively narrow coastal zone, which includes the foothills of the Aurés Mountains. The Algerian population stood at an estimated 29,276,767 in 1998 and has been rapidly urbanizing as well as growing by 3 percent per annum, one of the highest growth rates in the world. The economy is narrowly based, with over 90 percent of export-related hard-currency earnings being derived from the sale of oil and natural gas, which accounts for Algeria's high annual per capita income of approximately $1,600.

When compared with other Arab/Islamic states, Algeria's population is relatively homogeneous, but divisions exist between the majority Arabs and the substantial minority of Berbers (Amazighs), which most recently led to severe civil unrest in the spring of 2001. Virtually all Algerians, Arabs and Berbers alike, are Muslim, and the literacy rate in the country grew rapidly after independence, from 10 percent in 1962 to 53 percent in the late 1990s, although rural and female rates were lower. Overall life expectancy in the early 1990s was 67.1 years (68.3 years for women and 66.0 years for men).

HISTORY

Before achieving independence from France in 1962, Algeria had long been a crossroads for foreign occupiers, including the Phoenecians and the Empire of Carthage. After the Roman Empire vanquished Carthage, it ruled Algeria for several centuries, bestowing many of the attributes of an advanced civilization on the area, including cities and towns, important public works, and an abundant food supply. After Rome's displacement by Byzantium, Arab armies from the east took control of the North African coast in about 700 C.E. and gradually converted the indigenous Berbers to Islam. Several dynasties established themselves in the territory during the period from 700 to the early 1500s, and starting around 1518, Ottoman Turkish rule put an end to political participation by Arabs and Berbers, with a succession of Turkish naval officers exercising most of the authority.

Concurrent with the gradual eclipse of the Ottoman Empire in the early nineteenth century, France became steadily more involved in Algeria's fate, as disputes between some of the remaining native leaders and French commercial and governmental interests eventually led to the capture of Algiers by Paris in 1830 and the whole territory's annexation as a French *département* four years later. From that point onward, European settlement became inexorable: By the late 1840s, over 100,000 Europeans had moved to Algeria. There, they enjoyed a privileged status above ordinary Muslims and steadily occupied the best agricultural land, in spite of the strong armed resistance mounted against the French from 1839 to 1847 by the prominent religious leader Emir Abdel Qadir, who was finally defeated and forced into exile by the early 1850s. Having suffered a great loss of life (mostly Muslim), Algeria remained quiet until after the end of World War I.

After World War I had punctured the myth of the moral superiority of the European powers, Algerian nationalist sentiment began to develop, although the people at first rejected full independence in favor of better civil rights for Muslims under French rule. World War II, by contrast, led to increased demands for equal treatment, and after the Sétif Massacre of May 1945 and the associated brutal reprisals by the French army and its settler supporters, a full-scale anticolonial revolt was probably inevitable. After the formation of a revolutionary movement, the Front de Libération Nationale (National Liberation Front, or FLN), in the early 1950s, a rebellion against Paris was finally launched on November 1, 1954, with the announced goal of achieving full Algerian independence. For the next four years, a bloody war was waged by the French against the FLN, with the Algerians also engaging in acts of indiscriminate urban terrorism. So deep had the Algerian crisis become for France that Premier Charles de Gaulle was recalled to power in June 1958. Exercising his power virtually by decree, de Gaulle quietly sought to neutralize the FLN while at the same time exploring some form of political compromise, eventually recognizing that a war-weary France needed to be released from its obligations in Algeria. To that end, he negotiated with Ahmed Ben Bella and other prominent (and imprisoned) FLN leaders, weathered a serious revolt by elements of the French army, and brokered the so-called Evian Accords, which provided for the granting of independence under FLN governance. Algeria finally achieved independence on July 5, 1962.

The country faced grave difficulties as a member of the international community from the start. A shortage of civil servants and skilled workers and a traumatized populace all hampered efforts at economic development. President Ben Bella, for his part, felt that a state-centered economy was best suited to Algerian needs, but he increasingly appropriated most power to himself. Partly for that reason, he was overthrown in June 1965 by his defense minister, Col. Houari Boumedienne, a prominent guerrilla leader. Boumedienne continued the socialist orientation of Algeria during his term in office (from 1965 to 1978) but still kept the country in the hands of a trusted group of military officers. Boumedienne's death in December 1978 and the accession to the presidency by Col. Chadli Benjedid several weeks later brought a considerable loosening of the bonds of dictatorship but also an increase in corruption and inequality among Algerian citizens. In this environment and parallel with the rise of Islamic fundamentalism elsewhere, Algerian Islamists rapidly acquired a higher profile, taking advantage of broadly based and violent protests against the Benjedid government in October 1988 to press for the institution of "Islamic" norms, based on the *sharia,* the Muslim legal code.

President Benjedid reacted to the unrest and the Islamist upsurge by briefly making Algeria probably the most democratic Arab country in the world between 1989 and 1992. But the military establishment—unwilling to face the prospect of an Islamist regime after the primary Muslim fundamentalist group, the Front Islamique de Salut (Islamic Salvation Front, or FIS), achieved notable successes at the ballot box in elections in 1990 and 1991—forced Benjedid to resign in January 1992 and canceled all further elections. Political power

devolved to the Haut Conseil de l'Etat (High State Council, or HCE), an improvised body without constitutional or popular legitimacy. The Islamist groups refused to accept being deprived of power and driven underground, and so, over the following decade, they waged a war of extreme brutality against the Algerian security forces, which responded with atrocities of their own. Over 100,000 Algerians were thought to have been killed by 2001, often in horrific circumstances—particularly in rural areas, where whole villages were sometimes wiped out, whether by the Islamists or the army few outsiders could know. Gen. Liamine Zéroual, the HCE leader in the late 1990s, recognized the utter despair of his compatriots (and the relative weakness of the Islamists) and therefore facilitated—in controversial electoral circumstances—the election of former foreign minister Abdelaziz Bouteflika to the presidency in April 1999. High hopes were generated by Bouteflika's election, and a "civil harmony" program of amnesty and disarmament for the fundamentalists raised expectations further. However, a continued high level of violence, renewed Berber protest, and an endemic lack of true democracy all made Algeria's plight in 2001 as seemingly intractable as it appeared to be ten years earlier.

LEGAL CONCEPTS

Algeria is a unitary republic in which authority flows directly from the central government in Algiers down to the provincial and local levels. Its legal system, like those in certain other Arab countries, is a mixture of traditional Islamic law and French-influenced secular jurisprudence, with the latter affecting nearly all areas of the law except those relating only to personal status. There are a total of 48 provinces *(wilayaat)* of greatly varying size, which are further subdivided into 214 administrative districts *(dairaat).* Both provinces and districts possess their own courts, with differing powers depending on their jurisdictions. Military and special antiterrorist tribunals also existed at various times after independence, but they were abolished (most recently in 1995) in an effort to curb the abuses inherent in the use of these courts; another reason for their abolition was the government's greatly increased confidence that it would eventually prevail against the Islamist insurgency. Also provided for by the Constitution of Algeria are the Higher Judicial Council, the Constitutional Council, and a financial court that tries cases of malfeasance by civil servants.

Historically, the laws of Algeria have been imposed by outsiders: first by the Ottoman Turks and then by the French from 1830 to 1962. The French, for their part, consciously supplanted the traditional, Quran-based Muslim laws in favor of their own, especially in the case of European settlers, who from the beginning had their own legal code wholly divorced from Islamic law. However, since the average Muslim Algerian under colonial rule (especially in rural areas) had little or no contact with the French administration and usually desired none, Islamic law as applied by the local *qadi (qazi)* courts was nearly always the furthest extent of their interactions with any type of legal system. These informal tribunals dealt with personal-status questions and with criminal law and civil matters, as well as family law areas such as marriage, divorce, and inheritance. The Berbers always expressed a preference for their own customary laws—not necessarily wholly Islamic in character—and the small Jewish population that lived in Algeria during Ottoman and French times was governed by rabbinical courts until 1842, when they were officially abolished by Paris. Algerian Jews, though, continued to utilize their own dispute resolution processes until 1870, when France's Crémieux Decree conferred full French citizenship to all Jewish residents. In terms of Islamic law, moreover, the qadi (qazi) courts were never quite as autonomous as they might have appeared at first glance. French colonial officials appointed all the qadis, and French courts sometimes took it on themselves to interpret Islamic law, a practice that deepened anticolonial resentments over time.

After Algerian independence was achieved in July 1962, the new government faced a dilemma in the legal sphere. On the one hand, the new state's identity was self-consciously Muslim; on the other hand, it was just as self-consciously socialist and thus secularist, at least on the official level. The Ben Bella regime, perhaps unsurprisingly, attempted to "split the difference": It paid what turned out to be lip service to Islam while at the same time retaining the French legal and judicial structure, all the while promising a thorough revision of legal codes to incorporate both Islamic and secular principles. In any case, judges were explicitly required to safeguard the socialist revolution in their work, and tensions remained between traditionalists and secularists on family law issues, particularly on the status of women in society. It was not until July 1975, under President Houari Boumedienne, that new civil and criminal codes were promulgated and Arabic made the official language of the justice system. Even then, however, some controversial matters were either sidestepped or eliminated entirely from the new laws. In January 1982, the new Penal Code was introduced, but the government continued to avoid family law questions until 1984, when the new Family Code was put into effect over the vociferous protests of women's groups, secularists, and international public opinion.

It is the Family Code, more than any other document or segment of Algerian law, that bears the imprint of Islam most clearly. Under the code, women occupy a subordinate position in relation to men in that they owe a husband a duty of obedience, cannot marry non-Muslims (although Muslim men can marry non-Muslim women), cannot inherit property to the same extent as a male, and are subject to divorce by simple repudiation and having a husband take one or more additional wives (polygyny, however, is exceedingly uncommon in Algeria). Women do have the right to sue for divorce in the event of desertion or nonsupport, and the Family Code also has eliminated—ostensibly, at any rate—the former practice of arranged marriages or marriages to child brides. A woman must be at least eighteen years of age to marry, as opposed to twenty-one years for men.

CURRENT STRUCTURE

At the apex of Algeria's system of courts and tribunals is the Supreme Court, sitting in Algiers. Aside from hearing individual cases, it has a supervisory role to ensure the uniform application of the laws. When the Supreme Court reviews the acts of the lower courts, it does so through the French-derived mechanism of *pouvoir en cassation* (power of abrogation), which is considerably more circumscribed than U.S. concepts of judicial review in that it is limited to questions of procedure only and not issues of both law and fact. Also unlike its U.S. counterpart, the Algerian Supreme Court is not generally permitted to pass on the legality or constitutionality of governmental actions, a fact that underscores the judiciary's lack of real independence from the executive branch. Substantively, the Supreme Court has shown a decided preference in its decisions in favor of Islamic law over secular law, and it is divided into four chambers for the purpose of deciding specific cases. The first chamber, which deals with private law, encompasses civil and commercial matters; the second, handling social law, covers labor laws and regulations and related ordinances; the third addresses criminal law matters; and the fourth chamber deals with administrative law and has jurisdiction over the workings of the civil service.

Below the Supreme Court, Algeria also has 48 Provincial (*wilaya*) Courts, one for each province, with three judges each. These courts also consist of four chambers: the civil, criminal, and administrative law chambers and the Chamber of Accusation, performing a function similar to a grand jury in the United States in criminal cases. Indeed, the Provincial Courts have original jurisdiction in cases of serious crime and appellate jurisdiction in the balance of cases. Once the provincial Chamber of Accusation indicts a person, a trial is held before the three judges and four nonlawyer "jurors." The 214 District (*daira*) Tribunals, with a single judge each, stand at the lowest level of the Algerian judicial hierarchy. Known to rely less on legal formality than on the country's other courts, the tribunals function more as dispute resolution forums for ordinary citizens. Islamic, rather than secular, law is the primary area of expertise of these bodies, and they have original jurisdiction over most civil and many criminal cases, particularly for offenses defined as misdemeanors in Anglo-American law and called *délits* and *contraventions* in Algerian jurisprudence, the latter offenses being less serious and punished only by very small fines.

SPECIALIZED JUDICIAL BODIES

Over and above the array of regular courts in Algeria, several other courts or law-related bodies, some still functioning and others abolished, have directly impacted the administration of justice. Aside from military courts-martial (which were under the control of the president of the republic and the minister of defense and which judged only infractions committed by active military personnel) and the Administrative Court for Financial Accountability (which sanctioned civil servants accused of finance-related offenses), the State Security Court and the Anti-Terrorist Courts provided the most intrusive means for the Algerian government to prosecute and imprison those suspected of involvement in antistate activities. These courts were not abolished until 1995, when reform legislation supported by President Liamine Zeroual eliminated both tribunals.

The State Security Court was the oldest of the special courts; it was established by President Boumedienne, sat in the city of Médéa, and was composed of high-ranking officers in the armed forces in addition to senior civilian judges. The competence of the court, from whose decisions there was only a very limited right of appeal, extended to a certain class of crimes or conspiracies directly affecting national security, including sabotage, espionage, some economic offenses, and attempts to overthrow the government. Defendants had only limited rights: the right to defense counsel, the right to confront their accusers, and the rights of cross-examination and calling their own witnesses. During the 1975–1992 period, relatively few trials were conducted—it was, after all, a period of stability in Algerian affairs—but after the January 1992 abolition of the democratic process by the armed forces, the State Security Court's three civilian and two military judges sentenced hundreds of Islamists and other regime critics to long terms of imprisonment after summary proceedings that drew extensive international criticism.

The Anti-Terrorist Courts, set up in early 1992 after the start of the antigovernment insurgency by the FIS (and later the Groupe Islamique Armé [GIA; Armed Islamic Group]), used similar procedures and had a composition parallel to that of the State Security Court, except that all judges in these three courts were civilians. They, too, sentenced countless Algerians to long jail terms, often after pretrial detentions that lasted many months. As with the State Security Court, defendants found themselves at a crippling disadvantage, and the government's security departments, including the regular police (Sûreté Nationale) and the powerful and secretive military security agency (Securité Militaire), found their work obtaining convictions considerably simpler. However, trials were generally open to the public, and the abolition of these courts in February 1995 placed all the cases formerly heard by the Anti-Terrorist Courts onto the dockets of the regular civilian-run criminal court system (although many abuses continued).

Two other legal/judicial bodies, the Higher Judicial Council and the Constitutional Council, could not be considered courts because they did not hear specific cases, yet they played a significant role in the administration of justice. The Higher Judicial Council, set up in 1976, assumed some of the Ministry of Justice's supervisory functions over the courts and also made recommendations to the president of the republic concerning judicial appointments. The council is made up mainly of judges on leave from their regular duties, and both the president and the minister of justice are ex officio members. Finally, the Constitutional Council performs some quasi-judicial review functions: It deliberated on the constitutionality of laws, regulations, and treaties with foreign states. It possessed little real autonomy and is a recent innovation, dating from the late 1980s.

STAFFING

Notwithstanding the fact that the legal system in Algeria bears the mark of its French counterpart in many ways, the country, since independence, has not acquired a dynamic and autonomous legal profession, at least as understood in the West. When independence was achieved, the FLN declared socialism to be the guiding principle of the state, and everyone, especially those employed by the government, were expected to place the state's interests ahead of all others. This expectation extended to the judges: Until 1989, the Algerian Constitution stipulated that a major obligation of the judiciary was to uphold and protect the "Algerian Revolution," and moreover, judges did not enjoy guaranteed tenure. In addition, Algerian judges are still appointed directly by the president, and only the High Judicial Council has the authority to challenge his choices. In this single-party, authoritarian environment, a fully independent bar could not develop. Yet an accused person's right to have a defense attorney is officially guaranteed, and lawyers could usually be found to defend criminal cases, as well provide representation in civil matters. And despite the duty of loyalty required of judges, most do have a reputation for fairness, at least in cases in which the state has no direct interest and that do not have political ramifications.

In the past, with Algerian politics and law structured on centralized and socialist lines for much of its history, the legal profession was not seen by most Algerians as a desirable occupation. Algerian women and men who were pursuing higher education generally believed that fields

Legal Structure of Algeria Courts

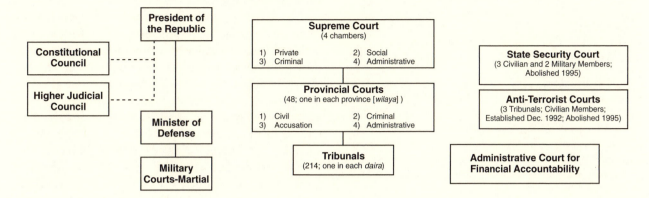

such as engineering, medicine, and the social sciences would offer better opportunities for advancement. This situation began to change in the 1980s with the general opening of Algerian society, the country's drift away from socialism, and the growth of the private economic sector and the consequent demand for attorneys skilled in commercial law. In 2001, there were law schools at the University of Algiers (the country's most prestigious institution), the University of Badji Mokhtar in Annaba, the University of Batna, the University of Constantine, the University of Oran, the University of Ferhat Abbas in Sétif, and the University of Tlemcen. Of course, students have also had the option of pursuing legal education outside the country, particularly in France.

IMPACT

The conditions of intense civil strife and random violence in Algeria during the 1990s gravely impeded the development of legal norms. The court system usually supported the actions of the army-backed Bouteflika government, and the police and other security organs showed few signs of respecting those laws and regulations that existed, further weakening the entire legal structure. Even more ominously, reforms that were intended to ameliorate the severity of the punishments meted out to criminal defendants sometimes had the effect of increasing the level of abuse. For example, the U.S. Department of State, in its *Country Report on Human Rights Practices in Algeria* for the year 2000, reported that the abolition of the State Security Court and the Anti-Terrorist Courts in 1995 (both being notorious for their slant toward the prosecution) made the security forces even more reluctant to release defendants into the regular courts, since those bodies functioned under somewhat more equitable procedures. Consequently, it was believed that long-term pretrial detentions did not measurably decrease in the late 1990s.

By 2001, public confidence in the Algerian legal/judicial process was at its nadir. With judges either beholden to the state or unable to enforce their rulings against the armed forces and the police and with defense attorneys subject to death threats, harassment, and even arbitrary arrest and detention (especially if they represented members of proscribed Islamist groups), it was no surprise to find a growth of militias, vigilante-type groups, and other private means of dispensing "justice." Perceived governmental unfairness toward the Berber population also continued to be an enormous problem, resulting in the Berbers' establishment of armed "self-defense" units that often targeted not only the Algerian government but also the Islamist militants the Berbers had so long opposed. In sum, legal norms were of decidedly secondary importance in Algeria at the start of the twenty-first century. The legal system's difficulties were symptomatic of the troubles of a young nation with few established institutions, an authoritarian regime immune from most public oversight or restraint, and insurgent groups whose activities reached new heights of cruelty during the 1990s. Only the restoration of peace in Algeria, coupled with the inauguration of a government more representative of and responsive to the wishes of its people, will offer Algeria the opportunity to evolve into an authentically law-based society.

Anthony G. Pazzanita

See also Adversarial System; Appellate Courts; Civil Law; Commercial Law; Constitutional Review; Criminal Law; Criminal Procedures; Family Law; Government Legal Departments; Islamic Law; Jewish Law; Judicial Independence; Judicial Misconduct/Judicial Discipline; Judicial Review; Jury Selection; Legal Education; Legal Professionals—Civil Law Traditions; Magistrates—Civil Law Systems; Qadi (Qazi) Courts; Trial Courts

References and further reading
Christelow, Allan. 1985. *Muslim Law Courts and the French Colonial State in Algeria.* Princeton, NJ: Princeton University Press.
Lawless, Richard I. 1995. *World Bibliographical Series: Algeria.* Oxford: Clio Press.

Metz, Helen Chapin, ed. 1994. *Algeria: A Country Study.*
Washington, DC: U.S. Government Printing Office.

Nelson, Harold D., ed. 1985. *Algeria: A Country Study.*
Washington, DC: U.S. Government Printing Office.

Reudy, John. 1992. *Modern Algeria: The Origins and
Development of a Nation.* Bloomington: Indiana University
Press.

Salacuse, Jeswald W. 1975. *An Introduction to Law in
French-Speaking Africa.* Vol. 2, *North Africa.* Charlottesville,
VA: The Michie Company.

Stora, Benjamin. 2001. *Algeria, 1830–2000: A Short History.*
Ithaca, NY: Cornell University Press.

U.S. Department of State. 1995–2001. *Country Reports on
Human Rights Practices.* Washington, DC: U.S. Government
Printing Office.

Willis, Michael. 1996. *The Islamist Challenge in Algeria: A
Political History.* New York: New York University Press.

ALTERNATIVE DISPUTE RESOLUTION

The term *alternative dispute resolution* (ADR) describes
processes used to resolve disputes, either inside or outside
the formal legal system, without formal adjudication and
decision by an officer of the state. The term *"appropriate"
dispute resolution* is used to express the idea that different
kinds of disputes may require different kinds of
processes—there is no one legal or dispute resolution
process that serves for all kinds of human disputing.
ADR includes a variety of different processes, including
mediation, which is a process in which a third party (usually neutral and unbiased) facilitates a negotiated consensual agreement among parties without rendering a formal
decision, and arbitration, which is the most like formal
adjudication and in which a third party or panel of arbitrators, most often chosen by the parties themselves, renders a decision in terms less formal than a court, often
without a written or reasoned opinion and without formal rules of evidence being applied. As noted below, the
full panoply of processes denominated under the rubric
of ADR now includes a variety of primary and hybrid
processes, with elements of dyadic negotiation and facilitative, advisory, and decisional action by a wide variety
of third-party neutrals, sometimes combined with each
other to create new formats of dispute processing.

ADR: WHAT IT IS

In an era characterized by a wide variety of processes for
resolving disputes among individuals, organizations, and
nations, process pluralism has become the norm in both
formal disputing systems, such as legal systems and
courts, and in more informal, private settings, such as
private contracts and transactions, family disputes, and
internal organizational grievance systems. There are a
number of factors that determine the kinds of processes
that parties may choose or may be ordered to use under
rules of law, court, or contract.

The primary processes consist of individual action
(self-help, avoidance), dyadic bargaining (negotiation),
and third-party facilitated approaches (mediation) or
third-party decisional formats (arbitration and adjudication). Hybrid or secondary processes combine elements of
these processes and include mediation-arbitration (facilitated negotiation followed by decision), minitrials (shortened evidentiary proceedings followed by negotiation),
summary jury or judge trials (use of mock jurors or judges
to hear evidence and issue advisory verdicts to assist in negotiation, often conducted within the formal court system), and early neutral evaluation (third parties, usually
lawyers or other experts, who hear arguments and evidence and advise about the issues or values of the dispute
for purposes of facilitating settlement or structuring the
dispute process). Increasing judicial involvement in dispute settlement suggests that judicial (and often mandatory) settlement conferences are another form of hybrid
dispute mechanism. Retired judges provide a hybrid form
of arbitration or adjudication in private "rent-a-judge"
schemes that are sometimes authorized by the state.

Dispute processes are also characterized by the extent
to which they are voluntary and consensual (whether
they are predispute contract agreements or are voluntarily undertaken after the dispute ripens) or whether they
are mandated (by a predispute contract commitment) or
by court rule or referral. The ideology that contributed to
the founding of modern mediation urges that mediation
should be voluntarily entered into and all agreements
should be arrived at consensually. Nevertheless, as courts
have increasingly sought to "manage" or reduce their
caseloads and have looked to ADR processes as a means
of diverting cases to other forums, even mediation may
be "mandated," although it is usually participation in,
not substantive agreement, that is required.

The taxonomy of different dispute processes also dif-
ferentiates between binding and nonbinding processes.
Arbitration, for example, can be structured either way.
Under some contractual and statutory schemes (such as
the American Federal Arbitration Act), decisions by private arbitrators are final and binding on the parties and
subject to very limited court review, including only such
claims as fraud, corruption of the arbitrator, or, in a few
jurisdictions, serious errors of law or extreme "miscarriages of justice." Nonbinding processes, including nonbinding decisions in some arbitrations, allow appeals or
follow-through to other processes, such as mediation or
full trial. Many "court-annexed" arbitration programs
(mandated and voluntary arbitration of cases, usually by
lawyers, which have been filed as lawsuits and are pending for decision in a court but may be assigned by court
rule or judicial order to a court-sponsored arbitration

program), for example, allow a de novo trial following an arbitration if one party seeks it, often having to post a bond or deposit for costs. The process of mediation itself is nonbinding, in that a party may exit at any time, but once an agreement in mediation is reached, a "binding" contract may be signed, which will be enforceable in a court of law.

Finally, dispute processes are often subject to different requirements depending on whether they are used in private settings (by contract or in employment or other organizational settings) or in public arenas like courts. Court-related or court-annexed ADR programs, now encompassing the full panoply of dispute processes, may be subject to greater legal regulation, including selection, training, and credentialing of the arbitrators or mediators; ethics, confidentiality, and conflicts of interest rules; and greater immunity from legal liability.

ADR processes are frequently differentiated from each other by the degree of control the third-party neutral has over the process (the rules of proceedings), the substance (decision, advice, or facilitation), and the formality of the proceeding (whether held in private or public settings, with or without formal rules of evidence, informal separate meetings, or "caucuses" with the parties, and with or without participation of more than the principal disputants). ADR processes are increasingly being applied to diverse kinds of conflicts, disputes, and transactions, some requiring expertise in the subject matter (such as scientific and policy disputes) and spawning new hybrid processes such as consensus building that engage multiple parties in complex, multi-issue problem solving, drawing on negotiation, mediation, and other nonadjudicative processes.

HISTORICAL BACKGROUND

The modern growth of arbitration, mediation, and other ADR processes can be attributed to at least two different animating concerns. First, scholars, practitioners, consumers, and advocates for justice in the 1960s and 1970s noted the lack of responsiveness of the formal judicial system and sought better-quality processes and outcomes for members of society seeking to resolve disputes with each other, with the government, or with private organizations. This strand of concern with the "quality" of dispute resolution processes sought de-professionalization of judicial processes (a reduction of the lawyer monopoly over dispute representation) and greater access to more local institutions, like neighborhood justice centers, which involved community members, as well as those with expertise in particular problems, with the hope of generating greater participation in dispute resolution processes. Others sought better outcomes than those commonly provided by the formal justice system, which tend toward the binary, polarized results of litigation in

which one party is declared a loser, whereas the other is, at least nominally, a winner. More flexible and party-controlled processes were believed to deliver the possibility of more creative, Pareto-optimal solutions that were geared to joint outcomes, reduction of harm or waste to as many parties as possible, improvement of long-term relationships, and greater responsiveness to the underlying needs and interests of the parties rather than to the stylized arguments and "limited remedial imaginations" of courts and the formal justice system. Some legal and ADR processes (like arbitration) are rule-based, but other forms of ADR (negotiation and mediation) are thought to provide individualized solutions to problems rather than generalized notions of "justice."

A second strand of argument contributing to the development of ADR was based more on concerns of quantity or efficiency. Judicial officers, including those at the top of the U.S. and English justice systems, argued that the excessive cost and delay in the litigation system required devices that would divert cases from court and reduce case backlogs, as well as provide other and more efficient ways of providing access to justice. The emphasis on efficiency behind ADR encouraged both court-mandated programs like court-annexed arbitration for cases with lower economic stakes and encouraged contractual requirements to arbitrate any and all disputes arising from services and products provided in banking, health case, consumer, securities, educational, and communications industries.

Modern ADR structures are only loosely related to their historical antecedents. In many countries, arbitration had its origins in private commercial arbitrations outside the formal court structure and used principally by merchants when disputing with each other. In the United States, labor arbitration developed to secure "labor peace," as well as to develop a specialized, substantive "law of the shop floor."

Early use of mediation or conciliation occurred in some courts and communities seeking both to reduce caseloads and provide more consensual agreements in ethnically or religiously homogeneous areas. Indeed, mediation and other consensual processes are thought to work best in regimes where there are shared values, whether based on common ethnicity or communitarian or political values. In Asian and other nations with more communitarian cultures emphasizing harmony (as contrasted to more litigious or individualistic cultures), mediation is often the preferred form of dispute resolution, but it too has been used for system or political regime purposes beyond resolving the disputes of the parties. Thus, most political regimes have had to deal with both public and private forms of dispute resolution that often supplement, but sometimes challenge or compete with, each other.

KEY CONCEPTS AND USAGE

Each of the ADR processes has its own logic, purposes, and jurisprudential justifications. Mediation and conciliation are often used to improve communications between parties, especially those with preexisting relationships, to "reorient the parties to each other," and to develop solutions to broadly defined conflicts that may recur in the future. Arbitration, however, being more like adjudication, is used more often to definitively resolve a concrete dispute about an event that has transpired and requires fact finding, interpretation of contractual terms, or application of legal principles.

These basic forms have been adapted to a number of subject areas and dispute sites. As regular use of these formats of dispute resolution becomes more common, mediation seems to be overtaking arbitration as a preferred method of dispute resolution (because of the ideology of party self-determination and the flexibility of agreements). Arbitration, still most commonly used in labor disputes, is now the method of choice in form contracts signed by consumers as well as merchants. Arbitration has, thus far, been the mode of choice for resolving international commercial, investment, and trade disputes, such as in the World Trade Organization (WTO) and its predecessor, the General Agreement on Tariffs and Trade (GATT). Arbitration has also been deployed in new forms of disputes developing under both domestic and international intellectual property regimes. Various forms of mediation and arbitration are also increasingly being used to resolve transnational disputes of various kinds (political, economic, natural resource allocation, and ethnic violence) and are employed by international organizations like the United Nations and the Organization of American States, multinational trade and treaty groups (North American Free Trade Agreement, the European Union, and MERCOSUR), and nongovernmental organizations in human rights and other disputes.

Beginning in the United States but now in use internationally, mass injury (class action) cases involving both personal and property damages have been allocated to ADR claims facilities, which use both arbitral and mediative forms of individual case processing. In legal regimes all over the world, family disputes are increasingly assigned to mediative processes, both for child custody and support and maintenance issues. In many nations, this growth in family mediation has spurred the development of a new profession of mediators, drawn from social work or psychology, who sometimes compete with lawyers in private practice and as court officers.

In many jurisdictions, some form of referral to ADR is now required before a case may be tried. Increasingly, however, parties to particularly complex disputes, such as environmental disputes, mass torts, or governmental budgeting conflicts, may convene their own ADR processes, with a third-party neutral facilitating a new form of public participatory process that combines negotiation, fact finding, mediation, and joint problem solving. Such consensus-building processes have also been applied to the administrative tribunal processes of both rule making and administrative adjudication in a new process called "reg-neg" (negotiated rule making or regulation).

Although ADR was considered, until quite recently, principally an alternative to courts in the United States, it is slowly spreading around the world and is used to relieve court congestion; provide expertise in various subject matter disputes (e.g., construction, labor matters, family law); build transnational dispute systems for economic, human rights, and political issues; and offer alternative justice systems where there is distrust of existing judicial institutions. The use of ADR across borders and cultures and raises complex questions about intercultural negotiations and multijurisdictional sources of law or other principles for dispute resolution.

CONTROVERSIES

The use of mediation, arbitration, and ADR processes in lieu of more traditional adjudication has not been without its controversies, which are reviewed briefly in this section.

Privatization of Jurisprudence

With the increased use of negotiated settlements, mediation, and private arbitration, there has been concern that fewer and fewer cases will be available in the public arena for the making of precedent and debate about and creation of rules and political values for the larger community. As settlements are conducted in private and often have confidentiality or secrecy clauses attached to them, others will not learn about wrongs committed by defendants, and information that might otherwise be discoverable will be shielded from public view. Settlements may be based on nonlegal criteria, threatening compliance with and enforcement of law. Claims are more likely to be individualized than collectivized.

Related concerns about the privatization of the judicial system include increased indirect state intervention in the affairs of the citizenry through more disputing institutions, at the same time that the exit of wealthier litigants gives them less stake in the quality and financing of public justice systems. The debate centers on whether dispute resolution systems can simultaneously serve the private interests of disputants before them and the polity's need for the articulation of publicly enforced norms and values.

Inequalities of Bargaining Power

A number of critics have suggested that less powerful members of society, particularly those subordinated by race, ethnicity, class, or gender, will be disproportionately disadvantaged in ADR processes where there are no judges, formal rules, or in some cases, legal representatives to protect the parties and advise them of their legal entitlements. Responses from ADR theorists suggest that there is little empirical evidence that less advantaged individuals or groups necessarily fare better in the formal justice system and that sophisticated mediators and arbitrators are indeed sensitive to power imbalances and can be trained to correct for them without endangering their "neutrality" in the ADR process. Many private ADR organizations have begun developing standards for good practices and due process protocols to protect the parties and ensure the integrity of the process.

Evaluation and Empirical Verification of Effectiveness

There are few robust research findings with respect to the effectiveness of ADR in meeting its claimed advantages. Recent findings from studies of ADR in the U.S. federal courts have been contradictory about whether or not arbitration, mediation, and some forms of early neutral evaluation do decrease case processing time or costs, either for the parties or the system, and preliminary studies from England demonstrate low usage of mediation schemes. Yet studies continue to demonstrate high satisfaction rates of users of arbitration and mediation programs and higher compliance rates with mediated outcomes than traditional adjudication. In light of the variation in ADR programs, it is too early for there to be sufficient databases for accurate comparisons among processes.

Distortions and Deformations of ADR Processes

Within the nascent ADR profession, there is concern that the early animating ideologies of ADR are being distorted by their assimilation into the conventional justice system. Within a movement that sought to de-professionalize conflict resolution, there are now competing professional claims for control of standards, ethics, credentialing, and quality control between lawyers and nonlawyers. Processes like mediation that were conceived as voluntary and consensual are now being mandated by court rules and contracts. Processes that were supposed to be creative, flexible, and facilitative are becoming more rigid, rule- and law-based, and judicialized as more common law about ADR is created by courts and more laws are passed by legislatures. The overall concern is that a set of processes that were developed to be alternative to the traditional judicial system are themselves being co-opted within the traditional judicial process and its overwhelming adversary culture. Policymakers and practitioners in the field are concerned about whether a private market in ADR is good for disciplining and competing with the public justice system or whether there will be insufficient accountability within a private market of dispute resolution.

THE FUTURE OF ADR

There is no question that the use of a variety of different processes to resolve individual, organizational, and international problems is continuing to expand. New hybrid forms of ADR (as in mediation on the Internet) are developing to help resolve new problems with greater participation by more parties. Large organizations are creating their own internal dispute resolution systems. There are clearly trends in favor of mediation and arbitration in the international arena, where globalization of enterprises and governmental interests requires creative and simple processes that are not overly attached to any one jurisdiction's substantive law to promote goals of efficiency, fairness, clarity, and legitimacy, particularly in regimes with underdeveloped formal legal systems. It is also clear that there is competition over who will control such processes and which processes will dominate in which spheres of human disputing and deal making. The likely result is that the creative pluralism and flexibility of ADR will be increasingly subject to its own forms of formality and regulation in an effort to keep its promises of efficiency, participation, better-quality outcomes, and justice.

Carrie Menkel-Meadow

See also Adversarial System; Arbitration; Civil Procedure; International Arbitration; Legal Pluralism; Mediation; Neighborhood Justice Centers; United States—Federal System; United States—State Systems; World Trade Organization

References and further reading
Fisher Roger, William Ury, and Bruce Patton. 1991. *Getting to Yes: Negotiating Agreement without Giving In.* 2nd ed. New York: Viking Penguin.
Fiss, Owen. 1984. "Against Settlement." *Yale Law Journal* 93: 1073–1090.
Fuller, Lon. 1971. "Mediation: Its Form and Functions." *Southern California Law Review* 44: 305–339.
Menkel-Meadow, Carrie. 1995. "Whose Dispute Is It Anyway? A Philosophical and Democratic Defense of Settlement (In Some Cases)." *Georgetown Law Journal* 83: 2663–2696.
———. 1997. "When Dispute Resolution Begets Disputes of Its Own: Conflicts among Dispute Professionals." *UCLA Law Review* 44: 1871–1933.
Palmer, Michael, and Simon Roberts. 1998. *Dispute Processes: ADR and the Primary Forms of Decision Making.* London: Butterworths.
Sander, Frank, and Stephen Goldberg. 1994. "Fitting the Forum to the Fuss: A User Friendly Guide to Selecting an ADR Procedure." *Negotiation Journal* 10: 49–68.
Susskind, Lawrence, Sarah McKearnan, and Jennifer Thomas-Larmer. 1999. *The Consensus Building Handbook: A Comprehensive Guide to Reaching Agreement.* Thousand Oaks, CA: Sage.

ANCIENT ATHENS

COUNTRY INFORMATION

Located in the Attica region of central Greece, Athens was the leading *polis* (city-state) among the ancient Ionian Greeks, most of whom lived on the islands of the Aegean Sea and the west coast of Asia Minor. Athens was thus a natural competitor for Sparta, in southern Greece, which led the Dorian Greeks. During the classical period (479 to 323 B.C.E.), Athens's citizen population, including women and children, probably varied between 120,000 and 200,000. There were likely half as many resident non-Athenians (*metics*) and an equal number of slaves and citizens.

HISTORY

By 700 B.C.E., Athens had assumed control over Attica, creating a single polis that included many villages (*demes*) as well as its urban core, the marketplace (*agora*) situated near the Acropolis. A hereditary kingship gave way to a proliferation of annually elected magistrates (*archons*), whose number was eventually fixed at nine. Disparities in wealth led to social strife, culminating in the attempt to establish a tyranny under Cylon in 631 B.C.E. Perhaps in response to this attempt, Athens's first law code was formulated by Draco around 621 B.C.E. In 594, Solon attempted more extensive legal reforms, which superseded those of Draco except with regard to homicide. He earned historical recognition as *the* lawgiver of Athens, as a counterpart to (the probably legendary) Lycurgus of Sparta, Zaleucus of Locri, and Charondas of Catana. The tyrant Peisistratus and his sons who succeeded him preserved Solon's legal framework through much of the sixth century, until they were toppled in 511.

The constitutional settlement conceived by Cleisthenes that emerged from the power struggle of 511 to 508 is recognized as the world's first democracy. It made Athens's Assembly (*ekklesia*) of all citizen males the sovereign political body, at least formally. Modifications introduced by Themistocles in 487, Ephialtes in 463, and Pericles in 451 wrested practical decision-making power away from the Areopagus, the council of (wealthy) former archons, giving it to the Assembly , the (representative) Council of 500, and the Popular Courts, and defined citizenship more narrowly. Under Pericles' leadership, Athens enjoyed unparalleled prosperity from 446 until the great Peloponnesian War broke out in 431. It eventually lost this war to Sparta and its allies and suffered under the despotism of the "thirty tyrants" for close to a year from 404 to 403 before a rebellion reestablished the democracy.

Most of the evidence for Athenian law derives from speeches composed by a group of ten speechwriters, the most important of whom are Antiphon, Lysias, Isaeus, and Demosthenes, who wrote in the late fifth and much of the fourth centuries B.C.E. Political domination over Athens by Philip of Macedon (d. 336), his son Alexander the Great (d. 323), and his successors led to the enervation of Athens's democracy and its judicial system. We have little evidence from after 320 B.C.E.

LEGAL CONCEPTS

Athens did not have a constitution in the modern sense of a discrete set of rules dictating its governance and judiciary, though Aristotle (or one of his students) did write an account of the history and practices of the Athenian polis—*Politeia,* a title usually translated as *Constitution* or *Republic.* The central concept was *nomos,* meaning "law" or "custom." During the classical period, a written nomos was established by the Assembly on the recommendation of a board of lawmakers. Solon had earlier established the tradition of inscribing laws on stone pillars that were put on axles and exhibited openly in a portico, or *stoa,* off the marketplace. These could be rotated and easily consulted. A magistrate was not allowed to bring forward a case that was not governed by a written nomos, and Athenian judges had to swear an oath to decide cases on the basis of the written laws.

An action in law was known as a *dikê* (which also means "justice") and could only be brought by the alleged victim of an act of injustice or in the case of homicide by a member of the victim's family. Both parties to the suit had to represent themselves in court, though some individuals could have their presentations composed for them by professional speechwriters and some cases allowed for the participation of a co-pleader. Women, slaves, and children were represented by their *kurios,* usually a husband or father, who was legally competent. Solon introduced the opportunity for "the one wishing," a voluntary prosecutor, to intervene on behalf of a victim through an action called a *graphê.* Though the term suggests that a graphê was written, in practice there seems to have been no additional requirement surrounding the writing down of the charge. Solon allowed for the appeal of any decision by a magistrate to a *dikastêrion,* or popular court, in which all adult male citizens could participate through a random selection process. This reform was one of the most important for the development of Athens's democracy.

Although the Athenians had no term to describe it, redress usually took the form of restitution of the original amount under dispute plus as much again as punishment, that is, a doubling of the damages. Failure to pay the court-ordered restitution resulted in another suit, a further doubling, and eventually a loss of civic rights. Except for this denial of civic rights, the Athenian polis did not assist in recovering court-ordered settlements.

Major crimes against the state, such as treason or

malfeasance by a general, were addressed through a suit called an *eisangelia* (impeachment), which was brought initially to a political body, such as the Assembly or the Council of 500, before being passed on to the courts. Less serious cases of misadministration could be tried at a magistrate's examination (*euthynai*) before the Council as the magistrate's year of office came to an end.

STRUCTURE

Ancient Athens had a large body of substantive law, but because it was preserved on stone, most of which has long since been diverted to other uses that have obliterated its legal information, little evidence survives about the structure of Athens's laws as the Athenians may have understood them. However, the Peripatetic philosopher Theophrastus (ca. 371–287 B.C.E.) wrote a twenty-four-volume comparative treatise on law, for which Athens's laws must have served as a template. Surviving fragments of this work suggest that the first six volumes dealt with laws regulating Athens's government, several covered legal procedure and the status of resident non-Athenians, several dealt with homicide and assault, at least one dealt with commercial matters, and another addressed regulations concerning public contests and dramatic festivals. Other sources inform us about laws on theft, inheritance, and the financing of maritime trade.

Since most of our evidence stems from speeches written for delivery before Athens's Popular Courts—the last stage in sometimes long and acrimonious legal disputes—it is easiest to understand the structure of its law by looking at its procedures. Disputants were socially encouraged to settle issues privately among themselves. Accompanied by witnesses (free adult males), a man confronted his opponent, spelled out his complaint, and sought adequate redress. If the dispute turned on a matter of fact rather than law, one party might offer through a challenge (*proklêsis*) to let the matter be determined by, for example, having a woman swear an oath to what she knew or by bilaterally torturing a knowledgeable slave. There could also be recourse to private arbitration (*diaita*), whether by one person or by a panel of three. Private settlement entailed a formal procedure of *aphesis* and *apallagê* (dismissal and release), whereby the two sides released each other from further claims.

Failing these attempts at resolution, the dispute moved from the private into the political realm when one of the disputants summoned the other to appear before one of the nine civic magistrates. It was the magistrate's job to conduct an *anakrisis,* a question-and-answer session designed to clarify what the parties were disputing and what laws applied. Since in the classical period the magistrate was selected by lot, he need not have had any legal expertise, and he had no power to render a judgment. In private disputes (*idiai dikai*), he generally passed the mat-

ter on to a panel of forty judges (the Forty), who were empowered to render judgments in disputes involving less than ten drachmas. Larger disputes were passed on to a public arbiter, a fifty-nine-year-old man selected by lot. If he was unable to bring about a mutually acceptable settlement, he rendered a judgment, which ended the dispute as long as both parties acceded to it. If either side appealed, however, the case was decided finally by the Popular Court. The public abiter had added authority, however, because the disputants could only produce evidence before that court if it had first been produced before him. In some cases, especially those involving contracts, the accused might bring a demurer (*paragraphê*), claiming that the original suit was inadmissible. This procedure had the result of turning the defendant into a prosecutor, so that he spoke first before the Popular Court.

The size of the Popular Court (which was chosen by lot each day from an annually selected panel of 6,000 citizen volunteers) and the length of the proceedings depended on the amount of money at stake. In private cases, the court size could vary from 200 to 500 people. In public cases, the citizen volunteers generally served in multiples of 500, up to 1,500. Each side was given the same amount of time to speak during the court proceedings; the time was measured by a water clock, which was stopped during the reading of evidence by the court secretary. That evidence consisted of the written pleas submitted by each side; excerpts from relevant laws; witness testimony from free, adult males that had been recorded before the public arbiter or earlier in the dispute; contracts; and challenges (*proklêseis*) that either side had made at preliminary points in the dispute. In cases in which there was a statutory punishment, each side spoke twice. When the court had to decide the punishment, each side spoke once and then again concerning the punishment, if needed. The judges (*dikastai*) then voted by secret ballot, a simple majority being sufficient for victory.

JUDICIAL BODIES

Together with their secretary, the nine annually selected magistrates represented each of Athens's ten tribes, and it fell to them to administer the court system. Of these, the six *thesmothetae* took on this role as their principal duty and steered most of the cases through the judicial structure. Three magistrates, however, had special responsibilities. The eponymous archon (so called because Athenians referred to his year in office by using his name) had special responsibility for ensuring the property rights of Athenians. Cases regarding citizens' obligations to perform civic responsibilities thus came before him. (Wealthy citizens were called on to finance festivals or military equipment but could escape that obligation by claiming that another man had more financial ability.) Likewise, he handled cases regarding the estates of elderly

Legal Structure of Ancient Athens

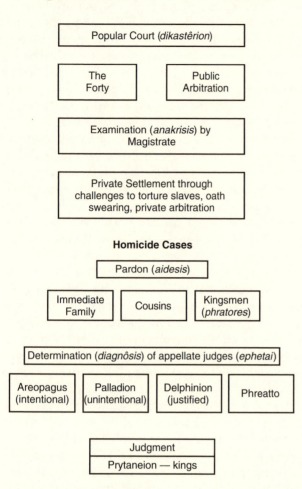

parents, orphans, heiresses, and the mentally unstable. The *archon polemarchos,* whose title suggests that his position once had a military function, handled all cases involving non-Athenians.

The *archon basileus,* or king magistrate, had responsibility for all those cases touching on religion. This category included disputes not only over impiety and the distribution of priesthoods but also homicide and intentional wounding, which entailed a religious pollution. Depending on the circumstances of the homicide or wounding, the case might go to one of five courts, all of which were located away from the central core of Athens and in the open air because of the pollution associated with the killers. Cases of alleged intentional homicide went before the Areopagus, the board composed of former magistrates. When there was a claim of unintentional homicide, an attempted homicide, or the killing of a slave or foreigner, the case was heard at the court at the Palladion. When the killer claimed justifiable homicide, the trial was held at the Delphinion. When an exiled killer wished to plead innocence of intent, the case was heard at the court of Phreatto, with the defendant on a raft off the coast so as to remain in exile. When the killer's

identity was unknown or when an animal or inanimate object seemed to have caused a death, a court at the Prytaneion, the town hall, assigned responsibility; the animal was slaughtered or the inanimate object removed from Athenian territory. Aside from the Areopagus court, a committee of fifty-one *ephetai* (appellate judges) heard the cases at the homicide courts; they appear to have been members of that council. In homicide cases, the charges had to be sworn three times in succeeding months and the witnesses had to swear not only to a particular fact but also to the accused's guilt or innocence. This requirement meant that the homicide courts had the highest reputation for the relevance of the argumentation, since no testimony was presented before it that was not directly material to the point at issue.

An epigraphic document known as Draco's Law, which appears to be the reinscription made around 409 B.C.E. of a law from two centuries earlier, gives further evidence for the operation of the homicide courts. According to it, the "kings" made an initial judgment (*dikazein*) of who or what was responsible (*aitios*) for a homicide. The appellate judges then made a determination of intention (or justification). Lastly, members of the deceased's family, in ever widening circles depending on survival, had the option of reconciling with the killer, if all agreed.

IMPACT

Athens's democracy was manifest as much in its legal system as in its deliberative assembly. Its large, randomly selected panels of judges had enormous power to police the state. Pay for serving in the democratic courts became a hallmark of democratic reformers and a lightning rod for democracy's critics. Likewise, the right of volunteer prosecutors to seek redress for those who suffered wrongdoing was seen as both a significant democratic principle and as a vehicle for *sykophantia,* or vexatious litigation, as the courts were manipulated for the pursuit of political feuds and judicial extortion. Let alone "beyond a reasonable doubt," the standard for proof was simply the conviction of a majority of judges. These individuals were sworn to rule according to the law and are likely to have been largely faithful to their oath, but in practice, there was no accountability for the judges. They were as free to determine issues of law as to decide issues of fact. In addition, although some men made a trade of writing speeches for others to deliver in court (the *logographoi*), there was no professional class of lawyers and judges to control and regulate Athens's legal system. Each accused man spoke for himself, ostensibly without expert help, and called on witnesses who, like the defendent, were free adult males. No witnesses were classified as experts; their only qualification was having "thorough knowledge" of the matter they testified about.

David C. Mirhady

See also Greece; Juries
References and further reading
Aristotle. *The Constitution of the Athenians.*
Carey, Christopher. 1997. *Trials from Classical Athens.*
    London,: Routledge.
Gagarin, Michael. 1986. *Early Greek Law.* Berkeley, CA:
    University of California Press.
Harrison, A. R. W. 1968–1971. *The Law of Athens.* Oxford:
    Clarendon.
MacDowell, Douglas M. 1978. *The Law in Classical Athens.*
    London: Thames and Hudson.
Todd, Stephen C. 1993. *The Shape of Athenian Law.* Oxford:
    Clarendon.

ANDORRA

COUNTRY INFORMATION

Andorra—officially known as the Principality of Andorra—is located on the southern slopes of the Pyrenees, bounded on the north by France and on the south by Spain. It is a landlocked country of narrow valleys, gorges, and defiles surrounded by mountain peaks, covering an area of 179 square miles (464 square kilometers). The population of Andorra in 2000 was 65,844 people, the majority of whom live in and around the capital, Andorra la Vella. Native Andorrans are a minority, accounting for only 34.4 percent of the population. Most residents are Spanish (roughly 50 percent of the population), French (8 percent), and Portuguese (7 percent). The country is administratively divided into seven districts, or "parishes." Each parish has a local body—the Comú—that manages the municipal budget and the public policies. The official language of Andorra is Catalan, which belongs to the group of western neo-Latin languages, although Spanish, French, and Portuguese are also widely spoken.

HISTORY

Remnants of the ancient feudal system have been preserved for centuries in Andorra. In 1278 and 1288, two judgments (the *pareatges*) established that two coprinces would rule Andorra: the bishop of Seu d'Urgell (Catalonia) and the French count of Foix. In 1589, when the count of Foix and Navarre became King Henry IV, the rights of the counts of Foix passed to the French monarchy and, after a temporary suspension during the French Revolution, to Napoleon Bonaparte and the successive heads of the French republic.

Since 1419, the main institution of government has been the Consell de la Terra (at present, the General Council of the Valleys), a syndic-led council composed of the heads of the leading Andorran families. The economic and political power of these prominent families has traditionally prevailed in the government of Andorra. Until 1970, only third-generation Andorran males had the right to elect their local representatives. And prior to 1993, Andorra had no formal constitution (the two pareatges still remained in force), there was no separation between legislative and executive powers, and political parties and trade unions were not legalized. Even now, under the political framework of the 1993 democratic constitution, the Andorran electorate is small in relation to the total population, since citizenship remains hard to acquire for foreign-born residents. (Only Andorran nationals are able to transmit citizenship automatically to their children, and lawful residents may obtain citizenship only after twenty-five years of residency.)

Since 1991, Andorra has been a member of the European Union (EU) Customs Union and is treated as an EU member for trade in industrial goods (but not agricultural products), and in 1994, it joined the European Council and became a member of the United Nations. Until the 1950s, the Andorran economic was traditionally based on farming (tobacco, grains, corn, and grapes), wood cutting, and duty-free shopping (jewelry, perfumes, leather goods, and so forth), since consumer goods have traditionally been tax free. The European Union countries—primarily Spain and France—are Andorra's major trading partners (accounting for 88.5 percent of imports and 92 percent of exports in 1999). Today, tourism is a major source of revenue, comprising nearly 80 percent of the economy, and tourist facilities, including winter-sports resorts, attract roughly 1 million visitors every year.

The financial and banking sectors have also contributed substantially to the Andorran economy. A reduced group of seven banks (three of them fully owned by Andorrans) dominate the financial activities of the country. The level of capitalization and the solvency ratio (ranging from 18 to 37 percent) of Andorra's banking institutions are very high. In addition, Andorran banks have a strict code of secrecy by which they may only divulge information on the identity of their clients if required to do so by an Andorran judge. Numbered accounts (available only to top-quality clients) may be opened in any currency, and no taxes are imposed. General accounts are equally protected by the code of secrecy. These policies have attracted a great number of foreign depositors and investors since the 1960s.

LEGAL CONCEPTS

Andorra is a civil law country whose courts have traditionally applied customary laws, supplemented by Roman law and customary Catalan law. Andorran civil law is also based on French and Spanish civil codes. Judicial decisions play a major role in the evolution of the legal system. At present, the enactment of a new criminal code is being debated in the Parliament.

The taxation regime is one the most salient features of the Andorran legal system. The Organization for Eco-

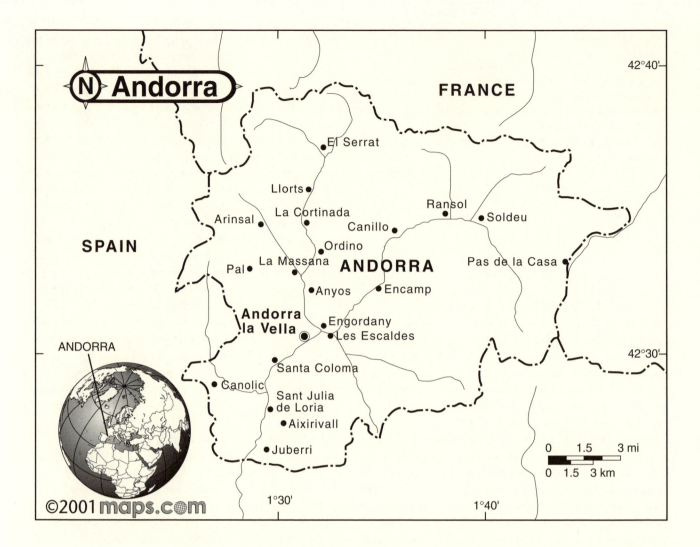

nomic Cooperation and Development (OECD) has identified Andorra as a tax haven in some of its reports (FATF Annual Report 1998–1999). To date, there is no direct income tax, corporation tax, or wealth tax in Andorra. The only taxes are minor government levies on consumption, property transactions, and business license fees. Indirect taxation—accounting for approximately 12.6 percent of the gross national product (GNP)—applies to the production, manufacture, and import of all products (the rates ranging from 1 to 12 percent of the value of goods).

CURRENT STRUCTURE

The 1993 Constitution, following recommendations of the Council of Europe, provided Andorra with a new political structure. It formally established the principle of separation of powers and conferred on Andorra the status of a "democratic," "constitutional," "independent," and "welfare" state. Under this framework, Andorra has addressed many long-awaited reforms, such as the legalization of political parties and trade unions, the regulation of the banking system, and the adjustment of internal legislation to international treaties on crime prevention and money laundering.

The executive branch of the Andorran state is composed of the chief of state (a position shared by the president of the French republic and the Catalan bishop coprince) and the head of government, or executive council president. The 1993 Constitution maintained the unique system of coprinces yet greatly curtailed their powers. Essentially, their role consists of guaranteeing respect for the constitution, calling general elections at the request of the head of government, accrediting the diplomatic representatives of Andorra and receiving foreign accreditations, and appointing one representative to the Constitutional Tribunal and one to the Superior Council of Justice (Consell Superior de la Justícia). The head of government is elected by the Parliament. The government directs the domestic and foreign policies of Andorra and has the power to issue decrees. In 1994, Marc Forné became the head of the Andorran government.

The legislative branch consists of the General Council of the Valleys, a unicameral body of twenty-eight members elected in general elections for a period of four years (fourteen from a single national constituency and fourteen representing the seven parishes). The General Council issues decrees (uniquely referred to as "laws"), approves the annual budget of the state, and controls the government's political activities. The parties represented in the General Council after the 2001 general elections were the Liberal Party, the Social Democratic Party, and the Democrat Party.

The judicial branch is composed of judges (*batlles*), the Tribunals of Judges (Tribunals de Batlle), the Tribunal of the Courts (Tribunal de Corts), and the Supreme Court of Justice of Andorra (Tribunal Superior de la Justícia de Andorra). The governing body of the judicial branch is the Superior Council of Justice. Finally, the Constitutional Court (Tribunal Constitucional) judicially reviews legislative acts. At the international level, the country accepted the jurisdiction of the International Criminal Court in 2000. Andorra also introduced the institution of the ombudsman in 1998; with a mandate to guard the rights and liberties granted by the constitution and deal with violations of rights committed by public authorities and bodies.

SPECIALIZED JUDICIAL BODIES
The Andorran judicial system is divided into civil, criminal, and administrative courts. Civil cases are heard before the batlles (sitting as either single or college courts), and decisions may be appealed to the Supreme Court of Justice. Criminal cases are heard before the batlles, the Tribunal de Batlles, and the Tribunal de Corts, depending on the severity of the crimes and offenses at issue. Administrative law cases are heard by the batlles and may also be appealed to the Supreme Court of Justice. Since industrial relations, employment law, and work conditions have traditionally been deprived of regulation, there are no labor courts in Andorra; labor disputes are heard before the civil jurisdiction.

The Constitutional Court is an independent institution that, strictly speaking, does not belong to the ordinary jurisdiction. According to Article 95 of the constitution, this court is the "maximum interpreter of the Constitution," and it deals with the adjustment of laws to the constitution, violations of fundamental rights, and conflicts between the public bodies of the state.

STAFFING
Contrary to the situation in European civil law countries, judges, magistrates, and prosecutors in Andorra are not tenure-track civil servants. According to the Andorran Constitution (Articles 90 and 93), all judges and public prosecutors, whatever their rank, are appointed for a renewable six-year term; each is an academically qualified lawyer.

The four magistrates of the Constitutional Court are appointed from among persons of known juridical or in-

Legal Structure of Andorra Courts

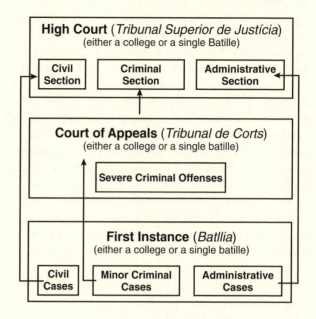

stitutional experience (as required by Article 96 of the constitution), and they hold office for a maximum period of two consecutive eight-year terms. Currently, Spanish and French law professors serve on the Constitutional Court. To practice law as a private attorney, a candidate must successfully complete a law degree either in France or in Spain and obtain a license to practice from the Andorran Law Society.

IMPACT
Andorra underwent a remarkable transformation of its political system during the 1990s. The 1993 Constitution opened the door to full democratization, international recognition as an independent country, and membership in international organizations such as the UN. The ongoing process of democratization, nevertheless, will require the gradual adjustment of Andorran institutions to the standards that the nation's own legislation establishes (protection of fundamental rights, social welfare, prevention and prosecution of money laundering, and so on).

From an economic point of view, Andorra will have to face several challenges in the short term, such as the introduction of the euro as the single European currency (Andorra has no national currency), the growing harmonization of European financial systems, and the adoption of new international standards of criminal justice. The Andorran Parliament has already passed legislation to combat money laundering (the 1995 Act for the Protection of Banking Secrecy and for the Prevention of Laundering of Money or of Assets Deriving from Crime) and has recently ratified the Vienna and Strasbourg conventions concerning international cooperation to prevent and prosecute money laundering. However, the internal regulation of the Andorran financial system still casts some doubts regarding the prevention of money-laundering operations. The banking sector, one of the pillars of the Andorran economy, is currently facing pressures from OECD countries to eliminate the existence of numbered accounts. To date, foreigners can make unlimited deposits in Andorran banks, which maintain their high standards of secrecy and customer confidentiality. The opening up of the highly restricted Andorran financial system to international competition is also envisaged in the short run.

Although it is not expected that Andorra will petition for full EU membership in the near future, political parties are currently debating a major integration of Andorra into the European Union. Perhaps this is the major upcoming challenge Andorra will have to face.

Marta Poblet

See also Catalonia; Civil Law; France; Spain

References and further reading

"Andorra," A Special International Report, *Washington Times,* http://www.internationalspecialreports.com/archives/99/andorra/6.html.

Barril, J. 1994. *Andorra.* Barcelona: Banc Internacional d'Andorra, Banca Mora.

FATF Annual Report (1998–1999). http://www.oecd.org/fatf

Figareda i Cairol, P. 1996. *Las instituciones del Principado de Andorra en el nuevo marco constitucional.* Madrid and Barcelona: Civitas, Institut d'Estudis Andorrans.

Iglesia Ferreirós, A., ed. 1994. *El "Ius Commune" com a dret vigent: L'experiència judicial d'Andorra i San Marino—Actes del I Simposi Jurídic Principat d'Andorra/República de San Marino.* Andorra: Institut d'Estudis Andorrans.

Pou, V. 1994. *El GATT i la nova organització mundial del comerç: Anàlisi i documentació sobre la situació d'Andorra en el nou ordre comercial internacional.* Andorra: Crèdit Andorrà.

Román Martín, L. 1999. *El nou estat andorrà: Un estudi jurídic.* Andorra: Institut d'Estudis Andorrans.

ANGOLA

COUNTRY INFORMATION

Angola is located on the western coast of southern Africa bordering the South Atlantic, between Namibia and the Democratic Republic of the Congo (Zaire). With a total area of 1,246,700 square kilometers, it has 1,600 kilometers of coastline and a 200-nautical-mile exclusive economic zone. The main cities are Luanda (the capital), Huambo, Beneguela, and Lobito, and eighteen provinces are established as administrative divisions. A separate province, Cabinda, is enclosed by the Congo and covered by equatorial jungles.

The Namib Desert occupies the coastal plain above Mocamedes. The climate is semiarid in the south and along the coast to Luanda; the region to the north has a cool, dry season (from May to October) and a hot, rainy season (from November to April). Forests and woodland cover 43 percent of the land; another 23 percent is devoted to permanent pastures. In terms of the environment, the overuse of pastures and the subsequent soil erosion contribute not only to water pollution attributable to population pressures but also to desertification and the deforestation of the tropical rain forest.

In 2000, the total population of Angola was 10,145,267, distributed by age group as follows: 0 to 14 years, 43 percent (2,215,706 males and 2,172,106 females); 15 to 64 years, 54 percent (2,792,313 males and 2,692,790 females); and 65 years and over, 3 percent (124,404 males and 147,948 females). Angola's population growth rate is 2.15 percent; the birth rate is 46.89 per 1,000 people; and the death rate is 25.01 per 1,000. The net migration rate is 0.34 migrants per 1,000 people; the infant mortality rate is 195.78 per 1,000 live births; the total fertility rate is 6.52 children per woman; and the ratio of males to females in the total population is 1.02.

Traditional indigenous religions prevail in Angola, but there is a large Roman Catholic minority (38 percent of the population) and a smaller Protestant minority (15 percent). The overwhelming majority of Angolans are of African descent, and most of the people speak Bantu, among other African languages. The official language, however, is Portuguese. The country has a 42 percent literacy rate.

The composition of the gross domestic product (GDP) by sector, based on 1998 estimates, is as follows: agriculture, 13 percent; industry, 53 percent; and services, 34 percent. Angola's primary industries are the production of cement and basic metal goods, fish processing, food processing, brewing, the manufacture of tobacco products, sugar refining, and textile manufacturing. The main natural resources are petroleum, diamonds, iron ore, phosphates, copper, feldspar, bauxite, uranium, and gold. Angola's economy is in disarray because the country has endured nearly continuous warfare for a quarter of a century. Today, despite the nation's abundant natural resources, output per capita is among the lowest in the world. Subsistence agriculture provides the main livelihood for 85 percent of the population. Oil production and supporting activities are vital to the economy, contributing about 45 percent to GDP and 90 percent of all exports.

The army is by far the largest military branch, accounting for 91.5 percent of the country's armed forces, whereas the air and air defense forces comprise 6.7 percent and the navy 1.8 percent. There is also a national police force. The military age is eighteen years old. Mili-

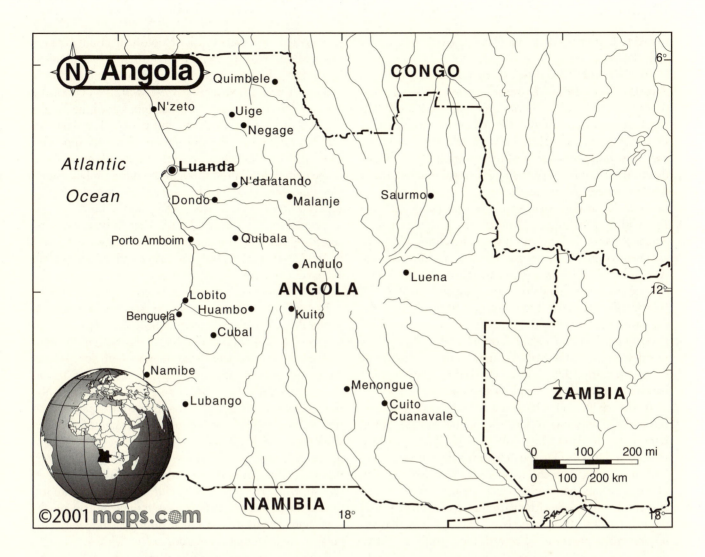

tary expenditures account for 23.9 percent of the gross national product (based on 1986 sources).

HISTORY

The first inhabitants of the area that is now Angola are thought to have been members of the hunter-gatherer Khoisan group. Bantu-speaking peoples from West Africa arrived in the region in the twentieth century, partially displacing the Khoisan and establishing a number of powerful kingdoms. The Portuguese first explored coastal Angola in the late fifteenth century, and except for a short occupation by the Dutch (from 1641 to 1648), the region was controlled by the Portuguese until they left the country in 1974.

Although they failed to discover the gold and other precious metals they were seeking, the Portuguese found in Angola an excellent source of slaves for their colony in Brazil. Portuguese colonization of Angola began in 1575, when a permanent base was established at Luanda. By that time, the Mbundu kingdom had established itself in central Angola. After several attempts at subjugation, Portuguese troops finally broke the back of the kingdom

in 1902, when the Bié Plateau was captured. Construction of the Benguela railroad followed, and white settlers arrived in the Angolan highlands.

The modern development of Angola began only after World War II. In 1951, the colony was designated an overseas province, and Portugal initiated plans to develop industries and hydroelectric power. Although the Portuguese professed the aim of establishing a multiracial society of equals in Angola, most Africans still suffered repression. Inspired by nationalist movements elsewhere, the native Angolans rose in revolt in 1961. When the uprising was quelled by the Portuguese army, many people fled to Congo (Kinshasa) and other neighboring countries.

Angola was a Portuguese colony for 450 years. Although most of the countries of Africa gained independence between the late 1950s and early 1960s, Portugal refused to grant independence to Angola. The Portuguese treated Angola (as well as their other African territories) as part of Portugal, but the Angolans wanted to join the rest of the African continent in gaining independence. As a result of the ongoing guerrilla warfare, Portugal was forced to keep more than 50,000 troops in Angola by the early 1970s.

In 1972, the Portuguese National Assembly changed Angola's status from an overseas province to an "autonomous state with authority over internal affairs." Portugal retained responsibility for defense and foreign relations. One year later, elections were held for a legislative assembly. Independence was finally won in 1975, mainly due to the 1974 military coup in Portugal that overthrew the Portuguese government.

After Portugal granted Angola independence in 1975, the MPLA (Movimiento Popular para la Liberación de Angola), one of the country's three nationalist movements, assumed control of the government in Luanda, and Agostinho Neto became president. However, the FNLA (Frente Nacional de Libertação de Angola) and UNITA (União Nacional para Independência Total de Angola), the other prominent movements, proclaimed a coaliton government in Nova Lisboa (now Huambo). In spite of this development, the MPLA gained control of the whole country by early 1976. When Neto died in 1979, José Eduardo dos Santos succeeded him as president.

In the 1970s and 1980s, the MPLA government received large amounts of aid from Cuba and the Soviet Union. In the late 1980s, the United States provided military aid to UNITA and demanded the withdrawal of Cuban troops and an end to Soviet assistance. As a result of negotiations between Angola, South Africa, Cuba, and the United States, the withdrawal of Cuban troops began in 1989. Also in the late 1980s, Marxist Angola implemented programs of privatization under President dos Santos. In 1985, South Africa signed a formal withdrawal accord, although sporadic incursions over the border continued until August 1988. Cuba consented in 1988 to withdraw its troops, and the warring factions agreed to a cease-fire on June 22, 1989. In March 1991, the Angolan ruling party relinquished its commitment to Marxism, opening the way for peace negotiations, and at the end of May, the Cuban troop withdrawal was completed. One month later, a peace treaty was signed in Lisbon, followed by a multiparty election that was won by the MPLA. However, UNITA did not consider the election results valid, and the civil war resumed with increased severity.

Supervised elections were held in September 1992, and early the next month, the former rebel movement UNITA, led by Jonas Savimbi, withdrew from Angola's new joint armed forces in protest over alleged electoral fraud; Savimbi refused to accept the results of the vote, and another civil war ensued, destroying many cities and much of the country's infrastructure.

In late October 1992, UNITA and the ruling government (MPLA), led by dos Santos, agreed to halt troop movements in an attempt to negotiate a power-sharing arrangement and avert further bloodshed, although fighting continued to escalate. On May 19, 1993, the United States officially recognized the MPLA government. A year and a half later, in November 1994, with UNITA on the verge of defeat, dos Santos and Savimbi signed the Lusaka Protocol, a new agreement to end the conflict. The two sides committed to the integration of several thousand UNITA troops into the government armed forces, as well as the demobilization of thousands more from both sides. UN peacekeeping troops began arriving in June 1995 to supervise the process. Troop integration, however, was suspended in 1996, and UNITA's demobilization efforts lagged. A new government of national unity was formed in 1997, including several UNITA deputies; Savimbi had declined a vice-presidency in 1996.

With renewed fighting in 1998, Angola's ruling MPLA put the country's coalition government on hold, saying that UNITA had failed to meet its peace treaty obligations. It suspended all UNITA representatives from Parliament and declared that it would no longer deal with Savimbi, instead recognizing a splinter group known as UNITA Renovada. In 1999, the United Nations voted to pull out all remaining troops stationed in the country, while continuing its humanitarian relief work with over 1 million refugees. UNITA was able to finance its activities, including the stationing of an estimated 30,000 troops in neighboring Zambia and Congo (Kinshasa), with some $500 million a year in diamond revenues from mines it controlled in the country's northeast region. Fighting continued through 1999, with Angola's army inflicting several defeats on UNITA.

Today, the pattern of military offensives followed by talks and peace agreements (cease-fires) persists, and the fierce fighting continues. Violence is a fact of life, millions of land mines remain buried in the earth, and farmers are reluctant to return to their fields. As a result, much of the country's food must still be imported.

LEGAL CONCEPTS

The Republic of Angola is a unitary, democratic, lay, independent, indivisible, and rule-of-law state. It exercises its sovereignty over an independent nation, with a legal system based on both the Portuguese civil law system (which itself is founded on Roman law) and customary, or traditional, law. Angola has a transitional government, nominally a multiparty democracy with a strong presidential system. Recently, modifications have been made to accommodate political pluralism. Apart from MPLA and UNITA, five minor parties occupy a small number of seats in the National Assembly. There has also been an increased use of free markets.

The Angolan Constitution, which dates from November 11, 1975, has been revised four times: on January 7, 1978; August 11, 1980; March 6, 1991; and August 26,

1992. Five precepts among its 166 articles are especially significant:

1. The attribution, acquisition, loss, or reacquisition of Angolan nationality shall be determined by law, as will be the life, freedom, personal integrity, good name, and reputation of every citizen.
2. The death penalty is prohibited.
3. Citizens over eighteen years of age have the right to vote.
4. Citizens may contest and take legal action against any acts that violate their rights.
5. Taxes may be created or abolished only by law, and issues regarding the applicability, rates, and benefits of taxation, as well as guarantees for taxpayers, shall be determined by law.

Most recently, legislation has been passed in the fields of telecommunications, foreign investment, foreign exchange, and the environment; other measures enacted include a law on the special statute granted to the chairman of UNITA and another law delimiting the sectors of economic activity. In addition, two parliamentary resolutions have been passed—one declaring Jonas Savimbi a war criminal and another expressing solidarity between the Angolan armed forces and the Angolan people.

The rights provided for in the international instruments on human rights to which Angola is a party are in force in the country and have the status of fundamental rights. The relevant international instruments include the Universal Declaration of Human Rights (1948), the African Charter of Human and Peoples Rights (1981), the International Covenant on Civil and Political Rights (1966), the International Covenant on Economic, Social and Cultural Rights (1966), the Convention on the Rights of the Child (1989), and the Convention on the Elimination of All Forms of Discrimination against Women (1979).

CURRENT STRUCTURE

Angola's legal structure features four sovereign branches: the president of the republic, the National Assembly (that is, the political heads of ministries), the government (that is, the prime minister and Cabinet), and the courts. In establishing this structure, emphasis was placed on the separation but interdependence of powers, local autonomy, administrative decentralization and deconcentration, and unity of governmental and administrative action. Angola's executive branch is headed by a president and includes a prime minister and a council of ministers. The legislature is unicameral, and the judicial branch has a supreme court.

The president of the republic is the head of state, elected for a five-year term of office by universal, direct, equal, secret, and periodic suffrage extended to all citizens residing in the national territory. He or she appoints the prime minister and presides over the National Defense Council. The National Assembly is the representative body for all Angolans, composed of 223 members elected by universal, equal, direct, secret, and periodic suffrage for four-year terms of office. The assembly has sole legislative powers. The government, as the the highest public administrative body, conducts the country's general policy and has political, administration, and legislative duties. Its composition is established by an executive law. Finally, Angola's courts are sovereign bodies with the power to (1) administer justice on behalf of the people in order to ensure compliance with the constitutional law and all other laws and legal provisions in force, (2) protect the rights and legitimate interests of citizens and institutions, and (3) determine the legality of administrative acts.

In general, the Constitutional Court administers justice on legal and constitutional matters. It is also charged with determining the constitutionality of laws, executive decrees, ratified international treaties, and any other rules. It also consideres questions including noncompliance with constitutional law caused by failing to take the requisite measures to make constitutional rules executable. It considers appeals in regard to the constitutional nature of all decisions of other courts that refuse to apply any rule on the grounds that it is unconstitutional, as well as appeals in regard to the constitutional nature of all decisions of other courts that apply a rule whose constitutional nature was evoked during the trial.

Apart from the Constitutional Court, Angola's legal system includes the Municipal Courts, the Provincial Courts, and the Supreme Court. According to Angolan law, all crimes with a penalty of less than two years of imprisonment fall under the jurisdiction of the Municipal Courts, with a right of appeal at the level of the Provincial Courts. In practice, the majority of trials occur in the Provincial Courts.

The High Council of the Judicial Bench is the highest body managing and disciplining the judicial bench; it regulates the professional abilities and conduct of the judges. The Judicial Proctorate is an independent public body whose purpose is to defend the rights, freedoms, and guarantees of citizens, ensuring by informal means the justice and legality of the public administration.

Judges may not be removed from office and may not be transferred, promoted, suspended, retired, or dismissed except in accordance with the law. They are responsible for the decisions they make in the discharge of their duties, except for restrictions imposed by law. The presiding judge of the Supreme Court, the vice-president of the Supreme Court, and other judges of the Supreme Court and the Constitutional Court may be arrested only if charged with an offense punishable by a prison sentence; trial court judges may not be arrested without being charged unless caught in flagrante delicto committing a felony punishable by imprisonment.

Angola has several specialized judicial bodies. These include military, administrative, auditing, fiscal, maritime, and arbitration courts constituted in accordance with the law.

STAFFING

To become an advocate (a barrister or solicitor), a law graduate must acquire added training by working at a law firm approved by the Angolan Bar Association (Ordem dos Advogados de Angola). No lawyer can practice law in Angola without being registered with the bar association, which acts as a self-regulating body for the profession.

As of 2001, there were almost 100 judges in the country. The Office of the Prosecutor General had around 200 magistrates covering the Supreme Court, the Provincial Courts, and the Municipal Courts. Of the country's 157 Municipal Courts, just 5 percent had fully functioning justice systems with judges, prosecutors, police investigators, and detention facilities, and only one-third of all provinces had one fully functioning municipal justice system. A serious lack of human resources persists.

IMPACT

The ongoing conflict in Angola has undermined the government's ability to establish a functioning legal system and enforce the law, which has retarded the country's economic and democratic growth. In addition, common practices such as nontransparent regulation, arbitrary decision making, corruption, and bureaucratic inefficiency are pervasive, creating an environment in which legal businesses find it nearly impossible to operate. Since investors cannot be assured of legal protections—obviously, laws and procedures as nontransparent as these are unlikely to offer real protection to investors in the event of a dispute with politically influential persons—Angola is closed to most foreign investment. Particularly onerous labor regulations are also a severe hindrance to business, and Angola has not adhered to any of the principal international conventions on intellectual property rights.

Although the constitution provides for an independent judiciary, the reality is that the judiciary, where it functions, is not independent of the president and the MPLA. In practice, the court system lacks the means, experience, training, and political backing to assert its independence from the president and the ruling party. Moreover, the judicial system was, to a great extent, destroyed during the civil war and did not function in large areas of the country.

Violations of the freedom of expression are also very common. Any journalist who writes an opinion article critical of the government or reveals news the leaders want suppressed is either arrested or expelled from the country. Such legal circumstances obviously have a strong impact on private and public affairs.

UNITA forces either control or are present in large portions of central, eastern, and southern Angola. Economic data are extremely suspect as a result of the ongoing conflict, and they do not encompass economic activity in the roughly one-third of the country over which the government has little or no control. Likewise, the government's economic policies are applicable only in areas of relative peace, where they can be reliably enforced. The government consumes 34.7 percent of the GDP. Progress toward privatization has been minimal, and the government continues to maintain monopolies in the telecommunications, insurance, and banking sectors.

Alexandre Miguel Mestre

See also Arbitration; Civil Law; Constitutional Review; Human Rights Law

References and further reading
www.cia.org
www.encyclopedia.com
www.fe.doe.gov
www.graphicmaps.com
www.heritage.org
www.jurist.law.pitt.edu
www.lawresearch.com
www.reliefweb.int/w/rwb.nsf
www.uni-wuerzburg.de

ANTIGUA AND BARBUDA

COUNTRY INFORMATION

The nation of Antigua and Barbuda lies to the north of the Leeward Islands chain in the eastern Caribbean, some 30 miles north of Guadeloupe, an overseas department of France. Although Antigua and Barbuda is one of the four double-named jurisdictions in the Anglophone Caribbean—St. Vincent and the Grenadines, Trinidad and Tobago, and St. Kitts-Nevis being the others—it actually consists of three islands: Antigua, which occupies an area of 280 square kilometers (110 square miles); Barbuda, which lies 40 kilometers (25 miles) north of Antigua and is 160 square kilometers (60 square miles) in area; and uninhabited Redonda, lying 40 kilometers (25 miles) southwest of Antigua and a mere 1.6 square kilometers (0.6 square miles) in size.

Antigua boasts of 365 beaches, "one for each day of the year," and pink and white sand covers the beaches on Barbuda. It is not surprising, therefore, that the country's main source of income is leisure tourism. The island of Antigua is relatively flat, its highest point being Boggy Peak, which rises to 399 meters. There are no rivers and

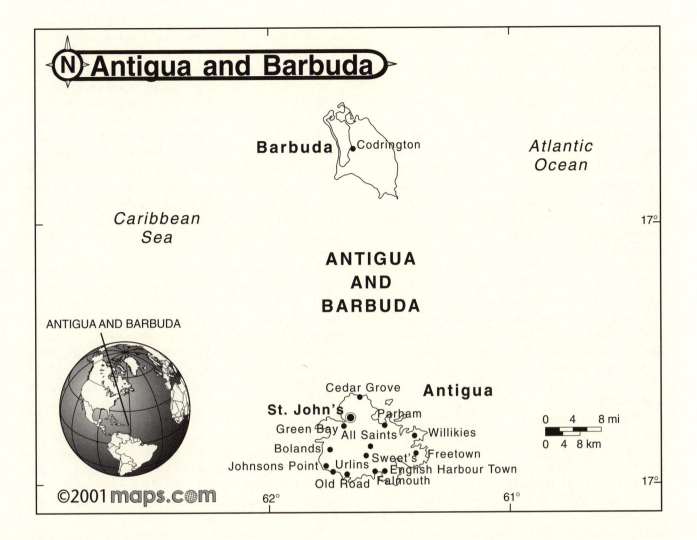

few springs in this dry country. Barbuda is totally flat and has a large mangrove lagoon on the west, and Redonda is rocky and dry.

There is only sparse vegetation on Antigua, a former sugar-producing country, and very little forest area, although some fruit trees—mangoes, guavas, coconuts, and bananas—may be found. Barbuda, by contrast, is thickly forested and provides a haven for wildlife, such as deer, wild pigs, duck, guinea fowl, and a large colony of frigate birds. Redonda is home to species such as the burrowing owl. The climate is tropical, though drier than elsewhere in the region. Rain falls mostly during the hot season from May to November, and the country lies within the hurricane belt. It suffered extensive damage from Hurricane Luis in 1995.

The 1991 census gave the population of the country as 62,911, a figure that was adjusted to 64,166 in a mid-1994 estimate. A more recent estimate is 65,647 persons, with a density of 384 people per square mile. Life expectancy is seventy-one years for men and seventy-five years for women, and the population growth rate over the ten-year period from 1985 to 1994 was 0.5 percent per annum. The majority of the people are of African descent, 21,500 of whom reside in the capital, St. John's. According to a 1992 estimate, Antiqua and Barbuda has a 90 percent literacy rate.

The developing economy is classified as upper-middle income, with a gross national product (GNP) per capita of U.S.$6,970. In 1993, tourism accounted for $277 million out of a total gross domestic product (GDP) of $400 million. The unit of currency is the eastern Caribbean dollar, which is valued at about $2.70 to U.S.$1, and the main exports are agricultural produce and manufactured items such as rum, clothing, household appliances, and assembled electronic components.

The main religion is Christianity, with the Anglican denomination being in the majority. Roman Catholics, Methodists, Lutherans, Moravians, Pentecosts, Baptists, Seventh-Day Adventists, and members of the Salvation Army are also found among the population. The legal system is based on English common law, supplemented by legislation. The official language is English, though the local variety of this, a form of patois, is widely spoken among the resident population.

HISTORY

Scholars believe there was an Arawak settlement in Antigua from about the first century C.E. Christopher Columbus sighted the large island in 1493 and named it after a church in Seville, Spain—Santa Maria de la Antigua. The Spanish and the French tried to colonize Antigua but failed. In 1632, however, the island was colonized by Sir Thomas Warner, and it became a British colony in 1667. Barbuda was annexed by Britain in 1628 and was subsequently granted to the Codrington family, who held it until it was annexed to Antigua in 1860. When sugar became the country's chief crop, supplanting tobacco, African slaves were imported to work on the plantations. They continued to work in the fields until slavery was abolished; they were emancipated in 1834.

The labor movement became the driving force in the political development of Antigua after the disturbances of the late 1930s. The first trade union was formed in 1939 by Vere C. Bird. This organization evolved into the Antigua Labour Party (ALP), a political group that has formed the government of the country for all but a few years since the first elections under universal adult suffrage in 1951.

Antigua and Barbuda has been a member of two regional federal groupings in its history—the Leeward Islands group, which started in the nineteenth century, and the West Indies Federation (from 1958 to 1962). In 1967, Antigua and Barbuda became an associated state with Britain. Under this arrangement, Antigua was responsible for its internal self-government, but Britain retained responsibility for its foreign affairs and defense. In 1980, the ALP administration called elections in order to seek a mandate to make the country fully independent of Britain, a goal that was achieved on November 1, 1981.

Antigua and Barbuda is now a member of the Organization of Eastern Caribbean States (OECS). This group provides member states with a common currency and a central bank, as well as a common judiciary. Proposals for political integration are under consideration, but little has been done in this regard. The country is also a member of the Caribbean Community (CARICOM), which is essentially an economic grouping of the independent Anglophone Caribbean states. A movement is underfoot to create a single market and economy, and suggestions for a common regional currency are being weighed.

LEGAL CONCEPTS

The supreme law of Antigua and Barbuda is its constitution, which is actually titled the Schedule to the Antiguan Independence Order and was made by royal prerogative under the 1981 Antiguan Independence Act of the United Kingdom. The constitution guarantees fundamental human rights, including the right to free speech and a free press, the rights to freedom of religion and association, the presumption of innocence, and freedom from discrimination on the grounds of race, creed, religion, political opinion, national origin, and so forth. The document also recognizes the separation of powers between the executive, legislative, and judicial branches, and it is read as permitting the judicial review of legislation in order to ensure its compliance with the fundamental rights provisions of the constitution. The primary source of law in Antigua and Barbuda is legislation. Of course, the common law tradition is very much alive, and thus there is a heavy reliance on the doctrine of judicial precedent, especially in the areas of civil obligations. Customary law does not play any significant role in Antiguan jurisprudence.

Antigua and Barbuda chose to retain the British monarch as head of state when it became independent in 1981. However, by constitutional provision, the monarch's executive authority is exercised by a local representative (as of 2001, this post was held by Sir James Carlisle, who became governor-general in June 1995). The legislature is bicameral, and elections are held approximately every five years. The lower chamber, the House of Representatives, comprises seventeen members, and the upper chamber consists of an equal number of nominated members. Eleven of these individuals are appointed by the governor-general on the prime minister's recommendation, four on the recommendation of the leader of the opposition, one on the recommendation of the Barbuda local government council, and one at the governor-general's discretion.

The governor-general is appointed by the British monarch, on the recommendation of his or her prime minister. With a largely ceremonial role, the governor-general usually acts on the advice of the cabinet. Antigua and Barbuda's prime minister is appointed by the governor-general at his or her own discretion and is usually the person judged by the governor-general to command the support of the majority of the members of the lower house. Generally, then, the prime minister is the leader of the victorious party in the elections, unless he or she fails to win a seat; in that case, the deputy leader will be appointed. The leader of the opposition is similarly chosen—that is, he or she is the person considered by the governor-general to command the support of the majority of those who do not support the prime minister. The leader of the opposition will typically be the head of the losing party in the general elections or, if there is more than one such party, head of the most successful of the losing parties.

As a member of the OECS court system, Antigua and Barbuda is staffed by a resident puisne judge of the Eastern Caribbean Supreme Court; appeals of his or her decisions are heard by the itinerant Eastern Caribbean Court of Appeal. The Judicial Committee of the Privy Council in London is at the apex of the judicial system. There is also a magistrates' court system in Antigua. These courts hear matters mainly of criminal law. The magistrates can also hear certain types of more serious cases ("triable either way offenses") at the option of the accused, the prosecution, or the court. Magistrates also hold preliminary inquiries into indictable offenses in order to ascertain whether a prima facie case of guilt has been made. Magistrates are generally chosen from among counsel employed by the state; alternatively, they may be selected from among those responding to an advertisement.

The Industrial Court in Antigua and Barbuda is charged with the resolution of industrial disputes, and its jurisdiction is exercised by a president, who is legally trained, and two other members of the court selected by the president. Inter alia, the Industrial Court is empowered to order the reinstatement or reemployment of an employee who has been dismissed in circumstances that are harsh and oppressive or not in accordance with the principles of good industrial relations practice.

In Antigua and Barbuda, the attorney general is chief legal adviser to the government and is a member of Parliament. However, the director of public prosecutions (DPP) has general supervision of criminal prosecutions. The DPP is appointed by the governor-general, acting on the advice of the Judicial and Legal Services Commission, and may be removed from office only (1) if he or she is unable to exercise the functions of the office, or (2) for misbehavior, once a specially appointed tribunal has recommended removal to the governor-general. In respect to certain offenses relating to official secrets, mutiny, or any law involving the nation's rights or obligations under international law, the attorney general is constitutionally permitted to give the DPP directions of a general or special nature regarding the latter's power of prosecution.

The constitution also provides for an ombudsman to investigate allegations of maladministration. This individual is an officer of Parliament and is appointed by resolutions of each parliamentary chamber. Like the DPP, he or she can only be removed from office for an inability to exercise the functions of that office or for misbehavior. The independence of the ombudsman is further entrenched by a provision stipulating that, in the exercise of his or her constitutional functions, the ombudsman shall not be subject to the direction or control of any other person or authority.

One other important office is that of the supervisor of elections. This person enjoys a security of tenure similar to that of the ombudsman and the DPP and is appointed by the governor-general on a resolution of both houses of Parliament.

CURRENT COURT SYSTEM STRUCTURE

The highest court in the Antigua and Barbuda system is the Judicial Committee of the Privy Council, which sits in England. A defendant has the right to appeal a lower-court decision to this body under certain circumstances: (1) in a civil proceeding in which the matter in dispute has a prescribed value of at least $1,500; (2) in a civil proceeding involving a question of property rights; (3) in a proceeding on the dissolution or nullification of a marriage; (4) in any civil or criminal proceeding that involves a question of constitutional interpretation; and (5) in such other cases as may be prescribed. A decision made in any civil proceeding may be appealed to the Judicial Committee with the permission of the Eastern Caribbean Court of Appeal if that court determines that the issue in dispute involves great general or public importance. In addition, the Judicial Committee may, at its own discretion, decide to hear an appeal of a decision issued by the Eastern Caribbean Court of Appeal in any civil or criminal matter.

The Eastern Caribbean Court of Appeal is the second highest court in the judicial hierarchy of Antigua and Barbuda. It is the court to which appeals lie from the High Court and the Magistrates' Courts. In addition, private dispute resolution systems are gradually gaining ground in Antigua and Barbuda, though they have not been formalized by legislative provision.

SPECIALIZED JUDICIAL BODIES

The sole specialized judicial body or court in Antigua and Barbuda is the Industrial Court, established under the Industrial Court Act (1976). This is a superior court of record, and it has jurisdiction (1) to hear and determine trade disputes referred to it under the act; (2) to enjoin a trade union or other organization, an employee, or an employer from taking or continuing an industrial action; and (3) to hear and determine any complaints brought in accordance with the act. The Industrial Court is empowered to act without regard to technicalities and legal form and is not bound to follow the rules of evidence. However, it may inform itself on any matter in whatever way it deems just, and it may take into account opinion evidence and such facts as it considers relevant or material. The court also determines its own procedure, and its decisions are appealable to the Court of Appeal on limited grounds—namely, that the Industrial Court had no jurisdiction or that it exceeded its jurisdiction, that the award or order was obtained by fraud, that any finding or decision of the court in any matter was erroneous in point of law, or that some other specific illegality was committed. An award of the court is binding on all parties to the dispute, relevant employers and their successors, all relevant trade unions and their successors, and all pertinent employees.

STAFFING

As of 2001, there were about eighty practicing attorneys in Antigua and Barbuda. There was one resident puisne judge of the Eastern Caribbean Supreme Court and three

Legal Structure of Antigua and Barbuda Courts

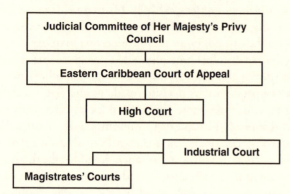

officers and may be appointed on contract or seconded from the civil service, usually from the DPP's chambers.

The law program at the only regional university, the University of the West Indies, began offering classes in 1970 and by 2001 had about 350 students and a full-time faculty of about 20, with some 10 adjunct staff members. The region's three law schools are located in Jamaica (the Norman Manley Law School, which commenced operations in 1973); in Trinidad and Tobago (the Hugh Wooding Law School, which also began in 1973); and in the Bahamas (the Eugene Dupuch Law School, which was established in 1998). Increasingly, the graduates of these regional institutions are assuming prominent positions in the judiciary, public service, and the academy.

magistrates. There were four counsel in the attorney general's chambers, and the offices of the director of public prosecutions had three attorneys-at-law and support staff. Three other attorneys were assigned to various state departments—Marine Affairs, Home Affairs, and the Constitution Review Commission. From time to time, in important matters, the state engages private attorneys. Magistrates do not enjoy the same security of tenure as judges, being essentially public service employees.

Under the regional treaty establishing the Commonwealth Caribbean Council of Legal Education, attorneys-at-law are required to undergo two years of professional training at one of the three regional law schools, leading to the award of the Certificate of Legal Education (CLE). Before entering this training, the student must complete a three-year academic undergraduate program at the University of the West Indies, earning a Bachelor of Laws (LL.B.) degree. If the LL.B. or equivalent qualification has been obtained elsewhere, the prospective attorney is required to successfully complete a competitive exam to gain entry to law school. There is no general system of continuing legal education, but some of the international agencies have, from time to time, sponsored projects or staged conferences on legal matters of importance to the region, such as drug offenses, money laundering, judicial reform, legislative drafting, and alternative dispute resolution.

There is no formal selection procedure for judges in Antigua and Barbuda: essentially, this is considered a matter for the Eastern Caribbean Court system. The president and vice-president of the Industrial Court are appointed by the governor-general after consultation with the Judicial and Legal Services Commission; the other members are appointed by the governor-general from among persons experienced in industrial relations or qualified as economists, accountants, or attorneys with no less than five years' standing. The president and vice-president must be attorneys-at-law of not less than ten and five years' standing, respectively. Magistrates are public

IMPACT OF LAW

The legal system of Antigua and Barbuda is critical to the country's social and economic development. The courts are jealous guardians of the fundamental freedoms of citizens, and legislation has been used as a tool of economic development (for example, by facilitating the use of the jurisdiction as an offshore tax center and offering tax incentives to qualifying investors). Like many of its neighbors in the region, the country is beset with a spiraling crime rate, fueled in large part by the ubiquitous drug trade. This situation has led to populist calls for a more frequent use of the death penalty, although efforts in that direction have been stymied by human rights considerations in judgments rendered by the Judicial Committee of the Privy Council. This development has, in turn, increased political fervor for the establishment of a regional final court of appeal as soon as possible, the preparations for which are already at an advanced stage. Recent international condemnations of Antigua and Barbuda as a tax haven have also caused an extensive reexamination of the country's legislation pertaining to offshore banking and money laundering.

Jefferson Cumberbatch

See also Alternative Dispute Resolution; Appellate Courts; Capital Punishment; Common Law; Constitutional Review; Legal Education; Magistrates—Common Law Systems; Privy Council

References and further reading
Antoine, Rose-Marie. 1998. *Commonwealth Caribbean Legal Systems.* London: Cavendish.
Augier, F. Roy, S. C. Gordon, Douglas G. Hall, and M. Reckord. 1970. *The Making of the West Indies.* London: Longman Caribbean.
Famighetti, Robert, ed. 1997. *The World Almanac and Book of Facts.* Manwah, NJ: World Almanac Books.
Gunthorp, Dale, ed. 1997. *The Commonwealth Yearbook.* London: Hanson Cooke.
Williams, Eric. 1970. *From Columbus to Castro: The History of the Caribbean, 1492–1969.* London: Andre Deutsch.

APEC
See Dispute Resolution under
Regional Trade Agreements

APPELLATE COURTS

"The appellate tradition dates back some four to six thousand years to several highly developed civilizations in that fecund area of the world we call the Near East" (Coffin 1994, 328). With the evolution of law and jurisprudence, the appellate traditions of early civilizations have developed into formally organized judicial entities. Today, appellate courts occupy vital positions within judicial systems. Their existence forms the upper echelons of a legal hierarchy through which disputes receive final adjudication. To better understand how appellate courts function, the following sections will explore their purposes, organizational structures, and jurisdictions.

PURPOSES

Appellate courts serve two fundamental purposes. First, they provide an additional remedy to individuals seeking recourse for a perceived wrong that was not resolved by a trial court. In general, courts serve the basic function of allowing two individuals engaged in a dispute to resolve their conflict via an impartial third party. The logic behind the triad for conflict resolution is so compelling that courts "have become a universal political phenomenon" (Shapiro 1981, 1). However, it is possible for the loser of the initial conflict to feel as though the other two members of the triad conspired in his or her defeat. Without additional recourse, the loser may attack the legitimacy of the judicial system because he did not receive a "fair deal." Thus the ability to appeal a dispute allows the loser to continue to assert his or her rightness without attacking the legitimacy of the legal institution. Additionally, through the avenue of an appellate court, the loser's frustration is channeled into the legal system, thereby reinforcing the system's legitimacy (Shapiro 1981, 49).

Second, appellate courts provide centralized supervision of local courts to ensure the uniform application of laws within a geographical boundary (e.g., nation, state, province, etc.). Centralized supervision becomes more essential as the geographical boundaries increase. Without a supervisory structure, the development of law would occur in a haphazard fashion with local judges—often isolated from legal developments in other geographical areas—rendering decisions that are potentially inconsistent with other areas.

Countries vary regarding the degree of supervisory power granted to appellate courts. In most common law countries, appeals are limited only to questions of law. Petitioners cannot request appellate judges to examine factual disputes. Those issues are solely under the authority of the trial courts. Common law appellate courts are thereby constrained in their supervisory capacity. In contrast, most civil law appellate courts possess the authority to review factual questions disputed from a trial. The review is usually accomplished through a trial de novo, and this authority provides "far more general supervisory power" (Shapiro 1981, 39).

Appellate courts fulfill these two purposes through a variety of mechanisms. Though the specific duties of appellate courts vary across (and within) individual countries, these tasks can be classified into four broad categories. Fundamentally, the *raison d'être* of appellate courts is to provide a forum for review of trial court decisions (Abraham 1998, 102). Thus, the primary duty is to correct any errors committed by trial courts. Second, appellate courts are often responsible for reviewing actions by governmental agencies/ministries. Several agencies/ministries possess quasi-judicial authority and render decisions on certain disputes. Losing litigants often appeal agency decisions to appellate courts, as they would file appeals from trial courts. Third, these courts offer additional clarification and interpretation of legislative statutes. Finally, appellate courts often provide legal insights into the meanings of constitutional provisions. These last two categories facilitate the development of uniform legal principles within geographic regions. Often statutes and constitutional provisions are crafted using vague and ambiguous language. When disputes arise, the local trial courts present an initial interpretation that may or may not coincide with other legal principles. Appellate courts have the opportunity to review these initial interpretations and provide additional clarification. Often the decisions rendered by appellate courts codify prior interpretations from several local courts, thereby elucidating previous explanations.

ORGANIZATIONAL STRUCTURES

Appellate courts come in many different shapes and sizes. Identifying the organizational structure of these courts is essential in understanding a country's particular judicial system. This structure contains two components: a hierarchical facet, which arranges the different courts into a single system, and a compositional facet, which determines how judges are organized within specific courts.

At the top of the hierarchical structure are *courts of last resort*. These courts serve as the final stage of the judicial process and many derive their authority directly from the country's constitution. National courts of last resort normally handle only the most important, most complex, or most controversial issues. Decisions by such courts as the U.S. Supreme Court or the Court de Cassation in France are usually final and cannot be appealed to a higher authority. Some countries, however, allow litigants to ap-

Legal Structure of Appellate Courts

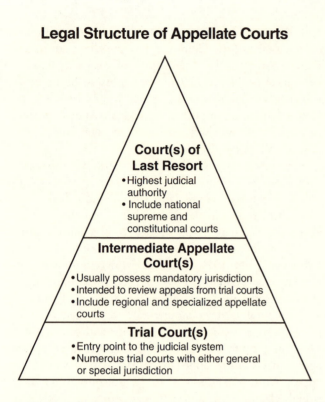

Court(s) of Last Resort
- Highest judicial authority
- Include national supreme and constitutional courts

Intermediate Appellate Court(s)
- Usually possess mandatory jurisdiction
- Intended to review appeals from trial courts
- Include regional and specialized appellate courts

Trial Court(s)
- Entry point to the judicial system
- Numerous trial courts with either general or special jurisdiction

peal decisions from their courts of last resort, usually to a specialized oversight committee within the legislature.

Below the courts of last resort are *intermediate appellate courts,* whose authority is often derived from legislation. These tribunals usually handle appeals from trial courts, and their purpose is often to ensure that the trial courts do not make mistakes. Examples of intermediate appellate courts include the U.S. Courts of Appeals and England's Court of Appeals. Decisions of these courts can be reviewed by higher judicial entities, such as courts of last resort (in England, the court of last resort is the House of Lords). Often intermediate appellate courts preside over specific geographical areas and regions.

Some countries possess specialized appellate courts to handle disputes in specific legal areas. In Russia, for example, specialized arbitration courts—with the Supreme Court of Arbitration at the apex—handle the majority of economic disputes. In the United States, the Federal Circuit Court of Appeals handles the majority of patent, trademark, copyright, and trade disputes. The Family Court of Australia is an intermediate appellate court with jurisdiction over marital and child custody issues. Many European and civil law countries utilize constitutional courts to resolve questions regarding the constitutionality of legislation and governmental actions.

The composition of appellate courts also varies by country, although two patterns exist that are common to most judicial systems. The U.S. Supreme Court and French Court de Cassation are examples of the first category in which judges preside in a *single court.* Here, a specific number of judges render decisions as a single, colle-

gial body, thereby ensuring greater uniformity of the law. Often single courts issue one opinion, although in some cases—such as the U.S. Supreme Court—individual justices can issue separate opinions. In contrast to the single court is the second category in which appellate courts are organized into *rotating panels.* In this system, a certain number of judges from the appellate court combines into a judicial panel to resolve disputes. Creation of rotating panels allows the judges on these courts to review a larger number of appeals. Examples of rotating panels include the U.S. Courts of Appeals, in which three-judge panels resolve disputes, and the Estonian Supreme Court, in which five judges from the seventeen-member court form the Constitutional Chamber to resolve questions of constitutionality. The Australian High Court consists of seven justices who can sit en banc on important constitutional questions but can also sit in panels of five or three or even as a single justice, depending on the statutory provisions involved in the case. The High Court issues opinions seriatim, with each justice expressing her or his reasoning for the decision in the case.

JURISDICTIONS

The jurisdictional authority of appellate courts involves several aspects. First, jurisdiction determines when appellate courts review cases. Second, it also determines which cases come before appellate courts. Finally, jurisdiction influences the ability of appellate courts to review legislation. Understanding these different aspects provides insights into how appellate courts operate.

By definition, most appellate courts possess *appellate jurisdiction,* that is, they review decisions rendered by a previous judicial entity. The exercise of appellate jurisdiction varies depending on the type of legal system. In many common law countries, an adversarial system is employed. In this system, attorneys argue the merits of their client's case before judges who are limited to only answering questions of law; factual questions are the province of trial court judges. In contrast, several civil law countries utilize an inquisitorial system. Appellate courts in these countries often possess the authority to review factual and legal questions. This review is accomplished through a trial de novo, in which the judges become active participants and can, along with the attorneys, question witnesses.

Some appellate courts also possess *original jurisdiction,* in which the judges are the first to preside over a particular dispute. In these instances, the appellate court actually conducts a trial to determine guilt or liability in addition to applying legal principles. For example, the U.S. Supreme Court possesses appellate jurisdiction to review cases decided by the federal Courts of Appeals or by state courts of last resort. Additionally, the U.S. Supreme Court possesses original jurisdiction over disputes between states or over disputes involving foreign diplomats.

The second aspect of jurisdictional authority involves docket control (i.e., which cases can appear before the appellate court). Some courts possess *mandatory control* and must review all appeals. Other courts possess *discretionary control* and can choose which cases to review. With discretionary control, judges can become gatekeepers by choosing only the most important cases. However, the exercise of discretionary control varies across countries. In some countries, the court below can grant a "leave to appeal." An example is the English Court of Appeal granting leave to litigants to present cases before the House of Lords. Conversely, other countries provide the reviewing court with the authority to control its own docket. In the United States, losers at the Courts of Appeals stage can apply for writs of certiorari to the Supreme Court. The justices possess the authority to grant or deny these writs, and thus they control which cases to review. Determining the judicial agenda thus becomes an important stage of the decision-making process, and the judicial behavior of judges often reflects this important power.

The final aspect of jurisdictional authority pertains to an appellate court's ability to review legislation. Most appellate courts possess *concrete judicial review*, also called *a posteriori review*. Under this category, appellate courts render decisions based on actual cases or controversies. A dispute occurs whereby litigants appear before the court to argue their positions. The logic behind concrete judicial review is that the judges do not rule on hypothetical situations. Instead, they apply existing laws to specific case facts when issuing decisions. In contrast, some appellate courts possess *abstract, or a priori judicial review*. In this category, legislatures request an advisory opinion from the appellate court (usually from a court of last resort). The judges are asked to provide their opinions on the constitutionality of a statute before the legislation becomes law. The rationale for abstract judicial review involves conservation of resources. Judges have the opportunity to eliminate blatantly unconstitutional statutes before the government invests resources to implement the law.

CONCLUSION

Appellate courts occupy vital positions within contemporary societies. Although the organizational structures and jurisdictions may differ depending on geographical boundaries, the fundamental purposes remain similar. Appellate courts enhance the legitimacy of the legal system by providing individuals an additional recourse to resolve disputes and ensuring the uniform application of laws by local judges. These courts often comprise the upper echelons of a formal judicial hierarchy and render decisions that affect political, social, economic, and cultural norms.

Kirk A. Randazzo
Reginald Sheehan

See also Adversarial System; Australia; Certiorari, Writ of; Civil Law; Common Law; Constitutional Review; England and Wales; Estonia; France; Judicial Review; Russia; Trial Courts; United States—Federal System; United States—State Systems

References and further reading
Abraham, Henry J. 1998. *The Judicial Process: An Introductory Analysis of the Courts of the United States, England and France.* New York: Oxford University Press.
Coffin, Frank M. 1994. *On Appeal: Courts, Lawyering and Judging.* New York: W. W. Norton.
Murphy, Walter F., and C. Herman Pritchett. 1986. *Courts, Judges and Politics: An Introduction to the Judicial Process.* 4th ed. New York: McGraw-Hill.
O'Brien, David M. 1997. *Judges on Judging: Views from the Bench.* Chatham, NJ: Chatham House.
Shapiro, Martin. 1981. *Courts: A Comparative and Political Analysis.* Chicago: University of Chicago Press.
Songer, Donald R., Reginald S. Sheehan, and Susan B. Haire. 2000. *Continuity and Change on the United States Courts of Appeal.* Ann Arbor: University of Michigan Press.

ARBITRATION

INTRODUCTION

Arbitration is a legal proceeding in which a neutral party, the arbitrator, conducts a hearing and issues an award resolving a dispute between parties. Arbitration is one of the three primary forums used worldwide to adjudicate disputes. The other two forums are judicial court trials and administrative hearings.

Parties may resolve their differences by negotiating with each other and reaching a compromise, by having lawyers or other representatives settle their disagreements, or by hiring a mediator to help them reach a settlement. If the parties cannot resolve their dispute using one of these approaches, then they will submit their case to an arbitrator, judge, or jury who will decide who wins and who loses.

Businesses, individuals, consumers, companies, employers, employees, organizations, and governments with a dispute can agree to choose to arbitrate their dispute instead of litigating it. Arbitration is usually must faster, far less expensive, and just as fair as litigation, which is why many parties prefer to use it.

Arbitration provides an economical, effective, and fair way to resolve local, regional, and global disputes. The United States Supreme Court and the United States Congress have recognized that arbitration is a very effective way to resolve disputes. Arbitration is the only universally recognized forum available in every country. The growth of national and international trade, Internet transactions, and global agreements makes arbitration the ideal way to resolve all types of disputes.

ARBITRATION PROCEEDINGS

An arbitration proceeding involves several steps:

1. An agreement to arbitrate.
2. The selection of an arbitration organization or arbitrator.
3. The filing of a claim and a response.
4. The exchange of information.
5. The arbitration hearing.
6. The issuance of an arbitration award.
7. The enforcement of the award.

Agreement to Arbitrate

Parties can agree before or after a dispute arises to use arbitration. Many parties to a contract include in it a predispute arbitration clause so that they both know how a potential dispute will be resolved. Predispute arbitration clauses are routinely included in all sorts of agreements: financial, construction, brokerage, employment, Internet transactions, credit card sales, real estate, international contracts, commercial cases, labor-management, and many others. Parties may also wait until a dispute arises and then agree to arbitrate. This is more common in major disputes between commercial companies, government agencies, or international parties. A typical predispute clause reads:

> The parties agree that all claims and disputes between them arising out of or relating to this agreement and relationship, including the validity of this agreement, shall be resolved by final, binding arbitration by [name of arbitration organization] in accord with its Code of Procedure. Judgment on the award may be entered in any court with jurisdiction.

Arbitration Organization

Professional arbitration organizations provide arbitration services in the United States and throughout the world. Among the largest are International Arbitration Forum, National Arbitration Forum, arbitration-forum.com, American Arbitration Association, International Chamber of Commerce, and London Court of Arbitration. These organizations maintain arbitration rules of procedure and panels of experienced professionals who arbitrate cases. The forum has an International Code of Procedure and a panel of arbitrators who are located throughout the world to conduct arbitration proceedings.

Claims and Responses

An arbitration case begins with the filing of a claim by a claimant with an arbitration administrative organization and the service of the claim against a respondent, who re-

sponds to the claim. The arbitration administer appoints an expert, neutral arbitrator to decide the dispute.

Discovery

The parties may exchange information before the arbitration hearing through the process of discovery. Parties may request documents from each other, take depositions, or undertake other means to gain relevant information from each other about their dispute.

Arbitration Hearing

The arbitrator conducts the arbitration hearing, usually scheduled some months after the case has begun. Parties may select from a document hearing (wherein all evidence is submitted in writing to the arbitrator), an online hearing (wherein evidence is submitted to the arbitrator electronically by computer), a telephone hearing (wherein witnesses testify and the parties present their case over the telephone), a video conference hearing (wherein the parties and witnesses appear on a video monitor), a participatory hearing (wherein parties and witnesses appear in person, as in a court hearing), or a combination of these types of hearings. Parties may represent themselves or have an attorney represent them.

A hearing usually includes an opportunity for each party to make an opening statement, conduct direct examination and cross-examination of witnesses, introduce exhibits and other evidence, and make a closing statement. The entire hearing may take an hour, a day, a week, or longer, depending on the number of parties and witnesses. A participatory hearing is usually held at a convenient location in the community where one or more of the parties do business or live. Arbitrations are commonly conducted and decisions reached by one arbitrator. More complex or significant cases are decided by a panel of three arbitrators.

Arbitration Award

The arbitrator usually issues an award within a month after the hearing. The award may be a short, summary decision or a detailed explanation of findings, conclusions, and reasons. The award may be binding or nonbinding, depending on the agreement of the parties and the law. A binding arbitration award is a final award with which the parties must comply. A nonbinding award is an advisory award to which the parties may agree or which they may ignore and proceed to litigation.

Enforcement

An arbitration award is usually self-enforcing, and the losing party does what the award requires. If a losing party refuses to comply with an award, the winning party can bring a confirmation action in a court that has jurisdiction over the losing party and obtain a civil judgment enforcing the award. Any party may challenge the award and ask that it be modified or vacated by bringing a court action for such relief. A judge reviews the award and determines whether it complies with the law or ought to be vacated or modified because of manifest injustice, fraud, or other statutory grounds. The federal or national laws of the country or state that governs the arbitration determine the scope of these rulings. In the United States, the Federal Arbitration Act governs all arbitrations between parties engaged in interstate commerce. In other countries, the arbitration laws of those countries may govern.

TYPES OF ARBITRATION

This general explanation of arbitration covers common disputes between parties for money damages and other civil relief. Businesses, individuals, companies, employees, and consumers may all have their disputes resolved through these general procedures. Common disputes that are arbitrated include business, consumer, commercial, contract, financial, property, investment, corporate, employment, construction, health, tort, and related problems.

Arbitration is these types of disputes is usually "binding," that is, the award is final and binds all the parties, both winners and losers, to adhere to its terms. Some cases may result in "nonbinding" awards that the parties may reject or accept.

There are several other types of arbitrations that are conducted under different rules and procedures.

Labor-Management Arbitrations
A collective bargaining agreement between a labor union and a company may include an agreement to arbitrate work-related disputes between employees and the company with a set or arbitration rules and a panel of arbitrators.

Sports Arbitration
Agreements with sporting teams and players may include an arbitration agreement. Professional baseball in America has an arbitration procedure in which the arbitrator is to select the salary proposal of either the player or the club as the final arbitration award.

Compulsory Arbitration
The law in some countries and states mandates that certain types of disputes must be arbitrated. Some insurance disputes between an insurance company and a policyholder may have to be arbitrated under a set of rules established by law.

Court Arbitration
Some courts require parties to arbitrate their disputes before they may obtain a court trial. An arbitrator selected by the court conducts a hearing and issues a nonbinding award. Any party may reject the award and choose to go to trial.

OTHER DISPUTE RESOLUTION METHODS
The most common alternative to arbitration is mediation. Parties in a mediation mutually negotiate a compromise settlement with the help of the mediator. Participants in a mediation include the parties, their lawyers, and the mediator, who facilitates a compromise. Mediation is a confidential process. The agreement that results from it is final and binding when the parties voluntarily agree to a settlement. The mediator cannot impose a final decision on the parties.

ARBITRATION DISADVANTAGES AND ADVANTAGES
Not all parties may want to arbitrate a dispute, and not all cases can or should be arbitrated. There are several reasons why parties may choose not to arbitrate:

1. *Juries.* Parties often prefer to have a jury decide the case. The United States is the only country where juries are still commonly used to resolve a wide range of civil disputes.
2. *Procedures.* Arbitration does not have as detailed a set of procedures as litigation, which affords more opportunities to seek discovery, bring motions, and have rules of evidence apply to a case before a judge.
3. *Publicness.* Litigation and administrative forums are more public than arbitration and may more easily establish legal precedents for the future.
4. *Familiarity.* Arbitration procedures may be less familiar to parties and lawyers than those governing litigation, and they may prefer litigate in their own local courts.
5. *Appeals.* Judicial and administrative decisions are more appealable. Courts have limited reasons to review and overturn arbitration awards.

Arbitration has several advantages over other forums:

1. *Cost.* Obtaining an arbitration award is far less expensive than obtaining a judgment through litigation. The costs associated with arbitration include filing fees, which are proportional to the amount of the dispute, and hearing fees, which can be minimal, especially if document, telephone, or online hearings are used.
2. *Speed.* Arbitration documents are simple to complete, discovery is limited, the hearing is held at a scheduled time and efficiently conducted, and the award is promptly granted. Many arbitrations can be completed within a few months.

3. *Flexibility and Adaptability.* Parties can choose in their arbitration agreement the organization that will conduct the arbitration and the rules that will govern it. They can review the code of procedures of available arbitration administrators and select the code that best meets their needs.

4. *Participation.* The simplicity of arbitration proceedings allows a party in many cases to decide to represent itself without the need to retain a lawyer. Or a party may prefer to have a lawyer represent it, especially in complex cases or multiple-party cases.

5. *Comprehensibility.* The uniform rules of an arbitration organization provide parties with an understandable and predictable process. Parties who may have disputes with companies or individuals located in different states or countries may have the same uniform arbitration rules apply, rather than the many diverse and complicated regional litigation procedures and rules.

Roger Haydock

See also Alternative Dispute Resolution; Dispute Resolution under Regional Trade Agreements; International Arbitration

References and further reading

American Arbitration Association, http://www.adr.org (cited March 29, 2001).

Arbitration-Forum.com, http://www.arbitration-forum.com (cited March 29, 2001).

Born, Gary B. 1994. *International Arbitration in the United States: Commentary and Materials.* Boston: Kluwer and Taxation Publishers.

Coe, Jack J., Jr. 1997. *International Commercial Arbitration: American Principles and Practice in a Global Context.* New York: Transnational Publishers.

Domke, Martin. 1990. *Domke on Commercial Arbitration.* Saint Paul: West Group.

International Arbitration Forum, http://www.arb-forum.com (cited March 29, 2001).

London Court of International Arbitration, http://www.lcia-arbitration.com/lcia (cited March 29, 2001).

MacNeil, Ian R., Richard E. Speidel, and Thomas J. Stipanowich. 1999. *Federal Arbitration Law: Agree, Awards, and Remedies under the Federal Arbitration Act.* New York: Aspen Law and Business.

National Arbitration Forum, http://www.arb-forum.com (cited March 29, 2001).

Oehmke, Thomas. 2000. *Commercial Arbitration.* Revised ed. Saint Paul: West Group.

ARGENTINA

COUNTRY INFORMATION

Argentina is located at the extreme southeast of the South American continent, bordering Bolivia and Paraguay to the north; Uruguay, Brazil, and the Atlantic Ocean to the east; the Atlantic Ocean to the south, and Chile to the west. It covers some 3.8 million square kilometers (1.5 million square miles), about one-third the size of the United States. It is the eighth largest country in the world and the second largest in South America after Brazil. The Andes mountain range forms a natural boundary between Argentina and Chile to the west. East of the Andes, the land is almost an entirely flat plain. The middle plain section is known as the Pampas and is the most productive agricultural section. The southernmost part of Argentina is called Patagonia, where the terrain is a mostly large arid steppe. There are numerous lakes, especially among the foothills of the Patagonian Andes. Most of the climate is moderate except for a small tropical area in the northeast and the tropical Chaco region in the north. It is generally colder in the higher Andes, Patagonia, and Tierra del Fuego in the south. The most important cities are: Buenos Aires, capital and largest city; Córdoba, major manufacturing and university city; Rosario, important river port; Mendoza, in the wine-growing region; La Plata, capital of the province of Buenos Aires; San Miguel de Tucumán, where the declaration of independence took place; and Mar del Plata, resort city on the Atlantic Ocean. Argentina has a population of 36.6 million, a third of which live in the city of Buenos Aires and the suburban Buenos Aires area. About 85 percent of the population are of European descent, mostly of Spanish or Italian heritage. Argentina has few mestizos compared to other Latin American countries. Spanish is the official language. Free mandatory education is provided from ages six to fourteen. Argentina's literacy rate is about 95 percent and is one of the highest in Latin America. Argentina has twenty-four national universities, as well as many private universities. Roman Catholics make up 92 percent of the populations. The country's legal system is based on European civil law.

HISTORY

In 1516, the Spaniards discovered the Río de la Plata. In 1536 Pedro de Mendoza founded Buenos Aires. After the initial settlers were expelled by the indigenous population, Juan de Garay finally settled Buenos Aires on a permanent basis in 1580. Argentina remained a Spanish colony until 1816. In 1776, Spain created the Virreinato del Río de la Plata (Viceroyalty of the Río de la Plata), a viceroyal type of governing jurisdiction. It entailed what today is Argentina and neighboring countries. In 1783, the Audiencia of Buenos Aires was created. The *audiencia* had supreme judicial and administrative authority. It was a unique political and jurisdictional institution ranking hand-in-hand in importance with the viceroy. Both were the direct representation of the Spanish king and therefore acted in his name. These two institutions were

meant to control each other. The *audiencia* was acting as a supreme court. Normally all cases were tried and settled in the West Indian colonies, but there was a measure of last resort before the king, through the Consejo de Indias (West Indias Council). Another institution was the *regente* (superintendent), who had coordinating functions and was also acting as a lower court. The creation of such a position had been the first attempt to separate the administration of justice from political affairs. In 1794, the Consulado of Buenos Aires was created. This institution was in charge of administering justice only in commercial matters. It also promoted trade, industrial and agricultural development, and public works. There were also other courts with specialized jurisdiction, like the ecclesiastic courts, and the Protomedicato, a court handling malpractice cases and other cases related to trades and professions. By the early 1800s, there was a clear distinction between administrative and judicial courts.

Napoleon's conquest of Spain prompted Argentina to declare temporary independence in 1810. On May 25, an assembly meeting at Buenos Aires's City Hall (Cabildo) overthrew the Spanish government and installed a provi-

sional governing council. Part of the legislation that had been enacted by Spain was derogated. Nevertheless, some of the old bodies of law (Ordenamiento de Alcalá, Fueros, Partidas, Novísima Recopilación) were still applicable provided they did not contradict the new regulations.

After several unsuccessful attempts by Spain to regain control, independence was declared in 1816 at Tucumán. Fighting quickly broke out among the provinces, which refused to be ruled by Buenos Aires. Most of the following decades were characterized by civil war between Buenos Aires and the rest of the provinces. This period of anarchy ended in 1852 and the following year the present constitution was adopted. A period of great stability followed. Argentina was fully united in 1880. When the constitution was enacted, the Castilian legislation was still in force. The constitution provided for the sanction of federal codes. In 1862, the commercial code of the province of Buenos Aires, the work of Eduardo Acevedo and Dalmacio Vélez Sarsfield, was adopted by the whole country as a federal code. In 1871 the civil code by Dalmacio Vélez Sarsfield was enacted, and is still in force at present. The main sources for this code were the Castilian legislation (modified by the national legislation after 1810), the Napoleonic Code of 1804, and the Esboço by the Brazilian author Freitas. The first penal code, by Carlos Tejedor, was enacted in 1886. It was replaced in 1921 with the penal code authored by Rodolfo Moreno. The latter is still in force at present, with some amendments. In general, there is a great influence of the European law tradition in Argentina, especially from France (in civil law) and Germany (in criminal law). There have been many amendments since the original codes, particularly in the field of commercial law, where special legislation has been enacted to deal with the growing complexity of modern trade and industrial enterprise.

In the half century following 1880, Argentina made remarkable economic and social progress and attracted millions of immigrants from Spain, Italy, and other countries. Farmland was very cheap and there was a huge expansion of farming. British investors pumped hundreds of millions of dollars into agricultural investments and set up the railroads to serve them. It was like an economic miracle. In 1900 Argentina was the fifth richest country in the world (today it ranks fifty-fifth).

The 1929 world economic crisis had serious repercussions in Argentina. In 1930, seventy years of uninterrupted democracy ended and were replaced by a period of fifty years during which military governments alternated power with democratic governments.

In 1983, democracy was reinstated and Raúl Alfonsín of the Radical party took office as president. Since the end of the last military government in 1983, Argentina has enjoyed a period of uninterrupted civilian rule. In 1989 Carlos Saúl Menem of the Justicialista party was elected president. In 1994, the constitution was amended, shortening the presidential term to four years and allowing one consecutive reelection. Mr. Menem was reelected in 1995 and his term expired in 1999. The current president, Fernando de la Rua, of the Radical party assumed office in December 1999.

LEGAL CONCEPTS

Argentina is organized as a federal republic with a democratic political system. The Argentine Constitution, established in 1853, provides for a tripartite system of government consisting of an executive branch headed by the president, a legislative branch, and a judiciary. The constitution expressly provides for fundamental civil rights such as equality before the law, freedom of speech, peaceful assembly, and the right to private property. The executive branch has been the dominant branch at the federal level. The president is elected by direct vote and may serve a maximum of two consecutive, four-year terms. He appoints the justices of the Supreme Court with the consent of the Senate by two-thirds of its members present, in a public meeting convoked to this effect. The

president appoints the other judges of the lower federal courts, with the consent of the Senate, from a binding proposal of three candidates submitted by the Council of Magistracy. After the 1994 constitutional amendment, a chief of cabinet is appointed by the president and can be removed by him or by Congress.

The Argentine Congress comprises two houses (a 72-seat Senate and a 257-seat Chamber of Deputies), which constitute the legislative branch. Senators are elected for six-year terms upon a staggered basis, with one-third of the Senate being elected every two years. Deputies are elected for four-year terms upon a staggered basis; one-half of the Chamber is subject to election every two years. Congress has exclusive power to enact laws concerning federal legislation, including international and inter-provincial trade, immigration and citizenship, patents and trademarks. The constitution entitles the Congress to enact the codes concerning civil, commercial, criminal, mining, labor, and social security matters, which are applicable throughout the country. Each province enacts its own constitution, elects its own governor and legislators, and appoints its own judges to the provincial courts. Judges at all levels are appointed for life.

The judges are bound by the abstract provisions of the civil code, the statutes, the decrees of the executive power, and administrative regulations, but not by the decisions of other judges rendered in similar cases. The system in Argentina is not one of stare decisis, and therefore, the rulings of the higher courts are not binding upon the lower courts. The case law therefore basically provides guidelines in respect of the general principles to be applied; the authority of the precedent is only persuasive. But even though the judges are not bound to follow the precedent, in fact they do in most of the instances. In certain situations where there are no statutory laws to follow, the courts have developed an important body of case law through numerous precedents applying general principles of law. The constitution provides for jury trials, but they have not been established so far.

Labor rights are of special concern in the Argentine constitution, although since the early 1990s the laws and regulations articulating those rights have granted more flexibility to labor contracts to promote the creation of jobs. There are laws for both collective labor agreements and for individual labor contracts. Collective agreements require the approval of the Labor Ministry and then become binding to the labor union and its employees. Individual labor contracts may be on a temporary basis or infinite. Indefinite labor contracts are regulated by labor contract law and can be disrupted by either party in certain circumstances. Salaries can be set on a monthly, daily, or hourly basis, but monthly is more customary. The minimum salary is $200 per month as of June 2000, plus an additional bonus, *aguinaldo,* which is paid 50 percent in June and 50 percent in December. Vacation benefits vary between fourteen and thirty-five days, depending on period of service with the firm. Other types of leave are maternity (ninety days), marriage (ten days), study, and illness.

Employers dismissing employees with indefinite contracts must give from one to two months' prior notice (depending on whether the period of service is less or greater than five years), and pay compensation of a month's salary for each year of employment, or fraction of a year (over three months). Two months' salary is the minimum compensation. No compensation is due if gross misconduct can be proven. The employer may dismiss personnel in the case of force majeure or an involuntary reduction of the employer's operations. Those to be dismissed first will be those with the shortest periods of service, and severance payments will amount to 50 percent of the normal rates applicable. There are severe penalties for dismissing pregnant women or new mothers. All workers must be protected against injuries on the job by Aseguradora de Riesgos del Trabajo (ART), which is a work risk insurer. Any necessary medical aid is financed by employers' monthly payments.

At present, 40 percent of all workers are in the black economy. Employers use a lot of temporary labor supplied by contractors, which they can take or dispose of at will. Employers negotiating with the unions find them more flexible than they look.

Argentine legal culture, as in the other Latin American countries, is legalistic and formalistic. As a consequence of bureaucracies ever expanding to administer the growing and confusing mass of regulations, the result is exaggerated concern with legal formality, the need to establish the existence of formal legal authority for almost any act, and the tendency to honor form over substance. More than 26,000 laws have been enacted so far, but only 3,500 are in force. The abundance of legislation and regulations reflects a mistrust of those administering and interpreting laws, and a belief in the effectiveness of legal enactment, without ever asking the question, Will it work? At present, most Argentines do not place any trust in the law, since their perception is that everything can be manipulated by bribes and power. Even lawyers and their professional integrity are under question. Public confidence in the judiciary is weak. Especially during President Menem's time, the judges were widely seen as bent. After the Supreme Court was enlarged by Mr. Menem, it seldom ruled against the regime. The Council of the Magistracy was finally established in 1999 to name new judges, but so far, its size and honest but laborious rules have delayed new nominations. At present, under President de la Rua's rule, the same old judges are in place. Rightly, the new government has not tried a purge.

CURRENT STRUCTURE

The judicial system is divided into federal and provincial courts, and each system has lower courts, courts of appeal, and supreme courts. The supreme judicial power of Argentina is vested in the Supreme Court of Justice, which has nine members. At a national level, there are the following tribunals, among others.

National Chambers:
- National Chamber of Criminal Cassation: 4 divisions; 13 judges.
- National Electoral Chamber: 3 judges.
- National Court of Appeals in federal civil and commercial matters: 3 divisions; 9 members.
- National Court of Appeals in civil matters: 13 divisions; 39 members.
- National Court of Appeals in commercial matters: 5 divisions; 15 members.
- National Court of Appeals in criminal matters: 5 divisions; 16 members.
- National Court of Appeals in federal criminal matters: 2 divisions; 6 members.
- National Court of Appeals in criminal matters related to tax evasion, accounting fraud, illegal business practices, and so on: 2 divisions; 6 members.
- National Court of Appeals in labor matters: 10 divisions; 30 judges.
- National Court of Appeals in social security matters: 3 divisions; 9 judges.
- National Court of Appeals in federal administrative matters: 5 divisions; 15 members.

Federal Trial Courts:
- Criminal courts: 12 departments.
- Criminal courts for oral proceedings: 43 departments in the capital area; 35 in the rest of the country.
- A single criminal courts in charge of enforcement of judgments.
- Criminal courts in charge of preliminary proceedings: 41 departments.
- Criminal courts in charge of sentencing: 8 departments.
- Criminal courts for misdemeanors: 14 departments.
- Juvenile courts: 7 departments.
- Criminal rogatory courts: 1 department.
- Courts in criminal matters related to tax evasion, and so on: 8 departments.
- Labor courts: 80 departments.
- Social security courts. 10 departments.
- Administrative courts: 12 departments.
- Trial court in electoral matters: 24 departments.
- Civil courts: 110 departments.
- Commercial courts: 26 departments.

Military courts are limited to military crimes committed by military officials. But civilians may become subject to military jurisdiction for offenses committed during conditions defined as states of siege.

Mandatory mediation and conciliation have been instituted with the objective of reducing the great number of new cases filed every year. As of April 1996, and for a period of five years, mediation will be an obligatory step prior to the initiation of any lawsuit, except those relating to: criminal actions; divorce, separation and other family matters; lawsuits where the state is involved, including its decentralized entities; probate; bankruptcies and receiverships; and labor lawsuits (There are specific conciliation proceedings in this area, known as the SECLO.) Mediation is optional for the plaintiff in cases such as debt collection. The mediator encourages direct contact between the parties with the purpose of reaching an out-of-court settlement. The mediator must be a lawyer registered with the Ministry of Justice. Information supplied to the mediator is strictly confidential and may not be revealed for any reason whatsoever, nor used as evidence or as precedent in any future judicial or out-of-court action. The mediator's remuneration is a fixed amount predetermined by a government decree, and it is shared equally by the parties, or as the parties better decide to do.

Regarding conciliation, Law No. 24.573 also establishes a mandatory hearing with the intention of reaching an agreement, before any evidence is submitted. The judge starts the hearing by stating the legal considerations leading to it, and listens to both parties in their claims and allegations. The parties and the judge may propose an agreement. Approval by the competent judge makes it binding and enforceable.

SPECIALIZED JUDICIAL BODIES

The Defensor del Pueblo and the Ministerio Público are among the most important institutions created upon the reform of the constitution in 1994. The institution of the Defensor del Pueblo (People's Defender), similar to the Scandinavian ombudsman, was included in the last reform of the constitution in 1994. It protects the rights of the people in issues related to human rights, social security, public services, health, education and the environment. It is an institution that operates with full independence and functional autonomy, receiving no instructions from any authority whatsoever. Its basic goal is the defense and protection of human rights, as well as those rights, guarantees, and interests protected by the constitution and the law. It also supervises the public administration. To this effect, the Defensor del Pueblo has the power to conduct investigations in order to clarify actions and omissions on the part of the public administration and its agencies, in the following situations:

Legal Structure of Argentina Courts

Supreme Court

National Chambers/Courts of Appeal
Criminal   Electoral   Civil   Commercial
Labor   Social Security   Administrative

Trial Courts

- Human rights infringement.
- Illegitimate, irregular, abusive, biased, discriminatory, negligent, seriously inconvenient, or untimely exercise of official functions, including those acts that may jeopardize individual or collective interests.

The office has judicial standing, that is to say, is party to the judicial proceedings. The Defensor is appointed by Congress with the vote of two-thirds of the members present of each house. He is elected for a term of five years and may only be reelected for another consecutive term. The Defensor del Pueblo enjoys all the immunities and privileges of legislators. The Ministerio Público (Public Ministry) is an independent body with functional autonomy and financial autarky. Its function is that of promoting the defense of the public interests of society, in coordination with the other authorities of the republic. It is led by the attorney general and the General Defender of the Nation. Its members enjoy functional immunities.

STAFFING

Registration in a local bar association is required for the active practice of law in a given jurisdiction, although there is no examination required. The Buenos Aires Bar Association has more than 60,000 members current on their dues. The bar associations have disciplinary powers over the practicing attorneys.

Regarding professional designations, there are no specific categories such as advocates. Any attorney can argue a case for a client in court. To become a notary public (*escribano público*), a law degree is required. However, a notary cannot practice law simultaneously.

According to the constitution, judges in the federal system are named for life by the president, with the advice and consent of the Senate. There is no prior investigation on the legal and other relevant history of the nominees. All the Senate gets is a résumé drafted by the nominees themselves. There are no public hearings or bar association reports; the nominations are discussed in a closed session by the relevant committee and its recommendations are then voted on by the entire chamber with no further discussion. Most observers criticize the selection process as highly politicized, resulting in a judiciary that cannot be said to be independent, despite some very competent and dedicated judges at both trial and appellate levels.

Regarding selection of judges, the reform of the constitution in 1984 created a new institution, the Council of Magistracy (Consejo de la Magistratura) with the purpose of improving the selection of judges and preserving the independence of the judiciary as a branch of government. This new institution has administrative, budgeting, and disciplinary functions, among others. Law no. 54 (August 1998) provided for the creation of the Jurado de Enjuiciamiento (Disciplinary Jury) to remove judges and members of the Public Ministry.

The Buenos Aires area is home to fourteen law schools, of which the National University of Buenos Aires School of Law is the most prestigious. As of 1999, it had 27,000 active students and 902 members in the school faculty. It is currently in charge of the creation of the Argentine Law Digest, which aims at comprising the laws and regulations that are in force. Most of the other thirteen schools are private.

Regarding the rest of the country, there are public and private law schools in each province. One of the most reputable is the University of Córdoba School of Law, which is public.

In general the curricula for law covers five years of studies. High school graduates join a preparatory program during one year, after which they go into law school. Just before graduating, the law students are required to work during one year for a public legal aid service run by the courts or the bar associations, depending on the jurisdiction. All the schools and bar associations offer Continuing Legal Education programs, although these programs are only optional.

IMPACT

The lack of judicial independence is a chronic problem in Argentina. There are many reasons that may have contributed to this problem. First, the legitimacy of the judiciary, like that of the legal order, stems from the constitution. Unfortunately, the Argentine Constitution was violated many times. Each coup d'état ruptured the pre-existing constitutional order, leaving the judiciary in the unenviable position of trying to maintain a de jure institutional authority in a de facto regime. One ineluctably clear lesson from the Argentine experience is that constitutional guarantees of judicial independence do not by themselves produce an independent judiciary. Second, the Argentine Constitution provides for the suspension of many important guarantees during states of emergency. The most abused of these states of emergency has been the state of siege. Declaration of a state of siege does not necessarily prevent the judiciary from functioning independently, but its practical effect has been the considerable reduction of the judiciary's sphere of action in protecting constitutional rights from governmental abuse. Consequently, long-term usage of the state of siege has substantially hindered judicial independence in Argentina by making the protection of individual constitutional rights impossible. Over many decades, the exceptional measure became the rule. This was especially true under military rule, but also during certain democratic governments. Third, the Argentine political tradition is rather authoritarian. The pattern of executive domination is not accidental. Despite extensive constitutional rhetoric, the principle that the government should be subject to the rule of law has not been easy to apply in Argentina. Fourth, corruption is an endemic problem. Judicial independence ceases to exist when the quality of justice is dependent on the wealth of the briber.

And last, although the formal legal system is universalistic and egalitarian, the true commitment to equality under the law is quite superficial. The Argentine courts are arenas where elites have been zealously fighting rearguard battles in order to preserve their power and privileges.

At present the courts, using antique procedures and equipment, are bogged down. Most proceedings take written form. Civil lawsuits can last forever, and there is no speedy small claims system. Criminal cases can take twelve months to reach court. As a result, although not all accused are locked away, two-thirds of prison inmates are people awaiting trial. The result is gross overcrowding and frequent mutinies. The worries of activists for human rights and justice join those of public opinion, but both are very different. Few Argentines care much about the rights of criminals, real or alleged. Many, hearing of armed robberies and hostage taking, care about crime. Disregard of law, fear of crime, and distrust of the police and the courts go hand-in-hand.

Nora Knudsen

See also Civil Law; Human Rights Law; Judicial Independence; Law and Society Movement; Legal Aid; Legal Education; Magistrates—Civil Law Systems; Judicial Selection, Methods of; Military Justice (Law and Courts); Napoleonic Code

References and further reading
Bushnell, David, and Neil Macauley. 1988. *The Emergence of Latin America in the Nineteenth Century.* New York: Oxford University Press.
"Digesto Jurídico Argentino: En una ley, todas las leyes." 2000. *Revista del Colegio Público de Abogados de la Capital Federal* 32: 23–28.

"Fortalecer la imagen de la profesión." 1998. *Revista del Colegio Público de Abogados de la Capital Federal* 17: 10–11.

Lambert, Jacques. 1967. *Latin America: Social Structure and Political Institutions.* Translated by Helen Katel. Berkeley: University of California Press.

Moriconi, María de los Milagros, and Graciela L. Storni. 1999. "El Jurado de Enjuiciamiento: Custodio de la idoneidad e incorruptibilidad en el poder judicial." *Revista del Colegio Público de Abogados de la Capital Federal* 27: 14–17.

Pinto, Mónica. 1999. "Abogados para el nuevo siglo: Estudiar abocacía en la Facultad de Derecho de la UBA." *Revista del Colegio Público de Abogados de la Capital Federal* 30: 23–30.

Rosenn, Keith. 1987. " The Protection of Judicial Independence in Latin America." *University of Miami Inter-American Law Review* 19: 1–35.

Tau Anzoátegui, Víctor, and Eduardo Martiré. 1980. *Manual de historia de las instituciones argentinas.* Buenos Aires: Ediciones Macchi. (Strongly recommended for its complete and clear coverage of Argentina's political and historical institutions from the 1500s until the early 1900s).

ARIZONA

GENERAL INFORMATION

Arizona covers 114,000 square miles of the American Southwest. In the northern part of the state are mountains, canyons, forests, and Indian reservations; in the central and southern portions of the state are desert, mountains, Indian reservations, and scattered cities. Arizona's population is approximately 4.9 million people, who live in the state's fifteen counties. Maricopa County is the most populous, with 2.9 million people. Some 67 percent of the population are white; about 21 percent are white and of Hispanic descent; 2 percent are Hispanic; 5 percent are Native American; 3 percent are African American; and less than 2 percent are Asian. The average per capita income in 1999 was $25,189. The Navaho Indian constitutes the largest population of Native Americans in the state.

Arizona in recent years has been ranked among the fastest-growing states in the nation. Much of that growth has been attributed to high-tech industries, such as computers, electronics, and electronic devices including semiconductors. The state's proximity to markets in Mexico and Latin America contribute to its economic base.

The Arizona Territory, formed in 1865, was composed of three judicial districts. Practicing lawyers created the first statewide bar association in 1895, and a few years later that organization led the rewriting of a civil code for the territory and advocated the admission of Arizona into the union. In 1912, Arizona became the forty-eighth state. Perhaps the most famous court case in Arizona history is *Miranda v. Arizona* (1966), a close decision by the U.S. Supreme Court, which specified that police must advise suspects of certain legal rights, including the right to remain silent and the right to have counsel present during interrogations. These warnings became known as the Miranda warnings; they are meant to protect the rights of the accused and place limits on police interrogation tactics.

EVOLUTION AND HISTORY

Although Arizona has always had Republican leanings, the state is not as conservative as most people think. As in many other American states, the ideological composition varies by county and city, with Tucson among the most liberal cities in Arizona. Arizonians' emphasis on individualism and direct democracy embraces such notions as accountability and popular participation, themes that often characterize the state's political and legal systems. These principles of direct, popular influence contributed to the initial process for selecting judges through nonpartisan elections, and encouraged the adoption of term limits for state legislators and governors. Arizona's original judicial system also reflected those themes. The state's legal system has numerous access points and an enhanced, direct role for the citizenry; these are traditions that still prevail today.

CURRENT STRUCTURE

Legal Profession and Legal Training

Through an act of the legislature, the State Bar of Arizona was created as a mandatory-membership organization in 1933. At the time, it consisted of 654 attorneys and 22 judges. In 1997, there were 11,571 in-state licensed attorneys, more than 10,000 of whom actively practiced law in Arizona. Most active attorneys are in private practice or practice alone in what is known as "solo practice." According to 1993 estimates, approximately 51 percent of the attorney population practice in private firms, about 32 percent practice alone, and some 16 percent work for public or government practices. Today almost 65 percent of all attorneys licensed in Arizona are men. The attorney population in Arizona has reported fluency in more than sixty languages, including Apache, French, Spanish, and Urdu. Legal training in the state is provided by two law schools: the University of Arizona in Tucson, and at Arizona State University in Phoenix.

Legal Aid and Criminal Defense Services

Most of the funds for legal services programs for the poor are provided by the Arizona Bar Foundation, which was created more than twenty years ago for this purpose. The foundation also funds a K–12 education program that teaches youth about conflict resolution, peacemaking, the creation of public policy, the Constitution, and the

Legal Structure of Arizona Courts

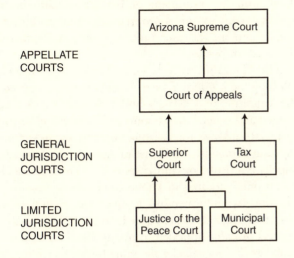

In 1988, the state legislature established the Arizona Tax Court, which has jurisdiction over all questions of law and fact that involve the imposition, assessment, or collection of Arizona taxes. This tax court, which is a department of the Superior Court in Maricopa County, handles cases from throughout the state. For certain cases, a taxpayer may choose to use the small claims division of the Tax Court for resolution of the dispute. These disputes involve the valuation or classification of "class five" property (for example, one's home), or where the full cash value of all real and personal property does not exceed $300,000. Judges in this small claims division also hear cases in which the monetary value of the taxes, interest, or penalty does not exceed $5,000. A taxpayer does not have the right to appeal a decision of the Tax Court's small claims division.

Judicial System

The structure of Arizona's judiciary has three levels: (1) limited jurisdiction courts, (2) general jurisdiction courts, and (3) appellate courts. These three levels are composed of municipal courts, justice of the peace courts, the Superior Court, the Court of Appeals, and the Supreme Court, arranged in a three-tiered hierarchy (see figure).

Municipal courts are limited jurisdiction courts that have criminal jurisdiction over misdemeanor crimes and petty offenses committed in the city or town where the court is located. Judges (magistrates) on these courts hear misdemeanor criminal traffic cases—such as driving under the influence of alcohol, hit-and-run, and reckless driving—in which no serious injuries have occurred. Additionally, these judges resolve civil traffic violations and violations of city ordinances, and issue orders of protection and injunctions prohibiting harassment. Municipal courts do not hear civil lawsuits between citizens. Municipal courts are also known as city courts or magistrates' courts, and they share jurisdiction with justice of the peace courts over violations of state law committed within their city or town limits.

Justice of the peace courts also are limited jurisdiction courts located in each county. The board of supervisors in each county sets the geographical boundaries for these courts, creating what are known as precincts. Most justice of the peace precincts are larger than city or town limits and typically incorporate an entire city or town. The boundaries can be changed, but the precincts cannot be altered until the four-year term of the current justice of the peace expires.

These courts hear cases involving traffic violations and certain civil and criminal cases. Civil jurisdiction is limited to cases involving claims of $10,000 or less. Disputes involving amounts greater than $10,000 must be heard by a superior court. A justice of the peace can issue search

Bill of Rights. Today, the Arizona Bar Foundation distributes almost $800,000 in grants to legal services programs that provide free legal representation to the poor. The Arizona Supreme Court must approve organizations and attorneys wishing to provide free legal assistance to indigents in civil matters. Primarily court-appointed attorneys provide criminal defense for indigent defendants.

Arbitration

Statutory law requires arbitration in civil cases not exceeding $50,000. Arbitrators, who are appointed by the Superior Court, act as judges in these cases. The arbitration process is relatively informal and proceeds in a manner that is meant to save money and reduce the number of cases reaching trial courts. While appeals of arbitration decisions are rare, if an appeal is made the case is heard from the start (that is, trial de novo) in Superior Court.

Administrative Hearings

Disputes involving state administrative agencies are heard by administrative law judges. The Industrial Commission of Arizona resolves disputes involving workers compensation claims. The scope of this commission has expanded over the years to include responsibility for youth employment claims, vocational rehabilitation for injured workers, and resolution of other similar disputes. Twenty-two judges conduct prehearing conferences and formal hearings at commission headquarters and at the Tucson district office. The same judge who conducts the prehearing conference conducts any subsequent formal hearing. The Department of Economic Security handles unemployment compensation disputes. Arizona has no administrative appellate body. Upon request by either party, however, the presiding judge reviews the decision. Further appeal is taken to the Court of Appeals and ultimately the Arizona Supreme Court.

warrants and handle domestic violence and harassment cases. Justice of the peace courts share jurisdiction with superior courts in landlord/tenant disputes in which damages are between $5,000 and $10,000. These courts can also hear cases regarding possession of, but not title to, real property.

For matters involving small claims (that is, less than $2,500), the Superior Court's presiding judge in each county appoints special hearing officers to resolve the dispute. In these cases, a judge or hearing officer decides the case, without attorney representation. Defendants who wish to have attorney representation must move the case from the small claims division to the civil division of the Justice of the Peace Court.

Justice of the peace courts have criminal jurisdiction over petty offenses and misdemeanors; assault or battery, when not committed on a public officer or committed with intent to make the offense a felony; breaches of the peace and committing willful injury to property; misdemeanors and criminal offenses punishable by fines not in excess of $2,500 or imprisonment for less than six months in county jail, or both fine and imprisonment; and felonies, for the purpose of issuing warrants and conducting preliminary hearings.

The Superior Court has both original and appellate jurisdiction and serves as the state's general jurisdiction trial court. Each of the fifteen counties in Arizona has at least one superior court judge. One additional judge is granted for every thirty thousand county residents. Currently there are more than one hundred Arizona superior court judges, most of whom serve in Maricopa and Pima counties. Judges operate in numbered divisions in counties with more than one superior judge. Counties with more than one superior court judge also have a special juvenile court. One or more of the superior court judges hear all juvenile cases involving delinquency, incorrigibility, and dependency. If the presiding juvenile court judge permits, a juvenile traffic case may be heard by a court other than a juvenile court.

Superior court judges are the state's main trial court judges, with jurisdiction over all types of cases except small claims, minor offenses, or violations of city codes and ordinances. The Superior Court also acts as an appellate court for justice of the peace and municipal courts.

Specifically, these judges hear cases and proceedings in which jurisdiction is not vested by law in another court; equity cases that involve title to or possession of real property or the legality of any tax, impost, assessment, toll, or municipal ordinance; other cases in which the value of property in question is more than $5,000, exclusive of interest and costs; criminal cases amounting to a felony, and misdemeanor cases not otherwise provided for by law; forcible entry and eviction of renters; proceedings in insolvency, with the exception of bankruptcy; actions to prevent or stop nuisances; matters of probate; dissolution or annulment of marriages; naturalization and the issuance of appropriate documents for these events; and special cases and proceedings not otherwise provided for by law.

The Court of Appeals was authorized by voters in 1960 by the Modern Courts Amendment and created by the legislature in 1965 as a buffer between the courts of limited and general jurisdiction and the Arizona Supreme Court. To address the Arizona Supreme Court's increasing case demands, the Court of Appeals has mandatory appellate jurisdiction and is split into two divisions. Division one is located in Phoenix and has sixteen judges. Division Two is located in Tucson and has six judges. The Court of Appeals hears cases in three-judge panels on matters properly appealed from Superior Court. The appeals process is generally the same for both criminal and civil cases; however, there are filing fees in civil cases, but not for criminal cases. Statewide responsibility for appeals from the Industrial Commission, unemployment compensation rulings of the Department of Economic Security, and rulings by the Arizona Tax Court are handled by Division One of the Court of Appeals.

The Arizona Supreme Court has discretionary appellate jurisdiction, which gives justices on this court the ability to refuse to review the findings of the lower court. However, cases involving capital punishment automatically go the Supreme Court for mandatory review. The Supreme Court has original jurisdiction of habeas corpus (in which a prisoner challenges the legality of detention) and other extraordinary writs to state officers. The Modern Courts Amendment, passed in 1960, increased the number of justices serving on the Arizona Supreme Court from three to five. One chief justice is selected by fellow justices to serve as chief justice for a five-year term. The chief justice handles case work like the other justices, as well as overseeing the administrative operations of all the courts in Arizona.

The Supreme Court in Arizona is the highest court in the state, with primary responsibility to review appeals and provide rules of procedure for all courts in Arizona. The Modern Courts Amendment gave the Arizona Supreme Court administrative supervision over all Arizona courts and the authority to make all rules regarding procedural matters in any court. Other duties of the Arizona Supreme Court include the regulation of the State Bar of Arizona, including overseeing admission of new attorneys to practice law, and reviewing charges of misconduct against attorneys, including the authority to disbar attorneys. The Arizona Supreme Court also serves as the final decision-making body when the Commission on Judicial Conduct files disciplinary recommendations against Arizona judges.

STAFFING

Most of the judges in Arizona were selected through non-partisan elections until 1974, when the voters of Arizona approved merit selection and retention election of justices for the Supreme Court and judges for the Court of Appeals. In this system, the governor appoints judges from a list submitted by judicial nominating commissions. At the completion of each four-year term, voters choose whether to retain state supreme court justices in a retention election. The merit selection and retention election system also applied to judges for the Superior Court in counties with 150,000 or more people (currently, Maricopa and Pima counties). The other counties elect their judges, but they can use the merit selection process if they wish. Judges serving in the Supreme Court, the Court of Appeals, and the Superior Court must retire at the age of seventy.

In 1992, the voters of Arizona passed proposition 109, which made some additional changes to the rules governing the selection and retention of judges. First, they changed the population cutoff for merit selection of Superior Court judges from 150,000 to 250,000 people, though this change still limited merit selection and retention election of Superior Court judges to Maricopa and Pima counties. Proposition 109 also requires public input and the establishment of a process to review judges' performance. Additionally, the number of persons involved in the merit selection process increased from 21 to 127 committee and commission members. Nine nonattorney members serve on the statewide Appellate Nominating Commission and ten committees of seven members each serve on the Judicial Nominating Commissions for Pima and Maricopa counties.

A Supreme Court justice must be of good moral character, must have been a resident of Arizona for at least ten years immediately prior to taking office, must be admitted to the practice of law in Arizona, and may not practice law while a member of the judiciary nor hold any other political office or public employment. Justices serving on this state's highest court also may not hold office in any political party and may not campaign except for themselves. A judge on the Court of Appeals or the Superior Court must be at least thirty years of age, of good moral character, admitted to the practice of law in Arizona, and a resident of Arizona for the five years immediately prior to taking office.

Superior Court judges serve four-year terms. City or town councils appoint their municipal court judges, with the exception of Yuma, where these judges are elected. Municipal court judges serve at least two years, with the number of years beyond the mandatory two being determined by the city or town council. City charters or ordinances establish the qualifications of municipal court judges. These judges do not have to be attorneys. A justice of the peace is elected to a four-year term, must be at least eighteen years of age, an Arizona resident, must read and write English, and must be a qualified voter in the precinct in which the duties of office will be preformed; however, a justice of the peace is not required to be an attorney.

Laura Langer

See also Administrative Law; Capital Punishment; Indigenous and Folk Legal Systems; Legal Aid; Magistrates—Common Law Systems; Merit Selection ("Missouri Plan"); Judicial Selection, Methods of; Native American Law, Traditional; Trial Courts; United States—Federal System; United States—State Systems

References and further reading
Administrative Office of the Court. 2000. *A Guide to Arizona Courts.* Phoenix, AZ.
Council of State Government. 2000–2001. *The Book of the States.* Lexington, KY.
Duncan, Philip D., and Christine C. Lawrence. 1997. *Congressional Quarterly's Politics in America 1998: The 105th Congress.* Washington, DC: CQ Press.
Hall, Melinda Gann. 1999. "State Judicial Politics: Rules, Structures, and the Political Game." Pp. 114–138 in *American State and Local Politics: Directions for the 21st Century.* Edited by Ronald E. Weber and Paul Brace. New York: Chatham House Publishers.
Klinker, Marsha. 1982. *The Arizona Judiciary.* Phoenix, AZ: Office of Administrative Directories of Courts.
Reincke, Mary, and Jeaneen C. Wilhelmi. 2000–2001. *The American Bench.* Minneapolis, MN: Reginald Bishop Forster and Associates.
1981 Arizona Judicial Plan. 1981. *Phoenix: Arizona Judicial Coordinating Committee.*

ARKANSAS

GENERAL INFORMATION

Arkansas entered the union in 1836. Modest in terms of population, geography, and economic circumstance at the time, it remains so today. Approximately 2.5 million people occupy the state's more than 53,000 square miles, with a per capita income of just over $20,000, making it the thirty-third most populous, the twenty-sixth largest, and the fifth poorest of the fifty American states. Although at one time the proportion of Arkansas residents of African-American heritage was roughly 25 percent, the portion today is not quite 16 percent. Hispanics represent a much smaller but rapidly growing component of the state's ethnic mix, constituting approximately 2 percent of the population in 2000. The state is still quite rural in character, its largest metropolitan statistical area (MSA) being in and around its capital city, Little Rock, which has a population of 550,000 people.

As a direct consequence of its early "slave state" status and its participation in the Confederacy during the Civil War, the state has ratified five separate constitutions. The first was a relatively short declaration of rights and principles that lasted until 1861 when, although Arkansas originally voted not to throw in its lot with the Southern cause, the actions at Fort Sumpter prompted a change of heart and a new constitution. The revisions were few but significant, as the state shored up its institutional mechanisms for maintaining slavery and inserted a reference to the "Confederate States of America." The defeat of the Confederacy ushered in a new, and equally short-lived, governing document in 1864, one that abolished the practice of slavery. The period of "Radical Reconstruction" brought yet a fourth constitution to Arkansas, in 1868. Congress insisted that the recalcitrant states institute new civil governments (that excluded former confederates), ratify the 14th Amendment to the U.S. Constitution, adopt universal male suffrage, and require all voters to take an oath of allegiance to the United States upon registration.

If such actions were not popular among much of white Arkansas, neither was the highly centralized government produced under the accompanying state constitution. Unable or unwilling to rely upon the local-level administration of state law, the Republican Reconstructors granted tremendous power to the governor, including the power to appoint tax assessors, prosecuting attorneys, and numerous other local officials, as well as the chief justice of the state's Supreme Court and all lower-level judges. A direct reaction to this situation, the state's fifth constitution, was adopted in 1874. Sometimes called the "Redeemer" constitution—a label that bespeaks the attitude of the white, Southern majority that returned to power after "Radical Reconstruction"—the Arkansas constitution of today is noteworthy for the very specific constraints it places on government activity, the high number of elective posts for which it provides, the frequency of elections it mandates (until 1986, the gubernatorial term of office was just two years), and the general fragmentation of political power it achieves. Such features remain quite evident in the more than 125-year-old document, though the judicial article has recently undergone major change.

EVOLUTION AND HISTORY

Arkansas's judicial system is distinguished by two key traits. First, authority within the system traditionally has been quite dispersed. For example, until Arkansas voters adopted sweeping reform of the state's judicial article in the fall of 2000, the state divided trial court activity into courts of equity and courts of law with substantial rigidity. Another source of fragmentation that colored the Arkansas legal landscape for many years was the fact that the state's legal infrastructure included six distinct types of minor courts, each of which was presided over by various city and county officials. To illustrate, county executives (known as county judges) heard matters of juvenile

justice until 1987, and presided over cases involving disputed paternity until 2000; county legislative officials known as justices of the peace took part in other minor civil cases for many years. The mayors of Arkansas towns and cities (or their designates) also have partaken in the administration of justice in the recent past, adding to the state's maze of jurisdictions. This fragmentation of authority was accompanied by a relatively low degree of professionalism and the virtual absence of consistent record-keeping among jurisdictions, features no doubt attributable to the discretion left to local governments by the "Redeemer" constitution. Many of the presiding officers in courts of limited jurisdiction, for example, were not required to have any form of legal training until the recent reforms. With respect to poor record-keeping, it may suffice to say that a legislative survey by the Arkansas General Assembly in 1957 could only estimate the number of courts within state boundaries.

The second key trait of the Arkansas judicial system—a history of attempts at legal reform—grows out of the overlapping jurisdictions and varying levels of professionalization long witnessed in the state. Just a glance at the efforts of subsequent generations to ameliorate the worst effects of the "Redeemer" constitution bears out this relationship. The state legislature established the Judicial Department and appointed as its head the chief justice of the Supreme Court in 1965 in an attempt to consolidate and standardize record-keeping. Eight years later, in 1973, legislators gave the Supreme Court the power, for the first time, to promulgate uniform statewide rules of evidence and procedure. At least two broader efforts at judicial reform were made in 1970 and 1980 at the state constitutional conventions convened in those years. Both of the proposed constitutions produced at those gatherings contained revised judicial articles that would have dramatically overhauled the structure of the court system. In both instances, however, the new constitution failed to garner the required majority of state voters. Decades later, in the fall of 2000, voters approved a state bar association–backed amendment aimed only at altering the judicial article of the state's constitution. The measure significantly transformed the Arkansas judiciary by consolidating the numerous courts of limited jurisdiction, merging the courts of law and equity, changing the method of judicial selection, and generally bringing the Arkansas judiciary into line with the court systems of other U.S. states.

CURRENT STRUCTURE

Arkansas's current judicial system, like that of most other American states, is four-tiered; at the bottom are the courts of limited jurisdiction (municipal, city, police, county, and justice of the peace courts), not all of which are operational. These are followed by the trial courts (cir-

Legal Structure of Arkansas Courts

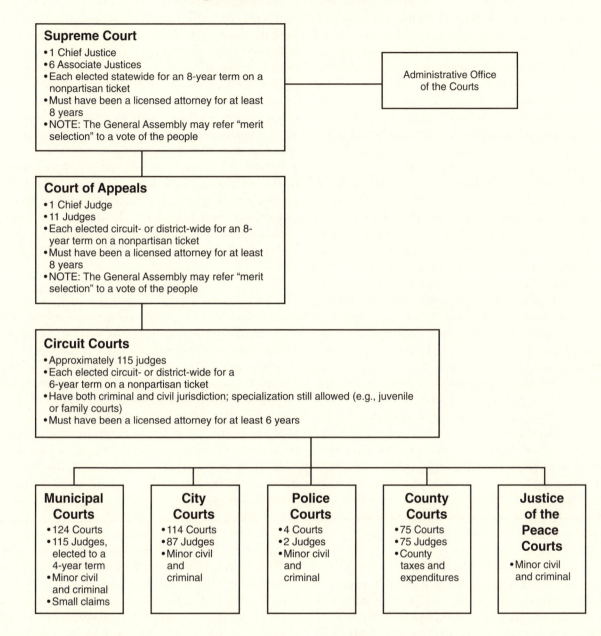

Supreme Court
- 1 Chief Justice
- 6 Associate Justices
- Each elected statewide for an 8-year term on a nonpartisan ticket
- Must have been a licensed attorney for at least 8 years
- NOTE: The General Assembly may refer "merit selection" to a vote of the people

Administrative Office of the Courts

Court of Appeals
- 1 Chief Judge
- 11 Judges
- Each elected circuit- or district-wide for an 8-year term on a nonpartisan ticket
- Must have been a licensed attorney for at least 8 years
- NOTE: The General Assembly may refer "merit selection" to a vote of the people

Circuit Courts
- Approximately 115 judges
- Each elected circuit- or district-wide for a 6-year term on a nonpartisan ticket
- Have both criminal and civil jurisdiction; specialization still allowed (e.g., juvenile or family courts)
- Must have been a licensed attorney for at least 6 years

Municipal Courts
- 124 Courts
- 115 Judges, elected to a 4-year term
- Minor civil and criminal
- Small claims

City Courts
- 114 Courts
- 87 Judges
- Minor civil and criminal

Police Courts
- 4 Courts
- 2 Judges
- Minor civil and criminal

County Courts
- 75 Courts
- 75 Judges
- County taxes and expenditures

Justice of the Peace Courts
- Minor civil and criminal

cuit courts), an intermediate appellate court (Court of Appeals), and a court of last resort (Supreme Court). The limited-jurisdiction courts serve as the forum for minor civil cases (traditionally defined in Arkansas as disputes over sums less than $5,000) and misdemeanor criminal cases (including those involving penalties of less than one year's confinement). The judicial reform measure adopted in 2000 stipulated that the various minor courts be consolidated by 2005 into "district courts." The measure also stipulated that at least one such court be located in each of the state's seventy-five counties and that the courts' jurisdiction be countywide. Proceedings will continue to be subject to the right of appeal to the trial-court level, although arguments and evidence are heard de novo.

In addition to conducting reviews of lower court rul-

ings, circuit courts are the courts of original jurisdiction in the state. Although they are no longer split into courts of equity and courts of law, the judges of any circuit may divide into subject matter divisions that allow for specialization (criminal, civil, juvenile, probate, and domestic relations). As of 2000, there were 115 circuit court judges serving twenty-eight judicial districts.

On the appellate end of the Arkansas legal system lie the Court of Appeals and the Supreme Court. The intermediate appellate court was adopted in 1978 (via Amendment 58) in response to the fact that the Arkansas Supreme Court had the highest workload of any court of last resort in the country. The six judges originally assigned to help reduce the Supreme Court's caseload eventually themselves became overwhelmed, prompting state legislators to double the appellate court's size in the 1990s. Since 1983, the twelve judges generally have heard cases in panels of three, sitting en banc only if a panel decision is not unanimous. Members of Arkansas's Court of Appeals are ostensibly elected on the basis of regional circuits, but when legislative sessions in 1995, 1997, and 1999 failed to agree to the recrafting of district lines necessitated by the court's increased size, the task was formally handed over to a specially constituted commission, the members of which will make recommendations currently slated to be adopted in the legislative session of 2003.

Finally, at the top of Arkansas's judicial pyramid is the Arkansas Supreme Court. Endowed early on with just three justices, today it is composed of six associate justices and one chief justice. Despite the adoption of an intermediate appellate court, it has continued to maintain an unusually large number of original jurisdiction cases, though recent a constitutional amendment and administrative maneuvering have streamlined its docket somewhat. Among the more significant issues over which it yet retains original jurisdiction are the sufficiency of state initiative and referendum petitions, the issuance of writs quo warranto, and questions of certification posed by a court of the U.S. court system. The Supreme Court exercises appellate jurisdiction over cases involving interpretation of the state constitution, cases in which the death penalty or life imprisonment has been imposed, petitions for quo warranto, appeals pertaining to elections and election procedures, the discipline of attorneys, the discipline and disability of judges, and appeals following an appeal that has been decided in the Supreme Court. The high court also is charged with prescribing rules of pleading, practice, and procedure for the lower courts, and it possesses superintending control over them.

LEGAL PROFESSION AND LEGAL TRAINING

There were seventy-eight hundred licensed attorneys in the state of Arkansas in the year 2000. A large portion of these lawyers were trained at one of two law schools in the state: the main campus of the University of Arkansas in Fayetteville, or the University of Arkansas at Little Rock.

STAFFING

Arkansas has selected its judges by a variety of methods over the years, including legislative election, gubernatorial appointment, and partisan public contests. Today, all of the state's judges and Supreme Court justices are selected in nonpartisan elections, a product of the sweeping reforms adopted in 2000. Amendment 80 also conferred upon the General Assembly the option of referring to the voters an initiative that would, if passed, provide for the merit selection of all appellate court judges and justices. The governor fills all midterm judicial vacancies. However, judges may not stand for election for a position to which they have been appointed.

The length of judicial terms varies, as do the qualifications required to fill each post. Specifically, members of both the Supreme Court and the Court of Appeals must have been licensed attorneys in the state for eight years prior to taking office; once having taken office, they serve eight-year terms. Circuit court judges must have been licensed attorneys in the state for six years, a period equal to their term of office. District court judges must have been licensed attorneys for four years, and they serve four-year terms. Amendment 80 also provided for the appointment of referees, masters, and magistrates to assist with the caseload in the Arkansas judicial system. Such persons may be appointed either by a circuit court judge or a district court judge (with the consent of a majority of circuit court judges in that circuit), and they are limited to the duties prescribed by the Supreme Court.

LEGAL AID AND CRIMINAL DEFENSE SERVICES

Defense for criminal misdemeanors (for which one could serve time in jail) and felonies is provided to indigent defendants by county public defender's offices, which are funded jointly by the counties and the state of Arkansas. In capital cases, courts will appoint and pay for attorneys in private practice who are certified by the state to handle such cases if the local county public defender does not have an attorney on staff who is certified for capital defense work. Six private nonprofit legal firms provide representation to individuals who meet eligibility requirements in such areas as family law, housing disputes, benefits claims, and debt problems. Both law schools at the University of Arkansas, Fayetteville, and the University of Arkansas, Little Rock, maintain legal clinics in which law students are assigned cases under the supervision of a staff attorney. They provide representation in various state civil matters, federal benefits and bankruptcy cases, and criminal defense. The clinic at the Fayetteville campus was founded in part by Hillary Rodham Clinton while a professor at the U of A.

NOTABLE FEATURES

There are several features of Arkansas's legal system that merit mention. First, its position as a state of Western/Midwestern, as well as Southern, heritage is well demonstrated by the fact that it is the only Southern state in which the citizens have two of the three mechanisms of direct democracy at their disposal. Specifically, Arkansans may play a direct role in crafting public policy through both initiative (the use of popular petition to submit a proposal—either constitutional or statutory—to the voters) and referendum (the use of popular petition to subject a measure already approved by the legislative and executive branches of government to the voting public). The state judicial system has been an active referee in this process, stepping in to evaluate the sufficiency of ballot titles and the means of signature collection, as provided for by Amendment 7 to the state's constitution.

Second, Arkansas courts, together with about half of the state judicial systems in the country, have been quite involved in legal disputes surrounding the disparity in public education funding from district to district. The reliance on locally generated property taxes as the central source of K–12 monies has resulted in within-state per pupil expenditure imbalances as high as 2:1. The basis for legal challenge has generally centered upon the state constitution's requirement that the state "shall ever maintain a general, suitable and efficient system of free public schools and shall adopt all suitable means to secure to the people the advantages and opportunities of education." Although the passage of Amendment 74 in 1996 ameliorated the situation slightly, resource-poor districts continue to sue for equal treatment. The matter stretches back to the 1970s and remains unresolved.

Finally, Arkansas's method for resolving matters of alleged malfeasance among members of the legal community has received an unusual amount of attention in recent years. The Arkansas Judicial Discipline and Disability Commission was adopted in 1988 to conduct investigations and make recommendations to the Supreme Court regarding allegations of misconduct or incompetence/disability among members of the bench. With the impeachment of President Bill Clinton by the House of Representatives in early 1998, detractors of the state's "native son" turned to the body to which the state's lawyers are held accountable: the Supreme Court Committee on Professional Conduct. Although critics took issue with the unusual speed with which the complaint was handled and other irregularities, the disciplinary committee recommended disbarment.

RELATIONSHIP WITH NATIONAL SYSTEM

Arkansas has been home to several important court cases that have traveled up the U.S. chain of legal authority to the U.S. Supreme Court. It was, for example, a 1992 popular initiative instituting term limits for all Arkansas state legislators, state executives, and members of Congress that prompted the U.S. Supreme Court to nip in the bud at least the latter category nationwide (see *U.S. v. Thornton* [1994]). The state also joined the creation-evolution fray with two nationally significant court cases: *Epperson v. Arkansas* (1968), in which the U.S. Supreme Court struck an antievolution law adopted by public referendum in 1928; and *McLean v. Arkansas* (1982), in which a federal district court invalidated a law mandating equal time for the teaching of "creation science" in the public schools. Abortion, too, has generated much legal conflict in the state, generating a 1988 popular initiative (Amendment 68) prohibiting the use of public funds in

paying for abortions, except to save the mother's life. The U.S. Supreme Court rejected this position in *Dalton v. Little Rock Family Planning Services* (1995).

William D. Schreckhise
Janine Alisa Parry

See also United States—Federal System; United States—State Systems

References and further reading
Administrative Office of the Courts. 2000. *Arkansas Judiciary Annual Report, 1998–1999.* Little Rock, AR.
Blair, Diane D. 1988. *Arkansas Politics and Government: Do the People Rule?* Lincoln: University of Nebraska Press.
Gingerich, James D. 1984. "Arkansas' New Court and Its Effect on the Arkansas Appellate System." *Arkansas Political Science Journal* 5: 20–37.
———. 1989. "Voting Rights Litigation and the Arkansas Judiciary: Getting What You Didn't Ask For." *Midsouth Political Science Journal* 10, no. 1: 43–57.
Greenebaum, Edwin H. 1964. "Arkansas' Judiciary: Its History and Structure." *Arkansas Law Review* 18: 152–166.
Rosenzweig, Jeff. 1991. "The Crisis in Indigent Defense: An Arkansas Commentary." *Arkansas Law Review* 44: 409–423.
Watkins, John J. 1995. "Division of Labor between Arkansas's Appellate Courts." *University of Arkansas at Little Rock Law Journal* 17: 177–214.
———. 2000. "Law and Equity in Arkansas: Or Why to Support the Proposed Judicial Article." *Arkansas Law Review* 53: 401–438.

ARMENIA

COUNTRY INFORMATION

Armenia is located in southwest Transcaucasia, between Europe and Asia. It is bordered by Georgia to the north, Azerbaijan to the east, Iran to the south, and Turkey to the west. The smallest republic of the former Soviet Union, it covers some 11,500 square miles and has a population of approximately 3.8 million people. It has no access to the sea, and its natural resources are sparse, but it is also a nation with an ancient history and culture, blessed with a vast and supportive diaspora and an industrious and hardy people.

The population is homogeneous and is approximately 94 percent ethnic Armenian. Small, officially recognized national communities include Russians, Jews, Kurds, Yezidis, Georgians, Greeks, and Assyrians. After the Karabakh conflict erupted between Armenia and Azerbaijan in 1988, almost all the ethnic Azeris living in Armenia at the time (some 185,000 persons) fled to Azerbaijan. Of the 400,000 ethnic Armenians then living in Azerbaijan, 330,000 fled and gained refugee status in Armenia. The majority of the remaining refugees went to Russia, and small numbers remained in Azerbaijan. As a result of the protracted Karabakh conflict, there is no significant Azeri minority in Armenia today.

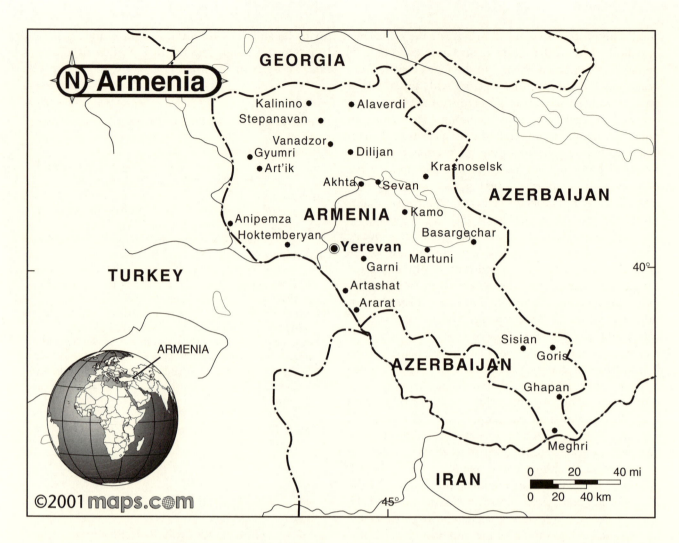

At various times during the past 2,000 years, Armenia claimed lands from the Mediterranean to the Caspian Sea, territory that now belongs to Turkey, Iran, Georgia, Azerbaijan, and other nations. In different periods, Armenia was subjugated by Russia, Persia, and the Ottoman Empire. Armenians had lived continuously in large parts of what is now Turkey and established what is considered to have been the first Christian state in 301 C.E.; indeed, several of the Byzantine emperors were Armenian.

In 1375, shortly before the fall of Constantinople, the Armenians no longer had a territorial homeland, and most of their domain was partitioned between Persia and the Ottoman Empire. Armenians in that period enjoyed considerable religious and cultural autonomy. They were recognized as a semiautonomous community within the Ottoman Empire and were led by the Armenian patriarch of Constantinople. In 1863, an Armenian national constitution in the form of an imperial edict, providing for a more representative form of self-government, was promulgated. However, in the 1890s, attacks on the Armenian communities in Turkey ensued, during which many Armenian cultural centers were destroyed. Toward the close of the nineteenth century, young Armenian intellectuals

educated in the west founded resistance groups—the Hintchak (1889), the Dashnak (1890), and the Ramgavar-Azadakan (1890)—in the hope of enlisting the aid of the western powers against Ottoman oppression. Between 1915 and 1918, more than 1.5 million Armenians perished at the hands of the Turks in what is referred to in Armenia as "the genocide." Indeed, according to some estimates, one in three Armenians out of the total Armenian population in the world died during that period.

Following World War I, for the first time in 600 years, an independent Armenian republic was established in 1918 under the protection of the western Allies. However, Armenia soon found itself under simultaneous attack by both Turkey and Soviet Russia. In 1920, Bolshevik troops occupied the nation and declared Armenia a Soviet republic. In the ensuing civil war between Armenian Bolsheviks and Nationalists, the Red Army helped crush the Nationalists. Ultimately, Armenia acceded to Soviet domination without massive resistance, in part because it looked to the powerful Soviet Union for protection from its enemies just across its borders. Armenia continued to enjoy a limited degree of autonomy, allowing its culture, language, and church to survive under Soviet rule.

As the former USSR crumbled, Armenia, along with the other Soviet republics and nations under Soviet domination, moved toward independence. From the outset, the nation's leadership was committed to establishing, through existing legal norms, a new republic based on the rule of law. In 1990, by a vote of 183 to 2, the Armenian Supreme Soviet adopted the Declaration on Armenia's Independence, forming the basis for a new constitution. In 1991, in full compliance with the Soviet constitution, 99 percent of the voters adopted a referendum for secession. Just one month later, Levon Ter-Petrossian, leader of the Armenian National Movement (ANM), was overwhelmingly elected president of the republic, and a constitutional commission headed by the president was constituted to draft a new constitution. The constitution was to guarantee individual rights and freedoms, as well as to promote the prosperity of Armenia's economy.

A general consensus was achieved by all political factions on secession and the formation of a new, independent nation. However, shortly after independence was achieved, the Armenian National Party split into a number of smaller political parties; one of those parties was made up of the core of the original group, and it kept the Armenian National Movement name. In addition, historical political parties, which had been banned during the Soviet era, returned. The ANM and the opposition parties disagreed on fundamental issues confronting the new nation, such as the status of the diaspora and the pace and magnitude of economic reforms. In addition, the opposition and the president disagreed on the structure of government that was to be established by the new constitution. The president favored a strong executive, whereas the opposition called for a strong parliamentary system. Further, the president favored a two-step process for drafting the constitution. He proposed enacting broad blocks of legislation that could be tested and then, if successful, embodied in the new constitution. The opposition instead proposed that a constitutional convention be formed in a more open process to draft the constitution, which would then be submitted directly to the people. Efforts to convene a constitutional convention failed, and after a five-year process, the draft prepared by the Constitutional Commission and supported by the president was approved by the National Assembly. In July 1995, a referendum on the constitution was held, and the measure carried 68 percent of the votes cast. In addition, members of progovernment parties were elected deputies in overwhelming numbers.

However, the election process was widely criticized by international observers, primarily because, prior to the scheduled vote, the leading opposition party was banned on charges of carrying out terrorist activities. Since the ban expired the day after the balloting, the opposition party was effectively prevented from participating in the election.

The following year, President Ter-Petrossian was returned to office in an election that once again was criticized by international observers for serious breaches, including ballot tampering and discrepancies in vote calculation. In February 1998, Ter-Petrossian, weakened by allegations of fraud and persistent suspicions that his 1996 election victory was illegitimate, resigned. A month later, Robert Kocharian was elected president, but once again, serious irregularities were recorded and the election was characterized as deeply flawed by international observers. Finally, the stability of the government was weakened by numerous assassinations, including an attack in the National Assembly in 1999 that killed the prime minister, the speaker of the assembly, and six other government officials. In addition, it is widely believed that a number of the high-profile murder cases involving government officials may have been related to corruption or criminal activities within the government.

LEGAL CONCEPTS

The Constitution of the Republic of Armenia, adopted in 1995, is the fourth constitution in the country's history; it was preceded by the constitutions of 1922, 1937, and 1978. The Armenian Constitution provides for a system of government based on the separation of power. However, the Armenian presidency as empowered by the new constitution has been characterized as the strongest in the world.

The president is directly elected by the citizens for a term of five years and may serve no more than two terms. He or she must be a citizen, must have resided in Armenia for ten years preceding the election, and must have the right to vote. The president is responsible for the execution of the nation's laws and controls the agenda of the legislative body. In addition, the president manages foreign policy, confers citizenship, and both appoints and maintains control over government officials and the prime minister. Moreover, after consulting with president of the National Assembly and the prime minister, the president can dissolve the assembly at any time prior to the last six months of his or her term and call for a special election.

The Government of Armenia is composed of the prime minister and other subordinate ministers appointed by the president. It develops and implements financial, economic, and tax policies as well as state policy regarding science, education, health and culture, national security, and foreign relations. Although both the Government and the individual delegates to the national assembly may initiate legislation, the Government to a large extent controls the process by setting the agenda for discussing draft laws. In addition, the Government presents the budget to the National Assembly for certification. The assembly oversees the implementation of the budget.

Legislative authority is vested in the National Assembly, a unicameral body composed of 131 deputies elected for four-year terms. Each delegate must be at least twenty-five years old and a citizen of Armenia for no less than five years preceding his or her candidacy. In addition, the delegate must be a permanent resident for at least five years and have the right to vote.

The powers of the National Assembly are fixed by the constitution, and as established in the constitutional framework of the United States, the legislature acts only pursuant to powers specified in the constitution. There are no inherent powers in the legislative body and no equivalent of a "necessary and proper" clause that might broaden the power of the legislature. The National Assembly can act in three instances: (1) at its own initiative in matters such as the creation of commissions to draft legislation, (2) on the proposal of the president, after which it can request a new discussion of a law, and (3) on the proposal of the Government.

The legislative branch is weakened by the controversial provision that enables the president to dissolve the National Assembly and require that new members be elected through special elections. The president may also veto actions of the National Assembly, but the assembly, in turn, may override the veto by a majority vote of the overall number of delegates. Finally, the president may convene an extraordinary session of the National Assembly and set its agenda.

Armenia's constitution protects the fundamental rights, liberties, and duties of individuals. These protections reflect the western traditions of inalienable rights and individual autonomy as well as the socialist traditions of collective economic and social rights. Specifically, the constitution includes the following: the rights of privacy and expression; the right to form political parties; due process; and certain procedures in criminal matters, such as the rebuttable presumption of innocence. Furthermore, the constitution affirms family values, calls for the payment of taxes, and requires participation in the national defense. Most important, it affirms the rule of law and declares that "everyone shall uphold the Constitution and the laws."

Armenia is a party to the major human rights treaties, including the Covenant on Economic, Social and Cultural Rights; the Covenant on Civil and Political Rights; the International Convention on the Elimination of All Forms of Racial Discrimination; the Convention on Elimination of All Forms of Discrimination against Women; the Convention against Torture and Other Cruel, Inhumane or Degrading Punishments or Treatment; and the Convention on the Rights of the Child.

CURRENT STRUCTURE

The 1995 Constitution establishes a three-tiered court system of general jurisdiction, composed of the Courts of First Instance, the Courts of Appeals, and the Court of Cassation. The constitution also provides for economic courts and a military court, but such bodies have not been created to date. Instead, economic and military matters are heard by the Courts of First Instance. The three Courts of Appeals hear criminal, military, and civil and economic cases. The Court of Cassation began functioning in the summer of 1998, and the Court of First Instance and the appellate courts began functioning in 1999. Although the constitution refers to trial by jury, legislation to establish a jury system has not been enacted. Judges are appointed for life and cannot be members of a political party. The Justice Council, headed by the president, oversees judicial nominations and discipline. The Council of Court Chairs, which is responsible for financial and budgetary issues for the courts, includes twenty-one court chairs (the senior judges of multijudge panels) at all levels.

The Constitutional Court consists of nine judge who are appointed for life and serve until they are seventy years of age. It rules on the conformity of legislation with the constitution, approves international agreements, and decides election-related legal questions. It also rules on cases involving the impeachment or incapacity of the president. However, its jurisdiction is limited. It can only accept cases proposed by the president or by two-thirds of all parliamentary deputies or election-related cases brought by candidates for Parliament or the presidency. Due to these limitations, the Constitutional Court has been limited in its ability to influence or implement the human rights guarantees in the constitution.

Three new codes—the Civil Code, the Code of Civil Procedure, and the Code of Criminal Procedure—entered into force in January 1999. The Civil Code, consisting of more than 1,200 articles, and the Code of Civil Procedure are substantially different from the previous civil codes and are designed to facilitate a market economy. However, under the Code of Criminal Procedure, prosecutors still retain substantial influence.

All trials are public except when government secrets are at issue or when, in the discretion of the judge, it is necessary to protect the privacy interests of the participants. Defendants are required to attend their trials and are entitled to lawyers of their own choosing. When requested by the court or at the pretrial stage, the bar association appoints an attorney for any defendant who cannot afford one. The constitution provides that those accused of crimes shall be informed of the charges against them. Defendants may confront witnesses and present evidence, and defendants and prosecutors both have the right of appeal.

The new Code of Criminal Procedure is an improvement on the Soviet model. For example, arrest warrants and search-and-seizure warrants can only be issued on a judicial order from the Court of First Instance. The court, in effect, oversees the investigative procedure. The right of defendants and victims are spelled out in detail. In addition, impartial observers participate in some investigative procedures (such as searches), and they must certify that a given procedure was done in accordance with the law. Rulings of the prosecutor in pretrial matters may be appealed to the Court of First Instance. Under the new code, the police may detain individuals for up to twelve hours before notifying family members, and detainees must seek permission from the police or procuracy (prosecutor's office) to obtain a forensic medical examination in order to substantiate a report of torture. During the pretrial or investigative stage, the prosecutor effectively controls the investigation. At the trial stage, prosecutor and defendant are more evenly matched.

Civil and criminal matters involving military personnel take place in the civil Courts of First Instance and are handled by military prosecutors, who perform the same functions as their civilian counterparts. Pending passage of a new criminal code, they operate in accordance with the Soviet-era criminal code. A new criminal code that has been proposed to Parliament is intended to clarify contradictory provisions of the law and create a more unitary, modern, and workable legal system. In addition, a new code for administrative procedure and administrative offenses are now in the drafting stages.

STAFFING

The judiciary of Armenia has been characterized as feeble and lacking judicial independence. Two facts are central to this problem: (1) The judiciary is subject to considerable political pressure, and (2) the constitutional provisions, which govern the judiciary, do not insulate the judiciary from such pressure. Under the constitution, the Council of Justice (headed by the president, the prosecutor general, and the justice minister) appoints and disciplines judges for the Courts of First Instance, Courts of Appeals, and the Supreme Court. The president appoints the other fourteen members of the Council of Justice and four of the nine Constitutional Court judges. This authority gives the president a dominant influence in appointing and dismissing judges at all levels. In addition, judges are subject to review by the president through the Council of Justice after three years. Thereafter, their tenure is permanent until they reach the age of sixty-five.

The two lower-level courts, the Courts of Appeals and the Courts of the First Instance, began functioning in January 1999. Judges were selected for nomination on the basis of multiple-choice tests covering the new legal codes as well as interviews with the minister of justice. Next, the list of nominations was approved by the Council of Justice and finally by the president. About 55 percent of the appointed judges were judges under the old

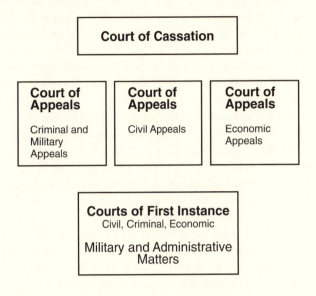

Legal Structure of Armenia Courts

Court of Cassation

Court of Appeals — Criminal and Military Appeals

Court of Appeals — Civil Appeals

Court of Appeals — Economic Appeals

Courts of First Instance — Civil, Criminal, Economic — Military and Administrative Matters

structure. Unless they are found guilty of malfeasance, their tenure is permanent until they reach the age of sixty-five.

In June 1998, the Constitutional Reform Commission was established, with one of its stated goals being to strengthen the independence of the judiciary and give the courts more authority in safeguarding human rights. The following year, the commission submitted its suggestions for constitutional amendments to the president. The president disbanded the commission and appointed new members to amend the constitution's chapter on the judiciary. Such constitutional revisions must pass both Parliament and a national referendum.

DISPUTE SETTLEMENT

According to the Foreign Investment Law of 1994, all disputes between a foreign investor and the Republic of Armenia must be settled in Armenian courts. All other commercial disputes may be heard by the Armenian courts or other bodies entitled to settle economic disputes unless otherwise provided for by international law or by preliminary agreements of the parties involved. The bilateral investment treaty, however, provides that in the case of a dispute between a U.S. investor and the Republic of Armenia, the investor may choose to submit the dispute for settlement by binding international arbitration. The provisions governing the resolution of commercial and other disputes are contained in the Civil Code, the Code of Civil Procedure, and the law on enforcement of court verdicts and decisions. There is no separate law governing arbitration or the arbitration process.

Effective January 1999, commercial disputes can be resolved either in the Courts of First Instance or through alternative dispute resolution mechanisms. All Courts of

First Instance can rule on cases involving commercial or economic disputes, and their verdicts can be appealed to the Court of Appeals and then to the Supreme Court. An arbitration service has been formed for independent dispute resolution.

Although the law recognizes that business and commercial organizations such as chambers of commerce and bank associations can create panels of experts authorized to settle disputes should the parties agree, this procedure is rarely followed. Alternatively, the parties may specifically write into their contract that any dispute between them should be settled by an ad hoc arbitration panel. The decision of the arbitration panel is final and may be revoked by the Court of First Instance only if the court finds that legal procedures were not properly observed. If one side fails to implement the verdict of the arbitration panel, the other may appeal to a state court with a request to enforce the decision; thereafter, the court may issue an order to a marshal, mandating enforcement of the decision.

IMPACT

The law and the legal system in Armenia continue to be in transition, and they have yet to gain the confidence of the citizens. Elections, including the constitutional referendum of 1995, have been monitored and criticized by the international community for failing to meet international standards. Corruption in government is prevalent, and numerous political figures have been assassinated. Governmental response to these problems has been slow and in many instances ineffective. Although constitutional reforms have been proposed to realign the separation of powers and to strengthen the independence of the judiciary, such reforms have been stalemated. However, significant first steps have been taken toward the establishment of a rule-of-law state.

Elizabeth F. Defeis

The author wishes to thank Vahe G. Yengibaryan and Hrair H. Ghukasyan of the Yerevan State University School of Law for their assistance with this article.

See also Soviet System

References and further reading
Defeis, Elizabeth F. 1995. "Armenian Constitutional Referendum: Towards a Democratic Practice." *Temple International and Comparative Law Journal* 9: 269–290.
———. 1995. "Constitution Building in Armenia: A Nation Once Again." *Parker School Journal of East European Law* 2: 153–200.
———. 1998. "Elections and Democracy: Armenia—A Case Study." *Loyola of Los Angeles International and Comparative Law Journal* 20: 455–474.
Khachatryan, Henrik M. 1998. *The First Constitution of Armenia*. Yerevan, Armenia: United Nations Commissioner for Refugees.
Kurkjian, Vahan. 1958. *A History of Armenia*. New York. Armenian General Benevolent Union.
Libaridian, Gerard J. 1991. *Armenia at the Crossroads: Democracy and Nationhood in the Post-Soviet Era*. Cambridge, MA: Harvard University Press.
Pipes, Richard. 1954. *The Formation of the Soviet Union.-* Cambridge, MA: Harvard University Press.
U.S. State Department. 1998. *Armenian Country Report on Human Rights Practice for 1998, Bureau of Democracy, Human Rights and Labor*. Washington, DC: U.S. Government Printing Office.
———. 1999. *Armenian Country Report on Human Rights Practice for 1999*. Bureau of Democracy, Human Rights and Labor. Washington, DC: U.S. Government Printing Office.

AUSTRALIA

GENERAL INFORMATION

Bounded by the Pacific and Indian oceans, Australia is an island continent that forms one of the political linchpins of the Oceania region in the Southern Hemisphere. The population is approximately 19.1 million people, who reside in a land area of 7,692,030 square kilometers (approximately the size of the United States excluding Alaska). Migration remains an important source of population for Australia. In 1999, according to the Australian Bureau of Statistics, 24 percent of the population of Australia had been born in another country and a further 27 percent had at least one parent born overseas. Until the 1960s, migration to Australia had primarily been from the United Kingdom and western Europe, but this pattern has since changed to reflect greater awareness of the geographical proximity of the country to Asia as well as the political role of Australia in Oceania. Seven percent of the population is of Asian origin. It is estimated that more than 1 million indigenous people lived in Australia prior to white settlement in 1788, and indigenous people now constitute 2.2 percent (approximately 427,000 persons) of the Australian population.

Australia is a constitutional monarchy. The queen of Australia (who is also the British monarch) is the head of state. It has a federal legal system, under which the powers of government are divided between democratically elected federal and state or territorial governments. The federal government is known as the Commonwealth. There are six states (New South Wales, Victoria, Queensland, South Australia, Western Australia, and Tasmania) and two self-governing mainland territories (the Northern Territory and the Australian Capital Territory, which is the seat of the Commonwealth government). Australia also has eight external territories, only three of which, the Cocos Islands, Norfolk Island, and Christmas Island, are permanently settled. The largest external territory is the Australian Antarctic Territory. With the exception of Norfolk Island, which has self-government arrangements,

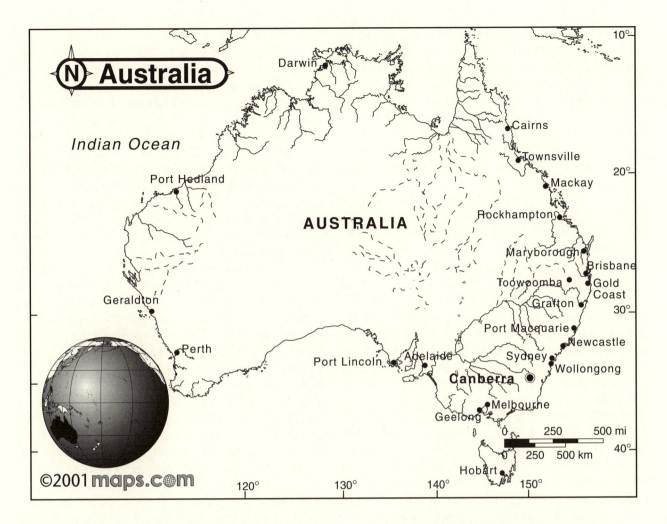

Indian Ocean

AUSTRALIA

©2001 maps.com

the external territories are directly subject to Commonwealth lawmaking powers.

CREATION OF THE COMMONWEALTH OF AUSTRALIA

The Australian constitution, which creates a federal system of government under which powers are distributed between the central and regional governments, was passed as part of a British act of Parliament (the Commonwealth of Australia Constitution Act 1900 [Imp], clause 9) on July 9, 1900. Before 1900, Australia was a collection of six self-governing British colonies, ultimate power over which rested with the British Parliament acting in its capacity as legislature for the British Empire. However, the constitution of Australia was the work of Australians. It was drafted by representatives of the colonies at a series of conventions held during the 1890s, and its terms were approved by the people of New South Wales, Victoria, Queensland, Tasmania, South Australia, and (belatedly) Western Australia in a series of referendums in 1898, 1899, and 1900. On the commencement of the British act on January 1, 1901, the Commonwealth of Australia came into being, and the six existing colonies became the six states of Australia.

HISTORY OF THE AUSTRALIAN LEGAL SYSTEM

Despite the fact that Australia has been inhabited for more than 40,000 years, the legal system and political institutions of Australia are based on the British legal tradition. In 1770, the explorer James Cook proclaimed sovereignty over the land of Australia on behalf of the king of England, George III. On January 26, 1788, the First Fleet arrived in Botany Bay (part of modern Sydney), and Governor Arthur Phillip formally claimed the territory for the British Crown.

Traditionally, international law recognized three ways for a country to acquire new territory: conquest of the proprietors of the territory; cession by those proprietors to the new power; or settlement of an uninhabited territory. In contrast to the first two methods of acquisition, which allowed for the preservation of elements of the existing laws of the land, in respect to settlement of an uninhabited territory the laws of the new power immediately came into force. Despite the presence of a large, highly visible indigenous population, the British asserted that Australia was *terra nullius,* or uninhabited, and could therefore be settled. This assertion was based on a contemporary concept in international law whereby a nomadic indigenous population with no apparent political organization or legal system was not regarded as the proprietor of the land. The idea that Australia was originally deemed to be a settled territory, as opposed to a conquered or ceded one, had two significant consequences in British law. First, Aboriginal native title to land was not recognized. Secondly, Aboriginal custom or law was deemed not to exist, so that British law, including common law, equity, and statute law, was immediately transplanted to Australian soil.

The applicability of the doctrine of *terra nullius* to the Australian situation was not overturned until 1992, by a ruling of the High Court of Australia in *Mabo v. Queensland (No. 2)*. In that decision, a majority of the High Court rejected the notion that Australia was practically unoccupied and without settled inhabitants or law when the First Fleet arrived. Further, it held that the common law would recognize that Aboriginal people had native title to lands if they could show that they had exercised traditional rights over the land since British colonization. Their native title could only be extinguished by the Crown's conveying the land to someone else or by reserving the land to its own use.

In 1828, to erase any doubt about the applicability of British law in the colonies, the Imperial Parliament (the British Parliament legislating for the empire) passed the Australian Courts Act. The act provided that all laws and statutes in force in Britain on July 25, 1828, that were applicable to the conditions in New South Wales (which at the time included what are now the states of Victoria and Queensland) and Van Diemen's Land (which later became the state of Tasmania) were deemed to be in force there. Under the act, the Supreme Courts of the colonies (which had been established under the New South Wales Act [Imp] in 1823) were given the authority to determine whether a given law was applicable to colonial conditions. As new states and territories came into being during the remainder of the nineteenth and early twentieth centuries, they too "received" British law.

The New South Wales Act also provided for the beginnings of constitutional government in the colonies. It conferred on the governor of New South Wales the power to enact laws for the colony, as long as they were not "repugnant" or inconsistent with British laws, and created the Legislative Council, which had the power (except in certain circumstances) to veto the governor's legislation. In a series of later acts, the Imperial Parliament legislated to increase the membership of the Legislative Council, to allow for popular election of a portion of its members, to increase its power in relation to the governor, and to give it a measure of fiscal responsibility. The repugnancy doctrine (which was clarified in the Colonial Laws Validity Act 1865 [Imp] to require consistency with legislation of the Imperial Parliament) continued to apply to the laws

of the Commonwealth of Australia until the Statute of Westminster Adoption Act (Cth) was passed in 1942. The states continued to be bound by the doctrine until the passage of the 1986 Australia Acts (Cth and Imp).

In 1850, the Imperial Parliament passed the Australian Constitutions Act (No. 2), which created the separate colony of Victoria and provided for the eventual creation of Queensland. In addition, the act conferred on the colonial legislatures the power (subject to the approval of the Imperial Parliament) to rewrite their constitutions to accommodate full responsible government. Each of the colonies passed acts to establish constitutions that the Imperial Parliament approved, with some amendments. Those amendments removed clauses limiting Britain's power to disallow the legislation of the colonial parliaments and required that certain acts be reserved to the British Crown for assent. The enactment of these constitutions meant that the colonial legislatures now had considerable autonomy. The Imperial Parliament retained, however, a residual governance over the affairs of the colonies.

Although a new nation of Australia and a new Federal Parliament were created when the Australian constitution came into force on January 1, 1901, the Commonwealth of Australia was still a colonial polity. Under the constitution, certain federal acts were to be reserved for royal assent (which, during the early years of the Commonwealth, would have been given or withheld on the advice of the British government). Further, the power to disallow federal and state legislation for repugnancy remained until 1942 and 1986, respectively. In practice, Britain's role in the governance of Australia became increasingly nominal (no such federal or state legislation was disallowed during the course of the twentieth century), it was not until 1986, when the Australia Acts (Cth and Imp) were passed, that Australia gained full independence from the Imperial Parliament. The acts provided that henceforth no act of the Parliament of the United Kingdom would extend or be deemed to extend to the Commonwealth or to a state or territory of Australia.

THE AUSTRALIAN CONSTITUTION

In the tradition of the constitution of the United States of America, the Australian constitution is a succinct document of eight chapters composed of 128 short sections. The constitution establishes a federal system of government and sets out the relationship between the Commonwealth and the states. Chapters 1, 2, and 3 provide for the separation of Commonwealth powers between three different bodies and confer legislative power on the Parliament, executive power on the Commonwealth executive, and judicial power on the federal judicature. The boundaries of the lawmaking power of the Commonwealth are defined in section 51. The constitution also establishes the Commonwealth of Australia as a constitutional monarchy, with the British monarch as the head of state. Under section 1, the queen or king is part of Parliament and is empowered to appoint the governor-general of Australia as the Crown's representative under section 2. Under section 61, the executive power of the Commonwealth is vested in the monarch and is exercisable by the governor-general.

The constitution is predicated on the Westminster model, whereby Parliament is the supreme arm of government. However, the High Court is the final arbiter on the constitutionality of laws made by the Parliament, and it can render invalid legislation that does not conform with the constitution.

Legislature

Section 1 of the Australian constitution creates the Federal Parliament, which (in addition to the Queen) consists of a Senate and a House of Representatives. Section 58 requires that there must be royal assent (through the governor-general) to all laws that have passed through both chambers of Parliament. The constitution also enshrines the fundamental principle of representative democracy by requiring (in sections 7, 24, and 28) that there be regular elections for the House of Representatives and the Senate and that all members of the Federal Parliament be directly chosen by the people.

The Senate was conceived as a state house and was to be entirely composed of popularly elected senators directly chosen by the people of each state voting as a single electorate. The original Senate had six senators from each state, but since 1983 that number has stood at twelve senators from each of the the six states and two senators from each of the two mainland territories, for a total of seventy-six senators. Under section 7 of the constitution, senators are chosen for a term of six years, but section 13 provides for the rotation of Senate places so that half the senators from each state are elected every three years. The Senate was given equal power with the House of Representatives except in one important respect: under section 53, the Senate cannot originate laws appropriating revenue or moneys or imposing taxation. Nor can it amend such laws, although it can return them to the House of Representatives with a request for amendments or omissions, which the House, at its discretion, may or may not adopt.

Under section 24 of the constitution, the House of Representatives is composed of popularly elected members who have successfully contested elections in a set electoral district or "division." Section 24 also requires the total number of members of the House to be approximately twice the total number of senators. As of 2001, the House of Representatives has 148 members, each of whom, under section 28, serves for a maximum term of three years. The

people of the Northern Territory have two representatives, and the people of the Australian Capital Territory also have two. As convention in Westminster-based systems dictates, the majority party of the House of Representatives is charged with forming a government.

Commonwealth Legislative Powers

The Constitution does not confer on the Federal Parliament the power to make laws on all subjects but instead enumerates a list of areas in which the Commonwealth can legislate. Section 51 lists thirty-nine subjects in relation to which the Federal Parliament has the power to make laws. These include taxation; defense; external affairs; interstate and international trade; foreign, trading, and financial corporations; marriage and divorce; immigration; bankruptcy; postal service and telecommunications; copyright; and interstate industrial arbitration. In addition to the powers conferred by section 51, grants of exclusive power are found in section 52 in relation to the seat of government and government departments. Since federation, section 51 powers have formed the basis of most High Court cases involving questions of constitutionality.

Section 51 (xxxix) confers incidental powers on the Federal Parliament whereby legislative power can be exercised in relation to any matter necessary to the execution of a power vested in the Parliament by the constitution. The Federal Parliament has used these incidental powers, along with other specific powers, to extend its legislative reach into new areas. For example, the external affairs power has been interpreted by the High Court as allowing Federal legislation on any subject if such legislation will give effect to an international agreement.

State Legislative Powers

Under sections 106 and 107, the constitutions and powers of the states are preserved but must be read subject to the Australian constitution. With few exceptions, the Australian constitution does not affect the plenary powers of legislation enjoyed by each state legislature under their own constitution, and state parliaments continue to be able to make laws on any subject of relevance. The most important exceptions are that the states cannot impose duties of custom and excise (section 90), nor can they raise defense forces without the consent of the Federal Parliament (section 114).

The Relationship between the Commonwealth and the States

The federal government is regarded as the dominant partner in the Australian federation, for a number of reasons. First, although its powers are restricted to those specifically granted in the Australian constitution (in contrast to the plenary legislative powers enjoyed by the states), those powers are numerous and have been interpreted quite broadly.

Second, the states have traditionally not raised sufficient revenue to perform all their functions, and Commonwealth legislation (made in the 1940s under the head of power contained in section 51 [ii]) effectively excludes the states from imposing income tax. In addition, under section 90 of the constitution the states are unable to impose duties of custom or excise. Consequently, the states are dependent on grants of financial assistance from the Commonwealth. Section 96 allows the Federal Parliament to attach to such grants any conditions and terms it wish. Although most grants are made unconditional, the power to impose conditions on how money is spent by the states allows the Commonwealth to influence areas over which it has no direct power to legislate. For example, the Commonwealth has exerted significant control over higher education through conditional grants, even though it has no specific legislative power in relation to education.

Third, in providing for the situation where the states and the Commonwealth may make laws on the same subject matter, the constitution clearly establishes that the legislative powers of the federal government are predominant. Section 109 provides that in the extent to which a state law is inconsistent with a law of the Commonwealth, the Commonwealth law shall prevail.

The Relationship between the Commonwealth and the Territories

Under section 122 of the constitution, the Federal Parliament may make laws on any subject in relation the territories. However, the Commonwealth has conferred self-government on the people of the Australian Capital Territory, Norfolk Island, and the Northern Territory.

Executive

Section 2 of the Australian constitution creates the office of the governor-general, who is appointed by the queen (or king) to serve as her representative in Australia. Section 5 vests in the governor-general various powers in relation to summoning and dissolving the Federal Parliament. Section 61 provides that the executive power of the Commonwealth is vested in the monarch and is exercisable by the governor-general, and section 68 vests in the governor-general the command of the military forces.

Notwithstanding these broad constitutional powers, the governor-general, by convention, acts in accordance with the principle of responsible government. Under this principle, the Crown acts on the advice of its ministers, who are in turn members of and responsible to the Federal Parliament. Accordingly, under Section 64 of the constitution, ministers are required to be current members of the House of Representatives or the Senate and are appointed by the governor-general (in practice acting on the advice of the prime minister) to administer gov-

ernment departments. By their appointment ministers become members of the Federal Executive Council (established by section 62), whose role is to advise the governor-general. Although they are vital to the actual operations of the Executive Government, neither the prime minister (who is the head of the government) nor the cabinet (which is made up of senior government ministers and serves as the principal decision-making body of the government) is mentioned in the constitution.

JUDICIARY

Chapter 3 (sections 71–80) of the Australian constitution lays out the power of the third branch of the Commonwealth government, the judiciary. Under section 71, judicial power is vested in the High Court of Australia, as a federal supreme court consisting of a minimum of three justices, and in other new federal courts as created by the Federal Parliament. By application of section 5 of the High Court of Australia Act 1979 (Cth), the High Court consists of six justices and a chief justice. Under sections 73, 75, and 76 of the constitution and sections 30–35A of the Judiciary Act 1903 (Cth), the High Court exercises both original and appellate jurisdiction. Its original jurisdiction pertains to certain defined matters, including disputes between state governments and between a state government and the Commonwealth. Most notably, under section 76, the High Court has original jurisdiction in relation to matters arising under the constitution or involving its interpretation. This jurisdiction cannot be devolved to any other court. In addition, under section 73, the High Court has jurisdiction, at its discretion, to hear appeals on matters that have been heard by a single High Court justice exercising original jurisdiction and on matters that have been heard by other federal courts and by state supreme courts. The High Court is the final court of appeal in Australia.

In addition to vesting Commonwealth judicial power in the High Court, section 71 empowers the Federal Parliament to create other federal courts and to vest existing courts with federal jurisdiction. Accordingly the Federal Parliament has vested state supreme courts with federal jurisdiction and has also created a system of federal courts. The Federal Court of Australia, established under the Federal Court of Australia Act 1976 (Cth), was created to resolve disputes arising out of the application of federal laws, notably in the areas of bankruptcy, trade, administrative law, and industrial law. It has both original and appellate jurisdiction. Other section 71 federal courts include the Family Court of Australia, which was established under the Family Law Act 1975 (Cth), and the Federal Magistrates Service, which was established under the Federal Magistrates Act 1999 (Cth). Between March 1994 and May 1997, there was also an Industrial Relations Court of Australia, but the jurisdiction of this court has now been transferred to the Federal Court.

Under section 72 of the constitution and the legislation establishing each court, justices of the High Court, judges of the Federal Court of Australia, and judges of the Family Court are commissioned by the governor-general in council (that is, on the advice of the Executive Council). Before an appointment is made to fill a vacancy on the High Court, the Commonwealth attorney-general must consult with the attorneys-general of the states. Justices of the High Court and judges of the Federal Court, as well as a majority of the judges of the Family Court, are selected from the legal profession. The Family Law Act 1975 allows appointment to the Family Court of other experts in family law, and several academics with such expertise have been appointed to that court. A report in 1993 by the Commonwealth attorney-general suggested alternative means of appointment of judges to the Family Court—creating advisory commissions, formalizing a public consultation process, selecting judges by election or confirming the appointment of judges through legislative ratification—but the system of appointment currently remains unchanged. Although the constitution originally gave federal judges life tenure, an amendment to section 72 made in 1977 means that federal court judges now have tenure only until they reach the age of seventy. However, the only means of removing a federal judge from office before tenure has lapsed is provided in section 72 (ii), which stipulates that the governor-general in council, on an address from both chambers of Parliament in the same session, may request removal on the grounds of "proved misbehaviour of incapacity." Under section 72, judges of federal courts are entitled to receive remuneration as fixed by Parliament. Such remuneration cannot be diminished during a judge's continuance in office.

Amendment Procedure

The procedure for amending the Australian constitution is set out in section 128. It is a complex and demanding process that requires two stages. First, a proposed amendment must gain the support of a majority in both the Senate and the House of Representatives. Second, the proposal must be placed before the people in a referendum. In order for the constitution to be amended, not only must the referendum receive the support of a majority of voters nationally, it must also gain the support of a majority of states. The difficulty of meeting this requirement has limited the number of amendments that have been enacted. To date, only eight out of forty-four proposed amendments have been passed in referendums. The latest unsuccessful attempt was made in 1999, when a proposed amendment that would have led to Australia's becoming a republic was put to the people in a referendum and failed to receive the required majorities.

PROTECTION OF INDIVIDUAL RIGHTS

Although the framers of the Australian constitution investigated the operation of the U.S. constitution in the years leading up to 1900, they did not incorporate in the Australian document any equivalent to the Bill of Rights. The Australian constitution does, however, afford some protections against overreaching Commonwealth legislative and executive action (although not against equivalent action by state governments). Under section 51 (xxxi) the acquisition of property by the Commonwealth must be "on just terms," and under section 116 the Commonwealth can neither establish nor prohibit the free exercise of any religion. In addition, section 80 grants a positive right to a jury trial for certain criminal offenses. In relation to state power, section 117 of the constitution effectively prohibits a state legislature from discriminating against persons who are not residents of that state. The question of whether section 117 applies to Commonwealth law is unresolved, having been left open by the High Court in *Leeth v. Commonwealth* (1992).

Since the 1990s, the High Court has found that, in addition to these express protections and grants of individual rights, further restrictions on legislative power are implicit in the fabric of the constitution. For example, in *Australian Capital Television v. Commonwealth (No 2)* (1992) and *Nationwide News v. Wills* (1992) a majority of the High Court found that there was implied in the constitution a protection of free speech in relation to political matters.

COURT STRUCTURE

The Australian legal system, which has grown out of the British model, is based on the common law. Accordingly, the central tenet of the Australian system is the doctrine of precedent, whereby the decisions of higher courts are binding on lower courts hearing cases involving similar facts and legal issues.

All jurisdictions in Australia have a clear and well-established hierarchy of courts. There are nine jurisdictions in Australia (the federal jurisdiction and the jurisdictions of the six states and two mainland territories), each with its own hierarchy. In accordance with the Australian constitution, state supreme courts have been vested with the power to hear federal matters and, when doing so, fall within the federal hierarchy.

The High Court of Australia is at the top of both the federal and the state hierarchies. However, there is no automatic right of appeal to the High Court from a state supreme court unless the matter comes within the original jurisdiction of the High Court under section 75 (v) of the constitution. Appeals to the High Court from the Federal Court of Australia or from one of the state supreme courts exercising federal jurisdiction are by leave of the High Court only. Likewise, an appeal from a deci-

Legal Structure of Australia Courts

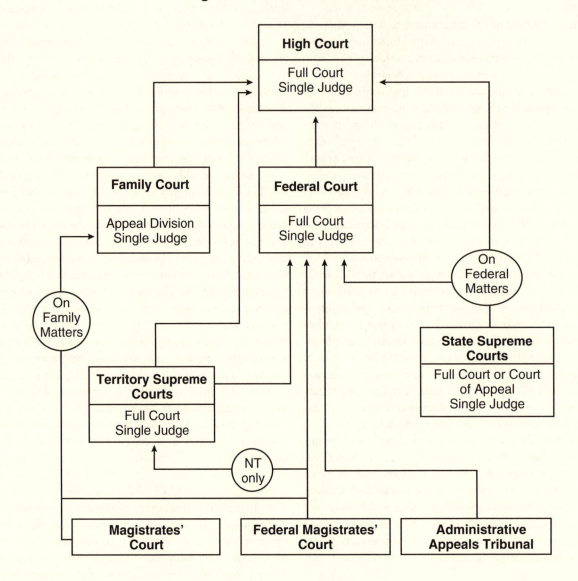

sion of a state supreme court on a state matter may be brought to the High Court only with the High Court's leave.

Until the passing of the Australia Act in 1986, though, it was still possible to appeal from state supreme courts on matters of state jurisdiction to the Judicial Committee of the Privy Council in London. However, appeals from the High Court to the Privy Council on matters of federal and territorial jurisdiction were abolished in 1968 and on matters of state jurisdiction were abolished in 1975.

In addition to its courts, each jurisdiction has a number of tribunals that supplement the work of the courts. These tribunals deal with a wide variety of specialist matters. The Commonwealth Administrative Appeals Tribunal is such a body.

The accompanying diagram shows the Australian fed-

eral court structure, including state supreme courts exercising federal jurisdiction.

Miriam Gani
Scott W. Barclay

See also Australian Capital Territory; New South Wales; Northern Territory of Australia; Queensland; South Australia; Tasmania; Western Australia

References and further reading

Attorney-General's Department. "Australia's Legal System." http://law.gov.au/auslegalsys/auslegalsys.htm (21 August 2001).
Blackshield, Tony, and George Williams. 1998. *Australian Constitutional Law Theory: Commentary and Materials.* 2nd ed. Sydney: Federation Press.
Booker, Keven, Arthur Glass, and Robert Watt. 1998. *Federal Constitutional Law: An Introduction.* 2nd ed. Sydney: Butterworths.
Castles, Alex C. 1982. *An Australian Legal History.* Sydney: Law Book Company.

Cook, Catriona, Robin Creyke, Robert Geddes, and Ian Holloway. 2001. *Laying Down the Law.* 5th ed. Sydney: Butterworths.

Coper, Michael. 1988. *Encounters with the Australian Constitution.* Sydney: CCH Books.

Crawford, James. 1993. *Australian Courts of Law.* 3rd ed. Melbourne: Oxford University Press.

Hughes, Robert, and Geoffrey Leane. 1996. *Australian Legal Institutions: Principles, Structure and Organisation.* Sydney: FT Law and Tax.

Kercher, Bruce. 1995. *An Unruly Child: A History of Law in Australia.* Sydney: Allen and Unwin.

Lumb, Richard D. 1991. *The Constitutions of the Australian States.* 5th ed. Brisbane: University of Queensland Press.

Parkinson, Patrick. 2001. *Tradition and Change in Australian Law.* 2nd ed. Sydney: Law Book Company.

Waller, Louis. 1995. *An Introduction to Law.* 7th ed. Sydney: Law Book Company.

AUSTRALIAN CAPITAL TERRITORY

GENERAL INFORMATION

The Australian Capital Territory (ACT) is located in eastern Australia. It lies approximately 300 kilometers southwest of Sydney and approximately 650 km northeast of Melbourne. The ACT is 80 km long, from north to south, and about 30 km wide, from east to west. Canberra is the capital of the ACT and is the only capital city in Australia that is situated inland. The population of the ACT is approximately 313,000.

EVOLUTION AND HISTORY

The origins of the law of the ACT differ due to historical and political reasons. The source of the law in the ACT is both parliamentary and common law. The geographical area that constitutes the ACT was originally a part of the State of New South Wales. The area was founded as a federal territory on 1 January 1911. In 1913 Canberra was formally named as the official capital. The federal Parliament House moved from Melbourne to Canberra in 1928.

Prior to self-government, the Commonwealth Parliament by virtue of section 122 of the Australian Constitution passed legislation exclusively for the ACT.

The Commonwealth Parliament passed the Australian Capital Territory (Self-Government) Act in 1988, which established self-government in the ACT. The ACT attained self-government on 11 May 1989. The ACT has only a single legislature, the Legislative Assembly, which both makes laws and approves delegated legislation. The Legislative Assembly has seventeen elected members. The crown is not represented in the legislature (note that in the Northern Territory the crown is represented by an administrator); however, under section 35 of the Australian Capital Territory (Self-Government) Act 1988

(Cth), the governor-general of the Commonwealth Parliament may disallow ACT legislation.

CURRENT STRUCTURE

Like the Northern Territory and Tasmania, the ACT has a two-tiered court system, which includes the Magistrates' Court and the Supreme Court. There are also a number of tribunals, which operate throughout the ACT.

Supreme Court

The Supreme Court is the highest court in the ACT and is usually presided over by a single judge. It has general civil and criminal jurisdiction, both original and appellate. An appeal from the Supreme Court is to the Full Court of the Federal Court of Australia and thereafter to the High Court of Australia. In limited circumstances there exists a right to seek special leave to appeal directly to the High Court. The Supreme Court of the ACT has both all original and all appellate jurisdiction necessary to administer justice in the ACT, and any jurisdiction that is conferred by a commonwealth act or a law of the territory. Where there is a conflict between the rules of equity and the rules of law, the rules of equity prevail.

Unless so required by or under a commonwealth act or a law of the ACT, the court is not bound to exercise its powers where it has concurrent jurisdiction with another court or tribunal.

Magistrates' Court

The Magistrates' Court exercises jurisdiction in the ACT and sits at Canberra, Jervis Bay, and such other places as are notified in the Government Gazette. By implication, the Magistrates Court Act 1930 extends to Jervis Bay.

The court's criminal jurisdiction covers any offense that is punishable on summary conviction or any offense, act, or omission that attracts a penalty, punishment, or fine; where there are no other provisions for the trial of a person who has committed the offense, then the matter may be heard and determined by the court. The jurisdiction is deemed to be conferred on and may be exercised by the court.

In civil matters, the court has jurisdiction to hear and determine any personal action at law where the amount claimed does not exceed $50,000 (Australian dollars).

Children's Court

The Children's Court is a specialist court dedicated to dealing with children's matters. It attempts to provide for and promote the care, protection, and wellbeing of children and young people in a way that recognizes their right to grow in a safe and stable environment and that takes into account the responsibilities of parents and others for them. It also has the power to hear and act on matters relating to children and crime.

Legal Structure of the Australian Capital Territory Courts

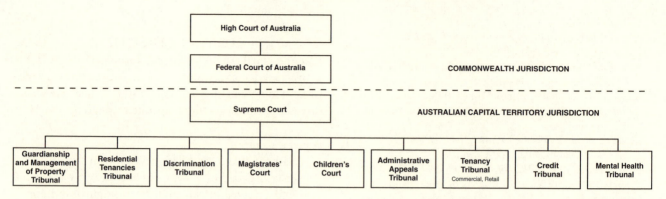

Tribunals

The Tenancy Tribunal (Commercial/Retail) hears disputes in relation to retail premises. The Tribunal consists of the president, or the president and two other members nominated by president. There is a right of appeal from the Tenancy Tribunal (Commercial/Retail) to the Supreme Court if the appeal is based on a matter of law.

The Administrative Appeals Tribunal allows review of some of the administrative decisions made by ACT ministers, departments, and agencies in a wide range of jurisdictions. The tribunal can only review decisions that it has been given specific jurisdiction to review. These decisions are therefore known as reviewable decisions. The tribunal is divided into two divisions for the exercise of its powers. They are the Land and Planning Division and the General Division. There is a right of appeal on questions of law from the Administrative Appeals Tribunal to the Supreme Court.

The Discrimination Tribunal hears complaints referred to it by the discrimination commissioner or by individual complainants concerning a range of topics including sexual discrimination, racial discrimination, racial vilification, sexual harassment and other unlawful forms of discrimination. The Discrimination Tribunal consists of a president. There exists a right of appeal to the Supreme Court on questions of law.

The Credit Tribunal hears matters concerned with credit sale contracts, contracts of guarantee, goods mortgages, contracts of insurance, home finance contracts, contracts of sale, and loan contracts. The tribunal will often have concurrent jurisdiction over matters with the Magistrates' Court, but an action must be brought in one forum or the other, not both. The tribunal consists of a chairperson and two other members. There exists a right of appeal to the Supreme Court on questions of law.

The Mental Health Tribunal hears applications for orders for the treatment and care of people who may have a psychiatric illness or mental dysfunction. It has the power to determine whether a person charged with a criminal offense is equipped to please and may also pro-

vide a court with advice in relation to sentencing. The tribunal consists of the president, the deputy presidents, and the nonpresidential members. There exists a right of appeal to the Supreme Court on questions of law and also a right of appeal with the leave of the Supreme Court.

The Residential Tenancies Tribunal is an independent body that has exclusive jurisdiction to hear and determine all matters arising from both private and public residential tenancy agreements. The tribunal aims to resolve disputes in an informal environment and, unlike a court, may inform itself in any way it considers necessary. It is the policy of the Residential Tenancies Tribunal to manage all cases from the moment initial contact is made with it. The tribunal is currently comprised of a president, an acting president, four members, and two referees, who sit independently as required. A decision of the tribunal may be appealed to the Supreme Court on a matter of law.

The Guardianship and Management of Property Tribunal has the power to make orders relating to the guardianship of persons who have a disability and orders relating to the management of their property. The tribunal consists of a president and two other members as chosen by the executive. There exists a right of appeal on a matter of law and on any other question with the leave of the court to the Supreme Court.

NOTABLE FEATURES OF THE LAW AND LEGAL SYSTEM

By virtue of Schedule 1 of the Seat of Government Acceptance Act (1909) Cth, the Commonwealth of Australia and the State of New South Wales agreed that the state would surrender to the commonwealth the land of the territory. Under the Seat of Government (Administration) Act of 1910, no crown lands in the ACT are allowed to be sold or disposed of for any estate of freehold, except in pursuance of some contract entered into, or of the right to enter into, which existed before 1910 and except for the purpose of giving effect to some right that existed before 1910 of any law of the State of New South Wales that has continued in force in the territory. Leasehold arrangements currently allow for a maximum term of fifty years in relation to farming leases and a maximum term of ninety-nine years for all other leases.

In 1994, the ACT Legislative Assembly passed the Domestic Relationships Act, which recognizes domestic relationships other than marriages. A domestic relationship is defined as "a personal relationship (other than a legal marriage) between two adults in which one provides personal or financial commitment and support of a domestic nature for the material benefit of the other, and includes a de facto marriage." Thus, homosexual relationships and nonsexual relationships fit under ACT's ambit. A party to such a relationship is able to apply to the court (either Magistrates or Supreme, depending on jurisdictional limits) for an order adjusting the interests in the property of either or both of the parties that seems just and equitable with respect to the nature, duration, and circumstances of the relationship. A court does not have the power to make such an order unless it is satisfied that a domestic relationship has existed for at least two years.

STAFFING

In 1970 the Commonwealth Government passed the ACT Legal Practitioners Ordinance, which since self-government has been called the Legal Practitioners Act. It outlines the requirements for legal practice in the ACT.

Once a person's name is, or is taken to be, on the Roll of Legal Practitioners, that person is considered a legal practitioner entitled to practice in the territory as a barrister or a solicitor or both. The legal practitioner also has the right of audience in any court of the territory.

For admission as a legal practitioner, an applicant must either complete a course of studies leading to the degree of Bachelor of Laws at an Australian university. There are also provisions for recognizing degrees from outside of the country. After receiving the degree, an applicant is required to have satisfactorily completed the course of professional training in law in the Legal Workshop within the Faculty of Law in the faculties within the Australian National University or another course of a similar nature recognized in a state or the Northern Territory as satisfying in that jurisdiction an admission requirement for practical professional training.

A magistrate is required to be a legal practitioner and to have practiced as such for at least five years. The children's magistrate is declared by the chief magistrate and must be a magistrate. Although there are some members of tribunals who are not legally trained, a number serve the dual role of magistrate. The Tenancy Tribunal (Commercial/Retail), the Discrimination Tribunal, the Guardianship and Management of Property Tribunal, the Credit Tribunal, the Residential Tenancies Tribunal, and the Mental Health Tribunal are all presided over by presidents who are also magistrates.

Nonpresidential members of the Mental Health Tribunal must be appointed from among psychiatrists and psychologists as well as from among other persons who, in the Executive's opinion, have skills and experience in providing clinical mental health services, including nurses, occupational therapists, and social workers.

The president of the Administrative Appeals Tribunal must be either a judge or have been a legal practitioner for a minimum of five years. Deputy registrars and senior members must have been legal practitioners for not less than five years, although a person may also be appointed a senior member if in the opinion of the Executive the candidatehas special knowledge or skill relevant to the duties of a senior member. Nonpresidential members other than senior members are required to be either legal practitioners or have had experience, for not less than five years, at a high level in industry, commerce, public administration, industrial relations, the practice of a profession, or the service of a government or of an authority of a government;

A judge of the Supreme Court is required to have been a judge of a superior court of the commonwealth, a state, or a territory or have been a legal practitioner for not less than five years.

Melanie R. Senior

See also Administrative Tribunals; Australia; Common Law; Criminal Law; Equity; New South Wales; Northern Territory of Australia

References and further reading
Bradbrook, Adrian J. (1991) *Australian Real Property Law.* The Law Book Company, Sydney.
Morris, G. Cook, C. Creyke, R. and Geddes, R. (2001) *Laying Down the Law.* Butterworths, Sydney.
Withycombe, Susan Mary Woolcock (1993) *Ethos and Ethics. A History of the Law Society of the Australian Capital Territory.* The Law Society of the Australian Capital Territory, Canberra.http://www.courts.act.gov.au.

AUSTRIA

GENERAL INFORMATION

Austria is situated in central Europe, bounded in the north by Germany and the Czech Republic, in the northeast by Slovakia, in the east by Hungary, in the south by Slovenia and Italy, and in the west by Switzerland and Liechtenstein. It comprises a territory of about 83,859 square kilometers (32,378 square miles). Two-thirds of its surface is covered by mountains, the Alps. Among the central ranges is the Hohe Tauern, which culminates in the highest elevation of the country, the Grossglockner (3,798 meters/12,460 feet). The main and longest river is

the Danube, which flows from east to west across northern Austria, passing through the largest city and seat of the federal government, Vienna. Austria possesses two especially beautiful landscapes of mountain lakes: the Salzkammergut and Carinthia. The climate is temperate and continental, with warm, rainy summers and moderately cold winters.

Austria is an economically prosperous and stable country. In 1996, its gross national product (GNP) amounted to approximately U.S.$226.5 billion and its per capita GNP was about U.S.$28,210. Exports consists primarily of machinery and transportation equipment, chemicals, iron and steel, and paper and paper products. Germany is the major trading partner (43.6 percent of the total volume of combined imports and exports), followed by Italy (8.8 percent) and Switzerland (5.4 percent).

Austria has a population of approximately 8.15 million (2001 estimate). Almost all Austrians (98 percent) speak German. Three-quarters (75.1 percent) of the population declare themselves to belong to the Roman Catholic church, and 5.4 percent are affiliated with various Protestant churches. There is also a small Muslim minority of 2.1 percent and an even smaller Jewish com-

munity of approximately 0.1 percent concentrated in the Vienna area. The remaining Austrians are nonreligious or of undeclared affiliation.

HISTORY

The first state in central Europe was the Celtic state Noricum, established around the fourth century B.C.E. in parts of the territory of present-day Austria. At the beginning of the sixth century C.E., Bavarian influence became dominant in the region between the Alps and the Danube. But in the following centuries these territories experienced under the dynasty of the Babenbergs (976–1246) and the house of Habsburg (1282/83–1919) a history rather different from that of the duchy of Bavaria and the rest of Germany, although all these regions were united under the Habsburgs in the Holy Roman Empire till the appearance of Napoleon at the turn of the nineteenth century. After Napoleon's final defeat at Waterloo in 1815, the Congress of Vienna decreed a general social and legal restoration under the leadership of Austria's chancellor Prince Metternich. For more than thirty years, the Holy Alliance of the old monarchies prevented any democratic reform in this prolongation of absolutism.

The revolutionary year 1848 held out the promise that Austria would develop into a constitutional monarchy, but the transformation was never successfully completed. In 1867, after a series of military defeats and financial disasters, Austria formed its first democratically elected parliament, but without women's suffrage, which was not attained until 1919. The dissolution of the Austro-Hungarian Empire at the end of World War I brought an end to the reign of the Habsburgs, and gave birth to the First Republic.

Against a backdrop of social unrest and violent confrontation between rival political factions, the governments of the First Republic were unstable from the beginning. As a result of civil war in the spring of 1933, the victorious Christian Social Party established an authoritarian government. The destruction of the Austrian workers movement in the following years increased Austria's political vulnerability to the growing Nazi movements. Hence when German troops invaded Austria on March 12, 1938, they met with no substantial resistance. Under German occupation (the Anschluss), the Austrian government was forced to resign, and a period of suppression and persecution began. Austria ceased to exist as an independent state. Unfortunately, many Austrians approved of the German annexation and opportunistic supporters, if not outright accomplices, of Hitler's Third Reich. Thus Austrians participated in terrible crimes against humanity such as the persecution and murder of the European Jews (the Holocaust).

In the Moscow Declaration of 1943, the Allied powers of Great Britain, the Soviet Union, and the United States pronounced Germany's annexation of Austria to be null and void and supported the reestablishment of a free and independent Austria.

After the fall of Hitler's Germany in 1945, Austria came under control of the four Allied powers (including France). International financial aid (such as U.S. assistance under the Marshall Plan) during the ten-year Allied occupation helped Austria to restore its economy and political life. By the Vienna International Treaty of May 15, 1955, Austria regained its independence and sovereignty. That same year, on October 26, in the midst of the simmering East-West conflict, Austria proclaimed "permanent neutrality"—a condition that the Soviet Union had demanded in exchange for its agreement to the Vienna Treaty.

In 1960, Austria joined the European Free Trade Association, and in 1994, after the association's demise, it became a full member of the European Union.

LEGAL CONCEPTS

The Austrian constitution that came into force in October 1920 had some obvious resemblances to the Weimar constitution promulgated at the same time in Germany. It was substantially modified in 1929 for example to introduce the election of the president by popular vote instead of by parliament and to grant the president emergencypoweres. In 1934, this liberal constitution was replaced by an authoritarian constitution and did not come into force again until after 1945.

Separation of Powers

Like other Western countries, Austria's fundamental law is laid down in its constitution, which must be seen in the tradition of the separation of powers dating back to such legal theorists as Locke and Montesquieu. The Austrian constitutional document provides for the separation of executive, legislative, and judicial branches of government, but in a rather unique manner. As opposed to the U.S. model of checks and balances of principally equal powers, Austrian constitutionalism is hierarchically structured in a steplike arrangement. The legislature is preeminent because of its exclusive prerogative to create legal rules. The judiciary is on equal footing with the executive branch insofar as they both are conceived as executors of law and therefore are strictly bound to acts of legislation.

Legal Positivism

The present Austrian constitution is above all the creation of the legal philosopher Hans Kelsen. Together with other members of the Viennese school of law, Kelsen elaborated a version of legal positivism that excludes extralegal arguments from judicial and administrative decision making. Kelsen was a part of the vigorous intellectual life that in prewar Austria gathered around Moritz Schlick and his ideas about logical positivism. This strand of legal thinking was highly influential in academic life as well as in the practice of the courts, especially the Constitutional Court.

Austria's constitution is based on a few leading principles that cannot be changed except by plebiscite. Primary among these principles are democracy and federalism.

In consequence of the federal principle, Austria consists of nine provinces, called federal states, which are endowed with parliamentary bodies and governments of their own. But a state jurisdiction does not exist apart from jurisdiction that is exclusively federal. All competencies are distributed among state and federal authorities according to the general rule that any matter not explicitly delegated to the federation by the constitution remains the purview of the particular state.

The legislative organization reflects the federal principle, too, in that the legislature is divided into two chambers: the National Council and the Federal Council, the latter being the proper representative of the federal states. The Federal Council has a right to veto decisions of the National Council but with none other than suspensory effects.

The first house of the Federal Parliament, the National Council, serves for a term of four years. Legislation is passed by an absolute majority vote (50 percent plus one), except for constitutional amendments, which require a qualified majority vote of two thirds.

Human Rights

The constitution guarantees basic and fundamental human rights such as freedom of expression, the right to a fair trial, the right to respect for private and family life, freedom of thought, conscience, and religion, freedom of assembly and association, presumption of innocence, and security of private property. Those rights were originally laid down in the constitution of 1867 and were incorporated into the 1920 constitution as catalog of human rights. This catalog has been extended and completed by the European Convention for the Protection of Human Rights and Fundamental Freedoms (ECHR) ratified by Austria in 1958. All these legal provisions are part of Austria's constitutional law and therefore have the highest priority in the country's legal structure.

The Austrian law embraces the protection of minority rights as well. Such guaranties are to be found in the Saint-Germain Treaty of 1919 and in the Vienna Treaty of 1955.

Pursuant to special constitutional provisions, generally recognized rules of international law are regarded as integral parts of federal law. Such rules do not need special implementation, as they are valid Austrian law.

Furthermore, Austria is a signatory to other international rights treaties, including the European Social Charter, the Universal Declaration of Human Rights, and the International Covenant of Civil and Political Rights.

Labor law in Austria provides workers with rights similar to those of other European countries. For example, vacations and sick benefits for employees are legally guaranteed. Pregnant women have the right to eight weeks of paid leave prior to giving birth and eight weeks following delivery, as well as a special right of vacation for up to eighteen months after the child is born. There are corresponding rights for fathers.

The Austrian labor market is among the strongest in the European Union. Austria's coordinated macroeconomic policy and unique system of social and economical partnershiphave resulted in a labor market that provides flexibility for companies and security for the workforce.

Because of the constitution's grounding in legal positivism there is only one legitimate source of law: parliamentary legislation. In principle, neither judicial precedents nor customs may constitute law in their own right. In the field of private actions and transactions, however, the law acknowledges a kind of individual autonomy. References in regulations to customary rules make some of these customs legally binding. Among merchants, unless otherwise agreed, commercial customs are applicable according to Article 346 of the Code of Commerce.

Private Law

The Austrian Civil Code (ABGB) was enacted as private law in 1811 and has ever since been respected as the main source of civil law. Even under Nazi rule, this code was not repealed. In some branches of civil law, such as tenant law, labor law, and provisions regarding liability, the older code has been modernized. But generally speaking, in the framework of the ABGB, which is justly held to be one of the great European codifications and a true product of the Enlightenment, a substantial part of the Roman law tradition still survives.

In 1938, after the annexation the German Commercial Code of 1897 together with just scant accommodations this was enacted by the then legislator for the territory of former Austria without being replaced after 1945.

Criminal Law

In 1974, the Austrian legislature passed a radical reform of its criminal law. The reform did away with retaliation and expiation as aims of punishment and emphasized the idea of punishment as a preventive measure to protect the values of society. One of the reform issues is the strict principle of legality, by which only the legislature defines what is to be regarded as a criminal offense and at the same time represses other viewpoints such as the natural-law definition of malice. Thus, metaphysical or speculative ideologies are put aside in favor focusing on real social circumstances.

In 1968, the minister of justice abolished the death penalty (although in fact no one had been executed in Austria in decades), a move that contributed to the enactment of the sixth protocol of the ECHR.

Austria's criminal procedure code is based on the principle of accusation, which entails separate, independent roles for the public prosecutor and the judge, on the official duty of ascertaining the truth, and on several principles: legality, immediacy, public trial, the presentation and free evaluation of evidence through oral proceedings, and the presumption of innocence.

Regional Court I (court of first instance), as a criminal court, forms divisions for serious criminal offenses in order to let citizens participate as lay judges. These lay assessors divisions (*Schöffengerichte*) consist of two regular judges and two lay judges. Jurors divisions (*Geschworenengerichte*) are made up of three regular judges and eight jurors.

STRUCTURE

Austria's courts of final jurisdiction are the Supreme Court, for civil and criminal cases, the Constitutional Court, and the Administrative Court. This difference originates in the fundamental distinction in ancient Roman law between *ius publicum* (public law) and *ius privatum* (private law). Constitutional Court and Administrative Court are active in the field of public law only.

The understanding of the term "civil rights" within the Austrian legal tradition is very different from that within the common law system of many European nations. This difference caused serious problems when fitting Austrian judicial practices to those of the European Union. and required adjustments of the Austrian constitution, especially with respect to Article 6 of the ECHR, which demands a tribunal for civil rights cases.

The Supreme Court sits in senates (panels) normally consisting of five judges. When treating questions of special importance, the senate includes eleven judges. The Supreme Court has a first and a second president, There is no fixed terms for court presidents; they serve until retirement or removal from office. As of 2001, the Supreme Court consists of fifty-seven judges, sixteen senates, thirteen senate presidents, and forty-one other members.

A separate Constitutional Court with twenty members, including six alternates, reviews the actions of administrative authorities against individuals for possible unconstitutionality. The Constitutional Court also has the right to repeal unconstitutional provisions in parliamentary acts and to decide matters of elections. Members are appointed for life by the federal president upon the advice of the president of the court and the vice president of the court. Nine nominations are to be proposed to the federal president by the government, five by the National Council, and four by the Federal Council. The members have to be judges, senior civil servants, or law professors.

A separate Administrative Court reviews unlawful notices, acts, orders, and delays by administrative authorities. Members are appointed for life by the federal president in accordance with proposals from the federal government and the plenary assembly of the court. The competence of the Administrative Court depends on the exhaustion of any administrative legal remedies and technically constitutes jurisdiction a posteriori. Therefore, as a rule, it is not possible to take direct action against measures of administrative authorities even if they affect civil rights.

Independent Administrative Senates

In order to comply with the terms of the European Convention on the Protection of Human Rights and the rulings of the European Court of Human Rights, Austria has created independent administrative senates. These tribunals deal with appeals and motions of individuals against administrative acts or delay of acts. Independent administrative senates consist of a presiding chairman, an alternate chairman, and an arbitrary number of other members who are appointed by the respective provincial government for six-year term.

Ordinary Courts

In Austria there are four basic types of ordinary courts: county courts, Regional Courts I and II (courts of first

Legal Structure of Austria Courts

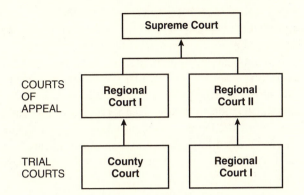

and second instance), and the supreme court. The Supreme Court has appellate jurisdiction against judgments of the regional courts.

The Supreme Court is the highest body within the ordinary judiciary, serving as the forum of last (third) instance in civil and penal law cases.

Regional Court I has first-instance jurisdiction in all civil litigation, apart from those matters assigned to the county courts and in more serious criminal matters. It also has appellate jurisdiction against most judgments of the county courts. Appeals from decisions of first instance of Regional Courts I lie with Regional Courts II, which are seated in Graz, Innsbruck, Linz, and Vienna.

The county court is the lowest court of record in Austria. Its civil jurisdiction includes matters not exceeding a litigation value of 130,000 Austrian schillings, landlord and tenant cases, maintenance claims, possessory actions, and other minor matters. Appeals from most decisions of the county courts lie with Regional Courts I.

In criminal matters, the county courts have jurisdiction over certain misdemeanors, that is, offenses for which the regular minimum punishment is a fine or less than one year of imprisonment.

Arbitration

In Austria private dispute resolution is regulated by law and has achieved importance particularly for cases in commercial law. Private dispute resolution and arbitration offer advantages by reducing the length of proceedings, but sometimes at a high financial cost. The most important of the arbitral bodies are the Court of Arbitration of the Austrian Chamber of Commerce and the Court of Arbitration of the International Chamber of Commerce, in Paris, whose function is the settlement by arbitration of international business disputes.

Legal Counsel

In civil proceedings that concern matters exceeding 52,000 Austrian schillings litigants must be represented by a qualified lawyer. Exception is made for some special matters, such as labor disputes.

In criminal cases concerning juvenile offenses and offenses that entail imprisonment for longer than three years, the accused must be represented by a qualified lawyer.

In-court legal aid is granted by the courts themselves in criminal cases when a defendant is unable to afford the costs of the judicial procedure or of a lawyer. The most indigent defendants receive legal counsel free of charge. Counsel for the defense is appointed by the court. They must be granted furthermore in case of complicated factual and legal position where representation by a lawyer is a statutory requirement.

A similar service is offered in civil matters. Litigants can make application for legal aid and are allowed to let the court itself draw up records of certain legal actions. Furthermore, as a public service the courts offer, on fixed dates and free of charge, information on points of law.

STAFFING

Austria's constitution guarantees that magistrates enjoy independence of the judiciary and tenure for life. They cannot be removed, suspended, transferred, or made to retire except under limited circumstances and only by means of a court's judgment.

Preconditions for nomination as judge are a law degree and experience in the practice of law. Law study can be started by candidates who have got a University entrance qualification or completed legally acknowledged exams.

Selection of judges is competitive. Candidates for the position of judge or public prosecutor must go through a training course at the court, which includes a short traineeship as a lawyer. After passing their final examination they can be nominated for judge and have to decide whether they want to become judges or public prosecutors. After nomination the courts' personnel divisions collect data to evaluate the performance of judges and prosecutors against objective criteria.

The appointment of judges in Austria is complex. Staff senates for the judicial authorities prepare lists of candidates for the Ministry of Justice. Judges are ultimately appointed by the president of the republic (federal president).

Attorneys are self-employed and have legally unlimited access to all courts. To become a lawyer, one must have completed legal studies, spent five years as a lawyer's trainee, and passed an examination for entrance into the profession. Registration in the Chamber of Lawyers is required for the active practice of law. According to the chamber, in 1999 there were 3,857 practicing lawyers, of whom 431 were women.

Lawyer's trainees must complete continuation courses during their traineeship in order to obtain authorization to represent clients in less serious trials.

The constitution also provides for a people's counsel (*Volksanwaltschaft*), which closely corresponds to the Scandinavian office of ombudsman. Counsellors are elected by the National Council and are independent from the government. They serve a five-year term and can be reelected one time. Ombudsmen make recommendations and conduct investigations. They have the right of recourse to the Constitutional Court to appeal against statutory instruments, and they enjoy privileges similar to those of a judge.

Austria has five universities with law faculties. The largest and oldest, the University of Austria, was founded in Vienna in 1365 and is the oldest university in the German-speaking world. The other Austrian universities having law faculties are in Innsbruck (founded 1562), Graz (1585), Salzburg (founded 1622, refounded 1962), and Linz (founded 1492, refounded 1962). In the academic year 1998–99, there were 23,958 students enrolled in Austrian law faculties.

In 2000, the judicial branch, not including the Supreme Court, had 1,654 judges, 198 public prosecutors, 1,305 trainees, and 5,489 persons working as support staff for judges and prosecutors.

SPECIALIZED JUDICIAL BODIES

A number of special courts have been created that are organizationally separate from the courts of record. Special juvenile courts in Vienna, Graz, and Linz have comprehensive jurisdiction over juvenile delinquency and related matters.

A special commercial regional court and a special commercial county court in Vienna exert ordinary jurisdiction in cases of commercial law. Elsewhere, commercial jurisdiction lies with the competence of the general judiciary, which in such cases is differently staffed, with mixed senates.

There is a special labor court in Vienna. Outside the capital, in matters of labor law Regional Courts I of ordinary jurisdiction organize divisions consisting of regular and lay judges and have to apply special rules of procedure. Appeals against these courts are heard by Regional Courts II in mixed senates consisting of three regular judges and two lay judges.

IMPACT

The fundamental function of judicial authorities is to guarantee the peaceful coexistence of citizens based on commonly shared values. Despite recent disputes over populism and far-right trends in politics that led to temporary sanctions from other European Community members, there is no doubt that Austria is a country with a solid democracy based on the supremacy of law.

The planned extension of the European Community toward the east and southeast has emerged as a contentious political issue in Austria. The enormous advantages that a greater European market will present to Austrians are likely to outweigh the possible disadvantages. In any case, because of its geopolitical position in the center of Europe, Austria will be more affected by the move than most other European countries will. For the enlarged European community there will be a greater need for legal adaptations, possibly ending in a truly European legal system, especially in the fields of civil and commercial law.

Johann J. Hagen

See also Commercial Law; Constitutionalism; Criminal Law; Legal Positivism; Legal Professionals—Civil Law Traditions; Private Law; Public Law; Roman Law

References and further reading
Bundesministerium für Bildung, Wissenschaft und Kultur. 2000. *Universitäten, Hochschulen. Statistische Daten 1999.* Vienna. Available at http://www.bmwf.gv.at.
Bundesministerium für Justiz. 2001. *Leistungskennzahlen Personalstand im Justizressort.* Vienna. Available at http://www.bmj.gv.at/index.html.
Council of Europe. 1950. *Convention for the Protection of Human Rights and Fundamental Freedoms.* ETS No. 005. Strasbourg. Available at http://conventions.coe.int.
Dimmel, Nikolaus. 2000. *European Data Base on Judicial Systems: Working papers.* European Research Network on Judicial Systems (Istituto di Ricerca sui Sistemi Giudiziari Consiglio Nazionale delle Ricerche IRSIG-CNR). Bologna.
Evans, Robert John Weston. 1979. *The Making of the Habsburg Monarchy, 1550–1700: An Interpretation.* New York: Oxford University Press.
Hausmaninger, Herbert. 2000. *The Austrian Legal System.* 2d ed. Boston: Kluwer Law International.
Österreichischer Rechtsanwaltskammertag. 2001. *Leistungsbericht.* Vienna. Available at http://www.oerak.or.at/.
Rhyne, Charles S. ed. 1978. *Law and Judicial Systems of Nations.* Washington, DC: World Peace Through Law Center.
Walter, Robert, and Heinz Mayer. 2000. *Grundriß des österreichischen Bundesverfassungsrechts.* Vienna: Manz.

AZERBAIJAN

COUNTRY INFORMATION

Azerbaijan is located at the crossroads between Europe and Asia on the southwestern shore of the Caspian Sea. Sharing borders with Georgia, Russia, Iran, Armenia, and Turkey, Azerbaijan is the largest of the three Caucasian countries (Azerbaijan, Armenia, and Georgia) at 86,600 square kilometers. With nine climatic zones ranging from sea level to almost 15,000 feet in the Caucasus Mountains, the territory ranges from woods and rich agricultural areas to barren, desert-like conditions. Approximately 8 million people live in Azerbaijan, more than 40 percent residing in and around the capital city of Baku.

More than half the population lives in poverty, and 40 percent are under eighteen years of age. The adult population is well educated and has a high literacy rate. The population has become increasingly homogeneous but still includes a number of ethnic minorities. The majority of the population are ethnic Azeris, a Turkic people who emanate from central Asia. They are Shiite Muslim, although most are highly secularized. In addition, both the Russian Orthodox and the Jewish religions are practiced freely. Since independence evangelical Christians and fundamentalist Muslims have made some inroads. The official language is Azeri, which is closely related to Turkish. Written in Cyrillic during the Soviet era, the government has decreed that Azeri should now be written in a Latin alphabet. Many Azerbaijanis, particularly among the most educated, speak Russian and prefer it for educational and professional enterprises. Much of the younger generation is learning English. Azerbaijan is rich in oil and gas reserves and is a major producer of caviar from the Caspian Sea. In addition, it has rich agricultural land with significant export potential. Cotton, tobacco, fruit, and flowers are major crops. The economy has declined since independence as the country tries to adjust to the loss of the guaranteed markets among the republics of the former Soviet Union and seeks to move to a market economy. The legal system of Azerbaijan is in transition from a Soviet to a civil law system. The new constitution, adopted in 1995, and the statutes passed to implement it reflect an effort to adopt the legal standards of the Council of Europe.

HISTORY

Ancient Azerbaijan is alleged by some to have been the site of the biblical Garden of Eden and was certainly inhabited early in human history. Early Stone Age carvings are found outside Baku, and Zarathustra, founder of Zoroastrianism, spent time on the Apsheron Peninsula, where natural gas flames may have influenced the fire worship of that religion. Over the centuries, the land now known as Azerbaijan was the subject of numerous invasions, military conquests, and population migrations. Conquered by the Persians in the sixth century B.C.E., it became a center for trading in silk and oil. Azerbaijan has also been invaded or inhabited by Greeks, Romans, Albanian Christians, Arabs (who brought Islam), Turks, Mongols, Ottoman Turks, Persians, and Russians. Under the terms of the Treaty of Turkemenchai in 1828, Persia and Russia divided the land of Azerbaijan between them. The northern third of modern Iran, including the city of Tabriz, remains ethnically Azeri and is coveted by some Azerbaijani nationalists.

Under Russian rule, the Azerbaijan economy expanded as its oil reserves were exploited. It is said that at the turn of the twentieth century, Azerbaijan supplied

half the world's oil. Baku became a boom town and attracted investors and workers from many lands. The oil economy contributed to the wealth of the Nobel brothers and the Rothschild family and created numerous local millionaires. The magnificent buildings, opulent cultural life, and cosmopolitan city that emerged around 1900 can still be seen in Baku, though they now coexist with Soviet-built structures, great poverty, and a crumbling infrastructure.

An Azerbaijan Democratic Republic was declared in 1918, but it was short-lived. In 1920, as the Red Army marched into Azerbaijan, the local leaders signed over their government to the Soviets. Initially part of the Transcaucasian Soviet Federated Socialist Republic, Azerbaijan became a full republic of the Soviet Union in 1936. In drawing boundaries, the Soviets differed little from the tsars who preceded them, as they adopted policies that seemed designed to exacerbate Armenian-Azerbaijani ethnic tensions. The current conflict over the territory of Nagorno-Karabakh dates back at least to this time.

The Soviets ruled Azerbaijan for seventy years and strongly influenced every aspect of Azerbaijani life. Mosques and other religious institutions were closed, and

Azerbaijani nationalists were eliminated. Russification included the imposition of the Cyrillic alphabet and the adoption of Slavic endings to family names. Russian became the language of government, commerce, and the best educational institutions, and a Soviet legal system was adopted. Oil and other resources were taken to serve Russian interests. There was extensive repression, and the government was dominated by Russians for many years. The position of first secretary of the Azerbaijani Communist Party was filled in 1967 by Heydar Aliyev, a local leader of the Soviet secret police (KGB) who moved on to become a member of the Politburo in Moscow and would later become president of independent Azerbaijan.

With the collapse of the Soviet Union in 1991, Azerbaijan again became an independent state. In just a few years there were three governments, including that of the popularly elected president, Abulfaz Elchibey, who was forced out of office as Azerbaijan continued to suffer reverses in the war over Nagorno-Karabakh (a region of Azerbaijan) and the economy failed. Heydar Aliyev assumed power in 1993 and was reelected in 1998 in a controversial election. He is widely credited with returning stability and security to Azerbaijan. Aliyev and his closest associates, many from his home region of Nakhchivan, retain power and tight control over the government. With independence came a rise in nationalism and in policies that reflect fear of Russia and Iran, two powerful neighbors. The government's decision to turn toward the west has had important implications for the legal system in Azerbaijan. In seeking to join the Council of Europe, Azerbaijan has been required to meet standards of democracy and the rule of law that are foreign to its history and cultural traditions.

The unrest surrounding the Azerbaijan government in the early years of independence cannot begin to be understood without consideration of the Armenian-Azerbaijan conflict that erupted in war in 1988. The conflict over Nagorno-Karabakh has its roots in deep-seated historical enmity, probably as far back as the sixteenth century. It appears that the territory was dominated by Azeris and became heavily populated with Christian Armenians who were fleeing the Turks during the time of the tsars. By the 1980s, the majority of the population in this territory was of Armenian descent, and the Soviets continued to take advantage of ethnic conflict. Although the exact role of the Russians in the armed conflict is subject to much debate, several things are clear. As a result of the war from 1988 to the ceasefire in 1994, between 800,000 and 1 million Azerbaijanis have become refugees and internally displaced persons (IDPs). The ethnic Armenian population fled areas of Azerbaijan where they were in the minority, and the Karabakh Armenians now control 20 percent of the territory of Azerbaijan. The continuing drain on the Azerbaijan economy has been enormous, particularly at a time when it has not recovered from the economic impact of the collapse of the Soviet Union. Much of the humanitarian aid for the refugees and IDPs comes from international relief organizations. Beyond the direct economic and humanitarian effects of the war, efforts to move to a market economy, and the legal system it requires, have been severely hampered. In particular, aid from the United States is restricted by one provision (Section 907) of the Freedom Support Act (FSA), which was adopted in 1992 to provide assistance to former Soviet republics in their efforts at democratization. That section, incorporated at the behest of the Armenian lobby, imposes an embargo on Azerbaijan until it takes "demonstrable steps to cease all blockades and other offensive uses of force against Armenia and Nagorno-Karabakh." At the same time, the Security Council of the United Nations has adopted several resolutions condemning Armenian aggression and demanding withdrawal of Armenian armed forces from occupied territory. The economic and political impact of the conflict on the Azerbaijan Republic remains far-reaching and will continue to affect progress toward both a market economy and a democratic state.

The legacy left by the Soviet legal system was one of authoritarian politics over legal regulation. Bureaucratic arbitrariness was facilitated by ambiguous laws that often overlapped and were sometimes contradictory. The government was characterized by a strong executive and centralized authority with a reputation for corruption. The courts only served to enhance executive authority, and the prosecutor was perceived to be the most powerful person in the courtroom. After independence these practices began to be examined when, as part of its efforts to join western nations, Azerbaijan applied for membership in the Council of Europe, an organization that develops agreements to standardize social and legal practices across eastern and western Europe and seeks to promote pluralistic democracy, the rule of law, and the protection of human rights. In addition, if Azerbaijan is to attract the foreign investment and generate the entrepreneurial activity necessary to move to a market economy, it must provide a legal system that enforces contracts and protects private property. It is to those ends that significant efforts at legal and judicial reform are underway.

LEGAL CONCEPTS

The constitution of the Azerbaijan Republic envisions a law-based democratic secular state with three branches of government. It provides specific guarantees of a broad range of human and civil rights and freedoms and makes clear that the courts are to play a vital role in their enforcement. It acknowledges that for this to be effective, the courts must be independent: "Judges shall be autonomous; they shall be subordinate only to the Constitution and the Laws." The legal system is a civil law system. The legislative power rests with the National Assembly, whose deputies are elected to five-year terms. The president is also elected to a five-year term and is limited to two terms. Although the constitution envisions power sharing among the branches, the executive branch continues to dominate. The judges of the Constitutional Court, Supreme Court, and highest Economic Court are appointed by the National Assembly on the recommendation of the president. All other judges are appointed by the president, with the Judicial Council created in 1998 now screening candidates and making recommendations to the president. The constitution also affirms the autonomous status of the Nakhchivan Autonomous Republic, a noncontiguous territory of Azerbaijan that has its own constitution and laws (though they must not contradict those of the Azerbaijan Republic) and its own legislature, ministers, and courts.

The constitution of the Azerbaijan Republic is the basis for the transformation of Azerbaijan from a Soviet socialist republic controlled from Moscow to an independent state with a market economy. Such a transformation is complicated, and the adoption of a new constitution is only a first step. Realization of the vision set out in the constitution requires writing new laws and regulations across all aspects of the legal system. Until those are fully implemented, old statutes remain in force. In addition, unless all parts of the government follow the laws consistently and there is coordination among the acts and decrees of the president's office, the ministries, and other agencies, confusion can prevail. With a legal legacy that included vague laws that allowed for maximum discretion by officials, the transition to legal specificity is a work in progress.

A series of legislative acts have been passed in support of the constitutional framework. These include the Law on the Constitutional Court, the Law on Courts and Judges, the Law on the Election of the President, and the Law on the Election of the National Assembly. The Constitutional Court interprets the constitution and the laws of the Azerbaijan Republic. It began issuing decisions in 1999. Cases can be brought by the president, the national assembly, the cabinet of ministers, the general prosecutor's office, and the assembly of the Nakhchivan Autonomous Republic. Individuals can gain access to the Constitutional Court only if the claim is brought on their behalf by the Supreme Court.

The Law on Courts and Judges was adopted in 1997 and establishes a new court structure for Azerbaijan, including the establishment of a new court of appeals. It reaffirms judicial independence and reiterates numerous constitutionally protected guarantees, including the presumption of innocence. It defines the jurisdiction of each of the courts along with the duties and obligations of the judges.

In the same year, in the context of Azerbaijan's application for full membership in the Council of Europe, the Bureau of the Parliamentary Assembly of the council requested a report on the extent to which the legal order of Azerbaijan conformed with the council's fundamental principles. While noting considerable progress toward democracy, the report observed that most of the relevant legislation lacked the clarity necessary for the rule of law to prevail; frequent "cross-references to other undefined or future legislation" were identified. In addition, the report noted the government's lack of tolerance for opposition and the need for the courts to actually operate independently. A number of specific suggestions followed: improve the procedure for selection of judges, draft new codes of civil and criminal procedure, increase the budget of the Ministry of Justice to provide for improving the courts, and adopt new legislation on the role and operation of the prosecutor's office. All these suggestions have been pursued, but real progress has been slow.

In anticipation of the wealth that is expected to be generated when oil production reaches projected levels, it is understood that a broad array of public sector reform is required. To that end, a 1999 conference on implementing public sector reform was held in Baku. Attendees included Azerbaijani officials and representatives of the World Bank, the United Nations, the United States, and Germany. It was observed that the government's intention to reform the public sector had moved slowly and that more accountability was required. It was noted that the 1997 Law on Courts and Judges had not yet been implemented. Again it was noted that investors require the certainty of law, and that the process of selecting judges is critical to judicial independence and public perception thereof. Some of the recommendations focused on reforming and effectively diminishing the traditional power of the office of the prosecutor, which provides oversight of the judiciary and is involved in civil and administrative cases in addition to prosecuting criminal cases. Similarly, the Ministry of Justice retains broad powers over the judicial branch that, it was suggested, should be transferred to the judiciary.

Legal and judicial reform in Azerbaijan has been actively assisted by a number of international organizations. The World Bank has been particularly active in encouraging reform and in reviewing draft legislation. Deutsche Gesellschaft für Technische Zusammenarbeit (GTZ), a German aid organization, has assisted in drafting new civil codes and codes of civil procedure in a number of former Soviet republics, including Azerbaijan. It is now providing financial and technical support for the commentaries on these new laws. The German Constitutional Court has provided assistance to the new Constitutional Court of Azerbaijan. Ultimately, it is the responsibility of the Azerbaijanis themselves to finalize appropriate legislation and to see that it is implemented. A civil code, criminal code, code of civil procedure, code of criminal procedure, law on prosecutors, and law on advocates were newly adopted in 2000. While these await full realization, there remains a need for additional legislation to implement the constitution and achieve the law-based society that is desired.

It is a difficult and arduous process to implement so much significant change in a short period of time, and these structural changes must ultimately be accompanied by a good-faith commitment of public officials to the principles that these changes seek to establish. Although considerable progress has been made in conforming some of the written laws to the principles of the rule of law, there remains considerable public skepticism that the rule of law is being sufficiently implemented in Azerbaijan. The Soviet legacy included corruption, which has not disappeared. Surveys of those who do business internationally continue to rate Azerbaijan among the most corrupt countries. This has substantial implications for the potential for achieving the rule of law envisioned by the constitution.

CURRENT STRUCTURE

The constitution of the Azerbaijan Republic establishes a Constitutional Court, Supreme Court, and Economic Court and recognizes the existence of the courts in the Nakhchivan Autonomous Republic. The Law on Courts and Judges created a Court of Appeals, so that the judicial system is now essentially a three-tiered hierarchy.

The courts of first instance are divided according to the type of case they handle, with separate courts for criminal, military, economic, and civil and administrative cases. In addition, there is a trial court that specializes in grave crimes, and another in military heinous crimes, both of which were added to the original court structure. An economic court specializing in trials of disputes arising out of international agreements has also been added. The juror courts that appear on the diagram of court structure have not yet been implemented. Local trial courts are designated as either city or regional courts, depending on their geographical jurisdiction.

The appellate courts (the Court of Appeals, the Supreme Court of the Nakhchivan Autonomous Republic, and the Supreme Court) are divided into panels that specialize in certain types of cases. Each court has a Bench on Civil Cases and a Bench on Criminal Cases and Administrative Delinquencies. The Nakhchivan Supreme Court has an additional panel that serves as the court of first instance for grave crimes. The Court of Appeals and the Supreme Court also have specialized panels that hear appeals of military cases. The Supreme Court has a panel that hears appeals of economic disputes from the Economic Court of the Azerbaijan Republic.

Litigants are guaranteed the right to representation by an attorney, and criminal defendants are provided representation by the state if needed. Cases must be heard in the appropriate court as designated by law and sitting in public session, although there are exceptions. Legal proceedings are conducted in Azeri, the official language of the Azeraijan Republic, or in the language of the majority of the populace in a particular area. Litigants are entitled to interpreters for legal proceedings if their own language differs from the language of the court.

STAFFING

The bar is nominally independent but functionally quite monopolistic, at least as to representation in court, which is generally restricted to members of the Collegium of Advocates. While a limited number of independent attorneys have been granted licenses to represent clients in civil and economic cases, representation in criminal cases is assigned exclusively to members of the Collegium. The Collegium assigns cases and receives a percentage of the lawyers' fees. It also assigns lawyers to pro bono work for indigent litigants. There are lawyers who do not belong to the Collegium, but with few licensed exceptions their practices are outside the courts. These include local practitioners, some of whom practice in firms, and a number of foreign-based law firms that have followed the oil companies to Azerbaijan. There are a few independent bar associations, but like other associations in Azerbaijan they must register with the Ministry of Justice if they are to operate legally. As before national independence, the prosecutor's office remains extremely powerful. The prosecutor general is appointed by the president with the consent of the national assembly. The prosecutor's office is in charge of investigations and brings prosecutions, and it can appeal court decisions. Law is an undergraduate curriculum, and there is no bar examination required for admission to practice.

The courts are funded from the state budget and overseen administratively by the minister of justice. The number of judges has increased from 200 to more than 300, as new courts were created and some courts were expanded. The constitution establishes minimal qualifications for judges. They must be thirty years of age, citizens of the Azerbaijan Republic with a university degree in law, and must have five years of legal experience. The Law on Courts and Judges adds further requirements: judges are prohibited from holding another elected or appointed position and from affiliating with a political party or engaging in political activity. Remuneration beyond their judicial salary is limited to that derived from "scientific, teaching, and creative work." These requirements are designed to acknowledge the importance of an independent judiciary. In fact, an entire chapter of the Law on Courts and Judges is devoted to the independence of judges. Members of the Supreme Court, Economic Court, Court of Appeals, and Supreme Court of the Nakhchivan Autonomous Republic serve for ten-year terms; the term for other judges is five years. Judges' salaries are tied to the salary of the chairman of the National Assembly, with salaries decreasing the lower the level in the hierarchy of courts. At each level, the chairman of the court receives a higher salary than other members of the court, and salaries increase with judicial experience. In addition, if needed, subsidization of housing is provided for judges. All public sector salaries in Azerbaijan are extremely low, and the salaries of judges are no exception. These new increased salaries, which were written into the 1997 Law on Courts and Judges and implemented with the selection of new judges in 2000, are designed to enhance judicial independence and diminish corruption on the bench.

Judges of the highest courts are appointed by the National Assembly upon nomination by the president. Although the constitution gives the president the power to appoint all other judges, at the end of 1998 a judicial council, chaired by the minister of justice, was established that recommends candidates to the president. The council's other members are the chairmen of the appellate

Structure of Azerbaijani Courts

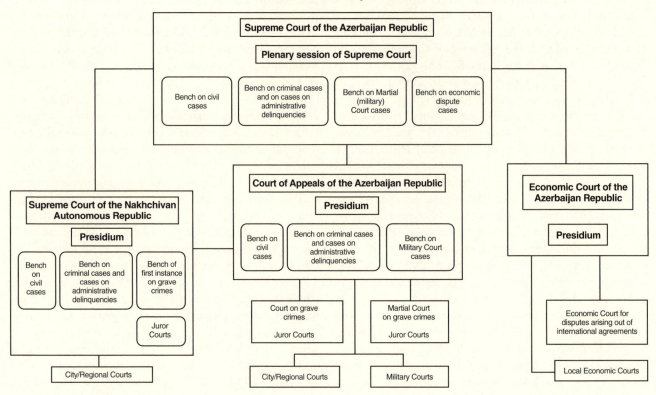

courts. Previously, judges were selected solely on the basis of an interview. In an effort to increase the professional competence of the judiciary, in 2000 all judicial candidates were required to pass a competitive written examination before reaching the interview stage. All sitting judges, except for the members of the Constitutional Court and the chairmen of the appellate courts, were also required to take the exam. The result was an infusion of new judges into the judicial system. Although the Law on Courts and Judges does provide the basis for discipline and removal of judges, procedural protections are lacking and there is no code of ethics to which judges must conform their behavior.

With so much new legislation and so many newly appointed judges, attention is turning to judicial training. An institute that had been providing courses for prosecutors, investigators, and notaries has been renamed the Minister of Justice Center of Training Courses, and its mission has been redirected to provide judicial training. A number of international organizations have also offered to provide training for judges. These include the Open Society Institute, funded by the financier George Soros, the American Bar Association Central and East European Legal Initiative (CEELI), funded by USAID, and GTZ, the German assistance organization. All these organizations have provided support for judicial reform and training throughout eastern Europe and the former Soviet Union. Thus far, Azerbaijan has been less active in taking advantage of this assistance than have neighboring countries.

IMPACT

Azerbaijan is in the midst of a significant restructuring of its government as it seeks to transform itself from a Soviet socialist republic to an independent state operating under the rule of law. After three generations of Soviet rule, and foreign rule before that, it will take some time before the transition is in effect. Implementation of the far-reaching institutional change that is anticipated in the constitution and many new statutes will require significant cultural change as well. Both the leadership and the public are inexperienced in operating in a system under the rule of law, and the transformation will not be easy. Since the rule of law limits the power of the rulers, a strong commitment by the country's leaders to operate within the letter and spirit of the law is requisite. Only then will the people come to respect the law and reap its benefits. To a great extent, the changes that have occurred have been driven by the desire to create a market economy so that the country can take full advantage of its oil riches. That will be possible only if investors are confident that the legal structure provides the predictability that is characteristic of the rule of law. The basic written documents are in place; the realization of the legal system that they anticipate is a work in progress that will take time and commitment to achieve.

Frances Kahn Zemans

See also Civil Law; Corruption in the Law; Marxist Jurisprudence; Soviet System

References and further reading
Azerbaijan International, http://www.azer.com.
Bernhardt, Rudolf, and Marek A. Nowicki. 1997. "Report on the Conformity of the Legal Order of Azerbaijan with Council of Europe Standards." Strasbourg: Council of Europe.
Curtis, Glenn E., ed. 1995. "Armenia, Azerbaijan and Georgia." In *Country Studies.* Washington, DC: Library of Congress.
Goltz, Thomas. 1998. *Azerbaijan Diary: A Rogue Reporter's Adventures in an Oil-rich, War-torn, Post-Soviet Republic.* Armonk, NY: M. E. Sharpe.
Van der Leeuw, Charles. 1999. *Azerbaijan: A Quest for Identity: A Short History.* New York: St. Martin's Press.
Virtual Azerbaijan (VAR) Major Links and Resources, http://scf.usc.edu/~baguirov/var/links.htm.
Yergin, Daniel. 1993. *The Prize: The Epic Quest for Oil, Money, and Power.* Video. Boston: Public Media Video.

B

BAHAMAS

COUNTRY INFORMATION

The Bahamas, a nation composed of 700 islands, is located in the Caribbean. It is a coral archipelago with over 2,000 cays, totaling 5,400 square miles. The whole archipelago extends for about 600 miles southeast from the Mantanilla shoal off the coast of Florida to 50 miles north of Haiti. The population of 285,000 is mainly Protestant and of African origin. A large number of expatriates, largely from North America, live in The Bahamas. The islands are more flat than mountainous, and the sea is a prominent feature of the landscape. Most of the smaller cays are uninhabited, but some are privately owned. The main tourist areas are Paradise Island and Cable Beach, on New Providence, and Freeport, on Grand Bahama, characterized by huge resorts. The other islands, known as the "Family Islands" or "Out Islands," are largely unspoiled and include Bimini, the Berry Islands, Abaco, Eleuthera, the Exumas, Andros, Cat Island, Long Island, San Salvador, Rum Cay, Inagua, Acklins, and Crooked Island. The capital is Nassau.

The Bahamas is a stable democracy with a distinct North American flavor. Its economy, mainly based on tourism and offshore financial services, is perhaps the most successful in the Caribbean and one of the best in the developing world. The gross domestic product (GDP) is currently $3.4 billion. Primary school education is free, and most residents also have secondary-school educations. Many Bahamians seeking postsecondary schooling enroll in U.S. colleges (unlike citizens in the rest of the Commonwealth Caribbean, where the country of choice for a university education is still England). The Bahamas is a member of the regional entity known as the Caribbean Community (CARICOM), established primarily to promote trade and economic cooperation. However, because it is farther from other Caribbean islands than most countries in the region and also because of its proximity to North America, The Bahamas is less closely linked with its neighbors—socially and otherwise. In some respects, this reality is reflected in the country's legal psyche. And perhaps its outward-looking character and its affinity for expatriates explain, at least in part, why The Bahamas is one of the first countries in the world to have developed as a tax haven and then as an offshore financial sector.

HISTORY

The Bahamas was rediscovered by Christopher Columbus in 1492, after which the indigenous population of Amerindians was quickly displaced. The island of Guanahani, called "San Salvador" by Columbus and renamed Watling Island in 1926, holds the distinction of being the first land in the New World on which Columbus disembarked. The Spanish seem not to have been very interested in The Bahamas; there is no evidence of permanent settlement.

The strong North American presence in The Bahamas began with its first inhabitants, believed to be the Siboneys—fishermen who migrated from Florida and the Yucatan. In 1781, after the American War of Independence, Americans who remained loyal to the British Crown settled in the islands with their slaves. As elsewhere in the Commonwealth Caribbean, slavery was abolished by the Emancipation Act of 1834. After that point, liberated Africans captured by the British from Spanish, Cuban, and U.S. ships were settled on the islands.

Like the rest of the Commonwealth Caribbean, The Bahamas was a British colony until the granting of independence in 1973. Because of their proximity to the United States, the islands had strategic importance for the British. In 1629, the country was granted to Sir Robert Heath by King Charles I, and it received its first constitution. In 1648, Capt. William Sayle and the Puritans of Bermuda settled the islands, forming a colony free of the religious dictates of the British Crown. The House of Assembly was established as early as 1728; thus, The Bahamas is one of the oldest representative governments in the region.

The traditions of English common law and equity were brought to The Bahamas during the early seventeenth century when the country was settled by the British. In 1779, the Declaratory Act officially assessed the reception of the common law in The Bahamas and clarified the scope of this reception. Although passed between imperial powers during the colonial era, The Ba-

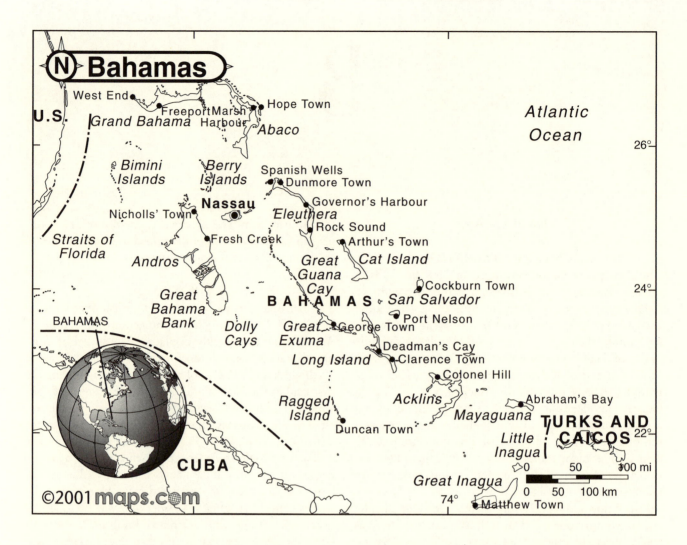

hamas did not, like some other Caribbean nations, retain strong links with the French, Spanish, or Dutch.

African slavery as a legal institution was a significant feature of the legal, political, and social framework of early Bahamian society. Slaves were viewed as chattel and inferior to whites. The racist biases in the legal system were manifested in several ways; for example, black slaves were not allowed to give evidence against whites or even to corroborate evidence more generally. These inherent prejudices were difficult to eradicate from the legal system. In one early case (in 1887), a circuit magistrate was dismissed for sending a white man to jail for slapping a black girl.

A significant feature of The Bahamas is its colorful history of piracy during the colonial period, beginning in the late seventeenth century and continuing into the early twentieth century. Piracy, like other aspects of life and the economy in The Bahamas, was greatly influenced by the country's proximity to the North American mainland and its place on the sea routes. Piracy fed off the needs, misfortunes, and wars of the neighboring United States, at one time even supplying the U.S. mainland with illegal slaves after emancipation.

The early court system was modeled closely on the British system. Prior to 1896, a plethora of courts existed, including the Courts of Chancery, Error, and Admiralty; the Ordinary Court; the General Court; the Inferior Court; the Court for Divorce and Matrimonial Causes; and the Court of Bankruptcy. These courts were often staffed by persons unqualified in the law. The establishment of the Supreme Court in 1897 marked the foundation of the modern court system in The Bahamas. The Supreme Court united several courts and also incorporated the law of equity. Of the courts just mentioned, the Inferior Court, dating from 1796, was the predecessor of today's Magistrates' Court, having jurisdiction over all summary matters, such as debts. The early court of record was the General Court; appeal matters went to the Court of Error.

At the advent of independence in 1973, The Bahamas embraced a written constitution that encompassed a bill of rights. The form of political and legal governance also changed from a colonial framework under a monarchy respecting parliamentary sovereignty to one based on constitutional supremacy.

LEGAL CONCEPTS

The English monarch is the head of state in The Bahamas, for it is a constitutional monarchy. A Bahamian national, in the office of the governor-general, represents the Crown and is appointed by the monarch. The governor-general is viewed as a symbol of statehood rather than a source of power; although he or she is given wide powers of appointment and dissolution, these powers are usually effected in consultation with the prime minister. The notion of consultation has usually meant that the governor-general cannot disagree with the recommendation of the prime minister, who occupies the real seat of power. However, recent developments in another Commonwealth Caribbean nation—Trinidad and Tobago, whose governor-general has attempted to act unilaterally—now place this assumption in question for The Bahamas and for all countries where such arrangements exist. Nevertheless, it is accepted that if the prime minister is absent or has effectively lost power in times of emergency or when national security is at risk, the governor-general can make certain political decisions. He or she can, for example, dissolve Parliament or invite peace forces into the country.

The Bahamian form of government is essentially based on the Westminster system. Accordingly, there are two houses of Parliament—the Lower House comprised of elected members and the Upper House (or Senate) consisting of senators appointed by the governor-general, who acts on the advice of the prime minister and the leader of the opposition. This arrangement means that individuals without party affiliation can be appointed to the Senate.

The power to make laws is given to Parliament. Executive or political power is assigned to the cabinet, which is made up of the prime minister and his or her ministers. Although ministers do not have to be elected members of Parliament, most are. Elections are held every five years and tabulated according to a geographic distribution of seats. There are two major political parties. A party supported by the black majority first came to power in 1967, replacing the "Bay Street Boys"—the merchant elite who had previously held the reigns of political and economic power in the country. This party, the Progressive Liberal Party (PLP), ruled The Bahamas until 1992. However, in the 1980s and early 1990s, the PLP was disgraced because several of its ministers and the prime minister himself were involved in financial scandals that rocked the nation. A number of public officials were also removed from office during that period. Further allegations involving drug offenses were never proved. As a result of these allegations and scandals, however, the PLP was conclusively defeated in the 1992 elections. Several well-publicized court cases and commissions of inquiry ensued, as well. The practical result was an imbalance in the seats in

Parliament, skewed in favor of the party in power. In 1997, the number of seats in the House of Assembly was reduced from forty-nine to forty because new electoral boundaries were established to give a more equitable distribution vis-à-vis the population.

As in the original Westminster model, a separation of powers exists in the Bahamian legal structure, and the judiciary, executive, and legislature branches are independent of each other. Although the executive branch does, in fact, take part in the law-making process, its powers in that regard are buttressed and safeguarded by the presence of the Upper House and the possibility of opposition by members of Parliament. The independence of the judiciary is a revered principle in The Bahamas, although, because of its small size, there are fears that political interference may, in practice, take place.

The constitution is the supreme law in The Bahamas, and all other laws must be measured against it and be declared null and void if they do not conform to the principles therein. The powers, fundamental principles, and parameters of governance are located in the constitution. Thus, the ground rules for the three arms of governance—the executive, the legislature, and the judiciary—are found in that document. The constitution also lays down the defining rules on citizenship, public finance, and state elections. In two significant deviations from the Westminster prototype, the written constitution also defines the terms and conditions of employment for the public service and the judiciary, and it addresses the substance of human rights. Further, fundamental features of the constitution are entrenched, meaning that they cannot be changed unless a majority vote is obtained in each house of Parliament.

The main sources of law in The Bahamas are the written constitution, judicial precedent, legislation, custom and convention, and international and regional law. The first source, due to the notion of constitutional supremacy, may be viewed as the most important. However, in terms of the quantity of principles imported into the legal system, precedent and legislation are more influential. Regional law sources derive mainly from the nation's membership in CARICOM and the precedents arising from other Commonwealth Caribbean countries and the Privy Council, which are viewed as highly persuasive.

Much of the law that was inherited from Britain remains intact. The Bahamas does not as yet have a strong indigenous jurisprudence except in certain aspects of commercial law, most notably in law and legal policies relating to the offshore financial sector. That sector, one of the most successful of its kind in the world, is an immensely important aspect of the country's legal system; for example, there are more than 400 offshore banks with assets over $150 billion. Thus, The Bahamas may be viewed as having something of a dual system in relation to its commercial legal framework, catering separately to domestic commercial matters and the needs of foreign offshore investors. In addition, The Bahamas has no direct system of taxation, a fact that benefits both residents and nonresidents alike.

What can be described as the offshore legal system encompasses a complex, innovative, and dynamic body of laws that define offshore trusts, banking, international business companies, mutual funds, shipping, insurance, and other commercial entities and structures. Since 1997, the government, now led by the Free National Movement (FNM), has enacted new legislation in a bid to improve the financial underpinnings of the legal system. These measures include laws to establish a stock exchange, improve regulation of the insurance industry and management of pension funds, and increase the role of The Bahamas Development Bank. The innovativeness and originality of the legal system are evident largely in the offshore sector.

Going hand in hand with these legislative measures are new and far-reaching mutual assistance statutes that attempt to address the problems related to commerce, such as money laundering and fraud. In addition, some believe The Bahamas is particularly susceptible to drug problems—a situation that may be explained, at least in part, by the difficulty of policing such a large group of islands with several hiding places at sea (the same circumstances that encouraged piracy in the past). The government, through its legislative programs, has demonstrated a commitment to fighting such problems.

There is little evidence of local custom being incorporated into the law. However, certain social practices (such as having children out of wedlock) have now been recognized by the legal system in affirmative ways (such as abolishing the negative effects of illegitimacy).

The Bahamas is not a heavily litigious society, although legal challenges, particularly those relating to the constitution, are on the increase. Litigation is expensive in a system that does not allow legal counsel to be paid from costs awarded, so many people find it difficult to afford litigation. Legal aid is scarce and devoted to more serious criminal matters, such as murder cases.

CURRENT STRUCTURE

At the top of the hierarchy of courts in The Bahamas is the Judicial Committee of the Privy Council, a court located in Britain and manned largely, but not exclusively, by British judges. This arrangement is a relic of the colonial past and is enshrined in the constitution. The Privy Council hears a select number of appeals, as its jurisdiction is confined under the constitution. Appeals may be as of right or by special leave. Constitutional motions enjoy an appeal as of right.

Next in the hierarchy is the Court of Appeal, a superior court with appellate jurisdiction. The superior court of original jurisdiction is the Supreme Court. Established under the constitution, its jurisdiction is defined by the Supreme Court Act of 1996, and it has unlimited jurisdiction in both criminal and civil cases. The Supreme Court hears constitutional motions in the first instance, and appeals go to the Court of Appeal. Under Section 28 of the constitution, appeals from the Supreme Court lie as of right to the Court of Appeal. An appeal from the Supreme Court to the Court of Appeal is made on a point of law. Indictable offenses go directly to the Supreme Court. The Court Martial may be considered an intermediate court. It hears cases involving alleged breaches of discipline by the defense forces.

Established under the Magistrates' Court Act, Chapter 42, the Magistrates' Courts, of inferior jurisdiction, make up the bulk of the court system in the country. In fact, magistrates hear and determine over 85 percent of all legal matters in the Bahamas. They have both criminal and civil jurisdiction, hearing summary offenses defined by monetary limits (currently U.S.$5,000) and the seriousness of the offense. Unlike other courts, the Magistrates' Court has circuit judges who travel around the Family Islands to hear matters—a feature related to the unique geography of The Bahamas. Apart from these traveling magistrates, however, magisterial jurisdiction is confined to geographically defined districts. The Coroner's and Juvenile Courts are actually Magistrates' Courts with specialized jurisdictions. The former, which sits with seven jurors, investigates the circumstances of suspicious deaths; the latter is confined to the exclusive determination of matters relating to children and young persons as established under the Children and Young Persons (Administration of Justice) Act. The chief magistrate has the power to establish a juvenile court in any magisterial district. Such a court consists of a magistrate as chairman and a panel of at least six members appointed by the chief justice and the prime minister.

In the Family Islands, the Commissioners' Court (also known as Local Government and Administrators) is made up of laypersons who hear minor matters. Justices of the peace also play an important role in civil matters. Appeals from the Magistrates' Courts go to the Supreme Court, except for certain more serious cases that, under Subsection 49-72 of the Magistrates' Act, may go directly to the Court of Appeal. A person convicted of a criminal offense in the Magistrates' Court has a right to appeal to the Supreme Court. Magistrates have appellate jurisdiction over Family Island Courts. The Family Island Courts are localized courts of summary jurisdiction that operate in the Family Islands. The Magistrates' Court may also hear traffic and parking violations or minor family matters, such as child maintenance cases. In The Bahamas, under Section 210 of the Criminal Procedure Code, certain offenses are treated as "hybrid" matters, meaning that an accused individual can choose whether to be tried in one of the Magistrates' Courts or in the Supreme Court.

A specialized function of note in the legal system is the Industrial Tribunal, a quasi-judicial body established in 1997 under the Industrial Relations and Fair Labor Standards Act. Dispute resolution is initiated in the Department of Labor and forwarded to the Industrial Tribunal if no settlement has been reached. The Bahamas has a highly regulated format for resolving industrial disputes and matters, including a limited form of compulsory arbitration. The Industrial Tribunal has original jurisdiction in such matters (with an appeal lying to the Court of Appeal), as well as other employment matters. The tribunal is characterized by a nonliteral approach to the law, relying heavily on the principles of good industrial practice.

The constitution establishes the general jurisdiction and powers of the superior courts but allows Parliament to set out more details in individual legislation, specifically, the Supreme Court and Court of Appeal Acts. The former, for example, unites the courts for admiralty, probate, and matrimonial matters; outlines practice and procedure, including the notion that law and equity will be concurrently administered; provides for judicial review of lower courts and procedures for court sittings; and establishes modes of trial and adjournments.

STAFFING

The key actors in the Bahamian legal system include the attorney general (who is a minister), the minister of legal affairs, and the director of public prosecutions (who holds a public office and is akin to a superior court judge). The Privy Council sits with an uneven number of judges, usually five. A peculiar aspect of this body is that its judges are often simultaneously judges in other courts, such as the House of Lords in Britain or superior courts in the Commonwealth. The Court of Appeal staff consists of six judges, including a chief justice who serves as the chairperson and the head of the judiciary; a president heads this court. The Supreme Court has the chief justice and up to eleven additional judges. Currently, the number of judges who sit on the court is twelve, having been increased from seven in 1994. Sixteen justices of the peace were appointed as lay magistrates to help alleviate the backlog in the Magistrates' Courts. The Industrial Tribunal consists of a panel of three. The number, qualifications, and power of judges in the superior courts are set out under the Supreme Court Act of 1996 and the Court of Appeal Act.

The governor-general appoints judges of the superior courts, registrars, magistrates, and justices of the peace on the recommendation of the Judicial and Legal Services Commission, established under the constitution. Under

Legal Structure of Bahama Courts

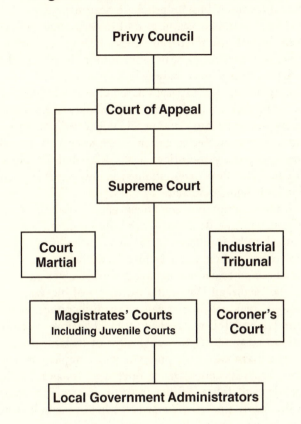

Articles 94 and 99, the appointment of the chief justice requires the recommendation of the prime minister after consultation with the leader of the opposition.

The offices of the superior court judges are defined by the constitution, and the appointment and removal of these individuals are subject to the deliberations of the Judicial and Legal Services Commission, in accordance with the constitution. They are independent and enjoy security of tenure. For example, the salaries and terms of employment cannot be altered to the judges' disadvantage. A justice of the Supreme Court may only be removed from office for infirmity of body or mind or misconduct. Removal must be done at the request of the governor-general to the Privy Council, which advises the governor-general on its decision. The matter is then referred to a tribunal. Thus, a distinct difference between the tenure of magistrates and the tenure of Supreme Court and Court of Appeal justices is that the former is not defined or protected by the constitution. Consequently, magistrates may be appointed or dismissed with ease.

Neither judges nor magistrates are trained to be specialist judicial officers in The Bahamas. However, attempts have been made recently to choose persons with a suitable sociological bent for juvenile matters, allowing them to specialize in that area. Similarly, persons in the Industrial Tribunals are appointed for their expertise in labor matters. A notable feature of these tribunals is that they also employ businesspeople to hear matters.

To be appointed as a magistrate, a person has to have been a member of the bar for at least five years. In accordance with Article 99 of the constitution, justices of the Court of Appeal must have held high judicial office before appointment. The age of retirement for Supreme Court justices is sixty-five, with a possibility of extension to sixty-seven; Court of Appeal judges retire at sixty-eight, with a possible extension to age seventy. Police officers carry out prosecutions in the Magistrates' Courts. Often, such officers are untrained in law, but this situation is changing gradually.

Jurors are important components in the administration of justice in The Bahamas. Indeed, the country is distinguished in the Caribbean by the fact that its constitution protects the right to a trial by jury. Nevertheless, the juries have been critized as ignorant and impartial by some.

The Faculty of Law at the University of the West Indies—a regional institution with full campuses in Trinidad and Tobago, Barbados, and Jamaica—recently introduced the first-year component of its law program in The Bahamas. This program will complement the other first-year courses being offered in Jamaica and in Trinidad and Tobago, although the main faculty remains in Barbados. Similarly, a new law school to supplement the two existing schools (in Trinidad and Tobago and in Jamaica) opened in 2000 in The Bahamas to offer practical and professional qualification in law.

IMPACT

Since the 1990s, the most pressing problem relating to the legal system in The Bahamas has been the need to defend the offshore financial legal infrastructure. This need has arisen in response to several challenges and pressures from international bodies, such as the UN's Financial Action Task Force (FATF), which seeks to eradicate money laundering, and the Organization for Economic Cooperation and Development (OECD). The latter organization has launched an attack on so-called "tax havens" and offshore financial sectors, particularly in developing countries, accusing them of engaging in unfair tax competition.

Due to the huge contribution that the offshore sector makes to the Bahamian economy, the FATF and OECD challenges have been met with considerable debate. Consequently, there has been much reorganization of the sector by the policy makers in The Bahamas. The most instructive response has been the dramatic reform of key laws and legal policies relating to the offshore sector, in an attempt to meet the guidelines laid down by the international organizations. Many of the new statutes have dealt with the relaxation of financial confidentiality rules in the interest of disclosure for criminal matters, in par-

ticular money laundering and fraud. (Financial confidentiality is a key ingredient in the offshore legal framework and is protected by statute in The Bahamas.) Mutual legal-assistance mechanisms, including procedures relating to the proceeds of crime, have also been revised in favor of disclosure. The Bahamas was recently given a clean bill of health by the FATF for its efforts to assist in the initiative against such international crime.

The response to the OECD's complaints about unfair tax competition has not been as positive. Many offshore countries, including The Bahamas, feel that the OECD's position is ill defined, without international justification, and simply unjustified. The threat to impose sanctions on countries that rely on offshore investment is seen as particularly unjust. The criticism is even more credible for The Bahamas, for it has no taxation regime for either residents or nonresidents. Consequently, the OECD's complaint—that offshore countries compete unfairly by offering tax incentives for *nonresidents*—is not applicable to The Bahamas. Furthermore, The Bahamas also relies on well-established international principles of noninterference and refusal of assistance for fiscal offenses in other countries. The fact that most offshore investment is considered not tax evasion but tax avoidance—which is traditionally viewed as legal in most countries—also supports the Bahamian view.

The severe delays in the administration of justice, in particular for serious crimes, are also cause for concern in The Bahamas. There is a major backlog at all levels of the court system, with over 18,000 delayed cases in the Magistrates' Courts alone. One practical consequence in relation to murder cases is that people are held on death row for lengthy periods of time. If The Bahamas were to follow the lead of a recent decision from Jamaica, which has found resonance throughout the Caribbean, capital punishment would be viewed as cruel and inhumane punishment; as such, it would be deemed unconstitutional and impermissible—despite the fact that, in The Bahamas, it is a constitutional penalty. This prospect has met with considerable opposition from the society at large, although a vocal Bahamian minority supports the abolition of capital punishment.

Other problems are related to deficiencies in the administration of justice, including the inadequacy of legal aid, both in quantity and quality; difficulties with the jury system; the inadequate preparation of records; the inability of accused individuals to post bail; and the fact that many counselors are unready to present their cases.

An interesting point to be noted about the Bahamian people's attitude toward the legal system relates to the rather different approach they have taken on the question of whether Commonwealth Caribbean countries should retain the British Privy Council as the final court of appeal. The Caribbean neighbors of The Bahamas have struggled to find a satisfactory answer to this question, engaging in hot debate; as a result, several governments have expressed a commitment to establishing a regional Caribbean court of justice. In contrast, the Bahamian government and people have stated from the outset that they are not interested in such a move. Ironically, The Bahamas is one of the few countries in the region that would have little difficulty contributing to the financing of the court (and cost has been one of the main obstacles to its establishment). To some, this reluctance in regard to a Caribbean court of justice might signal a hesitation about establishing independent legal structures and jurisprudence, yet The Bahamas's courage in defining its legal and social destiny in commercial areas challenges that view. Nevertheless, this issue does underscore the perception that The Bahamas is not in the habit of looking toward the rest of the Commonwealth Caribbean for guidance.

Rose-Marie B. Antoine

See also Antigua and Barbuda; Barbados; Jamaica; Labor Law; Legal Education; Magistrates—Common Law Systems; Privy Council; Trinidad and Tobago

References and further reading

Antoine, Rose-Marie B. 1999. *Commonwealth Caribbean Law and Legal Systems.* London: Cavendish Publications.
Cash, Phillip, Don Maples, and Allison Packer. 1978. *The Making of The Bahamas.* London: Longman Caribbean Publishing.
Crayton, Michael. 1992. *A History of The Bahamas.* Ontario: San Salvador Press.
Department of Archives, Bahamas Government. 1993. *Important Facts to Know about the Commonwealth of The Bahamas.* Nassau, The Bahamas: Government of The Bahamas.
Knowles, L. P. 1989. *The Bahamian Law of Real Property.* Nassau, The Bahamas: Nassau Guardian Printing.
Patchett, Keith W. 1973. "The Reception of Law in the West-Indies." *Jamaica Law Journal* 17.
Powles, L. D. 1996. *Land of the Pink Pearl.* Nassau, The Bahamas: Media Publishing.
Rolle, Ralph. 1999. *The Judicial System of The Bahamas.* The Bahamas: Bahamas Government Printing.

BAHRAIN

GENERAL INFORMATION

Bahrain is an archipelago of small islands in the Arabian Gulf with an area of approximately 706 square kilometers. The population of Bahrain is 675,000, which includes a sizable population of foreigners working and doing business. Islam is the religion practiced by the overwhelming majority in Bahrain. The country is currently going through an educational revolution, with more and more youngsters opting for higher education. There are two universities, the University of Bahrain and the Arabian Gulf University.

The literacy rate in Bahrain is around 90 percent. A high proportion of women take jobs, and it is not uncommon for women to occupy executive and professional positions. Legislation is being drafted to allow women equal rights with men, pursuant to the Bahrain National Charter and the Constitution. The diversified economy of Bahrain is robust, with a per capita gross domestic product (GDP) of about US$9,508. The major industries are petroleum refinery, aluminum, and ship repair. Tourism and offshore banking bring in considerable revenue. Inflation is minimal. There are no taxes and no exchange control. Bahrain is the regional hub for financial services. Many offshore banks, joint stock companies, and limited liability companies are registered in Bahrain, and shares are actively traded in the stock exchange. The Bahrain Monetary Agency closely supervises the financial activities of of the country, and the Bahrain Chamber of Commerce and Industry plays an active role in the national economy. The currency is the Bahraini dinar (BD), in 2001, one dinar was equal to approximately US$2.65. The country has an extensive system of well-laid and well-maintained roads. The official and court language of the country is Arabic. English and Hindi are also widely spoken and understood. Bahrain is a modern nation, yet it embraces traditional values and systems. Pursuant to the National Charter and Constitution, Bahrain is transforming itself into a constitutional kingdom by means of a series of democratic reforms. The country is an interesting mixture of old and new culture, both Arab and Western, with shooks and malls, narrow alleys and broad highways. The climate is mild and pleasant in December, January, and February and very hot and humid from May to September. The standard of living is high, and poverty is practically nonexistent. The country has reclaimed land from the sea and hopes to continue increasing its area by such reclamation in the future.

Bahrain is ruled by a hereditary monarch, called the amir. The executive branch of government consists of the amir, the prime minister, and the council of ministers appointed by the amir. The National Assembly enacts laws, and the Shura Council plays an advisory role. The country follows the civil law system and *sharia*, or Islamic law.

HISTORY

The original occupants of Bahrain and surrounding areas of the gulf were tribesmen and villagers, and justice was rendered by the tribal chiefs or the religious *khadi* (judge). Bahrain was repeatedly invaded by Persians, Portuguese, Wahabis, Omanis, and mainland tribes. In 1631, the Persians, with the assistance of British forces, attacked the Portuguese in the Gulf. The people of Bahrain sought the protection of Shah Abbas I of Persia, who sent an army to

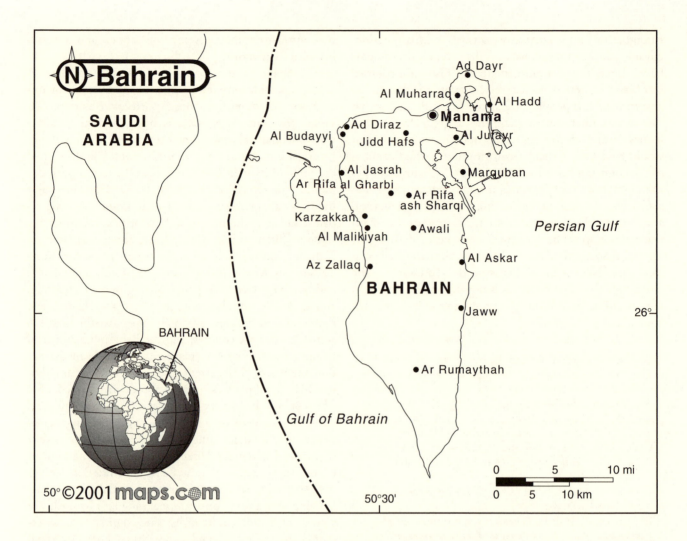

Bahrain, freed it from Portuguese occupation, and brought it under his control. The Persian domination of Bahrain under the Safavids and their successors continued until 1783, when they were ousted in by the Utub tribes under the leadership of the tribal chief Al-Khalifa, the ancestor of the present rulers of Bahrain.

During the Persian Safavid domination, most Bahrainis adopted the Shi'a sect of Islam. Judges played a vital role, wielding enormous authority and independence, which extended over executive poweras well. Jurists were expected to be learned in the Quran. Bahrain was considered an intellectual center, and Persian jurists sometimes sought the opinion of their Bahraini colleagues.

Beginning in the seventeenth century, the British had established factories in the gulf, in competition with the Dutch and the French, who were already in the region. Britain's purely commercial interest was replaced by new political and strategic considerations. It started signing treaties and agreements that confirmed its direct political presence in the gulf and in Bahrain. The British forced the Bahraini shaikhs to sign a treaty of nonaggression, in 1820, and a "Friendly Commission," in 1861, by which Britain reserved the right to settle maritime disputes. The

British political resident, established by the commission, was responsible for keeping security in the gulf. This agreement was the beginning of British concern about judicial matters in Bahrain and its intention to intervene in them. The ruler of Bahrain was deprived of his judicial competence over British subjects.

The rule of Al-Khalifa and British intervention coincided with the migration to Bahrain of peoples from Persia, India, Iraq, and other regions. There thus emerged in Bahrain a population of various origins, beliefs, customs, and even uniforms. Britain gave judicial protection to its subjects and dependents in Bahrain. By the early twentieth century, there were several judicial institutions in Bahrain, namely the Sharia Sunni Judicature, the Sharia Shi'a Judicature, the ruler, the amirs, Salifat al-Goas and Al-Majlis al-Urfi. The British government's Foreign Jurisdiction Act gave impetus to British interference in the administration of justice in Bahrain. Subsequently, at the insistence of the British, the ruler was forced to relinquish judicial jurisdiction over non-Bahrainis in favor of the British authorities. The Bahraini Order in Council, which became effective in 1919, established six courts: the Chief Court, the District Court, the Joint Court, the

Majlis al-Urfi, the Salifah Court, and the Khadi's Court, without the approval of Shaikh Isa, the ruler of Bahrain.

In 1922, there was widespread unrest among the Bahrainis, who presented a petition to Shaikh Isa. The shaikh's reply, called the Declaration of 1922, laid the basis for the Bahrain judiciary's independence from the Bahrain Order in Council and created the nucleus of the Shaikh's Court, later known as the Bahraini Law Court.

The following year, the British removed Shaikh Isa and appointed his son, Hamad, as ruler, ushering in a new era in Bahrain's administrative and judicial history. Britain appointed an adviser to the ruler, whose principal responsibility was the judicial system. In 1938, the adviser restructured the courts and thereby achieved complete stability of the judicial framework. In 1954, an intellectual movement called the National Movement Organization, led by its High Executive Committee, made demands for political and judicial fortification, insisting on the introduction of reforms to the Law Courts and establishing a just judicial system. In 1956, differences arose between the adviser and the High Executive Committee, followed by demonstrations and meetings fueled by the conflict in Egypt regarding sovereignty over the Suez Canal. The adviser tendered his resignation, but continued violence and rioting resulted in the arrest and imprisonment of key leaders. The year 1956 also witnessed the start of administrative reforms, which eventually led to constitutional reforms and the creation of the state of Bahrain on a modern constitutional basis.

Persia, and later Iran, persisted in claiming that Bahrain was part of its territory. In 1970, a United Nations envoy visited Bahrain on a fact-finding mission and concluded that it was the unanimous desire of the Bahrainis to form an independent Arab state. On August 15, 1971, the independence of Bahrain was declared and decrees were issued that overhauled the administrative and political structure of the country. The ruler of Bahrain, Khalifa bin Salman Al Khalifa, became the amir, the State Council was transformed into the Council of Ministers, and its chairman was made prime minister. On December 16, 1971, Bahrain's National Day, the amir expressed his determination to introduce a constitution ensuring the enforcement of the proper democratic principles. The Constituent Assembly then drafted the Constitution of the State of Bahrain, which was promulgated by the amir on May 26, 1973. New legislation, beginning with Legislative Decree No. 13 of 1971 and continuing under the provisions of the new constitution, have firmly established the judiciary of Bahrain on a sound and modern basis.

The process of democratization in Bahrain received a boost at the turn of the twenty-first century, when the amir set up a committee of experts to suggest a blueprint for Bahrain's political development. The committee adopted the National Charter, reaffirmed the hereditary monarchy and functional democracy, and recommended the introduction of more democratic reforms and an increase in political participation by citizens. The amir accepted the committee's recommendations, and in a referendum on the National Charter held in February 2001 an overwhelming majority of Bahraini citizens exercised their franchise and approved the charter.

LEGAL CONCEPTS

Article 1 of the constitution declares that Bahrain is an independent and sovereign Arab Islamic state. It provides for hereditary succession by the eldest son of the amir, although power is vested in the amir to appoint another son as successor. The system of government is democratic; sovereignty resides with the people, who are the source of all power. The citizens have the right to participate in the public affairs of the state and to vote. Islam is the religion of the state, and Islamic law, *sharia,* is the main source of legislation. Justice is the basis on which government functions. The state guarantees liberty, equality, security, tranquility, education, social solidarity, and equal opportunity to all citizens. The national economy is based on social justice founded on fair cooperation between the public and private sectors. There is freedom to form associations and to hold private and public meetings.

The system of government is based on the principle of separation of legislative, executive, and judicial powers, which function in cooperation with each other. Executive power is vested in the amir, the cabinet, and the ministers. Judicial decrees are passed in the name of the amir, in accordance with the provisions of the constitution.

The amir is the head of state. He exercises his powers through his ministers, who collectively report to him. Each minister is responsible for the affairs of his ministry. The amir, after traditional consultations, appoints first the prime minister and then other ministers upon the recommendation of the rime minister.

The activities of the executive branch are overseen by the Council of Ministers, supervised by the prime minister. The council formulates the general policy of the government, pursues its execution, and supervises the functioning of the government departments. The prime minister is responsible for the council's decisions and for coordination among the various ministries.

The National Assembly, also known as Parliament, consists of forty members, elected directly by universal suffrage and secret ballot, and the ministers. Members serve for a term of four years. They have freedom to express any views or opinions in Parliament or its committees. Pursuant to the National Charter, however, the constitution is to be amended to adopt a bicameral parliamentary system.

No law may be promulgated unless it has been passed by Parliament and ratified by the amir. The amir has the right to initiate laws, and the amir alone ratifies and promulgates laws. A bill passed by Parliament is sent to the amir for ratification. The amir may either ratify it or return it within thirty days for reconsideration. If Parliament reconfirms the returned bill by a majority vote, the amir shall ratify and promulgate the law. The amir may issue decrees in matters of urgency when Parliament is not in session or has been dissolved. Such decrees are referred to Parliament for confirmation. If they are not referred or not confirmed, they will cease to have the force of law retrospectively.

The constitution declares that the honor of the judiciary and the integrity and impartiality of judges are the bases of the rule of law and a guarantee of rights and liberties. Judges shall not be subject to any authority in the administration of justice. No interference whatsoever is allowed in rendering justice. The law guarantees the independence of the judiciary. Court hearings, barring exceptions, are held in public.

Those provisions of the constitution relating to the hereditary rule, the principles of liberty and equality, Islam as the religion of the state, Islamic sharia as a main source of legislation, and Arabic as the official language are unamendable under any circumstances. Also, the powers of the amir may not be proposed for amendment when a deputy amir is acting for him. Other provisions may be amended by two-thirds majority vote of Parliament and ratification by the amir.

The Supreme Judicial Council is the overall supervisor of the judiciary. It is empowered to give necessary directives for rendering accomplished justice.

The Court of Cassation consists of a president, a puisne judge, and three other judges. They are appointed, and may be removed, by an amiri decree. The Court of Cassation is an appellate court (not in sharia jurisdiction) and is assisted by a technical office headed by one of its judges and a sufficient number of judges with the rank of at least a high court judge.

A public prosecutor, appointed by the minister of interior, supervises all criminal prosecution. However, the transfer of this authority to the Ministry of Justice is under serious consideration.

The Judiciary Act declares that judges are independent and that there is no authority above them in carrying out their powers except the law. It also defines the gradual steps to be followed by a judge in rendering judgments. The first source is the provisions of the law, meaning the constitution and the various duly enacted laws. The second source is the principles and rules of Islamic sharia. With respect to criminal matters, however, many laws have been enacted and many regulations and proclamations issued by virtue of ministerial orders, so that in such cases the judge never refers to sharia. Likewise, many laws have been enacted that deal with civil matters,

and the civil courts do not refer to sharia except in cases relating to inheritance, as estates must be divided in accordance with Islamic law. Third, the courts take into account prevailing special customs. Fourth, the courts rely on general customs and usage that prevail in the country as a whole. Fifth, the courts rely on the rules of natural law, equity, and good conscience.

Labor law attempts to balance the rights and obligations of both the employer and the employee. The law mandates payment of an amount called end-of-service leaving indemnity to expatriate workers, and a pension scheme is available for Bahraini nationals. If an employee is removed from service, he can file a petition with the Ministry of Labor, which will call a meeting for conciliation. If conciliation is unsuccessful, the matter will be referred to the courts, which usually direct compensation to be paid for unjustified termination. Maternity leave is available for women employees, who also get rest periods during working hours up to two years after childbirth for breastfeeding the infant. Employment conditions for women and juveniles have been regulated. Compensation and leave are available to redress employment injuries and occupational diseases. There is no minimum wage in Bahrain, although one is under consideration.

Bahraini law recognizes the rights of corporations and individuals to include clauses whereby agreements and contracts may be subject to foreign law, foreign jurisdiction, and arbitration. Bahrain is a signatory to most international conventions and regional cooperation agreements. Recent amendments permit foreign companies to own real property in Bahrain. Laws to augment the rights of intellectual property owners, regulate e-commerce, and introduce a new civil law code are on the table.

CURRENT STRUCTURE

The judiciary consists of two branches: courts of general jurisdiction and sharia courts. Neither branch has competence to examine acts of sovereignty. Courts of general jurisdiction have jurisdiction over all civil and commercial matters, disputes relating to personal status of non-Muslims, and all criminal cases other than those excepted by special provisions, military crimes, and disputes relating to members of the ruling family. The sharia courts have jurisdiction over all disputes relating to personal status for Muslims irrespective of nationality, such as marriage, divorce, family relations, inheritance, custody, wills, and gifts.

Sharia law courts consist of the Junior Sharia Court, Senior Sharia Court, and High Sharia Court of Appeal. Each has two departments, one for the Shi'a sect and the other for the Sunni sect. The Junior Sharia Court is a court of first instance. The Senior Sharia Court is a court of first instance and hears appeals from Junion Sharia Court judgments. Appeals from judgments with respect to first instance cases rendered by the Senior Sharia Court are filed in the High Sharia Court of Appeal. There is no provision for filing an appeal in the Court of Cassation against the appellate judgments of the Sharia courts.

The general jurisdiction courts are the Junior Court, Senior Civil Court, High Civil Court of Appeal, and Court of Cassation. The Junior Court is competent to hear civil and commercial claims up to BD5,000 in the first instance, labor and certain other matters irrespective of the value of the suit, and minor criminal matters. It also acts as the executing court and as a summary proceedings court to hear and act on urgent matters.

The Senior Civil Court has original as well as appellate jurisdiction. It is competent to hear civil cases not falling within the competence of the Junior Court, all disputes concerning the personal status of non-Muslims, and every case that any law stipulates. It also hears appeals against the judgments rendered by the Junior Court and the Court of Execution. In criminal matters it has original jurisdiction to hear felony matters and appellate jurisdiction against the judgments rendered by the Junior Court with respect to misdemeanors and other offenses.

The High Civil Court of Appeal hears appeals from judgments rendered by the Senior Civil Court. It also hears appeals against arbitration awards. It has no jurisdiction to hear appeals against an appellate judgment of the Senior Civil Court. It has original jurisdiction to hear matters under the State Security Law.

Appeals may be filed by litigants before the Court of Cassation against final judgments rendered by the High Civil Court of Appeal or by the Senior Court in its appellate capacity if (1) the judgment is based on a breach of the law or an error in its application or the interpretation thereof, or (2) there is any invalidity in the judgment or if the invalidity of procedures has a bearing on the judgment. In criminal matters, the public prosecutor or a convicted litigant may appeal in criminal matters on the first two grounds enumerated above. A judgment inflicting capital punishment automatically comes before the Court of Cassation for review. The Court of Cassation reviews all cases on questions of law, not of fact.

The Court of Cassation has exclusive jurisdiction to resolve disputes arising from contradictory judgments rendered by two sharia courts, or by a sharia court and a civil court, and to refer it to the appropriate court for adjudication. It does not have jurisdiction, however, to sit in appeal against a single sharia court judgment.

There are two special courts. Military Court deals with offenses committed by members of the armed forces. The Ruling Family Council deals with matters among members of the ruling family.

Lawyers represent their clients in the courts. In both civil and criminal cases, when a litigant or an accused is indigent and unable to pay for a lawyer, the court ap-

Legal Structure of Bahraini Courts

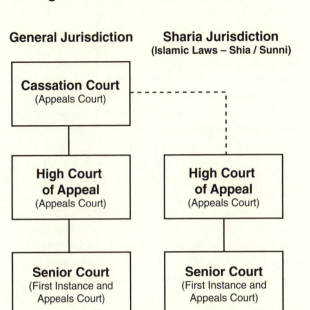

points one to render assistance. It is possible for a close relative to represent an accused or a litigant in court.

STAFFING

There are approximately 300 lawyers currently practicing law in Bahrain. In order to practice law before the courts, one must hold a law degree and must pass a sharia examination if sharia was not one of the subjects in the law curriculum. New lawyers are expected to clerk for two years under a lawyer with at least five years' experience.

To be appointed to a sharia court as a judge, one must have an advanced degree in sharia sciences. A bachelor's degree in law is a prerequisite for appointment as a judge to a civil court. For appointment to the Junior Court, a candidate must have practiced law before the Junior Court for at least two years; the prerequisite for appointment to the High Court is six years' legal practice or three years' experience as a Junior Court judge; appointment to the High Court of Appeal requires ten years' legal practice or three years' experience as a Senior Court judge; and fifteen years' legal practice or four years' experience as a judge on the High Court of Appeal is required for appointment to the Court of Cassation. Lawyers, experts, clerks, and translators are judges' assistants in the resolution of disputes.

In 2001, there were three judges on the Junior Court, nine judges on the High Court, nine judges on the

High Court of Appeals, and five judges on the Court of Cassation.

IMPACT OF LAW

Bahrainis are generally law-abiding citizens, and consequently there are few criminal cases. When civil cases are filed, essential details must be published in the Official Gazette, with the result that citizens are acutely aware of the dispute resolution mechanism. In the rare instances in criminal trials that a person is sentenced to death, newspapers pick up the story and closely follow the appeals. The amir has the power to reduce the sentence and has in fact done so in many cases. The amir has also granted pardons with respect to political crimes, thereby enabling banished citizens to return to Bahrain and those imprisoned to be released from jails. Awareness of human rights is evidenced in the fact that prisoners and convicts are not subjected to inhuman or unusual treatment.

Hassan Ali Radhi

See also Islamic Law

References and further reading
Al Rumaihi, M. G. 1975. "Bahrain: Study on Social and Political Changes." Ph.D. dissertation. University of Kuwait.
Belgrave, Charles. 1960. *Personal Column.* London: Hutchinson.
Kelly, J. B. 1964. *Eastern Arabian Frontiers.* London: Faber and Faber.
Palgrave, W. G. 1865. *Narrative of a Year's Journey through Central and Eastern Arabia.* London: Macmillan.
Radhi, Hassan Ali. 2001. "The Bahrain Judiciary System: A Historical and Analytical Study." Ph.D. dissertation. University of London.

BANGLADESH

GENERAL INFORMATION

Situated in south Asia (latitude 22 degrees 30 minutes north, longitude 90 degrees east), the People's Republic of Bangladesh borders on India from all sides except the south, where it opens to the Bay of Bengal and to the Indian Ocean. Once a province of Pakistan, Bangladesh (then East Pakistan) broke away to form an independent and sovereign state in 1971 after it had fought a war of liberation for nine months. A country of hot and humid summers and moderate winters, Bangladesh has an area of 144,000 square kilometers and a huge population of 130 million. The literacy rate is around 50 percent. The country possesses a developing economy predominantly based on agriculture, only recently making some inroads into the world market with the products of its flourishing garments industry.

Bangladesh prides itself on its rich cultural heritage, going back to the ancient Hindu and Buddhist period and stretching over many centuries. Located at the Ganges delta, Bangladesh has traditionally been a fertile land of rich biodiversity, abundant agricultural, and enchanting scenic beauty. Unfortunately, this natural richness is often disrupted by natural calamities, which is one of the reasons for the country's poverty.

A distinctive feature of the people of Bangladesh is their remarkable cultural and linguistic homogeneity. More than 99 percent of its people are Bengalees, speaking the Bengalee language as their mother tongue. The rest are sparsely populated in the northern and northeastern hilly regions of the country as various tribal and ethnic groups such as Chakma, Marma, Tonchonga, Lusai, Murong, Bom, and so forth. Although they have their native dialects and cultures, most of them speak Bengalee. Relative homogeneity is marked in the religious belief of the people. Some 85 percent of the people of Bangladesh are Muslims, 14 percent are Hindus, and the rest are Buddhists, Christians, and of other religious sects.

As is evident from the country's history, the legal system of Bangladesh has been greatly influenced by political developments and political systems prevailing at various times. In the ancient period (roughly 1000 B.C.E. to C.E. 1000) this region was ruled by Hindu and Buddhist rulers; the Muslims ruled the region between C.E. 1100 and 1757; the British rule spanned from 1757 to 1947. So far as the legal system is concerned, British influence proved to be the strongest and most far-reaching. Despite the fact that the legal system of Bangladesh still contains in itself traditions and customs that go back to the ancient times of the Hindus and Buddhists, and to the medieval period that belonged to the Muslims, and also despite the fact that the personal laws of the Hindus and the Muslims are still regulated by their respective religious norms, the legal system of Bangladesh is predominantly modeled on the common law system. Hence the legal system of Bangladesh can be characterized as belonging to common law as practiced in the U.K. and in its former colonies, including the United States. This stands in marked contrast to the civil law system of Europe.

HISTORY

In a sense, Bangladesh attained political independence twice—once in 1947 as a province of Pakistan when the British left the subcontinent, and again, as noted earlier, in 1971 when it severed links with Pakistan to form independent Bangladesh. Preceding historical and political developments greatly molded the legal development and legal system of Bangladesh.

Ancient Hindu and Buddhist Period

Present Bangladesh formed an integral part of ancient Indian civilization. For many centuries before and after the birth of Christ, this part of India was ruled by Hindu and

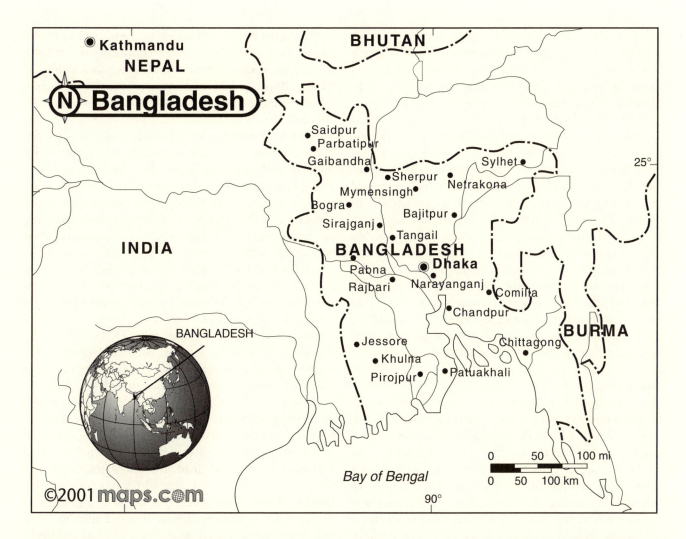

Buddhist rulers—rajas (kings) and maharajas (super kings). Often there was more than one kingdom. Kings had absolute power over their subjects. They were regarded as the fountainheads of justice. The king in the court heard appeals from other courts and also exercised original jurisdiction in very serious cases. There was also a chief court with the chief justice at the head. At district levels, justice was administered by the representatives of the king, while justice in the rural areas was administered by *panchayet,* a very effective form of local self-government. Local disputes were settled amicably by village eldermen. Traditionally their decisions received patronage from the top. Remnants of the panchayet system are still found in the territories that once composed ancient India. This also includes present Bangladesh. The laws prevalent in those times were predominantly religious in character, with occasional pronouncements of edicts and orders by the kings.

Muslim Period

Muslims invaded western India as early as the eighth century. But their presence was short-lived. They finally made a strong foothold in India in the thirteenth century. Present-day Bangladesh came under Muslim rule almost at the same time. A sultanate, a form of Muslim monarchy, was established, continuing until the advent of the Mughals in India in 1526. The Mughals established a huge empire and ruled India for about three hundred years. They were Muslims and established a wide network of justice systems based on Islamic law. The Mughal emperor was considered the fountainhead of justice. A gradation of courts with well-defined powers and jurisdictions existed all over the empire.

The emperor-in-court was the highest judicial authority as well as the highest executive and legislative authority. The Emperor's Court had original and appellate jurisdictions to hear both civil and criminal cases. There was also a capital city Delhi-based Chief Court of the Empire, presided over by the *Qazi-ul-Quzat* (chief justice). Besides exercising original and appellate jurisdictions in civil and criminal cases, he also supervised the workings of the provincial courts. There was a Chief Revenue Court in the capital to hear revenue appeal cases. Correspondingly, there were courts in the provinces, namely: (1) the Governor's Court, (2) the Chief Court of the province, and (3) the Chief Revenue Court. There were also civil and criminal courts of varying jurisdictions at district and subdivisional levels (*parganahs*). Judges at different levels were called *qazis*. Qazis in the course of time became a symbol of justice throughout the empire. In the rural areas, the Mughals retained the ancient system of panchayet for the settlement of petty local disputes.

The Mughals in India administered both civil and criminal justice, mostly applying Islamic law, with the important exception that personal laws of the Hindus were honored and applied. The system of justice administered by the Mughals continued to be effective until central Mughal control over the provinces started to loosen in the early eighteenth century. Almost simultaneously the British and other European overseas traders began to knock at the doors of the Mughal Empire. The British proved stronger than other outsiders. They infiltrated not only commercially but also militarily and politically. In the course of time, their influence increased so much that they could colonize all of India, taking in their hands the reins of full political power. Subsequently, they brought common law to the subcontinent.

British Period

The English started coming to India in the early seventeenth century as traders. Under a charter from Elizabeth I, in 1600 the East India Company got a monopoly of eastern trade. The charter also gave the company the power and authority to make, ordain, and constitute such laws, constitutions, orders, and ordinances as may be necessary for the good governance of the company and for better administration of their trade, and furthermore to impose "such pains, punishments and penalties, by imprisonment of body, or by fines and americants or by all or any of them" as might seem requisite and convenient for the observation of such laws, considerations, orders, and ordinances.

The English proved very successful traders, and by a series of concessions from successive Mughal emperors they established absolute trading influences in the areas around the towns of Calcutta (Kolkata), Bombay (Mumbai), and Madras (Chennai). In 1726 the British Crown granted letters patent creating Mayor's Courts in the presidency towns of Calcutta, Bombay, and Madras. They were not company's courts, but the courts of the King of England. In these courts both civil and criminal justice was required to be administered according to English law. That was how the king's courts were introduced in India, though the king of England had not yet established sovereignty over any Indian soil. Establishment of these courts raised the question of jurisdiction over Indians. Accordingly, by a new charter in 1753, the Mayor's Court was forbidden to try action between Indians who did not submit to its jurisdiction.

In 1757, after the English defeated the *nawab* (ruler) of the eastern provinces of India (Bangla, Bihar, and Urissa) in the Battle of Plassey, they assumed virtual control of those provinces of the Mughal Empire. In 1767 the English obtained *diwani* (revenue administration) of Bangla, Bihar, and Urissa from the Mughals and established revenue and administrative control as well as judicial authority there. The company used the existing institutional network for revenue collection as well as for the administration of civil and criminal justice, gradually reforming and adjusting it to their own needs. They strengthened their administrative and judicial control beyond the territorial jurisdiction of the presidency town of Calcutta into the *mufassil* (rural) areas, mainly operating on the existing system. Primarily, criminal courts applied Islamic law with occasional and necessary changes made under the influence and dictates of English law. In civil courts the personal laws of the Muslims and Hindus were administered with the aid and advice of *moulvis* (Muslim clerics) and *pundits* (Hindu clerics).

Under the Regulating Act of 1773, passed by the British Parliament, the Supreme Court of Judicature was established in Calcutta in 1774, which replaced the Mayor's Court. It had the jurisdiction of a common law court as well as the Court of Equity—that is, the Court of Chancery that once existed in the U.K. The Supreme Court of Judicature was a court of record and consisted of a chief justice and three judges. The court exercised both civil and criminal jurisdiction and in some cases also acted as a court of appeal. In civil matters an appeal lay from its decisions to the Privy Council in Britain. The Supreme Court applied English law, and advocates and attorneys were admitted to appear and plead before it. The Regulating Act, in fact, brought into existence two distinct systems of court in Bengal—one was the company's own court system with pre-existing *Sadar Diwani Adalat* and *Sadar Nizamat Adalat* at the top of the hierarchy, and the other the British Crown's Supreme Court of Judicature in Calcutta. Initially there was some confusion over the jurisdictions of these courts, which was resolved by the Act of Settlement in 1781. In the meantime there took place further gradation and diversification of civil and criminal courts in the mufassil areas outside the presidency of Calcutta.

In the middle of the nineteenth century, both the company's courts, predominantly modeled on the pre-existing Mughal court system, and the Crown's Court—that is, the Supreme Court of Judicature—were in existence in the provinces of Bangla, Bihar, and Urissa. As they applied different substantive and procedural laws, it became necessary that a single system of courts and law be introduced in the country. Thus it was under these circumstances that the British embarked on a program of massive law reforms. The process actually started with the creation of the All India Legislative Council in 1833 under the Charter Act of 1833. Law reform commissions were set up in 1833, 1853, 1861, and 1879. These commissions did wonderful work in codifying a large body of substantive as well as procedural laws.

Consolidation of civil procedural laws was attempted in the Code of Civil Procedure of 1859, but the code did not apply to the Supreme Court of Judicature at Fort William in Calcutta. Ultimately a complete Code of Civil Procedure was adopted in 1908, which with amendments is still operative in Bangladesh.

In 1861, the Indian High Courts Act was passed by the British Parliament for the creation of such courts in the presidency towns. Accordingly, under letters patent of 1865 issued pursuant to the above act, the High Court of Judicature was established in Calcutta. This court replaced the Supreme Court of Judicature as well as the Sadar Diwani Adalat and Sadar Nizamat Adalat, assuming at the same time the original and appellate powers and jurisdictions of all three courts. Subsequently, under the Civil Courts Act of 1887, a hierarchy of subordinate civil courts was established. Criminal courts were reorganized under the Criminal Procedure Code of 1898. The High Court exercised power of superintendence over all civil and criminal courts. These reforms, which systematized the courts in India in a unified hierarchy and which took a few decades in the latter half of the nineteenth century to take final shape, form the core of the system of courts in these territories even today.

The latter half of the nineteenth century also witnessed the codification and enactment of some very important substantive and procedural laws, which with necessary amendments are still operative in Bangladesh, India, and Pakistan (the former British India). Some of these laws are: Indian Penal Code, 1860; Police Act, 1861; Court Fees Act, 1870; Contract Act, 1872; Evidence Act, 1872; Majority Act, 1872; Specific Relief Act, 1877; Arms Act, 1878; Negotiable Instruments Act, 1881; Transfer of Property Act, 1882; Easement Act, 1882; Charitable and Religious Trust Act, 1882; Court of Admiralty Act, 1891; Prisons Act, 1894; General Clauses Act, 1879; Code of Criminal Procedure, 1898; Code of Civil Procedure, 1908; Limitation Act, 1908; Registration Act, 1908; and Companies Act, 1913.

The above-mentioned law reforms commissions played a historic role in drafting these laws. They have been mostly borrowed from written and unwritten common law of England and marvelously blended with local laws and conditions in India, to make a codified Indian version of common law. These laws are gems of legal mastery that, owing to their technical, procedural, and substantive perfection, have made a lasting impact on the legal system of the region of South Asia. It was never possible for the countries of the region to part with them, nor was it necessary to do so. Only the personal laws of the Muslims, Hindus, and Christians remained mostly untouched and uncodified, and continue to operate as before.

As it stands, the British in India, mainly in the latter half of the nineteenth century and the early twentieth century, brought about a revolutionary change in the legal and judicial system in India by the codification and enactment of substantive as well as procedural laws, and also by introducing a definite system of courts to administer those laws. The British had long left the Indian subcontinent, but their law has remained. It has predetermined the common law character of the legal system of the region. It explains why the legal systems of Bangladesh, India, Pakistan, and Sri Lanka bear marked similarities, despite the fact that they have made many amendments to suit the laws to particular situations in their respective countries.

LEGAL CONCEPTS

Adversarial System of Adjudication

As is characteristic of all common law countries, adjudicative process in Bangladesh is adversarial or accusatorial in nature, rather than inquisitorial as is the case in civil law countries in Europe. The litigation process is party-controlled and confrontational, and presupposes lesser initiative and the relative passivity of the judges.

Case Laws

Another fundamental characteristic of the common law system of justice is the predominance of the law of precedents or case law. In Bangladesh all subordinate courts are bound by the decisions of the Supreme Court in deciding similar cases and in the interpretation and application of laws. The High Court Division of the Supreme Court of Bangladesh is bound by its own decisions and the decisions of the Appellate Division. The Appellate Division, while in principle bound by its own previous decisions, can in extraordinary situations deviate from them. Judicial decisions, therefore, along with enacted laws and customs, are important sources of law in Bangladesh. This system of adjudication is called stare decisis, which means "to abide by authorities and cases already adjudicated upon." It may be mentioned that in the civil law countries of continental Europe, where litigation is inquisitorial in nature, entailing greater initiative on the part of the judges in the judicial process, courts are not bound by previous decisions. Hence the judicial decisions in those countries have only persuasive value as sources of law.

Absence of a jury in deciding civil as well as criminal cases is another important feature of the justice delivery system of Bangladesh. Jury trial exists in some common law countries, such as the United States. Trial by jury existed for a few years in Bangladesh after the British had left the subcontinent, but it no longer exists in the countries of the region.

Judicial Review

Judicial review is a fundamentally important characteristic of the legal system of Bangladesh. It provides enormous power to the higher judiciary to protect the fundamental rights of citizens, to prevent executive arbitrariness, and to compel governmental officials to act according to law and the principles of natural justice. Acts of the Parliament of Bangladesh (Jatiya Sangsad) also have to pass the judicial test if challenged on their constitutionality. The power of judicial review is so strong that the legislature is barred from amending the constitution—even by strictly following the relevant provisions of the constitution—if, according to the Supreme Court, the impugned amendment is repugnant to the basic structures of the constitution [*Anwar Hossain Chowdhury vs. Bangladesh,* 1989, BLD (Spl)1, Dhaka].

The power of judicial review, which has been recognized and declared by the U.S. Supreme Court in *Marbury vs. Madison* in 1803 and developed and nourished by subsequent practices of the highest court of the United States, has been enshrined in Art. 102 of the Constitution of Bangladesh. This provision of the constitution is a fundamental principle of the entire constitutional scheme of the country and has been rightly characterized as safeguard of liberty. The right of any citizen to resort to the shelter of Art. 102 has also been recognized as a fundamental right in the constitution (Art. 44). On the other hand, the High Court Division of the Supreme Court can also move *suo motu* to stop any violation of law or to meet the ends of justice. In a parliamentary democracy, Parliament has often been characterized as sovereign. In the U.K., sovereignty of the Parliament is a much talked about constitutional issue. In parliamentary democracy as it exists in Bangladesh, such sovereignty, if it exists at all, is greatly qualified and conditioned by the power of judicial review, which lies with the highest court of the country.

CURRENT STRUCTURE

After independence in 1971, Bangladesh opted for parliamentary democracy. Its Constitution of 1972 was an ideal model for democratic governance. But extraordinary political developments three and half years after independence, military takeovers, and military-guided democracy defaced the original constitution. Presently, Bangladesh has again been able to return to parliamentary democracy, restoring in many respects its original Constitution of 1972.

The constitution that Bangladesh adopted in 1972, along with thirteen amendments made so far, is the supreme law of the land. Art. 7 of the constitution declares:

1. All powers in the Republic belong to the people, and their exercise on behalf of the people shall be effected only under, and by the authority of, this Constitution.
2. This Constitution is, as the solemn expression of the will of the people, the supreme law of the Republic, and if any other law is inconsistent with this Constitution, that other law shall, to the extent of the inconsistency, be void.

There is a chapter in the constitution that provides for the fundamental rights of citizens (Arts. 26–44). These are basic human rights that reflect many of the provisions of the International Covenant on Civil and Political Rights, 1966. These rights are justiciable under Art. 102 of the constitution.

Bangladesh is a unitary sovereign republic. The constitution defines the relationship between the three organs of the state—legislature, judiciary, and executive—and provides for a reasonable balance of power between them. The Jatiya Sangsad (House of the Nation), the Parliament of Bangladesh, consists of three hundred members elected for five years on the basis of universal adult franchise. Thirty more women members are specially elected by the Parliament itself. The Parliament is responsible for making laws under the constitution.

The constitution provides for a Supreme Court as the highest court of justice, consisting of a High Court Division and an Appellate Division. The Supreme Court works as the highest court of appeal, interprets the constitution and the ordinary laws, exercises power of judicial review, and acts as the guardian of the constitution. The High Court Division of the Supreme Court exercises superintendence, administration, and control over the subordinate courts and tribunals (Art. 109). The independence of the Supreme Court is provided for by its constitutional position and power. The appointment of judges to the Supreme Court, the terms and conditions of their service and tenure, are all regulated by the constitution. Judges can be removed only by a special procedure provided for in the constitution. Yet their independence is only relative, for they are appointed by the executive. The president of the republic, who acts on the advice of the prime minister, appoints the judges of the Supreme Court, conventionally in consultation with the chief justice, and the chief justice himself is appointed by the president from among the most senior judges of the Appellate Division. Art. 116(A) of the constitution guarantees the independence of subordinate judiciary. This is also very relative. Judges of the subordinate judiciary and the magistrates performing judicial functions are appointed by the executive on the recommendation of the Public Service Commission. The executive also exercises control as regards their promotion, posting, leaves, and other administrative and disciplinary

Legal Structure of Bangladesh Courts

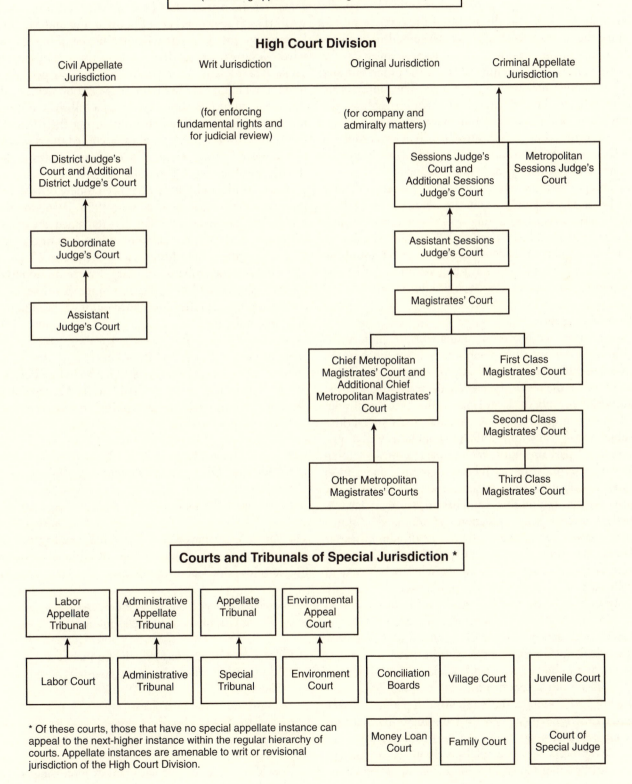

The Supreme Court

Appellate Division
(for hearing appeals from the High Court Division)

High Court Division

Civil Appellate Jurisdiction   Writ Jurisdiction   Original Jurisdiction   Criminal Appellate Jurisdiction

(for enforcing fundamental rights and for judicial review)

(for company and admiralty matters)

District Judge's Court and Additional District Judge's Court

Sessions Judge's Court and Additional Sessions Judge's Court

Metropolitan Sessions Judge's Court

Subordinate Judge's Court

Assistant Sessions Judge's Court

Assistant Judge's Court

Magistrates' Court

Chief Metropolitan Magistrates' Court and Additional Chief Metropolitan Magistrates' Court

First Class Magistrates' Court

Second Class Magistrates' Court

Other Metropolitan Magistrates' Courts

Third Class Magistrates' Court

Courts and Tribunals of Special Jurisdiction *

Labor Appellate Tribunal   Administrative Appellate Tribunal   Appellate Tribunal   Environmental Appeal Court

Labor Court   Administrative Tribunal   Special Tribunal   Environment Court   Conciliation Boards   Village Court   Juvenile Court

Money Loan Court   Family Court   Court of Special Judge

* Of these courts, those that have no special appellate instance can appeal to the next-higher instance within the regular hierarchy of courts. Appellate instances are amenable to writ or revisional jurisdiction of the High Court Division.

matters, although this control is exercisable in consultation with the Supreme Court. Another constraint on the independence of the lower judiciary is that the magistrates, who are primarily the members of the executive branch of the government, and are subject to its exclusive control, also exercise judicial power in criminal cases.

The president of the republic is the nominal head of the state, always acting on the advice of the prime minister, who exercises real executive power. The president appoints the leader of the majority party in the Parliament as the prime minister, and uponthe advice of the prime minister appoints other members of the cabinet. The ministers are responsible to the Parliament and resign if they loose the confidence of the majority of members in the Parliament. On the other hand, the executive branch of government is obliged to perform its duties strictly under law, observance of which is ensured by the Supreme Court.

The president, when circumstances so demand, may declare a state of emergency in the country on the advice of the prime minister, during which time certain fundamental rights can be suspended. When the Parliament is not in session, the president has the power to promulgate ordinances, and the same must be placed in the first session of the Parliament after such promulgation.

Laws of Bangladesh

All constitutional provisions, along with the judicial decisions of the Supreme Court on constitutional issues, make up the constitutional law of Bangladesh. Parliament enacts the necessary laws for the republic under the authority of and in accordance with the constitution. There are innumerable parliamentary acts on various subjects that deal with the affairs of public as well as private life. A parliamentary act empowers various executing authorities, ministries, local bodies, corporations, and so forth to adopt by-laws, if necessary, to implement the provisions of the mother act. These subordinate laws or by-laws are delegated legislation and are called administrative law. The volume of the norms of administrative law is constantly on the rise. Delegated legislation would be declared *ultra vires* by the higher judiciary if it were to contradict the provisions of the mother act.

Laws enacted during the British and Pakistani period were made effective in the territories of Bangladesh by the Laws Continuance Order of 1972, subject to the fact that they shall not contradict the constitutional provisions, ideals, and public policy of independent Bangladesh.

With certain amendments, the Code of Civil Procedure of 1908, adopted during the British period, remains to date the fundamental law in Bangladesh for civil procedure. Amendments were aimed at expediting the adjudicative process—for example, provision for second appeal to the High Court Division of the Supreme Court has been waived, although there is provision for revision

by the High Court Division in appropriate circumstances.

The British, while introducing major changes in the legal system of the Indian subcontinent, did not interfere with the personal laws of the natives—the Muslims and the Hindus. The personal laws under British rule continued to be based predominantly uponreligion and customs. Yet the British brought some vital and progressive reforms to the personal laws of both Hindus and Muslims by way of legislation. The religious custom of burning of wives along with their dead husbands was abolished in 1830. The remarriage of Hindu widows was permitted under the Hindu Widows Remarriage Act of 1856. Widows along with their sons were given a full share of their husband's property, although only during their lifetime (1937). In Muslim law, a wife was accorded the power to seek divorce in some extraordinary circumstances under the Muslim Marriage Dissolution Act of 1939.

While in India Hindu law has been totally revised and modernized by a series of acts in 1955–1956, for the Hindus in Bangladesh the law has remained the same. Muslim law has also remained unchanged, with the single exception that the Muslim Family Law Ordinance of 1961 limited the scope of arbitrary divorce pronounced by the husband, and of his having more than one wife, and also recognized the inheritance rights of the children of a deceased father.

Subordinate Civil Courts and Procedures

Subordinate courts in Bangladesh, both civil and criminal, owe their origins to the Civil Courts Act 1887 and the Code of Criminal Procedure, 1898, respectively.

Civil courts are as follows:

- District Judge's Court
- Additional District Judge's Court
- Subordinate Judge's Court
- Assistant Judge's Court

The above courts have definite pecuniary and territorial jurisdictions. District Judges and Additional District Judges enjoy appellate jurisdictions.

Subordinate Criminal Courts and Procedures

Subordinate Criminal courts are as follows:

- The Court of Sessions, which also includes Additional Sessions Court and Assistant Sessions Court
- Magistrate of the First Class
- Magistrate of the Second Class
- Magistrate of the Third Class

In view of the need to cope with rapidly increasing crime in the metropolitan areas, Metropolitan Magistrates'

Courts have been set up in four large cities. The chief metropolitan magistrate and other metropolitan magistrates have the power of the magistrate of the first class. Recently, Metropolitan Sessions Courts have been established in the capital city of Dhaka and in the second largest city of the country, Chittagong.

The above courts have their respective territorial jurisdictions and the power to impose penalties and sentences of varying degrees. Death sentence cases can be tried only by sessions judges, including metropolitan sessions judges. Magistrates' Courts try offenses of lesser magnitude.

Other Courts and Tribunals

Besides regular civil and criminal courts, there are many other courts and tribunals in Bangladesh that deal with specific issues, both civil and criminal. While these courts and tribunals generally follow the Code of Civil Procedure or the Code of Criminal Procedure, they enjoy certain procedural simplifications for expeditious disposal of suits. Their proceedings are more summary in nature.

There are labor courts in Bangladesh that deal only with labor and industrial disputes. Each labor court consists of a chairman who is either a High Court Division judge or a district judge and two members to be nominated by the government, one representing the employees and the other the employers, after due consultation with the respective sides. There is also a Labour Appellate Tribunal constituted by a judge of the High Court Division. There are also administrative tribunals and an Administrative Appeal Tribunal for the resolution of disputes arising out of the implementation of the terms and conditions of the services of government employees. There is a provision for Money Loan Courts (Aurtho Rin Adalat) in Bangladesh, for the recovery of bank loans from defaulters. These courts are presided over by subordinate judges.

By the Family Courts Ordinance of 1985, provision has been made for the creation of family courts for the resolution of disputes relating to dissolution of marriage, restitution of conjugal rights, dower, maintenance, guardianship, and custody of children. Under the ordinance, Assistant Judge's Court shall act as a family court within its local jurisdiction. Under the Children Act of 1974, a Juvenile Court has been established to try cases connected with juvenile delinquency. The main characteristic of this court is that its approach is corrective rather than punitive. The law prohibits the use of the words *conviction* and *sentence* in relation to offenders dealt with under the law. There is now only one Juvenile Court in the country. But there is provision for establishing more such courts.

Under the Village Court Ordinance of 1976, Village Courts have been set up throughout Bangladesh for adjudicating petty civil and criminal matters in rural areas.

A Village Court consists of the Union Council (parishad) chairman and four members equally nominated by both parties to the dispute. These courts do not follow statutory procedural laws, nor can any advocate appear and plead before them. Unanimous decision or decision by four is final. But decision by three members can be appealed to the Magistrates' Court of the area in criminal matters, and to Assistant Judge's Court in civil matters. Under a separate ordinance (1979), conciliation boards have been set up in the municipal areas with powers and jurisdictions similar to those of Village Courts.

STAFFING

The Public Service Commission, a constitutional agency, conducts periodical examinations among willing law graduates for recruiting members of the judicial service. Those who qualify in the examinations are recommended by the commission for appointment by the government as assistant judges. In the course of time and experience, they may be promoted to the position of district judge. Some of the senior district judges are also appointed as the judges of the High Court Division of the Supreme Court. The government also appoints some capable senior practicing lawyers as the judges of the High Court Division. While the judges of the subordinate courts retire at the age of fifty-seven, the judges of the Supreme Court retire at sixty-five. Magistrates who work as executives as well as judicial officers are also recruited by the Public Service Commission, but to become a magistrate one need not possess a law degree.

In 1996 the government set up a Judicial Administration and Training Institute (JATI) for the training of judges for the subordinate courts. But no compulsory and regular system of training for the newly appointed judges has yet been introduced. At best the newly appointed assistant judges undergo a few weeks of training in the Institute. Otherwise, newly appointed judges are required to watch a senior judicial officer at work for a few months before starting to decide cases. The magistrates undergo training in the Public Administration Training Centre (PATC) where, inter alia, they undergo intensive courses on criminal law and procedures.

There is a Bar Council for Bangladesh. It is a statutory body elected by the advocates throughout the country. It exercises regulatory and disciplinary powers over all the advocates in Bangladesh to ensure good professional conduct and ethics. The council conducts examinations among willing law graduates for enrollment in the bar and awards licenses to successful candidates to practice law as advocates. For qualifying to appear at the bar examinations, the law graduate is required to undergo a period of pupilage for at least six months under a practicing lawyer. After passing the bar examination, prospective advocates are required to undergo a newly introduced Bar

Vocational Course for forty-five days before they are finally awarded Bar Council certificates. For the first two years, the advocates can practice only in the subordinate courts. Then they become entitled to appear also at the High Court Division. Seven years' experience qualify them to appear as advocates in the Appellate Division.

There are several bar associations at different levels and in different territorial jurisdictions. These are the professional homes of the lawyers whose numbers now stand around twenty-five thousand. Each bar association is required to be registered with the Bar Council.

The Bangladesh Bar Council is also partially responsible for providing quality legal education in Bangladesh. This the council does by collaborating with the law faculties and law colleges of various universities and by endorsing the curriculum of those institutions. There are now about forty law colleges in the country under the administrative control of the National University that admit general graduates to their colleges, in which students are required to undergo a two-year course before they can sit for final examinations for obtaining the LL.B. degree. Four public universities offer four-year LL.B. (honors) and one-year LL.M. courses. These universities admit students after they have passed the Higher Secondary Certificate examination. Presently, judicial officers and brighter sections of the young advocates come mostly from LL.B. (honors) and LL.M. courses.

There is a Law Commission in Bangladesh established under the Law Commission Act of 1996. It is engaged in making recommendations for law reforms and, accordingly, makes drafts of necessary amendments to existing laws or of new laws and presents them before the government for enactment. The commission has recently done some very useful work in reforming intellectual property laws. On the commission's recommendation, the Parliament during 2000 passed bills amending laws relating to arbitration, copyright patent, design, trademark, and the Court of Admiralty, in order to make them more responsive to the needs of modern trade and commerce and dispute resolution.

There has been a longstanding demand by the people of Bangladesh for the creation of an independent Human Rights Commission in the country. A draft bill for the creation of such a commission is awaiting final approval of the government before it can be laid before the Parliament. Functions of the commission would be to monitor human rights situations in the country and to make effective recommendations for the prevention of human rights violations.

There is a provision for an ombudsman in Art. 77 of the constitution. An act was passed in 1980 for creating the Office of the Ombudsman, but it was never made effective. Recently, a fresh move has been taken with a few amendments to the existing act to make it effective. The final draft is also awaiting government approval. When made effective, this law is expected to become a landmark in overseeing bureaucratic practices and malpractices.

There are many nongovernment organizations (NGOs), lawyers groups, and private institutions in Bangladesh engaged in promoting and developing human rights; providing alternative dispute resolution through negotiation, mediation, and conciliation; and providing legal aid to the needy. The Parliament has passed the Legal Aid Act (2000) to provide for legal aid to the poor. The act describes legal aid as a right of the people who need it, and an institutional framework has been provided in the act to allocate and distribute government funds as legal aid to the people.

IMPACT

Bangladesh inherited a developed and effective legal and judicial system. Despite the economic and social turmoil that the country underwent after it obtained independence, its legal system has stood the test of time. It greatly has contributed to the process of nation building as a factor of stability.

The public and private life of the country is well regulated by the laws of the land. While people in general abide by the laws, there are also massive violations of law. In case of such violation, aggrieved private individuals, public or private establishments, and businesses have access to the system of justice, which is administered by a network of courts that exists to provide legal remedies. The people have a strong feeling that as a last resort they can always have recourse to the courts of justice, although various socioeconomic constraints often impede access to justice.

It is encouraging to note that with gradual improvement of socioeconomic conditions and increasing literacy among the people, their consciousness about their rights and the various laws of the land is increasing. This is very important for proper implementation of law by law-enforcing agencies, including the courts.

M. Shah Alam

See also Common Law; Islamic Law; Pakistan
References and further reading
Ahmed, Naimuddin. 1998. "The Problem of Independence of Judiciary in Bangladesh." *Bangladesh Journal of Law* 2, no. 2: 132–151.
Alam, M. Shah. 2001. "Alternative Dispute Resolution by Early Judicial Intervention: A Possible Way Out of Delay and Backlog in the Judiciary." *Law Vision,* no. 6: 5–7.
Chodesh, Hiram K., Stephen A. Mayo, A. M. Ahmadi, and Abhishek M. Singhvi. 1997–1998. "Indian Civil Justice System Reform: Limitation and Preservation of the Adversarial Process." *New York University Journal of International Law and Politics* 30, nos. 1 and 2: 1–77.
Chowdhury, Badrul Haider. 1983. *Evolution of Supreme Court of Bangladesh.* Kamini Kumar Dutta Memorial Law Lecture. Dhaka: Dhaka University.

Halim, Md. Abdul. 1998. *Constitution, Constitutional Law and Politics: Bangladesh Perspective*. Dhaka: Md. Yousuf Ali Khan.

Hoque, Azizul. 1980. *The Legal System of Bangladesh*. Dhaka: Bangladesh Institute of Law and International Affairs.

Hoque, Kazi Ebadul. 1998. *Bichar Babasthar Bibartan* (*Evolution of Administration of Justice*). Dhaka: Bangla Academy.

Index of Bangladesh Laws. 1991. Compiled by M. R. Hassan. Chittagong: Basic Law Series.

Jain, M. P. 1990. *Outlines of Indian Legal History*. 5th ed. Nagpur: Wadhwa and Company.

Kamal, Mustafa. 1994. *Bangladesh Constitution: Trends and Issues*. Kamini Kumar Dutta Memorial Law Lecture. Dhaka: Dhaka University.

Kulshreshtha, V. D. 1995. *Landmarks in Indian Legal and Constitutional History*. 7th ed. Lucknow: Eastern Book Company.

Patwari, A. B. M. Mafizul Islam. 1991. *Legal System of Bangladesh*. Dhaka: Humanist and Ethical Association of Bangladesh.

Rahman, Ghazi Shamsur. 1977. *Bangladesher Ain Babastha* (*The System of Law in Bangladesh*). Dhaka: Bangla Academy.

BARBADOS

COUNTRY INFORMATION

Barbados, the most eastern Caribbean island, measures 21 miles by 14 miles and features a flat limestone and coral topography. Surrounded by generally calm seas and white sand beaches, it has a tropical climate, with temperatures ranging between 75 and 90°F. Its mainly Protestant population of approximately 254,000 is largely of African origin, but approximately 15 percent of the people come from European ancestry (mainly British) or are a blend of these two races.

A democracy with a stable political environment, Barbados has a healthy economy, described by the United Nations as one of the best in the developing world. It boasts a high level of literacy and offers free primary schooling; many Barbadans also have secondary educations. The capital is Bridgetown, and the official language is English. Barbados belongs to a regional entity established primarily for trade entitled the Caribbean Community (CARICOM), and it is part of the Commonwealth.

HISTORY

Since Barbados was a British colony until independence was granted in 1966, its legal system closely follows that of the United Kingdom. The English common law and equity were received in Barbados on settlement by the British colonists in 1627. This reception was smooth, unlike the experience in other Commonwealth Caribbean islands, for Barbados was not the subject of fierce battles waged by imperial powers and did not change hands like conquered Caribbean territories did. This background perhaps accounts for its relatively uniform legal system and the strong English traditions that persist even today. The Spanish had taken the island from the indigenous peoples, the Amerindians, in 1492, but they did not maintain a presence and displace the native population.

From settlement onward, a slave system serviced a sugar- and tobacco-based plantation economy until the emancipation of the slaves in 1834. There followed a four-year apprenticeship period for newly freed slaves, during which they were still legally and financially tied to the plantation. Slaves were primarily drawn from Africa, but white indentured servants, today known as Red Legs, also served the plantations.

The preemancipation court system largely resembled the British model, including the Court of the Exchequer and the Court of Common Pleas. However, one significant deviation was the establishment of unique courts to accommodate the slave society, among them the special courts set up to try slaves. The legal system was not equitable, dictated as it was by the slave economy and the needs of the plantation. Long after emancipation, the legal system, particularly the courts, failed to fulfill its mandate as an independent dispenser of justice: Early courts such as the courts of the stipendiary magistrates were compromised by their dependence on the planter elite, either due to lack of financial means or the requirements of staffing these bodies.

The House of Assembly was established in 1639, making Barbados the third parliamentary democracy in the world. Until the mid-1970s, the principal industry was still sugar production. Today, the leading industries are tourism and international financial services.

One important development after independence was achieved in 1966 was the advent of the written constitution, influenced by the UN Declaration on Human Rights and the European Human Rights Charter. Self-rule under the independence constitution meant a transfer of power into the hands of the black majority. Since 1974, sporadic changes have been made to the constitution. The most significant modifications involve matters of citizenship, senate and judicial appointments, the establishment of the Teaching Service Commission, and increases in the governor-general's powers of appointment.

Between 1958 and 1962, Barbados experimented with a political union known as the Federation that involved other Commonwealth Caribbean countries. That effort subsequently failed, but calls continue for a return to some form of political union in the region in order to enhance the chances of survival of small Caribbean states in today's globalized world.

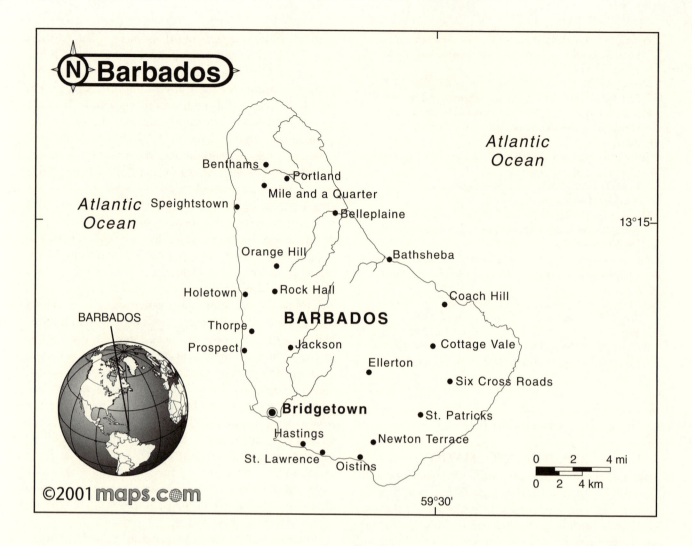

N Barbados

Atlantic
Ocean

Atlantic
Ocean

Benthams
Portland
Mile and a Quarter
Speightstown
Belleplaine
Orange Hill
Bathsheba
Holetown
Rock Hall
Coach Hill
BARBADOS
Thorpe
Cottage Vale
Jackson
Prospect
Ellerton
Six Cross Roads
BARBADOS
Bridgetown
St. Patricks
Hastings
Newton Terrace
St. Lawrence
Oistins

13°15'

0   2   4 mi
0   2   4 km

©2001 maps.com

59°30'

LEGAL CONCEPTS

The Barbados Constitution deviates from the traditional Westminster model of parliamentary sovereignty and conforms to the concept of constitutional supremacy. It is, therefore, the supreme law against which all others must be measured under a process of judicial review; laws that violate the constitution may be declared ultra vires. The constitution lays down the framework for government and defines the relationship between the state and its citizens, in particular providing for fundamental human rights and their protection. The constitution is also the authoritative base for matters involving treaty-making powers, the judiciary, public finance, state elections, public service, and citizenship. Certain provisions are entrenched, such as those on the judicature, and cannot be changed unless at least a two-thirds majority vote is obtained in each parliamentary house.

The sources of law in Barbados are judicial precedent, custom, legislation, the constitution, and international and regional law. The doctrine of precedence is prominent, but increasingly, legislation occupies much of the legal landscape. Custom is not an important legal source

except in labor law matters, for it is difficult to establish under the common law and it can only become law if it is judicially recognized. Critics argue that certain common law rules regarding custom are inappropriate to Barbados—for example, the requirement that a custom must have long usage before being enshrined in law is unrealistic in such a relatively young country. Some have also called for a greater utilization of the indigenous customs and social norms important to Barbadian society in the law. This call has been answered mainly by legislation: For instance, the legal concept of illegitimacy has been abolished, since Barbados has a high percentage of unwed mothers and is viewed as a matrifocal society.

Elections are held every five years, and the winning party must obtain a majority of seats, which are geographically distributed. The two major political parties, the Democratic Labor Party and the Barbados Labor Party (which was in power in 2001), have tended to share political power equally, as the reins of government have changed hands approximately every two terms.

Barbados is a constitutional monarchy, with the king or queen of England as the head of state, represented by a Barbadian national holding the post of governor-general. It is a bicameral model of government. Based on the British political system, the legislature is made up of two chambers known as the Houses of Parliament. This body is composed of the monarch (represented by the governor-general), an appointed Senate (or Upper House), and the House of Assembly (or Lower House), consisting of elected representatives. Executive power is vested in the cabinet, which comprises the prime minister and the other ministers of government. Thus, Barbados conforms to the separation-of-powers doctrine—that is, the executive, legislature, and judiciary are independent of each other.

The members of the Senate are appointed by the governor–general, who acts on the advice of the leader of the opposition and the prime minister. In practice, Senate members represent both political parties and may also be persons independent of either of the parties. The prime minister usually, but not necessarily, appoints ministers from among the members of Parliament who have been elected to office.

Under Section 28 of the Barbados Constitution, the governor-general is appointed by the British monarch, and he or she has authority to dissolve Parliament in certain circumstances. The attorney general, a minister, is in charge of the Ministry of Legal Affairs and, traditionally, the police and security forces. The director of public prosecutions, a public officer appointed under Section 101 of the constitution on recommendation by the Judicial and Legal Services Commission, is responsible for executing the prosecution of litigation on behalf of the state and must be qualified for appointment as a judge.

Final appeals for most of the Commonwealth Caribbean countries are still heard by a representative body of the previous colonizing power—the Judicial Committee of the Privy Council, which sits in London. Due to this fact, Barbadian and, indeed, West Indian (Caribbean) jurisprudence in general may sometimes be viewed as being out of sync with the countries' social, economic, and political realities. Perhaps the best example of this observation is the 1993 Privy Council decision in *Pratt and Morgan v. A G of Jamaica,* which had ramifications all over the Caribbean. Since that decision, there has been turmoil in relation to the state's ability to effect capital punishment for prisoners on death row, despite the fact that the death penalty is a legal punishment in Barbados and determined by case law to be permissible under the constitution. In *Pratt and Morgan,* the court held that prisoners who had been on death row for more that five years (the term has since been shortened) had suffered cruel and inhumane punishment—a constitutional violation—and should be freed. Although this case was from Jamaica, the fact that the Privy Council also hears such matters for Barbados means that the decision is viewed as binding on Barbados. Because of the difficulty of completing appeals in such cases within the allotted time period, the death penalty, in effect, is now in abeyance.

The majority of Barbadians are in favor of the death penalty, so the Privy Council's ruling has not been a popular decision. There is a strong feeling in many quarters that Britain, which itself has abolished the death penalty, is attempting, through the Privy Council, to force its legal policies onto independent Caribbean nations by "unconstitutional" means. The fact that the legal principle upheld in the decision was promulgated by international jurisprudence and, more particularly, by the UN Human Rights Committee even before *Pratt and Morgan* is not discussed or even well known in Barbados. Consequently, the decision has been seen as an interference with Barbados's sovereignty.

Barbados is a signatory to major human rights conventions, such as the UN Declaration on Human Rights, the Convention on the Elimination of All Forms of Discrimination against Women, and several International Labor Organization (ILO) conventions (including those on freedom of association and othe basic labor rights). As a member of the Organization of American States, Barbados is also a party to that body's human rights instruments.

The labor rights regime in Barbados is notable. The voluntary model of the common law is emphasized, albeit with some statutory intervention (for example, on maternity benefits, occupational health and safety, and social security). Indeed, Barbados is one of the few countries in the region with unemployment benefits. Significantly, an efficient, tripartite code of practice exists that encourages a relatively stable industrial relations climate. Efforts are under way to strengthen labor laws, including unfair-dismissal legislation. One other concern relates to the recent demonstration that some of the customary practices may be inadequate in the changing labor environment. Certain foreign firms have refused to recognize unions, for instance, although voluntary recognition was the long-standing tradition. It was the custom that once a union could demonstrate that it had a majority of workers in a bargaining unit, it would be recognized.

Constitutional reform is now being discussed in Barbados. One hotly debated topic is a proposal to change the form of government from the present monarchy to a republic. Another significant subject is the judiciary. Changes were made in regard to the appointment of judges in 1974, removing the role of the independent Judicial and Legal Services Commission and placing more autonomy in the hands of the executive; as a result, some fear, the independence of the judiciary may be undermined and opened up to partisanship and governmental interference. The Constitution Commission has recommended a reversal of the 1974 changes.

Similarly, there are concerns about the fact that magistrates are not part of the judiciary but mere civil servants and are consequently not accorded the same constitutional protection as judges—protection that is necessary to preserve judicial independence. Additionally, although the Magistrates' Act of 1996 imposes monetary limits on jurisdiction, they may have a discretion under other legislation, such as the Drugs Abuse (Prevention and Control) Act, CAP 131, whereby such limits can be exceeded. This is seen by some as an encroachment on the jurisdiction of the High Court. Other potential constitutional changes include a strengthening of certain rights in the constitution (for example, the inclusion of specific protections for gender rights).

Although Barbadians are generally satisfied with the workings of the legal system, problems do exist, such as the paucity of indigenous law, the sparseness and poor quality of legal aid entitlements, and the high cost of litigation, which restricts access to the courts. One particularly severe problem is the case backlog, exacerbated by the institution of quarterly assizes (which further slow the administration of justice). This problem, in fact, fueled the death row crisis mentioned earlier. There are also difficulties with the conditions in the prisons and recent lapses in security that resulted in dangerous criminals escaping.

Since 1998, an important debate on the need to establish a regional court of appeal, rather than directing appeals to the Privy Council in London, has raged in Barbados and elsewhere in the area. This prospect is on the way to becoming a reality with the CARICOM proposal for the Caribbean Court of Justice, although many West Indians, comforted by a distant, apparently impartial British justice, are resistant to the change. Another concern is the high burden that funding a regional court will place on the already financially challenged Caribbean states.

Barbados is one of several countries in the Caribbean offering international financial or offshore services. This financial legal regime is important to the economy. Specific, unique legislation and institutions requiring changes in domestic trust and company law, which cater primarily to nonresident investors, have been created for such investments and banking purposes. An important and somewhat distinctive element of the Barbadian international financial sector is the system of double-taxation treaties, which are designed to encourage investors from beneficiary countries to take advantage of tax incentives in Barbados.

Of concern are recent attempts by the Organization for Economic Cooperation and Development (OECD) to blacklist Caribbean financial centers and denounce them as engaging in unfair tax competition. Barbados views these attempts as a violation of sovereignty. In addition, Barbados's international financial system, like that of other Caribbean countries, follows examples set in Switzerland and other parts of the world, which have not attracted such hostility. Barbados considers itself a responsible offshore regime, and, indeed, it has modern regulatory mechanisms and legislation on money laundering (enacted in 1998) in accordance with international standards. Furthermore, the sector has not suffered any financial scandals.

CURRENT JUDICIAL AND QUASI-JUDICIAL STRUCTURE

The Judicial Committee of the Privy Council, which sits in England, is the final court of appeal. Next in the hierarchy is the Supreme Court of Judicature, comprising the High Court and the Court of Appeal, with superior jurisdiction. Below them come the Magistrates' Courts, of inferior jurisdiction in both civil and criminal law.

Magistrates' Courts perform a dual function—investigative, for inquiry into indictable offenses for trial at the High Court; coroners' inquests; and trial, of summary, or less serious, offenses. Their jurisdiction, including the sentences they can hand down, is limited by financial factors. Magistrates are also responsible for juvenile matters. Magisterial jurisdiction, which is divided into six geographic districts hosting approximately twelve courts, obtains its authority from the Magistrates' Act of 1996.

The Supreme Court derives its authority directly from Section 80 of the Barbados Constitution, supplemented by the Supreme Court of Judicature Act, CAP 117A. This court has unlimited jurisdiction in both civil and criminal matters. The High Court is primarily a court of original, or first-instance, jurisdiction, addressing constitutional matters; indictable offenses such as murder and treason; serious civil matters such as libel and slander; property matters above a certain monetary limit; and marriage and divorce issues. Significantly, it can judicially review the decisions of administrative tribunals and bodies. There are three divisions of the High Court: the Civil Division, the Family Division, and the Criminal Division. This court hears civil matters thoughout the year and criminal matters during one of the four criminal assizes (in January, April, July, and October).

The Court of Appeal has a solely appellate function, hearing appeals from the Magistrates' Courts and from the High Court. It must sit with an uneven number of judges (a minimum of three). Appeals are as of right (meaning that one is entitled to an appeal automatically)only in exceptional cases, such as an alleged violation of constitutional human rights. Other cases require leave of the court.

The Privy Council is reserved for selected appellate matters as outlined under the constitution. Appeals are as of right or with leave or special leave. For example, under Section 87 of the constitution, appeals are of right from the Court of Appeal in matters alleging a violation of constitutional rights. The conditions for leave are also spelled out, such as the requirement that the matter be one of considerable public importance.

The Barbadian Court Martial has superior jurisdiction for matters relating to the defense forces. Specialized courts include the Juvenile and Traffic Courts, which are actually ordinary Magistrates' Courts carrying out specialist functions. Juvenile matters are informed by special legislation that seeks to protect and rehabilitate youngsters and that conforms in the main to the principles laid down in the UN Convention on the Rights of the Child. Such matters are tried in a less formal manner than adult offenses. A number of specialized administrative tribunals and boards also exist, including the Ministry of Labor Department, which functions as a labor tribunal.

SPECIALIZED JUDICIAL BODIES

Commissions of inquiry to investigate particularly sensitive political matters are becoming increasingly popular in Barbados. These are merely investigatory bodies, and their work is carried out in public. Two recent commissions investigated alleged corruption relating to a national hospital and the third-time escape from prison of a notorious convict.

Barbados has an ombudsman's office established under the Ombudsman Act of 1980. The office is independent and can inquire into administrative misconduct and malfunction. The current office is particularly vibrant and has ventured into areas not previously covered, such as human rights and the preservation of the public beaches. These actions have led some to complain that the ombudsman's investigations are without jurisdiction; in fact, the statute is not entirely clear on these matters.

A growing number of active nongovernmental groups, such as Caribbean Rights, address social concerns that impact on the legal system. Their efforts are devoted, in particular, to children's rights, drug-related juvenile delinquency, women's issues, and human rights matters. On another front, private dispute resolution and arbitration are only now becoming well known in Barbados (although in labor law matters, there is a healthy tradition of arbitration and negotiation). Such means of solving disputes are applied on a noninterventionist basis, that is, by consent.

STAFFING

As dictated by Section 4 of the Supreme Court of Judicature Act, CAP 117A, there are currently no more than six High Court judges. The chief justice is also ex officio a judge of the High Court. Five justices man the Court of Appeal. Supreme Court judges in Barbados enjoy security of tenure, protected by Section 84 (3) of the constitution. Such judges, including the chief justice, are appointed under Section 81 of the constitution by the governor-general (by instrument under the public seal), on the recommendation of the prime minister and after consultation with the leader of the opposition. To qualify for

Legal Structure of Barbados Courts

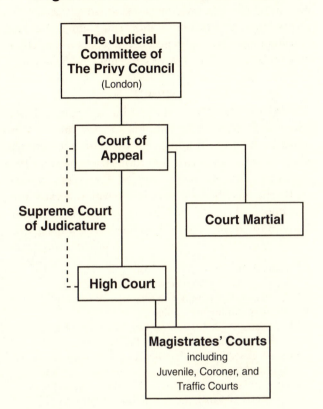

appointment, a judge must have been practicing for a period of no less than ten years. Judges may only be removed for misbehavior, inability, infirmity, or like cause. There are strict processes for removal. For example, the governor-general, after a decision to remove a judge, must refer the matter to the Privy Council. When the prime minister wishes to remove a judge, he or she must make a request to the governor-general, who must then refer the matter for investigation by an independent tribunal. The age of retirement is sixty-five for regular judges and seventy for the chief justice.

Under Section 3 of the Magistrates' Court Act of 1996, the governor-general appoints magistrates by warrant under the public seal on the advice of the Judicial and Legal Services Commission. This commission is also responsible for the discipline and control of the magistrates. Eight magistrates currently serve Barbados.

As a general rule, there is a lack of continuous legal training for judicial and quasi-judicial personnel in Barbados. Approximately 435 attorneys are registered with the Barbados Bar Association, about 35 of whom work in the Attorney General and Director of Public Prosecution Offices. Since the advent of the University of the West Indies—a regional entity with campuses in Trinidad, Jamaica, and Barbados (which houses the law faculty)—persons trained in law are qualified to be both solicitors and barristers (called attorneys-at-law). The faculty's enrollment is currently over 320 students. The bar examination, which measures the law graduate's practical and professional qualifications after completing the legal training program, is administered in separate law schools in Trinidad, Jamaica, and, very recently, the Bahamas.

IMPACT

The legal system is viewed as an integral part of Barbados's proud democratic tradition. Despite the problems noted earlier, there is a high approval rating for the type of system overall and the commitment of the country as a whole to maintaining that system. The system complements that in other countries in the region, with whom, it is hoped, there will be greater political and economic unity in the future, for the benefit of the entire region.

Rose-Marie B. Antoine

See also Antigua and Barbuda; Bahamas; Constitutional Law; Corporal Punishment; Jamaica; Legal Education; Magistrates—Common Law Systems; Privy Council
References and further reading
Alexis, Francis. 1983. *Changing Caribbean Constitutions.* Bridgetown, Barbados: Antilles Publications.
Antoine, Rose-Marie Belle. 1999. *Commonwealth Caribbean Law and Legal Systems.* London: Cavendish Publications.
Beckles, Hilary. 1990. *A History of Barbados: From Amerindian Settlement to Nation State.* Cambridge: Cambridge University Press.
Carnegie, A. N. R. "General Outline and Comparison of Some Main Features of the Constitution of the Barbados." In *Constitution Review Commission—1978.* Barbados: Government Printing Office.
Georges, Telford. 1985. "Is the Jury Trial an Essential Cornerstone of Justice." In *Proceedings and Papers of the Seventh Commonwealth Law Conference.* Hong Kong.
Goveia, Elsa V. 1970. *The West-Indian Slave Laws of the 18th Century.* Barbados: Caribbean University Press.
Hall, Neville. 1970. "The Judicial System of a Plantation Society." *Groupe Universitaire de Recherches Inter-Caraibes,* no. 7.
Patchett, Keith W. 1973. "The Reception of the Law in the West-Indies." *Jamaica Law Journal* 17.
Report of the Constitution Review Commission. 1998. Barbados: Barbados Government.
Williams, Eric. 1964. *Capitalism and Slavery.* London: Andre Deutsch.

BARRISTERS

THE STRUCTURE OF THE BAR

Barristers are members of the oldest legal profession in England and Wales (Scotland has its own legal system and professions). Their principal role is to represent clients in the civil and criminal courts. Although barristers no longer have a monopoly on advocacy in the courts—they share it with solicitors—they do have the weight of tradition and an organizational structure that maintains their dominance.

At the end of 2000, there were just over 10,000 barristers in practice, two-thirds of whom practiced in London, the primary location of the major British courts. The bar is a predominantly male and white institution. Only 26 percent of its members are female, and a mere 9 percent are of nonwhite ethnic origin. The smallest group in the bar is composed of women of color, who number 322.

There are two major functional groups of barristers, namely, junior barristers and Queen's Counsel, often known as QCs or silks (because they wear silk gowns in court). On call to the bar, all barristers are known as junior barristers. After a number of years in practice (perhaps ten or fifteen), barristers are entitled to apply to the lord chancellor for silk—that is, to seek a position of seniority that increases the barrister's fees and making him or her eligible for appointment to the judicial bench. Not all applicants are successful. There are approximately 1,000 QCs in practice, 900 of them situated in London. The proportion of QCs in the barristers' total number has always hovered around 10 percent. Eighty-two QCs are women, and only 25 come from ethnic minorities.

The organization of the bar is different from that of other legal professions in England and Wales. Nominally, barristers are self-employed and forbidden to form partnerships or companies. They typically work in chambers—suites of offices or cooperative associations, often located in the Inns of Court (the set of buildings in London near the Royal Courts of Justice that were the traditional lodging and dining places of barristers), with expenses-sharing arrangements. The administration of the chambers is run by the barrister's clerk who, though not a lawyer, has considerable influence over the career trajectory of a barrister. Chambers used to be small enterprises with a handful of barristers and a senior and junior clerk. Nowadays, they have grown to the extent that some of them contain up to 100 barristers and 20 clerks, practice managers, and information technology (IT) assistants. Chambers also tend to take corporate decisions on who should receive pupillages (apprenticeships) and tenancies (memberships).

The governance of the bar has changed significantly in recent years. Whereas the Inns of Court (the Inns) used to be the main gatekeepers of the bar, much of that role has now been taken over by the Bar Council. The Inns still call new entrants to the bar, but matters of entry qualifications and discipline are handled by the Bar Council. There are four Inns of Court—Middle Temple, Inner Temple, Lincoln's Inn, and Gray's Inn—and virtually all barristers belong to one of them. The role of the Inns concentrates on fostering a collegial mentality among its members by bringing them together for dining and other social events. The Inns are, however, significant owners of property in central London, where many chambers are situated. The Bar Council is now the representative body of the bar, determining what the entry requirements to the bar should be, how minority issues within the bar should be addressed, and how professional misconduct cases should be handled; it also presents the bar's case to government and functions as the regulatory body of the bar.

The sole route into the bar is through the academy. A law degree is the usual prerequisite, although graduates of other disciplines can do conversion courses to bring them to a comparable level. Following the law degree, the aspirant takes a one-year bar vocational course (BVC). The BVC is a mix of theoretical and practical skills, including advocacy. After successfully completing the BVC, the novice can be called to the bar. However, to practice as a barrister, a pupillage must be undertaken. Each set of chambers will determine how many pupils it wishes to take each year. The one-year apprenticeship under the supervision of a senior barrister is designed to instill the principles of the craft of being a barrister. In the second six months of the pupillage, the prospective barrister can do his or her own work, which may mean appearing in court on small pretrial matters or writing opinions for the pupil master. A stipend is usually paid to the pupil, who is also under scrutiny for his or her likely prospects of obtaining a tenancy with the chambers. There are always far more pupils than tenancies.

BARRISTERS' WORK

The working arrangements of the bar are unusual. The bar is largely a referral profession in that barristers are hired by solicitors on behalf of clients for specific tasks. With a few exceptions, public clients cannot approach barristers directly. (Outside England and Wales, however, barristers' rules of conduct permit them to establish full-service law firms.) The philosophy behind this arrangement is that the barrister can bring a disinterested mind to the legal problem and suggest the most efficient and effective outcome, whether that be settlement or litigation. Barristers are additionally bound by the bar's "cab-rank rule" (although just how far they are bound is debatable). The rule states that barristers are not permitted to select cases according to personal whim; if the matter is their field of practice, they are obliged to accept the case.

Because barristers have few or no pastoral duties in connections with clients (unlike solicitors), they are, in theory, able to concentrate on the legal consequences of the case at hand. They are meant to be experts in the law and experts in trial advocacy. A large part of the advocacy expertise has depended on the bar having a monopoly on rights of audience in the higher courts. In 1992, the government decided to widen audience rights to include so-licitors who had undergone advocacy training and become solicitor-advocates. Although not many solicitors have yet taken this route, the numbers are growing and therefore will pose a threat to the bar's hegemony in advocacy.

Advocacy is the core of the barrister's work. Preparing a case and presenting it in court is perhaps the most public demonstration of a lawyer's work. The British tradition of advocacy has always been one of orality, unlike the situation in the civil code countries. But with the growth of European Union law, the emphasis on oral presentation is beginning to decline. Courts expect briefs to be submitted in advance of trial and are willing to impose limits on advocates' freedoms to extend arguments for as long as they desire.

Increased specialization in the law has resulted in the formation of a number of specialist bar associations (SBAs). For example, the Commercial Bar Association (COMBAR) is the commercial and international barristers' SBA. Comprising 900 barristers, COMBAR represents an elite segment of the bar, one that, in effect, has its own court, the Commercial Court, staffed by specialist judges. To understand the extent of that court's influence, consider that 80 percent of the caseload in the Commercial Court has at least one non-British party and that in 50 percent of its cases, both parties are non-British. Quite understandably, English law and lawyers are desirable commodities in a globalized world.

HISTORICAL BACKGROUND

Barristers began to constitute a recognized professional group around the end of the sixteenth century. Their main distinction from other groups, such as attorneys and solicitors, was social. Barristers were members of the Inns of Court, whereas attorneys belonged to the minor Inns of Chancery (now no longer extant). At that time, they did a mix of work, including conveyancing and advocacy for a range of clients, not merely the rich elite. Common law was not taught within the universities; neophyte barristers entered the Inns for their study of the law. Certain comprehensive texts on the common law, such as the magisterial *Blackstone's Commentaries,* began appearing in the eighteenth century. These works assisted students in learning the law, but legal education was largely ossified until the Inns of Court created their own law school in the nineteenth century. Both nepotism and expertise played significant roles in a lawyer's advancement, and on occasion, judgeships could be purchased.

During the eighteenth and nineteenth centuries, divisions between attorneys and solicitors and barristers hardened. Property conveyancing became the monopoly of attorneys, and advocacy became the province of the bar. Barristers also reluctantly relinquished direct contact with clients, instead receiving their instructions from solicitors. From conflict emerged an uneasy, symbiotic alliance. Yet barristers maintained one significant advantage: They provided the senior figures who became the judges. Solicitors only began to breach this barrier in the second half of the twentieth century.

SIGNIFICANCE AND FUTURE

With their wigs and gowns, the trappings of the eighteenth century, barristers might seem an anachronism, yet they have survived, and despite a regime of restrictive practices, they have grown in number. Barristers have flourished in the world of politics; many members of government cabinets have belonged to the bar. However, in the twentieth century, the bar came under attack for being elitist, snobbish, and out of touch with modern legal life. Gradually, various restrictive practices disappeared, such as the tradition of the junior, as of right, receiving two-thirds of the fee when a silk was hired. In the 1990s, solicitors were given, under certain constraints, rights of audience in the higher courts. And solicitors' firms hired barristers as in-house advocates.

Perhaps the biggest change was the division of the bar into two hemispheres. The growth in legal aid in the second half of the twentieth century allowed a large class of barristers to sustain careers through state subsidy. Virtually every criminal defendant was legally aided; most divorces were done with legal aid. By the end of the century, it was evident to governments that open-ended, exponential growth in the legal aid budget was not viable. The result was a switch from legal aid to contingent fees on the civil side, with greater conditions being attached to the granting of criminal legal aid. This has made a barrister's career more parlous for many. For those in the commercial bar, however, the rewards have grown hugely as businesses litigate at an ever increasing rate.

It is unlikely that the bar will fuse with the solicitors' profession, as there is no real necessity to do so. There will always be a need for independent counsel and expert advocates, but their numbers will probably decline. However, much of the routine work of barristers is now being undertaken by solicitors, and they, too, are keen to take on the advocacy. It is more likely that, as legal education for solicitors and barristers converges, their career trajectories will increasingly intertwine. Each will spend time in the other's profession: Barristers will join solicitors' advocacy departments; solicitors will join barristers' chambers as advocates. These developments are presently occurring and will intensify in the years ahead.

John Flood

See also Common Law; England and Wales; Judicial Selection, Methods of; Law Firms; Legal Aid; Legal Education; Legal Professionals—Civil Law Traditions; Scotland; Solicitors

References and further reading

Abel, Richard. 1988. *The Legal Profession in England and Wales.* Oxford: Basil Blackwell.
Bar Council Website. http://www.barcouncil.org.uk.
Boon, Andy, and John Flood. 1999. "Trials of Strength: The Reconfiguration of Litigation as a Contested Terrain." *Law and Society Review* 33, no. 3: 595–636.
Director of Fair Trading. 2001. *Competition in Professions.* London: Office of Fair Trading (OFT).
Flood, John. 1983. *Barristers' Clerks: The Law's Middlemen.* Manchester, England: Manchester University Press.
Hazell, Robert, ed. 1978. *The Bar on Trial.* London: Quartet.
Lord Chancellor's Department Website. http://www.lcd.gov.uk
Morison, John, and Philip Leith. 1992. *The Barrister's World and the Nature of Law.* Buckingham, England: Open University Press.
Prest, Wilfrid R. 1986. *The Rise of the Barristers: A Social History of the English Bar, 1590–1640.* Oxford: Oxford University Press.

BASQUE REGION

GENERAL INFORMATION

Exactly what constitutes the Basque region (or Euskaldunak, meaning "land of the Basques") has long been disputed. Culturally, it is the western area of the Pyrenees along the Bay of Biscay where the Basque language (Euskera) is or has been spoken. Historically, seven territories comprised the Basque region: the old Kingdom of Navarre and its part of the Basse-Navarre area in France; the Provinces of Labourd and Soule in France; and the Provinces of Vizcaya, Alava, and Guipúzcoa in Spain. In a contemporary political sense, the Basque Country (Euskal Herria) constitutes only the three historical provinces that Spain includes in the Basque Autonomous Community (Pais Vasco-Euskadi), although ardent Basque nationalists also claim Spain's Province of Navarre. Linked to the legal tradition of the Basque Country's three provinces, the Navarrese Foral Community became a separate autonomous community (AC) in Spain's contemporary democracy.

With ancestors that predate most modern Europeans, about 2 million Basques live in Euskadi on the Spanish side of the border, and another 200,000 live in France. The Basque language motivates much of their continued sense of identity and cultural distinctiveness. Euskera is linguistically unrelated to other European languages, having survived the Indo-European and Roman influences. The invading cultures that characterized the history of the Iberian Peninsula, including the Romans, the Visigoths, and the Muslims, had little contact with the Basques. The isolation afforded by the mountainous terrain protected the Basque language, promoted the development of a distinct identity, and facilitated the creation of some unique public institutions.

The Basque region's political roots are found in the ancient Kingdom of Vasconia. In the Middle Ages, the

Kingdom of Navarre was created from part of that entity. The Reconquest began in the western Pyrenees, which testifies to this area's long-acknowledged strategic importance. Many of the people in the contemporary Province of Navarre speak Basque and feel an affinity with the Basque provinces to the west.

With agriculture at the heart of its traditional economy, the area began, in the early nineteenth century, to be transformed into one of Spain's principal industrial and financial regions. In close cooperation with nearby Asturias and its coal, the Basques used their iron ore to build a powerful iron and steel industry that, in turn, provided a strong economic base for other trade. The resultant demographic growth produced large urban centers in Bilbao and San Sebastian. The Basque Country's industrialization and economic activity has made it, like Madrid and Catalonia, a magnet for Spain's internal migration, urbanization, and socioeconomic inequalities. With 295 inhabitants per square kilometer, its three provinces are second only to Madrid in terms of population density in Spain.

EVOLUTION AND HISTORY

No distinct Basque legal system exists, if by this term one means a complete set of judicial and legal norms, laws, and structures. Nor does the Basque region possess an autonomous system of law such as Scottish law in the United Kingdom. Special laws in France's Basque region were abolished during the French Revolution and, consequently, are not considered in this analysis. The rest of the Basque region is fully integrated into the Spanish judicial system.

However, such observations do not mean that no Basque law exists. Although most law in the southern part of the Basque region is Spanish, a distinct body of law is applied in the Basque Country and Navarre. Two major components of Basque law can be identified: private law, which is primarily customary civil law known as "foral law," and public law, created and applied by the Autonomous Communities in the Basque Country and Navarre.

Local customs are a major component of specifically Basque law. At the beginning of the Reconquest, customary laws were neither homogeneous nor highly developed in the Basque region. They tended to be quite localized, reflecting the many dialects of the language. During the medieval period, the Crown of Castile controlled much of the Basque region. The Cortes of Castile, however, did not have complete law-making authority over the Provinces of Vizcaya, Alava, and Guipúzcoa. The laws these Basque territories followed were derived from several different sources. First, nonwritten customary law coexisted in rural areas alongside the laws and privileges the king of Castile granted to city dwellers. Second, in the fourteenth century, city inhabitants organized associations called brotherhoods (*hermandades*) and councils (*juntas*) with the power to dictate rules (*ordenanzas*) to judge and punish crime. Individual assaults, violent robberies, and other crimes had increased to such an extent that they impeded movement and trade between the different territories. Third, Basque customary laws were compiled in writing in the fourteenth and fifteenth centuries, in part to prevent their extension beyond the Basque region. These compilations included the Fuero de Ayala (1373) in Vizcaya, the *Fuero Viejode las Encarnaciones* (1394), and the *Fuero Viejode Vizcaya* (1452). As customary laws that originate from society rather than from the state, these *fueros* and the general rules of the different brotherhoods and councils provide the main body of Basque customary law.

In Navarre, local customs and fueros were later incorporated into a general law for the entire kingdom, called the Fuero General de Navarra. Castilian monarchs historically tended to respect these laws; they agreed to honor their traditional basis and consequently passed little legislation to challenge them. In fact, the Royal Council of Navarre (Consejo Real de Navarra) was created to serve as a system of prior control known as *pase foral*. In this procedure, the council had to approve all dispositions of the Spanish monarchy prior to their application in Navarre. This system was also practiced in the Basque Provinces of Vizcaya, Alava, and Guipúzcoa until the nineteenth century.

Following the unification of Spain in 1492, Castile's centralization of power had important legal implications for the Basque region. During the sixteenth and seventeenth centuries, the Spanish Crown ruled over numerous kingdoms on the Iberian Peninsula, many with their own systems of law. Under Philip IV and thereafter, the political institutions of Castile were extended to the other territories, threatening their distinct histories, unique political and legal constitutions, and different sources of laws. Resistance to Castile's centralizing tendencies, including the protection of their particular laws, was uneven. Important to the long-term preservation of some, the Cortes of Burgos established a formula in 1379 that acknowledged the king's authority to legislate but also delayed the application of such legislation until the king, once informed of its incompatibility with foral laws, resolved the conflict. Many areas nevertheless saw their foral laws abolished following the Spanish War of Succession (1701–1713) as a consequence of siding with those who were eventually defeated. This effectively unified civil law throughout these parts of Spain. However, the extension of Castilian law did not include the Basque provinces and Navarre. Their leaders' skills in the politics of alliance formation helped preserve their foral laws.

Postabsolutist Spain (and many other European countries) advanced the notion that equality before the law meant the existence of a single system of law applied to all. The Napoleonic Code of 1804 began the implementation of this important legal legacy of the French Revolution. Its codification and recompilation of local norms and customs limited judicial decisions to law. In Spain, numerous attempts to create a civil code, including an important initiative in 1851, met with opposition from those wishing to preserve local norms and laws. Efforts to force recognition of foral laws delayed the creation of a unified code in Spain. Finally, in 1880, a royal decree stipulated that a general code commission had to include local representatives. Breaking a political stalemate, the commission recognized the local laws and made specific provision for the inclusion of foral laws as appendixes to the code. The resultant Civil Code of 1889 (clearly influenced by France's 1804 Code Civil) remains the basis of Spanish civil law and is applied in the Basque Country and Navarre. The code systematizes Spanish civil law while also preserving the use of foral law. The appendixes containing foral laws acknowledge, among other things, Spain's regional culture and heritage. For the Basque region, these appendixes to Spain's civil code are the Navarrese foral law (Compilación del Derecho Civil Foral de Navarra, March 1973), foral civil law in Vizcaya and Avala (Compilación del Derecho Civil de Vizcaya, June 1959), and accommodations for Guipúzcoa's special customary norms. The Civil Code's general yet supplementary nature in regard to foral laws gives it a certain common law element not normally found in highly centralized civil law systems.

Public law is the second major component of Basque law. Spanish public law is applied in the Basque Country and Navarre in the areas of constitutional, criminal, procedural, tax, and general administrative law. However, the institutions of the Autonomous Communities in the Basque Country and Navarre now add new elements to Basque public law. Spain's process of regionalization gave impetus to these more recent developments in Basque law.

Throughout the late nineteenth and entire twentieth centuries, autonomy for Spain's Basque region depended on the political winds blowing from Madrid. Regime changes—including the short-lived First Republic, the dictatorship of Miguel Primo de Rivera, the Second Republic, the Spanish civil war of 1936–1939, the Francisco Franco regime, and the transition to democracy following Franco's death in 1975—have determined the possibilities for Basque autonomous government. The end of the Franco regime and Spain's transition to democracy were quite significant in advancing this regionalization of governance.

The Spanish Constitution of 1978 and the subsequent Basque Statute of Autonomy provide the framework for the Basque Country's contemporary legal system. The constitution created a multinational state in an attempt to balance the unity of the Spanish state with the regions' uneven centrifugal tendencies. It provided three routes to autonomy, including an accelerated route (Article 51) for the historical regions of the Basque Country, Catalonia, and Galicia. Contemporary Spain has seventeen autonomous communities, varying considerably in size, population, diversity of people, and languages. The three historical provinces of the Basque Country comprise one AC. The Province of Navarre separately constitutes another. Since being established, these two ACs have, consistent with their respective statutes of autonomy, produced laws that apply only within their own territories. Constitutionally grounded and central to the development of regional autonomy in Spain, the institutions of the Basque Autonomous Community are now contributing to contemporary Basque public law.

CURRENT STRUCTURE

Basque law's public and private components generally emanate from distinct structures. As already discussed, Basque private law is quite complex, given its origins in local custom. In terms of common structure, the Basque farmhouse (casério) as an institution (and the freedom of action to preserve it) is at the center of the early development of customary foral civil law. Reflecting this institution's centrality in Basque culture, the legal protection of the farmhouse means, for example, that family and inheritance laws ensure its integrity, rather than benefiting specific individuals. Such foral laws in the Basque Country and Navarre tend to conflict with Castilian law regarding inheritance and marital property.

In terms of Basque public law, governing institutions in the Basque Autonomous Community are grounded in the constitution (Article 152) and detailed in the Basque Statute of Autonomy. The Basque Parliament (Eusko Legebiltzarra) and the executive—that is, the Basque government and administration (Eusko Jaurlaritza)—make and apply norms and laws for the Basque Country within their specified powers. Also, each of the three Basque provinces or "historical territories" (lurralde historikoak) has its own elected legislature (the Junta General or Foru Biltzarrak) and executive (the Diputación Foral or Foru Aldundiak) that enact legal norms consistent with their competencies as defined in the statute (Article 37). The provincial governments' foral decrees and orders are hierarchically secondary to the provincial legislatures' foral norms, and the legislatures norms, in turn, are secondary to Basque AC laws. Though complex, these structures suggest a unique Basque legal order does exist in each province as well as in the autonomous community.

The Spanish Constitution of 1978 and the Basque Statute of Autonomy provide the negotiated framework from which these public institutions' powers are derived. Their competencies are central to their exercise of regional autonomy. Historically, public foral law in the Basque region has included the following: (1) a requirement that Spanish monarchs take an oath of loyalty to the fueros; (2) the pase foral, discussed earlier; (3) the system of provincial government just described; (4) freedom of trade exempt from custom duties; (5) exemption of Basque men from military service; (6) a special tax system; and (7) the rule of law and individual rights, including due process in regard to arrest, a ban on torture, the right to defense, and equal civil rights. The Constitution of 1978 recognized the Basques' historical institutions and special powers and reinforced Basque rights when it referred to "the historic rights of the foral territories" and "the right of autonomy of nationalities and regions." The Basque Statute of Autonomy gives exclusive power to the Basque Country for the preservation, modification, and development of its foral law. With regard to public law, the statute specifically mentions particular local administrative and military arrangements, and it contains provisions for police and education and for special financial, tax, and budgetary relations with the central state (the Concierto Económico). Judicial authority is noticeably absent from this list.

The nonexistence of unique Basque judicial structures reflects Spain's unitary political system, despite its strong federal tendencies. The current constitution's notion of autonomy remains secondary to its principle of unity. Article 149 clearly includes justice and the judiciary in this regard—regionalization in Spain has had little effect on the judiciary. The Basque Country and Navarre remain fully integrated into the overarching Spanish judicial system, whose structures continue to be highly centralized and hierarchical. From the top down, Spain's ordinary court system includes the Supreme Court, which serves as the ultimate appellate court, the National Audience (since 1977), Superior Courts of Justice, and Provincial Audiences. In addition to hearing original cases, the last two types of courts serve as appellate courts for lower courts, including the Courts of First Instance. The Superior Court of Justice replaced the Territorial Audience in the late 1980s; a change of structure more than judicial substance, the move was a small territorial adaptation to democratic regionalization. Corresponding to Spain's division into separate autonomous communities, these courts hear civil, criminal, administrative, and social cases at the regional level. Applicable to all of Spain and not just the Basque Country, Superior Courts of Justice address judicial matters in each AC territory.

STAFFING

Throughout the Spanish judicial system, including the Basque Country and Navarre, judges are recruited at all levels by a judicial corps of nonpolitical civil servants. New judges gain entry into the judiciary through a na-

tional system of competitive exams. As the administrative organ of the Spanish judicial corps, the General Council of the Judiciary determines assignments, promotions, and, if necessary, judicial discipline. Furthermore, no associations of Basque judges, attorneys, or prosecutors exist, given the lack of a separate Basque judiciary or distinct legal identity.

The Basque Autonomous Community has staffed some areas that work with the judiciary, the most visible being law enforcement and public security. In 1980, the Basque government created the Ertzaintza, a Basque police force. Reflecting Spain's unitary structure, however, these security forces remain linked to the Ministry of Home Affairs in Madrid. Its Security Council (Junta de Seguridad) coordinates all regional security forces (Navarre and Catalonia also have autonomous police), despite the Ertzaintza's administrative and financial dependence on the Basque regional government.

RELATIONSHIP TO THE NATIONAL SYSTEM

The Basque Country and Navarre are both substantively and structurally integrated into the Spanish judicial system in most areas of the law, including criminal, civil, administrative, and labor law. Although no separate Basque legal system exists, two distinct but symbiotic components of Basque law are now applied in the Basque Country and Navarre. First, Basque foral civil law adds complexity to Spain's legal system. As noted earlier, the Basque Country's foral law is mostly private law, and the historical particularities of the foral territories contribute distinct legal norms in different areas of the Basque region. Despite their unique origins, these fueros share many common characteristics. Second, foral law has public law elements, many of which are deeply rooted in the history of the Basque region. Recently, a new legal order has begun to develop based on the Basque Statute of Autonomy and the powers it grants to make public law. The shared constitutional framework within which the institutions of the Basque provinces and the Basque AC operate provides a degree of coordination that is new to the region, despite the particularities of foral law and differences in institutional powers.

The Spanish judiciary—not Basque courts—apply this legal diversity in the Basque Country and Navarre. The relationship of Basque law to the Spanish legal system and judicial structures is laid out in many constitutional, statutory, and legal texts. Three examples suggest how this works. First, the Spanish Constitution of 1978 and the Basque Statute of Autonomy delineate the relationship of the central state and the Basque Country. Second, to clarify the complex civil law, Articles 13 through 17 of Spain's Civil Code spell out which laws are to be applied. For example, Article 13 states that the central legal system applies in (1) the application of legal rules and sources of law; (2) marriage certification and related issues, except economic issues; (3) the organization of registries and public documents; and (4) the bases of contractual obligations. In all other areas of civil law, the foral laws apply, with the Civil Code acting as a supplementary source of regulation. Third, the concept of civil domicile governs the application of foral laws. The Civil Code regulates legal residency, with personal choice being central. Individuals in Spain identify themselves as being from a specific place, and they officially register as such. Official residency determines whether an area's foral laws are to be applied to an individual. If none are applicable in the matter, Spain's Civil Code remains in force.

With questions of institutional competencies and the division of power crucial to the application of law in the Basque region, democratic Spain's Constitutional Court has played an important role in resolving such matters since its creation in 1979, specifically in two broad areas. First, the Basque Parliament (or government) and the Spanish Parliament (or government) can challenge the others' acts, legislative decrees, and regulations in the Constitutional Court. Through this process, the court has greatly defined central-regional relations in democratic Spain. In a steady stream of cases, the court has determined the legal delineation of powers between the central government and the Basque AC. Despite having a tilt toward central government control, the Constitutional Court has handed down some important rulings favoring the Basque Country. Second, the court's defense of constitutionally based individual rights has frequently focused on cases originating out of the Basque Country. For example, it has often defended the Basque Country's regulation of bilingualism regarding Euskera and Castillian Spanish.

Finally, Basque and Spanish law are increasingly becoming intertwined with the emerging European Union (EU) legal system. As a consequence, three issues of this complex legal system are noteworthy. First, additional layers of a hierarchy of laws are now applied in the Basque region: All Basques live under EU law and the Convention on Human Rights, in addition to foral civil law, Spanish private and public law, provincial public law, and Basque AC public law. The matching of issue to law depends on different institutions' spheres of legal competence. Second, the Spanish Constitutional Court has repeatedly asserted that within the areas of their legally defined powers, AC governments are responsible for the implementation of EU law. The third question concerns the degree of AC participation in EU decision making. Basques want a more active role in this process than the Spanish authorities would like. Though this issue is not fully resolved, the Basque Country has unquestionably benefited from the Treaty of Maastricht's highlighting of the special position of such regions.

Through the Committee of the Regions and other institutions, the Basque Country is increasingly participating, albeit slowly, in the creation, elaboration, and implementation of European law.

Thomas D. Lancaster

See also Catalonia; Civil Law; Customary Law; European Court of Justice; Federalism; Spain

References and further reading

Castán Tobeñas, José. 1991. *Derecho civil español, omún y foral.* 10th ed. Madrid: Reus.
Díez-Picazo, Luís, and Antonio Gullón. 1997. *Sistema de derecho civil.* 7th ed. Madrid: Tecnos.
Heiberg, Marianne. 1989. *The Making of the Basque Nation.* Cambridge: Cambridge University Press.
Merino-Blanco, Elena. 1996. *The Spanish Legal System.* London: Sweet and Maxwell.
Tomás y Valiente, Francisco. 1997. *Manual de historia del derecho español.* 4th ed. Madrid: Tecnos.
Villiers, Charlotte. 1999. *The Spanish Legal Tradition.* Brookfield, VT: Ashgate/Darmouth.

BELARUS

GENERAL INFORMATION

Belarus is a landlocked nation in eastern Europe. It borders on Latvia and Lithuania to the north and northwest, Poland to the west, Ukraine to the south, and Russia to the east. Belarus's 80,100 square miles (207,600 square kilometers) contain mostly flat terrain and vast marshlands. This area, which is slightly smaller than Kansas, has a transitional climate between continental and maritime, and experiences cold winters and cool, moist summers. Twenty-nine percent of the land is arable. Natural resources include forest, peat deposits, and small quantities of oil and natural gas. In the early 1930s, Belarus—then within the Soviet Union as the Belorussian Soviet Socialist Republic—was designated an industrial region by Soviet administrators. This industry concentrated around production of military materiel. Although the Belarus economy became one of the most developed among the Soviet republics, manufacturing and industrial activity depleted natural resources and raw materials. Since the collapse of the Soviet Union the market for manufactured goods has disappeared.

Belarus's primary trading partner is Russia, which in 1998 received 66 percent of its exports and accounted for 54 percent of its imports. In keeping with "market socialism," President Alexander Lukashenko reimposed administrative controls over prices and currency exchange rates and expanded the state's right to intervene in the management of private enterprises.

Belarus is heavily polluted. Seventy years of heavy industrialization had deleterious effects, and fallout from the nuclear disaster at Chernobyl, in Ukraine, contami-

The map shows Belarus and surrounding countries (Latvia, Lithuania, Poland, Ukraine, Russia), with cities including Polatsk, Navapolatsk, Vitsyebsk, Orsha, Pastavy, Vilnius, Maladzyechna, Barysaw, Mahilyow, Krychaw, Minsk, Hrodna, Baranavichy, Slutsk, Babruysk, Salihorsk, Homyel, Rechytsa, Pinsk, Kalinkavichy, Mazyr. ©2001 maps.com

nated nearly 25 percent of the state's land mass. Bio-genetic disorders as well as a host of other illnesses including leukemia and other cancers plague up to 20 percent of the national population as a result of exposure to nuclear radiation. Due to few environmental regulations during the Communist era and continuing lack of enforcement, run-off from mining has contaminated much land and water, and toxic chemicals and petrochemicals used primarily for defense, heavy industry, transportation, and agricultural purposes, as well as industrial effluent, have caused acute environmental problems.

Belarus's demography provides for a nearly homogeneous culture. More than three-quarters (77.9 percent) of the country's 10.4 million citizens were ethnic Belarusians in 2000. Russians made up 13.2 percent of the population, and Poles and Ukrainians accounted for most of the remaining 9 percent. The death rate exceeds the birth rate, which, along with emigration, contributes to negative population growth (–0.17 percent in 2000). Belarus boasts a 98 percent literacy rate among persons age 15 and over. The official language is Belarusian, but Russian is the predominant language in the workplace because it was the official language under Soviet rule.

POLITICAL HISTORY

The first recorded settlements in Belarus date back to the six century C.E. The princes of Kiev began to rule Belarus late in the ninth century when there emerged the first East Slavic state, Kievan Rus. Polatsk, which formed the center of modern-day Belarus, was a principality that resulted from the splinter of Kievan Rus when its ruler, Prince Yaroslav the Wise, died in 1054. The Mongols destroyed most of the towns of Belarus when they invaded in 1240.

Belarus entered Lithuanian control in 1386, under the Lithuanian-Polish Jagiellonian Dynasty. Some historians speculate that the name Belarus, which literally translates as "white Rus," originally meant "free Rus," free from domination by Kievan or "black" Rus, a small territory in the western part of modern Belarus. After converting from paganism to Roman Catholicism, in 1385 the Lithuanian grand duke married the queen of Poland and thus became king of Poland. Lithuania and Poland were joined as a single state, the Polish-Lithuanian Commonwealth, in 1569 by the Union of Lublin. The religious conversion of the new king and the Union of Lublin resulted in the conversion of Lithuanian and Belarusian nobilities from Orthodoxy to Roman Catholicism, as well as to their assimilation of Polish culture. The Union of Brest in 1596 reconciled part of the Orthodox church with the Roman Catholic church. This new, "Uniate" church retained traditional Orthodox rites and customs and preserved autonomy in nondoctrinal matters in exchange for acknowledging the ultimate authority of the Catholic church. However, bitter struggles ensued between the Orthodox church and the Uniate church on account of the former's concerns that latinization and polonization would erode Belarusian identity. Between 1648 and 1654, widespread revolts were launched against Polish landowners. Subsistence farming became the dominant economic endeavor. Belarus remained part of Poland until Russia, Prussia, and Austria carried out three partitions of Poland in 1772, 1793, and 1795. Nearly all of Belarus went over to the Russian Empire in the last partition, except for a small portion of western territory maintained by Prussia. Tsar Nicholas I of Russsia abolished the Uniate church and forced Belarusians to reconvert to Orthodoxy.

For much of the nineteenth and twentieth centuries Belarus was once again a battleground of Europe. Napoleon fought there in 1812, and the Germans fought the Soviets there in World War I. The Belarusian People's Republic was crushed between the warring Soviet and Polish armies in 1921 and divided between Soviet Russia and Poland. The Soviets took the greater portion of Belarusian territory and made its largest city, Minsk, the capital of the Belarus Soviet Socialist Republic. Western Belarus was joined to Poland. During the first years of Soviet Belarus, the Communist regime encouraged Belarusian cultural development in the hope of gaining the population's loyalty. In the early 1930s, however, the Soviet dictator Joseph Stalin reversed policy and repressed any signs of nationalism in Belarus and the other constituent republics.

Belarus suffered heavy losses in World War II. Between the German invasion of the Soviet Union in June 1940 and the defeat of Nazi Germany in May 1945, 2.2 million Belarusians perished. The country experienced a kind of economic rebirth during the postwar period, although it remained a backwater of Russia, the dominant Soviet republic.

On August 25, 1991, after seven decades as a constituent Soviet republic, the Belarusian Supreme Soviet, Belarus's parliament, declared the nation's independence from the Soviet Union. After numerous drafts, the Supreme Soviet adopted a new constitution, which went into effect on March 30, 1994. Alexander Lukashenko won the quickly organized presidential election of 1994. Although Lukashenko initially appeared to support an independent Belarus, his position changed as he pursued closer ties with Russia. In April 1996, despite substantial public opposition, Lukashenko joined Russia in signing the Treaty on the Formation of a Community of Sovereign Republics. The purpose of this treaty is to bind the two nations politically, economically, and militarily.

Lukashenko sought to consolidate his power over other branches of government, as well as the media. In fall 1996, a constitutional referendum was proposed to increase the president's powers, including extending the president's term and giving him the authority to appoint the judiciary. The chairman of the Central Election Commission refused to approve the referendum and was dismissed. The chairman of the Council of Ministers then resigned, and Lukashenko successfully stifled media coverage of these events. Foreign observers and providers of assistance criticized both the substance of the proposed constitutional amendments and the president's muting of the media and political opposition.

Soon after Lukashenko's election, a well-planned attack on the independent media, which did not always approve of his actions as president, was launched. The editor in chief of Belarus's most popular newspaper, *Narodnaya Gazeta,* was fired by decree of Lukashenko. The opposition newspaper, *Svaboda,* was forced out of Minsk and soon out of Belarus; it is now printed inVilnius, the capital of neighboring Lithuania. The Supreme Soviet began presidential impeachment proceedings, but they were halted after Lukashenko won the referendum by a 70 percent majority. Lukashenko's supporters then abolished the Supreme Soviet and established a bicameral parliament that is subservient to Lukashenko, who essentially rules by decree. Lukashenko-appointed loyalists dominate the Constitutional Court, which by the end of 1996 had shown tremendous bravery in ruling that seventeen of nineteen presidential decrees were unconstitutional. It similarly declared the referendum and new amendments to the constitution to be unconstitutional. Lukashenko ignored the decision, and in January 1997, seven members of the court were dismissed or resigned. In April 1997, the court, newly packed with Lukashenko appointees, abrogated its 1996 referendum decision and held that the court would no longer examine the constitutionality of presidential decrees.

Belarus maintains closer economic and political ties to Russia than do any of the other independent states formed from the Soviet republics. Not only did Belarus host the signing of the agreement between Russia, Ukraine, and Belarus that created the Commonwealth of Independent States in 1999, but it signed several treaties with Russia on a two-state union with a view toward political and economic integration. Despite Lukashenko's active support for integrating Belarus into Russia, Russia has been slow in implementing these accords. Little changed with the 2001 reelection of President Lukashenko. Belarus remains a nation in limbo, mired in autocratic rule, political uncertainty, international isolation, and economic policies from the Communist past. Lukashenko's mismanagement of the economy, rather than his poor record on democracy and human rights, may be his downfall. Consumer prices have increased from 1994 to 1998 at an average annual compound rate of 143 percent. In 1999, the inflation rate was 295 percent. Living standards for many segments of society have declined precipitously since independence. Belarusian authorities reported that average monthly wages were just over U.S.$70 a month by the end of 2000, but independent analysts suggest the true figure is even lower. Foreign investors have steered clear of Belarus. As the Belarusian foreign minister, Ural Latypau, observed, "Belarus is the only country in the post-Soviet area without any branch of the West's leading banks, without any hotel or shopping center built by foreign investors, and without any office of the world's major companies." (Interfax Report, November 16, 2000). Whether Lukashenko's decision to ignore the West and look eastward to Russia for its future will bring Belarusians what they desire politically and economically remains doubtful.

Since 1999, the tension between Lukashenko and the opposition has not abated but rather has become palpable even within the government. Lukashenko blasted the cabinet for not controlling inflation in 1999, and he dismissed his prime minister in February 2000. In the 2001 presidential elections, the suppressed and fractious opposition was unable to effectively unify and communicate its message to the people, due in part to its lack of access to the state-controlled mass media.

HISTORY OF THE LEGAL SYSTEM

The Belarusian legal system has for several centuries been greatly influenced by the Russian legal tradition. Belarus follows the German civil law model yet retains many characteristics of Soviet jurisprudence. This combination of civil law and socialist law is the common heritage of Communism in the countries formed after the demise of the Soviet Union in 1989. Because few democratic and free market reforms have been implemented since independence, many of the freedoms and guarantees contained in the Belarusian constitution are meaningless and Belarus has become increasingly isolated from the international community.

Under Soviet rule, the basic legal document governing the judicial system of Belarus was the Decree on the Judiciary No. 1. When the decree was enacted in 1917, Belarus was a part of the Russian Federation. Local courts were established to try civil and common criminal cases placed in their jurisdiction. Revolutionary tribunals were instituted to try cases of counterrevolutionary (or state) crimes and other crimes of particular danger to the new Soviet state. Decree on the Judiciary No.2, enacted in the following year, called for district people's courts to try

cases that exceeded the jurisdiction of local people's courts. Other decrees on the organization of general courts and revolutionary tribunals included the Regulations of the People's Court of the Russian Federation of Socialist Republics, which instituted a uniform people's court throughout the federation. Under these regulations the people's court existed in three versions: a people's judge, a people's judge with two people's assessors, and a people's judge with six people's assessors. Councils of people's judges sat in every judicial district to hear appeals against judgments and sentences made by people's courts. The councils exercised judicial control functions as well.

In 1922, fundamental restructuring further developed the Soviet judicial system in the Belarussian Soviet Socialist Republic. The first Regulation of the Judiciary established a three-tier judicial system consisting of the People's Court, the High Court, and the Supreme Court.

Under Joseph Stalin, from 1926 until his death in March 1953, the Soviet regime ruled in Belarus by a combination of law and terror. Where political life was stable, law was introduced. When the regime felt threatened, terror, sometimes in the guise of law, took over. The 1936 Soviet constitution provided the grounds for the promulgation of all-union codes to replace the codes of the separate constituent republics. In 1938, a new Judiciary Act was promulgated to bring about more orthodox trial procedures.

The legal scholar Harold J. Berman has describe seven major tendencies in law reform during the decade following Stalin's death:

> First, there was a tendency toward the elimination of political terror; Second . . . the liberalization both of procedures and of substantive norms; Third . . . the systematization and rationalization of the legal system; Fourth . . . decentralization and democratization of decision-making; Fifth . . . popular participation in the administration of justice; Sixth . . . severe threats and crackdowns on those who did not cooperate in building communism; and Seventh . . . a new Soviet theory of state and law which rejected some of the Stalinist innovations in Leninist doctrine. (*Justice in the USSR*, 56)

In the economic realm, Soviet law provided a legal system for a planned economy. This required making the plan law, developing a socialist concept of property and contracts, and creating economic crimes such as profiteering. In the political and civil spheres, Soviet law provided for greater rights and freedoms, including economic rights, than the U.S. Constitution. The gap, however, between what was promised and what was delivered only grew with time and contributed to the downfall of the Soviet Union.

After independence, Belarus made attempts at judicial and legal reform. The objectives of these reforms included ensuring the rule of law, establishing an independent judiciary as the principal guarantor of individual rights and freedoms, promoting the effectiveness of laws, and fixing in the law democratic principles that meet the standards of international law and the recommendations of modern legal science. Although these objectives helped form Belarus's 1994 constitution, they have not been realized. Belarus has implemented little structural reform since Lukashenko came to power.

LEGAL CONCEPTS

Belarus is a republic consisting of a powerful executive branch, a bicameral parliament, and a judicial branch that places jurisdiction over constitutional issues solely in a Constitutional Court separate from the courts of general jurisdiction and other courts. The executive branch includes a prime minister, who serves as head of government and is appointed by a strong president, who serves as chief of state. The entire executive branch is sufficiently subject to the president's authority that it is under his effective control.

Both the 1994 constitution and the 1996 referendum provide that the president may participate in the legislature and its subordinate bodies, but they are silent about what such participation should entail. The president selects many members of the legislative branch and has extensive control over the course of legislation. The president may appoint one-third of the Senate. As with nearly all other areas of government, Alexander Lukashenko, the only person to serve as president under the constitution, exerts enormous influence over the judiciary despite constitutional provisions for judicial independence.

Belarus is a unitary state. It has no federalism. Lower levels of government are uniform; they have no constitutions of their own and enjoy no autonomy. Under article 123 of the constitution, the Senate may dissolve local soviets, effectively stifling any independent-mindedness.

Constitution

The first constitution of the newly independent Belarus was radically transformed by the referendum of 1996. Both documents contain provisions to protect negative and positive individual rights, but such protections may be rendered empty against the greater interest of the state.

Under the referendum the president may eliminate the legislature and may suspend the constitution entirely by declaring martial law whenever he or she believes it is warranted. In such circumstances the president would be free to run the country according to his or her discretion. The central theme of the 1996 referendum is enhancement of the presidential powers and weakening of the

powers of the other branches, in violation of the principle of separation of powers.

The Constitution of the Republic of Belarus as adopted on March 15, 1994, proclaims independence of the judiciary as a prerequisite for the rule of law in the state. In practice, however, the judiciary of Belarus is not independent. The 1996 referendum provides the president the power to appoint six of the twelve members of the Constitutional Court, including its chairman. The Council of the Republic, which is itself composed of presidential appointees and members elected by individuals under the president's influence, appoints the remaining six justices of the Constitutional Court. The court, as defined in the 1994 constitution, is the sole agency empowered to settle legal disputes. Article 61 guarantees protection of individual rights and freedoms by a competent, independent, and impartial court. Individuals are entitled to sue at law for both property and personal damages. Article 25 guarantees the right of a detained or arrested person to appeal the detention or arrest. Article 26 reaffirms the provision on the presumption of innocence contained in the Universal Declaration on Human Rights. According to article 27, one cannot be forced to give evidence against oneself, one's own family, or one's close relatives, and illegally obtained evidence is inadmissible.

Chapter five of the constitution elaborates nine principles of judicial organization. First, judicial power rests with the courts. Second, judges are independent and obey the law when administering justice. Third, judges may not engage in any other activities except teaching and research, and may not engage in teaching or research when those positions entail holding a staff position. Fourth, the administration of justice must be based on the constitution, laws, and statutory acts of the republic. Fifth, related court cases are heard together or, where allowed by law, individually. Sixth, all court proceedings must be public except for instances prescribed by law. Seventh, justice is to be administered on the basis of the adversarial system and the equality of parties in a trial. Eighth, parties have the right to appeal court decisions. Ninth, higher court judges are elected; all other judges are appointed.

The passage of the Law on the Judicial System and the Status of Judges, which further elaborated these principles of judicial organization and operation, was heralded as a positive step toward democratic judicial reform when it passed on January 13, 1995. Yet under the 1996 referendum these attempts at reform have been essentially abandoned.

STRUCTURE

The Belarusian judiciary is organized into general, economic, and specialized courts. The general courts include the Supreme Court, regional courts, district and city

Legal Structure of Belarus Courts

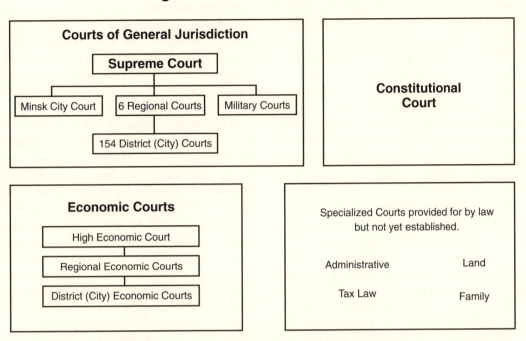

*An *International Court of Arbitration* sits at the Belarussian Chamber of Commerce. It serves as a permanent and independent court of arbitration, but does not form part of the national judiciary.

courts, and military courts. The Minsk city court is on the same level as the regional courts.

Constitutional Court

The Constitutional Court, established on April 28, 19994, has since 1996 consisted of twelve justices. As part of the 1996 reforms, the Constitutional Court may no longer on its own initiative review the validity of acts of other branches of government nor participate in the impeachment process. Perhaps most important, judicial immunity has been eliminated. The president's ability to appoint members of the Constitutional Court, as well as other judges, without legislative confirmation undermines the development of an independent judiciary. The president now appoints half of the Constitutional Court, including the chairperson, and the other half is appointed by the Senate, one third of which is chosen by the president. This ensures that the reformed Constitutional Court does not stray too far from the president.

Before the reforms, the court decided more than thirty cases concerning the constitutionality of laws, presidential decrees, government resolutions, and other statutory acts. However, President Lukashenko ignored many of those decisions and they probably prompted the reforms of 1996. The Court may, however, submit proposals to parliament and other government agencies on amendments to the constitution and other statutory acts. Each year, it sends a message to the president and the Supreme Soviet on the state of constitutional law and order in the republic. Judgments of the Constitutional Court are final and may not be appealed.

Courts of General Jurisdiction

The highest court of general jurisdiction in Belarus is the Supreme Court. The Supreme Court is composed of a chairman, deputy chairman, and justices. It may hear appeals from judgments of the regional courts and the Minsk city court that have yet to enter into legal force. The Supreme Court may also act as a court of supervision over judgments that have entered into legal force. In certain cases it may act as a court of first instance.

Six regional courts and the Minsk city court, which is of equal status with the regional courts, form the second level of the judicial system. The regional courts and the Minsk city court hear cases within their original jurisdiction as courts of first instance. They also function as appeals courts with respect to judgments of district courts that have not yet come into legal force. The regional and Minsk city courts also exercise supervision, as prescribed by law, over court judgments that have entered into legal force and revise cases after new circumstances have become known.

The regional courts consist of a chairman, deputy chairman, and approximately 150 judges. The chairman, deputy chairman, and judges are organized into boards of justices and the court presidium. The board of justices of the regional courts and Minsk city court hear civil and criminal cases within their jurisdiction as courts of first appearance. The board also hears appeals and cases where new circumstances have become known.

The presidium of the regional and Minsk city courts is composed of the chairman of the court, deputy chairman, and judges. It hears cases within its jurisdiction by way of supervision and when new facts become known. It also examines judicial practices, conducts judicial statistical analyses, renders assistance to district courts on the proper application of laws, upgrades judges' professional skills, and exercises other powers as prescribed by legislation.

District courts are the lowest-level primary courts in the general court system. They are established in urban districts, and in districts and cities of regional jurisdiction that are not divided into urban districts. In 2001, there were 154 district courts employing some 600 professional judges. These courts consist of a chairman and judges. Where there are five or more judges in the district, a deputy chairman of the court is appointed. District courts hear most of the first-instance civil, criminal, and administrative cases and also examine materials related to the execution of judgments.

The republic's system of general courts includes the military courts. Their jurisdiction embraces criminal cases where the accused is a member of the armed forces, civil cases in law suits involving military service relationships, and complaints by servicemen and servicewomen against unlawful acts and decisions of military officers and other military authorities. The system of military courts is based on the principles of general court organization and activities. There is also, however, regard for the specific structure of the armed forces, which consists of intergarrison military courts and the Belarusian military courts headed by the Military Board of the Supreme Court.

Economic Courts

In accordance with the Law on the Economic Court of 1991, the system of economic courts consists of the High Economic Court and regional economic courts. At the recommendation of the chairman of the High Economic Court, the Presidium of the Supreme Soviet can establish economic courts in cities and major industrial areas. The system of economic courts has been complemented by economic courts in cities and districts, in accordance with article 1 of the Law on the Judicial System and the Status of Judges.

From 1922 to 1991, state bodies of arbitration, which were administrative and judicial institutions, exercised jurisdiction over economic issues. The department commissions of arbitration set up in the 1930s were even more administrative in their nature. The procedure used in economic courts is governed by the Code of Economic

Procedure of the Republic of Belarus, adopted in 1991. Economic courts have jurisdiction over disputes between legal entities and natural persons, including aliens, that arise in concluding, changing, terminating, and executing contracts or carrying out any other economic activity, as well as disputes over invalidation of acts by government and other agencies that contravene legislation and affect the interest of economic entities.

On account of difficulties in determining which cases should be referred to either general or economic courts, on March 23, 1995, the Plenary Sessions of the High Economic Court and the Supreme Court adopted a resolution entitled "On the Delimitation of Jurisdictions Between General and Economic Courts." The resolution prescribes the jurisdiction of economic courts to include economic disputes arising between legal entities as well as natural persons engaged in business activities, economic actors in particular; any dispute over a contract the conclusion of which is governed by legislation or which the parties agree to submit to an economic court; disputes over a change of terms or cancellation of contracts, nonfulfillment or improper fulfillment of obligations, recognition of the right of property, recovery by the owner or another lawful possessor of property held unlawfully by another person, damages, denial of government registration of economic entities, liquidation, reorganization of legal entities, breach of antimonopoly law, and bankruptcy.

Specialized Judicial Bodies

The Law on the Judicial System and the Status of Judges permits the creation of specialized courts including family, administrative, land, and tax law courts. However, these courts have not yet been established.

An International Court of Arbitration that does not form part of the state judiciary has been functioning at the Belarussian Chamber of Commerce and Industry since 1994.

JUDICIAL SELECTION

The Law on the Judicial System and the Status of Judges defines the principal requirements for becoming a judge. A successful candidate must be at least twenty-five years of age, have received a legal education, passed a qualifying exam, and completed two years of practical study, and have a spotless moral reputation.

Similar to the former Communist party control of judicial selection, the president of the republic effectively controls judicial selection. The president appoints six justices of the constitutional court, as well as the chairperson. The remaining six justices are appointed by the Council (Senate) of the Republic, which is composed primarily of individuals appointed by the president.

Under article 84 of the constitution, the president appoints the members of the Supreme Court with the consent of the council. The president can also dismiss the chairman of the Supreme Court.

The president appoints the judges of regional, Minsk city, district, military, regional economic, specialized, town, and district economic courts.

LEGAL PROFESSION

Article 62 of the constitution grants citizens the right to an advocate not only in criminal cases but in all legal matters, and forbids interference with the offering of legal assistance. It also provides for legal assistance expenses to be paid for by the goverment under certain circumstances.

These rights exist only to the extent that there are qualified advocates who can provide the legal services needed, that individuals have the resources (where not provided by the state) to pay for such services, and that the law is not subject to governmental abuse. As is the case in most countries formed from the former Soviet republics, in Belarus there is a shortage of attorneys because under communism, there was little need for them. This shortage will take a number of years to address, as state law schools are slow to change and private law schools, which respond much more quickly to market needs, have not proliferated owing to the government's control of business.

Because of the poor economy in Belarus, many citizens cannot afford lawyers and so must represent themselves if they to settle civil disputes in the courts. Yet owing to widespread corruption of the judiciary, another legacy of Communist rule, the courts are not the preferred means for settling most legal disputes. Moreover, the government abuses the legal representation process. In May 1997, Lukashenko issued a decree that subordinated all lawyers to the Ministry of Justice, which now controls the licensing of all lawyers. Several lawyers, including a number of the president's opponents, have been stripped of their licenses. This has made Belarusian lawyers more and more unwilling to accept the growing number of political cases. and any case that challenges a governmental decision may be considered political.

As in most civil law countries, in Belarus the legal profession is regulated primarily by law, not by an independent bar association. The Law of the Bar details the organization, admission, discipline, and practice of the legal profession. Instead of creating the environment for democratically elected independent bar associations, the law grants favored status to the holdover organizations from the Communist era, the collegia of advocates and the Union of Advocates, which rely heavily on the old, established networks. Like many of the provisions in the Belarus constitution, the law promises more than it can possibly deliver. Article 4 of the Law of the Bar asserts that the state "shall provide legal counsel to anyone who needs it, without any limitation." Even a government truly interested in achieving this goal would fail miserably. As it now stands, President Lukashenko's appointees at the Ministry of Justice preside over the legal profession, pursuant not to the Law of the Bar but to his presidential decree.

IMPACT OF THE LAW

The legal landscape in Belarus combines with an unstable political climate that presents numerous concerns about human rights for ordinary citizens. Nearly all power is concentrated in the president, in which office Alexander Lukashenko has remained long after his term was scheduled to end in 1999. The fact that, in practice, the judiciary is not independent severely inhibits the protection of individual rights against the power of the state. The Presidential Guard acts against President Lukashenko's political enemies without judicial or legislative oversight. The Law on the State Guard provides the president with the right to subordinate all security forces to his personal command. According to human rights reports, members of the security forces have committed numerous human rights abuses. Police and prison officials beat detainees and prisoners, despite the 1996 constitution's prohibition of torture and provision for the inviolability of the person. Human rights monitors report coerced confessions through beatings and psychological pressure from investigators. The government seldom punishes such abuses, despite their illegality under Belarusian law.

Soviet-era laws on detention have been amended only slightly. Security forces arbitrarily arrest and detain citizens. The code of criminal procedure provides that police may detain a person suspected of a crime for up to twenty-four hours without a warrant, within which time the procurator is notified. The procurator then has forty-eight hours to review the legality of the detention. If the procurator deems the detention legal, a suspect can be held for a maximum of ten days without formal charge. However, usually once the decision is made to hold a suspect, a formal charge is entered. Once a suspect is charged, a trial must be initiated within two months, although in some cases the procurator general can extend pretrial detention to eighteen months to allow for further investigation. In late 1998, some 64,000 persons were held in detention according to the Belarussian-Helsinki Committee. Under the current legal code there is no provision for bail. Detainees are at the mercy of investigators. Suspects' appeals to have their detentions reviewed by the courts are frequently suppressed, as detention officials are unwilling to forward appeals.

When the state may arbitrarily ignore laws drafted to protect individual liberty and there are no effective checks against the power of the president, the president's will dictates the meaning of all individuals' rights. This presidential prerogative, although derived from the text of the 1996 constitution, which is the supreme law of Belarus, is contrary to international norms regarding human rights and abhorrent to the rule of law.

John C. Knechtle
Russell L. Weaver

John Knechtle wishes to thank his research assistant, David Hamm, for his invaluable work.

See also Soviet System

References and further reading
American Bar Association, Central and East European Law Initiative legal assessments and reports:
1. Analysis of the Draft Constitution of the Republic of Belarus, August 28, 1992.
2. Analysis of the Draft Statute of the Bar of the Republic of Belarus, Feb. 16, 1993.
3. Analysis of the Draft Professional Code of Ethics of Lawyers for the Republic of Belarus, Feb. 21, 1996.
4. Analysis of the Draft Constitution of the Republic of Belarus with Alterations and Amendments, October 15, 1996.
5. The Judiciary of the Republic of Belarus, 1996.
"Belarus Overview, Freedom in the World." 1999. http://freedomhouse.org/survey/2000/reports/country/belarus.html.
"Belarus Overview, Nations in Transit." 1998. Freedom House. http://freedomhouse.org/nit98.
Berman, Harold. 1982. *Justice in the U.S.S.R.: An Interpretation of Soviet Law.* 2d ed. Cambridge: Harvard University Press.
"Constitution Watch." 1999. *East European Constitutional Review* 8, no. 4 (Fall).
"Constitution Watch." 2000. *East European Constitutional Review* 9, no. 1/2 (Winter/Spring).
Country Profile: Belarus, 1999–2000. London: Economist Intelligence Unit.
Reshatau, Jahuen. "Notes From the History of Belarus." www.hf.uib.no/Andre/vesti/belohist.htm (cited December 5, 2001).
United States Central Intelligence Agency. 2001. "The World Factbook—Belarus." http://www.odci.gov/cia/publications/factbook/geos/bo.html (cited December 5, 2001).
United States Department of State. 1996. *Background Notes: Belarus* (March).
———. 1999a. *Annual Report on International Religious Freedom for 1999: Belarus.* (September 9).
———. 1999b. *International Narcotics Control Strategy Report.*
———. 2001. *Belarus Country Report on Human Rights Practices for 2000* (February).
International Narcotics Control Strategy Report, U.S. Department of State, 1999.

BELGIUM

COUNTRY INFORMATION

Belgium is located in Western Europe, between France and the Netherlands. Its northern part consists of flat coastal plains bordering the North Sea. Moving southward, rolling hills appear and gradually grow into the rugged mountains of the Ardennes Forest. The total area covered by the country is 30,510 square kilometers. The capital is Brussels (population 954,460), one of the few officially bilingual cities in the world. Other major cities are Antwerpen, Gent, Liège, Charleroi, Brugge, and Namur.

The Kingdom of Belgium's population was 10,263,414 on January 1, 2001. From a territorial point of view, the majority of Belgians are either Flemings (58 percent) or Walloons (32 percent). The remaining 10 percent of the people are located in the Brussels area.

Regarding nationality, 91.27 percent of the inhabitants carry Belgian passports; the rest form a very heterogeneous group. Most immigrants come from one of the European Union member states (mainly Italy, which is the homeland of nearly 2 percent of the total Belgian population), and significant minorities descend from non-European countries (the largest group being Moroccans, who account for 1.22 percent of the total population in Belgium).

Almost two out of three Belgians are native Dutch-speakers (referred to as Flemings), and the mother tongue of about one of every three Belgians is French (these individuals are known as Walloons). Around 9 percent of the people are (legally) bilingual, and 1 percent speak German. Actually, Belgium is bisected by a linguistic border between the Germanic north and the Latin south, leading some observers to speak about the country's cultural split personality; others prefer to describe Belgium as a melting pot of different cultures. The predominant religion is Roman Catholicism, although the number of Belgians practicing their faith is declining. Belgium has a civil law system, together with a written constitution. Legal acts are judicially reviewed, and compulsory jurisdiction by the International Court of Justice is accepted, albeit with reservations.

HISTORY

Belgium derives its name from a Celtic tribe, the Belgae. Although described by Caesar as "the most courageous" of all the tribes of Gaul, the Belgae ultimately had to yield to the Roman troops. Their land became a Roman province, which flourished until Attila the Hun invaded Germany and pushed fleeing Germanic tribes into the northern region of present-day Belgium. A century later, about 400 C.E., the Germanic tribe known as the Franks took possession of Belgium. The north was Germanized, whereas people in the southern part continued to be Roman and speak derivatives of Latin. This cleavage would determine the German-Latin duality in Belgian identity forever.

The area of modern Belgium continued to exist under foreign rulership—by the dukes of Burgundy, the Haps-

N Belgium

burgs, Spain (1519–1713), Austria (1713–1794), France (1795–1815), and the Netherlands (1815–1830). With the exception of Germany's temporary occupations in both world wars, the Netherlands was the last foreign power to rule Belgium.

The Belgian state was created in 1830, following an uprising by the people that ultimately led to independence from the enlightened despotism of King Willem I of the Netherlands. A monarch was invited into the country from the House of Saxe-Coburg Gotha in Germany. By 1831, the Belgian Constitution was created. In Belgium, unlike Britain, the constitution took a written form. The Constituent Assembly was inspired by two essential principles: national sovereignty and the separation of powers. The work of those who framed the constitution was heavily influenced by the French Constitutions of 1791 and 1830 and the 1815 Constitution of the United Kingdom of the Netherlands. However, it is the way these constitutional provisions were combined that made the Belgian Constitution unique. One innovation was the establishment of a constitutional monarchy in which the king (before 2001, no women were allowed to ascend the throne) has no political responsibility.

The constitution was not the product of a united nation or a particularly free one. Even the form of government, the constitutional monarchy, was chosen more to please the great neighboring powers than out of popular desire. Nevertheless, the rule of law has been succesfully preserved ever since the state was founded. Personal liberties have been safeguarded in all but a few cases, and there have been no dictatorships or military coups. This situation can be explained by the careful constitutional guarantees for the independence of the judiciary, the relative stability of the constitution (it has changed only six times since 1831), and the people's willingness to compromise when necessary.

Belgian law is modeled on the Napoleonic Code, modified and brought up to date. In criminal law, for example, the French Penal Code of 1810 was replaced by the Belgian Penal Code of 1867. The civil tradition of Belgian law means that Belgian courts decide cases by referring to the legal principles and rules contained in the codified and statutory law. In principle, therefore, they are not bound by previous decisions of other courts ruling in similar cases.

The 1831 government declared French to be the official language of the newborn nation. A sole language was seen as the cement of Belgian society, and since the revolution was anti-Dutch and the upper classes spoke French, it was obvious that this language would become the only official language in independent Belgium. Flemish—a dialect of Dutch—was the mother tongue of the often illiterate masses in the impoverished north, who had neither political rights nor socioeconomic power. However, a gradually increasing number of Flemish intellectuals protested against the subordination and neglect of their language. This led to the birth of the Flemish movement, which achieved its first success in the early 1880s when Flemish was recognized as an official language in certain policy domains within the Flemish provinces. A landmark political victory for the Flemish movement was the passing of a law in 1898 recognizing Flemish as an official language of the kingdom, along with French. But the true rise of the Flemish people cannot be attributed to these political activities alone. Rather, it was the growing consciousness of the Flemish sociocultural and linguistic identity, supported by a general political and economic emancipation, that finally gave birth to the present-day Flemish people.

LEGAL CONCEPTS

Belgium is a hereditary constitutional monarchy. The constitution provides for basic and fundamental human rights, including free speech and press, the presumption of innocence, guarantees of private property and individual freedom, the right to gather peaceably and to enter into associations or partnerships, the confidentiality of letters, and so on. Belgian citizenship is acquired, preserved, and lost according to rules determined by civil law. Belgians are equal before the law, and enjoyment of the rights and freedoms recognized for them is to be ensured without discrimination. To this end, laws and decrees guarantee the rights and freedoms of ideological and philosophical minorities. Education is free, and the community gives parents the freedom of choice (within certain bounderies) between different kinds of education for their children. The community also provides a neutral, nonconfessional education, which implies respect for the philosophical or (non)religious conceptions of all parents and pupils. Everyone has the right to lead a life in conformity with human dignity. Consequently, the laws and decrees guarantee economic, social, and cultural rights (for example, the right to employment, social security, health care, decent accommodation, cultural and social fulfillment, and social, medical, and legal aid).

As in many other countries, the constitution provides for the separation of power between the executive, legislative, and judicial branches of government. In the Belgian context, a distinction has to be made between the federal (or national), the regional, and the local levels of power.

At the federal level, the legislative power is exerted by the monarch and the Parliament (which consists of the Chamber of Representatives and the Senate); the executive power belongs to the king or queen (as the head of state), the prime minister, and the federal government. In practice, however, the power of the monarch is very restricted. The person of the king or queen (Albert II since August 9, 1993) has immunity: The ministers are liable for the monarch before Parliament, and not a single pronouncement by the king or queen can have any consequence without being countersigned by a minister. One of the monarch's main political functions is to designate a politicial leader when forming a new federal government after an election or the resignation of the existing government. The king or queen plays a symbolic and unifying role, representing a common national Belgian identity. The central state is responsible for national defense, foreign policy, social security, and monetary and fiscal affairs.

At the regional level, a further distinction has to be made between communities and regions. The communities (Flemish-, French-, and German-speaking) have authority over cultural matters, education, use of language, and "person-related matters" such as health policies, policies related to the disabled, and the protection of youths. The regions (Flanders, Wallonia, and Brussels) deal with socioeconomic matters, such as urban planning, housing, environment, economic development, employment, energy, public works, and transportation, as well as the administrative supervision of the local authorities. The legislative power belongs to the Flemish Parliament (which handles community and regional matters), the Walloon Regional Council, the Brussels Regional Council, the Francophone Community Council, and the German-speaking Community Council. The executive power is exercised by corresponding executive bodies.

At the local level, there are 10 provinces (Antwerp; the Flemish Brabant, West Flanders, East Flanders, and Limburg; and the Walloon Brabant, Hainaut, Liège, Luxembourg, and Namur) and 589 municipalities. Although they all fall under the supervision of the regional government, they have some degree of autonomy within their competences. They also have their own legislative and executive entities.

To understand the functions of these political institutions and to explain why the (originally unitarian) Belgian Constitution became such a curious mix of federal and confederal elements, a crucial period in the constitutional history of Belgium has to be reconstructed here. Historically, nations had developed through a process of centralization, but the Belgians took a unique approach and created their federal state through a process of *de-*

centralization. In addition, the enduring conflicts between the Flemings and the Walloons gave birth to a new and complex kind of federalism: The devolution of power to representative institutions for both nationalities offered an effective way to deal with these tensions. Between 1970 and 1993, the Belgian Constitution was changed four times (in 1970, 1980, 1988, and 1993). These constitutional reforms changed Belgium into a federal structure.

As noted, the first constitutional reform dates to 1970. The Flemings wanted to have more cultural power because they were unsatisfied with the dominance of the French language and culture in Belgium. The Walloons, for their part, wanted more regional economic power. The main political problem was that the two nationalities could not agree about the exact borders of the new entities (especially as they would affect Brussels). The result was the formation of communities and regions.

To honor Flemish aspirations, communities were created. As Belgium had already opted for monolingual regions in the 1930s, the logical consequence (in 1963) was to draw a linguistic border between monolingual Flanders, monolingual Wallonia, and bilingual Brussels (except for a number of villages along the borderline and around Brussels, which became monolingual Dutch or French but obtained linguistic facilities for the minority language group). The next step (taken in 1970) was the establishment of the constitutional principle that Belgium should contain four language areas. Unfortunately, the linguistic regions could not be used as a basis for regional authority because both the Flemings and the Walloons claimed Brussels as their own. The technical problem was the constitutional obligation to secure two-thirds of the votes in the Parliament. To resolve the problem, the communities, which had no borders and corresponded to linguistic population groups (as opposed to regions), were created. With respect to its competences, the Flemish Community assumed responsibility for all the inhabitants of Flanders and also for all the schools and cultural institutions in Brussels, where Dutch was the working language. A similar legal construction was set up for the French and the German Communities. The communities were given the power to promulgate laws, which required that each have its own parliament and its own government. For the time being, these bodies were populated with people who also took part in the national government, or Parliament.

Meanwhile, as mentioned, the Walloons sought more regional economic power. Here, the trick used to resolve the Brussels problem, which was used to form the communities, could not be repeated. Economic competences could not as easily be linked to linguistic population groups as education or culture. Consequently, the introduction of regional institutions based on geographic entities became un-

avoidable. Because the Brussels problem persisted, the parties finally decided to create three (instead of two) regions: one for Flanders, one for Wallonia, and one for Brussels. The intention was written into the constitution, but the implentation was left for future governments.

In 1980, the Flanders and Wallonia Regions were made operational, but Brussels remained a problem. A provisional border between Flanders and the Brussels Region was drawn around the capital and its municipalities, and the bilingual area remained, at least temporarily, under the custody of the national government. The two other regions devolved competences regarding the environment, housing policy, regional aspects of economic policy, retraining of the unemployed, and supervision of local authorities. The regional governments were also made completely independent of the national one. Regional ministers were to be responsible to their regional assemblies, although the possibility of bringing them down was largely reduced by the introduction of the system of the constructive motion of confidence (according to which a motion can only be filed if a majority of the parliament has lost confidence and can present a candidate as a possible successor).

The communities were given the same structures as the regions, and matters of health and specific aspects of social policy were added to their competences. To finance their activities, regions and communities were allotted a fixed part of the national tax revenues, and they were granted a marginal authority to raise their own taxes. After the constitutional reform, the Flemish Community and the Flemish Region immediately decided to merge. Both governed about 6 million citizens, the sole difference being the 150,000 Flemings in Brussels over whom only the community exercised power. A similar merger did not take place on the francophone side.

In 1988, Brussels, the third region, finally became operational, with its own government and a directly elected parliament. It remained within the limits of its nineteen municipalities, and specific institutions for a bilingual entity were set up. Depending on the matter, the Brussels Parliament could split up into both a French and a Flemish community commission. The Flemish minority in Brussels could claim two of the five minsterial seats in the Brussels government, and each decision on regional matters had to be approved by a majority in both language groups of the Parliament. Also, new competences were transferred to the communities and the regions. The former were given overall responsibility for education, the latter for public works and industrial policy. The regional authorities were given a greater (but still minimal) fiscal competence, and the structures of conflict prevention were made stronger. The Court of Arbitration received the power of a constitutional court, at least in terms of three key articles in the constitution (Articles 10, 11, and

24). The system of cooperation agreements between the different levels became obligatory for several matters. In 1989, the first direct elections for the Brussels Parliament took place.

The last reform in the process of federalism occurred in 1993. The major change was the creation of directly elected parliaments for Flanders and Wallonia. As a result of this change, the number of members of Parliament (MPs) in the federal assemblies was reduced, from 212 to 150 in the Chamber of Representatives and from 184 to 71 in the Senate. The Chamber was given the exclusive competence of voting on the budgets and motions of confidence involving the federal government. The Senate saw its competences reduced, but it was to function as a moral authority on constitutional affairs. The reform contained new transfers of competences, as well. Part of the agricultural and environmental policies were transferred to the regions, and most of the supervision of local welfare institutions went to the communities. The main transfer was in the field of foreign policy: Each authority became entitled to pursue its own foreign policy, including the signing of treaties. The communities also obtained a lager part of the federal tax revenues. The number of ministers in the federal government was limited to a maximum of fifteen. The Parliament also proclaimed a completely rewritten text of the constitution.

CURRENT STRUCTURE

Belgium is divided into 27 judicial districts and 225 judicial cantons. The district courts include the Tribunals of First Instance, the Labour Tribunals, and the Tribunals of Commerce. The courts in the judicial cantons are the Justices of the Peace and the Police Courts.

The Tribunal of First Instance has jurisdiction in both civil and criminal matters. It has general jurisdiction in all civil matters and also hears appeals from decisions in civil matters addressed by the Justices of the Peace. The tribunal's rulings in civil matters are subject to appeal to the Court of Appeal. The president of the tribunal has the power to act alone in certain matters, such as the commissioning of experts to assess damages; provisional orders (especially in disputes between spouses); and injunction, attachment, and sequestration proceedings. In criminal matters, the Tribunal of First Instance has jurisdiction over all violations that are not reserved to the Police Courts or the Court of Assizes. It hears appeals from the decisions of the Police Courts. Decisions issued by the tribunal can be appealed to the Court of Appeal. Finally, a special section of the Tribunal of the First Instance has jurisdiction over juveniles.

The Labour Tribunal consists of a professional judge, assisted by two lay judges representing employers and employees. It decides matters related to individual labor disputes, accidents at work, and the application of work-

ers' compensation laws, as well as litigations with respect to social security. If one is not pleased with a decision of the Labour Tribunal, he or she can appeal to the Labour Court of Appeal.

The Tribunal of Commerce is composed of a professional judge, assisted by two lay judges, merchants. It decides on all litigation between businesspeople and on some other claims concerning acts of commerce. It also hears appeals of decisions in commercial matters originally issued by the Justices of the Peace. Bankruptcy and corporate matters are in this tribunal's purview. Appeals of its decisions are taken to the Court of Appeal.

There is one Justice of the Peace for each judicial canton. This court is composed of a single judge, assisted by a clerk, who acts in civil and commercial matters in which the value of the claim does not exceed Ä1,859.20 The judge has sole jurisdiction over a number of matters, such as leases and alimony, and also acts in family disputes. His or her decision can be appealed to the Tribunal of First Instance or the Tribunal of Commerce, if the value of the claim exceeds Ä1,239.47.

There is also one Police Court in every judicial canton. This court is presided over by one judge, assisted by a clerk, and it deals with minor offenses, such as traffic offenses. The Police Court has both a criminal branch (in which prosecutors bring offenders before the court) and a civil branch (which deals with insurance disputes). Appeal lies to the Tribunal of First Instance if the value of the matter in dispute exceeds Ä1,239, 47

Belgium's judiciary system incorporates several other types of courts, as well. Cases involving major criminal offenses (murders, homocides) as well political and press offenses are heard by the Court of Assize; there is one such court in each province. The Court of Assize is presided over by a member of the Court of Appeal, assisted by two judges from the Tribunal of First Instance. The defendant's guilt or innocence is decided by a jury of twelve laypeople.

The Court of Appeal consists of three sections: the civil section (handling civil and commercial matters), the criminal section, and the juvenile section. Belgium's five appellate courts are located in Antwerpen-Hasselt, Brussels, Gent, Luik and Bergen. The Labour Court of Appeal is presided over by a professional judge who, like the Labour Tribunal judge, is assisted by two lay judges. This court decides on appeals from the Labour Tribunal. The Court of Cassation in Brussels has the power to quash judgments that infringe on the law or misapply substantive law or procedural provisions. The Constitutional Court decides whether there is discrimination between different applications of a law. Finally, there is an administrative court, known as the Council of State, whose main judicial function consists of annulling illegal regulations issued by administrative authorities. A legislative section advises the executive and Parliament on bills, draft decrees, and regulations.

European Courts and Their Impact on Belgian Legislation and Jurisdiction

The European Community (EC) has used the rule of law to unify the nations of Europe. The Court of First Instance and the Court of Justice, created in 1989, comprise the judicial institution of the EC, and they effectively safeguard the juridical system when EC law is challanged or when it must be applied.

The Court of First Instance has jurisdiction to rule at first instance on all actions for annulment, for failure to act, and for damages brought by individuals and organizations/companies against the EC. It also rules in competition proceedings, in EC cases, and in disputes between the EC and its officials and other servants.

The Court of Justice has jurisdiction to rule on actions for failure to fulfill treaty obligations (brought by the European Commission against a member state or by one member state against another), actions for annulment (judicial review of the legality of EC acts), actions for failure to act (against the European Parliament, European Council, or European Commission), actions for damages (against EC institutions or servants), preliminary rulings on the interpretation or validity of EC law, and appeals against judgments of the Court of First Instance.

The EC law and its jurisdiction have a great impact on Belgian law, especially with regard to the free movement of persons, goods, and capital and the provision of services. A decision of the European Court of Justice forces the Belgian government and legislators to adapt their legislation or jurisdiction to that of the EC.

The European Court of Human Rights

The Convention for the Protection of Human Rights and Fundamental Freedoms was drawn up within the Council of Europe. It was signed in Rome on November 4, 1950, and entered into force in September 1953. Belgium ratified the convention in 1955. The convention set up a system to enforce the obligations entered into by contracting states. Three institutions were entrusted with this responsibility: the European Commission of Human Rights (set up in 1954); the European Court of Human Rights (set up in 1959); and the Committee of Ministers of the Council of Europe, composed of the ministers of foreign affairs of the member states (or their representatives). Under the convention, contracting states and, if the contracting states had accepted the right of individual petition, individual applicants (individuals, groups of individuals, or nongovernmental organizations) could lodge complaints against contracting states for alleged violations of convention rights.

Since the convention's entry into force, eleven proto-

Legal Structure of Belgium Courts

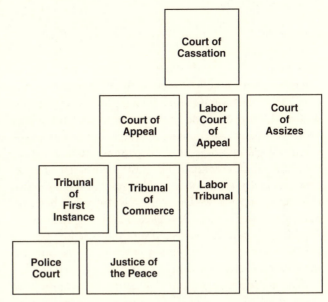

cols have been adopted. Protocols 1, 4, 6, and 7 augmented the rights and liberties guaranteed in the convention, and Protocol 2 conferred on the European Court of Human Rights the power to issue advisory opinions. Protocol 9 enabled individual applicants to bring their cases before the court, subject to ratification by the respondent state and acceptance by a screening panel. Protocol 11 restructured the enforcement machinery. The remaining protocols concerned the organization of and procedure before the convention institutions.

Any contracting state or individual may lodge a complaint alleging that a contracting state has breached one of the convention rights. The state or individual application that initiates this process is filed directly with the court in Strasbourg. Each individual application is assigned to a section, whose president designates a rapporteur. After a preliminary examination of the case, the rapporteur decides whether it should be dealt with by a three-member committee or by a chamber. All final judgments of the court are binding on the respondent states concerned.

Responsibility for supervising the execution of judgments lies with the Committee of Ministers of the Council of Europe. Thus, the committee must verify whether a state found to have violated some provision of the convention has taken adequate remedial measures to comply with the specific or general obligations arising out the court's judgments.

The court may, at the request of the Committee of Ministers, give advisory opinions on legal questions concerning the interpretation of the convention and protocols. Advisory opinions are given by the Grand Chamber and by a majority vote. Any judge may attach to the advisory opinion a separate opinion or a bare statement of dissenting opinion.

STAFFING

Advocates

There are about 40,000 law graduates in Belgium. In the past, a large number of them joined the bar or another traditional legal occupation as notary or magistrate; today, however, many law graduates enter nontraditional—whether legal or nonlegal—occupations, such as education and inhouse counsel. Have the traditional occupations reached a saturation point? Or are they less attractive to young people now? Unfortunately, there has been no research on this subject. It is likely that law graduates are unwilling to join the bar because of the very low pay attorneys receive at the beginning of their careers, but also the future earnings and employment are not predictable.

Bars are given legal status by statute in Belgium and are established in every judicial district. The Order of the Bar has statutory legal status and can intervene in any matter concerning the administration of justice and operational procedures. The general assembly of the bars is called the Council of the Order. The Head of the Bar (bâtonnier, stafhouder) is the appointed leader and representative of the order. The National Order of Advocates united until 2001 the twenty-seven local bars. But problems between the Flemish and Waloon Bars have paralyzed the workings of the order, and leaders of the Flemish and the Walloon Bars have installed their own institutes, the Order of Flemish Bars and the Order of Walloon and German Bars, recognised by statute.

After a three-year training period, a lawyer can be accepted as advocate. They have numerous privileges, such as the right to bear the title of advocate and the right to wear a toga. They also have monopoly rights (which means that they can represent people before the courts), as well as the right of audience, freedom of communication, and the right to documents. Advocates are well endowed with prerogatives, but they also must submit to rules of conduct defined in the Judicial Code and the bar regulations and usages.

A special group of sixteen advocates, known as "the Advocates at the Court of Cassation," are entitled to plead civil cases before the Court of Cassation.

Notaries

Recently, the act on notaries has been changed. Anyone who has a special notary degree can enter the profession after completing a three-year training period and passing an exam. There are only 1,221 notaries in Belgium, assisted by clerks called "candidate notaries."

Notaries are exclusively responsible for receiving and assembling formal documents and deeds that must be au-thenticated. Their duties are related to matters of all sorts, including succession, testamentary, matrimonial, and property issues, as well as the sale of land. The notaries are organized in a general assembly, headed by a syndic.

Bailiffs

There are about 580 bailiffs in Belgium, who are exclusively responsible for the service of writs and judgments of the Belgian courts and tribunals and the enforcement of those judgments against anyone who resides in Belgium. They only act at the request of an advocate, notary, judge, or public servant.

IMPACT

As everywhere in the industrialized countries, the law in Belgium is conceived as a mechanism to regulate private and public affairs. However, in the field of private and business affairs, Belgian litigation rates are significantly lower than those in the United States. The prevalence of informal and extralegal means of handling conflicts and thereby avoid excessive legal action can be attributed, in large part, to the Belgian people's willingness to compromise.

With regard to the impact of law on society and, more specifically, the use of law as an instrument for social change, it is noteworthy that legislative evaluation is a salient topic on Belgium's current political agenda. Academic and political debates now center on the question of implementing and institutionalizing a system to evaluate the nation's laws. In addition to investigating the formal qualities of the laws, such a program would incorporate the systematic study of the social adequacy of law giving in Belgium.

Francis Van Loon
Gerrit Franssen
Steven Gibens
Koen Van Aeken

See also Common Law; Constitutional Law; Constitutional Review; Federalism; Judicial Review; Napoleonic Code

References and further reading
Alen, André, ed. 1992. *Treatise on Belgian Constitutional Law.* Deventer and Boston: Kluwer.
Belgian Constitution, http//www.fed-parl.be/constitution_uk.html (cited October 10, 2000).
Boudart, Marina, Michel Boudart, and René Bryssinck, eds. 1990. *Modern Belgium.* Brussels: Modern Belgium Association.
Deprez, Kas, and Louis Vos. 1998. *Nationalism in Belgium: Shifting Identities,* 1780–1995. Basingstoke: MacMillan.
Federal Government of Belgium, http//www.fgov.be (cited October 4, 2000).
Huggett, Frank E. 1969. *Modern Belgium.* London: Pall Mall Press.
Jan, Impens, and Guy Schrans. 1972. "Belgium." In *The Legal Systems of the World: Their Comparison and Unification.* International Encyclopedia of Comparative Law. Vol. 2, Edited by R. David. Tubingen, Germany: Mohr.

Tyrrell, Alan, and Zahd Yaqub. 1993. *The Legal Professions in the New Europe.* Oxford: Blackwell.

Van Houtte, Jean, and Steven Gibens. 2000. *The Traditional Occupation of Jurists and The Non-Traditional Occupation of Jurists: In Which Jobs Do Law Graduates End Up?* Paper presented at the International Working Group of the Legal Profession, Peyresq, 2000, 23p.

BELIZE

GENERAL INFORMATION

Population and Geography

Belize, formerly British Honduras, is bordered on the east by the Caribbean Sea, on the west and south by Guatemala, and on the north by its second largest trading partner, Mexico. The United States is Belize's main trading partner. The country's population is today nearing the 250,000 mark, with population shifts over the last fifteen or so years caused mainly by emigration of Central American refugees fleeing their countries in the 1980s because of civil unrest and by the migration of Belizeans to destinations abroad, such as the United States. With this shift in the population makeup, the Hispanic sector now exceeds the Creole sector. The multiethnic populace is composed mainly of Mestizo, Creole, Garifuna, and Maya Indian people, with a smaller segment that includes East Indians, Chinese, Arabs, and Mennonites. Although there is bilingualism, English is the main language and Spanish is considered a second language. A Creole dialect is spoken in the country as well.

There are six districts in Belize: the northern half of the country is low-lying, while the southern portion is for the most part hilly. The Maya Mountains lie to the south, with Victoria Peak their highest point. Belize's climate is subtropical, and the rainy season begins in May and lasts for a few months.

Constitution and Government

Belize was colonized by the British but gained its independence from Great Britain on September 21, 1981. She holds membership in the Commonwealth, the Caribbean Community, the United Nations, and the Organization of American States, among others.

Belize has inherited the Westminster model of parliamentary democracy, and she has three main branches of government—namely, the executive, the legislature, and the judiciary. The constitutional head of state is the Queen of England, and she is represented in Belize by a Belizean governor general. Currently, the governor general is Sir Colville Young.

Elections and Political Parties

The last general election took place in 1998, and the next election is scheduled for the year 2003. These are held every five years, although they can be called, and have been called in the past, before that time by the party in power. Currently, the People's United Party (PUP) is the party in power, and its members dominate both the House of Representatives and the cabinet. The other major political party in Belize is the United Democratic Party (UDP). In 1993 the UDP, together with the National Alliance for Belizean Rights (NABR), won the general elections, and that coalition formed the government. Since independence, no one party has held power for more than one term.

HISTORY

The Maya Indians were the first people in Belize, and today descendants of that ancient civilization populate the southern districts. Also in the southern region are the Garifuna people, descendants of the Carib Indians who emanated from the eastern Caribbean islands of St. Vincent and the Grenadines.

Belize, formerly known as British Honduras, went from being a settlement where logwood and mahogany cutters were prevalent in the seventeenth century, to being a British colony in 1871, and later a sovereign country in 1981 after achieving independence in 1964.

A very important period in Belize's history was the Battle of St. George's Caye in 1798, when, on September 10 of that year, the British defeated the Spaniards and gained full control of the settlement now known as Belize. That is why Belize's National Day, celebrated and revered to this day, is September 10.

Despite the victory in 1798 and independence in 1981, Guatemala still maintains her claim to Belizean territory, allegedly pursuant to rights acquired from Spain. Belize stands steadfast in her assertion that all 8,864 square miles of her territory belong to her by virtue of the rights she acquired from Britain. Presently the two countries are seeking to resolve the dispute through negotiations and have sought the assistance of the Organization of American States.

LEGAL CONCEPTS

Belize's legal system is that of the common law, and the doctrine of separation of powers and the rule of law obtain. There is a written constitution. The court system is composed of Alcalde Courts (Mayan community courts) at the lowest level, and the Privy Council in London for constitutional appeals at the highest. Magistrates' Court decisions may be appealed to the Supreme Court, and those decisions, in turn, can be appealed to the Court of Appeals.

The attorney general is the minister in charge of the Attorney General's Ministry. Areas of responsibility for this

ministry include the Registrar General's Office, the Solicitor General's Office, the Office of the Chief Parliamentary Counsel and Law Revision, as well as the Family Court.

To assist in the improvement of Belize's judicial system, the Attorney General's Ministry has undertaken a three-year ambitious program called Delivering Justice.

One of Delivering Justice's goals is to augment the efficiency and effectiveness of legal services as a whole. To achieve that end, the program aims to implement ongoing training sessions in all areas of practice. This endeavor will not only maintain the profession on the cutting edge locally but is designed to enhance competition internationally as well.

Legal Aid Services: The Delivering Justice program seeks to enhance legal aid services, both in terms of access and effectiveness, since a lack of resources limits the reach of the program. The only cases for which such services are mandated are murder cases. Most law firms are located in Belize City rather than in the districts, and private attorney pro bono services are hortatory.

Director of Public Prosecutions: The director of public prosecutions has responsibility for all criminal prosecutions.

Ombudsman: The ombudsman is charged with investigating and exposing allegations of governmental irregularities.

The Judiciary: The judiciary is composed of the Court of Appeals, the Supreme Court, and the Magistrates' Courts. The Alcalde courts and the Family Court fall under the purview of the executive. The Privy Council in London is the final decision-making body in constitutional appeals. The duties and responsibilities of the justices of the Supreme Court and the Court of Appeals are delineated in the constitution of Belize, as amended.

CURRENT STRUCTURE

As stated earlier, separation of powers exists constitutionally, and the judiciary is one branch of government. The Belizean legal system is that of the common law. In its foremost legal authority, the constitution, the laws through which the country is governed are detailed. These encompass the rights and duties of Belizeans.

The structure of the court system shows that the Maya Alcalde courts are located in the two districts inhabited by the Mayan Indian—that is, the Stann Creek and Toledo

Districts. In addition to the Alcalde courts in those two districts, and in all districts and the capital, Belmopan, there exist Magistrates' Courts or Courts of First Instance.

The next tier in the court system is the Supreme Court, which has original jurisdiction in cases too serious for the Magistrates' Court, and appellate jurisdiction for appeals emanating from courts below. Supreme court decisions, in turn, can be appealed to the Court of Appeals. Constitutional cases may be appealed to the Privy Council in London, which, to date, is still the last resort for such types of cases.

SPECIALIZED JUDICIAL BODIES

Family Court

Areas of responsibility for the Family Court focus on children's rights and such as guardianship; custody; support; parentage; foster-care placements; adoption; and protection.

Magistrates' Court

Other than the Alcalde courts described below, the Magistrates' Court is generally the court of first instance, and it maintains jurisdiction for crimes bearing penalties of fines and six months or less imprisonment. Otherwise, the case goes to the Supreme Court for jury trial. The Supreme Court has original jurisdiction in such cases and appellate jurisdiction for appeals from below.

Alcalde Jurisdiction

The positions of Alcalde and deputy Alcalde are elected ones, and this communal system of justice applies only in the Maya societies. This type of court maintains civil and criminal jurisdiction for disputes of $25 or less, although it may, in some instances, deal with disputes totaling no more than $100.

Commissioners of the Supreme Court

These officers of the court can be granted limited judicial authority, and they can also certify Supreme Court documents.

Justices of the Peace

Justices of the peace are appointed by the attorney general, and these lay officers are granted the important powers of maintaining the peace, administering oaths, and, like magistrates, issuing certain warrants.

STAFFING

Justices of the Supreme Court

The chief justice and four puisne justices compose the Supreme Court. The constitution details the powers and tenure of these honorable individuals.

Legal Structure of Belize Courts

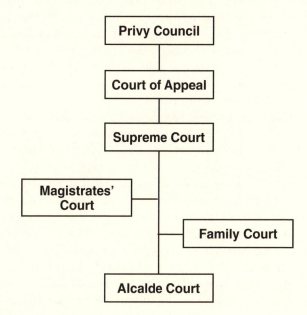

Justices of Appeal

There are three justices of appeal, and they hear matters on appeal from the Supreme Court. Like the justices of the Supreme Court, these justices of appeal derive their powers from the constitution.

Director of Public Prosecutions

There is a director of public prosecutions, together with one senior crown counsel, three crown counsel, and support staff.

Attorney General's Ministry

In this ministry, there is an attorney general, a solicitor general, senior crown counsel, and crown counsels. There is also a chief parliamentary, a law revision counsel, and a parliamentary counsel. The Family Court has two magistrates, one coordinator, and four counselors.

Magistrates' Court

In Belize City, there are five magistrates: a chief magistrate and four magistrates.

Lawyers

There are fewer than one hundred lawyers in Belize, and statistics for members of the Belize Bar Association may be sought from the Supreme Court Registry, through the Attorney General's Ministry and the Belize Bar Association itself. A listing of law firms is also available at the embassy of Belize to the United States of America in Washington, D.C., and information on practicing lawyers can be found both on-line and in hard copy from Martindale-Hubbell, and on-line from *Hieros Gamos* and others.

IMPACT

Of the thirty chief justices that Belize has had, only four—Sir Albert Staine (deceased), Sir George N. Brown, George Bawa Singh (deceased), and Manuel Sosa—have been Belizeans. The other chief justices have been recruited from Commonwealth countries. The first chief justice in Belize was Robert Temple, who was appointed in 1843. He served until 1861.

Under the able and wise guidance of the chief justices, the judiciary has evolved and progressed over the years. They have made constant and diligent efforts to continue to effectively manage an ever-increasing caseload. In keeping with the notion of ongoing evaluation and the crafting of innovative methods and solutions for the maintenance of law, order, and justice in Belize's developing and dynamic society, the Attorney General's Ministry—separation of powers notwithstanding—has undertaken an ambitious program called Delivering Justice, designed to assist with the improvement of Belize's justice system. Delivering Justice's comprehensive mandate encompasses, among others, the traditional functions of the Attorney General's Ministry, the judiciary, the legal profession, and certain aspects of the legislature.

The consolidation of the administration of justice in Belize has been furthered by the publication of certain guides, such as *Justice of the Peace Manual* and *Judge's Rules,* together with *How We Are Governed,* information for the general public on the mechanics of governance in Belize.

Furthermore, the annual Bench and Bar Summits encourage dialogue among the key players in Belize's justice system. A topic of particular significance to the legal community is the advent of a Caribbean Court of Justice. The *Amandala* newspaper reported that some bar associations in the Caribbean, including that of Belize, are against the establishment of such a court, which would replace the Privy Council as the Court of Final Appeal in certain cases. The government, however, has not to date decided that issue.

Conferences similar to the Human Rights Training Seminar for the Commonwealth Caribbean show the progressive nature and dynamism of the legal community in Belize. A shift in the thinking on capital punishment, an important topic for Belizean citizens, is evidenced by Attorney General Smith's statement at that seminar, which essentially stated that focus should no longer be on the death penalty aspect of human rights law, but rather should be on the development aspect, in its many forms—economic, social, and political.

All in all, it can be readily concluded that Belize is making positive strides in this new era of globalization to provide the utmost protection to Belizeans and non-Belizeans alike in law, order, and justice.

Georgia Brown Gillett

See also Capital Punishment; Common Law; Human Rights Law; Magistrates—Common Law Systems; Privy Council

References and further reading
Amandala. 2000. "Bar Associations, Regionally, Reject Caribbean Court of Justice." Amandala, Dec. 10. http://www.belizemall.com/amandala/.
Bar Association of Belize. *The Creation Continues—A Review of the Belize Constitution (On the Occasion of the Xth Anniversary of Independence, 1981–1991).*
Brown, Sir George N. 1996, 1997. *Address at the Opening of the Supreme Court.*
———. 2000. Interview on December 25, 2000.
CIA Factbook. "Belize." http://www.odci.gov/cia/publications/factbook/geos/bh.html.
"About Belize." http://www.belize.gov.bz/belize (cited November 30, 2001).
Fairweather, Stephen. 1992. *The Baymen of Belize.* London: Society for Promoting Christian. Knowledge.
Government of Belize. "Feature Address of the Human Rights Training Seminar for the Commonwealth Caribbean." http://www.belize.gov.bz/pressoffice/press_releases/12–09–2000–658.shtml.
Library of Congress. "Belize—A Country Study." http://lcweb2.loc.gov/frd/cs/bztoc.html.
Lumor, Fred. 1999. *Law and Order in Belize.*
Shoman, Assad. 1994. *Thirteen Chapters of a History of Belize.* Belize: Angelus Press.
Smith, Godfrey. 2000. "Facing the Challenges of the Millenium." *Reporter* 33, no. 39 (September 21): 1, 7.

BENIN

GENERAL INFORMATION

The Republic of Benin, formerly the Republic of Dahomey, is a West African country that originally gained its independence on August 1, 1960. The name change came about in November 1975, when the Marxist-Leninist regime introduced a new flag. With the restoration of democracy in 1990, the country remained Benin but returned to the flag flown in 1960.

Some 112,622 square kilometers in area, Benin is bordered on the north by the Niger River, which separates the country from the Republic of Niger; on the northwest by Burkina-Faso; on the west by Togo; on the east by Nigeria; and on the south by the Atlantic Ocean. Apart from an area of hills and low-lying mountains in the northwest, the country's terrain is mostly flat or undulating plains, stretching from the coastal region through plateaus with wooded savannah to the fertile Niger plains.

The population of Benin totaled 4,915,555 according to a general census conducted in February 1992 and is growing at an annual rate of 2.8 percent. Its current population is estimated at over 6 million.

Benin has three major cities with more than 100,000 inhabitants:

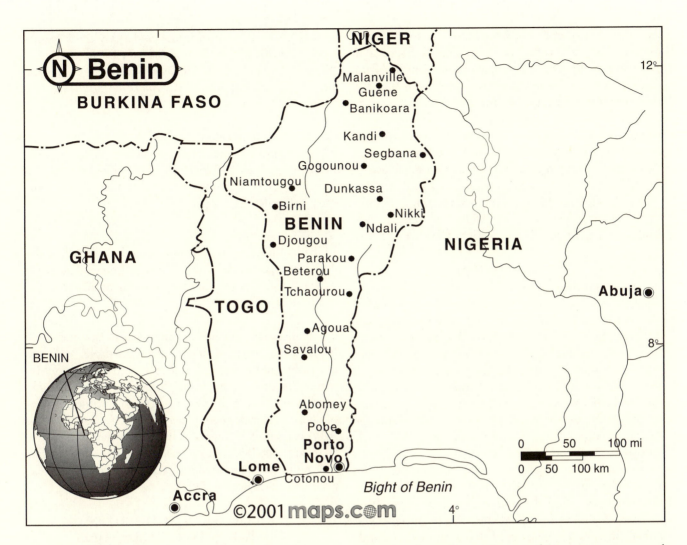

- Cotonou (the economic capital, seat of government, and largest port), with more than 750,000 inhabitants;
- Porto-Novo (the official capital and a historic city, located on the Porto-Novo Lagoon), with more than 200,000 inhabitants;
- Parakou, with more than 120,000 inhabitants.

The majority of Benin's population are young; more than half are less than twenty years of age.

A land of ancient tradition and culture, Benin is considered the birthplace of Voodoo. Both traditional and revealed religions (particularly Christianity and Islam) are embraced by the Benin people. Because of the phenomenon of religious syncretism, Catholics, Protestants, and Muslims readily take part in Voodoo rites.

Some twenty socioethnic groups each have a territorial base, creating more or less homogenous entities. From a linguistic and cultural point of view, the most significant groups are the Adja, Fon, Yoruba, Batonu, Dendi, and Bètamandibè.

This cultural and ethnic diversity extends to the Beninese judicial system, which is characterized by a dualism stemming from the coexistence of customary norms and modern principles inherited from French colonization. It is thus a hybrid system of customary law and French law, the latter based on Romano-Germanic law. Although Muslims make up nearly a quarter of the population, there is no autonomous Islamic system of law. However, certain customs are influenced to a certain extent by Islamic law.

Despite its hybrid nature, the entire Beninese judicial system is perceived to be, and functions, like the Romano-Germanic system of law.

HISTORY

As previously noted, Benin has a dual system of law, consisting of so-called modern law and customary or traditional law (these terms will be used interchangeably).

Customary law is oral, ethnic, and religious law. It is itself pluralist, the product of a multiethnic society. In existence from precolonial times, its main focus today is family and property law.

The history of modern law in Benin begins with the introduction of the civil code in the colony of Dahomey and its acceptance by the newly independent state. In effect, the colonial policy of assimilation led to the introduction of the civil code, first in the colony of Senegal in 1883 and then in the other French possessions in Africa. Colonial France did not preoccupy itself with the existence of indigenous legal systems.

The application of the civil code, initially intended to be the only law in force, was extended to the colonies, including present-day Benin, by "orders of introduction" that applied "the civil, commercial, and criminal laws of Senegal" to the other colonies. In the case of Benin, the civil code was introduced for the first time by Article 23 of the order of December 18, 1896, and subsequently confirmed by Article 17 of the order of August 6, 1901.

LEGAL CONCEPTS

It may be said that Benin's legal system today is basically liberal. Its long experiment with Marxism-Leninism (1974–1989) failed to shake its legal foundations or undermine the acceptance of the French colonial model of Romano-Germanic law. This system, rooted in Judeo-Christian values of individualism, private property, and fundamental human rights, is embodied in the Declaration of the Rights of Man and Citizen of 1789, the Universal Declaration of Human Rights of 1948, and the African Charter of Human and Peoples' Rights of 1981, ratified by Benin on January 20, 1986.

Moreover, with the restoration of democracy in 1990, Benin adopted a constitution on December 11, 1990, that forcefully affirmed the ideal of a state governed by the rule of law in which fundamental human rights and public liberties are guaranteed and protected. Accordingly, private property, the role of the judiciary, basic human rights, and the presumption of innocence are constitutionally recognized and guaranteed by law.

Private Property

Private property receives constitutional protection. The right to own property, one of the pillars of liberal society, is inviolable, and every individual has the right to own property (Article 22 of the constitution). Naturally, the government may expropriate property in the public interest. Expropriation deemed to be in the public interest must adhere to a strictly regulated administrative and judicial procedure, violation of which invalidates the expropriation. (See, for example, *A. Codjo Dado v. Etat Béninois,* Administrative Chamber of the Supreme Court, April 15, 1999, published in the Supreme Court *Reporter,* 1999, p. 234; and *Allagbe Sossou v. Maire de Sê,* Administrative Chamber of the Supreme Court, May 20, 1999, ibid., p. 379.)

The Role of the Judiciary

The role of the judiciary is governed by the principle of the separation of the political and judiciary powers. The principle of independence of the judiciary is ordained by

Article 25 of the constitution, and the Constitutional Court upheld the principle on May 7, 1997. (See DCC 97-024 of May 7, 1997, *Bulletin de Droit et d'Information de la Cour Suprême* (*Supreme Court Bulletin*) No. OO2, 1997, p. 57.)

Equality of Citizens before the Law

The principle of equal treatment before public authorities is recognized in Article 26 of the constitution. Numerous judicial decisions have sanctioned the government for violating this principle.

Individual Liberties

Individual liberties are guaranteed and protected by the judiciary, particularly the Constitutional Court, to which any citizen may have recourse by means of a simple request.

The Presumption of Innocence and Right to Defense

It may seem unremarkable to affirm principles so inherent as the presumption of innocence and the right to defense. Yet these basic principles were so abused only decades ago that their revival by the constitution of December 11, 1990, merits mention. Protection of these rights is ensured by laws and by the judiciary.

In sum, the Beninese judicial system draws on the liberal tradition, the product of its colonial past, and its experience as a sovereign state.

RESOLUTION OF DISPUTES (CURRENT LEGAL STRUCTURE)

As in all societies, conflicts of all types arise in a variety of domains (property, work, obligations, family, and so forth). The means of resolving these conflicts are equally varied. Alongside the judicial forums are alternative methods of dispute resolution, such as conciliation, mediation, and arbitration. Conflicts are still settled by traditional chieftains under "the council tree" (*l'arbre à palabre*), but the extent of this practice is difficult to assess in light of its informal structure.

Recourse (or right of recourse) to state tribunals and courts is the officially accepted means to redress citizens' grievances. The government renders justice through courts and tribunals whose organization is defined by the constitution and special statutes. There are three types of jurisdictions: courts and tribunals of ordinary jurisdiction, the High Court of Justice, and the Constitutional Court.

COURTS AND TRIBUNALS OF ORDINARY JURISDICTION

This section will review the fundamental principles governing their organization, as well as the various courts and tribunals of ordinary jurisdiction themselves. This

Legal Structure of Benin Courts

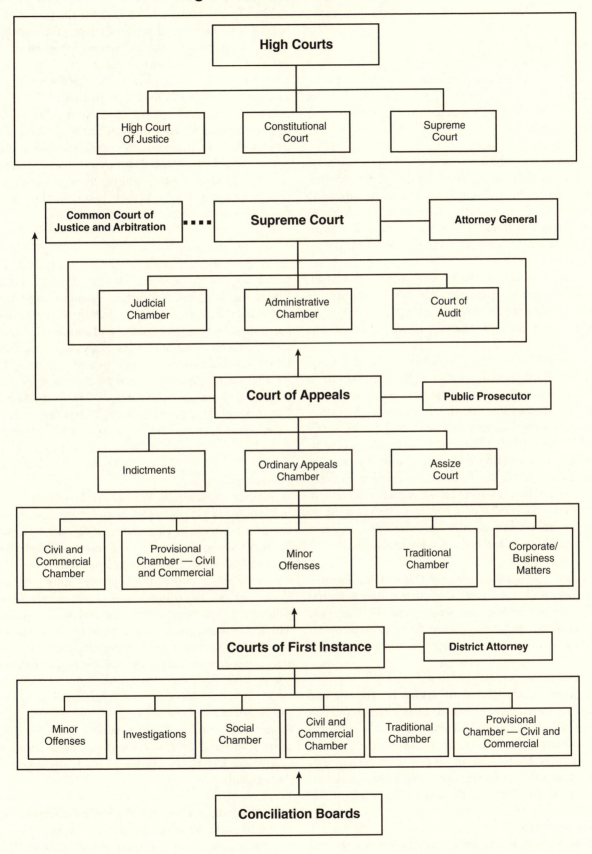

term will be used to mean all courts of law other than the High Court of Justice and the Constitutional Court.

General Principles

The organization of ordinary courts and tribunals is guided by two basic principles: exclusive jurisdiction and the right of appeal. However, the right of appeal does not apply to matters heard by the chambre de compte.

Exclusive Jurisdiction

This concept is twofold. First, it signifies the elimination of dual jurisdiction arising from the distinction between persons subject to traditional law and those subject to modern law. The ordinary court or tribunal before which a matter is brought now has jurisdiction regardless of the subject matter or personal status of the parties involved.

Secondly, it indicates the absence of independent administrative courts. There is only one administrative chamber, within the Supreme Court, which serves as the court of first instance whose decisions are not appealable.

Right of Appeal

The right of appeal is the parties' right to a trial on the merits of their case (that is, both facts and law) by two successive jurisdictions, the second considered hierarchically superior to the court that renders the initial decision. This principle is illustrated by the opportunity afforded litigants to bring their case before the court of appeal if they are not satisfied with the decision rendered by the court of first instance. However, the availability of appeal to the Supreme Court does not imply a third jurisdiction in the same sense, because the Supreme Court decides questions of law but not questions of fact.

The Various Courts and Tribunals of Ordinary Jurisdiction

These include the ordinary courts that render decisions on the merits, the Supreme Court, and the Common Court of Justice and Arbitration of the Organization for the Harmonization of Business Law in Africa (OHADA).

The Ordinary Courts

These courts decide all disputes arising between natural persons or legal entities under civil law (traditional or modern civil law), commercial or corporate law, as well as all violations of criminal law other than those specifically reserved to the High Court of Justice. In ascending hierarchical order, they constitute the conciliation boards, the courts of first instance, and the court of appeal.

Conciliation Boards

Conciliation boards are distributed throughout the national territory. They are competent to decide all matters, except as provided by law—one notable exception being individual labor disputes. Their decisions consist of the record of conciliation proceedings (or the record of failure of conciliation, depending upon the outcome). When efforts at conciliation fail, a copy of the record, certified by the president of the board, is transmitted with the case file to the court of first instance, which immediately assumes jurisdiction over the case. When conciliation is successful, the record is submitted to the court of first instance for confirmation. If the decision is confirmed, the conciliation record acquires the force and effect of a final judgment. Thereafter, the only means by which to challenge the decision is through an appeal *en cassation* (appeal to the highest court, in this case the Supreme Court, limited to questions of law).

Courts of First Instance

Since 1964, Benin has had only eight courts of first instance, located in Cotonou, Ouidah, Abomey, Lokossa, Kandi, Parakou, and Natitingou. A single judge decides the cases before these courts, and their jurisdiction is based on subject matter. In civil and commercial matters, their decisions in actions in personam and actions to recover movable property up to a certain value (60,000 CFA francs in principal or 10,000 CFA francs per annum in revenues) are not appealable, except to the Supreme Court, where the appeal is limited to points of law. In other types of actions, their decision may be appealed (on factual or legal grounds) to the court of appeal.

Court of Appeal

A single court of appeal, having jurisdiction over the entire country, is located in Cotonou. It hears cases brought before it by litigants who consider themselves wronged by the decisions rendered by the courts of first instance. Its findings of fact are final, and its conclusions of law may be appealed only to the Supreme Court.

In addition, the court of appeal includes two special panels: the indictments chamber and the assize court. The indictments chamber conducts a second investigation, following that of the investigating judge. The assize court tries serious violations that are legally defined as crimes.

The Supreme Court

As its name implies, the Supreme Court is the highest court in the land, against whose decisions no appeal may lie (Article 131 of the constitution). It is composed of three chambers:

1. The Judicial Chamber, the highest court of law
2. The administrative chamber, the highest administrative tribunal, and
3. The *Chambre des Comptes* (Court of Audit), which serves as the country's auditor-general

Its organization, powers, and functions are prescribed by the constitution and by order No. 21/PR of April 26, 1966.

The Judicial Chamber. This chamber hears appeals in cassation from decisions of the court of appeal and both final and appealable decisions of the courts of first instance. However, appeals involving disputes as to the enforcement and interpretation of the Uniform Acts of the OHADA are heard by the Common Court of Justice and Arbitration of the OHADA. An appeal must be brought within five months for civil, commercial, and corporate matters, and within three calendar days for criminal matters. In principle the filing of an appeal does not suspend enforcement of the decision, except in matters involving civil status, title to real property, crimes, and authenticity of documents.

When the judicial chamber sets aside a decision of the court of appeal, the case is remanded to the court with instructions. The court of appeal, constituted as a different panel, must render a new decision in accordance with the instructions of the judicial chamber.

Finally, in certain cases provided by the law, the Supreme Court convenes as the full panel of the court. The full panel is composed of all the judges of the High Court and is presided over by the first president of the Supreme Court. Its decisions carry special weight, since the full panel is convened when a case presents a question of principle or its resolution is likely to result in conflicting rulings.

The Administrative Chamber. As stated above, this chamber of the Supreme Court serves as a court of first instance whose decisions are not appealable. The administrative chamber is the court of ordinary jurisdiction for administrative disputes. Such disputes, defined by Article 31 of the law concerning the organization of the judiciary, comprise:

- Appeals to set aside decisions of administrative authorities on grounds of abuse of power
- Appeals involving the interpretation or findings as to the legality of acts by those same authorities, upon referral of the judicial authority if the petitioner raises a threshold issue
- Litigation involving public entities
- Individual claims for damage caused by the personal actions of contractors, licensees, or agents of the government
- Tax litigation
- Challenges to municipal election results

However, actions for damages remain under the jurisdiction of the judicial chamber.

Any citizen who considers himself wronged by the government may bring action before the administrative chamber. On an exceptional basis, representation by an attorney is not required in cases involving abuse of power.

The Chambre des Comptes (Court of Audit). This chamber of the Supreme Court oversees the proper use of public resources. It also receives the declarations of property and assets submitted by the president of the republic and of members of government upon assuming and leaving public office. In addition, it audits the accounts of election campaigns in national and local elections.

The Office of Documentation and Research. To support its mission of rendering justice, the Supreme Court is provided with a specialized technical department under the direct authority of its first president, the Office of Documentation and Research. Headed by university professors, magistrates, and senior civil servants, it provides support to all three chambers of the court. Specifically, the department:

- assists the court's decision-making; it is responsible for referring cases to the various chambers according to the nature of the case
- with the help of data records alerts the court to potential conflicting decisions through research memoranda
- combines cases of a similar nature, identifies fundamental questions, and prepares documentation as required for designated counsel

Since 1997, the Office of Documentation and Research has systematically published all judgments rendered by the Supreme Court, as well as a bulletin of doctrine, case law, and legislation entitled *Bulletin de Droit et d'Information.*

The Common Court of Justice and Arbitration (CCJA)

The CCJA, located in Abidjan, Côte d'Ivoire, was created by the October 17, 1993, Treaty of Port Louis, which established the OHADA.

The CCJA provides uniform interpretation and enforcement of the OHADA treaty, its implementing regulations, and the Uniform Acts within the state parties. The courts of each state party decide cases and appeals regarding enforcement of the uniform acts. However, jurisdiction over the imposition of criminal sanctions provided under the Uniform Acts is reserved to the state parties by the Port Louis treaty, which dared not relinquish that remnant of sovereignty.

Cases are brought before the CCJA by means of an appeal *en cassation* (supreme appeal procedure). The CCJA is also empowered to transfer cases to itself and render a decision on the merits. It also administers arbitration within the OHADA area.

The Constitutional Court and the High Court of Justice

These two jurisdictions occupy a special position within the Beninese judiciary.

The Constitutional Court

This is Benin's highest court in constitutional matters. It rules on the constitutionality of laws and protects fundamental human rights and civil liberties. It also regulates the institutions of the republic and the activities of the public authorities.

In addition, the Constitutional Court reviews the legality of presidential elections and hears cases brought concerning legislative elections. Its decisions are not subject to appeal and are binding on public authorities and on all civil, military, and judicial authorities (Article 124, paragraphs 3–4).

The High Court of Justice (High Political Court)

This is a court of special jurisdiction that was created by the Beninese Constitution of December 11, 1990. Its jurisdiction is limited to cases brought against the president of the republic and the members of government for actions defined as high treason and violations of the criminal code committed in the exercise or in the course of exercising their duties. In cases involving high treason, it also tries accomplices.

Problems in Enforcing the Law

In any state governed by the rule of law, it is essential that appropriate mechanisms exist to sanction illegal acts and redress harm. These mechanisms should be readily accessible to citizens. In Benin the legal and judicial security that exist under the rule of law have yet to be fully realized. This section will review certain problematic aspects of law enforcement in the Republic of Benin, such as the judiciary charter, legislation, independence of the judiciary, delays in deciding cases, and respect of fundamental human rights.

The Judicial Structure of Benin

The judicial structure established by the law of December 9, 1964, concerning the judiciary has not been extended to date, despite increasing demographic changes and various institutional, economic, and political changes. The judicial apparatus must be decentralized in order to bring justice to the citizens.

The State of Legislation in Benin

Despite the intensive legislative activity that accompanied the advent of democracy, many fundamental laws in effect today date back to the colonial period or find their roots in the early years of independence. Among them are the civil code (from 1804, applicable in its 1958 version), the criminal code (1877), the code of criminal procedure (1967), and the law on real property (1965). These laws are outdated and in need of reform. Some effort has been made in this direction in the last ten years, and a half-dozen draft laws have been transmitted to the National Assembly for adoption.

Independence and Impartiality of the Judiciary

It is acknowledged today that citizens are increasingly skeptical of the justice rendered by courts and tribunals. This crisis in confidence has resulted in a search for extrajudicial solutions (alternative modes of settling conflicts). At times, populations deprived of justice find an outlet in public outcry.

Delay in Deciding Cases

Benin suffers from a quantitative and qualitative shortage of judicial personnel. The findings of the 1996 Etats Généraux de la Justice (General Assembly of the Judiciary) in Cotonou aptly describes the situation: for a population estimated then at 5 million people, Benin had a ratio of one magistrate per twenty-eight thousand people. Little has changed since; the courts are inundated with case files, and personnel are overburdened. Justice is seldom rendered within a reasonable time, and in certain respects, this is tantamount to a denial of justice.

Respect for Fundamental Human Rights

The constitution guarantees the sacred rights of defense and due process. This principle is respected for the most part by the courts and tribunals. However, the number of persons languishing in prisons awaiting trial as a result of the provisional detention system instituted by the code of criminal procedure is disturbing in the eyes of many observers. In recent years, many voices have been raised in favor of reforming the criminal and prison systems to introduce alternatives to imprisonment (community service work, for example).

JUDICIAL PERSONNEL

Judicial personnel include magistrates (or judges), lawyers, *notaires, huissiers* (officials who combine the roles of bailiff and process server), bailiffs, and clerks, to name but a few.

Magistrates (Judges)

The power to decide litigation in Benin belongs to professional magistrates who serve as judges.

In general, admission to the ranks of the judiciary is open to those who have studied at the Ecole Nationale d'Administration (ENA) or any other educational institution and majored in judicial studies, or who hold a master's degree in law or an equivalent degree (level I of the ENA judicial studies major). Clerks holding a master's in law and having ten years' professional experience may also become judges. The same applies to police commissioners.

Judges are civil servants appointed by the president of the republic upon recommendation by the minister of justice or the president of the Supreme Court (for Supreme Court judges), after receiving the favorable opinion of the Conseil Supérieur de la Magistrature (Supreme Council of Magistrates).

There is currently an Ecole Régionale Supérieure du Magistrature in Benin, created under the auspices of the OHADA, which has been providing ongoing and professional training for judges for the past several years.

Lawyers

Lawyers are officers of the court, registered with the bar, who serve as counsel in legal or litigation matters, assist or represent those who so request, and argue or plead in court.

In order to be a lawyer in Benin, one must hold a master's degree in law and a certificate of aptitude for the legal profession (Certificat d'Aptitude à la Profession d'Avocat). Candidates must then be admitted, by decision of the bar association, to a two-year internship to prepare for the practice of law. Admission to the internship entitles the candidate to be sworn in as a lawyer. Certain categories of individuals, such as magistrates who have practiced for five years and certain senior-level professors, are exempt from the requirement of a certificate of aptitude.

On August 28, 2000, the Centre International de Formation en Afrique des Avocats Francophones (CIFAF) (International Center for the Training of French-Speaking Lawyers in Africa) was created in Cotonou to provide professional training.

There is one bar association in Benin, established near the court of appeal in Cotonou. Lawyers who belong to this bar may appear before any court in the country.

Clerks

Clerks are officers of the court responsible for assisting judges at hearings held by courts, tribunals, and investigating courts, and in all proceedings aimed at regulating lawsuits. They are public officials having the status of permanent government agents, and play an essential role in judicial administration.

There is no specialized institution that trains clerks, but seminars are arranged for them in the context of continuing education.

Huissiers and *Notaires*

The positions of *huissier* and *notaire* (solicitor) are professional occupations. They are ministerial, public officers whose services are indispensable to the proper administration of justice. The *huissier* is responsible, inter alia, for judicial and extrajudicial service of documents and the enforcement of judgments, decisions, and notarial acts.

The primary role of the *notaire* is to authenticate documents and provide expert counsel in all areas in which individuals typically require legal documents, such as contracts, wills, real estate transactions, and taxes.

There is no specialized school for the training of *notaires* in Benin. Candidates are admitted to the profession after taking a professional examination jointly arranged by the corporation concerned and the court of appeal.

SPECIALIZED JUDICIAL BODIES

Benin has undergone a turbulent political history since its independence in 1960. With the advent of pluralist democracy in 1990, the country broke new ground by incorporating the African Charter of Human and Peoples' Rights—whose provisions have greater force and effect than national laws—into its constitution. Thereafter, a number of institutions were established with the objective of defending human rights and informing citizens of their rights and duties. Among them are:

Institut des Droits de l'Homme et de Promotion de la Démocratie (IDH) (Institute for Human Rights and Promotion of Democracy)

Created in 1993, the IDH works under the auspices of UNESCO for the protection and the popularization of human rights.

As is often demonstrated today, war and insecurity are born in the hearts and minds of men, and so the IDH has decided to act at the root, on men, to eradicate these scourges. It has organized a three-year program of courses intended for the literate sectors of the population, as well as occasional campaigns to raise awareness and inform the illiterate and rural population.

Ligne pour la Défense des Droits de l'Homme (LDH) (League for the Defense of Human Rights)

The LDH was created on May 20, 1990, following the Association des Anciens Détenus Politiques et Victimes de la Répression (ASSANDEP) (Association of Former Political Detainees and Victims of Repression). It is a broad-based organization welcoming any person wishing to defend these rights, without regard to race, social origin, or philosophical opinions. It is affiliated with the International Federation of Human Rights and is the Beninese arm of the International Observatory of Prisons.

ASSANDEP is involved in a wide range of activities, such as providing legal assistance to victims of human rights violations, providing moral and material support to detainees, combating torture, defending the reputations of persons shot or killed other than by torture, settling conflicts through its intervention and good offices, and serving as election observer.

IMPACT OF THE LEGAL AND JUDICIAL SYSTEM

With democracy has come a resurgence of interest in legal affairs, no doubt resulting from the expressed wish of citizens and authorities that Benin be a nation governed by the rule of law. Political figures and prominent members of society are concerned with issues of constitutional legality. Numerous conflicts have been resolved by the Supreme Court, and the parties—despite recriminations—bow before the High Court's decisions. While confidence in the rule of law has been shaken at times by the difficulties that courts face in rendering justice, it persists in the expectation of judicial reform and legislative changes. Of course, access to modern law and justice on the part of disadvantaged and rural sectors remains an area of great concern, given the continued high level of illiteracy.

Noel Gbaguidi

With the collaboration of William Kodjoh-Kpakpassou, L.L.M., and Theodore H. Zinflou, esq.

See also African Court/Commission on Human and Peoples' Rights; Civil Law; Magistrates—Civil Law Systems; Notaries

References and further reading
Beynel, Jean. 1973. *L'organisation judiciaire du Dahomey.* Penant.
Conac, G. 1981. *Dynamique et finalités des droits africains.* Paris: Economica.
Cornevin, R. 1981. *La République Populaire du Bénin: Des origines à nos jours.* Paris.
Darbon, Dominique, and Jena du Bois de Gaudusson, eds. 1997. *La création du droit en Afrique.* Paris: Karthala.
Egharevba, Jacob U. 1949. *Benin Law and Custom.* 3rd ed. Benin City: J.U. Egharevba.
Gbago, Barnabé Georges. 2001. *Le Bénin et les droits de l'homme.* Paris: Harmattan.
Gbaguidi, A. N. 1997a. "Principes fondamentaux d'identification du droit positif béninois." *Bulletin de Droit et d'Information de la Cour Supreme* 1.
———. 1997b. "Quelques aspects de l'application du droit en république du Bénin." *Bulletin de Droit et d'Information de la Cour Supreme* 2.
———. 1999. "Les conflits de compétence nés de la présence d'actes administratifs dans les contestations de droit de propriété foncière entre particuliers: Reflexions à propos de l'arrêt du 6 mars 1998 de l'Assemblée Plénière sur deux arrêts contradictoires de la chambre judiciare de la Cour Suprême du Bénin." *Law in Africa* 2.
Mensah, Nathanaël G. 1982. *Evolution politique et constitutionnelle de la République populaire du Bénin: l'Ère de la politique nouvelle d'indépendance nationale.* Cotonou, République populaire du Bénin: Centre de formation administrative et de perfectionnement.
Palau-Marti, M. 1965. *Problemes juridiques du Dahomey moderne: In études de droit africain et malgache.* Paris: Cujas.
l'Union Interafricaine des Droits de l'Homme. 1996. *Les droits de l'homme en Afrique: Historique, réalités et perspectives.* Burkina Faso: l'Union Interafricaine des Droits de l'Homme.

BHUTAN

COUNTRY INFORMATION

Bhutan is located in the Himalaya Mountains between China (Tibet) in the north and India in the west, south, and east. The land area is approximately 46,500 square kilometers, or half the size of Indiana. The terrain is characterized by hills that begin from a narrow strip of plains almost at sea level and grow into the high Himalayas, which rise to an altitude of over 21,000 feet and are cut by deep, generally north-south, river valleys. The country has forest cover of 72 percent, and the Bhutanese government has a policy to maintain at least 60 percent of the total area under forest cover for all time. Bhutan is known to contain a wide range of flora and fauna, including more than 5,000 species of plants, 700 species of birds, and 165 species of mammals.

The majority of Bhutan's population, officially estimated at 658,000, are dependent on agriculture and livestock raising and live in widely scattered villages and farms. Only 7.7 percent of the country's land is under cultivation. Urbanization is increasing rapidly, however, and approximately 21 percent of the people live in the towns. Thimphu, the capital, and Phuentsholing, a town on the border with India, together have 40 percent of this urban population. Based on 1999 statistics, the average per capita income is estimated to be $551 in absolute terms and $1,534 in purchasing power parity.

Bhutan's economically most important natural resources are its forests and its hydroelectric potential. For the sake of environmental preservation, exploitation of forests is strictly controlled, and hydroelectric projects that would damage the environment are not permitted. So far, only about 2 percent of the country's estimated 20,000 megawatt capacity has been tapped in several hydroelectric dams. Most of the electricity is sold to India. Between 1998 and 1999, 48 percent of the total national revenue came from the electricity sector. There are plans to develop natural resource–based processing industries that can take advantage of the country's electricity production. Other exports include cement, calcium carbide, apples, canned fruit, jam, and mushrooms.

Since Bhutan's king decided to end the country's isolation and embark on a program of planned development, impressive gains have been made in education and health. In 1958, the education system consisted of 11 Western-style primary schools with 440 students, as well as a monastic or religious system that had been relied on for centuries. By 1999, the total number of Western-style schools increased to 343, and the number of students was 107,792. English has been the language of instruction in the schools at all levels since the 1960s.

Bhutan's health care system provides free medical treatment to all citizens through a network of clinics

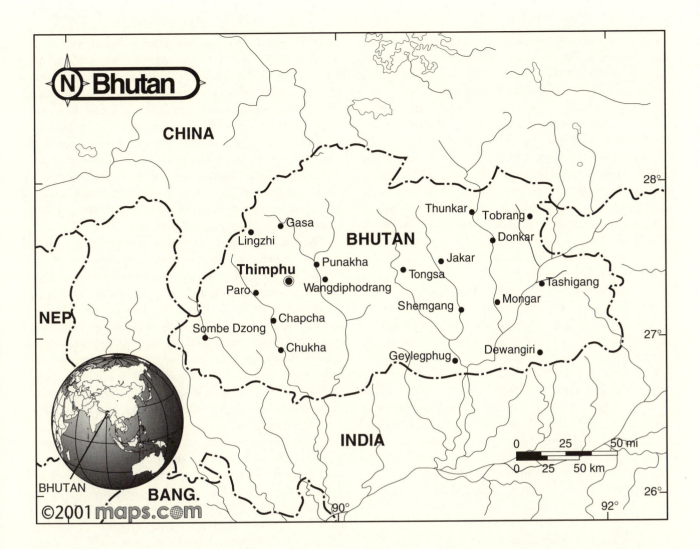

across the country along with a village health worker program. Difficult medical cases are referred to district hospitals, and special cases are sent to hospitals in India. There also is a network of indigenous medicine and traditional healers.

HISTORY

The founder of Bhutan was the Zhabdrung Ngawang Namgyal, a Tibetan incarnate lama (*rinpoche*) of the Drukpa sect who formed a state in 1616 from a collection of principalities in Bhutan's valleys. From 1616 to 1907, the system he established was a theocracy with a dual system of authority under the Zhabdrung, a position that was filled by identifying the person believed to be the reincarnation of the deceased Zhabdrung. The Zhabdrung selected two lamas to administer the country, the Je Khenpo, who was the head of the Central Monastic Body, and the Druk Desi, who was chiefly responsible for temporal affairs. Eventually, the position of Druk Desi was filled by laymen, but the primary function of the state remained the support of the religious establishment. The country's government was centered around fortresses

called *dzongs,* which were shared by the monastic and temporal administrations. On December 17, 1907, an assembly of the princes (*penlops*) of the four provinces and other leading persons of Bhutan recognized Ugyen Wangchuck, the Trongsa Penlop, as hereditary king. Since 1907, Bhutan has had four kings of the Wangchuck line.

Zhabdrung Ngawang Namgyal promulgated laws that were codified in 1652. The Code of Zhabdrung was based on the fundamental teachings of Buddhism and addressed the violation of spiritual and worldly laws alike. The code exhorted observance of the ten pious acts (*lhachoe gyewa chu*) and devotion to the sixteen virtuous acts of social piety (*michoe tsangma chudrug*). These acts range from "not taking life" to "not engaging in worthless chatter." This same legal code was amended in the mid-eighteenth century, again after 1907 under the first and second kings, and, in a substantial way, by the National Assembly (Tshogdu) in 1957. It is still in effect as the Supreme Law of Bhutan (*thrimzhung Chhenmo*). Bhutan only began to end its isolation from most of the world at the beginning of the 1960s. Because of religious and cultural similarities and well-established trade, Bhutan had been more oriented toward its northern neighbor Tibet than toward India. However, as a result of the Tibetan uprising against the Chinese in 1959 and the Sino-Indian border war in 1962, Bhutan's border with China (Tibet) was closed. Bhutan then began to reorient itself by increasing contacts and trade with India and the rest of the world. Nevertheless, it was only in 1961, under the First Five-Year Development Plan, that construction of the first road in Bhutan—the east-west national highway—was begun, with UN assistance. After that, Bhutan became a member of the most important regional and international organizations, including the Colombo Plan in 1962, the United Nations in 1971, the International Monetary Fund in 1981, and the Asian Development Bank in 1982.

Despite Bhutan's previous orientation toward Tibet, the country's relations with India have always been important. Until India gained independence from Britain in 1947, Bhutan's rulers were careful to avoid giving the British government in India any excuse to seek to incorporate Bhutan in British India. In 1865, the Indian and Bhutanese governments signed a treaty under which Bhutan ceded certain territory to India in exchange for an annual payment. Revised treaties signed in 1910 and 1949 provided, among other things, for such payments and other assistance to continue, and they affirmed India's right to advise Bhutan on foreign affairs. A trade and commerce treaty was signed by India and Bhutan in 1972.

LEGAL CONCEPTS

Law in Bhutan is symbolized by a knot and a yoke. Spiritual laws are said to resemble a silken knot (*dargye duephue*) that is easy and light at first but gradually becomes tight; worldly laws are compared to a golden yoke (*sergyi nyashing*) that grows heavier with the degree of the crime. The combination is expressed by the intertwining of the two. The symbol of this combination appears, among other places, in the seal at the center of the wall of the High Court (Thrimkhang Gongma) chamber, behind the panel of judges.

Gross national happiness (GNH), rather than gross national product, is the key measure of development success in Bhutan. This point of view pervades official political and legal discourse in the country. The core of the concept is that there must be an equilibrium of economic and noneconomic factors in order to achieve the goal of development that is the purification of the human character. The concept was proposed by the current king and has been the subject of a conference and other discussions in the UN system, particularly in an effort to compare the concept to the UN's Human Development Index.

The Supreme Law of Bhutan was intended to cover the field of law comprehensively, including both civil and criminal provisions and encompassing both substantive

and procedural matters. Subsequent legislative enactments can be viewed as amendments to the Supreme Law. In the area of civil law, provisions in the basic areas of contracts and damages are limited to a few essentials. The parties' broad freedom to formulate their own contracts is recognized, and provisions in the Supreme Law of Bhutan and other laws permit suits for certain kinds of tort damages. In settlement of disputes outside of court, including marital disputes, customary law relevant to the ethnic group or religion of the parties sometimes is used, and these customary laws provide for various types of compensatory and liquidated damages.

The Supreme Law of Bhutan and other laws, such as the Police Act, contain provisions requiring respect for the rights of citizens and other persons in Bhutan, but they also limit those rights. The right of assembly exists, for example, but can be limited by the Council of Ministers in case of necessity. Similarly, an arrest ordinarily requires a warrant from a court, but this requirement is subject to a list of fourteen exceptions. Searches also require a court-issued warrant except in specified circumstances, and in case of such an exception, the search must be conducted in the presence of two respectable and disinterested witnesses.

An arrested person must be brought before a court within 24 hours of arrest, excluding travel time (which may amount to days in some remote areas), and may be detained for up to 49 days during investigation of a crime (or 108 days for a heinous crime). Arrested individuals have the right to assistance for their defense, especially by *jabmis,* who are persons knowledgeable in the law and possibly eloquent speakers. When a suspect is going to be interrogated, he or she should be informed of his or her right to consult a jabmi before any such interrogation occurs. Currently, there are no fully trained lawyers working as defense attorneys. Capital punishment, except for treason, was eliminated in 1965.

The independence of the judiciary from the executive and the legislature is a key concept in the Bhutanese legal system. Its roots can be found in the Code of Zhabdrung, which assigned the responsibility of adjudication to law lords (*drangpoen*) separate from the Druk Desi who administered the country and the district heads (*dzongdas*) who administered districts both before and after the monarchy was established. Nevertheless, the king and his court continued to have a role in mediating or adjudicating cases until the 1950s. The National Assembly confirmed the independence of the judiciary in its early resolutions and in the Supreme Law of Bhutan. The judiciary continued to be dependent on the Royal Civil Service Commission, however, for the transfer of officials to be appointed to judicial office and for the budget of the court system. Beginning in 1990, a separate career path was established for judges and other officials of the courts. The Civil and Criminal Procedure Act now provides for the complete independence of the courts from the rest of the Bhutanese government, except in regard to approval of the budget.

The king and the Bhutanese government have begun to promote the development of a private sector, and they recognize the need to promulgate an appropriate legal framework for private business activity. These moves will be required, in part, by the commitments Bhutan must make to join the World Trade Organization (WTO), which it expects to do in 2002. Much of the necessary legal framework for the private sector can be found among the almost 100 laws approved by the National Assembly since development planning began in the early 1960s, including laws such as the Commercial Sale of Goods Act (which closely follows Article 2 of the U.S. Uniform Commercial Code), the Financial Institutions Act, the Income Tax Act, the Copyright Act, and the Industrial Property Act.

Despite the rapid rate of legal development, gaps in the private sector legal framework remain. For example, there is as yet no legal provision for direct foreign investment. The existing foreign investments—such as the foreign share of the Bhutan National Bank (20 percent Citibank, 20 percent Asian Development Bank)—have been approved by the relevant ministers on an ad hoc basis.

Bhutan has acceded to or ratified the four Geneva Conventions of August 12, 1949, for the protection of war victims, including the convention related to the protection of civilians in a time of war. The country has also ratified the Terrorism Convention of the SAARC, the Convention on Elimination of Discrimination toward Women, the Convention on the Rights of the Child, the Convention on Bio-Diversity, and the UN Framework Convention on Climate Change.

CURRENT STRUCTURE

The king (*Druk Gyalpo*) is at the apex of the Bhutanese state. He is the supreme authority in all matters of law and justice. Although the current king and his predecessor have devolved some of the monarch's power onto the National Assembly, the Council of Ministers, the judiciary, and local development bodies, the king ultimately has the final word in legal matters, if he wants it. The king, in fact, is formally above the law, as the Supreme Law of Bhutan indicates that it applies to all equally except for the king, to whom it does not apply.

The Royal Advisory Council (Lodey Tsogdey) was created in 1965 and consists of representatives of the Council of Ministers, the Monk Body, and the people. The council advises the king on legal cases appealed to him and on matters before the Council of Ministers and the National Assembly.

Legal Structure of Bhutanese Courts

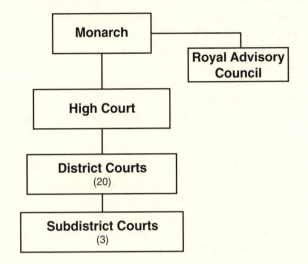

The Drukpa-Kagyupa school of Mahayana Buddhism is the state religion, and the Monk Body has a role in public affairs through its representatives in the National Assembly and the Royal Advisory Council. The Je Khenpo is elected by senior monks with the assent of the king, and he has social status at the same level as the king.

Legislative

The king, the National Assembly, and the Council of Ministers are the sources of legislation. The king legislates by issuing orders called *kasho,* which are compiled in collections called *kadyon.* They do not require the approval of the National Assembly, but they can be annulled or amended by it.

The National Assembly was established in 1953 by the kasho on the that topic, which comes as close as any document to being a constitution for the country. The National Assembly is responsible for approving laws, including the budget and the five-year development plans. It consists of 150 members, including 105 *chimis,* delegates elected from constituencies for three-year terms; 10 Buddhist clergymen; 1 representative of the Bhutan Chamber of Commerce and Industry; the 9 members of the Royal Advisory Council; and 25 others who are representatives of the ministries and agencies and nominated by the king.

An election for the position of chimi is held whenever a chimi's term ends or there is a vacancy for another reason. Voting is by household, usually at an open assembly. The votes are cast in various ways, including voice vote, balloting, and acclamation. The Bhutanese government discourages the formation of political parties, and there are none in the country at the present time.

The king formerly had the right to veto decisions of the National Assembly, but he gave up that right in 1968. The third king introduced the concept of expressing confidence in the king by a two-thirds vote of the National Assembly in 1969, but in 1974, at the coronation of the fourth king, the National Assembly gave up its right to take such a vote. In 1998, the National Assembly acquired the right to require the king to abdicate to permit his heir to ascend the throne.

Since the National Assembly now legislates without the formal decision of the king, the speaker of the assembly is the one who signs that body's decisions. The king nevertheless often still attends sessions of the National Assembly and may participate in debate. The speaker, who is elected by the National Assembly from among its members, plays a very powerful role in debates in terms of stating the issues, in determining what the consensus is on any particular point, and in revising the texts of laws after passage to reflect that consensus. Formal votes by ballot are rare. Rather, discussion continues on a point until the speaker enunciates a consensus position that finds no objection among the members.

The National Assembly itself has the right to draft legislation, but in practice, almost all laws are drafted by ministries and agencies, discussed by the Council of Ministers, and circulated for public comment before they come to the floor of the National Assembly. Some laws are implemented by a decision of the Council of Ministers in advance of consideration by the National Assembly. For example, the Department of Legal Affairs, which is responsible for carrying out certain prosecution and advisory functions and which could evolve into a Ministry of Justice and/or Attorney General's office, was implemented in April 2000, although the draft law providing for the department was still being discussed by the Council of Ministers. Draft laws previously also were reviewed by the High Court. This is no longer the case because of the sharpening of the separation of the judiciary from the rest of the Bhutanese government.

Executive

The Council of Ministers (Lhengyal Shungtshog), also called the Cabinet, was formally constituted in 1968 with five ministers, three representatives of the king, and the nine members of the Royal Advisory Council. The council now includes eight ministers, namely, the home, foreign affairs, planning, finance, agriculture, health and education, trade and industry, and communications ministers. The execution of laws, including the issuing of regulations (chatrim) to implement them, is in hands of the ministries and other executive agencies. However, the king has strongly advocated decentralization, which is implemented mainly in the formulation and execution of the country's development plans.

Until 1998, the king appointed the ministers and served as head of government and chairman of the Council of Ministers. In that year, on the king's proposal, the National Assembly made ministers answerable to the assembly, which now elects them for five-year terms. These ministers are nominated by the king and chosen from among officials at the rank of secretary or above. The position of head of government is filled for one-year terms by ministers in the order of the number of votes each received in their election in the National Assembly.

Judicial

Bhutan has a multitiered court system. At the peak of the system, the king is the ultimate decision maker on legal cases. In addition to the usual executive powers of pardon and commutation, the king has the right to set aside a decision of the High Court if that decision is considered by him not to be in accordance with the law. Below the king is the High Court, which hears appeals from lower courts and has original jurisdiction in certain types of cases. The District Courts in each of the country's districts have general jurisdiction as the courts of first instance. However, three districts also have Subdistrict Courts that have general jurisdiction within their geographic areas. (An appeal from a subdistrict court is heard by a district court.) Where there is no subdistrict court, the subdistrict head, or dungpa, is empowered to preside over and settle cases.

The High Court was established in 1968. The chief justice was first appointed in 1985 to be the first among equals on the High Court and the administrative head of the judiciary. The High Court's jurisdiction is defined as including:

1. Offenses against the state, for example: treason, terrorism, or any act against tsa wa sum (king, country, people); cases of the sale and purchase of arms and ammunition involving foreigners; matters related to international treaties; government officials accused of criminal acts; and disputes between two or more dzongkhags
2. Appellate jurisdiction over the judgments of a district court
3. Appeals concerning interlocutory orders of a district or subdistrict court

Traditionally, disputes in Bhutan have been resolved by mediation and arbitration with the assistance of arbiters (barmi). The courts strongly encourage the use of these methods in cases that come before them. The jabmis, who are licensed to appear in court on behalf of parties, are also available to act as mediators or arbiters. A decision reached through mediation or arbitration generally is concluded with an agreement (genja) between the parties and an undertaking providing for a bond (bah) of a specified amount to implement the agreements. These resolutions can be registered with the court. (Many disputes concern land, and the courts also have responsibility for the registration of land transfers.)

The encouragement of mediation and arbitration by the courts occurs in appeals to the king and the High Court as well as in the District and Subdistrict Courts. In the case of an appeal to the king, the monarch's first response is to issue a royal decree to the parties, jabmis, and witnesses in the case, directing them to consider reaching a settlement. During the preliminary hearing at all levels of the courts, it is mandatory for the judge or judges to invite the litigants to explore the possibilities of the settling the case out of the court. At any stage of the proceeding, the parties can request an adjournment within the limits specified in the law in order to pursue settlement. At the High Court level in a recent year, 27 percent of the cases submitted were settled between the parties without a decision by the court. Parties to construction contracts are encouraged to provide, in their contracts, for arbitration conducted according to the rules formulated by the Construction Development Board under the Ministry of Communications.

The cases before the District Courts mainly concern land, loan repayment, and crime. Before the High Court, most of the cases concern land. The land cases at both levels frequently arise out of prescriptive rights claims and intrafamily disagreements. There are also some business cases at both levels. Very few criminal cases are appealed.

The rules of procedure for the courts were streamlined and codified in the Civil and Criminal Procedure Act approved by the National Assembly in July 2001. When a case is filed, it is received by a registrar (*rabjam*), who makes an initial review of residence in the district and other jurisdictional issues and may make an initial investigation. If the case is an appeal of an administrative decision, the court will take jurisdiction only if administrative remedies have been exhausted.

At the point of intake, the registrar and/or the judge will contact the parties and encourage settlement through mediation or arbitration. Such alternatives will also be suggested by the court at an initial appearance and in a calendar hearing. The procedural steps in general are very similar to those in trial courts in the United States. The registrar is supposed to monitor time limits carefully. Usually, at each level, the court is expected to reach a decision within 108 days.

At trial, a case is heard by a judge. There are no juries. Both testimonial and documentary evidence can be presented to the court. The parties have a right of confrontation, that is, to see and hear the other party's evidence, to cross-examine, and to rebut. If any item of testimony or other evidence is disputed, a bond can be required of the parties such that the party whose evidence on the point is not accepted will be required to pay the amount of the bond. Oral testimony does not have precedence over written evidence; if a witness makes a mistake in oral testimony, the mistake can be corrected in a written submission. Although the system is adversarial, the judge is entitled to conduct an investigation or to summon his or her own experts if the parties do not develop the case adequately. Since many parties appear without jabmis and since the jabmis who do appear are not fully trained lawyers, the judge often needs to help the parties clarify their positions and their evidence. In a criminal case, since there is no position of prosecutor in Bhutan, the prosecution has usually been carried on by the ministry or agency with a substantive interest in the crime.

A court's evaluation of a case must follow the standards of the Civil and Criminal Procedure Act. The court is required to ensure that its consideration of the case at trial is "complete and exhaustive." In a civil case, the plaintiff/appellant must prove his or her case by a preponderance of the evidence. In a criminal case, a judgment of conviction is to be entered only if the "prosecution to the full satisfaction of the Court has established a proof beyond reasonable doubt."

The court's judgment (*thruenchoe*) in a case must be written, reasoned, and limited to the issues raised by the case. Judgments are announced in open court and are available to the parties in written form. They are public documents and may be referenced in other proceedings. Significant judgments are sometimes published in the newspapers, and there is a plan to publish judgments on a regular basis when funds become available. In a civil case, the parties have ten days to sign the judgment or to appeal. A party can be held in contempt for not doing either. On signing the judgment, each party agrees to implement the judgment unless it is appealed successfully and to pay the amount of a bond and be held in contempt if he or she fails to so so. Judges are responsible for supervising implementation of judgments.

In the case of an appeal of a judgment to the High Court, the matter will be heard by a panel of judges—usually the two judges of one of the three divisions, but larger panels are also used in important cases. Procedure in the High Court is similar to that in the District Court except that the lower court judge may be contacted by the High Court panel to provide information on the case. The High Court hears the case de novo, that is, it hears the arguments and the evidence of the parties all over again; new evidence is admissible, and the High Court is not bound by any aspect of the decision of the District Court.

The High Court's judgment can be appealed either to an expanded panel of three to five High Court judges, including the chief justice, or to the king. As with the District Court's decision, the High Court's judgment must be signed or appealed within ten days of being handed down, and signing involves an agreement by each party to implement the decision and to pay the amount of a bond and be held in contempt in case of failure to so so.

An appeal of a judgment to the king usually is not handled by the king himself but is referred to the Royal Advisory Council. The council's responsibility is to review the judgment to ensure that it is "in accord with the law." The council will meet with the relevant judges of the High Court and the parties, and it can rehear any evidence or even the entire case if it chooses to do so. The result of the council's consideration can be a recommendation to the king for an affirmation, reversal, or revision of the judgment. A revision will be drafted with the involvement of the High Court.

The court system is being modernized rapidly. Dockets have been computerized since 1990, and there is a plan to make them available online. Judges are now able to research case precedents by computer, and publication of a court reporter is likely in the future. Educational requirements to enter the judicial profession have been raised. Continuing education for judges and staff also has been instituted. An advocates act is being drafted to provide for the development of a private bar to represent parties before the courts.

SPECIALIZED JUDICIAL BODIES

All judicial authority in Bhutan is allocated to the court system. There are no specialized judicial bodies.

STAFFING

The standards of the judicial profession in Bhutan have been increasing with the modernization of the laws. Under the Judicial Service Act, judges and court officials now have a career path separate from the civil service generally. To be appointed, judges must have a law degree from a Western country and complete the National Legal Service Course, an eighteen-month training program in Bhutanese law offered by the High Court through the Royal Institute of Management. (Bhutan's only degree-granting institution, Sherubste College, does not offer a program in law.) Judges usually begin their careers serving as registrars or other court officials. However, lateral entry to judicial office from government and private positions is also possible.

Since 1991, promising students have been sent to India to study for law degrees, and some have studied in the United States and Europe as well. As of 2001, 89 had returned with LL.B.'s to fill positions in the courts and in the ministries and other agencies where law graduates are increasingly in demand.

There are as yet no fully trained private lawyers in Bhutan. The legal representatives of parties in litigation, the jabmis, have a wide variety of backgrounds. The basic requirement traditionally was eloquence in Dzongkha, the national language, coupled with knowledge of the

law. Many jabmi have been village elders, headmen, or retired officials, including former judges. Beginning in 1996, jabmis have been required to be licensed by the High Court after completing a one-month training course. Approximately 180 had been licensed by 2001, mostly on a part-time basis. The mix of cases handled by the jabmis is similar to that of the courts except that the jabmis also handle a significant number of family law cases, such as divorces that they settle or mediate without filing in court.

As of 2001, there was no law society, bar association, or association of jabmis. There has been an annual judicial conference for the judges, however, since 1976.

IMPACT

The legal system is developing in Bhutan at an extremely rapid pace, along with the rest of the society. Law and systematic planning are two key tools that the king and the Bhutanese government are using to foster change throughout the society in accordance with their vision of Bhutan's future. Since the Supreme Law of Bhutan maintains in effect Buddhist and cultural values set forth in the Code of Zhabdrung, enhancement of the status and functions of legal institutions such as the courts potentially can allow these values to be asserted in modern contexts where those values might otherwise not find a role.

John R. Davis

See also Alternative Dispute Resolution; Appellate Courts; Arbitration; Buddhist Law; Capital Punishment; Judicial Independence; Jury Selection; Mediation
References and further reading
Hainzl, Christian. 1998. *The Legal System of Bhutan: A Descriptive Analysis.* Vienna: Ludwig Boltzmann Institute of Human Rights.
Planning Commission, Royal Government of Bhutan. 1999. *Bhutan 2020: A Vision for Peace, Prosperity and Happiness.* Thimphu, Bhutan: Planning Commission, Royal Government of Bhutan.
———. 2000. *Bhutan National Human Development Report 2000.* Thimphu, Bhutan: Planning Commission, Royal Government of Bhutan.
United Nations Development Program. 2000. *Bhutan: Moving toward a Common Understanding—Common Country Assessment 2000.* Thimphu, Bhutan: United Nations Development Program.
Ura, Karma. 1995. *The Hero with a Thousand Eyes: A Historical Novel.* Thimphu, Bhutan: Centre for Bhutan Studies.
Winter, Renate. 1999. *Juvenile Justice in Bhutan: Report on the Workshop on Juvenile Justice, 12–16 April, 1999.* Strengthening the Bhutanese Legal Framework Report 2 (BHU/98/002). Thimphu, Bhutan: United Nations Development Program.

BOLIVIA

COUNTRY INFORMATION

Bolivia is a landlocked country in central South America, lying entirely within the Tropics. It borders Peru to the northwest, Chile to the southwest, Argentina and Paraguay to the south, and Brazil to the north and east. Bolivia continues to have border disputes with Chile and Peru, having lost its outlet to the sea due to a conflict with Chile at the end of the nineteenth century. Two cities are actually recognized as the capital of Bolivia. Sucre is the home of the Supreme Court and therefore serves as the constitutional capital. La Paz is the de facto capital, with the executive and legislative branches each operating out of that location. The population, estimated at 8.1 million in 1999, is about 90 percent Catholic, although in the indigenous communities, characteristics of the pre-Columbian pantheistic religion have survived and, in some cases, become integrated into the Catholic faith. About 40 percent of the population is fourteen years old or younger. Life expectancy is about sixty-five years, and illiteracy is about 17 percent. The gross national product per capita is about U.S.$800, making Bolivia one of the poorest countries in the Western Hemisphere.

The country has 424,165 square miles (1,098,581 square kilometers), about three-fifths of which consists of vast low plains, mainly in the east and north. Here are found low alluvial plains, giant swamps and flood lands, and forest regions, which constitute the western portions of the Amazon Basin. The western section of Bolivia is one of the highest inhabited areas of the world, and it represents the heart of Bolivia. The Andes Mountains cross the western part of Bolivia in two parallel ranges, east and west. Between the ranges lies the high plateau known as the Altiplano. The Altiplano is a nearly flat depression about 500 miles (800 kilometers) long and 80 miles (130 kilometers) wide. The elevation there runs between 12,000 and 12,500 feet (3,600 to 3,800 meters). The Altiplano is windswept, cold, bleak, hostile, and barren. On the western border with Peru lies Lake Titicaca, the highest large navigable lake in the world. Extremely high mountains, some over 21,000 feet (6,400 meters), are found in the northeast. To the extreme south is the Chaco. The Chaco is a plain, lowland area, approximating a swamp in the three-month rainy season or a hot semidesert in the dry season of the rest of the year.

Because of differences in altitude across Bolivia, the country has temperatures equivalent to everything from arctic cold to Amazon jungle hot. Temperature deviation is determined by altitude, since the entire country is within the Tropics. Rainfall is nearly as varied as temperature. To the east of the eastern mountain range, rainfall is nearly constant all year. In the elevated plains, limited amounts of rain fall. In La Paz, there are only about 23 inches (584 millimeters) of rain a year, falling only during the summer months. At times, the Altiplano becomes absolutely barren of vegetation. To the west of La Paz, near Lake Titicaca, brief but immensely strong thunderstorms cut across the northern plain during summer months.

Bolivian ethnicity is often broken down into three separate groups. Those in the largest group, the indigenous population, are descendants of the Aymara or Inca. Other groups include people descending from Spanish ancestry and those from a mixed indigenous and European ancestry (the mestizos, or, as they are known particularly in Bolivia, the *cholos*). However, definition of race in Bolivia has come about in social rather than strictly genetic terms. Peasants are usually referred to as indigenous people. The urban lower and lower-middle classes and the rural freehold farmers wear European clothing and are often called "the mestizos." The upper class of elites are assumed to be of European ancestry. Intermarriage has caused new subgroups to emerge over time. Today, ethnicity is increasingly a question of self-identification and class, rather than genetics.

HISTORY

Population in the Andean region dates back some 20,000 years. Bolivia today traces its roots to ancient civilizations. The Altiplano was densely populated for several hundred years prior to the arrival of the Spanish in the 1500s. The Tiahuanaco Empire, with a complex customary legal system, began in the seventh century and reached its high mark by the eleventh century. At that time, although centered in the Altiplano, the empire extended over the Peruvian highlands and coast. Later, the empire was broken into smaller, regional states. Civilization was characterized by advanced technologies in agriculture and irrigation systems. After the collapse of Tiahuanaco, various groups of Aymara-speaking Indians emerged, comprising twelve separate nations. These groups then became competitors to the Quechua-speaking nation, the Inca, centered in Cuzco (today, in Peru). After years of fighting, the Quechuan groups eventually gained the upper hand. However, the Aymara retained their language, culture, and local customary legal system within the broader Incan Empire. Later, when the Spanish Conquest arrived both the Quechua and Aymara retained their cultural and linguistic heritage, despite brutal oppression. Today, Bolivia officially recognizes Spanish, Quechua, and Aymara as national languages. Guarani is also spoken in Bolivia among lowland indigenous groups.

During the era of the Spanish Conquest, Spain quickly began to mine the abundant mineral wealth of the region, using forced indigenous labor. The largest silver mine in the western world, located in the high, arid town of Potosí, was founded in 1545. Some authors claim that more than a million indigenous slaves died in the Potosí

mine alone. Starting in the sixteenth century, as a result of mining operations, Upper Peru (as Bolivia was then known) was one of the wealthiest and most densely populated areas of Spain's empire in the Americas. By the middle of the seventeenth century, Potosí was the largest city in the Americas, with a population of over 150,000. At the close of the eighteenth century, the best mines had been exhausted, and the region began a decline.

In 1809, revolts in Chuquisaca and La Paz ignited wars of independence across South America. With historical irony, Upper Peru was the last major region in South America to gain independence from Spain, which was accomplished with Antonio José de Sucre's defeat of the Spanish in Peru in 1824. At the time, Simon Bolívar was pressing the countries of South America to remain united as Greater Colombia. Nevertheless, he allowed Upper Peru to declare itself an independent republic on August 6, 1825. The fact that the new republic would be named after him was no doubt a helpful factor in his decision. Bolívar himself drafted Bolivia's first constitution, approved in 1826.

Antonio José de Sucre became Bolivia's first president. Declining mining income and war expenses pushed the new nation into an economic depression. By 1846, Bo-

livia had more than 10,000 abandoned mines. To compensate, it began to heavily tax its indigenous population, estimated at 1.1 million as of 1825. Taxation of the indigenous was the largest single source of income for the government until late in the 1800s, in contrast to the situation in other South American countries, which relied almost exclusively on import and export taxes to produce public revenue. Bolivia, once the premier South American state, became its most backward nation.

Beginning in the 1840s, Chile began to expand mining operations along the Pacific coast, through treaties and concessions with the Bolivian government. The English provided Chile with needed capital for the ventures. With discovery of nitrate deposits in the 1860s, investment became more active. To stave off the Chileans, the Bolivians entered into a treaty with Peru in 1873. When Bolivia increased the tax on nitrate companies, Chile invaded. The War of the Pacific (1879–1884) had begun. In the end, Bolivia lost its access to the sea to Chile. At about this time, world silver prices dropped. The dual effects of the price drop and the military defeat led to a shift in power to the new tin-mining entrepreneurs. It is worth noting that the loss of access to the sea remains a sore point between Chile and Bolivia. As of 2000, Bolivia remained in discussions with Chile about access rights, with the threat of pursing international judicial action if Chile refused to compromise.

In June 1932, a border conflict with Paraguay resulted in the Chaco War, a long, costly disaster for Bolivia. After three years of fighting and with 100,000 Bolivians dead, deserted, or captured, Bolivia lost a great deal more territory than Paraguay had ever demanded. The defeat was made more tragic for Bolivia because, at the start of the conflict, it was the better-equipped and better-trained force.

In April 1952, Bolivia experienced one of Latin America's most important revolutions, also having a regional impact on postrevolutionary constitutional frameworks. Mine workers rose against the tin-mining industry. In October 1952, the state nationalized the three biggest tin-mining operations. In August 1953, a major land reform program began (predating similar reforms in nearly all of Latin America, with the exception of Mexico). At the same time, universal suffrage was set in motion, and literary requirements for voting were abolished. Indigenous people were freed from labor obligations and given land, the right to vote, and arms, making the indigenous peasantry a major force from then on in Bolivian politics. From 1964 to 1985, there were a number of governments, some elected and some military. In 1967, the Argentine revolutionary Ernesto (Che) Guevara arrived in Bolivia, with support from Cuban president Fidel Castro, in an attempt to overthrow the Bolivian state and spread revolution across South America. Guevara failed largely because he was unable to attract or mobilize any significant peasant following. In 1971, Col. Hugo Banzer Suarez assumed power and ushered in the most repressive regime of this period, suppressing the labor movement, suspending all civil rights, prohibiting peasant organization, and sending in troops to occupy the mines.

Politically, when one thinks of Bolivia, the stereotype that comes to mind is that of a country plagued by military dictatorship and political and economic instability. At one point, Bolivia had gone through 78 different governments over a period of just 169 years of independence. At another point, inflation topped 23,000 percent. All that has changed. Military dictatorship came to a close in August 1982 with the election of Hernan Siles Zuazo as president and Jaime Paz Zamora as vice-president. Prior to 1982, the military had been supported and advised by the Argentine military and foreign fascists such as former Gestapo leader Klaus Barbie and terrorist Pier Luigi Pagliari. With the change in 1982, demilitarization began, but the economy defied control. Between 1980 and 1984, money in circulation increased 1,000 percent. In 1985, the newly elected president, Victor Paz Estensorro, implemented an austere economic package. He devalued the national currency, established a free-floating exchange rate, eliminated price and wage controls, cut public spending and public employee wages, and raised prices for public services. By 1989, there was broad political consensus for a continuation of the economic package. Once heavily protectionist, Bolivia now has a maximum tariff of 10 percent, and it allows free entry and exit of capital. Further, since 1985, Bolivia has enjoyed a multiparty political system. This system tends to encourage the creation of ever more new parties, with older parties splintering, resulting in complex electoral alliances.

From 1993 to 1997, President Gonzalo Sanchez de Lozada initiated reforms designed to privatize industry, reform education, promote participation, and decentralize government. Though controversial in their enactment, the reforms are revolutionary. The privatization program, actually called "capitalization," sells off a 50 percent interest in state enterprises and invests the proceeds into retirement funds for all adult Bolivians. All new private investment is plowed back into the company to expand or upgrade service. Education reforms are geared to providing basic education and adult education to citizens in their native language. These measures seek to correct the previous practice of teaching only in Spanish even though the majority of Bolivians are indigenous people, speaking languages other than Spanish. The reformers also hope to address centuries of discrimination against indigenous groups and women, providing them with more-equal opportunities for advancement through education.

The new Popular Participation program promotes a decentralization of fiscal authority and responsibility from central government to the municipal level. Previously, decision making was highly centralized at the nation's capital. Budgets were allocated primarily to the big three cities: La Paz, Cochabamba, and Santa Cruz. Today, this is no longer true: All 314 municipalities receive coparticipation funds under the Popular Participation Law. Finally, a new decentralization law seeks to cement control of government at the local level. It provides for strong municipalities but stops short of federalism by denying much power to the state level. Taken as a whole, these measures are the most exciting legislative changes in Bolivia since the agrarian reform of 1953. They are a model for other countries to evaluate as they confront similar challenges.

In 1997, former military dictator Hugo Banzer Suarez was elected president. Although many predicted a return to strong-arm rule, Bolivia has stayed the course of democratization, albeit with political, economic, and social turbulence.

LEGAL CONCEPTS

As in most countries, Bolivia's supreme law is found in its constitution. Under the constitution, Bolivia is considered a "unitary" republic, which means that governmental authority rests entirely in the capital, rather than in departmental or state governments as might be the case in a "federalist" system such as Brazil or the United States. Under Article 85 of the constitution, the resident heads the executive branch and presides over the ministers of state. He is elected for a nonrenewable four-year term of office. Beyond the executive branch, there are also legislative and judicial branches of government. An attorney general is separate from each of the other branches of government and operates with independence.

Like the United States, Bolivia has a two-chamber Congress. Congress is responsible for all legislative acts. An upper chamber, the 27-member Senate, is elected through a direct, universal voting system. There are three senators serving four-year terms concurrently from each of Bolivia's nine departments. The lower house, the 130-member Chamber of Deputies, includes members elected for four-year terms by direct voting as well as a system providing for proportional representation of minorities. Legislation requires an absolute majority in both houses for passage. As a historical note, a July 1980 military coup suspended the Congress, but it reconvened in October 1982, and fresh elections were held three years later.

If a presidential candidate does not receive a majority of votes, the national Congress serves to elect a national president. In some cases, the Congress has selected one of the losing candidates to become the next president. For example, in 1989, Gonzalo Sanchez de Lozada finished first in the elections with a plurality. However, the second- and third-place parties linked forces in Congress, and Jaime Paz Zamora, the third-place winner, was elected president. If the president dies, the vice-president takes power. If the vice-president is also unable to assume power, the president of the Senate becomes the head of state on an interim basis.

Although Bolivia is a unitary republic, for administrative purposes, Article 108 of the constitution divides the country into departments (under the authority of prefects, representing national executive authority), provinces (under subprefects) and provincial sections, and cantons (under magistrates, or, in Spanish, *corregidores*).

In terms of legislation, Bolivia, like most civil law countries, has specific codes for civil law, civil procedure, commercial law, family law, mining, tax, criminal law, and criminal procedure. Other significant pieces of legislation include the Judicial Organization Law, Municipal Law, Political Organization Law, Customs Law, Social Security Code, and Aeronautic Code.

One of the most important areas of legislation concerns labor issues. The constitution provides for a right to employment and to a fair wage. Bolivia also has a system of social security. The maximum workweek is forty-eight hours. Except for apprenticeships, work by minors under the age of fourteen is prohibited. Since 1997, social security participation has been compulsory. Women enjoy

particular rights under the law, including the right not to be fired as a result of pregnancy or within one year after giving birth. The age of majority is twenty-one.

In the environmental area, the legal framework recognizes the need for conservation and protection of the environment. The Bolivian National Secretariat for the Environment carries out a function similar to that of the Environmental Protection Agency in the United States. Bolivia is one of the first Latin American countries to require environmental impact statements in public works and in any activity that may damage the environment. Bolivia refuses the entry of radioactive materials.

In the intellectual property rights area, Bolivia affords legal protection to copyrights, patents, and trademarks. As in most of Latin America, the real question is one of enforcement. Bolivia is a signatory to a number of intellectual property rights conventions, including the Montevideo Convention of 1889, the Buenos Aires Convention of 1910, the Caracas Agreement of 1911, the Washington Convention of 1946, the Rome Convention of 1961, and the Stockholm Convention of 1979. National legislation was updated in the 1990s. Bolivia also belongs to the World Trade Organization and the World Intellectual Property Organization.

In 1999, Bolivia passed monumental reforms in the area of criminal procedure. Like the Guatemalan reform of 1994, the Bolivian change radically reformed criminal justice, moving from a mainly written civil law, inquisitorial system to a mainly oral, adversarial system. As in Guatemala, the hope is that this will provide for increased transparency of process, greater public scrutiny and victim participation, and lowered rates of impunity and corruption. The new Procedure Code, which entered into effect on May 31, 2001, allows police to use undercover agents and to participate in sting operations.

CURRENT COURT SYSTEM STRUCTURE

The Supreme Court is the highest body within the judicial branch. The twelve-member body is appointed by the Chamber of Deputies of the national Congress; its members serve ten-year terms. The Supreme Court is divided into four chambers, with three justices assigned to each. Two of those chambers review civil cases. Another chamber oversees criminal justice. The last chamber reviews administrative, social, and mining cases. The president of the court chairs meetings between chambers and directs the court in appeals cases.

Beyond its adjudication functions, which include opining on the constitutionality of laws, the Supreme Court has the administrative functions of preparing the budget and supervising procurement for the judicial branch. Under the Judicial Organization Law of 1993, the Supreme Court hears select cases on appeal from lower courts. It also has original jurisdiction in cases such as accusations against high-ranking government officials and government contract disputes. Supreme Court justices enjoy tenure in office. They cannot be removed or suspended without cause and then only with a two-thirds majority vote of the Chamber of Deputies. In 2000, the Bolivian Supreme Court upheld the drug conviction of Oscar Eid Franco, a deputy party leader of the Movement of the Revolutionary Left (MIR), which linked former Bolivian President Jaime Paz Zamora to drug trafficking.

Superior District Courts hear appeals from trial judges. The trial judges have original jurisdiction over civil, family, commercial, and labor matters, as well as matters involving minors, criminal cases, and misdemeanors. An independent Constitutional Court was created under the constitution and has national jurisdiction (Law 1836 of April 1, 1998). The Constitutional Court reviews habeas corpus actions, resolves conflicts between the branches of government, and has original jurisdiction over the constitutionality of legislation, presidential decrees, and international treaties and conventions.

Despite the presence of the formal legal structure, private systems of dispute resolution exist, through traditional indigenous legal mechanisms, in a number of countries in the Americas—Bolivia, Ecuador, Peru, Mexico, and Guatemala. Prior to the arrival of the Spanish in Bolivia, the main governmental unit was the *kollasuyo,* or community. The kollasuyo included complex market and trade arrangements among different towns located at differing altitudes, assuring diversity of production and therefore a self-insurance system. The basic social unit of the kollasuyo was the *ayllu* (neighborhood), which contained a number of smaller population units. Each community specialized in the production of certain produce (corn, potatoes, fish, coca, and so forth), in accordance with its ecological location. The area that is now Bolivia was part of the old Inca kollasuyo, with its center at Cuzco (now in Peru). The economic system relied on barter—there was no monetary system.

Spanish rule radically changed the legal structure. Mining became the dominant industry, and emphasis was placed on production at the fastest, cheapest rate possible. Working conditions were harsh. Forced labor, called the *mita,* was imposed, and stiff taxes were levied on the indigenous labor force. Evangelism also made inroads on traditional culture and religion. Despite the influence of Spanish rule and the experience of years of liberalism and westernization, indigenous culture and legal concepts remain relevant and important today. The Andean system of values, sometimes called the Andean Code, revolves around six basic values—*ama quilla* (no laziness), *ama llulla* (no lying), *ama shua* (no stealing), love for the land, reciprocity, and the presence of the sacred.

Traditional indigenous values are still very relevant to political discourse in Bolivia. A rediscovery of indigenous heritage is under way, and we can expect customary dispute settlement practices to gain renewed importance, especially in the face of a dysfunctional formal legal system.

SPECIALIZED JUDICIAL BODIES

In January 1998, President Hugo Banzer Suarez announced a $1 billion, five-year plan to combat narcotics production, with Bolivia picking up about 15 percent of the cost and the rest split between the United States and Europe. Much of the money went to farmers to encourage them to produce "alternative" crops—this is, crops other than coca. At the time, Vice-President Jorge Quiroga noted that there was nothing more damaging to Bolivia's international image than drug trafficking and nothing more corruptive to Bolivia's public institutions.

That same year, 1998, Bolivia created the new Judicial Council to professionalize the nomination of candidates for the judiciary. The council also serves as a vehicle for disciplining judges. Some of its powers were subsequently taken away by the Constitutional Court, which ruled that judges could not be removed on suspicion of corrupt practices until convicted by a criminal court.

Bolivia has developed specialized Controlled Substances Courts for trying drug cases, complete with special antinarcotics police. These courts have had mixed results. Although Bolivia's judicial organization otherwise appears similar to that of a European country, it nevertheless has to operate within a national context that includes high levels of corruption, in large part due to the expansive cocaine production. In March 1999, six judges were suspended on allegations of corruption: The judges specialized in narcotics cases and had been compromised by defendants. Five ended up resigning as a result of the probe. In April 2000, reputed drug kingpin Marco Marino Diodato (an Italian who was married to the niece of the president) was acquitted of drug charges in Santa Cruz, leading to a cooling of the relationship between La Paz and Washington in terms of the international war on drugs. Marino remained in detention, however, on other charges, including operating illegal casinos and cloning mobile phones (charges related to money laundering and drug trafficking). In 1999, Bolivia eliminated about 14,000 hectares of coca production, and it was expected to end coca production a few years later.

Law 1770 (March 10, 1997) provides for the arbitration of disputes. The law distinguishes between domestic and international arbitration proceedings. For national arbitration, the parties can select the arbiters, the place for arbitration, and even the language to be used. The process is supposed to take less than six months. Normally, the parties enter into an arbitration agreement to spell out the terms of settlement for the dispute. In the case of international arbitration, enforcement of a foreign arbitration award requires the use of a specific interna-

Structure of Bolivian Courts

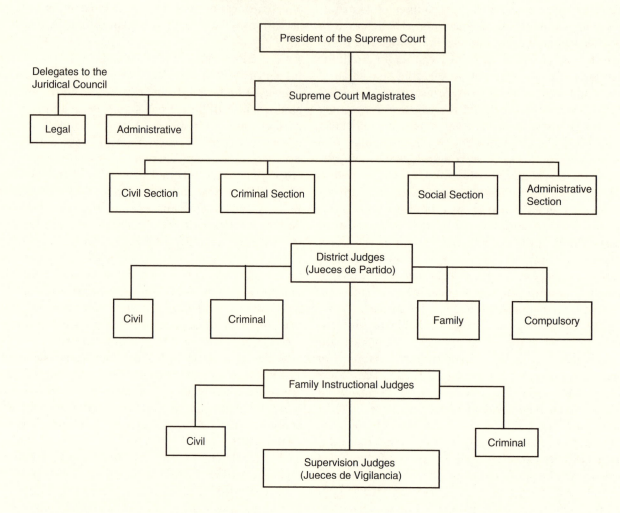

Chart adapted from U.S. Agency for International Development. 2000. "Plan Nacional de Implementación del Nuevo Código de Procedimiento Penal Avanza en Seis Areas Principales."

tional convention or agreement, or can be done according to the terms of the Civil Procedure Code. While awaiting a decision in arbitration, the parties are free to seek mediation or conciliation. Bolivia is a signatory to the Convention on Recognition and Enforcement of Foreign Arbitral Awards, the Convention on the Settlement of Investment Disputes between States and Nationals of Other States, the Inter-American Convention on International Commercial Arbitration, and the Extraterritorial Validity of Foreign Judgments and Arbitration Awards.

In 1997, Bolivia passed new legislation to advance a "people's defender," or human rights ombudsman, as a high commissioner of the Congress. The defender is actually an entire institution, as contemplated in the constitution, to make sure the public administration gives its citizens a fair shake. It also performs a watchdog function in terms of human rights.

STAFFING

A student must study for five years in an accredited law school to become a lawyer. The law degree is awarded at the undergraduate level, as in most Latin American countries. Most business leaders and politicians are lawyers, so a law degree is certainly considered prestigious, especially in a country with a high illiteracy rate where any university degree sets one apart from the majority.

Officially, Bolivia has about 650 judges and 300 prosecutors, though over one-quarter of the prosecutor positions are vacant. An ambitious training plan is currently under way for police, prosecutors, judges, and other formal sector actors to gear up for the oral, adversarial procedures called for in the new Criminal Procedure Code. In part with support from the U.S. Agency for International Development, comprehensive training is being carried out in a concerted effort with public and private universities, as well as the various public sector institutions. A separate police academy has been established and includes training on human rights.

Bar associations exist in each department of Bolivia, with the largest being in the Department of the Capital City of La Paz. That association has 3,800 members. There is also a national bar association. One of the typical services of these associations is to provide continuing legal education for members. Annual conferences and prestigious academic journals are also part of the bar associations in the Departments of La Paz and Santa Cruz de la Sierra. Continuing legal education, though not mandatory, is viewed by practitioners as a way to network, develop new practice areas, and keep on top of developments. In 2000, the Bar Association of La Paz inaugurated new teaching facilities, and in 2001, graduate degree programs for its members were initiated.

Steven E. Hendrix

See also Adversarial System; Civil Law; Constitutional Law; Criminal Law; Criminal Procedures; Customary Law; Human Rights Law; Indigenous and Folk Legal Systems; Napoleonic Code

References and further reading
"Bolivia." 1988. *Encyclopedia Britannica* 15: 160–171.
Curtis, Mallet-Prevost, Colt, and Mosle, LLP. 2000. "Bolivia Law Digest." *Martindale-Hubbell International Law Digest.*
Fernandez de Cordova, Miguel Urioste. 1992. *Fortalecer las comunidades.* La Paz, Bolivia: AIPE/PROCOM/TIERRA.
Hendrix, Steven E. 1997. "Advancing toward Privatization, Education Reform, Popular Participation, and Decentralization: Bolivia's Innovation in Legal and Economic Reform, 1993–1997." *Arizona Journal of International and Comparative Law* 14: 679–713.
Leons, Madeline Barbara, and Harry Sanabria. 1997. *Coca, Cocaine, and the Bolivian Reality.* New York: State University of New York.
Patch, Richard. 1960. "Bolivia: The Restrained Revolution." Land Tenure Center Reprint no. 33, University of Wisconsin.
U.S. Agency for International Development. 2000. "Plan nacional de implementación del nuevo código de procedimiento penal avanza en seis areas principales." La Paz, Bolivia.

BOSNIA AND HERZEGOVINA

HISTORY

The Republic of Bosnia and Herzegovina declared its independence from the former Yugoslavia in October 1991. Following a four-year armed conflict between Bosnians, Croats, and Serbs, the country has been divided into two separate republics functioning together as a single sovereign nation. Bosnia and Herzegovina is now in the process of rebuilding from the shambles of war and ethnic cleansing.

Bosnia and Herzegovina (BiH), like the entire Balkan region, has had a bellicose past. The nation traces its history back more than two thousand years, to when the Illyrians settled the area. In 395 C.E., when the Roman Empire was divided, the present border between BiH and Serbia became the border between the eastern empire of Byzantium and the western empire, centered in Rome. In the fifteenth century, after Byzantium fell to the Ottoman Turks, BiH became part of the Ottoman Empire. Many of BiH's inhabitants, including Roman Catholic Croatians and Eastern Orthodox Serbs, gave up Christianity and converted to the conqueror's religion, Islam.

As the Ottoman Empire declined in the nineteenth century, Russia backed the Hapsburg claim to the Balkans, allowing the Austro-Hungarian Empire to take control of BiH by force. Resentment of Hapsburg rule in BiH spawned resistance movements. In 1914, a Bosnian Serb assassinated Archduke Franz Ferdinand, heir to the Hapsburg throne, an act that sparked World War I. The defeat of the Central Powers in 1918 brought about the collapse of the Austro-Hungarian empire. BiH became a spoil of the war and was awarded to Serbia. In 1941, when Nazi Germany dominated the region, BiH was attached to a fascist Croatia. The alliance, whether willing or forced, of BiH with the Axis powers in World War II led to the slaughter of thousands of Serbs—an eerie portent of the ethnic cleansing of Bosnians by Serbs that would follow half a century later.

With the assistance of Soviet and British forces, by 1944 Yugoslavian nationals led by Josip Broz Tito pushed the Germans out of BiH. Under Soviet protection, Tito took control of BiH as well as Croatia, Serbia, Slovenia, Macedonia, and Montenegro, uniting them in one sovereign state of Yugoslavia. BiH held the status of a constituent republic. Although Yugoslavia was communist, Tito managed to hold the Soviets at arms' length, keeping Yugoslavia on friendly terms with the Soviet Union but achieving a measure of independence in domestic and foreign policy. Political conditions in Yugoslavia were never as severe as in the Soviet republics or the satellite countries of eastern Europe, and Tito was able to quash ethnic disturbances.

Bosnian War

Following the death of Tito in 1980 and the fall of the Soviet Union in 1989, ethnic nationalism began to foment in the republics of Yugoslavia. The first free elections in BiH, held in November 1990, spelled the political death of communism in the region. The Communists were opposed by a largely Muslim party advocating a multiethnic BiH, but nationalist Serbian and Croatian parties were also launched to represent their communities' exclusive interests. Within a year, the Croatian and Muslim parties united and, despite Serb objections, on

Bosnia & Herzegovina

BOSNIA & HERZEGOVINA

©2001 maps.com

October 15, 1991, BiH declared its independence from Yugoslavia. When the United Nations hastily recognized BiH as a separate country, the Bosnian Serbs withdrew in protest. Spurred on by nationalists in Serbia, they declared war on the Muslim population and began a campaign of ethnic cleansing, forcefully removing the Bosnian Muslims, or Bosniacs, from the north and east of BiH to unite Serb populations from western BiH with a greater Serbia.

The Bosnian conflict of 1991–1995 is sometimes called a civil war, as Bosnian Serbs, Croats, and Muslims fought for control of the country. But more properly, the war was a campaign of Serbian aggression. The Bosniacs undoubtedly made a fatal political calculation in declaring an early independence from Yugoslavia, but that hardly justified the brutality and depravity that followed. And while each side committed its own share of war crimes, it would be a misreading of history to ignore the organized campaign of terror that Serb nationalists inflicted on Bosnian Muslims and to a lesser extent Croats. The Serbs systematically killed, raped, and burned the homes of Bosniacs, and even after the United Nations set

up "safe areas" for Bosnian Muslims, the Serbs massacred as many as 6,000 Bosniac men in the town of Srebrenica, unceremoniously dumping the bodies into mass graves. The violations of humanitarian law during the war were so great that the United Nations established an international tribunal to prosecute these crimes against humanity. To date, the vast majority of suspects and defendants have been Serbs, whether Bosnian Serbs who carried out the atrocities or leaders from Serbia proper who are said to have supported and inflamed the Serb aggressors.

Dayton Accord and Beyond
By 1995, the Bosnian Serbs were on the defensive, and President Clinton floated a peace plan at a conference in Dayton, Ohio. The resulting peace agreement, called the Dayton Accord, declares that BiH shall retain its prewar boundaries, but the country is now composed of two separate entities: a joint Muslim-Croat Federation of Bosnia and Herzegovina (the Federation) and the Serb Republic of Bosnia and Herzegovina, also known as the Republic of Srpska (RS). Each comprises about half the country. In a nation with such a convoluted history, the current

framework for Bosnia's government is no less complex. The country's head of state, called the chairman of the presidency, is a rotating position, first held by Alija Izetbegovic, a Muslim. The chairman shares the office with two copresidents, one a Croat (the first was Ante Jelavic) and the other a Bosnian Serb (first Zivko Radisic). Each copresident is elected by his own people. Together, the presidency has nine official functions: conducting foreign policy for BiH; appointing ambassadors and international representatives, no more than two-thirds of whom may come from the Federation; representing BiH in international organizations and institutions; negotiating, refusing, and, with the consent of the Parliamentary Assembly, ratifying treaties for BiH; executing decisions of the Assembly; proposing an annual budget; reporting to the Assembly at least once a year on expenditures of the presidency; coordinating with international and nongovernmental organizations in BiH; and performing other functions as necessary to carry out these duties.

The presidency also nominates the chairman of the Council of Ministers and submits the candidate's name to the BiH House of Representatives for approval. The chairman in turn appoints a foreign minister, a minister of foreign trade, and any other ministers deemed appropriate or necessary. The Council of Ministers has responsibility for the day-to-day functioning of the Bosnian government.

The Bosnian legislative power is endowed in the Parliamentary Assembly, which is composed of two houses: the House of Peoples and the House of Representatives. The House of Peoples includes fifteen delegates, two-thirds of whom come from the Federation and the other third from the RS. The House of Representatives is comprised of 42 members and, like the House of Peoples, is split 2:1 between the Federation and the Republic of Srpska. Federation representatives are elected directly by the voters of the Federation, and Srpska representatives are selected by the RS National Assembly.

In addition to the national government, both the Federation and the Republic of Srpska have their own presidencies, with regional governments existing within each of the two provinces. Municipal governments are organized among cantons, the rough equivalent of counties or parishes in other governmental ystems.

Although the Bosnian War ended in 1995, ethnic tensions remain just below the surface. More than 30,000 NATO troops are stationed in BiH to keep the peace, and a large number of international development professionals are helping to rebuild the country. Indeed, the Dayton Agreement established the international Office of the High Representative with responsibilities to oversee the implementation of civilian aspects of the pact. Annex 10 of the Dayton Agreement gives the High Representative final authority in BiH on matters of civil im-

Legal Structure of Bosnia and Herzegovina Courts

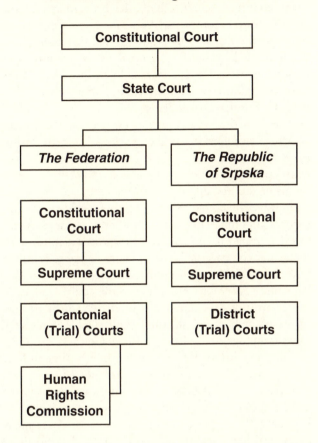

plementation of the peace settlement, including the power to pass and enforce laws (at least on an interim basis) on matters of state reconstruction. Although since 1995 there has been progress within BiH, the country is still very much divided along ethnic lines. Refugees attempting to return, and municipal officials attempting to assume their posts, have been subject to attacks and harassment. Under these circumstances, reconciliation is still far away.

STRUCTURE OF THE JUDICIARY

Even prior to the breakup of Yugoslavia, BiH had its own constitutional court, an unusual situation in a socialist legal system. Yugoslavia maintained a national constitutional court, and under the Constitution of 1963 BiH, as well as each of the other six republics and two autonomous provinces (Kosovo and Vojvodina), had constitutional courts to interpret the legality of statutes, regulations, and provisions as against their own constitutions.

National Constitutional Court

Since independence and the conclusion of the war, BiH's national government has been determined by the Constitution of Bosnia and Herzegovina, adopted on December

14, 1995. Article 6 of that constitution establishes a Constitutional Court, with binding legal authority across the entire country, including both the Federation and the RS. The court is comprised of nine members. Four are selected by the Federation's House of Representatives, two are appointed by the RS National Assembly, and three non-Bosnian members are named by the president of the European Court of Human Rights after consultation with the Bosnian copresidents.

The Constitutional Court is chaired by a president and three vice presidents, who are elected by secret ballot from among the judges. These positions rotate, with the court's president to hold that position for twenty months. Terms of the first appointees to the court are five years, with judges ineligible for reappointment. However, subsequent appointees may serve until the age of seventy unless they resign or are removed for cause. Later appointments may be governed by a different law of selection, a responsibility the constitution gives to the Bosnian Parliamentary Assembly. According to the court, "judges of the Constitutional Court are required to be distinguished jurists of high moral standing. Any eligible voter may serve as a judge of the Constitutional Court."

The Constitutional Court sat for the first time in May 1997, when it wrote its own rules of procedure, which have been amended at least twice since then. Among the court's rules is the prohibition on judges from serving in Bosnian political parties or organizations or as members of any legislative, executive, or other judicial authority in BiH as a whole or in either the Federation or the Republic of Srpska.

The Constitutional Court has exclusive jurisdiction to decide any dispute that arises under the constitution between BiH and any other entity, or between the Federation and the Republic of Srpska. In addition, the court has exclusive power to decide if the constitution or laws of the Federation or the Republick of Srpska are consistent with the Bosnian constitution. To reach the court, a dispute may be referred by a member of the presidency, by the chair of the Council of Ministers, by a chair or deputy chair of either chamber of the Parliamentary Assembly, by one-fourth of the members of either chamber of the Parliamentary Assembly, or by one-fourth of either chamber of a legislature within the Federation or the Republic of Srpska.

Besides its exclusive jurisdiction, the Constitutional Court has appellate jurisdiction over issues arising under the national constitution decided by any other court in BiH. Moreover, such lower courts may refer to the court issues concerning the European Convention for Human Rights and Fundamental Freedoms or matters of public international law.

From its inception the Constitutional Court went three years before issuing its first decision. But then, in 2000, eleven members of the House of Representatives for the Parliamentary Assembly filed a case challenging the constitutionality of the Law on State Border Service imposed by the high representative in January of the same year. Ruling in November 2000, the Constitutional Court concluded that it had jurisdiction to review the constitutionality of the law and that the law was itself constitutional.

State Court for BiH
At the time of the Constitutional Court's decision, there were no other courts in BiH at the national level. Given the large schism in the country between the Federation and the Republic of Srpska, the lower courts were found exclusively at the provincial level, specific either to the Federation or the RS. The Dayton Accords, however, recognized the need for "judicial institutions at the State level" to deal with such matters as "criminal offenses perpetrated by public officials of Bosnia and Herzegovina in the course of their duties," not to mention "administrative and electoral matters" at the national level. Since the jurisdiction of the Constitutional Court is limited essentially to questions of the national constitution, Bosnian leaders recognized the need for a separate court to handle other serious legal questions related to the carrying out of the national state power. In October 2000, a working group composed of members of the Ministry for Civil Affairs and Communication, the Ministries of Justice from the Federation and the RS, and the Office of the High Representative agreed on a draft law for a State Court for BiH. But because of national elections on November 11, 2000, the Bosnian Council of Ministers and the Parliamentary Assembly were unable to pass the law through regular legislative procedures. In response, the high representative invoked his powers from the Dayton Accord to implement the draft law and, with it, to establish the new State Court for Bosnia and Herzegovina. It seems clear that BiH is on its way to creating another national court to handle serious matters of state outside of the national constitution.

Provincial Courts
The Dayton Accords put much of the judicial power in the hands of the two provincial authorities, the Federation and the Republic of Srpska. In fact, most cases are heard in the cantonal courts. Nonetheless, the structure and proceedings of these courts vary between the Federation and the RS. Within the Federation, there are three levels of courts: the cantonial, or trial, courts; a supreme court; and a constitutional court.

As at the national level, the Federation's constitutional court handles questions concerning the constitution of the Federation. Its supreme court, then, retains ultimate authority for other legal matters, but with a significant limitation. A loophole in the enabling legislation allows Croat-majority cantons to ignore the Federation's supreme court. The significance of this limitation is that, at least in Croat cantons, there is no appeal beyond the cantonal courts. Unfortunately, this arrangement opens court decisions to the influence of ethnic bias. For example, a Bosnian Muslim convicted of a crime in a Croat-majority canton has no opportunity to challenge the impartiality and fairness of the judicial decision, a right he or she would retain before the Federation's Supreme Court if the trial were held in a Bosniac-majority canton.

Apart from the province's court system, federation litigants retain the right to appeal to the provincial Human Rights Commission after they have exhausted their options in the courts. It is not yet clear which powers the Commission has, although it is said to offer a check on the court system to ensure that judicial decisions comport with European and international principles of human rights. The Federation has also created a separate judicial police force, to operate at both the federation and cantonal levels. The judicial police are supposed to offer protection to litigants, judges, and witnesses, as well as enforcing court orders. At present the judicial police have been created at the federation level and in two cantons, but questions of jurisdiction have arisen, particularly the extent to which the judicial police may duplicate the work of the cantonal police.

The Republic of Srpska also has three levels of courts, including a constitutional court, a supreme court, and the district courts. They operate roughly like their counterparts in the Federation, but there is no loophole that limits cases that may be heard in the higher courts. The RS constitutional court has exclusive jurisdiction over questions of constitutional law and is the recourse for litigants who seek annulment of administrative measures. The supreme court is the highest appellate court in the RS, with the district courts handling matters of general jurisdiction. It is not surprising that the Republic of Srpska, given its Serb majority, has borrowed extensively from the legal system of the Federal Republic of Yugoslavia (FRY), including Serbia and Montenegro, when formulating its new laws. For example, the RS has essentially adopted the FRY criminal code in full.

THE LEGAL PROFESSION

Much of the Bosnian legal system is a holdover from the FRY structure, including the organization of the legal profession. The Bosnian bar is a single system, with attorneys permitted to advise clients and appear before the bench. College graduates who received their first-level degree in law are qualified to practice under the tutelage of a seasoned attorney.

FAILURES OF THE JUSTICE SYSTEM

Arising out of a horrific five-year war, the emerging Bosnian judicial system has many weaknesses, a number of them related to the still-evolving political balance. Many prewar judges are missing and are presumed dead—victims of wartime atrocities. As a result, experienced, impartial judges have been replaced by untrained jurists appointed largely to represent "their" ethnic group on the bench. Indeed, the separation of the country into Serb, Muslim, and Croat areas encourages, if not ensures, that governmental functions—including the judiciary—operate on an ethnic basis.

A culture of lawlessness also survives the war. The shortages during the hostilities led to a Mafia-style black market, and the paramilitary operations themselves were part of a atmosphere of gangsterism that pervaded Bosnian society in the 1990s. Although the war is now over and reconstruction is underway, there remains a lack of respect for institutional authority throughout the country, a problem that makes it all the more difficult for the courts to command adherence to their decisions. Moreover, too many police officers are reluctant to enforce the law. In some jurisdictions, political leaders are intertwined with organized crime, bribing or threatening officers to look the other way while on the beat. Especially when police operate in uni-ethnic areas and are associated with a local strongman, they are reluctant to arrest friends of the black market dealers. In still other areas, alleged war criminals remain as powerful political or police officials, making it all but impossible for fair-minded public officials to do their jobs.

Even where ultranationalists do not hold power, the judicial system remains under the direct control of political leaders. For example, Alija Izetbegovic, former chairperson of the BiH presidency and president of the SDA political party, held a meeting of judges in the Federation to criticize their operations, including specific cases. As many human rights groups correctly pointed out, Izetbegovic had no constitutional authority to place political pressure on the judiciary, a practice that would be eschewed in most democratic nations. Political influence also extends to the Republica Srpska, where the ongoing struggle between moderates and hard-liners results in considerable political pressure on judges to rule "the right way."

The fact that political leaders control the appointment of judges severely restricts the courts' independence, for in such an ethnically divided country politicians usually appoint those jurists whom they are sure will rule for "their" people. For example, as the International Federation for Human Rights has noted, the president of the Sarajevo cantonal court could only appoint judges with the approval of the mayors of the local municipalities. Reports suggest that the mayors had almost exclusive influence, for no other judges or lawyers were consulted in the appointment process.

Such influence also extends to financial matters, where judges are dependent on politicians for their courts' budgets as well as their own salaries. Most courts lack basic resources, including such essential items as telephones or photocopies. As a result, there is a backlog in cases. In addition, judges' salaries are so low that judges may be tempted to supplement their income by taking bribes. Although the judiciary is nowhere near as contaminated by corruption as before the war, the culture may unfortunately be turning.

FUTURE OF THE BOSNIAN JUDICIARY

The Bosnian judiciary is fortunate to have a friend in the Office of the High Representative. As part of the office's judicial reform program, the high commissioner is working to encourage witness protection in the Bosnian courts, to promote uniform norms for court procedure, and to implement reforms on judicial selection, promotion, and remuneration. But most important is the office's goal to create a political constituency for judicial reform, as well as teaching the general public that they can use legal means to challenge political decisions. In a country with such a tortured political history, the future of the Bosnian judiciary depends on the country's prospective political culture. If political leaders can rise from the fire of ethnic warfare to pioneer a stable civil society, a fair and independent court system seems likely to follow. But if Bosnia's future lies in an ethnically divided country led by ultranationalist politicians, the rule of law seems destined to be buried alongside the many victims of the Bosnian War.

Jon B. Gould

See also Croatia; Macedonia; Serbia and Montenegro; Slovenia; Yugoslavia

References and further reading

Bosnia Constitution, http://www.uni-wuerzburg.de/law/bk00000_.html.
Bosnian Constitutional Court, http://www.ustavnisud.ba/home/en/index.html.
Constitutional Court of the Republic of Srpska, http://www.ustavnisud.org/index_e.html.
International Crisis Group, http://www.crisisweb.org
Office of the High Representative, http://www.ohr.int.

BOTSWANA

GENERAL INFORMATION

Botswana is a landlocked country in southern Africa that shares borders with Zimbabwe, the Republic of South Africa, Namibia, and Zambia. It covers an area of 581,730 square kilometers, slightly smaller than the state of Texas, and straddles the Tropic of Capricorn in the center of the Southern Africa plateau. Much of the country is flat, with gentle undulations and occasional rocky outcrops. Two distinct topographical regions exist, the hilly grassland in the east and the Kalahari Desert in the west, which accounts for more than two-thirds of Botswana's land area. Most of the country's population, estimated at 1,464,167 in 1999, belong to one of the eight major polities (*merafe*) that speak Setswana, although other groups exist, including San-speaking peoples (often referred to as Basarwa), Bakgalagadi, Bakalanga, and Baherero, together with a small number of people of Asian and European origin. Since the mid-1990s there has been a decline in the population growth rate due to falling fertility levels brought about by better education and more effective family planning services. It is predicted, however, that in future years population growth will be reduced much further as a result of deaths from AIDS. A high proportion of the population is made up of children and young people. Literacy has gradually been increasing in the years since independence in 1966. By 1995, an estimated 69.8 percent of the population fifteen years of age and older was able to read and write; the figures are disappointing, however, in relation to the sexes, for only about 60 percent of women were considered literate, as compared to some 80 percent of men.

At independence, Botswana was one of the poorest countries in Africa. Since then the country has experienced a remarkable economic transformation that in the past has been unmatched by any non–oil producing country in Africa. Botswana's main exports are diamonds, copper, nickel, and beef. Diamond mining alone represents about 30 percent of the country's gross domestic product (GDP). According to the United Nations Development Program (UNDP), in 1998 Botswana ranked fourth among African countries in terms of its Human Development Index (HDI), after the Seychelles, Mauritius, and South Africa. Nonetheless, not all citizens have benefited equally from the country's development, and it has been recognized that the gap between the better-off and the very poor is growing, so that it is estimated that half of all Batswana (as the dominant Bantu people of Botswana are called) live below the poverty line. In part, this is because subsistence agriculture, which provides a livelihood for more than 80 percent of the population, supplies only about 50 percent of food needs and accounts for only 4 percent of GDP. While unemployment is officially set at 21 percent, unofficial estimates place it closer to 40 percent.

Gaborone, the capital city, with a population of 133,468 in the 1991 census, straddles the north-south railway. It is located in the eastern part of the country where many Batswana live owing to climate, terrain, and enhanced access to resources.

Religious affiliation within Botswana ranges from Christianity (as espoused by mainstream churches as well

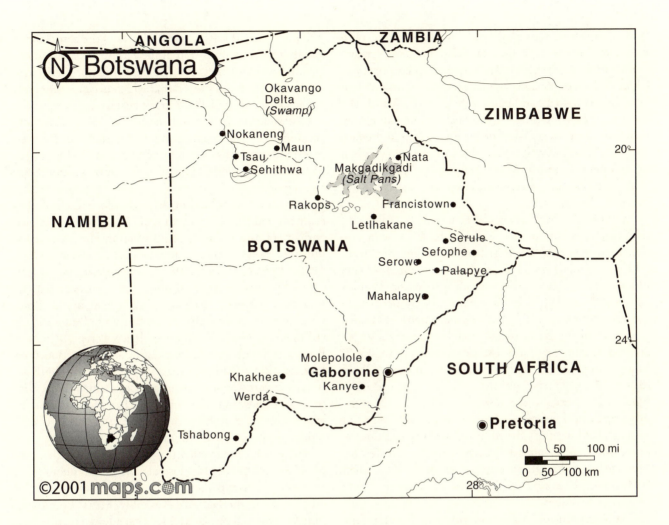

as by more evangelical and prophetic sects) and Islam to indigenous belief systems. Botswana's legal system incorporates both western-style and indigenous law in the form of common and customary law. It has two official languages, Setswana and English, although other languages, especially those connected with other Bantu-speaking peoples in southern Africa, are spoken. Botswana has a dry season from May to September and a rainy season from October to April, although drought is a recurring hazard. The climate is generally temperate, but temperatures may occasionally dip below freezing and reach upwards of 40° Centigrade.

HISTORY

Before independence in 1966, Botswana was known as the Bechuanaland Protectorate and subject to indirect British rule from 1885 onward. In the early nineteenth century, the territory that is now Botswana experienced the effects of warfare that restructured the geographical and political map of southern Africa. Such warfare included attacks by Amandebele under the leadership of Mzilikazi (who operated out of what became Southern Rhodesia, now Zimbabwe) as well as Boer aggression. When the Boers broke away from the British in 1842 and undertook the Great

Trek to settle in the Transvaal (that became the Southern African Republic) they had a great impact on the lives of Africans. They imposed land and labor policies that altered the social, economic, political, and demographic status quo within their extensive areas of settlement. The creation of a Protectorate saved the country that is now called Botswana from outright incorporation into the South African Republic. This was not the only threat that Africans faced, however, as they also had to deal with the expansionist tendencies of Cecil Rhodes, a prominent politician in the Cape Colony, and of the British South Africa company that he established. His aim was to take over the Protectorate and rule it. He had the support of powerful politicians in Great Britain but the plan failed due to vigorous opposition mounted by Batswana, assisted by their supporters, including the influential London Missionary Society. Three prominent chiefs, Khama, Bathoen and Sebele went to England and successfully protested against incorporation into Rhodesia.

The threat of incorporation arose once again when the Union of South Africa was formed as a British colony in 1910. This was because the South Africa Act establishing the Union provided for the future incorporation of the three British High Commission territories of Bechuanaland, Basutoland (Lesotho), and Swaziland along with Rhodesia. However, the act provided for consultation, and Batswana vociferously opposed incorporation. Chiefs Tshekedi Khama and Bathoen II threatened to take their case to London and fight it in the British law courts. At the same time, Britain became more and more unwilling to go ahead with the transfer owing to the race laws that were being introduced into the Union. When the Union of South Africa became a republic, this marked the end of any serious attempt to transfer the territories to South Africa.

In 1960, the Bechuanaland People's Party (BPP) was founded, maintaining close links with the African National Congress (ANC) of South Africa. The BPP soon split into two factions, which later became the Botswana Independence Party (BIP) and the Botswana People's Party (BPP). In 1961, Seretse Khama, the former heir to the chieftainship of the Bamangwato polity (*morafe*), gained a seat on the legislative council and was also appointed to the territory's executive council. In 1962, Khama formed the Bechuanaland Democratic Party (BDP). Many white settlers also gave their support to the BDP, in preference to the more radical BPP. In the territory's first direct legislative election under universal adult suffrage, held in 1965, the BDP won twenty-eight of the thirty-one seats. Khama duly became prime minister. Independence followed on September 30, 1966, when Bechuanaland became the Republic of Botswana, with Khama as president.

The constitution that underpinned the republic adopted a Westminster model of government establishing a parliamentary democracy within the country. The legislative branch consists of a parliament comprised of the House of Chiefs and the National Assembly. The House of Chiefs is primarily an advisory body consisting of Bangwato, Bakgatla, Bangwaketse, Bakwena, Batlokwa, Balete, Barolong, and Batawana chiefs plus six members appointed by these chiefs, four of whom are from four other administrative regions in the country and two of whom are specially elected members. The House of Chiefs is not part of the legislature. Its main duty is to advise the government on *merafe* and customary matters. Bills before the National Assembly dealing with such matters must be sent to the House of Chiefs for its advice, although the National Assembly is not bound to follow it. The National Assembly, which is directly elected, is a unicameral legislature. All citizens are eligible to vote from the age of eighteen. The presidential candidate whose declared supporters form the majority of directly elected members of parliament takes office as president and selects his ministers from among members of the National Assembly.

A commission (known as the Balopi Commission, after its chairman) was empowered by the president in 2000 to review those sections (77–79) of the constitution specifying the composition of the House of Chiefs to determine whether they contain discriminatory language. The language in question is that which declares the chiefs of the eight traditionally central Tswana polities to be the only permanent ex officio members of the House. The commission recommended that the sections be rewritten to extend representation beyond the eight centrally recognized polities to include all the country's administrative regions.

The president is head of the executive branch of government and presides over the cabinet. He must dissolve parliament and hold a general election after five years, but may do so sooner. National elections were held in 1965, 1969, 1974, 1979, 1984, 1989, 1994, and 1999. The BDP was returned to power on each occasion, although it has been challenged in the past by the Botswana National Front (BNF), the Botswana People's Party (BPP), The Botswana Independence Party (BIP), the Botswana Progressive Union (BPU), and the Botswana Freedom Party (BFP). In the 1994 election the BNF attracted strong support in urban areas, and for the first time an opposition party emerged from an election (in which over 70 percent of the electorate voted) to offer a serious challenge to the ruling party.

There is an independent judiciary with a high court presided over by the chief justice. The government's principal legal adviser is the attorney general, who has an ex officio seat on the National Assembly. He is also responsible for criminal prosecutions. Legal advice is centralised within the attorney general's chambers, whose staff service all government ministries and departments. All suits for or against government are instituted by or against the attorney general.

The main components of central government shown in the accompanying table. It is represented in each of the districts by the district administration, headed by a district commissioner. There are ten districts and nine district councils. There are city councils for the capital city, Gaborone, and for Francistown, as well as town councils for Lobatse and two major mining centers, Selebi-Phikwe and Jwaneng. District, city, and town councils have elected councillors, but the minister of local government and lands may nominate additional councillors. The civil service is headed by the permanent secretary to the president, and each ministry is headed at official level by a permanent secretary.

At independence, Botswana was surrounded by Southern Rhodesia, South Africa, and Nambia, countries that were ruled by white elites who refused to share power with their African citizens. Unable to challenge its neighbors directly, Botswana assisted the struggle for African liberation by providing sanctuary and indirect support for nationalist guerrilla movements until South-

Legal Structure of Botswana Courts

National Court of Appeal	

National High Court	

Chief Magistrates' Courts (District Level) Principal Magistrates (District Level)	National Customary Courts Commissioner
Senior Magistrates' Courts (District Level)	Customary Courts of Appeal (National Level)

Magistrates' Grade One (District Level)	Higher Customary Courts (Chiefs, District Level)
Magistrates' Grade Two (District Level)	Lower Customary Courts (District and Local Levels)

ern Rhodesia acquired independence as Zimbabwe in 1980, Namibia in 1990, and the Republic of South Africa became a post-apartheid state with the adoption of an interim constitution in 1994 and a new constitution in 1996. Botswana was a founding member of the Southern African Development Co-ordination Conference (SADCC), formed in 1979 with the aim of encouraging regional development and reducing members economic dependence on South Africa. This organization was superseded in 1992 by the Southern African Development Community (SADC). In the interests of broader international co-operation Botswana is a member of the Organisation of African Unity (OAU), the United Nations (UN) and the Commonwealth. From October 1997 it participated in a Commonwealth Ministerial Action Group, which investigated human rights abuses in member states with military governments and worked to restore democratic civilian rule in Nigeria. Botswana's principled stand over apartheid, its enviable political stability and democratic record, and its reputation for moderation of approach have given the country a minor but effective voice in many international deliberations.

LEGAL CONCEPTS

Like many African countries subjected to colonial rule, Botswana inherited a legal tradition that it retained on independence. Thus western-style law was upheld through the recognition of common law that was defined as "any law, whether written or unwritten, in force in Botswana, other than customary law" (Customary Law [Application and Ascertainment] Act No. 51 [1969], sec-

tion 2). This form of law covers Roman-Dutch law received into the Protectorate in 1885 by proclamation via the Cape, then a British colony (often referred to as Cape colonial law), and legislation emanating from the National Assembly. However, this law was received law and did not reflect the customs and practices of the indigenous people, which became encapsulated under the heading of customary law, defined in the 1969 act as being "in relation to any particular tribe or tribal community, the customary law of that tribe or tribal community so far as it is not incompatible with the provisions of any written law or contrary to morality, humanity or natural justice." The proviso to the 1969 act, often referred to as the repugnancy clause, is a common feature of legal systems associated with former British colonies.

There is disagreement about the extent to which Tswana law and custom (*mekgwa le melao ya Setwana*), viewed by some as "living law," is congruent with the customary law recognized by the state, as well as about the extent to which customary law is a product of the colonial encounter. Whatever the position, the distinction between common and customary law gave rise to a legal pluralism that at its inception was intended to provide one law, common law, for the colonizers and another, customary law, for the colonized, thus marking a clear divide between those of European descent and Africans. In these terms pluralism represented separate or dual systems of law. The rationale behind this was that the Africans were to be left to run their own affairs except where these might come into conflict with colonial powers. In keeping with this approach common and customary law operated through different institutions and personnel. While they were never totally separate and some Batswana—namely, elites—were able to utilize common law, the rationale clearly became redundant when the Protectorate gained independence and Botswana became a postcolonial state. Since then, all Batswana have in theory had access to and are governed by a range of institutions and personnel incorporating both common and customary law.

STRUCTURE OF COURT SYSTEM

The customary courts in Botswana are successors to an elaborate system of courts that existed prior to the colonial period and have survived in a different form since then. These courts were tied to the sociopolitical organization of precolonial Tswana societies. Such organization was predicated around a hierarchy of progressively more inclusive coresidential and administrative groupings, beginning with households and expanding to cover wards, extended family groups in *kgotlas*. A kgotla is the assembly center (both the physical location and the body of members) of a group of households presided over by a male headman or ward head. In the past, all heads of household were related through the male line, but this is rarely the case today. Nonetheless, men continue to hold power as headmen and ward heads. Wards are the major units of political organization of a Tswana village; they are still presided over by men. The most powerful ward is called *kgosing*. The word derives from *kgosi*, typically translated as "chief." Kgosing refers both to the chief's ward and to the chief's kgotla (often, loosely, called the chief's court), which is the apex of the administrative and political structure through which a kgosi exercises his power.

Customary courts today are governed under the Customary Courts Act (Cap. 05:05), which recognizes three categories of courts. These include lower customary courts, which roughly correspond with the traditional ward courts under a headman but may also be courts convened by a headman in a small outlying village. Further up the chain come higher customary courts, normally the chief's courts, which serve as courts of appeal from lower customary courts, and in some cases as courts of first instance. Appeal lies from lower to higher customary courts, and provision is also made under the Act for cases to be reviewed by the customary courts commissioner, an official who plays a supervisory function, but who also has the authority to act in the same manner as a subordinate court. At the highest level come the customary courts of appeal. Although provided for since 1968, the first customary court of appeal did not come into existence until 1986. The court, which is mainly based in Gaborone but also operates from Francistown, also sits on circuit in other parts of the country and has original jurisdiction in certain cases that are beyond the jurisdiction of the lower and higher customary courts. It also possesses appellate jurisdiction in matters on appeal from the ordinary customary courts below. Appeals from the court go straight to the High Court.

General principles for the application and ascertainment of customary law are contained in the Customary Law (Application and Ascertainment) Act (Cap.16:01) passed in 1969. (It has since been consolidated and is called the Common Law and Customary Law Act.) The Customary Law Act lays down the general rule that customary law is the system primarily applicable between "tribesmen" in civil matters, but with three exceptions. These exceptions provide that customary law will not apply if the parties to the dispute expressly or impliedly intended the matter to be regulated by common law; where the transaction out of which the case arose is one unknown to customary law; and where the parties themselves have excluded its application by executing a written document specifying that common law is to apply instead. It is important to note that while customary law could not be applied to non-Africans during the colonial era, today non-Africans may expressly or impliedly bring it into operation in cases where they are involved with "tribesmen."

Common and customary institutions vary in rank according to the statutory powers that they possess. Chiefs' courts, although at the apex of power within *merafe*, nonetheless find themselves operating as a low-ranking institution in terms of the national legal system, with their authority that extends to common law confined to minor civil and criminal matters under the Customary Courts Act and the Customary Courts (Procedure) Rules. This process of curtailing chiefs' powers has been ongoing for many years beginning with the colonial period. By the mid-1930s, for example, most areas of public law had been removed from the jurisdiction of traditional authorities and brought within the sphere of colonial law, with the result that many areas of law such as constitutional, criminal and labor law today fall exclusively within the domain of common law.

Magistrates' Courts are constituted and governed by the Magistrates' Courts Act (Cap.04.02) as amended by the Magistrates' Courts Amendment Act 1992, which provides for five grades of magistrate. The lowest grade covers magistrate grade 2, moving up to magistrate grade 1 until reaching the higher echelons of senior magistrate, and on to principal magistrate until arriving at the most senior grade of chief magistrate. These Magistrates' Courts exercise jurisdiction within the district within which they are situated, and like the customary courts they are subject to restrictions in certain civil and criminal matters. Although they mainly apply common law, they potentially have jurisdiction to apply customary law although the extent of their jurisdiction in this area remains unclear.

The constitution provides for the High Court of Botswana, which is regulated by the High Court Act. It is a court of record and has unlimited original jurisdiction in civil and criminal matters, under any law and in all cases arising within the country. Most cases that come before this court under its original jurisdiction involve homicide and the dissolution of civil marriages that fall outside the scope of the subordinate courts. The court also has appellate jurisdiction in cases from all subordinate courts and exercises review functions. It mainly applies common law, although it may apply customary law in the rare situations where it hears an appeal on a point of customary law. Jurisdiction is also vested in the high court to decide any question as to interpretation of the constitution. Given the size of the country, the court has a permanent presence in two sites, Francistown in the north and Lobatse in the south, although a judge may take the court on circuit.

The constitution also provides for a court of appeal, which is constituted under the Court of Appeal Act. Like the High Court, the court of appeal is a court of record with appellate jurisdiction over all High Court decisions in both civil and criminal matters. Unlike the high court,

Structure of Botswana's Government

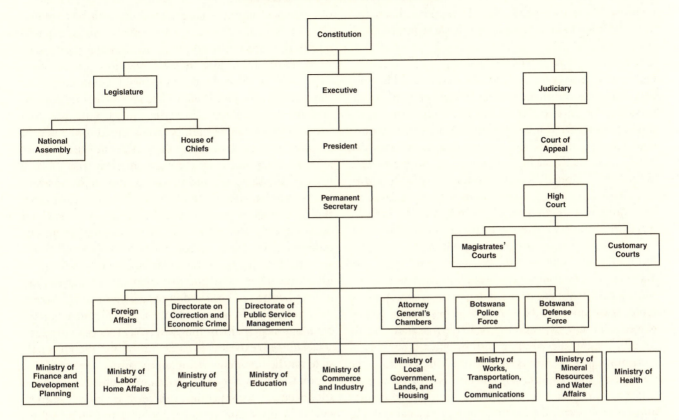

however, it has no original jurisdiction (although certain questions of law may be reserved for it). Its decisions are binding on all other courts in the country. The court comprises a president, the chief justice (ex officio), any number of justices of appeal as the national president may prescribe, and the judges of the high court (ex officio). In practice high court ex officio judges have not sat in the court of appeal since the 1980s. Normally three members sit as a court of appeal, except in certain important cases, where a quorum of five is required. High Court judges may not sit on appeals from their own decisions, and the final decision of the court is based on that of the majority. The court has jurisdiction over common and customary law, although it deals primarily with the former in practice.

SPECIALIZED JUDICIAL BODIES

The office of the ombudsman was established by the Ombudsman Act in 1995. The responsibility of the ombudsman is to implement and administer the act with a view to preventing maladministration in connection with government affairs. The ombudsman investigates any improper conduct by persons performing a public function and, where necessary, recommends action to remedy the situation.

The Industrial Court was established by the Trade Dis-

pute (Amendment) Act of 1992 to replace the office of "permanent arbitrator" created by the 1982 act. The court was established "for the purpose of settling trade disputes, and the furtherance, securing and maintenance of good industrial relations in Botswana" (s.17[10]). The court has therefore been given jurisdiction over a wide range of labor matters, but it can only hear a dispute once the matter has been properly referred to it. The court has no power to intervene in a dispute on its own initiative.

The Industrial Court may generally be considered as having equivalent status to the High Court in that Industrial Court judges are appointed by the President from among persons possessing the qualifications to be judges on the High Court (s. 17[3]). Section 25(2) of the act similarly provides that any decision of the Industrial Court shall have the same force and effect as a judgement or order of the High Court. The only qualification to this general rule is that where a question concerning the interpretation of the constitution arises, the Industrial Court is classified as a "subordinate court" and may therefore be required to refer the question to the High Court.

The status of the Industrial Court may soon change. The Constitution (Amendment No. 2) Bill of 1999 proposed to amend the definition of the term "subordinate court" contained in section 127 (1) of the constitution by providing that the Industrial Court is not a subordinate court. Although this bill was not passed before Parliament was dissolved in the 1999 election, it is likely that a similar bill will be introduced in the near future.

STAFFING

Customary courts are run by local government. The minister of local government and lands may, on behalf of the president, establish or recognize an already existing customary court by warrant. Official warrants are granted mainly, in practice, to chief's courts in the various districts, traditionally the highest courts of appeal. However, lower-level customary courts, administered by headmen and chiefs representatives' courts in outlying villages are also sometimes granted official recognition. It was estimated that there were around 361 customary courts in the country in Botswana's latest development plan (NDP8). But it is difficult to state with any accuracy how many customary courts exist overall, because not all operating customary courts are recognized by the state. In some cases unwarranted courts exist because headmen perceive of themselves as fulfilling a role that traditionally would have included dealing with disputes. Thus formal and informal perceptions of justice clash regarding the number of courts dispensing justice daily to Botswana's rural majority. Within these courts no legal representation is permitted and personnel have no formal training as lawyers but hold office on the basis of their genealogical connections within a morafe. Proceedings are conducted in Setswana and are recorded only in the chief's court. Appeals to the Magistrates' Court are translated into English.

During the colonial period, magistrates were drawn from a class of administrative officers (including district commissioners) who had no legal training but were invested with powers to carry out judicial functions. Today qualifications are prescribed by the president acting in accordance with the advice of the Judicial Service Commission (JSC), and it is only professionally trained lawyers who are appointed to act as magistrates. According to NDP8, there are currently fifteen Magistrates' Courts throughout Botswana. Whereas in the past, magistrates tended to be drawn from among former British or colonial judges or from other African countries such as Uganda or Tanzania, there are now a high number of Batswana in post, several of whom are women. Proceedings at all levels take place in English (with an interpreter being provided where necessary) and are recorded. Legal representation is competent but not always adhered to, especially in civil cases concerning family matters.

The High Court consists of the chief justice and such number of judges as the president may appoint. The court is conducted in English by a single judge, but provision is made for the summoning of assessors to assist the court in an advisory capacity. Such assessors do not have a decision-making role, although their agreement or disagreement with the judge's decision must be noted on the court's record. Assessors are normally only called in to advise the court on questions of customary law. Like magistrates, there was a tendency to appoint non-Batswana to judicial appointments in this court, although the first Motswana to become a chief justice was appointed in 1990. Since the late 1990s, the first Motswana woman has also been appointed to the bench.

Both the chief justice and the president of the court of appeal are appointed by the state president, that is, by a political figure. Other judges are appointed by the president acting on the advice of the JSC, which also advises the president on discipline and removal of judges and other judicial officers. Once appointed, a judge cannot be removed from office except under constitutional provision. Before a judge can be removed from office, the president must refer the matter to a tribunal for investigation. Once a person has been appointed a judge, she or he is entitled to remain in office until the age of sixty-five or such other age as parliament may prescribe. On attaining such age, a judge is expected to vacate office, although it is possible for the president, acting on the advice of the JSC, to appoint or allow a judge to continue in office beyond the stipulated age for a period of three years. However, most judges in Botswana are not appointed but are hired on contract, so that the procedure set out in the constitution is little used. In practice the contract tends to be for a period of three years and is renewable at the recommendation of the JSC. Such practice raises questions about whether a voluntary contractual arrangement can supersede a constitutional provision and the status of provisions relating to removal from office. In doing so, it raises questions about the independent status of the judiciary.

LEGAL EDUCATION AND QUALIFICATIONS

The Legal Practitioners Act 1996 introduced three sets of qualifications applying to citizens, commonwealth citizens, and noncitizens. Citizens must have obtained their L.L.B. degree from the University of Botswana (or its predecessors) or from a "specified university." Such universities are mainly in the United Kingdom, Ireland, and South Africa but also include Syracuse University and American University in the United States and universities in Australia, Zambia and Ghana. In addition, a citizen must pass a form of traineeship called pupillage. It takes one year to serve pupillage and this must be done under a pupil master who has practiced law for seven years. As far as Commonwealth citizens are concerned, they must have an L.L.B. degree and have been admitted to practice law either as a barrister/advocate or attorney/solicitor in the United Kingdom, Ireland, South Africa, or Zimbabwe. They must also have served pupillage in their own country. Commonwealth citizens must also be ordinarily resident in Botswana or intend to permanently reside in Botswana and their own country should extend reciprocal provisions to Batswana wishing to practice there. Noncitizens must either have qualified from the University of Botswana or have a degree from a recognized foreign university. Where the latter is the case, they must also sit prescribed examinations and serve pupillage. In addition, they are required to be ordinarily resident in Botswana or to intend to be permanently resident there.

Both advocates and attorneys have rights of audience before all the courts and may, therefore, choose whether or not to appear before a particular court. However, if admitted to practice as an advocate, that person is expected to act as one and not to deal directly with the public as clients in the way that attorneys or solicitors do.

So far there is only law school in the country, at the University of Botswana, which runs a five-year program taught by staff drawn from Africa, the United Kingdom, and Botswana. In 2001, the enrolment was around 185 students, 15 percent of whom represented international students from all over the world.

IMPACT

The extent to which women are placed at a disadvantage in terms of their access to and use of, the legal system has been the subject of debate, highlighted by the case of *Unity Dow v. The Attorney General* (High Court Misca. No. 124/90). Unity Dow, a prominent lawyer (and now a High Court judge), challenged changes made by the Citizenship Act in 1984 restricting the categories of persons who could become citizens of Botswana through birth or descent, with the effect that children born to Tswana women married to foreigners no longer had rights to citizenship. These restrictions did not apply to the children of Tswana men married to noncitizens or to the children of unmarried Tswana women whose fathers were noncitizens. As Dow had married a U.S. citizen and subsequently had two children, these children were denied citizenship. Dow argued that the 1984 act's provisions violated some of her fundamental rights, because as a female she was prevented from passing citizenship to her children, which denied her the equal protection of the law and the right not to be discriminated against on the basis of her sex (guaranteed under sections 3 and 15 of the constitution).

This was the first time in Botswana's history that a woman challenged the government in court. When Dow raised her action she was a leading member of the feminist organization Emang Basadi (Stand Up Women) and a participant in the Women and Law in Southern Africa Research Project. In its response to Dow's challenge, the state argued society in Botswana upholds a patrilineal structure that is male oriented, and that this had been taken into account when the constitution was enacted. This meant that section 15, which deals with discrimina-

tion, expressly declined to cover sex because it was alleged that the whole fabric of customary law revolves around the notion of a patrilineal society, which by its very nature discriminates on the basis of sex. The High Court rejected this argument on the grounds that it would be offensive to modern thinking and the spirit of the constitution to find that the constitution was deliberately framed to permit sex discrimination. In reaching this decision, the judge was heavily influenced by the provisions of the Convention on the Elimination of All Forms of Discrimination Against Women, although at the time Botswana was not a signatory to the convention. On appeal, the court of appeal reaffirmed the High Court's decision in *The Attorney General v. Unity Dow* (Court of Appeal, Civil Appeal No. 4/91), once again relying on international human rights instruments upholding nondiscrimination, equal protection of the law, and the elimination of discrimination against women in reaching its judgment. Under pressure the government passed the Citizenship (Amendment) Act 1995, which altered the law to provide that children acquire citizenship from either parent, by birth if they are born in Botswana and by descent if born outside the country.

Anne Griffiths

See also Alternative Dispute Resolution; Customary Law; Feminist Jurisprudence; Human Rights Law; Indigenous/Folk Legal Systems; Jurisdiction; Legal Pluralism; Parliamentary Supremacy; Public Law; Trial Courts
References and further reading
Ayeni, Victor, and Kershav Sharma. 2000. *Ombudsman in Botswana.* London: Commonwealth Secretariat.
Botswana, Republic of. *National Development Plan 1991–1997 (NDP7).* Ministry of Finance and Development Planning, Central Statistics Office. Gaborone: Government Printer.
———. *National Development Plan 1997/98–2002/03 (NDP8).* Ministry of Finance and Development Planning, Central Statistics Office. Gaborone: Government Printer.
Botswana Budget Speech 1999/2000 at http://www.newafrica.com/profiles/Botswana.htm.
Report of the Presidential Commission of Inquiry into Sections 77, 78 and 79 of the Constitution of Botswana. 2000. Gaborone: Republic of Botswana.
Briscoe, Andrew. 2000. *The Labour Laws of Botswana.* Business School of Botswana: Morula Press.
Dow, Unity, ed. 1995. *The Citizenship Case: The Attorney General of the Republic of Botswana v Unity Dow: Court Documents, Judgments, Cases and Materials.* Gaborone: Lentswe La Lesedi (Pty) Ltd, on behalf of Metlhaetsile Women's Information Centre, Mochudi.
Griffiths, Anne. 1997. *In The Shadow of Marriage: Gender and Justice in an African Community.* Chicago: University of Chicago Press.
Otlhogile, Bojosi. 1994. *A History of the Higher Courts of Botswana, 1912–1900.* Gaborone: Mmegi Publishing House.
Molokomme, Athaliah. 1991. *"Children of the Fence": The*

Maintenance of Extra-Marital Children under Law and Practice in Botswana. Research Report No. 46. Leiden: African Studies Centre.

Quansah, Emmanuel Kwabena. 1993. *Introduction to the Botswana Legal System.* Gaborone: University of Botswana.

Tlou, Thomas, and Alec Campbell. 1984. *History of Botswana.* Gaborone: Macmillan Botswana.

BRAZIL

Brazil is the fifth-largest country in the world in terms of land mass, and with 170 million inhabitants, it is the sixth most populous. Its gross domestic product of U.S.$588 billion makes it the tenth-largest economy in the world as well.

Unlike the other countries of Latin America, Brazil was colonized by the Portuguese. In 1808, when Napoleon's armies invaded, Portugal's royal family moved the throne to Brazil, and seven years later, Brazil was officially proclaimed a kingdom coequal with Portugal. Even after the French threat to Portugal subsided, King João VI remained in Brazil until 1821, when he reluctantly returned to Portugal. He left behind his minor son, Dom Pedro, as the regent prince. In 1822, Dom Pedro declared Brazilian independence. The reality, however, was that Brazil had ceased to be a colony years earlier. Unlike its Spanish neighbors, it did not have to fight a war to secure independence. Dom Pedro became Brazil's first emperor, and he and later his son, Dom Pedro II, ruled the country as a constitutional monarchy until 1889.

GOVERNMENTAL STRUCTURE

Brazil's first constitution, promulgated in 1824, divided the nation into provinces with limited autonomy. In 1891, the military overthrew the monarchy and established a federal system of government modeled on the U.S. Constitution. Unlike the United States, the Brazilian states have never been sovereign entities. From the country's inception, power has been heavily concentrated in the central government. During certain historical periods, the autonomy of state and local governments has increased; during other periods, particularly military dictatorships, such autonomy has sharply decreased. The present constitution, promulgated in 1988 as a reaction to twenty-one years of military rule, substantially augmented the autonomy of state and local governments.

The federal government (the Union) is headed by a president and vice-president, elected by direct popular vote for four-year term that is renewable for a single subsequent term. The bicameral federal legislature consists of the Senate, with 81 members, and the Chamber of Deputies, with 513 members. Each state and the Federal District elect three senators for eight-year terms. Members of the Chamber of Deputies are popularly elected in the states and Federal District for four-year terms. The number of deputies from each state is theoretically proportional to population. But the small states are overrepresented because each is entitled to a minimum of eight deputies, whereas the populous states are underrepresented because of a cap on the number of deputies they can elect.

The traditional civil law notion that the Congress has a monopoly over legislation requires qualification for Brazil. The constitution specifically authorizes the president to enact provisional measures with the force of law on any matter he or she deems urgent and relevant. In theory, provisional measures were void ab initio if not ratified by Congress within thirty days, but Brazilian presidents routinely reissued unratified provisional measures every month. This practice, which has been upheld by the Supreme Federal Tribunal unless the measure has been specifically rejected by Congress, essentially allowed presidents to govern by decree. Between September 1988 and August 24, 2001, presidents issued 601 original provisional measures and reissued 5,474. A total of 464 were converted into law, 29 were revoked, and 22 were rejected. To curb abuse of the provisional measure, a constitutional amendment was adopted on September 11, 2001, making provisional measures valid for sixty days. If Congress fails to act on the measure within this period, it may be extended only once for another sixty days. A provisional measure that has been rejected or has expired may not be reissued during the same legislative session. A lapsed provisional measure is no longer void ab initio; any legal relations constituted under it are to be regulated by legislative decree, or, in default thereof, by the provisional measure itself. Provisional measures may no longer be issued with respect to a number of subjects, such as political rights and parties; criminal, procedural, or electoral law; or budgets. Nor may they be used to detain or sequester private property.

Each state has its own constitution and a governmental structure that resembles the Union. The executive is headed by a governor and a lieutenantgovernor, elected by direct popular vote for a four-year term that can be renewed once. The size of the unicameral legislature is three times each state's representation in the federal Chamber of Deputies, but if a state has more than twelve federal deputies, each deputy over that number increases the state legislature's size on a one-to-one basis. Representatives are popularly elected for four-year, renewable terms. Each state also has its own judiciary.

States are further subdivided into more than 5,500 counties (*municípios*), each with its own organic law and quasi-autonomous system of government. Each county is headed by a prefect and vice-prefect, elected by direct popular vote for a four-year term that can be renewed

one time. County legislatures have a minimum of nine popularly elected aldermen, in the least populated counties, to a maximum of fifty-five, in counties with more than 5 million inhabitants. Counties do not have their own judiciaries.

Brazil's current constitution contains a complex scheme for dividing powers and revenues among the Union, the states, the Federal District, and the counties. It specifically provides for exclusive, joint, and concurrent powers and permits delegation of exclusive powers. Unfortunately, there is considerable overlap and redundancy among the different categories of legislative powers.

The Union has exclusive powers to regulate a great many areas, such as international relations, war, defense, declaration of states of siege, currency, broadcasting, postal service, interstate and foreign commerce, and expropriation. It also has the power to legislate as to civil, commercial, penal, procedural, electoral, agrarian, maritime, aeronautical, space, and labor law, which means that the basic codes are federal. Nevertheless, states may be authorized by complementary laws, which require approval by an absolute majority, to legislate on particular

subjects within certain areas of exclusive federal power. The Union, states, Federal District, and counties have joint powers in twelve areas and concurrent authority in sixteen. The Union may enact only general rules in areas of concurrent powers. Once federal rules are enacted, the states may adopt only supplementary legislation. If no federal rules have been enacted, the states are free to regulate, but a supervening federal law prevails over any inconsistent state law. The constitution's residual clause provides that powers not forbidden to the states by the constitution are reserved to the states. Counties may legislate about subjects of local interest and supplement federal and state laws. Counties are also assured political, legislative, administrative, and financial autonomy. The Union may intervene in the states to deal with serious threats to public order, to restore the credit of states that fail to pay their debts, to guarantee a republic form of government, to enforce federal law and court orders, and to protect county autonomy. States may intervene in the counties to ensure that government debts are paid, that public accounts are lawfully rendered, and that court decisions are enforced.

BRAZIL'S CIVIL LAW TRADITION

Brazil is a civil law country, which means that its legal system and legal culture are heavily influenced by Roman law. The heavily Romanized legislation that the Portuguese colonizers brought to Brazil remained in force as the governing rule for private disputes until 1917, when Brazil's first civil code went into force. At the heart of the Portuguese legislation was the Ordenações Filipinas, promulgated for the Portuguese in 1603 by Philip III of Spain (Philip II of Portugal). Although often referred to as the Código Filipino, the Ordenações was not really a code but rather a compilation of prior compilations, which, in turn, amalgamated the Roman law of Justinian's Corpus Juris, the *forais* (municipal charters granted to reconquered towns that contained detailed rules and special privileges), customary usage, the Visigothic Code, the Siete Partidas (the Spanish codification of 1265 adopted as supplementary legislation), canon law, and the general legislation of Portugal since 1211. Despite being a hodgepodge of overlapping and inconsistent amendments, the Ordenações remained at the heart of Brazil's private law for almost a century after independence and a full fifty years after Portugal had discarded it.

The Ordenações specifically directed that Roman law should be utilized to fill any gaps in domestic law. Because Portuguese law was so omissive and technically inferior, lawyers and judges often went directly to Roman law for the applicable rule. In 1769, as a reaction to this practice, Portugal enacted the Law of Right Reason (Lei de Boa Razão), which directed the judiciary to apply Roman law only to fill legislative lacunae and only when Roman law accorded with "right reason": in other words, when it was consistent with natural law (meaning Roman ethical ideals formally recognized by the legal rules and practices of Christian nations). The Law of Right Reason also made decisions of Portugal's highest court a source of law with binding precedential value—a distinct departure from the civil law tradition, which does not regard judicial decisions as a source of law.

THE BASIC LEGAL CODES

Brazilian law is heavily codified. In the civil law tradition, a code is not merely a compilation or consolidation of prior laws. Rather, it is a systematic and comprehensive treatment of a large body of law meant to endure for a long period of time. A code's provisions are the distillation of years of comparative study of the legislation of other countries and scholarly treatises in an attempt to select the best system of regulation. Brazil's basic codes are the Civil Code, the Commercial Code, the Penal Code, the Code of Civil Procedure, and the Code of Criminal Procedure. All are federal laws, and all apply uniformly in the twenty-six states and Federal District.

The Civil Code

At the heart of Brazilian private law is the Civil Code. The task of drafting a civil code was initially entrusted to Teixeira de Freitas, one of Brazil's greatest jurists. He never completed the project, largely because he insisted on combining civil and commercial law into a single code. The legislature refused and eventually canceled his contract. Nevertheless, his rough draft (*esboço*) heavily influenced the drafters of other Latin American civil codes, particularly the Argentine Civil Code. In 1899, the task of codification eventually fell to Clôvis Beviláqua, who completed a draft code in one year. Congressional approval required an additional sixteen years.

The substance of the Civil Code is based primarily on Roman, French, Portuguese, and canon law. Yet its structure reflects the influence of the German Civil Code of 1896. Brazil's code is divided into three parts: (1) an introductory section dealing with general principles of interpretation and conflicts rules; (2) a general part dealing with persons, things, and juristic acts; and (3) a special part dealing with family law, property, torts, contracts, and inheritance.

Beviláqua's code has been much amended. In 1941, the conflicts-of-laws principles were replaced by the new Law of Introduction to the Civil Code. Its heavy emphasis on freedom of contract and individualism has been modified by a series of laws restricting contractual freedom. Family law has been extensively revised, replacing a decidedly patriarchal view of the family with greater gender equality. A law permitting absolute divorce was adopted in 1977. Discrimination against illegitimate and adoptive children has been eliminated.

In 2003, a new civil code, drafted by a commission of law professors chaired by Miguel Reale, will go into force. The draft fulfills Teixeira de Freitas's vision of unifying private law by including the regulation of most commercial activity within the Civil Code. It also incorporates the great bulk of the amendments made to the present Civil Code by subsequent supplemental legislation. After lingering for twenty-six years in Congress, the new code was finally approved on August 15, 2001. Because of the long delay, the new code begins with signs of obsolescence, failing to deal with current problems such as protection of human embryos, artificial insemination, and custody shared by separated parents.

The Commercial Code

Brazil's original Commercial Code, adopted in 1850, is still formally in effect but is hopelessly obsolete and largely irrelevant. The code regulates mercantile contracts, bankruptcy, admiralty, transportation, commercial agency, financing, banking, commercial companies, and negotiable instruments. Most of its important provisions, however, have been replaced by supplemental legislation.

Business entities are regulated by specific statutes, such as the 1976 Corporation Law and the 1919 Limited Liability Companies Decree. Bankruptcy, air transport, antitrust, intellectual property, capital markets, banking, franchising, accounts receivable financing, foreign investment, and negotiable instruments are all regulated by specific federal laws. Moreover, much commercial activity is supervised by federal agencies such as the Central Bank, the Securities Commission (CVM), and the Administrative Council for Economic Defense (CADE).

Penal Code and the Code of Criminal Procedure

Brazil's current Penal Code and Code of Criminal Procedure were both adopted by decree during the dictatorship of Getúlio Vargas (in 1940 and 1941, respectively). Serious tension exists between the liberal individual rights guarantees of the 1988 Constitution and the Code of Criminal Procedure. The code is excessively formalist and obsolete. In many cases, it assures that the defendant will be subject to extensive, secret interrogation and long periods of pretrial detention rather granted than his or her constitutional right to due process. Its archaic and dilatory written procedure is widely blamed for the huge delays in resolving criminal cases.

With the exception of intentional homicide cases, criminal cases are tried solely by judges in Brazil. There are no grand juries. The decision to prosecute public criminal actions is made by the Public Ministry, an autonomous institution responsible for defending the legal order. Generally, members of the Public Ministry regard their duty to prosecute as mandatory, although in certain cases, the victim must file charges. A criminal conviction also acts as a civil judgment against the defendant in favor of the victim or the victim's family.

A government-appointed commission recently submitted a substantial set of revisions to the present Code of Criminal Procedure. These reforms place greater emphasis on orality and due process, permit cross-examination of witnesses, prevent use of illegally obtained evidence, and eliminate any inference of guilt from exercising the constitutional right to remain silent. Draft legislation significantly amending the Penal Code is also pending before Congress.

Code of Civil Procedure

The Roman-canonical system of civil procedure in the Ordenações Filipinas governed civil cases in Brazil until the 1891 Constitution authorized each state to adopt its own civil procedure code. The 1934 Constitution allocated the power to promulgate a code of civil procedure to the federal government, which enacted the first national code in 1939. The present Code of Civil Procedure replaced this code in 1973, making numerous improvements. Nevertheless, it still suffers from excessive formalism and is largely responsible for the huge delays so common in civil litigation.

Brazil does not use juries in civil cases. All findings of fact and law are made by judges, although experts frequently help the judges determine complicated factual or technical questions. Except for small claims courts and summary proceedings, the entire pleading stage is entirely written. In certain cases, the judge may enter judgment without even holding a hearing. Evidence is introduced piecemeal in the pleadings, in a series of written submissions to the court clerk, and in a public hearing before the judge. The actual questioning of witnesses is done by the judge, who will generally ask questions that counsel request. There is no opportunity for cross-examination or redirect examination as in common law procedure.

The losing party in Brazilian litigation generally has a right to de novo redetermination on appeal of both law and facts without posting a supersedeas bond. Normally, judgments on appeal may not be executed. Execution of a judgment requires bringing a separate action, but certain kinds of debts are treated by Brazilian law as the functional equivalent of a judicial judgment. Hence, one can bring an executory action directly on negotiable instruments; debts secured by a mortgage, pledge, or bond; tax debts; and in other cases expressly provided for by statute. A 1985 law created a limited class action for the protection of environmental, cultural, and consumer interests. This has been considerably expanded by the Code of Consumer Protection of 1990.

THE BRAZILIAN JUDICIAL SYSTEM

After adoption of the 1891 Constitution, Brazil instituted a dual judicial system of federal and state courts. As in the United States, state courts are courts of general jurisdiction, and federal courts are courts of limited jurisdiction. Federal court jurisdiction is generally limited to cases in which (1) the Union has a patrimonial interest, (2) a crime involves federal property or services, (3) an international concern is present, or (4) Indian rights are disputed. Brazil also has three specialized court systems within the regular judiciary: the Labor Courts, the Electoral Courts, and the Military Courts. Outside the regular judiciary, the Union, states, Federal District, and counties have Tribunals of Accounts, with responsibility for supervising the legality of governmental expenditures.

Brazil has a career judiciary, with opportunities for lateral entry. A percentage of the seats (usually one-fifth) in the higher state and federal courts are reserved for distinguished lawyers and members of the Public Ministry. A Brazilian who has practiced law for two years starts a judicial career by passing written and oral tests. Those who pass start in entry-level judicial districts and eventually are promoted to the higher courts, either on merit or seniority. After a two-year probationary period, judges have life tenure but must retire at age seventy. Judicial salaries may not be reduced, and judges may not be involuntarily transferred.

The Public Ministry is an autonomous parallel institution to the judiciary, with responsibility for defending the legal order, prosecuting crimes, and instituting certain types of public actions to defend public patrimony, the environment, and other collective interests. It is headed by the procurator general, who is appointed by the president for a two-year term and removable only by the president with the prior approval of an absolute majority of the Senate. Like the judiciary, members of the Public Ministry are career officers, with guarantees of life tenure, nonreducibility of salary, and nontransferability. Members of the Public Ministry often submit nonbinding legal opinions to the courts. The Union is represented in the courts by a separate institution, the advocacy general, which also furnishes legal advice to the executive.

THE FEDERAL COURTS

The Supreme Federal Tribunal

Brazil's highest court is the Supreme Federal Tribunal (STF), which consists of eleven justices (*ministros*) and normally sits in panels of five. Except for a few types of cases, only one member of the panel, designated as the rapporteur for the case, actually reviews the briefs and record and prepares a written report and vote. The other members of the panel vote orally. The procurator general sits with the justices and has the right to be heard but not to vote. The president of the republic appoints the justices, with the approval of an absolute majority of the Senate. The presidency of the STF rotates every two years according to seniority. The first female justice was appointed to the STF in 2000.

The 1988 Constitution restructured the STF's jurisdiction to make it largely a constitutional court. In addition to its powers of judicial review through the exercise of appellate jurisdiction, the STF has original jurisdiction over a variety of direct actions involving constitutional challenges. For example, a direct action challenging the constitutionality of any federal or state law or act in the abstract can be brought by a limited group of individuals and entities, such as the president of the republic, the procurator general, certain congressional committees, state governors, the Federal Council of the Bar Association, and any political party represented in Congress. Direct actions of unconstitutionality require a quorum of eight, with a minimum of six votes needed to declare a law unconstitutional. The STF's decision in a direct action of unconstitutionality is binding *erga omnes*.

Superior Tribunal of Justice

Immediately below the STF is the Superior Tribunal of Justice (STJ), the court of last resort for much of the appellate caseload formerly decided by the STF. The STJ has thirty-three judges appointed by the president from nominees by the courts, the bar association, and the Public Ministry. The tribunal is divided into six chambers with five judges each.

The STJ functions almost entirely as an appellate court. Its ordinary appellate jurisdiction includes denials of habeas corpus or writs of security and cases in which the party on one side is a foreign state or an international organization and the party on the other side is a county or a person residing or domiciled in Brazil. It has jurisdiction to decide on special appeal cases decided by the lower tribunals if the appealed decision is contrary to a treaty or federal law or if it denies the effectiveness of a treaty or federal law, if it upholds a law or act of local government challenged as contrary to federal law, or if it interprets federal law differently from another tribunal.

The Council of Federal Justice, which supervises the administration of justice in the lower federal courts, functions together with the STJ. The council consists of the president and vice-president of the STJ, three other judges elected from the STJ, and the presidents of the five Federal Regional Tribunals.

Federal Regional Tribunals

Below the STJ are five Federal Regional Tribunals (TRFs) whose primary function is to hear appeals from cases decided by federal judges and by state judges exercising federal jurisdiction within their particular regions. Each TRF has at least seven judges, who are appointed by the president of the republic. To assure lateral entry, one-fifth of each TRF must be selected from lawyers and Public Ministry members with more than ten years of professional activity. The other four-fifths are appointed by the promotion of federal judges, alternating between seniority and merit. The five TRFs have a total of 101 judges (22 of them women), with 38 vacancies.

Federal Judges

The federal judges are courts of first instance, primarily for cases in which the Union has an interest. Federal judges are career judges, chosen by competitive examinations. If there is no federal judge in a particular judicial district, a state law judge may be permitted to decide federal cases. The few intentional homicides committed in areas of federal jurisdiction are tried by federal jury tribunals similar to state tribunals (which will be discussed). Brazil has a total of 766 federal judges (including 231 women), with 337 vacancies.

Federal Small Claims Courts

A law of July 12, 2001, created federal small claims courts along the lines of those already in operation in the state judiciaries (see the subsequent discussion). These courts have jurisdiction in civil matters involving up to sixty times the minimum monthly wage and for crimes punishable by up to two years of imprisonment or fine.

Labor Courts

The Labor Courts are regular members of the Brazilian federal judiciary, but their jurisdiction is limited to labor matters. Until recently, they were made up of professional judges and lay representatives of labor and management, but a 1999 constitutional amendment abolished the lay judges. The Labor Court system is exclusively federal. Federal labor legislation, inspired by Italian corporatism during the Vargas dictatorship, is collected in the Consolidation of Labor Law, first published in 1943. The 1988 Constitution made many changes, guaranteeing workers' rights, establishing principles of self-organization of unions, and encouraging collective bargaining.

The Labor Courts have jurisdiction to conciliate and adjudicate individual and collective labor disputes. If collective bargaining negotiations fail to produce an agreement, the Labor Courts set the rules and conditions of employment and umpire grievances. Brazil has 2,070 labor judges (978 of them women), with 218 vacancies. Appeals are initially heard by the Regional Labor Tribunals (TRTs). Brazil has 287 judges (including 95 women) on the TRTs, with 28 vacancies. The highest Labor Court is the Superior Labor Tribunal (TST), with seventeen judges appointed by the president with Senate approval. Eleven must be selected from career labor judges, three from the lawyers, and three from members of the Labor Public Ministry. The TST sits in panels of three judges.

Electoral Courts

The electoral courts are responsible for supervising the integrity of elections. Unlike other Brazilian courts, they are staffed by members of other courts who serve two- to four year-terms. The highest electoral court is the Superior Electoral Tribunal (TSE), which has seven judges selected by secret ballot. Three are chosen from members of the STF, two are from the STJ, and two are appointed by the president from a list of six lawyers nominated by the STF. Decisions of the TSE may be appealed only to the STF on constitutional issues or if they deny a writ of habeas corpus or writ of security.

Directly below the TSE are the Regional Electoral Tribunals (TREs). Each state capital has a TRE, whose jurisdiction is statewide rather than regional. Each TRE has seven judges: Two are elected from the Tribunal of Justice, two are law judges chosen by the Tribunal of Justice,

one is a judge of the TRF in the state capital, and two are appointed by the president from a list of six lawyers nominated by the Tribunal of Justice. Judges serve two-year terms but never more than two consecutive terms.

The baseline courts for the electoral justice system are the electoral judges, who sit alone. Usually, the state law judge in the electoral district acts as the electoral judge; if a district has several judges, the TRE designates one. Election returns are supervised by election boards. The boards consist of a law judge, who presides, and two to four citizens nominated by the presiding judge with the approval of the TRE.

Federal Military Courts

The Military Courts try military personnel (and those equated with such personnel) for military crimes. This court system consists of the Superior Military Tribunal (STM), the Councils of Justice, and professional military judges.

The highest military court is the STM, whose fifteen judges are appointed for life by the president with Senate approval. Ten must be selected from the highest ranks in active service: three admirals, four army generals, and three air force generals. The balance must include three experienced lawyers, a military judge, and a member of the Military Public Ministry.

The military judges of first instance, called *auditors,* are lawyers and career judges, chosen through competitive examinations. They perform many of the functions of an investigative magistrate or prosecutor. Trials are held before Councils of Justice, made up of one auditor and several military officers. The number and rank of the officers vary with the rank of the accused.

THE STATE JUDICIARIES

Tribunals of Justice

The highest court in every state is called the Tribunal of Justice (TJ). The number of judges, called *desembargadores,* on the TJ varies from as few as 7 in Roraima and Amapá to as many as 145 in Rio de Janeiro. Every TJ with at least 25 judges has a special division that performs administrative and jurisdictional functions and resolves conflicts in the case law. Sitting in panels, the TJ hears appeals directly from courts of first instance; appeals from panels are heard by TJ chambers or groups. Brazil has a total of 888 state supreme court judges (81 of them women), with 15 vacancies.

Tribunals of Alçada

Three states have an additional appellate court with limited jurisdiction called the Tribunal of Alçada (TA). The busiest court system, São Paulo, has two civil and one criminal TA, and Paraná and Minas Gerais each have

Legal Structure of Brazil Courts

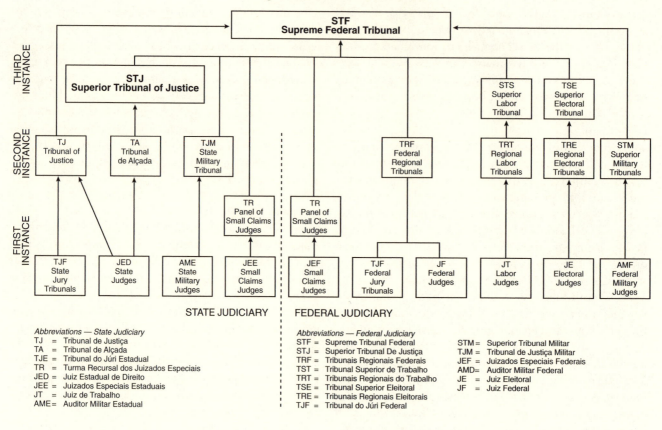

one. The TA divides jurisdiction with the TJ, hearing appeals relating to leases, labor accidents, fiscal matters, most summary proceedings, and less serious criminal offenses. Appeals from the TA go directly to the STJ on issues of federal statutory interpretation or the STF on federal constitutional issues. There 302 judges (including 17 women) on the TA, with 4 vacancies.

State Military Courts

States also have their own systems of military justice. The court of first instance is the Council of Military Justice, which tries military police and firefighters for military crimes. In some states, appeals are heard directly by the Tribunals of Justice; other states have Tribunals of Military Justice to hear such appeals. These tribunals usually have seven judges: four colonels in active service in the military police and three civilians.

Judges of First Instance

Every state is divided into judicial districts, each with at least one titular state judge. The baseline courts are single professional judges with jurisdiction over all matters not specifically allocated to the exclusive jurisdiction of other courts by the constitution or statute. In the larger cities, judges are assigned to specialized divisions—civil, criminal, juvenile, consumer, tax, on so forth. The states and

the Federal District have a total of 7,231 first-instance judges (2,162 being women), ranging from only 15 in Roraima to 1,345 in São Paulo, with 2,463 vacancies.

Jury Tribunals

Intentional crimes against human life are tried by the Jury Tribunal, which consists of one presiding professional judge and seven lay jury members chosen by lot from an array of twenty-one persons. The jury decides whether a crime was committed, the nature of the crime, its gravity, and who committed it. The jury is always sequestered and does not deliberate as a group. Jurors may not communicate with anyone, including each other. They simply mark their secret ballots in response to the issues formulated by the presiding judge. Decisions are by majority vote. In nonjury criminal cases both acquittals and convictions may be appealed, and the appellate tribunal has ample freedom to review both issues of law and fact. Verdicts of the Jury Tribunal may also be appealed, but the appellate tribunal can only modify the decisions of the presiding judge and only to correct an error or injustice in his or her application of the penalty. The appellate tribunal may only make the judgment correspond to what the law establishes and what the jury found. If it determines that the jury's decision was manifestly contrary to the evidence on the record, the appellate court will vacate the jury verdict and remand for retrial by the same Jury Tribunal. A second appeal may not be taken after a retrial.

Small Claims Courts

Since authorizing legislation was passed in 1984, many states have created Small Claims Courts to decide less complex civil cases and minor criminal infractions. A 1995 statute mandated creation of such courts by the Union, the Federal District, and all states, and it changed their name to Special Courts. Their civil jurisdiction has been expanded to cover all disputes involving not more than forty times the minimum monthly wage (including actions to execute on extrajudicial executory instruments up to the same amount), ejectment of a tenant for the owner's personal use, rural leases, expenses owed to a condominium, suits for damages from buildings or auto accidents (including suits against insurers), and suits for attorneys' fees. Disputes can be resolved inexpensively through conciliation, arbitration, or trial before a law school graduate. Many states have established appellate divisions of small claims judges to hear appeals from these courts.

Justices of the Peace

At the bottom of the state judicial system are justices of the peace, who do not enjoy the constitutional guarantees of the regular judiciary. They are nominated by state governors from a list of three prepared by the president of the Tribunal of Justice. Justices of the peace perform marriages and attempt conciliations, but they have no real jurisdictional functions.

SOURCES OF LAW AND JUDICIAL DECISIONS

The principal source of law is legislation. When legislation is silent, both the Law of Introduction to the Civil Code and the Code of Civil Procedure direct the courts to decide cases in accordance with analogy, customs, and general principles of law. Brazilian courts also rely heavily on doctrinal writing and prior cases.

Although judicial decisions generally have no precedential value in civil law jurisdictions, Brazil has developed three types of binding precedents. In direct actions of unconstitutionality or constitutionality, the STF's decision is binding on everyone. If the STF has firmly taken the position that a law or decree is unconstitutional in a decision binding only on the parties, the STF president can send its decision to the federal Senate for enactment of a resolution suspending the norm. (The Senate does not have to suspend the norm but generally does so.) Finally, Brazilian appellate courts have a set of numbered black letter rules firmly settled by several decisions of a higher court, called *súmulas*. Until a súmula is modified, the issuing court and all judges lower in the hierarchy are

expected to adhere to it. This practice began in the STF in 1964 and has spread gradually to other tribunals. Although a súmula is technically binding only on the tribunal that has created it, failure to follow it virtually ensures summary reversal. Any appellate judge or party who sees a conflict between the interpretation of the law in a case before the court and a prior interpretation can ask the tribunal to resolve the conflict by an en banc decision. The interpretation by an absolute majority will then be binding on the tribunal and will be entered into its súmula.

In practice, none of these precedential devices has done much to alleviate Brazil's badly congested judicial system. Most courts have huge caseloads and huge backlogs. For example, in 2000, the STF received 105,307 new cases and decided 86,138 cases. Despite the súmula, it is estimated that about 85 to 90 percent of these appeals present issues that the STF has previously decided. Resolution of cases frequently takes six to eight years in major urban centers in Brazil. More resources need to be allocated to the judiciary, and more judges are needed, particularly in urban areas. In almost all of the lower courts, a substantial percentage of the judgeships are vacant. Excessive formalism and the plethora of dilatory appeals need to be pruned from the procedural codes. The entire judicial system badly needs major streamlining in order to cope with the expanded volume of cases.

ARBITRATION

Brazil has long permitted arbitration, but the institution has been little used as a means of resolving private disputes. One reason is that prior to 1996, clauses in contracts agreeing to arbitrate any disputes that might arise in the future were not specifically enforceable. The 1996 Arbitration Law made such clauses judicially enforceable. It also eliminated the troublesome requirement that foreign arbitral awards be reduced to judgment in the country where rendered before they may be enforced in Brazil, as well as permitting a Brazilian party to a foreign arbitration proceeding to be served by registered mail rather than by letter rogatory. Unfortunately, the constitutionality of the new law has been under a cloud since 1997 because of a controversial vote of the former president of the STF in a case still pending before that tribunal.

LEGAL EDUCATION

Students who successfully complete the entrance exam enter law school directly after high school. Legal education is provided in a five-year program, with a minimum curriculum prescribed by the Ministry of Education. The number of law schools has mushroomed since 1967, and the overall quality of legal education has declined precipitously. There are now more than 160 public and private law schools, one fourth of which are in the state of São Paulo. Most operate only in the evening, and only about

15 percent offer postgraduate programs. About 80 percent of the faculty are practicing lawyers or judges who teach part-time for little remuneration. With few exceptions, law schools have minuscule libraries, and the usual teaching method is the lecture. Students must pass a bar exam, administered on a regional basis by the Bar Association, the Ordem dos Advogados do Brasil (OAB), to be able to practice law. Although the top schools had passing rates close to 100 percent, the overall rate in 2000 was only 40 percent. The pass rate for judicial entrance exams was even lower.

Keith S. Rosenn

See also Civil Law; Federalism; Juries; Jury Selection; Portugal; Roman Law; Small Claims Courts

References and further reading
Dolinger, Jacob, and Keith S. Rosenn, eds. 1992. *A Panorama of Brazilian Law.* Miami and Rio de Janeiro: North-South Center/Editora Esplanada.
Pinheiro Neto Advogados. 2001. *Doing Business in Brazil.* Yonkers, NY: Juris.
Pires Filho, Ivon D'Almeida. 1985. "The Legal System of Brazil." In *Modern Legal Systems Cyclopedia.* Edited by Kenneth Robert Redden. Buffalo, NY: William S. Hein and Co.
Rosenn, Keith S. 1986. "Civil Procedure in Brazil." *American Journal of Comparative Law* 34: 487–525.
———. 1998. "Judicial Reform in Brazil." *NAFTA: Law and Business Review of the Americas* 4 (Spring): 19–37.
———. 2000. "Judicial Review in Brazil: Recent Developments." *Southwestern University Journal of Law and Trade* 7 (November): 291–319.
———. 2001. "An Annotated Translation of the Brazilian Constitution." In *Constitutions of the Countries of the World,* vol. 3. Edited by Gisbert H. Flanz. Dobbs Ferry, NY: Oceana.
Velloso, Carlos Mário da Silva. 1995. "Do poder judiciário: Organização e competência." *Revista de Direito Administrativo* 200 (April–June): 1–19.
———. 1998. "Do poder judiciário: Como torná-lo mais ágil e dinâmico: Efeito vinculante e outros temas." *Revista de Direito Administrativo,* 212 (April–June): 7–26.
Wald, Arnoldo, Patrick Schellenberg, and Keith S. Rosenn. 2000. "Some Controversial Aspects of the New Brazilian Arbitration Law." *University of Miami Inter-American Law Review* 31: 223–252.

BRITISH COLUMBIA

GENERAL INFORMATION

British Columbia, the third-largest province in Canada, is situated on the west coast. It measures 1,200 kilometers from north to south, is as wide as 1,050 kilometers, and has 7,000 kilometers of coastline along the Pacific Ocean. It is larger than any of the states in the United States, except for Alaska. Over 90 percent of this mountainous province comprises provincial forests and parks.

More than half of its 4.1 million people (13.2 percent of the Canadian population) live in the southwestern corner of the province: Vancouver and its surrounding cities (often referred to collectively as the "Lower Mainland," or "Greater Vancouver") and Victoria (the capital of the province, which is located on Vancouver Island). BC Ferries operates twenty-six routes between the Lower Mainland, Vancouver Island, other local islands, and coastal points. Historically, interior, northern, and coastal settlements away from the southwest corner were very difficult to reach, and these geographical barriers probably had some influence on how the legal profession developed in the province.

The provincial economy is based on forestry, mining, tourism, agriculture, fisheries, transportation, communications, manufacturing, high technology, retail trade, and energy. Recently, the province has become known as "Hollywood North" for the number of film projects it attracts. The mountains surrounding the port city of Vancouver and the skiing facilities at Whistler have made it a destination for many international tourists.

The people of British Columbia are quite diverse. There are 197 First Nations, representing 3.8 percent of the population. The top five languages spoken at the last census in 1996 were English, Chinese (Cantonese/Mandarin), Punjabi, German, and French. Only 6.7 percent of the population know both of Canada's two official languages, English and French.

EVOLUTION AND HISTORY

Prior to becoming a province of Canada in 1871, the land now known as British Columbia was governed largely by the Hudson Bay Company (during the fur-trading period). When the British colony of Vancouver Island was formed in 1849, the British Crown gave trading rights to the Hudson Bay Company and delegated other powers to it. In 1851, James Douglas was appointed the governor of Vancouver Island while also acting as chief factor for the Hudson Bay Company. The Mainland became a separate colony in 1858 as a result of the gold rush and a demand for a more public, rather than private, interest in the enforcement of laws. Douglas was appointed governor and resigned his position with the Hudson Bay Company. In the same year, Matthew Baillie Begbie, a Cambridge-trained barrister from England, was appointed judge of British Columbia. His preference for British-trained barristers and his control over admissions to the bar may have been one reason that notaries survived in British Columbia to provide legal services, unlike in other provinces.

The Royal Proclamation of 1763 by King George III stated that aboriginal peoples "should not be molested or disturbed" in their possession of land that had not been "ceded or purchased" by the Crown. James Douglas made fourteen purchases of First Nations lands between 1850 and 1854. However, Joseph Trutch, chief commissioner of lands and works before the province joined confederation and the province's first lieutenant-governor, took the position that aboriginal title did not exist, and so he did not enter into any treaties. This decision resulted in years of protest by First Nations in British Columbia and negotiations and court battles extending into the 1990s. The governments of Canada and British Columbia are presently negotiating treaties with First Nations people.

Some credit the early gold rush, which pushed economic expansion northward in the province, with keeping the province from joining the United States to the south. When the two colonies were joined in 1866, however, the earlier economic expansion left the new colony with a debt of $1.5 million. Much debate and negotiation over whether the province should join the United States or Canada resulted in the Dominion of Canada absorbing the debt and promising to build a transnational railway if British Columbia joined confederation. Although Chinese immigrants were initially welcomed to work in the gold rush and later on the railroad, they and other Asian immigrants soon became the target of hostility. British Columbia has a sordid history of racism, and the legal profession played an active part in that racism.

In 1918, Gordon Won Cumyow, the son of the first Chinese person to be born in British Columbia, applied for admission to the Law Society, which had the power to admit and enroll students and lawyers. The Vancouver Law Students Society requested that the benchers of the Law Society ask the provincial government to amend the Legal Professions Act "so that Japanese, Chinese or East Indians, or any such persons of Asiatic origin, whether of British Birth or otherwise, be prohibited from being enrolled as Articled Clerks and Students-at-Law, or being admitted as Solicitors or called to the Bar of British Columbia." The Law Society introduced a new rule that required its members to be entitled to vote provincially. Since Asians were prohibited from voting in British Columbia under provincial legislation, they could not be members of the Law Society. The Law Society turned down Cumyow's application on the basis that he did not qualify under the new rule. The rule was used to exclude Asians from practicing law in British Columbia until the legislature removed the barriers to their voting in the late 1940s. Aboriginals were also disenfranchised until 1951, and the first aboriginal lawyer in British Columbia, Alfred Scow, was called to the bar in 1962.

When Mabel Penery French, the first woman called to the bar in New Brunswick, applied to the Law Society of British Columbia for admission in 1911, her application was rejected because the Law Society and the courts did not considered her to be a "person" under the Legal Pro-

fession Act. She and other women lobbied the legislature to pass a special act so that women could practice law, and in 1912 French became the first woman called to the bar in British Columbia. French practiced law on her own for about a year and then moved to England. The second woman called to the bar, Edith Louise Paterson (in 1916), practiced law until suffering a stroke in 1970. Barriers that prevent women's full participation in the legal profession, such as harassment and discrimination, still exist today.

RELATIONSHIP TO THE NATIONAL SYSTEM

Areas of provincial jurisdiction under the Constitution Act of 1982 (which incorporated the British North America Act of 1867) are governed by the provincial legislative assembly, composed of the lieutenant governor and seventy-five elected members. There are also 154 municipal governments in the province. British Columbians are represented in federal politics by thirty-four elected members of Parliament and six senators, who are appointed by the federal government.

Although criminal laws are legislated at the federal level, the administration of that law falls within provincial jurisdiction. Provinces also have the power to create offences within their sphere of jurisdiction (e.g., securities law, motor vehicle regulations, etc.), and administrative boards and tribunals are either federally appointed or provincially appointed, depending on their jurisdiction. Civil law (family law, tort, contracts, etc.) is within the jurisdiction of the provinces.

Bills (the first step in creating a statute) are introduced into the provincial legislature, mostly by government members (a government bill) but occasionally by an individual member (a private member's bill). After the bill is debated and passed by vote on three separate occasions, it still requires approval by the lieutenant governor (royal assent) before it becomes law. Many statutes also allow the lieutenant governor in council to add detail to enacted legislation through regulations.

Judges of the British Columbia Supreme Court and British Columbia Court of Appeal (superior courts) are appointed by the federal government. The Supreme Court (consisting of approximately 100 judges) hears the more serious criminal cases and civil matters throughout the province. The Court of Appeal, which sits in panels of three or five, hears criminal and civil appeals. Appeals from this court go to the Supreme Court of Canada. The Canadian Judicial Council deals with complaints against federally appointed judges (see figure).

The Provincial Court of British Columbia, which sits in ninety-seven different locations and comprises approximately 130 judges, hears the less serious federal criminal cases, all provincial offences, and cases involving young offenders, family law, small claims, and child protection.

Legal Structure of British Columbia Courts

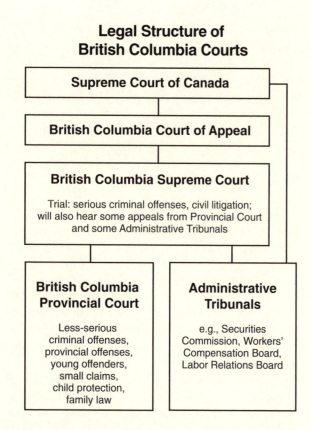

Supreme Court of Canada

British Columbia Court of Appeal

British Columbia Supreme Court

Trial: serious criminal offenses, civil litigation; will also hear some appeals from Provincial Court and some Administrative Tribunals

British Columbia Provincial Court

Less-serious criminal offenses, provincial offenses, young offenders, small claims, child protection, family law

Administrative Tribunals

e.g., Securities Commission, Workers' Compensation Board, Labor Relations Board

Its decisions can be appealed to the Supreme Court of British Columbia or the British Columbia Court of Appeal and, in some instances, to the Supreme Court of Canada. The Judicial Council of British Columbia (the chief judge of the Provincial Court and members of the public, the legal profession, and the judiciary) deals with complaints about provincial court judges and screens applicants before they are appointed to the Provincial Court. Lawyers with ten years of practice or related experience may apply to the Judicial Council for the position of provincial court judge. The council considers the lawyer's legal reputation (through letters of references from the Canadian Bar Association and judges before whom the lawyer has appeared and his or her professional record with the Law Society of British Columbia), general knowledge of the law, health, compassion, humility, appreciation for cultural diversity, and other factors. The council then interviews selected candidates, and if it determines that the applicant is acceptable for the job, his or her name is forwarded to the attorney general, who has the discretion to appoint the person to the Provincial Court. Candidates who do not hear from the attorney general within three years may apply again.

MAJOR DIMENSIONS OF VARIATION

Legal Services: Notaries and Lawyers

Notaries play a unique role in the delivery of legal services in British Columbia. Although they do not attend law school, they are allowed to provide some legal services to the public (e.g., to convey property and draft simple wills), which are provided exclusively by lawyers in all other provinces (except Quebec, where notaries are trained through law schools). In 1929, there were more notaries (1,000) than lawyers (600) in British Columbia. Through court action and changes to the legislation over the years, the number of notaries has dwindled, and the number of lawyers has increased. By 1981, when there were approximately 4,500 lawyers in the province, the two professions reached an agreement (incorporated into legislation) that the number of notaries would be limited to 322, which was the number of notaries practicing at that time.

Today, the number of possible notaries in British Columbia is limited by statute to 323 (they forgot to count one in 1981), although the number practicing is only around 280. The number of practicing lawyers is around 9,000. The notaries have made several unsuccessful attempts to expand their jurisdiction, and the lawyers have won several major victories in their recent courtroom and legislature battles. The courts have determined that notaries cannot incorporate companies, keep corporate records, or probate wills. Recently, changes to adult guardianship legislation have excluded notaries from certain activities to the benefit of lawyers. It is unclear whether notaries will survive these major reductions to their practice.

In effect, lawyers have a monopoly on legal services in British Columbia, but they must share a small number of these services with notaries. Lawyers are required to have a bachelor of laws degree from an accredited university (usually after obtaining another bachelor's degree, although some law schools do not require a completed degree). Then, they must article (serve an apprenticeship) with a member of the Law Society for one year (there are some variations), during which they take a ten-week professional legal training course and write examinations. The lawyer they article with (their principal) must certify that the student is of good repute before he or she can be called to the bar as a barrister and admitted to the rolls as a solicitor. There is no formal distinction between barristers and solicitors in the province.

Both the Law Society and the notaries are self-governing, as are most professions in this province and others. Self-regulation involves the delegation of government regulatory powers to professional bodies, which allows them to set entry standards (some might refer to these as entry barriers) and to regulate the behavior of their members through disciplinary hearings and penalties. In 1999, the Law Society opened 1,557 complaint files. In over half of these complaints, the Law Society staff investigations found that misconduct was not established. Thirty-five citations were issued in 1999, commencing a formal hearing, and the following penalties were imposed: four disbarments, nine suspensions, seven fines, and seven reprimands. Four lawyers resigned from the Law Society, and nine cases were resolved by admissions of wrongdoing and publication of the facts.

There are a number of trends in professional self-regulation that appear to be changing its nature. An increasing number of public representatives are being appointed to the governing bodies, and many disciplinary hearings are now open to the public, with the results increasingly available to the press and the public through professional websites. These changes may lead the proceedings to become more formal and technical.

Securities Law

British Columbia was the home of the Vancouver Stock Exchange from its formation in 1907 until it merged with the Alberta Stock Exchange at the end of 1999 to form the Canadian Venture Exchange (CDNX). This interprovincial merger was unusual in that securities law falls under provincial jurisdiction, and provincial securities commissions oversee the various stock exchanges in Canada. Presently the CDNX, which has split its headquarters between Calgary, Alberta, and Vancouver, British Columbia, is overseen by the British Columbia Securities Commission and the Alberta Securities Commission. At the time of this writing, the Toronto Stock Exchange is considering buying the CDNX. Although there has been talk about a national securities commission in Canada for years, it still appears unlikely to be created, as doing so would have to involve the federal government. The various provincial securities commissions as a group (known as the Canadian Securities Regulators) have been moving to harmonize laws and even rely on each other for certain regulator tasks. Given the split in constitutional powers between the federal and provincial governments, coordination might be the most workable solution.

Joan Brockman

See also Administrative Tribunals; Appellate Courts; Barristers; Canada; Constitutional Law; Federalism; Legal Education; Judicial Selection, Methods of; Notaries
References and further reading
British Columbia Superior Courts, http://www.courts. gov.bc.ca (cited July 5, 2001).
Brockman, Joan. 1997. "'Better to Enlist Their support Than to Suffer Their Antagonism,' The Game of Monopoly between Lawyers and Notaries in British Columbia, 1930–81." *International Journal of the Legal Profession* 4, no. 3: 197–234.
———. 2001. *Gender in the Legal Profession: Fitting or Breaking the Mould.* Vancouver: University of British Columbia Press.
Government of British Columbia, "BC Stats," htpp://www. bcstats.gov.bc.ca/index.htm (cited July 5, 2001).

Law Society of British Columbia. 1999. *Annual Report, 1999.* Vancouver: Law Society of British Columbia.
Loo, Tina Merrill. 1994. *Making Law, Order, and Authority in British Columbia, 1821–1871.* Toronto: University of Toronto Press.
Ormsby, Margaret. 1958. *British Columbia: A History.* Toronto: Macmillan.
Pue, W. Wesley. 1995. *Law School: The Story of Legal Education in British Columbia.* Vancouver: Faculty of Law, University of British Columbia.

BRUNEI

BACKGROUND INFORMATION

Brunei Darussalam (Brunei) is a small southeast Asian sultanate located on the northwestern coast of the island of Borneo. It has a land area of 5,765 square kilometers, and is bordered by the South China Sea. It consists of two sections, approximately 30 kilometers apart, which are separated and surrounded by the Malaysian state of Sarawak. The eastern section of Brunei, Temburong, is covered by virgin equatorial rainforest with a rugged mountainous area. It is sparsely populated with a small town at Bangar. The western section is predominately hilly lowland and consists of the other three districts of Brunei—Belait, Tutong, and Brunei Muara. The oil and gas industry is located in Belait, Tutong is largely rural, and in Brunei-Muara the administrative and commercial capital of Brunei, Bandar Seri Begawan, is located. The capital is situated on the Brunei River and is the site of the famous landmark, the *Kampong Ayer* (water village), which has existed since the fourteenth century. It is referred to in travel books as the "Venice of the East" and is home to 30,000 people. In Brunei there are four main rivers, with numerous tributaries, which serve as the principal means of communication in the interior, with water taxis and boats being the main form of transport for residents in the water villages.

Brunei has an equatorial climate, characterized by high temperatures of 23° to 32° C, high humidity, and high rainfall. The population in 2001 was 342,000. Malays form the majority of the population (67 percent), with the term *Malay* encompassing Brunei Malays as well as the indigenous Kedayan, Tutong, Belait, Bisaya, Dusun, and Murut peoples, who are classified as Malay to accord with the Brunei Nationality Enactment (1961). There are an additional 20,000 indigenous people (6 percent) such as the Iban, Kadazan, Punan, and Melanau who have come to Brunei in search of work and stayed. The Chinese community makes up 15 percent and there is a mix of Indians, Filipinos, Thais, Indonesians, and European expatriates who comprise the 12 percent Other Races category in the official census data. Bahasa Malaya is the na-

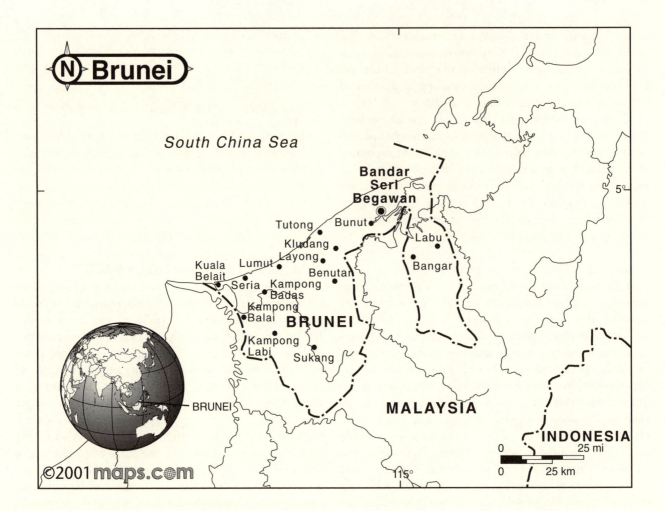

Brunei

South China Sea

Bandar Seri Begawan

Tutong • • Bunut
Kludang •
Layong
Kuala Lumut • Benutan • Labu
Belait • • Kampong
Seria • Badas Bangar
Kampong
Balai **BRUNEI**
Kampong
Labi • Sukang

MALAYSIA

BRUNEI

INDONESIA

0   25 mi
0   25 km

©2001 maps.com

tional language for Brunei. Chinese is spoken throughout the Chinese community, but English is the second language in the country and is used widely within both the legal system and the commercial sector.

The legal system is pluralistic, with common law courts and laws operating alongside Islamic courts and laws. The jurisdiction of the latter extends only to Muslims. To be a Brunei Malay is to be Muslim. Islam is the state religion, but the constitution provides that other religions can be practiced in peace and harmony. When non-Malays convert to Islam, the process is known as *masuk Melaya* (becoming Malay). There are considerable advantages to being a Malay in Brunei and conversions by Chinese and indigenous people are a documented trend. The official adoption of Melayu Islam Beraja (MIB), or the Malay Islamic Monarchy, as the national ideology has strengthened the role of Islam. Teaching MIB is compulsory for students at school and at the University of Brunei, Darussalam. Islamic banking and financial institutions are promoted. The Department of Religious Affairs exert considerable political influence. Government departments close during the daily Islamic prayer times. Ensuring that *halal* food is provided for Muslims is a national priority. Under the MIB ideology,

loyalty to one's country, to the sultan, and to Islam are one and the same.

The economy of Brunei is largely based on revenues from the oil and gas industry. Brunei is the third largest oil producer in Southeast Asia, and the world's fourth largest producer of liquefied natural gas. Income from investments abroad, which are managed by the Brunei Investment Agency, contributes significantly to the national revenue. Awareness of the nonrenewable nature of oil and gas and the uncertainty in world oil prices has made economic diversification a national development goal. Despite some economic downturn in the wake of the Asian economic crisis in 1997 and 1998, the citizens of Brunei continue to enjoy one of the highest per capita gross national products in the world, second only to Japan in the Asian region.

HISTORY

The official history of the country holds that Brunei has been an independent kingdom for nearly 1,500 years. It first became a sultanate in the mid-fourteenth century when its raja, Awang Alak Betatar, converted to Islam, and changed his name to Sultan Muhammad Shah in honor of the Prophet. The present sultan is his descendent. It was during the reign of the fifth sultan, Bolkiah, from 1524 that Brunei was at the height of its influence as its sovereignty extended to all of Borneo and the Philippines. The description of Brunei by Antonio Pigafetta, who came with Magellan in 1521, is of a regal, organized, and affluent court and society. This is acknowledged as the first official visit of westerners in Brunei, although Portuguese, Spanish, and Italian sailors were in the region also. From the seventeenth century Brunei was in a state of decline and its territory began to contract. The Spanish made inroads into the territory in the Philippines. The island of Borneo was an arena for a power struggle between the British, Dutch, Portuguese, and the Americans.

In 1888, Sultan Hashim signed a British Protectorate Treaty entrusting Brunei's defense and foreign affairs to British administration. As a protectorate, Brunei would continue to be governed and administered by the sultan and his successors. This treaty was intended to deter other European powers from pursuing territorial claims on the island. The treaty did not protect Brunei against Sarawak, which continued to expand at the expense of Brunei's territory. To preserve the sultanate, a supplementary treaty was signed in 1905 that introduced the British Residential System. The British Resident was to advise the sultan on all matters, excluding "those affecting the Mohammedan religion." Effectively the administration of Brunei was in the hands of the resident, who was accountable ultimately to the British Colonial Office.

Among the measures introduced by the first resident in 1906 was the establishment of common law courts and the implementation of English laws. Courts of the *Kathis* (also spelled *qadis* or *qazis*) were also established with jurisdiction over matters concerning Islamic religion, marriage, and divorce as defined by the Qur'an, plus limited criminal jurisdiction for breaches of Islamic tenets, such as nonattendance at compulsory Friday prayers, and for offences against morality, such as adultery. Prior to the residency, there had been no formal Islamic courts in the sultanate. At that time, the sultan personally played a significant role as mediator and adjudicator, maintaining control on the implementation of Islamic law while the day-to-day administration of law was dealt with at the local level by district rulers. The majority of disputes that involved people at the community and village (*kampong*) level were resolved by the arbitration of the village headman. These informal processes continued through the residency.

Along with the imposition of an English legal system came British administrative reforms that undermined the traditional roles and power of the Brunei nobles and chiefs. A British style civil service was introduced, including the establishment of a police force and a jail. Despite opposition, traditional Brunei forms of land ownership were replaced by English land titles through the Land Code (1908). Customs, excise duties, and taxation replaced the traditional monopolies rights.

At the turn of the twentieth century Brunei was bereft of any resources save agriculture and fishing. The discovery of oil in Seria in 1929 was to transform the economic situation, although full development of the industry was delayed by the Japanese occupation of 1941–1945.

When Sultan Haji Omar Ali Saifuddien III ascended the throne in 1950, nationalism was growing in Brunei. Fundamental changes occurred in 1959 when the Treaty of 1906 was abrogated and Brunei received internal self-government under the sultan. In place of the resident was a British high commissioner, responsible only for Brunei's defense and external affairs. The first written constitution was promulgated in 1959. It vested the sultan with supreme executive authority, and provided for five councils: the Privy Council, the Council of Ministers, Legislative Council, Council of Succession, and the State Religious Council. The Legislative Council was to include elected as well as nominated members. The concept of a federation with either Malaysia, or with Sarawak, Sabah, and Kalimantan, was debated at this time. Ultimately, federation was rejected by the sultan. In 1962, in the country's first election, the People's Party of Brunei won all but one of the sixteen elected seats. Later that same year an armed rebellion involving the members of the People's Party erupted and was quashed with the assistance of British and Gurka troops. An immediate state of emergency was declared, which has been renewed every two years since 1962.

In 1967, the sultan abdicated in favor of his son, the current monarch, Sultan Hassanal Bolkiah. Full sovereign status and independence from Britain was gained in 1984, when Negera Brunei Darussalam (Brunei the Abode of Peace) was proclaimed. A new revised constitution was promulgated, which further consolidated the power of the sultan by suspending certain parliamentary institutions such as the Legislative Council. The country retained the common law legal system postindependence.

LEGAL CONCEPTS

Brunei is an absolute monarchy. Unlike the United Kingdom where the reigning monarch governs in accordance with the decisions of the elected government, in Brunei there is no democratically elected legislative body, and executive power vests in the prime minister, a position also held by the sultan. While the sultan in council has ultimate executive and legislative authority, he is advised and assisted by a cabinet of eleven ministers. Each minister is nominated and appointed by him. In addition to his post as prime minister, the sultan also is minister of Defense and minister of Finance. The sultan's younger brother, Prince Muda Haji Jefri, had held the latter position until the scandal of 1998, which culminated in a $25 billion suit brought against Prince Jefri in 2000, for misappropriation and breach of fiduciary duties (*State of Brunei v. HRH Prince Jefri Bolkiah,* 2000). The sultan's other brother, Prince Muda Haji Mohammad, is minister for Foreign Affairs. Thus the key posts in government have been retained by the royal family, with the sultan's control over the prime minister's department giving him key areas of responsibility including the petroleum unit, internal security, the police force, and the judiciary. Until 1999, there had been a separate Ministry of Law. With its abolition, all judicial administration was resumed by the prime minister's Department of the Judiciary.

The attorney general acts as the principal legal adviser to the government and represents the government in civil and criminal cases, being vested with the power to institute, proceed, and discontinue once instituted, all criminal proceedings. In these tasks there is assistance from the solicitor general and the public prosecutors. The Department of the Attorney General also drafts all legislation in consultation with the relevant ministries and departments.

Although Brunei has a common law system there are some traditional features that are absent. One of these is the absence of trial by jury for either criminal or civil offences. In the first years after independence, there was a provision, now abolished, for two (lay) assessors to sit with the judge in criminal trials before the High Court. The current requirement is that two judges of the High Court hear and determine all cases involving the death penalty. Where the two judges cannot agree on the guilt of the accused, he or she is acquitted. Capital punishment is prescribed for murder, culpable homicide, possession of firearms, trafficking of controlled drugs, gang robbery, and rape.

Another feature is the absence of democratic institutions. It is paradoxical that in the Abode of Peace all legislation is by way of emergency order due to the continuance of the state of emergency since 1962, almost forty years after the rebellion was suppressed and order returned. These are not matters ever to be questioned; they certainly are not issues that would be raised by the local media or academia, or be challenged in the courts. The one registered political party is cautious in its demands for democratic reform, given that earlier parties have been short-lived. The Brunei National Democratic Party, which was formed in 1985, was banned three years later and its leadership detained. Without representative government, there are no elections and little scope for informed public debate.

As an Islamic sultanate, legal concepts derived from Islam are equally important especially in personal and family matters. During the reign of Sultan Omar Ali Saifuddin III, his conservative but pro-Islamic stance re-

sulted in the enacting of The Religious Council, State Custom and Kathis Courts Act (1955). This was a turning point for Islam and for the application of Islamic law in Brunei, as the importance of both has grown steadily since then. The religious council (Majlis Ugama Islam) is the designated authority on Islamic law and has a close nexus with the sultan as head of the Islamic faith. This council through its office of the State Mufti issues fatwas that bind and guide Muslims of the Shafeite sect resident in Brunei.

CURRENT STRUCTURE
At the apex of the court hierarchy is the Judicial Committee of the Privy Council in London. The right of final appeal to this court was maintained in the 1984 postindependence revision of the courts. The right of appeal has subsequently been reduced, with all criminal appeals to it from Brunei abolished in 1995. In 1997, legislation modified appeals pertaining to civil matters by limiting the avenue of appeal to cases where there was agreement of both parties prior to the hearing of the appeal in the Court of Appeal of Brunei. The effect is to have this court as the final appellate court for the country, although not totally closing the door where parties voluntarily agree to a further appellate option prior to trial. The option was retained, so that foreign investors would have confidence in the judicial system.

The Supreme Court of Brunei was established in 1963, after the dissolution of the joint Sarawak, North Borneo, and Brunei Supreme Court. It is a court of record and consists of the Court of Appeal, which has only appellate jurisdiction, and the High Court, which has both original and appellate jurisdiction. The Court of Appeal is constituted by the president and two judges or commissioners. This court sits twice during each legal year, usually in April and November, and hears between twenty and thirty appeals. The court is comprised of judges and commissioners from other commonwealth jurisdictions. The High Court has unlimited original civil and criminal jurisdiction. The court usually hears civil and criminal cases that exceed the jurisdiction of the intermediate and Magistrates' Courts, including those with provisions for the death penalty or a life sentence.

The intermediate court's original criminal jurisdiction excludes cases punishable with death, or imprisonment exceeding twenty years. Its civil jurisdiction includes civil cases where the amount claimed or the value of the subject matter in dispute is more than B$30,000 but does not exceed B$100,000, or a sum prescribed by order of the chief justice in the Gazette. Appeals from this court are to the Court of Appeal.

The Magistrates' Court was established under the Subordinate Courts Act (1983). This court hears and determines the majority of cases. It has the power to try any

Legal Structure of Brunei Courts

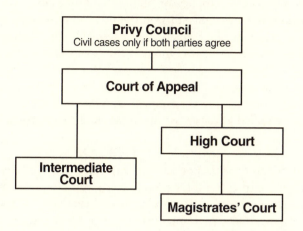

offence that is punishable by a term of imprisonment not exceeding seven years, or a fine not exceeding B$10,000. These powers may be extended by specific legislation. For example, the Prevention of Corruption Act (1981) and Drugs Misuse Act (1978) give special jurisdiction to a magistrate to impose a higher imprisonment term or fine. Civil jurisdiction is limited to where the amount claimed or the value of the subject matter in dispute does not exceed the prescribed limit currently of B$30,000. This limit extends to B$50,000 where a senior magistrate, chief magistrate, or chief registrar is presiding. Appeals from the Magistrates' Court are heard by the High Court. The accused may appeal against judgment and sentence, for any error in law or in fact, or on the ground of excessive severity in the sentence. In civil matters, appeal is of right from any proceedings for the recovery of immovable property or where the amount claimed or the value of the subject matter in dispute exceeds B$500. Leave is otherwise required.

At present legal aid is available only to defendants in criminal trials and only where the death penalty may be imposed. Following a successful application, the chief registrar of the Supreme Court makes a grant of legal aid. These are not means- or merit-tested, but are determined on the sole ground of the seriousness of the offence. In 1999, legal aid was granted to one applicant, with the highest number of grants being six, in 1997. Even in the small number of cases where legal aid is granted, the fees paid to defense counsel are not in accordance with the current fee scales. There have been calls for an increase in the fees paid under legal aid, and for the establishment of a public defender's office to cover all criminal cases heard in the High Court and the intermediate court.

The government of Brunei cannot be sued. The Succession and Regency Proclamation (1959) allows for it but no law has yet been enacted to provide the mechanism for such a proceeding. The result is that anyone who is injured or suffers a loss has no legal recourse to the courts for redress where it involves the government of Brunei or one of its employees. Instead, an application can be made to the attorney general, whose generosity must be relied upon, with the claimant having no alternative but to accept what is offered. The sultan enjoys absolute sovereign immunity provided for in section 25(1)(b) of the constitution.

There is no law society in Brunei, but there have been calls by the chief justice and practitioners for one to be established. The absence of a law society means there is no regulatory or supervisory body to deal with complaints and concerns about individual practitioners. It is left to the inherent jurisdiction of the court to deal with such matters. The senior registrar and the chief justice can undertake a taxation of the lawyer's bill for services to ensure that the fees charged were reasonable. It also means there are no continuing legal education programs operating in Brunei, nor, importantly, is there any organization to represent or to speak on behalf on the lawyers in the country.

SPECIALIZED JUDICIAL BODIES

Since 1955, the religious courts for Muslims were the *qadi (qazi)* courts. The Emergency (Sharia Courts) Order (1998) was enacted to upgrade their role, and the transition from *qadi* to *sharia* courts has been occurring during 2001. Thus far, the new *sharia* courts retained similar jurisdiction to that of the *qadi* courts. Civil matters extend to disputes arising out of betrothal, marriage, divorce, nullity of marriage, judicial separation; disposition of property arising from such proceedings; maintenance of dependents, legitimacy, guardianship, or custody; division of or claims to *sapencharian* property (derived from *adat,* the customary Malay law on the division of matrimonial property on divorce; it provides that the wife should normally receive either a one-third or one-half share of property acquired during the marriage); the validity and entitlement from deceased estates of Muslims; wills or deathbed gifts; gifts inter vivos; and trusts. Criminal cases are confined to offences against Islamic tenets that would not be punishable in the secular courts. These range from the eating of food during fasting hours of Ramadan to the offence of *khalwat* (suspicious proximity), where there has been intimate contact between an unmarried man and woman. Appointments of *qadis* and *sharia* judges are made by the sultan.

STAFFING

Judges in the common law courts are also appointed by the sultan. The qualifications for judicial appointment are either judicial experience in a court with unlimited jurisdiction in civil and criminal matters in another commonwealth jurisdiction, or a commonwealth appellate court; or, alternatively, seven years' experience as an advocate or solicitor in such a court. Appointment is until sixty-five years, although this can be extended by the sultan. There are provisions detailing removal from office when there is an inability to perform the function of the office or for misbehavior. Such matters are determined by the Judicial Committee of the Privy Council in England. Commissioners can also be appointed to the Supreme Court. Their qualifications are the same as for judges, but commissioners are appointed on an ad hoc basis, while a judge holds office for a fixed term.

The judiciary in Brunei has a reputation for maintaining independence from the executive, and none of the concerns that have plagued the judiciary in the neighboring countries of Malaysia and Indonesia have surfaced in Brunei. Although the courts have made decisions that have not been to the liking of various government departments, the former chief justice Sir Denys Roberts (1988–2001) frequently emphasized that there had been no attempts to interfere with the courts, or to influence them, except in ways permissible in open court. This, together with the efficiency in the court processes, has meant that other forms of alternative dispute resolution, such as mediation and arbitration, have not developed as necessary adjuncts to adjudication.

There are approximately seventy lawyers in private practice and just over fifty lawyers employed by the government mainly in the Attorney General's Department. This is a ratio of private practitioners to the general population of 1:4724. Lawyers in private practice are mostly in partnership firms, and there are approximately eighteen firms of advocates and solicitors. Most are situated in or around the capital Bandar Seri Begawan.

Brunei did not retain the traditional common law separation of solicitors and barristers, mainly because of the small population and the initial scarcity of trained professionals. Brunei does not have a law school or faculty, or any other system of professional training through a bar or solicitors' board. Admission to practice is dependent on overseas legal training that meets the requirements set out in the local legislation. To be admitted and to practice one has to be a "qualified person," which requires firstly that you hold a law degree from one of the prescribed universities or have been admitted as a barrister or solicitor in England, Northern Ireland, Scotland, or Malaysia, or Singapore. The second requirement is to be of good character and diligence. A petition of admission is made to the chief justice, and also to the attorney general, who may raise an objection to an admission. However, the final determination lies with the chief justice. Those who have been admitted are issued with a practicing certificate that must be renewed annually. A third requirement was introduced in 1999. It requires Brunei citizenship, a residency certificate, or seven years' prior experience in legal practice immediately preceding ad-mission as a prerequisite for admission. This recent addition is part of a policy of promoting Bruneians, which was seen as necessary to stop the tide of non-Bruneians practicing law in Brunei. A perception is that Chinese practitioners, some of whom lack citizenship, dominate the profession. Provisional admission for limited periods also can be given, and this occurs mainly where a complex case requires an experienced Queen's Counsel or other skilled advocate for the duration of that hearing.

IMPACT OF THE LAW

Although the common law system and courts remain entrenched, the increasing prominence given to Islamic law is having the greatest impact on the legal landscape of Brunei. At the proclamation of independence in 1984, the sultan's address (*Titah*) declared MIB to be the national ideology that must be honored and practiced by all the people of Brunei. He formalized it as "a concept which upholds Islamic principles and values based on the Quran and Hadith as the basis of all activities concerning the racial necessity, language, Malay culture and the monarchy institution as the governing system and administration of Brunei." The result has been that reforms to the legal system have been guided by this ideology, and there has been a directional change toward Islamization and Bruneization of the legal system. The latter can be seen in the changes to admission requirements and in the appointment of Bruneians to the courts.

The aim to return Islamic laws to what the sultan described in his 1984 *Titah* as "their rightful place as the principal legal system in the country and not the colonial system as practiced today" has accelerated in the last decade. Apart from the prohibition on the sale and importation of alcohol in 1991, laws were introduced into the financial sector to provide for Islamic banking and finance that prohibit the giving and taking of interest, speculative investments, and any other activities forbidden in Islam. The first Islamic Bank of Brunei opened in 1993 and the Development Bank of Brunei converted from conventional banking to an interest-free full Islamic system. Legislation has also provided for an Islamic trust fund and Islamic insurance. Furthermore, MIB policy has recently been manifested in the implementation of Islamic family law and laws of evidence.

This expansion of *sharia* law necessitated the reorganization of the courts. The Syariah Courts Order (1998), which is more than a terminology change from *qadi* (*qazi; kadi* in Brunei) to *sharia* (*Syar'ie* in Brunei) judge. Unlike the *qadi* courts, the *sharia* courts are hierarchical, which allows for an appellate process to a *sharia* appeal court. This is a powerful symbolic reversal of the standing of Islamic courts, making them equal not subordinate to the common law courts. These changes also make possible the implementation of more *sharia* law, including criminal law, which is specifically referred to in section 6(3) of the order. This is consistent with the sultan's 1996 statement that *sharia* courts would not be confined to the implementation of family laws, but would extend to the application of Islamic criminal law in its entirety. To date, further Islamic criminal law has not been enacted.

The Islamization of the legal environment can be further seen in the introduction in 2000 of a diploma course in Islamic Law and Practice at the University of Brunei. This provides accreditation for practice as a counsel or judge in the new *sharia* courts, or as a *sharia* lawyer. Admission to this course is for graduates with either Islamic law or common law qualifications. This will both increase the numbers of lawyers able to operate in the new system and also enhance the standing of Islamic law generally. These initiatives are consistent with MIB, and with the policy direction that Brunei become a center of excellence in Islamic studies, Islamic banking and finance, and technology for the Asia Pacific region.

Ann Black

See also Appellate Courts; Common Law; Criminal Law; Government Legal Departments; Islamic Law; Judicial Independence; Judicial Selection, Methods of; Juries; Legal Aid; Legal Education; Legal Pluralism; Magistrates—Common Law Systems; Privy Council; Qadi (Qazi) Courts; Sharia Court

References and further reading
Chiew, James. 1990. "Brunei, Abode of Peace (Negara Brunei)." Pp. 1–17 in *Constitutional and Legal Systems of ASEAN Countries.* Edited by Carmelo V. Sison. Manila: The Academy of ASEAN Law and Jurisprudence.
Borneo Bulletin. 2000. *Brunei Yearbook* (2000). Bandar Seri Begawan: Brunei Press Sdn Bhd.
Braighlinn, G. 1992. *Ideological Innovation under Monarchy: Aspects of legitimation activity in contemporary Brunei.* Amsterdam: VU University Press for Centre for Asian Studies Amsterdam.
Gunn, Geoffrey C. 1997. *Language, Power and Ideology in Brunei.* Athens: Center for International Studies, Ohio University.
Saunders, Graham. 1994. *A History of Brunei.* Kuala Lumpur: Oxford University Press.
Singh, D. S. Ranjit. 1990. "Executive Power and Constitutionalism in ASEAN States: the Brunei Experience." Pp. 18–44 in *Constitutional and Legal Systems of ASEAN Countries.* Edited by Carmelo V. Sison. Manila: The Academy of ASEAN Law and Jurisprudence.
State of Brunei and Brunei Investment Agency v. HRH Prince Jefri Bolkiah & anor. 2000. HC of BD Civil Suit No. 31.

BUDDHIST LAW

From Korea in the north to Sri Lanka in the south and from Afghanistan in the west to Japan in the east, Buddhism has been a significant cultural presence. The nineteenth-century poet Edwin Arnold summed this up by referring to Buddhism as the "Light of Asia," or *Lux Asiae.* Across this wide region, Buddhism has very obviously influenced architecture, literature, sculpture, and painting. At a more abstract level, it can be shown to have influenced ethics, philosophy, and statecraft. What about law? Buddhism is a remarkably legalistic religion, in that its central text, the *Vinaya,* is a code that defines and regulates its central institution—the *sima* (defined as all the monks who live in a particular monastery, together with all the hermits who live in the nearby forests). In this entry, I examine the suggestion that we should think of the *Vinaya* as *Lex Asiae,* the common element that unifies Asian law.

The Urals, equidistant between Lisbon and Vladivostok, mark the halfway point between Eurasia's eastern and western extremities. The 60° east line of longitude, which descends from the Urals to the Iran-Afghan border, divides Eurasia into two spheres of legal influence. West of that line, the unifying theme has been Roman law; to the east, it has been Buddhist law. In Tibet and Southeast Asia, the influence on local legal literature has been as powerful and direct as was Roman law on Spanish and French law. In Afghanistan, India, and Indonesia, the influence has been obscured by the arrival of a more recent but equally legalistic religion. But if legal historians can still find evidence of Roman law in Egypt and Algeria, we cannot rule out the possibility that a layer of Buddhist law survives beneath the thousand-year presence of Islam east of the Urals. On the east Asian seaboard, the question of influence is even more complicated. The cultures that have borrowed China's writing system—principally Korea, Vietnam, and Japan—also borrowed Chinese attitudes to law. And China's attitudes to law were formed a century or two before the arrival of Buddhism. During Buddhism's period of maximum influence in China (300 to 1000 C.E.) did it change Chinese legal attitudes as, during the same period, Christianity changed the way Europeans thought about Roman law? If we could answer all these legal historical questions, we could organize the story of east Eurasian law around a single theme—varied cultural responses to the challenge posed by Buddhism—to match the west Eurasian legal history organized around responses to the challenge of Roman law. In recent years, we have begun to get some answers from Tibet and Southeast Asia. Elsewhere, however, the work has scarcely begun. Why is Buddhism the least known of Eurasia's written legal cultures?

Europeans have been ignorant about Buddhism for millennia. It was not until the mid-nineteenth century that the various "idols" worshiped in Japan, China, Southeast Asia, and Sri Lanka were recognised as Buddha images. It took fifty more years for the existence of a massive, Asia-wide library of texts associated with the Buddha to be revealed. The serious study of these texts, along with their associated practices and traditions, was largely a twentieth-century phenomenon. Where Europe colonized Buddhist cultures, mostly between 1850 and 1914, the imposition of European law was facilitated by playing down the importance of Buddhist law. Max Weber, having read all this early colonial literature, generalized it into his conclusion that Buddhism's preoccupation with conscience and ritual formalism left no room for specialized legal learning. This is approximately the opposite of the truth, but Weber's immense influence has ensured that his distortions are still accepted among nonspecialists. For very different reasons, twentieth-century Chinese scholars were reluctant to investigate the question of Buddhist influence on Chinese law. After its humiliation at the hands of European traders, China spent the twentieth century trying to recover its pride. Suggestions that China's legal culture has been influenced by a foreign doctrine fell foul of this nationalist agenda. Since 1948, Buddhism has also fallen afoul of the dialectical materialist agenda: As mere idealistic superstructure, Buddhism could have had no significant effect on the techniques China developed to fill the nation's rice bowl. Given these obstacles, can we say anything about Buddhist legal history with confidence?

Over 2,500 years, many Buddhist traditions have risen to fame, and nearly as many have drifted back into obscurity. Each tradition preserved its own particular literature, often in its own language and script. Islamic, Chinese, and Jewish law texts prefer to be written in Arabic, Chinese, and Hebrew: Buddhism can display no such preference. The common core of Buddhist literature, which ranges from the legalisms of the *Vinaya* and the dry psychological lists of the *Abidhamma* to such literary masterpieces as the *Sutta of the Great Decease,* is preserved in about fifteen different languages and twice as many different scripts. We Buddhologists have had to adopt a postmodern disregard for absolutes in our discussions of this common core. Were we to claim that the Buddha's message is conveyed better in a Devanagri script than in Chinese ideograms, we would soon be arguing rather than cooperating. And cooperation is essential—many of the texts that tell us what Buddhism was like in its Indian phase are only available in Chinese translation. Typically, each Buddhist tradition seems to have preserved a literature that was three parts common core to one part unique texts. But we can only be certain of this for the living traditions. All we know of the dead traditions is the few texts we dug up from the desert sand: How big is the invisible part of the iceberg? Thus, there is plenty of scope for controversy on which texts should be included in Buddhism's common core. Two generalizations seem safe: First, traditions that preserved their own *Vinaya* text survived longer than those that didn't. Second, the highest level of difference into which the Buddhist common core subdivides is the three-way split between the Tibetan, Chinese, and Pali traditions.

Gautama Buddha lived, meditated, preached, and died in southern Nepal and the eastern Ganges Valley some time between 550 and 350 B.C.E. Southeast Asian Buddhists think he lived earlier within that period, whereas most European scholars now put him toward the end of it. During his lifetime, north India was undergoing profound social change, as new technologies and new agricultural techniques allowed the development of urbanization, state formation, and maritime trade. Buddhism soon came to be associated with these three processes, which the upholders of Vedic wisdom shunned as unpleasant innovations. Since these three processes are associated with the development of law, it is plausible to think of a Buddhist input to the law administered by the first north Indian emperors. Unfortunately, this conjecture cannot be proved. Buddhists are interested in history, so Buddhist literature has preserved some historical information on the Mauryan Empire (321 to 185 B.C.E.). But the accounts are one-sided because Vedic experts were quite uninterested in recording contemporary events. The greatest of the Mauryan emperors, King Ashoka (265 to 238) left a series of inscriptions across north India. They show that he was, in some sense, a Buddhist, but they provide few legal details, other than confirming the existence and importance of *Vinaya* texts.

LAW FOR MONKS—THE *VINAYA*

The Pali version of the *Vinaya* is shorter and more ordered than the others. During the first half of the twentieth century, this was taken as showing its fidelity to the Buddha's original intentions. Nowadays, we take it as showing that a vigorous editorial policy was adopted when the Pali scriptures were committed to writing around 75 B.C.E. in the *Alu* monastery in Sri Lanka. In this recension, the canon divides into three baskets (*pitaka*), of which the first is the *Vinaya*. The six volumes of the *Vinaya* basket divide into three separate works: the *khandhaka* (rules telling monasteries how to act collectively), the *suttavibhanga* (rules telling monasteries how to deal with offending monks), and the *parivara* (analysis and specimen problems for students). The parivara, a late work written by a Sri Lankan monk called Dipa, is known only to the Pali tradition, but the khandhaka (meaning "heaps of stuff") and the suttavibhanga (meaning "rule analyzer") vary but little between the various recensions. Behind the khandhaka is an ill-defined list of between twenty and forty *kammavaca* (deed-speeches). Kammavaca are the verbal formulas put to the monastic community in formal assembly for their approval. They provide templates for how various issues and tasks are to be discussed and carried out. Only when the sima follows a specific kammavaca described in the khandhaka, using the right words and having the right quorum, are its collective actions valid. The list behind the suttavibhanga is the recitation of 227 offenses known as the *patimokkha,* which the sima must recite together aloud twice a month. Each of the 227 forms of individual misbehavior is classified into eight groups of accusation. We start with the most serious accusations (the four *parajika,* which lead automatically to the end of monastic status—killing, having sex, thieving, and misclaiming meditative prowess). We end with the least serious (the seventy-five acts of rudeness, which don't merit any specified punishment—such as "Don't tiptoe in public" or "Don't urinate standing up.")

To what extent may we call the *Vinaya* law? For legal positivists such as Jeremy Bentham and Hans Kelsen, the crucial question is whether it is enforced by sanctions. Given the Buddhist commitment to nonviolence and given that monastic status and membership in a sima are voluntary and can be reliquished at will, this approach is unhelpful. The nub of the matter is this: The two most powerful *Vinaya* sanctions depend not on brute force but on the stipulative definitions framed by the inventor of the institution. In both the khandhaka and the suttavibhanga, the Buddha's power to define the institution of monasticism is his ultimate sanction against miscreants. The moment a monk commits theft, he becomes, by the Buddha's definition, an ex-monk. The moment the sima mispronounces a kammavaca, their discussion, by the Buddha's definition, becomes null and void. If you want to be one of the Buddha's monks, as opposed to a Jain monk or a Daoist monk, you have to comply with his definitions. This power of institutional definition is different from the powers wielded by such code-mongering kings as Hammurabi and Justinian. In some respects, the Buddha had more power than they did. Whether or not we regard the *Vinaya* as law depends on how we weigh these distinctions.

BUDDHIST LAW SPREADS
BEYOND INDIA AND SRI LANKA

A *Vinaya* text was first translated into Chinese around 250 C.E., but the Chinese did not get a complete *Vinaya* until the late fourth or early fifth century. China's pilgrim monks continued to import other *Vinaya* recensions, and it was not until the seventh century C.E. that the *Dharmagupta Vinaya* was recognized as authoritative on Chinese monks. Did *Vinaya* influence the broad Chinese legal tradition? This possibility is not yet proven, but three suggestions need to be investigated: that the Chinese *Vinaya* experts provided a model for specialists in other areas of Chinese law, that the *Vinaya's* emphasis on intention sharpened the Chinese distinction between mens rea and negligence, and that the *Vinaya* served as a model for the Tang dynasty's modifications to the legal and bureaucratic structure.

Buddhism spread across Southeast Asia during the first millennium, but there is little detailed evidence until the Pagan (Burma) and Angkor (Cambodia) civilizations of the eleventh century. The kings and monks of Pagan mixed the Pali *Vinaya* with other Buddhist sources and with a pinch of Hindu legal material to create new legal genres that applied to ordinary, lay rice farmers. These genres—known as *dhammasat* and *rajasat*—spread across all the Pali kingdoms of mainland Southeast Asia. By the eighteenth century, they were found in profusion in Burma, Laos, Thailand, and—as the heirs of Angkor embraced Pali Buddhism—even in Cambodia. It was this law that captured European attention in the late nineteenth century and that Weber dismissed as Hindu law modified in the direction of Buddhism. This Pali Buddhist law took a battering during the colonial period, but it still seems to survive in Burma and Cambodia, where the postcolonial state has failed to provide an acceptable postcolonial legal system.

Tibet acquired an interest in Buddhism in the eighth century, then again in the eleventh century. The Mulasarvastivadin *Vinaya* became Tibet's recension of choice, and Tibetan monks busied themselves producing the usual *Vinaya* commentaries, manuals, and textbooks. In Tibet, as in Southeast Asia, the *Vinaya* formed the basis of law codes binding the Tibetan farmers and herdsmen. The chronology of these Tibetan codes is not yet clear, but thanks to a recent study, we have a clear picture of how Tibetan law operated in the final decades before the Chinese invasion and the exile of the Dalai Lama in 1959.

THE CORE CONCEPTS OF BUDDHIST LAW

The Buddhist diagnosis of human suffering is that need (or grasping or desire) causes our illusion of ego (or consciousness or subjective personality). We suffer because we mistakenly think we have an ego. The Buddhist cure reverses this causal chain: To end suffering, we must remove the ego. We do this by switching off the need functions in our mind. This psychosurgery requires intense meditation, impeccable moral behavior, and total chastity. In the Confucian and Aristotelian traditions, virtue takes most of a lifetime to acquire. Buddhism goes further: It takes several lifetimes to switch off these brain functions completely and thereby achieve nirvana.

Notice the importance of causation to this analysis. If the practice of Buddhism is largely meditation, doctrinal Buddhism (if it did not sound so paradoxical, I would refer to Buddhist theology) is largely the analysis of causation. The Buddha's theory of multifactored causation (codependent origination) is at the heart of his message. Of the several causes that coalesce to bring about an effect, none can be singled out as *causa efficiens* or *causa sine qua non.* One cause of Abraham Lincoln's demise was that John Wilkes Booth pulled the trigger. Another cause was the president's decision to go to the theater that night. The

Buddha will not allow us to evaluate the relative strengths of these causes. The reality of the moment can only be grasped by appreciating all its effective causes (and all the effective causes that gave rise to John Wilkes Booth and theaters and guns and so on in infinite recursivity). One can see the need for meditation: We've got a big job to do, and we must cut out as many distractions as we can. No one, I can safely say, ever achieved nirvana while landing a jumbo jet or day-trading on the futures market.

This fundamental Buddhist attitude to causation leads Buddhist lawyers to prefer situations over rules. Everyone agrees on the general ethical principles: killing, lying, stealing, and bad sex are forbidden, and so are drink or drugs, which encourage us to the other four. But when it comes to applying these principles to actual cases, reasonable people can disagree. It depends on how many of the operative causes we can identify, and this, in turn, depends on how much meditation and morality we have practiced in this and previous lives. A persistent theme in Buddhist legal literature is that every rule is defeasible. Rules are, at best, rules of thumb, that is, a summation of past experiences that, for one cause or another, may not apply in the instant case. There is no such thing as Buddhist equity because there is no such thing as Buddhist strict law. This premise has two repercussions. It reduces the possibility of dogmatic claims to legal knowledge, since only a fully enlightened Buddha can know the "one right answer" to a specific hard case. And it shifts the focus of the legal literature from rules to case law. By reading case law (the history of what actually happened in actual disputes), we can build up our own situation-sense and learn how to appreciate more of the covalent factors that impinge on each moment.

If we think of the Buddha as Albert Einstein, multi-factored causation is his General Theory of Relativity applying to all events in the world, whereas karma is his Special Theory of Relativity applying just to sentient beings and the ethics of their actions. The doctrine of karma holds that all sentient beings are reborn as higher or lower forms of life, depending on the state of their karmic balance at death. Our universe is constructed in such a way that violence, however justified, gets its dessert. By a natural process of causation, karma will punish the rapist in his next incarnation. This idea is comparable, but much wider, than European ideas of natural law. Karma goes further than any natural law theory, since nature does not just proclaim what good behavior is but also punishes bad behavior. This has led to a series of typically Buddhist confusions over the respective role of king and karma. Why should a king bother punishing rapists if they will be punished inexorably by nature itself? A rough boundary between the respective jurisdictions is provided by death. Broadly speaking, the king could only punish you in this life, and karma could only punish you in the next life. But Buddhist law allows exceptions to both of these statements.

Andrew Huxley

See also Bhutan; Burma; China; Japan; Laos; Sri Lanka; Thailand; Tibet

References and further reading
French, Rebecca. 1995. *The Golden Yoke: The Legal Cosmology of Buddhist Tibet.* Ithaca, NY: Cornell University Press.
Hinüber, Oskar v. 1995. "Buddhist Law According to the Theravada Vinaya—A Survey of Theory and Practice." *Journal of the International Association of Buddhist Studies* 18: 7–45.
Holt, John C. 1981. *Discipline: The Canonical Buddhism of the Vinayapitaka.* Delhi: Motilal Banarsidass.
Huxley, Andrew, ed. 1996. *Thai Law: Buddhist Law Essays on the Legal History of Thailand, Laos and Burma.* Bangkok: White Orchid Press.
Lee, Luke T., and Whalen W. Lai. 1978. "The Chinese Conceptions of Law: Confucian, Legalist, and Buddhist." *Hastings Law Journal* 29: 1307–1342.
Prebish, Charles S. 1994. *A Survey of* Vinaya *Literature.* Taipei: Jin Luen Publishing House.

BULGARIA

GENERAL INFORMATION

Bulgaria is a Balkan state in southeastern Europe that controls the land routes from Europe to the Middle East and Asia. Occupying 110,910 square kilometers, making it slightly larger than the state of Tennessee, Bulgaria borders the Black Sea between Romania and Turkey, with Greece and Turkey to the south and the former Yugoslav Republic of Macedonia, Kosovo, Montenegro, and Serbia to the west and northwest. Bulgaria's terrain is mountainous, with lowlands in the north and southeast regions of the country.

There are slightly more than 8 million Bulgarians, with a declining population growth rate of –0.52 percent as of 1999 and a life expectancy for men of 68.2 years and for women of 76.03 years. Eight-five percent of the population is composed of ethnic Bulgarians; 9 percent are ethnic Turks; and the remaining 6 percent are Gypsies (Roma), Jews, and others. Bulgaria's current constitution declares Eastern Orthodox Christianity the traditional religion, and indeed, most Bulgarians (85 percent) are said to be identified with the Bulgarian Orthodox Church, while 13 percent are Muslims, 0.8 percent are Jewish, 0.5 percent are Roman Catholic, 0.2 percent are Uniate Catholic, and a remaining 0.5 percent are members of Protestant, Georgorian-Armenian, and other churches. Bulgarian is the official language, although the various ethnic groups employ secondary languages. With a 98 percent literacy rate, Bulgarians are well educated. The climate is temperate, with cold, damp winters and hot, dry summers. Sofia is the nation's capital, with twenty-

eight administrative provinces in a unitary form of government. The country's legal system is rooted in the European civil law tradition.

HISTORY

Bulgaria's struggle for a constitutional democracy founded on rule of law principles is a recurring theme in its history. For five hundred years (1396–1878), Bulgarians were subjected to the rule of the Ottoman Empire governed by Turkish sultans that often ruled harshly and arbitrarily. Despite many indigenous uprisings, it took the intervention of a Russian army with aid by volunteers from elsewhere in Europe to liberate Bulgaria from what Bulgarians typically characterize as the "Turkish yoke."

Beginning in the late nineteenth century, Bulgaria was ruled by monarchs or by a communist dictatorship, although in the 1920s there was a brief experience of democracy that ended in bloodshed. During November 1989, when the authoritarian communist regime was toppled in a bloodless coup d'état, events were placed in motion that led to the transition toward a constitutional democracy with an emphasis upon the protection of human rights.

Bulgaria's first constitution, adopted in 1879, was by the European standards of the day an advanced basic document that included a limited monarchy, a unicameral legislature based upon universal male suffrage, and protections of civil liberties and rights. While it is doubtful that the foreign-born monarchs were ever comfortable with democratic principles, including an independent judiciary, the intelligentsia and professional classes supported democracy and organized competitive political parties. When, however, democracy became too inconvenient for the monarchy and its supporters in the military and the business community, coups and other extralegal tactics served to deter the consolidation of democratic institutions.

Marxist ideology was employed by Communist Party leaders in the late 1940s to proclaim courts and judges instruments of the party in the service of socialist justice, including collectivization of agricultural lands and state ownership of the means of production and the distribution of services. In Bulgaria, however, private ownership of some real property, such as the widely owned country cottages, remained undisturbed. Opponents of the regime maintain that during the communist era, telephone justice was widely practiced—party functionaries let judges know their desires for particular case outcomes, and the judges complied with their wishes. Although some telephone justice no doubt took place, it is likely that in most instances such direct communication was unnecessary if the judges wanted to continue to practice their profession. During the 1950s and 1960s, the government used the judiciary to place opponents into forced labor camps. Back in the mid-1940s, the People's Courts had been used not only to eliminate Nazi wartime collaborators but, in addition, to convict opponents of the Communist Party—all told, 12,000 persons were convicted, 2,730 of whom were executed.

The leaders that seized control in a November 1989 coup d'état pledged to reverse the use of the judicial system for political purposes by promoting political pluralism and the rule of law. Significantly, they halted the persecution of the Turkish ethnic minority that had been going on for some time. Within a few years after the coup, 77 members of the judiciary took voluntary retirement, and 243 persons left the judicial system without offering an explanation—none was required. Forty-four others were dismissed.

Between January and May of 1990, a series of meeting were held between the leaders of the Bulgarian Communist Party (who changed the organization's name to the Bulgarian Socialist Party) and a loose coalition of opposition leaders that came to be known as the Union of Democratic Forces. Held in Sofia, these Roundtable Meetings, as they were called, created the framework for the principles that guided the Grand National Assembly (GNA), the body that drafted and ratified the new constitution on July 12, 1991. The four hundred members of the GNA that served as both a working parliament and a constitutional convention were elected in June 1990. They produced a ten-chapter document with human rights and constitutional supremacy as central features. The 1991 constitution provides for separation of powers with a unicameral legislature, a council of ministers, a president, and a judiciary capable of exercising independent power.

LEGAL FRAMEWORK

The belief that law should be a set of objective rules that are applied to particular disputants in a relatively neutral manner is a central organizing concept deeply and firmly imbedded in the 1991 Bulgarian Constitution. This concept of a rule-of-law state, sometimes called a law-governed state, is viewed as the alternative to the authoritarian ways of the past and points toward the greater observance of democratic values in a new Bulgarian society.

The Bulgarian Constitution features human rights as its central theme. The preamble pledges "loyalty to the universal human values of liberty, peace, humanism, equality, justice and tolerance." It purports to do so by "elevating as the uppermost principle the rights, dignity and security of the individual." Chapter one of the constitution formally renounces the suggestion that Bulgaria should return to its monarchal past by declaring the state a republic with a parliamentary form of government. The 1991 constitution is declared the "supreme law, and no other law shall contravene it." Moreover Article 5(2) commands that provisions of the constitution shall "apply directly," meaning that rights exist independent of and are superior to ordinary acts of parliament or of the executive branch of government. The constitution also contains a provision that international agreements to which Bulgaria is a party are part of internal domestic law, and such agreements shall supersede domestic legislation stipulating otherwise. Consequently, international conventions on human rights of which Bulgaria is a party, including the European Convention for Human Rights and Liberties, and various other international conventions and protocols, serve as additional civil liberties and human rights protections and guard against the resurgence of a repressive government.

Articles 25 through 61 found in chapter two of the constitution contain specific human rights protections, including well-known political protections such as freedom of speech and press and protections against repressive police tactics, including the right to legal counsel and the presumption of innocence until proven guilty. These enumerated rights also name specific positive rights including, for example, paid maternity leave for mothers, social security, health insurance, and the right to an education.

The framers of the 1991 constitution made an explicit attempt to avoid the ethnic unrest and separatist movements that plague the Balkan region of the world and thereby to encourage the creation of a pluralist democracy. Article 6(2) located in chapter one of the constitution specifically prohibits "privileges or restrictions of rights on the grounds of race, nationality, ethnic self-identity, sex, origin, religion, education, opinion, political affiliation, personal or social status or property status." This provision may be viewed as well as an article of peace among the nation's diverse populations, which include Bulgarians, Turks, Jews, Armenians, Gypsies, and other minorities.

Government authority is further limited by the constitution's explicit separation of power design. Article 8 of chapter one divides power among the legislative, executive, and judicial branches of government. The National Assembly is a unicameral legislature with 240 members elected for four-year terms. Members of the National Assembly selected for another state post, including, for example, government ministers, judges, prosecutors, and investigators, must cease to serve as parliamentarians and be replaced for the period they function in that capacity.

The National Assembly is responsible for making laws that impact the lives of citizens in their everyday affairs.

The Council of Ministers is responsible for guiding the implementation of domestic and foreign policy consistent with the constitution. It consists of a prime minister, deputy prime ministers, and other ministers. It is responsible for public order and national security as well as the overall leadership of the state administration and of the armed forces. It directly implements the state budget, organizes the management of state property, and concludes, ratifies, and rescinds international treaties consistent with acts of the National Assembly. The Council of Ministers promulgates governmental rules and regulations by means of decrees.

Because the constitutional framers created a parliamentary and not a presidential system of government, the president of the republic is in large measure consigned to the position of head of state. In that capacity, the president embodies the unity of the nation and represents it on the world stage; a vice president is elected on the same ballot with the president, for no more than two five-year terms. Among the president's most significant powers is the ability to veto an act of the parliament, but such action may be overridden by more than half of the members of the National Assembly. The president may also refer laws to the Constitutional Court for constitutional review.

The judicial branch is created to protect the rights and legitimate interests of citizens, juridical/legal persons, and the state. As is the practice in other countries with a civil law tradition, judges, prosecutors, and investigators are regarded together as part of the judicial branch of government. Importantly, the constitution mandates that the judiciary be independent, and in the exercise of their various functions law must guide judicial personnel in all their official actions. The 1991 constitution guarantees the judiciary a separate budget, and whereas the National Assembly may establish specialized courts such as those for labor, juveniles, or bankruptcy cases, no extraordinary courts are permitted such as the People's Court of the 1940s, which conducted political trials for offenses involving Bulgaria in World War II.

The Supreme Judicial Council (SJC) is designed as an additional safeguard to guarantee judicial independence. Article 129 of the constitution provides that justices, prosecutors, and investigating magistrates are elected, promoted, demoted, and reassigned by this body. The president of the Supreme Court of Cassation, the president of the Supreme Administrative Court, and the prosecutor general are appointed or dismissed by the president of the republic after nomination by the SJC. Article 129 further provides that the president shall not deny an appointment or dismissal on a repeated motion of the SJC. The council consists of twenty-five members, eleven of whom are elected for five-year terms without immediate renewal by the parliament, and bodies of the judicial branch elect eleven additional members. Three additional council members are seated by virtue of their official positions: the chair of the Supreme Court of Cassation, the chair of the Supreme Administrative Court, and the chief prosecutor. The minister of justice of the Council of Ministers chairs the meetings of the SJC but without voting privileges.

By the end of 1999, there were a total of 1,296 judicial posts in all jurisdictions. There are 1,002 postings for investigating magistrates and 822 positions for prosecutors. Life tenure for most judges in the judicial system is an additional constitutional protection designed to promote judicial independence. The SJC is also authorized to appoint junior judges and junior prosecutors for two-year terms of office that may be extended by six months. Available to the ordinary law court judges but not to constitutional court justices, Article 129(3) provides that after the third year in office, justices, prosecutors, and investigating magistrates may be removed only for retirement, to serve a criminal sentence, or for a disability. The Law on the Judiciary (LJ) of 1994 as amended in 1996 makes operational these protections by providing that judges, prosecutors, and investigators may not be detained and criminal proceedings may not be instituted against them except as provided by law. Moreover, these legal professionals may not be called to military training or service. Further, to avoid excessive political entanglements, Article 12 of the LJ prohibits their membership, for as long as they are judicial system functionaries, in political parties or organizations and movements or coalitions that have political ends. Moreover, professional organizations of judges, prosecutors, and investigators may not associate with trade union organizations from another branch of government or sector of the economy at either the national or the regional level.

CURRENT COURT SYSTEM STRUCTURE

Chapter six of the Bulgarian Constitution provides for five regular courts that resolve legal disputes. Reflecting the historical tradition of conceptualizing the judicial system broadly, the constitution and statutory law also provide for the establishment of prosecutors' offices and investigation services within the judicial branch of government.

During the first three years under the 1991 constitution, parliamentarians debated the details of a judiciary act that would establish the new courts, but they were distracted from the task by a number of other pressing matters. In the meantime, the old court system was kept intact, although a good number of former Communist Party–appointed judges resigned or took early retirement. The current judicial structure is spelled out in the 1994

Law on the Judiciary as amended in 1996 and subsequent years.

Article 15 of the LJ provides for three types of legal proceedings: first-instance, appeal on the merits, and cassation proceedings. In first-instance proceedings, the court resolves both factual and legal disputes. An appeal on the merits reviews how the first-instance lower court resolved both factual and legal matters. In cassation proceedings, the high court decides only questions of law brought before it, and it has the option to affirm or to quash (*casser*) the decision below and remand the case for reconsideration by the lower court. The following regular law courts currently exist in Bulgaria, and the diagram below expresses in general the jurisdiction of each court within the system:

(1) Regional courts: Cases tried by one judge plus two lay jurors in criminal cases unless otherwise specified by law; prosecutorial offices, bailiffs, and in some instances notaries are connected to these courts; these courts also try civil cases and administrative matters such as those relating to agricultural land ownership and use;

(2) District courts: Adjudicate first-instance civil and criminal cases as provided by law and serve as courts of review for the regional courts with established civil, criminal, commercial, and administrative sections; acts of municipal councils may be appealed before district courts; cases are tried by three judges unless specified by law, one of whom may be a junior judge, and in first-instance criminal cases jurors participate in deliberations; prosecutorial and investigative magistrate offices are present at these courts;

(3) Courts-martial: Cases tried by one judge plus jurors or by three judges, one of whom may be a junior judge; military prosecutor and military investigative magistrate offices serve at this jurisdictional level;

(4) Appellate courts: In civil, criminal, and commercial sections, three-judge panels hear cases on appeal by private litigants or prosecutors objecting to decisions of courts below as well as disciplinary cases against junior judges and junior prosecutors; appellate prosecutorial officers are connected to the appellate court, but this court does not hear appeals concerning administrative law matters; currently these courts examine appellate cases on the merits; reviewing matters of both fact and law, these courts do not simply review and reverse first-instance judgments concerning interpretation of law alone;

(5) Military Appellate Court: Three-judge panels hear appeals from first-instance military courts; it has same powers relative to the military courts that the regular appellate courts have in relation to the district courts;

(6) Supreme Administrative Court: The final appellate court for all administrative law matters within Bulgaria; this court sits in Sofia, pronouncing judgments in three-judge panels in cases appealed from courts below; only five-judge panels may rule on disputes concerning the legality of acts of the Council of Ministers and of the individual ministers, as well as other acts that can be appealed as dictated by law; five-judge panels also hear disputes on final appeal from decisions of the court's three-judge panels, and in some instances a general assembly of the respective bodies (colleges) of the Supreme Administrative Court hear cases; a prosecutor's office is connected to this court, and it is presided over by a deputy chief prosecutor;

(7) Supreme Court of Cassation: A court of final appeal with a total of sixty-seven judges sits in Sofia in three-judge panels to hear cassation appeals from the civil, criminal, and military courts about matters of law alone and not of fact, and to settle jurisdictional disputes involving courts of appeal; cases involving questionable judicial practices require a general assembly of colleagues to render opinions; when this court identifies a discrepancy between law and the constitution, it suspends the proceedings in such cases and refers the matter to the Constitutional Court; there is a prosecutorial office associated with this court, chaired by a deputy chief prosecutor.

As provided by law, the National Investigation Service exists to conduct investigations of cases when certain factual or legal matters are at issue within the territorial limits of Bulgaria, as well as cases involving criminal acts committed abroad or fines under legal assistance treaties with other countries. This agency is associated with the courts to ferret out the facts in criminal cases and to provide equal justice under law. Assuming greater independence from the central authority, these services have been decentralized with the creation of the Specialized Investigation Service and district investigation services.

Article 4(1) of the 1994 Law on the Judiciary mandates that all civil, criminal, and administrative disputes fall within the jurisdiction of the courts. Consistent with the constitutional mandate, the LJ dictates that citizens and legal persons have a right to mount a defense in court and that no court may deny them an adequate defense, subject to the limitations set forth in the statute. The LJ empowers courts to exercise control over the legality of the acts and measures of administrative bodies.

Ordinary Bulgarian courts may not adjudicate constitutional issues with binding effect applicable to all persons (*erga omnes*), but they are nonetheless binding on parties to the suit in question. Nor may ordinary courts bring matters directly to the attention of the Constitutional Court. However, Article 150(1) of the constitution provides that the Supreme Court of Cassation and the Supreme Administrative Court may refer constitutional matters to this court. Under paragraph 2 of this same provision these courts possess the authority to refer both abstract and concrete issues wherein they suspend the proceedings and await the decision of the Constitutional Court. Further, Article 13 of the LJ provides, in the event

Legal Structure of Bulgaria

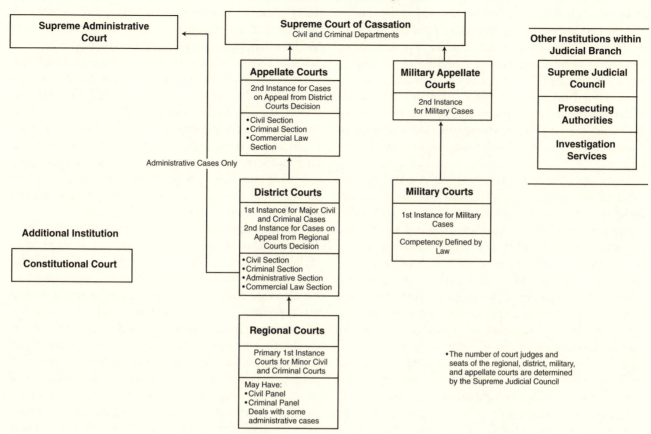

Supreme Administrative Court

Supreme Court of Cassation
Civil and Criminal Departments

Other Institutions within Judicial Branch

Supreme Judicial Council

Prosecuting Authorities

Investigation Services

Appellate Courts
2nd Instance for Cases on Appeal from District Courts Decision
• Civil Section
• Criminal Section
• Commercial Law Section

Military Appellate Courts
2nd Instance for Military Cases

Administrative Cases Only

District Courts
1st Instance for Major Civil and Criminal Cases
2nd Instance for Cases on Appeal from Regional Courts Decision
• Civil Section
• Criminal Section
• Administrative Section
• Commercial Law Section

Military Courts
1st Instance for Military Cases
Competency Defined by Law

Additional Institution

Constitutional Court

Regional Courts
Primary 1st Instance Courts for Minor Civil and Criminal Courts
May Have:
• Civil Panel
• Criminal Panel
Deals with some administrative cases

• The number of court judges and seats of the regional, district, military, and appellate courts are determined by the Supreme Judicial Council

---

a lower court estimates that a law contravenes the constitution, that court shall notify the Supreme Court of Cassation or the Supreme Administrative Court so that the Constitutional Court may exercise jurisdiction over the matter. Likewise, prosecutors and investigators shall notify the chief prosecutor, who in turn may refer the matter to the Constitutional Court.

The constitution provides that the National Assembly shall determine the organization of the courts and the status and conditions of employment of judicial personnel. Article 126 of the LJ sets out the following requirements for judicial appointments. First, prospective judges, prosecutors, and investigating magistrates must complete a legal education in an institution of higher learning. Second, they must undergo some form of postgraduate practical training. Third, they must not have been convicted of a premeditated crime for which they have been imprisoned, regardless of rehabilitation. And lastly, they must possess moral and professional qualities befitting the legal profession.

The requirement for the attainment of a law degree dates from the end of the nineteenth century. Presently, law faculties at ten different institutions of higher education confer law diplomas. By special statute, students may be granted the diploma after ten semesters of course

work, and they must pass state-administered examinations in the final stages of their education in Public Law, Civil Law (substantive and procedural), and Criminal Law (substantive and procedural). Unlike France, for example, there is no particular training offered by law faculties or specific diplomas for those desiring to become judges, prosecutors, or investigating magistrates. Yet, because of a wide range of elective courses, students may plan their course of study with a view toward becoming a judge, prosecutor, investigating magistrate, or private attorney. With the growing privatization of the economy, many young professionals are setting their sights on the relatively lucrative private practice of the law rather than the once more prestigious public-service occupations in the judiciary. Some law faculties are now offering legal clinics that are designed to give students practical training in the law before graduation. Further, in April 1999, a training center was created to facilitate practical education in the law and to provide a program of continuing education for judges, prosecutors, and investigators.

Members of the judiciary are required to take an oath that is recited orally and must also be signed. Reflecting the emphasis upon impartial justice and the rule of law, the oaths articulate the national rejection of both socialist law principles and the class bias evident in earlier eras.

Lay jurors sit with judges in first-instance criminal cases. Municipal councils nominate prospective jurors, and they are appointed by the general meetings of judges in the respective district courts for the regional courts, and by the general meetings of the judges in the respective court of appeals for the district courts. Jurors in court-martial cases are appointed upon the nomination of the commanders of military units by a general meeting of the judges in the court-martial appeals court. Jurors in court-martial cases may be generals, admirals, and other officers.

Ordinary lay jurors are summoned to participate in court deliberations for no more than sixty days in a calendar year, unless a trial in which they are sitting lasts for a longer period of time. Under law, lay jurors are afforded unpaid leave of absence from their jobs, and they are remunerated for their time from the budget of the judicial system. The Ministry of Justice and the Supreme Judicial Council are charged with the regulation of the terms and procedures for nominating jurors and other such matters pertaining to the inclusion of jurors in the judicial process, including appropriate remuneration.

Indicating the special legal role and political influence of the Constitutional Court in the life of the republic, it is provided for in chapter eight and not in chapter six of the constitution, as is the case for the regular courts. The constitution grants to the Constitutional Court the authority to pronounce binding interpretations of the constitution. It rules on challenges to the constitutionality of laws and other acts passed by the National Assembly and acts of the president. This court adjudicates conflicts between and among the National Assembly, the president, the Council of Ministers, and the bodies of local governments and the central executive branch of government. Constitutional Court justices are empowered to rule on the constitutionality of international agreements before they are ratified and on the compatibility of domestic laws with universal norms of international law and treaties and other international obligations to which Bulgaria is a party. The court may also rule on the constitutional status of political parties and associations and on the legality of the election of the president, vice president, and members of the National Assembly. Finally, the Constitutional Court may rule on impeachment controversies involving the president or the vice president of the republic. In the event that the Constitutional Court convicts the president or vice president of high treason or a violation of the constitution, the prerogatives of each shall be suspended.

Unlike the U.S. judicial system, Bulgaria's constitution allows for abstract judicial review wherein there need not be an actual case or controversy before a case may be brought before it. If a promulgated act of parliament is suspected of containing constitutional defects, the Constitutional Court may rule on the matter resulting from the petition of no fewer than one-fifth of all members of the National Assembly, the president, the Council of Ministers, the Supreme Court of Cassation, the Supreme Administrative Court, or the chief prosecutor. Unlike ordinary statutes, however, international treaties are reviewed by the Constitutional Court before their ratification by the National Assembly. Consequently, unlike the U.S. system, it is possible to dispose of an unconstitutional law or treaty before it damages persons unnecessarily. Important to maintaining the independence of the Constitutional Court, Article 149(c) of the constitution provides that no law may be enacted that would suspend its authority to hear cases.

The Constitutional Court is a twelve-member body. The president of the republic appoints one-third of its members, while the National Assembly is responsible for appointing an additional one-third. The remaining four members are elected by a joint meeting of the justices of the Supreme Court of Cassation and the Supreme Administrative Court. Unlike the judicial officials of the regular courts, who have lifetime tenure, Constitutional Court justices are elected or appointed for nine-year nonrenewable terms. Although the justices that have served on this court since the adoption of the 1991 constitution share good reputations, they are not household names. Yet members of this court have been willing to exercise their authority, and by virtue of their written opinions they have been central actors in helping to resolve through the use of legal concepts many important political conflicts during the first decade of the new democratic republic.

IMPACT OF LAW

Opinion polls reveal that the judiciary suffers from relatively low public esteem. This is due in part to the high crime rate in postcommunist Bulgaria and the widespread perception that public officials of all sorts are responsible for this sad state of affairs. Then, too, there is general ignorance among the population about how the judicial system works. Currently, leaders of a judicial reform movement have established joint committees with media representatives and magistrates to help inform the population about the judiciary. Some contemporary judicial reform advocates seek to revise the requirement for practical training. They seek to focus it and give it greater definition, so that the existing practical training requirement becomes more meaningful and useful to future legal professionals.

A group of leading jurists has established the Judicial Reform Initiative. They have offered a series of concrete reform proposals. These proposals include changes in the criminal, civil, and administrative codes, changes in the structure of legal education, court administration initiatives, the creation of a judicial ombudsman, and a host of other ideas intended to create greater public support for the judicial system as a whole.

Albert P. Melone
Mariana Karagiozova-Finkova

See also Administrative Law; Appellate Courts; Civil Law; Constitutionalism; European Court and Commission on Human Rights; France; Judicial Review; Judicial Independence; Juries; Marxist Jurisprudence; Judicial Selection, Methods of; Soviet System; Trial Courts

References and further reading
Bell, John D., ed. 1998. *Bulgaria in Transition.* Boulder, CO: Westview Press.
Judicial Reform Initiative. "Judicial Reform Initiative: Program for Judicial Reform in Bulgaria: Sofia 2000," http://www.csd.bg/jri/RROGRAM_april_E.html (cited October 6, 2000).
Karagiozova-Finkova, Mariana. 1997. "La Justice constitutionalelle en Bulgarie." Pp. 5–52 in *La Justice constitutionnelle en Europe centrale,* Edited by Robert Badinter. Bruxelles: Center d'etudes constitutionnelles et administratives sous la direction de Verdussen, M. Bruylant.
Melone, Albert P. 1994. "Bulgaria's National Roundtable Talks and the Politics of Accommodation." *International Political Science Review* 15 (July): 257–273.
————. 1996. "The Struggle for Judicial Independence and the Transition toward Democracy in Bulgaria." *Communist and Post-Communist Studies* 29 (June): 231–243.
————. 1998. *Creating Parliamentary Government: The Transition to Democracy in Bulgaria.* Columbus: Ohio State University Press.
Melone, Albert P., and Bradley Best. 2000. "Creating the Institutions for a Law-Governed State: The Constitutional Politics of Bulgaria's Grand National Assembly." Pp.167–178 in *Handbook of Global Legal Policy.* Edited by Stuart S. Nagel. New York: Marcel Dekker.
Melone, Albert P., and Carol E. Hays. 1994. "The Judicial Role in Bulgaria's Struggle for Human Rights." *Judicature* 77 (March–April): 248–253.
Trendafilova, E., and T. Hinova. 1999. "Bulgaria." Pp. 18–31 in *International Encyclopedia of Laws.* Edited by R. Blanpain. The Netherlands: Kluwer Law International.

BURKINA FASO

COUNTRY INFORMATION

Burkina Faso, formerly Upper Volta, is a landlocked Sahelian nation in West Africa. It is bordered by six countries: on the north and west by Mali, on the east by Niger, and on the south by Ivory Coast, Ghana, Togo, and Benin. The country's area is about 274,200 square kilometers, and its population is roughly 12 million, not including the 6 million citizens who live outside the country, particularly in Ivory Coast. This latter figure reflects the poverty of the country, which is generally ranked at the bottom in the United Nations Development Pro-

gramme (UNDP) reports on human development.

About half of the population are from the Mosse ethnic group, which is characterized by a centralized authority, and the other half represent a mosaic of about sixty ethnic groups, most of them lineage or village societies. Every ethnic group has its own culture, including its own language and customs. About 50 percent of the population are Muslims, and 20 percent are Christians (mainly Roman Catholics). The remainder are Animists. However, traditional religious practices still influence widely the followers of imported religions, either Islam or Christianity. Generally speaking, the cohabitation between followers of diverse religious groups is exemplary, and there is no real tension between them. Three main languages are used in Burkina Faso: More, the Mosse language; Fulfude, the Fulani language; and Jula, which is more a common language than a language of an ethnic group. The official language of the country is French, the tongue of the former colonial power, but it is spoken by less than 20 percent of the population (generally, the well-read individuals). The legal system of Burkina Faso is based on French civil law. But as in many African countries, customs still regulate the lives of the great majority of the population.

HISTORY

An independent state since August 5, 1960, Upper Volta, renamed Burkina Faso in 1984, was colonized by France at the beginning of the twentieth century. After subjugating the local populations and pacifying their territories, the French set up a colonial administration that ruled the colony of Upper Volta until it became independent. The colony faced some vicissitudes, and in 1932, the French decided to dismantle Upper Volta because it was too poor and had insufficient resources to meet its own needs. Neighboring colonies benefited from this situation, particularly the Ivory Coast, where thousands of Burkinabe people emigrated to work on plantations. But in 1947, the colony was reestablished for different reasons. First, many local lobbies particularly the Mosse traditional authorities, demanded reestablishment in order to preserve the identity of their groups. Second, the French sought to weaken the African Democratic Rally, an anticolonial political party whose main base was established in Ivory Coast, by isolating it from its northern base.

Before the colonial era, each of the sixty ethnic groups of Burkina had its own legal and judicial system, based on customs. But the colonizing French initially didn't want to recognize those systems and instead introduced their own legal system. However, French colonial legislation was not necessarily identical to the French law at home. To be applicable to colonial territories, it must contain a provision which mentions expressly this assumption. In fact, a decree could extend the application of French leg-

islation to colonial territories and even modify some of its provisions. Thus, in most of its aspects, colonial legislation departed from the principles of the rule of law.

Because they failed to suppress the local customs, the French in time decided to allow indigenous populations to practice their own traditions in civil matters, marriages, inheritances, and settlements. The legal dualism that resulted from this situation was based on the distinction between "citizens" and "subjects." Implicit in this dualism was the coexistence of two legal systems, one based on the home-country (French) law and the other based on customs or Islamic law. The former system involved the citizens and matters of public law; the latter involved only subjects, or indigenous people, and their private matters. In criminal law, indigenous populations were subject to a repressive special code, which was later recalled.

As a consequence of this dualism, a two-track judicial system developed, based on the application of home-country law, on one hand, and customs or Islamic law, on the other. In the lattercase, people were subjected to indigenous justice rendered by courts presided over by a colonial administrative officer, with the possibility for appeal in some cases to another indigenous court. In fact, the indigenous justice applied not only customs and the

"custom statute" written by colonial legislators but also the French law if there was a gap or "silence" in the customs. French legislation was also applied when a judge felt that the application of customs would be contrary to "law and order," a concept that represented the idea of civilization as perceived by the colonizer. After 1946, the discrimination between citizens and subjects was progressively abolished, and African people increasingly enjoyed French citizenship as colonies moved toward their independence.

As in other former French colonies, the new Burkinabe regime did not really challenge the legal and judicial system established by the former colonizer when the country became independent. Indeed, the constitutions of French-speaking countries state that the legislation inherited from the colonizer shall remain in force, provided that it is not contrary to the country's constitution or that it is not replaced by new legislation. However, the new African authorities did make some major changes. Indeed, new legislation was adopted to organize the state and its apparatus. In addition, many codes and laws were adopted in diverse fields—addressing, among others, matters of nationality, civil law, and agrarian and land tenure, as well as judicial, fiscal, and social issues. Many laws and governmental regulations were also passed to regulate the economy (prices, investments, state-owned enterprises, and the like). As in many francophone countries, customs lost their weight in the legislation and were replaced by measures adopted by Parliament or other arms of the government.

Beginning in 1983, a radical change occurred in Burkina Faso after a revolutionary elite seized power. The new rulers renamed the country in 1984 to symbolize their strong desire to radically transform society. So Upper Volta became Burkina Faso, a name formed from a combination of a More word signifying integrity and a Jula word signifying homeland, which is also defined by the constitution as the "Republican form of the State." The revolutionary government decided to reform the legal and judicial system, which was perceived as "bourgeois" and colonial and one that oppressed the people. The major reforms were related to agrarian and land-tenure law, the family and citizen code, and the judicial system. Concerning the agrarian and land-tenure matters, the revolutionary government abolished the customs and the customary authority on land and replaced them with new governmental legislation and committees of revolutionaries. Lands were nationalized through the creation of a "national land domain," defined as the set of lands of the national territory, including those acquired abroad. These lands were not subject to the right of private property. Indeed, private individuals had no right to sell land. However, they did enjoy certain other rights, among them the right of use and the right of usufruct. But since the wind of economic liberalization blew in Burkina, the authorities, under pressure from donors, agreed in 1991 to reform the land legislation in order to secure property ownership. Concerning family and personal law, the most remarkable dispositions related to the abolition of customs. However, certain undying practices (such as polygamy) were recognized by the new legislation, with some restrictions.

The main changes that occurred in the mid-1980s involved the judicial system. The revolutionary elite justified these changes by stating that the judicial was an instrument of domination for the former ruling class; they contended that it had to be transformed in order to better serve the masses and become more accessible and effective for them. In that context, popular courts were established, with nonprofessional judges chosen from among militants of the committees for the defense of the revolution. The president of Faso himself maintained in a January 3, 1984, speech that there was no need for revolutionary judges to know the old laws; deriving from the people, they only had to be guided by their own sense of popular justice. The new revolutionary courts were supposed to replace the courts based on the French model. The most spectacular revolutionary courts were the Popular Courts of Revolution (TPR) and the Popular Courts of Conciliation (TPC). The former were composed of both professional and nonprofessional judges; the latter were made up of nonprofessionals, chosen from among members of the defense committees of the revolution or the local populace. The TPR were competent to judge matters such as cases of bribery and corruption, and their judgments were broadcast. The TPC were deemed competent to judge some minor matters but were not allowed to pronounce prison sentence. Instead, they provided social mediation and conciliation for the people. In fact, the TPC were established to replace the traditional justice rendered by customary authorities that were targeted and fought by the revolutionary elite.

The new regulation did not allow a person subject to revolutionary courts to be assisted by a lawyer. Indeed, the law profession was suppressed by the government and replaced by another, similar profession, whose members were appointed from among magistrates and former lawyers and paid by the government as public servants. The "public lawyers," as these individuals were known, could only practice in courts based on the French model. Finally, it should be noted that the judicial system was extremely politicized, and it submitted to the revolutionary regime.

On October 15, 1987, Capt. Blaise Compaoré, the military junta's number-two man, and the minister in charge of justice seized power in a bloody coup and progressively ended the Burkinabe revolution. When Burkina Faso adopted a new constitution and began a process of democratization and economic liberalization in 1991, the government suppressed the revolutionary courts and rehabilitated the legal and judicial system based on the French model.

LEGAL CONCEPTS

The Constitution of Burkina Faso, adopted in June 1991, is at the top of the hierarchy of legal norms. No statute or law can be applied if it is contrary to the constitution. Under the constitution, the country subscribes to the main international legal instruments, such as the Universal Declaration of Human Rights, the International Covenants on Civil and Political Rights, and the International Covenants on Economic, Social and Cultural Rights. Citizens have some duties, among them the duty to respect the constitution, laws, and acts of the republic. In fact, each category of rights recognized by the constitution is accompanied by specific obligations.

The constitution defines the state of Burkina Faso as a democratic and secular republic, one and indivisible. The sovereignty belongs to the people, who can exercise it in the ways stated in the constitution. A semipresidential regime is established in the constitution, based on the French Fifth Republic. However, the president, who can only serve two terms of five years each, determines the main orientations of state policies instead of the prime minister and the National Assembly. This is true whether or not the president has a majority in that body. The prime minister, who is appointed by the president, has only the role of leading and of coordinating the action of the government.

The Parliament established by the constitution is bicameral. It is composed of the National Assembly, whose members are elected, and the Chamber of Representatives, whose members are appointed as representatives of civil society components, organizations, and associations. However, the legislative power is in the hands of the National Assembly, which passes laws. The Chamber of Representatives has only consultative powers, which do not bind the assembly.

The Constitution of Burkina Faso, like that of many francophone countries, takes up the French constitutional distinction between the domain of the law and that of the executive acts. The former domain belongs to the National Assembly, which intervenes through laws that determine the rules or general principles involving certain matters strictly listed by the constitution. Other matters, which are not mentioned by the constitution, are negatively defined as the domain of the executive acts. Several institutional mechanisms have been set in place to enforce this separation. Among them is the Constitutional Council, based on the French model. This body is composed of a president, appointed by the president of Faso, and nine counselors, six of whom are appointed by the president of Faso and three of whom are appointed by the president of the National Assembly. One-third of the council is renewed every three years. As its name implies, the Constitutional Council reviews the constitutionality of bills, interprets the constitution, regulates the functioning of the powers, and stands as an electoral tribunal.

The judiciary is defined by the constitution as being independent from the executive and the legislature. The constitution upholds, among others, the principle of the separation of powers between the executive, legislative, and judicial branches. The judiciary is the guardian of individual and collective liberties. The constitution specifies that justice is to be dispensed in Burkina Faso through the judicial and administrative courts. To enforce the independence of the judiciary, the constitution states that magistrates, when exerting their function, are subject only to the authority of the law. In addition, magistrates of the bench cannot be removed. According to the constitution, the president of Faso is responsible for ensuring judicial independence. As such, he or she presides over the Upper Council of the Magistracy. As a management body, the council is involved in the nomination and assignment of judges who sit on the bench on the basis of advice given to the minister of justice. The

council also decides on the promotion of judges at different levels of the judicial hierarchy and is consulted by the head of state in relation to the exercise of his right of pardon. As a disciplinary body, it rules on matters involving judges, without input from political authorities.

For many jurists, there is a contradiction between the constitutional provision that makes the president responsible for judicial independence and the fact that the executive, the ruling party, and the regime's dignitaries are the main threat to this independence. The provision, which reflects the specific constitutional history of France, brings to mind the conflicts that occurred between the two branches of power in that country. To avoid the "government of judges," institutional arrangements have been established, and the judicial branch has been treated as a simple authority, instead of a real power equal to the executive or the legislative branch. Many constitutions of francophone countries such as Burkina Faso imported the French perception of the judiciary, although they formally established a "judicial power." In fact, the judiciary is often treated as an appendix of the state apparatus, subordinate to the executive. In the case of Burkina Faso, many factors can explain this situation. Among them are the politicization of the judicial apparatus, political patronage, and the fear of executive retaliation. In reality, the fate of the judiciary depends partly on the political situation of the country. Indeed, despite some progress made on the long road to democratization, the political regime is still authoritarian. A wide system of patronage built by President Compaoré and his party runs across the Burkinabe political system. In that context, many judges, like most of the senior civil servants, feel that it is prudent to join the presidential party to protect themselves or to make their careers.

For many people, the judiciary in Burkina is neither independent nor impartial. The lack of confidence in the judiciary power is, in fact, so deep that the government held a meeting in October 1998 to find some solutions to the crisis. The diagnostic established by the participants states that the crisis was caused by the frequent violations of professional ethics by judges and attorneys, the weaknesses of hierarchical control, the slowness of trials and even the failure to apply judicial decisions, the interferences of politicians and other powerful people, and the militancy and incompetence of some magistrates, not to mention the insufficiencies of human, financial, and material resources. Under these circumstance, wealthy people, particularly the dignitaries of the regime, enjoyed total impunity. Although the human rights situation in Burkina Faso is not as bad as it is in many African countries, the increasing number of murders committed by the presidential guard, with complete impunity, has become a threat to the people's security.

The demonstrations led by civic organizations and political parties of the opposition and the political crisis that ensued have provoked various political changes and commitments to deal with the problem of impunity. To handle the judiciary crisis, the government designed a strategy and an action plan. However, the problem is not only technical or institutional but also political and ethical. Without a genuine commitment from the government and the judicial bodies to promote and respect the independence of the judiciary, the problem of its credibility will remain.

The body of regulatory and legislative texts is composed of codes—among them, the Civil Code, Code of Commerce, Civil Procedure Code, Family and Citizens Code, Labor Code, and Penal Code. The first two codes date back to the Napoleonic era and are not suited to the present social, economic, and political context, particularly as shaped by liberalism. So the government established a commission of codification to review the old laws, with the support of donors. The courts also apply a corpus of rules established by regional organizations to which Burkina Faso belongs. Among these rules are six uniform legislations of business law adopted by the Organization for the Harmonization of Business Law in Africa (OHADA). This community business law is applicable to the fifteen members states (Benin, Burkina Faso, Cameroon, Central African Republic, Comoros, Congo, Ivory Coast, Gabon, Equatorial Guinea, Mali, Niger, Senegal, Chad, and Togo), all of which are French-speaking countries, except for Equatorial Guinea. The uniform acts supersede any legislation of a member state. A common court of justice and arbitration was established to ensure a common application and interpretation of these uniform acts. The constituent treaty also established an upper regional school of magistracy to train and perfect magistrates and representatives of the law in the members states.

CURRENT STRUCTURE

Burkina Faso's jurisdictional structure comes from the dispositions of the Constitution of June 2, 1991, which instituted two jurisdiction orders in particular: the judicial order and the administrative order. Both address the exercise of judicial power, which is entrusted to the judges. In addition, there are exception jurisdictions created by special laws.

Current justice is rendered through the following judicial courts: the Departmental Courts (Tribunaux Départementaux), Magistrates' Courts (Tribunaux d'Instance), High Courts (Tribunaux de Grande Instance), Labour Courts (Tribunaux de Travail), Courts of Appeal (Courts d'Appel), and the newly established higher jurisdictions that replaced the Supreme Court (Cour Suprême).

Each of the 322 departments of Burkina Faso has its own Departmental Court, composed of three nonprofessional judges appointed for two years by an order of the justice minister. In each court, the judges are the department prefect (or another authorized representative) and two assessors. The Departmental Courts have limited authority. They deal with petty offenses, small civil and commercial cases involving sums of no more than CFA 100,000 under the Penal Code, suppletory judgments, and judgments ordering rectification of civil status. Their decisions are opened to appeal at the Magistrates' Court.

The Magistrates' Courts are single-judge courts established wherever the High Courts are located. They deal with civil and commercial cases of average importance (between CFA 100,000 and 1,000,000). They also serve as police courts.

The High Courts are the ordinary jurisdiction in commercial, civil, and correctional cases. They also hear appeals from decisions made by the Magistrates' Courts. Only twelve High Courts have been established, whereas the legal provision allowed for one such court in each of the forty-five provinces of Burkina Faso. They are, in principle, collegial courts and are composed of three specialized chambers (civil, commercial, and correctional). Their decisions may be appealed to the Court of Appeal.

The Courts of Appeal are the second-highest level of jurisdiction in Burkina Faso. They render decisions concerning civil, commercial, and correctional cases previously submitted to the High Courts and the social questions judged by the Labour Courts. They are also competent to hear criminal matters without appeal. Each Court of Appeal comprises six chambers: civil, commercial, social, correctional, accusatory, and criminal. They are two such courts in the two most important cities of Burkina, Ouagadougou and Bobo-Dioulasso.

At the top of the judicial pyramid are three structures based on the French model—the Court of Cassation, the Revenue Court, and the Council of State. They were created to replace three chambers of the Supreme Court at the same time as the Constitutional Council, which replaced the constitutional chamber. The Court of Cassation is defined by the constitution as the higher court for the judicial order, the Council of State is the higher court for the administrative order, and the Revenue Court is the higher court for the control of finances.

As in France, administrative litigations are judged in Burkina Faso by ordinary administrative courts, which, in principle, are created in the head office of each judicial higher court. Currently, however, except for the administrative courts of Ouagadougou and Bobo-Dioulasso (whose judges serve on a full-time basis), the other administrative courts are presided over by the presidents of judicial high courts, regarding administrative litigations matters. The Council of State serves as the administrative higher court. It issues decisions sometimes without any possibility for appeal, and sometimes as a court of appeal for judgments passed by administrative courts.

The Revenue Court has ordinary law jurisdiction over all public and de facto accounts. It is supposed to control the regularity and the fairness of the financial operations executed by public accountants and by any entity that receives financial aid from the state. It also acts as a consultative organ on bills, ordinances, or decrees regarding the organization and functioning of the state financial services, the decentralized communities, and public establishments. The effectiveness of the Revenue Court is so far weak, due to a lack of personnel and resource and to competition with other state structures whose mission is also to oversee the management of public finances.

Nonjurisdictional justice plays a key role in the regulation of conflicts in Burkina Faso. It is rendered through customary and religious authorities, state institutions, and ad hoc commissions. As in many African countries, the majority of the people perceive the modern justice system as a western institution that does not fit traditional African societies or is only understandable by some city dwellers. Thus, customary and religious authorities continue to play an important social and regulatory role. In the past, particularly during the revolution (from 1983 to 1987), traditional authorities were especially denigrated and forbidden to play a judicial or political role. But since the beginning of the process of democratization in 1991, they have been rehabilitated by President Compaoré's regime, with which they maintain good relationships. In that context, they took part in different ad hoc structures set up by the government to manage conflicts, investigate crimes, rule on a process of national reconciliation, manage elections, and so forth. In villages, they mostly rule on conflicts in family and land matters. Unfortunately, the law does not recognize their judicial role and jurisdictional authority.

The ombudsman of Faso (médiateur du Faso), a post established in 1994, it is not a judicial position. The ombudsman's role is to settle disputes between the administration and the citizens. Those who use public services and have grievances can submit a request to this individual for an out-of-court settlement. The ombudsman is defined as an independent authority who receives no instruction from any other authority. He or she cannot examine a request if a given case has already been submitted to a court. The ombudsman's office is a successful institution, particularly in the most important cities of the country, because it is easy to access, free, and appropriate for African societies, which value mediation as a mean to solve disputes. Several hundred requests have been submitted to the ombudsman, and most of the cases have been resolved. This successful activity has prevented some of the disputes from degenerating into conflicts and helped to safeguard social peace in Burkina Faso. However, much can be done to make the institution better known and more widely used by rural people.

SPECIALIZED JUDICIAL BODIES

The Labour Courts are specialized courts that deal with social disputes stemming from the execution of a work or apprenticeship contract. These courts have been established in the three most important industrial cities of Burkina Faso—Ouagadougou, Bobo-Dioulasso, and Koudougou.

The High Court of Justice, another specialized judicial body instituted by the Constitution of June 1991, is composed of parliamentarians and professional judges. It handles the impeachment of the president of Faso, and deals with acts comitted by the president when in office and described as high treason, violation of the constitution, or misappropriation of public funds. It also handles acts qualified as crimes and offenses committed by other government members while in office. These members are obliged by the constitution to list their personal property when they enter and leave office and transmit the lists to the Constitutional Council. But as of late 2001, neither the constitutional chamber of the Supreme Court nor its substitute, the Constitutional Council, has called a member of government to account, despite some suspicions or even actual evidence of public corruption.

Armed forces courts are also specialized judicial institutions. They apply the Military Code under the supervision of the judicial chamber of the Supreme Court, now replaced by the Court of Cassation. Military courts are composed partly of magistrates from the judicial order and partly of military judges. Each court is competent for one or for several military districts. They can sit in any place within their domain and can be established anywhere in the event of war. They hear cases involving common violations of law committed by military personnel, as well as attacks against the reputation of the armed forces or breaches of the peace. In some cases, civilians can be tried by military court.

STAFFING

The functioning of the judiciary requires a variety of professionals. Among them are magistrates and representatives of the law—lawyers, clerks of the court, bailiffs, and notaries—who assist judges or people subject to trial. Only one body of professional judges is responsible for applying the law through judgments, judicial orders, decisions, arbitral awards, and proceedings that have the force of res judicata. The number of professional judges in Burkina Faso is insufficient. As of 2001, about 200 judges had been recruited since independence, whereas the number required is about 600 judges. Efforts have been made in recent years to recruit additional personal, but the ratio of judges to inhabitants—about 1 judge for every 100,000 inhabitants—is still low in Burkina Faso.

As public servants, magistrates must complete the general requirements stipulated in the civil service statute,

Legal Structure of Burkina Faso Courts

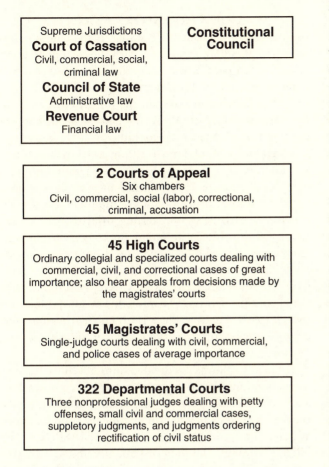

Supreme Jurisdictions
Court of Cassation
Civil, commercial, social, criminal law
Council of State
Administrative law
Revenue Court
Financial law

Constitutional Council

2 Courts of Appeal
Six chambers
Civil, commercial, social (labor), correctional, criminal, accusation

45 High Courts
Ordinary collegial and specialized courts dealing with commercial, civil, and correctional cases of great importance; also hear appeals from decisions made by the magistrates' courts

45 Magistrates' Courts
Single-judge courts dealing with civil, commercial, and police cases of average importance

322 Departmental Courts
Three nonprofessional judges dealing with petty offenses, small civil and commercial cases, suppletory judgments, and judgments ordering rectification of civil status

and they are recruited through competition among individuals who hold at least a bachelor's degree in law. Today, the National School of Administration and Magistrature trains magistrates for two years, including a period of in-service training.

Some of the legal occupations perceived by the revolutionary regime as bourgeois were suppressed, replaced, or severely restricted during the revolutionary era (1983 to 1987). They were, however, rehabilitated at the beginning of the 1990s, when the country began a process of political and economical liberalization. The lawyer's profession is relatively young in Burkina Faso: The first lawyer in Burkina Faso took an oath in 1973. The country has only one bar, and it is composed of around 115 lawyers, most of them established in the capital. Their profession is defined as a liberal and independent one, and it may be practiced alone or in association. Lawyers are selected from among applicants who must be citizens of Burkina Faso, have good moral character, hold a bachelor's or a master's degree in law, and pass the exam certifying his or her ability to join the profession. Those who are selected are trained in the chambers of other lawyers or judges. New professional regulations require that trainees be given practical and theoretical training in a

professional center. Unfortunately, the structure to support this requirement has not been created as yet.

Unlike lawyers, notaries are not well known in Burkina. Applicants are supposed to be selected in the same way as lawyers are, but there is neither a special exam nor a truly professional training program available in in the country; consequently, applicants are either selectively trained on the job for long periods or trained abroad, in France, by passing a one-year postgraduate diploma program in the notary profession. Thus, there are only around ten notaries in Burkina Faso.

IMPACT

Generally speaking, the judicial system in Burkina suffers from many dysfunctions, stemming from the insufficiencies of human resources, infrastructures, and equipment. Hundreds of matters are pending, hundreds of judgmnts are unwritten, and files inexplicably disappear. Moreover, there is often a lack of discipline in the judiciary, as well as a lack of respect for the obligation to remain very reserved, impartial, and neutral.

It has been acknowledged for years that Burkina's judicial system is really in the throes of a multiple crisis. In addition to the lack of resources, other contributing factors include violations of professional ethics by magistrates and other representatives of the law, weaknesses of control and the failure to sanction careless agents, slowness in the review of cases, poor execution of judicial decisions, political and social pressures on magistrates, and fear of the regime in power. Because magistrates carry out their duties under poor conditions and for low pay, they are exposed to pressures and temptations. At the same time, they are bound by strict ethics rules—calling for dignity, loyalty, conscience, and impartiality—that are applicable to their professional and extraprofessional lives.

For the majority of citizens, the judicial system is perceived as unattainable, expensive, and slow. Due to the weak decentralization of the relevant structures, the judicial coverage of the country is inadequate. In addition, many established jurisdictions are not yet functional because of the lack of human and material resources. Thus, full access to justice is limited for the majority of the population, particularly in rural areas, and most citizens cannot afford the costs of justice. Indeed, although free access to the courts is recognized in principle, it is, in practice, subject to the payment of various fees. Furthermore, people generally ignore their rights, and the subtleties of the judicial system (to the extent that customs and traditional justice have been replaced by a westernized law and judiciary) are understood only by a minority of the populace.

The judiciary's dependence on the regime is also an obstacle to the normal exercise of legal authority. Since the country achieved independence, the regimes in power have tried to subjugate the judiciary. And none has challenged the independence of the judiciary more than the revolutionary regime. Magistrates who disagreed with the revolutionaries' concept of justice were considered enemies and tracked down.

Since the 1990s, when the country began a process of democratization and economic liberalization, the situation has improved. However, the independence of the judiciary remains precarious. The magistrate's career advancement is, in fact, dependent on the executive, who dominates the Upper Council of the Magistracy. Thus, the principles of the independence and irrevocability of a judge are uncertain. On the pretext of "operational requirements," the executive can remove or transfer judges perceived as too independent, and chief prosecutors and attorneys generals, whose careers closely depend on the executive will, generally protect the regime's dignitaries and guarantee them impunity. By contrast, political opponents are sometimes subject to expeditious trials, and ordinary citizens are generally suspicious toward the modern judicial system.

In fact, the Burkinabe judiciary has suffered from many weaknesses, which led the government to convene in October 1998 a forum to address the problem. Several solutions were recommended to deal with the judicial deficiencies. Among them was an improvement in magistrates' living and working conditions; an additional recruitment of personnel; an effort to decentrialize the judicial courts in order to improve coverage across the entire country; the review of legislation, particularly the texts relating the magistracy and its Upper Council, in order to reinforce the independence of the magistracy; and increased respect for discipline and ethics rules within the body. However, it is important for political authorities to prove their attachment to a free, independent, effective, and impartial judiciary. Without this political will, it is hard to see how the Burkinabe judiciary will come out of the crisis that has affected it for years.

Augustin Loada

See also Côte d'Ivoire; Islamic Law

References and further reading
Ibriga, Luc, and Amidou Garane. 2001. *Constitutions burkinabè.* Namur, Belgium: Amitiés Belgo-Burkinabè.
Meyer, Pierre. 1988. *Introduction à l'étude du droit burkinabè.* Namur, Belgium: Andre Boland.
Yonaba, Salif. 1997. *Indépendance de la justice et droits de l'homme: Le cas du Burkina Faso.* Leiden, the Netherlands: Pioom.

BURMA

COUNTRY INFORMATION

Burma, recently renamed Myanmar, is the largest country in mainland Southeast Asia with the total population of 47 million people. It has a total land area of 676,577 square kilometers and shares a border of 5,858 kilometers with Bangladesh and India on the northwest, China on the northeast, Lao P.D.R. on the east, and Thailand on the southeast. It has a total coastline of 2,832 kilometers and stretches 2,090 kilometers from north to south and 925 kilometers from east to west at its widest points. Geographically, Burma is surrounded by a series of mountains. It has three parallel chains of mountain ranges that run from north to south, starting from the eastern extremity of the Himalayan mountain range. These mountain ranges are Rakhine Yoma, the Bago Yoma, and the Shan Plateau. These ranges divide the country into three river systems. They are Irrawaddy (Ayeyarwady), the Sittaung, and the Selween (Thanlwin). The most important river system, the Irrawaddy, is about 2,710 kilometers long. Its major tributary, the Chindwin, is 960 kilometers long.

Politically, Burma is divided into seven states and seven divisions. Each division and state has townships and each township governs villages and wards. Currently, Burma is controlled by the ruling military council known as State Peace and Development Council (SPDC). The SPDC maintains the judicial structure and system that was operational under the Burmese Socialist Programme Party (BSPP), which governed the country from 1974 to 1988. However, since the fall of the BSPP government, the judicial branch in Burma is not an independent branch of the government. At present it is under the absolute control of the military council. Judges are "readers at court" of opinions written or ordered by the military council. The most powerful general of the ruling council, Secretary One of the council, once stated, "martial law means no law at all" in Burma. Therefore, to talk about a *legal system* in Burma at present is misleading, as there really isn't one. Under the current military regime no rule of law exists, as was admitted by the Secretary One of the ruling council.

POLITICAL HISTORY

Burma gained its independence from Britain on January 4, 1948. After it gained independence, Burma embraced a parliamentary democratic system. Burma was a respected leader in the developing world and had wide international influence, a position furthered by such figures as the late United Nations General Secretary U Thant and the late Prime Minister U Nu. Burma's parliamentary democratic system survived only a little over decade, from 1948 to 1962. In 1962, the then Burmese army

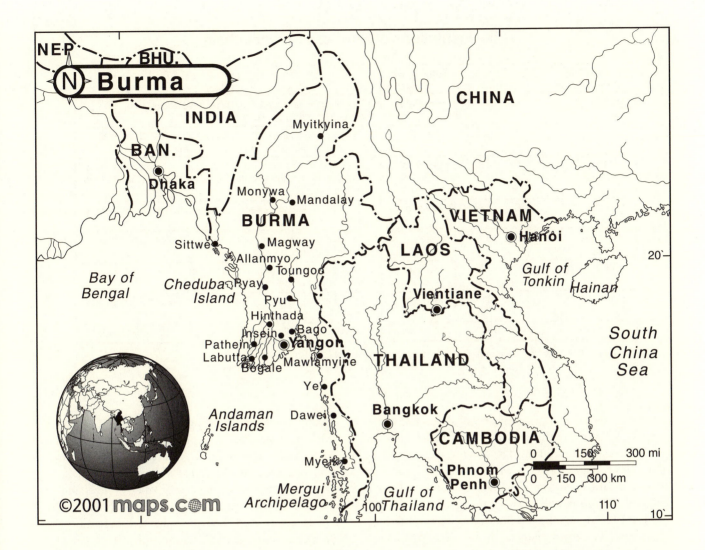

general U Ne Win took power by a military coup from the civilian government led by Prime Minister U Nu. This political drama was a turning point of Burmese history at which the country was transformed from a parliamentary democratic system to an authoritarian system of government. This turning point had great impact on the existing Burmese political and legal system. Under the rule of the BSPP government from 1974 to 1988, Burma became a least developed country (LDC) in the list of UN members in 1987.

In 1988, the student-led movement to overthrow the BSPP government emerged. On August 8, 1988, the whole Burmese population took to the streets and called for the abolition of the one-party system in favor of a multiparty democratic system. This popular movement, known as 8888 People Movement, ended the era of the BSPP socialist government. However, the new generation of the Burmese army took political power by a brutal military coup on September 18, 1988, and the movement was crushed by the newly emerging military regime then known as the State Law and Order Restoration Council (SLORC). The regime changed its name in 1997 to the

State Peace and Development Council. As of 2001, the SPDC is institutionally above the law in Burma and governs the country with absolute authoritarian rule.

HISTORY OF LEGAL DEVELOPMENT

Burmese legal development began with the emergence of the first kingdom in 1044 C.E. Before King Anawratha conferred different dynasties to establish the first Kingdom of Pagan in 1044, Burma passed through eras of dynasties for thousands of years. Pagan is also known as the Kingdom of Temple Builders for its great number of temples built during the Pagan era. After Anawratha had established Pagan's power, his grandson, King Alaungsithu, began the formalization of a legal system based on customary law in 1112–1165 (Aung 1962, 9). However, while legal disputes were decided according to native customary law, it was also in accordance with the spirit of Buddhist ethics. When Alaungsithu died, his decisions were collected as a work called *Alaungsithu's Pyat-hton (or Alaungsithu's Judgment),* which served as a code of precedent for later generations up until the nineteenth century (Aung 1962, 9).

Nine Institutions of Burmese Dhammathats

Name of Dhammathat	Date	Reign of the King	Remarks
Manu	C.E. 540—560	First Pagan	The introduction states that it was presented to King Mahathamada by the Rishi Manu.
Dhammavilasa	C.E. 1200	Fifth Pagan	The introduction states that it was an abridged edition of the Manu Dhammathat by Shinn Dhamavilasa.
Wagaru	C.E. 1270	Martaban	This Dhammathat at the introduction states that it was rooted in Manu Dhammathat, written at the instance of Wagaru, King of Mataban.
Pasadha	C.E. 1468	Taungoo	This Dhammathat has been considered to be high authority in Burmese law.
Manusara	C.E. 1549	Pegu	Twelve legal scholars in 1549 composed this Dhammathat under King Sinbyumyashin.
Dhammathat Kyaw	C.E. 1581	Taungoo	This Dhammathat, according to its preface, is a combination and analysis of previous Dhammathats.
Pyanchi	C.E. 1614	Taungoo	This Dhammathat was written by an individual named Maung Pe Thi.
Myingun	C.E. 1650	Konebaung	It is named after the town where the Dhammathat was written.

Sources: Kinwun Mingyi U Gaung, *A Digest of Burmese Buddhist Law.* Rangoon: Govt. Print.
Justice E. Maung, *The Expansion of Burmese Law.* Ithaca, NY: Cornell University Press.

In 1173, Narapatisithu, grandson of Alaungsithu, became the king of Pagan. Like all kings of Pagan he was a great patron of Buddhism. The king wanted a young monk named Shin Ananda, who was then educated in India, to be the royal tutor. The king gave a great feast in honor of the monk and offered him the title of Dhammavilasa (Great Scholar of Buddhist Scriptures). Shin Dhammavilasa became famous all over the region as a teacher of other monks. He later wrote a treatise on law, which became to be known as Dhammavilasa Dhammathat and is one of nine highly regarded institutions of law out of thirty-six Dhammathats in Burma (see figure). The Dhammavilasa Dhammathat is the oldest surviving Burmese law book today, although it is not a pioneer work among thirty-six Dhammathats (E Maung 1951, 6).

Burmese legal scholars have followed the Dhammathats and attempted to trace the legal development of Burma beginning from the first Manu Dhammathat, which was written at the time when this world emerged, according to Burmese mythical tales and stories. The earliest written work by Western scholars about the sources of Burmese law and legal concepts was the Jardine Prize essay entitled "On the Sources and Development of Burmese Law from the Era of the First Introduction of the Indian Law to the Time of the British Occupation of Pegu" by learned British scholar Dr. Emanuel Forchammer. It was published in 1885, one year before the British invaded the last Kingdom of Burma. Dr. Forchammer in his essay observed:

The development of law in Burma has not been a steady devolution. Every great Burmese or Talaing Monarch endeavored to preserve existing laws and to enact and enforce new ones suitable to the customs and usages of the people for whom they were intended. But subsequent weak rulers, or a change of dynasty, reduced the body of law promulgated by predecessors or members of subverted dynasties to a dead letter; it was set aside and then forgotten. (p. 91)

The scholars, including Burmese legal historians and judges, rejected Dr. Forchammer's observation. Former Justice U E Maung of Burma, in his series of lectures given at Cornell University and published in 1951, stated that Burmese law in its descent to the latter part of the nineteenth century had no breaks and catastrophes. He argued that: "Dynasties passed away to be succeeded by other dynasties; kings waged war with supplanted other kings; rebellion on many occasions reared its head and pretenders had come to the rule; but there never was a revolution in the growth of Burmese law" (E Maung 1951, 1). This view was supported by the Letters Patent of the appointment of judges in the last days of Burmese monarchs in 1885:

In case of dispute they must, in accordance with all thirty-six Dhammathats, enquire into the causes of the people and decide between them and for this purpose they are appointed to the Courts as judges. In a lawsuit or dispute any of our subjects apply to a Judge, the Judge shall decide the matter with the

Manu Dhammathat in hand first. If the required rule is not to be found therein, follow all other Dhammathats. (Maung 1951, 2)

Therefore, the development of Burmese law is rooted in all Dhammathats written by different legal scholars appointed by different kings throughout eras of Burmese kings. These Dhammathats were restored one dynasty after another and observed by one king after another. By this observance, the kings gained people's support and respect throughout Burmese history.

LEGAL THEORY

Among the Burmese Dhammathats, the Manu Dhammathats is the first of thirty-six Dhammathats. Throughout Burmese history, the Dhammathats are the fundamental sources of laws. In the introduction of Manu Dhammathat, the foundation of the source of law in Burma is written:

When this universe had reached the period of the firmly established continuancy, the original inhabitants of this world conjointly entreated the great king Mahasammata to become their ruler. King Mahasammata governed the world with righteousness. Now the king had a wise nobleman called Manu, who was well versed in the law. This nobleman called Manu, desiring the good of all human beings, and being also opportuned by King Mahasammata, rose into the expanse of heaven, and having arrived at the boundary wall of the world, he there saw the natural law, Dhammathat, he committed them to memory and having returned, communicated the same to the King Mahasammata, stating eighteen branches of law.

"Burmese laws on the whole seem wise, and evidently are calculated to advance the interests of justice and morality" (Vincent 1874, 16). The value of justice or truth is seriously upheld in Burmese culture. The worst insult that one could do to oneself and society is giving lies or making false statements to harm others. This is reinforced by the belief in the concept of karma. To be able to capture the mentality of the Burmese in regard to law and justice, I present the oath of witness used in court during the Ava dynasty in 1782 (cited in Vincent 1874, 18) as follows:

I will speak the truth. If I speak not the truth, may it be through the influences of the laws of demerit—passion, anger, folly, pride, false opinion, immodesty, hard-heartedness, and skepticism—so that when I and my relations are on land, land animals—as tigers, elephants, buffaloes, poisonous serpents, scorpions, and etc.—shall seize, crush, and bite us, so that we

shall certainly die. Let calamities occasioned by fire, water, rulers, thieves and enemies oppress and destroy us, till we perish and come to utter destruction. Let us be subject to all the calamities that are within the body, and all that are without body. May I be seized with madness, dumbness, blindness, deafness, leprosy, and hydrophobia. May we be struck with thunderbolts and lightning, and come to sudden death. In the midst of not speaking truth may I be taken with vomiting clotted black blood, and suddenly die before assembled people. When I am going by water may the water nats [goddesses] assault me, the boat be upset and then property lost; and may alligators, porpoises, sharks, and other sea monsters seize and crush me to death; and when I die and change worlds may I not arrive among human or nats, but suffer unmixed punishment and regret, in the utmost wretchedness, among the four states of punishment, Hell, Prita, Beasts, Athurakai.

If I speak the truth, may I and my relations, through the influence of the ten laws of merit, and on amount of the efficacy of truth, be freed from all calamities within and without the body, and may evils which have not yet come be warded far away. May the thunderbolts and lightning, the nat of waters, and all sea animals love me, that I may be safe from them. May my prosperity increase like the rising sun and the waxing moon; and may the seven possessions, the seven laws, and the seven merits of the virtuous be permanent in my person; and when I change worlds [life after death] may I not go the four states of punishment, but attain the happiness of men and nats, and realize merit, reward, and perfect calm.

This oath of witness illustrates how serious the Burmese are about upholding the truth in order to help the machinery of justice at the court. In addition, the oath conveys the root of the social philosophy of the Burmese people, the concept of karma, in such ideas as wishing to gain good things as a result of the good deed of telling the truth and willing to accept the bad that comes as a result of one's lie or bad acts.

BURMESE LAW AFTER INDEPENDENCE

After Burma gained independence from Britain on January 4, 1948, it established a parliamentary democratic system in which the rule of law became an important parameter for keeping the system working. The first Burmese prime minister, U Nu, speaking to the whole nation on March 12, 1948, said, "The first essential condition for making democracy secure in our lives is to base all our activities firmly on the rule of law." With this ideology, the postcolonial government introduced the "rule of law" system by explicitly copying almost all rules of the governing system from the British. A Burmese legal scholar J. S. Furnivall, in his book *Colonial Policy and Practice,* pointed out that "judicial interpretation in British Burma was to favor private interest over social welfare. This was a heritage from the British legal system, which had been transplanted in Burma by judges and lawyers. But judicial traditions that fortified the national solidarity of England furthered the disintegration of social order in Burma" (Maung Maung 25).

A similar sentiment was expressed in a note of dissent, which a Burmese political leader wrote for the report on reorganization of the administration in 1949:

> It has been found that the introduction of the rule of law, which is alien to Burmese tradition, has led to the disintegration of Burmese social life. Any unalloyed continuance of the rule of law will further disintegrate Burmese social life. Hence any measure to reintegrate Burmese social life will have to depend more on social sanction than on the rule of law. I do not recommend that the rule of law should be dispensed with. But the rule of law should be adjusted in such a way that it should leave the largest possible scope to the play of social sanction. (Administration Reorganization Committee 1949)

The parliamentary system of postcolonial Burma, based on the rule of law, lasted just over twelve years, from late 1948 to early 1962. In 1962, Burma fell into the hands of the Burmese army led by General Ne Win. General Ne Win created a political system called "Burmese Way to Socialism" and implemented a new rule *by* law system to replace the rule *of* law system. In the new rule by law system, law is made by the authoritarian power. Meanwhile, General Ne Win sorted out social norms and traditional practices outside of the political boundaries in which rule by law is practiced. Therefore, social norms and traditional practices are left to be dealt with by village headmen and abbots of Buddhist monasteries throughout the country. This dual system of rule by law and rule of the social and traditional practices exists today. This, from the legal scholars' point of view, is a challenge for the next generation of government in Burma. The fundamental question is how can a newly emerged government in Burma integrate social norms and traditional practices into the rule of law system?

LEGAL SYSTEM FROM 1988 TO 2001

The military regime has committed widespread human rights violations, forced labor practices recorded by the International Labor Organization (ILO), and brutal oppression against its political opposition since it took power by the military coup on September 18, 1988. None of those military officers who ordered or took charge of committing these crimes were prosecuted in Burma under the current regime. This is another clear indicator that the military regime sits above the law. The regime uses military tribunals to issue prison sentences to its political opposition. However, in principle it maintains the legal structure and processes of the BSPP government to hear less political criminal cases such as robbery and theft.

A BURMESE LEGAL SYSTEM IN THE MAKING

Burma now is at the cusp of transition to modernization and change. The quest for this modernization and change began in 1988 after the student-led popular uprising challenged the Burmese Way to Socialism under General Ne Win's government. The military government known as State Peace and Development Council promised to transform the country to a "modern and developed" nation. In 1990, it held democratic elections. The National League for Democracy (NLD) led by Daw Aung Suu Kyi won the election by gaining 392 out of 485 parliamentary seats. The military government refused to transfer power to the elected government on the grounds that the emergence of a new constitution was a priority before the transfer of power could take place.

As of 2001, Burma was in a period that might be viewed as a constitutional moment. The military regime in Rangoon has been convening the National Convention since 1992 to write the constitution. The opposition party, the National League for Democracy, has its own version of the constitution. In addition, two constitutions still exist in Burma. The first is the 1947 Constitution nullified by the 1962 military coup, and the second is 1974 Constitution ended by the 1988 military coup. Therefore, there are at least two challenges at the frontier of legal transformation in Burma.

First is the challenge for the emergence of a constitution. What kind of constitution should be implemented to meet the desires of the population—a liberal democratic system of government? The general public and many politicians in Burma view the constitution as the foundation for a political system rather than for a legal system within which a political system should be framed. Legal and political systems are, by nature, different. Legal systems clearly outline a set of rules that society as a whole view as parameters of civic behaviors, whereas political systems are based on the level of civic education and the scale of the economy. However, these two systems are dependent upon each other. The progress or change of one can have a significant impact on the other.

For the constitution to set parameters for civic behaviors, it is important in the Burmese context that the rule of law framed by the constitution not deviate from the traditional and social elements of the society. The challenge for the constitutional framers, therefore, is to sort out current social and traditional values that dominate the daily life of people in Burma and to incorporate them into the constitution.

The second challenge is to introduce the rule of law system in Burma so as to plug the Burmese social and economic systems into the global economy while it encompasses traditional values. The rule of law system is important to maintaining political and economic stability as well as to fostering economic and social progress. Burma had a short history of parliamentary democracy from 1948 to 1962, in which the rule of law system began to emerge. However, the system failed due to the lack of political will and the failure of the then legal system to frame rule of law in accordance with the social elements of the society. The difficulty was, however, encountered in discovering what the Burmese social elements and customary laws were (Maung Maung 1963, 27). The new government in the future has to deal with this difficulty.

Tun Myint

See also Buddhist Law
References and further reading
Administration Reorganization Committee. 1949. *The First Interim Report.* Bo Khin Gale's note of dissent. Rangoon.
Aung, Htin, 1962. *Burmese Law Tales.* Oxford: Oxford University Press.
———. 1970. *Burmese History Before 1287: A Defense of the Chronicles.* Oxford: Oxonian.
Forchammer, Emanuel. 1885. *On the Sources and Development of Burmese Law from the Era of the First Introduction of Indian Law to the Time of the British Occupation of Pegu.* The Jardine Prize Essay. Rangoon: Rangoon Government Press.
Furnivall, J. S. 1948. *Colonial Policy and Practice: A comparative study of Burma and Netherlands India.* Issued in cooperation with the International Secretariat, Institute of Pacific Relations. Cambridge: Cambridge University Press.
Gaung, Kinwun Mingyi U. 1893. *A Digest of the Burmese uddhist Law.* Rangoon: Superintendent, Government Print.
Maung, E. 1951. *The Expansion of Burmese Law.* Ithaca, NY: Cornell University Press.
Maung, Maung. 1963. *Law and Custom in Burma and the Burmese Family.* The Hague: Mo Nijhoff.
Myint, Tun. 2000. "Evolution of Law and Legal Concept in Burma: Challenges at the Transition." Paper presented at the Burma Studies Conference at the Northern Illinois University, October 13–15.
Sangermano, Revnd. 1833. *A Description of Burmese Empire: Compiled Chiefly from Native Documents.* Rome: Oriental Translation Fund of Great Britain and Ireland.
Vincent, Frank, Jr. 1874. *The Land of the White Elephant: Sights and Scenes in Southeast Asia.* New York: Harper and Brothers Publishers.

BURUNDI

GENERAL INFORMATION

Burundi is located between 2 degrees 20 minutes and 4 degrees 27 minutes latitude south, and 28 degrees 53 minutes longitude east. To the east it borders Tanzania, to the west the Congo (R.D.C.) and Lake Tanganyika, and to the north Rwanda.

In 1998 the population of Burundi was estimated at 6.1 million. Population density was 220 persons per square kilometer, with an annual increase of 3.2 percent. Like Rwanda, the population of Burundi contains three ethnic groups: the Hutu, the Tutsi, and the Twa. Since 1961 ethnic struggles for government control have grown progressively worse, culminating in cyclic crises, including those of 1972, 1988, and 1993, during which thousands of citizens were massacred or exiled.

HISTORICAL BACKGROUND

According to oral tradition, Burundi has been a nation since the fifteenth century. It was a centralized kingdom directed by a king, assisted by noblemen.

On June 6, 1903, King Mwezi Gisabo, after having resisted the Germans, accepted the treaty of Kiganda and recognized the protectorate. After countless hesitations, the Germans inaugurated an indirect government based on the maintenance of traditional local authorities.

Belgium occupied Ruanda-Urundi beginning in 1916. Its administration was followed by a mandate from the League of Nations, supported by the local central government and based on the ancient monarchical structures. The law under the administration of Ruanda-Urundi from August 21, 1925, permitted the administrative union of Ruanda-Urundi with the Belgian Congo.

On June 27, 1962, the UN commission on protectorates abrogated the agreement of protectorship signed in 1946, and independence was solemnly proclaimed on July 1, 1962, with a constitution based on that of Belgium. The government was then characterized by a succession of coups in 1966, 1976, 1987, 1993, and 1996. The current regime issued from the coup d'état of 1996. Negotiations are in process at Arusha between the rival factions to re-establish a constitutional regime recognized by all.

AN INSTITUTIONALIZED JUDICIAL PLURALISM

As in Rwanda, judicial pluralism is without a doubt the most striking characteristic of Burundian law. It was created under the Belgian period of administration and was instituted into law in an effort to open society to new rules without upsetting the practices of the Burundian people. The population, more than 90 percent rural, had continued to apply the traditional laws, which were better known, better understood, and still capable of gov-

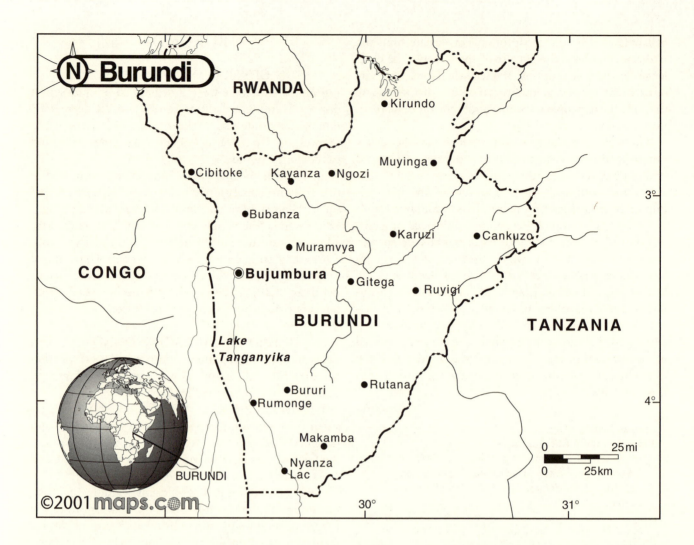

erning social interactions. Leadership reverted to the magistrate, who was tasked with helping the traditional law evolve according to new exigencies and mentalities, with respect to universal public order and the laws (Lamy 1960, 111–116).

JUDICIAL PLURALISM UNDER THE BELGIAN PROTECTORATE

Article 4 of the law of October 18, 1908 (*Moniteur belge* 1908, 5887–5894) reads:

> Natives who are not citizens of [Congo] enjoy the civil rights recognized for them by the legislation of the colony and by their customs as long as they are not contrary to either the legislation or the public order.

Thus, unlike France, Belgium did not impose its own civil code on Burundi; it adopted a colonial code elaborated by an ad hoc commission and supposedly better adapted to the desires of the local populace. In matters civil and commercial, the ordinance of the general ad-

ministrator of Congo of May 14, 1886, predicted: "[W]hen the matter is not foreseen by a decree, a check, or an ordinance already promulgated, the disputes which fall under the purview of the Congo tribunal will be judged according to local customs, the general principles of law and equality" *(Bulletin Officiel* 1886, 188). In penal or criminal matters, only the imported law was applied, but the customary jurisdictions could see customary infractions and impose penalties extending up to a month of penal service. The customs survived despite the interests that represented the written imported law and continued to impose themselves on private relations.

EFFORTS AT CONCILIATION FROM HETEROGENEOUS SOURCES OF LAW FOLLOWING INDEPENDENCE

After independence, the Burundian constitution did not establish a hierarchy between the applicable norms but remained silent on the judicial value of customs followed by the populace. Given that no single criterion of choice between applicable rules imposed itself anymore in a general and obligatory manner, conflicts between these rules were inevitable. However, it seems that in the Burundian departments the lines between the two systems had been permeable, and that the borrowing of written laws to resolve problems of a customary order had been frequent, especially since the judges had to follow the written rules of procedure.

It is thus that one must understand the exposition of issues of personal and family law, which make it possible for this code to "bring clarity and serenity to the decisions of justice" (Law of January 15, 1980, Exposition of Motifs, 17). Another defect in jurisprudence based on two systems is the fact that it is necessary to issue hypotheses while ensuring that the eventual conflicts between the two may be resolved without preferring one over the other. A single constant was revealed in this doctrine: the fundamental rules are found in customs, while procedure follows written law. However, as R. David has concluded, the people continue to live according to their traditional way of life, without worrying about the body of artificial laws imposed by the legislator (David 1973, 32). The practices of the populace correspond to the economic needs, the religion, and the whims of the people, by which the law must be ruled.

Unification of Law and Plurality of Sources

The unification and the codification of Burundian law that followed the movement toward global modernization and the establishment of a uniform law was considered an element of national integration. In effect, judicial pluralism, that which had been consolidated by the colonial powers, was perceived as discriminatory, since the same laws were not applicable to all citizens. The Europeans and the natives who became naturalized citizens followed the written law, while the rest of the indigenous people followed their customary laws.

In the beginning, certain leaders wanted to introduce a truly national law, at the heart of which the elements of popular law would be conserved and integrated, but the desire for modernization and a break with the past pushed for the pure and simple suppression of popular law and its replacement by a "modern" judicial system, especially in public law. Traditional law was considered a symbol of stagnation by one opinion. In private law, the resistance to tradition is more obvious.

The Burundian judicial system is thus based on law, customs, international conventions, and the general principles of right, jurisprudence, and legal doctrine.

THE LAW

The Domains of the Law

The law is sovereign in all matters. These include the domain of the law; the fundamental guarantees and obligations of citizenship; the statute of persons and goods; the

political, administrative, and judicial organization; the protection of the environment and the conservation of natural resources; financial and patrimonial questions; nationalization; the denationalization of businesses and the transfer of business properties in the private and public sectors; the realm of education and scientific research; the objectives of economic and social actions of the state; and the regulation of work and social security (Law No. 1/008, 1998), bringing about the promulgation of the constitutional act of transition of the Republic of Burundi. Other matters are regulatory in nature. Almost all the domains are ruled by one law, with the exception of successions and matrimonial regimes.

The Institutional Evolution and Public Law

Analysis of the constitutional evolution of Burundi presents an interesting case, in that the country finds itself in a quasi-permanent situation of institutional insecurity. According to M. Massinon, the first constitution of Burundi, called the "Provisional constitution of Burundi" was instituted by the ordinance of Ruanda-Urundi on January 30, 1962, retroactive to January 15, 1962. This was replaced by the definitive Constitution of the Kingdom of Burundi of October 16, 1962, retroactive to July 1, 1962, the date of independence. This constitution was itself suspended by the Decree of the Royal Prince No. 001/2, on July 8, 1966 (*B.O.B.* 1966, 315). A military coup a few months later proclaimed the country a republic, but the new authorities waited until November 28, 1974, to institute a new constitution, which would be suspended in 1976 (*Déclaration du Conseil suprême révolutionnaire* 1976; *B.O.B.,* 207).

In 1981 the second constitution of Burundi was approved by popular referendum and instituted a few days later (*B.O.B.* 1981, 407). It was suspended at the command of the Armed Forces on November 20, 1987.

A constitution was adopted in 1992, establishing a semipresidential, semiparliamentary rule characterized by several political parties and respecting human rights and the guarantees of public liberty (*B.O.B.* 1992, 4: 95). This process resulted in the popular election of a president who was then assassinated in a military coup on October 21, 1993. The blockading of political institutions and the violence that followed lasted until the coup of July 25, 1996. A legal statute established the transitionary institutional system currently in place (Law No. 1/001/96 of September 13, 1996, *B.O.B.* 1996, 4: 95). It summarily returns to the main ideas of the Constitution of 1992, especially with regard to human rights.

The constitutional act of transition of June 6, 1998, abrogated the Constitution of 1992 and organized the functions of the institutions of transition while waiting to put in place a new constitution. The negotiations are in process at Arusha in Tanzania to put an end to the conflict between the different political and military factions that pretend to power. The conclusion of these negotiations will give Burundi a platform permitting the establishment of another constitution.

The penal code, administrative law, and fiscal law are ruled entirely by the written law.

Private Law

Matters of private law are regulated by written law with the exception of marital relationships, gifts, and inheritances. The still vital patrilineal tradition and the varying evolution of the culture in urban and rural locales make the establishment of a sole, universally applicable legislation difficult to imagine.

Two new pieces of legislation illustrate this difficulty well: the family and personal law and the civil code. The resistance to imported laws is the most marked in these two domains. The Burundian legislator must face two exigencies: respecting international conventions signed and ratified by the country, and the elaboration of universally applicable laws. The compromise obtained does not always achieve a perfect harmony between local needs and the demands of modernism. The laws will remain torn between tradition and modernity until they recognize equality for all while at the same time imposing limits to this equality, unified by the law but conserving a diversity of sources.

One example taken from family and personal law illuminate this point: the civil code imposes the attachment of a child to an individual and no longer to a family lineage. Also, the abandoned child will have no familial attachment, contrary to the custom of placing it in the care of the maternal family. This situation was inconceivable under traditional law, in which the child belonged to a family, by reason of the dowry agreement.

With regard to civil matters, one of the most important innovations was the recognition and the identical protection of civil rights guaranteed by a legal writ and those exercised by tradition or a property title delivered by competent authorities (Law No. 1/008 of September 1, 1986, *B.O.B.* 1986, 7–9: 12). The difference is in size. The customary civil rights are considered as a simple right of occupation. Only those holding certificates of registration and property titles delivered by competent authorities can lay claim to the rights of ownership. Lands entailed by customary laws or obtained by a property title delivered by a competent administrative authority can be ceded and used for the general good without a single indemnity of expropriation. In effect, before the institution of the civil law, these lands belonged to the public domain and could be taken by the state.

Commercial law, labor law, contract law, and family and personal law are subject to the written law, retaining certain integrated traditional elements.

Customs

The Burundian customs that exist throughout the country are an ensemble of continued practices respected by Burundians as social necessities and considered by them as having obligatory force. The customs impose themselves in daily life mainly in the branches of law that are nearest to the populace's everyday world: inheritance law, marriage, gifts, and the acquisition of nonregistered property. As in Rwanda, Burundian customs follow a long ancestral tradition that has evolved with the times and social mores.

Traditional law issues equally from decisions by customary courts of Ruanda-Urundi and from instances in which courts of written law have affected the traditional law in creating new rules or forbidding traditional behavior (Sohier, 1953). One finds some examples of decisions that have been accepted as custom, notably the interdiction against marriage by kidnapping (*Bulletin des jurisdictions indigènes du Congo Belge et du Rwanda-Urundi* 1949, 412) and the interdiction against usury interest, which are considered contrary to universal public order. These decisions were adopted bit by bit by traditional courts in the same way that the customs were brought about by the practice of the people.

Contrary to Western law, traditional law is not everywhere a discipline distinct from religion, morality, and other mechanisms of social control. The rights of each person are determined according to the responsibilities he or she assumes in the group. Moreover, these rights are not established definitively, and the protection of the individual is sometimes precluded by the necessity of ensuring the cohesion of the group. The rule of law often bends before the imperatives of collective security. The feeling of belonging to a group and its near magical hold on each group member attenuates, to a certain degree, any individual claims.

Traditional Burundian law is essentially conciliatory. The Burundians fear the law, because they do not allow it to regulate conflicts but to mediate between them. Thus bringing someone before the court constitutes a severe injury to his position and the position of his family, for this is interpreted as refusing the principle of conciliation. Instead of aiming at social harmony, it crystallizes positions, giving each his right at the cost of his social group, his family, and his state. However, it equally perpetuates the rancor of conflicting parties in determining the winner and the loser and in fixing the limits of reparations to be reclaimed.

Other Sources

Burundi has ratified several international and regional conventions, notably the different pacts of the United Nations relative to human rights and the African charter of the rights of man and peoples. The internal legislation does not have the ability to determine the hierarchy between the internal norms and international norms. However, one can not say that the Burundian legislator gave magistrates and legal practitioners the right to violate these commitments to the international community. Even if the cyclical conflicts did not permit the cementing of this agreement with Burundi in the protection of persons and their property, the constitution refers to this in its preamble and thus intends to mark the attachment of a country to its values. The same goes for the general principles of law that act as a source for Burundian law.

Burundian jurisprudence has not been systematically published since 1953 (Sohier 1953). Court decisions have thus been poorly known. Judges can learn from them, but these decisions are neither unanimous nor consistent enough to form a jurisprudence, a source for law.

The doctrine of law is principally constituted of articles published before and after independence. Burundian law inherited from colonial Belgian law many dispositions in civil and penal matters. The Belgian doctrine constitutes a significant source of inspiration.

ORGANIZATION OF JUSTICE AND AUXILIARY INSTITUTIONS

Burundi has a school of law at the center of the University of Burundi. For more than twenty years this school had issued licenses to practice law. Graduates of this university and others educated in foreign universities carry out the duties of magistrates. They are assisted in inferior courts by assessors, assistant judges who are not necessarily schooled in the law. The case of Burundi is not unique in Africa. The lack of trained magistrates obliges the authorities of some African countries to name magistrates who have not studied law but who often judge fairly nonetheless.

THE JURISDICTIONS OF THE JUDICIARY

The Supreme Court contains three chambers: an administrative chamber charged with the appeals formed against the decisions of the administrative courts, a chamber of appeals responsible for the petitions against the decisions given of last resort by the court of appeals, and a judiciary chamber that deals with infractions committed by public representatives under the jurisdiction of the Supreme Court, notably the president of the republic and his ministers. Together the chambers of the Supreme Court deal with magistrates of lower courts and provide recourse against decisions rendered by the individual chambers and, for demands of revision.

A constitutional court able to rule on the constitutionality of laws and regulations interprets constitutional law, rules over the regulation of disputed elections, swears in the president of the republic, and declares when the office of president becomes vacant.

The court of accounts, established in 1989, deals with final review errors in public documents, embezzlement of public funds, bribery, and corruption carried out by public agents and representatives. It checks the inconsistencies of public agents and representatives as well as the origins of their holdings.

Burundi has three courts of appeal able to handle appeals of judgments rendered in first resort by the higher courts, the courts of labor, and the courts of commerce. They deal in final review of infractions committed by judges and magistrates of lower courts. Each court of appeals contains two chambers: a criminal chamber and a civil chamber.

The seventeen higher courts are responsible for all civil and criminal actions that the law does not attribute to another jurisdiction. They deal with a degree of appeal providing recourse against judgments of courts of first instance made by local district courts.

The local district courts handle criminal infractions with penalties of no more than two years in prison and fines of no more than 300,000 Burundian francs, as well as questions relating to the state and capacity of persons. There are 123 district courts in Burundi.

SPECIALIZED JURISDICTIONS

The Court of Commerce was established by law on January 14, 1987. It deals with commercial litigation for cities and the rural Bujumbura province. Other cases related to commercial litigation are decided by the higher courts.

The Court of Labor was established by legislative ordinance on June 2, 1966. It presides over the first resort of infractions of labor and social security laws, of individual or collective work-related disputes, and of quarrels between contributors of social security, the employers and the workers. The country has two courts of labor, in Bujumbura and in Gitega. The higher courts are responsible for these cases in the other provinces.

Administrative litigation, mainly cases against public figures, is within the province of the two administrative courts.

MILITARY COURTS

The court-martial was established by law on April 28, 1917. It handles the first resort cases of infractions committed by military personnel during military service. The country has five courts-martial.

The military court was established by law on June 16, 1960, to replace the court-martial of appeals. The military court deals with final review cases of infractions committed by superior officers having a rank of major or higher and of appeals to decisions given by the court-martial. Appeals against the decrees of the military courts can be introduced before the Chamber of Appeals of the Supreme Court.

The law organized a public ministry charged with petitions against infractions before the various courts and tribunals. At the head of the public ministry is the office of the general public prosecutor, directed by a national attorney general (Law No. 1/4 of January 14, 1987, pertaining to judiciary reform, *B.O.B.* 1987, 87), whose jurisdiction extends throughout the nation's territory. The same law established a general prosecutor over the courts of appeal, directed by an attorney general and a national prosecutor over the higher courts. The public ministry presides over the military courts and controls a designated subdivision of the military auditing office. The military auditor and its substitutes, under the direction of the national attorney general, researches, instructs, and prosecutes infractions committed by the military courts.

AUXILIARY JUDICIAL INSTITUTIONS

The Council of Nobles
With the goal of privileging conciliation over contention, the Burundian legislature instituted over all of Burundi the Council of Nobles of the Hill, responsible for counseling parties in litigation. The mandate for members of the council and the procedure are free. This council can give its advice on all civil affairs under the jurisdiction of the district courts. The decision of the council of nobles is recorded from a verbal process before the concerned parties, containing their identification, the object of the litigation, the testimonies heard, and the arrangement proposed. This arrangement is not binding for the district court judge, but it provides him or her with a better understanding of the case and furnishes testimonies.

Before examining a case, the district court verifies if a settlement was attempted and decided; if not, it may return the case to the council of nobles or rule on the case itself. Even if the decision of the council has no authority over judgment, it directs the testimonies of the persons immediately concerned and related parties. The district court judge can not render judgment without a serious motivation. This obligation of conciliation before judicial action stands as an example of custom resisting imported law.

The Institution of the Bashingantahes
The accord of the political platform of the transitional regime of June 6, 1998, instituted the Council of the Bashingantahes for Unity and Reconciliation as an organ of conciliation (*B.O.B.*, No. 7/1998, 491 (art. 5, al. 2).

The Bashingantahes, an institution of judicial and social mediation made up of men of proven integrity and morality, are charged with settling disputes at the heart of the population and are recognized by the customary leaders. These men have strongly affected the community life of Burundi and have kept the high regard of the people,

who still solicit their arbitration because they have remained honest and are well informed on the daily incidents that often become sources of litigation.

The Ubushingantahe is based on a communal faith in the valor of the person of the Umushingantahe, an honest man, an apostle of peace, exercising both social and judicial power. The preparation of these men was very exacting, but the society lived with a certain harmony that is difficult to find in Burundi today, because of the cyclical conflicts that have plagued Burundi for more than twenty years.

The application of the law gives way to the search for equitable arbitration, which demands that the parties involved have total confidence in the Umushingantahes, along with an understanding that the law bends before the imperatives of collective security and social harmony. The procedures before the Bashingantahes follow local customs. Even if the facts can be exactly reported, the council is under no obligation to accept advice that is not authoritative on the subject under judgment.

According to tradition, the choice and preparation of the Bashingantahes guarantees their credibility before the people. It is necessary to be married, to have reached the customary age of majority, to be respectable, to be of legitimate birth, to come from a credible family, and to be trained for several years. The people are informed of a man's candidacy, so they can observe his deeds and his general manner of living. After a certain time, in the presence of a sponsoring council member, candidates must be accepted by a secret vote (*gutaramuka*). After admittance to the council, the new member remains watched by all and cannot, without risking loss of membership, commit any serious error, such as drunkenness, chasing women, behaving unjustly, and so forth. The training period and these social controls guarantee the morality of the Bashingantahes. It remains to be seen if their social value is still respected today.

The Ubushingantahe of Burundi represent a small fraction of family chiefs, chiefhood being one of the requirements of membership. "The integrity of the Bashingantahes, their knowledge of customary law, assures their credibility before the people who consider them their natural representatives." An official inauguration (*kwatigwa*) is also required before the sponsors and the people.

Since the Constitution of March 13, 1992, the Ubushingantahe has been proposed as a criteria of eligibility for community councils. While this may be considered beneficial as a means of moralizing government, it may have a flaw—namely, that giving a salary to the position may breed corruption, competition, or pressure to gain the position, which would result in candidates getting elected without truly meeting the customary requirements. Thus while constitutional recognition, at the voice of the people, may give added weight to the council's decisions, it also gives it an additional burden.

One might say that the institution of an Ubushingantahe could be an alternative to the inadequate solutions proposed by the imported laws, which were maladapted to the lives of the people, because the council would be reclaimed by the population itself. However, it is still necessary to establish fixed laws to avoid arbitration that could bring about the dislocation of the traditional family and to establish standards, such as the respect for life, the respect for a man's word, and the sense of honor.

While civil suits can find appropriate solutions, penal cases pose more of a problem, in the sense that the public interest is not appeased by the conciliation of parties as in traditional cases. Furthermore, the fixed laws do not recognize the customary spirit of seeking conciliation, even to the point of not necessarily heeding established laws. The establishment of a constitutional Ubushingantahe would also be faced with the growing role of women, who do not yet have a place in customary institutions.

THE BAR ADMINISTRATION OF BURUNDI

Since the time of the Belgian administration, Burundi has had a bar association. It is made up of lawyers, mainly schooled at the University of Burundi. The bar association is independent and practices before the courts and tribunals.

THE IMPACT OF LEGISLATION ON THE LIVES OF THE POPULACE

More than 90 percent of the Burundian population is rural. The literacy rate is very low. Knowledge of the laws and their application poses a real problem. Thus unification and the struggle against anachronisms, inscribed as objectives to be attained when Burundian personal and family law were elaborated, remain a goal of the effective application of the law. In effect, the popular customs are still in force in family and civil matters, and could survive the adoption of a unified system of law. This includes cases related to dowries, marital relations, family relations, and so forth. The state law serves as a guide, but it still remains an objective to be reached, not an applicable law. As in many African countries, the populace supports the legislative law developed in other places and imported for the needs of "modernization."

There is a real risk that the measures imposed would not apply, as during the period of the Belgian protectorate, or that certain measures taken against customary law would be ineffective, creating only an "illusion of civilization" (Massinon 1983, 135).

An in-depth study of the laws and their current applications helps one appreciate the effects of changing from a communal conception of law to an individualist one, and from a conciliatory judicial system to a contentious one. In order to avoid turning everything upside down, Etienne Leroy proposes an approach different from the one the Burundian legislature has followed: "It consists of borrowing from the past the fundamental principles of African judicial thought and adapting it to the modern techniques of economic and social development." This is even more true than the idea that "if the law can forbid an ancient custom that no longer has reason to exist, it cannot be hindering the adaptation of tradition."

CONCLUSION

This brief overview of the Burundian judicial system has surveyed the progressive imposition of Western law and the reduction of domains subject to traditional law. If this situation is already accepted in public law, it does not go as well for private law, where one still encounters the resistance of traditional law in the practices of the people. A more in-depth study is needed to understand the extent of this resistance and the capacity of the people, especially in rural areas, to adopt the principles of the imported law.

Negotiations are in process at Arusha between the various political factions of Burundi. It is hoped that the product of these negotiations will bring to pass changes that will be sensitive to the needs of current institutions.

Charles Ntampaka
Translated by Gayle Toone

References and further reading
Bourgeois, R. 1954. *Banyarwanda et Barundi: La coutume.* Bruxelles: Institut royal colonial belge.
David, R. 1973. *Les grands systèmes de droit contemporains.* Paris: Dalloz.
De Lespinay, Charles, and Emile Mworoha. 2000. *Construire l'etat de droit Le Burundi et la Région des Grands Lacs.* Paris: L'Harmattan.
Lamy, Emile, ed. 1960. "Possibilités actuelles de codification du droit coutumier au Ruanda-Urundi." Journal des Tribunaux d'Outre-mer (1960): 111–116.
Lemarchand, R. 1970. *Rwanda and Burundi.* London: Pall Mall Press.
Massinon, René. 1981, 1983, 1986. "L'illusion civilisatrice dans les actes législatifs de la période coloniale: Trois exemples burundais." In *Culture et Societe Revue de Civilisation Burundaise.* Edited by C. S. Bujumbura. Vol. 4: 135–161; vol. 6: 66–104; vol. 8: 100–134.
Mworoha, Emile. 1987. *Histoire du Burundi des origines à la fin du XIXe siècle.* Paris: Hatier.
Sohier, J. 1953. *Répertoire de jurisprudence du Congo belge du Ruanda-Urundi jusqu'au 31 décembre 1953.* Bruxelles: Larcier.
Trouwborst, Albert. 1962. "Le Burundi." In *Les anciens royaumes de la zone interlacustre méridionale.* Edited by Marcel d'Hertefelt, Albert Trouwborst, and J. H. Scherer. Rwanda, Burundi, Buha, Tervuren: Musée royal d'Afrique Centrale.
Verstraete, Maurice. 1956. "Les personnes et la famille." Vol. 1 of *Droit civil du Congo belge.* Edited by Antoine Sohier. Bruxelles: Larcier.

C

CALIFORNIA

GENERAL INFORMATION

California occupies roughly two-thirds of the Pacific coast of the United States between Mexico and Canada. It is bordered on the north by Oregon, on the south by Mexico, on the east by Nevada and Arizona, and on the west by the Pacific Ocean. It is the third largest state in the Union (158,706 square miles) and has the largest population of any state, with more than 33 million inhabitants. Its capital is Sacramento, and Los Angeles is its largest city. Among the better known public figures who came from California have been Earl Warren, who served as governor from 1943 to 1953 and was later appointed by President Eisenhower as chief justice of the U.S. Supreme Court, and presidents Ronald Reagan, who served as governor from 1967 to 1975, and Richard Nixon.

California leads the states in agricultural production, and it is near the top in manufacturing, mineral and lumber production, and tourism. Its other major industries include high technology, biomedical research, entertainment, and telecommunications. If California were a country, its gross domestic product would rank eighth in the world. The state also, however, suffers from pressing and complex problems, such as growing racial tension among its minority groups; diminishing supplies of clean air, water, electricity, and open space; chronic congestion on its freeways; and growing fiscal demands, especially in public education and crime control.

The history of the state can be divided into three eras: the era prior to European colonization (pre-1768), the era of Spanish-Mexican tenure (1769–1848), and the era following its acquisition by the United States in 1848. The Gold Rush of 1849 led to a dramatic increase in California's population. In 1846 it was only 9,000, but by 1852 it had grown to 264,000. On September 9, 1850, California was admitted as the thirty-first state in the Union. Over the next century its population on average doubled roughly every twenty years. California currently has fifty-two seats in the U.S. House of Representatives, and it has the largest bloc of electoral votes of any state—54.

EVOLUTION AND HISTORY

Since the early 1900s, California has been a forerunner in political reform. At that time the reform-oriented Progressive Party came to political power, seeking to promote open, efficient, and responsive government. Progressives, who believed in the wisdom and public-mindedness of voters against the influence of party bosses, corrupt officials, and special interests, sought to place greater power in the hands of voters.

Key to the Progressive movement was the institution of political reform devices that strengthened the voters' ability to affect government. One such device was the direct initiative, which enables voters to pass any law or constitutional amendment without recourse to the legislature. Another reform device is the referendum, used to repeal laws with which voters disagree. Another is the recall, whereby voters can remove elected officials before the expiration of their terms. Since their adoption, these devices have been used by Californians in almost every election to make important decisions affecting government. Many of the constitutional amendments affecting the judiciary were passed by direct initiative. While the wisdom of direct democracy is still debated, these devices will likely continue to be popular among Californians seeking to improve their government.

CURRENT STRUCTURE

Overview of the Court System

The California court system settles civil disputes and prosecutes defendants for violating state criminal laws. It is the largest and busiest judicial system in the nation, with almost nine million cases filed and nearly $2.4 billion in total operating costs (constituting 2.7 percent of the state's budget) during the 2000–2001 fiscal year. Like other states, California has two types of courts: trial courts, which in California are called superior courts; and appellate courts, consisting of a supreme court and courts of appeal, which review primarily the decisions of superior courts. The state has more than two thousand judicial officers (including judges, commissioners, and referees) and eighteen thousand court employees (see figure).

235

Legal Structure of California Courts

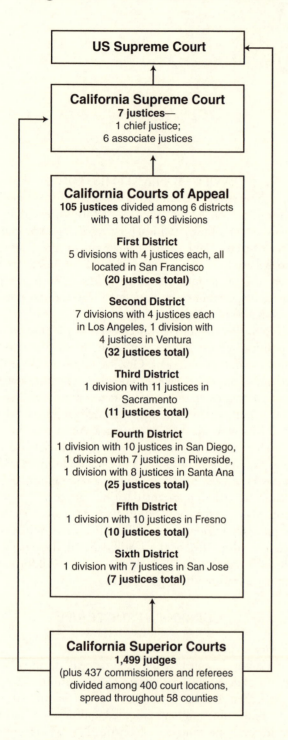

US Supreme Court

California Supreme Court
7 justices—
1 chief justice;
6 associate justices

California Courts of Appeal
105 justices divided among 6 districts
with a total of 19 divisions

First District
5 divisions with 4 justices each, all
located in San Francisco
(20 justices total)

Second District
7 divisions with 4 justices each
in Los Angeles, 1 division with
4 justices in Ventura
(32 justices total)

Third District
1 division with 11 justices in
Sacramento
(11 justices total)

Fourth District
1 division with 10 justices in San Diego,
1 division with 7 justices in Riverside,
1 division with 8 justices in Santa Ana
(25 justices total)

Fifth District
1 division with 10 justices in Fresno
(10 justices total)

Sixth District
1 division with 7 justices in San Jose
(7 justices total)

California Superior Courts
1,499 judges
(plus 437 commissioners and referees
divided among 400 court locations,
spread throughout 58 counties

Trial Courts—Superior Courts

The superior courts are the courts with which citizens are most likely to have contact. Their jurisdiction covers the whole range of human activity: business contracts, family law (for example, divorce, child custody), personal injury, real estate transactions, probate (that is, wills), and law enforcement. Nearly all of the cases filed in the state court system are filed first in the superior courts. Of the 8.7 million cases filed in the superior courts during the 2000–2001 fiscal year, 44 percent involved criminal misdemeanors, 43 percent were civil cases, and 13 percent involved felony and juvenile delinquency cases combined.

On June 2, 1998, California voters approved Proposition 220, a constitutional amendment allowing for the voluntary unification of the trial courts, which previously had been divided into superior and municipal (also called inferior) courts, each with its own jurisdiction and judges. Proposition 220 enabled the municipal and superior courts in each county to consolidate into a single court system if a majority of the superior court judges and a majority of the municipal court judges in the county approved. Proponents argued that unification would eliminate much of the duplication and delay leading to congestion in the trial courts. As of January 2001, all fifty-eight counties had voted to unify their trial courts, with some still in the process of changing signs and forms and reorganizing court personnel. Under unification the municipal courts were abolished, and municipal court judges became superior court judges. Now all trial courts in California are called superior courts, with a single court administration in each county.

Appellate Courts—Courts of Appeal

Established in 1904 by constitutional amendment, the courts of appeal review the vast majority of appeals from the superior courts, as well as decisions made by a number of state administrative agencies, such as the Workers' Compensation Appeals Board and the Agricultural Labor Relations Board. During the 1999–2000 fiscal year, more than twenty-five thousand cases were filed in the courts of appeal.

California is divided into six appellate districts, three of which are subdivided into divisions: the First District, with three divisions all located in San Francisco; the Second District, with seven divisions in Los Angeles and one in Ventura; the Third District, with one division in Sacramento; the Fourth District, with one division in San Diego, one division in Riverside, and one division in Santa Ana; the Fifth District, with one division in Fresno; and the Sixth District, with one division in San Jose. The legislature can create new districts or divisions as it sees fit.

Appellate Courts—Supreme Court

The Supreme Court is the state's highest court. Its decisions cannot be appealed, unless the case involves the U.S. Constitution, in which case it may be appealed to the U.S. Supreme Court. The supreme court has discretionary jurisdiction over most appeals, which means that it need not review all, or any, of the cases appealed to it. The exception is death penalty cases, which are automatically appealed from the superior courts following a conviction. In those cases the court has mandatory jurisdiction, which means that it must review the case. It also reviews recommendations regarding disciplinary action against judges and attorneys for misconduct. The only other matters that come directly to the Supreme Court are appeals from decisions made by the Public Utilities Commission. The court regularly hears appeals in San Francisco, Los Angeles, and Sacramento, but it may hold special sessions elsewhere. During the 1999–2000 fiscal year, more than ninety-four hundred cases were filed with the California Supreme Court.

Judicial Council

In addition to the courts, the constitution also establishes several judicial administrative agencies, one of which is the Judicial Council (JC), which oversees the operation of the court system. (Three-quarters of the states have established similar councils.) The JC sets administrative policy for the courts, gives annual recommendations to the governor and the legislature, and adopts and revises court rules and procedures to improve the administration of the judicial system. It also holds orientations for new judges and seminars to keep judges updated on the law. The JC has twenty-seven members, including the chief justice, fourteen other judges appointed by the chief justice, four attorneys, a member from each house of the legislature, and six advisory members drawn from court administrative executives and the California Judges Association.

NOTABLE FEATURES OF LAW/LEGAL SYSTEM

"Three Strikes" Law

Crime, especially concern over recidivism (that is, repeat criminals), has been a leading public issue in California and elsewhere. In 1994 two highly publicized criminal cases, each involving the murder of a young girl, one by a man with a long record of previous crimes, the other by a man recently released from prison, galvanized public support for the "three strikes and you're out" law, signed in March 1994 by Governor Pete Wilson. Prior to that time, most states already had statutes increasing the punishment of repeat offenders, but California, following Washington in 1993, was the second state to enact so-called three strikes legislation. Although twenty-four states and the federal government had enacted similar laws between 1993 and 1995, California's has been called the most controversial and restrictive.

Defendants convicted under the California law must serve 80 percent of their sentence (unlike most other offenders, who must serve 50 percent) before becoming eligible for parole. On the second conviction for a serious or violent felony, the law doubles the length of the sentence. On a third felony conviction, even if it is not a serious or violent felony, the law imposes a minimum sentence of twenty-five years to life, if the defendant has two or more prior convictions for serious or violent felonies. The Supreme Court, however, has handed down several decisions that limit the application of the three strikes law.

Community Property

Because of its Spanish heritage, California is one of eight states that recognize community property. In community property states, property acquired before marriage is generally treated as the separate property of each spouse, but property acquired after marriage is generally presumed to belong to both spouses equally. Modern statutes often modify this presumption, specifying under what conditions and what kinds of property can be maintained as a spouse's separate property. Further, spouses may freely contract with each other, either before or after marriage, delineating how they will hold their property. Usually, however, the legal status of a couple's property becomes an issue only in the case of divorce.

No-Fault Divorce

California, along with a minority of states, has adopted a no-fault divorce system that permits either spouse to seek a divorce for basically any reason, the grounds of which are usually stated as physical separation, breakdown in the marriage, or "irreconcilable differences." Although California is a community property state, when dividing a couple's property upon divorce, the court usually seeks a "fair and equal" distribution, taking into account property held separately as well as in community.

STAFFING

Practice of Law and the State Bar

There are more than 125,000 lawyers licensed to practice in California. To practice law in the state, one must meet the registration and education requirements set by the state bar and pass the state bar exam. The state bar is a public corporation to which all attorneys practicing law in the state must belong. It formulates and enforces rules of attorney conduct, investigates allegations of attorney misconduct, and makes recommendations for disciplinary action, including temporary suspension of license or even permanent disbarment.

While one need not attend law school in the state to take the bar exam, most state bar applicants graduate from one of the many California law schools, which range from the most prestigious in the nation—for example, Boalt Hall at the University of California at Berkeley, UCLA Law School, and Stanford Law School, the last from which U.S. Supreme Court justices William Rehnquist, Sandra Day O'Connor, and Anthony Kennedy graduated—to many lesser-known schools that offer part-time and evening programs to almost anyone desiring to enter the legal profession.

Superior Courts

As set forth in the state constitution, to be eligible to serve as a judge on either the superior or appellate courts, with the exception of former municipal court judges in the unified courts, one must have been licensed to practice law in the state for ten years prior to election or appointment. The number of superior court judges in each county is set by the legislature, the number ranging from 2 judges in sparsely populated counties to more than 240 in Los Angeles County.

Superior court judges are either elected by a majority of the county voters to a six-year term, or appointed by the governor for an interim term to fill a vacancy caused by the retirement, resignation, removal, or death of a judge. The vast majority of judges obtain their office initially through appointment. Superior court appointees, unlike appellate court appointees, do not serve out the remainder of the original judge's term, but only until the next election is held to fill that vacancy, as specified in the constitution. At that time, the interim superior court appointee, along with any other eligible candidates, may run for the office.

Judges run on nonpartisan ballots (that is, the judge's political party is not identified), and they are elected in county elections by majority vote. Most incumbent superior court judges run unopposed and are easily elected, though contested elections occasionally arise. If an unopposed candidate fails to receive a majority of the county votes, or if no one runs for the office, the governor makes another interim appointment to serve until the next election. There are currently 1,499 judges on the superior courts.

Appellate Courts

The current method of selecting justices for the Supreme Court and the courts of appeal was established in 1934 by constitutional amendment. That amendment sought to insulate the appellate courts from political influence by abolishing contested elections, making appellate justiceships obtainable only through appointment or nomination by the governor. While the governor must first consult the state bar's Commission on Judicial Nominees when choosing potential appointees to the appellate courts, it is the Commission on Judicial Appointments (CJA) that has the authority to either approve or veto the appointment. At least two persons on the three-member CJA—on which sits the chief justice, the attorney general, and a senior presiding justice from the courts of appeal—must approve an appointment.

Appointments are made to fill vacancies, and appellate appointees serve the remainder of the regular twelve-year term of the justice they replace. To serve out that term, however, the appointee must be approved at the next gubernatorial election (also called a judicial retention election) by a majority of the voters of either the state or the appellate district, depending on whether the appointment was for the Supreme Court or the courts of appeal. An appointee approved by the voters serves the remainder of the original justice's twelve-year term, at the end of which the appointee may choose to run for a full twelve-year term. If the appointee chooses not to run for re-election, the governor nominates a candidate to run on the ballot. Appellate justices run unopposed in elections and are approved by receiving more "yes" votes than "no" votes. If a justice fails to receive voter approval, the governor makes another vacancy appointment, who is then subject to voter approval at the next judicial retention election.

The courts of appeal currently have 105 justices. Each district or division of the courts of appeal has a presiding justice and two or more associate justices who rotate sitting on three-judge panels to hear appeals. A judgment in an appeal case requires that at least two of the three justices on the panel agree on the decision. The California Supreme Court is composed of one chief justice and six associate justices who hear appeals as a single body. A judgment there requires that at least four justices agree on the decision.

Controversial Elections: Rose Bird

For most of the history of California's judicial elections, Supreme Court justices have always won voter approval, though it was common to receive 9 to 12 percent negative votes in any judicial election. That number increased during the late 1970s, perhaps because of controversial court decisions in the areas of school busing, abortion, and the rights of criminal defendants. That period also coincided with an increase in the percentage, albeit still extremely small, of contested elections at the superior court level. Then, in 1986, Californians voted to reject three liberals from the Supreme Court—Chief Justice Rose Bird and two associate justices. Bird's appointment by Governor Jerry Brown as the first woman chief justice had been marked by controversy, beginning with concern over the fact that she had never served as a judge. She won her first voter approval in 1978 by the narrowest margin of any justice (51.7 percent), and she drew much fire when, during her tenure, the Supreme Court reversed fifty death sentences based on what critics viewed as legal technicalities. The rejection of three Supreme Court justices in a single election remains unprecedented in California history. Since then, the disapproval rating of Supreme Court justices has leveled off to between 20 and 40 percent, still higher than before, and the percentage of contested superior court elections has also declined. The current court is clearly more favorable to law enforcement authorities and the death penalty than was the Bird court.

Removal from Office

There are several ways that judges or justices may be removed from office: they may be recalled by the voters, impeached by the legislature, dismissed by the Supreme Court if found guilty of a felony or any crime involving "moral turpitude" and the conviction is upheld by a higher court, or removed on the recommendation of the Commission on Judicial Performance (CJP). The CJP was created in 1960 by constitutional amendment to investigate charges of judicial misconduct or incompetence. It can remove, retire, and censure judges for a disability interfering with their judicial duties or for willful misconduct (for example, racial or gender bias, substance abuse, verbal abuse in court, accepting bribes). The CJP has eleven members, made up of judges, attorneys, and members of the public, who are appointed for four-year terms. While hundreds of complaints are filed each year, one-third of which lead to formal investigations, only a few judges have been censured or removed, largely because they usually resign before the investigation can lead to disciplinary action.

RELATIONSHIP TO THE NATIONAL SYSTEM

National Prestige

The California Supreme Court is one of the most prestigious state supreme courts, although its prestige has waned a bit since earlier decades. During the 1950s and 1960s, its decisions in the areas of civil rights and the rights of the accused were followed by the U.S. Supreme Court. Other areas in which California Supreme Court decisions have influenced the decisions of other state and federal courts have been in abortion, product liability, and school finance.

Independent State Grounds Doctrine

The independent state grounds doctrine, which has been incorporated into U.S. constitutional law, was originally advocated by California Supreme Court Justice Stanley Mosk, who has sat on the court since 1964. It holds that state courts, when interpreting their state constitutions, may read them as affording greater but not weaker protections of constitutional rights than the protections required by the U.S. Constitution, even if the language of the state constitution is identical to that of the U.S. Constitution.

The *Bakke* Case

A landmark affirmative action case that came out of California is *Regents of the University of California v. Bakke* (1978). Alan Bakke, who was white, claimed that he had been denied admission to the U.C. Davis Medical School because of an unconstitutional quota system favoring minority applicants. The U.S. Supreme Court held that U.C. Davis's quota system was unconstitutional, but said that race could be a legitimate criterion for admission to assist minority applicants.

Federal Courts in California

The state and federal court systems exist side by side in every state, handling different types of cases but having some overlapping jurisdiction. The United States is divided into ninety-four federal judicial districts, four in California: the Northern Federal Judicial District, with courts in San Francisco and San Jose; the Eastern Federal Judicial District, with courts in Sacramento and Fresno; the Central Federal Judicial District, with a court in Los Angeles; and the Southern Federal Judicial District, with a court in San Diego.

Paul Chen

See also Alternative Dispute Resolution; Appellate Courts; Arbitration; Arizona; Canada; Criminal Law; Incarceration; Judicial Selection, Methods of; Mediation; Mexico; Napoleonic Code; Nevada; Oregon; Probate Succession Law; Trial Courts; United States—Federal System; United States—State Systems

References and further reading

Blume, William W. 1970. "California Courts in Historical Perspective." *Hastings Law Journal* 22: 121–195.

Bogan, Deborah. 2001. *California Courts and Judges Handbook.* Costa Mesa, CA: James Publishing.

California Judges Association. "CalCourts.org: The California Judicial System," http://www.calcourts.org (accessed May 18, 2001).

Field, Mona, and Charles P. Sohner. 1999. *California Government and Politics Today.* 8th ed. New York: Longman.

Gerston, Larry N., and Terry Christensen. 1999. *California Politics and Government: A Practical Approach.* 5th ed. Forth Worth, TX: Harcourt Brace College Publishers.

Hyink, Bernard L., and David H. Provost. 1998. *Politics and Government in California.* 14th ed. New York: Longman.

Nunis, Doyce B., and Gloria R. Lothrop, eds. 1989. *A Guide to the History of California.* New York: Greenwood Press.

Rolle, Andrew F. 1998. *California: A History.* 5th ed. Wheeling, IL: Harlan Davidson.

Ross, Michael J. 2000. *California: Its Government and Politics.* 6th ed. Fort Worth, TX: Harcourt College Publishers.

Scheiber, Harry N. 1993. "Innovation, Resistance, and Change: A History of Judicial Reform and the California Courts, 1960–1990." *Southern California Law Review* 66: 2049–2121.

State of California. Administrative Office of the Courts. "California Courts: The Judicial Branch of California," http://www.courtinfo.ca.gov (accessed May 18, 2001).

CAMBODIA

GENERAL INFORMATION

Cambodia (Kampuchea), officially the Kingdom of Cambodia, is a country in Southeast Asia. It is bordered on the east and the southeast by Vietnam, on the northwest by Laos, on the west and northwest by Thailand, and on the southwest by the Gulf of Siam and Thailand. From north to south Cambodia spans 450 kilometers (280 miles) and from east to west about 580 kilometers (360 miles). Its total area is approximately 182,000 square kilometers (70,000 square miles). The central part of the country consists of plains spreading out from the Mekong River delta. To the north are the Damgrek Mountains. To the south are Cardamon (Kravanh) Mountains, and the Damrei Mountains form the highland area covering the region between the great freshwater lake Tonle Sap and the Gulf of Siam.

Cambodia's population in 1998, according to official figures, was 11,437,657, with females comprising 52 percent of the population. One-quarter of Cambodian women are heads of household. Approximately 42 percent of the population is under the age of fifteen, and 50 percent is under the age of eighteen. The vast majority of the people, 85 percent, live and work in rural areas. Out of this rural population, 83 percent of women and 72 percent of men work in agriculture.

Cambodia has twenty-one different ethnic minorities. Seventeen are ethnic tribes; the other four are Thais, Chinese, Vietnamese, and Laotians.

The rate of annual population growth, 2.5 percent, is the highest in the region. Population density is at 64 persons per square kilometer. The rapid population growth affects the growth of gross domestic product (GDP), which was at 4 percent per year in 1999. In 2000, GDP per capita was US$274.

The official language of Cambodia is Khmer. The capital city is Phnom Penh.

HISTORY

Cambodia today is a small remnant of what was once a large Khmer empire that peaked in the twelfth and thirteenth centuries. Archeological evidence is that Khmer habitation in Southeast Asia dates back about 600,000 years and Khmer civilization may have begun as early as two thousand years ago.

Following the demise of the Khmer empire in the mid-fifteenth century, Cambodia experienced invasions by its neighbors as well as internal conflicts. In 1863, France established a protectorate over the country.

Cambodia promulgated its first modern constitution in 1947, establishing democratic governance and a multiparty system largely modeled on the constitution of the French Fourth Republic. Cambodia gained its independence in 1953 under the leadership of King Norodom Sihanouk. In 1955, King Sihanouk abdicated the throne in favor of this father, Norodom Suramaritr, so that he might involve himself in national politics. At this stage in Cambodian history, the 1947 constitution relegated the role of the monarch to that of symbolic rather than actual power—it became a constitutional monarchy. For Sihanouk to play an actual political role, he had to abdicate the throne, as a monarch could not also participate in the political governance of the state. Sihanouk became the country's political leader, and the country was under his authoritarian rule until he was ousted from his position as prime minister/head of state by Lon Nol in a military coup on March 18, 1970.

Following the 1970 coup, the country became embroiled in civil war. Cambodian Communist forces, widely known as the Khmer Rouge, gained increasing power both by taking over Cambodian territory and through popular support and support by Shanouk. After his ouster, Sihanouk allied himself with the Khmer Rouge, thus boosting the influence and popularity of the Communist movement. The nation was further destabilized because of the United States' extension of the Vietnam War into Cambodia in pursuit of enemy guerrillas. Carpet bombing of the countryside killed some 700,000 Cambodians.

On April 17, 1975, the Khmer Rouge took over the country. Soon they established the most repressive and brutal regime in Cambodia's history. They emptied the cities and forced the urban population into the countryside. In their reign of terror about 1.7 million people died; more than 100,000 were executed; and the rest perished from diseases, malnutrition, and exhaustion.

In 1979, as a result of long-simmering border disputes and with military assistance from the Soviet Union, Vietnam invaded Cambodia and drove the Khmer Rouge from power. In their place, the Vietnamese army installed a group of ex–Khmer Rouge officers, including Hun Sen, the current prime minister of Cambodia. Remnants of the Khmer Rouge regrouped along the border with Thailand. Other non-Communist groups also organized resistance to the Vietnamese-backed regime.

The resistance continued for ten years. In September 1989, Vietnam pulled out its troops, and in October 1991, the four warring factions—the Khmer National Liberation Front, FUNCINPEC (an acronym of the French name for the National United Front for an Independent, Neutral, Peaceful, and Cooperative Cambodia), the State of Cambodia (representing the incumbent Vietnamese-backed government), and Democratic Kampuchea (known as the Khmer Rouge)—reached a United Nations–brokered peace agreement in Paris. Under this agreement, Cambodia was put under the administration of the United Nations Transitional Authority in Cambodia (UNTAC). One of UNTAC's main duties was to administer general elections held in 1993. The factions converted into political parties to compete in the election. Despite political vio-

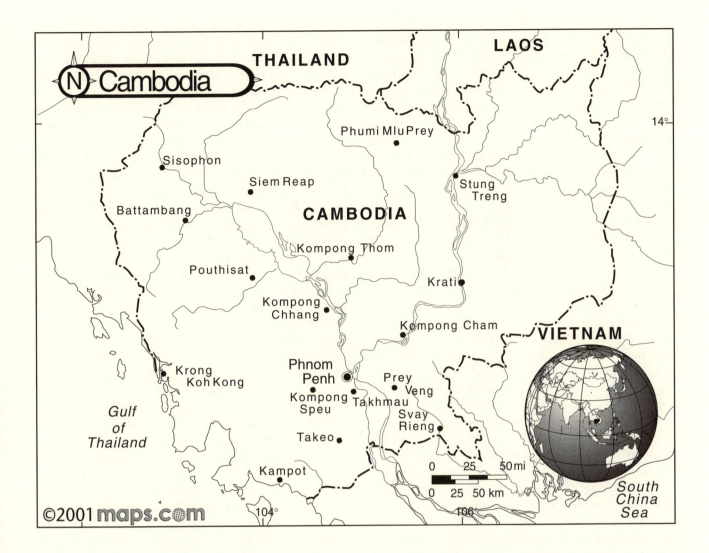

lence and intimidation by the Cambodian People's Party (CPP), representing the former Communist regime, and by the Khmer Rouge guerrillas, approximately 90 percent of Cambodians voted. The royalist FUNCINPEC party, headed by Prince Norodom Ranariddh, won the election.

The CPP refused to accept FUNCINPEC's victory and threatened to plunge the country back into civil war if power was not shared with them. Ultimately, a power-sharing agreement was reached between Ranariddh, who became first minister, and Hun Sen, vice president of the CPP, who became second prime minister.

In 1997, Sen staged a coup in which hundreds of FUNCINPEC members and members of opposition parties were killed or injured. Ranariddh was ousted as first prime minister. Hun Sen of the CPP currently heads the government of Cambodia.

LEGAL SYSTEM

Pre-Angkorian Era
Details about the legal system of the pre-Angkorian era are sparse. The memoirs of two Chinese diplomats, dat-

ing from 225 C.E., show that Cambodia (called Funan) had a system of laws modeled on the Indian system. The Cambodian system, which survived until the thirteenth century, as reported by another Chinese diplomat, included trials by ordeal such as throwing the accused to wild animals. Trials by ordeal exist unofficially in the country to this day, although they are very rare.

Angkor
The stability of the Khmer Empire (Angkor), beginning in 802, allowed for reform and elaboration of the legal system. The ancient Khmer society was hierarchical; personal status flowed from function or position held in the administration, titles, names, and wealth. The system of ownership of land was well developed.

The court of law was called *vrah sabha* or *dhamadhikarona*. There were central or municipal courts of law called *vrah sabha nagara* and provincial or territorial courts called *vrah sabha sruk*. The sovereign was the ultimate authority of law and had the power to grant amnesty or pardon.

The officials associated with the administration of justice were given the title *sabhapati* (later *sopheathipdey*), president of the court of the presiding judges; *guna-dosadarsi*, inspector of qualities and defects; *svat vrah dharmasastra*, reciter of the sacred legal text; *vyavaharadhikarin* or *ranvan*, usher; *care*, emissary; *vrah sarvadhikarin*, judicial land surveyor; *mahasresthi* or *sresthimukhya*, chief of merchants; *ta cam likhita kamvuvansa nu anga vrah rajakaryya*, records keeper; *Pratyaya* or *rajapratyaya*, royal confidante or representative; and *pratyaya mrtakadhana* or *amrtakadhana*, administrator of property received by inheritance.

Indian legal textbooks such the *Manu*, the *Dharmasastras*, and other *sastras* or law were studied and practiced in the royal courts. Legal terminology, both that used for speaking in court and that used in writing, was mainly in Sanskrit, but Khmer was used in descriptions of material facts.

The litigation process commenced with a complaint by the plaintiff, a response by the defendant, and examination by the court. The steps in the proceeding were also modeled on the *vyavahara matyka*. The procedure of examination of witnesses *(saksin)* and evidence was also modeled after the Indian practice of the time.

In the late sixteenth century, in the aftermath of invasion by the Siamese, which resulted in looting and destruction of legal texts and records, King Chey Chettha focused on law reform. He created a royal law commission and appointed six people to revise and collate legal texts that remained in the country. As a result, twelve volumes of law were promulgated. Two of the most important laws were the *Kram Sopheathipdey* or Law of the Presiding Judges and *Kram Chor* or Crimes Act. The death penalty was abolished, and the severity of sentences was reduced.

French Influence on the Cambodian Legal System
In 1863, Cambodia became a French protectorate. By the French-Cambodian treaty of 1884, a French administration of justice was established, under the supervision of a French resident. By royal ordinance of February 7, 1902, the provincial court of first instance, the Sala Khet, and a court of appeal, the Sala Outor, were established on the basis of Cambodian law. A royal ordinance of June 26, 1903, established the Supreme Court, the Sala Vinichay. At this stage, indigenous laws were still applicable. By royal ordinance of September 7, 1910, formal law courses were established in Khmer for judicial officials.

Royal commissions were created by a royal ordinances of May 5 and August 11, 1905, and by ordinances of September 3, and October 21, 1908. The royal ordinance of November 20, 1911, the Code of Criminal Instructions and Judicial Organization, Penal Code, Book I, of the French Civil Code were promulgated and came into force on July 1, 1912.

In 1915, the French took complete control over the Cambodian judiciary. In the early 1920s, indigenous laws were replaced by French laws and the French legal system. A civil code, a law on judicial organization, a judicial personnel statute, and a law on the control of the judiciary were promulgated. A court of petty crimes Sala Lahu, court of first instance (Sala Dambaung or Sala Lukhun in Phnom Penh), the Court of Appeal (Sala Outor), and the Supreme Court (Sala Vinichay) were established. Book I, previously promulgated, was recodified and came into force on July 1, 1920. It was now divided into four books regulating person, property, obligations (contracts and torts), and procedure. By royal ordinance of April 5, 1948, an administrative chamber was established with the jurisdiction to hear administrative matters. Appeals are submitted to the Council of Ministers. In 1953, an administrative appeal tribunal was established to hear appeals. This entire legal system was abolished in April 1975 when the Khmer Rouge took power.

After the Vietnamese invasion in 1979, which ousted the Khmer Rouge regime, and the installment of a puppet regime officially known as the People's Republic of Kampuchea, a legal system was reestablished, but modeled on that of the Soviet Union. Despite constitutional reform in 1993, the Soviet system and practice still define, in part, the Cambodian legal system today.

LEGAL CONCEPTS
The Cambodian legal system has suffered as a result of the various political influences since Cambodian independence in 1953—authoritarianism, military dictatorship, the total annihilation of the French-based legal system by the Khmer Rouge, and the introduction of Soviet-style communism under the Vietnamese-backed regime established in 1979. The current regime, which took power in 1993, bears many hallmarks of Soviet-style practice.

Only ten lawyers remained in Cambodia after the Khmer Rouge were ousted. Thousands of lawyers were killed, died of starvation or disease, or fled the country. The legal infrastructure was also destroyed and has had to be rebuilt from scratch.

As a result of 1993 elections sponsored by the United Nations, Cambodia adopted a new constitution. The 1993 constitution stipulates liberal democracy and a multiparty system. It provides for a separation of powers between the three branches of government—the legislature, executive, and judiciary. The legislature is composed of the National Assembly and the Senate. The constitution states that a free-market economy is the foundation of state's economic system. It restores the monarchy, but with the stipulation that the monarch reigns but does not rule. It recognizes and respects human rights as defined in the U.N. Charter, the Universal Declaration of Human

Rights, and all other treaties concerning human rights, women's rights, and children's rights. It also provides for due process of law and prohibits enacting laws with retroactive force. It provides for checks and balances on the branches of government. It allows citizens of both sexes over twenty-five years of age to run for office.

Despite the liberal terms of the constitution, in reality Cambodia is dominated by a powerful executive and a judiciary composed of generally unqualified political appointees.

JUDICIARY

Article 109 of the constitution enshrines, for the first time in Cambodian history, the principle of the independence of the judiciary. The judiciary comprises four separate legal entities: the Constitutional Council, the Supreme Council of Magistracy, the courts, and prosecutors. The court system is divided into courts of first instance, the Court of Appeal, and the Supreme Court.

The judiciary has the constitutional power to review the executive branch. Citizens are entitled to lodge complaints with the court for judicial redress of violations of the law by the executive, by organs of the executive, or by members of a particular organ. It is also empowered to determine administrative law matters, which traditionally were the competence of the executive, the administrative chamber, which is a separate administrative law structure with the Council of State as the supreme court. The 1953 constitution provided for the establishment of a council of state, perhaps to act as the highest administrative law review body; but an organic law was never passed and so this body was never created. Accordingly, not a single administrative law case has been heard in Cambodia since 1970.

Supreme Council of the Magistracy

To guarantee the independence of the judiciary, the 1993 constitution provides for the establishment of an independent body, the Supreme Council of the Magistracy, with the power to appoint, transfer, suspend, and remove judges and prosecutors. In December 1994, the National Assembly adopted the Law on the Organization and the Functioning of the Supreme Council of the Magistracy. During debate of the draft law, the minister of justice, who had previously acknowledged that the constitution prohibited him from sitting on the council, insisted on being included as a member of it. Over opposition, and with the Constitutional Council not yet formed to review the constitutionality of his membership, the law was passed and the justice minister became a member.

The Supreme Council of the Magistracy is composed of nine members: the king, who presides over the council; the minister of justice; the president of the Supreme Court; the prosecutor general attached to the Supreme Court; the President of the Court of Appeal; the prosecu-

tor general attached to Court of Appeal; and three judges selected from among all sitting judges. All members except the king are political appointees of the ruling CPP. The Law on Political Parties allows members of the council to maintain their party ties and engage in such political activities as campaigning during elections. Without a clearly defined term of office and a requirement of legal qualifications, the members are vulnerable to political manipulation, and the ability of the Supreme Council to ensure judicial independence comes under question.

The new law assigned to the council powers beyond those permitted by the constitution. The council has, for example, not only the power to discipline judges and prosecutors but also to remove and dismiss them.

Constitutional Council

The 1993 constitution provides for the creation of a Constitutional Council to interpret laws passed by the National Assembly and to rule on their constitutionality. Although the constitution fails to assert that this council is to be independent from any other governmental body, the Law on the Organization and Functioning of the Constitutional Council does so.

In providing for a constitutional council, the Cambodian constitution of 1993 mirrors the French constitution of 1958, which included the constitutional review body in order to curb excesses of legislative or executive power. This is an example of appropriating French law and institutions where they may not be appropriate to the Cambodian context, where the executive has always dominated the other branches.

The Constitutional Council consists of nine members, each appointed for a nineyear term. The terms are staggered, so that one-third of the council members are replaced every three years. Three of the members are appointed by the king, three by the National Assembly, and three by the Supreme Council of the Magistracy. The president of the Constitutional Council is appointed by the members of the council. The president, who must be a CPP member, has the prevailing vote in case of ties.

There is no guarantee of tenure—the king, the National Assembly, or the Supreme Council of the Magistracy can remove a member at will before the member's nine-year term is completed—although such a guarantee would facilitate members' impartiality and independence. Neither is there a requirement that members have legal qualifications or undergo legal training following appointment. Rather, any Cambodian with a degree in law, administration, diplomacy, or economics and at least fifteen years of work experience to be appointed to the council.

The jurisdiction of the Constitutional Council is broader than that of its French counterpart. It automatically reviews the constitutionality of "organic laws, National Assembly's Internal Regulations, amendments to the organic law and National Assembly's Internal Regulation" after passage by the National Assembly but prior to promulgation, and any enacted law or promulgated law submitted for review by the king, the president of the National Assembly or one-tenth of its members, or the prime minister. Ordinary Cambodians may also seek review of any law by petitioning the president of National Assembly or an assembly member. In addition, the law grants litigating parties the right to submit for review by the council any provision of a law at issue in the litigation or any administrative decision that affects the party's rights or liberties. Applications for such review are to be lodged at the Supreme Court. Arguably, this provision is in violation of article 109 of the constitution, which vests the competence of the review of administrative decisions in the courts.

Unlike its French counterpart, however, the council does not have the power to review executive decrees, decree-laws, subdecrees (regulations), and international treaties. The council therefore serves as a check against abuses by the legislative branch while allowing the executive to enact decrees with impunity.

It appears that it was the intention of the National Assembly that the council be an independent body. The Constitutional Council Act requires members to be impartial and to recuse themselves from consideration of any case that presents a conflict of interest. Deliberations and votes must be secret. Members are prohibited from making public statements. Like the Supreme Council of the Magistracy, however, the Constitutional Council is dominated by the CPP. Six of the council's nine members belong to the ruling party, and only a simple 5–4 majority vote is required for a decision. There are no council members from the other political parties. The CPP members of the council are encouraged to maintain their party affiliation, although council rules require that a leave of absence be granted if a member wants to work on an election campaign or seek elective office.

An example of the politicization of the council is that it declined to hear eighty-five complaints regarding recent elections lodged by an opposition party, the Sam Rainsy Party. These complaints were rejected outright by clerks and were never reviewed by council members.

Structure of the Judicial System
In civil and criminal matters, cases are initiated at the court of first instance, the municipal court, or the provincial court. Appeal is a matter of right in both civil and criminal matters, and the Court of Appeal will hear an appeal de novo on both factual and legal issues. A further right of appeal, on legal grounds, can be made to the Supreme Court, the highest court for general cases unrelated to constitutional law issues. The structure of the Cambodian court system is shown in the accompanying figure.

Legal Structure of Cambodia Courts

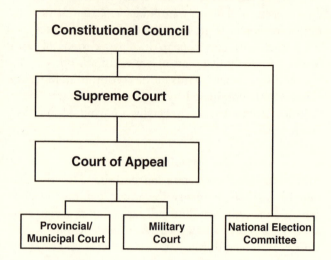

The Military Court was established in 1981 under Decree-Law No. 05 (12/08/81), which gives the court jurisdiction to try members of the military, civilians who work in the Ministry of National Defense, and civilians who have committed military offenses with members of the military.

Specialized Judicial Bodies
Cambodia is in a process of setting up a special tribunal, officially known as the Extraordinary Chamber in the Courts of Cambodia. The draft law, called the Law on the Establishment of the Extraordinary Chambers in the Courts of Cambodia for the Prosecution of Crimes Committed under the Period of Democratic Kampuchea ("The Khmer Rouge Law"), was passed by the National Assemby in January 2001 and has been promulgated. As of November 2001, the next steps for setting up the tribunal had not been taken by the Cambodian government. Some international observers are concerned about an apparent reluctance on the part of the Cambodian government to set up the tribunal after years of discussion with the United Nations and the international community.

This tribunal, if successfully established, will have the jurisdiction to hear charges of genocide, crimes against humanity, and war crimes levied against Khmer Rouge members who are believed responsible for the death of about 1.7 million people during their period of their rule, from April 17, 1975, to January 7, 1979.

National Elections Committee
The National Elections Committee (NEC) is a body established in 1997 to administer the election of members of the National Assembly and commune elections and to adjudicate electoral disputes. The Constitutional Council

is its final appellate body. Although the NEC was supposed to be an impartial body composed of representatives of all parties that contested the 1993 elections, in reality its ten members were appointed by the CPP.

Staffing

There is no requirement for members of the judiciary to have a law degree or a particular level of legal training. The Royal Faculty of Law in Phnom Penh, closed in 1975, reopened only in 1993, and its first class graduated in 1997.

As of 2001, only two of nine Supreme Court justices held a bachelor's degree, and only one of those two degrees was in law. Two judges had a diploma in law, having studied law for one year. Of the remaining judges, two had graduated from high school, one from primary school, one held a teacher's certificate, and one was a graduate of the Ecole Royale d'Administration.

Of the Court of Appeal judges, six held Bachelor of Law degrees, and one had a bachelor's degree in another field. Of the remaining three judges, two had graduated from high school and one from primary school.

The accompanying figure shows the number and disposition of judicial personnel in Cambodia.

LEGAL PROFESSION

After twenty years without a law regulating the legal profession, the Law on the Bar was adopted on June 15, 1995. As a result, the Bar Association was established on October 6, 1995. On that day, thirty-eight lawyers were admitted to legal practice before the Court of Appeal. The new members later elected a president of the association and nine members of the Bar Council, a body that regulates the association as a whole. The Bar Council has the power to grant and revoke licenses to practice law. As of 2001, there are 221 members of the bar, of whom only 176 hold a license to practice and are practicing.

Apart from its responsibility to train, professionalize, and discipline its members, the Bar Association plays an integral role in establishing democracy and the rule of law in Cambodia. Unfortunately, the association has become politicized and has been accused of corruption. Its members have been known to act in an unprofessional manner as brokers between judicial officials and their clients.

There are two internationally funded legal aid organizations in Cambodia that have been providing free legal assistance to the poor: Legal Aid of Cambodia, created in 1995, and the Cambodian Defender Project, created in 1994. Most practicing lawyers in Cambodia work for these two organizations.

IMPACT OF THE LAW

Cambodia has a civil law tradition, but the administration of justice still bears the hallmark of the old Soviet

Cambodia Judiciary

Category	Judges	Prosecutors	Clerks
Constitutional Council	9		15
Supreme Court	9	4	59
Appeal Court	10	4	43
Provincial/Municipal Court	89	46	372
Military Court	11	4	36
Total in Judiciary	128*	58	525

*Includes 7 judges in the Ministry of Justice.

practices. The government, dominated by the CPP, does not regard legal reform as a priority. Nevertheless, Cambodia has moved beyond the years of brutal repression and is beginning to rebuild social and governmental institutions and the national economy. The 1993 constitution provides for the protection of human rights and for the establishment of the democratic institutions. Although not always followed in practice, the constitution can supply the legal framework for the gradual evolution of Cambodia's political system from authoritarianism to democracy. The determining factor, however, will be whether future governments of Cambodia accept the principle of democracy and the rule of law.

Bora Touch

See also France; Vietnam; Laos

References and further reading
Chakravarti, Adhir. 1978. *The Sdok Kak Thom Inscriptions: A Study in Indo-Khmer Civilization*. Part 1. Calcutta: Sanskrit College.
Donovan, Dolores A., Sidney Jones, and Robert J. Muscat. 1993. *Rebuilding Cambodia: Human Resources, Human Rights, and Law*.
Initial Report of States Parties Due in 1993: Cambodia. 23/09/98. CCPR/C/81/Add.12 (State Party Report). Cambodia's Report to the International Covenant on Civil and Political Rights Committee.
Marks, Stephen. 1994. "The New Cambodian Constitution: From Civil War to Democracy." *Columbia Human Rights Law Review* 26(5): 45.
Sok, Siphana, and Denoran Sarin. 1998. *The Legal System of Cambodia*.
Ricklefs, M. C. 1967. "Land and the Law in the Epigraphy of Tenth-Century Cambodia." *Journal of Asian Studies* 26(3): 411.

CAMEROON

GENERAL INFORMATION

Cameroon is located in Western Africa, bordering the Atlantic Ocean, Equatorial Guinea, Gabon, and the Re-

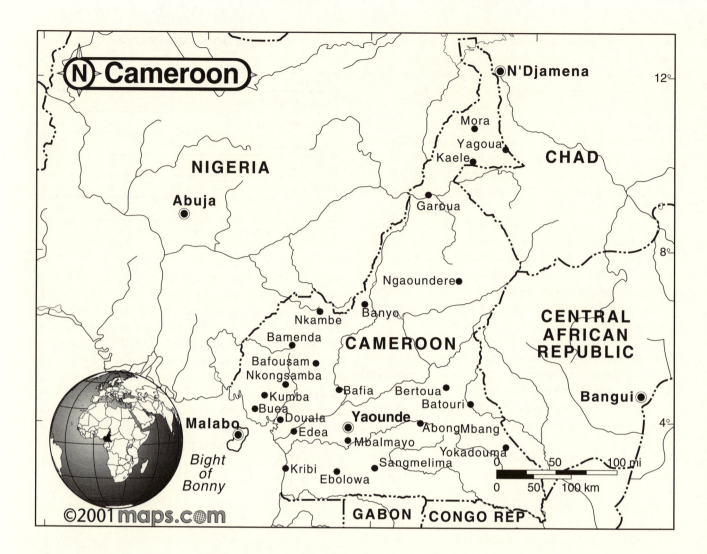

public of Congo to the south; the Central African Republic and Chad to the east; Lake Chad to the north; and Nigeria to the west. The climate varies considerably from hot and humid along the Atlantic coast, to cool in the dissected plateau in the center, and hot in the semiarid north. With a total land area of 475,440 square kilometers, about 78 percent of the country is covered by forests and woodland, much of which are documented centers of endemism for many species of animals and plants. The uncontrolled exploitation of these forests has become a matter of international concern in recent years.

The population of 15,456,092 (as of 1999) is made up of an extraordinary diversity of about 250 tribes speaking at least 280 different indigenous languages. To this complex mix is superimposed a bicultural division between a minority Anglophone community from the former British trust territory of Southern Cameroons, who make up about 20 percent of the population and occupy two of the ten administrative provinces in the country, and a dominant Francophone community from the former French Cameroun, who make up 80 percent of the population and occupy the remaining eight administrative

provinces. The English and French languages are constitutionally recognized as the official languages, though most official communications are usually in the dominant French language. However, Pidgin English, a common lingua franca in English-speaking West Africa, is widely spoken in the Anglophone provinces and in some of the major towns in the Francophone provinces that have a substantial Anglophone community. About 33 percent of Cameroonians are Christian and 16 percent are Muslim, while a majority, 51 percent, practice a wide variety of indigenous beliefs.

The legal system, like most in Africa, is a relic of the colonial era. However, it is unique in that it consists of two distinct and often conflicting legal systems, the English common law and the French civil law, operating in some sort of tenuous coexistence. This makes Cameroon one of the few examples in the world of a bijural system.

HISTORY

The Portuguese are thought to be the first Europeans to have arrived on Cameroon's coast, in the 1500s, but malaria prevented any significant settlement and conquest of the interior until the late 1870s. The country's name is derived from the word *camaroes,* meaning "shrimps," so called by the Portuguese explorer Fernando Po, who named the River Wouri the Rio dos Camaroes ("shrimp river"). It was at the Berlin Conference of 1884 that all of what is now Cameroon and parts of several of its neighboring lands became the German colony of Kamerun. The German presence lasted until 1916, when, during World War I, a combined British and French expeditionary force defeated the Germans and proceeded to divide the territory into two unequal parts. The British took control of two disconnected portions, which they labeled Northern and Southern Cameroons, while the French took the larger portion, constituting about four-fifths of the territory.

This arbitrary division was later recognized by the League of Nations, which on June 28, 1919, conferred mandates on the two powers to administer the territories. The mandates were later superseded by trusteeship agreements upon the creation of the United Nations in 1945. The British administered their portion as part of their neighboring colony of Nigeria, while the French made theirs part of their colony of French Equatorial Africa. In a U.N.-conducted plebiscite of February 11, 1961, the Southern Cameroons voted in favor of gaining independence by reuniting with the French Cameroun, which had already become independent on January 1, 1960. The Northern Cameroons voted in favor of remaining a part of Nigeria. On September 1, 1961, the Southern Cameroons and the newly independent French Cameroun were formally reunited as the Federal Republic of Cameroon. Three major periods can best explain the nature and evolution of the legal system—namely, the precolonial, the colonial, and the postindependence periods.

In precolonial Cameroonian society there existed diverse unwritten indigenous laws and usages that applied in varying degrees to the different ethnic groups. The only exception was in the north, where the Foulbe tribes, who had originally invaded the territory from North Africa in the early nineteenth century, had introduced Islamic laws. Despite the differences in the structures, content, and institutions that applied these indigenous and Islamic laws—or traditional laws as they are referred to today—there were many similarities. A German attempt to ascertain and codify the different traditional laws was frustrated by the outbreak of World War I, but the results from the six tribes that were studied showed that there were substantial similarities in basic concepts and practices. The traditional system of justice was administered by a series of ad hoc bodies including the family head, quarter head, chief, and the chief's council. Perhaps the most remarkable and controversial aspect of this system of justice was the extensive use of trial by ordeal. The commonest examples of this involved drinking poisonous concoctions, putting the hands in boiling palm oil or water, or holding a red-hot iron bar. If the accused came to no harm, then his innocence was considered as proven.

During the German colonial period, a rudimentary system of administration was established. Two parallel systems of courts existed: one exclusively for Europeans, in which German law was applied, and the other exclusively for Cameroonians, in which traditional law under the control and supervision of the Germans was applied. Article 9 of the Mandates Agreement gave the British and French the right to introduce their respective laws and legal systems into Cameroon, although they had already done so since 1916 by extending to it the laws of their contiguous colonial territories. There were significant differences in the policies they pursued in introducing their respective systems of justice. The British, like the Germans and French, also operated two parallel systems of courts, but, unlike them, the two were not separated on racial lines. One structure was for the traditional sector of the population, mainly Cameroonians, and the other was for the modern sector, mainly Europeans or those Cameroonians who opted for it. The applicable law was based on Section 11 of the Southern Cameroons High Court Law (SCHCL) of 1958, which provided for the application of English common law, the doctrines of equity and statutes of general application that were in force in England on January 1, 1900. On that basis, a number of English statutes as well as Nigerian laws and ordinances were made applicable to Southern Cameroons. Through the system of "indirect rule," traditional institutions and laws were retained, provided they were not repugnant to natural justice, equity, and good conscience, nor incompatible with any existing laws.

In French Cameroun, the French, in line with their policy of assimilation, made a strict distinction between citizens, who were defined as either French nationals or Cameroonians who had evolved and were honored with that status (and there were hardly any), and the ordinary Cameroonians, who were derogatorily referred to as *sujet* (indigenous people). Based on this, two systems of justice were administered, one for the Cameroonian population in accordance with traditional laws, and another for French nationals in accordance with French law. French administrators presided over the traditional courts and used the local chiefs and notables merely as assistants or assessors.

The federal system that came into existence in 1961 was based on a two-state federation consisting of West Cameroon, made up of the former Southern Cameroons, and East Cameroon, made up of the former French Cameroun. Until the country became the United Republic of Cameroon in 1972, when a unitary system of government was introduced, the two federated states had each retained their inherited colonial system of justice, although that was under the control of a Federal Ministry of Justice. However, the early history of the independent and reunified Cameroon was marked by strides toward complete political and legal unification. By 1964, two Federal Law Reform Commissions had been created to draw up a penal code, a criminal procedure code, and several other codes. Its only achievement was the 1967 Penal Code, which remains the only reasonably successful legislation that reflects the country's dual legal culture, although it was substantially based on the French Penal Code. Based on the unitary Constitution of 1972, Ordinance No. 72/4 of August 26, 1972, which has since been amended several times, created a civilian-style unitary system of courts to replace the different court structures that had operated in the two states. Nevertheless, Article 38 of the constitution provided for the continuous application of the different laws that were in force in the two legal districts, provided that these were not inconsistent with any new laws. As a result, despite the unified court structure, the two preindependence legal systems continued to operate. The 1972 Constitution has been amended on several occasions, though the most significant and substantial was in 1996, in response to prodemocracy nationwide strikes and demonstrations that had started in the early 1990s.

LEGAL CONCEPTS

Several changes were brought in by the 1996 amendment to the constitution. For the first time, certain basic, fundamental human rights—including freedom of speech, freedom of worship, the right to life, and the prohibition of torture and cruel, inhumane, or degrading treatment—were recognized. The country's attachment to the fundamental freedoms enshrined in the Universal Declaration of Human Rights, the Charter of the United Nations, and the African Charter on Human and Peoples' Rights, as well as any other international conventions signed and ratified on the subject, were affirmed. Although they appear only in the preamble, Article 65 of the constitution makes it clear that the preamble is an integral part of the constitution.

An attempt was made to introduce a regime of separation of powers. However, the government remained a highly centralized system, dominated by a president elected by universal suffrage who holds office for seven years and is eligible for re-election once. The present incumbent, President Paul Biya, has been in power since 1982 and was reelected under this constitution in 1997. The control that the government has over the electoral process and the repeated rejection of demands for the creation of an independent electoral commission to supervise elections makes another term for the incumbent likely. The president has exclusive powers to appoint and dismiss cabinet ministers, judges, generals, provincial

governors, and all senior government officials, as well as the heads of parastatals. In addition, the president can approve or veto any newly enacted legislation and has the power to legislate and rule by decree. Such checks to control presidential power as exist are minimal and practically ineffective, especially with respect to illegal administrative acts that violate the constitution.

Provisions of the amended constitution that provide for a senate to operate as a second chamber of parliament and for some deconcentration of power through the creation of regional and local authorities have not yet been implemented. Legislative power continues to be exercised, as in the past, by a 180-member National Assembly. In the last legislative elections, held in 1997, the ruling Cameroon Democratic Peoples' Movement (CPDM) secured 116 seats in an election process that many national and international observers consider to have been marred by wide-ranging procedural flaws. The constitution restricts the legislative powers of the National Assembly to certain clearly defined matters. But even within this restricted domain, the powers of the National Assembly to initiate or influence the content of legislation are quite limited, since all legislation is usually prepared by the government.

A key innovation in the constitution was the purported elevation of the judiciary to the status of a "judicial power," on the same par as the executive and the legislature. This bold attempt to break with the inherited French tradition, which relegates the judiciary to a mere department of government under the supervision of the Minister of Justice, is compromised, however, by other provisions that make the president the guarantor of this judicial power. There is unlimited scope for political interference with the judiciary, because the president has the power to appoint, promote, transfer, and dismiss judges and other judicial personnel, although the "opinion" of the Higher Judicial Council is required. Occasionally some judges have refused to be intimidated. The most remarkable instance of this occurred in 1992. The Supreme Court, in exercising their power to proclaim the results of the presidential elections of that year, which saw the reelection of President Biya, went out of their way to itemize a series of irregularities that had marred the process, but it pointed out that it had no power to pass any judgment on those irregularities.

Although Article 68 of the amended constitution follows the previous pattern in recognizing the bijural legal system, there remain problems with identifying the law applicable in many areas. It is a problem that has not been diminished by the increasing adoption of "unified" laws applicable in the two legal districts, such as the Penal Code and the Labor Code. There is no consistency in the interpretation or application of these unified laws, because Anglophone and Francophone judges adopt sometimes diametrically opposed methods of statutory interpretation. For instance, Anglophone judges rely heavily on judicial precedent, whereas that is either disregarded or treated as of minor importance in the decision-making process adopted by Francophone judges. Perhaps the most serious problem is that there are no settled, clear, and predictable rules to govern the conflicts that often arise between the laws in the two legal districts. The uncertainly over legal rules has encouraged some form of "forum shopping," with litigants resorting to the legal district that will best serve their interests.

The new constitutional dispensation provided for the creation of a Constitutional Council to take over the functions of controlling the constitutionality of laws from the Supreme Court, as well as ensuring the "regularity of presidential and parliamentary elections." Because of its essentially political nature, it is likely to be less effective than the Supreme Court as a means for ensuring that legislative and administrative acts do not violate the constitution. Despite this, litigants in the Anglophone provinces have on a number of occasions been able to invoke the English common law principles of judicial review to persuade courts there to invalidate illegal administrative acts under circumstances in which no similar remedy can be obtained in the Francophone courts.

CURRENT COURT SYSTEM STRUCTURE

Six main principles underpin the organization of courts and the structure of the system for the administration of justice in the country:

1. Justice must be administered in public. This is to ensure transparency, impartiality, and that justice is not only done but is also seen to be done.
2. Judgments must set out the reasons upon which they are based in fact and in law.
3. Justice is rendered free of charge. This is designed to prevent litigants from bribing judges, but it does not exempt them from paying court and other official fees.
4. Judicial decisions and orders are enforceable throughout the country. This serves to dispel any doubts as to whether court decisions, and orders delivered by the courts in one legal district, are enforceable outside the district.
5. There is unity of criminal and civil courts. This takes account of the fact that due to the shortage of judicial personnel, the same judges sitting at different times in the same court can handle civil and criminal matters but still operate as different divisions of that court.
6. Finally, there is decentralization of the system of administering justice, to make justice quick, inexpensive, and as close to the people as possible.

Based on these principles, courts fall into two categories: courts with ordinary jurisdiction, and courts with special jurisdiction. The former have powers to hear all matters, including civil, criminal, and labor disputes. Save for the Supreme Court, which has jurisdiction over the whole national territory, the ordinary courts are highly decentralized. Within this category there are two types. The first are courts that have original jurisdiction, in the sense that they have the power to hear matters at first instance. These consist of

1. Traditional Law Courts, which operate at village or tribal level;
2. Magistrates' Courts, which operate at subdivisional level, although they usually cover several subdivisions; and
3. High Courts, which operate at divisional level, but they also often cover several divisions.

The second type consists of courts with appellate jurisdiction. While the High Court has limited appellate jurisdiction, the main appellate courts are the courts of appeal, which are located in the headquarters of each of the ten provinces. The Supreme Court sometimes operates as an appellate court, in the sense that, on an application to it, it can quash a judicial decision that it considers to have mistakenly interpreted the law. It does not decide the matter itself, but usually instructs a lower court of standing similar to that of the one from which the matter came to do so. Nevertheless, the Supreme Court has exclusive jurisdiction over all administrative, institutional, and constitutional disputes. Since it is usually saddled with a heavy backlog of administrative and institutional disputes, and has generally been slow and inefficient, a party who "appeals" a matter from the provincial courts to the Supreme Court usually does so more to delay and frustrate the other party than to achieve anything else.

Courts with special jurisdiction deal with either specific matters provided for by law, or a particular class of persons. Besides the Constitutional Council, the amended constitution also provided for the creation of a set of administrative and audit courts, decentralized along the lines of the ordinary courts. With the perennial problem of shortage of qualified personnel, it is not surprising that no steps have been taken to create any of these courts. Perhaps the most that can be expected is that administrative and audit matters might be added to the list of responsibilities that the ordinary courts handle. However, three courts with special jurisdiction operate. First is the Court of Impeachment, which has powers to try the president for treason, as well as ministers and some senior pubic officials for conspiracy against the security of the state. Second is the Military Court, located

Legal Structure of Cameroonian Courts

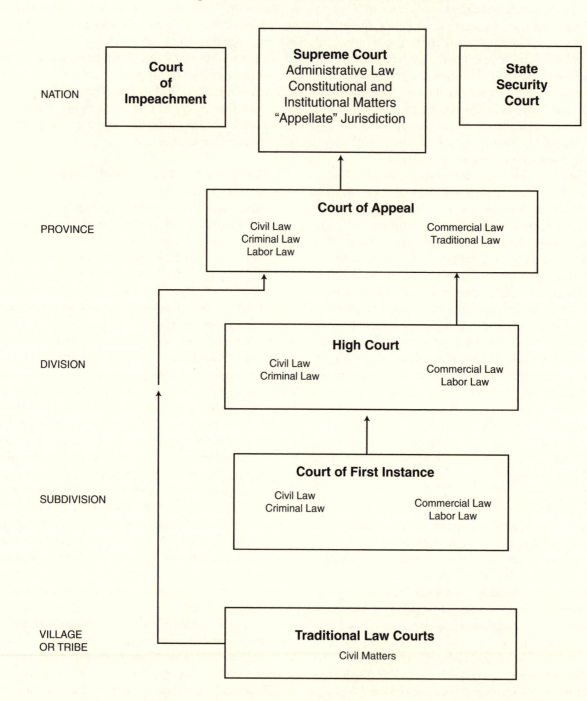

in Yaounde. Its jurisdiction is defined in such broad and vague terms that civilians have been brought and convicted by it under circumstances in which their cases would have been dismissed by the ordinary criminal courts. Finally, there is a State Security Court, which has exclusive jurisdiction to try felonies and misdemeanors against the internal and external security of the state, and related offenses (see figure).

An ongoing economic crisis, rising costs, and the uncertainties of litigation, compounded by judicial corrup-

tion, have led an increasing number of Cameroonians to use the ordinary courts only as a last resort, when private attempts at settlement of their disputes have failed. Disputes within the family are usually brought before the family head, and those within a village or clan before the chief or peer groups within the village or clan. In villages or towns in which clan or tribal links are weak or nonexistent, efforts to resolve disputes are often made through informal mediation by relatives, friends, neighbors, or quarter heads. So far, neither the government nor any of the five national universities that have law programs have initiated any research or studies into alternative dispute settlements mechanisms.

SPECIALIZED JUDICIAL BODIES
No specialized judicial bodies exist. However, the government, in response to repeated criticisms of its human rights record, created the National Commission on Human Rights and Freedoms (NCHRF) in 1990. The NCHRF has conducted many investigations into human rights abuses and has organized several human rights seminars for the training of public officials. While it has rarely publicly condemned the government's human rights abuses, its staff has intervened in many sensitive cases. Since it is prohibited by law from publishing information on specific human rights cases that it has investigated, the NCHRF often submits reports on such abuses to the government, along with its recommendations for improving the situation or punishing violators.

Since 1990, numerous domestic and international human rights NGOs have been authorized to operate in the country. Their activities have consisted mainly of holding seminars and workshops on various aspects of human rights, or issuing press releases or reports on aspects of human rights violations The activities of the local NGOs have been hampered by shortages of funds and the absence of trained personnel.

STAFFING
The Ministry of Justice directs, coordinates, and supervises government policy with regard to the administration of justice, as well as overseeing and supervising its key actors. The latter are made up of persons who dispense or demand justice, such as judges of the bench and prosecuting judges, and the auxiliaries of justice who ensure the smooth operation of the administration of justice by either assisting the judge (for instance, court registrars and judicial police officers) or assisting the parties (such as advocates and notaries).

The judges who preside over traditional law courts are usually appointed by the minister of justice from among notables and other persons knowledgeable in the customs and traditions of the area to be served. Other judges are appointed from among persons with at least a master's degree in law who have undergone a two-year training at the National School of Administration and Magistracy (ENAM) in Yaounde. Entry into the school is by competitive examination, and upon graduation, the intending judge may be appointed either to the bench or to the prosecution department. A judge's career progress depends on seniority and the ability to impress senior judges, although political loyalty and reliability are increasingly beginning to count.

An intending advocate must be a Cameroonian with a law degree who has obtained a certificate of proficiency to practice. This certificate is issued only after two years of study followed by passing a qualifying examination. All advocates are members of the Cameroon Bar Association, which, among other things, maintains discipline among members of the profession.

As regards the auxiliaries of justice, court registrars, who are appointed after studies at ENAM, assist judges by authenticating their acts as well as by keeping a minutes book in which they record all incidents that take place during judicial hearings. Judicial police officers, who may be either police or gendarme officers, help the judge in carrying out criminal investigations. Besides advocates, other auxiliaries of justice who are primarily there to assist the parties in legal proceedings include notaries, who draft legal documents that are then regarded as authentic and enforceable; process-servers, who are responsible for judicial and nonjudicial notifications; and auctioneers, who appraise and value property for sale.

There are no statistics on the number of legal personnel in the country. While it is clear that there is an acute shortage of judges, because only twenty graduate from ENAM each year, there have been attempts in the last few years by the Bar Association to restrict the number of advocates called to the bar, because of a feeling that the market is saturated. Most lawyers are concentrated in the major towns, leaving the rural areas without easy access to legal representation.

IMPACT OF LAW
The coexistence of English and French law in two distinct legal districts, and the multiplicity of traditional laws in an underdeveloped and complex country like Cameroon, which is grappling with a severe economic crisis, have not been easy to deal with. Enormous challenges exist. Many citizens today prefer to resort to self-help measures such as burning or beating suspected thieves to death. Traditional law courts, which still play a very important role in settling disputes in rural areas, still subject suspects to trial by ordeal, such as by drinking poisonous concoctions. There are many Anglophone jurists who feel that there is a trend toward the elimination of the English legal tradition from the Cameroonian system. Confidence in the judiciary has been steadily undermined by incidents of corruption and inefficiency. On October 29, 1999, the minister of justice organized an information week designed to "end the rift between the judiciary and citizens." It is not yet clear how that has helped.

The Cameroon legal system remains a comparative-law melting pot and a potential laboratory for ideas on how the common and civil law can coexist or cross-fertilize. It is hoped that the present struggle to establish a more participatory democratic system will open the vistas to a more scientific process of law reforms in which the best of the inherited bijural culture can be brought together in a more sustainable manner.

Charles Manga Fombad

See also Alternative Dispute Resolution; Constitutional Review; Constitutionalism; Customary law; Judicial Independence; Legal Pluralism; Legal Professionals—Civil Law Traditions

References and further reading
Anyangwe, Carlson. 1987. *The Cameroonian Judicial System.* Yaounde: Ceper.
Enonchong, H. N. A. 1967. *Cameroon Constitutional Law: Federalism in a Mixed Common-Law and Civil-Law System.* Yaounde: Centre d'Edition et de Production de Manuels et Auxiliaires de L'Enseignement.
Fombad, Charles M. 1991. "The Scope for Uniform National Laws in Cameroon." *Journal of Modern African Studies* 29, no. 3: 443–456.
———. 1996. "Judicial Power in Cameroon's Amended Constitution of 18 January 1996." *Lesotho Law Journal* 9: 1–11.
———. 1998. "The New Cameroonian Constitutional Council in a Comparative Perspective: Progress or Retrogression?" *Journal of African Law* 42, no. 2: 172–186.
———. 1999. "Cameroonian Bi-Juralism: Current Challenges and Future Prospects." *Fundamina: Journal of Legal History* 5: 22–43.
Kamto, M. 1996. "Revision constitutionnelle ou ecriture d'une nouvelle constitution?" *Lex Lata* 23/24: 17–20.
Monie, J. N. 1970. *The Development of the Laws and Constitution of Cameroon.* Unpublished Ph.D. thesis. University of London.
———. 1973. "The Influence of German Law in Cameroon." *Annuaire de la Faculte de Droit du Cameroun* 5: 3–12.
Olinga, A. D. 1996. "Le pouvoir executif dans la constitution revisee." *Lex Lata* 23/24: 29–32.
Riou, A. M. 1969. "L'organisation judiciaire du Cameroun." *Penant* 79: 33–86.

CANADA

GENERAL INFORMATION

At 2.1 million square miles, Canada is the second-largest country in the world. Because of its harsh northern climate, only 12 percent of the land is arable. As a result, most of Canada's 31 million people live along the long border with the United States. In 1996, the "mother tongue" of 59 percent of the population was English and for 23 percent it was French; the vast majority of Francophones live in Quebec, one of Canada's ten provinces. Visible minorities make up slightly more than 11 percent of the population. Approximately 900,000 Aboriginal or "First Nations" people are included in Canada's population. Canada has two official languages, French and English, and language is one of two main lines of political cleavage, the other being regional divisions, primarily the western provinces versus the eastern provinces. The economy is advanced and highly integrated with that of the United States, on which Canada is primarily dependent for trade. Automotive products, natural gas and oil, wheat, and timber products are among Canada's major exports to the United States.

Canada, a former colony of Great Britain, is a federal state with a Westminster parliamentary form of government and the queen of England as its head of state. Canada has a system of common law except in the province of Quebec, where the private law is governed by the province's Civil Code. Persistent struggles over public policy authority between the federal government, located in the city of Ottawa, and the provinces and territories characterize Canadian politics. The most intense conflict has been over Quebec's quest for autonomy from English-speaking Canada and its efforts to secede and become an independent country. However, even western, English-speaking provinces like British Columbia and Alberta periodically voice resentment over Ottawa's policies and occasionally express desires for independence. In addition, native peoples and aboriginals have fought both provinces and the federal government over land claims and the administration of native lands. These disputes raise fundamental constitutional issues about the nature of the Canadian federal system, the meaning of citizenship in Canada, and even the future of Canada as a political entity.

Regional conflicts in Canada stem in part from its sprawling size, which historically impeded communication and interprovincial trade while simultaneously encouraging local, isolated views. The interests of the Atlantic provinces of Newfoundland, Prince Edward Island, New Brunswick, and Nova Scotia often differ from those of the western provinces of British Columbia and Alberta. Economic and political resentment of Ontario, the country's largest, richest, and most powerful province, is longstanding. And Quebec's demand that it be recognized as a "distinct society" within Canada and its threats to secede exacerbate and complicate national and provincial politics. It is indicative of the provincial hesitancies with which Canada was formed in 1867 that Newfoundland, preferring to wait for independence as a colony of Britain, reluctantly and narrowly voted in a referendum to join the confederation eighty years later, in 1949.

Canada's current fractured party system reflects these various divisions and the country's recent constitutional turmoil. The Liberal Party, centrist to moderate-left in orientation but primarily pragmatic in governance, won majorities in the past three national elections by capturing almost every federal seat in Ontario. Quebec, at one time pivotal to the success of the Liberals or the Progressive Conservative Party, now votes predominantly for the Bloc Quebecois, an avowedly separatist party formed after the defeat of the Meech Lake Accord in 1990.

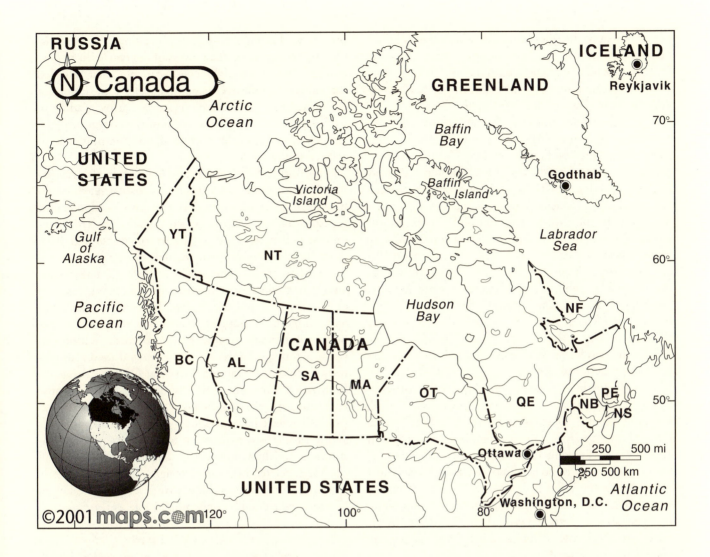

Meech Lake was an attempt by the Progressive Conservative government to reconcile Quebec to the constitutional reforms inaugurated by the Liberal Party in 1982 over the French-speaking province's objections. Two years after the Meech Lake debacle, in 1992, the Progressive Conservative government, through a more comprehensive package of reforms known as the Charlottetown Accord, tried to placate Quebec while broadening support in the rest of Canada for constitutional change. The proposal met defeat in a national referendum. As a result, the Progressive Conservative Party ("Tories"), formed at the time of Canada's confederation in 1867 and over the years the Liberals' chief competitor, virtually disappeared in the next federal election, winning only two seats in Parliament.

The Canadian Alliance has taken the place of the Progressive Conservatives and is currently the Official Opposition in Parliament. A decidedly more conservative, right-wing party than the Tories, and with strong support from the "religious right," the Canadian Alliance is based primarily in Alberta and British Columbia. A fourth party, the New Democratic Party, whose origins were in

a socialist party based in the prairie provinces, has strong ties to labor unions but has slipped at the polls in the past three elections, claiming roughly a dozen seats in the prairie provinces and the maritime province of Nova Scotia. The party system in Canada is thus regionally fractured and ideologically divided. In no small part this is the result of Canada's constitutional crisis over Quebec and historic regional rivalries between the provinces and the federal government.

HISTORY

The first European nation to explore Canada was France, beginning in 1534. By the 1600s, the colony, known as New France, encompassed what is now Quebec and Ontario. French law accompanied colonization and was officially adopted in 1663 in the form of the Coutume de Paris, which remained in force until Quebec, following the example of the Napoleonic Code, codified its laws beginning in 1857. In 1866, the Civil Code of Quebec came into existence, and with modifications it remains in force today. In the areas of property and private law as well as civil procedure, the law of Quebec is very different from that of the rest of Canada. With regard to criminal, constitutional, and administrative law, however, Quebec follows the English common law.

Several years after the conclusion of the Seven Years War between France and Britain, the Treaty of Paris (1763) ceded New France to Britain, which then imposed English common law on the former French colony. Popular resistance by French-speaking Canadiens forced the British to reinstate the Coutume and French civil law with the Quebec Act (1774), although English criminal law remained in force as French criminal law was seen as too harsh. In the Constitution Act of 1791, Britain divided Quebec into two provinces, a predominantly French-speaking Lower Canada and a predominantly English-speaking Upper Canada. Lower Canada retained French civil law while Upper Canada's assembly adopted the English common laws then in effect. After civil unrest in both Canadas in 1837, the two were rejoined through the Union Act (1840). The Act did not alter the laws of the two halves of the united province; this situation continued until confederation in 1867.

Canada became a dominion through negotiations among representatives of the United Provinces of Canada East and Canada West, New Brunswick, Nova Scotia, Prince Edward Island, and Newfoundland that began in 1864 and concluded in 1867. The British Parliament ratified the results of these negotiations through the British North American Act of 1867). The act combines guarantees, details, vague terms, and omissions into something that resembles a treaty between the new federal government and the former colonies rather than a conceptual blueprint for governance.

The British North American Act did not establish a common system of law. Instead, the laws of the provinces at the time they entered confederation continued as law, with the exception of those areas assigned to the federal government. Nor did the act include anything similar to the American Bill of Rights. Protection of Canadian civil liberties and rights rested instead in the guarantee that Canada would have a "Constitution similar in principle to that of the United Kingdom." Over time, "conventions" have filled in the constitutional blanks. Although conventions are a vital part of Canadian constitutional law, they lack the force of law and gain strength only as a result of the political consequences of ignoring or violating them.

Until 1949, the Judicial Committee of the Privy Council in London, which served as the final court of appeal for Britain's colonies including Canada, was the final interpreter of the British North American Act. The Judicial Committee had a major role in changing the balance of authority between the federal government and the provinces. The 1867 act was intended to centralize authority in Ottawa, while limiting the powers of the

provinces. Through a series of decisions, the Judicial Committee separated the powers of the two levels of government into "watertight compartments" that reflected the Judicial Committee's expansive views of the powers of the provinces and its correspondingly narrow reading of federal powers. As a consequence of the committee's decisions, Canadian federalism is among the most decentralized in the world.

The British North American Act remained in Parliament's hands until 1982, when Canada patriated it—renaming it the Constitution Act of 1867—adopted the Constitution Act of 1982, which amended the 1867 document, and entrenched a Charter of Rights and Freedoms. Quebec, feeling that the new charter undermined its ability to preserve the province's language and culture, argued that convention required the unanimous consent of the provinces to these changes. In a controversial reference opinion, the Supreme Court disagreed, stating that only "substantial agreement" was needed. Within ten years, two major efforts, Meech Lake and the Charlottetown Accord, were mounted to meet Quebec's demands. Both failed. One irony of these failures is that because both included changes in how Supreme Court justices would be selected, unanimous agreement by the provinces and territories was required in order to amend the Constitution Act. In October 1995, Quebec held a second provincial referendum on sovereignty that was narrowly defeated. Out of several million votes cast, the breakup of Canada was averted by only 50,000 "no" votes.

LEGAL CONCEPTS

The Charter of Rights and Freedoms marked a shift in Canadian constitutional values. The Constitution Act of 1867 is a governments' constitution resting on the premise of legislative supremacy. It did not include a bill of rights or an enumeration of Canadian civil liberties. Shortly before the start of World War II, Canada's Supreme Court embarked on an effort to develop an implied bill of rights based on an organic view of the written and unwritten elements of Canadian constitutionalism. The ensuing decisions challenged the premise of the "governments' constitution" as the Supreme Court imposed limits on provincial legislative authority. When the Court abruptly ended this project in the late 1970s, popular support grew for constitutional reform that would limit both provincial and federal authority through guaranteed rights enforced by the judiciary. Adding to this support was the weakness of the statutory Canadian Bill of Rights (1960).

The Charter of Rights and Freedoms guarantees "fundamental freedoms," such as religion, belief, expression, assembly, and association. It identifies "democratic rights" like the right to vote and mobility rights. It protects "legal rights" relating to the rights of criminal defendants. It offers protections against discrimination based on various grounds. Official language rights are guaranteed. The charter also provides for the rights of linguistic minorities to a publicly funded education in the language of their choice "where numbers warrant." It includes an equality clause but not a provision protecting property. The charter emboldened the Supreme Court to take a more creative and active role. Judicial review was well established before the Charter of Rights and Freedoms, but it centered on the distribution of legislative powers between the federal government and the provinces. Judicial review is now broader and more policy-oriented.

Reference questions are a distinctive feature of judicial review in Canada. Reference questions are an exception to the general rule in common law that there be an actual dispute for courts to resolve. Instead, references ask courts for advice or guidance on often fundamentally political questions. References occur with some frequency in Canada's Supreme Court. Between 1867 and 1986, slightly more than a quarter of the 351 constitutional cases heard by the Court (or before 1949 the Judicial Committee of the Privy Council) arose first as references. Although the Supreme Court has the discretion not to answer a question posed by a reference, it infrequently declines to use this discretion and in some notable instances, such the Patriation Reference in 1981, has chosen to address questions that have only political content and consequences. As in the instance of Patriation Reference, these advisory opinions have had a notable impact on Canadian politics and society. In 1998, for example, the Supreme Court rendered an advisory opinion that Quebec could secede from Canada through a democratic referendum as long as certain conditions were met, which included Parliament's review of the clarity of the question put to Quebec's citizens.

The Charter of Rights and Freedoms includes two provisions that reflect Canadian politics and history. Section 1 includes a limitation clause that authorizes the courts to balance individual rights against competing societal values. Laws may impose "reasonable limits" on guaranteed rights or freedoms as long as they "can be demonstrably justified in a free and democratic society." Because of this section, judicial review involving the charter has two steps. First, the Supreme Court must decide if the law violates a right. If it does, the court moves to the second stage to decide if the limitation is justified and reasonable and whether the law should be upheld. A less restrictive version of this section, which effectively defines the scope and content of the charter's guarantees, was offered to provincial leaders during negotiations over the charter to win their support. When the provinces refused the compromise, Prime Minister Pierre Trudeau turned to organized interests and minorities as allies to push for

the more stringently worded limitation clause that was included in the charter.

A second feature of the charter is its "notwithstanding" or override clause. In Canada, either Parliament or a provincial legislature can by majority vote overcome any judicial decision involving the charter, although this authority is limited to certain sections of the charter. A legislative majority may suppress the guarantee of a right for a renewable maximum of five years. The clause was inserted at the insistence of provincial premiers who opposed the charter. The notwithstanding clause has been used only once. When the Supreme Court ruled that Quebec's language laws violated the charter, the Quebec National Assembly invoked the clause. The ensuing controversy across the rest of Canada has stilled legislative enthusiasm for the clause. Subsequently, however, a Supreme Court decision reading homosexuality as a prohibited ground for discrimination into Alberta's human rights law prompted calls for the provincial legislature to invoke the clause and override the Court's decision.

Quebec has both common law and civil law. The coexistence of these systems has modified the classic distinctions between them. For example, Quebec judges place considerable importance on stare decisis, a common law concept respecting precedent, which draws them closer to the English system. This tendency reflects the strong influence of the common law, the practice of individual judgment writing (also a common law tradition), and the firm desire of Quebec judges to preserve their province's legal customs through the use of precedent.

STRUCTURE

The Supreme Court of Canada was created by statute in 1875. Unlike the U.S. Supreme Court, Canada's Court does not have constitutional grounding. There are three broad categories of courts in Canada corresponding to the sections of the Constitution Act of 1867 authorizing their establishment. The Supreme Court, the Federal Court of Canada, and the Tax Court were created by Parliament under section 101 of the act. These are "pure" federal courts in that Parliament is solely responsible for staffing, financing, and organizing them. Under section 96, however, the federal and provincial governments share responsibilities for the provinces' appellate courts and superior trial courts.

In Alberta, for example, the Court of Appeal, the province's highest appellate court, and the Court of Queen's Bench, which hears trials in civil and criminal matters and appeals from the lower Provincial Court, are organized and financed by the province. The federal government, however, appoints and pays the salaries of the judges to these section 96 courts. Alberta's Provincial Court, as a section 92 court, is the responsibility solely of the province. In general terms, the provinces, through

Legal Structure of Canadian Courts

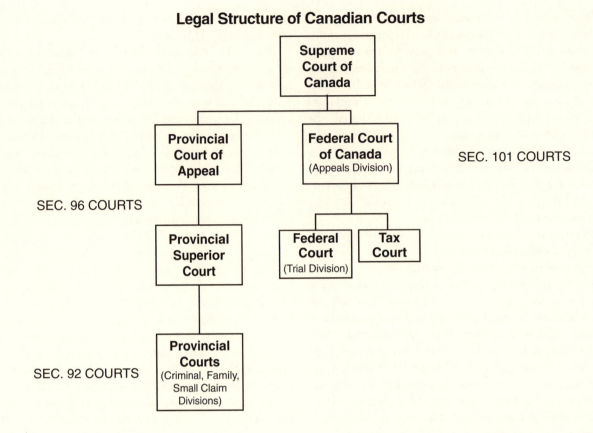

section 96 and section 92, have authority over the administration of justice in the provinces; this includes civil procedure in these courts. Parliament, however, has, as part of its criminal law power, exclusive authority over the procedure in courts of criminal jurisdiction.

Canada's Supreme Court has final authority over the entire body of Canadian law, making the Court the center of a single, national court system. At the same time, the composition of the Supreme Court, comprising a chief justice and eight puisne (lower-ranking) justices, reflects Canada's regional politics. By law three of the justices must come from Quebec, and by convention three come from Ontario, two from Western Canada, and one from the Atlantic provinces. Lowercourt decisions generally may be appealed to the Supreme Court only by leave of the Court. The Supreme Court annually receives between 550 and 650 requests of leave to appeal, and it grants leave to 15–20 percent of those applications.

The provinces divide their court systems into two levels: provincial courts and superior courts. Superior courts are the highest level of court in a province, with power to review the actions of the lower provincial courts. Superior courts have both trial and appellate functions. There may be single court, generally called the Supreme Court, with a trial division and an appeal division. Or, the superior court may be divided into two separate courts, with the trial court named the Supreme Court or the Court of

Queen's Bench, and the appeal court called the Court of Appeal. The trial court hears the more serous civil and criminal cases and has authority to grant divorces. The appeal court hears civil and criminal appeals from the superior trial court. The names and structures of the superior courts and their divisions vary from province to province. The jurisdiction of these courts includes disputes arising in many areas involving federal law, such as criminal law and banking.

Provincial courts, the lowest courts with limited jurisdiction, deal with most criminal matters and in some provinces with civil cases involving smaller amounts of money. The provincial court level may also include certain specialized courts, such as youth and family courts. There are numerous judicial officers in the provincial courts who operate as judges under certain circumstances. They include hearing officers, magistrates, adjudicators, and justices of the peace, commissioners, "masters," or "prothonataries." These officials perform many pretrial, informal, and formal court proceedings. They may assess penalties under summary conviction on criminal code offenses, set bail, release prisoners on bail, or issue search warrants.

SPECIALIZED JUDICIAL BODIES
Because of their impact on public policies, the Canadian Human Rights Commission and Human Rights Tribunal

Panel are especially significant bodies. In 1977, Parliament passed the Canadian Human Rights Act. The legislation covers distinctions based on race, national, or ethnic origin, color, religion, age, sex (including pregnancy and childbirth), marital status, family status, mental or physical disability (including previous or present drug or alcohol dependence), pardon of conviction of a crime, or sexual orientation. The provinces have similar but not necessarily identical legislation and have established provincial human rights commissions.

The Canadian Human Rights Commission investigates complaints of rights violations. If it decides an inquiry is warranted it forwards the complaint to the Human Rights Tribunal for adjudication. Between 1988 and 1997, the commission received about 7,450 complaints (excluding pay equity complaints) and made final decisions on some 6,550 of them. About 6 percent of the complaints were forwarded to the tribunal for inquiry. The commission tries to settle complaints through conciliation, and the tribunal tries to mediate complaints when the commission forwards them for inquiry. Since 1996, about 18 percent of the complaints have been settled through early resolution or conciliation.

A final note should be taken of aboriginal circle courts. Unlike traditional courts, in circle courts the judge, police, social workers, tribal band officials, victims, and convicted person meet to consider an appropriate sentence. Circle sentencing arose out of a Supreme Court of the Yukon case in 1992 and has become increasingly popular in native communities and cities with large native populations. Circle courts attempt to integrate native culture with Canadian law by emphasizing "balance," through the participation of those included in the circle court, and "responsibility," by recognizing the relationships of the offender to the community. Circle courts attempt to heal the relationships disrupted by the offender instead of merely meting out punishment, which from the native perspective relieves the offender of responsibility for the crime.

STAFFING

There are about 2,300 judges in Canada. All of them are appointed either by the federal government or by the provinces. The federally appointed section 101 and section 96 judges totaled 1,014 (as of April 2000), while there were roughly 1,300 provincially appointed section 91 judges. Federally appointed judges must have at least ten years of experience as a lawyer or provincial judge. All judges are subject to mandatory retirement. For some federally appointed judges, the age of retirement is fixed at seventy-five by the Constitution Act of 1867. For all other judges, both federally and provincially appointed, the age is fixed by statute at either seventy-five or seventy depending on the court.

Ottawa's appointment authority centralizes Canada's court system. In the instance of the section 101 courts, the governor general, the titular representative of the Crown, on the advice of the cabinet appoints the nine judges of the Supreme Court, the twenty-five judges of Federal Court, and the ten judges of the Tax Court. In the minutes of a cabinet meeting in 1896, however, the prime minister was granted the prerogative to appoint with the formal approval of the cabinet all the Supreme Court justices, the chief judge of the Federal Court of Canada (at that time the Court of Exchequer), and the chief justices of the section 96 appellate and trial courts.

The basic process of federal judicial appointments has existed since 1988. This process, with the exception of Supreme Court and chief judge appointments, applies to the appointment of judges to the superior courts of the provinces and territories, the Federal Court of Canada, and the Tax Court of Canada. Qualified lawyers seeking an appointment apply to the commissioner for federal judicial affairs. Other interested persons and organizations can nominate candidates for judicial office. The commissioner then forwards the candidate's file to the appropriate provincial or territorial committee for assessment. Advisory committees exist in each province and territory; Ontario has three regionally based committees and Quebec has two. Four of the seven positions on the committees are filled on the basis of nominations made at the provincial level, and the justice minister appoints the other three representatives. The committees rank candidates as "recommended," "highly recommended," or "unable to recommend." The ranking is advisory only. The committees review only persons not currently holding judicial office and do not assess current provincial or territorial judges seeking promotion to a higher court, although they may comment on their candidacy.

The minister of justice consults with the appropriate provincial chief judge as well as the attorney general or minister of justice of the jurisdiction involved. Cabinet involvement in the appointment process is often significant. Individual ministers, especially those responsible for patronage in a province where an appointment is being made, may intervene and even veto the justice minister's recommendations. The prime minister's influence, of course, extends considerably beyond the appointment of chief judges. The role of the justice minister in turn depends greatly on the support of the prime minister and the goals and concerns that the prime minister hopes to achieve through the appointment of judges.

The appointment process for judges in section 92 courts varies somewhat across the provinces and territories. Most employ some form of screening committee or nominating commission as a preliminary stage. The attorney general in each province has final authority to appoint judges. Judicial councils in British Columbia and

Alberta, for example, interview and screen all candidates for judge or justice of the peace to determine their qualifications. In Ontario, the Judicial Appointments Advisory Committee has these responsibilities. The committee includes seven lay members appointed by the attorney general and six lawyers, two of them appointed by the chief justice of the Ontario Court of Justice (the province's section 92 court) and one each by the Law Society of Upper Canada, the Ontario Judicial Council, the Canadian Bar Association, and the County and District Law Presidents' Association.

The Canadian Judicial Council, created by Parliament in 1971, is a statutory body composed of the federally appointed chief justices. The purpose of the council is to promote efficiency and quality of judicial service in the superior courts and the Tax Court of Canada. The chief justice of the Supreme Court chairs the council. The other members are drawn from those courts whose judges are federally appointed. The council works with the Canadian Judges Conference, an association of all federally appointed judges, to develop proposals. The provinces in most instances have similar judicial councils to hear complaints against provincially appointed judges. The Office of the Commissioner for Federal Judicial Affairs has responsibility for paying the salaries, allowances, and other benefits to federally appointed judges. The National Judicial Institute, established in 1988, coordinates and provides training programs and continuing education services to all of Canada's judges.

The council makes enquiries and investigates complaints of misconduct made against members of the federally appointed judiciary. Under the Constitution Act of 1867, judges "shall hold office during good behavior" and can only be removed by Parliament. Only five petitions for the removal of a superior court judge have ever been filed with Parliament, and in none of those cases did Parliament vote on the petition. Between 1992 and 2000, an average of 170 complaints a year were filed with the council. Nearly 95 percent of the cases were closed as inappropriate or groundless.

The Canadian Association of Provincial Judges is a federation of provincial and territorial judges' associations. Founded in 1973, its membership now includes most of the provincial and territorial judges. The purpose of the association is to promote the interests of the provincially appointed judges. It is involved in law reform, continuing education, and especially issues regarding judicial independence in the courts. The association has an extensive committee structure throughout Canada to press its concerns on specific issues.

In 1995, there were approximately 61,500 lawyers (*advocats* in Quebec) in Canada with more than one-third (24,400) located in Ontario. The individual law societies of the provinces and territories license and regulate the attorneys in their respective jurisdiction. All lawyers must be members of a law society. The distinction between barrister and solicitor is no longer meaningful in Canada and the title Queen's Counsel is mostly honorific and does not necessarily indicate special trial or appellate skills. Lawyers may receive training in either the common law or civil law, although most lawyers with degrees in civil law practice in Quebec. Six universities offer legal education in civil law; five are located in Quebec and one is in Ottawa.

IMPACT

For more than forty years after Quebec's "Quiet Revolution" and the rise of Quebec nationalism, Canada has engaged in broad constitutional reform. It patriated its constitution and added the Charter of Rights and Freedoms, in part to create a pan-Canadian identity transcending provincial allegiances, and then tried to amend its constitution through the Meech Lake initiative and the Charlottetown Accord in ways that would end Quebec's self-imposed exile from the Constitution Act of 1982. These efforts failed, and in October 1995 Quebec nearly seceded from Canada. The impact of constitutional politics on the unity of Canada is thus mixed. On the one hand, the country remains intact; on the other hand Quebec separatism, while waxing and waning, has not been decisively thwarted by the legal framework constructed by the charter, by Supreme Court decisions and reference opinions, and by Parliament's actions. Moreover, a contributing factor to alienation in the Western provinces (particularly Alberta), all of which see Ottawa as treating them in a high-handed, possibly exploitive manner, is the enhanced power of the Supreme Court of Canada under the charter.

The vast majority of Canadians, both anglophone and francophone, nevertheless express strong support for the charter, although there are significant regional differences in this support as well as differences between political elites and citizens across the provinces. The inauguration of the charter, however, reflected ongoing, preexisting changes in Canadian values. Organized interests concerned with the rights eventually entrenched in Canada's constitution emerged before 1982 and the adoption of the charter. When combined with a growing, increasingly professional legal community, these two factors fostered an infrastructure for the lobbying, publicizing, and litigation that eventually shaped the charter's content. Deference to authority also has declined in Canada while rights consciousness has increased. Very probably, even if the constitutional moments in Canada centering on the unity question had not occurred, rights discourse in the media and law schools still would have increased during the 1990s because of the charter and Supreme Court decisions.

Roy B. Flemming

See also Alberta; British Columbia; Civil Law; Common Law; Manitoba; New Brunswick; Newfoundland and Labrador; Northern Territories of Canada; Nova Scotia; Ontario; Prince Edward Island; Quebec; Saskatchewan

References and further reading
Heard, Andrew. 1991. *Canadian Constitutional Conventions: The Marriage of Law and Politics.* Toronto: Oxford University Press.

Hogg, Peter W. 1997. *Constitutional Law of Canada. 4th ed.* Toronto: Carswell.

McRoberts, Kenneth, and Patrick Monahan, eds. 1993. *The Charlottetown Accord, the Referendum, and the Future of Canada.* Toronto: University of Toronto Press.

Monahan, Patrick J. 1991. *Meech Lake: The Inside Story.* Toronto: University of Toronto Press.

Moore, Christopher. 1997. *1867: How the Fathers Made a Deal.* Toronto: McClelland and Stewart.

Morton, F. L., and Rainer Knopff. 2000. *The Charter Revolution and the Court Party.* Peterborough, NH: Broadview Press.

Russell, Peter H. 1987. *The Judiciary in Canada: The Third Branch of Government.* Toronto: McGraw-Hill Ryerson.

Sheppard, Robert, and Michael Valpry. 1984. *The National Deal: The Fight for a Canadian Constitution.* Toronto: Macmillan of Canada.

Sniderman, Paul M., et al. 1996. *The Clash of Rights: Liberty, Equality, and Legitimacy in Pluralist Democracy.* New Haven, CT: Yale University Press.

Strayer, Barry L. 1988. *The Canadian Constitution and the Courts.* 3rd ed. Toronto: Butterworths.

CANADA, NORTHERN
See Northern Territories of Canada

CANON LAW

Canon law—a term derived from the Greek word meaning "rule or measurement"—refers to the body of ecclesiastical law proper to the Roman Catholic Church. Regulating the external and visible life of the institutions and members of the community of faith, canon law is an essential part of the church's nature and mission. The church has both a divine and a human dimension, and it is believed that the human side must be regulated and structured in order to achieve the church's purpose and carry out its mandate to proclaim the gospel, celebrate the sacraments, and be of service to all who search for truth and holiness.

Like all legal systems, canon law is designed to assist in the attainment of the common good of society, and to afford stability and order. In addition, it is intended to protect and defend the rights of church members and to remind all of the values and standards that the church upholds. Unlike other legal systems, the ultimate purpose of canon law is the sanctification and salvation of those who belong to the Catholic faith.

THE HISTORICAL DEVELOPMENT OF CANON LAW

Church law has a long and detailed history. For many centuries, it was a collection of legislative acts and decisions derived from the writings of popes, the rulings of local, provincial, and general councils, and the opinions of learned jurists. Custom also played an important role in the legal history of the church. All of these elements would combine to become the rule (canon) for the administration of justice in the community. The historical development of canon law can be divided into five basic periods.

From the Apostles to the Time of Gratian
Within this long span of time can be found several subperiods. The first (beginning between 30 and 60 C.E.) lasted nearly sixty years and saw the establishment of the Christian religion in the Roman Empire. A new way of thinking evolved with the advent of Christianity's hierarchical structure and community practices, especially in terms of worship, discipline, finances, and relations with the non-Christian world. In the second subperiod (from 100 to 325 C.E.), the primitive structures of the early church gained in prominence with the publication of new sources of doctrine contained in the ancient writings of the Patristic Fathers. It was during this time that the oldest known canonical document, *The Apostolic Tradition,* was written by Saint Hippolytus. Ecclesiastical structures in terms of church organization and disciplinary law continued to develop despite harsh persecutions. The importance of local church councils and the development of penitential practices were significant in regard to disciplinary matters during this time. In the third subperiod (from 325 to 600 C.E.), the first canonical collections began to be gathered, especially the legislation of popes and the decrees of ecumenical councils such as those of Nicaea and Constantinople. Important juridical texts, including the *Apostolic Constitutions, Codex Ecclesaie Africanae,* and *The Dionysiana,* were major contributions to the development of canon law. During the fourth subperiod (from 600 to 850 C.E.), universal norms in terms of directories for clerics were introduced, and collections on various matters of worship and discipline were exchanged. Moreover, the impediments inherent in Roman law were acknowledged, and the political supremacy of the Roman pontiff was recognized. In addition, this period produced one of the more influential authors of the seventh century in the person of Saint Isidore of Seville. The fifth subperiod (from 850 to 1075 C.E.) witnessed the writings of reformers in regard to legislation, collections, and institutions. It was during this subperiod that efforts to establish episcopal authority over monarchs and the Oriental churches occurred. As well, the period saw an ongoing struggle against the practice of simony and

clerical excesses. The so-called *False Decretals* and the specialized canonical collections on marriage and sexual questions gained a place of eminence in the church of the ninth and tenth centuries, and one of the most long-standing institutions in the church, the College of Cardinals, was finally recognized. The sixth subperiod (from 1075 to 1140 C.E.) was greatly influenced by Pope Gregory VII, who saw to it that he and his successors became the source of all canonical authority in the church. In addition, numerous canonical collections continued to surface, many based on the *False Decretals* of the previous centuries. Furthermore, a number of traditions and procedures that would become institutionalized over time developed in this period, such as the election of bishops by cathedral chapters, the founding of religious brotherhoods, and the increasingly popular practice of indulgences. Perhaps the most profound contribution of this period in canon law was the establishment of the great universities of Rome, Bologna, and Paris, which engaged in the study of both canon and civil law.

From the Twelfth Century to the Sixteenth Century

During this 400-year period, perhaps the most significant era in the history of canon law, three significant developments occurred. First, over an 18-year span (from 1140 to 1158 C.E.), the contribution of the Camaldolese monk Gratian lead to the systematic and scientific approach to canon law. His classic achievement, *Concordia Discordantium Canonum* (The Decretum of Gratian), provided the first detailed exposition and synthesis of all canonical matters up to that time. Gratian's collection contains over 3,000 texts, dealing with various dogmatic, pastoral, and disciplinary subjects. Although essentially a private work, containing many omissions and uncertainties, it remains to this day an important and significant document in the study of canon law. Second, what has become known as the "golden age" of canon law produced yet another important collection, the *Corpus Iuris Canonici,* which was the main source of canonical law until the promulgation of the 1917 Code of Canon Law. Under the diligent guidance of four popes—Alexander III, Innocent III, Gregory IX, and Boniface VIII—five classical canonical works were undertaken. The first of these, the *Quinque Compilationes Antiquae,* parts of which had been officially promulgated, was followed by the *Decretals of Gregory IX* in 1234. Pope Gregory's work contained an authentic and universal collection of law in five books. In 1298, Pope Boniface promulgated the *Liber Sextus,* which contained the rules of law and an authentic canonical collection. Other major works included the *Clementinae* (from the constitutions of Pope Clement V) and the *Extravagantes* of John XXII, both published in 1317, as well as the *Extravagants Communes,* published from 1303 through 1484. Finally, the second period also saw the development of judicial procedure in the practice of canon law.

From the Council of Trent to the Promulgation of the 1917 Code of Canon Law

Two significant developments occurred in this period. First, as the church and canon law in general attempted to adapt to the modern age, anintense activity in the development of canon law took place over the course of 300 years. Under the great legislator Pope Benedict XIV, all ecclesiastical institutions were renewed and great canonical collections were published, among them the *Magnum Bullarium Romanum* and the *Acta Sanctae Sedis.* Furthermore, encyclical letters were used extensively, Roman congregations were established, many religious congregations were founded, the office of the defender of the bond was set up, and the use of mandatory appeal was introduced in canonical trials. Second, papal leadership in the church was further developed. During the nineteenth century in particular, centralization of authority in the church and papal infallibility were promoted to counter the effects of the decline of the papal states.

Ultimately, as the nineteenth century drew to a close, it was recognized that many of the church's canonical regulations had lost their relevance. In addition, they had multiplied dramatically over time. It became clear that a substantial revision was needed.

From 1904 to 1959

The fathers of Vatican I requested a codification of all existing laws in the church, and on March 19, 1904, Pope Pius X began the long process of preparing for this codification by appointing the scholarly canonist Cardinal Pietro Gasparri as head of a special commission. After 13 years of consultations and various draftings, Pope Benedict XV promulgated the first official Code of Canon Law in one volume on May 27, 1917 (it went into effect on May 19, 1918), and roughly four months later (on September 15, 1917), the first official pontifical commission to interpret the code was established. Influenced by both Roman and Germanic sources, the code consisted of 2,414 canons organized in 5 books: (1) *General Norms,* (2) *Persons,* (3) *Things,* (4) *Procedures,* and (5) *Crimes and Penalties.* It would be the official law of the church until 1983.

Subsequent legislation followed, such as a partial promulgation of canon law for the Oriental churches in terms of marriage legislation, procedural law, law for religious and temporal goods, and persons in the church. Both Pope Pius XII and Pope John XXIII provided further changes in the law by introducing legislation on such things as the Eucharistic fast, the minister of confirmation, cardinals, time for the celebration of the Mass, and the form of marriage, to list but a few.

From January 25, 1959, to January 25, 1983
On January 25, 1959, Pope John XXIII announced the revision of the Code of Canon Law, along with the convocation of a synod for the Diocese of Rome and the convening of an ecumenical council, Vatican II. However, after the first session of Vatican II, Pope John died and was succeeded by the cardinal-archbishop of Milan, who became known as Paul VI. One of his first acts was to recall the council and continue the work begun by his predecessor. Soon after the conclusion of the council, Pope Paul began the daunting task of revising the existing Code of Canon Law. The revision would be the last of the council documents to be officially proclaimed. A committee of cardinals, bishops, canonists, and others diligently undertook the actual work of revision, after adopting the ten guiding principles approved by the 1967 Synod of Bishops. Finally on January 25, 1983, Pope John Paul II promulgated the new Code of Canon Law for the Latin church.

WHAT CAN BE FOUND IN THE 1983 CODE OF CANON LAW?

The 1983 Code of Canon Law can be described as a minilibrary of sorts, with its varied literary forms ranging from exhortations and admonitions to directives, precepts, and prohibitions. It is divided into seven books, each dealing with a specific subject. Using the theology and language of Vatican II, the present code concentrates on the three functions of the church: teaching, sanctifying, and governing. Book 1, entitled *General Norms,* consists of 203 canons dealing with terms, persons, tools, and structures found throughout the other canonical books. This book is a key to understanding the very background of canon law. Book 2, *People of God,* takes its title from Vatican II's image of the church. Within the covers of this most important book of the code can be found the basic constitution of the church. In 542 canons, topics such as rights and obligations, the Christian faithful, the hierarchy, and religious, universal, diocesan, and parish structures are addressed. Book 3, *The Teaching Office of the Church,* has 86 canons and covers topics such as the ministry of the word, catechetical formation, missionary activity, Catholic education, social communication, and the profession of faith. In Book 4, *The Sanctifying Office of the Church,* 419 canons are devoted to the sacraments, sacramentals, sacred places, and sacred times. The shortest book of the Code of Canon Law is Book 5, entitled *Temporal Goods of the Church,* which deals with the rules and regulations guiding the acquisition, administration, and alienation of church funds and property. In addition, canons on wills and bequests are included. With 88 canons, Book 6 is entitled *Sanctions in the Church.* The final book in the 1983 Code of Canon Law, *Processes,* deals with procedural law in the church. In 352 canons, it outlines the processes to be employed in church tribunals. These tribunals most often deal with marriage nullity cases as well as other administrative processes.

ARE ALL THE LAWS OF THE CHURCH FOUND IN THE CODE OF CANON LAW?

The Code of Canon Law promulgated for the Latin church on January 25, 1983, is only one part of the whole collection of laws for the universal church. In addition to the 1983 code, the twenty-one autonomous churches in union with Rome also have a code. As early as 1929, work on a code common to all these churches began, but it was not until October 18, 1990, that Pope John Paul II issued the apostolic constitution *Sacri Canones,* promulgating the *Codex Canonum Ecclesiarum Orientalium* (The Code of Canons of the Eastern Churches). This work is divided into 30 titles, with a total of 1,546 canons dealing with matters such as the rights and obligations of the Christian faithful, authority in the churches, the teaching office of the church, divine worship, temporal goods of the church, procedural law, and penalties. Each of the autonomous churches develops its own particular law.

In addition to the two Codes of Canon Law, another source of law in the church is to be found in the apostolic constitution *Pastor Bonus.* Issued on June 28, 1988, by Pope John Paul II, this constitution spells out the law pertaining to the various departments of the Roman Curia, such as the secretary of state, the nine Vatican congregations, the three tribunals, the twelve pontifical councils, and a variety of other offices. These three laws constitute the main body of church law.

Many other laws govern specific matters, including the vacancy of the apostolic see and the election of the pope, the procedures to be followed for the canonization of the saints, and the spiritual care of military people. In addition, particular laws for individual countries have been promulgated by the Bishops Conferences on a wide variety of matters, such as diocesan consulters, the term of office for pastors, the catechumenate, the minimum age for the lawful celebration of marriage in the church, the celebration of Holy Days of Obligation, and the days of fast and abstinence, among many others. Unlike other legal systems, canon law is never static—it continually develops in order to adapt itself to the ever changing needs of the church in a particular time and place.

Michael D. McGowan

See also Vatican
References and further reading
Beal, John, James Coriden, and Thomas Green, eds. 2000. *New Commentary on the Code of Canon Law.* New York: Paulist Press.
Coriden, James. 1991. *An Introduction to Canon Law.* New York: Paulist Press.

De Agar, Joseph M. 1999. *A Handbook on Canon Law.* Montreal: Wilson and Lafleur Limitée.

Huels, John. 1995. *A Canon Law Handbook for Catholic Ministry.* Quincy, IL: Franciscan Press.

McKenna, Kevin. 2000. *A Concise Guide to Canon Law: A Practical Handbook for Pastoral Ministers.* Notre Dame, IN: Ave Maria Press.

Sheehy, Gerald, Ralph Brown, Donal Kelly, Aidan McGrath, eds., and Francis G. Morrisey, consultant ed. 1995. *The Canon Law Letter and Spirit: A Practical Guide to the Code of Canon Law.* Collegeville: Liturgical Press.

CAPE VERDE

COUNTRY INFORMATION

The Republic of Cape Verde is one of the smallest of the African countries. It consists of a group of islands situated in the Atlantic Ocean about 650 kilometers west of Senegal, with a total area of only 4,035 square kilometers. The population is 407,000 persons, about 80 percent of them Creoles (mixed-blood descendants of African slaves and Portuguese settlers). Some 17 percent of the population is Black and only 3 percent White. Cape Verde became independent in 1975, but the cultural inheritance from Portugal remains strong: the official language is Portuguese, almost all inhabitants are Roman Catholics, etc. The same applies to the legal system, which is strongly entrenched in the civil-law tradition inherited from Portugal. The continued poverty of the country (the GNP is about U.S.\$1,000 per capita) and the high rate of unemployment are the two main reasons for substantial emigration of Cape Verdeans, mainly to Portugal and the United States. The number of Cape Verdeans living abroad is said to be substantially higher than the whole resident population of the country. Remittances from the emigrant workers account for a great part of the country's income, as does foreign aid (some 20 percent of GNP originates from foreign donors). The export of labor has successively become much more difficult, due to the increasingly restrictive immigrations policies in European and North American countries.

HISTORY

The islands were uninhabited prior to the arrival of the Portuguese in 1462. The Portuguese turned the islands into a bastion of their slave trade between Africa and the New World. The termination of the slavery activities in the nineteenth century led to an economic decline, but it seems that the Portuguese considered their continued control of the islands to be more important than the control of some of the richer colonies, maybe because of the relative geographical proximity to Portugal. Being light-skinned, Portuguese-speaking (although the everyday communication takes place in a local Creole dialect), and partly of Portuguese stock, the inhabitants of Cape Verde benefited from the first school for higher education in any Portuguese colony, and they were often employed as minor officials in the administration of the various parts of the Portuguese colonial empire. Nevertheless, it seems that the population of the islands developed a sense of national identity oriented toward Africa rather than Portugal. This resulted in the formation of PAIGC (African Party for the Independence of Guinea-Bissau and Cape Verde), and participation in the struggle for independence launched in the other Portuguese colonies in Africa. The guerrilla tactics employed with some success in the jungles of Angola, Guinea-Bissau, and Mozambique were, however, hardly suitable for small, isolated islands far out in an ocean. In spite of a unilateral declaration of independence in 1973, Cape Verde did not achieve real sovereignty until 1975, after a revolution had taken place in Portugal itself, replacing a conservative dictatorship there with a left-wing regime.

The original aim of PAIGC was to create a union of Guinea-Bissau and Cape Verde, but this aim has not been materialized. Cape Verde became a one-party state led by a successor of PAIGC, the Marxist-oriented African Independence Party of Cape Verde (PAICV). Over some fifteen years, the country was under the influence of the Soviet Union and other Marxist-Leninist states such as Cuba. The one-party system, which was entrenched in the 1980 Constitution, was abandoned in 1990. This democratic revolution was peaceful and orderly. The first democratic multiparty elections were held in 1991, when a right-wing party, the Movement for Democracy (MPD), took over after winning about 70 percent of the seats in the Parliament and began to implement a number of political and economic reforms (this perestroika went under the name of Mudança). The process of economic transition, aiming at replacing the socialist-oriented economy with an open market economy based on a dominant and dynamic private sector, has not yet been quite terminated, in spite of many important steps that have been taken during the 1990s (a comprehensive tax reform; liberalization of prices; reversal of the socialist agrarian reform enacted in 1981; increased flexibility of the labor market by means of a revision of the labor legislation; new law protecting foreign investments; creation of tax-free export-processing zones; transformation of the Cape Verde escudo into a convertible currency; creation of a stock market, etc.). In particular, the privatization of certain state enterprises has been delayed due to, inter alia, the resistance of the management and the trade unions. However, it must be added that Cape Verde has never been a truly socialist country of the Soviet type with a dominant centrally planned, state-owned economy. In 1990, just before the abandonment of the so-

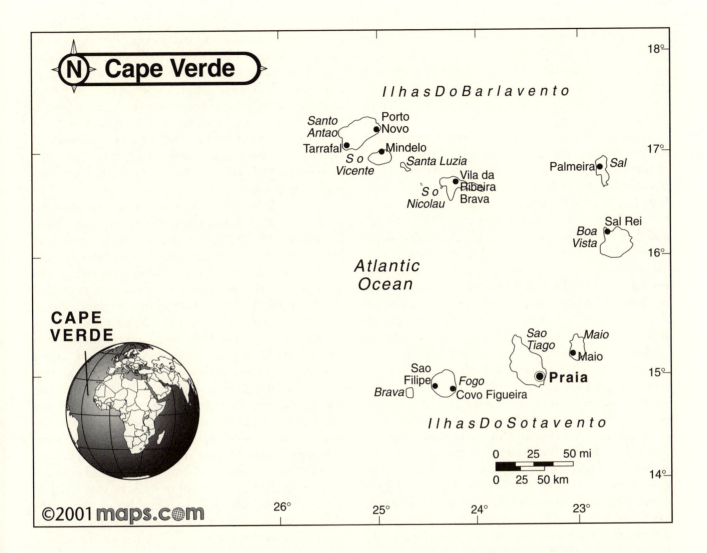

cialist model, the state enterprises accounted for less than half of the total economy, although the figures varied between the various sectors.

LEGAL CONCEPTS

The present Constitution of Cape Verde, in both structure and contents strikingly similar to the Constitution of Portugal, was promulgated on September 4, 1992. It replaced the Marxist-oriented political constitution of 1980, and introduced a democratic system of government, based on political pluralism and the balancing of powers among the various organs of state power, including an independent judiciary. The constitution was amended in 1999, although most of the changes are of a technical nature. Among the more important substantive changes is the creation of the institution of ombudsman and of the Constitutional Court.

The preamble of the constitution mentions that the previous (pre-1992) organization of state power had followed the philosophy and principles characteristic of one-party-rule regimes. The preamble also gives an indication of why this previous system had to be abandoned, apparently hinting at the dramatic changes that had taken place in Eastern Europe and elsewhere: "New ideas spread out around the world bringing down structures and conceptions, which seemed to be entrenched, and changing completely the course of international political events."

Article 1 of the constitution defines Cape Verde as a sovereign, unitary, and democratic republic, guaranteeing respect for the dignity of the human person and recognizing the inviolability and inalienability of human rights as the foundation of the whole human community, peace, and justice. The same article recognizes the equality of all citizens before the law, without distinction as to social origin or economic status, race, sex, religion, or political or ideological convictions. Article 2 declares the state to be based on, inter alia, the rule of law, pluralist democracy, separation and interdependence of powers, separation between the church and the state, and the independence of the courts. In particular, the rule of law is repeatedly stressed in several articles, for example in Article 3, providing that the state shall be subordinated to the constitution, abide by the principle of democratic legality, and respect the law.

The constitution contains an impressive list of rights and freedoms—and even some duties—of citizens, including all the standard provisions on the freedom of expression, religion, association, assembly, etc. It is important to note that in contrast to many other African countries, the constitutionally protected rights and freedoms appear to be intended to be more than mere political declarations without real legal value. First of all, the constitution provides for judicial review of the constitutionality of inferior legal norms. Furthermore, it stipulates that the state and other public entities shall bear civil liability for violations of these constitutional provisions, and that the officials shall bear criminal and disciplinary responsibility for such violations. The constitution grants each citizen the right to disobey any order that offends his rights and freedoms, and to resist by force any illegal act, when the recourse to the public authority is not possible. The citizens are given extensive rights to petition and complain, including the right to institute court proceedings pursuant to the provisions on habeas corpus.

Only a small part of the many other constitutionally protected substantive rights and freedoms can be mentioned here, the focus being on those provisions that are of particular legal interest. Article 21 protects every citizen's right of access to justice for a reasonable price, and the right of defense and counsel. The same article obligates the courts to provide redress within a reasonable period of time. Article 27 prohibits the death penalty and Article 32 does the same with regard to imprisonment for life: No penalty depriving a person of liberty shall be of a permanent character or of an unlimited or indefinite duration. The maximum prison sentence imposed by the penal code is presently twenty-four years, under especially aggravating circumstances thirty years, with the possibility of parole after having served about half of the time. Retroactive application of penal law to the detriment of the accused is forbidden. In penal procedures, any evidence obtained through illicit means "shall be null and void."

Article 253 contains since 1999 a description of the newly created Provedor de Justiça, which is an ombudsman-like institution copied from the Portuguese Constitution. It is an independent organ, elected by the Parliament, and all state organs and instrumentalities are under an obligation to cooperate with it. Everyone has the right to present complaints regarding acts and omissions of public authorities to the ombudsman, who does not have the power to make any binding decisions but may make recommendations to competent organs in order to prevent and correct illegalities and injustices. More detailed regulation of the activities of the ombudsman is to be enacted by Parliament.

Cape Verde's constitution follows the example of Portugal and prohibits the utilization of computerized means for registration and treatment of data that are individually identifiable, relative to political, philosophical, and ideological convictions or to religious faith, party, or trade union affiliation and private life, unless the person concerned has explicitly consented to it. A special form of action, *habeas data,* gives every citizen a right of access to information stored in files, archives, or computerized records concerning him, as well as to be informed of the objective of such information and to demand a correction or updating of it.

Articles 90–94 deal with the economic system of the country. It follows from these provisions that Cape Verde has a mixed public-private economy. The coexistence of both sectors is explicitly guaranteed, as is "the equality of conditions for the establishment, realization and competition of all economic actors." This seems to mean that the state must not discriminate against the private sector, for example by excessive taxation. The state shall support foreign investments and the integration of Cape Verde into the world economic system. A number of articles support the creation of a market economy by protecting its various preconditions, such as the right to free economic initiative, the right to private property, and the right to choose freely one's occupation, work, or profession. Less compatible with the principles of market economy appears to be the provision of every citizen's right to work, although it follows from the wording that this is more an ambition on the part of the state than an actually enforceable legal right of citizens. In fact, the constitution grants quite a few social rights that the state can hardly afford to provide.

The Parliament of Cape Verde (the National Assembly) is elected for five years through an electoral system based mainly on the principle of proportional representation. It has some exclusive legislative powers, but many legislative tasks can be and are entrusted by the Parliament to the government, which is the supreme organ of public administration. Even such important pieces of legislation as the new Code on Commercial Enterprises or the new edition of the civil code have been enacted by executive orders on the basis of parliamentary authorization. This practice, which seems to have Portuguese roots, is not considered controversial; local lawyers are of the opinion that legislation requiring legal expertise should not be left in the hands of politicians.

The government is politically responsible to and must enjoy the confidence of the Parliament. The head of state is the president of the republic, who is elected by direct ballot for a period of five years. He has many important functions, among them to appoint and dismiss the prime minister and other members of the government, but he must consult the political parties and take into account the results of parliamentary elections. As in the United States, he has power to veto legislation, although his veto can be overridden by an absolute majority of all members of Parliament.

The constitutional reform of 1999 created the Constitutional Court. However, until the establishment of a functioning Constitutional Court, which may take some time, its duties are discharged by the Supreme Court of Justice. The future Constitutional Court shall consist of three professional judges, elected by the Parliament for nine years and not eligible for reelection. The constitution recognizes both an abstract and a concrete judicial review of the constitutionality of laws. The abstract review, which may even take place preventively, that is, before the law in question is adopted, can only be performed by the Constitutional Court (at present the Supreme Court) at the request of some specified state bodies and representatives, whereas the concrete review takes place whenever a court (not necessarily the Constitutional Court or the Supreme Court) considers to refuse, on the basis of unconstitutionality, to apply any norm in a specific case.

As mentioned above, the islands were uninhabited prior to the arrival of the Portuguese, who could bring in their law to fill the vacuum without conflicts with any preexisting legal culture. The Portuguese authorities had full control of the islands until independence. In contrast to some other colonies, there were thus no substantial parts of the territory controlled for many years by a guerrilla army fighting the Portuguese authorities and operating a competing administration of its own.

Upon achieving independence, Cape Verde decided to continue to apply Portuguese law as it was at that time, provided it was not contrary to the national sovereignty, laws of the new republic, and the principles and objectives of PAIGC (the only permitted political party at that time). The present Constitution of 1992 preserves this continuity by stipulating that the law valid prior to this constitution's entry into force shall remain in force, unless it is contrary to the constitution or to the principles enshrined therein. These Portuguese roots place Cape Verdean law firmly into the civil law family of legal systems. As a true member of this family, Portuguese law consisted at the time of Cape Verdean emancipation of statutory law, in the first place large-scale codifications such as the civil code, the commercial code, the penal code, the code of civil procedure, and the code of criminal procedure. These codes constituted, consequently, the starting point of the subsequent Cape Verdean legal development.

Of course, the old Portuguese rules continue to apply merely to the extent they have not been amended by or replaced with new legislation of the Republic of Cape Verde. Only one of the codes has been totally replaced so far, namely the Commercial Code of 1888, but it seems that the new Code on Commercial Enterprises mainly reflects and follows similar modernizations of commercial law in Portugal. It focuses on the legal regulation of corporations, partnerships, cooperatives, and other commercial entities, including unincorporated individual businesses that are the most widely used form of carrying on business in the country. The new code does not provide complete coverage of all legal issues in the field and the existing gaps are to be filled by applying the civil code.

Current legislative projects include a new penal code and a new code of criminal procedure. The government has commissioned a prominent local lawyer, who used to teach penal law in Portugal and Macao, to write drafts of these codes. A draft penal code was submitted by him a few years ago but the legislative process seems to have stopped in order to wait for the procedural draft, which is due shortly. There is also a draft of a new code of civil procedure. All these projects follow openly in many (albeit not all) respects legal developments in Portugal.

The Portuguese Civil Code of 1966, as amended by Cape Verde legislation, was reedited in 1997 and reprinted in the official gazette. This new edition of the civil code again contains family law, which previously (since the enactment in 1981 of the family code) was regulated separately. The family law that in 1997 was reintroduced into the civil code is, however, similar to the relatively modern legislation of 1981. As could be expected, it is based on the principles of equality of the sexes and equal rights of all children, whether born in or out of wedlock. A more surprising element is the recognition since 1981 of de facto cohabitation, defined as the monogamous and serious communion for at least three years of "bed, table and residence" of two persons of opposite sexes having the capacity to marry and intending to create a family by means of fully sharing their lives. The couple can make a joint application for registration of their relationship, which can be granted if there are no marriage impediments and their common life guarantees the stability and seriousness that are typical of marriage. The requirement of three years of cohabitation does not apply if the couple have common children. The cohabitation, thus registered, has all the legal effects of a regular marriage and this applies retroactively from the time of the beginning of the relationship, that is, from the time when the relationship acquired the above-mentioned qualities. A registered cohabitation terminates in the same way as a marriage (death or divorce). The civil code gives certain important effects even to a nonregistered cohabitation if it fulfills the other requirements. In such cases, any of the parties can apply to a court for maintenance or property rights under the rules applicable to marriage, provided the application is made within three years after the termination of the relationship.

Pursuant to the constitution, international law including valid international treaties shall be an integral part of the Cape Verdean legal order and in case of conflict shall prevail over all domestic normative acts with the exception of the constitution. Cape Verde has acceded to a number of treaties in the field of human rights, including the 1966 UN Covenant on Civil and Political Rights, the 1966 UN Covenant on Economic, Social and Cultural Rights, the 1966 Convention on the Elimination of All Forms of Racial Discrimination, the 1979 Convention on the Elimination of All Forms of Discrimination against Women, and the 1984 Convention against Torture and Other Cruel, Inhuman or Degrading Treatment or Punishment. Furthermore, the Universal Declaration of Human Rights (which is not, as such, an internationally binding legal document) is made part of the legal order of Cape Verde, since the constitution provides that the constitutional and legal norms concerning fundamental rights shall be interpreted and the gaps filled in conformity with the said Declaration.

CURRENT COURT SYSTEM STRUCTURE

The judiciary of Cape Verde consists mainly of courts of first instance and the Supreme Court of Justice, but there are also military courts (which may seem to be a surprising luxury considering the very limited size of the armed forces), fiscal and customs courts, and a Court of Audit. The Supreme Court of Justice is the highest instance in civil and penal as well as in administrative matters. The constitution permits the creation of intermediate courts of appeal and of administrative courts, but no such courts exist at present.

The Supreme Court of Justice consists of at least five judges, but most cases are decided by a panel of three (in the courts of first instance all cases are decided by a sole judge). Court hearings are normally public and court decisions shall be substantiated. Judicial precedents are not considered to be a source of binding law, but they are published, albeit with a considerable delay. The style of the judgments differs in some respects from the judicial style in most other countries of the civil-law family, for example by containing dissenting opinions and references to previous decisions and legal writing. The court procedure follows the Portuguese model, including such outer attributes as the style of gowns worn by judges and attorneys.

SPECIALIZED JUDICIAL BODIES

There are no judicial bodies other than the courts. The so-called *tribunais de zona,* with competence in very minor matters and composed of nonprofessional judges, have been abolished as a result of the dismantling of the one-party system, since they were considered to be an extended arm of the PAICV. The same fate was met by the special commissions for labor disputes, created in 1983.

Legal Structure of Cape Verde Courts

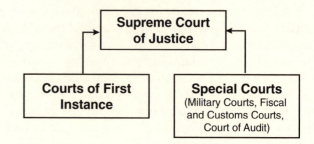

STAFFING

Since there is no higher legal education available in the country, a vast majority of legal professionals have Portuguese law degrees (the few existing graduates from Cuban and eastern European law schools do not work in the legal professions, although they may be active in the public administration). Numerous scholarships are made available by Portugal for Cape Verdean students wishing to study law. Many younger judges have even undergone postgraduate judicial training in Portugal, while some of the older legal professionals did in fact even work as Portuguese magistrates in various parts of the Portuguese colonial empire prior to 1975. There are several cooperation agreements between Cape Verde and Portuguese legal institutions, including law faculties.

One of the Supreme Court judges is appointed by the president of the republic, one is elected by the Parliament and the rest are appointed by a special organ, the Supreme Council of Magistrates, which in addition deals with the promotion and placement of all judges, as well as with disciplinary actions against them. The mandate of the Supreme Court judges is limited to five years, which seems to be a rather short period of time from the point of view of judicial independence.

The constitution stipulates that judges shall be independent and subject only to the law and their conscience; they cannot be suspended, transferred, retired, or dismissed except in cases specified by law. The judges on active duty shall not be members of any political party and must not exercise any other public or private functions, with the exception of legal teaching and research. Some 40 percent of the country's judges are women, but there is presently only one woman among the judges of the Supreme Court. The remuneration of judges is decent by African standards. Consequently, Cape Verde's judiciary does not seem to suffer from serious corruption problems, and there is a sufficient number of young and promising law graduates who prefer working in the court system rather than in the much more lucrative private practice.

The constitution deals even with prosecutors and advocates. The prosecutors represent the state in both criminal and civil proceedings. With regard to the advocates, the constitution stresses the confidentiality of documents and other objects, as well as of communications between an advocate and his client. Pursuant to the procedural codes, the accused and the parties must normally be represented by advocates. Unfortunately, there is at present no functioning bar association controlling the activities of its members.

IMPACT

Contemporary Cape Verde is, in fact, a state ruled by law and it seems that the legal system has been accepted by the population as expressing the proper rules of conduct. In this respect, Cape Verde differs from many African countries, where the official legal system of European origin is often disregarded and replaced in everyday life by elders or chiefs applying customary law.

Michael Bogdan

This entry constitutes an abbreviated and modified version of the article, "The Law of the Republic of Cape Verde after 25 Years of Independence," published in *Journal of African Law* 44: 86–95 (2000).

See also Portugal
References and further reading
There is practically no modern literature in English about the legal system of Cape Verde. Cape Verdean legal writing is necessarily limited. A hopeful sign is the founding in 1997 of a good-quality journal, *Direito e Cidadania,* which appears three times yearly and seems to have attracted both subscribers and contributors from all parts of the Portuguese-speaking world plus a number of other countries. In their daily work, Cape Verdean jurists widely use Portuguese materials (textbooks, manuals, journals, etc.).

CAPITAL PUNISHMENT

Capital punishment is best conceptualized as the legal process by which those accused of capital crimes are convicted, sentenced, and put to death by state entities. Although state actors may perform what amount to executions, even in the furtherance of state interests, in a number of extralegal ways (for example, shooting looters during a riot), capital punishment is more narrowly characterized as a sanctioned legal procedure that begins with an adjudication process and ends with the infliction of the death sentence. Capital punishment may be used in the case of "ordinary" crimes, such as murder, rape, robbery, drug trafficking, and various property offenses (depending on the jurisdiction) and for military offenses and offenses against the state, such as treason.

Even though capital punishment was a long-standing practice in the majority of jurisdictions worldwide and was a central component of most state penal regimes through the eighteenth century, it has steadily declined in significance in a number of regions since then. Most significantly, western European nations steadily lessened their reliance on the practice as the prison and other non-corporal sanctions were developed, culminating in the complete abolition of capital punishment across the region by the late twentieth century.

By the end of 1999, less than half of the world's nations still practiced capital punishment: seventy-one countries retained the death penalty, seventy-four had completely abolished it, and eleven had abolished it for ordinary crimes. An additional thirty-eight states are considered de facto abolitionist, since no judicial executions have taken place in each of these countries for at least ten years. The rate of abolition has been somewhat accelerated since the late 1980s: a total of forty-five countries completely abolished the death penalty between 1987 and 1999. This large number is likely due to several key international developments. First, beginning in 1997, the United Nations Commission on Human Rights annually adopted a resolution urging all UN member nations to implement a moratorium on executions and consider total abolition, and second, the European Union made abolition a prerequisite for membership, which prompted a number of formerly active retentionist states in eastern Europe to abolish capital punishment. A number of countries in central and southern Africa have also abolished capital punishment in recent years, including South Africa—which had been one of the more prolific executing nations in the world—by a landmark Constitutional Court decision in 1995.

The countries that continue to use the death penalty tend to be concentrated in the Middle East (for example, Iran, Iraq, Saudi Arabia), North Africa (for example, Egypt, Libya, Sudan), and Asia (from Pakistan and India through the People's Republic of China, Japan, Thailand, and Malaysia). There are also scattered nations in the Americas and the Caribbean that continue to practice capital punishment, including Guatemala, Cuba, Trinidad, and the United States. The continued retention by the United States is particularly notable, in that it is the only Western industrialized democratic nation to continue to execute citizens, and it is quite out of step with its peer nations. It is also somewhat unusual in that capital statutes have been enacted independently at both the state and the federal levels, so some jurisdictions do not allow for capital punishment at all, and others utilize it with great frequency. This peculiarity may have played a part in capital punishment's revitalization after the U.S. Supreme Court decision in *Furman v. Georgia* (1972) declared most state capital statutes unconstitutional. A state legislative backlash to that decision resulted in the enactment of new death penalty statutes in jurisdictions around the country. Since then, the United States has experienced a steady increase in death sentences and executions each year.

In countries that retain capital punishment, the definitions of capital crimes and eligible criminals vary considerably from jurisdiction to jurisdiction. For instance, although most retentionist states bar the execution of juveniles, in accordance with the International Covenant on Civil and Political Rights (ICCPR), and of the mentally retarded (implied by the ICCPR), several do not. In the past ten years, only six countries have executed those who were under the age of eighteen at the time of their offenses: Nigeria, Pakistan, Saudi Arabia, Iran, the United States, and Yemen, which has since adopted a bar on executing juveniles. The United States, which allows sixteen- and seventeen-year-olds to receive the death penalty, has executed the highest number of juveniles worldwide in the past fifteen years. Twenty-six states in the United States, as well as Japan and Togo, are also known to allow the execution of mentally retarded offenders. The United States has, over the past two decades, led the world in the number of mentally retarded people executed as well.

Among ordinary crimes punishable by death, murder is the most universally condemned offense. Many retentionist nations execute only those convicted of murder, either by law or by normative practice (as in the United States and Japan); however, almost half of the retentionist countries mandate or allow the death penalty for convicted drug traffickers, and in a number of Middle Eastern and Asian nations such as Singapore, China, Saudi Arabia, and Iran, such offenders have been regularly executed in recent years. Other ordinary crimes that are legally eligible for death in jurisdictions across the globe include rape and child sexual assault (in twenty-five nations), kidnapping, armed robbery, and even blasphemy or apostasy in several Middle Eastern nations. China has perhaps the broadest list of death-eligible crimes, with seventy death-eligible offenses, including murder, rape, bribery and various forms of political corruption, counterfeiting, smuggling, distributing obscene material, robbery, drug trafficking, and selling women into prostitution.

Although the death penalty has historically been a mandatory sentence for those who are convicted of capital crimes, the contemporary norm in retentionist countries is discretionary sentencing, depending upon the adjudicator's assessment of the facts and circumstances of the case. Nonetheless, some nations, such as Barbados, Lebanon, Turkey, Zimbabwe, and Grenada, still do mandate death in the case of murder convictions, and Kuwait, Malaysia, Thailand, and Taiwan mandate death for various drug-related convictions. In the majority of death penalty countries, a judge (or panel of judges) makes the guilt and sentencing determinations in capital cases in a formal court proceeding. Most (but not all) death penalty states in the United States, however, rely upon a jury to determine guilt and sentence in a bifurcated proceeding.

According to the United Nation's ongoing research on the status of capital punishment worldwide, all retentionist countries for which information is accessible describe legal procedures in capital cases that at least minimally meet the UN standards and safeguards for the protection of capital defendants' rights, including the requirement of proof by evidence that is subject to cross-examination to establish guilt, a presumption of innocence for the defendant (except in Bahrain), resources for the defendant to prepare a defense, the right to legal representation, and for the most part, some provision for automatic or discretionary appellate review. However, the realities of these procedural safeguards are likely far from the ideal, especially because a number of nations, including China, Pakistan, the United States, and Ethiopia, have been engaged in a "speedy trial" movement that severely limits access to appeals. Further, the quality of legal representation is often questionable in capital cases, with particular problems in the southern United States, a region responsible for most of the U.S. death sentences and executions, and in a number of Caribbean countries.

Most nations have a mechanism for seeking pardons and reprieves, either by governmental agents or by private parties, as in Islamic nations where the system of Diya allows victims' relatives to grant reprieves, but their actual frequency is relatively unknown for most countries. In the post-*Furman* (1972) era of capital punishment in the United States, death sentence commutations are extremely rare, as they are in Indonesia and Singapore. In Japan, pardons are virtually unheard of in practice, although the prime minister does hold the power to commute death sentences.

Execution frequency varies considerably across death penalty nations. In raw numbers, China has carried out the most executions in recent years, although estimates are generally rough because of lack of access to accurate data. That nation was responsible for over 90 percent (12,338) of the approximately 13,500 executions that took place between 1994 and 1999. Iran and Saudi Arabia were second and third in number of executions, with 505 and 465 executions during the five-year period, respectively. The United States executed the sixth-largest number—274—during the same period, with the state of Texas responsible for over one-third of that total. Turkmenistan, which in 1999 completely abolished capital punishment, had in the mid-1990s been the world leader in per capita rate of execution, at almost 15 per million citizens. Singapore was second (13.73 per million), in large part because of drug convictions. In contrast, the rate for China during the same period was just over 2 per million population, and the rate for the United States was 0.2 per million.

In both the United States and Japan, condemned prisoners tend to spend multiple years and even multiple decades on death row awaiting execution. The average period between sentencing and execution in the United States is almost twelve years and may exceed two decades in many states. In Japan, some prisoners spend twenty-five to thirty years on death row, often under stark solitary confinement conditions. In contrast, China and several countries in the Middle East have occasionally executed condemned persons within days of their conviction, raising international concern about whether such persons had any form of appellate review or opportunity to seek pardons or sentence commutations.

The two most common methods of execution worldwide are firing squad, which is the sole execution method in forty-five countries, and hanging, which is used exclusively in thirty-eight countries. China, which generally conducts public executions in an effort to enhance their deterrent value, primarily uses the firing squad, although it has recently adopted lethal injection as a second method. Japan, which probably has the most secretive execution ritual—even the condemned's family and legal counsel are not notified until after the death—relies solely upon hanging for its method. The ancient method of stoning is still used in six nations, and beheading is still practiced in the United Arab Emirates and Saudi Arabia. The United States authorizes the largest variety of execution methods—lethal gas, electrocution, hanging, firing squad, and lethal injection—but lethal injection is quickly replacing the other methods as the only option in most jurisdictions. Only three states still mandate electrocution as the sole method, and in only one of those has the chair been active in the last several years. In all other jurisdictions, lethal injection is either mandated or one of the options available, so well over 90 percent of executions in the United States in recent years have used lethal injection.

As indicated above, the trend toward global abolition of capital punishment has intensified in the 1990s, and more and more nations are experimenting with moratoriums or are outlawing the practice completely. For retentionist states, there is growing pressure to abolish, which emanates from a variety of sources. For instance, tensions over international human rights laws, issues raised by the newly established International Criminal Court, and the increasing influence of the European Union have all placed capital punishment as a legal practice under intense scrutiny and have put countries that continue to use the death penalty on the defensive in a global arena, especially in cases where there are serious breaches of internationally recognized safeguards that aim to protect human rights, such as when juveniles or the mentally incompetent are executed. That states as diverse as Chile, Malawi, the Philippines, Georgia, and Russia have all moved to moratorium or total abolition status at the end of the twentieth century is a testament to this global trend.

Within death penalty nations, concerns about miscarriages of justice and discriminatory imposition of the punishment have also recently resulted in renewed social and political movements to reconsider its use. The United States is a prime example. Through a series of happenstance discoveries, investigations, research endeavors, and legal actions, numerous troubling aspects of the U.S. death penalty practices came to light in the 1980s and 1990s. Dozens of wrongly convicted persons who had been sentenced to death have been discovered through the use of new DNA technology, patterns of serious police and prosecutorial misconduct have been uncovered in a number of capital cases, and continued patterns of sentencing disparities based on extralegal factors such as the race of the victim and offender have been documented. As a result, officials in a number of death penalty states are evaluating their capital procedures, and in one of the most well-known instances, the Illinois governor ordered a moratorium on executions because of the extremely high rate of innocent men on death row who have been discovered in his state. Whether this means that the United States will join the worldwide trend in abolishing capital punishment is unclear; however, from the standpoint of many abolitionist groups and scholars, U.S. abolition is key to global abandonment of this anachronistic punishment.

Mona Lynch

See also Appellate Courts; Constitutional Law; Criminal Law; Criminal Procedures; Habeas Corpus, Writ of; Human Rights Law; International Criminal Court; Retribution; Trial Courts

References and further reading

Boulanger, Christian, Vera Heyes, and Philip Hanfling, eds. 2001 *Zur Aktualität der Todesstrafe: Interdisziplinäre und globale Perspektiven.* Berlin: Berlin Verlag Arno Spitz.

Fine, Toni. 1999. "Moratorium 2000: An International Dialogue toward a Ban on Capital Punishment." *Columbia Human Rights Law Review* 30: 421–438.

Furman v. Georgia, 408 U.S. 238 (1972).

Hood, Roger. 1996. *The Death Penalty: A World-wide Perspective.* 2nd ed. Oxford: Clarendon Press.

Prinzo, Kristi. 1999. "The United States—'Capital' of the World: An Analysis of Why the United States Practices Capital Punishment While the International Trend is Towards Its Abolition." *Brooklyn Journal of International Law* 24: 855–889.

Schabas, William. 2000. "Life, Death, and the Crime of Crimes: Supreme Penalties and the ICC Statute." *Punishment and Society* 2: 263–285.

United Nations. 2000. *Capital Punishment and Implementation of the Safeguards Guaranteeing the Protection of the Rights of Those Facing the Death Penalty: Report of the Secretary-General.* Economic and Social Council. Crime Prevention and Criminal Justice (March).

CATALONIA

GENERAL INFORMATION

Catalonia is an autonomous community of Spain. It is located in the northeast corner of the Iberian Peninsula and covers an area of 31,895 square kilometers, about 6.5 percent of Spain's total peninsular land area. Catalonia is divided into four provinces—Barcelona, Girona, Lleida, and Tarragona—each of which is further divided into counties and municipalities. In 1997, the population of Catalonia was 6.12 million, of whom 4.6 million lived in the densely populated Barcelona province. The population density in 1997 was 192 inhabitants per square kilometer. Catalonia's capital city is Barcelona. The official languages are Spanish and Catalan. Catalan is one of the group of western neo-Latin languages that includes Spanish, Portuguese, and French.

EVOLUTION AND HISTORY

Throughout the centuries, Catalonia has had various political and legal institutions and has enjoyed varying degrees of sovereignty. The medieval Catalan-Aragon crown was born in 1137 and included at various times the Balearic Islands, Valencia, Sicily, Sardinia, Naples, and some portions of Greece. Among the many local laws and privileges (*costums*) given by the kings to the different localities, the most important Catalan legal code to emerge in the Middle Ages is the *Usatges de Barcelona* (Usages of Barcelona, 1060–1064), a compilation of feudal laws. Nevertheless, since its early reception, the *ius commune*—an adaptive law using fragments of the *corpus Iuris*—had a pervasive influence as applicable supplementary law throughout the Catalan territory. The evolution toward a mercantile society in the following centuries resulted in the publication of another celebrated code, the *Llibre Del Consolat De Mar* (1494), a collection of ancient maritime customs and ordinances of the Mediterranean cities that also includes a code of procedure for the guidance of the consular courts.

In the late fourteenth century, the marriage of Ferdinand II of Aragon and Isabella of Castile, the so-called Catholic Kings, brought together the crowns of Castile and Catalonia-Aragon. However, the Catalan-Aragon crown kept most of its laws and political institutions until the establishment of the French dynasty of the Bourbons after the War of Succession (1702–1714). With the Decree of Nova Planta (1716), Catalonia lost all political and legislative power, to the detriment of Castilian law. Catalan private law was maintained, but it was deprived of amendment or renewal for the next two centuries. Except for the brief period of the Second Republic (1931–1939), this situation came to an end only with the coming of the democracy in 1978, after the end of the Francoist dictatorship. The Autonomous Community of Catalonia recovered its legislative power in 1979, and since then the Catalan Parliament has passed since then many acts and statutes on a wide variety of subjects, such as family law, law of succession, and property law.

CURRENT STRUCTURE

Political System

According to the 1978 Spanish Constitution (EC), the Statutes of Autonomy are the "basic institutional rules" of each autonomous community (article 147.[1] EC). The Catalan Statute of Autonomy (CSA) establishes that the Catalan government, or Generalitat, shall be composed of three essential bodies: the Parliament, the president, and the Executive Council (article 29 CSA).

The scope of the legislative powers attributed to Catalonia depends on the CSA, which establishes the matters over which the Generalitat holds sole jurisdiction, concurrent jurisdiction, or shared jurisdiction with regard to legislative power. The exclusive legislative domains granted to the Generalitat in article 9 of the CSA are:

- organization of the institutions of self-government
- Catalan civil law
- procedural laws
- culture
- historical, artistic, monumental, architectonic, archaeological, and scientific heritage
- archives, libraries, museums, and conservatories of music
- research
- local government
- territorial and urban planning
- forests, protected natural areas, and the special treatment of mountainous areas
- hygiene
- tourism
- public works that only affect Catalonia
- roads whose routes are entirely contained within Catalonia
- transportation, ports, and airports
- exploitation of hydroelectric energy, facilities for the production, distribution and transportation of energy
- fisheries
- crafts
- pharmaceuticals
- centers dealing in commodities and securities
- co-operatives
- real estate chambers and chambers of commerce, industry, and shipping
- professional associations
- foundations and other charitable associations
- social services

- youth
- women's affairs
- guardianship of minors
- sports
- advertising, entertainment, casinos, gaming, and betting
- statistics

Taxes

The autonomous community of Catalonia may adopt tax measures only with respect to assets situated inside its territory. Other tax-raising entities bearing on Catalonians are the Spanish state and the municipalities. Among other procedures, the legislation governing local finance regulates the criteria for distribution of revenue, which consists of a share in the revenue of the state and the Generalitat.

Judicial System

With regard to the judicial system, and except for the military jurisdiction, whose competence belongs exclusively to the judicial power, the CSA (article 18) establishes a shared jurisdiction between the Spanish state and the autonomous community, according to which the Generalitat has the power to exercise all the powers that the organic acts of the judiciary recognize or assign to the government of the state; establish the boundaries of the regional divisions of the Catalan jurisdictional agencies and determine their seat; and organize and maintain court facilities. The Generalitat is responsible for providing all the material and budgetary means for the functioning of the justice administration and for the management of all the judicial administrative staff. The division of Spain into autonomous communities does not, however, affect the unity of jurisdiction of the state, so that the court structure of both Catalonia and the Spanish state is the same.

Alternative Dispute Resolution

Mediation, arbitration, and other mechanisms of alternative dispute resolution (ADR) have been developing in Catalonia. While private law firms normally handle mediation, institutions such as the chambers of commerce, the bar associations, and the city councils participate in the management of the thirteen commercial arbitration courts in Catalonia. Instead, consumers' complaints—and the network of consumer courts—are organized by the public administration at the local, council, and autonomic levels, making a total of seven courts in Catalonia.

FEATURES OF THE LAW SYSTEM

The area in which legal regulation presents the most particularities in Catalonia is civil law. The traditional civil law institutions had been scattered for centuries and were only partially coded in the 1960 Compilation Act. The Catalan Parliament is in the process of updating these traditional institutions by means of different codes. The broader contemporary reforms are the Catalan Code of Family Law (1998) and the Catalan Code of Successions (1991). Among the specific features gathered in these laws, some basic principles may be considered:

Family Law

With regard to family law, there are several institutions and principles to be considered. First, concerning economic relations between spouses, Catalan civil law establishes a separate property regime (*separació de bens*) if spouses do not make other matrimonial stipulations. Some supplementary traditional regimes of several Catalan counties are also regulated. Second, spouses married under the separation of marital property regime may establish a survival agreement (*pacte de supervivència*) by which the surviving spouse inherits all common goods jointly purchased. Among the basic principles of Catalan civil law are free investigation of parentage in affiliation processes and the equal right of married and unmarried couples to adopt.

Succession

The basic principle of Catalan law is the universality of the heir. The intestacy regime applies only when the deceased has instituted no heir. The most genuine institution of Catalan law is the tenements (*heretaments*), which is a postnuptial agreement regarding the future state made in favor of spouses, spouses' sons, or regarding their mutual wills.

Patrimonial Law

There are two characteristic institutions of patrimonial law in Catalonia. One is a special rescission of contract, *actio ultra dimidium*. This consists of the personal action of a real estate seller (transferable to heirs) who suffered economic losses exceeding half of the "fair price" of the property. The other is the sale with agreement of repurchase (*venda a carta de gràcia*), which is the personal right (transferable to heirs) to recover a good by repurchasing it.

In Catalonia since 1998, for the first time within the Spanish state, two acts regulate the legal regime of unmarried heterosexual and homosexual couples and other stable relationships based on mutual help (10/98 and 19/98 Acts).

STAFFING

The administration of the Generalitat employed 129,041 persons in 1999. Although access to public service employment is through official exams, a large proportion of employees are hired through standard labor contracts.

With regard to legal professions, in 1999–2000, 18.9 percent of Spanish graduates in law (from 10,000 to 12,000 every year) obtained their degree from a Catalan law school. The basic requisite to practice law is to obtain the degree of *llicenciat* in a law school, upon completion of a four- or five-year program. To become a practicing lawyer, it is necessary to register with one of the fourteen Catalan bar associations; no examination is required, although a two-year postgraduate training has now been established to access public practice. In 1997, however, 24.4 percent of the lawyers registered in Catalan bar associations were nonpracticing.

Access to both careers as judges or public prosecutors requires passing competitive entry examinations. Judges, magistrates, and prosecutors share the same rights of independence and irrevocability, and they are all integrated within the judicial power.

Judicial secretaries, who must hold a law degree, are in charge of the *officinal judicial* (the basic organizational unit) and assist judges in all judicial activities. They are part of the justice administration of the state. In contrast, members of the auxiliary staff of the justice administration (officials and agents) do not need to hold a law degree and are, by dint of having passed a competitive exam, civil servants of the administration of the Generalitat.

Notaries are legal professionals whose basic role is to give "public faith" or to confer certainty on the documents that legal parties present before them. The Generalitat appoints notaries—they constitute a *numerus clausus*—in accordance with the laws of the state. Because of their public function, notaries have a special dependency on the Ministry of Justice. Access to this profession is also by means of a competitive examination.

RELATIONSHIP TO THE NATIONAL SYSTEM

In practice, the distribution of matters designed by both the 1978 Spanish Constitution and the 1979 Catalan Statute of Autonomy (concise, vague, and flexible enough to allow for different alternatives of competence distribution) results frequently in so-called conflicts of competences between the Spanish state and the Catalan autonomous community when both declare themselves competent to exercise a particular power. In those cases, both entities (its governments or legislative assemblies) are entitled to file an appeal of unconstitutionality or to initiate a conflict of competences before the Constitutional Court, which issues a final decision on the conflict. With thirty cases pending at the end of 1999, Catalonia has been the most litigious autonomous community of the state.

Marta Poblet

See also Basque Region; Civil Law; Magistrates—Civil Law Systems; Spain

References and further reading
Generalitat de Catalunya. "Competències de la Generalitat en

Legal Professionals in Catalonia (2000)

Category	Number
Lawyers, Practicing*	14,986
Lawyers, Nonpracticing*	4,216
Judges	104
Magistrates	451
Prosecutors	227
Judicial Secretaries	453
Officials	1,654
Auxiliaries	2,460
Agents	1,139
Notaries	324

*The Barcelona Bar Association, in particular, reports a total of 15,527 registered lawyers.

material d'Adninistració de Justícia." http://www.gencat.es/justicia (cited August 21, 2000).
Generalitat de Catalunya. "The Political Autonomy of Catalonia." http://www.gencat.es/autonom/aindex.htm (cited August 2, 2000).
Generalitat de Catalunya. Institut d'Estadística de Catalunya. "Figures of Catalonia 1999." http://www.idescat.es (cited August 2, 2000).
Martín Casals, M. 1995. "Catalan Civil Law and its Main Institutions." In Jürgen Gödanand Bernard Reams, eds., *Catalonia, Spain, Europe, and Latin America: Regional Legal Systems and their Literature.* Buffalo: William S. Hein, pp. 87–106.
Merino-Blanco, Elena. 1996. *The Spanish Legal System.* London: Sweet and Maxwell.
Oleart, Oriol. 1995. "An Outline on Catalan Legal History Sources." In Jürgen Gödan and Bernard D. Reams, eds., *Catalonia, Spain, Europe, and Latin America: Regional Legal Systems and their Literature.* Buffalo: William S. Hein, pp. 77–86.
Villiers, Charlotte. 1999. *The Spanish Legal Tradition.* Aldershot: Dartmouth.

CAUSE LAWYERING

DEFINITION

Cause lawyering is a concept that gathers under a single terminological umbrella a number of modes of legal practice—including public interest lawyering, civil rights and civil liberties lawyering, feminist lawyering, poverty lawyering, and the like. What distinguishes cause lawyers is their determination to devote their professional lives to and deploy their capabilities on behalf of social and political causes in which they believe. This determination also distinguishes them from and puts them ethically at odds with the vast majority of lawyers who see their primary responsibility as serving individual clients, not causes. Thus, the best way to understand cause lawyering is to explore its similarities to and differences from conventional modes of legal practice.

RELATIONSHIP TO CONVENTIONAL LAWYERING

To begin with, it is important to acknowledge that both cause and conventional lawyers have ideals: It is not true, as some might claim, that conventional lawyers are simply cynical maximizers of their own wealth and status, while cause lawyers are altruistic and self-abnegating. Yet there *is* a dramatic difference between the ideals of conventional and cause lawyering—a difference, in effect, between *ethics* and *morals*. The ethical code of the legal profession is supposed to guide the behavior of conventional practitioners. According to this code, which is accepted by legal practitioners around the world, it is the duty of lawyers to provide vigorous representation to all comers. In the United Kingdom, this duty is referred to as the "cab-rank rule." Irrespective of whether a lawyer approves of a client's moral stance, he or she is supposed to provide zealous advocacy on the client's behalf.

Accordingly, conventional lawyers are to have no qualms about switching sides; indeed, it is supposed to be a point of professional pride to do just that. Thus, British barristers are readily prepared to both prosecute and defend in criminal cases—according to the aforementioned cab-rank rule. And similarly, the noted U.S. "litigator" David Boies probably considers it a hallmark of his professionalism to have represented the U.S. Justice Department in an antitrust suit brought against Microsoft not long after he successfully represented IBM in an antitrust suit brought by the Justice Department. More broadly, politically liberal U.S. lawyers, including Boies, think nothing of working on behalf of corporations, on the one hand, and serving left-wing causes or even serving *in* Democratic administrations, on the other. Anyone who challenges this behavior as inconsistent or cynical would be seen by conventional practitioners as confusing ethics with morals.

The rationale for this bedrock of professionalism is simple and straightforward and is readily embraced by members of other professions—as, for example, by doctors or police officers. Professionalism is, in this framing, measured largely in terms of technical expertise put at the disposal of clients, patients, or, in the case of police officers, the public. According to this view, emotional involvement—whether positive or negative—is likely to compromise effective representation. Thus, detachment and distance are deemed the most probable route to service excellence.

Cause lawyers reject this way of thinking about the professional project, choosing instead to privilege their moral aspirations even if that leads to violations of the profession's ethical code. They expressly seek clients with whom they agree and causes in which they believe. They are not only eager to take sides in social conflict; they are also determined to construct their legal practices around this taking of sides. They deny that their effectiveness will be put at risk by the values that they share with their clients. Indeed, some cause lawyers argue that the more closely they identify with their clients' values, the better advocates they will be. Shared values, according to this perspective, are conducive to a deeper understanding that will enable them to engage in context-sensitive advocacy that can be both reasoned and compelling.

Nonetheless, in so doing, cause lawyers tend to transform the nature of legal advocacy—becoming advocates not only (or primarily) for their clients but also for causes and, one might say, for themselves. Indeed, cause lawyers will often recruit clients in order to pursue a cause with which they themselves identify. In short, for cause lawyers, clients are more means than ends—thereby reversing the priorities of legal professionals around the world.

Although cause and conventional lawyers might thus seem to inhabit different and mutually antagonistic professional worlds, this is not the case in practice. Many conventional lawyers tend to represent primarily (perhaps exclusively) those with whom they agree; this certainly seems to be true of many (perhaps most) lawyers who represent corporations. Consider also personal injury lawyers in the United States. They are divided between a plaintiffs' bar and a defense bar. The plaintiffs' bar exclusively represents individuals or classes of individuals who have been injured—consumers, workers, victims of police abuse, and so forth. Conversely, the defense bar represents *only* the targets of such suits—typically, business corporations and insurance companies. Further muddying the professional waters is the cause lawyer who uses a lucrative conventional legal practice to finance low-fee or no-fee representation of causes in which he or she believes—a modus operandi that can be found, for example, in the United States, Japan, and the United Kingdom.

RELATIONSHIP TO THE ORGANIZED LEGAL PROFESSIONS

Note also that cause lawyering is not entirely unwelcome to either the leadership of legal organizations or the vast majority of lawyers who are indifferent, at least as lawyers, to political and social causes. Bar leaders see cause lawyers as fortuitous allies in the defense and enhancement of the profession's social capital. To the public, after all, lawyers typically appear to be no more than hired guns—using suspect means to defend often unsavory clients and profiting handsomely in the process. Put another way, the public finds it easier to grasp and identify with widely shared *moral* truths rather than the counterintuitive *ethical* principles of legal practice. Accordingly, cause lawyers, with their penchant for doing good, can add some luster to the often tarnished public image of the legal profession. There is also a kind of tacit quid pro quo between cause lawyers and conventional practitioners. Cause lawyers generally represent the impecunious and in so doing assume a burden that mainstream professionals are, according to their own ethical precepts, supposed to shoulder but are often more than happy to leave to others.

The acceptance of cause lawyers by the professional mainstream is, however, decidedly conditional, extending most readily to those involved with noncontroversial causes. After all, the more controversial the cause, the less likely are its advocates to be seen as doing *good.* Thus, insofar as the public associates cause lawyering with causes deemed subversive or clients who are perceived as unworthy or dangerous, cause lawyers put the profession's social capital at risk. It is, in other words, one thing for cause lawyers to vindicate widely accepted rights and quite another for them to become advocates in political struggles over hotly contested issues such as the death penalty, the status of immigrants, abortion, or euthanasia.

The alliance between cause lawyering and the organized legal profession is, in short, contingent and frequently contested. The more sweeping their aspirations, the more professionally embattled cause lawyers are likely to be. This helps explain why, as will be discussed, the affinities between cause lawyering and democracy are largely confined to *liberal* democracy. Only in exceptional circumstances have cause lawyers proven to be effective advocates of *social and economic* democracy.

APPLICABILITY

Cause lawyering has flourished in the United States at least since the 1960s. This growth has been due, in large part, to the successes of the civil rights movement and to the work of a number of well-established social advocacy organizations such as the National Association for the Advancement of Colored People (NAACP) Legal Defense Fund, the Environmental Defense Fund, the Center for Constitutional Rights, and many others. In recent years, cause lawyering has been documented in parts of Europe, Asia, Latin America, the Middle East, and Africa, as well.

The expansion of cause lawyering throughout the world can be traced to a combination of factors, including the spread of written constitutions and constitutional courts, the neoliberal values driving globalization, and the development of transnational human rights networks. All of these factors can, for example, be readily observed in the development of the European Union. To stabilize this intrinsically economic undertaking, a legal regime was constructed to enforce what were initially rules to govern trade, industrial organization, and (later) capital flows. Although restricted to these economic matters at the outset, both the rules themselves and the jurisdiction of the European Court of Justice have spilled over into the social realm. A comparable kind of dynamic is at

work elsewhere. That is, the emergence of civil society, the establishment of a rule of law, and the development of varying degrees of electoral accountability in hitherto authoritarian settings have been, albeit to varying degrees, among the ancillary and unintended consequences of economic globalization.

VARIATIONS

To say that cause lawyering exists all over is not, however, to say that it is the same all over. Indeed, the most striking finding to emerge from research on cause lawyering is how much it varies from time to time and from place to place. The research record reveals cause lawyers associated with different causes, functioning with varying resources and degrees of legitimacy, deploying a wide variety of strategies, and seeking diverse goals. Cause lawyering has also been traced to the full range of professional venues: to large and small private firms, to salaried practice in national and transnational nongovernmental organizations (NGOs), and to government and publicly funded lawyering.

Irrespective of all of this indeterminacy, one can usefully plot variation among cause lawyers along a continuum, with *traditional* cause lawyers at one end and *transgressive* cause lawyers at the other. Traditional cause lawyers tend to pursue so-called first-generation rights primarily through litigation. These first-generation rights are closely linked to the rule of law and to liberal social contract theory. Although traditional cause lawyering has, until recently, been almost exclusively a creature of the liberal Left, right-wing cause lawyering has, at least in the United States, become increasingly prominent. Right-wing cause lawyers serve conservative causes such as the property rights and right-to-life movements, and they tend to work for and on behalf of relatively well-funded foundations such as the Manhattan Institute or the Mountain States Legal Defense Fund. Conversely, transgressive cause lawyering is associated with so-called second-generation rights—minimum income, health care, and housing, for instance—and is often combined with grassroots organizing and other unconventional tactics. Whereas traditional cause lawyers can achieve significant prestige within the legal profession, transgressive cause lawyers are likely to be marginalized professionally. Indeed, because second-generation rights are rooted in social democratic traditions with redistributive implications, transgressive cause lawyers are sometimes deemed subversive and find themselves marginalized politically as well as professionally.

CAUSE LAWYERING AND DEMOCRACY

As was indicated at the outset, a constant of cause lawyering is its affinity with liberal democracy. Generally speaking, liberal democratic states tend to sustain and be sustained by cause lawyering; elsewhere, cause lawyering is a more precarious enterprise. But this observation is only part of the story because there is evidence that cause lawyering can be useful in less hospitable settings and that even in liberal democratic settings, support for cause lawyering is conditional.

Consider, to begin with, the neocorporatist democracy of the Israeli state, with its racialized inflection of citizenship and the long-standing life-and-death conflict with the Palestinian-Arab other. In this setting, Israeli insiders tend to practice a collaborative form of cause lawyering and are generally reluctant to confront the state, particularly on matters of security. Still, Palestinians, Bedouins, and other outsiders are not without legal recourse when their rights are violated. Rule-of-law institutions are in place, and some cause lawyers are willing to operate from beyond the corporatist compact. Other cause lawyers, working within the corporatist compact, will oppose human rights abuses that are regarded as incompatible with their vision of Israeli democracy.

In autocratic and/or dangerously unstable polities, even the pursuit of minimal rights puts cause lawyering and cause lawyers in serious jeopardy. Consider the Sri Lankan cause lawyer Neelam Tiruchelvam, who became a martyr to rule-of-law values and to human rights in 1999. Certainly, there are many states—present-day China, to name just one—where to claim basic human rights is ipso facto deemed a confrontational and hostile *political* act. Thus, even the most modest imaginable forms of cause lawyering may be deemed intolerable.

Still, the record of apartheid South Africa suggests that cause lawyering in fundamentally hostile settings can sometimes make meaningful, if marginal, contributions. Insofar as South Africa and other such states are seeking to play a role in the global political economy, they are pressured to accept the rudiments of liberal democracy, including the rule of law and civil society. To that degree, there is space and potential for cause lawyering—perhaps *only* for cause lawyering—working in concert with transnational human rights organizations to provide some sustenance for liberal democratic values.

As for states where liberal democratic values are well entrenched, it is useful to distinguish between cause lawyering on behalf of these established values and cause lawyering in pursuit of egalitarian and redistributive social and economic democracy. The latter is likely to result in professional as well as political marginalization. To thus politicize legal practice is to put in jeopardy the discursive cover that insulates the legal profession (or that is seen to insulate the profession) from partisan scrutiny and from the threat of an unregulated market for legal services.

Conversely, insofar as their ambitions are confined to the rule of law, an independent judiciary, due process,

and first-generation rights, cause lawyers effectively align themselves with both the professional mainstream and the incentives and institutions of globalization. In so doing, they anchor their democratic advocacy in a combination of supportive structures and allies that provide both legal and political routes to a relatively safe harbor for their cause-lawyering enterprise.

Stuart Scheingold

See also European Court of Justice; Human Rights Law; Law Firms; Legal Aid

References and further reading
Auerbach, Gerald S. 1974. *Unequal Justice: Lawyers and Social Change in Modern America.* New York: Oxford University Press.
Halliday, Terrence C., and Lucien Karpik, eds. 1997. *Lawyers and the Rise of Western Political Liberalism: Europe and North America from the Eighteenth to Twentieth Centuries.* New York: Oxford University Press.
Lopez, Gerald P. 1992. *Rebellious Lawyering: One Chicano's Vision of Progressive Law Practice.* Boulder, CO: Westview Press.
Sarat, Austin, and Stuart Scheingold, eds. 1998. *Cause Lawyering: Political Commitments and Professional Responsibility.* New York: Oxford University Press.
———. 2001. *Cause Lawyering and the State in a Global Era.* New York: Oxford University Press.
Scheingold, Stuart A., and Anne Bloom. 1998. "Transgressive Cause Lawyering." *International Journal of the Legal Profession* 5, no. 2-3: 209–253.
Simon, William H. 1998. *The Practice of Justice: A Theory of Lawyers' Ethics.* Cambridge, MA: Harvard University Press.

CENTRAL AFRICAN REPUBLIC

GENERAL INFORMATION

Almost exactly in the center of Africa, the Central African Republic (République Centrafricaine) is one of the world's least developed countries. Landlocked, it is bound by Cameroon, Chad, the Democratic Republic of the Congo, the Republic of the Congo, and Sudan. It covers an area of 622,984 square kilometers, slightly smaller than Texas. The country's terrain is dominated by a vast plateau about 600 meters above sea level. Scattered hills cover the northeast and southwest. Its climate is hot and tropical, ranging from humid in the south to semiarid in the north, with dry winters and wet summers. Threequarters of the country is forested. About a tenth of the land is cultivated or pasture. Floods, desertification, deforestation, and lack of potable water are environmental difficulties, which profoundly affect national life.

The Central African Republic's demographically young population was estimated to be 3.5 million in 1999. Annual population growth is 1.77 percent (2000 est.). Infant mortality is high, and life expectancy is only

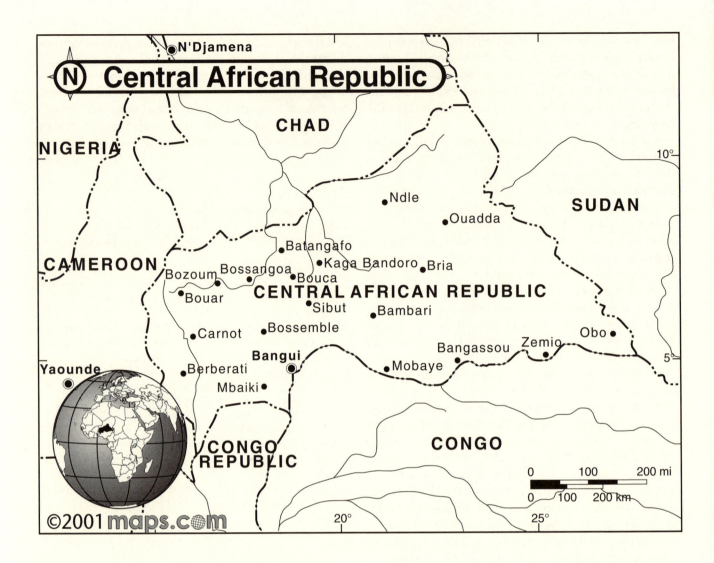

Central African Republic

N'Djamena

CHAD

NIGERIA   10°

                                        Ndle   SUDAN
                                    Ouadda

CAMEROON   Batangafo
            Bozoum   Bossangoa   Kaga Bandoro Bria
                        Bouca
            Bouar   CENTRAL AFRICAN REPUBLIC
                    Sibut   Bambari
        Carnot   Bossemble   Obo
                                        Zemio
Yaounde   Bangassou
        Bangui   Mobaye   5°
    Berberati
    Mbaiki
                                    CONGO
    CONGO
    REPUBLIC

©2001 maps.com

0   100   200 mi

0   100   200 km

20°   25°

44 years. More than 55 percent of inhabitants live in sparsely populated rural areas. The capital, Bangui, with an estimated population of 690,000, is by far the largest city. Other major towns are Berberati, Bouar, Bambari, Bangassou, Bossangoa, Mbaiki, and Carnot. The country has more than eighty ethnic groups, each with its own language. About half of all Central Africans are from western Gbaya-Mandja groups. The Banda, a large group in the north and center, comprise around 28 percent of the population. The Sara, near the border with Chad, account for another 10 percent. Other important groups include the Yakoma, Mboum, M'Baka, Zande, and some 6,500 Europeans. The national language, Sangho, which is the common language along the Ubangui River, is spoken by a majority of Central Africans. Many have only a basic knowledge of the official language, French. Literacy is about 45 percent. Approximately half the population is Christian, and affiliation is evenly divided between Roman Catholicism and various Protestant sects. Fifteen percent are Muslim. These imported faiths are strongly influenced, however, by the traditional indigenous beliefs of the remainder of the population.

With a per capita annual income equivalent to U.S.$300 (2001), the overwhelmingly agrarian Central African Republic is very poor, indebted, and aid-dependent. The country's gross domestic product (GDP) in 2001 was estimated to be U.S.$1.052 billion, with an annual growth rate of 5 percent. Inflation averaged 6.4 percent in 2000. Most Central Africans live in poverty and are engaged in subsistence farming. Fifty-five percent of GDP arises from agriculture. Principal crops are cotton, cassava, yams, bananas, maize, millet, coffee, and tobacco. Livestock is also a source of income. The country has rich but largely unexploited resources of diamonds, uranium, timber, gold, oil, and hydroelectric power. Exports, mainly of diamonds, timber, cotton, coffee, and tobacco, were valued in 1999 at $195 million, while imports cost $170 million and included food, textiles, fuels, machinery, electrical equipment, vehicles, chemicals, pharmaceuticals, consumer goods, and industrial products. The country's principal trading partners are France, Côte d'Ivoire (Ivory Coast), Cameroon, Germany, Japan, Spain, Egypt, and Belgium. Most export income comes from extractive industries. Uncut diamonds make up close to 60 percent of export earnings, and timber accounts for 16 percent. Dominated by diamond mining and timber operations, industry contributes less than 20 percent of the country's GDP. Smaller industrial sectors include brewing, textiles, footwear, soap, and bicycle and motorcycle assembly. Services account for a quarter of GDP, owing to oversized bureaucracy and high transportation costs resulting from the country's lack of an open-water port.

Transportation and communications networks are limited. The country has no railways, and less than 2 percent of its 23,810 kilometers of roads are paved. Trade and transportation on some 800 kilometers of navigable rivers are carried on mainly by small dugout craft. The most important river, the Ubangui, is impassable from April to July because of high water from heavy rains, and much of the country is fragmented by numerous unnavigable rivers running north to south. Only three of the country's fifty-two airports have paved runways. International air service is limited, and domestic service is irregular. Eighty percent of the country's limited electrical supply is provided by hydroelectric facilities in Boali. Fuel supplies are subject to chronic shortages and must be barged in on the Ubangui River or trucked overland through Cameroon. Regional instability has sometimes halted shipments. Newspapers and other publications are published regularly, but electronic media are sparce. A limited telephone system functions with only 8,000 mainline and 79 cellular customers. Five radio stations and one television station are in operation. Only one company has initiated Internet service. Medical facilities are limited and sanitation levels are low.

On August 13, 1960, the former French colony of Ubangi-Shari became independent as the Central African Republic. Since independence, political, military, economic, and cultural ties with France have remained strong. French troops have been based in the country, which is a member of the French Community and regional Francophone organizations. The Central African Republic's currency, the Communaute Financiere Africaine (CFA) franc, is pegged to the euro. The Central African Republic has made slow progress toward economic and political development. The country's land-locked position, mismanagement, poor infrastructure, limited tax base, largely unskilled work force, scarce private investment, and adverse external conditions have caused budgetary and trade deficits and a net decline in per capita GNP since 1970. The central government's budget of $170 million (2001) is bolstered by traditional subsidies from France. The country received $172.2 million in economic aid, mainly from France, in 1995. By 1999, its considerable external debt burden has grown to around $790 million. World Bank and International Monetary Fund structural adjustment programs and

credits have had limited impact. After three decades of misrule, a civilian government was installed in 1993. As a result of international pressure, many state-owned businesses have been privatized and efforts have been made to standardize and simplify labor and investment codes and to combat corruption. The country's legal system is based on French codified law and influenced by local traditions and the experience of abusive dictatorial rule.

HISTORY

The territory of the Central African Republic was settled from the seventh century onward by overlapping empires, including Kanem-Bornu, Ouaddai, Baguirmi, and Darfur. From 700 to the mid-1800s, various sultanates claimed the area, using the Oubangui region as a source of slaves, who were traded north across the Sahara and to western Africa. Migrations in the 1700s and 1800s brought new peoples into the area, including the Zande, Banda, and Baya-Mandjia. In 1875, Sultan Rabih governed large parts of present-day Central African Republic and Chad. Europeans, primarily French, Germans, and Belgians, arrived in the region in 1885. An 1887 agreement with the Congo Free State granted France possession of Oubangui-Chari, areas north of the right bank of the Ubangui River. In 1889, they established an outpost at Bangui. By 1894, Oubangui-Chari became a French territory, but Paris did not consolidate its control and establish an administration until the defeat of Rabih's forces in 1903. By 1906, the Oubangui-Chari territory was united with Chad. Four years later, it became part of French Equatorial Africa (AEF), along with Chad, Congo (Brazzaville) and Gabon. The next three decades were marked by brief revolts against colonial rule and the development of plantations. In August 1940, the territory sided with the Free French forces of General Charles de Gaulle and the Chadian governor, Felix Éboué. After World War II, France's 1946 constitution brought reforms granting all AEF inhabitants French citizenship and seats in the French National Assembly and local assemblies. These reforms eventually led to independence for French territories in western and equatorial Africa. The Central African Republic's Territorial Assembly was led by Barthelemy Boganda, a Roman Catholic priest known for advocating independence in the French National Assembly. In 1956, French laws eliminated some voting inequalities and provided limited self-government. A September 1958 constitutional referendum dissolved AEF, and on December 1 of that year the National Assembly declared the Central African Republic independenct.

The first Central African constitution was approved by the Territorial Assembly on February 9, 1959. A lengthy, handwritten preamble by Boganda thoroughly affirmed fundamental human rights, just procedures, equality before the law, and representative democracy. The constitution provided for parliamentary government with a legislative assembly elected for five years, a president invested by the assembly, and ministers named by the president, whose terms were to match the assembly's. More like a prime minister than a president in the usual sense, the Central African president could dissolve the assembly, which could turn out the government by a motion of censure. Revisions that infringed on the system's republican form of government and democratic principles were specifically prohibited. Hoping to facilitate African unity, the 1959 constitution held that the country could accept partial or total abandonment of sovereignty. After Boganda died in a plane crash in March 1959, his cousin, David Dacko, replaced him and oversaw the country's independence on August 13, 1960. Under the 1960 act of independence, the Central African Republic was permitted to join the French Community as an independent nation. The following day, the assembly named Dacko president of the republic. Four laws (passed in December 1960, May 1961, September 1962, and November 1963) suppressed civil liberties and mandated a single party and pure presidential system. Law No. 64/37 of November 26, 1964, promulgated a new constitution that retained few traces of democracy.

On New Year's Day, 1966, a swift, almost bloodless coup brought Colonel Jean-Bedel Bokassa to power. Dacko fled the country. Bokassa abolished the already suspended 1959 constitution, dissolved the National Assembly, and issued decrees giving him all legislative and executive powers. A new constitution, enacted on January 8, 1966, was inspired by the 1940 constitution of Vichy France. The country became a dictatorship directed by a military officer, who as president for life placed himself above the law. On December 4, 1976, imitating his hero, Napoleon Bonaparte, Bokassa proclaimed himself Emperor Bokassa I. The republic became a hereditary monarchy with an "Imperial Constitution." In theory the new regime was a parliamentary monarchy and had reinstated the liberties proclaimed in the 1959 constitution. A national assembly and independent judiciary were guaranteed. But the Imperial Constitution was written only so that Bokassa could continue to receive aid from Western democracies, who were troubled by the regime's totalitarian character. Only Bokassa's own political party was recognized. None of the institutions called for was created, and all the proclaimed democratic principles were ignored. Bokassa's regime was marked by numerous atrocities, which went far beyond his decimation of political opponents, military officers, and the press. On September 20, 1979, following riots in Bangui and the murder of scores of schoolchildren, former president Dacko led a successful French-backed coup and ended Bokassa's fourteen-year reign.

Once back in power, however, Dacko was ineffective in promoting economic and political reforms. Exactly two years after ousting the Bokassa regime, Dacko was overthrown by General André-Dieudonné Kolingba on September 20, 1981. Kolingba, a Yakoma, led the country as head of the Military Committee for National Recovery (CRMN). Signaling a return to civilian rule, in 1985 the CRMN was dissolved and Kolingba named a cabinet with increased civilian participation. The process of democratization accelerated in 1986 with the creation of a new political party, the Rassemblement Démocratique Centrafricain (RDC), and the drafting of a new constitution that was subsequently ratified by national referendum. This constitution established a 52-member National Assembly, which was elected in July 1987. In 1991, under mounting pressure as president under the new constitution, Kolingba created a national commission to rewrite the constitution to provide for a multiparty system. Multiparty presidential elections were conducted in 1992 but were canceled due to irregularities. Ange-Félix Patassé won the rescheduled elections in October 1993 and was reelected president in September 1999. Throughout 1996 and 1997, however, pay arrears, living conditions, political representation for the military, and unequal treatment of military officers from different ethnic groups led to army mutinies. Violence between government and rebel elements in the army destroyed many businesses in Bangui. Economic difficulties caused by this destruction, fuel shortages, and mismanagement reduced tax revenues and led to a 2 percent drop in GDP. The French succeeded in quelling the rebellions, and an African peacekeeping force (MISAB) occupied Bangui until 1998, when it was relieved by a United Nations peacekeeping mission (MINURCA), which departed in March 2000.

On May 28, 2001, military units loyal to Kolingba attacked the presidential residence and other government and military installations. The mutineers were supported by some 300 mercenaries from Rwanda and Angola. The eleven days of fighting, limited to Bangui and its eastern suburbs, cost between 250 to 300 lives and temporarily displaced a minimum of 50,000 people. Kolingba's revolt was repulsed by loyalist units, supported by Libyan troops and a 700-strong battalion from the Mouvement pour la liberation du Congo (MLC), a rebel movement from the Democratic Republic of the Congo, whose leader, Jean-Pierre Bemba, was concerned that the Central African Republic's insecurity would spill over into his territory. The mutineers were driven out of Bangui into the bush. Summary executions and attacks against Yakomas ensued. Some 25,000 citizens, mainly Yakomas, fled across the Ubangui River to the Congolese town of Zongo to escape reprisals. In July 2001, the government closed border crossings with the Democratic Republic of the Congo in an effort to

Legal Structure of Central African Republic Courts

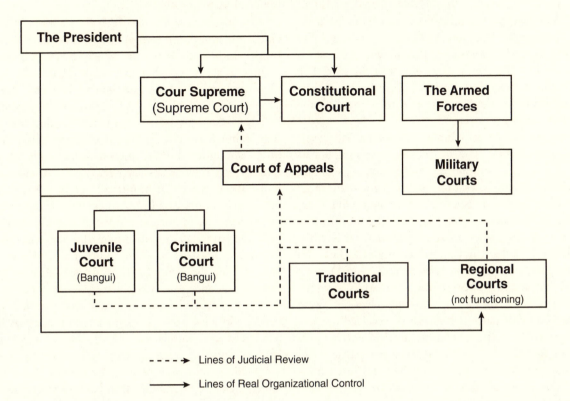

Lines of Judicial Review

Lines of Real Organizational Control

stop the flow of arms and dissidents. A bounty of 25 million CFA francs was offered for Kolingba, dead or alive. Responding to widespread accusations that their troops attacked and looted Bangui residents, the MLC subsequently arrested one of its officers, whose troops had been seen looting, and withdrew its forces. Appointed as special envoy by UN Secretary-General Kofi Annan, former Malian president General Amoudou Toumani Toure met with President Patasse and others in an effort to restore calm. Instability continues to plague national life and prevents any further establishment of legal institutions.

LEGAL CONCEPTS

The legal system of the Central African Republic is based on French models of codified civil law. All law is national. Six constitutions since 1959 have altered government structures and legal procedures greatly. The country's current constitution was approved by referendum on December 29, 1994, and adopted on January 7, 1995. It provides for a republican form of government comprised of a strong executive branch and weaker legislative and judicial branches. The president's powers of appointment are very broad. Voting is based on universal suffrage for all citizens over age twenty-one. Traditional customary law effectively dominates court proceedings outside of the capital.

CURRENT STRUCTURE

The Central African Republic has an active civil society, with numerous political parties and professional, labor, and local associations. Parties with significant national roles are the Christian democratic Mouvement pour la Libération du Peuple Centrafricain (Liberation Movement of the Central African People or MLPC), the authoritarian Rassemblement Démocratique Centrafricain (Central African Democratic Rally or RDC), the authoritarian Mouvement pour la Démocratie et le Développement (Movement for Democracy and Development or MDD), the social democratic Front Patriotique pour le Progrès (Patriotic Front for Progress or FPP), the conservative Parti Social Démocratique (Social Democratic Party or PSD), the progressive Alliance pour la Démocratie et le Progrès (Alliance for Democracy and Progress or ADP), the Parti de l'Unité Nationale (Party for National Unity or PUN), the liberal Parti Libéral Démocratique (Liberal Democratic Party or PLD), the Forum Démocratique pour la Modernité (Democratic Forum for Modernity or FODEM), the conservative Forum Civique (Civic Forum or FC), and the Union Populaire pour la République (People's Union for the Republic or UPR).

Influenced by French models, the Central African Republic's executive branch is composed of a president, prime pinister, and Council of Ministers (cabinet). The head of state is the president, who is directly elected by universal suffrage to a term of six years. In October 1993, the MLPC's Ange-Félix Patassé was elected president with 51.6 percent of the vote. Other candidates included the RDC's André-Dieudonné Kolingba, the MDD's David Dacko, and seven others. Patassé was reelected on September, 19, 1999, with 56.4 percent of the vote. The head of government is the prime minister, who is appointed by the president and who in turn appoints the Council of Ministers.

The republic's legislative branch has seen much development since 1998. The unicameral Assemblée Nationale (National Assembly) has 109 members, who are directly elected for five-year terms from three- and four-seat constituencies. The National Assembly is advised by the Conseil Economique et Regional (Economic and Regional Council); when these bodies sit together they are collectively called the Congrès (Congress). The National Assembly elections on November 22 and December 13, 1998, led to the formation of an MLPC government allied with the PLD, but the elections were contested by other parties. The MLPC received 43 percent of the vote, the RDC 18 percent, the MDD 9 percent, and the FPP 6 percent. Seven other parties who won seats got less than 5 percent of the vote. Seven nonpartisan independents also were elected. In the election's aftermath, heated debates and motions for censure underlined the National Assembly's slowly growing independence from executive control. After attempts by opposition parties and independents to form a coalition government, five independents and one opposition deputy had joined the MLPC. In early January 1999, opposition members of the existing Council of Ministers resigned in protest and an MLPC-dominated coalition government, led by Anicet Georges Doleguele, was appointed on January 15. Doleguele was reappointed after the October 1999 presidential elections and formed a Council of Ministers, which included members of the MLPC, PLD, CN, PUN, and PSD, as well as the military. In 2001, Martin Ziguélé of the MLPC replaced Doleguele as prime minister and Luc Apolinaire Dondon Konamabaye was named president of the National Assembly.

The judicial branch includes the Cour Supreme (Supreme Court), constitutional court, criminal court, court of appeals, and juvenile court, all located in the capital. Some of these courts have insufficient resources and personnel to operate on a regular basis. In contrast to their broader past roles, military courts are currently used only to try military personnel for crimes committed in the course of duty. Despite provisions for regional courts, there are no formal courts currently functioning outside Bangui. Traditional arbitration and negotiation play major roles in administering property, probate, and domestic law. All judges are appointed by the president, and

the country has a history of executive influence impeding judicial independence.

Administratively, the Central African Republic is divided into the commune of Bangui and sixteen prefectures: Bamingui-Bangoran, Basse-Kotto, Gribingui, Haute-Kotto, Haute-Sangha, Haut-Mbomou, Kemo-Gribingui, Lobaye, Mbomou, Nana-Mambere, Ombella-Mpoko, Ouaka, Ouham, Ouham-Pende, Sangha, and Vakaga. The prefectures are further divided into some sixty subprefectures. The heads of these administrative units, appointed by the president, are called prefects (*prefets*) and subprefects (*sous-prefets*). Local elections in mid-1988 created 176 municipal councils, each headed by a mayor appointed by the president. Traditional ethnic leaders play important but varying local roles.

In December 1999, armed forces of the Central African Republic numbered between 4,000 and 4,500 personnel and included the Central African Armed Forces (Republican Guard and Air Force), Presidential Security Unit (UPS), National Gendarmerie (land and naval), National Police, and local police personnel. The military is highly politicized and influences all branches of government. Under military restructuring plans formulated in 1999–2000, the minister of defense controls all armed forces, including the UPS, which had previously been seen as the president's personal militia. With French assistance, the military is attempting to provide professional training and decentralize its troops to combat banditry, poaching, and other crimes. Plans are also underway to encourage greater professionalism and ethnic balance through recruitment and voluntary demobilization. Defense accounted for U.S.$9.7 million or 5.7 percent of the budget in 2001.

The Central African Republic is an active member of several pan-African, Francophone African, and central African organizations as well as the United Nations. The country's close ties to France have been considerably reduced since the early 1990s. In the late 1990s, France withdrew its forces stationed in the Central African Republic and cut assistance. The remaining ties to France, however, as well as diplomatic relations with about eighteen other countries, have insured some contact with, respect for, and support for international norms of democratic governance and human rights.

SPECIALIZED JUDICIAL BODIES

Human rights issues have been the subject of special judicial bodies domestically. In late 1986 and early 1987, the former dictator Jean-Bedel Bokassa was tried for human rights violations by a special court. Bokassa was found guilty and sentenced to life imprisonment. In an attempt to deal with the country's history of ethnic discord and accompanying human rights violations, the National Conference of Reconciliation, which included all sectors of government and society, convened on February

25, 1998, and adopted a National Reconciliation Pact on March 4, 1998. Efforts toward democratization have proceeded from this agreement. Internationally, the Central African Republic's internal stability and respect for human rights have been the focus of attention by the UN High Commission on Human Rights and other world bodies and advocacy groups.

STAFFING

All judicial personnel in the Central African Republic are appointed by the president. Their tenure in office is dependent on presidential political considerations and the president's own tenure in office. Their levels of education, training, and experience vary, but all have some knowledge of French legal and local customary norms. Some legal education is available at the country's only university in Bangui. A few lawyers are French-educated. Officials in traditional courts outside the capital have little if any formal training and are recruited by and closely linked to local traditional leaders, if they are not in fact the leaders themselves.

IMPACT

The lack of formal courts in most areas outside the capital is the most striking example of the profound limitations of the Central African government in general and the justice system in particular. The central government's control and ability to enforce legal and administrative norms is limited but growing. Although the police and courts have had success in reducing crime in some regions, armed robbery in rural areas is common, especially in the dry season. The system is limited by poverty in ways unimaginable in most of the world. For example, crime victims often have to pay to send taxis or other vehicles to pick up police officers owing to the shortage of police vehicles. In October 1997, because of its inability to provide security for foreigners traveling outside the capital, the Central African government closed all border points for travelers seeking to enter the country.

The Central African Republic also bears the legacy of its dictatorial past. Its human rights record is flawed by continued reports of arbitrary detainment, torture, and extrajudicial killings. Journalists have been threatened. Prison conditions remain harsh.

Randall Fegley

See also Civil Law; Customary Law; France; Human Rights Law; Napoleonic Code

References and further reading
Bureau of Consular Affairs. 2001 (June 5). *Central African Republic: Consular Information Sheet.* Washington, DC: U.S. Department of State.
Bureau of African Affairs. 2001. (July) *Background Note: Central African Republic.* Washington, DC: U.S. Department of State.
"Central African Republic." 2001. (January 1). In *People in Power.* Cambridge: Cambridge International Reference on Current Affairs.
"Central African Republic." 2001. In *The World Factbook.* Washington, DC: Central Intelligence Agency.
Derksen, Wilfried. 2001. "Elections in Central African Republic." In *Elections around the World,* at http://www.electionworld.org.
IRIN News Briefs. Nairobi: UN Office for the Coordination of Humanitarian Affairs/Integrated Regional Information Networks. http://www.reliefweb.int/IRIN/index.phtml (cited December 11, 2001).
Kalck, Pierre. 1980. *Historical Dictionary of the Central African Republic.* Metuchen, NJ: Scarecrow Press.
O'Toole, Thomas. 1986. *The Central African Republic.* Boulder, CO: Westview Press.

CERTIORARI, WRIT OF

A writ of certiorari (cert) is an order of an appeal or appellate court "directing a lower court to deliver the record in the case for review." (*Black's Law Dictionary,* 320.) The appellate court decides whether to grant the writ at its discretion. Thus the writ of certiorari is one of the ways by which an appellate court exercises jurisdiction that is discretionary in nature (i.e., where the court has the discretion to decide whether to hear a case). In many judicial systems, this type of discretionary jurisdiction is exercised through a process of granting "leave to appeal." Writ of certiorari is the common method of exercising discretionary jurisdiction by courts in the United States.

The U.S. Supreme Court was first given the power to grant cert by the Judiciary Act of 1891, an act passed by Congress. But cert was not widely used by the Court until the passage of the Judiciary Act of 1925. This statute substantially increased the Court's discretionary appellate jurisdiction (or power) by replacing most mandatory writs of appeal with discretionary writs of cert. Finally, in 1988, Congress eliminated all the mandatory appeals except for those that came from the three-judge (federal) district courts. As a consequence of this act, virtually all the cases decided by the Court come to the Court after it has granted cert.

THE CERTIORARI PROCESS

A party to a lawsuit in the U.S. Court of Appeals, in a specialized federal appeals court, or in the highest state court has ninety days after the entry of a judgment in a case to file a petition for a writ of cert with the clerk of the U.S. Supreme Court. He also files a brief in support of that petition. The party on the other side (i.e., the respondent) has thirty days to file a brief in opposition to the petition. The petitioner in turn may submit a reply brief. Outside groups (i.e., groups that are not parties to the lawsuit) are usually given permission by the Court to submit amicus curiae (friends of the court) briefs either in support of or in opposition to the petition.

At present, eight of the nine justices on the Court (all the justices except Justice John Paul Stevens) participate in a "cert pool" in which they pool their law clerks for the purpose of evaluating the cert petitions. The law clerk who is assigned to evaluate the merits of a given cert petition writes a memo summarizing the facts, legal issues, and the court decisions in the case and presents one or more arguments regarding whether cert ought to be granted or denied by the Supreme Court. If the cert pool law clerk is not from a given justice's office, a law clerk from that office reads the cert petition and indicates whether she agrees or disagrees with the recommendation in the cert pool memo and the reason or reasons for her position. Justice Stevens's law clerks review all the cert petitions and prepare memos for those cases (1) for which they believe the cert ought to be granted, (2) for which cert is requested by the solicitor general on behalf of the U.S government, or (3) for which the petition is subsequently included in the Court's Discuss List.

The Chief Justice circulates a list of cases to be discussed and voted on in conference. Any justice can add any case to the Discuss List. Any case that is not listed on the Court's final Discuss List is automatically denied cert. The justices then meet in conference to decide whether to grant or deny cert for the cases on the Discuss List. The justices present their views and vote in order of seniority, with the chief justice presenting his view and voting first. It takes four votes to grant cert.

Rule 10 of the rules of the U.S. Supreme Court sets forth the guidelines for granting cert. These rules focus on conflict in the law and the importance of the issue in the case. But Rule 10 also states that the reasons listed are "neither controlling nor fully measuring the Court's discretion." Most scholars believe that these rules are insufficiently precise to inform the parties regarding whether cert is likely to be granted or denied.

Cert petitions are of two kinds: paid petitions in which the petitioner pays the required fees, submits the required number of copies of the petition and brief, and follows the other guidelines, and "in forma pauperis" (in the form of pauper), in which the fees and most of the other requirements are waived. Most of the in forma pauperis petitions are submitted by federal or state prisoners.

Since 1925 the number of paid petitions has increased dramatically, from 586 (1926) to 927 (1956) to 2,324 (1976) to 2,456 (1995). Not surprisingly, the percentage of cases granted cert has decreased dramatically, from 20 percent (1926) to 15 percent (1956) to 10 percent (1976) to 4 percent (1995). A similar pattern has occurred regarding petitions in forma pauperis. In 1935, for example, 59 petitions were submitted and 14 percent were granted, whereas in 1995, 5,098 were submitted and three-tenths of 1 percent were granted.

Certiorari is not the only method of review from the lower courts. A writ of appeal is also available and was used extensively in the earlier periods of the Court's history, particularly prior to 1925. Although this writ is officially mandatory, the Court, in fact, rejects many petitions. In addition, the Court at times receives and reviews certified questions from the lower courts.

THE CERTIORARI STRATEGIES

Some Supreme Court scholars have investigated the strategies pursued by the individual justices when voting to grant or deny cert. S. Sidney Ulmer (1972) compared cert voting by the individual justices from 1946 to 1956 with their subsequent voting at the final vote on the merits (i.e., the vote set forth in the Court's various opinions, which indicates whether a given justice wants the Court to reverse or to affirm the decision of the lower court). Ulmer discovered a statistically significant relationship for eight of eleven justices between their votes to grant cert and their subsequent vote to reverse the decision of the lower court and their vote to deny cert and their subsequent vote to affirm the decision of the lower court. Ulmer argued that this relationship exists because the justices were pursuing an "error correcting strategy." Ulmer investigated only those cases in which cert was granted by the Court, for no researcher knows whether a given justice wants the Court to reverse or affirm when the case is denied cert by the Court.

There is, however, a second possible strategy that the individual justices might be following. This strategy is called the "outcome prediction strategy." Saul Brenner (1979) discovered a relationship between voting to grant cert by the individual justices and their subsequent winning at the final vote on the merits and voting to deny cert and their subsequent losing at the final vote on the merits. But this relationship was only present for justices who wanted the Court to affirm the decision of the lower court, not for justices who wanted the Court to reverse that decision. The justices who wanted the Court to affirm the decision of the lower court had already won on the lower court. They did not want to risk losing at the Supreme Court level unless they believed that there was a good chance that it would not happen. Their subsequent win at the final vote indicates that they were able to predict the Court's final vote fairly accurately. The justices who wanted the Court to reverse the lower court decision, however, had already lost in the lower court. They were willing to gamble that the outcome they favored would win at the Supreme Court level. As a consequence, they did not bother to calculate whether they were likely to win or lose at the final vote. Indeed, the rationality of the actions by the two kinds of justices is reinforced by the fact that the Court (at least in the period of my study, i.e., 1946–1956) was significantly more likely to reverse the decision of the lower court than to affirm it.

VARIABLES ASSOCIATED WITH APPROVAL AND DENIAL OF CERTIORARI

No scholar has argued that the cert strategies are the most important determinant of the cert voting. All the scholars recognize that a host of other variables play a major role in whether cert is granted or denied. Much of the research on this topic concerns the cert decision by the Court as a whole. Gregory Caldiera and John Wright (1988) conducted the most important study on this topic. They examined both the cases granted cert and the cases denied cert during the 1982 term of the Burger Court. They discovered that the following variables are associated with the granting of cert by the Court:

1. The U.S. government petitioned the Court for a writ of cert. (The U.S. government is the most important litigant before the Court and has a high success rate in getting its petitions granted by the Court. In the 1998 term, for example, its success rate was 52 percent, compared with less than 1 percent for the other petitioners.)
2. There were one or more amicus briefs in support of granting cert. (The presence of these briefs indicates that the case is important.)
3. There was an *actual* conflict between
   a. Two or more U.S. Courts of Appeal;
   b. Two or more state courts;
   c. A federal court and a state court;
   d. The court immediately below the Supreme Court and a Supreme Court precedent.
   (The Court apparently sees its role as that of resolving conflicts of law.)
4. The case was decided in a liberal direction in the court immediately below the Supreme Court. (Caldiera and Wright were examining the conservative Burger Court, and it is hardly surprising that this Court was more likely to want to hear liberal decisions, most of which it reversed.)
5. There were one or more amicus beliefs in opposition to granting cert. (Apparently, the presence of an amicus brief in opposition also indicates that the case is important.)
6. The court immediately below decided the case by a split vote, or the court immediately below reversed the decision of the lower court. (This result, of course, also suggests that the law is unclear.)
7. The petitioner *alleged* a conflict among the courts. (This variable suggests that the Court may be fooled by petitioners or, perhaps, that there is some uncertainty between "actual" conflict, as judged by Supreme Court scholars, and "alleged" conflicts.)

One can also identify a host of variables associated with the denial of cert:

1. The converse to the variables associated with the granting of cert.
2. The Court does not wish to exercise jurisdiction (e.g., there is no federal question involved).
3. The Court does not believe that the case is appropriate for decisions for one or more of following reasons:
   a. The petitioner does not have standing to sue (e.g., the case does not involve an issue that concerns the petitioner).
   b. The controversy is not ripe (i.e., not yet ready for decision) or moot (i.e., it has already been resolved).
   c. The controversy constitutes a political question (e.g., one that ought to be decided by the president or Congress).
   d. The petition seeks an advisory opinion (i.e., an opinion that gives advice instead of resolving a controversy).
   e. It is a "friendly suit" (i.e., one in which both parties want the same decision by the court).
4. The facts are inappropriate for review by the Court.
5. The issue or issues in the case need more percolation (i.e., they need to be heard and decided by additional lower courts or by others).
6. The Court seeks to avoid the issue in the case (e.g., the constitutionality of the Vietnam War).

WRIT OF CERTIORARI IN OTHER COURTS

The foregoing discussion focuses on how certiorari functions in the U.S. Supreme Court. Many state supreme courts also use a certiorari process. However, the nature of process may differ from that used by the U.S. Supreme Court. For example, some states make certiorari decisions using panels of justices; others rely upon staff attorneys to review petitions and make recommendations to the justices. What factors influence these processes is unknown because of the lack of any significant research on certiorari processes in state courts.

Saul Brenner

See also Appellate Courts; Law Clerks
References and further reading
Baum, Lawrence. 1997. *The Puzzle of Judicial Behavior.* Ann Arbor: University of Michigan Press, chap. 3.
———. 2001. *The Supreme Court.* 7th ed. Washington, DC: Congressional Quarterly, chap. 3.
Black's Law Dictionary, 1999. 7th ed. St. Paul: West Group.
Brenner, Saul. 1979. "The New Certiorari Game." *Journal of Politics* 41: 649–655.
Caldiera, Gregory A., and John R. Wright. 1988. "Organized Interests and Agenda Setting in the U.S. Supreme Court." *American Political Science Review* 82: 1109–1128.

Perry, H. W., Jr. 1991. *Agenda Setting in the United States Supreme Court.* Cambridge: Harvard University Press.

Stern, Robert L., Eugene Gressman, and Stephen M. Shapiro. 1993. *Supreme Court Practice.* 7th ed. Washington, DC: Bureau of National Affairs.

Ulmer, S. Sidney. 1972. "The Decision to Grant Certiorari as an Indicator to Decision 'on the Merits.'" *Polity* 4: 429–448.

CHAD

GENERAL INFORMATION

Landlocked in central Africa, Chad is bordered by Libya to the north; Cameroon, Nigeria, and Niger to the west; the Central African Republic to the south; and Sudan to the east. It is about three times the size of California, with deserts in the north; broad, arid plains in the center; tropical lowlands in the south; and mountains in the northwest. Lake Chad, which borders Nigeria and Cameroon, is the largest body of water in the Sahel region, although it has been drying up rapidly in recent years, in part because of overuse of its waters and tributary rivers. The country is plagued by severe drought, a shortage of potable water, and increasing desertification.

Some 85 percent of the population is involved in agriculture, primarily subsistence farming, herding, and fishing. Only 3 percent of the land is considered arable, and 36 percent is in permanent pasture. Annual per capita income is estimated to be $239, although that figure does not reflect a fairly thriving informal sector of the economy. Chad has proven petroleum resources that have thus far been unexploited, but the World Bank recently approved a pipeline project to Cameroon over the objections of environmental and human rights groups. While this should boost the overall economic picture, many predict that the benefits will be limited to the country's elite.

The capital, N'Djamena, is located some fifty miles southeast of Lake Chad. French and Arabic are the official languages, although more than a hundred different languages and dialects are spoken. The population is 50 percent Muslim, 25 percent Christian, and 25 percent indigenous beliefs such as animism. Ethnicity and regional background are more frequently used to identify Chadians than religion, however. Muslims are concentrated in the north, while non-Muslims live mostly in the south. Commonly inhabitants are referred to as "northerners" or "southerners," which also connotes differentiation along religious and ethnic lines.

Transportation and communication are primitive in Chad. Roads are few and poorly maintained. There are no railways, and only 267 kilometers of paved roads. The telephone system is primitive, with only seven thousand lines in use. There are one television station, five radio stations, and five short-wave stations. There are only ten thousand televisions in use, and one thousand Internet users, out of a population estimated at 8.7 million. There were 1.67 million radios in use in 1997. Fifty airports are scattered throughout the country, although only seven have paved runways. Some 48 percent of the population is literate—that is, able to read and write either French or Arabic by age fifteen.

HISTORY

The land of Chad was originally peopled by scattered agricultural communities, but the spread of Islam through much of the region led to the rise of a series of states, kingdoms, and suzerainties between the eighth and nineteenth centuries. The Muslim states were located primarily in the north, prospering off slave raiding at the expense of the animist populations to the south and their key location as a trans-Saharan trade route. By the end of the nineteenth century, Chad had fallen under Sudanese control, and in 1900 it came under French control. In 1910, Chad became part of French Equatorial Africa. A treaty between France and Italy would have ceded the northern Aozou Strip to Italian-controlled Libya, but the treaty was never ratified. It did, however, serve as a pretext for the 1973 Libyan invasion of Chad. This territorial dispute would lead to Libya's annexation of the northern territory, which it would continue to occupy until 1994, when the International Court of Justice (ICJ) would rule in favor of Chad in an arbitration proceeding. Libyan troops withdrew under UN observation, and in May 1994, Libya and Chad signed a cooperation agreement.

Chad became an autonomous republic within the French Community in 1958, and it moved on to full independence on August 11, 1960, with François Tombalbaye, a southerner, the first president. Discontent soon grew, however, and a northern-based rebellion broke out in 1965. Libya provided support to various rebel groups and factions, and the French intervened in support of the government. So began a period of rebellions, coups, insurgencies, and factional fighting that continues to this day. For most of this period Chad's neighbors, Libya and Sudan in particular, supported and harbored various rebel groups, including the 1990 invasion from Sudan that would bring Chad's current president, Idriss Deby, to power.

Under Deby, relations with Libya and Sudan have improved. Deby, a former army chief of staff, declared early on his intention to provide Chad with a new constitution and introduce multiparty elections. Opposition movements were permitted to register and compete in elections, but coup attempts and violent clashes between rebel groups and government forces continued through the 1990s. The Deby government continues to reaffirm

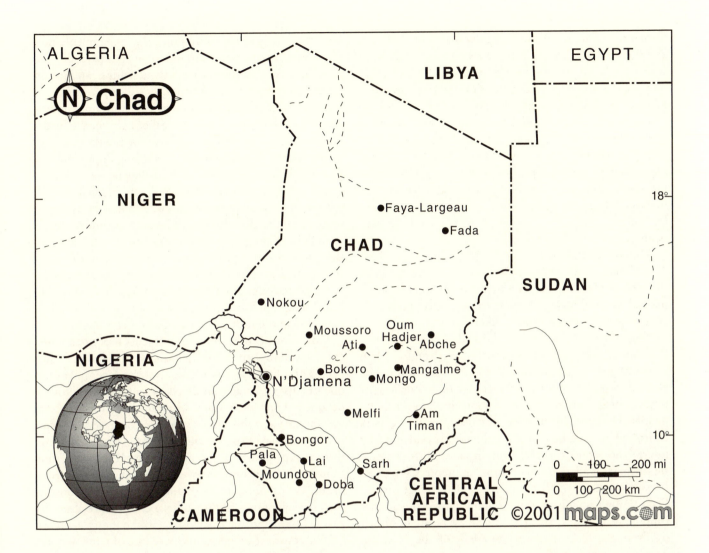

its commitment to democratization despite widespread abuses of government power, such as summary executions of criminals and suspected rebels, and libel charges brought against critics of the government.

In 1994 the transitional council approved a draft constitution that provided for an elected bicameral legislature, a constitutional court, and a president who would be elected for a five-year term. Administrative structures would also be decentralized. As preparations were underway for legislative and presidential elections, violent clashes continued, with government troops killing scores of civilians and rebel factions attacking government forces. A reconciliation agreement allowed Chad's first election to proceed, even though many of the armed factions rejected the cease-fire agreement. On March 31, 1996, the new constitution was approved by 63.5 percent of the voters, and Idriss Deby emerged in July as the winner of the presidency from a field of fifteen candidates. The election was marred, however, by boycotts and charges of corruption. In 2001, Deby was re-elected to a second five-year term from a field of seven candidates.

GOVERNMENT STRUCTURE

Chad is a centralized republic with a strong executive branch as the dominant political force. There is a unicameral, multiparty legislature, and a nominally independent judiciary, although the courts are highly subject to outside political interference. The country is divided into fourteen prefectures, with each provincial capital hosting administrative and judicial institutions. Local governance is either canton- or village-based. The northwestern part of the country remains outside of effective government control, as rebels continue in power there. Despite progress toward democratic reform, control remains firmly in the hands of a northern ethnic oligarchy, and political abuses are rampant.

LEGAL SYSTEM

Chad's legal system is based on a hybrid of French legal codes and Chadian customary law. Chad has not accepted compulsory ICJ jurisdiction. Applicable law and questions of jurisdiction can be confusing, and seemingly arbitrary, as courts often blend the French and traditional legal philosophies in unpredictable ways. In rural areas formal courts are usually unavailable, and most civil cases are handled by traditional courts. These traditional courts might be presided over by a village chief, a sultan, or a tribal elder. Technically, decisions from these informal, traditional courts may be appealed to the formal courts, but in practice the availability of such courts is scant. Many circuits go unserved simply because the judicial branch doesn't have enough money to serve remote areas. Each provincial capital has a magistrate and a criminal court, and ideally the N'Djamena Court of Appeals is supposed to travel to provincial capitals to hear cases, but thus far a lack of money has prevented that from happening.

Military courts are no longer functioning in Chad. The Military Code of Justice has not been enforced since the 1979–1980 civil war, and there are no longer courts-martial or military tribunals for security personnel charged with crimes against civilians.

Since 1999, Chad has established and sworn in a Supreme Court, a Constitutional Court, and a High Court of Justice, as mandated by the constitution. The constitution also calls for a Superior Council of Magistrates, which is charged with guaranteeing judicial independence, but so far that has not been created. Chad's courts are plagued by political influence, as evidenced by interference from the president in cases with political significance, and the demotion of Supreme Court justices who voted against the interests of the chief justice. Even though members of the High Court of Justice are supposed to be elected, so far they have been appointed by President Deby and the president of the National Assembly.

IMPACT

While political and governmental institutions in Chad have remained relatively stagnant and ineffective, by comparison civil society has flourished. Despite threats of legal action or extralegal repression, newspapers continue to criticize the government and test the limits of its tolerance. Development and human rights organizations operate with a high degree of independence, and they serve as an institutional link between government and civil society. The National Commission on Human Rights (CNDH) is modeled on the French advisory commission on human rights, and while it is formally attached to the office of the prime minister, in practice it enjoys a good deal of autonomy. It is prevented, however, from investigating cases pending before the courts, except in cases in which there is "a manifest denial of justice."

The CNDH has resisted offers to move its offices into spaces provided by the national assembly, and in general it is vigorously assertive of its autonomy. International human rights organizations also operate, and while government officials allow these groups to present their find-

ings, they are generally unresponsive or even openly hostile. Some human rights groups are seen as partisan, and there have been incidents of arrest, detention, and intimidation of human rights workers by security forces.

The presence of these human rights groups, despite their limitations, sheds a great deal of light on the inadequacies of the Chadian legal system. While the constitution contains a bill of rights that is strong in principle, in practice these guarantees are routinely ignored. Arbitrary arrest and detention are prohibited, and judicial officials are required to sign arrest warrants, but security forces often do not respect those requirements. Political and extrajudicial killings are often sanctioned officially, although sometimes members of security forces who commit such acts are brought to court on charges. It is commonplace for no action to be taken in response to such killings, however, especially in or near the Tibesti region, where the northwestern rebellion continues.

Government officials and influential persons often enjoy immunity from judicial sanction. Individuals suspected of subversive activities against the government frequently disappear, are murdered by security forces, or are detained. Long detentions without charges or trial are commonplace, with some suspects going several years without a trial. Prisons and jails are overcrowded, and torture, rape, and beatings are commonplace. One rural canton chief was found last year to be operating a private prison with more than one hundred inmates, all outside the purview of any formal judicial court proceeding. By year's end this prison was closed and the inmates freed.

The constitution guarantees freedom of religion and a secular state. In general the government respects freedom of religion, but it requires religious groups to register with the government. Despite the prevalence of Muslims in high positions of government, it seems to be fundamentalist Islamic groups that suffer the most direct repression, to the extent that they are seen as contributing to instability. Some Islamic groups have been sanctioned and their members imprisoned, and several imams have been detained, placed under house arrest, or restricted from preaching. Generally, there is a high level of religious tolerance and coexistence, with the exception of tensions between proselytizing Christians and fundamentalist Muslims.

Discrimination against women is widespread. Traditionally wives are subject to their husbands and have little or no legal protection. Polygamy is legal, and female genital mutilation is common. Theoretically, female genital mutilation is prosecutable as a form of assault, and charges can be brought against parents of victims, medical practitioners, and others involved. In reality, though, the practice is deeply rooted in tradition, and no charges have ever been brought to court. The government does cooperate with the NGO community in trying to edu-

Legal Structure of Chad Courts

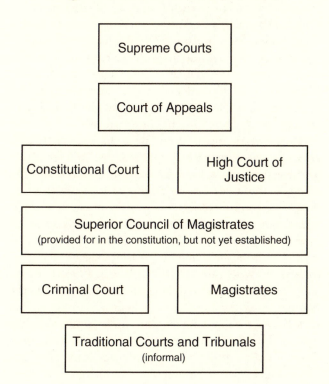

cate the public against this practice. Women have theoretically equal status in property, inheritance, education, and job opportunities, but traditional practice heavily favors men in all of these areas. Forced and arranged marriages are commonplace.

The constitution forbids slavery, child labor under age fourteen, and trafficking in persons. There are reports, however, of forced labor in the formal economy, and even more widespread abusive labor practices in the countryside, especially of children. The military routinely rounds up criminals and forces them to fight on the front lines, and it has been known to conscript young boys to join the ranks, although that practice currently appears to be more rare. Freedom of association is recognized in the constitution, and in general the government has respected both the right to organize unions and the right to strike.

In general, Chad's constitution provides for sound guarantees of a wide range of political and human rights, and in theory it calls for institutions to safeguard those rights. In practice, however, the judicial system has far too few resources to guarantee these standards, and the government's commitment to advancing basic rights seems minimal at best.

Ralph Durham

See also Civil Law; Islamic Law
References and further reading
CIA. *The World Factbook—Chad, 2001.* http://www.odci.gov/ cia/publications/factbook/geos/cd.html (accessed November 9 2001).
Human Rights Watch. *Protectors or Pretenders? Government Human Rights Commissions in Africa: Chad, 2001.* http://www.hrw.org/reports/2001/africa/chad (accessed November 9, 2001).
NewAfrica.com. "Chad History." http://www.newafrica.com/ history (accessed November 9, 2001).
U.S. Department of State. *Country Reports on Human Rights Practices 2000: Chad.* Released by the Bureau of Democracy, Human Rights, and Labor, February 2001. http://www. state.gov/g/drl/rls/hrrpt/2000 (accessed November 9, 2001).

CHANNEL ISLANDS

GENERAL INFORMATION

The Channel Islands of Jersey, Guernsey, Alderney, and Sark, are well known for their cows, their temperate climate, their picturesque scenery, and their status as an offshore banking and financial center. The islands occupy a unique position in the British Commonwealth; they are not part of the United Kingdom or Great Britain, nor are they sovereign states. They are British Crown dependencies that have never been subject to the British Parliament and have always been self-governing units under the direct rule of the Crown acting through the Privy Council. Jersey, Guernsey, Alderney, and Sark have their own insular legislature, judicial system, and administration.

The Channel Islands are located in the Bay of Mont St. Michel off the coast of Normandy, closer to the northwest coast of France than to England. The four main islands—Jersey, Guernsey, Alderney, and Sark—total 194 square kilometers (km). The two main administrative areas are the Bailiwicks of Jersey and Guernsey, each with its own unwritten constitution, local laws, and customs. Guernsey's dependencies include the smaller islands of Alderney, Sark, Herm, Jethou, Lihou, and Brecqhou. Both English and French were the official languages until the mid-twentieth century, but now English is the only official language, although many Channel Islanders are bilingual and some of the older people still speak the Jersey French or Guernsey French languages.

Jersey, at 116 square kilometers, is the largest and most southerly of the islands, only 22 km northwest from the Normandy coast of France, but 160 km from the English coast. Jersey's main source of income is its financial services sector. The population is approximately eighty-seven thousand, with very restrictive immigration controls. The second largest island, Guernsey, is well known for horticulture, especially the export of tomatoes and fresh-cut flowers to the United Kingdom. Guernsey lies 35 km northwest of Jersey and has a total area of 65 square km and a population of approximately sixty-five thousand people. Alderney and Sark are smaller in both area and population. Alderney's population is approximately two thousand people, and the island is 8 square km, lying 11 km west of mainland France. Sark, with its approximately five hundred inhabitants, is considered the last bastion of feudalism in the Western world. Sark has a total area of 5.5 square km and lies 11 km east of Guernsey.

EVOLUTION AND HISTORY

The history of the Channel Islands has led to a judicial system and body of laws that are distinct, yet related, to both England and France. To understand the law of the Channel Islands, it is necessary to understand its roots in the medieval Duchy of Normandy, which held land in what is now modern-day England and France. The Channel Islands were part of the Duchy of Normandy before William's conquest of England in 1066. When William the Conqueror became King of England, the islands became English dependencies. In 1204, upon the loss of continental Normandy to France, the islands remained sovereign to England. At this early period, the two bailiwicks of Jersey and Guernsey were created and received successive royal charters with England that secured important rights and privileges for the Channel Islands' inhabitants.

After 1204, Norman customary law evolved in Jersey, Guernsey, and Normandy in parallel, but not identical, developments. The basis of modern-day Channel Island law is the ancient and customary law of Normandy, collected in the *Ancienne Coûtume,* which probably dates to the time of Henry III in the thirteenth century. A Jersey commentator, Poingdestre (1609–1691), in his *Commentaires sur l'Ancienne Coutume de Normandie,* found that seventeenth-century Jersey still looked to contemporary Norman law. But by that time, the Normans were moving away from the ancient *coutume* and toward a more modern French, or civil, law modeled on the law that prevailed in Paris. French law changed greatly after the French Revolution, when the *Codes Napoléon* superseded the French customary law in 1804.

The influence of English and French law on present-day Channel Island law is not clear, but both have played a role in the development of the laws of the islands. In Jersey, English legal doctrines have shaped both criminal and civil law. Two nineteenth-century reports, *The Criminal Report* (1847) and *The Civil Report* (1861), documented the status of the contemporary Jersey laws. *The Criminal Report* found that criminal law derived from the laws of Normandy as cited in the ancient commentaries and considered by the Royal Court, but in practice the authorities extensively cited English criminal law and cases. Civil examples of English influence on Guernsey and Jersey law are the adoption of English principles of negligence law

and the use of English authority in commercial matters. Modern French law as such is not authoritative in the islands, but French law after the introduction of the *Codes Napoléon* has been much cited in the Jersey courts when it is shown to be continuous with the customary law before codification. A degree of uncertainty about some Channel Island legal doctrines has resulted from the courts' melding of elements from both the English and French legal systems without consistent rules.

The Norman origins of the law of the Channel Islands are still a force. The Jersey Court of Appeal will refer back to the earliest sources in the *Ancienne Coûtume* and the commentaries to determine the law of Jersey today when there is no established Jersey law. Many question whether a legal system based in medieval Norman concepts can meet the demands of modern-day finance. Jersey showed that it can meet the changing needs of society when it reformed the Wills and Successions Law in 1993. The new laws changed testate and intestate succession from the Norman *conservation du bien de la famille* and made the laws of succession simpler and more equitable. The changes include an improved position of women upon the death of a spouse or divorce, the abolishment of primogeniture, and a simpler inheritance design of immovable property (realty) to replace the complex Norman-based *partage.* Similarly, Sark revised its property laws in 1999 to grant women the right to inherit property where previously property could be handed down to women only if no male heirs existed.

Until 1771 the Royal Court was the only legislative body in Jersey. All laws passed by the Royal Court were collected in the Code of Jersey. The States of Jersey (the island parliament) legislate primarily by way of laws, with subordinate legislation taking the form of regulations and orders. The laws form part of the *Recueil des Lois,* dating from the Code of 1771, with the regulations and laws published together in a separate series. Judgments of the Royal Court are recorded in the Public Registry, and judgments from 1885 to 1978 are indexed in the *Tables des Décisions.* They are not a true report or published opinion in the American sense, but a very brief synopsis of the pertinent points. The Jersey Judgments that ran from 1950 to 1984 were the first formal law reports. Since 1984 there has been an official reporter series for case opinions, the Jersey Law Reports, published on the authority of the Royal Court of Jersey by Law Reports International in England.

CURRENT STRUCTURE

The Bailiwicks of Guernsey and Jersey each have a Royal Court, the principal court in each Bailiwick, that exercises criminal and civil jurisdiction. Alderney and Sark have local courts with the right of appeal to the Royal Court of Guernsey.

Legal Structure of Channel Islands Courts

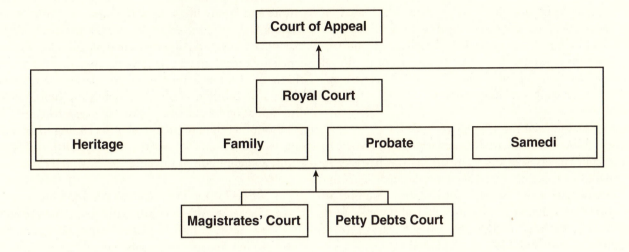

Jersey Judicial System

The Jersey judicial system consists of the Jersey Court of Appeal, the Royal Court (which has both superior and inferior courts), Magistrates' Court, and Petty Debts Court. There are four divisions of the superior court: Héritage, Family, Probate, and Samedi. The jurisdiction of the Héritage division is the determination of the following actions: ownership of immoveable property, division of immoveable property, annulment of hereditary contracts, fixing of boundaries, and assignment of *rentes*. Family division jurisdiction involves matrimonial matters including divorce, separation, maintenance, and custody issues, as well as legitimacy, paternity, and adoption matters. Probate division jurisdiction is concerned with estate administration, and the jurisdiction of the Samedi division is the determination of all matters not within the jurisdiction of the Héritage, Family, or Probate divisions.

The jurisdiction of the inferior Royal Court is both civil and criminal. In civil matters it is a court of first instance, and in criminal matters it is a court of first instance for serious offenses and the appeal court from the Magistrates' Court where that court has exercised summary jurisdiction in lesser offenses. The Inferior Number of the Royal Court may impose imprisonment for a period not exceeding four years; only the Superior Number of the Royal Court can impose sentences greater than four years. The Magistrates' Court deals with most criminal cases at first instances, and the Petty Debts Court with small claims and a number of specific civil matters.

The head of the judiciary is the bailiff, who is also president of the States of Jersey. The bailiff has a deputy, and they are assisted by full- or part-time judges known as commissioners. Unique components of the Jersey courts are jurats, men and women of experience and social standing who are elected to serve as lay assessors of fact and only receive a small payment from monies raised by stamp duty on contracts. Unlike members of a jury, jurats are not drawn at random from members of the community to serve for a short period. Jurats are permanent judges appointed by an electoral college. Normally two jurats will sit with the bailiff as the Inferior Number, or in certain cases as the Superior Number comprising between five and twelve jurats. All law judges (bailiff, deputy bailiff, and commissioners) will sit with jurats unless the matter before the court is one of law only, or in the case of a criminal trial, the judge is sitting with the jury. The Magistrates' Court is presided over by a magistrate and assistant magistrates, together with several part-time relief magistrates as necessary.

Juries are not used with civil trials and may or may not be used in criminal trials. Historically, offenses in Jersey have been divided into two separate classes: common law offenses called crimes and *délits* (crimes less serious in nature) and statutory offenses called contraventions. A defendant charged with a statutory offense has no right to a jury trial and instead will be tried by one law judge (the bailiff or deputy bailiff) and two jurats. The law judge casts the deciding vote in cases where the jurats are divided in opinion. Anyone committed by the Magistrates' Court for a common law offense can request a trial by judge and jury but has no right to such a trial.

The Jersey Court of Appeal was created in 1964. The three-judge appellate court assumed jurisdiction to hear and determine civil and criminal appeals from both the Inferior and Superior Numbers of the Royal Courts. It is, in this sense, the supreme court of Jersey, but the final court of appeal is to the Privy Council in England.

Other judicial players of the modern-day judicial system in Jersey include the attorney general and the solicitor general, who are Crown appointees that represent the

Crown and States in both civil and criminal matters. There is also the viscount, the chief executive officer of the island's courts and the States of Jersey, who may sit in a quasi-judicial capacity when hearing bankruptcy matters and inquests. The judicial *greffier,* the clerk and registrar of the court and keeper of the records of the Royal Court, can sit in a judicial capacity and hear certain applications in civil and family matters.

Legal Profession and Legal Training

Jersey lawyers are either advocates who are qualified to appear in all Jersey courts (comparable to a barrister in England) or solicitors who have more limited rights but otherwise have a similar role. Until 1860 the number of advocates was limited to six, and the bailiff chose them without any testing. In 1860 the Jersey Bar was thrown open to any British subject who had lived ten years in Jersey and possessed the necessary English or French diplomas, or had passed a local law examination. Today, the majority of Jersey lawyers study law in England and obtain a professional qualification as a barrister in England or Wales prior to training in the Channel Islands. A small minority qualify locally without outside study. Currently, prospective advocates and solicitors must pass a qualifying exam to practice law in Jersey. Ten persons passed the qualifying exam in April 2001.

The legal aid system in Jersey is administered and financed by practicing lawyers, both advocates and solicitors. By custom and practice all Jersey lawyers are on the roster, called the *Tour de role,* for fifteen years after qualification. They do not receive any payment for their services other than what the client can afford and are obliged to comply with the client's instructions, except in exceptional circumstances.

NOTABLE FEATURES OF LAW/LEGAL SYSTEM

The *Clameur de Haro* is an interesting vestige of feudal law still extant in the Channel Islands. Each island practices a slightly different version, but all derive from the Norman custom that a person can obtain immediate cessation of any action he or she considers to be an infringement of personal rights. In one version, the harmed person must, in front of witnesses at the scene, recite the Lord's prayer in French and cry out *"Haro, Haro, Haro! A mon aide mon Prince, on me fait tort!"* The *Clameur* must be registered at the *Greffe* (Court Clerk's office) with a fee of approximately ten dollars. All actions must end until the matter is heard by the Royal Court, and if, after investigation, the complaint is disallowed, the complainant can be liable to a claim for damages.

In 2000 the European Convention of Human Rights was assimilated into a Human Rights Law of Jersey. The Articles of Convention are evocative of the U.S. Bill of Rights. Articles include a right to life; a right to liberty and security; a right to a fair trial; a right to respect for private and family life; a right to marry; no punishment without law; a right to education; a right to free elections; freedom of thought, conscience, and religion; freedom of expression; freedom of assembly and association; a prohibition of torture; a prohibition of slavery and forced labor; a prohibition of abuse of rights; a prohibition of discrimination by sex, race, color, language, religion, political or other opinion, national or social origin, association with a national minority, property, birth, or other status; and abolition of the death penalty.

RELATION TO NATIONAL SYSTEM

Jersey, Guernsey, Alderney, and Sark have a unique constitutional relationship with the United Kingdom because of their history as the only remaining remnants of the Duchy of Normandy possessed by the English Crown. The Channel Islanders owe allegiance to the sovereign (Queen Elizabeth II, who to them is the successor of the Duke of Normandy), but they are not incorporated into the United Kingdom. The involvement of Great Britain is generally limited to defense matters and international affairs, never local affairs. The Guernsey and Jersey States legislate on domestic matters, including taxation. It is generally accepted that the Parliament of the United Kingdom can legislate for the Bailiwicks of Guernsey and Jersey, but in practice no laws are imposed against the wishes of the respective bailiwicks. The United Kingdom has negotiated special arrangements with the European Economic Community regarding the Channel Islands to protect their constitutional rights and preserve their fiscal autonomy.

Karen Gottlieb

See also England and Wales; France; Napoleonic Code; Privy Council

References and further reading
Bell, Brian, ed. 2000. "Insight Guide Channel Islands." 3d ed. Singapore: APA Publications.
Jersey Law Review. 1997, 1998, and 1999 issues. http://www. jerseylegalinfo.je/publications/jerseylawreview/index_frames. htm (accessed May 16, 2001).
Jersey Legal Information Board. "Jersey Legal Information." http://www.jerseylegalinfo.je (accessed May 16, 2001).
Seigneur of Sark. "Sark Government." http://www.sark.gov.gg (accessed May 2, 2001).
States of Alderney. "The States of Alderney." http://www. alderney.gov.gg/govern (accessed October 30, 2001).
States of Guernsey. "The States of Guernsey." http://www. gov.gg (accessed May 2, 2001).
States of Jersey. "Judicial Greffe." http://www.judicialgreffe. gov.je (accessed October 30, 2001).

CHILE

COUNTRY INFORMATION

Chile is a thin, lengthy strip of land running down the west coast of southernmost South America. It borders on Peru to the north, Bolivia to the northeast, Argentina to the east, and the Pacific Ocean to the west. It is some 2,006,096 square kilometers in area, including Easter Island and Antarctica. Due to its length, Chile's climate, geography, and landscape run the entire gamut—from the world's driest desert on the north to cold forests, lakes, fjords, and archipelagos on the south, with tall mountains, active volcanoes, and deep valleys throughout. In central Chile, home to most of the population, the climate is temperate Mediterranean. While summer officially runs from December to March, warm weather often extends from November through May.

Fully one-third of Chile's 15,211,300 inhabitants live in Santiago, the nation's capital. Two-thirds are over eighteen.

About 65 percent of the population is of mixed descent—a combination of Spanish and native stock. European backgrounds other than Spanish account for another 25 percent. Indigenous groups account for 10 percent. The largest of these are the Mapuche, the first inhabitants of the south of Chile. While Spanish is the official language, many native peoples still maintain their language and culture.

According to the 1992 census, literacy is high. The illiterate population stands at some 575,176 people, with women accounting for slightly over half (304,986). The rate is higher in rural areas—14 percent of the population, affecting men and women equally.

Of the population over age fourteen surveyed in the 1992 census, 7,409,520 (77 percent) reported being Roman Catholic, followed by 1,198,385 Evangelicals, and 80,259 Protestants. Some 409,910 were members of other denominations and 562,285 nonbelievers were registered. About 27.7 percent of the population lived below the poverty line. Chile's legal system is based on the civil law tradition prevailing in continental Europe.

HISTORY

At the time of the arrival of the Spanish conquistadors, part of the Chilean territory was under the rule of the Inca Empire. The Mapuche inhabited the south and parts of current-day Argentina. The Spanish reached central Chile in 1541 and founded Santiago, the nation's capital. The colonial period began in earnest around 1598 and ended in 1810, when Chile declared independence. The Mapuche fiercely fought the Spanish for 200 years, successfully preventing settlement south of the Bío-Bío River.

Colonial Chile was administratively dependent on the viceroyalty of Peru, and its legal system had a mix of sources, including Spanish law and special edicts—*las leyes indias*—enacted for the colonies. After independence in 1810, the sources of private law continued to be Spanish law, old colonial ordinances, and from then on, local statutes. This brought about an often inconsistent body of laws, with some newly enacted local laws contradicting Spanish ordinances. To deal with this issue, in 1831 the government commissioned Venezuelan-born legal scholar Andrés Bello to draft a civil code. He accomplished this task in several stages and brought it to completion in 1855. The code came into effect in 1857. Bello's sources were eclectic: Roman law, canon law, torts and contracts from the French civil code, and even the civil code of Louisiana and Sardinia. In the area of family issues he followed canon law, which disallows divorce.

The Chilean civil code subsequently served as a model for Latin America. Ecuador and Colombia adopted it in its entirety, while Argentina, Nicaragua, El Salvador, Venezuela, Paraguay, and Uruguay used it as a source in drafting their own civil laws.

Over the years the civil code underwent important reforms, mostly in the area of family law. The most recent, adopted in 1999, provided equal rights to children born out of wedlock. Still, Chile remains the only country in the western hemisphere to have no provision for divorce. While a divorce bill did clear the Lower House in 1997, Senate approval remains pending. The bill is bitterly opposed by the Church and some conservative members of the legislature.

The code of commerce was adopted in 1865 and came into effect two years later. A criminal code was enacted in 1894 and civil and criminal procedure codes were introduced ten years later. In the 1880s the government obtained passage of a body of laws known as *liberal or lay laws* because they provided for religious freedom, lay cemeteries, and the preeminence of civil over religious marriages. In 1931 Chile enacted a labor code, which essentially assembled in one place all statutes governing labor relations.

After independence, governments moved quickly to draft a constitution, with several attempts starting in 1811. Some scholars claim that the first constitution was that enacted in 1822. Others counter that these were inexperienced attempts at constitutional drafting that had little to do with political and cultural developments in the country. In the end, a true constitution was enacted in 1833 and stayed in effect for nearly a century. Although there were no constitutional reforms as such through 1871, an 1865 bill interpreted the constitution to the effect that the country's official religion was Roman Catholic and that others could not worship in public places. A rapid series of reforms followed, to the extent that some commentators wrote that amendments effected through 1874 amounted to a true rewriting of

the constitution. The 1833 Constitution was replaced in 1925. This constitution, which declared Chile a secular state, was in effect until 1980. Prior to that year, the military government under General Augusto Pinochet had reformed important segments of the 1925 Constitution and suspended others, notably constitutional rights.

In 1973 a bloody coup d'état overthrew the democratically elected government of President Salvador Allende. The country was ruled until 1990 by a military junta led by General Augusto Pinochet. Unlike other Latin American dictatorships, the Chilean military built a new institutional order that involved introduction of far-reaching economic, cultural, and legal reforms—notably enactment of a new constitution with built-in provisions designed to thwart amendment.

Much has been said about the legitimacy of the 1980 Constitution still in effect. While approved by referendum, the vote was held in a climate of massive human rights abuses and major restrictions to freedom of expression, the right of assembly, and political participation. This constitution has a strong presidential orientation, giving the executive branch a virtual monopoly on leg-

islative initiatives. It also stacks the Senate with nine "appointed senators," including four former commanders in chief of the Armed Forces and Police appointed by the National Security Council; two former Supreme Court justices and one former comptroller-general appointed by the Supreme Court, and one former cabinet minister and one former university president, both appointed by the president. It also included a recently repealed clause entitling former presidents having served a full six-year term to become "life senators." The constitution bestows upon the military the role of guarantors of institutional order and national security and provides for a National Security Council where Armed Forces heads sit as equals with Supreme Court justices, the comptroller-general, the speaker of the Senate, and the president. Finally, it provides for a binomial electoral system effectively guaranteeing the (right-wing) minority an important block of seats in Parliament even if defeated at the ballot box.

In 1988, as provided in the constitution, the government called a Yes-No referendum asking whether General Pinochet should continue to rule for another eight years. The No side won a resounding victory in a vote the junta could not fix, and the de facto ruler reluctantly stepped down. As some writers have noted, the opposition, having failed to defeat Pinochet through civil disobedience or military means, in the end did so under his own rules of the game. The referendum result was a mixed blessing, as the new government inherited the tailor-made social, economic, and constitutional order designed by the military and their right-wing civilian supporters. General Pinochet stayed on as army commander-in-chief through March 1998, when he became a life senator. Although members of Parliament moved to impeach him, they failed to force the general to retire from political life.

An otherwise peaceful return to democracy was marred by tension over past human rights abuses. In 1990 President Patricio Aylwin set up a Truth and Reconciliation Commission to look into human rights under Pinochet. In 1978 General Pinochet issued a blanket amnesty covering the time when most such cases—notably disappearances—took place, and the Pinochet-appointed judiciary showed little interest in investigating or prosecuting cases that were not covered by the amnesty. As a result, the commission mandate was based on what came to be known as "transitional justice." There was an urgent need to find out the truth of human rights abuses under Pinochet and to investigate and prosecute cases of murder and forced disappearance to the extent permitted by legal constraints. Although the commission was not mandated to deal with other abuses such as torture and exile, it did produce a fairly accurate record of what transpired in Pinochet's Chile. The Commission Report and subsequent investigation by a successor commission established that nearly 3,200 people were murdered or made to disappear. Murders and murder attempts took state agents as far afield as the USA, Italy, and Argentina.

In October 1998, General Augusto Pinochet, recuperating from back surgery at a London clinic, was arrested on a warrant from Spanish judge Baltasar Garzón requesting his extradition. The warrant alleged that Pinochet was responsible for the murder of Spanish citizens in Chile when he was president. Pinochet spent more than a year in detention in England, until the British Home Secretary allowed him to return to Chile on humanitarian grounds. Not without irony, much of Pinochet's defense was based on international human rights law and the need for due process. After his return, in what became a milestone in Chile's democratic transition and judicial history, a Chilean judge lifted his senatorial immunity and indicted him in Chile.

LEGAL CONCEPTS

The basis of Chilean law is the country's constitution. Article 1 of the civil code defines the law as "a manifestation of the sovereign will which enjoins, forbids, or permits in the manner prescribed in the Constitution." The consti-

tution provides for a division of powers into executive, legislative, and judicial branches. It also protects fundamental human rights such as free speech, equality before the law, presumption of innocence, and the right to counsel in criminal proceedings. It also protects private property and the right to live in a pollution-free environment. Although the constitution recognizes a long list of fundamental rights, not all of them can be enforced by constitutional means, notably such social and economic rights as education, health care, or employment. Yet, consistent with its social and economic orientation, the constitution does entrench such rights as to choose between the public and private health care systems and to organize private schools, to name a few.

Legislation is the only source of law. As stated in the civil code, judges do not make law. Their rulings only apply to the case at hand and set no precedent. Custom is recognized as a source of law if referred to and complemented in legislation. To use customary practice as a rule, the practice must first be proven. Article 63 of the constitution requires a different quorum for approval of legislation, depending on its nature.

Current president Ricardo Lagos took office in March 2000. Presidents serve a six-year term and cannot succeed themselves. Election requires a majority of votes cast; if no candidate receives a majority a runoff election is called, as was the case in the past presidential election. Although the president has veto power, he can be overruled by a two-thirds vote in Congress.

The bicameral legislature consists of a 49-member Senate and a 120-member Chamber of Deputies. Senators are elected to an eight-year term. Excepting appointed members, the Senate is renewed in alternate elections held every four years. Deputies serve a four-year term.

The Supreme Court has twenty-one members appointed by the president from a list submitted by the Court itself. These appointments are subject to Senate approval. If the Senate declines, the Supreme Court must nominate new candidates. Justices serve through the age of seventy-five. The Supreme Court elects a president from among its number to a single three-year term. Its members include five prominent lawyers or scholars drawn from outside the judiciary.

A seven-member Constitutional Tribunal reviews statutes that interpret or complement the constitution as well as treaties submitted to Parliament for ratification. If requested by the president, either chamber of Congress or one-quarter of its members, the tribunal can also rule on the constitutionality of Executive Decrees or bills presented to Parliament. Its members include three Supreme Court justices plus four prominent lawyers or scholars named by the National Security Council (2), the president (1), and the Senate (1).

A five-member Electoral Tribunal rules on referenda

and presidential, parliamentary, and municipal elections. The Supreme Court appoints four members from among its current or former members and a fifth from among former speakers or deputy-speakers of the Chamber of Deputies or the Senate. Members serve a four-year term.

The recent reforms in Chile's criminal justice system have created the independent Ministerio Público or Office of the Public Prosecutor. This agency sets global prosecution policy and oversees regional prosecutors. A National Prosecutor is appointed by the president to a ten-year term from among five candidates submitted by the Supreme Court. Appointment is subject to approval by a two-thirds Senate majority. Regional prosecutors are appointed by the National Prosecutor from lists submitted by appellate courts.

The constitution was amended in 1989 to provide that international human rights treaties and conventions prevail over domestic law. Most legal scholars concur with the position that human rights instruments hold constitutional rank as a result. Chile is a signatory to key international human rights covenants, including the Universal Declaration of Human Rights, the American Declaration of the Rights and Duties of Man, the International Covenant on Civil and Political Rights, the International Covenant on Economic, Social and Cultural Rights, the International Convention on the Elimination of All Forms of Racial Discrimination, the Convention on the Elimination of All Forms of Discrimination Against Women, the Convention Against Torture and Other Cruel, Inhuman or Degrading Treatment or Punishment, the Convention on the Rights of the Child, the Inter-American Convention to Prevent, Punish, and Eradicate Violence Against Women, and the American Convention on Human Rights, among others.

Although collective bargaining and labor relations are regulated by the labor code, civil contracts are often used to disguise labor agreements. The code provides for a forty-eight-hour working week. Although it bans gender discrimination, recent studies by the government's own Department on the Status of Women found that on average women earn 65 percent of men's wages for work of equal value. Women are entitled to paid maternity leave from six weeks prior to birth to twelve weeks after. A working parent can take paid leave if a child under the age of one is seriously ill. If both parents work, the mother chooses who uses this benefit. Nursing mothers are entitled to two half-hour breast-feeding breaks per day. Employers of twenty women or more must provide or subsidize day-care service for children until the age of two. The minimum wage—currently set at about U.S.$173 per month—is legislated following negotiations between unions, government, and employers.

Ever since November 2000 the Chilean code of criminal procedure has been undergoing radical reform modeled after the Ibero-American code of criminal procedure. Based on the German tradition, this code was adopted by many countries in the region in the 1980s and 1990s. The reform does away with the inquisitorial system, a document-based scheme whereby judges investigate, lay charges, then act as trial judges. This burdensome system is being replaced by oral hearings, an adversarial system, pretrial judges, and a three-member trial court.

Criminal justice system reforms are now being phased in in two of Chile's administrative regions, with the rest of the country soon to follow. This is part of a major legal reform drive that includes family courts providing oral hearings and institutionalized mediation, as well as significant changes to civil and labor court procedures.

Although there are few formal public opinion studies of the old justice system, the public perception is one of near collapse. The clearest symptom was the failure of the judiciary to prevent human rights abuses under the military government. The Truth Commission Report concluded that the judiciary failed not only to prevent, but also to punish gross human rights violations. As President Aylwin stated in an interview, " . . . it lacked the moral courage to protect human rights." Indeed, at the inauguration of the 1975 judicial year, the president of the Supreme Court had rebuffed reports that people were disappearing and that torture was being widely used. Polls have ranked the state of the justice system among the top three concerns of Chilean citizens. In a joint survey by the University Development Corporation and the Catholic University of Chile, fully 83 percent of respondents reported having a negative opinion of the justice system, which they perceived as inefficient, discriminatory, and arbitrary.

Democratic governments since Pinochet have striven to modernize the justice system by improving salaries and court infrastructure. A new Judicial Academy trains new members of the judiciary and provides refresher courses for sitting judges and court clerks.

In the 1990s four Supreme Court justices, including the court president, were impeached by Parliament. One such action resulted in the removal of the individual in question for gross dereliction of duty. Since then the Supreme Court has made a major effort to rid the justice system of corrupt or influence-peddling magistrates and court clerks, ranking members of the appellate and Supreme courts included.

CURRENT COURT SYSTEM STRUCTURE

The Supreme Court is the highest body. It is a forum of last resort with additional oversight powers over all courts, save for the Constitutional and Electoral Tribunals and Wartime Military Courts. Supreme and appellate court justices can be removed by Parliament, with the Lower House declaring the charges pertinent and the Senate acting as a jury.

Chilean courts are organized as follows:

1. Appellate courts: Primarily review trial and lower court rulings. They act as courts of first instance for habeas corpus and other constitutional rights actions; also adjudicate on administrative decisions and dispute resolution cases.
2. Trial courts: Ordinary courts with civil or criminal jurisdiction, including over some family law issues.
3. Minor courts: They handle alimony, guardianship, and adoption cases and certain issues related to young offenders and other children at risk.
4. Labor courts: Oversee labor issues; only available in larger urban centers.
5. Military courts: They handle offenses involving members of the military and police, whether as plaintiffs or defendants, whether in time of peace or war.
6. Local courts: In charge of motor vehicle offenses and consumer and small claims.

In general, litigants must be represented by an attorney, although participants in family, domestic violence, and constitutional cases—for example, habeas corpus and constitutional protection writ—are allowed to litigate on their own.

Since the right to counsel is guaranteed in the constitution, Chile meets this obligation by requiring graduating law students to perform an unpaid, compulsory six-month legal aid internship. This arrangement is criticized for its predictably poor service quality and its inability to meet demand from the poor for legal services. In response, national and local governments have implemented programs to improve access. As the new code of criminal procedure provides that only trained lawyers can act as counsel in criminal matters, important changes to the structure of the legal aid system should result. Legal aid often allocates significant human resources to criminal defenses, to the detriment of family, labor, and other cases. Legal aid also provides mediation services designed to encourage out-of-court settlements, however the services are rendered in one center in Santiago.

Military courts investigate and prosecute indictable offenses committed by members of the armed forces or Carabineros police or by civilians against them, whether in time of peace or war. These prerogatives are strongly criticized because of the armed forces's track record of direct involvement in massive human rights violations that were never prosecuted or punished by military courts, as well as because of these courts' lack of impartiality in such cases. In the past decade lawyers and scholars have de-manded a major overhaul of the military justice system, essentially to rein in its peacetime jurisdiction.

In addition, certain government agencies and departments are empowered to adjudicate on matters such as tax and antitrust law and telecommunication and public utility rate schedules, to name a few. These decisions remain subject to review, especially by appellate courts.

STAFFING

The judiciary employs 136 appellate court magistrates, 402 lower court judges, 402 court clerks or deputy judges, and more than 3,800 support staff.

Early on the military government did away with membership in a professional association as a requirement for practicing a profession. This still stands. As a result, there are no accurate figures on the number of practicing lawyers. The Santiago Bar Association alone has some 11,000 registered members, with close to 7,700 in good standing. There are seventeen regional bar associations throughout the country. In 2000 more than 1,000 lawyers were admitted to the bar. The title of attorney is granted by the Supreme Court.

Since a criminal justice reform is currently being phased in, no final figures on the numbers of prosecutors and public defenders are available. Appointment to these posts is competitive.

Judges and court clerks can be removed by the Supreme Court if their conduct or performance fail to meet standards or if found guilty of an indictable offense. Upper-court magistrates can be removed by Parliament if found guilty of dereliction of duty.

The judge selection process has changed substantially since creation in 1999 of a Judicial Academy. This arm's-length agency is administered by a governing board consisting of three members of the Supreme Court, one appellate court magistrate, the chair of the Santiago Bar Association, two legal scholars, and the minister of Justice.

Chile has twenty-seven law schools. The University of Chile Law School, founded in 1843, is the oldest and largest, with some 2,400 students.

IMPACT OF LAW

Chile is a highly legalistic society where the law plays a pivotal role in conflict resolution. However, the traditional administration of justice is widely regarded as merely an application of the statutes that leaves little room for innovative interpretation.

Lidia Casas

See also The Spanish Empire and the Laws of the Indies
References and further reading
Alvarez, Hernán. 2001. "Inauguration of the 2001 Judicial Year." *Official Gazette* (March 6).
Campos, H. Fernando. 1997. *Historia Constitucional de Chile.* 6th ed. Santiago: Editorial Jurídica de Chile.

Correa, Jorge. 1992. "Dealing with Past Human Rights Violations." *Notre Dame Law Review* 67, no. 5: 1455–1494.

Correa, J., and M. A. Jiménez. 1995. "Acceso de los pobres a la justicia en Chile." In *Acceso de los pobres a la justicia.* Edited by Franz Vanderschueren and Enrique Oviedo. Santiago: Ediciones SUR. Colección Estudios Urbanos.

Figueroa Yáñez, Gonzalo. 1989. *Curso de Derecho Civil.* Vol. 1. 2nd ed. Santiago: Editorial Jurídica de Chile.

Horwitz, María Inés. 1998. "La Justicia Militar: Justificación, competencia y organización en el derecho comparado. Los principios de independencia e imparcialidad en la organización de los Tribunales Militares chilenos." In *Justicia Militar y Estado de Derecho.* Edited by Jorge Mera. *Cuadernos de Análisis Jurídico* 40. Santiago: School of Law, Diego Portales University.

Jocelyn-Holt, L. Alfredo. 1998. *El Chile Perplejo: del avanzar sin transar al transar sin parar.* Santiago: Editorial Planeta.

———. 1992. *La Independencia de Chile: tradición, modernización y mito.* Madrid: Editorial Mapfre.

Mera, Jorge. 1998."Razones justificatorias y ámbito de la jurisdicción penal militar en tiempos de paz." In *Justicia Militar y Estado de Derecho.* Edited by Jorge Mera. *Cuadernos de Análisis Jurídico* 40. Santiago: School of Law, Diego Portales University.

Peña, G. Carlos. 1993. "Informe sobre Chile. Situación y políticas judiciales en América Latina." *Cuadernos de Análisis Jurídico,* Serie Publicaciones Especiales No. 2. Santiago: School of Law, Diego Portales University.

Riego, Cristián. 1998. "The Chilean Criminal Procedure Reform." *International Journal of the Sociology of the Law* 26: 437–452.

CHINA

COUNTRY INFORMATION

China is situated in eastern Asia, bordering the East China Sea, Korea Bay, Yellow Sea, and South China Sea, Afghanistan, Bhutan, Burma, India, Kazakhstan, North Korea, Kyrgyzstan, Laos, Mongolia, Nepal, Pakistan, Russia, Tajikistan, and Vietnam. Its land mass is 9,326,410 square kilometers. China is the third largest country in the world after Russia and Canada. The population is about 1.3 billion people, more than any other country. China is largely culturally homogeneous, over 90 percent of all Chinese are Han. There are also Zhuang, Uygur, Hui, Yi, Tibetan, Miao, Manchu, Mongol, Buyi, Korean, and other nationalities. The official language is Mandarin Chinese. China's legal system is an amalgam of custom and statute, largely criminal law. A rudimentary civil code has been in effect since January 1, 1987. The state is giving high priority to improvement of civil, administrative, criminal, and commercial law.

HISTORY

China has a longer recorded history than any other nation on earth. The present nation is based on the unifi-cation of diverse principalities by the first emperor of the Qin Dynasty in 221 B.C.E. The English name China has its origins in this ancient imperial state. Qin is pronounced like the English word *chin,* hence "China." The name of the country in Chinese is *Zhongguo,* literally "the Middle Kingdom."

The Chinese emperor was referred to as the Son of Heaven. Through ritual, Chinese emperors legitimated their rule as divinely ordained. The emperor was the sole legitimate temporal power over all the earth ("all under heaven"). The emperor thus had authority over all foreign sovereigns (who were regarded as little more than tribal heads).

China as the Middle Kingdom thus traditionally saw itself as the center of the world, with culture and civilization radiating in concentric circles from its emperor's imperial throne. The further people lived from the Chinese capital, the less cultured and civilized they were seen to be. The Chinese emperor sent officials to the limits of the civilized areas, but for areas inhabited by barbarians the emperor considered it acceptable that their leaders simply acknowledge China's preeminence by sending tribute missions to China every third year to bow in obeisance and bring the emperor gifts of their local products. To discourage China's armies from invading them, the neighboring nations, including Korea, Japan, and Vietnam, cooperated in the bearing of tribute (for which their leaders were richly rewarded by return gifts from the Chinese emperor). Indeed the Chinese cosmology of being the Middle Kingdom and sole civilization was affirmed by the reality that the Koreans, Vietnamese, and Japanese adopted classical Chinese as their written language and accepted Chinese Confucianism as their state ideology.

As Latin, Christianity, and Greek and Roman thought played an important unifying and determinative role in Europe's identity and the development of political and legal institutions, classical Chinese and Chinese philosophy had a corresponding function in East Asia.

Chinese philosophy has two main threads: Confucianism and Daoism. The latter encouraged a laissez-faire approach. As the *Dao De Jing* (*Tao Te Ching* or *Classic of the Way*) put it: "Ruling a large country is like cooking a small fish." The *Analects of Confucius* defined a feudal hierarchy wherein the maintaining of social roles was the basis for political stability. Emperors should rule benevolently. Officials should defer to those above them in the hierarchy and treat those below them with compassion. Within families the sons should defer to their fathers and younger brothers defer to elder brothers. The virtue of the emperor was the key link in the social system. If the emperor became morally corrupt then the corruption would penetrate throughout society. Officials would greedily extract unjustly heavy taxes to maintain their corrupted lifestyles. The natural order would similarly go

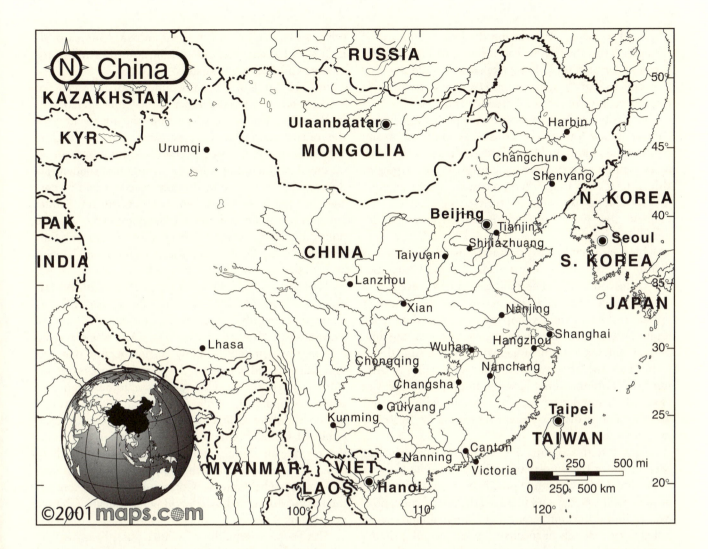

awry, with floods and pestilence bringing suffering on to the people (from a rational perspective corrupt regimes tended to sell grain reserves, meaning that a year with poor harvest had disastrous consequences of mass starvation). Responding to a corrupt regime, it was written that women would give birth to cows and birds would fly backward as indications of heaven's displeasure with the breakdown in the temporal order. Then a popular rebellion fueled by the peasantry's discontent with a corrupt, rapacious, and ineffective government would challenge the existing dynastic regime and a new dynasty would eventually take its place. China had twenty-four imperial dynasties that followed this general pattern of rise and fall over the period from about 2100 B.C.E. up to 1911 C.E. when the Republic of China was promulgated.

For most of its long history China was (up until only a few hundred years ago) without question the most advanced nation in the world. In his famous account of his travels in China, the thirteenth-century Venetian merchant, Marco Polo, commented on all aspects of Chinese life in a highly laudatory manner. The standards of architecture, commerce, art, governance, cuisine, clothing, agricultural technology, and so on, all compared favorably to those prevailing in Europe at the time. Chinese products, particularly silk cloth and porcelains, were much in demand abroad as the European cloth and chinaware were for inferior due to the relatively primitive technologies in use in the West.

In the eighteenth century there began large-scale export of Chinese products into Europe. This was intensified by Europeans acquiring a taste for Chinese tea. Because there was virtually no European product able to compete in the Chinese market, this one-sided trade led to a major outflow of silver from Europe into China. At the time Europeans were not permitted to enter China. All trade was done at limited times of the year from the docks of the city of Guangzhou (known then as Canton). Missions were sent to China by European governments with a view to an exchange of embassies and the establishment of normal trading relations. But these were consistently rebuffed by the Chinese emperors, who saw European trade as akin to the tribute missions of barbarian tribes, not something that should be equal and reciprocal. One British mission returned bearing an imperial edict addressed to George IV advising the British king in the strongest terms that China had no need of British products and threatening military retaliation should any further ambassadors attempt to enter Chinese territory. It terminated with the words, "Tremble and Obey!"

Eventually a foreign product that appealed to Chinese consumers was found. The British East India Company resolved the serious problem of a trade deficit with China by engaging in a triangular trade involving the export of British textiles to India, the purchase of opium in India that was shipped to China in return for the much coveted Chinese silks, porcelains, and tea that were in such demand in Britain.

This eventually led to a serious problem of opium addiction in China. Opium was made illegal in China, but the trade continued. The Chinese emperor eventually wrote Queen Victoria asking her to ban the export of opium by the East India Company, but received no reply. Opium was not a banned substance in Britain at the time as the Chinese government had wrongfully assumed.

In 1839, the Chinese government took action by seizing British opium stored in warehouses on the docks at Guangzhou and destroying it by mixing it with lime and pouring it into the sea. Britain responded by declaring war on China.

China lost this opium war. The Qing Dynasty had been in power for almost 200 years by this time and was in decline. Chinese cultural proclivity to stress the study of philosophy, poetry and fine arts, the liberal education, over technical learning meant that China's military technology was woefully inadequate in the face of Britain's naval power, which had been tempered by many decades of colonial conquest.

By the Treaty of Nanjing of 1842, China was obliged to cede the island of Hong Kong to Britain and open "treaty ports" to foreign residents. Soon thereafter the Japanese, Americans, Russians, Germans, French, and so on, followed suit and set up "foreign concessions" on the eastern coast of China and inland. The largest of these were Shanghai, Tianjin, Guangzhou, and Wuhan (Hankow). Foreign embassies were allowed to be established in Beijing. Foreign nationals resident in the treaty ports were not subject to Chinese law but were only subject to prosecution by foreign courts set up on Chinese soil under the principle of "extraterritoriality."

Over the later part of the nineteenth century there was increasing support for the perception that the Qing government had sold out China to the foreign imperialist powers. The increased exposure to Western ideas engendered by Christian missionary enterprises in China and associated opportunities for Chinese to study abroad led to new concepts of nationalism and republicanism and demands for rule of law infiltrating Chinese intellectual discourse. The fact that the Qing emperors were ethni-cally Manchu and not of the predominant Han nationality further hastened the tide turning against them by progressive Chinese intellectuals.

In 1911, Dr. Sun Yat-sen became the first president of the Republic of China as leader of the Chinese Nationalist Party (known as the KMT from the abbreviation of the romanization of its Chinese name). The new regime attempted to establish democratic institutions modeled on the West, including a legislature and independent judiciary. However these institutions failed to gain acceptance as legitimate instruments of government. China lapsed into an almost four-decades-long period of severe political breakdown with shifting areas of control by diverse warlords, Japanese invaders, rival Republics, and areas under control of the Chinese Communists.

After victory over the Japanese in 1945, with American assistance the KMT led by Chiang Kai-shek attempted to reunify China by vanquishing the Chinese Communists. However because the KMT was perceived by many to represent a highly corrupt regime that had only half-heartedly resisted the Japanese incursions on Chinese territory, the Communists enjoyed significant popular support. By 1949, the KMT had been pushed out of Mainland China and established a remnant Republic of China regime on the island of Taiwan. Today the regime on Taiwan controls territory occupied by about 21.5 million or less than 2 percent of the Chinese population. The Chinese Communist regime controls the territory occupied by over 98 percent of the Chinese population.

The People's Republic of China was proclaimed by Chairman Mao Zedong from the rostrum of the Gate of Heavenly Peace (Tiananmen) at the entrance of the former imperial palace in Beijing, the Forbidden City. Mao noted in his speech that from henceforth "the Chinese people have stood up!" The new regime adopted a strong stance against "western imperialism and colonialism." By the early 1950s nearly all the foreign residents in China had left. China's support for North Korea in the Korean War led many Western nations to abandon plans to establish diplomatic relations with the government in Beijing. The Beijing authorities were not able to assume China's seat at the UN until 1971. Full diplomatic relations with the United States did not come until 1979.

The People's Republic of China was mostly modeled on Soviet-style political and judicial institutions. Industry and agriculture were nationalized. The ideology of Marxism-Leninism and Mao Zedong Thought was intensively applied. There was no freedom of expression allowed. The regime set about preparing China to achieve utopian communism.

Practically speaking the move to communism was implemented through the application of mass campaigns against "anti-socialist elements." Ex-landlords, ex-capitalists, and liberal intellectuals were all targets of political persecution. By the late 1950s, contrary to the expectations of the regime, the economy started to stagnate.

In response, the Chinese Communist Party launched the Great Forward Campaign with a view to "exceeding the living standard of Britain within 15 years." This campaign involved attempting to make steel by microsmelters in backyards throughout the country. Steel was, after all, considered the primary ingredient of the Stalinist economic system. Ordinary citizens were pressed to donate their pots and pans to this end. Agricultural production was to be accelerated through triple cropping, where double cropping had been the custom, and by plowing deeper. The citizenry were made to eat communally in common dining halls and children were moved into twenty-four-hour day care to increase time available for productive labor. The upshot was a massive famine in the early 1960s. Over 3 percent of the exhausted population of China consequently perished of starvation and disease. Estimates vary but at least 20 million people and perhaps as many as 40 million died.

The Great Leap Forward measures were quietly abandoned and agricultural production returned to sustainable rates in 1964. However the Chinese Communist Party launched its last major mass campaign, the Great Proletarian Cultural Revolution in 1966. This campaign was based on the premise that the revolution was being sabotaged by capitalist agents who were secreted inside the Chinese Communist Party. A massive purge of pragmatic Party members and liberal intellectuals ensued. The economy again experienced low or even negative growth.

In April 1976, spontaneous demonstrations with a strong antigovernment cast broke out in Tiananmen Square. The demonstrations were held on the date of the Chinese Qingming Festival supposedly to commemorate the death of Premier Zhou En-lai. Banners were put up expressing discontent with the Party's "ultra-leftist" leadership. One banner read "mouthing empty words about communism will not satisfy the people's needs."

By December 1978, more than two years after the death of Chairman Mao, the Chinese Communist Party abandoned Marxist ideology in favor of the new pragmatic official doctrine of "seek the truth from facts." The revolutionary goal of a rapid transition to utopian communism was deferred in favor of China's sole priorities: economic development and maintaining the political leadership of the Chinese Communist Party.

Mao's successor, Deng Xiaoping, promoted the notion of a new policy of "reform and openness to foreign things." This initiative has been extraordinarily successful. Over the past twenty-five years China has achieved economic growth rates that are unprecedented in human history. The proportion of the Chinese population living in absolute poverty has been drastically reduced. In the cities along China's east coast (including Beijing, Shanghai, Guangzhou) a significant proportion of the citizenry have achieved a standard of living comparable to that of the advanced industrialized nations.

Chinese nationalism is on the ascendancy. Many Chinese yearn to see China reassume great power status. A major challenge facing China today is how to accommodate the contemporary inexorable trend of globalization. China, a permanent member of the UN Security Council, recently signed the International Covenant on Civil and Political Rights and has ratified the International Covenant on Economic, Social, and Cultural Rights (albeit reserving important clauses). The challenge of Chinese entry into the World Trade Organization is writ large in China's future. Chinese domestic laws and practices still fall short of international standards for protection of contractual obligations and the protection of individual and collective rights. As China's economy continues to grow and the Chinese middle class consolidates its economic, social, and political role, demands that China adopt effective rule of law and a truly democratic political system become more and more pressing.

LEGAL CONCEPTS

The rule of law has not been a feature of China's system of state control until relatively recently. Under the imperial system, the rule of virtuous men was considered more than just codified law. Similarly the Chinese Communists regarded "redness," that is a consolidation of Marxist ideological norms and ethics, as of preeminent importance in the selection of political leaders at all levels. Codified law was officially suspect as it was seen as the protector of bourgeois property rights. Lawyers ceased to practice altogether in the Cultural Revolution, only being allowed to resume the practice of law in a highly restricted way in 1982.

In ancient times, China maintained social order though the *baojia* system. Under this system the head of every family was responsible for the conduct of the members of his extended family. Each hundred households formed a *jia* with one head of household as its head. Ten *jia* formed a *bao* with a designated head. Each head was responsible to those above in the hierarchy for the conduct of those below. Punishments were meted out to the incumbents for breach of responsibility if there was misconduct by those in their unit.

The equivalent institution in the People's Republic of China was the neighborhood committees, which consisted of local unpaid people with a mandate to ensure that order is maintained in their small territory. They reported regularly to the police and work units. Chinese citizens were also controlled by the personal file maintained on all citizens that contained records of major life events (marriage, birth of children), school records, work reports, political assessments (including materials elicited from coworkers, neighbors, and acquaintances in the course of political campaigns), and any police involvement. These files were kept at the work unit and were not open to perusal by their subject. Negative notes in a personal file were career limiting and even affected decisions with regard to allocation of state housing (which impacted on the possibility of marriage). The files thus performed an effective means of controlling deviant behavior.

Since the phasing out of the planned economy in favor of the market-based system, the neighborhood committees and system of personal files no longer play such a definitive role in controlling deviance. Fewer and fewer Chinese have a work unit as such these days and housing is now largely privately owned. The result has been soaring rates of all kind of crimes (including drug use and prostitution that had been almost completely wiped out through political campaigns in the early years of the Communist regime).

Similarly, with a large proportion of the population now engaged in some form of private enterprise, there is increasing awareness of the need for an effective rule of law to allow for the enforcement of business contracts and to create a fair, predictable, stable, and safe environment to do business in. As China's economy becomes more oriented to foreign trade and investment, it is increasingly appreciated that the arbitrary rule of corrupt and readily bribed communist officials, instead of the rule of predictable and effective law, discourages foreign investment.

Nevertheless, as there is little consolidated culture of law in China, there are serious difficulties in implementing the rule of law. While China's legislatures at the various levels have promulgated vast bodies of codified law, these laws are often not implemented. Similarly, people have difficulty in seeking recourse through law. Courts will often simply refuse to take up a "difficult" case. Judges are too often amenable to bribery or subject to political pressure in their rulings. An adversarial approach by lawyers is culturally dissonant. The Chinese traditionally prefer to resolve conflict through mediation and conciliation. Lawyers who defend accused persons too vigorously may themselves be subject to legal sanctions. Nevertheless, as the nation rapidly modernizes, traditional legal concepts are rapidly being replaced by a more modern Chinese approach that more and more closely approximates international legal norms.

CURRENT STRUCTURE

The Chinese court system is responsible to China's parliament, the National People's Congress. The court system is a unitary one so that courts at the provincial and local levels are responsible to the courts above them in the hierarchy. Expressive of this is that all death sentences are subject to review by the Supreme People's Court.

There is a separate system of military courts. Members of the Communist Party are often exempted from prosecution in favor of "internal Party discipline."

The Supreme People's Procuratorate is also responsible to the NPC and, parallel to the Supreme People's Court, the Supreme People's Procuratorate supervises local procuratorates.

The function of the procuracy is to examine charges brought by the police and to decide whether to bring a case before a court for trial. Cases that do come to trial tend to be well established as a consequence. According to statistics given by the Supreme People's Court, guilty verdicts occur in over 93 percent of cases brought to trial.

STAFFING

Presently there are only something in the order of 100,000 lawyers in China. For a nation of 1.2 billion people, 100,000 lawyers is a very small number in proportion to the huge population of China. Lawyers largely prefer to work in lucrative corporate law. This means that it is relatively difficult for those accused of criminal offenses to find a lawyer. Similarly, use of lawyers in civil matters is limited by the small numbers of lawyers working in these areas.

There is a requirement on the books that Chinese law firms perform some hours of pro bono work yearly. Practically speaking, however, there seems to be little in the way of effective sanctions against law firms who fail to fulfill their limited obligations to assist those who cannot afford to pay them. The minister of Justice is currently developing a network of legal aid centers, but there are problems of funding. The All-China Women's Federation and All-China Federation of Labor (both NGOs answerable to the Chinese Communist Party) have separate but modest networks of legal aid centers.

The range of services able to be undertaken by foreign law firms in China is largely limited to foreign trade-related matters. However, China's entry into the World Trade Organization will lead to liberalization of access to the service sector, including legal services by foreign firms.

The profession of judge is not particularly prestigious in China. Many judges are retired military officers with little or no legal training. Some judges are surprisingly youthful. Steps are being taken by the government to improve the professional qualifications of judges. However this is a long term project. The continuing problem of judges and procurators taking bribes is major concern of the government.

Some minor offenders are sent to Reform Through Labor camps by the police without reference to the courts. However, this extrajudicial mechanism for addressing minor criminal deviance is the subject of debate

Legal Structure of China

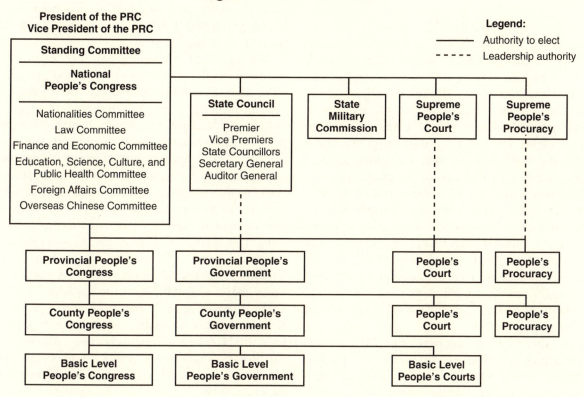

in China. As it is inconsistent with the requirements of the International Covenant on Civil and Political Rights, which was signed by China in 1998, it is expected that the Reform Through Labor camps will be phased out in the years ahead.

IMPACT

The role of law in the social and political life of the country remains relatively low in China. The Chinese Constitution of 1982, amended in 1988, 1993, and 1999, reads more as a review of medium-term political and economic policy proposals than a statement of sacred and immutable principles for a nation based on the rule of law. The Supreme Court does not review Chinese laws passed by the National People's Congress for constitutionality. In making their rulings, Chinese judges do not cite legal precedents.

There is also the well-based perception that Chinese legal rulings are subject to political interference, so many Chinese believe that codified law as such is not so meaningful in determining justice.

Nevertheless the general trend is toward further consolidation of the rule of law in China. This process is expected to be hastened by the need for China to become in compliance with WTO rules that demand transparency and fairness in commercial transactions.

Charles Burton

See also Adversarial System; Capital Punishment; Civil Law; Constitutional Review; Criminal Law; Criminal Procedures; Human Rights Law; Judicial Independence; Judicial Selection, Methods of; Law and Economics; Legal Aid; Marxist Jurisprudence

References and further reading

Brown, Ronald C. 1997. *Understanding Chinese Courts and Legal Process: Law with Chinese Characteristics*. Cambridge, MA: Kluwer Law International.

Cohen, Jerome, R. Randle Edwards, and Fu-mei Chang Chen, eds. 1982. *Essays on China's Legal Tradition*. Princeton, NJ: Princeton University Press.

Keith, Ron C., and Zhiqiu Lin. 2001. *Law and Justice in China's New Market Place*. New York: St. Martin's Press.

Keller, Perry, ed. 2001. *Chinese Law and Legal Theory*. Burlington, VT: Ashgate Publishing Company.

Lubman, Stanley. 1999. *Bird in a Cage: Legal Reform in China after Mao*. Stanford, CA: Stanford University Press.

———, ed. 1996. *China's Legal Reforms*. Oxford: Oxford University Press.

Turner-Gottschang, Karen, James V. Feinerman, and R. Kent Guy, eds. 2000. *The Limits of the Rule of Law in China*. Seattle, WA: University of Washington Press.

CITIZENS ADVICE BUREAUX

WHAT THEY ARE

Citizens advice bureaux (CABx) are charitable bodies that provide a national network of advice agencies to help citizens solve a wide range of problems. Their services are available at no cost to all citizens, regardless of their means. Legal assistance is but one part, albeit a very significant part, of the business of the CABx. Their objective is to help resolve the kind of everyday problems that can affect the members of any local community, and they function as a first port of call for the great number of people who face legal and other difficulties. As of 2001, there were almost 700 CABx in England and Wales, handling over 6 million inquiries each year. CABx are located in all major towns and cities and operate in some rural areas as well, although on a much more limited basis. In addition to these CABx, there are countless similar agencies throughout the Commonwealth world. For the sake of simplicity, however, this discussion will focus on those that exist in England.

Despite their generalist character, the CABx are now among the major providers of legal assistance in England and Wales. Indeed, no other voluntary agency offers more extensive coverage than the CABx. A survey of the work done by the CABx in England and Wales, conducted by the Royal Commission on Legal Services (1979), found that a third of all the inquiries handled had a legal component and that the legal assistance offered by CAB workers typically involved filling out forms, writing letters, and conducting negotiations. Much less frequently, representation was provided for clients in courts or tribunals.

Professional lawyers and other experts are employed within some of the larger CABx, and it is common for firms of lawyers (perhaps working on a rotating basis) to make themselves available for consultation for a limited number of hours per week at a local CAB on a pro bono basis. The work of the CABx is, however, heavily dependent on unpaid volunteers, of whom there are now more than 28,000, working as advisers, administrators, and managers. These volunteers are, in the main, generalists who are expected to advise on a wide range of social and legal issues. They are trained by the National Association of Citizens Advice Bureaux (NACAB), which is also responsible for supervising staff, setting national standards for the service, and coordinating policy. NACAB has developed an elaborate database for its volunteers and an extensive information technology (IT) program to improve the quality of its advice, and it is in the process of developing its own Internet site to provide on-line advice for the CAB network. NACAB also acts as a pressure group, and on social policy issues such as landlord-tenant disputes, housing, and the provision of welfare benefits, it exerts a powerful influence on government policy. In addition, NACAB has become an increasingly important voice in debates about legal aid and the delivery of legal services.

Although CAB volunteers generally seek to resolve problems (legal and otherwise) on the spot, people with more intractable difficulties may well be referred to specialized agencies, particularly professional lawyers, law centers, and local government departments. Recognizing when such referrals are needed is an important part of the work of CAB volunteers, and knowing the appropriate agencies to which referrals should be made requires considerable legal judgment and expertise. Referrals by CAB volunteers are most commonly made when legal assistance is needed, especially in relation to problems stemming from matrimonial issues. Some idea of the scale of referrals is given in the survey conducted by the Royal Commission on Legal Services (1979), in which it was noted that about 250,000 of the inquiries made to the CABx each year were referred to lawyers in private practice. Nonetheless, the expectation is that most legal problems will be dealt with internally: The CABx provide, in the Royal Commission's words, "a para-legal service, based on laymen, with common sense, training and experience" (71).

Ever since the CABx were established, securing adequate funding has been a persistent problem, and this difficulty has inevitably limited the amount and the quality of the advice offered. The CABx are, after all, nonprofit agencies, and they are dependent on outside bodies for their continuance. The central government contributes to their efforts, as do nongovernmental sources such as charities, local business organizations, and individuals, but the principal source of CAB funding comes from local government departments. In some areas, inadequate funding by local government has made their existence precarious, and staffershave often complained about the difficulties they face in working in a financially unstable environment. Overall, it has been difficult to ensure sufficient funding to keep pace with the considerable increase in the number of cases dealt with annually by the CABx.

The rapidly changing situation surrounding the public funding of legal aid in England and Wales may, however, have a considerable bearing on this problem, and it is likely that the CABx will play a more prominent part in providing legal advice under the legal aid scheme than they have in the past. For many years, public expenditure on legal aid in England and Wales has been much higher than that in most other countries, and successive governments have struggled to contain its growth. Knowing that the CABx can offer routine, preliminary advice much more cheaply than professional lawyers can, governments have sought to induce the CABx to become involved in legal aid work. The blandishments of the Conservative government in the 1980s were not taken up by the CABx; however, the approaches of the Labour administration are beginning to change the situation. Instead of allowing any legal firm that wishes to undertake legal aid work to be remunerated for doing so, the government has contracted with a much smaller number of firms (and other organizations) in each area of the country to provide these services at fixed annual rates of payment. The importance of this change for the CABx is that they are themselves being actively encouraged to apply for legal aid contracts, and a number of them have already done so successfully. Although only the larger CABx have the resources and the expertise to carry out such work, the availability of legal aid will place the funding of contracted CABx on a much more secure basis in the future. But a change of this type will also alter the character of those CABx that are able to secure contracts, and a debate is currently taking place within the service about the extent to which legal aid work should be undertaken by the CABx and whether this will undermine the independence that they have traditionally enjoyed.

HISTORICAL BACKGROUND

The origins of the citizens advice bureaux can be traced to the period immediately preceding the outbreak of World War II. At that time, it became clear that people would need assistance in coping with the chaos and disruption of wartime conditions. Voluntary social services were gathered under an umbrella organization—the National Council of Social Service—that produced a blueprint for a national advice network to provide an emergency war service. The service grew rapidly, and by the outbreak of war, some 200 CABx, staffed entirely by volunteers and supported financially by local governments, were in operation. This number grew very rapidly over the course of the war.

A short extract from the records of one bureau in east London, capturing the words of one CAB client, provides a vivid picture of the kind of pressing, albeit mundane, problems created by social conditions at that time: "We were bombed out the night before last, and the pawn tickets went. Now the pawnbroker says that he can't give us our stuff back without them. He's got our blankets and our best clothes" (National Association of Citizens Advice Bureaux 1999, 5). The emphasis then was far removed from the provision of legal advice, as the CABx sought to deal with the immediate problems that the war created for local communities—evacuation, rationing, homelessness, missing relatives, establishing contact with prisoners of war, seeking compensation for war damage, and the like. In addition, advice about problems associated with debt caused by the drastic reductions in family incomes as a result of the war became a central part of the

work of the fledgling service. Social welfare (and related) issues have continued to predominate in the caseload of the CABx, and the main focus of their legal advice work has been, in rough order of frequency, social security payments, debt and consumer issues, housing, employment and disability, and sickness benefits. Although it has been the policy of the CABx to offer assistance to anyone who seeks it, it is clear that the great majority of clients have always been those with low incomes.

MAJOR VARIANTS

There are considerable variations among citizens advice bureaux in terms of their size, their facilities, their working practices, and the nature and quality of the work they do. In an organization that is so heavily dependent on unpaid volunteers (whose caliber is inevitably variable), the quality of advice offered will be inconsistent, as well. Consequently, individual bureaux are sometimes criticized for the amateurish approaches they adopt, particularly in relation to the provision of legal advice. Although the National Association of Citizens Advice Bureaux seeks to set national standards and to monitor the work done by its volunteers, practice and standards nonetheless vary widely. For example, it is clear that staffers at some bureaux are much more reluctant than others to refer difficult or complex legal matters to professional lawyers. In part, this is due to the differential availability of legal expertise within individual bureaux, but it also reflects the fact that it often requires a considerable amount of knowledge and judgment to recognize where legal complexity exists. And such skills are sometimes in short supply.

SIGNIFICANCE

In England and Wales, citizens' rights and access to justice have been major preoccupations of the government since the 1950s, and as a result, there has been an extraordinary expansion in the role of paralegals in the provision of legal services. Much has been written in recent years about the formidable barriers that inhibit ordinary people from pursuing legal remedies in resolving problems. The expansion of the role played by the CABx has been of great social and legal significance: In particular, it has meant that routine, free legal advice—as well as advice about many other matters—has become much more widely available to members of the general public. Indeed, NACAB (2000) itself has claimed that "the Citizens Advice Bureau Service is the world's largest independent advice-giving agency" (1).

Some indication of the significance of the role played by the CABx is given by the sheer number of cases they deal with annually—now in excess of 6 million, as noted earlier. Of the many voluntary agencies that offer legal advice, these bureaux are by far the most prominent, making a very significant contribution in sorting out the legal problems within the general population, especially those of the poor. In her survey of what people in England and Wales do when they face serious legal difficulties, Hazel Genn (1999) found that almost as many turned to the CABx for assistance (21 percent) as to lawyers in private practice (24 percent); other sources of legal advice were far behind these two main groups. It should be noted, however, that Genn's study also revealed widespread dissatisfaction with the service that was offered among those who had used the CABx. As she put it, "Prospective clients are discouraged as a result of limited opening hours, unanswered telephones, full offices, and queues" (Genn 1999, 78).

The expansion in the role of the CABx in offering legal advice has been, in large part, a reflection of the limited availability of lawyers in private practice (particularly those prepared to do work under the state system of publicly funded legal aid) and their lack of expertise in many of the areas about which the volunteers in the CABx are most frequently consulted. The policies of the Blair government with regard to legal aid have served to consolidate the position of the CABx in the provision of legal services. Agencies such as the citizens advice bureaus have tended to flourish because they have attempted to plug the gaps left by private practitioners, especially by focusing on areas that have been largely neglected by lawyers in private practice, including social welfare and consumer law. My own research in the 1980s showed that there was surprisingly little conflict between the CABx and local law firms, despite the real possibility of tension stemming from duplication in the kind of work they do; indeed, working relationships between the two groups were, on the whole, harmonious and symbiotic. Complaints by local lawyers about any overlap of work, still less the poaching of clients, were rare. Research conducted a decade later by Andrew Francis (2000) indicates that this situation has continued.

Despite the number and range of problems they seek to address, the CABx have been neglected, to a quite extraordinary extent, by legal writers and researchers in England. They tend to be viewed by academic commentators simply as part of the legal landscape. There is certainly no body of mainstream academic writing to which one can turn to learn more of the role that the CABx play in the provision of legal services. It is, however, important to remember that, because they offer frontline assistance to people who may be unwilling to turn to any other source of help, volunteers may be involved in matters that have a critical bearing on citizens' lives—including debt, deportation, eviction, and mortgage repossession.

John Baldwin

See also Law Firms; Paralegals
References and further reading
Baldwin, John. 1989. "The Role of Citizens Advice Bureaux and Law Centres in the Provision of Legal Advice and Assistance." *Civil Justice Quarterly* 8: 24–44.
Francis, Andrew. 2000. "Lawyers, CABx and the Community Legal Service." *Journal of Social Welfare and Family Law* 22: 59–75.
Genn, Hazel. 1999. *Paths to Justice: What People Do and Think about Going to Law.* Oxford: Hart.
National Association of Citizens Advice Bureaux. 1999. *The Inside Story.* London: National Association of Citizens Advice Bureaux.
———. 2000. *The NACAB Evidence Reports.* London: National Association of Citizens Advice Bureaux.
Royal Commission on Legal Services. 1979. *Final Report.* Vol. 1. London: Her Majesty's Stationery Office.

CIVIL LAW

Civil law is generally understood as one of the major legal formations in the world. Like *common law,* the term *civil law* is used by those who study comparative law to demarcate a group or family of laws in the global legal landscape. Broadly stated, the study of civil law relates to the legal orders that have developed on the European continent as well as in those parts of the globe that have been influenced by Europe's legal systems. These are distinct from the common law that has evolved in England and the United States.

However, the distinction between civil law and common law is not arbitrary. The concept of civil law is intricately linked to the concept of common law. It is in particular civil law that enables the common lawyer to develop an external view of his or her own order. In this sense, the field of civil law is, in fact, the product of common law debates. Furthermore, the concept of civil law does not necessarily reflect the view of lawyers practicing in a so-called civil law system. These practitioners might find other aspects more characteristic of their system than academic studies of civil law emphasize.

In the following, I shall first present the main features of civil law systems, which constitute common topics in conventional civil law studies. These include the specific characteristics of legal science and legal education; codification and statutory law; the civil code and statutory interpretation; constitutional law and judicial review; and courts, lawyers, and notaries. I shall conclude with some remarks on methods and the role of theory in civil law studies.

LEGAL SCIENCE AND LEGAL EDUCATION IN CIVIL LAW

Legal historians and comparative lawyers agree that Roman law had an equal impact on common law and civil law in early medieval legal development. Medieval Roman law influenced both the law and the scholarly legal writing in England and on the Continent alike. However, the situation changed during the Tudor period, after the British Inns of Court prevailed over academic education in the preparation of barristers, sergeants-at-law, and judges. The common law resisted further domination by Roman law, including the use of scholarly texts and interpretations to mold legal decision making.

In contrast, the development of civil law was closely linked to a rediscovery of Roman law and the creation of legal science in the eleventh century. The renaissance of classical Roman law on the European continent began in Italian law schools, of which Bologna was predominant. The scholarly approach of these schools spread quickly throughout Europe. Legal science had a historical function in developing a comprehensive system of rules in civil law countries. Thus, the rediscovery of the Justinian Corpus Juris and the scholastic method of analyzing and teaching law in universities created the basis of the western tradition of legal science.

The scientific character of law has shaped legal education in civil law countries from medieval times to the present. Legal education on the European continent and in Latin American countries is democratic, public, general, and scientific, whereas in common law countries, it is meritocratic, private, professional, and obsessed with teaching methods. However, there are certain disadvantages in civil law education. These relate to institutional factors that make the learning experience a rather anonymous affair. The reality of mass legal education on the European continent somewhat contradicts the general ideas of legal education in civil law countries. For example, despite the reform efforts in the 1970s, which were unfortunately abolished in the 1980s, German legal education continues to follow the traditional path of separating university studies and practical training. Legal education in both phases is centered on the abstract idea of studying for a judicial career. University education is almost entirely devoted to a "scientific" introduction to law and Supreme Court decisions. In the second stage, which is fully separated from the university, training mainly takes place in courts. The academic teaching of law in France seems even more theoretical and impersonal than that in the German law faculties. Mass lectures largely prevent students from being taught practical or critical perspectives on the law.

CODIFICATION AND STATUTORY LAW

The scientific approach to law encouraged the compilation of rules into comprehensive codes in civil law countries. We can distinguish three forms of codification. The early approach adopted in medieval times in Germany and elsewhere was to create codes by compiling existing customary law. A famous example is the Sachsenspiegel (Mirror of Saxon Law), which was written by a well-educated knight, Eike von Repgow, in the 1220s in order to document the laws of Saxony. A similar attempt to compile and codify customary law was undertaken in the north of France in the sixteenth century.

A different concept of codification emerged with the introduction of the great codes around 1800. The Preußische Allgemeine Landrecht (1794) of Saxony and the French Code Civil (1804) were clearly influenced by ideas of the Enlightenment period. Although these codes represented political attempts to create a rational society through law, they have been accused of revolutionary democratism and "rampant rationalism" (Merryman 1985). This is because they attempted to grant each citizen knowledge of his or her rights, as well as to provide a complete list of solutions for any legal complaint, thus reducing the role of the judge to the selection of the relevant provision and denying the jurist further powers of judicial interpretation.

A third approach was taken by the German Civil Code, the Bürgerliche Gesetzbuch (BGB). Historically oriented, scientific, and professional, it combined both Roman law traditions and German law developments. Its provisions appear to be rather abstract and scientific without, however, displaying a rationalist zeal. The BGB acknowledged that there must be scope for judicial interpretation by incorporating a number of general clauses.

The French Code Civil and the BGB differ fundamentally in the scope they grant for judicial interpretation. Whereas German judges enjoy wide powers to interpret legislative provisions of the BGB, French judges pay literal lip-service to their restrictions imposed by the Code Civil. Somewhat paradoxically, however, by adhering to a restrictive judicial style, the French judges also free themselves from the Code Civil. In cases not regulated by this code, they acquire quasi-legislative power.

Although both civil law and common law have "migrated" their manner of doing so has differed markedly. Whereas the common law migrated through principles of private and public common law and by exporting distinct legal institutions—the jury, the writ of habeas corpus, an independent judiciary, and an adversarial procedural system—mainly to other Commonwealth countries, the civil law penetrated other systems through its comprehensive, systematic codes. A remarkable example of such a migration of civil law was the adoption of the French Code Civil in Louisiana and the discussion of civil law as the basis for a particular U.S. jurisprudence. In general, the history of the migration of law seems to reveal that civil law had a greater potential for persuasion, while common law more often had to rely on coercion.

THE CIVIL CODE AND STATUTORY INTERPRETATION

From a common law perspective, a specific feature of civil law is the role and structure of statutes, codes, and codification in general. The common assumption is that the civil law systems are ruled by statutes, that these systems make an attempt to unify regulations in single codes for each area of law, and that codification dominates legal policies. In contrast, common law systems are said to be governed by case law, and statutes play only an auxiliary role to precedents established by courts.

Both generalizations need to be qualified. On the one hand, case law and judge-made law is a necessary feature of civil law systems. The meaning of provisions of the German BGB, for instance, is established by case law, and indeed, there are large areas of pure case law in the civil law system. On the other hand, statutes have become the dominant form of regulation in common law systems. This fact has led some commentators to speculate about a convergence between English and continental laws. Furthermore, there have been a number of attempts to systematize and "codify" common law. The U.S. Uniform Commercial Code and the (failed) British attempt to introduce a comprehensive code in the areas of contract law and landlord-tenant law are prominent examples of efforts to provide comprehensive legal frameworks. The common law of the United Kingdom in particular is faced with continuous pressure to introduce new legislation due to its membership in the European Union.

The lesson that common law can draw from the French and the German experience is that codification can occur at different levels of generalization. Furthermore, periods of codification are followed by periods of decodification and fragmentation into special statutes that, with increasing complexity, lead again to attempts to recodify in order to reduce the complexity. However, the idea of codification has been transformed and no longer rests on a rationalist philosophy that attempts to restructure society. Rather, it has become a bureaucratic device to facilitate administrative and judicial decision making.

CONSTITUTIONAL LAW AND JUDICIAL REVIEW

A distinct feature of civil law systems is their hierarchy of norms, with the written constitution at the apex. In a civil law system, any legislation can be scrutinized to determine if it is in accordance with the constitution. Furthermore, modern constitutions grant citizens human and civil rights, which require effective means of enforcement in order to guarantee real protection.

The postwar German judicial system enforces rights in five different court systems. In addition and most important with respect to constitutionally protected rights, there is the Federal Constitutional Court, the Bundesverfassungsgericht. Its far-reaching powers include not only the protection of human rights but also the arbitration of conflicts between organs of the federal state and judicial review of legislation. The Federal Constitutional Court is little constrained by law to act on its own volition. However, it would soon encounter opposition and implementation problems if it were to disregard the contemporary political climate. Thus, judicial self-restraint is actually a precondition for the court to be effective in its decision making.

The French system of judicial enforcement of rights is divided into two sections that have their own appeal structures: the judicial courts and the administrative courts. In addition, there is the Constitutional Council (the Conseil Constitutionnel). Its powers are limited and do not include a right to challenge a violation of human or civil rights. This French constitutional court is almost exclusively concerned with questions regarding the constitutionality of legislative and administrative acts.

COURTS, LAWYERS, AND NOTARIES IN CIVIL LAW SYSTEMS

The civil law and the common law differ most, perhaps, with respect to judicial practice and administration. In particular, the style of conducting a hearing and reaching a decision is linked to distinct general principles and functions of procedure. The main principles that govern criminal procedures are commonly referred to as "inquisitorial" in the civil law tradition and as "accusatorial" in the common law tradition. Whereas common law judgments concentrate on establishing premises, civil law decisions, particularly under French law, concentrate on the law.

The French legal profession was, for a long time, diversified, with a major distinction existing between legal practitioners who represented clients in court (*avocats*) and those who mainly communicated with clients in writing (*avoués*). This distinction certainly bore some similarity to the distinction between barristers and solicitors under English law. However, since 1972, this distinction has been abolished, and the French legal profession now appears more united than its English counterpart.

The German legal profession is probably the most diversified among the civil law countries. There are four major groups of jurists: judges, legal practitioners, administrative lawyers, and company lawyers. Three factors characterize German jurists from a comparative point of view: (1) an academic understanding of law through legal education and legal doctrine; (2) a special emphasis on and communication of experiences through written legal texts; and (3) a state-focused understanding of the role of the legal profession, with judges at its center. Somewhat surprisingly, these features also dominate the work and attitudes of legal practitioners, even including the powerful group of German corporate lawyers. There is still little lateral mobility between the various subgroups of German jurists. Becoming a judge means entering a separate judicial career immediately after completing legal education. Only to a limited extent do transfers occur between administrative lawyers working for regulatory agencies and practicing attorneys. The rule continues to be that a young jurist begins a judicial, an administrative, or a lawyer's career and stays in that chosen track.

A special role is performed by notaries in civil law systems. They serve, in effect, as a public record office, recording legal transactions and storing legal documents. The main function of notaries is to certify the accuracy of contracts and other legal issues. The number of notarial offices is limited. In some European countries (for example, France), notaries follow a career path separate from the rest of the legal profession, whereas in other parts of the European continent (for example, the northern German states), the tasks of a notary are fulfilled by a specialized advocate.

THE FUNCTION OF THEORY IN CIVIL LAW STUDIES

The study of civil law is closely linked to developments in comparative law. In particular, methods of comparison have been a topic of continued debate. These discussions have recently evinced a renewed interest in theory.

However, the degree of theoretical emphasis differs according to the comparative approach. We can distinguish four methods: the country studies, the use of benchmarks, the functional method, and theoretical or deductive approaches. In particular, the fourth method—the advanced theoretical approach—offers many possibilities to explore new dimensions in contrasting civil and common law. It enables the establishment of a comprehensive comparative framework; it allows analysis of the position of an external observer of a legal system; and it encourages criticism and self-criticism of the comparative frame.

A new commitment to theory transcends the rule-based comparative analysis of law and takes into account the inevitability of the mediating effect of the observer of another legal system. For some comparativists, the study of civil law appears as an attempt to "restage" that legal culture within the parameters of the common law. The observer only detects those legal aspects that his or her framework suggests it is relevant to analyze.

One response to these limitations is to broaden the basis of comparison. Notably, legal sociology offers a way forward in this regard by suggesting a comparison of legal cultures. From this perspective, future studies of civil law need to be interdisciplinary and theoretical in order to grasp diversity and detail of legal cultures, including their particularities and local deviations.

A similar reaction comes from comparative lawyers who emphasize the importance of case law, judicial practice, the study of specific legal problems, and the personalities of comparative lawyers as objects of comparison. By concentrating on these issues, civil law studies promise to attract a wider common law audience. This proposal to highlight fine detail in comparative law would seem to have advantages and disadvantages. It is convincing insofar as it contextualizes the comparative approach and focuses on the essence of an autonomous legal system, that is, recursive decision making and the development of binding case law. It opens comparative law to include particularistic aspects of legal history and the cultural context, thus promoting analysis at a concrete level as well as increased interdisciplinarity.

However, there is also a limitation to this approach, for it falls into the old trap of comparing common law and civil law by using common law and its particularities, most especially case law, as the mirror by which to view civil law. The only aspects of civil law that appear in this mirror are those that have a reference point in common law.

CONCLUSION

The origin of the concept of civil law lies in the comparison of notions of private law—hence the name *civil law*. However, in its semantic development, the concept has transcended the comparison of private law concepts and now comprises substantive public and private law as well as legal institutions. It incorporates all aspects of a legal system, including the specialized fields of law, the legal profession, judges, codification, procedural law, and legal scholars.

The history of civil law studies encompasses a number of self-critical debates. More specifically, legal historians have questioned the origin of the split between common law and civil law, with the traditional view blaming England for this divergence. This perspective attributes the dichotomy to a peculiar isolation of English law from the law that was developing in the rest of Europe during the Middle Ages. According to this view, common law deviated from the scholarly course of using Roman law to establish a unifying concept of law and resisted modernization. However, this traditional interpretation of the divergence thesis has always been questioned. Some continental scholars, among them R. C. van Caenegem, argue that the common law followed a "normal" path by modernizing the English judicial system through gradually building up case law without adhering to ancient Roman law principles.

Looking toward the future, we might see signs that the rules and principles of common and civil law will converge over time. Indeed, there might be scope for a "common law of Europe," administered by the European Union. However, diversity will always remain. In fact, it is the acknowledgment of the virtue of particularistic law that characterizes our modern (or postmodern) legal systems. The legal cultures and the legal mentalities of the people may not naturally move toward harmonization because there are vast differences in method and style of law making and legal argument. The study of civil law systems needs to focus on these cultural differences of continental legal institutions, judicial practices, and doctrinal approaches. However, to be successful, it also needs to develop appropriate theoretical frameworks that are able to encompass the origins and the virtues of discrepancies.

Ralf Rogowski

See also France; Germany; Inquisitorial Procedure; Louisiana; Magistrates—Civil Law Systems; Legal Professionals—Civil Law Traditions; Notaries; Quebec

References and further reading
Bell, John. 2001. *French Legal Cultures.* London: Butterworths.
Berman, Harold J. 1983. *Law and Revolution: The Formation of the Western Legal Tradition.* Cambridge, MA, and London: Harvard University Press.
David, René, and John E. C. Brierley. 1985. *Major Legal Systems in the World Today: An Introduction to the Comparative Study of Law.* 3rd ed. London: Stevens.
John, Michael. 1989. *Politics and the Law in Late Nineteenth-Century Germany: The Origins of the Civil Code.* Oxford: Clarendon Press.
Merryman, John H. 1985. *The Civil Law Tradition: An Introduction to the Legal Systems of Western Europe and Latin America.* 2nd ed. Stanford, CA: Stanford University Press.
Rogowski, Ralf, ed. 1996. *Civil Law.* New York: New York University Press.
Rudden, Bernard. 1974. "Courts and Codes in England, France and Soviet Russia.'" *Tulane Law Review* 48: 1010–1028.
van Caenegem, R. C. 1987. *Judges, Legislators and Professors: Chapters in European Legal History.* Cambridge, MA: Cambridge University Press.
von Mehren, Arthur T., and James R. Gordley. 1977. *The Civil Law System: An Introduction to the Comparative Study of Law.* Boston, MA, and Toronto: Little, Brown.
Zweigert, Konrad, and Hein Kötz. 1998. *An Introduction to Comparative Law.* 3rd ed. Oxford: Clarendon Press.

CIVIL PROCEDURE

Civil procedure is that part of the law that is concerned with the procedures by which litigation is conducted in the civil courts. In legal systems of the common law tradition, procedure in administrative law cases would be included under the heading of civil procedure, but in the civilian tradition such cases would be regarded as matters of public law and thus subject to a different procedural regime. Civil procedure may include procedures to be adopted before any litigation is commenced, and is also generally taken to include procedures for the enforcement of any judgment obtained. Civil procedural law is generally to be found in codes (in the civil law jurisdictions) or rules of court made under statutory powers (in the common law countries), in both cases supplemented by decisions of the appellate courts on the interpretation and application of the code or rules. Common law jurisdictions often acknowledge that civil courts (or in some cases merely the higher ones) have an *inherent jurisdiction* to regulate their own procedure in ways not explicitly covered by the statutory rules. It is also usually assumed by the common law that judges have to be invested with very broad discretionary powers in order to carry out their role in the procedural system, even though that role is in theory much more limited than that of judges in civil law systems.

In the legal systems in the common law tradition, procedure was historically based around a jury trial before a single judge and jury, with matters of law being reserved for the decision of the judge and matters of fact for the jury. Although jury trial is in practice of greatly reduced significance in modern common law systems, except in the United States, the procedural system is still largely premised upon the assumption that the main purpose of the procedural rules is to prepare the parties for a trial in which all issues of law and fact arising in the litigation will be decided at a climactic hearing. In systems of this kind the dominant principles are *party control* and *party presentation.* Party control expresses the notion that it is for the parties to the litigation and not the court to determine what issues are in dispute and require resolution by the court and to decide, within a framework set by the rules of court, the pace at which the litigation proceeds to trial. The court is conceived as holding itself aloof from these matters unless the parties choose to refer a question concerning them to the court for decision during the *pre-trial* (or *interlocutory*) procedure. Party presentation is the notion that it is for the parties to decide what evidence is to be presented to the court in order to decide the issues of fact that arise in the case and to present that evidence to the court in whatever manner they see fit, within the limits set by the rules of the law of evidence and the professional practices of the bar. Systems of this kind are sometimes said to adopt an *adversarial* procedure.

Consistent with these principles the commencement of litigation in the common law systems is usually by means of a document (the *originating process*) drawn up by the plaintiff (*writ, complaint, claim form*), which is then either validated by the court and served on the defendant or triggers the issue of a summons by the court. Service of the originating process may be effected by the plaintiff himself or by an officer of the court. There follows the exchange of pleadings between the parties in which, by means of somewhat formal documents, the parties set out their respective claims and defenses in order to define the issues to be determined at the trial. The rules may permit, or even require, the disclosure of certain types of evidence (particularly documentary or expert evidence) at this stage of the procedure.

Pleading is usually followed by *discovery* (*disclosure*) in which the parties reveal to one another certain types of evidence that is available to them and relevant to issues disclosed by the pleadings. Discovery was a procedure invented by the English Court of Chancery and was originally confined to discovery of documents and discovery by interrogatories (formal written questions submitted by one party to another). It often nowadays includes procedures for the pretrial disclosure of expert evidence and even, in some jurisdictions, all the oral testimony that a party is proposing to call at the trial. There are many differences of detail between the common law systems in relation to these matters. In the United States, considerable emphasis is placed upon discovery by *oral deposition* in which a party is permitted to question his opponent and his witnesses on oath during the pretrial procedure. This type of discovery does not exist, or exists only in a limited form, in most other common law jurisdictions.

These procedures may be short-circuited at any stage of the pretrial procedure by applications (*motions*) by the parties for summary disposal of the case without a trial. The plaintiff may apply for *summary judgment,* contending that the defendant has no defense to the claim worthy of trial; the defendant may move to strike out the plaintiff's claim by arguing that it has no basis in law or that it is inherently unlikely to succeed for other reasons.

Trial in the common law systems is usually preceded by some hearing before the court at which outstanding problems arising from the pretrial procedure can be determined, and attempts may be made by the court to encourage *settlement* (compromise) of the litigation.

In most common law systems trial is now by a single judge sitting alone who decides all issues of law and fact and delivers a reasoned judgment on these issues at the conclusion of the trial. Most jurisdictions retain jury trial for certain categories of case (such as defamation) and in the United States jury trial is still the norm, being constitutionally guaranteed in all cases worth more than $10.

American law also differs from most other jurisdictions, both common law and civil law, in its attitude toward the *costs* of the proceedings. Although it agrees that the winner of the litigation is in principle entitled to recover the costs from the loser (*the indemnity rule of costs*), American law (except in some cases) defines costs in such a way as to exclude lawyers' fees, which other jurisdictions do not. The result is that in the United States the parties bear their own costs, win or lose; but in claims for damages plaintiffs' lawyers will often act on a *contingency*

fee basis in which they recover no fee if the claim is unsuccessful and a fixed proportion of the damages recovered if successful.

At the trial itself considerable emphasis is usually placed upon oral evidence and the testing of the credibility of witnesses through a process of oral examination and cross-examination. The hearing, consisting of speeches by counsel, the presentation of evidence and submissions on the law, normally takes place in a continuous sequence, possibly over many days, in which all the issues to be decided are determined at the end of the trial.

The procedural tradition in the civil law countries is quite different from that of the common law. Trial by jury is unknown in civil cases and the litigation is usually conducted before a multijudge court acting in a collegial manner to arrive at a decision that is, on the surface, unanimous. The principle of party control is not recognized. It is for the court to decide, having received written pleadings from the parties and heard their submissions, what issues arise in the case, and for it to indicate what evidence it will require in relation to them. There is no process equivalent to discovery. It nevertheless remains for the parties, in most circumstances, to present the relevant evidence to the court in accordance with its directions. The court actively manages the case throughout the procedure, indicating what steps are to be taken and when. The procedure is sometimes said to be *inquisitorial,* but this should not be misunderstood. In practice, the court's ability to conduct independent fact-finding operations is very limited and is not much greater than that of common law courts. However, it is often the case that the court will appoint its own expert witnesses in cases where expert evidence is called for. This is sometimes done before the formal commencement of the litigation. There is no process directly equating to discovery.

There is often no trial in the sense in which that word is used in the common law, but issues of law and fact are resolved in a series of hearings. Systems of this kind often result in frequent short hearings. The emphasis is more on written evidence than oral presentation. The role of the judges is also significantly different. Although their role is a more active one, they often lack the broad discretionary powers that common law judges have; instead the theory is that a correct ruling on any question can be deduced by a logical process from the text of the procedural code or other statutory source. Although the concept of summary judgment is recognized, there has traditionally been a greater reluctance to apply nonstandard procedures in particular cases than in the common law systems. The indemnity rule of costs is generally recognized, but the costs recoverable are often rigidly linked to the amount of the claim and are frequently fixed at a low level.

In recent years there has been some convergence in the theory and practice of civil procedure of the common law and civil law systems. Courts in the common law world have moved away from the principle of party control and increasingly take a more interventionist role in deciding what issues are to be decided in the case, what procedures are to be followed, and the speed at which the case is to proceed. *Court management* of litigation has become a common feature of the procedural system. An example is the reforms of the English rules of civil procedure instigated by Lord Woolf LCJ, which took effect in 1999. Party presentation, however, remains dominant in both theory and practice, with only limited exceptions. Attempts have been made to limit the use of costly procedures, such as discovery, and to encourage the use of procedures likely to result in early settlement of the litigation, such as early disclosure of evidence and the use of alternative dispute resolution methods, such as mediation. Similarly, the civil law systems have taken steps to reduce the number of hearings before the court (such as the Stuttgart Reforms in Germany) and have given greater powers to judges to dispose of cases on a more individualized basis. They have also extended the use of single judges instead of the traditional multijudge court. Nevertheless, all civil justice systems remain in great difficulties in disposing of cases with reasonable expedition and at an affordable cost.

Keith Uff

See also Adversarial System; Civil Law; Common Law; Criminal Procedure; Inquisitorial System

References and further reading

Hazard, Geoffrey C., and Michele Taruffo. 1993. *American Civil Procedure: An Introduction.* New Haven, CT: Yale University Press.
Jacob, Jack I. H. 1987. *The Fabric of English Civil Justice.* London: Stevens.
Merryman, John Henry. 1969. *The Civil Law Tradition: An Introduction to the Legal Systems of Western Europe and Latin America.* Stanford, CA: Stanford University Press.
Stein, Peter. 1984. *Legal Institutions—The Development of Dispute Settlement.* London: Butterworths.
Zweigert, Konrad, and Hein Kötz. 1998. *An Introduction to Comparative Law.* Oxford: Clarendon Press.

COLOMBIA

GENERAL INFORMATION

Colombia is located in northern South America. With approximately 440,000 square miles of land, the country is about the size of Texas and California combined. It is the fourth largest country in South America. Colombia's northwestern corner shares a border with Panama, linking South America and Central America. It is the only country in South America with coastlines on both the Pacific Ocean and the Caribbean Sea. Moving clockwise from its northern mainland connection with the Isthmus of Panama, its other boundaries are with the Caribbean Sea to the north, Venezuela and Brazil to the east, Peru to the south, Ecuador to the southwest, and the Pacific Ocean to the northwest. Among the islands it claims are San Andres and Provencia in the Caribbean, and Malpelo in the Pacific.

Colombia's 2000 estimated population was approximately 40 million. Among Latin American countries, only Brazil and Mexico have larger populations. More than 75 percent of the total population is urban. Demographic estimates vary considerably, but according to one source, the major ethnic groups are mestizos, or mixed Spanish and indigenous (60 percent), Caucasians (20 percent), mulattos (14 percent), Afro-Colombians (4 percent), and indigenous peoples (2 percent). Vast social, economic, gender, racial, and ethnic inequalities have contributed to a culture characterized by many forms of extreme violence. Spanish is the primary language, and the major religion is Roman Catholicism.

The Andes Mountains split at the Ecuadorian border into three ranges that divide Colombia and create its extremely diverse climates and temperatures, including tropical jungles, snow-capped mountains, and temperate plateaus, plains, and valleys. Administratively, the country is divided into thirty-two departments. Bogotá, in the central Andean region, is the capital district and largest urban area. Other major cities include Medellín and Cali in the western Andean region, and Barranquilla on the Caribbean coast—the second, third, and fourth most populous cities, respectively.

Colombia's legal system was initially based primarily on the Roman law systems of Spain, France, and Germany. It is classified as a civil law system but also has been influenced in some respects by the constitutional model of the United States.

HISTORY

Colombia's indigenous population belonged to numerous tribes with varied customs and systems of government, including the highland Chibchas and the Taironas of the Sierra Nevadas. The Chicba or Muisca society had particularly well organized religious and civil systems based on a matrilineal system of succession to office and a patrilineal system of inheritance. The combined indigenous population was not as numerous as in some parts of Latin America, and their numbers diminished dramatically—because of war, disease, and intermarriage—after the first Spanish explorers arrived in 1499.

The first permanent Spanish settlement was founded in 1525, and Bogotá was established in 1538. Although the military rule of the conquerors was gradually replaced by civil administration, Spanish colonists enjoyed little opportunity to gain experience with self-government or an independent judiciary. While *cabildos,* a form of local

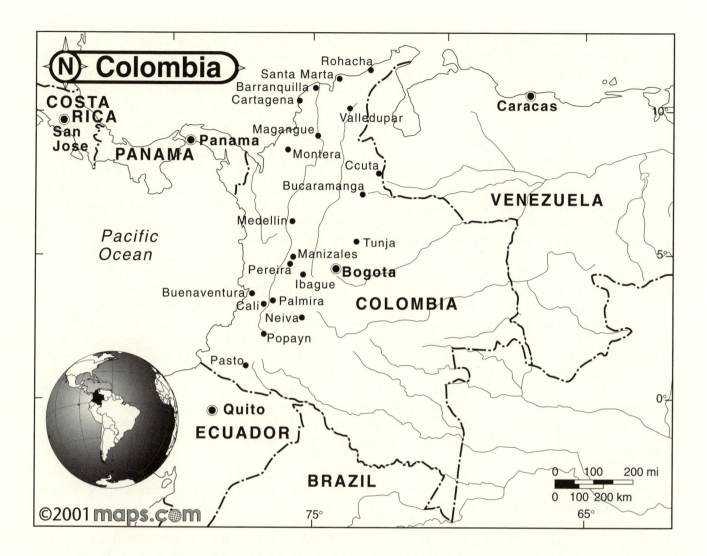

government similar to a town council, were established, the Spanish monarchy exercised tight control over all but the most local of matters through the Council of the Indies (appointed by the Crown and exercising legislative, administrative, and judicial powers from Spain) and through the governors or viceroys who carried out royal policy in the colonies. *Audiencias,* or high courts of justice, were established to review the acts of royal officers in the colonies, but they generally exercised their appellate power to protect royal prerogatives. Preindependence years were characterized by civil strife and repeated attacks by pirates and buccaneers.

In 1717, New Grenada (including the territories of the present countries of Colombia, Ecuador, Panama, and Venezuela) was elevated to the status of a vice-royalty. Resentment toward Spain intensified in the late 1700s, and mounting taxes led to an attempted revolt in 1791. When Napoleon invaded Spain in 1808, King Ferdinand VII was deposed and was replaced by Napoleon's brother Joseph. In Bogotá, colonists seized the opportunity thus presented to follow the example of resistance groups in Spain by forming an autonomous junta on July 20, 1810.

Absolute independence from Spain was formally declared in 1813 and finally won in 1819. Colombia and Venezuela then united to form the Greater Colombia Confederation headed by Simón Bolívar, as president, and Francisco de Paula Santander, as vice president. When Ecuador was liberated from Spanish control in 1822, it joined Colombia and Venezuela to become part of Gran Colombia until the confederation dissolved in 1830. Following independence, the Spanish law system was followed until replaced by later codes based on Napoleonic Codes.

By some counts, Colombia has had thirteen constitutions (not all of them coextensive with present territorial limits). The drafters of the first constitution followed the French model of a declaration of rights and the French understanding of separation of powers (with its concept of legislative supremacy), while following the U.S. model of the structure of the presidency and the courts. Early constitutions attempted to establish a centralist form of government. The 1863 Constitution established an extreme federal system, renamed the United States of Colombia, under which separate state constitutions also existed. The 1886 Constitution, though amended several times, remained in effect until 1991. It was characterized as "ultra-centralist" because it concentrated power in the presidency, including broad emergency powers. As a result, almost continuous states of emergency were declared. Beginning in 1910, the Colombian Supreme Court was granted a form of judicial review. While the judiciary includes many courageous and highly respected judges, it has continued to be viewed as the "Cinderella" among the three branches of government, plagued by perceptions of weakness, inefficiency, and corruption. Courts have been seen largely as pawns in the country's power struggles. The judiciary itself has been a frequent target of violence and this in turn has been pointed to as justification for the highly controversial use of so-called faceless judges in certain cases.

Rivalries between the followers of Bolivar and Santander eventually resulted in the formation of the two parties—the Conservatives and the Liberals—that despite the emergence of numerous smaller parties have dominated Colombian politics. After a period of civil war known as "La Violencia" in the 1940s and 1950s, these two parties formed a "National Front," lasting from 1958 until 1974, under which the presidency alternated between the two parties and those parties equitably shared other offices.

In the 1970s and 1980s, guerrilla insurgency, paramilitary activity, and drug trafficking increased. World attention focused on the escalating violence in November 1985, when the army's violent suppression of an assault by the Democratic Alliance/M-19 guerillas on the Palace of Justice led to more than one hundred deaths, including eleven justices of the Supreme Court.

After failed attempts at constitutional reform, a student-led movement, "We Can Still Save Colombia," was successful in placing the issue of whether to elect a constitutional assembly on the ballot in 1990. The assembly that was subsequently elected met for five months in early 1991, and the new constitution was promulgated on July 4, 1991. Strengthening the judiciary and establishing a more balanced distribution of powers were primary aims of the 1991 Constitution, which sought to bring peace to a nation long torn by violence—private and governmental, left-wing and right-wing. Among the important changes it made to the legal system were the creation of a separate Constitutional Court and the inclusion of provisions for a transition to a prosecutorial model instead of the country's traditional inquisitorial criminal system. In 2000 new Codes of Criminal Law and Criminal Procedure were adopted.

LEGAL CONCEPTS

The 1991 Constitution provides for three major branches of government—legislative, executive, and judi-

cial—as well as other autonomous and independent bodies to perform other functions of the state. The constitution provides that the branches have separate functions, but it also states that they are to collaborate harmoniously. The constitution proclaims that Colombia is a social state of law, organized as a unitary, decentralized republic with autonomous territorial entities and with participatory and pluralist democracy. It recognizes and protects the cultural and ethnic diversity of the nation, as well as a broad panoply of civil, political, social, and collective rights. Article 93 of the constitution provides that international conventions and treaties recognizing human rights that have been ratified by Colombia prevail in the internal order and that the rights and duties recognized in the constitution are to be interpreted in accordance with those international treaties. Spanish is declared the official language, but the languages and dialects of ethnic groups are also recognized as official in their territories, and bilingual education is required.

The executive branch is headed by a president who is head of state, head of government, and chief administrative authority. The president and vice president are elected by national popular vote for four-year terms. The current president is Andres Pastrana, who was elected in a runoff election in 1998.

The legislative branch is a bicameral congress elected through a system of proportional representation for four-year terms. The 102-member Senate has 100 members who are elected nationally and two who are elected nationally by indigenous communities. The House of Representatives has 161 members elected by departments or districts. The current Congress was elected in March 1998.

The judicial branch is composed of courts of ordinary jurisdiction (headed by the Supreme Court), administrative courts (headed by the Council of State), the Constitutional Court, special jurisdictions (indigenous peoples' jurisdiction and justices of the peace), the public prosecutor, and the Superior Council of the Judiciary. These entities and their personnel are described further in the sections that follow.

The National Electoral Council oversees elections. The constitution provides that its membership must reflect the political composition of the Congress. Members are elected for nonrenewable four-year terms from lists of three submitted by political parties and movements.

CURRENT STRUCTURE

The Supreme Court of Justice is the highest court of ordinary jurisdiction (including civil, commercial, criminal, labor, and family law matters). As in other parts of Latin America, the members of this and other higher courts are called *magistrados* (if they are men, as most higher-level judges are) and *magistradas* (if they are women); members of lower courts are called judges—

Legal Structure of Colombia Courts

Judicial Branch

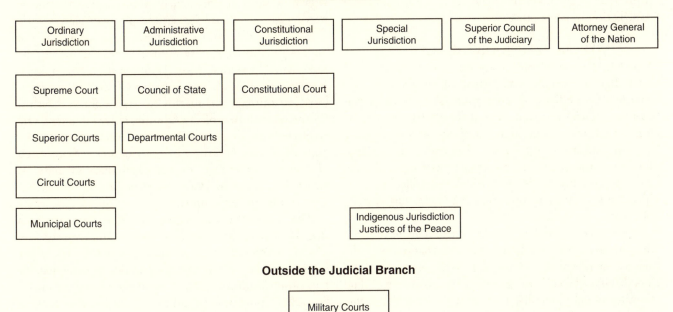

| Ordinary Jurisdiction | Administrative Jurisdiction | Constitutional Jurisdiction | Special Jurisdiction | Superior Council of the Judiciary | Attorney General of the Nation |

Supreme Court | Council of State | Constitutional Court

Superior Courts | Departmental Courts

Circuit Courts

Municipal Courts

Indigenous Jurisdiction
Justices of the Peace

Outside the Judicial Branch

Military Courts

juezas (if they are women, as many of them are) and *jueces* (if they are men). The Supreme Court currently is composed of twenty-three members who are divided into three chambers—civil and agrarian appeals (seven members), criminal appeals (nine members), and labor appeals (seven members)— who also sit as a full court for certain matters. The Supreme Court hears appeals in cases from the lower courts of ordinary jurisdiction and has authority to investigate and judge the president, members of Congress, and other high government officers. The nation is organized into twenty-nine judicial districts, each of which has a superior court that is divided into civil, penal, family, and agrarian chambers, which exercise appellate jurisdiction over the circuit courts within the district. There are also municipal courts and special territorial judicial zones.

The Council of State is the highest administrative tribunal and is composed of twenty-seven members who are divided into an adversarial administrative chamber (twenty-three counselors) and a consultation and civil service chamber (four counselors), and who sit as a full court for certain matters. Below the Council of State are administrative courts in each department. The Council of State decides controversies arising from administrative acts and acts of private entities performing public duties, and it also rules on constitutional challenges to governmental decrees that do not fall within the jurisdiction of the Constitutional Court.

The Constitutional Court is responsible for safeguarding the integrity and supremacy of the constitution. It is composed of nine members who sit as a full court but generally divide into panels of three when considering special protective petitions called *tutelas*. Among its additional functions, the Constitutional Court rules on the constitutionality of laws and of some decrees.

The Fiscalia General, or National Attorney General's Office, is part of the judicial branch but has administrative and budgetary autonomy. The national attorney general is the chief public investigator and prosecutor.

The Superior Council of the Judiciary is responsible for administration and disciplinary functions of the judicial branch. Its thirteen members are divided into two chambers: the administrative chamber (six members) and the disciplinary chamber (seven members). The administrative branch sets territorial divisions, handles the judicial budget, and administers the judiciary. The disciplinary chamber handles disciplinary matters against members of the judicial branch and against practicing attorneys and decides jurisdictional conflicts.

Colombia was a leader among Latin American countries in turning to alternative dispute resolution mechanisms as a means of alleviating judicial congestion and delay. Conciliation measures were strengthened in the 1980s and are explicitly recognized in Article 116 of the 1991 Constitution. Centers of Conciliation and Arbitration have been established by law schools, chambers of commerce, and nongovernmental organizations. A 2000 report by the Corporation for Judicial Excellence (CEJ) recommends greater development and regulation of alternative dispute resolution mechanisms, and Ministry of

Justice initiatives seek to strengthen extrajudicial conciliation measures. However, the Constitutional Court has ruled that it is unconstitutional to require mandatory conciliation in labor cases.

SPECIALIZED JUDICIAL BODIES

The 1991 Constitution recognizes special jurisdictions for indigenous peoples and justices of the peace. Under Article 246, indigenous communities' authorities can exercise judicial functions within their territory according to their own norms and procedures, so long as these are not contrary to the constitution and national laws. Justices of the peace may be created pursuant to Article 247 to equitably resolve individual and collective conflicts, and the law may provide for their election by popular vote.

Under the constitution, military tribunals have jurisdiction over service-related criminal charges brought against members of the armed services on active duty. The Military Penal Code governs these proceedings. The Constitutional Court has ruled that if convicted, members of the military may not only be sentenced to prison but may also be held personally liable to pay indemnification to victims and their families.

In addition, as part of its elusive peace process, the government has temporarily ceded control over portions of the nation's territory to armed guerrilla groups who exercise certain privatized forms of judicial powers.

STAFFING

Members of the Supreme Court are named by the court itself from lists sent to it by the Superior Council of the Judiciary. They serve single eight-year terms and cannot be reappointed. The members of the superior courts of each judicial district are appointed by the Supreme Court from lists sent to it by the Superior Council of the Judiciary. They and the lower judges within the ordinary courts are part of the judicial career system and, given good conduct and satisfactory performance, may serve until a mandatory retirement age of sixty-five. The judges of the district and municipal courts are appointed by the superior courts from lists sent to them by the Sectional Council of the Judiciary.

The members of the Council of State are appointed by the council itself from lists sent to it by the Superior Council of the Judiciary and are limited to a single term of eight years. The members of departmental administrative courts are appointed by the Council of State from lists sent to it by the Superior Council of the Judiciary.

The members of the Constitutional Court are appointed by the Senate from lists of three names for each seat submitted to it by either the president, the Supreme Court, or the Council of State, depending on the seat. Members serve eight-year terms and cannot be reappointed. On December 13, 2000, the Senate selected seven new members of this court, including the first woman to serve as a permanent justice. These new members replace members with terms expiring in March 2001.

The national attorney general is selected by the Supreme Court from a list of three names sent to it by the president. The term of office is four years and reappointment is not allowed. The Superior Council of the Judiciary has thirteen members who serve eight-year terms. Of the six members of the Administrative Chamber, one is elected by the Constitutional Court, two by the Supreme Court, and three by the Council of State. Each of the seven members of the disciplinary chamber is elected by the national Congress from lists of three names sent to it by the government.

The structure of the legal profession in Colombia is singular. Colombia's leading public and private law schools are highly regarded, and the publications of their faculty members are widely used throughout the region. Law students must complete a five-year undergraduate law school program, including required clinical education, and pass comprehensive exams. In order to graduate, students must also either complete a graduate monograph or complete a year of unpaid social service in the judicial system or other state entity. The 1991 Constitution guarantees educational autonomy, and in recent years the number of law schools and lawyers in Colombia has increased rapidly. The country has the most law schools and the most lawyers in Latin America. This has led to proposals for greater regulation of legal education and the legal profession.

IMPACT

Colombia is a country of paradox and extremes. It has long operated as a formal democracy (experiencing only three periods of formal military rule) and has been called a country of laws, with approximately ninety thousand lawyers and a well-developed formal legal culture. But the country is characterized by extreme wealth disparities and plagued by rampant violence and lawlessness. Operating amid almost continuous states of emergency for many years, its weak judicial system has long suffered from congestion, delay, inefficiency, and corruption. In recent years, the drug war has paved the way for extensive U.S. and international intervention in internal policies and priorities.

The 1991 Constitution raised hopes for reform that remain largely unrealized. Within the judicial branch, the most dramatic impact has been produced by the new Constitutional Court. Charged with safeguarding the constitution and its extensive guarantees of individual and collective rights, the new court has used the constitution's streamlined procedures to provide judicial access to marginalized groups and individuals who have never before seen the courts as an effective avenue for redressing their grievances. A new writ of protection called the *tutela* requires courts of ordinary jurisdiction to rule immediately (within ten days) to prevent violations of fundamental rights, subject to expedited appeal to higher courts of ordinary jurisdiction and to automatic transmission for discretionary review by the Constitutional Court. The avalanche of these citizen petitions has resulted in what some have described as an epidemic of *tutelitis* but others have depicted as a healthy sign of growth in protection for human rights. Additionally, any citizen can bring direct challenges to the constitutionality of laws in the Constitutional Court.

The 1991 Constitution explicitly embraces the concept of affirmative or positive action in behalf of marginalized groups. The Constitutional Court has provided special protection for certain groups, including women, children, the elderly, persons with disabilities, indigenous and ethnic groups, gays and lesbians, and prisoners. For example, in 2000 the court upheld many of the provisions of a Quota Law requiring that one-third of high public positions be filled by women, though it declared that a similar quota for electoral candidates (as now exists in several countries in Latin America as well as in several other parts of the world) conflicted with the associational rights of political groups.

Martha I. Morgan

See also Constitutional Review; Human Rights Law; Indigenous and Folk Legal Systems; Judicial Independence; Legal Pluralism; Legal Professionals—Civil Law Traditions; Magistrates—Civil Law Systems; Napoleonic Code; The Spanish Empire and the Laws of the Indies

References and further reading

Álvarez, Gladys S., and Highton Elena I. 2000. "Resolución Alternativa de Conflictos: Estado Actual en el Panorama Latinoamericano." *California Western International Law Journal* 30: 409–428.

Colombia Information Service. 1989. *A Sketch of Colombia.* New York.

Conference of Supreme Courts of the Americas. 1996. "Legal System of Colombia." *Saint Louis University Law Journal* 40: 1353–1356.

Judicial Branch of the Colombian State. http://www. ramajudicial.gov.co (accessed November 26, 2000).

Kline, Harvey F. 1995. *Colombia: Democracy under Assault.* 2d ed. Boulder, CO: Westview Press.

Monroy Cabra, Marco Gerardo. 1998. *Ética del Abogado: Régimen Legal y Disciplinario.* 2d ed. Bogotá: Ediciones Libería del Profesional.

Morgan, Martha I. 1999. "Taking *Machismo* to Court: The Gender Jurisprudence of the Colombian Constitutional Court." *University of Miami Inter-American Law Review* 30: 253–342.

Morgan, Martha I., with Alzate Buitrago and Mónica María. 1992. "Constitution-Making in a Time of Cholera: Women and the 1991 Colombian Constitution." *Yale Journal of Law and Feminism* 4: 353–413.

Nagle, Luz Estella. 1995. "Evolution of the Colombian Judiciary and the Constitutional Court." *Indiana International and Comparative Law Review* 6: 59–60.

———. 2000. "The Cinderella of Government: Judicial Reform in Latin America." *California Western International Law Journal* 30: 345–379.

Pearce, Jenny. 1990. *Colombia: Inside the Labyrinth.* London: Latin America Bureau (Research and Action); New York: U.S. distribution by Monthly Review Press.

Posada-Carbó, Eduardo, ed. 1998. *Colombia: The Politics of Reforming the State.* New York: St. Martin's Press.

Rodríguez R., Libardo. 1992. *Nueva estructura del poder público en Colombia.* Bogotá: Editorial Temis.

COLORADO

GENERAL INFORMATION

The state of Colorado is located in the center of the western half of the United States. The outline of Colorado approximates a rectangle and the state is bounded by Kansas and Nebraska on the east, New Mexico and Oklahoma on the south, Utah on the west, and Wyoming on the north. Colorado is the eighth largest state in area and covers 103,718 square miles. The center of Colorado is approximately 1,500 miles west of the east coast, 800 miles east of the west coast, 650 miles south of the Canadian border, and 475 miles north of the Mexican border.

Although Colorado has a diverse geography of mountains, plateaus, canyons, and plains; the state is best known for the Rocky Mountains. Colorado is the nation's highest state with an average elevation of 6,800 feet, ranging from 3,350 feet in the eastern plains to 14,431 feet at the top of Mount Elbert in the Rockies. The continental divide runs from north to south through west central Colorado and bisects the state into eastern and western slopes. Fifty-four mountain peaks in Colorado are over 14,000 feet and more than a thousand peaks are over 10,000 feet.

Colorado's 2000 population is 4,301,261, almost double that of the 1970 population of 2,209,596. The population density is 41.5 persons per square mile, compared to the United States' average of 79.6 persons. The 2000 racial makeup of the state is 82.8 percent White, 3.8 percent Black or African-American, 2.2 percent Asian, 1.0 percent American Indian and Alaskan Native, 7.3 percent Other, and 2.8 percent reported two or more races. Persons of Hispanic or Latino origin, who may be of any race, comprise 17.1 percent of the population.

Historically the economy of Colorado was based on mining, beginning with the discovery of gold in 1858 and later silver, uranium, coal, molybdenum, and petroleum. Much of the economy currently centers on high technology and the service industry. But agriculture is important in the eastern, western, and south central parts of the state. Colorado's main agricultural products are grains, beef, fruit, and vegetables.

EVOLUTION AND HISTORY

The first inhabitants of what is now the state of Colorado were Native Americans; the Ute, Cheyenne, Arapahoe, Kiowa, Comanche, Pawnee, and Sioux tribes. The United States acquired most of eastern Colorado through the Louisiana Purchase in 1803. Mexico ceded most of that part of Colorado not acquired by the Louisiana Purchase by the Treaty of Hildalgo in 1848. The present-day boundaries of Colorado were established in 1850 when the United States purchased Texas's claims in Colorado. The earliest permanent European settlement was founded in the San Luis Valley in the southwestern part of Colorado in 1851.

There was no established law or government in Colorado (then part of the Territory of Kansas) at the time of the discovery of gold near the present-day site of Denver, the future capital, in 1858. The gold rush brought large numbers of people, as many as 5,000 per week, to the area. Crime was rampant in the frontier mining town. Fourteen murder jury trials were held during 1859 and 1860; six of the men were sentenced to death by hanging. An 1860 editorial in the *Rocky Mountain News* called for some form of government and law to protect life and property. During that time Denver's attempt at self-government included a miners' court that took care of civil matters and a people's court that handled criminal matters.

The politics of the eve of the Civil War encouraged Congress to give the area a legal government. After Texas seceded in 1861 with the rest of the southern states, there was a move by the Republicans in Congress to establish territorial governments in areas not involved in slavery. On February 28, 1861, Congress created the Colorado Territory with William Gilpin as the first territorial governor. Colorado's territorial legislature laid out seventeen counties, chartered the city of Denver, organized courts including the Territorial Supreme Court of Colorado, and adopted a legal code. President Lincoln appointed the first three justices of the Territorial Supreme Court of Colorado. These justices were not from the territory but from the eastern United States, and there was concern that their rulings would not reflect the people's wishes. The ability of the Colorado people to elect their own judicial officers was one incentive to becoming a state.

The first attempt by the citizens to create a state happened not long after, in Denver in 1864. The attempt was unsuccessful and the Colorado Territory remained under the jurisdiction of the federal court system. Twelve years later, on August 1, 1876, Colorado became the twenty-eighth of the United States. Colorado is nicknamed the Centennial state because it became a state one hundred years after the signing of the Declaration of Independence. John L. Routt was elected Colorado's first governor after statehood in 1876. The first state legislature was convened the same year. The Colorado Constitution, modeled after the United States Constitution, also was completed in 1876. The constitution, which is very similar to Colorado's present constitution, established the state Supreme Court, district courts, and county courts. The Colorado Constitution also granted the Supreme Court supervisory power over the lower courts in the state, but that power was not exercised until 1953.

The original constitution did not establish an intermediate appellate court. But over the last century there have been three manifestations of the Colorado Court of Appeal. A three-judge court was created in 1891 to assist the Supreme Court in clearing its backlog. When the backlog was cleared in 1904, the intermediate appellate was abolished. The next year, the Colorado Constitution was amended to increase the number of Supreme Court justices from three to five to keep up with the appellate caseload. A second court of appeals was established in 1911 for four years to once again help with the backlog of cases. It was not until 1970 that the Colorado General Assembly again authorized the formation of a six-judge intermediate appellate court to help with the backlog of appellate cases. The court of appeals's jurisdiction originally was limited to civil matters, and criminal jurisdiction was added in 1974 along with the addition of four more judges. Six additional judges were added in 1987 bringing the court to its present number of sixteen judges.

CURRENT STRUCTURE

Judicial System

The Colorado court system consists of the Supreme Court, an intermediate court of appeals, district courts, and county courts. There are twenty-two judicial districts within the state. Each county has a district court, a general jurisdiction court, and a county court, a limited jurisdiction court. Specialized probate and juvenile courts exist in the City and County of Denver. Colorado statutes also authorize locally funded municipal courts with jurisdiction limited to municipal ordinance violations.

The Colorado Supreme Court is the court of last resort for all conflicts arising under the Colorado constitution or statutes. The Colorado Supreme Court is comprised of seven justices who sit en banc. The court has both appellate and original jurisdiction with mandatory jurisdiction in capital criminal, disciplinary, and interlocutory decision cases and discretionary jurisdiction in civil, noncapital criminal, administrative agency, juvenile, advisory opinion, and original proceedings cases. The head of the Colorado judiciary is the chief justice, who is elected by a vote of the other justices to serve an indefinite term as chief justice. Since 1959, the Supreme

Legal Structure of Colorado Courts

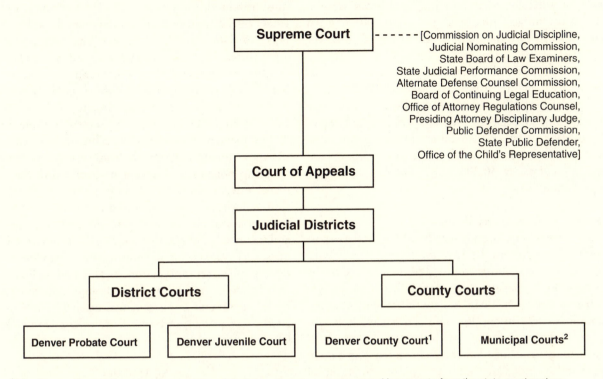

Supreme Court - - - - - - [Commission on Judicial Discipline,
Judicial Nominating Commission,
State Board of Law Examiners,
State Judicial Performance Commission,
Alternate Defense Counsel Commission,
Board of Continuing Legal Education,
Office of Attorney Regulations Counsel,
Presiding Attorney Disciplinary Judge,
Public Defender Commission,
State Public Defender,
Office of the Child's Representative]

Court of Appeals

Judicial Districts

District Courts   County Courts

Denver Probate Court   Denver Juvenile Court   Denver County Court[1]   Municipal Courts[2]

[1] The Denver County Court functions as a municipal as well as a county court and is separate from the state court system.
[2] Municipal Courts are created and maintained by local government, but are subject to Supreme Court rules and procedures.

Court has hired a state court administrator who serves at the pleasure of the chief justice and oversees the administration of all courts in the state.

The Colorado Court of Appeals is comprised of sixteen judges who sit in panels of three to hear cases that have been appealed from the district courts, Denver Probate Court, Denver Juvenile Court, and twenty-seven state agencies and boards. The court of appeals has mandatory jurisdiction in civil, noncapital criminal, administrative agency, and juvenile case appeals. There is no discretionary jurisdiction. The chief justice of the Supreme Court appoints the chief judge of the court of appeals, who serves at the pleasure of the chief justice. The Colorado Supreme Court hears appeals from decisions of the court of appeals.

As of July 1, 2001, there were 126 district court judges. In addition, thirty-six senior judges who have retired from the bench are available to handle cases in districts where there is a backlog of cases, conflict of interest, or vacant judicial positions. Quasi-judicial resources include 100 magistrates who perform duties as assigned by the chief judge of their judicial district and as authorized by rule. The general jurisdiction of the district courts include tort, contract, real property rights, estate, civil appeals, mental health, and miscellaneous civil cases, felony, criminal appeals, and miscellaneous criminal case types.

The district court has exclusive domestic relations jurisdiction as well as exclusive juvenile jurisdiction (except in the City and County of Denver). An adult drug court was implemented in Denver in 1994 and three districts implemented family courts in 1997. Colorado trial courts require a jury size of twelve jurors for felony cases and six jurors for misdemeanor and civil cases. Verdicts must be unanimous.

As of July 1, 2001, there were 101 county court judges in 62 counties. This does not include the seventeen Denver County Court judges. The county courts are courts of limited jurisdiction and hear tort, contract, and real property rights cases whose amount is less than $10,000, preliminary hearings for felony cases, criminal appeals, and traffic cases. The county courts have exclusive jurisdiction in small claims cases, misdemeanor, and driving while intoxicated/driving under the influence cases. Jury trials are possible except in small claims and appeals cases. The municipal courts also are limited jurisdiction courts and hear moving traffic, parking, and miscellaneous traffic cases and have exclusive ordinance violation jurisdiction.

Water rights have been important to Colorado since its inception and there are seven specialized water courts in the state. There is a water court in each of the major river basins: the Arkansas, Colorado, Gunnison, Rio Grande, San Juan, South Platte, and White Rivers. Seven part-time water referees adjudicate real property rights involving water. District court judges also can serve as water court judges. Jury trials are permitted in water court. Appeals of water court decisions are heard by the Supreme Court.

Probation is another responsibility of the judicial branch. Each of the twenty-two judicial districts has a chief probation officer whose staff provides presentence investigations and special program services, and supervises offenders sentenced to community programs. Probation has a total of 817 employees across the state, handling approximately 36,000 adults and 9,000 juveniles on probation.

Legal Profession and Legal Training

In 2001, there were approximately 20,000 active attorneys in Colorado, one attorney for every 215 residents. There are two ways to be admitted to the practice of law in Colorado: by passing the Colorado bar examination, or on a motion to the Board of Law Examiners if the candidate is licensed in another state and has work experience as an attorney for five of the previous seven years. Appellate, general jurisdiction, and limited jurisdiction judges and attorneys are required to complete 45 hours of continuing legal education, including seven ethics hours, every three years.

The two law schools in Colorado, the University of Denver College of Law located in Denver and the University of Colorado Law School located in Boulder, were established in 1892. Both schools draw students from all regions of the United States. The University of Denver College of Law is a private school with over 900 law students for a student/faculty ratio of 18.0 in 2000. The most recent Colorado bar passage rate for University of Denver College of Law students was 79.9 percent. The University of Colorado School of Law is part of the state university system with approximately 500 students for a student/faculty ratio of 12.5 in 2000. It has nationally recognized programs in natural resources and constitutional law and was recently ranked thirty-eighth in a survey of top law schools. The most recent Colorado bar passage rate for University of Colorado School of Law students was 96.5 percent.

NOTABLE FEATURES OF LAW/LEGAL SYSTEM

Colorado's voters have initiated constitutional amendments during the last decade to rein in the powers of government. For example, Colorado voters have limited the government's ability to impose taxes without the people's consent, known as the Taxpayer's Bill of Rights (art. 10, sec. 20). This 1992 amendment to the Colorado constitution sharply limits the amount of money that state and local government can collect by holding the spending growth to a rate that cannot exceed the sum of popula-

tion growth and inflation. Any revenue above the limit must be refunded to taxpayers. In 1994, a majority of the voters agreed to impose term limits for all local state officials to eight years in the House (four terms) and Senate (two terms) starting in 1998 (art. 18, sec. 11).

A recent landmark United States Supreme Court ruling, *Romer, Governor of Colorado et al. v. Evans et al.* (1996), struck down an amendment to the Colorado Constitution. The amendment, known as Amendment 2, was a statewide initiative prohibiting all branches of state government in Colorado from passing legislation or adopting policies prohibiting discrimination based on sexual orientation. The measure had been passed by a slim majority of Colorado voters in 1992 in response to municipal ordinances in Aspen, Boulder, and the City and County of Denver that banned discrimination based on sexual orientation in housing, employment, education, public accommodation, health and welfare services. In a 6–3 ruling, the United States Supreme Court held Amendment 2 was unconstitutional because it violated the Equal Protection Clause of the United States Constitution.

STAFFING

Until 1966, both trial and appellate judges ran for judicial office in partisan elections. In 1966, Colorado adopted the Missouri Plan, a merit-based selection and retention system for judges. The governor selects a potential judge from a list of judges submitted to him by a judicial nominating commission. The only exception is that the mayor of Denver appoints Denver County judges. The person chosen does not need to be confirmed by any other governmental body. Before the first retention election, the judge is said to be serving a "provisional" term. At the end of their first term, individual judges stand for retention or nonretention in the general election. Supreme Court terms are ten years, court of appeals terms are eight years, district court terms are six years, and county court terms are four years. Appellate court judges stand for retention in statewide elections, while district and county court judges stand for retention in their respective jurisdictions.

Qualifications to serve as an appellate judge include state residency and ten years of state bar membership. To serve as a district court or trial court judge, the person must be a resident of the district, possess a law degree, and have been a member of the state bar for five years. A law degree is required for county court judges in metropolitan areas, but is not required for rural county courts or any municipal court judgeships.

The State Commission on Judicial Performance for appellate judges and the District Commission on Judicial Performance for trial judges conduct judicial performance evaluations. The commissions prepare evaluation profiles on each judge standing for retention based on surveys of court participants and provides these profiles to the public.

RELATION TO NATIONAL SYSTEM

United States District Court for the District of Colorado, a limited jurisdiction court that hears civil and criminal cases brought under federal law, was established with statehood in 1876. Judge Moses Hallett was the first judge appointed to the court. His decisions on mining and water law were an important foundation for economic development in the west. Seven active judges, two senior judges, and three full-time magistrates currently serve in the court. Approximately 2,500 civil and 500 criminal cases are filed each year. Colorado was originally part of the Eighth Circuit that was established as part of the United States federal circuit court system in 1891. A new circuit, the Tenth, was carved out of the Eighth Circuit in 1929. The Tenth Circuit includes the states of Colorado, Kansas, New Mexico, Oklahoma, Utah, and Wyoming.

Karen Gottlieb

See also United States—Federal System; United States—State Systems

References and further reading
Colorado Courts. http://www.courts.state.co.us (accessed November 23, 2001).
Colorado State Archives, http://www.archives.state.co.us (accessed December 13, 2001).
Kania, Alan J., and Dian Hartman. 1993. *The Bench and Bar: A Centennial View of Denver's Legal History.* Chatsworth, CA: Windsor Publications.
Romer, Governor of Colorado et al. v. Evans et al. 1996. 517 U.S. 620.
Rottman, David B., Carol R. Flango, Melissa T. Cantrell, Randall Hansen, and Neil LaFountain. 2000. *State Court Organization 1998.* Washington, DC: U.S. Department of Justice.

COMMERCIAL LAW (INTERNATIONAL ASPECTS)

Defining international commercial law can be difficult. There is no consensus on which areas of law are included under that heading. Traditionally, international commercial law meant trade law or mercantile law. It encompassed the areas of law governing what merchants do: trade, or buy and sell goods. Under this definition, commercial law includes those legal matters and rules that affect importing and exporting. More recently, international commercial law has come to have a much broader meaning. For some, it includes any area of law that is of special interest to those who do business across national borders. Under this all-encompassing umbrella, international commercial law covers a wide range of laws relevant to any international business transaction. It spans laws affecting banking, consumer protection, contracts, corporations and partnerships, insurance, investment, employment and labor, the licensing of copyrights, trademarks and patents, taxation, and trade in services, to name only a few. It would be impossible to discuss all of these areas of law in a short article. Therefore, because importing and exporting are often a company's first step into international business, this article focuses on legal issues related to the more traditional definition of international commercial law. However, this discussion illustrates some common principles and emerging trends in other areas of international commercial or business law.

In order to begin to understand international commercial law, two questions must be answered. Is there an international agreement or treaty on the subject? And, how do national laws deal with the topic? These questions illustrate two broad sources of international commercial law: public international law and private international law. Public international law concerns the relationships between nation states. Treaties and other international agreements are examples of public international law. Unlike public international law, which concerns the rights and duties of countries, private international law deals with the rights and duties of private parties, individuals, or companies. Private international law is really national law. It focuses on how and whether the courts in one country apply another country's law. Private international law is sometimes called "conflict of laws," because it determines which law will apply to a particular business transaction, in which country a dispute might be heard, and whether one country will enforce a court's judgment from another country.

The laws concerning importing and exporting have roots in both public and private international law. For many years, countries have used bilateral treaties of Friendship, Commerce, and Navigation (FCN) to regulate trade between their nations. In addition, numerous multilateral trade agreements exist. These agreements regulate trade between more than two nations. During the 1990s, many new multilateral trade agreements came into force. For example, the North American Free Trade Agreement (NAFTA) set out a new trade relationship between Canada, Mexico, and the United States. In the mid-1990s, more than 100 nations signed the Uruguay Round of the General Agreement on Tariffs and Trade (GATT). This GATT created the World Trade Organization (WTO) and provided a framework for a worldwide trading system. There are now 142 members of the WTO. The GATT set out the rules on importing that WTO member countries must follow concerning goods from other WTO member countries. These international agreements affect the national laws in the countries that have signed them by determining how their national laws may regulate international commerce.

Every nation has laws or regulations governing importing and exporting. These rules vary greatly from one country to another. Some countries place restrictions on some or all exports. For instance, Australia controls the export of food, some animals, and goods destined for certain countries by requiring the exporter to obtain a license from the government. Russia regulates exporting by charging an export duty, or a tax, on the value of the goods leaving the country, and it requires exporters to obtain special permission to export technology and certain commodities. In South Korea, the law requires an exporter to register with the government and obtain a license for any goods to be exported. Countries also heavily regulate imports. One of the most common methods of doing so is taxing the goods that are imported into the country. The tax is called a tariff or duty. An importer must consult a country's tariff schedule to learn the amount of tax that will be imposed. Each tariff schedule will contain different rates the country will charge on the same goods depending upon which country they originally came from. Countries also regulate imports through nontariff measures, such as quotas. A quota will limit how much of a particular item may be imported or will restrict from which countries the goods may be imported. Some countries require licenses to import goods.

International trade agreements greatly influence a nation's import laws. As a general rule, a country that has signed the GATT has agreed to adjust its national import duties so that it charges the same tariff rate on the same category of goods, regardless of which other WTO nation the goods have come from. This is called the most favored nation (MFN) rate. In addition, once goods from one WTO nation have been imported into another, the GATT requires that the importing nation must treat them precisely as they would their own products. This national treatment standard means that once the tariff has been paid, a WTO nation cannot impose any additional taxes on the imported goods, unless it imposes the same tax on the same domestic products.

Bilateral and multilateral agreements may also impose requirements on national laws in areas other than trade. Many contain features that prohibit discrimination, such as MFN or national treatment. Bilateral treaties of FCN typically set out rules defining the rights of nationals of each country to invest in the other country and often require each nation to grant equal investing opportunities to nationals from the other country. NAFTA includes investment provisions that require MFN and national treatment for investors from the other NAFTA countries. The most recent GATT agreement included a special treaty dealing with intellectual property, the Agreement on Trade Related Aspects of Intellectual Property (TRIPs). This agreement requires all WTO members to ensure that their laws concerning copyright, trademarks,

and patents meet international minimum standards. As a result of TRIPs, many nations, including the United States, revised their national intellectual property laws to meet international standards. TRIPs also requires national treatment so that foreign intellectual property owners receive the same level of protection as nationals.

These international agreements and national laws serve as a backdrop against which merchants buy and sell goods. Certainly, whether two nations have a trade agreement and how national laws govern exports and imports will influence whether a merchant trades within a certain country. If tariffs are high or a national quota has been met, a merchant's ability to sell goods into a particular nation will be hindered. On the other hand, if there are no tariffs or other barriers, a merchant may more easily import its goods. Private international law, or the national law of contracts, is the law that most affects the actual agreement between the buyer and the seller. This agreement is the contract for the international sale of goods. Contract law is the general body of law that governs the rights and obligations of the private parties to this contract. Many nations have a separate body of law specifically for contracts for the sale of goods. Contract law is always a matter of national law. When buyers and sellers of goods trade within the same country, the contract law of that country will determine whether their agreement is valid and enforceable. It will also delineate the rights and obligations of the buyer and seller in addition to those specified in the contract. When buyers and sellers are in different countries and trading internationally, none may assume that the contract law of their home country will automatically determine all or any of their rights and responsibilities. When parties trade across borders, they will be subject to the laws of their own country as well as those of the other country. It isn't necessary for a party to physically enter the other country for the laws to be imposed. Consider a seller e-mailing an advertisement to a buyer in another country who orders goods, which the seller sends through the mail. The seller has probably done enough to be subjected to the laws of the buyer's country.

To complicate matters, national contract laws can differ vastly. Therefore, parties to international sales agreements may be exposed to laws and legal obligations quite different from those in their home countries. For instance, some socialist countries treat a breach of contract, in which one party fails to meet its contract obligations, as a criminal offense. The economic police investigate the breach of contract, and the matter can be prosecuted. This concept is foreign to the contract law in Western industrialized nations that treat a breach of contract as an economic matter. National laws also vary on the formal requirements necessary to create a sales contract. The Uniform Commercial Code (UCC), the state law that governs most contracts for the sale of goods within the United States, requires that any contract for the sale of goods worth more than $500 must be in writing, although that rule has exceptions. Great Britain had a similar rule but did away with it about fifty years ago. Most other western European nations have never required a written contract for the sale of goods. In those countries, a seller and buyer may agree on all of the details for the contract orally and have a valid contract even though there is no written document. National sales laws provide rules for what happens when a buyer or seller does not perform to contract specifications. If a seller does not perform, perhaps by delivering inferior goods, it is common for national laws to allow the seller to "cure" or fix a faulty shipment if the seller can do so before the date the contract requires for performance. In many European countries, the law will allow the seller to cure a faulty shipment even after that date. The law gives the seller an additional grace period in which to perform. This grace period is called *mise en demeur* in France and *nachfrist* in Germany. The UCC does not give the seller such a grace period.

Because national laws concerning the buying and selling of goods vary so widely, the United Nations created a uniform law to govern the international sale of goods. The UN's Convention on the International Sale of Goods (CISG) is one of the most important developments in the area of international commercial law. It sets out uniform rules that apply to contracts for goods sold internationally. The United Nations considered many very different rules from different legal and economic systems, such as common law and civil law, and tried to balance the needs of industrial and developing countries. As a result, the rules contained in the CISG are based on rules from different countries and legal systems. Fifty-nine countries have adopted the CISG and made it their national law governing contracts for the international sale of goods. In the United States, the UCC still governs purely domestic sales contracts, but the CISG is the national law governing contracts for the international sale of goods. If a buyer has a place of business in the United States and a seller has a place of business in Switzerland, another country that has adopted the CISG, the CISG will govern the contract.

The CISG provides a comprehensive set of rules for merchants who buy and sell goods internationally. The CISG delineates what parties must include in their agreement in order for it to be considered a valid and binding contract. It provides rules to follow in the event the parties leave something out of their contract. And it determines the rights and obligations of the buyer and seller in the event the contract is breached. Because the United Nations understood that international merchants are typically sophisticated business people, the CISG recognizes that these buyers and sellers have "freedom of contract."

They are allowed to change the rules in the CISG and even choose a law other than the CISG to govern their contract.

The CISG is an example of a trend in international law to develop uniform laws to ensure that nationals from countries with different local laws receive fair treatment in international transactions. It does so by ensuring that the same rules will apply to an international sales contract whether an international merchant located in a country that has adopted the CISG is contracting with a merchant in Argentina, Belarus, Canada, or another nation that has adopted the CISG. The CISG illustrates a broad trend in international law to harmonize national laws, or make them more uniform worldwide. This trend toward harmonization can be seen in other areas of international commercial law. For instance, the TRIPs agreement required nations to change their intellectual property laws. Under TRIPs, the national laws in every member of the WTO will be harmonized to the extent that they all provide the same minimum level of protection. Therefore, whether you register your patent in the United States or any other WTO member nation, it will be protected for a minimum of twenty years.

A key factor to researching any area of international commercial law, whether you follow the traditional or all-encompassing definition, is considering both public international law and the national laws in the countries the business transaction will touch.

Susan J. Marsnik

See also Civil Law; Common Law; Contract Law; Private Law; Public Law

References and further reading

August, Ray. 2000. *International Business Law: Text, Cases, and Readings.* 3d ed. Upper Saddle River, NJ: Prentice Hall.
Folsom, Ralph H. 2001. *Hornbook on International Business Transactions.* 2d ed. St. Paul, MN: West Group.
Folsom, Ralph H., Michael W. Gordon, and John A. Spanogel, Jr. 1996. *Gordon and Spanogle's International Business Transactions in a Nutshell.* 6th ed. St. Paul, MN: West Group.
Ramberg, Jan. 1998. *International Commercial Transactions.* Cambridge: Kluwer Law International.
Schaffer, Richard, Beverely Earle, and Filiberto Agusti. 2002. *International Business Law and Its Environment.* 5th ed. Cincinnati, OH: West Legal Studies in Business.
Shippey, Karla C. 1999 *A Short Course in International Contracts: Drafting the International Sales Contract.* San Rafael, CA: World Trade Press.
UN Convention on the International Sale of Goods. http://cisgw3.law.pace.edu/cisg/text/cisg-toc.html (accessed November 5, 2001).
Van Dervort, Thomas R. 1999. *International Law and Organisation: An Introduction.* Thousand Oaks, CA: Sage Publications.
World Trade Organization. http://www.wto.org (accessed November 5, 2001).

COMMON LAW

Reprinted from *Comparative Legal Systems in a Nutshell,* 2d ed. By Mary Ann Glendon, Michael Wallace Gordon, and Paolo Carozza, 1999, with permission of the West Group.

HISTORY

Origins

The common law's origins in England evolved from necessity. William, conqueror at Hastings in 1066, centralized judicial administration in London. This allowed governance of the Saxon population by comparatively few Normans. Conflicts of royal concern were decided in the courts at Westminster, leaving local issues to the rural courts. William's enduring legacy was the creation of a highly centralized legal system, the foundation being an "unwritten" constitution and orally rendered but reported decisions on specific issues, which accumulated as a body of decisional law, or *jurisprudence.* The common law developed insulated from the continental reception of Roman law, and the civil law's emphasis on codification.

The Early Law Courts

The first common law court, the Exchequer, was a judicial offspring of the king's advisory council, the *Curia Regis,* reflecting the king's interest in resolving tax disputes. Disputes involving land titles, and most personal actions, were heard by the Court of Common Pleas. Finally, the King's Bench resolved issues with a direct royal interest. Litigants usually preferred the fairer procedure in the common law courts over the rural courts. But the jurisdiction of the common law courts was limited by a *writ* system. A civil action was permitted only when a specific writ was available from the Crown. Writs authorized commencement of specific suits, later known as "forms of action." Fictions were invented to extend the limited writs. Procedure tended to precede substance, similar to the concentration in early Roman law on the form and facts of a case rather than the creation of substantive, abstract legal rules. Because a plaintiff without a writ was without a remedy, the king's chancellor accepted petitions for *equitable* relief. Equitable proceedings were heard in an inquisitorial fashion modeled on canon and Roman law, avoiding the strictures of the common law. The *trust* became equity's most important contribution. In the nineteenth century, law and equity would be merged.

The Magna Carta

The diminishing use of rural courts shifted revenue collected from court fees to the king from the barons, increasing their hostility to royal power. Joined by an aggrieved clergy, they forced King John to sign a charter in 1215, halting the loss of feudal privileges. The few provisions protecting ordinary citizens later endowed the charter with stature as a constitutional document of exceptional magnitude, and the name Magna Carta. Common law institutions were severely strained in the fifteenth and sixteenth centuries. Some preferred the allegedly more understandable civil law. But Chief Justice Edward Coke ruled persistently to preserve the autonomy of the common law courts. The common law survived this tumultuous era, and common law lawyers successfully protected their role. The threat of civil law notions of codification of the common law was ended.

DISTRIBUTION OF THE COMMON LAW

Involuntary Reception

The distribution of the common law throughout the British Empire was not a voluntary reception but an imposition of the law as part of British territorial expansion. English law was ruled effective when England colonized an area without a "civilized" local law. Civil law is the more easily received legal tradition. The convenience of codes rather than case law favors the civil law system in a voluntary adoption process.

Australia, Canada, and the United States

The distribution of common law where there was no well-established system of justice beyond tribal law occurred in Australia, Canada, and the United States. The English Parliament decreed that the Australian colony's legal system was the common law, including English statutes. Respect for English decisions is understandable by the peaceful growth of Australia as an independent nation, in contrast to the American Revolution. Australian law remains the most closely identified to English law of all the major nations that trace their legal systems to England.

Acquisition by Britain of the French area of Canada did not lead to a fusion of the legal systems. An expanded Canada was influenced largely by English government, economic, and social structures, although Quebec preserved its civil law system. A Canadian jurisprudence has developed that includes influences external to the historical affiliation to English law; particular notice is given to legal developments in the neighboring United States.

Unlike Australia and Canada, the United States broke with England by means of a bloody revolution, costly both in terms of human life and in the perceived need to adopt new executive, legislative, and judicial institutions. The United States replaced a hereditary monarch with an elected president, and a parliament with a bicameral legislature. It established a unique system of federal and state courts, and an allocation of powers between the states and the federal government. These changes are expressed in the U.S. Constitution, a document as venerated as the core of the American legal system as is the civil code in many civil law nations. Although much English law remained the foundation of U.S. law, being free of English dominance meant none of the slow and sometimes tortuous separation by stages necessary for Australia and Canada. But whenever choices were made between the form of legal system to be adopted in new states, including those of French and Spanish dominance, the decision-makers turned to the common law as developed in England.

India

The common law distribution in India illustrates that the expansion of English common law could contribute to the administration of justice in a diverse social system. But attempts to apply the common law in India to both English and Indian parties were resisted by the latter. Hindu and Islamic law were substituted for common law in land, family, and succession matters. Reform concepts promoted by Jeremy Bentham found greater reception in India in the early nineteenth century than in England. Little truly Indian precedent had developed, and there was insubstantial consistency among Indian courts in determining sources of law. The private law of India was codified at an early date. As in most common law nations outside England, India adopted both a written constitution and judicial review.

PROCEDURE

Civil Procedure—History

Common law civil procedure developed internally—that is, within the court system itself—to meet immediate needs. Rules that resolved questions of how the course of an action would proceed were established on the spot by the courts. The development of civil procedure, particularly since the sixteenth century, has been a process of periodic alterations to correct immediate deficiencies that distract a court from reaching a just result. It has evolved into written codes of procedure, but they are more codifications of the common law rules than civil law codes. The civil law has seen a more methodical, external development, in which procedure is guided by legislative enactments and by the writings of law faculty, detached from any particular, current dispute. The civil law lawyer consequently views his system of procedure as more logical and rational in development.

The Civil Trial

The common law trial remains an oral process, notwithstanding the increased use of written witness and expert statements. The common law nation trial is "an event." It begins with all parties present and proceeds to its conclusion while they remain. Successful trial advocacy requires rapid comprehension and response. The usual common law trial has counsel for the plaintiff making a statement of his client's case, then calling his witnesses, each of whom may be cross-examined by defense counsel and reexamined by the plaintiff's counsel. When the plaintiff's case has been presented, the defense initiates a similar presentation of witnesses, with cross-examination by the plaintiff. Both counsel give final summaries, and a decision is then rendered by the judge. In some common law systems the trial judge plays a role in directly questioning the parties, to clarify conflicting or unclear matters, or even to commence a new line of questioning that the judge perceives as important but that had been ignored by counsel. Greater latitude in the presentation of evidence is related to the predominance of bench trials versus jury trials.

The Civil Jury

The use of a civil trial jury varies throughout common law systems. The United States extends the right to trial by jury well beyond practice in England. The concept that the essence of the common law system is trial by jury appears to the English lawyer to be carried to an unnecessary extreme in the United States. The importance of the jury in the development of English common law is more correctly associated with the criminal legal process.

Criminal Procedure

Common law criminal process is accusatorial rather than inquisitorial. The case against an accused is investigated, prepared, and directed through the courts, usually by a public official representing the state rather than by a judge or magistrate, as in a civil law system. As issues have become more complex over the decades, common law judges have tended to leave questioning to the advocates, sitting more as silent umpires than an inquiring third party. The decision to prosecute is not reserved by the state; in most systems anyone, not only public prosecutors or other officials, or even those with an interest in the matter, may act as a prosecutor. Private prosecution is used rarely, however. It nevertheless illustrates the conceptual aspect of the common law criminal process, that a citizen, either public or private, must commence and pursue the action, and that the role played by the person or group that determines guilt or innocence is only a minor part in the preparation and presentation of the suit.

Appellate Review

The emphasis on an oral process carries over to the appeal, although briefs have reduced or replaced oral reading of the lower court record. The oral focus is most evident during the actual appellate argument before the court. It is another event, this time by the lawyers alone before the appellant bench, and mainly involving questions of law.

RULES

Divisions of Law—Public and Private Law

Division of common law systems into private and public law is an infrequent classification, in contrast to civil law tradition legal systems. A division is more often noted in terms of the law of torts or the law of property, all part of what is known as substantive, as opposed to procedural, law. Were the system to be classified as public and private law, private law would include the law of contracts, torts, and property. Additionally so categorized would be family law, succession, and trusts. Criminal law would constitute a major part of the public law, which would further embody constitutional and administrative law as well as procedure. Labor law arguably fits either the public or private division. Civil law nations often employ entirely separate hierarchies of courts for public and private law. The view is mixed in the common law nations. In England there are specific common law courts for criminal law, but in the United States, most federal and state courts of first instance assert both civil and criminal jurisdiction. The other major division of public law, the law of the constitution, is allocated in England primarily to administrative tribunals, but the common law appellate court system retains jurisdiction over most administrative appeals. U.S. constitutional law, both state and federal, is a major part of proceedings at all levels.

Divisions of Law—The Law Merchant

Commercial law is often separately administered in civil law nations. Evolving within the fairs and markets of the Middle Ages, it created what became known as the law merchant. Commercial law might have developed within England as a largely separate system existing parallel to the common law. But it substantially assimilated into the common law by the seventeenth century, although retaining a separate significance, because judges recognized that commercial rules were chiefly based on the practices of merchants and traders. By the late nineteenth century, most of the law merchant was incorporated into statutes. While the law merchant had its own separate origin, little of that isolation remains today in common law systems.

Sources of Law

Legal tradition separates sources of law into written and unwritten. Classification of sources is less important than their assigned values. Value allocation to sources within a system is a slow, evolutionary process. Common law system judges traditionally have been less inclined to defer unquestioningly to legislation, particularly social reform legislation. Although there is no dispute that legislation is the source of law that has authority over all other sources, the fabric of the common law is its precedent.

Precedent

The theoretical usefulness of prior case law should not be any less in a legal system in which judges do not have to follow earlier decisions, than where they are compelled to follow them. When the rules denominating sources of law in a system exclude precedent as the primary source of law, precedent nonetheless retains value. Where precedent becomes a primary source of law, as in common law systems, the case does more than teach judges something; it exists separately as law to be followed, or distinguished. Certainty, precision and flexibility are viewed as characteristics of precedent as a binding source of law. Once a decision has been rendered, there is some assurance that in a subsequent identical fact situation a similar conclusion will be reached. Common law system lawyers nevertheless are exceptionally skillful at distinguishing fact situations when a client's case seems disadvantaged by an earlier case of uncommon similarity. The aggregate of judicial decisions in common law countries often appear to constitute an extensive framework of variations on common themes. To the common law lawyer it is inconceivable that these variations could be foreseen, or included, in statutes. The most exhaustive civil code cannot offer solutions to all possible situations. It must of necessity have some measure of abstractness.

It is frequently very difficult to distinguish a legal principle in a case, or *ratio decidendi,* from additional rulelike statements that are ancillary to the decision and not binding, but considered only *obiter dicta.* If it is difficult for a civil law observer to separate law from dictum in reading a common law decision, some comfort should be found in the fact that persons trained in the common law often cannot agree on the distinction in a given case.

Legislation

The authority of legislation in common law nations is clear. It is primary authority. But most statutes are subject to different perspectives. The principal method is strict construction according to its literal meaning. But a literal interpretation may lead to an unjust result. The provision may thus be considered in the context of the entire enactment. A court may consider the social, political, and economic circumstances that led to the enactment. A purpose test may be used, involving inquiries about the state of the law before the act, what the act was intended to correct as an apparent defect in the common law, and the reason for the interest in such a change.

Michael Wallace Gordon

See also Adversarial System; Civil Law; England and Wales
References and further reading
Clark, David S., and Tugrul Ansay. 2001. *Introduction to the Law of the United States.* 2d ed. The Hague: Kluwer Law International.
Dicey, Albert Venn. 1924. *Introduction to the Study of the Law of the Constitution.* London: Macmillan.

Gilmore, Grant. 1977. *The Ages of American Law*. New Haven, CT: Yale University Press.

Glendon, Mary Ann, Michael Wallace Gordon, and Paolo G. Carozza. 1999. *Comparative Legal Traditions in a Nutshell*. St. Paul, MN: West Group.

Holdsworth, William Searle. 1913–1966. *A History of English Law*. London: Methuen.

Holmes, Oliver W. 1881. *The Common Law*. London: Macmillan.

Jackson, Richard Meredith. 1977. *The Machinery of Justice in England*. 7th ed. Cambridge: Cambridge University Press.

COMOROS

COUNTRY INFORMATION

The Federal Islamic Republic of the Comoros (République fédérale islamique des Comores, hereafter the Comoros) is composed of three out of four islands forming a small archipelago situated between Africa and the northern tip of Madagascar. The country's 1,660 square kilometers are inhabited by some 550,000 Black and mixed-blood descendants of African slaves, immigrants from Madagascar, Arab and Iranian traders, and French settlers. The country is staunchly Islamic, some 90 percent of the population being Sunni Muslims of the Shafi'i rite. The rest are mainly Roman Catholics. The official languages are French and Arabic, although the lingua franca is a local, Swahili-related language called Comorean or Shimasiwa. Arabic is, in fact, understood only by a tiny minority of the people, but remains the language of religious services and of the Koranic schools. About one half of the population, mainly women, are illiterate. As indicated by its official name, the Comoros is formally supposed to be a theocratic state whose leadership is vaguely expected to abide by the policies of Islam. The Comoros is, however, far from being fundamentalist in this respect: veiled women are rare, alcoholic beverages are legally available, and there is even a casino (which is, of course, intended for foreign tourists).

HISTORY

After centuries of being divided into several—as many as fourteen—small rival sultanates established by Arab and Iranian slave and spice traders, the Comoros came under French sovereignty in the late nineteenth century. The islands were for a long time governed through Madagascar but they became a separate territory in 1947. They were granted some internal autonomy in 1961 and, following considerable tension, mass demonstrations, and a referendum, became independent on July 6, 1975. The country is politically unstable, having endured almost twenty coups or attempted coups (some of them bloody) since receiving independence. The latest, bloodless, coup was staged on April 30, 1999, by Colonel Assoumani Azzali, who promised that democratic elections would be held within one year. No preparations have been made for such elections so far, however. There is also considerable tension among the four large islands of the archipelago; one island, Mayotte, has in fact successfully opted to remain a French territory, whereas Anjouan and Moheli have made attempts to gain independence from the Comoros, which is dominated by the largest island, Grande Comore, where the capital city of Moroni is situated.

LEGAL CONCEPTS

The most recent constitution of the Comoros was promulgated on October 20, 1996, but it was abolished after the 1999 coup and replaced by a very concise, temporary charter, which is of more political than legal interest. For the moment, the country has thus no constitution at all and it is run by a head of state who so far has not assumed the title of president. Pursuant to the now abolished constitution from 1996, the president, elected for five years in direct general elections, was the head of state. There was also a bicameral legislature consisting of a Federal Assembly whose forty-three members were elected for four years by direct popular vote, and of a Senate whose fifteen seats were occupied by representatives of regional councils. The government was headed by the prime minister, appointed by the president, and representing the party enjoying majority in the Federal Assembly. To what extent these traditions will be resuscitated in a future new constitution remains to be seen.

In connection with the attainment of independence by the Comoros in 1975, the Provisional National Assembly adopted Act no. 75-04/ANP, preserving the continued validity of legislation then in force until it is amended or replaced by new, Comorean legislation. An attempt to do away with the legal heritage from preindependence day was made during the thirty-three months of Marxist-Leninist dictatorship (1975–1978) of Ali Soleh, who planned, inter alia, to give the country a totally new revolutionary civil code. These plans were abandoned when Ali Soleh was overthrown and the law reverted to what it had been before, that is, a combination of French law (as it stood in 1975), Muslim law, and local customary law. This preindependence law deserves, therefore, a short presentation.

Prior to the French takeover, the life of the Comoreans was ruled almost exclusively by Muslim law, albeit combined with a number of local customs that at times deviated from the tenets of Muslim law known elsewhere. For example, it was and still is customary in parts of the country that when a new daughter is born, her family begins to construct a house, which is given to her when she marries and remains her property even if the husband dies or divorces her. As could be expected, polygamy is

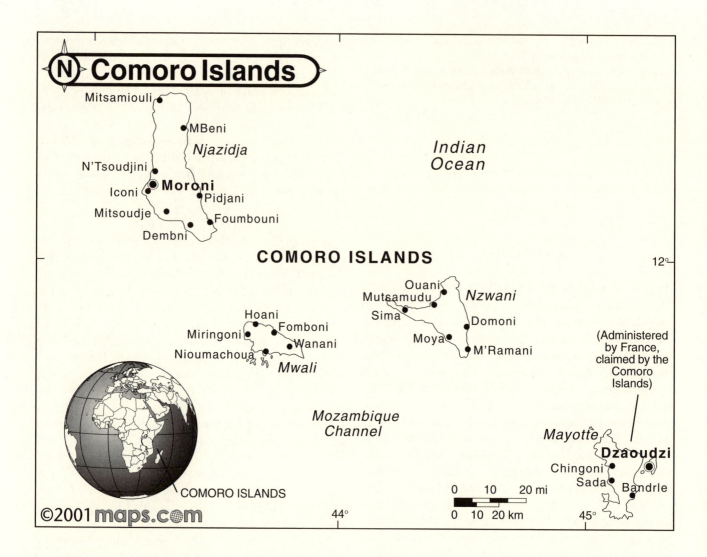

accepted and even today about 20 percent of Comorean men have more than one wife.

The French introduced step-by-step French law into the Comoros, without however attempting to replace Muslim law in fields such as personal status, family law, and the law of successions. Nevertheless, if there was a conflict between various rules of Muslim law and/or custom, French law was to be applied, which meant that French law started to influence even the above-mentioned areas of life.

By decrees of 1934 and 1939, one of the classic works of Islamic jurisprudence, the *Minhadj at Talibin,* written by An-Nawawi, a thirteenth century professor in Damascus, was declared to be the only official source of Muslim law in the Comoros. This book can be said to replace, for the Muslim majority of the population, those parts of the French civil code that pertain to personal status, family law, and inheritance law. It is not used in the Arabic original but in a French translation edited by Mr. Paul Guy, a French lawyer who used to be the president of the Superior Court of Appeals in Moroni. The close ties existing between the Comorean legal system and the Muslim faith are reflected, inter alia, in the fact that the present minister of Justice is at the same time responsible for Islamic affairs, the full name of the ministry being Ministère de justice et des affaires islamiques.

Although it is French law as it was in 1975 that forms the core and backbone of the Comorean legal system, even current Comorean legislation follows the French legal pattern and the legal developments in France. Thus, the postindependence Comorean Penal Code (Code pénal comorien) from 1982 follows the French model, although there are some Islamic influences, such as the provision requiring four eye witnesses for conviction for the crime of adultery (but the ensuing punishment is not death by stoning, as stipulated by *sharia,* but merely a short-term jail sentence). The penal code provides for the death penalty for murder, but executions are extremely rare and the death penalty will probably have to be abolished due to international treaties. The Comorean Commercial Code from 1982 was of such poor quality that it had to be abolished, whereupon the French Code de commerce was reintroduced. Other legislation worth mentioning is the labor code from 1984, inspired by both French law and a number of ILO conventions. At present, work is going on to produce a draft of a new family code, which in spite of all the intentions to modernize will probably preserve polygamy and other institutions typical of Islamic family law.

As could be expected of a legal system based on French traditions, the principal source of law in the Comoros is legislation, although due to the 1999 coup ordinances of the head of state are today used instead of Acts of the National Assembly as the main form for important new statutes. Because of the lack of resources, the publication of the *Journal Officiel des Comores* was discontinued in 1997, so that the spreading of knowledge about new legislation has to rely on the radio, local newspapers of general circulation, and simple word of mouth. Similarly, there is no organized publication of judicial decisions, which pursuant to the French tradition do not, of course, constitute a binding source of law (they are never openly referred to in judgments) but whose great real practical importance is clear to any French lawyer. Comorean legal professionals, including judges, have to search for relevant prior decisions in the court archives and it seems doubtful whether they do so; the value of previous case law may therefore be smaller than in France, where leading cases are readily available since they are published and commented in numerous legal journals. There is no Comorean legal science or research. An attempt to produce a simple law review was made a few years ago, but it failed.

CURRENT COURT SYSTEM STRUCTURE

Due to the lack of human and material resources, the ambitious court system provided for in the Comorean legislation is far from being fully implemented in practice. In reality, there are two levels of courts. There is a general court of first instance (*Tribunal de première instance*) in each of the three islands, and a court of appeals (*Cour d'appel*) in Moroni. The courts of first instance sit with one sole judge, while the court of appeals sits with three judges at a time. At the court of first instance in Moroni, which is the biggest one in the country, there are at present seven professional judges. Three of them work at the same time as investigating judges (*juges d'instruction*), who supervise and guide, pursuant to the French model, pretrial investigations in serious criminal cases. The court of appeals is at present staffed with six judges. State attorneys (*procureurs*) are attached to the courts and considered, even this time pursuant to French traditions, to constitute a part of the judiciary.

In matters pertaining to personal status, family law, and inheritance law, disputes are adjudicated in the first instance by justices of the peace (*justices de paix*), staffed by judges who are knowledgeable about Muslim and customary law. Appeal from their decisions lies directly to the court of appeals. The role of the justices of the peace,

Legal Structure of Comoros Courts

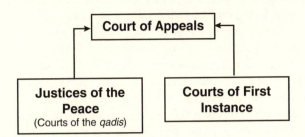

commonly also called the courts of the *qadis* (*qazis*), is in reality much more restricted than what follows from formally valid statutory provisions. On paper, the justices of the peace are supposed to deal not merely with the above-mentioned matters involving Muslim and customary law, but even with other disputes under general law concerning small amounts and petty offences punishable by fines. In customary law matters, the justices of the peace are supposed to sit together with two assessors. In reality however, the justices of the peace always adjudicate alone and do not deal with cases other than those pertaining to matters governed by Muslim and customary rules. Recently appointed Justices of the Peace have degrees in Islamic law from universities in other Muslim countries, while the older ones may lack formal legal education altogether.

Serious criminal cases are tried once and only by the Cour d'assises, composed of both professional judges from the court of appeals and lay jurors.

In contrast to France, there are no separate commercial and administrative courts, but merely commercial and administrative chambers at the general courts. Special chambers exist also for labor disputes and matters relating to minors. Due to the small number of judges, however, the same persons judge in all the chambers.

On paper, there is also supposed to be a superior court (Cour supérieure), with functions corresponding roughly to those of the French cassation court, but it has not yet been established and it is doubtful whether it ever will be.

There are no judicial bodies in the Comoros other than the courts.

STAFFING

The Conseil supérieur de la magistrature, which is a French-inspired body nominating judicial appointees and having disciplinary powers over judges, exists on paper only. The Comoros has no university and all post-secondary education, including that in the field of law, has to take place abroad. Among the very few Comorean judges, there are, for example, at present judges with legal degrees from France, Togo, Madagascar, Cameroon, Morocco, but even from nonfrancophone countries such as Egypt, Kuwait, United Arab Emirates, and the former

USSR. To create a real uniform national legal culture, shared by legal professionals with such varying educational backgrounds, is indeed a formidable task. It is, however, made easier by the fact that most of the countries in question share the French legal heritage, which undoubtedly dominates the country's legal life. The power of the French language should not be underestimated: All paperwork, including the judgments of the *qadis* (*qazis*), is done in French. Comorean is used merely for oral presentations. Furthermore, the procedure, including that in the courts of the *qadis,* follows French procedural rules.

There are, today, only two fully qualified advocates in the country (both in Moroni), but representation by an advocate in not compulsory in judicial proceedings. Furthermore, there are a number of other, less qualified, professional *agents d'affaires,* representing clients in courts. The limited number of legal practitioners makes specialization impossible, so that in complicated cases, for example those pertaining to maritime law, foreign attorneys have to be used. The functions of notaries public (*notaires*), who are a very important institution in French-inspired legal systems, are carried out partly by court secretaries (*greffiers*), partly by justices of the peace. Independent notaries are too few. There are five bailiffs (*huissiers de justice*), dealing mainly with execution of judgments and service of documents.

IMPACT

The most serious problem of the Comorean legal system appears to be the severe lack of financial and human resources. The court buildings are old and decrepit, there is very little functioning modern office equipment (even telephones and typewriters are rare), access to relevant legal literature is very limited, and so on. It has, in fact, occurred that a court has had its electricity supply cut off due to unpaid bills. Salaries of judges and other personnel are low (even if judges earn more than other civil servants) and are paid irregularly, with substantial delays. The country receives, however, some international assistance in the legal field, in particular from France and the World Bank.

Access to justice in the Comoros is seriously hampered by economic and geographical factors, in particular the distances between the capital city of Moroni and the two other islands. Very few people from the other islands can afford to travel to Moroni, for example to participate in proceedings before the court of appeals. But even for the population of the main island, justice may simply be too expensive. There is no state-operated or other legal aid scheme. It is, therefore, hardly surprising that most disputes are solved by amicable settlement and conciliation.

The ambitions of the Comoros to imitate the French court structure and other French legal traditions go far beyond the country's means, which has led to a situation where many of the French-inspired rules simply remain on paper with no relation whatsoever to the legal realities. This is a serious problem, endangering the rule of law, since it is not always clear which rules are followed and which are ignored; the weak authority of previous case law makes it difficult to develop a consistent practice. Even Comorean lawyers often have great difficulties when describing the current state of the law.

Michael Bogdan

With the kind permission of Kluwer Law International, the original copyright holder, this entry is based on the author's article, "Legal Pluralism in the Comoros and Djibouti," published in *Nordic Journal of International Law* 69:195–208 (2000).

See also Civil Law; Customary Law; Islamic Law; Legal Pluralism; Qadi (Qazi) Courts
References and further reading
There is practically no modern literature in English about the legal system of the Comoros. An interesting booklet regarding the marriage customs in one part of the country is Martin Ottenheimer (1985), *Marriage in Domoni. Husbands and Wives in an Indian Ocean Community,* Prospect Heights, IL: Waveland Press.

CONFEDERATE STATES OF AMERICA

COUNTRY INFORMATION

In 1860 and 1861 eleven slaveholding Southern states of the United States of America seceded from the Union. They formed the Confederate States of America. The Confederacy consisted of the states, in order of secession, of South Carolina, Mississippi, Florida, Alabama, Georgia, Louisiana, Texas, Virginia, Arkansas, North Carolina, and Tennessee. Montgomery, Alabama, was the first capital of the Confederate States. On May 24, 1861, the capital was moved to Richmond, Virginia. The population of the Confederacy was 9 million, including almost 4 million slaves. By contrast, the population of the states remaining loyal to the Union was approximately 22 million, including a half-million slaves. Four slaveholding states—Maryland, Delaware, Kentucky, and Missouri—remained in the Union. The Confederate Congress, however, accepted the latter two states as members because of acts of secession that they enacted in 1861. As a consequence, the Confederate flag carried thirteen stars. The Union Army, however, prevented Kentucky and Missouri from actually seceding, and public opinion was deeply divided in the two states between loyalty and disloyalty to the Union. The Confederate Congress made no attempt to set up courts in either state.

In 1861 the eleven Southern states constituted 662,032 square miles. The Confederate States (C.S.) also claimed sovereignty over Arizona Territory and exercised administrative control over the Indian Country, which after the Civil War became the State of Oklahoma. In 1861 the western counties of Virginia, opposed to slavery and faithful to the Union, separated. The U.S. Congress admitted the new state of West Virginia, 24,087 square miles in area, in 1863. The twenty-one Union states comprised 2,441,645 square miles.

The economy of the Confederate States was agrarian, while that of the Union was industrial and commercial. The South, for example, had 150 textile factories, compared with the North's 900. The South was dependent on exports of cotton and imports of machinery. In 1860 Southern imports were valued at $331 million, while those of the North were $31 million. Confederate railways were underdeveloped.

The population of the South was relatively homogeneous. The white population consisted largely of persons whose ancestors came from the British Isles. In contrast the white population of the North included large numbers of persons who had immigrated recently from the continent of Europe. The Southern people were overwhelmingly Protestant, while the population of the North included large numbers of Roman Catholics, as well as smaller numbers of Orthodox Christians and Jews. The Irish immigrants who settled in the South were mostly Protestant, while the Irish who settled north of the Mason-Dixon line, the line dividing the slave state of Maryland from the free state of Pennsylvania, were largely Catholic.

The legal system of nine of the states of the Confederacy was common law, while the legal systems of Louisiana and Texas were based on the Civil law. France had originally settled Louisiana and Spain had colonized Texas. Unlike the Constitution of the United States, the Constitution of the Confederacy accommodated the two legal systems.

HISTORY

In response to the election of Republican Abraham Lincoln to the U.S. presidency in November 1860, South Carolina seceded from the Union on December 20, followed by ten other slave states over the next six months. The Republican Party was opposed to the extension of slavery into the western territories. The president of the Confederacy, Jefferson Davis, envisioned the establishment of a great slave empire that would include not only Oklahoma, New Mexico, Arizona, and Southern California but also Mexico and Cuba.

Delegates from the six states that had up to that time enacted ordinances of secession met in Montgomery, Alabama, on February 6, 1861, to draft a provisional constitution. Many had represented their state in the United States Congress or had been executive or judicial officers of the United States government. On March 11, 1861, the Montgomery convention unanimously ratified a per-

manent constitution. Federal judicial authority passed from the United States to the state courts initially and, with the establishment of federal courts by the Confederate Congress, to the courts of the Confederacy. The Confederate district courts took up and resolved all cases pending in the U.S. district courts.

The Confederacy collapsed with the surrender of its armies in 1865. President Lincoln did not believe that states had the right to leave the Union and therefore regarded the Confederacy as simply a group of states in rebellion against the authority of the United States. He referred to civil officers of the Confederate States as persons of influence in the rebellious states and to military officers as leaders of the rebellion. Confederate diplomats failed to receive recognition for the new nation from any of the European powers.

LEGAL CONCEPTS

The framers of the Confederate constitution believed in the principles of the Declaration of Independence and the U.S. Constitution and sought to replicate the political and legal system with which they were intimately familiar. As a result, the provisional and permanent constitutions were nearly identical to the U.S. Constitution on which they were based. The principles adopted in Montgomery were that the main purpose of government is to protect individual liberty, and that government should operate by majority rule, with protection for the rights of the minority. The only real differences were a belief that sovereignty lay with the states and not the federal government and that slavery was a beneficent and permanent institution.

The Confederate courts exercised the power of judicial review. They declared several laws enacted in Richmond unconstitutional, including a federal tax on state bonds.

STRUCTURE

Article 3 of the C.S. Constitution provided for a Supreme Court and "such inferior courts as the Congress may, from time to time, ordain and establish." Article 1, section 9 directed Congress to establish "a tribunal for the investigation of claims against the government." The constitution observed the principle of dual judicial systems, with the hierarchy of state courts matched by a parallel hierarchy of federal courts. Appeals to the C.S. Supreme Court came from both the state supreme courts and the Confederate district courts. The state supreme courts were the final determiners of cases involving only state law. Appeals to the C.S. Supreme Court were only possible if one of the parties raised a federal question, such as interference with a right under a law of the Confederacy. The C.S. district courts were trial courts of original jurisdiction. No provision was made for Confederate circuit courts. The Confederate framers found the U.S. circuit courts to be redundant. The Judiciary Act of 1789

Structure of the Confederate States of America

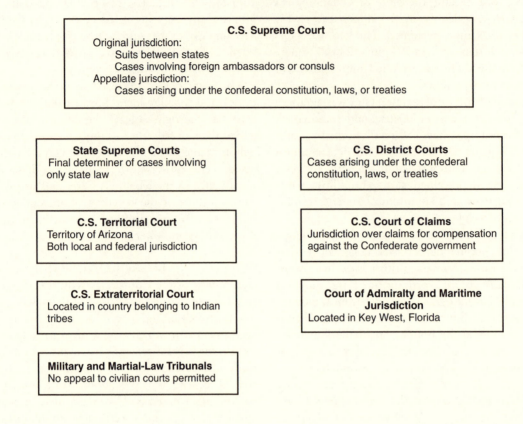

C.S. Supreme Court
Original jurisdiction:
    Suits between states
    Cases involving foreign ambassadors or consuls
Appellate jurisdiction:
    Cases arising under the confederal constitution, laws, or treaties

State Supreme Courts
Final determiner of cases involving only state law

C.S. District Courts
Cases arising under the confederal constitution, laws, or treaties

C.S. Territorial Court
Territory of Arizona
Both local and federal jurisdiction

C.S. Court of Claims
Jurisdiction over claims for compensation against the Confederate government

C.S. Extraterritorial Court
Located in country belonging to Indian tribes

Court of Admiralty and Maritime Jurisdiction
Located in Key West, Florida

Military and Martial-Law Tribunals
No appeal to civilian courts permitted

gave the circuit courts a limited appellate jurisdiction over the district courts but a much larger original jurisdiction. The act envisioned the circuit courts as three-judge tribunals, staffed by two Supreme Court justices and a district judge. The Supreme Court held, however, that the district judge alone could hold circuit court. The Confederate Constitution did away with these anomalies of two federal trial courts and the same judge sitting in judgment of his own previous decisions (Robinson 1941, 68). The U.S. Congress followed suit by establishing the courts of appeal in 1891 and finally abolishing the circuit courts in 1911.

The framers of the Confederate Constitution departed in a few ways from Article 3 of the U.S. Constitution. The motive behind each change was respect for states' rights. They denied the district courts jurisdiction over suits between citizens of different states. Out of respect for the civil law tradition of Louisiana and Texas, the Confederate framers omitted the distinction between law and equity found in the U.S. Constitution. In England separate courts of common law and equity had developed, with different principles and remedies. The French and Spanish civil law did not recognize any distinction between law and equity, and judges in that system could provide to plaintiffs both monetary and injunctive relief (Robinson 1936, 461).

To assure continuity, the Confederate Congress adopted all the laws of the United States except those inconsistent with the Confederate Constitution. The Congress felt compelled, nevertheless, to enact a judiciary act. Under United States statutes no appeal lay to the Supreme Court in criminal cases, but under the Confederate States judiciary act (section 38) appeals from a district court in all criminal cases where death or imprisonment were possible lay to the Supreme Court. The judiciary act also stated that to appeal a civil case to the Supreme Court, the amount in controversy had to be at least $5,000, ten times the limit in the U.S. judiciary act.

The Confederate Congress never instituted the Supreme Court, even though the constitution required it to do so and President Davis called on that body to organize the court at its first session. Several members of Congress objected to Supreme Court jurisdiction over the decisions of the state supreme courts involving federal questions. They viewed such power of review as inconsistent with the sovereignty of the states, acknowledged in the Confederate constitution. Chief Justice John Marshall had annoyed the Southern states' leaders by pointing out in *Cohens v. Virginia* (1821) that the state supreme courts no longer had the finality that they had enjoyed under the Articles of Confederation.

Article 3 of the permanent constitution differed in

several ways from the judicial article in the provisional constitution. The provisional constitution explicitly directed the Congress to establish district courts, one for each state. The permanent constitution left the establishment of federal trial courts up to Congress, which was free to divide the states into more than one district. The provisional document stipulated that the Supreme Court would consist of all the district judges. The permanent constitution did not prescribe or restrain the composition of the high court. Section 2 of the provisional Article 3 maintained the distinction between law and equity and extended federal jurisdiction over suits between citizens of different states. The drafters of the permanent instrument removed both clauses. The permanent constitution added to the federal court's jurisdiction cases in which the Confederate States were a party, as well as controversies "between a State or the citizens thereof, and foreign states, citizens, or subjects; but no State shall be sued by a citizen or subject of any foreign state." This last clause recognized the states' enjoyment of sovereign immunity. Federal judicial power was limited to suits between a state and citizens of another state where the state is plaintiff. The result was that no individual could sue a state in a Confederate court.

SPECIALIZED JUDICIAL BODIES

Article 3 of the Confederate Constitution authorized Congress to establish courts inferior to the Supreme Court. Congress not only established the district courts but also a Court of Admiralty and Maritime Jurisdiction, territorial courts, extraterritorial courts, and military tribunals. President Davis appointed a judge for the admiralty and maritime court, located in Key West, Florida, but the judge was forced to hold court on the Florida mainland because of Union occupation of the island. The territorial court of Arizona consisted of probate courts in each county, three district courts of general jurisdiction, and a territorial supreme court, whose decisions were subject to review by the Supreme Court in Richmond. The territorial court functioned until Union occupation of Arizona and New Mexico in 1862. The two extraterritorial courts in the Indian protectorate exercised the same functions as the district courts. In keeping with the foundation of the courts in treaty rights, the judges of the courts in Indian country only served four-year terms. Congress established the extraterritorial tribunals, but not until 1865. On the recommendation of General Robert E. Lee, Congress replaced courts martial with several permanent military courts composed of three officers with judicial experience. Appeals to the civilian courts from the decisions of courts martial or military courts were not possible. Congress never established the constitutionally mandated Court of Claims out of fear that it would drain the federal treasury at a time of the utmost financial exigency.

STAFFING

Approximately half the judges of the Confederate States district courts were former judges of the United States district courts. They sat on the bench in what had been federal courtrooms. Several U.S. district court judges in the South remained loyal to the Union. They continued as federal judges after the collapse of the rebellion, while their brethren who had served as Confederate judges lost their offices, and most returned to the private practice of law. The U.S. district judges in the South had been nominated by the president of the United States and confirmed by the U.S. Senate. The senator or senators from the president's political party had recommended them. They were lawyers or state judges, usually active in the nominating senator's party, from the district where the judicial vacancy arose. In his selection of nominees, the president was constrained by the custom of senatorial courtesy, in which senators refuse to vote for persons lacking the appropriate home-state senator's endorsement. Confederate president Jefferson Davis followed the same procedure as his U.S. counterpart. Typical of the Confederate district judges was Andrew Magrath, a Harvard Law School graduate and United States judge for the district of South Carolina. Following Lincoln's election, Judge Magrath resigned from the federal bench and was elected a delegate to the secession convention. The newly independent state of South Carolina appointed Magrath secretary of state, responsible for the conduct of its foreign relations. After the formation of the Confederacy, President Davis appointed Magrath Confederate States District Judge for the District of South Carolina. He resigned in 1864 after his election as governor of South Carolina. In May 1865 Governor Magrath was arrested by Union cavalry and imprisoned for being an officer of a rebel state government. After release from prison, Magrath returned to the practice of law in South Carolina.

The judges of both the United States and Confederacy received no special training. The Confederate and U.S. constitutions both described the tenure of federal judges as "during good behavior." Although in the U.S. constitution, removal could only be accomplished by impeachment of the House and conviction by two-thirds of the Senate, the Confederate Constitution authorized state legislatures to impeach federal judges sitting within their state. Judges of the Confederate Supreme Court, district courts, court of claims, and admiralty and maritime court were Article 3 judges appointed for life. Judges of the territorial and extraterritorial courts were considered Article 4 and Article 2 judges, respectively, and enjoyed only limited tenure. Article 4 empowered Congress to administer the territories, and Article 2 authorized the president to make treaties with foreign nations.

Several years before the United States Congress did so, the Confederate Congress established a Department of

Justice headed by the attorney general. One of the duties of this cabinet-level department was to administer the courts. The Confederate Department of Justice became a model for the U.S. Department of Justice, established in 1870.

IMPACT

The failure of the Confederate Congress to organize a supreme court limited the impact of the federal judiciary. The district court judges had the final word on issues within their jurisdiction. The state courts heard the vast majority of criminal and civil cases. The state supreme courts were the dominant tribunals during the Confederacy's brief life. The lack of judicial finality was mitigated by the fact that the district courts and state supreme courts unanimously supported the Confederate government on the most important issues, including the constitutionality of military conscription.

The U.S. government's position was that the government of the Confederate States lacked legitimacy and therefore its judicial decisions were a nullity (*Hickman v. Jones*). Because the federal judges of the Confederacy had no lawful authority, they lacked immunity against lawsuits after the war for depriving persons of their life, liberty, or property without due process of law. After 1865 no one could use a judgment of a Confederate court to lay claim to property and anyone convicted of a crime by a Confederate district judge was released from prison.

Kenneth Holland

See also Civil Law; Common Law; Federalism; Military Justice (Law and Courts); United States—Federal System; United States—State Systems

References and further reading

Cohens v. Virginia. 1821. 6 Wheaton 264.

Hamilton, J. G. de Roulhac. 1938. "The State Courts and the Confederate Constitution." *The Journal of Southern History* 4 (November): 425–448.

Hickman v. Jones. 1879. 9 Wallace 197.

Johnson, Bradley T. 1900. *Why the Confederate States of America had no Supreme Court*. Washington, DC: Southern History Association.

Lee, Charles Robert. 1963. *The Confederate Constitutions*. Chapel Hill, NC: University of North Carolina Press.

Robinson, William M., Jr. 1936. "Legal System of the Confederate States." *The Journal of Southern History* 2 (November): 453–467.

———. 1941. *Justice in Grey: A History of the Judicial System of the Confederate States of America*. Cambridge, MA: Harvard University Press.

Tilley, Nannice M., ed. 1940. "Letter of Judge Alexander M. Clayton Relative to Confederate Courts in Mississippi." *The Journal of Southern History* 6 (August): 392–401.

CONGO, DEMOCRATIC REPUBLIC OF (KINSHASA)

COUNTRY INFORMATION

The vast territory of the Democratic Republic of Congo (DRC)—some 2.4 million square kilometers—makes it the third-biggest country in Africa after Algeria and Sudan. Almost the entire territory lies in the basin of the Congo River, the largest in Africa. It is bordered by the Central African Republic, Sudan, Uganda, Rwanda, Burundi, Tanzania, Zambia, Angola, and the Republic of Congo (Brazzaville). DRC's population of approximately 47.4 million (according to a 1997 estimate) includes over 450 ethnic subgroups belonging to five major ethnic groups: the Bantus (80 percent of the population); the Sudanese, the Nilotes, the Pygmies, and the Hamites. The official language is French, but Kiswahili, Lingala, Kikongo, and Tshiluba are recognized as national languages. Some 46 percent of the population are Roman Catholics, while 16 percent follow Kimbanguism, an African adaptation of Catholicism. Other major religions include Protestantism (28 percent), Islam (1.3 percent), Judaism, Greek Orthodox, Jehovah's Witnesses, the Black African Church, and the Seventh-Day Adventists. Some 40 percent of the people live in urban centers. The capital city, Kinshasa, is home for more than 6 million persons. Other major cities are Lubumbashi, Kisangani, Matadi, and Goma.

The economic structures of the DRC have increasingly collapsed since the 1980s as the result of successive corrupt regimes. Once one of the most promising developing countries, the DRC now is among the poorest nations in Africa. The gross domestic product (GDP) per inhabitant has constantly fallen, dropping from $630 in 1980 to $200 in 1993 to $120 in 1995. The collapse of formal economic structures and of the administration has resulted in the development of an unprecedented network of informal economic activities. With the agricultural sector largely shut down, minerals have been the only exported products since the mid-1980s.

HISTORY

Like the majority of contemporary African states canvassed at the 1885 Berlin Conference, Congo is the product of successive colonial conquests in the early nineteenth century. From the beginning, however, it was always a colony with a difference. For over thirty years, the country was, in fact, a "private property" of its "creator," King Leopold II of Belgium. Since Belgium refused to embark on the colonial adventure because of financial difficulties, Leopold decided to create his own colony by funding the successive conquest missions that eventually led to the constitution of Congo. After being recognized by the United States on April 22, 1884, and by the Eu-

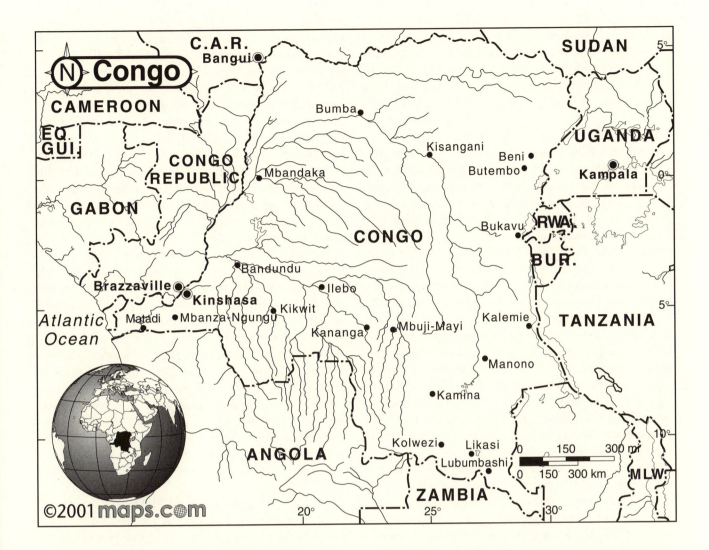

ropean colonizing powers at the 1885 Berlin Conference, the country Leopold had just created became known as the Congo Free State (Etat Indépendant du Congo).

The Congo Free State soon established a blatantly violent law-and-order apparatus, the legacy of which is still reflected in various areas of legislation in today's Congo. Leopold ruled the territory as a private investment corporation, with an administrative system designed to exploit the country's natural resources for his personal benefit. The indigenous population was denied the protection of basic rights.

The two pillars on which Leopold built his administration were the armed forces and the law. In 1888, he signed a decree structuring the Force Publique, the "national" army of the Congo Free State. It grew rapidly and soon became the most powerful army in colonial Africa. A multifunctional body, the Force Publique was assigned tasks that went beyond specific military functions. To compensate for the lack of qualified judicial personnel in the early years of the state, for example, the army was called on to perform judicial functions. Each army officer was also a police officer with extended prosecutorial pow-

ers. As an *officier de police judiciaire,* that is, a police officer with judicial authority, the army officer had the power to prosecute, detain, and issue warrants. The law provided that in remote areas with no career magistrate—which, due to the scarcity of such magistrates, meant almost the entire territory—an army officer could preside over a police tribunal (*tribunal de police*) with jurisdiction for offenses punishable by up to six months in prison. The army was, consequently, the primary law enforcer.

The law that was thus enforced was oriented toward maintaining strict "discipline" among the indigenous population, which meant repression. The administration was run by King Leopold himself, who held the title of king sovereign of Congo Free State. Belgian law was not automatically applicable in Congo because the Belgian Parliament had no jurisdiction over the "independent" state. Instead, the law of the land in Congo consisted of the Decrees of the King Sovereign (*Décrets du Roi Souverain*). In his role as Congo's legislator, Leopold consulted the Legislative Council (*Conseil de Législation*), composed of lawyers, investors, anthropologists, historians, and missionaries of diverse nationalities appointed by the king. Congo's legal system was, therefore, not a copy of the Belgian system, as was generally the case in other colonial territories. In French colonies, for example, the Napoleonic Code was directly applied, whereas King Leopold promulgated for Congo a whole range of particular laws, including the Civil Code of Congo, which was markedly different from the Napoleonic Code.

Even after King Leopold handed Congo over to Belgium in 1908 and a more classical colonial rule was established in the country (which was renamed Belgian Congo), very few changes were made to the king's legacy. On October 18, 1908, the Belgian Parliament passed the Law on the Government of Belgian Congo (*Loi sur le Gouvernement du Congo Belge*), also known as the Colonial Charter. The charter was an attempt to infuse more transparency in colonial affairs and regulate the structure of power in Congo as well as formalize the relationship between Belgium and its colony. It was thus a clearly positive step after the authoritative Leopold's administrative style. Yet the charter confirmed the core of Congo Free State's legal architecture. Article 1 stated that Belgian Congo and the Kingdom of Belgium were two legally separate entities and that the laws passed by Leopold II remained in force unless expressly abrogated. The Force Publique was also expanded during the fifty-two years of formal colonization.

Moreover, the charter and subsequent legislations formalized the apartheid regime of Leopold's era by formally dividing the population into different categories with different sets of legal privileges and rights. At the top of this structure were the whites, who enjoyed all the rights embodied in the civil code and were subject to Belgian laws. Members of races believed to be halfway "civilized," including natives of Asia, Arab traders, and *Arabisés* (Africans culturally assimilated to Arabs by Europeans), occupied a middle position. The civil code's provisions on marriage, divorce, and commercial law could be extended to them, and their grievances were admitted in modern courts. At the bottom of the apartheid structure was the entire indigenous population, believed not to be "civilized" enough to benefit from any of the civil code rights and thus not admitted in any circumstances into modern European courts. To them were applied customary laws enforced by indigenous tribunals presided over by traditional judges. However, for obvious reasons, the criminal code was the only European law applied to the indigenous population.

Because Belgian law did not automatically apply to Congo, the colonial judiciary was faced with the difficulty of identifying the applicable law or legal principle when a given case was not regulated by existing law. To resolve this difficulty, judges continued to apply a May 14, 1886, decree known as Principles Guiding the Issuing of Judicial Decisions (*Principes à Suivre dans les Décisions Judiciaires*). The decree prescribed that in the cases not regulated by a law, the courts should apply customary principles, the general principles of law, or equity. This decree was later interpreted as allowing judges to apply Belgian laws and laws from other European countries, reflecting general principles of law, whenever a case being litigated seemed to relate to a matter not yet regulated by a law. The decree was considered to authorize the usage, in some instances, of customary principles. But later jurisprudence set strict limits in this regard: Customary law not only had to be applied to cases involving two indigenous individuals but also had to be consistent with European law.

Although abuses of indigenous peoples' rights in Belgian Congo were much less cruel than in the Congo Free State, the Belgians continued to rely on the Force Publique and the law as the two pillars of the colonial regime. The legal fiction of Belgian Congo being a separate country perpetuated the scarcity of career judicial personnel by preventing Belgian magistrates from automatically serving in Congo. In turn, the shortage of magistrates allowed Force Publique officers and local administrators to continue to perform judicial functions. This system persisted long after independence was granted in 1960 because no Congolese had graduated from the law school established by the Belgians only a year earlier and because law schools in Belgium were not opened to Congolese.

LEGAL CONCEPTS

Congo has inherited a civil law system from the Belgian colonial rule. The judiciary is a united bloc under the administrative and moral authority of the Supreme Court, but each of the twelve Courts of Appeal is supposed to infuse a specific jurisprudential line to lower courts.

The first postindependence constitution, the Fundamental Law of February 1960, did not last long, thus setting a tradition for all subsequent constitutions. Only two months after independence, the president dismissed the elected prime minister, which prompted a dispute on the constitutionality of the president's decision. As if the constitution itself were to blame, the political parties agreed to draft a new constitution in 1964, which lasted less than a year before it was suspended in 1965 following Mobutu Sese Seko's coup d'état. The 1967 Constitution was amended more than ten times in thirty-three years, with each amendment being so sweeping that, according to some constitutional scholars, it amounted to a new constitution. From 1990 to 1997, three constitutions were enacted, the latest by President Laurent Kabila in May 1997.

All postindependence constitutions have asserted the principle of separation of powers and recognized three branches of government. But, despite clear references to judicial independence, the constantly growing power of the executive since President Mobutu's institutionalization of the single party in the mid-1970s has resulted in de facto subordination of the judiciary to the executive branch.

The hierarchy of laws is well defined. The constitution is the supreme law of the land. It indicates which matters can only be regulated under general laws passed by the legislative body and which matters may be regulated by the executive branch. The laws passed by the legislative assembly must be consistent with constitutional provisions, and the decrees issued by executive authorities must be consistent with the law. As a consequence, there are two types of judicial review: the "administrative" judicial review and the "constitutional" judicial review. Under the administrative judicial review, the courts assess the legality of the acts and decisions of the executive authorities (including the president of the republic, ministers of the cabinet, provincial and local authorities, and executives of administrative agencies) by examining whether a specific decision or order issued by a member of the executive branch is consistent with the law. Under the constitutional judicial review, by contrast, the judges examine whether the general laws are consistent with the constitution. Constitutional judicial review can be exerted either a priori, when the court is asked to issue an advisory opinion on the constitutionality of a draft law introduced before the assembly, or a posteriori, during a dispute over the constitutionality of a law already passed and entered into force.

The constitution contains a monist provision that makes international conventions and treaties automatically applicable, on ratification, as part of national legislation. The same provision, modeled after the French 1958 Constitution, states that such treaties rank higher than ordinary laws in the hierarchy of laws. Despite such a clear constitutional provision, however, Congolese judges have usually been reluctant to apply international treaties not "backed" by a specific domestic law. Acting as if they operate in a dualist system, the courts have consistently required that an international convention, even if regularly ratified, be formally "approved" by an ordinary law.

The more recent constitutions have contained carefully drafted bills of rights, providing basic guarantees of such freedoms and human rights, as the right of assembly, the guarantee of due process, and the freedoms of speech, press, religion, thought, and movement. But in a 1995 case, the Supreme Court held that the freedom of assembly guaranteed by the constitution could not be given effect in the absence of an ordinary implementing law. That ruling prompted a debate among human rights activists and constitutional lawyers on whether to extend the same standard to other constitutionally guaranteed human rights, which would result in these rights being rendered meaningless unless "confirmed" by an ordinary law.

The 1886 Principles Guiding the Issuing of Judicial Decisions decree is still applied by the tribunals, allowing judges to apply general principles of law, equity, or custom in cases not regulated by existing law. Since there are as many customary laws as there are ethnic groups, it has long been admitted that the custom to be upheld in a particular case must be the local custom in the area of the tribunal and that all the parties to the case must be familiar with the custom. Only in family disputes—involving divorce, paternal authority, inheritance, guardianship, and so forth—have customary principles been applied.

In the early 1970s, the government created the National Permanent Commission for the Reform of the Law, an expert commission composed of judges, law professors, and members of the bar. Its principal task is to undertake studies for the purpose of reforming and amending the law, with the special objective being to bring the law as close as possible to the African mentality. Among the efforts the commission has undertaken is the codification of the customary principles shared by most of the ethnic groups. That effort resulted in the passage of the Land Reform of 1973 and the adoption of the Family Code in 1981. The Family Code has proven a successful attempt to adapt the Napoleonic Code to the African notion and organizational principles of the family. In 1981, a commission study resulted in the creation of the Tribunals of Peace, which hear family matters with a single career judge assisted by two assessors who are not lawyers but have expert knowledge of the local customary law.

CURRENT STRUCTURES

Under the Organic Law of March 31, 1982, the ordinary, civilian judiciary consists of Tribunals of Peace (Tribunaux de Paix), Tribunals of Major Jurisdiction (Tribunaux de Grande Instance), Courts of Appeal, and the Supreme Court.

The Tribunal of Peace was created in 1979 to replace the Tribunal de Police and the customary court; the original intention was to have one such tribunal in each town or rural area. The Tribunal of Peace is a Magistrates' Court dealing with minor offenses punishable by up to five years in prison. In civil matters, it has primary jurisdiction on juvenile justice and family disputes involving the application of the Family Code and customary principles. Other important jurisdictions of the Tribunal of Peace include the control of the legality of pretrial detentions and the granting of habeas corpus. The Tribunal of Peace normally consists of a single judge; the exception is a tribunal involving family matters, wherein the presiding career judge is assisted by two assessors.

There are thirty-two Tribunals of Major Jurisdiction, located in all towns and subregions. Their criminal jurisdiction includes offenses punishable by over five years of imprisonment, as well as appeals against the decisions of

Legal Structure of the Democratic Republic of Congo Courts

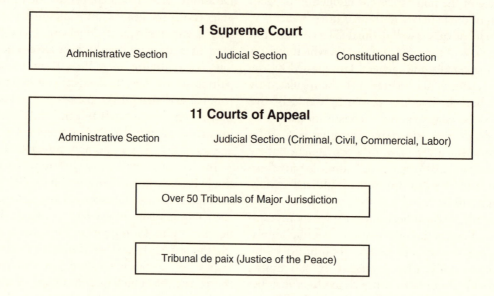

1 Supreme Court

Administrative Section   Judicial Section   Constitutional Section

11 Courts of Appeal

Administrative Section   Judicial Section (Criminal, Civil, Commercial, Labor)

Over 50 Tribunals of Major Jurisdiction

Tribunal de paix (Justice of the Peace)

This Chart does not include specialized bodies, such as the Military Court (Cour d'Ordre Militaire) and the Office des Biens Mal Acquis, which are not part of the normal judicial system.

the Tribunals of Peace. Their civil and commercial jurisdictions include all labor law and all commercial law.

The Courts of Appeal, with one in each of the eleven provinces, have second-degree jurisdiction to review cases in which judgment has been passed by the Tribunals of Major Jurisdiction. In addition, they function as courts of first instance for offenses committed by judges and public officials. They also have first-degree jurisdiction over the administrative judicial review of acts committed by provincial and local authorities.

The Supreme Court of Justice, sitting at Kinshasa, is a multifunctional court with constitutional, administrative, and judicial jurisdictions. As a constitutional court, the Supreme Court is the sole body to review the constitutionality of laws. As an administrative court, it reviews the legality of acts enacted by the central authorities and has a second-degree jurisdiction over administrative review judgments passed by the Courts of Appeal. Finally, as the highest judicial tribunal, the Supreme Court controls the legality of the judgments of all lower courts. In that sense, it is like the Court of Cassation (Cour de Cassation) in the French system. In addition, the Supreme Court is the sole court competent to deal with offenses attributed to ministers, regional governors, and members of Parliament.

Attempts to create new tribunals have not been successful. The 1967 Labor Code provided that special courts would be set up to deal with labor disputes, and it was foreseen that representatives of both unions and employers would be allowed to be seated as assessors in the

labor tribunals. However, these special tribunals have never come into the existence, essentially due to financial reasons. In 1992, delegates to the National Sovereign Conference passed a resolution that would abolish the Supreme Court and instead create three different courts, drawing on the French model: a constitutional court, an administrative court, and a high court (or cour de cassation). Although the majority of lawyers are in favor of such a reform, the government has repeatedly invoked the lack of money as a reason not to carry the reform to fruition. Recently, though, the government accepted a World Bank recommendation that special commercial tribunals be set up. The minister of justice has introduced legislation to the Parliament for that purpose.

In most civil law countries, criminal investigation functions are separate from prosecution functions: The sole mission of the prosecutor (*procureur*) is to lead the charge at the trial, whereas the prosecuting judge (*juge d'instruction*) investigates the crime. But the judicial system of the DRC has no prosecuting judge. Like the U.S. district attorney, the state prosecutor in the DRC both investigates and prosecutes. The term *opportunity of prosecution* (*opportunite de poursuite*) refers to the large discretionary power enjoyed by prosecutors, by which they can decide whether a particular crime warrants investigation. This discretionary power may only be overruled either by an injunction to prosecute (*injonction de poursuite*), issued by the minister of justice, or by a complaint filed directly before the court by the victim of the crime. In both cases, the prosecutor is obliged to open an investigation or join the victim in taking the accusation to the court.

SPECIALIZED JUDICIAL BODIES

The 1972 Code of Military Justice established the Military Courts to deal only with offenses committed by service personnel. For certain offenses, military jurisdiction could be extended for a period of five years beyond the date on which an individual's active duty came to an end. In addition, various categories of civilians could also be brought to the Military Courts, including: civilians accused of belonging to "rebel bands"; those who incited service personnel to commit offenses; coperpetrators or accomplices of service personnel; individuals accused of treason; and those accused of illegally possessing military weapons. Career magistrates presided over the Military Courts, and basic guarantees of due process were provided, including the right to appeal, the right to an attorney, the right to a fair trial, and so forth.

In 1997, on the fall of Mobutu, President Kabila abolished all military tribunals and replaced them by a single Special Military Court (Cour d'Ordre Militaire), which was later expanded by the creation of new permanent chambers in the countryside. This Special Military Court was the result of the widespread suspicion with which the new regime, sprung from the 1996–1997 military uprising, reacted to anyone who had previously worked in the justice system under Mobutu. Members of the new army preferred to handle arrest and adjudication directly, without passing through the courts. Since its establishment, the Cour d'Ordre Militaire has been characterized by a total violation of due process and basic guarantees of fair trial. A propensity to apply and carry out the death sentence, a denial of the right to appeal and to a counsel of one's choice, and abnormally prolonged delays are the daily commodities of this court.

After the fall of Mobutu in 1997, the Kabila government established the Commission of Illegally Gotten Wealth (Commission des Biens Mal Acquis, or CBMA) to investigate economic crimes committed by members of the Mobutu regime. The stated mission of the commission was to investigate the origin of the wealth accumulated by the most well-known officials of Mobutu's regime and to bring to court those found guilty of illegal enrichment. Unfortunately, the commission has been acting as a tribunal, administering justice without respect to due process and ordering the seizure of properties alleged to have been illegally obtained. Such abuses have been so widespread that human rights lawyers now joke about the need to investigate the commission's illegally gotten wealth.

STAFFING

A lack of sufficient and well-trained personnel has always been one of the most serious concerns of the Congolese judiciary. At independence in 1960, there was not a single trained lawyer in the country, and the government was forced to recruit foreign judges from Africa and Haiti to fill the vacuum left on the bench by the Belgians. Only between 1962 and 1963 did the first graduates of Congolese law schools joined the bench.

Like other systems derived from continental Europe, the Congolese judicial system is based on a career magistracy, including both judges and prosecutors. These individuals are appointed straight out of law school and consequently have no prior experience as lawyers. They enter a hierarchical corps in which they depend on their superiors for job assignments and promotions. For this system to work as it does in Western Europe, there must be specialized training for judges and a self-policing mechanism to oversee discipline and promotion. Such specialized training was provided in the early 1960s through the Ecole Nationale de Droit et d'Administration, a judicial college that did not last more than five years. The function of overseeing discipline and promotion has since been assumed by the Superior Council of the Magistracy. According to the constitution, the council is to be presided over by the president of the republic, assisted by the minister of justice. In the 1960s and 1970s, this infringement on the independence of the judiciary was not obvious: Neither the president nor the minister of justice seemed to be interested in conducting the council's business. But the 1975 constitutional amendment made the judiciary a "specialized branch" of the state party, the Mouvement Populaire de la Révolution (MPR), and the president of the Supreme Court and the general prosecutor became members of the MPR's political bureau. As a consequence, the judiciary lost the relative independence it had enjoyed in the late 1960s and the beginning of the 1970s. The democratic reforms of the earlier 1990s restated the separation of powers, and the judiciary showed significant signs of independence. In a celebrated ruling in1992, for example, the Supreme Court refused to apply the 1967 Mobutuist constitution as the president wanted it to do and held that the valid and applicable constitution was that approved by the National Sovereign Conference. On August 16, 1993, the president of the Supreme Court and the general prosecutor signed a joint statement declaring void the measures of dismissal and transfer of judges arbitrarily decreed by Prime Minister Faustin Birindwa.

But this demonstration of independence did not last long enough for the judiciary to fully recover from the damages inflicted during the Mobutu era. In 1997, President Laurent Kabila rose to power with a widespread suspicion of anything associated with the Mobutu regime, beginning with the judiciary. His minister of justice reduced the Council of the Magistracy virtually to the point of nonexistence, making no mystery of the government's will to exert a tighter control over the judiciary. In 1998, the minister of justice fired 315 judges and magistrates without even consulting the council.

The last figures released by the Ministry of Justice show that there were 1,448 judges and prosecutors in the entire country in 1998, with over 70 percent concentrated in the four biggest cities of Kinshasa, Lubumbashi, Kisangani, and Goma. The resulting caseload is such that it takes at least three years of trial for a decision to be reached. It is estimated that a minimum of 5,000 judges and magistrates are needed to significantly reduce the caseload.

THE LEGAL PRACTICE

In contrast to the judicial bodies staffed with state-appointed, state-paid judges and magistrates, private practitioners in Congo enjoy a relatively high degree of independence as compared to average African standards. Only private practitioners can become members of the bar, in exclusion of magistrates and judges. One of the oldest bars in Africa, the Congolese Bar was created by a colonial decree of November 7, 1930, and only Europeans were admitted. Since independence, however, only Congolese nationals have been admitted to the bar. In addition to the national bar, there is a bar association at each Court of Appeals. Each run its own business, including discipline and membership, independent of the national association. Disciplinary decisions against individual attorneys can be appealed before the Supreme Court.

IMPACT

The judiciary in Congo has been so discredited that the law has no impact on the social events and political life of the country today. No political crisis of a constitutional nature has been resolved by the judiciary, and politicians and businesspeople are reluctant to bring their disputes to the courts. There is an equally total lack of confidence in judges among the general population. Estimates are that less than 5 percent of all disputes end up in courts of law, not because the parties to the disputes have better options but because they are so suspicious of the judiciary that they prefer other venues, including the police, security services, the military, or, in rural areas, traditional arbitration. Even victims of human rights abuses are generally reluctant to resort to judicial mechanisms for redress. Recently, the crisis of the judicial system has led the population to the dangerous course of self-defense.

Since President Laurent Kabila's death in January 2001, the country has regained its 1990–1993 mood for reform. Lawyers who have been critical of the government's human rights abuses are working to craft the needed reforms, and an inter-Congolese dialogue has been called to decide the shape they will take. One can

only hope that the law will play a decisive role in the process of redefining the future of the country.

Pascal K. Kambale

See also Appellate Courts; Arbitration; Belgium; Capital Punishment; Civil Law; Commercial Law (International Aspects); Constitutional Review; Customary Law; Equity; Family Law; Government Legal Departments; Judicial Independence; Judicial Review; Juvenile Justice; Labor Law; Magistrates—Civil Law Systems; Military Justice (Law and Courts); Napoleonic Code; Prosecuting Authorities

References and further reading
Bayona ba Meya. 1973. "La mutation du droit judiciaire sous la deuxième République." *Revue Juridique du Zaire*, no 1: 16–47.
Djelo E. Osako. 1990. *L'impact de la coutume sur l'exercice du pouvoir en Afrique: Le cas du Zaire*. Brussels: Louvain-la-Neuve University Press.
Kabange Ntabala. 1971. *Production de la loi et restructuration du système juridique congolais, thèse de doctorat*. Brussels: Katholieke Universiteit Leuven.
Kalongo Mbikay. 2000. "La problématique des jugements iniques." *Revue de Droit Congolais*, no. 003: 1–25.
Lamy, Emile. 1980. "Le problème de l'intégration du droit congolais: Son origine, son évolution, son avenir." *Revue Juridique du Congo*, ed. spéciale.
Likulia Bolongo. 1981. *Droit et science pénitentiaires: Vers le traitement scientifique de la délinquance au Zaire*. Kinshasa: PUZ.
Lukombe Nghenda. 1999. *Droit congolais des sociétés.*Vol. 1. Kinshasa: Preses Universitaires du Congo.
Matadi Nenga Gamanda. 2000. *La question du pouvoir judiciaire en République Démocratique du Congo: Contribution à une théorie de réforme*. Kinshasa: Droits et Idées Nouvelles.
Nyabirungu M. Songa. 1989. *Droit pénal général zairois*. Kinshasa: Droit et Société.
Piron, Pierre. 1970 (1960). *Codes et lois du Congo*. Brussels: Larcier.
Rubbens, Antoine. 1965. *Le droit judiciaire congolais*. Brussels: Larcier.
Vudisa Mugumbushi. 2000. "Réflexions sur le contentieux administratif congolais: Analyse critique de quelques points de doctrine et de jurisprudence." *Revue de Droit Congolais*, no. 003: 26–54.

CONGO, REPUBLIC OF

GENERAL INFORMATION

The Republic of the Congo is a country of some 2.6 million people located on the West Central Coast of Africa on the Atlantic Ocean. It covers 132,600 square miles (342,000 square kilometers). It is bordered by Gabon to the west, Cameroon and the Central African Republic to the north, the Democratic Republic of the Congo (Congo Kinshasa) to the east, and the Cabinda strip of Angola to the south. The topography is divided into four

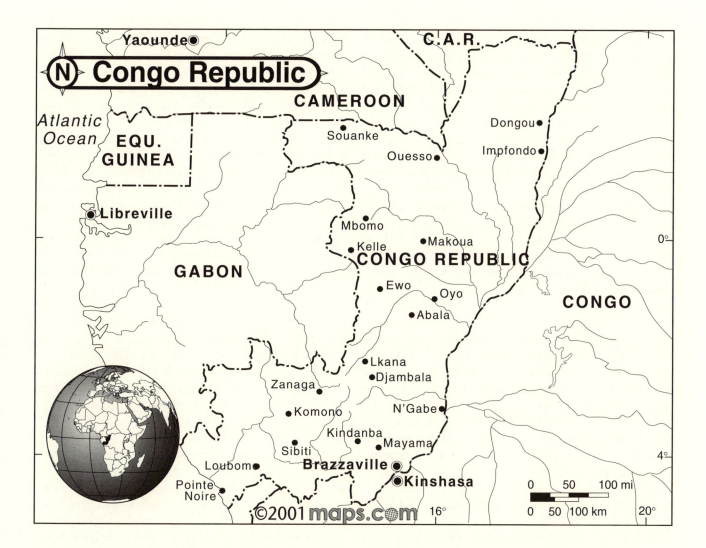

regions: coastal plains, fertile valleys, a central plateau, and forested plains. The climate is tropical.

The Republic of the Congo has an ethnically diverse population that is made up of some fifteen main groups and more than seventy subgroups. The Bakongo, who make up 48 percent of the population, is the largest ethnic group. It is followed by the Sangha at 17 percent, and the Teke with 14 percent of the population. Other major groups include the M'boshi, the Vili, and the Bateke. Significant numbers of Gabonese and French also live in the country.

The Republic of the Congo was one of Africa's high-growth economies during the late 1970s and early 1980s. Although it has a highly diversified economy, its growth was spurred mainly by oil. The fall in oil prices in the mid-1980s significantly changed the country's economic outlook. With less revenue coming in through oil, the entire government budget was reduced. Public investments were reduced, with negative effects on the industries that had depended on such investments. Exacerbated by corruption, a bloated bureaucracy (80,000 out of a population of 2.6 million), a Marxist economic philosophy that had in-

creasingly become outdated, an overvalued currency, and inefficiently managed parastatals, the fall in oil prices plunged the country into an economic crisis. Attempts to jump-start the economy—such as the devaluation of the country's currency, the franc CFA, in 1994—to stimulate economic growth through exports was slow to yield the desired results. Economic conditions have been further destabilized by a protracted civil war, discussed below.

In 1996 the Congo had a gross national product (GNP) of U.S.$1.813 billion, and a per capita income of $670. Its GNP had declined by 4.3 percent between 1990 and 1996. And although Gross Domestic Products (GDP) did better on average than GNP, its average increase of 0.7 percent between 1990 and 1997 disguised the inconsistency associated with the performance of domestic productivity. For example, the Congo experienced a 5.5 percent drop in GDP in 1994 while registering an increase of 2.2 percent in 1995 and 6.8 percent in 1996. The country also suffers from a debilitating debt burden that has been a major drain on its scarce resources. In 1997 it had a total debt of over U.S.$5 billion, which was 247 percent of GNP.

The Congolese economy is a typical Third World economy in the sense that it is highly dependent on primary production. Agriculture, forestry, and fishing are the primary industries, employing around 43 percent of the population. But the sector contributed only about 12 percent to GDP. Petroleum and petroleum by-products dominate productivity in the mining sector; they accounted for 38 percent of Congo's GDP. Despite a decline in extraction and refining that in 1995 was 1.8 percent of volume, petroleum is the leading foreign exchange earner, accounting for 84 percent of total export earnings, which in 1995 was $952 million. Because of increased exploration, petroleum's share to GDP and export earnings is projected to surpass the current level. Other exports include timber, diamonds, sugar, coffee, and cocoa.

HISTORY

The original inhabitants of the area known today as the Republic of the Congo were pygmies. They depended on hunting and gathering for their livelihood. Around 1000 c.e., Bantu-speaking peoples migrated to the area where, with their settled life based on agriculture, they were able to dominate the original people. Some of these same Bantu-speaking groups also settled in what are today Northern Angola, Gabon, and the Democratic Republic of the Congo (formerly Zaire). The new immigrants developed various forms of political organizations. Some, such as the Bakongo, the Loango, and the Teke, had highly centralized political structures and extensive empires. Others were organized mainly around lineage and clan lines and without a highly structured military, bureaucracy, or judiciary organization. That was the situation when Portuguese explorers made contact with the area in the fifteenth century. The outcome of these contacts was the establishment of trade relations between Portugal and the coastal kingdoms of the area. These trade relations degenerated from trade in tropical products to trade in human beings, with the coastal kingdoms serving as intermediaries, selling slaves captured from the interior to Portuguese slave merchants. These activities continued until the early nineteenth century, when French antislaving activities put an end to the trade.

In the European scramble for territory in Africa during the late 1800s, the Frenchman Pierre de Brazza in his efforts to secure the wealth of the area for his business ambition, signed treaties with the peoples on the West Bank of the River Congo, guaranteeing them French protection. He went on to found the city of Brazzaville (named after him), which presently is the Congo's capital. As a result of de Brazza's work, France claimed the area west of the River Congo. This was later recognized and affirmed by the Berlin Conference of 1884–1885, called by Otto von Bismarck to deal with various European countries' claims over various territories in Africa. The territorial arrangements at Berlin saw the dismemberment of various groups in Africa, one of which was the once extensive and powerful Bakongo kingdom, whose territory and peoples were divided between present-day Angola, the Democratic Republic of the Congo (formerly Zaire), and the Republic of Congo. In 1891, France turned the Congo into a colony, and later in 1910 made it part of French Equatorial Africa, comprising of the territories today known as Gabon, the Central African Republic, and Chad. The capital of this enlarged French-controlled area was Brazzaville.

France's attempts to impose its rule over the entire territory met with fierce resistance from various indigenous groups, some of which resistance lasted to the 1920s. The number of casualties in those battles was so high that the Congo is said to have lost some two-thirds of its population between 1914 and 1924 to what is reported as outright French slaughter of Congolese.

French colonial policy in the Congo was similar to her policies in her other colonies. It was a policy of Direct Rule, guided by the objective of assimilating the areas into metropolitan France economically, politically, territorially, and culturally. This policy was later discarded for that of association. The French in the Congo sought to make the colony pay for its own development, as well as help in accelerating the development of France itself. The latter was accomplished through extraction of natural resources, which during the initial years was through private firms, and then cash crop agricultural production. France ruled its colonies in Africa with an iron fist. Colonials were subjected to numerous human rights abuses, and deprived of various freedoms. Even principles such as due process were often circumvented to ensure the primacy of Europeans. Further, Africans were deprived of their basic political rights, including the right to hold public office and to have a say in the way in which they were governed. It was not until 1946, when the territories were made Overseas Territories of France, that the situation began to change. The French colonies were then entitled to representation in the French Parliament in Paris. In 1958, French Equatorial Africa was dissolved and the Congo, plus the three territories that had formed it, were given internal political autonomy within the French Union. In August of 1960 the Congo became fully independent, and in March of 1961, Fulbert Youlou of the Democratic Union for the Defense of African Interests (UDDLA) was elected the country's president.

Although brief, Youlou's term in office showed the willingness of the Congolese to resist attempts to establish dictatorial rule. It also revealed the willingness of elected officials to do whatever they could to accumulate power in the absence of an assertive public. In 1963, Youlou would be forced out of office in demonstrations when he tried to restrict the power of labor unions and to institute single-party rule. His replacement was Alphonse Massemba-Debat, who was supported by the military, which had temporarily seized power, and trade unions. In December 1963, the National Assembly elected him to a five-year term as president.

Massemba Debat and his National Movement for the Revolution (MNR) laid the foundation for what subsequent politics in the Congo would become, even if he himself was not very adept at it. It was a foundation based upon dependence on armed militias, one-party rule, anti-Western politics, a socialist agenda, and the establishment of closer ties with communist China. He was replaced by Captain Marien Ngouabi in 1968.

Ngouabi initiated a series of measures that transformed the Congo into a full-fledged Marxist-Leninist state. He changed the name to the Peoples Republic of the Congo, changed its flag, the national anthem, and replaced the MNR with a new Congolese Workers Party (PCT) and a new constitution. Rising oil prices helped the regime, as it was able to use oil revenue to finance its socialist programs. Although Ngouabi became very popular for his commitment to socialism, he was unable to avoid the sometimes overt and sometimes covert struggle for power or ideological purity and dominance that had become the hallmark of Congolese politics. He escaped a coup in 1972 and had to deal with a guerilla war until 1973. In 1977, he was assassinated. His assassination brought to power army chief of staff Joachim Yhombi-Opango, who in the mucky climate of Congolese politics lasted only for two years before being replaced by Colonel Sassou-Nguesso in 1979, on grounds that he had overstepped his authority in his attempt to reduce the influence of the PCT.

Sassou-Nguesso continued the radical leftist policies of Ngouabi, while working to cement his hold on the state. The former were marked by anti-Western rhetoric; an intensification of relations with Communist-bloc countries, especially China, North Korea, the Soviet Union, and Cuba through military and economic assistance; educational training; and cultural exchanges. Although these actions gave the impression that the Congo had separated itself completely from the West, the reality was that France continued to dominate economic activities in the country, from trade, to investment, to foreign aid. In 1986, unable to meet its obligations to its creditors and to its people, the Sassou-Nguesso government accepted the International Monetary Fund (IMF) Structural Adjustment Package, in return for help in rescheduling its debt repayment. The package ranged from privatization of parastatals, to downsizing the bureaucracy, reductions in government spending, elimination of various government subsidies, and greater emphasis on agriculture.

By 1990 the economic situation had not changed. Meanwhile, pressure from within the country and outside became focused not on economic change alone but also on political change. After trying to delay action in order to control any demands for political change, the government agreed to convene a national conference in 1991 to determine the country's future. The outcome of the conference was a new constitution for the country, the organization of a transition government led by Andre Milongo, a former World Bank official, to organize elections in 1992, and the return of exiles. Pascal Lissouba's Pan African Union for Social Development Party (UPAD) won the municipal elections held in June and July 1992, and also the National Assembly elections held in June and July.

In June 1997, in preparation for parliamentary and presidential elections scheduled for July, the Lissouba government moved to disarm the militia linked to Sassou-Nguesso. This led to renewed fighting between militias and supporters of Sassou-Nguesso, Lissouba, and Kolelas. Efforts at mediation were of no avail. As the conflict intensified, French troops evacuated foreign nationals and left the country themselves in mid-June. In October, Angolan troops intervened on the side of Sassou-Nguesso, enabling him to capture Brazzaville and Pointe-Noire, thereby giving him the victory. This led to the flight of Lissouba and Kolelas.

Upon seizing power, Sassou-Nguesso moved swiftly to reconstitute the Congolese political system. He convened a forum for unity and national reconciliation of the various political groups in January 1998 that was attended by 1,420 delegates to decide on a transitional period and to set up institutions for the transition. But Lissouba's party and others loyal to him refused to take part. The forum agreed to the establishment of the National Transitional Council, made up of seventy-five members, to serve as a legislative body during the transition. The Transitional Council was compiled from a list submitted by the government and political as well as legal commissions. The council also agreed to a transitional period of three years, during which a new constitution would be written and presidential and legislative elections organized. In addition to the Transitional Council, Sassou-Nguesso also set up a Council of Ministers to perform executive functions.

The transition has been everything but peaceful. In 1998 clashes between militias loyal to Kolelas and Lissouba against the new government of Sassou-Nguesso erupted. This new round of fighting saw a further internationalization of the struggle for the Congo on both sides. It involved Angolan rebels on the side of Kolelas, while Angolan government forces were fighting on the side of Sassou-Nguesso. In addition, France has also been linked to helping Sassou-Nguesso. France's involvement was said to be due to dissatisfaction over the marginalization of French oil interests in favor of American oil interests by the Lissouba government.

LEGAL CONCEPTS

The Republic of the Congo has a unitary system of government divided into executive, legislative, and judiciary branches. The executive branch is made up of the president as head of state and his Council of Ministers, or cabinet. The Transitional Council performs legislative functions, while a Supreme Court heads the judiciary branch. This setup came into effect in October 1997 following Sassou-Nguesso's seizure of power from the elected government of President Pascal Lissouba, with the help of Angolan troops. Prior to the 1997 incident, the Congo had a republican form of government based on the Constitution of 1992. That constitution had been written by a commission set up by the 1991 National Conference. The government under the 1992 setup was a republican system of government, unitary in organization with a bicameral legislature (the National Assembly and the Senate), an executive branch with the president as head of state and a prime minister (PM) as head of government, and an independent judiciary headed by the Supreme Court.

The 1992 Constitution had created a strong presidency directly elected by the people for a five-year term and eligible for re-election only once. The president appointed the prime minister, who had to be approved by the National Assembly. Cabinet appointments by the president had to be based on the suggestion of the prime minister. The president could dissolve Parliament, fire the PM and his cabinet, and submit issues to the people directly in a referendum. The PM's role was mainly to coordinate government business and to see to it that the government's programs as defined were well implemented. The people directly elected members of the National Assembly for five-year terms, while local councils, districts, regions, and communes elected members of the Senate to serve six-year terms. The Senate therefore was meant to represent geographical areas. The constitution had two separate judiciary setups, the High Court and the Supreme Court. The High Court served mainly to try high government officials including the president, cabinet members, legislators, members of the judiciary, and other officials for crimes and misdemeanors committed while they were exercising their official duties, and for high treason and other plots against the country. Parliament and the Supreme Court were responsible for selecting members of the High Court. The other judiciary setup was made up of the Supreme Court and lower courts. The Supreme Court was the highest court, and its members were elected from among magistrates by Parliament. They held office until retirement. However, they could be removed from office before retirement on account of insanity, death, indignity, resignation, definitive incapacity, or for crimes and misdemeanors.

The 1992 Constitution was a break from Congo's authoritarian past, which had been so often marred by rancorous personal and factional politics secured by militias and guided by Marxist-Leninist ideology. The constitution provided for a secular democratic state with guarantees of basic rights and freedoms to all citizens and noncitizens. Beside the more standard political and civil rights that are found in most constitutions—such as freedom of the press, freedom of speech, life, belief, freedom to petition the state, and so forth—the 1992 Constitution also identified various economic and social service rights that the state was obligated to guarantee. Among these were the right to peace, development, a clean and healthy environment, good health, and education. It addressed one of Africa's perennial problems, ethnicity and regionalism, as it declared that "every citizen shall have the right to freely choose his place of residence." Of note under the rights enumerated was the right of citizens to resist by civil disobedience any endeavors to overthrow the constitutional regime by a coup d'état, or the institution of tyrannical government. This was to eliminate from the Congolese body politic the use of coup d'états, which had become the standard process of bringing about governmental change. A further departure of the constitution was in what it identified as "duties of citizens." These included duties toward the family and the state. Among them were duties "to preserve the harmonious development of the family and to work in favor of its cohesion and its respect, to respect at all times [one's] parents, to nourish and to assist them in case of necessity." In another article, it states the requirement of all citizens to "respect and consider his equals without any discrimination, and to maintain with them relations which permit promotion, safeguard, and reinforcement of respect of reciprocal tolerance." Of the many other duties, it is worth mentioning the duty to be uncorrupt, in view of the rampant corruption and mismanagement that have characterized Congolese society over the years.

Separation of powers, judiciary independence, due process, equal protection, the rule of law—are all concepts identified with the Congolese legal system. The constitutional roots of these concepts in the Congo is the 1992 Constitution, which as discussed earlier was eliminated in 1997 when Sassou-Nguesso in an unconstitutional process seized power and declared himself president. But even under the current system, the spirit of the 1992 constitutional setup as far as the separation between legislative, executive, and judiciary powers has been retained. The Council of Ministers, which performs executive functions, is separate from the National Transitional Council, which serves legislative functions. The judiciary setup under the 1992 Constitution in its strictly legal functions remains the same under the 1997 transitional setup. For example, the 1992 Constitution prohibited, under articles 130 and 131, any of the other branches of government from interfering in the proceedings of the courts, or from modifying any rulings of the courts. Article 132 similarly prohibited the judiciary from incrementally intruding upon the "attributes" of the legislature and executive branches. Under the constitution, the president was elected separately from the legislature and could not sit in the legislature. The prime minister and the cabinet, however, had to be approved by the National Assembly. Under the Sassou-Nguesso transitional setup, the president and his Council of Ministers are separate from the National Transition Council—that is, the legislative body.

However, almost immediately, when put to the test, the 1992 Constitution failed to protect the integrity of some of these concepts. Upon constant bombardment from different angles, it collapsed. The president's choice of Maurice-Stephane Bongho-Nouarra of the Union Panafricaine pour la Démocratie Sociale (UPADS) to be prime minister, in September 1992, was rejected by the National Assembly in which the opposition coalition of the Union pour le renouveau democratique (URD)—the Parti Congolais du travail (PCT)—made up the majority. When President Lissouba dissolved the assembly, which he could do constitutionally, this caused a constitutional crisis. Using the provision of the constitution that called on citizens to use peaceful demonstrations to confront any challenges to the constitution, members of the opposition coalition URD-PCT in the assembly called on their supporters to protest and demonstrate against the president's act. This was the first indication that legal frameworks are only as good as they are made functionable. While the constitution did survive, it did so only after the unconstitutional intervention of the armed forces, whose chief of staff pressured the politicians to form a transitional government while working to hold new legislative elections.

The Republic of the Congo's legal system is based on the French Civil Code and indigenous African customary practices. This is a reflection of years of French colonial rule and its various assimilation policies. Even years after independence, the Congo still looks up to France's legal institutions as examples in restructuring its own institutions. The Constitutional Court is one such institution, in which France's example has been an influence to the Congo. However, it is important also to note that even with French legal influence, the Congo's legal system has borrowed from other countries, especially the United States. Because of the different ethnic and cultural groups in the country, and their territoriality, no uniform indigenously Congolese legal norms are applicable countrywide. But the design of a second legislative chamber to represent such interests ensures respect for cultural pluralism and customary norms.

CURRENT STRUCTURE

The Republic of the Congo was as of 2001 without a constitution, despite the fact that the National Forum set up the transitional period and institutions in 1998. In November of that year, Sassou-Nguesso installed a Constitutional Committee to draft the country's new constitution. As of October 2001, the Congo continues to be governed under the political institutions of the transition. A new constitution is not yet in place, and because presidential and legislative elections would have to be based on the type of constitutional arrangements devised, presidential and legislative elections have not been held. The latest information is that a draft constitution was submitted to the National Council this past September, and the council approved it. Because a new constitution has to be approved by the people in a referendum, it is unclear when that will be done. It should be noted, however, that the three-year transitional period approved by the 1998 National Forum was conditional, depending upon the security and economic situation in the country. Since 1997, neither the security situation nor the economic situation has improved significantly. The government has been under heavy attack from armed militias loyal to Sassou-Nguesso's opponents. The security situation has in turn had a negative effect on the economic situation, giving reason for Sassou-Nguesso to move slowly on the transition.

Because the National Forum of 1998 had dealt principally with political aspects of governmental institutions, the judiciary setup remained as it had been under the 1992 Constitution. The court system in the Congo is composed of Magistrates' Court, the High Court of Justice, the Constitutional Council, and the Supreme Court. The Supreme Court is the highest court in the country and hears appellate cases from lower courts. It is presided over by a president, whose appointment and the appointment of other members of the court under the 1992 Constitution were the responsibility of Parliament. The constitution also required appointees to the court to come from the ranks of magistrates. Supreme Court judges hold office until retirement. Below the Supreme Court are Magistrates' Courts, which are the lowest sets of courts (or courts of first instance) and have jurisdiction over civil and criminal matters. Magistrates must hold a university degree in law. Appointees also serve till retirement.

The appointment of magistrates is the responsibility of the president acting on the recommendation of the High Council. This council, which was mandated under the 1992 Constitution, is presided over by the president of the country and has responsibility for disciplining members of the judiciary, safeguarding judicial independence, and advising the president on appointments into the judiciary, promotion, and disciplinary actions. Its members include the president of the Supreme Court, and magistrates elected by Parliament.

Legal Structure of the Republic of the Congo Courts

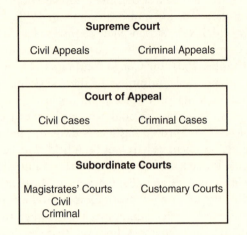

Supreme Court	
Civil Appeals	Criminal Appeals

Court of Appeal	
Civil Cases	Criminal Cases

Subordinate Courts	
Magistrates' Courts Civil Criminal	Customary Courts

Court registers constitute an important group in the legal system of the Congo, although they function mainly as administrators of the courts. Because of the specialized nature of the High Court of Justice and the Constitutional Court, they are discussed under specialized judiciary bodies (below).

Besides judges, members of the legal profession in private practice constitute a significant force in Congolese society. These include advocates known as *advocat* and *notaire* (solicitors). The latter prepare legal documents and perform other forms of legal activities, except for representing clients in court before a judge, unlike advocates who can do both.

SPECIALIZED JUDICIARY BODIES

Logically, the High Court of Justice should be the next layer of courts below the Supreme Court. But that is not the case, because the High Court of Justice was designed to deal only with crimes committed by high-level state officials, including the president, in the exercise of their powers. It also had jurisdiction over trying the president and other governmental officials for high treason or plots against the security of the state.

The Constitutional Council completes the list of special judiciary bodies. As its name suggests, the Constitutional Court was designed to ensure the constitutionality of the actions of the other branches of government. Thus, before all bills, treaties, and laws were to be ratified or promulgated, they were to be submitted to the Constitutional Council for a decision on their constitutionality. Beside the strictly legal constitutional matters that the Council had been designed to handle, it also had jurisdiction and responsibility over elections and referenda. It was responsible for ensuring the regularity of elections and for proclaiming their results. Membership in the council and the selection process of the members re-

flected the mix of political and legal roles it was designed to serve. Its members consisted of two magistrates elected by the High Council of the Magistrates; two law professors from the university; two lawyers elected by their peers; one member named by the president of the country; one member named by the president of the National Assembly; and one member named by the president of the Senate. The council was constitutionally mandated to have a total of nine members, and each member was to have at least fifteen years' experience. Service in the council is renewed every two years by thirds.

STAFFING

The legal system of the Republic of the Congo has been greatly affected by the insecurity and economic crisis that has wrecked much of the society. Until the economic crisis, and even thereafter, the members of the legal profession, especially judges and prosecutors, were among the most highly paid state officials. The World Bank's Structural Adjustment Programs and reduced wages have placed these employees in a situation of being easily swayed by kickbacks to raise their incomes. The insecurity and fear created by the country's raging war have affected members of the legal profession in the same way that they have affected much of society. The situation is even more difficult on judges and magistrates, because they may sometimes deal with issues not favorable to some of the groups involved in the conflicts, and in so doing might not be unmindful of their own security.

Other staffing issues pertain to legal education. There are a number of tracts in the legal profession in the Republic of the Congo. To be a magistrate, one must have a law degree, and spend two years in the program for magistrates in the School of Administration and Magistracy. Entry into the school is by competitive examination. After the two years of study, one becomes a magistrate. Upon entry into the School of Administration and Magistracy to pursue the magistrate's program, one is already an employee of the state. Another track in the legal profession is to become an advocate. Advocates also spend two years in training in the School of Administration and Magistracy. State advocates (prosecutors) and lawyers in private practice called *advocat* (advocates) are trained in the same program. Lawyers in private practice come out of the program and join law firms or open their own independent legal practice. There is also the registrar's track in the legal profession in the Republic of the Congo. To become a court registrar, one must have a high school diploma. A fair comparison with the U.S. system would be a high school diploma plus one or two years of college. One must then enter the registrar's track in the School of Administration and Magistracy and spend three years in the program. Entry into the program is by competitive examination. Upon completion, one is posted as registrar in the court system.

IMPACT

Any attempt to gauge the impact of the legal system of the Republic of the Congo is a futile enterprise. This is because of the armed conflict that has been going on in the country since 1997. The conflict has created a climate of fear and intimidation that has not been helpful to the application of the various principles adopted in 1992 to create a new political order based on the rule of law through institutions created to safeguard against the abuses of the past. The rulings of the Supreme Court involving the disputed elections of 1993 suggest that the Congo was again on its way toward creating a society based on laws and not of men. However, the seizure of power by force in 1997 by Sassou-Nguesso and his militia made the legal and constitutional order that had been established short-lived. It is thus not an overstatement to say that the legal system of the Republic of the Congo in 2001 is still of men and not of laws.

Moses K. Tesi

See also Civil Law; Congo, Democratic Republic of (Kinshasa); Customary Law; Human Rights; Indigenous and Folk Legal Systems; Judicial Independence; Legal Professionals—Civil Law Traditions; Notaries

References and further reading
Africa Confidential. 1990–2001. Various Issues.
Clark, John F. 1997. "Congo: Transition and the Struggle to Consolidate." In *Political Reforms in Francophone Africa.* Edited by John F. Clark and David E. Gardinier. Boulder, CO: Westview Press.
———. "Elections, Leadership and Democracy in Congo." 1994. *Africa Today* 41: 41–62.
———. "Socio-Political Change in the Republic of Congo: Political Dilemmas of Economic Reform." 1993. *Journal of Third World Studies* 10, no. 1 (spring): 52–77.
Decalo, Samuel. 1981. "People's Republic of the Congo." In vol. 1 of *Marxist Governments: A World Survey.* Edited by Bogdan Szjkowski. London: Macmillan.
Economist Intelligence Unit. *EIU Country Report: Congo.* Various issues, 1990–2000.
Gauze, Rene. 1973. *The Politics of Congo-Brazzaville.* Translated, by Virginia Thompson and Richard Adlof. Stanford, CA: Hoover Institution Press.
International Foundation for Electoral Systems (IFES). 1992. "IFES Observers' Reports on Elections in Congo." IFES Document. New York.
Legum, Collin, ed. 1980. *Africa Contemporary Record 1978–1979.* Vol 2. New York: Africana Press.
Marchés Tropicaux et Meditérranéens. 1990–2001. Various issues.
Massou, Assou. 1995. "Rente: La Nouvelle Donne." *Jeune Afrique,* no. 1803 (July 27–August 2): 38–39.
Officials at the Congo Embassy in Washington, D.C. 2001. Personal communication. Fall.
Okoko-Eseau, Abraham. 1995. "The Christian Churches and Democratisation in the Congo." In *The Christian Churches and Democratisation of Africa.* Edited by Paul Gifford. Leiden, Netherlands: Brill.
Radu, Michael S., and Keith Somerville. 1989. "The Congo."
In *Benin, the Congo, Burkina Faso.* Edited by Chris Allen et al. London: Pinter.
Republic of the Congo. 1992 Constitution.
World Bank. *World Development Report.* 1989–2000. New York: Oxford University Press.

CONNECTICUT

GENERAL INFORMATION

Connecticut stands today as an odd contradiction, a curious blending of the United States' primitive past and its progressive, aggressively capitalistic present. Much of Connecticut, the third-smallest state in area, remains a testament to the nation's rural roots. The northeast quadrant of the state has been aptly dubbed the "Quiet Corner," as its landscape and character are largely unchanged from two centuries ago. At the same time, Connecticut has the highest per capita income of any state and enjoys a reputation for technological innovation; Eli Whitney, inventor of the cotton gin, and Charles Goodyear, who discovered the method to vulcanize rubber, both came from Connecticut. Hartford, the capital city since 1875, is a center of the U.S. insurance industry. The state's population in the 2000 census was reported as over 3.4 million, and the rate of population growth, 3.6 percent, is below the national average. For the foreseeable future, state politics are likely to be a battleground between rural communities and industrial cities; between old-line AngloYankees, typically Protestant and Republican, and the mainly Catholic and Democratic Irish, Italian, and Hispanic constituencies; and between longtime New Englanders and newcomers settling in southwestern Connecticut suburbs along the commuter lines to New York City.

HISTORY

Connecticut was originally explored by the Dutch, but the first permanent European settlers were the English Puritans who arrived in 1633. The people of Connecticut are credited with having created, in 1639, the first written constitution of a democratic government. Connecticut delegates played a crucial role in the U.S. constitutional convention of 1787: by proposing the compromise between the interests of small and large states by which delegates to one legislative chamber (the House of Representatives) would be apportioned by population and the number of delegates to the other chamber (the Senate) would be the same for every state.

From 1703 to 1875, Connecticut maintained two capitals, with sessions of the General Assembly meeting alternately in Hartford and New Haven. The state was one of the last in the nation to maintain an established church (until 1818) and is one of the most recent to institute an income tax. Unlike most other states, Connecticut has no county government. Below the state level, the governing units are cities and towns.

The state's judicial system has evolved over the past two centuries. Prior to the creation of a Connecticut Supreme Court in 1784, the General Assembly assumed the power to review all lower-court rulings. Evidence of the high court's political character lay in its membership, which during the first two decades of its existence included (at various times) the governor, the lieutenant governor, and members of the upper chamber of the General Assembly. Additionally, the General Assembly retained the power to overturn the court's rulings. In 1806, the Connecticut Supreme Court of Errors (the phrase "of errors" was deleted in 1965) underwent an increas in size (from five to nine justices) and political officials were dropped from its membership altogether. The creation of an independent judiciary, however, had to wait until 1818, when the Connecticut high court was afforded the responsibility for interpreting the laws enacted by the legislative branch.

On July 1, 1978, the General Assembly passed bold legislation to create what is known as a unified trial court system. Until that time, Connecticut had had a multi-tiered court system featuring municipal courts or, after 1961, circuit courts. In 1974, the circuit courts were merged into the court of common pleas. The 1978 legislation took unification a step further by merging the court of common pleas and the juvenile court into the superior court. Currently, with the exception of probate matters, all disputes that require resolution by the state's judicial system are brought before the unified Superior Court.

STRUCTURE

The Connecticut judicial system is composed of probate courts, the Superior Court, the Appellate Court, and the Supreme Court.

Probate courts are concerned with such matters as wills, estates, guardianships, and the commitment of the mentally ill. Appeals of probate cases may be taken to the Superior Court, and from there they follow the same path as other cases. The day-to-day operation of the probate courts is the responsibility of the probate court administrator, who is appointed by the chief justice. Unlike all other courts in Connecticut, which are state operated and maintained, probate courts operate on a fee basis, that is, the probate judge receives compensation and reimbursement for court expenses from fees paid for services rendered by the court. Each probate court serves a probate district, which by statute consists of one or more towns.

The Superior Court is the sole trial court of general jurisdiction in Connecticut. It hears all legal controver-

Legal Structure of Connecticut Courts

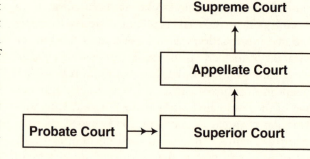

sies except those over which the probate courts have exclusive jurisdiction. The Superior Court has four principal trial divisions: civil, criminal, family, and housing. The state of Connecticut is divided into thirteen judicial districts. Courthouses serving these districts are referred to as judicial district courthouses. Most civil cases and family cases not involving juvenile matters are handled in the judicial district courthouses. Generally, major criminal cases are also handled in the judicial district courthouses. In addition to judicial districts, there are twenty-two geographical areas of the Superior Court. Each geographical area lies entirely within a judicial district. All minor criminal cases are handled in the geographical area courthouses, as are all arraignments, small claims, paternity, support, and housing matters. The state is also divided into fourteen juvenile districts. Receiving centers for the detention of children awaiting adjudication are maintained in each district. These facilities also include offices for the filing and hearing of cases involving juveniles.

The Appellate Court was created in 1982 by constitutional amendment approved by Connecticut voters in response to an overburdened Supreme Court docket. As the intermediate court of appeals, the Appellate Court reviews decisions made in the Superior Court to determine if errors of law have been committed. The Appellate Court is made up of nine judges, one of whom is designated by the chief justice to serve as chief judge. Generally, three judges hear and decide each case, although the court may also sit en banc, whereby the entire membership participates in the decision. The Appellate Court does not hear witnesses but renders its decision based on the record, briefs, and oral argument.

The Supreme Court is the highest court in the state of Connecticut. It consists of a chief justice and six associate justices. A panel of five justices hears and decides each case. When necessary, a judge of the Superior Court may be designated by the chief justice to sit as a member of the high court. The Supreme Court reviews selected lower court decisions to correct errors of law. It does not hear witnesses or receive evidence. It decides each case on the basis of the printed record of lower court proceedings, printed briefs prepared by counsel for each side, and oral argument based on the briefs. State law specifies which types of appeals may be brought directly to the Supreme Court from the Superior Court. These include cases involving the validity of constitutional or statutory provisions, capital punishment, judicial discipline, election or primary disputes, and convictions for the most serious felonies. All other appeals are heard initially by the Appellate Court. The Supreme Court may transfer any matter form itself to the Appellate Court or from the Appellate Court to itself. It may also agree to review a decision of the Appellate Court.

ADMINISTRATION

The head of the judicial branch in Connecticut is the chief justice of the Supreme Court, but its administrative director is the chief court administrator. The chief court administrator is responsible for the efficient operation of the judiciary, the expeditious dispatch of litigation, the prompt and proper administration of judicial business, and the assignment of judges. The court unification legislation of 1978 granted the chief justice the authority to appoint the chief court administrator. Prior to that legislation, appointments were made by the General Assembly from a nomination made by the governor.

The Connecticut Administrative Procedure Act (APA), which became effective in 1972, governs the actions of state boards, commissions, departments, or officers authorized by law to make regulations or determine contested cases. According to the rules of the APA, no regulation is effective in Connecticut until it has been made available for public inspection and notice has been published in the *Connecticut Law Journal.* Any person may petition an agency, or an agency may initiate a proceeding on its own, for a declaratory ruling about the validity of any regulation. The APA requires each agency to adopt regulations establishing procedures for making declaratory rulings. Although agencies are not required to hold formal hearings, if they elect to do so they much follow certain evidentiary and procedural guidelines stipulated by the APA for contested cases. If an agency decides not to issue a ruling, petitioners may seek a declaratory judgment in the Superior Court as long as they can successfully demonstrate that the statute, regulation, or final decision of the agency interferes with or impairs their legal rights or privileges. There is ordinarily no constitutional right to judicial review of administrative action. Appeals to the Superior Court are permitted only after the aggrieved party has exhausted all administrative remedies within the agency. In cases where appeals are permitted, the APA tightly restricts the scope of judicial review.

STAFFING

Connecticut's judiciary is composed of the seven justices of the Supreme Court, the nine judges of the Appellate Court, and, as of January 1, 1999, the 170 judges of the Superior Court. All judges (except for probate judges) are nominated by the governor from a list of candidates compiled by the Judicial Selection Commission and then are appointed by the General Assembly to eight-year terms of office. Probate judges are elected by the voters of the probate district to four-year terms of office, and unlike other judges they do not need to be lawyers and may serve part-time.

Not all legal controversies in Connecticut are heard by active judges. Judges who retire at the age of seventy become state referees. The chief justice of the Supreme Court may designate, from among state referees, state trial referees who conduct trials in cases referred to them. In addition to state referee, attorneys appointed by the chief justice or the chief court administrator hear some cases. These attorneys are called attorney state trial referees, fact finders, small claims commissioners, magistrates, and arbitrators.

In 1999, there were 16,918 practicing attorneys in Connecticut. To practice law in Connecticut, a person must earn a law degree and pass the state bar examination. There are currently three law schools that grant law degrees in Connecticut: Yale Law School, the University of Connecticut Law School, and the Quinnipiac College School of Law, which was established in 1995. Those three schools follow in a long tradition of legal education in the state: the Litchfield Law School, established in 1784, was the first law school in the United States; its graduates included such luminaries as John C. Calhoun, Aaron Burr, Horace Mann, Oliver Wolcott, Jr., and Noah Webster.

RELATIONSHIP TO NATIONAL SYSTEM

Connecticut includes within its boundaries one federal district court, whose thirteen judges preside in federal courthouses in Hartford, Bridgeport, New Haven, and Waterbury. Cases are appealed from the federal district court of Connecticut to the U.S. Court of Appeals for the Second Circuit, and from there to the U.S. Supreme Court.

Although a small state, Connecticut has enjoyed great influence in shaping the federal constitutional landscape. The law of all fifty states has been affected by litigation emanating from Connecticut courts. For example, in *Cantwell v. Connecticut* (1940) the U.S. Supreme Court considered the plight of Jehovah's Witnesses who were arrested in New Haven and convicted on charges of soliciting contributions without obtaining the proper approval from a state official. The Court invalidated their convictions on the grounds of free exercise of religion and in the process articulated what would later become a fundamental premise of constitutional jurisprudence: that although a state is free to regulate the time, place, and manner of constitutionally protected rights, it cannot prohibit their exercise altogether.

Additionally, the birth of modern privacy rights dates from 1965, when the U.S. Supreme Court first entertained a challenge to Connecticut's 1879 law criminalizing the use of contraceptive devices. Earlier, the Court had ducked the issue in *Poe v. Ullman* (1961), when it refused to review the Connecticut law on grounds that it was not being enforced and thus lacked "ripeness." Four years later, in *Griswold v. Connecticut* (1965), the Court invalidated that law on the grounds that it violated various provisions of the Bill of Rights, including the First Amendment right to freedom of association. The paramount significance of *Griswold* to the development of constitutional law is that the Court established the legal doctrine that certain fundamental "personal rights" not enumerated in the Bill of Rights could still enjoy full constitutional status. Eight years later, in *Roe v. Wade* (1973), the Court applied the doctrine in *Griswold* in order to protect a woman's right to an abortion during the first trimester of pregnancy and thus set off a storm of heated constitutional conflict that continues today.

Kristin Kelly
David Yalof

See also Administrative Law; Appellate Courts; Constitutional Law; Probate (Succession) Law; United States—Federal System; United States—State Systems

References and further reading

The Biennial Report of the Connecticut Judicial Branch. 1996–1999.
Bysiewicz, Shirley. 1987. *Sources of Connecticut Law.* Boston: Butterworth Legal Publishers.
Carson, Clara. 1999. *The Lawyer Statistical Report: The U.S. Legal Profession in 1995.* Chicago, IL: American Bar Foundation.
Kort, Fred. 1985. "Connecticut Administration of Justice: Common Law Tradition, Structural Innovation, and a Civil Law Perspective." *Connecticut History* 26: 145–155.
Lee, Joseph. 1990. "Administrative Law in Connecticut and Overview of the Administrative Procedure Act." *Connecticut Bar Journal* 64:259–276.
State of Connecticut Judicial Branch, http://www.jud.state.ct.us/external/supapp/suphist.html.

CONSTITUTIONAL LAW

The term *constitutional law* has three related meanings. First, it refers to a set of fundamental laws that determine the form, powers, and limits of a government, typically but not universally through a written constitution. Second, it refers to the process of adjudicating claims made under a constitution. And third, it refers to a particular law that is consistent with the constitution.

Constitutions ideally have several features: (1) They set the conditions of legitimacy for a government, (2) they specify the structure and powers of government, (3) they articulate limitations on what government may or may not do, (4) they provide mechanisms for their own modification, and (5) they claim some degree of supremacy over ordinary laws and the day-to-day proceedings of governance. Constitutional supremacy may come from different sources. In the United States, it is essentially contractual; by contrast, the basis of the supremacy of some Islamic constitutions is theological.

If we think of constitutionalism generally as the rules and practices that define the structure and practices of government, then every polity has a constitution. But that does not mean that every polity has constitutional law or that a document entitled "constitution" forms the real basis of political life. Two important points should be mentioned in this regard.

First, for there to be constitutional law, there must be a document (or documents) or sets of values that are widely recognized as establishing a fundamental law that is in some way superior to ordinary law. A polity's *nominal* constitution may serve that function, but it may also serve other functions, such as hiding the real structure of politics, serving as a symbol of unity, or calling on the people and the government to live up to high ideals. The political life of a society (its *effective* constitution) may be based on things other than its nominal constitution, such as corruption, patronage, or tradition. Only when nominal and effective constitutions overlap significantly is it possible to use the constitution to contest elements of day-to-day politics and thus to have constitutional law.

Second, a constitution need not be a single written document. Great Britain, for example, has what is often called an "unwritten" constitution—a collection of texts, common law precedents, doctrines, and customary practices that are routinely enforced by courts against the executive branch (although not against Parliament). And Israel's Basic Laws, which are intended to form a constitution superior to ordinary laws, are still being drafted and passed by ordinary majorities of the Knesset. To fill the void created by political stalemate, the Israeli Supreme Court, acting as a high court of justice, has increasingly provided constitution-like rules that limit the powers of government and its agents.

The most distinctive feature of constitutional law is constitutional review—the doctrine that laws passed or actions taken through the ordinary political process may be reversed (or prevented beforehand) if they are incompatible with the constitution. Scholars are widely agreed that the modern practice of constitutional review began in the United States, with the case of *Marbury v. Madison* (1803). However, the idea of judging ordinary laws by higher norms has a long history in western moral and political philosophy, with roots both in the Judeo-Christian divine law tradition and in Greco-Roman legal practice. Constitutional review became entrenched in European legal practice during the twentieth century, especially in the period of constitutional renewal after World War II. During that same period, many newly independent nations around the world wrote postcolonial constitutions that incorporated provisions for constitutional review. The most recent round of constitution making, following the collapse of communist governments in the Soviet Union and Eastern Europe in the early 1990s, has seen a further extension of constitutionalism and constitutional review.

The majority of countries today have written constitutions, and the majority of those constitutions provide for some form of constitutional review. But there are many variations in the practice of constitutional review. Perhaps most important are the degree of supremacy a constitution has over ordinary politics and the closely related issue of the ease or difficulty of constitutional change. In Great Britain, Parliament can change the unwritten constitution by an ordinary act, but it rarely does so because the body of tradition and custom built up around the constitution is quite strong. In the United States, by contrast, although a supermajority of the national legislature and the agreement of a supermajority of the states are required to formally amend the constitution, the Supreme Court routinely reviews and more than occasionally overturns acts of Congress and executive actions, in effect creating new constitutional law.

There is also an important distinction between rigid and flexible constitutions, which is best stated as a paradox. If a constitution is too flexible and unable to withstand ordinary efforts to change it, it will be of little use as fundamental law, but if it is too rigid, it will either invite informal change procedures or become dysfunctionally rigid and stagnant.

Another important variable is whether constitutional law is more the province of courts (judicial review) or of political bodies (political review). Constitutional review today is typically but not universally judicial review. Yet another important factor is whether constitutional review can be carried out by many entities (as, for example, in the United States, where any state or federal court of general jurisdiction or appeals can hear arguments on constitutional questions) or only by a single, specialized body (as with Germany's Constitutional Court).

Other questions help to highlight variations in the practice of constitutional review. Does the reviewing body focus exclusively on constitutional meaning in the abstract or do constitutional issues arise only out of adversarial cases? Does review occur before an action or the passage of legislation (proactively) or only after the act or legislation is complete (reactively)? Similarly, is the review

merely advisory or is it binding? In the case of reactive review, does the review affect only the parties directly involved or does it establish a more general precedent? Finally, is review initiated only by a case alleging a specific harm or can it be initiated by a special organ of government or designated individuals as a matter of principle? In other words, who has standing to activate constitutional law processes?

Since the role of constitutional law is to approve, overturn, or modify ordinary legislation or political acts, it is always open to the charge of subverting the will of the majority. Democracy and constitutionalism are necessarily in tension with one another. In the United States, this tension is often referred to as the "countermajoritarian difficulty." A related concern is the tension between pragmatism and principle. A constitutional review body is often confronted with the danger of making unpopular or unenforceable decisions, which might diminish the legitimacy or effectiveness of the body itself or of the government as a whole. It is thus often necessary to strike a balance between what the review body thinks it *ought* to do and what it thinks it actually *can* do. Finally, since constitutions are intended to specify the structure and powers of government, they tend to be quite general. If a constitution is too detailed, it runs the risk of becoming irrelevant as the society changes; if it is too general, its application will require extensive interpretation and lead to continuing controversy about its meaning.

Controversies about constitutional meaning are thus, to a greater or lesser extent, endemic and continuing, often prompted by disputes about particular constitutional interpretations or decisions but also reflecting deeper conflicts over meaning. Such controversies are part of the fabric of constitutional government and not necessarily unhealthy. But they place a strain on popular support for and the perceived legitimacy of both the constitution itself and its review mechanisms. In some cases, as in the United States, debates over constitutional interpretation form a major part of constitutional law scholarship and discourse.

Most of these debates focus on normative issues and competing modes of constitutional interpretation. The most common interpretive approaches are, from most restrictive to most open-ended: (1) *textualism,* which is the view that a constitution should be interpreted solely by considering the plain meaning of its text; (2) *originalism* or *legislative intent theories,* which argue that it is also legitimate to inquire about the intentions of the framers of a constitution; (3) *theories of general intent,* which hold that the meaning of an obscure passage should be interpreted in the light of the overall purposes and tenor of the constitution as a whole; (4) *theories of ideological coherence,* which contend that the meaning of the constitution should be interpreted in terms of the overall ideological commitments of its framers or so as to be as consistent as possible with the cultural traditions of the polity; and (5) "*living constitution*" *approaches,* which claim that, while respecting original intent (and in common law countries, the rule of precedent), courts have to interpret constitutions in light of historical developments and modern societal conditions to ensure the vitality of basic values and principles.

The practice of constitutional interpretation and the debates surrounding it vary significantly both among countries and within them. For example, while arguments from the overall tenor of the constitution are considered controversial in the United States, the German Constitutional Court has explicitly endorsed this approach as a valid method of interpretation and review. This difference reflects a fundamental variance in the roles of the constitutions in the two countries. Although both documents are intended as basic laws, the U.S. Constitution's "contractual" origin and its concern for individual rights leads to a general preference for restrictive interpretations, whereas the German Basic Law is intended to speak widely to fundamental legal and moral issues and thus encourages more expansive interpretations.

At the same time, there are significant divisions and debates within countries, especially in systems that permit multiple bodies to conduct constitutional review. For example, in the United States, Supreme Court decisions are often prompted by a need to harmonize conflicting constitutional interpretations emerging from lower federal courts. Overall, although debate and disagreement can signal problems within a polity, they are also a sign of a healthy constitutional culture, one in which the relationship of the fundamental law to day-to-day politics is continuously scrutinized and harmonized.

Although most constitutional law functions on a national level, there is also a growing international dimension. There are at least four examples of international or supranational constitutional law venues today, all established by treaty: the International Court of Justice, the Inter-American Court of Human Rights, the European Court of Justice, and the European Court of Human Rights. These metaconstitutional courts are empowered to find that actions or laws of members states are in violation of the relevant treaties or charters and to order remedies for violations. It remains to be seen how much influence they will have, not only on member nations but also on the role and form of constitutionalism in an increasingly globalized environment.

The idea and the practice of constitutional law have never before been as widespread as they are today. That development, however, poses a number of important challenges. How will constitutional law, which depends on a reservoir of goodwill and shared values, fare across national, cultural, and language boundaries? Is constitu-

tionalism an appropriate and sufficiently flexible model for governing increasingly heterogeneous but interdependent polities? The hope is that, at least for the foreseeable future, constitutionalism will continue to provide a structure and a set of common practices and procedures for maintaining and achieving stable and enlightened governance.

Joel B. Grossman
Matthew J. Moore

See also Civil Law; Common Law; Constitutional Review; Constitutionalism; European Court and Commission on Human Rights; European Court of Justice; International Court of Justice; Islamic Law; Judicial Review; Parliamentary Supremacy

References and further reading
Beatty, David. 1995. *Constitutional Law in Theory and Practice.* Toronto: University of Toronto Press.
Brewer-Carias, Allan R. 1989. *Judicial Review in Comparative Law.* Cambridge: Cambridge University Press.
Davidson, Scott. 1992. *The Inter-American Court of Human Rights.* Aldershot, England: Dartmouth.
Dinnage, James, and John Murphy. 1996. *The Constitutional Law of the European Union.* Cincinnati, OH: Anderson Publishing.
Finer, S. E., Vernon Bogdanor, and Bernard Rudden. 1995. *Comparing Constitutions.* Oxford: Oxford University Press.
Greenberg, Douglas, Stanley N. Katz, and Steven C. Wheatley, eds. 1993. *Constitutionalism and Democracy: Transitions in the Contemporary World.* New York: Oxford University Press.
Jackson, Vicki, and Mark Tushnet. 1999. *Comparative Constitutional Law.* New York: Foundation Press.
Lane, Jan-Erik. 1996. *Constitutions and Political Theory.* Manchester, England: Manchester University Press.
Stone Sweet, Alec. 2000. *Governing with Judges: Constitutional Politics in Europe.* Oxford: Oxford University Press.

CONSTITUTIONAL REVIEW

Constitutional review is the judicial power to impose constitutional limitations on government power. Although some early seventeenth-century English antecedents for that practice exist, constitutional review began as and is most commonly identified with judicial review in the United States. Shortly after the adoption in the late eighteenth century of written federal and state constitutions, federal and state courts began exercising the power to declare federal and state laws unconstitutional. Many democracies after World War II similarly ratified written constitutions and adopted some form of constitutional review. Courts are presently participating actively in the policymaking process and protecting constitutional rights throughout Europe and in Canada, the Middle East, and South Africa. The German and Hungarian constitutional courts are exercising constitutional review with particular vigor. The United Kingdom remains a rare democratic holdout, clinging to parliamentary supremacy and an unwritten constitutional order. Nevertheless, English law is subject to a form of constitutional review. The United Kingdom is a member of the European Union, and the European Court of Justice holds the treaties that formed and maintain the European Union to be superior to national law.

In many countries, constitutional review does not take the form of judicial review as practiced in the United States. Courts in the United States declare laws unconstitutional in the course of ordinary litigation, a practice described as concrete review. Other countries empower only a limited number of courts to declare laws unconstitutional, and constitutional review typically takes place outside the contours of ordinary litigation. Abstract review occurs in many European countries, when elected officials refer legislative proposals to the judiciary before those measures become the law of the land. Judicial review in the United Kingdom also differs from that in the United States. Unlike the form of constitutional review practiced across the Atlantic, judicial review in England concerns only judicial power to correct administrative rule making. English courts may not declare parliamentary legislation unconstitutional.

THE AMERICAN EXPERIENCE

Marbury v. Madison (1803) is generally regarded as the ruling that established judicial review in the United States. In that case, Chief Justice John Marshall declared unconstitutional a provision of the Judiciary Act of 1789 on the grounds that the jurisdictional rules set out in Article III, Section 2 of the U.S. Constitution forbade Congress from giving the Supreme Court original jurisdiction in matters where the Constitution assigned the Supreme Court appellate jurisdiction. This holding was accompanied by a long analysis of the judicial power to declare laws unconstitutional. Marshall placed particular emphasis on the nature of written constitutions and the traditional power of justices to say what the law is regarding constitutional review in the United States. *Marbury* established the power of judicial review in a legal sense. Marshall's claim that the constitution authorized judicial review was central to his decision. Significantly, however, Marshall declared an innocuous statutory provision unconstitutional in order to avoid handing down a ruling ordering the Jefferson administration to deliver a judicial commission to a Federalist appointed by President John Adams during his last days in office. That judicial order probably would have been disobeyed, demonstrating that in a political sense the Marshall Court did not have the power to impose its constitutional and legal understandings on hostile legal officials. Early exercises of constitutional review in U.S. states and many countries followed a similar pattern. Courts declared unconstitutional fairly obscure provisions, often dealing with jurisdictional issues of little interest to the general public, rather than first exercising the power of constitutional review to play a major role in a hotly partisan constitutional controversy.

Judicial review in the United States as that practice has evolved serves several political functions. First, judicial review provides a means for enforcing national constitutional values in outlying localities. Many decisions handed down by the Warren Court (1954–1968) required Southern or Catholic localities to respect the dominant constitutional understandings of the Northern elite that dominated the national government during the 1950s and 1960s. That Court's controversial decision in *Griswold v. Connecticut* (1965) declaring bans on birth control unconstitutional, from this perspective simply required two states to treat married couples the way those couples were being treated in the other forty-eight states. Second, judicial review in the United States has provided a means for elected officials to invite judicial officials to resolve hot political issues that crosscut existing partisan alignments. The Supreme Court made several controversial decisions before the Civil War protecting the rights of slaveholders only after being asked to do so by the leaders of both major political coalitions of the time. Since 1973, pro-choice forces in the United States have had the political power necessary to keep most responsibility for abortion policy in the federal courts. When courts impose national values on outlying localities or take responsibility for controversies elected officials would rather not resolve, the justices act as an agent of the dominant national coalitions. According to much conventional theory, the primary purpose of judicial review is to check elected officials, prevent the dominant national coalition from usurping power, and protect the rights of politically powerless minorities. In practice, however, justices almost always share values that resonant somewhere in the dominant national coalition. With the exception of numerous cases decided during the early New Deal and a few others, most judicial decisions articulate the constitutional values of at least some members of the dominant national coalition and do not seek to challenge consensual constitutional understandings among nonjudicial elites. Preliminary evidence from other countries suggests that judicial review is in general more likely to serve regime maintenance than countermajoritarian functions.

Judicial review is a distinctive form of constitutional review. All courts in the United States may declare any state or federal law unconstitutional in the course of ordinary litigation, but only in the course of ordinary litigation. The Supreme Court does not formally respond to official requests to determine the constitutionality of proposed government actions, although many justices informally advise legislators and executive branch officials. Only those persons who have suffered a legal injury may challenge the constitutionality of a federal or state law in court. No person or official may ask a court to declare a law unconstitutional simply because the law might be unconstitutional. Persons who claim legal injury may challenge the constitutionality of government action in any court with the jurisdiction to hear their claim. Constitutional attacks on federal policies may be made in the lowest criminal court in the country as well as in the Supreme Court. Indeed, the Supreme Court will rarely hear a constitutional case unless the party claiming legal injury made the constitutional claim in every previous appeal. With particular respect to prisoners making habeas corpus attacks on the death sentence, their constitutional claim will almost always have to be raised and decided by virtually every kind of court that exists in the United States before being adjudicated by the U.S. Supreme Court.

CONSTITUTIONAL REVIEW OUTSIDE THE UNITED STATES

A global explosion in constitutional review has occurred since 1950. During the nineteenth century, judicial review was the only form of constitutional review and the United States the only country whose judges frequently imposed constitutional limitations on elected officials. In the wake of World War II, many countries in Europe and elsewhere began ratifying written constitutions and moving toward some system of constitutional review. At present, England is the only country in western Europe that does not have some form of constitutional review. Japan, Singapore, India, and other Asian nations are experimenting with forms of constitutional review, and the practice is being urged on China as a condition of trade liberalization. The Canadian courts are exercising review powers, as are courts in Israel, South Africa, and several other African nations.

Constitutional review is flourishing for various reasons. Major political parties are weakening throughout the world. Weak political parties foster judicial review because such political coalitions are often incapable of resolving heated political controversies in electoral forums. Increases in the politics of rights are facilitating judicial power by fostering the impression that fundamental questions concern matters of individual rights best resolved by judicial officials rather than questions of public policy traditionally resolved by legislators. In many countries, constitutional review has become a means by which established elites both cede and maintain power. Elites in South Africa and Israel, Ran Hirschl (2000) notes, were able to accommodate insurgent forces by developing a judicially enforceable constitution. That constitution was then enforced by judicial elites whose values were far more similar to the established elites than to those insurgents whose political strength in the legislative branches of the national government was increasing.

Constitutional review as practiced in most countries differs from judicial review in the United States in numerous ways. Some countries, most notably Canada, constitutionally permit the national legislature to override judicial decisions declaring laws unconstitutional. In the United States and most other countries, judicial decisions can be changed only by judicial decision or constitutional amendment. In some countries, the written constitution declares specific features of the constitution unamendable. On the basis of such provisions in the basic law, constitutional courts in Germany have declared certain constitutional amendments unconstitutional. Many countries vest constitutional authority only in a specific constitutional court. Ordinary courts are not officially expected to make constitutional decisions in the course of ordinary litigation in most western European nations. When constitutional issues arise, they are noted. An appeal is then taken to a special court with jurisdiction to hear constitutional issues. The Supreme Court of France and the Constitutional Court of France, for example, are different institutions with different agendas.

In practice, however, the distinction between constitutional and other courts may be breaking down. Many constitutional courts make constitutional decisions that arise outside the course of normal litigation. Some are not concerned with ordinary litigation at all. Authoritative advisory rulings on the constitutionality of proposed legislation, called abstract review, is the most common form of constitutional review in western Europe. German law requires constitutional courts to resolve constitutional disputes whenever they are asked to do so by various elected officials. This practice enables political minorities in the legislature and sometimes in smaller jurisdictions to challenge proposed measures before they become law. Few countries adopt the U.S. practice of giving justices on the highest constitutional court life tenure. Justices in Italy sit for twelve-year terms and cannot be reappointed. Justices are similarly term-limited in the rest of Europe and most of the world.

Constitutional courts outside the United States frequently give more detailed constitutional instructions to elected officials than the U.S. judiciary. Justices in the United States often simply void laws, leaving a good deal of discretion to legislatures as to subsequent action. Abstract review in Europe seems to promote more proactive policymaking. The French and Italian constitutional courts often issue specific directives to legislatures as to how some subject matter must be regulated. These different practices when declaring laws unconstitutional may also be partly rooted in the difference between U.S. and continental notions of constitutional rights. Constitutional rights in the United States are generally conceived as almost exclusively negative. Government may not take certain actions that violate rights, but government inaction never violates rights. Constitutions in other countries set out certain positive obligations deemed necessary for protecting rights. Hence, constitutional review in those jurisdictions cannot simply specify what elected officials cannot do; it must also specify what they must do.

The European Court of Justice is presently practicing a supranational form of constitutional review. The justices on that tribunal have declared that the principles established in the treaties creating, revising, and expanding the European Union are higher law than or at least supercede the laws of those countries in the European Union. On matters as diverse as the advertisement of abortion clinics and the movement of soccer players in Europe, the European Court of Justice has declared national laws void in the name of the greater union. Efforts to confine that supraconstitutional review to economic cases failed. As in the case involving national control of star soccer players, the European Court of Justice invariably finds an economic dimension to the issues before the justices. This supranational tribunal also insists that national courts declare national laws unconstitutional that conflict with the rules set down by higher European authorities. This demand further promotes constitutional review within European countries.

CONTROVERSY AND PROBABLE EVOLUTION

Constitutional review is highly controversial. U.S. commentators tend to debate how such review should be done, although a number of commentators have recently challenged the very existence of the practice. Some commentators in Europe continue bemoaning the gradual abolition of legislative supremacy. Still, the sociological and political forces that foster written constitutions and constitutional review remain strong. Given the numerous regime functions courts play in most democratic societies, the immediate future is likely to witness more, rather than less, judicial efforts to impose constitutional limits on government.

Mark A. Graber

See also Appellate Courts; Constitutional Law; Constitutionalism; European Court of Justice; Judicial Review; Parliamentary Supremacy

References and further reading
Griswold v. Connecticut. 1965.
Hirschl, Ran. 2000. "The Political Origins of Judicial Empowerment through Constitutionalization: Lessons from Four Constitutional Revolutions." *Law and Social Inquiry* 25: 91–149.
Kommers, Donald P. 1989. *The Constitutional Jurisprudence of the Federal Republic of Germany.* Durham, NC: Duke University Press.
Kommers, Donald P., and John E. Finn. 1998. *American Constitutional Law: Essays, Cases, and Comparative Notes.* Belmont, CA: West/Wadsworth.
Marbury v. Madison. 1803.
Silverstein, Gordon. 1998. "Democracy and the Law: Can Judicial Institutions Pave the Way to Democratic Legitimacy?" Paper presented to the 1998 Annual Meeting of the American Political Science Association, Boston, Massachusetts.
Stone, Alec Sweet. 2000. *Governing with Judges: Constitutional Politics in Europe.* New York: Oxford University Press.
Tate, C. Neal, and Torbjorn Vallinder, eds. 1995. *The Global Expansion of Judicial Power.* New York: New York University Press.

CONSTITUTIONALISM

"Constitutionalism" is the principle that a legal system is based on and legitimated by a system of legal or lawlike principles that stand outside the lawmaking system itself. In a constitutionalist system, there are two distinct kinds of "law"—the law created by and administered through a set of political institutions and a system of higher legal principles that define the process and limits of legitimate lawmaking. This latter metalaw is "constitutional," whether it is contained in a single written document (as in the U.S., Russian, and Indian models) or not (as in the British model).

The idea of a constitution has two distinct elements. First, constitutionalist principles describe the arrangement of political institutions within the system. This kind of constitution goes back at least as far as the constitutions of Athens described by Aristotle. The second sense of constitutionalism is the idea of a system of supreme law that defines fundamental rights, prerogatives that are not subject to the processes of legislation and adjudication. Some of the first examples appeared in the seventeenth century among English dissenters, in documents such as the Massachusetts Body of Liberties of 1641. In effect, these rights are statements of the point of supremacy of law over politics, the limits to the permissible scope of the democratic process.

The U.S. Constitution is probably the best-known and may also be the clearest example of a certain model of constitutionalism in practice. There is a single, written text, subject to amendment by specified procedures. The text defines the structures of the national government, its powers, the outlines of the political process, and the relationship between that government and other levels of governance. There are also statements of fundamental rights, particularly in the first ten amendments, known as the Bill of Rights.

Two things are noticeably missing from the text of the U.S. Constitution. First, there is nothing in the text that tells a reader who is to have the authority to determine the meaning of the text in cases of disagreement. Second, there is nothing that clearly indicates the source of the authority for the creation of the constitution in the first place. The Preamble states that the constitution is formed by "the people of the United States," who "ordain and establish this Constitution for the United States of America." This language points to the obvious fact that both the nation and the people of the United States were in existence prior to the constitution. This makes the problem of authoritative interpretation acute; anyone who can claim to speak for "the people" can, in principle, claim authority to interpret the constitution, and any document or source that illustrates the will of "the people" may be taken to be inform its reading. Finally, what is also missing from the constitution is anything more than the barest statement of its overall purpose, of the principles that it is intended to articulate and that are to be served by the remainder of the text. "To form a more perfect union" and "to secure the blessings of liberty" are pretty much the entirety of the U.S. Constitution's statement on that score. This brevity, too, returns to the problem of authoritative interpretation, since the authority to interpret the text will imply the authority to define those guiding purposes.

Although an observer would hardly want to argue that these issues have been resolved, the manner in which they are to be determined was made clear in a remarkable piece of judicial bootstrapping. Supreme Court Chief Justice John Marshall, in an 1803 decision, *Marbury v. Madison,* declared that the Constitution is a legal document and that "it is emphatically the province of the Court to say what the law is." The implications of that statement were taken to their logical extreme by Justice Charles Evan Hughes in 1907: "We are under a Constitution, but the Constitution is what the Judges say it is." These words point to what is perhaps the most fundamental characterizing aspect of the U.S. Constitution: judicial supremacy. The U.S. Constitution is conceived of as a species of law and hence is subject to authoritative interpretation by the courts. The reason this concept is referred to as "judicial supremacy," as opposed to merely a statement of the principle of "judicial review," is that in the United States, an authoritative interpretation of a constitutional question by a court takes precedence over any contrary interpretation made in any other branch of the government.

The idea of a court taking upon itself to declare its own supremacy as an agent of constitutional interpretation did not end in the nineteenth century. An even more remarkable example comes from Israel in the past decade. At the time of the state's founding in 1948, Israel did not adopt a constitution. Over the ensuing forty-four years, however, the Israeli Parliament passed a number of "basic laws," culminating in 1992 with the enactment of the Basic Law of Freedom of Occupation (the term *occupation* refers to profession, not land) and the Basic Law of

Human Dignity and Liberty. Together, these two enactments come close to describing a bill of rights, a set of property and personal rights that are taken to define the limit of the reach of the democratic political process. In 1995, the Israeli Supreme Court declared that the two basic laws of 1992 defined a constitutional order and, moreover, found that Israel had implicitly adopted the principle of judicial review. In 1977, in the first ruling of its kind, the high court struck down a law governing the occupational qualifications of stockbrokers as violative of the fundamental rights found in the Basic Law of Freedom of Occupation.

The Indian Supreme Court similarly transformed itself by assuming substantive powers of constitutional review without formal changes in its political mandate. In 1975 it invalidated the election of Indira Gandhi. She responded by issuing a decree declaring a "civil emergency"; among other things, this removed national legislation from review by the court. In 1994, the Indian Supreme Court reasserted its authority when it overruled an exercise of executive authority called "president's rule" whereby the executive took over governance of one of the states. In the process, the high court declared that it had the authority to interpret the constitution. This decision may, in time, be looked upon as India's version of *Marbury v. Madison.* In fact, India may be tending further in that direction even than the United States. India's Supreme Court has invalidated amendments to its constitution and struck down social and environmental laws on the grounds that they are contrary to the public interest. This form of judicial review represents a level of constitutional supremacy that is rarely seen in U.S. jurisprudence. The U.S. Supreme Court, in fact, has generated self-imposed "prudential" restraints that require U.S. courts to refrain from issuing constitutional rulings on "political questions" and to show deference to other branches of government in specific areas such as foreign policy.

As the Israeli case demonstrates, a constitution need not be a written document. It is also the case that not all constitutional systems include judicial review, let alone judicial supremacy. Great Britain is an example of a constitutional system that has neither. Among the official volumes of British statutes in force, published by Her Majesty's Stationery Office, there are two volumes of "constitutional law," containing the texts of 138 acts of Parliament from 1297 to 1993. A separate volume on "rights of the subject" gives another 32 acts. These acts constitute the British Constitution, with the obvious result that what is or is not an element of that constitutional system is a matter of opinion and dispute. There are certain acts, to be sure, that are clearly fundamental to the organization of the state: the 1707 Acts of Union that created Great Britain out of England and Scotland, the 1800 Act of Unification with Ireland, and the Ireland Act of

1949 that finally declared the independence of the Republic of Ireland. Beyond those, however, the "text" is open to interpretation. The authority to engage in that interpretation, in turn, is vested not with the courts but with Parliament, comprising the Crown, the House of Commons, and the House of Lords. The result is that even the structural elements of the British Constitution are subject to considerable variation by the political process. For example, the Parliament Acts of 1911 and 1949 provide that a bill passed by the House of Commons and signed by the Crown can become law without action by the House of Lords. On questions of rights, moreover, the status of constitutional provisions has become even more complex since Britain's entry into the European Community (EC) in 1973. The pattern of constitutional development in the EC warrants particular mention.

In contrast to Great Britain, the post–World War II experience of most of the nations that make up the EC can be described in terms of a transition from a model of legislative supremacy, in which constitutional provisions and courts played little role in limiting the actions of governments, to one characterized by the idea of constitutions as the necessary source of state legitimacy and limit of state authority, with an emphasis on human rights and the guarantee of democratic elections. (Stone Sweet 2000, 37.) The fundamental force behind this "new constitutionalism" (31) has been a concern for the protection of fundamental rights, and the mechanism for the articulation of that concern has been judicial review. The dominant European model of judicial review, however, is different from the U.S. model. Specialized constitutional courts, separate from the ordinary judiciary, have been established and have been given powers to engage in the abstract review of legislation. Conversely, the jurisdiction of those courts has generally not included the adjudication of individual disputes. This model draws heavily on the writings of Austrian constitutional theorist Hans Kelsen, who distinguished between the "positive" legal role of the legislature and the "negative" role of a reviewing court. This model also reflects concerns by both left- and right-wing political parties that U.S.-style judicial review would unduly interfere with legislative autonomy. Initially, then, these specialized courts were conceived of as serving a limiting function over the exercise of government power but not as possessing the authority to interfere directly with the formulation of policies.

As in India and Israel, however, over time European constitutional courts have taken upon themselves the power of substantive invalidation of laws. One notable case occurred in France in 1982, when the major provisions of the Socialist government's plan to collectivize important sectors of the economy were ruled unconstitutional, based on an application of principles derived from the 1789 Declaration of the Rights of Man, the 1958

Constitution, and the statement of social and economic principles found in the preamble to the 1946 Constitution. Combining these texts into a source of motivating constitutional norms was entirely the work of the court (Stone Sweet 2000, 66–68).

The development of constitutional courts in individual European nations has taken place against the backdrop of the increasing constitutional importance of the 1957 Treaty of Rome that established the EC, of subsequent treaties (notably the 1992 Maastricht Treaty), and of the European Court of Justice (ECJ), "the most powerful and influential supranational court in world history" (Stone Sweet 2000, 153). Beginning in earnest in the 1970s, the ECJ has engaged in a process of fashioning a judicially enforceable supranational constitution out of international treaty law originally designed primarily for economic integration. In the words of a former justice of the ECJ, this process has turned the Treaty of Rome into "an open-ended charter of human rights" (Mancini 2000, 52.) The various EC treaties have established the principle that treaty law is superior to national law and directly applicable to national affairs, a principle that has been given substance by virtue of the fact that national court justices have been willing to enforce these principles in their own rulings and that national governments have been willing to accept the combined authority of international and national judiciaries (Mancini 2000, 17–29, 243–257). There remain unresolved tensions, however. In 1993, the German Federation Constitutional Court ruled that the Maastricht Treaty of 1992 did not violate the German Constitution. In doing so, however, the German Court announced the principle that actions taken by EC authorities could be found to be invalid if they directly conflicted with the German constitutional guarantees of direct elections (Article 38) or violated the fundamental sovereignty of the German state in the process of European economic integration (Stone Sweet 2000, 176–177; Mancini 2000, 55–56). As of this writing, these issues are still in flux in European courts and parliaments and in the halls of the European Court of Justice. To return to our first case, British courts have indicated that they recognize the supremacy of EC law over British law, but it remains unclear what the result would be if the British Parliament were to enact a law that clearly and specifically violated EC law as interpreted by the ECJ.

All the constitutions discussed so far share a common heritage in the Western legal tradition, and all, despite their variations, display a conception of constitutionalism as a system of law superior to that of ordinary legislation that stands close to the heart of the legitimating claims of the system of government. There are other models, however. In what Vicki Jackson and Mark Tushnet call "constitutions without constitutionalism" (1999), both the permanence and the supremacy of the constitutional order seem to be missing. In the old Soviet Union, the constitution was considered a mandate for the government to engage in projects of social, economic, and political improvement. As a result, one of the premises of the Soviet Constitution was that it would be temporary, and indeed, the Soviet Union replaced its constitution approximately every twenty years. The same is true of the Constitution of the People's Republic of China (PRC). The current (there have been five) constitution, for example, guarantees freedoms of speech, press, and assembly, but Article 51 of that constitution also states that "the exercise by citizens . . . of their freedoms and rights may not infringe upon the interest of the state, of society and the collective, or upon the lawful freedoms and rights of other citizens." In these communist models, a citizen's "right" is the freedom to act in the service of the community, not to restrict the actions of the political process.

It should be noted that although few Western constitutional systems go so far as the Soviet Union or PRC in subordinating claims of individual rights to social goods, such a theme appears in a variety of guises. Article 34 of the Irish Constitution establishes judicial review, but Article 28(3) excludes any law "which is expressed to be for the purpose of securing the public safety and the preservation of the State in time of war or armed rebellion" from being so tested. Article 33 of Canada's Constitution Act of 1982 declares a bill of rights and provides for judicial review but states that the federal or provincial government can make a law that "shall operate notwithstanding a provision" protecting a fundamental right. The government of Quebec used this authority in 1988 to restrict the rights of English speakers to display signs in English. At the other extreme, perhaps, one might situate the High Court of Australia, which in 1992 invalidated laws restricting campaign financing despite the fact that the Australian Constitution makes no mention of a right to free expression.

It has not always been the case that the Western model has survived export without strain. Numerous African nations, upon achieving liberation from colonial rule, adopted constitutions modeled on Western exemplars, a process that repeated itself in eastern Europe in the 1990s. In the 1970s, a number of these constitutions were replaced. The complaint was that they were artificial, importations of alien normative systems that did not jibe with local practices and understandings. In 1973, the king of Swaziland abolished the constitution that had been adopted at independence, declaring it to contain "undesirable political practices alien to and incompatible with the [African] . . . way of life," and similar arguments were raised in Lesotho, Tanzania, Zambia, Zimbabwe, Kenya, and the Central African Republic.

The same concern with authenticity that appeared in postcolonial Africa has become evident in the new democracies of eastern Europe. The preamble of the Constitution of the Russian Federation combines the clear inspiration of the U.S. text with uniquely Russian elements, speaking of "a common destiny on our land," the "historic unity of the state," "honoring the memory of our ancestors, who have passed on to us love of and respect for our homeland," and "reviving the sovereign statehood of Russia." This idea of constitutionalism as the principle that law must be autochthonous is in sharp contrast to the Anglo-American tradition of constitutionalism conceived as an arrangement superceding previous claims of authority. Nonetheless, like the constitutions of the United States, Germany, or India, these constitutions define the fundamental legitimating norms for any subsequent legal act.

Howard Schweber

See also Constitutional Law; Constitutional Review; Federalism; India; Israel; Judicial Review; Parliamentary Supremacy; Russia; United States—Federal System

References and further reading
Cappalletti, Mauro. 1989. *The Judicial Process in Comparative Perspective.* Oxford: Oxford University Press.
Finer, S. E., Vernon Bogdanor, and Bernard Rudden, eds. 1995. *Comparing Constitutions* Oxford: Oxford University Press.
Greenberg, Douglas, Stanley M. Katz, Melanie Beth Oliver, and Steven C. Wheatley, eds. 1993. *Constitutionalism and Democracy: Transitions in the Contemporary World.* Oxford: Oxford University Press.
Jackson, Vicki C., and Mark Tushnet. 1999. *Comparative Constitutional Law.* New York: Foundation Press.
Kelsen, Hans. 1942. "Judicial Review of Legislation: A Comparative Study of the Austrian and the American Constitution." *The Journal of Politics* 4: 183–200.
Mancini, G. F. 2000. *Democracy and Constitutionalism in the European Union.* Portland, OR: Hart Publishing.
Marbury v. Madison. 1803.
O'Brien, David M., ed. 1995. *Constitutional Law and Politics.* 2nd ed. 2 vols. New York: Norton.
Slaughter, A. M., J. H. H. Weiler, and A. Stone Sweet, eds. 1998. *The European Courts and National Courts: Doctrine and Jurisprudence.* Portland, OR: Hart Publishing.
Stone Sweet, Alec. 2000. *Governing with Judges: Constitutional Politics in Europe.* Oxford: Oxford University Press.

CONSUMER LAW

INTRODUCTION AND DEFINITION

Consumer law is a relatively recent phenomenon in most legal systems. Elements of consumer law have roots in better-established legal doctrines such as personal injury, product liability, invasion of privacy, and unconscionability. But the collection of laws specifically and explicitly devoted to the protection of consumers has existed for only a few decades in most developed nations, and generally for less time in many developing countries.

In most legal systems, consumer law can be thought of as an array of legislative and administrative measures designed to level the playing field between consumers and the entities that manufacture, market, and sell the goods and services that consumers purchase and use. Consumer law can also be viewed as a check on unfettered freedom of contract, because it recognizes that in many situations, particularly in modern industrialized economies,- the seller is in a far more advantageous position than the buyer. Moreover, consumer law often requires the flow of information from merchant to customer, under the theory that consumers have the right to make informed choices based on quality, safety, and price. In this way, consumer law reflects the global shift from "let the buyer beware" to "let the seller disclose."

The most common forms of consumer protection laws across legal systems are those that promote product safety and quality, prohibit misleading advertising and other misrepresentations by merchants, require certain disclosures, bar unfair trade practices, and improve access to justice for private citizens. In addition, in some developed countries, such as the United States, many consumer laws provide for the awarding of attorneys' fees to successful plaintiffs, thereby making it more likely that those laws will be used by consumers.

APPLICABILITY

The idea of consumer law is generally recognized in virtually all modern legal systems. In common law countries, consumer law is typically a combination of common law doctrines (such as fraud and misrepresentation), statutes enacted by the legislature, and judicial decisions interpreting those laws. In civil law systems, it is not uncommon to find a code containing consumer protection provisions. However, the specifics of what constitutes "consumer law" and the extent to which those laws are enforced by public entities and private parties varie greatly from country to country. Thus, while consumer rights are generally taken for granted and enforced in developed countries, those rights are frequently ignored or overshadowed by more pressing concerns in less developed countries. For example, in many developing countries so much attention and energy is devoted to the provision of basic human needs such as food, shelter, and health care that traditional consumer protection priorities fade into the background. In this way, consumer law, unlike more firmly established legal concepts, is something of a luxury reserved for more economically stable nations.

VARIATIONS

The discussion above suggests that the key variable relevant to consumer law across legal systems is the socioeconomic status of the country. Thus, consumer law in most developed countries focuses on ensuring the quality and safety of goods and services and on providing information to consumers about those goods and services. In less developed countries, consumer law has more to do with providing consumers access to basic goods and services. In this sense, consumer law in developing nations is more akin to basic economic justice than it is to information about products and services. Moreover, consumer protection law is far more specialized in developed countries. For example, consumer laws in the United States and western Europe are frequently dedicated to a single industry, marketing practice, or product, such as travel packages, health clubs, timeshare contracts, consumer credit, and contracts negotiated away from the merchant's place of business.

Other variations relevant to consumer law in different legal systems include:

- *The wealth of the consumer.* Wealthier consumers, regardless of the country in which they reside, are better able to take advantage of whatever consumer laws exist. They are more likely to be aware of their rights and the means by which they can assert them. They can afford to hire private attorneys or influence the public officials who enforce the laws. Indeed, it is frequently those consumers with the financial wherewithal to endure protracted legal or legislative battles who are responsible for key legal interpretations of consumer laws. In a related vein, the consumer laws with the strongest and most specific remedies are frequently those which benefit the wealthiest consumers. Thus, in the United States, lemon laws—which provide refunds or replacements, plus attorneys fees, for consumers who purchase poorly manufactured cars—are among the most effective consumer protection statutes. Conversely, there are few laws designed to protect lower-income consumers against the kinds of products or marketing practices directed primarily toward them, such as loans offered at exorbitant interest rates.

- *The extent of resources devoted to consumer protection.* This variable is related to the wealth of the country, but is also influenced by the ideology and philosophy of those who lead it. Legislators and executives who view consumer protection as vital to any civil society are more likely to direct significant resources to the enactment and enforcement of consumer laws. Those who view such laws as bothersome or unpatriotic impediments to capital accumulation and a corporatist economy are likely to reduce support for enforcement. Another important factor relevant to this variation is the extent to which violations of consumer laws are punishable as criminal offenses. Criminal penalties are likely to have a stronger deterrent effect than civil remedies, such as money damages.

- *Adequacy of administrative and legal mechanisms.* The inefficiency of the legal systems in many developing countries impedes the effectiveness of consume laws. Merchants in such systems can prevail simply by waiting out their consumer opponent, regardless of the merits of her claim. Procedural devices for enacting and enforcing consumer laws also differ from country to country. Thus, consumer laws tend to be more effective in systems that permit class actions and attorney's fees for successful plaintiffs. Under such systems, consumers have greater access to court and can thus become private attorneys general, enforcing laws that in other countries are the exclusive domain of public employees. The problem with the latter model is that public enforcement is frequently influenced by political consideration and resource limitations (and, frequently, the interplay between the two.

- *Corruption and cooptation.* Many legal systems throughout the world suffer from corruption, both open and covert. Indeed, citizens in some parts of the world regard their national judiciary as another form of repression rather than as a source of redress of grievances or protection of individual rights and liberties. The greater the corruption within the system, the less likely it is to enforce whatever consumer protection laws exist, since those in greatest need of consumer protection are the least likely to offer the kinds of incentives (financial and otherwise) that corrupt the judicial system. In a similar vein, the more that the administrative agencies charged with policing merchants and industries have been coopted by those very industries and merchants, the less likely they are to enforce the law.

EVOLUTION AND CHANGE

Perhaps because of its relative youth, as well as its relationship to ever-changing market forces, consumer law is one of the most dynamic concepts in modern legal systems.

Without question, the most significant development in consumer law since the 1980s is the internationalization of consumer protection. Individual countries and their legal systems are catching up with global capitalism, by which multinational corporations have come to employ production standards and marketing techniques on a global scale. Not coincidentally, the same kind of consumer frauds and scams once limited to a few of the more developed economies is now being experienced in the global arena. As free markets have multiplied after the fall of communism in eastern Europe and the demise of authoritarian regimes in Latin America and elsewhere, the need to protect consumers from accompanying commercial abuses has followed.

The globalization of consumer protection has taken many forms. One of the most obvious is the adoption by individual countries of international agreements. Most notable among these is the United Nations Guidelines for Consumer Protection, passed by the General Assembly in 1985 and adopted in various forms by numerous individual countries in the ensuing years. This was an important development because it marked the first time that many countries enacted a comprehensive series of consumer protection laws, as opposed to a patchwork of statutes aimed at specific problems such as price control, weights and measures, and food and drug regulation.

Another sign of the globalization of consumer law is the way in which many countries have consciously harmonized their consumer protection laws with neighboring states. This is perhaps most evident in Europe, where the European Union has entered into a series of agreements with the Baltic states, Slovenia, and Russia. In this way, consumer protection has cut across the borders of nations and legal systems, in some sense mirroring the way free trade has made national borders less relevant. This process is facilitated by the growing number of regional and global conferences on commercial and consumer law.

Of course, globalization has sometimes meant the erosion, rather than the strengthening, of consumer protection laws. Some newly developing countries (including those emerging from periods of political or military repression), eager to attract foreign investment, have discouraged and in some cases eliminated consumer and environmental protections. This is particularly true because some corporations based in countries with strong consumer and environmental regulations seek markets in countries that deemphasize such protections. In a similar vein, consumer protection has been slow to emerge in some eastern European countries where *any* government regulation is viewed as an unwanted vestige of the prior Communist regime.

Other developments in the area of consumer protection include:

- *Mandatory arbitration clauses in consumer contracts.* As large corporations, often doing business on a global scale, seek to reduce the costs associated with litigation, many (particularly banks and insurance companies) have made mandatory arbitration clauses part of their standard contracts. Under these clauses, if a consumer has a dispute with a business, she must seek redress through some form of alternative dispute resolution rather than the court system. The arbitration may be an internal grievance process or review by an outside mediator. In any event, such clauses raise significant concerns about access to the legal system and meaningful remedies, particularly because most consumers who utilize arbitration programs do so without the assistance of attorneys. Of course, in countries with weak, inefficient, or corrupt legal systems, bypassing litigation may not be much of an impediment to adequate relief.

- *Greater access to justice for more consumers.* It is one thing to pass a panoply of consumer laws; it is another to allow sufficient numbers of consumers to use those laws, thereby making them meaningful. An increasing number of countries are improving access to justice for consumers in a number of ways. One of these is the class action (or some derivation thereof), which permits large numbers of consumers to join together in a single lawsuit rather than having to file separate cases. Class actions are particularly helpful to consumers whose monetary loss is relatively modest and who therefore are unlikely to be able to retain legal counsel on their own. Class actions are also useful means to curb illegal conduct directed at large numbers of persons because they are less likely to be settled quickly. As such, class actions often result in injunctive relief that prevents a continuation of the unlawful activity, as well as monetary damages for injured consumers.

- *Statutory changes to fee-shifting rules* are another important development in increasing access to justice for consumers in the United States. Under these laws, if a consumer prevails in a lawsuit against a merchant, the merchant must pay the consumer's attorney's fees and costs, as well as her monetary damages. (In most countries a general loser-pays rule has long existed for civil litigation, including consumer cases.) Fee-shifting provisions make it more likely that aggrieved consumers can find attorneys willing to represent them in court, especially when the amount of monetary loss is relatively modest. (If the case is worth more money, it is more likely that the consumer will be able to find an attorney to represent her on a contingency fee basis.) Without such fee-shifting provisions, the consumer would frequently pay more to her attorney than she could ever hope to recover in the lawsuit. This economic fact makes it difficult for many consumers, particularly those of modest income, to hire an attorney regardless of the merits of their case.

The concept of consumer law has grown in scope, acceptance, and importance within most legal systems in recent years. Its increased prominence reflects the growth of global capitalism, as well as a recognition of the need to protect consumers from some of its excesses.

Stephen E. Meili

See also Administrative Law; Administrative Tribunals; Cause Lawyering; Civil Law; Commercial Law (International Aspects); Common Law; Public Law

References and further reading
Consumer Protection for Asia and the Pacific: Report of the International Conference on Consumer Protection: Consumers in the Global Age; New Delhi, 22–24 January 1997. 1998. New York, United Nations.
Cranston, Ross, and Roy Goode, eds. 1993. *Commercial and Consumer Law: National and International Dimensions.* Oxford, Clarendon Press.
Jaffe, David B., and Robert G. Vaughn. 1996. *South American Consumer Protection Laws.* Boston, Kluwer Law International.
King, Donald B., ed. 1986. *Commercial and Consumer Law from an International Perspective.* Littleton, CO: Fred B. Rothman.
Ramsay, Iain, ed. 1997. *Consumer Law in the Global Economy: National and International Dimensions.* Brookfield, VT: Ashgate Publishing.
Ziegel, Jacob S. ed. 1998. *New Developments in International Commercial and Consumer Law.* Oxford, Hart Publishing.

CONTRACT LAW

DEFINITION AND APPLICABILITY

Contract law governs promissory relations between individuals and institutions. It defines the content and enforceability of all agreements, including complicated, long-term arrangements between businesses and promises made by an individual to a family member or friend, as well as everything in between.

No legal system in history has enforced all promises. Yet dating back to the Roman Empire and the principle of *pacta sunt servanda* ("agreements are to be kept"), society has treated at least some promises as binding. Modern contract law has distinguished between enforceable and unenforceable promises on the basis of the process by which the parties reached an agreement and the reason each entered into the agreement.

Offer and Acceptance

Contract law generally requires that enforceable promises take the form of an offer by one party that is accepted without modification by the other party. The offer and acceptance operate as an objective manifestation of assent by both parties to be bound to an agreement. For example, if John offers to sell his car to Maria for $5,000 cash at the end of the month and Maria says she'll take it, then the parties have a contract. If, however, Maria proposes that John sell the car to her for less money or deliver the car immediately or accept monthly payments, then there is no contract. Maria has now made a counteroffer that John can accept only by agreeing to Maria's new terms.

As reflected in this example, the offeror is the "master of the offer" because he or she dictates the terms of any agreement and the proper manner and form of acceptance. The offeree accepts the offer by responding voluntarily in the manner requested by the offeror *before* the offer has been destroyed and with the apparent intent to create a contract. An offer is destroyed by direct or indirect revocation, lapse of time, death of the offeror or offeree, or rejection or counteroffer by the offeree. If the offeror seeks a return promise as acceptance, then the offeree's return promise must mirror the offer in order to be an acceptance rather than a counteroffer (the mirror-image rule). If, instead, the offeror seeks performance as acceptance, the offeree accepts by fully performing what is requested in the offer.

Consideration

Once accepted, the offer becomes a contract if the agreement is supported by consideration. The bargain theory of consideration stipulates that "[t]o constitute consideration, a performance or a return promise must be bargained for. A performance or return promise is bargained for if it is sought by the promisor in exchange for his promise and is given by the promisee in exchange for that promise" (Restatement [2d] Contracts, §71). The great American jurist and scholar Oliver Wendell Holmes, Jr., described bargain consideration as "reciprocal conventional inducement" (Holmes 1881, 227–30). The bargained-for exchange definition supplants an earlier benefit-detriment theory of consideration where the court found consideration if one party gained a benefit or the other suffered a detriment as a consequence of their agreement. The bargain theory, by contrast, looks at both sides of the agreement and requires a connection in the form of an exchange or inducement between the two parties' promises.

The requirement of a bargained-for exchange means many promises that parties intend to be enforceable are *not* legally enforceable contracts. For example, if a grandmother promises to pay her grandchild $100 on the grandchild's eighteenth birthday, the grandmother may have every intention that the promise be enforceable and that the grandchild rely on it. Yet because the grandchild is not required to do anything in exchange for the grandmother's promise, the promise is not enforceable. Such a gift promise, even if conditional (the condition in the foregoing example was the child's eighteenth birthday), is not supported by consideration and thus is not contractual. Likewise, a promise in recognition of a benefit previously received lacks consideration and thus is not a contract. If,

after an employee has retired, a company promises to pay that employee a pension in recognition of previous years of service, then the promise does not create an enforceable contract. In each instance, the promise either is not induced by a return promise (or performance) or is not the inducement for a return promise (or performance).

Defenses

An agreement to which both parties have assented and that is supported by consideration is a contract; however, the legal system will refuse to enforce an otherwise valid contract if the contracting process was flawed in some way. The party seeking to avoid enforcement points out the flaw by asserting it as a defense to enforcement. One set of defenses arises from the principal that courts should only enforce agreements that reflect informed, voluntary decisions by competent individuals. Thus, promises that are made under unfair pressure from one side, as a result of mistake about basic facts relating to the exchange, or owing to a misrepresentation by one party about the agreement can be canceled. Likewise, an individual who enters into an agreement while he or she is a minor or is suffering from some mental defect or illness that affects his or her mental capacities may withdraw his or her promise.

Contracts normally do not need to be reflected in a written document in order to be enforceable. In 1677, the English legislature adopted "An Act for the Prevention of Frauds and Perjuries," which prohibited the enforcement of certain types of contracts unless evidenced by a writing. Although Great Britain has abandoned this so-called Statute of Frauds, the American states still allow charged parties to avoid enforcement of certain categories of contract by asserting the lack of the requisite writing. The exceptions to the statute have, however, grown sufficiently to make most contracts enforceable without a writing.

Remedies

The legal system enforces contracts by giving a remedy to the injured party in the event of breach. In the Anglo-American tradition, the goal of contract remedies is to compensate the nonbreaching party for any loss resulting from the breach; thus, the goal is *not* to punish the breaching party or to deter breach (that is, to ensure performance).

The default remedy for contract breach is a sum of money intended to compensate the injured party for her loss; this sum of money is called *damages*. The standard measure of damages is an amount that will place the non-breaching party where she would have been had the contract been fulfilled as promised. This payment fulfills the injured party's expectations of the benefits she would have received from the contract. Damages can be measured instead by the amount of loss the nonbreaching party suffered owing to the breaching party's failure to fulfill the contract. This sum of money puts the injured party in the position she would have been if she had never entered into a contract with the defendant. A nonbreaching party can only recover for damages that were reasonably foreseeable by the parties at the time of contracting and that did not result from her own irrational or unfair behavior.

Another possible remedy for breach of contract is equitable relief in the form of an order compelling a defaulting promisor to perform. In contrast to civil law systems, common law courts will order specific performance only in exceptional circumstances. The plaintiff must prove both that monetary relief will be inadequate to compensate her for her losses and that she will suffer irreparable harm unless the court orders the breaching party to perform. Courts are most likely to order specific performance where the breaching party was to sell to the injured party a unique good (such as artwork or antique) or was to provide a service not readily available in the marketplace.

VARIATIONS

Statutory

The United States Congress as well as individual state legislatures have supplemented or modified common law approaches by the adoption of statutes governing certain types of agreements, such as sales of goods, employment contracts, and real estate transactions. These statutes often codify certain traditional contract rules while creating new approaches particularly appropriate for the subject matter at issue. For example, article 2 of the Uniform Commercial Code, which is promulgated and updated by the National Conference of Commissioners on Uniform State Laws, has been adopted by forty-nine states, with minor variations, and governs agreements for the sale of goods, defined as all "movable" things (§2–105). Article 2 in certain instances establishes different rules for professional buyers and sellers, labeled merchants, from those for inexperienced ones, such as consumers. It also substitutes bright-line rules for certain common law standards. In addition, article 2 has effectively abandoned the mirror-image rule.

Great Britain

American and English contract law share the same roots and for centuries developed along shared paths. In fact, it was at one time common for American judges to cite English court decisions to justify their rulings. But over the course of the twentieth century the two systems diverged. The growing independence of American contract law from English law reflects the maturity of the American legal system as well as the different social and economic values that emerged in each country in the modern era.

As previously noted, Great Britain no longer requires that any type of agreement be recorded in writing to be enforceable, whereas most American states continue to require that certain categories of contract be reflected in a signed, written document. This requirement is embodied in state statutes including the Uniform Commercial Code–Sales (UCC-S), a model statute adopted by nearly every state legislature to govern contracts for the sale of goods. The Great Britain has not adopted a similarly ambitious statutory scheme for sales contracts. The UCCS explicitly protects parties against unconscionable bargains (Uniform Commercial Code, §2–302[1]), allowing courts to void all or parts of a contract if one party was disadvantaged in the bargaining process and as a result agreed to an oppressive bargain. Great Britain has no comparably broad protection against unconscionable contracts. These are just a few examples of the distinction between these common law countries in the area of modern contract law.

EVOLUTION AND CHANGE

The single most significant event in contract law in the twentieth century was the development of *promissory estoppel*. The original doctrine provided that if the promisee has reasonably and predictably relied on a gratuitous promise, a promisor is estopped (prevented) from avoiding enforcement on the grounds of lack of consideration. Today, promissory estoppel is a cause of action (or legal claim).

How could promissory estoppel emerge after the widespread adoption of the rigorous bargain formulation of consideration? Indeed, Holmes had said, "It would cut up the doctrine of consideration by the roots if a promisee could make a gratuitous promise binding by subsequently acting in reliance on it" (*Commonwealth v. Scituate Savings Bank,* 137 Mass. 301, 302 [1883]). Nevertheless, the first Restatement of Contracts in 1932, in section 90 ("Promise Reasonably Inducing Definite and Substantial Action") recognized reliance as a basis for the enforcement of promises lacking consideration. Although the American legal community debated the Restatement's formal inclusion of a cause of action in reliance, a number of cases from the turn of the twentieth century awarded recovery on the basis of the injured party's reliance interest. Following the American Law Institute's promulgation of the first Restatement, judicial adoption of promissory estoppel increased.

The Second Restatement of Contracts, adopted in 1978, contains section 90 with only minimal variation: "A promise which the promisor should reasonably expect to induce action or forbearance on the part of the promisee or a third person and which does induce such action or forbearance is binding if injustice can be avoided only by enforcement of the promise. The remedy granted for breach may be limited as justice requires." The drafters of the Second Restatement sought to justify the continued recognition of promissory estoppel by asserting that "it is fairly arguable that the enforcement of informal contracts . . . rested historically on justifiable reliance on a promise" (Restatement [2d] Contracts, §90, comment a).

Despite these assurances, some scholars have argued that the rise of promissory estoppel has marked the decline of consideration as the primary basis of enforcing promises. Indeed, promissory estoppel now serves as a solution to errors in contracting beyond lack of consideration. "Promissory estoppel may be viewed as a mender of ailing contracts" (Calamari and Perillo 1998, 248). Grant Gilmore went so far as to declare, "Contract is dead," and to assert that promissory estoppel is the culprit (Gilmore, 1974).

Tracey E. George

See also Civil Law; Commercial Law (International Aspects); Common Law; England and Wales; Law and Economics; Private Law; Small Claims; United States—State Systems

References and further reading
American Law Institute. 1981. *Restatement of the Law, Second, Contracts*. Saint Paul: American Law Institute Publishers.
American Law Institute and National Conference of Commissioners on Uniform State Laws. 1963. *Uniform Commercial Code–Sales*. Philadelphia: American Law Institute.
Calamari, John D., and Joseph M. Perillo. 1998. *The Law of Contracts*. 4th ed. St. Paul, MN: West Group.
Chirelstein, Marvin A. 2001. *Concepts and Case Analysis in the Law of Contracts*. 4th ed. New York: Foundation Press.
Corbin, Arthur Linton. 1952. *Corbin on Contracts* One-volume edition. Saint Paul, MN: West.
Gilmore, Grant. 1974. *The Death of Contract*. Columbus: Ohio State University Press.
Holmes, Oliver Wendell, Jr. 1881. *The Common Law*. Boston: Little, Brown. Reprint, Dover, 1991.

CORPORAL PUNISHMENT

DEFINITION

Corporal punishment is the infliction of physical pain on the body as a penalty for a person's wrongdoing. The word *corporal* comes from the Latin *corpus*, "body," so *corporal punishment* means literally "punishment of the body." Corporal punishment may be administered in response to a rule violation at school, at home, in the military, and in prisons, as well as being applied as a sanction for criminal acts. It has, at various times and in different criminal justice systems, included beating, blinding, branding, caning, flogging, mutilation, paddling, pillory, and stocks. Many instruments have been used to inflict corporal punishment, among them the tawse (a leather strap resembling a belt), the cat-o'-nine-tails (nine lengths of whipcord or rope tied with three knots at different places along its length), the birch (a bundle of small sticks), and the rattan cane.

EVOLUTION AND CHANGE

According to the ancient *lex talionis* or law of retaliation, propounded in Babylonian and Old Testament law as the principle of "eye for an eye" justice, perpetrators deserved corporal punishment commensurate with the injury they inflicted on their victim. Through the eighteenth century, corporal punishment remained a common sanction for cases that did not call for execution or exile.

In seventeenth- and eighteenth-century America, whipping in the public square was the most common punishment for felonies and some misdemeanors. Many minor offenses were punished by an hour of pain and ridicule in the pillory or stocks. Prisons became increasingly common in the 1820s, as reformers believed incarceration (or "correctional" facilities) provided a more enlightened response to crime than corporal punishment. By the twentieth century, imprisonment had replaced corporal punishment as a criminal sanction in most countries.

POLITICS AND PURPOSE

In the criminal justice arena, corporal punishment is commonly considered to be a punitive tactic, not intended to rehabilitate but rather to exact vengeance and, when publicly administered, reaffirm community values and deter others from wrongdoing. The accompanying humiliation and stigmatizing of the offender are often deemed to be part of the punishment.

A different explanation, however, was offered by Michel Foucault in his book *Discipline and Punish* (1975). Foucault asserted that during periods when monarchs dominated in Europe, public corporal punishment (meted out for offenses ranging from minon infractions to murder) was primarily a spectacle aimed at displaying the supreme power of the sovereign, whom the perpetrator had in theory offended by violating the law. A similar intent may be seen in slave owners' frequent flogging of their slaves.

The means of corporal punishment often reflected social class. In England, for example, a nobleman convicted of murder would be beheaded whereas a commoner found guilty of the same crime would be hanged. In colonial America, individuals of high social status were subjected to the pillory in cases where lower-class offenders might be sentenced to the stocks. In addition, when a criminal lacked the resources to pay a fine, he was whipped instead. For this reason corporal punishment was most common applied against the nonpropertied classes, including slaves. Even after the growth of prisons in the nineteenth century, whipping remained popular in Southern U.S. states, perhaps because a jailed slave could pick no cotton.

CORPORAL PUNISHMENT IN THE TWENTY-FIRST CENTURY

Although the use of physical punishment diminished following the rise of prisons, whipping has remained a legal penalty in a number of countries to the present day. Singapore and Malaysia, followed by Brunei, have the highest reported rates of inflicting corporal punishment. In Singapore, thousands of canings are inflicted each year for a variety of offenses. The perpetrator is stripped naked and held with leather straps over a trestle, with buttocks elevated. A warder whips the offender with a pliable four-foot length of rattan no more than half an inch in diameter. The cane, soaked in water to increase its flexibility (so as to prevent its splitting during the caning) and its capacity to shear skin, performs like a lash. Although twenty-four can strokes is the maximum that can be ordered at a given trial, the usual number of strokes is three or four. Caning in Singapore is mandatory for more than forty offenses, including trafficking in fireworks and entering the country illegally, and is optional for such offenses as rioting. It is generally assigned in addition to a prison sentence. Moreover, caning is commonly used within prisons as a means of disciplining prisoners. Caning is usually imposed on males aged 16–50, most of whom are in their twenties and thirties. Caning is reported to be excruciatingly painful; the wounds require from a week to a month to heal.

Countries and regions that strictly observe Islamic law, or shar'ia, generally apply both amputation and flogging as punishments. In 2000–2001, in northern Nigeria, two teenaged women were each sentenced to 100 lashes for having had premarital sex that led to pregnancy. (The sentences were carried out after they gave birth.) Also in northern Nigeria, two men publicly received eighty lashes each for drinking alcohol and a third received eighty cane strokes for selling it. In Saudi Arabia, one man was sentenced to seventy lashes for placing a call on a mobile phone during a domestic flight, and another was sentenced to twenty lashes for answering a call on a mobile phone during a flight. Eight Saudi students who attacked teachers also were publicly flogged, receiving forty lashes each. In other countries, for example, Sri Lanka, caning is legal but rarely used, owing to worldwide criticism from such groups as Amnesty International.

In the U.S. criminal justice system, the last flogging as part of a criminal sentence was carried out occurred in Delaware in 1952; the punishment was not taken off the books there, however, until 1972.

APPLICABILITY

Prisons

In the United States, corporal punishment for even slight infractions took place in prisons as a means of controling inmates. In New York's Elmira Reformatory, for example, nearly 20,000 blows to more than 2,500 inmates were recorded between 1888 and 1893. Such beatings were administered with a whip that typically had a three-inch-wide leather lash.

Corporal punishment to achieve correctional disciplinary goals was effectively abolished by a 1992 ruling of the U.S. Supreme Court. In *Hudson v. McMillan* the Supreme Court declared that the beating of an inmate, Keith Hudson, by a correctional officer who was escorting him to a lockdown area for a disciplinary infraction had violated the Eighth Amendment prohibition against cruel and unusual punishment. Great Britain ended whipping as a judicial penalty through the Criminal Justice Act of 1948 and abolished its use for prison discipline in 1967.

Schools

Corporal punishment is still applied in schools in parts of the United States (particularly the South), most English-speaking countries in Africa, much of southeast Asia (Singapore, Malaysia, and Thailand), parts of the Middle East, some Canadian provinces, the more remote regions of Australia, and several countries in the Caribbean and the Pacific. A number of countries have, however, banned corporal punishment in schools. These include Ghana, Hong Kong, India, Kenya, New Zealand, South Africa, Thailand, Trinidad and Tobago, and the United Kingdom. It is estimated that schoolchildren in the United States are paddled or spanked between 1 million and 2 million times a year.

In *Ingraham v. Wright* (1977), the U.S. Supreme Court addressed the issue of corporal punishment in schools. The case involved an incident in which students at a Florida junior high school had received a severe paddling. Questions were raised as to whether the punishment violated the Eighth Amendment's cruel-and-unusual-punishment clause and the Fourteenth Amendment's requirement for due process. In its ruling, the Supreme Court maintained that such protections applied specifically to criminals, not to schoolchildren. This gives inmates of U.S. prisons more protection from corporal punishment than children have in U.S. schools.

Students who feel that their rights have been infringed by school corporal punishment can still seek redress in court if the punishment was so severe as to violate the "reasonable but not excessive" standard. To attain a criminal conviction against a teacher for school corporal punishment would require the state to prove beyond a reasonable doubt (not just by the preponderance of evidence, as in a civil suit) that the person who administered the punishment not only exceeded the standard—itself a difficult burden of proof—but also intended to harm the child beyond normal, sanctioned disciplinary measures.

Despite the 1977 *Ingraham* decision and the lack of federal laws prohibiting corporal punishment in U.S schools, it has now been banned in twenty-seven of the fifty states, most recently (1995) in West Virginia. Mississippi leads in paddling—12 percent of students are paddled each year—followed by Arkansas and Alabama. Most estimates, however, undercount incidents of corporal punishment, for many cases are not recorded, nor are numbers of incidents provided by private schools.

Typical guidelines provide that the punishment be carried out in a private setting (that is, without other children present) by a teacher, principal, or assistant principal using "reasonable" force, and that it be witnessed by a second school official. The punishment should only be used as a last resort, after alternative disciplinary means have failed. In some states, the child's parent or guardian must be informed that the punishment has occurred and may request a written explanation of why the punishment was administered. Other states obtain parental permission at the beginning of a school year and notify parents prior to a paddling. Schools often offer a suspension as an alternative discipline for children whose parents object to corporal punishment. Concerns about ensuing lawsuits, however, have curbed the use of corporal punishment in schools even in states that continue to allow it.

CORPORAL PUNISHMENT BY PARENTS

Parental use of corporal punishment in the United States waned throughout the course of the twentieth century, partly in response to Sigmund Freud's revolutionary claim that a child's emotional trauma, which may result from harsh physical punishment, could have a negative impact well into adult life. With the recognition of the "battered child" phenomenon in the early 1960s, both parents' and pediatricians' awareness of the dangers of excessive corporal punishment increased. By 1966, all states except Hawai'i had enacted laws making it mandatory to report the physical abuse of children by parents. The difficulty in differentiating physical punishment from child abuse has played a role in reducing corporal punishment in homes in the United States. Spanking and slapping are a form of discipline for about a third of infants, more than 90 percent of toddlers, and a third of those in their early teens. Americans continue to agonize over whether corporal punishment by parents is appropriate.

ATTITUDES TOWARD CORPORAL PUNISHMENT

After the government of Sweden prohibited corporal punishment of children by all caretakers in 1979, there followed a significant drop in Swedes' support for this punishment. In the United States, the debate over corporal punishment was revived in May 1994 when Michael Fay, a young American living in Singapore, was sentenced to six strokes (later reduced to four) with a rattan cane (as well as four months in prison) for vandalism. Reaction to this penalty in the United States was mixed, because of the long-standing practice of corporal punishment to discipline children as well as a body of research that links corporal punishment to depressed self-esteem, violence, and other negative outcomes.

It has been observed that the same activity constituting corporal punishment in schools would be deemed criminal assault if conducted on the street or child abuse at home. Opponents of corporal punishment assert that when children are struck, it has more to do with parents' or teachers' frustration about unrelated problems than it does about the child's misbehavior. They suggests tactics such as "time outs" and rational discussions with the child as substitutes. Others defend the practice as necessary for maintaining order and argue that alternative punishments are ineffective. Some turn to their religious beliefs for support. The adage "Spare the rod, spoil the child" has its origin in the Old Testament: "He that spareth his rod hateth his son: but he that loveth him chasteneth him betimes" (Proverbs 13:24). The debate will likely continue, as it is difficult to determine the extent to which possible benefits of corporal punishment are outweighed by its probable negative consequences.

Lauren Dundes

See also Brunei; England and Wales; Human Rights Law; Malaysia; Retribution; Saudi Arabia; Shaming; Singapore; Sri Lanka; Sweden.

References and further reading

National Center for the Study of Corporal Punishment and Alternatives. Archives. Temple University, Philadelphia.

Newman, Graeme. 1995. *Just and Painful: A Case for the Corporal Punishment of Criminals.* New York: Harrow and Heston.

Scott, George Ryley. 1996. *The History of Corporal Punishment.* London: Senate.

Straus, Murray A. 1994. *Beating the Devil Out of Them: Corporal Punishment in American Families.* New York: Lexington Books.

COSTA RICA

GENERAL INFORMATION

Costa Rica is a small Central American country that shares a 309-kilometer border with Nicaragua to the north and a 330-kilometer border with Panama to the south. It also has 1,254 of coastline along the Pacific Ocean and 212 kilometers of coastline along the Caribbean Sea. The country's total area, 51,022 square kilometers, is slightly smaller than that of the U.S. state of West Virginia. It contains four mountain ranges, many volcanoes, and a variety of topographical environments.

Most of the country's urban development and more than half its population are situated in the Valle Central, a highland valley. The total population is approximately 3.82 million (2000). The capital city, San José, had a population of 324,011 in 1996. Other major cities in the Valle Central are Alajuela (175,129), Cartago (120,420), and Heredia (74,857). One major urban center is situated on each coast: Puntarenas (102,291) on the Pacific coast and Limón (77,234) on the Caribbean coast. The climate is temperate for most of the year. Temperatures vary only slightly between the country's two seasons, dry (December to April) and rainy (May to November).

Costa Rica has a relatively homogeneous population. More than 95 percent of Costa Ricans are classified as white or mestizo (mix of Indian and Spanish heritage). The rest of the population is either black (3 percent), indigenous peoples (1 percent), or Chinese (1 percent). The official language is Spanish, although some Jamaican English is spoken in and around Limón. The exact breakdown of religious affiliation is in dispute. Estimates of membership in the majority religion, Roman Catholicism, range from a high of 95 percent to a low of 74 percent. The vast majority of the remaining population belongs to one of a number of Protestant denominations, which since the 1980s have experienced rapid growth in membership (especially evangelicals) at the expense of the Roman Catholic Church. Roman Catholicism remains the state religion.

Costa Rica is exceptional among the republics of the Central American isthmus in terms of economic development and social welfare. While most Central American countries have been wracked by civil wars and guerrilla insurrections, Costa Rica has not experienced a major violent insurrection since the end of a short, bloody civil war in 1948. Thereafter the ballot box has been the sole avenue of replacing the country's political leaders, in quadrennial elections. Costa Rica's legal system is based on European civil law.

HISTORY

Costa Rica, the "Rich Coast," received its name after Columbus came ashore in 1502 and believed that the area contained enormous deposits of gold. Once Columbus's early impression was proved incorrect, Costa Rica became a colonial backwater that few Spaniards chose to settle or explore. Thus, when Spain's colonial empire in Mexico and Central America collapsed on September 15, 1821, Costa Rica emerged as the poorest province in the whole region. A short-lived Mexican empire filled the power void created by the Spanish exit. With the collapse of the Mexican empire in 1824, the five provinces of the former Capitanía General de Guatemala—Guatemala, Honduras, El Salvador, Nicaragua, and Costa Rica—formed the Central American Federation (CAF). The constitution of the CAF, based on the U.S. Constitution of 1787, granted the individual states considerable political autonomy and created a weak federal executive branch. Each state was permitted to make and implement policies that diverged significantly from those of other CAF states. In reality, the CAF was more of a confederation than a federation. The ineffectual central government contributed to the CAF's political instability and eventual collapse. In 1838, in response to another conservative coup in Guatemala, Head of State Braulio Carrillo ceded Costa Rica, the poorest province in Central America, from the CAF. Thus, in 1838, Costa Rica became a fully independent state.

From 1821 to 1871 the political and legal life in Costa Rica was governed by a succession of ten constitutional documents. The Pacto de Concordia (Concord Pact) of 1821 is widely viewed as the country's first constitution. But it was the constitutional convention of 1824 that first proposed a separation of powers between the executive, legislature, and judiciary. This proposal was concretized by article 87 of the 1825 constitution, which mandated the creation of a Supreme Court composed of from three to five popularly elected magistrates. The judicial branch was further strengthened by the creation of an unspecified number of *tribunales* (appeals courts) and *juzgados* (courts).

The Supreme Court, for all the powers the new constitution granted it, played only a minor role in the immediate postindependence period. The court's inactivity was due in part to a lack of trained lawyers and the public's lack of familiarity with the concept of a high court. The court's ability to meet its constitutional obligations was further hampered by a fee that had to be paid by appointees to the court. Many people appointed by the Legislative Assembly refused to pay the fee, and magistracies remained vacant. Moreover, until the end of the CAF period, the vast majority of Supreme Court magistrates were not native Costa Ricans but citizens of Nicaragua or Guatemala. The first Costa Rican Supreme Court president, Juan Mora Fernández, did not take office until 1842.

The training of Costa Rican lawyers began in 1814

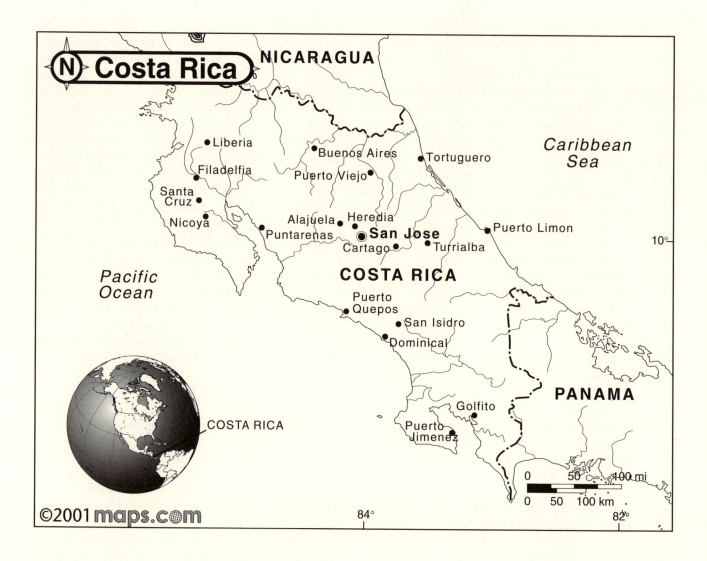

through a precursor institution, which by law in 1824 became the Casa de Enseñanza de Santo Tomás. This institution taught the rudiments of Roman, civil, and canon law as well as the history of law. In 1843, the institute converted into a public university and thus established the country's first and only law school. The creation of a Costa Rican law school helped alleviate the country's shortage of trained lawyers. When the university was closed from 1888–1940, the Colegio de Abogados (bar association) took up the university's function of training new lawyers. The university was eventually reopened, in 1940, by President Rafael Angel Calderón Guardia as the University of Costa Rica, and the faculty of law reentered the university, where it remains today.

The constitution of 1843 increased the number of Supreme Court magistrates to seven. A subsequent constitutional convention, in 1859, created the position of *co-juez nato,* precursor of the current *suplentes* (alternative magistrates). In 1869, after another military coup, the Supreme Court was reorganized and divided into two chambers (*salas*) and a plenary session, and the number of magistrates was increased to nine. The court was again

reorganized two years later, following another military takeover of the government and the writing of another constitution. As a result of the new constitution of 1871, the Supreme Court maintained its two chambers, but each chamber was expanded to seven magistrates. Also, the power to appoint Supreme Court magistrates moved from the office of the president to the deputies of the Legislative Assembly. A public prosecutor's office, controlled by the president of the Supreme Court, was created at the same time.

On January 1, 1888, the Ley Orgánica de Tribunales (Organic Law of Tribunals) granted independence to the judicial branch for the first time in Costa Rican history. The judiciary's independence was reaffirmed in 1937 in the Ley Orgánica del Poder Judicial (Organic Law of Judicial Power). The new law also replaced the existing two chambers of the Supreme Court with three chambers. Each of the new chambers was assigned a specific area of law—civil, cassation, and penal—as its remit. The court was expanded to seventeen magistrates in 1940.

The constitution of 1871 survived for almost seventy years with only two short breaks: from 1876 to 1882 and again during the Tinoco dictatorship, from 1917 to 1919. It was replaced by a new constitution in the aftermath of the short civil war of 1948. The current constitution, promulgated in 1949, was the result of a series of compromises. The initial draft, written by the victorious junta, was rejected by a popularly elected constituent assembly. Much of the new constitution drew heavily on the 1871 constitution, and many of the labor, social, and economic reforms of the defeated administration of Rafael Angel Calderón Guardia were maintained. The political institutional rules that the new constitution established remain in effect in Costa Rica today. The government is still divided into three branches: legislative (represented by the Legislative Assembly), executive (led by the president of the republic), and judiciary (headed by the Supreme Court). Although the postwar constitutional convention made extensive reforms to the legislative and executive branches, the judiciary remained largely intact.

A major constitutional amendment (article 177) in 1959 further enhanced the judiciary's immunity from political interference by affording it a significant level of financial autonomy. Article 177 mandates that at least 6 percent of the annual national ordinary budget should be earmarked for the judicial branch. In practice, however, the full 6 percent is not usually allocated. Even with its constitutionally grounded political and economic autonomy, the Supreme Court has shown considerable deference to the popularly elected branches of government and rarely challenged decrees or laws emanating from either of them. Many commentators argue that this behavior is largely due to the civil law tradition in which Costa Rican courts operate.

The most significant judicial reform since the 1948 civil war came in August 1989 when the Legislative Assembly passed Law No. 7128. This law amended articles 10, 48, 105, and 148 of the constitution and created a new constitutional chamber within the Supreme Court: the Sala Constitucional, commonly referred to as Sala Cuarta or Sala IV. The number of magistrates on the Supreme Court was expanded to twenty-two. Chambers I, II, and III each have five magistrates, and the new chamber, Sala IV, has seven. Each chamber also has a variable number of suplentes, who can be called in to hear specific cases as temporary replacements for sitting magistrates.

Contrary to Costa Rica's national mythology, the immediate postindependence period was not a bucolic, pacific, democratic one. Political violence was commonplace; the average tenure of civilian presidents between 1824 and 1889 was 1.5 years, and 44 percent of the period passed under military rule. Democratic political procedures and culture only gradually took hold. Between 1890 and 1920, the average length of a civilian president's tenure in office increased to 3.6 years, and only 7

percent of the period was under military rule. From 1921 to 1950, no military dictators ruled and civilian presidents generally served out their entire elected term in office. Since the 1948 civil war, which was ostensibly the result of electoral fraud, all presidents have served their full terms in office and all have been popularly elected in elections widely regarded as the fairest in Latin America.

In the second half of the twentieth century, Costa Rica's economic and social development outstripped that of its neighboring republics. In 1994, for example, poverty in Costa Rica stood at 6.6 percent, as compared to 28.5 percent in El Salvador and 44.4 percent in Guatemala. Life expectancies also reflect this development: in Costa Rica life expectancy at birth in 1994 was 76.6 years; in Guatemala it was 11 years less. According to the 1996 Human Development Index Report, issued by the United Nations Development Programme, Costa Rica ranked thirty-first among the nations of the world in overall human development. The index ranked the other Central American countries between 112th and 117th.

LEGAL CONCEPTS

The constitution is the supreme law of Costa Rica. The 1948 constitution (based on the 1871 constitution) concentrates political power geographically in the capital city of San José but disperses political authority widely among governmental bodies. It mandates a presidential system with a president, two vice presidents, a 57-member unicameral Legislative Assembly, a Supreme Court, an Electoral Tribunal, and various autonomous institutions. The 1948 constitution deliberately weakened the powers of the president by devolving them to the other branches of state, so as to hamper a return to *caudillo* (political strongman) politics of the pre–civil war years.

As a result of a 1969 constitutional amendment, presidents can serve only a single four-year term. An attempt in the late 1990s to push a constitutional amendment through the Legislative Assembly to permit an incumbent president to stand for reelection failed to gain sufficient backing from legislators, despite widespread popular support. Subsequently, a case was filed with the constitutional branch of the Supreme Court alleging the unconstitutionality of the assembly's handling of the amendment. On September 5, 2000, in a split vote, the court rejected the complaint (Sentencia No. 2000-07818). (There are plans to take the case to the Inter-American Court for Human Rights, which happens to be situated in San José.)

To win election as president, a candidate must receive at least 40 percent of the popular vote. The current president of Costa Rica, Miguel Angel Rodríguez Echeverría, was elected in February 1998 and took office in May of that year.

Presidential, assembly, and local elections are held simultaneously on the first Sunday of February, once every four years. All fifty-seven members of the Legislative Assembly, the president, and the two vice presidents serve concurrent four-year terms. Legislators may not serve consecutive terms in office. Although they are permitted to seek reelection after having sat out a term, most choose not to run again or fail to win reelection. Consequently, the Legislative Assembly is typically composed of more than 80 percent freshmen. The assembly is currently discussing a constitutional amendment to permit immediate reelection—an initiative that enjoys considerable support among legislators but is very unpopular with the public.

Elections and all election-related matters (including party registration, voter registration, registration of births, deaths, and marriages, election funding, ballot design, and vote counting) are controlled by the nonpartisan Tribunal Supremo de Elecciones (Supreme Electoral Tribunal or TSE), which has formal status as a fourth branch of government. In nonelection years, the TSE has three magistrates and six suplentes. In the year leading up to an election and for six months after the election, two more magistrates are added. To enhance the political autonomy of the TSE, magistrates are elected to staggered six-year terms by a two-thirds vote of the Supreme Court (article 100).

The Supreme Court resides within the judicial branch and enjoys considerable political and financial autonomy. Its twenty-two members are elected by a simple majority vote of the Legislative Assembly, except for the seven members of Sala IV, whose election requires a two-thirds majority. Supreme Court magistrates are elected for staggered eight-year terms to specific chambers within the court. In reality, magistrates effectively enjoy life tenure; they are automatically reelected unless a supermajority of two-thirds of the Legislative Assembly votes to remove them from office—an act that has yet to happen. The chief justice of the Supreme Court is elected by an internal vote of the other Supreme Court magistrates. The autonomy of the judicial branch is enhanced by its control of most judicial appointments. The Supreme Court appoints all appellate and superior court judges. A judicial council (Consejo Superior del Poder Judicial), composed of members of the judiciary, appoints all lower court judges.

The Costa Rican state has a large number of autonomous institutions (AI), government agencies charged with providing various goods and services, from insurance to health care to oil and gas. At the peak of the AI system in the early 1980s, there were more than 200 of autonomous institutions. The AIs enjoy considerable policymaking autonomy; some have financial autonomy, too, as they are guaranteed a percentage of the state's budget. The 1948 constitution specifically mentions several of these institutions and grants them absolute control over various functions. For example, the Instituto Costar-

ricense de Electricidad (Costa Rican Electricity Institute) enjoys a monopoly on telephone services.

In 1992, the Legislative Assembly created the Defensoría de los Habitantes (literally, Defender of the Inhabitants), which operates as an ombudsman's office. The Defensoría is part of the legislative branch. The defender and an assistant defender are elected by a simple majority of the Legislative Assembly to serve concurrent four-year terms. Because the Legislative Assembly decides who shall fill those posts, the Defensoría would seem to run the risk of becoming a partisan supporter of the government. Despite this threat to the office's political autonomy the two people who have served as defenders to date have been highly active in their pursuit of cases. This activity is encouraged, perhaps, by the fact that the terms cross two administrations. That is, the defender and assistant defender are elected in the final year of one administration and serve for the first three years of the subsequent administration, which frequently is controlled by a different party.

The function of the Defensoría is to protect the rights and interests of all Costa Ricans against actions of public agencies (or organizations that provide public services) and their functionaries. The Defensoría can act either on a complaint filed with its office by a citizen or at its own initiative if it discovers irregularities. The Defensoría also has an educational function: it conducts public forums and takes mobile offices to visit communities in remote parts of the country. The Defensoría employs these forums and visits to inform people of their legal rights and what actions they might take to resolve their problems. Much of the power of the Defensoría lies in the moral pressure it can exert by publicizing irregular actions of public officials. If public officials do not respond to the Defensoría's reports, the office can recommend sanctions against them or even advise that the official be fired.

The Defensoría is joined in its government oversight function by another autonomous agency, the office of the Comptroller General. This audit agency reviews all expenditures by the state or any of its autonomous institutions. The state is represented in any legal sistuation by the office of the Procurator General, which exercises a similar function to the U.S. Attorney General's office.

COURT STRUCTURE

As in the United States, the Supreme Court in Costa Rica is the highest body in the judicial branch. The Costa Rican court differs, however, from the U.S. court in its organizational structure. The Supreme Court consists of four chambers (*salas*) that sit independently for issues within their remit; it also meets to hear some cases in plenary session. There are five magistrates for each chamber, except the constitutional chamber, the Sala Constitucional, which has seven magistrates. The Supreme Court

Structure of Costa Rican Courts

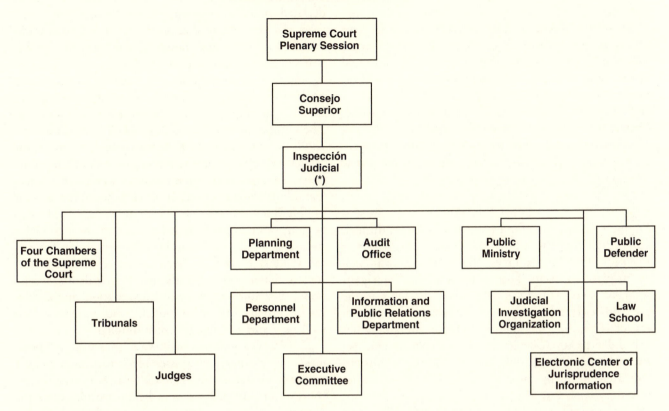

(*) The "Inspección Judicial" exercises control over all workers in the Judicial Branch. Its location in this figure does not signify any hierchial superiority, only that it covers the whole judicial branch

also has at least thirty-seven alternative magistrates (*magistrados suplentes*), who can be called on to hear cases but do not meet with the plenary court. The alternative magistrates for the first three chambers are elected at the same time by the Legislative Assembly and serve four-year terms. Sala Primera (Sala I) is responsible for family and civil cases; Sala Segunda (Sala II) labor issues, among others; Sala Tercera (Sala III) criminal matters; and the Sala Cuatra (Sala IV), or Sala Constitutional, constitutional issues and habeas corpus and amparo cases. The Supreme Court can, when requested, create commissions to investigate specific issues.

Within the judicial branch is the Office of the Judicial Inspection (*Inspección Judicial*), which exercises regular and constant oversight of all judicial employees.

The lowest level of court comprises *juzgados contraventionales, juzgados y tribunales de menor cuantía,* and *juzgados de asuntos sumarios,* which are effectively justices of the peace and are responsible for minor cases. There are more than 100 of these courts. Similarly, there are over 100 courts of first instance (*juzgados*), which are divided according to areas of law: juvenile, family, labor, civil, administrative, and so on. It is common to have more than one juzgado per district.

The middle level is occupied by the appellate or superior courts (*tribunales superiores*), which are also organized by case type. Some superior courts also operate as courts of first instance (trial courts) for criminal cases in which the maximum penalty is more than three years' imprisonment.

Whereas the lower courts are situated throughout the country, the appeals courts are located in major cities. The Supreme Court is seated in San José, the capital city.

SPECIALIZED JUDICIAL BODIES
There are no specialized judicial bodies in Costa Rica. This is in part a reflection of Costa Rica's democratic history and respect for human rights. The Inter-American Court of Human Rights is situated in San José, and the Costa Rican Supreme Court has on a number of occasions stated that it views the Inter-American Court's interpretation of the American Convention on Human Rights as binding on Costa Rica.

STAFFING
In 1995, there were nearly 350 judges and magistrates in Costa Rica. The Supreme Court, as stated earlier, has twenty-two magistrates and thirty-seven suplentes. In ad-

dition, each magistrate has two clerks (*letrados*), who are full-time lawyers.

There are eighty-nine judges employed in ten different offices of the superior court. Some 120 lower court judges are situated in eighty-four offices nationwide, and almost an equal number of *juzgados* work out of 103 offices across the country.

In 2000, the judicial branch employed 182 public defenders (*ordinarios*) and six supplemental public defenders (*extraordinarios*). There were also 243 public prosecutors (*fiscales ordinarios*) and 37 supplemental public prosecutors (*fiscales extraordinarios*).

IMPACT OF LAW

From the declaration of independence, in 1821, through 1989, the Costa Rican Supreme Court played a similar role in the life of its nation as other Latin American high courts played in theirs. That is, it was politically insignificant, unassertive, and showed extreme deference to the popularly elected branches of government. After the civil war of 1948, the court was granted more autonomy but still did little to challenge the acts of government. Between 1948 and 1989, only 347 cases of unconstitutionality were heard by the Supreme Court (327 were resolved), yet in every year since its creation in 1989 Sala IV has received 350 cases of unconstitutionality, with more than 330 being resolved each year.

One Costa Rican constitutional expert, Jaime Murillo Víquez, comments that many Costa Ricans believed that the reforms of 1989 brought to an end the "tyranny of the law" and ended 170 years of political leaders' disrespect for the constitution. The Supreme Court, though, even if it was previously interested in judicial activism, was limited in its actions by other institutional rules. For example, a ruling of unconstitutionality required a supermajority of two-thirds of the full court. Thus, it was possible that laws publicly declared unconstitutional by a majority of the court were still constitutional and still had the full force of law.

The magistrates' understanding of their own function compounded the difficulty of ruling a law unconstitutional. There was in Costa Rica, as in other Latin American countries, a general presumption that the Legislative Assembly was sovereign and that its laws were constitutional. Furthermore, while decisions of unconstitutionality made the relevant decrees and statutes "absolutely null," in other cases, such as amparo or habeas corpus, only the parties immediately involved were bound by the decision. That is, the decision was not viewed as a precedent affecting all similar cases.

Since the 1989 judicial reforms, the Costa Rican judicial system has become one of the most influential political institutions in the country, and an increasingly controversial one. In November 2000, for example, the procurator general and the assistant procurator general declared publicly what many had thought for many years, that it is Sala IV that makes the important political decisions in the country rather than the executive or legislative branches of government.

The easy, inexpensive access to Sala IV (litigants need no lawyers, except in cases of unconstitutionality, and there are no filing fees), has created a landslide of cases. The number of cases received by Sala IV increased from 2,296 in 1990 (its first full year of operation) to almost 10,000 in 1999. Other chambers of the Supreme Court have also experienced significant growth in their caseloads, but it is the actions of Sala IV that have the most profound political impact. The court has addressed issues ranging from amparo cases dealing with the rights of a shaved-ice vendor (ruled against the state and in favor of the vendor) to in-vitro fertilization (ruled unconstitutional), major political issues such as presidential reelection (ruled unconstitutional), privatization of the telephone system (unconstitutional), and limitations on workers' rights to strike (unconstitutional).

Sala IV also routinely replies to "constitutional hearings" from the Legislative Assembly. It requires the signatures of only ten deputies to ask Sala IV to rule on the constitutionality of legislation being considered by the Assembly. This procedure has introduced a new avenue for opposition parties to block or at least delay legislation that they do not like. Other constitutional consultations are mandatory; for example, all constitutional amendments and international treaties discussed by the Legislative Assembly must be sent to Sala IV.

Bruce M. Wilson
Roger Handberg

See also Civil Law; Constitutional Law; Constitutional Review; Habeas Corpus, Writ of; Inter-American Court and Commission on Human Rights; Judicial Independence; Judicial Review; Parliamentary Supremacy
References and further reading
Barker, Robert S. 1986. "Constitutional Adjudication in Costa Rica: A Latin American Model." *University of Miami Inter-American Law Review* 17: 249–272.
Giralt, Henry Q. 1995. "Costa Rica's Justice System: An Analysis of Costa Rica's Law System." In *World Factbook Of Criminal Justice Systems,* http://www.ojp.usdoj.gov/bjs/pub/ascii/wfbcjcos.txt.
Jiménez Aguilar, Manuel Fernando. 1994. *Estructura y funcionamiento del Poder Judicial.* San José: Corte Suprema de Justicia Escuela Judicial.
Ley de Reorganización Judicial (Ley No. 7728 de 15 de diciembre de 1997). San José: La Gaceta.
Murillo Víquez, Jaime. 1994. *La Sala Constitucional: Una revolución político-jurídica en Costa Rica.* San José: Editorial Guayacán.
Rodríguez Cordero, Juan Carlos. 2001. "Las reformas constitucionales en el diseño del sistema político costarricense: el caso de la consulta preceptiva de

constitucionalidad (1989–1997)." Master's thesis. University of Costa Rica, San José.

Sáenz Carbonell, Jorge Francisco. 1997. *Historia del Derecho Costarricense.* San José: Editorial Juricentro.

Solís Fallas, Alex. 1999. Dimensión política de la justicia constitucional." *Revista Parlamentaria* 7(2): 310–378.

Wilson, Bruce M. 1998. *Costa Rica: Politics, Economics, and Democracy.* Boulder: Lynn Reiner.

Wilson, Bruce M., and Roger Handberg. 2000. "Costa Rica's New Constitutional Court: A Loose Political Cannon?" *South Eastern Latin Americanist* 43(4), Spring: 58–79.

———. 1999. "From Judicial Passivity to Judicial Activism: Explaining the Change within Costa Rica's Supreme Court." *NAFTA: Law and Business Review of the Americas* 4, no 4 (Autumn): 522–543.

CÔTE D'IVOIRE

GENERAL INFORMATION

Côte d'Ivoire has a total area of 322,460 square kilometers and is located on the Atlantic coast of West Africa. It is bordered by Burkina Faso and Mali to the north, Ghana to the east, Guinea to the northwest, Liberia to the southwest, and the Atlantic Ocean to the south. The country is mostly flat with undulating plains, with mountains in the northwest.

Côte d'Ivoire has an ethnically diverse population estimated to number 16.3 million. The country has more than sixty ethnic groups divided into four major divisions as follows: Akan, 42.1 percent; Gur, also known as Voltaiques, 17.6 percent; Mandes, 26.5 percent; Kru, 11 percent; with 2.8 percent consisting of other minor groups. Of these groups, the Mandes have inhabited the country the longest.

The economy of the Côte d'Ivoire was among the leading economies in Africa on the index of growth during the 1960s and 1970s. In the 1980s, economic growth that had averaged 11 percent during the 1960s, and around 7 percent in the 1970s started a downward trend. The growth was fueled by both high prices for the country's main exports—cocoa and coffee—and good harvests. During the 1980s, however, low agricultural productivity caused by drought and a fall in commodity prices plunged the country into an economic slump. In 1991 the government adopted a World Bank/International Monetary Fund (IMF) Structural Adjustment Program in an effort to revive the stagnating economy. Key features of the program were fiscal austerity, market liberalization, and civil service retrenchment. Reforms were further boosted by the devaluation of the country's currency, the franc CFA. Although not as prosperous as had been predicted, the economy was on the way to recovery in the mid-1990s, with a growth rate of 6.8 percent between 1995 and 1997 and 6 percent in 1998.

Even after having gone through a debilitating economic stagnation, the Côte d'Ivoire remains one country in Africa with relatively high incomes. Average GNP per capita in 1998 was estimated to be $700, as compared with $480 for the rest of sub-Saharan Africa. Like that of most Third World countries, the economy of the Côte d'Ivoire is highly dependent on agriculture. Sixty-eight percent of the labor force in 2000 was employed in the agricultural sector, but agriculture's contribution to GDP was only 32 percent. The principal agricultural products are cocoa, coffee, bananas, palm products, pineapples, rubber, and cotton. The country also produces petroleum and tropical timber. Unlike many African countries—in which agricultural production is in the hands of small-hold farmers—plantations, most owned by foreign, mainly French and Lebanese, planters dominate Côte d'Ivoire's agricultural sector. This has led to a skewed distribution of incomes, especially during periods when commodity prices are high in the world market. Also worth emphasizing is the large immigrant population from neighboring countries working in Côte d'Ivoire's many plantations and the large settler population from Lebanon and France involved in economic activities. There are more than 3 million migrant workers employed in the agricultural sector of the country's economy, in addition to some 300,000 Lebanese (some engaged in agriculture, others engaged in commerce) and thousands of French settlers.

HISTORY

As is the case in most African countries, contemporary Côte d'Ivoire's political history and culture have been conditioned by indigenous African and European influences. As indicated already, more than sixty indigenous African groups inhabit the country. Upon signing treaties of protection with the indigenous people around the Atlantic coast in the 1840s, France's claim over the area and its hinterland was recognized by the Berlin Conference of 1884-1885, which had formalized European powers' partition of Africa among themselves. In 1893 it was formally declared a French colony, and after fierce resistance by indigenous African groups France succeeded in 1917 in exerting complete control over the territory. As in its other colonies, the colonial policy of assimilation guided France's activities in the territory, and with it French civil law. French rule was politically oppressive, economically exploitative, and legally discriminatory. It used forced African labor to build infrastructures, imposed excessive taxes on the people, excluded them from political activities, and allowed them no legal recourse. Even though Africans were made to cultivate cash crops, they were not accorded the same prices for their products that French farmers were paid. Nonetheless, the cash economy led to

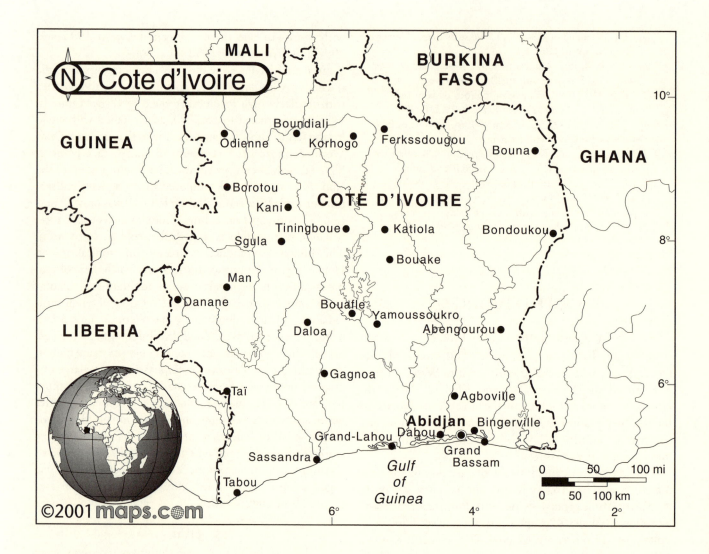

Cote d'Ivoire

MALI
BURKINA FASO
GUINEA
GHANA
COTE D'IVOIRE
LIBERIA

Boundiali
Odienne
Korhogo
Ferkssdougou
Bouna
Borotou
Kani
Tiningboue
Katiola
Bondoukou
Sgula
Bouake
Man
Bouafle
Danane
Yamoussoukro
Daloa
Abengourou
Gagnoa
Agboville
Taï
Abidjan
Bingerville
Grand-Lahou
Dabou
Sassandra
Grand Bassam
Tabou
Gulf of Guinea

10°
8°
6°
6°
4°
2°

0   50   100 mi
0   50 100 km

©2001 maps.com

the emergence of a new breed of wealthy African farmers who would use their union, the Syndicat Agricuture Africain (SAA), to agitate for changes in French policy through the Democratic Party of the Côte d'Ivoire (PDCI), led by Felix Houphouet-Boigny, himself a wealthy farmer. The PDCI was affiliated with the African Democratic Assembly (RDA), hence it was PDCI-RDA. Initially, the PDCI spearheaded a radical program that called for political participation for Africans and higher prices for their agricultural products, and used equally radical means, such as demonstrations, as happened in 1948–1949. Those demonstrations ended with fifty-two fatalities. By the 1960s, Houphouet-Boigny and the PDCI had made a turnabout, from a radical party to a very conservative party with a conservative agenda. For example, it opposed the French West African Federation as the basis through which the territories that made it up should gain their independence. It was also against immediate independence in the 1958 referendum that France had held in its territories to determine their future. Both the party and its leader would continue with the conservative stance after the territory became independent.

Under French colonial rule, Côte d'Ivoire was administered as part of French West Africa, which had its headquarters in Dakar, Senegal. It gained independence on August 7, 1960, with Felix Houphouet-Boigny as its first president. Houphouet-Boigny went on to lead the country until his death in December 1993, a record thirty-three years in office. He was able to transform the country both politically and economically in the conservative direction he had started in the 1950s, and that continued until his death. Politically, he converted the country into a one-party state tolerating no dissent and using a combination of coercion, patronage, and conciliation to win out opponents. And despite the much talked about indigenization of the country's administration and economy during the 1960s, French influence grew even stronger. For example, France continued to maintain a military base in the country, while French investments and aid were crucial to its rapid growth. As discussed earlier, his economic policy emphasized agriculture, building it around French plantation owners and foreign investments, again dominated by French businesses.

To the extent that the government's economic policies

produced unprecedented growth, created jobs, and raised incomes, Ivorians were willing to put up with the absence of political choice and freedom. But when the economy started its downward decline in the 1980s, unrest among workers, students, and university professors increased, with calls for constitutional reforms to establish a multiparty system and greater accountability. Houphouet-Boigny's decision to build a new capital for the country in his hometown of Yamoussoukro, and a Catholic basilica in the same town (which is today the largest church in the world, capable of seating 500,000 people at a cost of 40,000 million Francs CFA) shed light on the waste associated with poor economic management and only heightened resentment against the regime. Shortly after the dedication of the basilica by Pope John Paul in January 1990, students, professors, and civil servants took to the streets to protest waste within the government, especially when salaries had been slashed to deal with the economic crisis. The government's reaction—banning demonstrations and closing the university—was met on May 16, 1990, by an unsuccessful coup d'état.

In an effort to ward off further incidents, Houphouet-Boigny accepted the recommendations of a commission he had appointed to come up with suggestions on how to deal with the political and economic crisis the country was facing. Upon the commission's recommendation, he agreed to multiparty presidential and legislative elections. The presidential elections took place on October 28, 1990, with Houphouet-Boigny as the PDCI's candidate, facing his challenger, Laurent Gbagbo of the Front Populaire Ivoirien (FPI). Houphouet-Boigny won with 81.7 percent of the total votes cast, but the opposition claimed that the election was marred by inconsistencies and wanted it invalidated, though to no avail. On November 25, legislative elections were held with some seventeen parties and more than 500 candidates participating. The PDCI won 163 seats out of a total of 175. The years 1991 and 1992 punctuated the struggle for democracy in Côte d'Ivoire with student demonstrations, followed by government brutality in putting down the demonstrations; opposition and human rights advocates joined with the students to protest the government's handling of the incidents. In December 1993, Houphouet-Boigny died, and Henri Konan Bedie, president of the National Assembly, succeeded him as president, as required by the constitution.

After the death of Houphouet-Boigny, politics in Côte d'Ivoire remained very fragile. Internal division within the PDCI between Konan Bedie and Ouattara led to the split of the party, with supporters of Ouattara leaving to form a new party. In the effort to consolidate his power, Bedie moved to fill the government, judiciary, and other critical positions with his supporters. And in preparation for the 1995 presidential elections, he initiated an amendment to the constitution banning anyone from contesting the election's outcome if both parents were not Ivorian citizens—a reference to Ouattara, whose mother was said to be from Burkina Faso. The 1995 elections were held amid boycotts and violence, with Konan Bedie winning more than 95 percent of the vote. He continued his efforts to consolidate power by initiating changes in the various articles of the constitution. But in December 1999 he was overthrown by the military, with General Robert Guei, who had served as Bedie's minister of employment and minister of sports. Guei himself was forced out of office by the masses in October 2000, after he tried to declare himself winner in the presidential election, which he had lost. Laurent Gbagbo, who had actually won the election, with 59.4 percent of the vote against General Guei's 32.7 percent, was installed as president after Guei's flight.

LEGAL CONCEPTS

Côte d'Ivoire has a republican constitution with a unitary system of government made up of a legislature (the National Assembly), an executive branch headed by the president, and an independent judiciary at the head of which is the Supreme Court. The constitution also makes provision for a prime minister and an independent judiciary headed by the Supreme Court. The president, who is popularly elected to serve a five-year term, is head of state and chief executive. He appoints the prime minister (PM) and on the latter's advice appoints the cabinet. The office of PM is a weak one. The PM, for example, serves at the pleasure of the president, with responsibilities limited to the coordination of government functions and their implementation. Elections for the National Assembly are from single and multiple districts for five-year terms. New articles to the constitution provided for a Senate whose members were to serve six-year terms. Unlike the National Assembly, some of the members in the Senate would be elected by universal suffrage, while others would be the result of presidential appointment. Despite provisions for a Senate in the constitution, it has not been constituted. Like France, Côte d'Ivoire is administratively divided into departments, at the head of which are *prefets*. Another body, the Constitutional Council, with responsibilities for ensuring the constitutionality of government actions, is enshrined as a watchdog.

Côte d'Ivoire's constitution has been revised more than half a dozen times during the past four decades. It was significantly revised in 2000, only two years after the 1998 revision. Unlike a number of constitutions devised in the 1990s in other African countries, Côte d'Ivoire's constitution is very much lacking in depth. The detailed work is thus left to legislation. Typically, the abstract designs of constitutions tend to make them flexible, so as to be conducive to changing circumstances over time. But given that the political system of Côte d'Ivoire is built on a strong presidency and the president's influence on constitutional interpretation through legislation, the risk of its excessively flexile constitution generating abuse cannot be discounted. Another notable characteristic of the constitution has to do with the things it leaves out. It does not include a bill of rights, or such new concerns as the right to economic and social development and environmental protection, as found in the constitutions of many African countries that were devised in the 1990s. Key provisions emphasized in the constitutional setup include the separation of powers, the rule of law, an independent and impartial judiciary, the innocence of accused persons until proven guilty, electoral eligibility for candidates, and due process. However, these provisions have not always been respected in practice. For example, the Houphouet-Boigny regime used fabricated stories to gain convictions for political reasons during the early 1960s to neutralize enemies, including Ernest Boka, who was the very first president of Côte d'Ivoire's Supreme Court. Activities that undermined legal principles—among them the use of extrajudiciary measures including the detention of opposition activists without trial during election violence in 1995, and the use of press censorship to silence journalists considered sympathetic to the opposition (as occurred in 1995 and 1996 involving the paper *La Voie*)—continued unabated. Deviations from the principles of due process, the rule of law, and the rights of citizens irrespective of who they were suffered greatly under the presidency of General Guei, as summary execution of criminals by soldiers, and intimidation of journalists and human rights lawyers, made justice a mockery.

Côte d'Ivoire's legal system is based on the French civil code tradition. This is a direct result of French colonialism. In addition, Côte d'Ivoire has based some of its institutional setups, such as the Constitutional Court, on the French model. Indigenous African tradition and Islamic law have also influenced the legal system.

CURRENT STRUCTURE

The legal structure in Côte d'Ivoire is composed of the court structures, attorneys (*advocats*), and other legal professionals such as *notaires* (solicitors). The court system is composed of the Supreme Court, Courts of Appeal, and Courts of First Instance (Magistrates' Courts). The Supreme Court serves as the highest court and is presided over by a president. The Supreme Court sits in Abidjan, Côte d'Ivoire's capital, and is composed of four chambers: constitutional, judiciary, administrative, and auditing. Its jurisdiction is over cases on appeal from the Courts of Appeal, and whatever judgment it renders is final. The Courts of Appeal (one of which is in Abidjan and the other in Bouake) hear cases on appeal from courts of first instance. Courts of first instance are the lowest courts and have original jurisdiction over civil, criminal, commercial, and administrative cases.

Judiciary appointments, with the exception of members of the High Court of Justice, are the responsibility of the president, who makes such appointments from candidates proposed by the minister of justice and keeper of the seal, who himself is advised in the process by the High Council of the Magistracy. Once appointed, judges serve until retirement. With the exception of members of the High Court of Justice, all judges must have legal training, as discussed below.

The legal system of Côte d'Ivoire also has a strong private practice component made up of *advocats* (attorneys) and *notaires* (solicitors). Members of these groups have been at the forefront of much of the liberalization of the political system. They continue to suffer abuses as politicians seek to silence them.

SPECIALIZED JUDICIARY BODIES

In Côte d'Ivoire, the constitution separates crimes by members of the government committed while exercising their official duties from other crimes. The High Court of Justice has original jurisdiction in such crimes. In addition, the High Court of Justice is responsible to try the president on any charges of high treason brought against him. It also has responsibility for trying members of the government for treason or related charges. The National Assembly selects members of the High Court from among its members, and once constituted, the constitution gives members of the High Court the responsibility of choosing a president among themselves. In 1997 another special judiciary body, the Court of Arbitration, with jurisdiction over commercial disputes, was also inaugurated.

As discussed already, Côte d'Ivoire's constitution also had provisions for a Constitutional Council. Its role is to evaluate governmental actions to ensure their constitutionality. The council also has responsibility over referenda and electoral eligibility of candidates, the regularity of elections, and the validation of election results.

STAFFING

Key staffing issues in the legal system of Côte d'Ivoire cannot be divorced from those faced by the population in general. Low salaries, heavy workload, and political pressures have had the impact of generating low morale for state legal employees. The country's economic problems during the past two decades have led to cuts in salaries of state employees, including judges. Insecurity in the country caused by the heavy crime wave of the past decade, itself a factor in the economic crisis, and the politics of intolerance have also taken their toll on judges and the legal profession. As indicated earlier, human rights lawyers have been subjected to abuse from law enforcement offi-

Structure of Côte d'Ivoire Courts

Supreme Court			
Constitutional	Judicial	Administrative	Auditing

Courts of Appeal (Appellate)			
Civil	Criminal	Commercial	Administrative

Courts of First Instance (Original Jurisdiction)			
Civil	Criminal	Administrative	Commercial

cials loyal to the government. Meanwhile, judges see their workloads skyrocket at the same time that some judicial appointments are being used for political reasons.

A team of highly trained and competent legal professionals is critical to a well-functioning legal system. Legal training in Côte d'Ivoire is similar to that in many other French-speaking African countries. To become a lawyer in private practice, one must acquire a law degree from the university and then receive further practical training in advocacy. For judges, after earning a law degree from the university, the prospective judge must pass a nationally administered competitive examination into the magistrates program of the National School of Administration (ENA). After two years of training in magistracy, the prospective judge is then posted to an entry-level position as a magistrate.

IMPACT

The role of the courts and the law in the political and social life of Côte d'Ivoire is very difficult to assess. Obviously one cannot say that the law and the courts have not had an impact on the social and political life of the country, but such impact has been significantly compromised by the lack of respect for the various legal principles that are enshrined in the system's basic laws.

Moses K. Tesi

See also Barristers; Burkina Faso; Civil Law; Human Rights Law; Islamic Law; Legal Professionals—Civil Law Traditions; Notaries

References and further reading
African Confidential. 1990–2001. Various issues.
Amnesty International. "Côte D'Ivoire Human Rights Violations." http://www.amnesty.ie/act/wafr/ivc.shtml.
Clark, John F., and David E. Gardinier. 1997. *Political Reform in Francophone Africa.* Boulder, CO: Westview Press.
Gbagbo, Laurent. 1983. *La Côte d'Ivoire: Pour une alternative démocratique.* Paris: L'Harmattan.
———. 1989. *Côte d'Ivoire: Histoire d'un retour.* Paris: L'Harmattan.
Médard, Jean-François. 1991. "The Historical Trajectories of the Ivorian and Kenyan States." Pp. 121–185 in *Rethinking Third World Politics.* Edited by James Manor. New York: Longman.
Mundt, Robert J. 1997. "Côte d'Ivoire: Continuity and Change in a Semi-Democracy." Pp. 182–203 in *Political Reform in Francophone Africa.* Edited by John F. Clark and David E. Gardinier. Boulder, CO: Westview Press.
Official site of the presidency of the republic of Côte d'Ivoire. http://www.pr.ci/côte_d_ivoire/ci/index.html.
Quarterly Economic Report, Côte d'Ivoire. 1990–2001. Various issues.
West Africa. 1990–2001. Various issues.
World Bank. 1989–2000 (various years). *World Development Report.* New York: Oxford University Press.
Zolberg, Aristide R. 1969. *One Party Government in the Ivory Coast.* Princeton, NJ: Princeton University Press.

CRIMINAL LAW

DEFINITION

Criminal law is a body of rules and regulations that specify and define punishment to redress offenses committed against society or the state. Each country has its own criminal codes and statutes that regulate criminal or deviant behavior. In the United States, each state has its own criminal code, as does the federal government.

Criminal law is distinguished from civil law in that the latter is a term for private law that addresses private rights and remedies. In some countries, such as France, civil law denotes a family of law that is not limited to noncriminal issues. Other families of law are: common law (as in the United States and England), Islamic law (as in Saudi Arabia), socialist law (as in the former Soviet Union and China), and the hybrid system (as in Japan).

PURPOSES AND CHARACTERISTICS OF CRIMINAL LAW

Laws enacted by governments are intended to regulate the behavior of everyone, including those who enforce the law. The requirement that law is supreme and must be abided by is known as "the rule of law." Criminal law defines and classifies behavior. These notions are shared objectives in every system of law, even though they are illusory in some countries. In the socialist system, for instance, individual challenges to government action used to be vitiated, although many socialist countries are now endorsing and respecting the rule of law. Islamic nations accept the rule of law because their law is considered to have a supreme origin—Allah. Islamic countries rely on the conscience of the law enforcer to monitor his or her activities.

There are six main characteristics of criminal law:

1. It stipulates behavior that people may or may not engage in.

2. These stipulations are written into law by the legislature or by the judiciary.
3. For every crime, the law stipulates a corresponding punishment.
4. Laws apply to all in a given jurisdiction.
5. The community at large is affected by a crime, even if it is perpetrated on only one person.
6. The punishment meted out to a criminal symbolizes the sentiments of the community.

SOURCES OF U.S. CRIMINAL LAW

Criminal law in the United States is derived from several sources. These are listed below.

Common Law of England

The common law of England originated in unwritten laws developed from customs. These customs eventually became enforced in courts, and the subsequent court decisions that applied throughout the country became known as common law. These traditions and the court decisions that served as precedents were introduced to the United States by the founding fathers. Common law acted as a stimulus for subsequent development in written laws. Today, vestiges of common law can be seen in the names, definitions, and classification of certain crimes, although some definitions have been altered to suit contemporary times. The common law definition of a burglary, for instance, required that the crime take place at night. Although eighteen states still retain that requirement in their definitions of burglary, most states now view the nighttime requirement as an aggravating factor.

U.S. Constitution

Treason (Article 3 s.iii) is the only crime defined in the U.S. Constitution. Much of the Constitution, particularly the Bill of Rights, deals with procedural law, that is, matters of rules and practices that govern the criminal justice process. Matters of substantive law such as definition of offenses are found in various criminal codes.

U.S. Criminal Code

The U.S. Criminal Code lists federal crimes defined by Congress. The code exists because of the federal system of government, which allows power to be divided between a central government and the various states. Federal crimes are defined and adjudicated in federal courts. Some of the crimes included in this code are: crimes perpetrated against the United States government, its employees, and its property; and drugs and weapons crimes.

State Constitutions

Each state to some extent incorporates criminal law in its constitution. As the supreme law of the state, the state constitution is the dominant source of governmental power regulating the justice process by granting powers to law enforcement and judicial personnel, as well as by constricting those powers.

State Criminal Codes

Each state defines crimes applicable to its residents. These definitions are derived to a large extent from common-law crimes even though many of the definitions have been revised to suit contemporary times. Lower courts in each state enforce the laws through guilty verdicts and sanctions. In the event of a discord in the interpretation of the code, the state appellate court provides clarity

Municipal/Local Ordinances

Each municipality may enact laws unique to that jurisdiction. The laws entail definitions of a variety of minor infractions such as disorderly behavior in public places, traffic violations, vagrancy, and others. the definition of crimes and their corresponding punishments differ based on the type of municipality and the social and economic factors peculiar to that jurisdiction.

Administrative Law

Administrative laws are promulgated by administrative agencies. While many of the laws are civil in nature, violations of some may be enforced in criminal courts. Certain rules and regulations derived from administrative agencies such as the Internal Revenue Services may create legal duties. Omission or failure to act when there is a legal duty to do so—for example, the failure to file income tax returns—may constitute an offense that may be enforced in a criminal court.

Judicial Decisions

Modern court judges continue to make law by deciding cases and by applying the principle of stare decisis, which obligates them to follow precedents when the facts of cases are similar. When the case on trial has nuances in facts from previous cases, judges distinguish the cases and apply the law more suitable to the new case.

SOURCES OF CRIMINAL LAW IN OTHER COUNTRIES

The sources of English law are common law and legislative law. As mentioned, common law is derived from unwritten laws, although in the eighteenth century, William Blackstone compiled the laws prevalent at the time in England in a book known as *Blackstone's Commentaries*. Legislative law is enacted by Parliament, which also updates the common law.

In France, law is divided into two broad categories comprising private and public law. Criminal law is a branch of public law. The most dominant source of criminal law in France is the 1994 Code Penale, which replaced the 1810 code.

In Japan, the Diet is the most important body that enacts criminal laws as outlined in the country's penal code. The Japanese legal system is classified as a hybrid system because many of its laws are derived from China, France, Germany, and the United States.

In the former USSR, laws adopted in 1958 by the Supreme Soviet and various amendments to these laws made by the unions in the early part of the 1960s established the Soviet codes of criminal law and criminal procedure.

Islamic law is based on the *sharia,* whose main source is the Qur'an. Other sources of Islamic law are the Sunnah, which are compilations of traditions and proclamations of prophets, and the precedents of early Islamic lawyers. The sharia controls all institutions, including courts and other government establishments. It specifies legal principles deemed right or wrong, governs laws relating to contracts and succession, classifies crimes based on whether they are acts against God or private wrongs, and prescribes punishments for crimes.

CLASSIFICATION OF CRIMES

Crimes are classified differently. The basis for classification is to delineate the most serious offenses from breaches of public decency and morals, and to designate a corresponding form of social control.

Classification Based on Severity of Offense and Penalty

Most modern statutes classify offenses as felonies, misdemeanors, and violations/infractions. Capital felonies, such as aggravated murder and treason, may require a punishment of death or life imprisonment. Other felonies are typically punished by from one year in prison up to life imprisonment. Intermediate punishments may also be imposed. In the United States, it is noteworthy that the various state statutes stipulate the limits of the sentence for each type of offense; hence, classifications based on punishment are not uniform. Misdemeanors are lesser offenses that may be punished by a jail sentence, a fine, or both. A California statute, for instance, defines a misdemeanor in the following way: "Except in cases where a different punishment is prescribed by any law of this state, every offense declared to be a misdemeanor is punishable by imprisonment in the county jail not exceeding six months, or by fine not exceeding one thousand dollars ($1,000), or by both" (Schmalleger 1999, 5). By implication, the definition suggests that any offense punished with over six months of imprisonment is a felony. Violations are usually petty offenses and primarily consists of traffic infractions. The penalty for such offenses is usually a fine. The French have a similar method

of classification, and this classification indicates which court has jurisdiction over a given matter. They classify offenses as *crimes, delits,* and *contraventions.*

Classification Based on Degree of Evilness

Crimes that are inherently bad, such as murder, are referred to as *mala in se* crimes. Acts that become classified as criminal because a law in a jurisdiction prohibits them are called *mala prohibita* crimes.

Classification Based on the Subject Matter

This type of classification is based on the subject at issue; for instance, a crime of sedition may be classified as a crime against the state, while arson and burglary may be classified as crimes against habitation or dwelling.

In England, the 1967 Criminal Law Act abolished the distinctions of crimes based on the categories of treasons, felonies, and misdemeanors. Thereafter, a dual system of classifying crimes was introduced, with both substantive and procedural classifications. Substantive classification distinguishes an arrestable offense from a nonarrestable offense, whereas procedural classification determines which court hears a case and how the case is to be handled. The substantive distinction classifies crimes into two categories: arrestable and nonarrestable offenses (Terrill 1999, 49; Gardner 1989, 10). Arrestable offenses are serious offenses whose punishments are fixed by law, and they require a jury trial. English police may arrest without warrants those who perpetrate arrestable offenses. Arrestable offenses are normally tried in Crown Courts, and in some instances, the High Court may act as a court of original jurisdiction for very serious offenses. Nonarrestable offenses are less serious, and a warrant is required before an officer effects an arrest in such a case. Those accused of committing nonarrestable offenses are tried in Magistrates' Courts. For procedural purposes, offenses are classified as summary and indictable (Terrill 1999, 49–50; Gardner 1989, 10). Minor criminal offenses that are tried by a magistrate having summary jurisdiction are known as summary offenses. Examples of summary offenses are vagrancy, disorderly conduct, and a variety of traffic offenses. There are no jury trials for summary offenses. Indictable offenses are serious offenses tried in either Crown Courts or the High Court, and they are tried before a jury. In some instances, offenses may be classified as "hybrid" (Terrill 1999, 50). Hybrid offenses (also known as "either-way offenses") may be tried on indictment or summarily. When they are not tried on indictment, the prosecuting lawyer must apply to a magistrate to have the case tried summarily. Examples of hybrid offenses are cruelty to children and driving under the influence of intoxicants.

Islamic systems classify offenses into three categories: *Huddud, Quesas,* and *Ta'azir.* Huddad crimes are the most serious offenses committed against Allah. The punishments for crimes such as apostasy are listed in the Qur'an and the Sunnah. Quesas crimes are grave crimes against individuals, for which the victim or his or her family may seek revenge. Murder, for instance, is a Quesas offense, and based on the will of the victim's family, an accompanying sanction may be negotiated. Ta'azir offenses are lesser crimes that are not classified under the categories of Huddud or Quesas offenses. In addition, offenses classified under Huddud or Quesas that cannot be proven during trial may be relegated to the status of Ta'azir offenses.

The Japanese Penal Code does not classify crimes; hence, no obvious distinctions between a felony and a misdemeanor can be discerned. Although the code outlines the major offenses and the elements of the crime, the judiciary classifies crimes on a case-by-case basis. The Minor Offense Law of 1948 regulates minor offenses; a crime regulated by that act—for example, public drunkenness—is deemed a minor violation.

PUNISHMENT PHILOSOPHIES

The main purposes of criminal law are to redress criminal behavior and to maintain social order. Each country administers its own types of punishment based on the nature of the crime. The goals of punishment are retribution, deterrence, incapacitation, rehabilitation, and restitution. These punishment philosophies are emphasized differently across the world, and they vary over time. At different points in history, the punishment philosophy in the United States has shifted between retribution, rehabilitation, incapacitation, and deterrence. In socialist countries, theoretically, the emphasis of punishment is on rehabilitation; meanwhile, Islamic systems of justice, as exemplified by that of Saudi Arabia, and the hybrid system, as in Japan, stress retribution and rehabilitation.

LIMITATIONS ON CRIMINAL LAW

Each country determines how much control may be imposed on the government in the administration of criminal laws. Some of these limitations may be written in a constitution or other statutes. The U.S. Constitution, for instance, restricts the government from encroaching on the rights of the people. In France, the Constitutional Council deplores certain human rights violation; the supreme administrative court, which is the Council of State, monitors citizens' rights; and the penal code also has provisions that limit the government's powers. Although England does not have a codified constitution, the rights of citizens against whimsical governmental actions are protected by the Bill of Rights. In Russia, Article 2 of the 1993 Constitution expressly emphasizes the "observance and protection of human and civil rights" (see Terrill 1999, 425).

Some limits on the administration of criminal law in most countries are: the principle of legality, which bars the government from punishing someone for behavior that has not been defined as criminal (*nullum crimin sin lege, nulla poena sin lege*). Vague laws, laws that are too broad, retroactive laws (ex post facto laws), and cruel and unusual punishment are deplored by the United States, England, and France. But just what constitutes cruel and unusual punishment varies by country; England and France, for example, have abolished the death penalty, regarding it as cruel and unusual. Certain countries, including the United States and England, accord people the right to privacy, equal protection of the laws, and free speech and also stipulate that the government may not arbitrarily encroach on these rights. Some researchers contend that in Russia, many of these rights are not respected (see Terrill 1999, 473).

Article 76 of the Japanese Constitution grants judges judicial independence, but it nonetheless mandates judges to uphold the constitution and other laws. In addition, the Penal Code, the Code of Criminal Procedure, and the Prison Law of Japan act as checks on governmental powers. Prosecutorial practices are also checked by inquest committees and by internal court review hearings known as "analogical institutions of prosecution"(Terrill 1999, 390).

ELEMENTS OF A CRIME

There are certain elements of a crime that a prosecutor/procurator or magistrate has to prove in order to convict a defendant. In the United States, the elements of a crime are: the guilty act (*actus reus*), the guilty mind (*mens rea*), concurrence, attendant circumstance, causation, and result. These elements are consistent with those that must be proven in other western systems of law.

The Guilty Act

The guilty act is the wrongful act for which one gets punished. Evil thoughts cannot be punished, but possession of illegal items may be tantamount to a guilty act. To be considered a *guilty* act, the act must be willfully and voluntarily done. Therefore, acts committed beyond one's control (for instance, during a somnambulistic state) may not be punishable. People cannot be punished based on their condition or status because these are not actions; status refers to who we are. However, individuals can be punished for acts that *result from* their condition, as, for instance, those who rob banks because they are poor.

Words may be guilty acts if they constitute a terroristic threat, solicitation, conspiracy, sexual harassment, or incitement of a riot. An omission to act or failure to intervene may constitute a guilty act if: (1) one fails to act when required by law to do so, or (2) one fails to intervene to prevent death or harm when one has a legal duty to intervene. A legal duty can arise from statutes, from contracts, or from special relationships, such as the relationship between parent and child.

The Guilty Mind
Four different mental states are accepted as constituting mens rea: (1) general intent, which means having the mind-set to do something evil or criminal; (2) specific intent, which relates to the will to obtain a particular result from one's action; (3) transferred intent, which occurs when one intends to harm a certain person but harms another instead; and (4) constructive intent, which occurs when, even without a mind-set of doing something harmful, one's act becomes culpable because one should have known that one's behavior might result in harm to others. The U.S. Model Penal Code delineates four types of intent: purposeful, knowing, reckless, and negligent.

In Islamic law, although general intent is inferred when a crime is committed, culpability can only be proven in some instances if both general and specific intent coexist. The reasoning is that criminal responsibility may not attach to an act when committed under certain circumstances, such as necessity, wherein a person might have acted with a general intent but without the specific intent to achieve the end result (see Reichel 1999, 126).

For some types of crimes, the law holds people strictly liable even though no mens rea was present. For instance, in the United States, selling alcohol to a minor is a strict liability offense.

Concurrence
When the criminal act and the evil mind fuse, one is criminally responsible. In some instances, if there is a guilty act but no guilty mind, criminal responsibility may be reduced—for example, when a drunk driver kills a pedestrian, since a drunk person is presumed not to be able to form mens rea. In cases involving a guilty but accidental act (as, for instance, a loss of life during an auto accident), no criminal responsibility may ensue if the accident could not have been avoided.

Attendant Circumstances
Attendant circumstances relate to those facts that "surround an event"(see Reid 1998, 51). For some kinds of crimes, one cannot be found guilty if in addition to the other elements of a crime, a specific circumstance is absent. In statutory rape, for instance, the age of the victim would be the attendant circumstance; hence, if the victim is not a minor, the act cannot constitute statutory rape.

Causation
Causation refers to the requirement that for some crimes, the "criminal conduct [should] cause a particular result" (Samaha 1999, 128). There are two types of causation:

(1) factual/"but for" causation (sine qua non causation), that is, when one's act undeniable caused a particular injury, and (2) legal causation, which relates to the proximate cause of harm. Courts have to prove whether an initial act or an intervening act is more likely to have caused a particular result.

In Islamic law, there is a slight twist because "a person is held criminally responsible even if some contributing factors intervene to assist in bringing about the criminal result as long as these factors are insufficient to bring about the result by themselves and do not break the causal relationship between the result and the act or omission, which remains the principal cause" (Sanad 1991, 86, quoted in Reichel 1999, 126).

CRIMINAL LIABILITY/PARTIES TO A CRIME
The doctrine of complicity outlines circumstances under which two or more persons become liable for the criminal activities of another during every stage of the criminal venture. Sometimes, liability may ensue vicariously based on the relationship of the criminal and some nonparticipant; for example, an employer may be held liable for the crimes of an employee committed within the scope of employment. Common law classifies participants to a crime in four categories: (1) principals in the first, who carry out the crime; (2) principals in the second, who are present at the crime scene to aid and abet the principal; (3) accessories before the fact, who aid and abet before the crime is carried out; and (4) accessories after the fact, who provide assistance and comfort to those who carry out a crime. Various criminal statutes in the United States have merged the categories of principals in the second and accessories before the fact, and the participants are now known as accomplices.

In the French Penal Code, Article 121-4 defines the principal of a crime as anyone who commits an incriminating act or attempts to commit a crime, or delit. Article 121-7 defines an accomplice as anyone who knowingly aids or assists in the facilitation or preparation of a crime or delit-misdemeanor. The code further defines an accomplice as one who utilizes a promise, threat, order, or abuse of power to incite the commission of an infraction or gives instructions for it to be committed.

Each system of law has provisions to punish accomplices. In general, the law of complicity is quite complex, and even in the United States, how accomplices are handled in court varies from state to state and from case to case. In some instances, just aligning with the criminal venture suffices for a punishment equal to that given the principal. In other situations, the intent of the parties is at the core of punishment practices. In *Enmund v. Florida* (458 U.S. 782 [1982]), for instance, the U.S. Supreme Court ruled that the death penalty was cruel and unusual punishment for Enmund, a coconspirator, since he only intended to aid and abet a robbery, not the killing of the robbery victims. In *Tison v. Arizona* (95 L.Ed.2d 127 [1987]), by contrast, the U.S. Supreme Court upheld the death penalty for the coconspirator because according to the court, even though he had no specific intent to kill the victims, his conduct amounted to "reckless disregard for human life" and thus was tantamount to an intent to kill.

TYPES OF CRIMES

Each society determines what behavior is criminal, and with the rapid advance of technology, there are now several different types of crimes that were not envisaged in other centuries—software theft, Internet fraud, and cable theft, among others.

Besides some of the more common crimes that are successfully carried out, such as murder, criminal law also punishes incomplete or inchoate offenses. In order to have anticipatory offenses punished, most statutes following common law require that some action toward completing the crime be manifested, that a specific intent to commit that crime exist, and that the punishment be of a lesser magnitude than that meted out for a completed crime. Three inchoate offenses are distinguished: (1) attempt, (2) conspiracy, and (3) solicitation. Article 121-5 of the French Penal Code addresses the crime of attempt. Similar to the common law requirement, French law also requires the manifestation of an overt act and stipulates that for the offense to be punishable, circumstances that hinder the completion of the crime should be independent of a voluntary renunciation. The less likely the completion of an offense, the less severe its punishment would be. That is, the justification of punishing an offense weakens as the completion of the crime becomes more remote. Therefore, the crime of solicitation (requesting someone to commit a crime) receives less punishment than conspiracy (agreement to commit a crime) or attempt (taking substantial steps to carry out the crime).

Islamic countries, for instance, punish crimes such as apostasy, and statutes against blasphemy still exist in some states in the United States, but they are rarely, if ever, enforced. In Singapore, the list of minor violations includes letting the hair grow below the upper part of the shirt collar (for men), break dancing in public areas, and public spitting (see Austin 1987, 283–285).

DEFENSES TO CRIMINAL LIABILITY

Three broad categories of defenses to criminal liability are recognized in the United States. These defenses are common in other systems of law, as well, even though they may be classified differently, and the crimes for which they may be used may be dictated by cultural practices. First is the alibi, which negates one's physical presence at a crime scene. Second is the defense of justification, whereby the defendant admits responsibility but contends that under the circumstances, what he or she did was the right thing to do. Some of the defenses that fall under this category are self-defense, defense of home and property, defense of others, execution of duty, necessity/choice of evils, and consent. Third is the defense of excuse, whereby the defendant acknowledges committing an offense but shifts responsibility to something that overwhelmed him or her. That something could be duress, entrapment, intoxication, age, mistake, syndrome, or insanity.

In the Islamic system, a defendant facing charges for a crime of theft may raise a "destruction of the property" defense if the property involved is something prohibited by Islamic law. A defendant charged with theft of liquor, for example, may claim that the basis for the theft was to discard it since liquor is forbidden by Islamic law.

Victoria M. Time

See also China; Civil Law; Civil Procedure; Common Law; Criminal Procedures; England and Wales; France; Germany; Islamic Law; Japan; Private Law; Prosecuting Authorities; Public Law; Rehabilitation; Retribution; Russia; Saudi Arabia; Singapore; Soviet System; United States—Federal System; United States—State Systems

References and further reading
Austin, W. Timothy. 1987. "Crime and Custom in an Orderly Society: The Singapore Prototype." *Criminology* 25, no 2: 279–294.
Beermann, R. 1975. "The Role of Law and Legality in the Soviet Union." *Review of Socialist Law* 1: 97–111.
Cadavino, Michael, and James Dignan. 1997. *The Penal System: An Introduction.* 2nd ed. London: Sage.
Dean, Meryll. 1997. *Japanese Legal System: Text and Materials.* London: Cavendish.
Gardner, Thomas J. 1989. *Criminal Law: Principles and Cases.* 4th ed. St. Paul, NY: West Publishing.
Goutal, Jean. 1976. "Characteristics of Judicial Style in France, Britain, and the U.S.A." *American Journal of Comparative Law* 24: 43–72.
Hazard, John N. 1984. *The Soviet Legal System: The Law in the 1980s.* New York: Oceana Publications.
Rabenou, Jerome, "Code Penal," http://www.rabenou.org/divers/penal.html (cited October 23, 2000).
Reichel, Philip L. 1999. *Comparative Criminal Justice Systems: A Topical Approach.* 2nd ed. Upper Saddle River, NJ: Prentice-Hall.
Reid, Sue T. 1998. *Criminal Law.* 4th ed. Boston and Burr Ridge, IL: McGraw-Hill.
Samaha, Joel. 1999. *Criminal Law.* 6th ed. Belmont, CA, and Albany, NY: West/Wadsworth.
Sanad, Nagaty. 1991. *The Theory of Crime and Criminal Responsibility in Islamic Law: Shari'a.* Chicago: Office of International Criminal Justice.
Schmalleger, Frank. 1999. *Criminal Law Today.* Upper Saddle River, NJ: Prentice-Hall.
Souryal, Sam S., Dennis W. Potts, and Abdullah I. Alobied.

1994. "The Penalty of Hand Amputation for Theft in Islamic Justice." *Journal of Criminal Justice* 22: 249–265.

Terrill, Richard J. 1999. *World Criminal Justice Systems*. 4th ed. Cincinnati, OH: Anderson Publishing.

CRIMINAL PROCEDURES

The criminal justice system is structured around criminal laws, laws of evidence, and procedural laws. Criminal procedures are critical to the maintenance of law and order in any society, for they govern the method to be followed in deciding whether any individual or entity alleged to have committed a crime is guilty. With new developments in social and interpersonal behavior and the increase in the prevalence of organized crimes, transnational and international crimes, corporate criminality, and offenses affecting national security and territorial integrity (such as those perpetrated by terrorists), criminal procedure systems are undergoing changes around the world.

New developments in the fields of information technology have also had an impact on criminal justice systems and improved their efficiency and productivity. Increased awareness of social issues and the intrinsic behavior of human beings, developments in the science of criminology, and sensitivity to the rights of victims of crimes have all led to changes in procedural aspects. One example is systems wherein a trial is held in one location and the witness is questioned and his or her testimony is recorded at a different location and simultaneously played at the trial venue. In addition, the availability of new forms of assimilating, recording, and disseminating information has led most criminal justice systems to evolve to the extent that they accept as evidence not only human testimony but also alternative forms of proof— for instance, evidence of shoplifting recorded in a supermarket's closed-circuit video recording. Modern criminal justice systems facilitate the presentation of such evidence even in the absence of human testimony. Advancements in the field of forensic sciences (such as DNA technology and new techniques relating to establishing the identity of the dead) have also led to developments in various criminal justice systems aimed at admitting such evidence in new forms.

Developments in the field of human rights law and international criminal law have spawned new approaches that seek to broaden the basic scope of criminal justice systems. For example "universal jurisdiction" seeks to vest jurisdiction in national criminal courts, deviating from the principles of territoriality and nationality. Accordingly, a court may, in certain circumstances, assume jurisdiction to try a person accused of having committed an offense against humanity, genocide, or a war crime even though the offense at issue is alleged to have been committed outside its territorial jurisdictional limits and by an individual who is not a national of the country.

For most underdeveloped and developing countries, criminal justice systems continue to be a heavy burden. Typically, their systems are outdated, underresourced, and overloaded, and they tend to malfunction. Given the heavy workloads of such systems, delayed justice is a common occurrence: Indeed, it is not uncommon for criminal trials to be taken up as much as ten years after the offense was committed.

In the post–World War II period, the world has witnessed a new breed of criminal justice systems—the "international tribunals" established by the international community to investigate, inquire into, and determine specific incidents and situations relating to mass human rights violations. These tribunals, which possess punitive powers, are based on the concept of universal jurisdiction. As of 2001, three international criminal tribunals (also referred to as ad hoc international criminal courts), established under the authority of resolutions adopted by the UN Security Council, are functioning and empowered to inquire into human rights violations in the former Yugoslavia, Rwanda, and East Timor. Another tribunal is being established in relation to Sierra Leone, and negotiations are being conducted to establish yet another for the atrocities committed in Cambodia. In addition, the world community is on the verge of witnessing the birth of the International Criminal Court (ICC), which will be a broad, long-term international criminal court (as opposed to the ad hoc tribunals mentioned earlier), empowered by the community of states to investigate and try individuals alleged to have committed war crimes, crimes against humanity, and genocide.

Criminal procedure systems around the world takes various forms. These forms are generally based on the respective country's constitutional and judicial institutional framework, legal systems, principles relating to the burden of proof (in criminal cases), admissibility of evidence, and other concepts such as processes relating to criminal trials being heard by juries. However, as a basic concept, most criminal justice systems are founded on principles relating to rules of natural justice and due process of law. Basically, these concepts of procedural law are structured around a series of legal principles that seek to ensure a fair trial. While most countries have their own criminal justice systems, some that were once colonies have inherited the systems of their colonial masters. For example, most nations that were colonies of the British Empire have inherited basic structures of the British criminal justice system. After independence, these systems typically evolved and developed in accordance with the country's domestic needs but not to the extent of replacing the inherited legacy. Thus, most erstwhile British colonies possess a somewhat common criminal procedure system.

Due to limitations of space, it is impossible to describe the main strands of criminal procedure systems throughout the world. However, taking into consideration the fundamental classification of these systems (based on similarity in approach, procedure, and application of legal concepts), this short essay provides an overview of the basic features of criminal procedure systems of selected jurisdictions.

UNITED STATES

Unlike most countries, the United States does not have a single criminal justice system. Instead, systems vary from state to state.

The U.S. criminal justice system comes into play with the commission of an offense. In most instances, information relating to that act is received by the relevant law enforcement agency from indirect sources, including the victim of the offense, a witness to the crime, nongovernmental organizations such as neighborhood groups, or state agencies such as public health organizations. On other occasions, information is directly received by law enforcement agencies—for example, if the offense is committed in the presence of law enforcement officers. After the information relating to the commission of a criminal offense has been received and the relevant law enforcement agency has established that an offense was, in fact, committed, the law imposes a duty on the relevant agency to conduct a criminal investigation..

A vital milestone in that process is the apprehension (arrest) of the suspect. If the investigation reveals the innocence of the arrested suspect, the investigator releases him or her from custody even if the suspect has not been produced before a court of law. The suspect is so produced only if there are reasonable grounds to believe he or she was involved in committing the crime. At this stage, information relating to the criminal act and any evidence currently available are reported to the prosecutor, who uses that information to decide whether to file formal charges in court. The law requires that suspects in custody of the police be produced before a court of law without unnecessary delay. Once the suspect appears in court, the judge must decide whether to continue to detain the individual or to release him or her before trial. If the charge being leveled against the accused is of a minor nature, he or she may opt to plead guilty to the charge (without opting to proceed to trial); the judge will then be required to convict the accused based on the plea of guilt and decide on the penal sanctions to be imposed.

After the completion of the investigation and the initial appearance of the suspect in a court of law, there is a preliminary hearing, during which efforts are made to determine whether probable cause exists to believe the accused has committed the offense charged and whether that offense is within the jurisdiction of the relevant court. At this stage, a detailed inquiry is not envisaged, and courts are required only to consider the basic nature and reliability of the available material, enabling a decision on the justification of the charge. If the judge determines that no probable cause exists, the accused is dismissed from further proceedings. If not, the case is bound over to a grand jury. In the grand jury, the prosecutor presents the available evidence against the accused, which the jury then weighs in deciding whether there is sufficient evidence to try the accused. If the grand jury decides in favor of the prosecutor, it is required to submit to the court an indictment (containing details of the offense allegedly committed by the accused), together with a written statement of the essential facts of the offense at issue. After the presentation of an indictment, or "information" (generally issued in cases involving misdemeanors), the accused is arraigned in court. At the arraignment, the charges are read to the accused, and he or she is informed of his or her rights; then, the accused's plea of guilt or nonguilt is recorded. On this occasion, the accused has the option of (1) pleading guilty to the charge, (2) negotiating an amendment to the indictment by pleading guilty to a lesser charge, (3) pleading "nolo contendere" (an acceptance of penal sanctions without admitting guilt to the charge), or (4) pleading not guilty. If he or she pleads not guilty, the case will be set for trial. In all other instances, the court proceeds to convict and sentence the accused. On rare occasions when the judge believes that the guilty plea has been tendered by an accused who does not comprehend the consequences of such a plea or who has been coerced, the plea may be rejected and the case will be set for trial.

The U.S. system guarantees a trial by jury to every individual accused of having committed a serious crime. However, in some instances, the accused is entitled to elect a bench trial, wherein it is the judge and not the jury that serves as the finder of fact. In either circumstance, however, it is the judge who decides questions of law. The trial proceeds on the premise that the prosecution has to prove the guilt of the accused and that until such an obligation is fulfilled, the accused is not required to prove his or her innocence. At the conclusion of the trial, the accused is either acquitted or convicted of the original charges or lesser charges. If the accused is convicted, he or she may seek review of the conviction or the sentence through an appeal process.

UNITED KINGDOM

In the United Kingdom, as in the United States, the suspect is arrested and produced before a court (in the UK system, the Magistrates' Court). The decision to produce the suspect in the Magistrates' Court is taken by the Crown Prosecution Service, based on a realistic prospect of securing a conviction against that individual. In the

Magistrates' Court, if the allegation against the accused relates to a summary offense (an offense that the Magistrates' Court has the jurisdiction to try directly), the accused is tried immediately. Cases involving offenses that require the accused to be tried on indictment (that is, more serious offenses) are sent to the Crown Court. Cases relating to a third category of offenses—those over which both the Magistrates' Court and the Crown Court have trial jurisdiction—are considered separately by the magistrate, who determines whether the magistrates will try the accused or whether the case will be sent to the Crown Court.

Cases before the Crown Court are heard by a judge sitting with a jury. The trial process is generally similar in nature and procedure to that in the U.S. system, with the burden of proof lying with the prosecution—that is, the prosecutor must prove the accused has committed the offense contained in the indictment.

FRANCE

In the French system, investigations into crimes are necessarily conducted by the police under the direction of the public prosecutor. After the investigation is completed, either the public minister or the victim of the crime can take steps to initiate criminal proceedings in a court of law. During the first phase of the judicial process, the accused is presented before the Chamber of Accusation, where a magistrate examines the available material against the accused. This magistrate is empowered to examine and record the statement of the accused, and he or she also performs an investigative role. At the end of this process, a decision is taken to either prosecute the accused or discontinue the proceedings. If the accused is to be prosecuted, the prosecution is conducted by the public minister. An important and unique feature of the French criminal justice system is that accused individuals are not permitted to plead guilty to indictments: All criminal cases relating to serious offenses necessarily proceed to trial, in the Assize Courts. The Correctional Courts have jurisdiction to try persons accused of offenses that carry a term of imprisonment not exceeding ten years. Police Courts possess jurisdiction to try accuseds who are alleged to have committed minor offenses (termed *violations of the law*), which carry terms of imprisonment that do not exceed two months or a maximum fine of 25,000 francs. Trials in the Assize Courts are heard by a judge sitting with a nine-member jury. An important procedural feature relating to the decisions of the Assize Courts is that they are not subject to an Appeal and hence are final.

CHINA

The Chinese criminal justice system is defined as a typically "Marxist" system. All criminal offenses are classified into one of eight groups: crimes of counterrevolution, crimes of endangering public security, crimes of undermining the socialist economic order, crimes of infringing on the right of the person and the democratic rights of citizens, crimes of property violations, crimes of disrupting social order, crimes of disrupting marriage, and crimes of dereliction of duty. For purposes of prosecution, these offenses are regrouped into two other groups—crimes of public prosecution and crimes of private prosecution.

A unique feature in the Chinese system is that the accused has the right to be defended by a lay citizen (recommended by a people's organization or defender's unit), by a close relative or guardian, or by a professional lawyer.

ITALY

Judicial proceedings in Italy begin with a preliminary judicial investigation. In the case of flagrant offenses—those admitted by the suspect or demonstrated by clear evidence—the investigation is conducted by a magistrate of the Public Prosecutor's Office and is known as *istruzione sommaria*. In all other cases, the investigation is carried out by an investigating judge and is called *istruzione formale*. The public prosecutor decides which of these two procedures is to be followed, but a suspect may request that the investigating judge undertake the preliminary inquiry. If the suspect is in custody, the investigation must be carried out by the investigating judge if, after forty days, the public prosecutor has not asked for a discharge or a trial.

JAPAN

In Japan, after the completion of a criminal investigation by the police, the findings of the investigation are reported by the police to a public prosecutor. If the investigator seeks continued detention of the suspect pending trial, the matter must be referred to a public prosecutor within forty-eight hours.

In Japan, accused persons are not convicted on their own pleas of guilt; hence, all cases necessarily proceed to trial. In addition, there are no jury trials. Public prosecutors possess considerable power to control and direct criminal cases. Notwithstanding the availability of adequate evidence, they can suspend prosecutions. They are also empowered to investigate complex criminal offenses without the assistance of the police.

SRI LANKA

Being a former colony of the British Empire, Sri Lanka has a criminal procedure system similar to that of many Commonwealth countries. The law governing criminal procedure was enacted in 1979 and has remained in force, subject to certain modifications. At present, jury trials are limited to cases of murder, attempted murder, and rape. Even in these cases, however, the accused enjoys the right to choose to be tried by a judge sitting without a jury. In a unique system, certain cases can be heard by three judges of the High Court sitting without a jury. Cases in this category involve crimes relating to (1) waging war against the republic, (2) conspiracy to wage war, (3) collecting persons, arms, ammunition, and so forth for the purpose of waging war, and (4) other matters that, in the opinion of the chief justice, warrant commissioning a special court due to the nature of the offense or circumstances relating to the offense and in the interests of justice. This type of trial is referred to as a trial-at-bar. A recent innovation, following developments in India, provides for anticipatory bail—whereby a person can appear before a magistrate in anticipation of being arrested on the basis of a complaint likely to be made and thereby obtain bail.

This necessarily brief survey exemplifies the divergent approaches adopted by selected jurisdictions to regulate criminal procedures. Systems seek, by and large, to balance the rights of persons charged with crimes to be tried impartially according to a procedure with a degree of certainty, on the one hand, and the right of society to ensure that criminal proceedings are conducted without fear or favor, on the other.

Dayanath C. Jayasuriya
Yasantha Kodagoda

See also China; France; India; Italy; Japan; Juries; Sri Lanka; United Kingdom; United States—State Systems; War Crimes Tribunals

References and further reading
Cole, George F. 1995. *The American System of Criminal Justice.* 7th ed. Belmont, CA: Wadsworth.
David, R., and J. E. Brierley. 1985. *Major Legal Systems of the World Today.* London: Stevens.
Guangzhong, Cheng. *Science of Criminal Procedure Law.* Beijing Law Publishing House.
Hamilton, Hugh. M. 1956. *Hamilton and Addison Criminal Law and Procedure.* 6th ed. Sydney: The Law Book Company of Australia.
Hampton, Celia. 1977. *Criminal Procedure.* 2nd ed. London: Sweet and Maxwell.
Kalmanoff, Alan. 1976. *Criminal Justice: Enforcement and Administration.* Boston: Little, Brown.
Newman, Graeme, Adam C. Bouloukos, and Debra Cohen. 2001. *World Fact Book of Criminal Justice Systems.* http://www.ojp.usdoj.gov/bjs/abstract/wfcj.htm.
Peiris, G. L. 1998. *Criminal Procedure in Sri Lanka.* 2nd ed. Columbo, Sri Lanka: Stamford Lake.
Shkit, M., and S. Tsuchiya. 1992. *Crime and Criminal Policy in Japan.* New York: Springer-Verlag.
Sohoni. 1990. *The Code of Criminal Procedure (India).* 19th ed. Revised by R. Nagaratnam. Allahabad, India: The Law Book Company.

CRIMINAL SANCTIONS, PURPOSES OF

DEFINITION

Andrew von Hirsch (1976, 35) defined a criminal sanction as "the infliction by the state of consequences normally considered unpleasant, on a person in response to his having been convicted of a crime." Like most definitions of a criminal sanction, this statement consists of five key elements (Hart 1968). First, a criminal sanction involves the infliction of pain or some other unpleasant consequence. Second, it is given to an individual when the law is broken. Third, it is applied to the individual identified by the legal system as the offender. Fourth, it is intentionally given. Fifth, it is administered by an entity (such as the state) whose authority comes from the legal system against which the offense was committed.

APPLICABILITY

The concept of a criminal sanction as an unpleasant consequence given by the state to an individual for committing a criminal offense is incorporated in all judicial and legal systems of the industrialized world. In fact, Hyman Gross and von Hirsch (1981) argued that every legal system in the modern world specifies criminal sanctions for those who break the law; every system also has laws that prohibit certain behaviors and regulate the procedures of the legal system.

VARIATIONS

Though criminal sanctions are imposed by legal systems across the globe, the purpose of such sanctions may vary across place and time. Four major purposes of criminal sanctions are identified: deterrence, rehabilitation, retribution, and incapacitation.

Deterrence refers to the idea that criminal sanctions can prevent individuals from committing crimes by instilling in them a fear of punishment. The deterrence philosophy is based on the assumptions of the classical school of thought, which views individuals as rational, free-willed, and hedonistic beings. Individuals' behavior, both criminal and noncriminal, results from decisions that they make in attempting to increase their pleasure and avoid pain. Under these assumptions, it is believed that criminal behavior can be controlled with criminal sanctions that, if swift, severe, and certain enough, increase the costs of crime.

Deterrence theorists generally speak of two types of deterrence—individual and general. With individual deterrence, the purpose of the criminal sanction is to instill fear in a specific offender, thus reducing the likelihood that he or she will commit another crime. With general deterrence, the purpose of punishing an individual offender is to illustrate to the general public the costs of crime. Deterrence theory predicts that witnessing another being punished will reduce the likelihood that a member of the general public will ever commit a crime.

When it comes to rehabilitation, the purpose of the criminal sanction is to treat the offender. Rehabilitation as a justification for criminal sanctions is based on the assumptions of positivism. Contrary to the classical school of thought, positivism assumes that individual behavior is determined, that individuals who commit crimes are "sick," and that their "illnesses" are beyond their control. Under this set of assumptions, it is believed that punishment will not work. What will work to reduce crime is providing offenders with "cures" for their "illnesses."

The purposes of retribution and incapacitation as criminal sanctions are as straightforward as those of deterrence and rehabilitation. According to retributivists, offenders should be sanctioned because they deserve to be. Retributivists argue that when people commit crimes, they have harmed society. To restore the balance of justice, offenders must be punished. In terms of incapacitation, the purpose of the criminal sanction is to prevent offenders from committing further crimes through restraint, such as imprisonment. Although incapacitation is an important component of many individuals' thinking regarding the purpose of criminal sanctions, it is generally viewed as a supplement to one of the other purposes of sanctions rather than as the primary justification.

EVOLUTION AND CHANGE

Different periods in history are associated with the predominance of each of the four major purposes of criminal sanctions. The discussion begins with the development of the classical school of thought and deterrence.

Philosophers such as Thomas Hobbes recognized early on the state's need to control the behavior of hedonistic individuals. It was with the 1764 publication of Cesare Beccaria's *On Crimes and Punishments,* though, that the classical school of thought arose and with it a framework for understanding the role of criminal sanctions in deterring criminal behavior. Based on the idea of offenders as rational, free-willed, and hedonistic beings, Beccaria argued that the most efficient method of crime control was to set sanctions at a level at which they raised the cost of crime higher than the benefits. He argued that efficient sanctions would be characterized by severity, promptness, and certainty. For Beccaria, severity meant that sanctions should be proportionate to the harm caused by the crime; sanctions more severe than that would actually cause crime as offenders tried to avoid punishment. The promptness of a sanction was important, according to Beccaria, because it would connect the pain of the sanction with the pleasure of the crime in the offender's mind. Of the three characteristics, however, Beccaria argued that certainty was the most important. He believed that most people commit

crimes not because they do not fear the punishment but because they do not think they will be caught. In fact, he believed that if we increased the certainty of punishments, we would be able to reduce their severity and still control crime. Along with his support for the reduction of torture, for the publication of laws that were clear, and for the separation of judges who applied the laws from legislators who made the law, Beccaria's ideas about criminal sanctions changed the shape of criminal justice forever. Today, they remain at the heart of the criminal justice systems in all modern, industrialized nations.

Traditionally, proponents of deterrence as the justification for criminal sanctions are distinguished by their support for a number of policies, including determinate and mandatory sentencing. Determinate sentencing is one of the hallmarks of a system based on deterrence. With determinate sentencing, both the offender and the public know the cost of each crime because the legal code specifies the sanction individuals will receive if they break the law. Mandatory sentences, which set specific sentences for certain crimes as mandated by law, are also a common characteristic of sanctions under legal systems that center on deterrence.

For approximately 100 years, the classical school dominated legal thought, and deterrence was viewed as the primary justification for criminal sanctions. Criticisms were voiced, however, by those who believed the classical school was based on a simplistic theory of the cause of crime and a failure to consider the offender. These criticisms combined with the influence of the scientific revolution to lead to the emergence of a second school of thought—positivism.

The origin of positivism in criminology is most often associated with the work of Cesare Lombroso in the middle to late 1800s. In direct contrast to the classical school, positivism centers around the assumptions that human behavior is determined and that offenders, who are "sick," are different from nonoffenders. From that conception flows the belief that offenders should be "treated" on an individual basis rather than punished as rational individuals who made a free-willed decision to offend. Based on these assumptions, the positivist would contend, rehabilitation or treatment of offenders should be the primary justification for sentencing. Lombroso proposed the development and use of a number of programs and policies that continue today in legal systems across the world. These include penitentiaries to give offenders time for reflection and repentance, indeterminate sentencing, probation, vocational and educational programs in prisons, and special laws and courts for children, designed to keep them away from the influence of hardened offenders.

Rehabilitation as the primary justification for criminal sanctions dominated correctional philosophy across the world through the Progressive era. But as the United States entered the second half of the twentieth century, things began to change yet again. By the 1960s, criticisms of rehabilitation led, once more, to a discussion of deterrence as the primary justification for sanctions. Basic critiques of rehabilitation started with reports indicating that rehabilitative programs did not work to prevent crime. Critics also argued that the rehabilitative ideal was responsible for a great many inequities in sentencing, since two people committing the same crime could get two very different sentences. Such criticisms, combined with the perception that crime was on the rise, brought calls for increased "law and order." At that time, proponents of deterrence argued that sanction policies based on deterrence ideals would be both more effective at preventing crime and more just: more effective because they would increase the costs of crime and more just because sentences would not be allowed to vary based on offender characteristics.

By the 1980s, the emphasis that proponents of deterrence had placed on justice led to a greater consideration of the importance of justice itself as the primary rationale for punishment (von Hirsch 1985). Soon, proponents of retributivism arose to argue that justice, not deterrence, should be our main reason for sentencing. Further, they argued that neither rehabilitation nor deterrence worked as a primary justification, since both could foster injustice—rehabilitation because it required that sentences vary according to individual characteristics and deterrence because it could result in unjustly harsh punishments. These retributivists, however, did believe that deterrence was an important secondary justification for punishment because it limited the harm done to the offender by the sanction to an amount that would prevent further crimes (von Hirsch 1976).

Throughout the 1980s, there was an uneasy alliance between the proponents of deterrence and the retributivists, with neither side appearing to dominate policy. For some, the differences between the two approaches were not important, since in many ways, the policies that each mandated coincided. However, one area in particular clearly pointed to the difference between the two camps—selective incapacitation.

Selective incapacitation refers to policies in which certain offenders are selected to have their sentences lengthened because of the likelihood that they will commit future crimes. Those who argue for deterrence as the primary purpose of punishment support the use of selective incapacitation because of its potential for preventing crime. Those who argue for retribution as the primary purpose do not support the use of selective incapacitation for two reasons. First, they argue that it is unjust to punish people for crimes they have not yet committed. Second, they argue that selective incapacitation will not be

effective because we cannot accurately predict who will commit crimes in the future.

Throughout the 1990s, the United States renewed its emphasis on deterrence as the justification for criminal sanctions. Fear of crime was generated, in part, by the perception of substantial increases in all categories of crimes, the real increases in juvenile violent crimes, and several striking and highly publicized incidents of violence in schools. Combined with a return to conservatism in politics, public calls to "do something about crime" led to the popularity of a llaw-and-order approach that emphasized crime control through increased punishment. In particular, the 1990s were a time in which the United States became fearful that offenders, both adult and juvenile, were getting the message that crime would not be punished. Policy changes then revolved around sending the message that the country was, indeed, "tough on crime." The juvenile justice system in particular saw many changes aimed at just this goal. As a result of these policy changes, incarceration rates in the United States almost quadrupled between 1970 and the mid-1990s (Currie 1998).

According to Michael Tonry (1999), European countries and other modern industrialized nations have generally not followed the United States in terms of these policy changes. Today, the nations of Europe are much more likely than the United States to have and to use alternatives to imprisonment, such as day fines and community service. Western European countries also do not employ the death penalty. These differences in policy have resulted in a clear variance in the use of imprisonment. Incarceration rates and sentence lengths for the United States are higher than those of almost all industrialized countries (Currie 1998).

Every modern legal system describes laws defining actions that the society wishes to prohibit and punishments associated with those actions. Though there is variation across time and place in terms of the justification a society gives for punishment of offenders, justifications generally fall into one of four categories—deterrence, rehabilitation, retrubution, and incapacitation. Only time will tell where the legal systems of today's societies will lead us in the search for effective and just criminal sanctions.

Ruth Triplett

See also Capital Punishment; Corporal Punishment; Criminal Law; General Deterrence; Rehabilitation; Retribution; Specific (Individual) Deterrence
References and further reading
Beccaria, Cesare. [1764] 1963. *On Crimes and Punishments.* Indianapolis, IN: Bobbs-Merrill.
Currie, Elliott. 1998. *Crime and Punishment in America.* New York: Henry Holt.
Gross, Hyman, and Andrew von Hirsch. 1981. *Sentencing.* New York: Oxford University Press.

Hart, H. L. A. 1968. *Punishments and Responsibility*. Oxford: Oxford University Press.

Tonry, Michael. 1999. "Parochialism in U.S. Sentencing Policy." *Crime and Delinquency* 45: 48–65.

von Hirsh, Andrew. 1976. *Doing Justice*. New York: Hill and Wang.

———. 1985. *Past or Future Crimes*. New Brunswick, NJ: Rutgers University Press.

Wilson, James Q. 1975. *Thinking about Crime*. New York: Basic Books.

CRITICAL LEGAL STUDIES

During the 1970s and 1980s, orthodoxy in law was challenged by a school of thought seeking to transcend conditions of unfulfilled promise and continuing patterns of domination in the United States. This school of thought was known as critical legal studies (CLS), and it sought to understand law's role in reproducing or legitimizing oppressive conditions. This entry will explore the intellectual precursors of CLS, examples of the CLS scholarly project, and that project's failure and success.

A diverse intellectual field that includes theoretical insights from Max Weber, Marxism, "superliberalism," and poststructuralism, CLS focuses primarily on legal doctrine. What unites CLS is a common enemy—liberalism—which CLS understands as the theoretical foundation of U.S. law. Liberalism is a political and legal theory premised on the principle of the priority of the individual to society. Because freedom of the individual is prioritized, limits to the individual's freedom are only justified based on the individual's consent. In the familial realm, the child is not understood to possess a fully mature will, and hence the child may be governed only until it is capable of autonomous will formation. In the economic realm, the individual's obligations are legitimized through contracts to which the individual has consented. And in the political realm, governmental force is legitimate only to the extent that consent justifies it. Thus, the only legitimate governmental actions are those enacted through valid, formal laws, and governmental actions face certain limits with respect to individual and family life. So, state sovereignty is constrained from reaching inequalities within the familial realm because of the marriage contract and the right to privacy. Additionally, although all citizens theoretically enjoy an abstract equality vis-à-vis the state, inequalities in the economic realm are justified on the grounds that they are due to the merits or failures of individual contracting behavior. The government, moreover, is barred from tampering with these economic inequalities because that would transgress the norm of legal neutrality as preserved through the preeminent liberal right that the individual holds against the government, the right to property.

The legitimacy of this system is based on several grounds: that law and the state are neutral and do not affect the distribution of property among individuals; that law can be interpreted objectively; that judges can and do interpret the law objectively; and that all governmental activity is legally justified. CLS attacks the theory of law that legitimates liberalism, claiming that law does not function as objectively or as neutrally as the liberal legal orthodoxy claims. The implications of this critique include, for example, the insight that the present distribution of economic resources is neither random nor due to merit or desert but is political—a consequence for which humans bear some responsibility. CLS proceeds, then, to examine law's role in forestalling a political solution to the political problem of economic and other inequalities.

PRECURSORS AND THEORETICAL INFLUENCES

CLS locates itself as an offspring of legal realism, a U.S.-based legal theory of the 1920s–1940s that is itself informed by the philosophy of pragmatism. Legal realism attacks the notion that law is susceptible to objective interpretation (a criticism of legal positivism) and that law can be hermetically sealed off from social influence (a criticism of legal formalism). For example, this scholarship finds that law must distinguish between legitimate inequalities and those inequalities that shall count as "duress" and therefore serve to void a contract. Thus, law makes value judgments that cannot be accounted for legally. It does not remain fully value neutral toward an individual's subjective decision making in the act of contracting.

Because contradictory outcomes of a given case may be produced, depending on the judge's subjective interpretation of the situation and his decision to follow one legal rule rather than another, law is often said to be "indeterminate." Some legal realism tries to contain the subjective dimension of the legal process. Although this wing of legal realism acknowledges law's indeterminacy, it reintroduces objectivity as it makes law the functional output of positively determined inputs such as the behavior of judges or assessments of "efficient" public policy. Much of the work of political science, which attempts to describe scientifically judicial behavior, or the conservative law and economics school, which seeks legal rules to maximize the efficiency of markets, can be seen as the offspring of this wing of legal realism. Other realists, such as Felix Cohen, understand that in the domain of law, facts and values are not so neatly distinguished. We may think of CLS as deriving from this wing of legal realism politically, although CLS shares with legal realism an ambivalence toward indeterminacy. Is the criticism of law's objectivity a subset of a broader argument that everything is indeterminate? Or is the problem with law its indeterminacy, and thus we ought to re-anchor our politics and our analyses to more stable foundations?

LAW AND THE DISTRIBUTION OF ECONOMIC INEQUALITIES

CLS criticizes the notion that law is neutral or objective (hence not political) and investigates how the politics of law are hidden from public view in order to protect the system from egalitarian change. For many "crits," liberalism's public-private distinction helps to mask law's politics. These themes are notable in Morton Horwitz's award-winning legal history, *The Transformation of American Law 1780–1860*. Horwitz contends that constitutional law (i.e., public law) in the United States is overstudied, particularly if one seeks to understand the connection between law and the economy. He turns the reader's attention to private law at the state level in order to grasp the more regular ways in which law, economy, and society interact to facilitate capitalist socio-economic relations and to reflect commercial interests in this process.

For example, analyzing litigation arising from Massachusetts's 1795 "mill acts," Horwitz charts how legal standards changed for determining when one person's property rights are violated by another. Horwitz describes how earlier legal practices privileged those who established themselves as property owners first and allowed these first users to prevent conflicting uses of property by those who came later. This privileged first users as markets were being developed. Once development reached a certain point, however, the law limited claims it formerly allowed in order to promote efficiency through competition. The later legal standard asked merely whether the productive value of one's property had been damaged, thereby allowing more actors to become commercially involved (Horwitz 1977, chap. 2).

The change in the conception of property to the idea that an essential attribute of property is the right to develop regardless of consequences to others is basically a system of subsidy for economic development, according to Horwitz. This system of subsidy, however, works not through a legislatively enacted tax system but through the judicial system. By promoting certain property interests over others, this system is certainly political rather than neutral. Because it is promoted through private law rather than taxes enacted by legislatures, it is hidden and easy to disguise politically, Horwitz argues. It exacerbates inequality because those least organized and active are forced to bear the greatest burdens of industrialization (chap. 3). Thus, Horwitz demonstrates that private law has political and therefore public consequences. This conclusion undermines the liberal public-private distinction and its position that law—particularly private law—is neutral. In this way, Horwitz shows how liberalism shields the political aspects of economic questions from

democratic consideration in order to promote commercial interests.

LEGAL INDETERMINACY

In the first volume of his history of U.S. law, Horwitz presents law as functionally determined by capitalist economic development. The picture of law that appears in Clare Dalton's "An Essay in the Deconstruction of Contract Doctrine," however, is indeterminate: law is capable of being manipulated by judges to whatever conclusions they are interested in reaching. In her essay, Dalton draws from poststructuralism to "deconstruct" the pretension that contract doctrine produces outcomes determined by objective rules. Whereas Horwitz presents contract law as varying in relation to the needs of capitalism in a given historical period, Dalton finds significant points of tension in contract law reappearing throughout U.S. history. Contract law embodies contradictory values such as freedom and community. Liberalism covers over these contradictions with legal sleights of hand. So, on the one hand, for liberal law, judges should interpret contracts according to the parties' intentions; on the other hand, judges should determine these intentions through objective rules of interpretation or industry customs that help identify manifestations of intent. They could not, however, identify certain words or actions as manifestations without knowing beforehand what sort of intent they were looking for. Rules of interpretation seem to assist law's objectivity, and yet general rules can be applied by judges in a manner contrary to the unique intentions of the parties. Contract doctrine therefore "pretends to provide a determinate guide to decisionmaking" (Dalton 1985, 1052), but instead its rules are so open to contradictory application that the judge is largely free to do whatever she likes.

CRITICISMS OF CLS

Liberal legal scholars like Owen Fiss condemn CLS as threatening the "death of the law" for its rejection of objectivity and the possibility of law transcending political or economic interests. CLS is more successfully criticized by poststructuralism, which gathered strength in the United States during the 1980 and 1990s. The point of entry for the poststructuralist critique of CLS is the contrast represented here by Horwitz and Dalton, which some crits like Karl Klare and James Boyle recognize. Klare notes that the antiformalism of some CLS work collides with the systemic explanations for oppression in other CLS work. For example, if legal rules like contract doctrine are as indeterminate as Dalton argues, then why do we see predictable patterns in legal outcomes? Dalton, however, presents her work as "devaluing doctrine" in order to "clear the ground" for other explanations of legal outcomes (Dalton 1985, 1010), thus positioning her work as less poststructuralist and more as "ideology critique," despite her attempted use of poststructuralist theory. Stanley Fish takes up this criticism of Dalton and CLS, arguing that they use an epistemology organized through the two poles of subjectivity and objectivity. By engaging in ideology critique, CLS leaves open the possibility for an objective description of social life for which it cannot account. According to Fish, because we cannot perceive or evaluate "objects" without the training we receive as subjects through a variety of disciplinary institutions or "interpretive communities," the objectivity of any claim is always contingent upon the discursive rules of a particular interpretive community. Thus, we may *change* our understandings of events, but it is impossible to achieve an unbiased view of the world.

RIGHTS AND THE DEATH OF CLS

The practical influence of CLS is limited because it was a radical critique of the legal orthodoxy at a time of increasing conservatism in the United States. Why did CLS die? Some, like Pierre Shlag, emphasize that to identify oneself as a crit scholar in the 1980s was to put one's career in grave jeopardy. Although this statement is certainly true, the emphasis here is on intellectual developments to which CLS did not respond well. If we were to identify a mortal intellectual blow struck against CLS, it would have to be Patricia Williams's critique of the CLS critique of rights. Because of the indeterminate and formalistic nature of legal rights, CLS scholars like Mark Tushnet, Peter Gabel, and Duncan Kennedy reject their objective existence and criticize their usefulness for progressive social change, preferring to discuss "real experience" and "real needs." From a poststructuralist perspective, this critique of rights merely displaces the problem: questions of "experience" and "need" will encounter the same interpretive problems that rights encounter. There is no ground upon which to base a claim for justice that is not itself socially or legally constructed, so indeterminacy is inadequate as a reason for rejecting legal rights as a means for seeking justice.

Williams employs insights from both poststructuralism and critical race theory to defend rights on pragmatic grounds that acknowledge their indeterminacy. Pointing out that blacks have been describing their needs for years to no avail, she rejects the CLS argument for shifting from a rights discourse to a needs discourse. CLS, she contends, underestimates the importance of rights for minority struggles. Accordingly, Williams advances the analysis from a question of false consciousness among the dispossessed for "objective" rights that CLS argues do not "really" exist, to an analysis of choosing appropriate signs and employing an appropriate rhetoric that others within the social formation will recognize and comprehend as a mechanism for making a legitimate claim to justice. According to Williams, blacks do not find rights alienating; blacks find that having rights means that they are recognized as equal members of the community. Thus, Williams's critique of CLS on rights avoids the pitfalls of ideology critique while illustrating the benefits of a consideration of questions of race to an evaluation of law as a tool for mitigating oppression.

Although CLS is effectively dead in the United States today, it would be wrong to dismiss it as a failure. CLS gave birth to a number of continuing legal projects that deepen our understanding of the intersections of race and law, as well as the "intersectionality" of race, gender, sexuality, and legal subjectivity—schools such as critical race theory, critical legal feminism, "LatCrit" theory, and queer legal studies. CLS continues to be vital in Europe, particularly in Great Britain. CLS may no longer be as influential in the United States as it once was. Nevertheless, it helped create a space for a variety of critical legal studies that continue to flourish in the United States and around the world.

Paul A. Passavant

See also Feminist Jurisprudence; Law and Economics; Law and Society Movement; Legal Positivism; Legal Realism; Marxist Jurisprudence

References and further reading

Dalton, Clare. 1985. "An Essay in the Deconstruction of Contract Doctrine." *The Yale Law Journal.* 94: 997–1114.

Fish, Stanley. 1991. "The Law Wishes to Have a Formal Existence." Pp. 159–208 in *The Fate of Law.* Edited by Austin Sarat and Thomas R. Kearns. Ann Arbor: University of Michigan Press.

Fiss, Owen. 1986. "The Death of Law?" *Cornell Law Review.* 72: 1–16.

Horwitz, Morton J. 1977. *The Transformation of American Law 1780–1860.* Cambridge, MA: Harvard University Press.

Hutchinson, Allan J., ed. 1989. *Critical Legal Studies.* Totowana, NJ: Rowman and Littlefield.

Kairys, David, ed. 1990. *The Politics of Law: A Progressive Critique.* Rev. ed. New York: Pantheon.

Schlag, Pierre. 1999. "U.S. CLS." *Law and Critique* 10: 199–210.

Tushnet, Mark. 1984. "An Essay on Rights." *Texas Law Review.* 62: 1363–1403.

Williams, Patricia J. 1987. "Alchemical Notes: Reconstructing Ideals from Deconstructed Rights." *Harvard Civil Rights–Civil Liberties Law Review* 22: 401–433.

CROATIA

GENERAL INFORMATION

The Republic of Croatia is situated on the crossroads between Central Europe and the Mediterranean Sea. On the north the crescent-shaped country borders Hungary, on the west Slovenia, on the east the Federal Republic of Yugoslavia (Serbia and Montenegro), and Bosnia and

Herzegovina, and on the south it has 1,777 kilometers of coastline along the Adriatic Sea. Croatia has 21,830 square miles) of landmass but also controls nearly 13,000 square miles of intercoastal waters between the mainland and some 1,200 islands off the coast in the Adriatic.

According to official census, Croatia had 4.7 million inhabitants in 1991, but owing to the low birth rate and political instability in the region during the 1990s, it is estimated than by 2001 the population had dropped below 4.5 million. Before the 1991 war, the population consisted of about 80 percent of Croats (largely Roman Catholic) and 12 percent Serbs (by religion Serbian Orthodox). Other minorities (including Bosnian, Roma, Magyar, Italian, and Slovene) did not reach above 1 percent of the population each. It is thought that as a result of the ethnic conflicts that accompanied the dissolution of Yugoslavia, the minority shares of the population have further decreased. The capital of the country is its largest city, Zagreb, with a population of about 810,000 inhabitants. In spite of economic difficulties, the 20 percent unemployment rate, and the incomplete transition from a state to a market economy, Croatia's per capita gross domestic product (GDP) of U.S.$4,400 makes it the second most developed (after Slovenia) of all states that evolved from the former Yugoslavia.

In geography, culture, and climate, Croatia is highly diverse. Northern parts of the country have a continental climate, with warm summers and cold winters, whereas the coastal areas enjoy a mild and pleasant Mediterranean climate. The country has three general regions: the Pannonic plains of Slavonia in the north and the hills of central Croatia are separated from the coastal regions of Istria, Kvarner, and Dalmatia by the steep Dinaric Alps. Croatian culture is mainly influenced by cultural patterns of its Western neighbors and former rulers—Austrians, Germans, Italians and Hungarians—but some impact of Turkish and Byzantine culture can be seen as well.

HISTORY

Croatian history was marked by its position at a crossroads. In ancient times, it was a part of the border between the Roman Empire and the so-called barbarian peoples. This mixture can be seen in the preserved documents and legal sources, which reflect both the Roman legal tradition (mostly in Dalmatian cities such as Split, which was the residence of the Roman emperor Diocletian) and the customary law of Slavic tribes. After the breakup of Rome into two separate empires, Croatia found itself on the eastern edge of the western empire, on the border with the eastern, Byzantine empire. After invasions by the Ottoman Turks, Croatia was the borderland of the Christian provinces facing Muslim territories. After World War II, Croatia was not only a part of a union, Yugoslavia, that was viewed as a country between two political blocs (capitalist and communist) but also as a border between western and eastern section within Yugoslavia itself. Because of its strategic position, Croatia has seldom been fully independent, and several parts of its territory (such as the peninsula of Istria) were long separated from the rest of the country. In the course of centuries under various foreign rulers, however, at least the core areas of the today's Croatia enjoyed the privilege of having their own administration and making their own laws.

After the arrival of Croats and other Slavic tribes in the western Balkans in the sixth and seventh centuries C.E., Croatia was ruled for only a few centuries by its native kings, who accepted Christianity under the Roman Catholic church. From this period, several documents that witness the early feudal legal structures are preserved, such as statutes of medieval cities and deeds granting privileges to monasteries. After 1102, Croatia came under the Hungarian monarchy, although it retained a significant measure of autonomy. The place of Hungarian rulers was taken by the Austrian Habsburg dynasty in 1527, and from 1867 until World War I Croatia was part of the Habsburg Austro-Hungarian Empire. Throughout this period, Croatia, as one of the independent king's lands, was governed by the local assembly, or *sabor,* and the provincial governor, or *ban.* The lawmaking competence of these bodies was substantial. In most areas of law, Croatia had its own legislation, although it was often influenced by Austrian and Hungarian sources. In the late eighteenth and nineteenth centuries, when feudal legal concepts were gradually dismantled and the modern nation-state started to emerge, many of the Croatian lawyers studied law in Vienna and other European centers, bringing home the ideas and legal concepts they learned there. The legal elite was also educated in Croatia, at the Zagreb University faculty of law, founded in 1669, but in the same atmosphere of legal positivism characteristic of enlightened absolutism. The spirit of the reforms made in the system of administration and justice that evolved under Habsburg rule, beginning with the absolutist rule of Maria Theresa and her son Joseph and ending with the last Habsburg emperor, Franz Joseph I, can still be traced in many features of the state bureaucracy, for example, in the system of land registry. At the

same time, however, Croatian political and legal life was marked by permanent opposition to the attempts of Austrian and Hungarian rulers to reduce the level of autonomy and assimilate the population, and therefore local Croatian representatives often insisted on specific features of the national legal and administrative system. On the other hand, some regions of today's Croatia, such as Dalmatia, Medjimurje, Istria, and Krajina (Military Frontier), were under direct rule of Austria and other neighboring states (Italy and Hungary) and as such directly applied their legislation.

In 1918, after the defeat of Austria-Hungary, Croatia joined the Kingdom of Serbs, Croats, and Slovenes, which in 1929 was renamed Yugoslavia. Both Croatia and other constituent parts of the new state were legally quite diverse, applying not only different legal acts but also different legal systems, from modernist Central European to the Ottoman Turkish law of shari'a. The process of unification and harmonization of law went forward only gradually during the two decades of the existence of the first state of South Slavs. In many respects this process was not fully completed. At the same time, in Croatia there was a growing dissatisfaction with the centralist rule of the Serbian dynasties, which had not lived up to the expectations of the Croatian politicians that once vigorously advocated the pan-Slavic movement and the union of equally treated Slavic nations.

This dissatisfaction was skillfully used during the World War II by Germany and Italy. After occupation of Yugoslavia in 1941, they divided it and established an apparently independent Croatian state that was ruled by a satellite regime installed by the Axis powers. During a period of four years, Croatia had the experience of racist and anti-Semitic legislation borrowed from its fascist sponsors. At the same time, the partisan guerilla movement, led by Croatian-born communist leader Josip Broz Tito, issued a series of documents and declarations that anticipated the formation of a new federative union that was supposed to be rooted in the principles of national self-determination and equality of all constituent ethnic groups.

On the basis of such premises, Croatia rejoined Yugoslavia after 1945 as one of the constituent republics of the new people's federation. But although the new federation soon broke its ties with Stalin's Soviet Union, it retained the features of the one-party socialist regime with limited civil and political liberties. In certain respects the new state attempted to go its own way, asserting from the mid-1970s the doctrine of self-management that was supposed to introduce a level of flexibility and autonomy in the rigid socialist system of centralized economic planning. Although new doctrine brought more freedom to companies (officially called "organizations of associated labor") and their managers, it created a complex, incomprehensible, and often contradictory body of law that eventually tried to reconcile irreconcilable legal concepts (such as a market economy without private property) and introduced hardly conceivble legal notions (such as "social property," that is, ownership without an owner). The economic inefficiency and lack of transparency of such a system led to abandoning the doctrine of self-management and replacing it, until the end of 1980s, by more conservative efforts to bring both and law closer to traditional concepts of private ownership and market economy.

The Socialist Federative Republic of Yugoslavia fell apart in 1991, when the majority of its constitutive units declared independence in the face of the aggressive Serbian nationalism that disrupted the fragile balance of powers in the multiethnic state of largely autonomous federal units. Establishment of an independent Croatian state proceeded under the difficult conditions of war and instability, as Serbian-dominated units of the former Yugoslav army supported by segments of the local Serb population managed to bring under their control about one-third of Croatian territory. Only after consolidation of the state's territory in 1995 (achieved through a combination of international diplomatic initiatives and successful Croatian military actions) and the elections in 2000, which removed from power the autocratic regime of President Franjo Tudjman and his party were the conditions for peaceful democratic development finally created. Croatia joined the circle of prospective candidates for the enlargement of the European Union (EU). With about 80 percent of population in favor of joining the (EU), Croatia has one of the most pro-European attitudes of the states in the region. This perspective has an effects on attempts to bring Croation law into line with the standards of Western European states.

LEGAL CONCEPTS

According to the 1990 constitution (the so-called Christmas constitution), Croatia is defined as a democratic and unitary state. Among the highest values of the constitutional order are concepts such as freedom, equal rights of individuals and ethnic groups, social justice, respect for human rights, protection of private property, the rule of law, and the democratic multiparty system. As opposed to the system prior to 1990, government is now founded on the principle of the separation of powers. The constitution also provides an extensive list of human rights, sometimes directly borrowing the language of appropriate international instruments, for example, the European Convention for the Protection of Human Rights and Fundamental Freedoms of 1950.

Until the constitutional reforms of 2000 and 2001, Croatia had a semipresidential regime that, during the Tudjman presidency, revealed some totalitarian traits. To avoid such occurrences in the future, the constitutional amendments of 2000 weakened the role of the president and introduced a parliamentary system of constitutional democracy. The executive is now effectively in the hands of the prime minister, while the president preserves mostly duties of protocol, participates in the making of foreign policy, and acts as the supreme commander of the army. His position and political weight is, however, not insignificant, partly because he draws his legitimacy from direct elections. The presidential mandate lasts five years, and the same person may serve no more than two terms.

Legislative power is vested in a parliament, the Sabor. In 2001, constitutional changes abolished the Chamber of Counties and replaced it with a unicameral parliament consisting of about 220 representatives. Electoral laws often changed in the 1990s, ranging from radical majoritarian to the current proportional system.

Judicial power under the constitution, is exercised by an independent and impartial judiciary that is bound only by law. Primary sources of law are, as in other civil law countries, the constitution itself, statutes enacted by the parliament, and other written legal acts enacted pursuant to statutory provisions. Court decisions are generally not viewed as precedents, and although lower courts mostly tend to follow the opinion of the higher courts, there is no legal obligation on judges to pursue legal interpretation of the higher courts. An additional practical problem is lack of access to court decisions. Only decisions of the highest courts are published, and even then only in short excerpts and only those selected by anonymous administrative services of the courts.

"Transition" is an understatement to describe the paradigm shift in legislation that have taken place in the short period since 1990. It was certainly necessary to adjust the law to new circumstances, ranging from abandonment of the socialist political and legal regime to war conditions and finally the establishment of an independent state. A byproduct of the ever-changing acts and statutes was an increase in legal uncertainty. Although many new essential laws (such as the Company Act and Bankruptcy Law) received praise from international observers and experts, it is a matter of common knowledge that implementation of new legislation is far from perfect. Courts and judges often cannot keep pace with new rules, and either do not know them or do not know how (or do not wish) to apply them. The reaction to practical problems that arise out of such a situation is in many cases new change of legislation, which again has poor chances for success. The same discrepancy between law and reality may be noticed with respect to international instruments. Under the constitution, ratified international agreements are directly applicable and have legal force above that of regular statutory law; courts are still reluctant, however, to apply directly the provisions of international instruments unless they are expressly incorporated into internal law.

Croatia is one of the countries that have a separate Constitutional Court entrusted with the protection of constitutional order, whose position is formally outside of the judicial branch. The thirteen judges (eleven prior to the 2000 constitutional amendments) of the Constitutional Court, elected by parliament for a term of eight years, have power to rule both on abstract conformity of laws and regulations with the constitution and on concrete cases in which violation of constitutional rights is pleaded (constitutional complaint). Apart from these two tasks, the Constitutional Court supervises national elections, controls the constitutionality of programs and activities of political parties, decides jurisdictional disputes between various branches of government, and rules on the impeachability of the president of the republic. With the 2000 constitutional amendments, the Constitutional Court assumed jurisdiction to hear appeals of disciplinary rulings against judges, including their removal.

Recent widening of the powers of the Constitutional Court is partly due to the mostly positive role that it played, in the eyes of the democratic observers, during the regime of President Tudjman. The court showed independence and courage in striking down various acts and statutes issued by the Tudjman government for violations of human rights.

CURRENT STRUCTURE

Judicial power is exercised by the courts, which organized in a hierarchical, three-tiered structure. At the top of the judicial hierarchy is the Supreme Court, whose task under the constitution is not only to perform ordinary judicial tasks but also to ensure the uniform application of law and equality among citizens. The Supreme Court acts as court of instance for special, limited legal remedies (revision, petition for protection of legality) in civil actions, whereas in criminal suits it also has the appellate jurisdiction in cases decided in first instance by the county courts.

Lower courts are organized into courts of general jurisdiction (ordinary courts), commercial courts, and an administrative court. Courts of general jurisdiction have two tiers. The lower tier comprises municipal courts that adjudicate criminal offenses punishable by up to ten years' imprisonment and virtually all civil cases, including labor and housing cases. In 2001, there were 102 municipal courts. The higher tier is filled by county courts (nineteen in 2001), which rule on appeals against decisions made by municipal courts and decide in the first instance on cases involving major crimes punishable by more than ten years' imprisonment). The system of petty crimes courts is also included in the law that regulates judicial power. There are 109 petty offense tribunals, as well as a high petty offense tribunal that acts as the appellate body against decisions of petty crimes courts. Mil-

itary courts that were formed by presidential decree in 1991 were abolished at the end of 1996, and their competence is assumed by the ordinary courts.

In litigation, parties may either represent themselves or freely choose a representative, who need not be a lawyer. In practice, in 70–80 percent of cases parties in litigation are represented by lawyers. The Croatian Bar Association, which has more than 2,000 registered members, is putting pressure on the legislature to introduce, as part of its reform of the Code of Civil Procedure, mandatory court representation by licensed attorneys (at least in certain instances and certain types of cases). In criminal cases, legal representation is obligatory if a person is indicted for a more serious crime, has been arrested or detained, or is incapable of presenting his own defense. Both in criminal and in civil cases, if a party cannot afford a lawyer, the court may grant legal aid and engage a lawyer free of charge to the defendant. In such cases, legal fees and expenses are paid by the state. Lawyers also perform a limited amount of pro bono service.

Administrative matters are dealt with by various administrative bodies. In administrative proceedings, appeals to higher administrative bodies (such as various ministries) are also generally provided. However, if a party to an administrative proceeding is not satisfied by the final resolution of the case, it has the right of recourse to the Administrative Court of the Republic of Croatia. The Administrative Court may review the final administrative act and change it or annul it; however, the review is generally made only on the points of law, and no rehearing takes place in the court proceedings. This practice has been challenged as incompatible with the right to a fair trial protected by article 6 of the European Convention on Human Rights, and formation of administrative courts with full jurisdiction is being contemplated.

In addition to state courts, private methods of dispute resolution are utilized. The most popular alternative method of dispute resolution is arbitration, primarily in commercial cases, both between Croation parties and involving disputes with foreign companies and individuals. The most influential arbitral institution is the Permanent Arbitration Court of the Croatian Chamber of Commerce. Other alternative methods of dispute resolution, such as mediation and conciliation, are also permissible but so far have not widely utilized.

SPECIALIZED JUDICIAL BODIES

Aside from the system of regular courts, there are no important standing judicial bodies outside the judicial branch. Occasionally, parliamentary commissions are entrusted with clarifying some cases of general importance that may also currently be sub iudice, but so far without major results. Because after the end of the period of war and instability, the country was faced with an increase of

Legal Structure of Croatia Courts

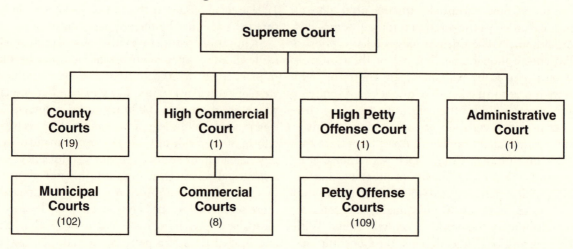

organized crime and corruption, in the beginning of 2001 a new body was formed within existing judicial structures: the Office for the Suppression of Organized Crime and Corruption (USKOK). A special department of the Public Prosecutor's Office, USKOK is composed of selected prosecutors, police officials, and judges that who investigate and prosecute offenses connected with corruption and organized crime in a special type of proceedings adjusted to meet the needs of combatting those specific forms of crime.

STAFFING

The legal profession is divided into several distinct career paths. All legal careers require completion of law school. Students may enroll in one of four law schools immediately after high school. After four years of study, students are granted the title "graduated jurist," *diplomatus iuris,* which is the equivalent of a Bachelor of Laws degree. In order to practice law, young jurists have to complete a traineeship in a court or prosecutor's office or in a law firm or solo practice, Training may also take place in legal positions within a state agency or a corporation, but in that case it generally takes longer than the usual term of one and a half years. Having completed training, the young jurist may apply to sit the state judiciary examination required for all positions in the judiciary and private practice.

In Croatia, lawyers may work either as private practitioners (attorneys) or as employees in corporations or the state administration. Attorneys obtain the right to practice law by become members of the Croatian Bar Association. Requirements for membership include Croatian citizenship and active knowledge of the Croatian language, a law degree obtained in the Republic of Croatia, legal training in a law office or in the judiciary of at least three years, and passing of the state judiciary examination. Attorneys can only be self-employed or be em-

ployed in a law firm; corporate lawyers cannot be members of the bar. Solo practitioners are still more prevalent in Croatia thanjoint law offices and law firms. Foreign law firms and lawyers do not have the right to practice law in Croatia, but they have begun to show their presence through cooperative arrangements with Croatian lawyers. Lawyers may not perform the duties of a notary public, which is a separate, private profession with its own rules and organization.

Judges and state attorneys typically start to prepare for their profession immediately after graduation from law school. Until 2000, any Croatian citizen who had completed studies at a faculty of law and passed the state judiciary examination could be appointed as a judge at the municipal or petty crimes court. Since that time, however, two years of practice after the examination isobligatory. For promotion to higher courts, more experience in practicing law (primarily before first-instance courts) is required.

The 1991 constitution provides that judges have life tenure until reaching the mandatory retirement age of 70. Their independence and impartiality are also constitutionally guaranteed. Judges are appointed by the State Judiciary Council (SJC), which consists of judges, lawyers, and law professors. The system was designed to provide a high level of autonomy and independence to the legal profession, but in the 1990s these guarantees were frequently disregarded and criteria for professional ability were often neglected. In the course of the appointments made by the SJC from 1995 to 2000, many judges of high reputation were quietly removed and others installed in their place, especially in the highest judicial ranks. The Constitutional Court on several occasions struck down these appointments as in violation of constitutional rights and, in 2000, ruled that the SJC had "twisted the constitutional idea of its tasks" and annulled many provisions of the statute that regulates its opera-

Human Resources in the Croatian Judicial Branch

Category	Number of judges
Supreme Court	35
Administrative Court	28
High Commercial Court	18
High Petty Offence Court	32
County Courts	322
Commercial Courts	131
Municipal Courts	867
Petty Offence Courts	363
Total number of Judges	**1796**
Support personnel (lawyers)	**604**
Support personnel (others)	**5678**

Source: Statistical data of the Ministry of Justice, July 2000

tion. This ruling led to the constitutional amendments of December 2000 and subsequent amendments to the laws regulating appointment of judges and the organization of the judiciary, among them being the introduction of a period of evaluation of five years for first-time judges, the separation of bodies competent to make appointments and and those charged with disciplinary responsibility over judges and state attorneys, abolition of the right of the SJC to appoint presidents of courts, and the establishment of new bodies of judicial self-administration. Reforms in the organization of the prosecution service are also under way.

IMPACT

The impact of law and courts on society is much greater today than it has been through much of Croatian history. During the socialist era, most social and political problems were resolved outside the legal system, within the party bureaucracy. With the transition to a market economy and multiparty democracy, many hotly contested issues are being submitted to the courts, which are often unprepared to handle them. Virtually all major issues of social and political life find wind up in court—from privatization and economic restructuring to organized crime and corruption and the consequences of war and ethnic conflict. The lack of preparation for these new challenges and the tampering with the judicial system that occurred during Tudjman's rule resulted in considerable inefficiency of the judicial system. From 1991 to 1997, the number of unresolved cases doubled. Some observers assert that the lack of efficiency and certainty in court proceedings poses one of the principal obstacles to foreign investment and economic revival in Croatia. Several foreign and international organizations, including the World Bank, the European Union, the Council of Europe, and USAID, have instituted programs in Croatia in support of the rule of law. Measures to promote efficiency and discipline in courts have brought a reaction from some judges appointed in the 1990s, who now claim that their independence has been placed in jeopardy. The ability to transform and adapt the judicial and legal system to the challenges of the new millennium will have great influence on the overall process of Croatian social and economic reforms.

Alan Uzelac

See also Bosnia and Herzegovina; Civil Law; European Court and Commission on Human Rights; Judicial Independence; Slovenia; Yugoslavia: Kingdom of and Socialist Republic; Yugoslavia: Serbia and Montenegro

References and further reading
Boban, Ljubo. 1993. *Croatian Borders, 1918–1993,* Zagreb: äkolska knjiga.
Branko Vukmir, ed. 1997. *Legal Framework for Doing Business in Croatia.* Zagreb: Croatian Investment Promotion Agency.
Carmichael, Cathie. 1999. *Croatia.* Oxford: Clio Press.
"Croatia." 2000. In *Judicial Organisation in Europe.* Strasbourg: Council of Europe Publishing, pp. 59–74.
Dika, M., A. C. Helton, and J. Omejec, eds. 1998. "The Citizenship Status of Citizens of the Former SFR Yugoslavia after Its Dissolution." *Croatian Critical Law Review* 3:1–351.
Doing Business in Croatia. 1998. London: Kogan Page.
Grdešić, Ivan. 1992. "1990 elections in Croatia." *Croatian Political Science Review,* 1:91–99.
Handbook Croatia. Prirucnik Hrvatska. 1992. Zagreb: HINA.
Republic of Croatia. 1999 and 2000. Central Bureau of Statistics. *Statistical Yearbook (1998/1999, 1999/2000).*
Republic of Croatia. 1999 and 2000. Ministry of Justice, Administration and Local Self-Administration. *Statistical Data on Courts (1998–1999, 2000 fragm.).* In Croatian.
Ustav (1990). The Constitution of the Republic of Croatia. 2001. Zagreb: Narodne novine.
Uzelac, Alan. 2001. "Role and Status of Judges in Croatia," In *Richterbild und Rechtsreform in Mitteleuropa,* ed. P. Oberhammer. Vienna: Manz.

CUBA

COUNTRY INFORMATION

The Republic of Cuba is an archipelago consisting of the main island of Cuba, the much smaller Island of Youth, and over 4,000 low-lying, uninhabited small islands and keys scattered along its coastline. Cuba's main island is the fifteenth-largest island in the world, extending 745 miles in length and from 124 miles at its widest point to 22 miles at its narrowest. Situated approximately 90 miles south of Key West, Florida, and 126 miles east of

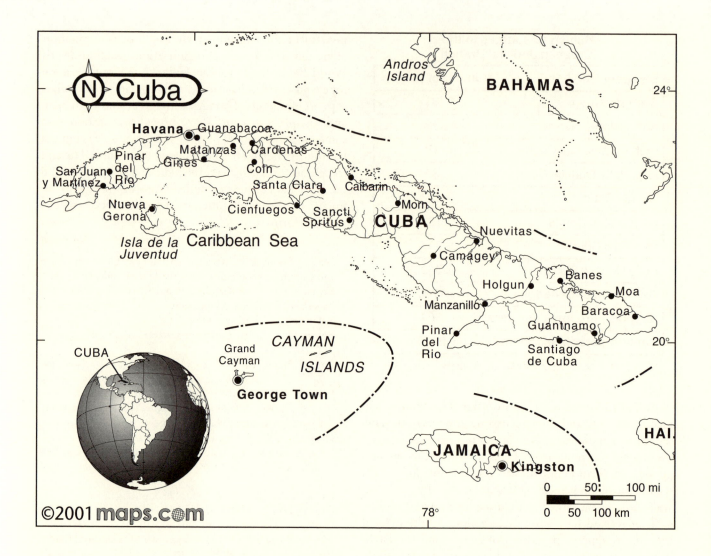

Mexico's Yucatán Peninsula, Cuba commands a central location in the Gulf of Mexico. Three-quarters of its landmass consists of flat terrain that is used primarily for grazing cattle and for cultivating tobacco, sugarcane, and vegetables. The remaining quarter of the island consists of mountain ranges whose lower elevations are often used for growing coffee. Cuba has a population of approximately 11 million people, about 10 percent of whom (2.2 million people) live in the capital city of Havana. The remainder of the population is distributed among several modest-size cities and numerous small rural towns. Cuba was a colony of Spain for 400 years, and as a consequence, Spanish remains the country's national language. During much of its colonial period, Cuba depended heavily on the forced labor of enslaved Africans, and so most Cubans today are of either Spanish or African descent—or, in many cases, both. About 45 percent of Cubans identify themselves as Catholic, and another 5 percent are Protestant, but these religions are less prominent in the daily life of many Cubans than Santeria, the Afro-Cuban spiritual practice that blends African beliefs and religious practices with Catholic ones. Cuba's

legal system is derived from the civil legal tradition of Spain. As the result of sixty years of U.S. domination followed by over forty years of socialist development that included decades of close political ties to the former Soviet Union, Cuban law today also incorporates a mixture of North American common law traditions and socialist conceptions of law and justice.

HISTORY

The modern history of Cuba began when Christopher Columbus claimed the island for the king of Spain in 1492. For most of the following 400 years, Cuba remained a Spanish colony. In the mid-1800s, Cuban nationalists began a series of armed struggles for independence. In 1898, as the revolutionaries were nearing victory, the United States inserted itself into the Cuban war of independence, inaugurating what came to be known as the Spanish-American War. As a result of winning this wider conflict, the United States obtained a peace treaty from Spain that gave the United States sovereignty over Cuba, as well as dominion over the Philippines and Puerto Rico. In 1902, the United States withdrew its armies from Cuba but only after a fledgling Cuban government accepted a constitution that gave the United States the authority to intervene in Cuba's domestic affairs whenever it determined that U.S. interests or political stability on the island was threatened. The terms of the U.S. withdrawal also granted the United States the right to use Cuba's Guantánamo Bay as a naval station. For the next sixty years, U.S. business and financial concerns dominated the economy and politics of Cuba, and the U.S. military returned to the island several times during the early part of the twentieth century to ensure that Cuba would be governed in ways that were hospitable to U.S. interests. In the late 1950s, a number of dissident groups opposed to the government of military strongman Fulgencio Batista joined together in an armed rebellion ultimately led by Fidel Castro. On January 1, 1959, this revolution toppled the U.S.-supported Batista government, beginning a political process that eventually led to the proclamation of Fidel Castro as president and the transformation of Cuba into a socialist state with a centrally planned economy.

Cuba's postrevolutionary history can be divided into five periods. The first period, extending from 1959 to the early 1970s, was characterized by revolutionary experimentation in all areas of social life and social organization, including government, economics, management, and law. Through a number of socialist initiatives, the revolutionary government made substantial headway in lowering infant and maternal mortality, increasing life expectancy, expanding literacy and employment, and providing universal free education for the island's children. The most notable experiment within the legal system during that time was the creation of People's Courts (Tribunales de Base). These courts emphasized informal procedures and used ordinary citizens rather than formally trained jurists as prosecutors, advocates, and judges.

At the same time that the revolutionary government was experimenting with new social and political structures, political dissidents both inside and outside Cuba began accusing the Castro government of communist leanings and political repression. Shortly after the revolutionary victory, many upper- and middle-class Cubans who were dissatisfied with the new government migrated to the United States, particularly to Miami, where they formed an influential anti-Castro lobby. In 1961, with the assistance and support of the U.S. government, anti-Castro Cubans in Florida sponsored an invasion force that landed at the Bay of Pigs on Cuba's southern coast. The invasion was based on the assumption that the landing of an anti-Castro force on the island would spark a spontaneous popular uprising that would remove Castro from power. Instead, local militia and the Cuban army rallied around the fledgling government and defeated the invading forces in days. The Bay of Pigs invasion led to

the first public declaration by Fidel Castro that the Cuban revolution was a socialist one. In response to his avowed commitment to socialism, the U.S. government committed itself to a path of fiercely anti-Castro foreign policy, a path that has been heavily influenced by the political power of anti-Castro Cubans in the United States since the 1960s.

In the early 1970s, the Cuban revolution entered a second phase, characterized by the institutionalization of Cuba's new socialist economic and political order. This phase included solidifying the social welfare gains made in the first period, approving a new Cuban constitution, reorganizing most administrative structures, and replacing the prerevolutionary legal system with one more suited to the ideology and practice of a socialist political economy. In 1973, the Cuban government implemented the new Law of Judicial Organization. This law transformed the experimental People's Courts into a formal, hierarchical court system that relied more on formally trained jurists, replaced the private practice of law with law collectives known as *bufetes colectivos,* and strengthened the emphasis on socialist legality. During this time, Cuba's penal code also began to focus more attention on the kinds of wrongdoing that often trouble centrally planned economies, particularly black-marketeering and the misuse of economic resources and political influence by government managers. The period of institutionalization was also characterized by closer political and economic ties to the Soviet Union, increased trade with the socialist trading bloc the Committee for Mutual Economic Assistance (COMECON), and modest but steady economic growth.

The third phase of Cuba's revolutionary history—the short-lived period of "rectification"—began in the mid-1980s. As the Soviet Union underwent a series of economic and political reforms, including significant reductions in its financial support for Cuba, the Cuban government began a program designed to correct what it saw as earlier errors in its efforts to build a socialist society, including a tendency to copy Soviet models of social organization too closely. One component of rectification was the passage of a new penal code in 1988 that decriminalized a number of political offenses, reduced penalties for crimes overall, and instituted a broader range of alternatives to incarceration, including Cuban equivalents of probation and parole.

By the early 1990s, the disintegration of the Soviet Union and the disappearance of the socialist trading bloc on which Cuba had depended for much of its foreign trade brought about the fourth phase of Cuba's revolutionary experience, the "special period not in time of war." This period was characterized by significant shortages of key imports such as food, fuel, and medicine as the Cuban government struggled to insert itself into capitalist world markets while preserving its socialist accomplishments in the areas of public health, education, and social welfare. During this period, the Cuban government made a number of legal changes to help stimulate its economy. These changes included legalizing the use of foreign currency by Cuban citizens, making it easier and more attractive for foreign companies to invest in Cuba, and expanding the number of areas of self-employment, such as operating private taxis, running restaurants, or providing repair services.

The fifth phase of Cuba's revolutionary experience can be characterized as a period of neosocialist exploration. Throughout the mid-1990s and into the first decade of the new century, the Cuban government continued to search for ways that would enable the country to retain its socialist commitments to provide universal and free health care and education, to take advantage of the opportunities offered by capitalist markets, and to minimize the economic instabilities and social problems such markets typically create. Cuba's attempts at economic recovery, however, were hampered by anti-Castro policies in the United States. In 1996, the United States enacted the Helms-Burton Law in the hopes of crippling Cuba's attempts at economic development and thereby bring an end to the Castro government. Among other provisions, the law imposed sanctions on nations that permitted trade with Cuba; it also authorized U.S. investors to sue foreign companies for using property that belonged to U.S. companies prior to the 1959 revolution but had long since been nationalized by the Cuban government. Although it was condemned by nearly every member of the United Nations as a violation of national sovereignty, the Helms-Burton Law remained in effect as of 2000.

LEGAL CONCEPTS

The concepts that inform Cuba's legal system reflect the island's history as a Spanish colony, a U.S. satellite, and a centrally planned socialist state. Cuba's history as a Spanish colony left the island with deep civil law traditions. Even after the 1959 revolutionary victory, the Cuban legal system continued to emphasize written codes rather than court-based precedent as the source of law. Although Cubans may win appeals in high-level courts, rulings of this type do not change existing law the way they can in common law systems such as that of the United States. Significant changes to Cuba's legal system, as in most civil law states, come about through the formal revision of legal codes. Cuba also utilizes an inquisitorial system of criminal procedure similar to that found in civil law state such as Spain and France, rather than the adversarial system of criminal procedure of the United States and Britain. Among other things, this means that prosecutors or plaintiffs, on one side, and attorneys for the defense, on the other, are supposed to determine the

truth of the matter at hand regardless of whether doing so will help them win their respective cases. To further this ideal, the Cuban prosecutorial system is organized according to a civil service model rather than an electoral one, thus reducing the significance of a prosecutor's win-loss record as a factor in career advancement.

Intermingled with Cuba's civil law traditions are elements of the Anglo-American adversarial system, such as habeas corpus and a greater separation of courts and prosecutors than was typical in many other socialist legal systems. Consequently, Cuban lawyers enjoy greater latitude in defending their clients that did attorneys in the former Soviet Union and its socialist allies. A key feature of this difference is that Cuban attorneys may submit evidence directly to courts without obtaining the prior approval of prosecutors, as was the case in most socialist countries in Eastern Europe. The result is that Cuban attorneys have typically achieved higher levels of acquittals for their clients in criminal cases than attorneys in other socialist countries.

In addition to these residues from its prerevolutionary history, the Cuban legal system has also been shaped by forty years of legal development guided by Marxist theory, as well as three decades of close relations with the former Soviet Union and its allies. These factors have produced a legal system that relies on concepts of *socialist legality.* First, Cuba's legal system gives as much weight to substantive measures of justice as it does to juridical ones. From this perspective, it is just as important to find outcomes through the legal system that fit with the reality of harms done and lives affected as it is to adhere to narrowly fixed legal definitions. This ideal was reflected in Cuba's 1988 Penal Code revision, which redefined a crime not just as an act that violated the law but as an act that *also* caused significant social harm. Acts that violated the law but caused only limited harm were redefined as infractions that could be handled by paying a fine, much as one might pay a parking ticket in the United States. Second, according to Cuba's conception of socialist legality, law should be used as a deliberate tool for socialist development rather than just a framework that individuals and institutions can use to can to protect or promote their own interests. Thus, revisions of Cuba's postrevolutionary legal codes were always shaped by the attention paid to how these revisions could move Cuba to its next stage of socialist development. Third, Cuba's socialist legality promotes the use of "social courts" rather than formal tribunals to resolve a variety of private disputes or conflicts that do not involve criminal matters. Fourth and very importantly, the Cuban legal system emphasizes direct citizen involvement in both the adjudication and the prevention of crime. This includes using citizens as lay judges in both lesser and superior courts and asking citizens to protect local safety by performing night-watch duties (*guardia*).

CURRENT STRUCTURE

The government of Cuba is divided into executive, legislative, and judicial branches. The executive branch consists of a Council of State and a Council of Ministers. The president of the Council of State serves as the president of Cuba. The national legislative branch consists of a unicameral body known as the National Assembly of People's Power. The Supreme Court of Cuba serves as the nation's highest judicial branch of government and as the court of last resort for all appeals from provincial-level courts. Below the national level, Cuba is divided into fourteen provinces and numerous municipalities, each with its own elected Assembly of People's Power.

Politically, Cuba is a one-party, socialist state organized according to Marxist-Leninist principles of *democratic centralism*. This means that primary political leadership is provided by the Communist Party of Cuba and that those elected to base-level representative bodies, such as a municipal assembly, choose from among themselves who will serve in the Provincial Assembly. This process is repeated as provincial representatives choose who will sit in the national assembly, while the National Assembly selects the executive officers of the government, including the president. Cuba's political system also includes a number of "mass organizations" such as the Young Communist League, the Cuban Federation of Women, the Association of Cuban Workers, and the National Association of Small Farmers. These associations are organized under the larger political umbrella of the Cuban Communist Party to provide a forum where citizens can discuss policies and laws proposed by the government and provide feedback to legislative and governmental bodies.

In addition to representative assemblies and mass organizations, each municipality and province in Cuba has a system of courts. Cuba's municipal-level tribunals serve as courts of first instance for lesser crimes and minor civil matters. Cases in these courts are heard by three-judge panels comprised of two lay judges—ordinary citizens elected to serve in a judicial capacity for a limited period of time—and one trained jurist with a formal legal education. Provincial Courts handle felony-level crimes, divorces, civil disputes involving values roughly equivalent to more than U.S.$50, and appeals from Municipal Courts. These higher-level courts utilize five-judge panels consisting of three trained and two lay jurists. Appeals from Provincial Courts will be heard in one of the sections (*salas*) of the Supreme Court. The Cuban legal system also includes a system of Military Courts that adjudicate offenses committed by members of the country's armed forces, including government officials who retain military commissions while serving in government posts.

While Cuba maintains an extensive system of formal courts to handle crimes and other problems, its commitment to socialist legality has also promoted nonjudicial forms of dispute resolution. Conflicts between neighbors, for instance, will frequently be directed to block-level Committees for the Defense of the Revolution for settlement. Similarly, disputes between workers and supervisors will typically be handled in workers' councils rather than courts, just as disputes resulting from Cuba's socialist system of housing allocation will typically be handled by municipal housing authorities rather than municipal or provincial civil courts. For much of Cuba's socialist history, private economic disputes between individuals were relatively rare and usually small in scale. Consequently, they were most often handled in social courts. Since the 1990s, however, the expansion of foreign investment and the growth in the number of Cubans pursuing self-employment or running their own businesses has led to an increase in the level and frequency of economic disputes directed to formal tribunals, rather than social courts. As of 2001, there were no specialized judicial bodies in Cuba.

STAFFING

Cuba has a well-defined system of legal education, with law schools at the University of Havana and throughout the country's university system. On graduation, law students are expected to perform two years of social service, such as providing legal counsel for poorer clients or working for some agency or ministry in an internship capacity. Graduating attorneys often attempt to arrange their social service in some area related to their career goals, such as working in a bufete colectivo or serving as legal counsel (*assesor*) to a ministry, agency, or economic enterprise. As in many civil law states, the role of providing legal counsel to the public and that of being a judge are relatively distinct career paths. Lawyers wishing to provide direct service to the public will orient their training in this direction and apply for positions in law collectives or other agencies. Those who seek a career path as jurists will work with and through the Ministry of Justice to obtain positions first in Municipal Courts or other lower-level dispute-resolving bodies and later in Provincial Courts.

The economic crisis experienced by Cuba as the result of the disappearance of the socialist trading bloc and the escalation of the U.S. embargo has had a serious impact on the career paths of some Cuban attorneys and jurists. As the country's domestic economy became increasingly tied to the U.S. dollar, some Cuban lawyers and law professors left their positions for less skilled but more lucrative jobs in the tourist industry or other sectors of Cuba's post-Soviet economy where they could earn at least a portion of their income in foreign currency.

IMPACT

Cuba's postrevolutionary legal system has played a fundamental role in shaping the reality of contemporary Cuba.

Legal Structure of Cuba Courts

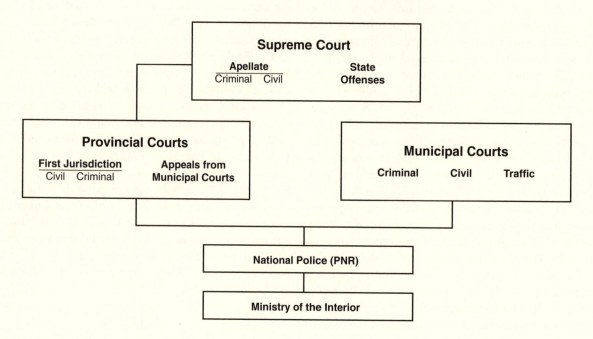

In the early years after the fall of the Batista regime, Revolutionary Courts and People's Courts helped create the basis for a socialist Cuba. Revolutionary Courts established to prosecute those accused of committing crimes under the authority of the former government helped solidify the power of the new government in two ways. By providing formal mechanisms for punishing those believed to be responsible for crimes such as torture, political killings, or false arrests, Cuba's Revolutionary Courts minimized the impulse for private vengeance that often follows revolutions, an impulse that can make it difficult for a postrevolutionary government to create a stable political climate. And by prosecuting operatives of the Bastista government and the Batista military, Revolutionary Courts effectively removed key potential sources of counterrevolutionary organization. The People's Courts also created a judicial process that was separate from Cuba's established court structure, which was steeped in prerevolutionary legal traditions and sometimes staffed by judges and attorneys who opposed the new government's plans for changing Cuban society. Freed from these constraints, People's Courts were able to develop and implement new, more socialist ideas about the nature and meaning of justice, some of which would eventually become part of the new court structure that was established in the 1970s.

The legal code promulgated in the early 1970s was also essential to the formation of a socialist Cuba. First, it provided a formal legal framework through which the government could manage economic production and guide distribution and future socialist development. Second, the general framework of socialist legality generated secondary structures to manage access to opportunities and commodities through mechanisms such as a rationing system to guarantee basic food needs, centrally planned construction and allocation of housing, and the distribution of highly desirable but scarce imported items such as cars, air conditioners, or color TVs through workers' councils rather than commodity markets. With the institution of these secondary legal frameworks, everyday life in Cuba became increasingly oriented to government bureaucracies. By the mid-1970s, these extensions of Cuba's legal system—whether housing authorities that allocated apartments, workers' council's that decided who would receive prized consumer goods, or local authorities that issued ration books—had replaced private markets as the places to seek fulfillment of routine material needs.

Third, Cuba's socialist system of production and distribution led to new categories of wrongdoing and new crime-control priorities. The system of rationed and planned distribution enabled Cuba to achieve higher overall levels of nutrition, public health, housing, and education than are found in many developing nations, but it also created barriers to satisfying desires that exceeded the minimum provisions. As a result, for over a generation, both private individuals and those in charge of economic operations often turned to black markets operating outside the planned distribution system in order to obtain things they could not acquire through that system. The manager of a clothing factory, for instance, might trade cloth for parts to repair a broken machine—parts that very well might have been stolen from another factory. A worker in a chicken-processing plant might routinely steal a few birds to sell to friends and neighbors. Or a street hustler *(jinetero)* might exchange Cuban pesos for U.S. dollars with foreign tourists and then use them to buy goods in tourist stores for personal consumption or for resale on the black market. In response, the Cuban legal system devoted considerable energy to identifying and prosecuting black-market offenders. Although the legal system focused more on those involved in organized black-market operations than on end consumers of black-market goods, the illegality of buying and selling in the black market meant that many otherwise law-abiding Cubans found themselves committing at least minor crimes on a regular basis as they tried to supplement what was available through the formal distribution mechanism. In the 1980s, the Cuban government established parallel markets to enable people with extra income to purchase some additional consumer goods, and in the post-Soviet years, markets offering goods that could be purchased with U.S. dollars were opened to the general public. While these dollar stores have minimized the need for routine black-market crimes, thus reducing the problem of turning large portions of the population into petty lawbreakers, this reintroduction of market distribution has also resulted in a growing disparity between those who have the foreign dollars to purchase goods and those who do not. As a result, the Cuban legal system has had to devote more attention to controlling crimes of inequality, such as theft, burglary, and robbery, and less to dealing with black-market economic crimes.

Cuba's system of socialist legality is in a state of flux. Some things that were once prohibited, such as having U.S. currency or running one's own restaurant, are now legal. Increasingly, in areas such as employment and consumption, Cubans are reorienting themselves to markets rather than government bureaucracies. At the same time, they continue to rely on their government for access to necessities such as an affordable basic diet, housing, health care, and education, and it is these provisions that keep many Cubans from falling into the kind of deep poverty that is typical in most developing nations. Whatever the outcome of this period of change, however, it is likely that Cuba will remain a civil law state whose legal system contains strong overtones of both socialist and common law traditions, even though the mix and relative influence of these elements may shift as the country adapts to new economic and political conditions.

Raymond Michalowski

See also Civil Law; Inquisitorial Procedure; Law and Society Movement; Lay Judiciaries; Marxist Jurisprudence; Napoleonic Code

References and further reading
Azicri, Max. 2000. *Cuba Today and Tomorrow: Reinventing Socialism.* Gainesville: University Press of Florida.
Codrescu, Andrei. 1999. *Ay, Cuba!: A Socio-Erotic Journey.* New York: St. Martin's Press.
Evenson, Debra. 1994. *Revolution in the Balance: Law and Society in Contemporary Cuba.* Boulder, CO: Westview Press.
Halebsky, Sandor, John M. Kirk, and Rafael Hernandez, eds. 1990. *Transformation and Struggle: Cuba Faces the 1990s.* New York: Praeger.
Michalowski, Raymond. 1995. "Between Citizens and the Socialist State: The Negotiation of Legal Practice in Socialist Cuba." *Law and Society Review* 29, no. 1: 65–101.
Miller, Tom. 1992. *Trading with the Enemy: A Yankee Travels through Castro's Cuba.* New York: Maxwell Macmillan International.
Pérez, Louis A. 1997. *Cuba and the United States: Ties of Singular Intimacy.* Athens: University of Georgia Press.
Pérez-Stable, Marifeli. 1993. *The Cuban Revolution: Origins, Course, and Legacy.* New York: Oxford University Press.
Salas, Luis. 1979. *Social Control and Deviance in Cuba.* New York: Praeger Publishers.
Smith, Wayne S. 1987. *The Closest of Enemies: A Personal and Diplomatic Account of U.S.-Cuban Relations since 1957.* New York: W. W. Norton.
Thomas, Hugh. 1998. *Cuba, or, The Pursuit of Freedom.* New York: Da Capo Press.
Zatz, Marjorie. 1994. *Producing Legality: Law and Socialism in Cuba.* New York: Routledge.

CUSTOMARY LAW

HISTORY

Unlike legal systems with more directly observable origins—such as the common law systems of the Anglo-American world, the legal systems derived from Roman civil law, or the socialist legal systems of the former Soviet Union and its satellites—it is not possible to trace the history of customary law. The designation *customary law* does not refer to a distinct legal system in historical terms at all, but rather to a type of legal system that has appeared in all historical eras in many parts of the world up to the present time.

Further, *customary law* has been used by many people to refer to the same type of legal system designated by such other phrases as *primitive law, unwritten law, indigenous law,* and *folk law.* This looseness in nomenclature results from a prevailing theoretical confusion among legal scholars and interested nonscholars (especially colonial administrators) but also the sheer diversity among the legal rules and practices with which these scholars and officials have been concerned.

So before moving on to discuss customary law in specific historical contexts, it would be wise to establish a set of working definitions. Customary law refers to the body of traditional rights and obligations that is binding on a distinct society or culture, the violation of which results in the application of prescribed sanctions that are themselves organic to the given society or culture. Customary law is originally oral, not written. This does not mean, though, that such law is haphazard, disorganized, and ephemeral. Many examples can be advanced—from the professional "law remembrancers" of early England to the *quipukamayojkuna* of the Inca empire, who used *quipukuna*, or knotted cords, to demonstrate laws—to refute the position that customary law lacks system or permanence.

Another source of confusion has been the tendency to make codification synonymous with the development of written law. Hence, unwritten customary law was thought to be inconsistent with codified law. But even if the majority of legal codes have been known to us through writings, codification does not necessarily mean to convert unwritten law to written law. Rather, the essence of codification is to make laws systematic, to arrange the prevailing understandings of rights and obligations into a coherent form so that they will achieve a measure of historical durability. The use of writing to accomplish this end has been a common and effective strategy across cultures and throughout history. Nevertheless, there is no reason that unwritten law cannot be codified. Indeed, the examples of the English law remembrancers and Inca quipukamayojkuna show that unwritten law has been codified at quite different times and places. Other codifications of customary law have been reported in Malaysia, Tibet, and Morocco.

Customary law has been found at many different levels of political organization, but it is most typically found in smaller levels, for example, districts, counties, or, even more commonly, villages. With very few exceptions, customary law is distinguishable from state law, which can be defined as the set of rights and obligations that is enforceable through the power of the maximal political unit such as the kingdom, city-state, principality, or, more recently, the nation-state. The major exception would be the common law of early England, which many would argue developed through the adoption of prevailing customary law at the highest levels.

It is difficult to say when the existence of customary law as distinct from state law was first noted. Historians of ancient Greece are divided over when a state law first emerged from the diversity of unwritten customary laws that regulated social life in districts and villages throughout the region. But by the classical period (ca. 400 B.C.E.), sources such as Aristotle and Euripides were already making the case that a written state law was a necessary precondition for general equality and justice and that unwritten customary law was too diverse to regulate the larger polities. And although this is a matter of some dispute, by the time of the greatest flourishing of Roman law, during Rome's classical period (ca. 150 B.C.E.–235 B.C.E.), scholars and government officials were making the distinction between *jus scriptum* and *jus non scriptum*. Thus it seems clear that at least in the West, the independent existence of customary law has been acknowledged since the early classical period.

But it was not until much later, after the age of exploration had begun in earnest in the late fifteenth century, that the true extent of the world's customary legal diversity became known and was made the object of formal inquiry. And it was not until the second wave of colonialism, after the first half of the nineteenth century, that customary law outside of Europe came to be seen as a distinct problem for European powers intent on consolidating their overseas holdings. With the spread of colonialism in Africa in particular, customary law became an object of interest for comparativelegal scholars, social scientists, and colonial officials seeking ways to lessen the inevitable social disruptions caused by the colonial encounter. Indeed, more is known about customary law in Africa than in any other part of the world.

The colonial era was important in the history of customary legal systems because during that time, state law and customary law often came into conflict in qualitatively different ways than they had before. When the colonial powers encountered customary law they reacted in one of two ways. Some, like the Spanish and Portuguese in the New World, attempted to eradicate customary legal systems by forcibly imposing the new state law at all levels. Others, like the British in Africa, sought to make customary law part of the emerging colonial legal order by permitting it to continue in carefully circumscribed areas. Neither of these strategies was as effective as intended. In the case of the Spanish, for example, customary law continued to regulate social life in rural areas throughout the colonial era. In the case of the British attempt to construct a de jure qualified legal pluralism in Africa, the resulting multilayered systems never functioned as smoothly as planned and the integrity of law suffered at all levels.

During the last third of the twentieth century, the colonial era came to an end. When the former colonies became independent nation-states, they typically adopted the law of the former colonial power as the law of the new state. Even so, the conflict between the state law and the many customary legal systems within the emerging nation-states did not disappear. Further, the ability of these nation-states to manage or eradicate customary law within their borders and replace it with a unified and universal state law, which would regulate social life in the smallest of political units, was as weak as that of the former colonial governments. Indeed, many postcolonial nation-states had by the turn of the twenty-first century begun experimenting with alternative notions of legal sovereignty that would allow the state to cede portions of its responsibility for social control to local customary legal systems. This movement had the potential to transform the distinction between state law and customary law, as well as to alter notions of the nation-state itself.

ESSENTIAL ATTRIBUTES

Customary legal theory and practice are as diverse as the many cultures and societies in which they are found. It is difficult, therefore, to identify one set of attributes that are essential to all customary legal systems around the world. Nevertheless, certain patterns in the shape that customary law takes have been observed cross-culturally. First, customary law is composed of a body of rules regulating social relations that has some degree of internal coherence, interconnection, and self-referentiality. This pattern allows us to distinguish customary law from both isolated rules of conduct and bodies of rules that lack those attributes that make such rules specifically legal. Second, customary law can be distinguished from other types of normative rules because a community that is subject to it both recognizes it as a distinct body of rules of conduct and agrees to regard the rules as obligatory. A set of rules that can be ignored by community members at will without sanction cannot be considered customary law. Third, customary law is always organic; that is to say, it is derived from the essential nature of the social group that it regulates. This attribute helps explain why externally imposed legal systems frequently meet with much resistance. Finally, customary law is, as already mentioned, typically unwritten. In some cases, legal knowledge is transmitted orally from generation to generation by a class of traditional legal specialists; in other cases, legal knowledge is not monopolized by a particular class but rather is passed on by members of communities who fulfill legal functions on a rotating basis.

LEGAL REASONING AND PROCEDURE

As with the essential attributes of customary law, there is not one type of legal reasoning and procedure that characterizes customary law in all places and at all times. But again, certain patterns to customary legal reasoning and procedure have been observed across cultures. Community members using customary law typically do not resolve disputes by applying to the facts of the case an ideal, general set of legal principles. Rather, customary legal reasoning is usually ad hoc, although patterns in dispute resolution exist and precedent does play a role in customary law, as in other legal systems. This case-by-case approach to resolving disputes means that customary legal reasoning is usually flexible and, above all, practical. Many observers have described legal reasoning in customary legal systems as common-sensical, as opposed to abstract or theoretical. Indeed, the legal reasoning style of the early English common law is a good example of customary legal reasoning. A type of legal reasoning that would stand in stark contrast to customary legal reasoning would be the highly abstract and formalized approach found in legal systems derived from the Roman civil law.

In terms of legal procedure, customary legal systems—because of their organic nature and the fact that the social unit they regulate is usually small and its level in the political hierarchy low—typically do not utilize adjudicatory or adversarial procedures. Rather, the application of customary law typically involves some version of mediation or arbitration. Rather than using professional advocates to argue cases in front of a neutral and supposedly impartial judge, most customary legal systems require that parties to disputes turn to family members or interested outsiders to aid in the presentation of the case, the goal being to achieve a result that is satisfactory to all involved. Other legal systems at the end of the twentieth century, particularly the common law in the United States, began adopting versions of these customary legal procedures because of the belief that adversarial procedures did not achieve lasting results.

GLOBAL SCOPE OF CUSTOMARY LAW

The first legal systems in human history were customary. Further, most scholars believe that all human societies have been subject to law, from the hunter-gatherer societies that characterized social life for some nine-tenths of human history to the very recent industrialized societies. Therefore, customary law existed and continues to be found in all societies in which other, noncustomary forms of law have not replaced it, either forcibly or through the voluntary adoption of noncustomary legal systems by states and communities. From a regional perspective, the customary legal systems of Africa have been most fully studied by scholars and interested nonscholars. But more and more, customary law has come to be studied and described in areas as diverse as Thailand, late-twentieth-century western Europe, India, Greece, Bolivia, and Israel.

Mark Goodale

See also Alternative Dispute Resolution; Arbitration; Civil Law; Common Law; Legal Pluralism; Mediation; Moots

References and further reading
Balzer, Marjorie Mandelstam. 1992. *Russian Traditional Culture: Religion, Gender, and Customary Law.* London: M. E. Sharpe.
Gluckman, Max, ed. 1969. *Ideas and Procedures in African Customary Law.* London: International African Institute and Oxford University Press.
Goodale, Mark. 1998. "Literate Legality and Oral Legality Reconsidered." *Current Legal Theory* 16, no. 1: 3–21.
Malinowski, Bronislaw. 1926. *Crime and Custom in Savage Society.* London: Routledge and Kegan Paul.
Moore, Sally Falk. 1986. *Social Facts and Fabrications: "Customary" Law on Kilimanjaro, 1880–1980.* Cambridge: Cambridge University Press.
Renteln, Alison Dundes, and Alan Dundes, eds. 1995. *Folk Law: Essays in the Theory and Practice of Lex Non Scriptum.* 2 vols. Madison: University of Wisconsin Press.

CYPRUS

GEOGRAPHY

The island state of Cyprus is one of the few remaining divided countries in the world. Since 1974 the island has been split almost in half, the northern and eastern parts controlled by the Turkish minority with help from the Turkish army. The southern and western portions of the island are controlled by the Greek majority and comprises the recognized state of the Republic of Cyprus. For over a quarter of a century of geographical division, the Republic of Cyprus has continued its development politically and economically.

The island of Cyprus sits in the eastern reaches of the Mediterranean Sea. With four portions of land poking out from each corner of the island and the Karpas Peninsula extending from its northwestern side, the island has been compared to a turtle. The topography of Cyprus includes a line of mountains, the Kyronian range, running along the northern and eastern coast. The southern half of Cyprus is dominated by the Troodos Mountains. The highest point of the island, Mount Olympus, stands in that range at 1,952 meters above sea level. In the middle of the island is the main agricultural plain or the Mesaria into which most of the rivers flow from the mountains and where the capital of the republic, Nicosia, is located. Cyprus's three main rivers, the Yealius, the Pehesis, and the Serakhis flow down the Troodos Mountains and into the Mediterranean.

As the third largest island in the Mediterranean, Cyprus does not suffer from the isolation attributed to lacking land borders with its neighbors. Instead Cyprus serves as the geographical link between the volatile Middle East region and Europe. Cyprus's closest neighbor is Turkey, only 75 kilometers to the north. Syria sits some 105 kilometers to the east, and Egypt is 380 kilometers to the south. The other main player in Cyprus, Greece, is a considerable distance, over 800 kilometers to the west of the island. These distances have affected the military and political policies of the country. The proximity of Cyprus and Turkey made the island a strategic region for the Turks and allowed for its rapid military intervention in 1974. It also made Turkish Cypriots feel closer to their ancient homeland. Contrarily, the extended distance from Greece made military intervention from that country less likely. It also made the Greek Cypriot more independent-minded and less willing to combine with the Greek homeland.

The 1974 division of the country split its northern and southern regions based on the ethnic composition of the areas. The capital and largest city, Nicosia, is similarly divided. With the largest city split into two pieces and its airport located directly on the line between the Turkish and Greek portions, the port city of Larnaca has become the major international city on the island. Located in the southeastern part, or Greek section, it has the sole international airport and the largest port facilities in the country. In the Turkish half of the country, the eastern city of Famagusta serves as the main port for the region. The airport at Ercan serves international flights for the northern sector of Cyprus.

HISTORY

Archaeological records have suggested that Cyprus has had human habitation for some 8,000 years. The main immigrants to the island came from Greece. Larnaca was one of the earliest and largest settlements for the descendants of the modern Turks. Because of their central location astride the trading routes of powerful empires, the Cypriots found themselves the target of invasion by the Egyptians, the Persians, the Greeks, and the Romans. It was the Roman empire that was the most constructive of all the invaders, building an infrastructure on the island. Cyprus also saw the major figures in the Christian movement visit including Paul and Barnabus, who set foot on the island on about 45 C.E.

As the Roman empire crumbled in the west, Cyprus's geography placed it in the more stable eastern half where it eventually became part of the Byzantine empire. This ended when Richard the Lion Heart captured the island while on his way to retake Jerusalem. Cyprus remained in European hands, used as a supply base for future crusades then falling under the control of the Lasignian family dynasty. During this period, the Orthodox Church found itself under attack, creating turmoil on the island until 1571 when the Ottomans seized Cyprus after a series of bloody sieges.

The island proved to be of little economic or strategic importance to the Ottomans and became one of the territories picked off of the dying empire during the nineteenth century. In 1878, during the Berlin Conference, the British were granted control over Cyprus as a balance to the Russian seizure of Ottoman lands in the Balkans. The Ottomans supported the takeover, seeking British support as they attempted to fend off Russian attacks. For the next eighty years, Cyprus remained a major naval base used to protect the Ottomans from Russian encroachment. Then during World Wars I and II the island provided valuable port facilities for the British, who established permanent military bases on the island. They also contributed in a more ominous manner, formulating a governmental system that divided power along ethnic and religious lines. During the twentieth century, the British presided over an island steadily dividing among the Greek and Turkish communities, who saw their concerns dictated according to their ethnic group.

The end of World War II witnessed agitation for Cypriot independence similar to conflicts breaking out

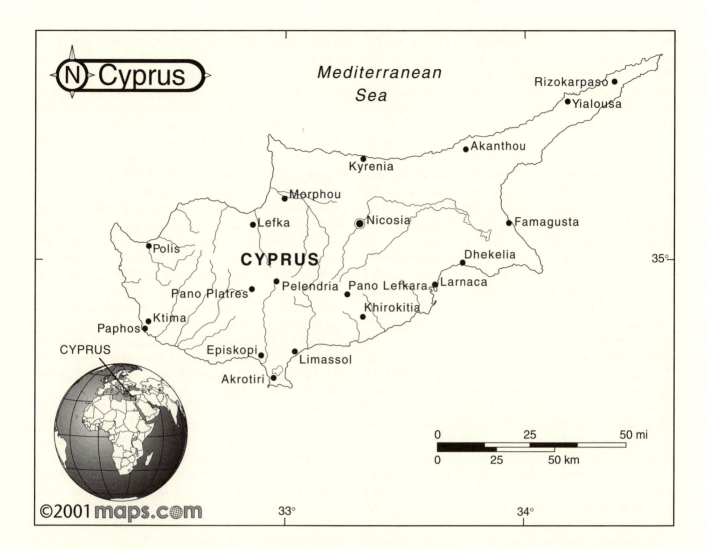

all over the British empire at the time. One of the main leaders of the movement, Bishop Makarios of the Orthodox Church, supported independence while other Greek leaders called for *enosis* or the Cypriot union with Greece. Such a demand created the expected response from Cypriot Turks, who would never accept Greek control over them. Suddenly Cypriot independence had to overcome the obstacle of centuries of conflict between Greeks and Turks. Terrorism from Greek independence groups including bombing attacks on most major cities and British military installations heightened tensions and the pressure for the British to leave. Yet independence could not be granted without the creation of a stable system agreeable to both Greek and Turkish Cypriots.

An agreement was reached in 1960. The British granted independence to the island while maintaining control over their military facilities on the island. The new government was formed under a constitution that granted Greek and Turkish representation at the executive, legislative, and judicial branch. Political power in these institutions was based on the ethnic proportions on the island. At the same time each ethnic group was granted veto power over any laws that would affect their status. Official independence for Cyprus came on August 16, 1960.

Almost immediately the Greek and Turkish sides began jostling for political and military advantage. The Cypriot army was segregated along ethnic lines, with each side acquiring ties with either the regular Greek or Turkish armies. By 1964 fighting between the two sides had broken out and a United Nations peacekeeping force was introduced to keep the combatants apart.

Bishop Makarios, the new president of Cyprus, maneuvered to create a separate Greek Cypriot army while holding back those who supported *enosis*. Greece and Turkey became involved in the dispute, threatening to go to war over attacks on Turks in Cyprus. Only American diplomacy and military pressure averted armed conflict. By the 1970s, though, the Greek Cypriots found themselves trapped between Greek demands for *enosis* and Turkish threats against a possible annexation of the island by Greece. The recently promoted Archbishop Makarios attempted to follow a middle course, one based on continued Cypriot independence with political domination by the Greek Cypriots. The result of this policy was the decision by the Turkish Cypriots to withdraw their political representatives from the government, calling into question the fairness of the ethnic divisions created under the constitution. By 1972 the country was partitioned in all but name between the two communities.

A military coup in Greece in 1973 led to a coup attempt against Makarios in July 1974 and the promise by the new military regime in Cyprus that *enosis* with Greece was forthcoming. This prompted an immediate Turkish response as its army intervened on the island on July 20, 1974. The Turks swept through the northern and eastern reaches, creating a military division of the island.

The lines separating the two were solidified by the arrival of United Nations peacekeepers to serve as a buffer between the groups and by the formation of the Republic of Cyprus in the south and the Turkish Republic of Northern Cyprus. The Republic of Cyprus is generally recognized as the official government of the island, whereas the northern sector is recognized only by the Turkish government in Ankara. Following the division there have been years of negotiations conducted at a snail's pace. The discussion has focused on how to end the partition. These occurred between the two sides with little involvement of the Greek or Turkish homelands. Instead the United States and the United Nations put forward various plans for a single multiethnic state. The negotiations foundered as neither the Turkish nor the Greek side would agree to a system that did not give them operating control of the government.

At the same time the two halves of the island thrived politically and economically. Both regions developed a democratic political system with multiple parties and an independent legislature and judiciary. The Republic of Cyprus became a mediator in the Middle East conflict, serving as a meeting place for summits. It also began discussions with the European Union for inclusion within that organization. While the Turkish republic lacked international recognition, it proved to be as democratic, though not as economically developed, as the southern half of the island.

As the partition of the country passes its quarter-century anniversary, the two sides appear farther apart on recreating a single Cypriot nation and a new constitution. The attempt to create a multiethnic state by protecting ethnic concerns failed and only a new, less ethnically based system appears likely to succeed.

LEGAL CONCEPTS

The 1960 Constitution stated with surprising specificity the roles of government officials in protecting the ethnic identities of Greek and Turkish Cypriots. Such identification became the operating legal basis for much Cypriot law during its early years. Instead of a legal system based

on the rights of all Cypriots, it was based on rights given to each ethnic group.

With its independence, the Republic of Cyprus operated under a constitution granting government positions on the basis of the island's ethnic composition. This guaranteed the Turkish Cypriots a vice-presidential office that could veto all presidential actions. The Turks were also granted twenty-four seats in the eighty-seat House. At the same time a majority of those Turkish representatives were required to support any legislation passed by the Parliament. This gave the ethnic minority a veto power in the Parliament and ensured that the majority Greeks would have many of their proposals blocked. The divisions along ethnic lines continued even when it came to the symbols of the country. The flag of Cyprus was to be of neutral colors so as not to make it appear overly Turkish or Greek. The president and the vice president of the country were given specific veto power over any change made to the flag. Because these two positions would be held by the two ethnic groups, it ensured that the Greeks and the Turks had an equal say in how the country was represented by its flag.

These same ethnically based mechanisms were found in the judiciary. The constitutional court was divided between a Greek, a Turk, and a neutral judge from another country. This judge would have two votes and hence could block any decision reached on those rare occasions when the Greek and Turkish judges agreed. At the same time, when those judges were in disagreement, the neutral judge would serve as a tiebreaker, with his two votes providing the winning margin in a dispute.

Almost immediately upon independence, there were strong disagreements over the ethnically based arrangement. Each side sought more power, believing that the constitution restricted their ability to wield control. In 1964 President Makarios proposed changes in the constitutional power-sharing structure to allow for smoother functioning of government. The Turks saw it as an attempt to eliminate their influence in each of the branches. They resisted by ending their participation in most governmental offices. Without the presence of Turkish representatives in Parliament or a Turkish vice president with veto powers, most of the special provisions in the constitution protecting Turks as an ethnic group were eliminated. This later resulted in the island's partition.

While both halves of the island run separate governments, the two judiciaries resemble each other. The Republic of Cyprus adheres to a constitutional system where basic rights are protected on paper and in practice. The constitution prohibits arbitrary arrests, and allows for regular trial procedures including the right to counsel, to question witnesses, and protection from involuntary self-incrimination. Under the constitution such liberties as free speech and association are guaranteed with

Cypriot authorities allowing for political debate without judicial interference. Cyprus has also proved to be easier on convicted criminals. Most receive fines and in the few serious cases where the death penalty was assessed, the president of the country commuted it.

The Turkish portion of the island also protects basic rights in its constitution. The judiciary serves as a buffer between government and the people rather than as a tool to be used against the population. Trial procedures are followed, and fair and open trials are the standard in the country.

While the governments on the two halves of the island have similar court systems and adhere to similar procedures, there is little cooperation between the two in criminal justice matters. Such issues as drug trafficking are handled differently by each government. The Republic of Cyprus has been aggressive, though not entirely successful, in preventing the southern half of the island from becoming a drug-processing center in the eastern Mediterranean. The Turkish half of the island has seen its government less active, with the result that northern Cyprus is known as a major drug transshipment point for illegal drugs in the region. Yet even with these differences, the similarity in approaches in court systems suggests that if the division of the island is ended, the judicial structure would be acceptable to either half of the island.

STRUCTURE OF THE COURTS

From the beginning of Cypriot independence, there was dissatisfaction over the division of powers created by the 1960 Constitution. This included the ethnic requirements established for the judiciary. While the current structure of the courts on the island does not resemble the ethnically based system created by the 1960 Constitution, knowledge of their establishment provides insight into how the ethnic composition of the government led to the eventual division of the island.

The Cypriot Supreme Constitutional Court was composed of one Turkish and one Greek justice with a neutral justice chosen from outside the island serving as the tiebreaking vote. The justices were approved by their ethnic representation in the parliament. It was given the power to rule on the constitutionality of all Cypriot law with particular emphasis on protecting the ethnic rights found in the constitution.

The second major judicial institution in the Republic was the High Court. Its membership was initially divided along ethnic lines with two Greek and one Turkish judge who were joined by an outside, neutral judge. The High Court had jurisdiction as the final appellate court for all questions of law. But its judicial functions were outweighed by its administrative duties. The High Court was given the role of determining the number and ethnicity of judges who conducted criminal and civil trials

where the litigants were of different ethnicities. The High Court also served as the Supreme Council of the Judicature with the power to appoint, promote, transfer, or dismiss lower court judges. The High Court also determined the composition of courts that tried treason cases involving violations of the constitutional order.

The Turkish intervention and the division of the island created two judiciaries on Cyprus. While the ethnic divisions run deep between Greeks and Turks, the structures of the two court systems are similar.

The Republic of Cyprus is divided into judicial districts, each containing its own court. These district courts hear minor civil and criminal cases. Cypriot law places constraints on the power of each of the judges in these districts to hear certain types of cases. A regular district court judge is limited to hear civil cases involving claims under 5,000 Cypriot pounds. A senior district judge can decide civil cases involving up to 10,000 Cypriot pounds. For cases above that amount, there must be at least two district judges, usually including the senior judge in that district. There are no such requirements for regular and senior judges hearing criminal cases. District courts decide criminal cases for crimes requiring less than three years' imprisonment. A single judge sits at the district court trial. Jury trials are not allowed at the district court level.

In 1991, a law created the permanent assize courts. These assize courts conduct criminal trials involving serious crimes with penalties exceeding a three year prison sentence. Each assize court has a three-judge panel presiding. Defendants may choose a jury trial. Criminal court case decisions by both courts can be appealed to the Cypriot Supreme Court, which has exclusive appellate power. Appeals to the Supreme Court would be heard by a minimum of three judges. The court could choose to uphold the lower court decision, overturn it and require a new trial, or modify the decision. This last choice included expanding the sentence, reducing it, or finding a defendant guilty in those cases where the prosecutor was appealing an acquittal. The Court also has the option of acquitting a defendant and preventing a new trial from occurring.

In 1964, two courts, the Supreme Constitutional Court and the High Court of Justice were combined into a single Supreme Court. The Supreme Court continued to have judicial review powers in deciding the constitutionality of laws and in overturning the laws found to be a violation.

This change in the judiciary's structure under the constitution led to the Turkish minority breaking away from the government. The new system abolished the neutral judge, allowing for Greek domination of the Court. The Supreme Council of the Judicature was retained but given different powers. The council was granted the power to hear the appeals previously decided by the High

Legal Structure of Cyprus Courts

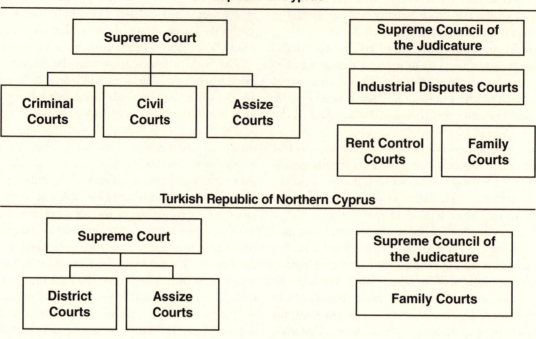

Republic of Cyprus

Supreme Court
- Criminal Courts
- Civil Courts
- Assize Courts

Supreme Council of the Judicature

Industrial Disputes Courts
- Rent Control Courts
- Family Courts

Turkish Republic of Northern Cyprus

Supreme Court
- District Courts
- Assize Courts

Supreme Council of the Judicature

Family Courts

Court. It also continued its role in the placement of judges. The new council was composed of the attorney general, three Supreme Court judges including the Court's president, a district court president, and a district court judge and a member of the bar, rotated in the position for a six-month term.

The 1983 declaration of a Turkish Republic of Cyprus included ratification of a constitution and establishment of a judiciary for that half of the island. The criminal courts in Turkish Cyprus resemble the Greek courts. A single district court judge hears minor criminal cases, those requiring under three years of imprisonment. There are also assize courts composed of three judges deciding the more important criminal cases. All decisions of these courts could be appealed to the Supreme Court. Unlike its Greek counterpart, though, the Turkish Cypriot Supreme Court also serves as the Supreme Council of the Judicature. In this capacity, the justices had the power to try high officials including the president, prime minister, and cabinet ministers for treason or other serious crimes.

SPECIALIZED COURTS

The specialized courts in Cyprus differ considerably from the northern half to the southern half of the island. In the Republic of Cyprus an Industrial Disputes Court operates like labor courts in many European countries or similar to the American National Labor Relations Board. The court hears disputes between workers and business or labor unions and business over unfair labor practices.

It also plays a role in settling disputes such as strikes. The Rent Control Court has a specialized duty in adjudicating claims involving the rent control laws that attempt to make housing affordable on the island. Finally the family court system is the most widely used in Cyprus. With several divisions handling such issues as divorce, wills, and juvenile crime, these courts are the ones more frequently used by citizens and have the most contact with Cypriots.

On the Turkish half of the island the only specialized judicial body is the family court system. Because the Turkish homeland is a secular government with an overwhelming Islamic population, it must handle many family disputes that would be settled under *sharia* law in other Islamic countries. The same is true for the Cypriot Turkish Republic. The family courts reject many of the Islamic features of family law and instead utilize government legislation on the subject.

SELECTION AND STAFFING

The selection of judges on both halves of the island is usually based on considerations of merit. On the Republic of Cyprus a separate judicial institution, the Supreme Council of the Judicature, is assigned the task of considering appointments and choosing judges for the lower trial courts and the Supreme Court. These decisions are less likely to be based on political motives. Rather the members of the council consider experience and proficiency in the law before choosing a judge. It also holds the power of moving judges around district courts to aid in the backlog of cases.

In the Turkish Republic of Cyprus, the Supreme Council of the Judicature is composed entirely of members of the Supreme Court of the country. The council retains appointment powers over lower court judges but surrendered its power to the president to appoint Supreme Court justices.

Legal training for both countries is conducted in the model of the Western civil law tradition. University-level legal training in both north and south Cyprus produces judges who can conduct trials using recognized legal procedures and have the training to interpret the law and the constitution.

IMPACT

The island of Cyprus, partitioned between the Greek Republic and the Turkish Republic, exemplifies the difficulty and eventual futility of creating a multiethnic state based on dividing power along ethnic lines. The original Cypriot judiciary, created to ensure equal representation for Greek and Turkish Cypriots, collapsed after less than five years. By equating justice with ethnic representation, the judiciary became one of the focal points of ethnic disagreements.

By 1974, with a militarily imposed division of the island between the Greeks and the Turks, the two countries established judiciaries along startlingly similar lines, considering the supposed division in their interests. In each the courts played an important role in protecting individual rights. Both sets of courts recognized legal procedures in their trials and judicial independence made them an effective buffer between government and the individual Cypriot. The smooth functioning of the court systems only highlights the weaknesses in the original Cypriot constitution. With the removal of ethnic considerations in structuring the courts and appointing judges, the judiciary functioned effectively in providing a measure of justice and protection of rights. The two court systems may provide the key to rejoining the two halves of the Republic. A functioning judiciary may be able to preside over a multiethnic Cyprus, protecting individual rights not through ethnic representation on the court but rather through the neutral application of the law and constitution without regard to ethnicity.

Douglas Clouatre

See also Greece; Turkey

References and further reading
Borowiec, Andrew. 2000. *Cyprus: A Troubled Island*. Westport, CT: Praeger Publishing.
Darke, Diana. 1995. *Guide to North Cyprus*. New York: Bradt Publishing.
Dodd, Clement, ed. 1999. *Cyprus: The Need for New Perspectives*. Cambridgeshire, UK: Eothen Press.
Hitchens, Christopher. 1997. *Hostage to History: Cyprus from the Ottomans to Kissinger*. New York: Verso Books.
Joseph, Joseph S. 1999. *Cyprus: Ethnic Conflict and International Politics*. London: Palgrave Publishing.
Kelly, Robert. 1998. *Cyprus: Country Review*. New York: Commercial Data Press.
O'Malley, Brendan, and Ian Craig. 2000. *The Cyprus Conspiracy: America, Espionage and the Turkish Invasion*. New York: St. Martin's Press.
Stafanidis, Ioannis. 1999. *Isle of Discord*. New York: New York University Press.
Streissgath, Tom. 1998. *Cyprus: Divided Island*. New York: Lerner Publications.

CZECH REPUBLIC

COUNTRY INFORMATION

The Czech Republic is located in East Central Europe, bordered by Austria on the south, Germany on the north and west, Poland on the north, and Slovakia on the east and southeast. Its territory of roughly 78,900 square kilometers (about the size of Maine) is divided into two main regions: the very hilly and largely agricultural Moravia to the east; and Bohemia, the historic industrial center of the Czech Republic, to the West. Administratively, the country is divided into seventy-three districts and four municipalities. Of the 10.3 million Czech citizens (as of 2000), 94.4 percent are ethnically and linguistically Czech, with small Slovak, German, Polish, and Roma enclaves. The principal languages are Czech and Slovak, although German is understood by the older population along the German and Austrian borders, and English is developing into the business language of choice in the cities. Seventy-five percent of Czechs live in cities, concentrated in the capital, Prague (1.2 million), Brno, Ostrava, and Plzen. Almost 40 percent of Czechs consider themselves atheist, about the same ratio as Catholics, with small Protestant (4.6 percent), Orthodox (3 percent), and Jewish (less than 1 percent) minorities.

Of the new democracies in Eastern Europe, the Czech Republic has one of the most developed industrialized economies, with a well-educated population and a sound infrastructure. As a result of Communist mismanagement prior to the fall of the Eastern Bloc in 1989, most of the industrial infrastructure is obsolete and the country had to undergo prolonged economic reforms. After the "shock therapy" proscribed by the International Monetary Fund (IMF) in 1991, and two austerity packages introduced in 1999 that cut government spending, prudent economic management has led to a significant modernization of the Czech economy, resulting in low unemployment, moderate budget deficits, low inflation, and shifts in the export market to Western Europe. As of 1999, GDP composition by sector was 42 percent industry, 53 percent services, and 5 percent agriculture. The

Czech Republic map showing neighboring countries GERMANY, POLAND, SLOVAKIA, AUSTRIA, and HUN. Cities labeled include Teplice, Liberec, Karlovy Vary, Kladno, Prague, Hradec Krlové, Pardubice, Krnov, Ostrava, Olomouc, Plsen, Rokycany, Prbram, Havlckuv Brod, Prosfejo, Kromerz, Zln, Tbor, Brno, Uherske Hradiste, Ceske Budejovice, Vienna, Bratislava.

©2001 maps.com

country's industrial output includes iron, steel, chemicals, wood and paper products, machinery, and motor vehicles. Chief agricultural crops are grains, corn, potatoes, hops, and cattle. Current major export goods are machinery, iron, steel, chemicals, raw materials, and consumer goods. Per capita GDP is $11,700 (as of 1999), and unemployment stands at 9 percent. The main problem, however, continues to be too much government influence on the privatized economy.

The Czech Republic is a constitutional parliamentary republic. President Vaclav Havel, a former dissident, human rights activist, and playwright, is head of state. Since the last national elections in June 1998, Prime Minister Milos Zeman has headed a center-left minority government (as of August 2001).

HISTORY

The historical record for what is now the Czech Republic dates back more than 2,000 years, as its strategic location in the heart of Eastern Europe made control over its territory highly desirable. It became part of the Holy Roman Empire, and under the kings of Bohemia, Prague devel-

oped into the undisputed center of culture and learning in fourteenth century East Central Europe. However, the Czechs lost their political independence to the Habsburg dynasty in the Battle of the White Mountain in 1620, and, for the next 300 years were ruled by the Austro-Hungarian Empire. The Austrians, who imposed their legal system and codes on the newly acquired territory, followed the civil law tradition, and their civil and criminal codes, such as they were, were heavily influenced by Catholic doctrine. No independent judiciary or rule of law existed at the time, with judicial proceedings arbitrary, and often devoid of even the most basic notions of fairness. Torture was frequent, and the death penalty was imposed for many offenses. However, as Austria proper reformed its judicial system under Emperor Joseph II (1780–1790), including the systematization and secularization of the codes as well as provisions for fair trials, the legal situation in the Kronländer, which included Bohemia, Moravia, and Slovakia, improved significantly.

After the defeat of the Austro-Hungarian Empire, the Czechs, Moravians, and Slovaks formed an independent united state on October 18, 1918, under the leadership of Thomas Masaryk and Eduard Benes. They adopted a modern constitution, instituted the rule of law, reformed the legal system—while retaining the basic structure and elements of the Austro-Hungarian codes—and included comprehensive guarantees for the protection of basic human rights.

Czechoslovakia was the only country in Eastern Europe to remain a democracy throughout the entire interwar period, despite its significant minority problems. The redrawing of political borders after World War I separated almost 3 million Sudeten-Germans, who lived concentrated in the Bohemian and Moravian border regions and formed almost 22 percent of the country's population, from their German homeland. Real and alleged discrimination led to an increase in support for the Nazi ideology by some Sudeten-Germans, and external pressures finally let France and the United Kingdom yield to Nazi demands in Munich to force Czechoslovakia to surrender the Sudetenland to Germany. Nazi Germany then invaded all of Czechoslovakia in 1939, turned Bohemia and Moravia into a protectorate, and established a puppet state in Slovakia.

In 1945, Soviet troops occupied almost the entire territory, and, after Germany's surrender, almost 3 million Sudeten-Germans were expelled following the so-called Benes Decrees. Czechoslovakia was to hold free national elections in 1946. The prodemocracy forces hoped that the Soviet Union would allow the country to choose its own political future. Yet after the Czechoslovak Communist Party won 38 percent of the vote, including key government positions, it soon managed to neutralize most anticommunist forces. In 1948 the Communists officially seized power. Extensive purges followed, and for more than a decade the country was frozen under the orthodox leadership of Antonin Novotny.

Rising discontent in the population and the leadership alike about the slow pace of economic reforms and stymied cultural liberalization caused the party leaders to overthrow Novotny and to replace him with the liberal-minded Alexander Dubcek, who, through extensive social, political, and economic reforms, wanted to give "socialism a human face." He tried to establish true civil and political rights, including freedom of religion, speech, assembly, and the press, and became a very popular political figure. Afraid that his liberal policies might threaten the coherence of the Eastern Bloc, Soviet troops, with the support of most members of the Warsaw Pact, invaded Czechoslovakia on August 20, 1968. The purges that followed saw Dubcek and most of his followers stripped of party functions, and Gustav Husak made First Secretary. Officially dubbed "years of normalization," the two decades that followed led, in fact, to almost complete economic, social, political, and cultural stagnation. The judges and the judicial system of communist Czechoslovakia was independent in name only. As the founding doctrine of the Czechoslovak state was Marxism-Leninism, all laws, civil and criminal, were written to conform to these standards, and interpreted according to the needs and whims of the Communist regime. Judges were often little more than puppets of the government, the sentences imposed arbitrary and harsh, with the most severe punishments meted out to dissidents and human rights advocates. In 1977, more than 250 human rights activists, among them the current president Vaclav Havel, signed a manifesto called the Charter 77, which criticized the government for failing to implement human rights documents it had signed, and aimed at inducing the government to observe the basic civil and political rights of its citizenry.

After the police violently dispelled a peaceful prodemocracy demonstration on November 17, 1989, the Charter 77 and other civic groups united to form the Civic Forum, led by Vaclav Havel. Faced with overwhelming popular opposition, the Communist regime collapsed almost immediately, and, as the leader of the Velvet Revolution, Vaclav Havel was elected president on December 29, 1989.

In the first free elections in June 1990, the Civic Forum won in a landslide and undertook forceful strides toward the democratization of Czechoslovak society. However, the Civic Forum was not an effective governing party and soon factions, or clubs, with different political agendas emerged—most notably the conservative Civic Democratic Party led by Vaclav Klaus, and the Czech Social Democratic Party—that weakened the Forum considerably. By 1992, Slovak demands for greater autonomy had effectively stymied the everyday work of the government. In the national elections of 1992, Vaclav Klaus won easily as an advocate of economic change, and the Slovak Vladimir Meciar won in Slovakia on a platform of Slovak autonomy. Realizing that the schism between the two regions had become too wide to be bridged, the federalist Havel resigned, leaving Klaus and Meciar to formulate an agreement of separation. This Velvet Divorce came into effect on January 1, 1993. The Czech Republic and the Republic of Slovakia each became independent states in their own right and won immediate recognition by all European countries as well as the United States. Aside from occasional disputes about border controls, the division of federal property and citizenship issues, often in the context of forced deportations of Roma without citizenship papers, the relationship between the two countries has been peaceful and cooperative.

In the national elections of June 1998, the left-of-center Czech Social Democrats under Milos Zeman obtained a plurality, but the right-of-center parties together obtained a majority of the votes. Consequently Milos Zeman formed a minority left-of-center government with the toleration of the conservative Civic Democrats under former prime minister Vaclav Klaus.

The Czech Republic became a full member of NATO on March 12, 1999, and has entered into membership negotiations with the European Union.

The Czech Republic's political system supports a wide spectrum of political parties, from Communists to right-wing nationalists. The Constitution of 1993 is the supreme law of the land, and establishes the principle of separation of powers. The legislative power is vested in a bicameral legislature, the Chamber of Deputies and a Senate. The 200 Chamber delegates are elected from seven districts and the capital, Prague, for four-year terms on the basis of proportional representation. The Senate is modeled after the U.S. Senate, with eighty-one senators serving six-year terms, with one-third being elected every two years in two rounds through majority vote. The first Senate was elected in 1996. There are no term limits.

The executive is composed of the president of the republic, the prime minister, and the cabinet of ministers. The president is elected for a term of five years (maximum two consecutive terms) by a joint session of both chambers of Parliament. He or she serves as the commander-in-chief of the Armed Forces, appoints the prime minister, has the right to veto any bill, and may, under certain circumstances, dissolve the Chamber of Deputies. The president, with the consent of the Senate, also appoints judges.

The judiciary consists of district, regional, high, and appeals courts, among them the Supreme Court as the country's highest court, the Supreme Administrative Court, and the Constitutional Court. Specialized judicial and semijudicial bodies are the Supreme Audit Court, the ombudsman, and the human rights commissioner.

LEGAL CONCEPTS

The present political, and, in particular, the legal system, reflect the desire of the vast majority of Czech citizens for a clear break with the communist past, a system that was viewed by many as arbitrary, inhumane, and a cynical violator of human rights. As a result, the Constitution and its correlative document, the Charter of Fundamental Rights and Freedoms, firmly establish the rule of law, an independent judiciary, and comprehensive guarantees of civil, political, economic, and social rights. Continuous monitoring by human rights organizations, the European Union, and the Commission on Security and Cooperation in Europe (CSCE) show extensive compliance with almost all constitutional provisions. Few attempts by officials to influence the judicial process are known, although cases of corruption emerge occasionally. Structural problems, such as lack of funding for the judicial system, lack of about 400 judges, sporadic incidents of police brutality, lengthy pretrial detentions, and the widespread discrimination, institutional, legal, and social, against the Roma minority, however, still remain.

The Constitution of the Czech Republic (adopted on December 16, 1992; in force since January 1, 1993) is the supreme law of the land. All domestic laws must conform to constitutional provisions. The Czech legal system follows the civil law tradition, and is based on Austro-Hungarian codes. International treaties, once ratified, are immediately binding, superior to domestic law, and enforceable through domestic courts (articles 10 and 88). Although the Czech Republic is a member of the UN, the Council of Europe, and the CSCE, it has not accepted compulsory jurisdiction by the International Court of Justice (ICJ). Nonetheless, it is party to a large number of international treaties, including the United Nations Declaration on Human Rights, the International Covenant on Civil and Political Rights, the European Convention on Human Rights, the Convention on Climate Change, the Genocide Convention, the Statute of the International Criminal Court, and the Nuclear Test Ban Treaty.

The Czech Constitution guarantees and protects all basic civil and political rights. The Charter of Fundamental Rights and Freedoms, which forms part of the Czech Constitution, guarantees, among other things, the right to life, equality, nondiscrimination, due process, fair remuneration, social security, free medical care, education, as well as freedom of thought, conscience, religion, expression, information, petition, assembly, and association. The Charter also guarantees the rights of national and ethnic minorities regarding language, education, and cultural matters. In the legal realm, everybody who claims that his or her rights have been violated by an official organ may request a review of that particular decision by a court. Everybody has the right to appeal a court ruling. Everybody enjoys the presumption of innocence, and has the right to assistance of counsel, with court-appointed counsel assisting the indigent. Every accused person who does not understand or speak Czech has the right to an interpreter.

CURRENT STRUCTURE

The judicial structure of the country is laid down in Chapter 4 of the Constitution of the Czech Republic.

The constitution provides for the independence of courts (Article 81), as well as the independence and impartiality of judges (Article 82). All judges are bound by the law (Article 95), and only courts are allowed to decide on the guilt and penalty for criminal acts (Article 90). The judiciary consists of the Supreme Court, the Supreme Administrative Court, and high, regional, and district courts. Articles 83–89 establish a Constitutional Court to oversee the constitutionality of laws and official acts (statute detailing operations Act No. 182/1993 Sb.).

Legal Structure of Czech Courts

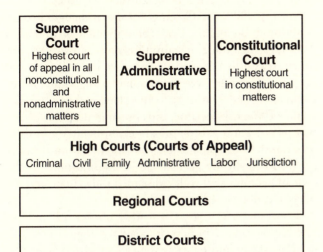

Supreme Court — Highest court of appeal in all nonconstitutional and nonadministrative matters	Supreme Administrative Court	Constitutional Court — Highest court in constitutional matters

High Courts (Courts of Appeal)
Criminal Civil Family Administrative Labor Jurisdiction

Regional Courts

District Courts

The Supreme Court is the highest court of appeals and supreme judicial body in all matters within the jurisdiction of the courts, civil and criminal, except for those under the jurisdiction of the Constitutional Court and the Supreme Administrative Court. The Supreme Court also has the power to review statutes for their compatibility with other laws.

The Constitutional Court rules exclusively on constitutional issues. It has jurisdiction over the following matters, among others:

1. Constitutional review of statutory law,
2. Constitutional review of decisions and official acts,
3. Cases concerning the impeachment of the president and his capacity to hold office,
4. Questions on how to implement decisions of international tribunals,
5. Questions incidental to a dispute concerning the violation of a constitutional right,
6. Election disputes.

The court acts in plenum or in three-justice chambers, but only the plenum has the right to annul an act of Parliament, decide on the impeachment of the president (supermajorities of nine justices required), or act on the dissolution of a political party. If the court finds a legal statute to be unconstitutional it annuls it in whole or in part. The Constitutional Court has no power to give advisory opinions. As of August 2001, the court has ruled on a variety of questions, including hate crimes, citizenship rights, the legality of the 5 percent electoral threshold, and the rights of conscientious objectors.

The constitution does not provide for institutionalized alternative dispute resolution, although the office of the Ombudsman can be considered to assume such a function, as discussed below. Nor does the constitution envisage a role for lay participants in the judicial system, such as juries, to assist in determining the guilt of an accused and the sentence to be imposed.

SPECIALIZED JUDICIAL BODIES
The Czech Republic has established a small number of specialized judicial bodies outside the court system.

Without question, the creation of the office of the Public Rights Prosecutor (Ombudsman) in December 1999 has been one of the most popular political acts of the last few years. Charged with enhancing the protection of citizens against improper treatment by state officials, the ombudsman is empowered to deal with complaints concerning the police, prisons, medical facilities, government ministries, and district offices. However, the ombudsman has no power to sanction the offending authorities, only to notify the government and to make the case public. In December 2000, Parliament elected former justice minister Otakar Motejl as ombudsman, and Charter 77 activist Anna Sabatova as deputy ombudsman.

To deal with the pervasive discrimination against Roma in the Czech Republic, Parliament created the post of Human Rights Commissioner in September 1997. The commissioner serves as the head of the Council for Nationalities and the middleman between the government and the Roma minority. The officeholder, currently Jan Jarab, analyzes government proposals concerning minorities, collects information and informs the Roma community about government programs, and recently has taken an active role in extrajudicial dispute resolution between the Roma minority and their non-Roma neighbors in towns, such as Usti nad Labem and Rokycany.

The Czech government also announced its intention to establish an independent state institution, the Office for Ethnic Equality, which will observe violations of the nondiscrimination laws and impose sanctions on the offending party.

The Supreme Audit Office is an independent controlling body entrusted with overseeing the management of state property and the fulfillment of the state budget.

STAFFING
All judges are appointed by the president of the republic, with the consent of the Senate, usually for unlimited terms, with the exception of Constitutional Court judges whose tenure is limited to ten years. The minimum qualifications for a judicial appointment are that the person be a citizen of integrity, must have reached the age of forty, be eligible to vote, have a law degree, and at least ten years experience in the legal profession (Article 84). While on the bench, a judge may not be a member of any political party and must not engage in any profit-making

activity. Justices are independent and enjoy immunity from criminal prosecution for the time of their tenure. They may be prosecuted for felonies only with the consent of the Senate. A justice may be removed from office only in case of a final conviction of a criminal offense, due to loss of eligibility for the Senate, or if the remaining judges on a particular court find, by majority vote, that a disciplinary infraction has been sufficiently grave to warrant expulsion.

The fifteen judges of the Constitutional Court are appointed by the president with the consent of the Senate and serve ten-year terms. Of the current justices, four were members of Parliament, four were justices of the Czecho and Slovakia Federation Republic (CSFR) Constitutional Court, four are professors, five were judges, and several had been lawyers in private practice.

Admission to legal practice requires a law degree, conferred after a minimum of five years of study (master's degree), and an additional rigorous examination (juris doctor). Academic standards are high, and current enrollment at the three law schools in the country (Charles University, Masaryk University, Palacky University) stands at approximately 7,000. All law schools have made forceful strides toward the Europeanization of their curricula. To bring the domestic legal education up to par with European standards, in light of the Republic's anticipated membership in the European Union (EU), the law faculties participate in almost all European educational programs, and actively encourage student exchange through partnerships with other European and American universities.

Approximately 6,000 Czech lawyers work in the public and private sectors and are organized in the Bar Association of the Czech Republic, located in Prague. The bar association functions as an effective lobby and also enforces the ethical standards of the profession. In general, the Czech legal market is characterized by its relative underdevelopment. Domestic firms are hardly present in the high-end commercial sectors (corporate, banking, finance)—dominated by big American, British, and German firms—instead restricting themselves to domestic civil, criminal, and commercial law.

IMPACT

While the government generally respects the human rights of its citizens, serious problems remain in certain areas. The judiciary in general is hampered by structural and procedural deficiencies and a lack of resources. Occasional incidences of police brutality, instances of corruption of the court system, lengthy pretrial detention, delayed judicial proceedings, and trafficking in women and children rank among the most prominent concerns. The lack in experienced police officers and qualified judges—in some estimates 400 posts remain unfilled—have led to a tremendous backlog in cases, and, according to the International Helsinki Federation for Human Rights, several instances of miscarriage of justice.

In early 2000, the Czech government inaugurated an ambitious program, the Concept of the Reform of the Judiciary, to streamline the administration and structure of courts, strengthen the independence of the judiciary, and carry out a complete recodification of civil, criminal, and commercial codes, which, to this date, still contain elements of Marxist doctrine, thus proving incapable of setting privatization efforts, private investment, and real estate transfers on predictable, consistent ground. Some progress has already been made in modifications to the civil and commercial codes, designed to facilitate and accelerate civil proceedings.

The European Union provided almost 22 million Czech crowns for a project designed to reform the Czech judicial system and to strengthen its independence. The funds will go to the Czech Judges' Association and the Czech State Attorneys' Association to improve cooperation between the Ministry of Justice and the professional organizations, as well as to strengthen the professional organizations so that they can become efficient partners in law enforcement.

The Czech Republic has been engaged in joint efforts with its neighboring countries to secure its borders against the influx of illegal drugs and illegal immigrants, and the rising influence of organized crime. Domestically, the Roma minority continues to suffer from widespread racial discrimination, institutional and civil, in areas such as housing, education, and employment, as well as sporadic physical attacks from skinheads, especially in the northwestern border regions. While some of these attacks have attracted widespread international attention and led the Czech government to enforce existing nondiscrimination laws more vigorously, much still needs to be done. Human rights organizations have criticized the reluctance of prosecutors to bring charges against those who physically assaulted Roma, the disinclination of lower courts to enforce nondiscrimination laws, and of local authorities to carry out unpopular policies designed to improve the social and economic situation of the Roma community.

As of August 2001, the Czech Republic is party to one international dispute. Liechtenstein demands restitution for 1,600 square kilometers of land that the Czech Republic confiscated from its royal family in 1918. The government rejects that claim, arguing that this expropriation happened before 1948, when the Communists seized power.

Since the Velvet Revolution of 1989, most areas of the justice sector have undergone substantial change. The judicial bodies have made great progress in expunging Marxist-Leninist doctrine from the legal codes, and more change is in store as the country brings its legal system in line with requirements of the CSCE and the Council of Europe, and prepares for membership in the European Union.

Sylvia Maier

See also Judicial Independence; Marxist Jurisprudence; Slovakia; Soviet System

References and further reading

Daubner, Robert. 1997. *Verfassungsumwandlung, Privatisierung und Privatrechtskodifikation in der Tschechischen Republik.* Berlin: Berlin Verlag A. Spitz.

Gillis, Mark. 1996. "Making Amends After Communism." *Journal of Democracy* 7: 112–134.

Kirchner, Emil J., ed. 1999. *Decentralization and Transition in the Visegrad: Poland, Hungary, the Czech Republic and Slovakia.* Basingstoke: MacMillan; New York: St. Martin's Press.

Marko, Joseph, ed. 2000. *Revolution und Recht: Systemtransformation und Verfassungsentwicklung in der Tschechischen und Slowakischen Republik.* Frankfurt am Main: Lang.

Saxonberg, Steven. 1999. "A New Phase in Czech Politics." *Journal of Democracy* 10: 16–23.

Vodicka, Karl. 1996. *Politisches System Tschechiens: Vom Kommunistischen Einparteiensystem zum Demokratischen Verfassungsstaat.* Munster: Lit.

http://www.czech.cz (Comprehensive webpage on the Czech political and legal system).

http://www.concourt.cz/justis.justis.html (Homepage of the Czech Constitutional Court).

http://www.usemb.se/human/human1999/czechrep.html (Annual Reports on Human Rights Practices in the Czech Republic).

D

DELAWARE

GENERAL INFORMATION

Delaware covers 2,400 square miles on the northeastern seaboard of the United States. Its population is 784,000, 75 percent of which is white and 19 percent of which is black. Europeans first settled the area during the 1600s and brought their English social and legal traditions. Among the top ten employers in Delaware, half are some unit of local, state, or federal government. The state government is the largest employer. Major private-sector employers include DuPont Co., a pharmaceutical interest, many banking and insurance concerns, and automobile manufacturers.

EVOLUTION AND HISTORY

The Delaware court system traces its origins to the 1600s, when Delaware was part of the British colony of Pennsylvania. The oldest of the Delaware judicial institutions is the justice of the peace courts, which were occupied by royal appointment. Justices of the peace decided misdemeanor, criminal, and small-claims civil cases, in addition to administering local government. The English monarch also established the Superior Court in 1669 to try a trio of Swedish loyalists for treason. During the Revolutionary War, this court's forebear, the Supreme Court, would try colonists still loyal to the crown for treason. As commercial and social life became more complex, royal proclamation created the Chancery, to resolve equity disputes. Chancery's cases were heard when the colonial governor thought that other courts had erred, or when other legal traditions would result in an injustice. These courts exist today, relying largely on the Anglo-American common law tradition.

Following the American Revolution, the Delaware court system largely became a localized judicial system, with the state's three county courts being quite diverse in structure, authority, and sources of funding. The 1792 state constitution divorced Chancery from the English common law tradition. This task however, did not replace standing decisions and British common law informed all of the state's civil proceedings through the 1800s. Delaware was unique among the U.S. courts in that Delaware kept its Chancery. Other states regarded these courts as having exercised arbitrary royal authority. Most judges of this time earned their incomes by charging court fees and imposing fines. This tradition remained intact until 1965, when the justices of the peace were at last paid from the state's treasury.

In the 1830s the constitution delegated civil disputes to the Superior Court, while a court of general sessions heard serious felony cases. The Court of Oyer and Terminer heard capital cases. The court of appeals became the court of last resort. There is little evidence that the court of appeals ever heard a case. The governor and members of the assembly sat in this court. The Constitution of 1897 abolished the court of appeals and gave final appellate authority to the Supreme Court. All of the Supreme Court's judges would be "learned in the law," and rather than the governor and legislators sitting on this court, "leftover" judges from the lower court would hear appeals. The chancellor or chief justice would preside at Supreme Court hearings. This leftover judge tradition remained intact until the 1950s.

At the end of the 1800s, other important changes came to the Delaware courts. The Superior Court would now try major criminal cases. The chancellor was given power to appoint several vice chancellors to help him with a growing caseload. Early in the 1900s, counties established courts of specific jurisdiction. Among the first is the family court, which traces its origins to 1911 in the city of Wilmington. Hearing mostly juvenile delinquency complaints, the family court later became a countywide court. The court of common pleas was organized in 1917 to relieve the Superior Court of small claims; it would issue criminal sentences. These were local courts, not part of a statewide system. Judges serving the local court of common pleas also sat on the state Superior Court system. Judges were paid a daily rate for their duty in common pleas. It was not until the 1930s that the court of common pleas in New Castle County took its modern form, with authority over cases worth up to $1,000 and a part-time judge assigned only to this court. In 1962, each of the three courts of common pleas was given trial authority and in 1969 the three county courts were merged into a unified, statewide court.

Structure of Delaware Courts

Under Article 4 of the State Constitution, Delaware courts are given their authority. The governor nominates and the Senate approves judicial nominees. They serve 12-year terms.

COURT OF LAST RESORT

Delaware Supreme Court
Authority to review virtually all lower court decisions, exercise judicial review, and issue rules affecting the administration of the courts.
Five judges dispose of 500–600 cases each year.

COURTS WITH GENERAL JURISDICTION

Superior Court
Serious Criminal and Civil Trials. Misdemeanor and Small Claims Appeals. Nineteen judges dispose of 17,000 cases per year.

Chancery Court
Court of equity, corporate, and contract law. Chancellor and 4 vice chancellors dispose of 4,400 cases per year.

COURTS WITH LIMITED JURISDICTION

Justice of the Peace Court
Minor Civil And Criminal Cases; Truancy; Fish and Wildlife Violations; and Landlord-Tenant Disputes. Nearly 60 judges hear 410,000 cases per year.

Aldermen's Court
Local Jurisdiction in Land Use or Local Ordinance Violations. Twelve aldermen hear about 15,000 cases per year.

Family Court
Civil and criminal domestic relations. Fourteen judges hear 58,000 cases per year.

Court of Common Pleas
Small-claims civil cases, preliminary hearings in criminal proceedings; sentencing in some criminal cases. Seven judges hear about 73,000 cases per year.

As a former British colony, Delaware judges applied English common law into the 1900s. Delaware court historian Paul Dolan writes that this tradition began eroding in the 1920s. This coincides with early twentieth century decisions in which the court cautiously exercised judicial review. Dolan wrote that during the first half of the twentieth century only twelve cases involved challenges to the constitutionality of state law. The state constitution and longstanding traditions discouraged this exercise of power.

The Delaware courts underwent their most significant shifts after World War II. In a series of divided opinions the Supreme Court shifted to American common law ideals in contract and tort. Chancery also would lead the way to abolishing the principle allowing separate, but equal facilities for Blacks. Chancery's 1952 opinion *Belton v. Gebhart* was consolidated on appeal to the U.S. Supreme Court in the *Brown v. Board of Education* case. This case fundamentally changed the meaning of the Equal Protection clause of the U.S. Constitution, so that local governments could no longer practice racial segregation. Vice chancellors also became separately appointed constitutional officers, no longer appointees of the chancellor.

In the 1950s, Delaware's courts would undergo changes, making it more like other state courts. The chief justice became the highest judicial officer, formerly a role of the chancellor. Rather than serving during "good behavior" the chief justice would serve for twelve years, like most other judges. The chief no longer sits on the Superior Court. A presiding judge now superintends the Superior Court. In 1965 the chief justice was given authority to appoint a chief magistrate to oversee the justice of the peace courts. In 1978 the number of Supreme Court justices was raised from three to five.

CURRENT STRUCTURE

Judges at all levels in Delaware are nominated by the governor, and require Senate approval. The governor does not have a completely free hand in making nominations. The constitution requires that membership on each of the courts be divided almost equally between the two political parties. One of the parties must have a one-member majority. Judges serve twelve-year terms and hold no other legal duties than those assigned by the constitution or state law. Rather than relying on court fees and fines for their income, their salaries are paid through the state treasury.

The state constitution authorizes a three-tiered court system, with the Supreme Court at its apex. Below it are two courts with general authority: the Court of Chancery (equity cases) and the Superior Court (criminal and civil cases). At the foundation are four courts of limited, original jurisdiction. Most cases have their origins in these courts. They are: family court, court of common pleas, justice of the peace courts, and the alderman's courts. There is also a court on the judiciary, which may reprimand and even remove judges from office for violations of law, bringing embarrassment to the judiciary, or failure to perform official duties.

The lower courts have authority in limited areas of law, such as small claims (common pleas), juvenile delinquency and divorce or child custody (family court), or misdemeanor offenses (alderman's and justice of the peace). The general authority courts have trial and appellate authority. In felony and major civil cases, these courts are the trial court. Individual judges may hear appeals from the lower courts. The Supreme Court only has appellate jurisdiction in almost all of the cases coming to it.

Court of Common Pleas

This court has limited original civil jurisdiction over disputes with a value of up to $15,000. It has authority in change-of-name filings. It has authority over preliminary hearings for felony matters, except narcotics cases. In 1995, this court assumed appellate responsibility for most traffic infractions and misdemeanor cases. After a criminal guilty plea, or finding of guilt, common pleas impose sentences. By 1999, common pleas saw case filings reach 137,000, up from about 5,000 in the early 1970s. Decisions by this court may be appealed to the Superior Court, where a single judge will review the standard of law applied.

Justice of the Peace Courts

Justices of the peace hear misdemeanor and civil cases with a monetary value of up to $15,000. Justices of the peace hear landlord-tenant disputes, truancy, limited fish and wildlife violations, local ordinance violations, and traffic cases. Justices' decisions can be appealed to the Superior Court. Justices impose bail in criminal matters that will later be tried in higher courts. Justices may issue search and arrest warrants for felony and misdemeanor criminal investigations. They may set bond in felony or misdemeanor criminal matters. Justices may subpoena witnesses. In 1999, the justice of the peace courts disposed of 367,000 cases.

Family Court

The family court has exclusive original jurisdiction in both civil and criminal matters as they relate to the family unit. This includes divorce, misdemeanor domestic violence, child custody, adoption, child abuse and neglect, and child support cases. It also hears criminal matters when a child is accused of a crime (except violent felonies). The family court appoints guardians and legal advocates for abused, abandoned, or neglected children. This court disposed of 58,000 cases in 2000.

Court of Chancery

The Court of Chancery has general trial authority in equity cases. Today these cases concern corporate shareholder issues, contracts and other financial topics. Chancery also hears cases involving trusts, real estate, and civil rights. Traditionally, equity cases arise when the law fails to offer a fair remedy. The court in practice does not hear appeals from lower courts, but has authority to review small claims cases.

The chancellor and vice chancellors sit in single-judge courts to hear and decide cases. It issues two types of opinions. A letter opinion traditionally is of interest to only the parties, while a memorandum opinion informs the opinions of others, such as other chancellors deciding similar cases. However, as both memorandum and letter opinions appear on the Internet, this distinction is becoming obsolete. This court disposes of about 4,400 cases per year.

Superior Court

The Superior Court has original and appellate jurisdiction. In both types of cases, one-judge courts issue rulings. This court has original authority in felony cases and in civil cases with values in excess of $50,000. Where a civil case has implications in equity, Chancery will advise the Superior Court.

The Superior Court has appellate jurisdiction in cases coming out of the family court, the court of common pleas, and the justice of the peace courts. Superior Court hears appeals from more than forty boards or executive agencies. The Superior Court has a special drug court that attempts to alleviate work in this area. The Superior Court has authority to commit individuals to mental institutions. The Superior Court disposes of about 17,000 cases per year.

Delaware Supreme Court

Since 1951, the Delaware Supreme Court has had five justices, with no other judicial or legal responsibilities. The Supreme Court has authority to exercise judicial review. The commonest process for judicial review is for someone to seek an advisory opinion. This questions the constitutionality of a law, though there need not be traditional parties who claim that they have been harmed by the statute. By contrast, the U.S. Supreme Court requires a "case and controversy" in which one party claims an injury.

In general, the Delaware Supreme Court reviews cases only after all proceedings in a case are finished in the lower court. The Court makes exceptions for interlocutory appeals, which clarify a central point of law, determine whether certain evidence can be presented so that a trial may proceed, or review orders placing a child in the care of someone during child-custody proceedings.

The Supreme Court can issue writs of certiorari and mandamus. The Court can establish rules governing "the administration of justice and the conduct of the business of any or all the courts in this State" (art. 4, sec. 1).

Though there are five justices of the Supreme Court, three justices review most cases. A three-justice decision is just as final as a five-justice ruling. It is conceivable that the three justices from a single political party will review any given case. Panels of the Supreme Court are chosen with the expertise of the justices in mind, rather than by lot. The full five-justice court will sit en banc to hear appeals only when litigants demonstrate that a case presents issues never before decided, when the validity of an established rule of law might be overturned, or when a criminal defendant is sentenced to death.

As a practical matter the Court allows all criminal defendants to bring their cases. Most criminal petitions are settled by the parties, or are dismissed without a hearing. In the Court's 2000 fiscal year, only fourteen appeals made to the Court were denied before briefs were filed. The vast majority of the Court's cases are disposed of by written order. The Court disposes of 500 to 600 cases per year. Nearly 300 of them are civil, about 240 are criminal, and a small number come under the Court's original jurisdiction. About half of the cases brought to the Supreme Court are affirmed, without modification.

STAFFING

The governor nominates judges for virtually all positions in the state judiciary. The state's Senate, by majority vote, either approves or rejects the nomination. Judges at most levels serve for twelve-year terms. Except for justices of the peace and aldermen judges, judges must be "learned in the law" and licensed to practice before the state Supreme Court.

Justices of the peace serve four-year terms and may be reappointed for a six-year term. A chief magistrate superintends the justice of the peace court. The chief magistrate may issue directives concerned with all matters related to the administration of the justice of the peace court. In addition, there is a deputy chief magistrate in each of the three counties. Along with judicial duties, deputies are responsible for scheduling proceedings, hearing initial complaints about justices in their branches, and answering questions of law for other justices (since they are not necessarily trained in the law).

In the family court, judges must have specific training in family law. The family court has a Foster Care Review Board, which monitors the progress of children who are in state custody and advises the court on matters pertaining to these children. The governor appoints a chief judge of family court. The chief judge is the court's administrative and executive officer. The court also has a staff of nearly 300 clerks and administrators. The governor, with Senate approval, appoints commissioners to four-year terms to set bail and accept pleas in criminal complaints in family court. When designated by the chief judge, a commissioner may hear civil trials and other proceedings.

As of 2000, the Chancery court did not have direct control over its own staff, and judges were petitioning the state's legislature to give the court greater control over personnel. By his office, the chancellor serves on the Court of the Judiciary, which may discipline any member of the state court system. Chancery renders verdicts without the aid of jurors.

Judges in the Superior Court and Chancery have judicially appointed masters who recommend case outcomes in less complicated litigation. Commissioners serve a similar role to the other court masters in the court of common pleas and in family court. The commissioners are gubernatorial appointees, unlike the masters.

The Superior Court is authorized to hire clerks, law clerks, staff attorneys, and other administrative assistants who serve at the pleasure of the Court. In the Superior Court, commissioners may accept pleas and make pretrial determinations including the suppression of evidence. Court masters may preside in postconviction proceedings. Presentencing officers inform judges about a convict's criminal history and tell judges when enhanced penalties apply. Within the Superior Court Clerk's office is the Prothonotary's Office, which prepares judicial orders such as warrants, summonses, indictments, and commitment paperwork. In the Superior Court, jurors may make factual decisions at trial. Jurors are drawn from voter and driver's license lists.

The Supreme Court has five justices, with the chief justice as the presiding officer. The chief may fill judicial vacancies with retired judges while the governor's appointments are being considered. The Supreme Court has several commissions answering to it. These agencies monitor licensing and education, discipline lawyers, and provide legal assistance to the poor. The chief justice serves on a commission that can transfer the governor's authority to the lieutenant governor when the governor is mentally or physically incapacitated.

Persons practicing law in Delaware must be licensed by the state Supreme Court. As of August 2001 there were 3,032 licensed attorneys in the state, with a lawyer to population ratio of about 1:259. About two-thirds are in private practice and about 30 percent are women. Lawyers must be recertified by the Commission of Legal Education every two years, to make sure that they undergo continuing legal education. The state's bar association conducts seminars and produces bulletins and videos to keep lawyers up to date. Individuals may represent themselves in court, though they are expected to comply with all court rules for filing paperwork and adhering to rules of oral argument. Businesses or other organizations must have a licensed attorney.

Sean O. Hogan

See also Common Law; Family Law; United States—Federal System; United States—State Systems
References and further reading
Allen, William T. 2000. "The Pride and the Hope of Delaware Corporate Law," *Delaware Journal of Corporate Law* 25: 70.
Fisch, Jill E. 2000. "Contemporary Issues in the Law of Business Organizations: The Peculiar Role of the Delaware Courts in the Competition for Corporate Charters." *University of Cincinnati Law Review* 68: 1061.
Holland, Randy J., and Helen Winslow. 2001. *Delaware Supreme Court, Golden Anniversary Book*. Wilmington, DE: Court Administrator's Office.
Macey, Jonathan R., and Geoffrey P. Miller. 1987. "Toward an Interest-Group Theory of Delaware Corporate Law." *Texas Law Review* 65: 469.

Quillen, William T., and Michael Hanrahan. 1993. "A Short History of the Delaware Court of Chancery." *Delaware Journal of Corporate Law* 18: 819.

Smith, D. Gordon. 1998. "A Tribute to Chancellor William D. Allen." *Seattle University Law Review* 21: 577.

Stempel, Jeffrey W. 1995. "Two Cheers for Specialization." *Brooklyn Law Review* 61: 67.

Walsh, Joseph T. 1999. "Judicial Independence: A Delaware Perspective." *Delaware Law Review* 18: 209.

DENMARK

GENERAL INFORMATION

Denmark (Danish: Danmark) is a western European state. It covers a territory of forty-three thousand square kilometers and in 1999 had 5,300,000 inhabitants. The language of Denmark is Danish, and the currency is the Danish crown (Danish: *krone*). Denmark consists of coastal lowlands. The peninsula of Jutland is connected to the European continent, and there are 406 islands, among them Zealand, with the capital of Copenhagen. The climate is temperate and humid, favoring a substantial agricultural sector. There is a considerable fishing industry. Denmark is poor in minerals and other natural resources, however, and consequently there is no mining industry, apart from the mining of North Sea gas and the open cast mining mainly of sand, stone, clay, and gravel. Denmark has an industrial sector that produces mechanical instruments. It also has shipyards and a chemical industry. In February 2001 the unemployment rate in Denmark was 5.8 percent. Denmark belongs to the Scandinavian welfare states, with traditionally a large public sector and a large middle class, and with a comparatively equal distribution of income. In 2000, some 93,000 persons were employed in the agricultural sector, 1,715,000 in the private urban sector, and 811,000 in public service. In 1999 the gross national product was 1,147.3 billion Danish crowns.

Denmark is a member of the European Union (from 1973) and NATO (from 1949). In 2001, Denmark entered into the Schengen, an agreement among the European Union countries to combat cross-border crime and to secure the free movement of persons inside the union. A consequence of the Schengen agreement is that travel inside the Schengen countries is free, while the control at the outside borders is strengthened. The control is tied to an electronic information system, the Schengen Information System (SIS).

Since 1901 Denmark has been a parliamentarian monarchy. The first democratic constitution went into force in 1849. The present constitution was enacted in 1953. The Danish head of state is the prime minister, who is responsible to the parliament (Danish: *Folketing*). The present monarch is Queen Margrethe II.

To the Danish realm also belong the Faeroe Islands (with 45,000 inhabitants) and Greenland (with 56,000 inhabitants). Both enjoy wide independence. In 1917 Denmark sold the then-Danish Virgin Islands to the United States. In 1944 Iceland gained independence of Danish rule.

Since the nineteenth century, the Danish population has been very homogeneous, consisting almost entirely of Danish nationals. At the present there has been a stop to immigration from outside the EU, except for situations in which the immigrant has special reasons for migrating (such as having family in Denmark, or cases of political persecution). In 1980 the percentage of immigrants in Denmark was 3.0 and in 2001 it was 7.4, the main groups having come from Turkey, Yugoslavia, Germany, Lebanon, Pakistan, and Iraq.

HISTORY

During the Bronze Age, Denmark acquired an elaborate culture. In the ninth century C.E., with the Norwegians and the Swedes, the Danes started to expand into Western and Eastern Europe, both pillaging and trading, and for a short time gained supremacy over a part of England. At the same time, a local dynasty from Jutland united some of the smaller kingdoms, and the country was christened around 1000.

A feudal society was founded around the twelfth century, influenced by the Roman Catholic Church and its officials. Simultaneously, a vast number of churches and monasteries were built. The crown was not hereditary, and therefore to gain power the king had to sign a coronation charter. In the contemporary Western tradition, in this charter he promised to respect the law. The period from 1157 to 1241 was one of high medieval culture. The rulers were the Valdemar kings, and a number of codes were enacted to guide the governance of the different regions. After that followed a period of economic and political weakening, the Danish strongholds in the Baltic and the Danish seas being threatened by the Hanseatic League. In the fourteenth century the Danish kingdom was under the reign of the daughter of Valdemar IV, Margrethe, who also governed Norway and Sweden in the so-called Calmar Union. In 1479 the University of Copenhagen was founded on a privilege from the pope. The subjects were Roman law and canon law.

The sixteenth century was a period of internal reform, and a rising bourgeoisie settled in the commercial port towns, enjoying privileges and self-governance granted by city laws issued by the king. The Calmar Union was terminated in 1523 with the Swedish struggle for independence, forming the Swedish state, while Norway and Denmark still both were governed by the Danish king. However, the southern part of the present Sweden (Scandia) stayed with the Danish crown, thus leaving Den-

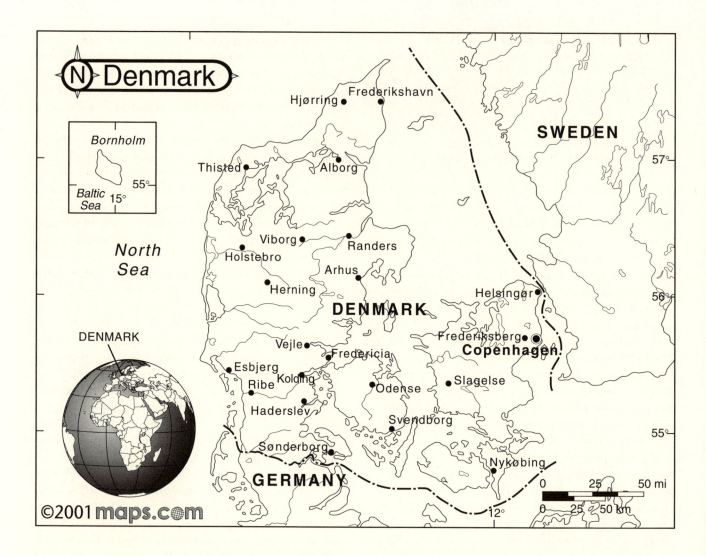

mark in control of access to the Baltic sea, a position that until 1857 would enable Denmark to force foreign ships to pay toll to the Danish crown for their passage. In 1536 the Lutheran Protestant religion was made the state religion, and churches and monasteries were transferred to the crown.

Denmark participated in the Thirty Years War, which ended in 1648. In 1658, the wars with Sweden resulted in the annexation by Sweden of Scandia, while Denmark kept control over Norway and the southern part of Jutland (Slesvig). The wars and the ravaging of Swedish troops left Denmark weak, and in 1660 the Danish king took the opportunity to gain control over what was left of the Danish nobility, establishing absolute power for the crown. In 1665 the position of the king was supported by the absolute constitution Lex Regia (Danish: *Kongeloven*), granting the king all powers and placing him above the law, contrary to previous tradition. Moreover, central power was strengthened by the promulgation of the Danish Code of 1683. This was followed in 1687 by a similar Norwegian code.

The eighteenth century was a period of reform. In

1736 the first regulation of the law degree was enacted, to facilitate the staffing of the courts with professional personnel. Commerce increased, inasmuch as Denmark benefited from her position of neutrality. However, after pressure from the British and the bombardment of Copenhagen in 1801, Denmark was forced into the French camp and sided with Napoleon. The Napoleonic Wars had a catastrophic effect on the Danish economy and crown, the country going bankrupt in 1813 and, in 1814, losing Norway.

In 1849 the Danish king, Frederik VII, peacefully abolished absolute reign and a democratic constitution was adopted. In 1848 a German nationalistic insurrection in the southern part of Jutland was crushed. In 1864, Prussia retaliated, Danish resistance was pushed back, and Prussia occupied the German national regions of southern Jutland, as well as a large part of the Danish national ones. The Danish language was abandoned from public life in those areas.

In 1901 the parliamentary system of government was established as a political practice. The industrialization of Denmark began during the second half of the nineteenth century, with worker unions gaining a major victory in 1899: they obtained the right to strike, collective bargaining, and the establishment of a system of negotiation and adjudication institutions governing the labor market.

During World War I, Denmark kept her neutrality. In 1920, Denmark recovered the Danish nationalist region of southern Jutland.

In 1924 the first Social Democratic government was established, and this party remained in government until 1970, although during that period it never gained control of a majority of the parliamentary seats. As in most other Western industrialized countries, the 1930s was a period of economic crisis and unemployment, as well as advancing public regulation both of external trade and of the domestic economy.

During World War II, Denmark was occupied by Germany. Since the war, the political history has been dominated by social democratic governments, in collaboration mainly with a social-liberal (nonsocialistic) party. The political program has been based on the building up of a welfare state, with a large public sector and a wide degree of public, tax-financed services. However, the election of 1973 produced some change in this picture of welfare state consensus, since a protest against the level of taxation was formed. Under nonsocialist governments in the 1980s there was a push for privatization of public activities and assets, just as in the 1990s Denmark has noted increased support for the abolishment of public monopolies.

LEGAL CONCEPTS

Denmark is a unitary monarchy. However, the 14 counties and 275 municipalities enjoy some independence from central rule. Each has a politically elected council and all have some power of taxation. Besides the counties, Denmark also has departments, organized under the Ministry of Interior. The distinction between county and department is not geographical, but lies in the tasks allocated to the different entities and the different management principles (the bureaucratic departments as opposed to the more closely politically governed counties).

The rule of law is embedded in the constitution with the division of powers between the legislative, the executive, and the judicial branches of government. The judges are independent and can be removed only through judgment by another judge. The judiciary is granted the right of constitutional review of government decisions and parliamentary acts. The Danish constitution has supremacy over all other law, and there is a hierarchy of laws according to which the statutory orders, regulations, and concrete decisions promulgated and issued by the ministries and the municipalities or counties must be within the authority of the law. In this respect the Danish legal tradition has adopted the theories of Hans Kelsen, as interpreted by the Scandinavian legal realists, among them the

Danish legal philosopher Alf Ross. The school of Scandinavian legal realism is related to the American school of legal realism, characterized by an empirical view of the law, as opposed to an abstract Continental concept of legal philosophy or of natural law.

In relation to conventions, Denmark adheres to the dualist position of law, which means that conventions must be incorporated before they become a part of Danish law. An exception is the law of the European Union, which in accordance with the principle of direct effect has been made part of Danish law.

The Danish constitution respects political and personal (including economic), as well as some social, rights. Denmark is commonly described as belonging to the Scandinavian legal family. Roman law never was adopted by Danish government, although Roman law can be seen in court decisions from the eighteenth century, as a part of the argumentation by judges. The Scandinavian legal family does not belong to the common law world, however. In a number of ways, the Danish legal tradition bears resemblance to the Continental tradition: there is no unified legal profession, legal training is directed in significant part toward positions as civil servants, and legal principles are organized around a number of codes, many of which were created collaboratively by the Scandinavian states. This collaboration on codes started as a reform project in the late nineteenth century. Among other fields it includes commercial law, the law of sales and trade, and family law. This use of regulation also has advanced a legal tradition with less emphasis on case law and more stress on regulation, although it should be noted that court judgments are considered as sources of law. The law of compensation has been developed almost entirely as judge-made law.

The position of the judge in criminal as well as civil procedure is that of the neutral party. In this the Danish court procedure distinguishes itself from the Continental inquisitorial system. In civil cases it is up to the parties to present the case, as in the American adversary system. In the criminal procedure it is the obligation of the police to investigate the case.

The European Union has been an object of concern for the Danish electorate, and in a number of referenda the Danish voters have displayed considerable skepticism toward it. In political debates, this takes the form of fear of losing national sovereignty, culture, and tradition through union harmonization.

CURRENT STRUCTURE OF THE COURT SYSTEM

The court system is regulated by the Danish Code of Procedure, the Administration of Justice Act (Danish: *retsplejeloven*). This act includes rules on civil as well as criminal procedure. Previously the courts were governed by the Ministry of Justice. However, in a reform enacted in 1999, this function was reorganized, and today it is found with a special agency (Danish: *Domstolsstyrelsen*) with an independent board.

The ordinary courts are organized in a three-tier system: city courts, courts of appeal, and the Supreme Court (Danish: *Højesteret*). Denmark has eighty-two city court districts, two high courts of appeal, an eastern division (Danish: *Østre Landsret*), and a western division (Danish: *Vester Landsret*). In Copenhagen there also resides a court dealing with matters concerning commerce and maritime conflicts in the greater Copenhagen area, the Maritime and Commercial Court (Danish: *Sø- og Handelsretten*). The Supreme Court is an appellate court for decisions made by the two appellate courts and the Maritime and Commercial Court. Hence Denmark does not have a court of cassation, as for instance is seen in France.

Judicial review is exercised by the ordinary court system. Outside the judiciary, Denmark has a number of agencies controlling the government, for example the parliamentary ombudsman, and a consumer ombudsman in consumer law (both ombudsmen hold law degrees). There are also the auditors of public accounts (Danish: *Statsrevisorerne*), who are politically elected, and the government Audit Department (Danish: *Rigsrevisionen*), which controls the lawful use of public funding. At present, Denmark does not have specific administrative courts, but a number of control measures directed to concrete decisions of the public authorities are found in administrative tribunals and boards, working within each ministry but as bodies independent of the minister (compare the English tradition in this field). As a rule, the proceedings of administrative tribunals are free of charge and carried out with an extended obligation of the civil service to give information to citizens about their rights.

The vast majority of cases, civil as well as criminal, are heard by the city court of first instance. However, some cases are tried by the appellate courts as a court of first instance. This applies to civil cases involving claims above a certain limit at the request of one of the parties, and cases against the state central authorities. Only a very small percentage of criminal cases are heard by the appellate court as first instance. Those may be cases that require trial by jury only, which would be very few cases involving only serious crimes. Capital punishment has been abolished.

In general the organizing principles encourage the Danish judges to be generalists rather than specialists, since a vast variety of claims will be brought before them and the court districts are too small to support a specialization. The judicial court system is based on the principle that a case may be tried in two instances, and that further appeal requires special permission. Permission may be granted if the case involves matters of principle, as for instance if the legality of a statutory order is involved, or if it concerns a question on which conflicting judgments exist from the two appellate courts, or if a review of established case law may be needed. Competence to grant permission does not lie with the courts, but with a specific board, presided over by a supreme court justice and consisting of judges from the lower courts, a professor in law, and a practicing lawyer.

Thus a judgment by a city court could normally be appealed to an appellate court only, and a decision by an appellate court in first instance could be appealed to the Supreme Court. The competence of the city court has been extended, and consequently, cases are less often brought before the Supreme Court. In civil cases the appellate court may try both the facts and the law. New evidence may be submitted by the parties, while new claims and allegations may be entered only after the consent of the other party.

Approximately 85,000 criminal cases and 130,000 civil cases are heard by the courts every year. The court procedure is marked by a considerable informality. Court hearings are public and may be reported in the press and other public forums. However, public broadcasting and television transmissions are not allowed. According to the constitution, proceedings must be conducted orally and be based on firsthand evidence. Hence witnesses must testify directly to the court. If an expert opinion is required, the court may appoint an expert. Normally the parties will recommend one from a public authority or institute. The court will be very reluctant to grant the appearance of a second expert, even though there may be a request from the party that was not satisfied by the opinion of the first expert.

The deliberations of a collegial court are not public. But the judgment will state the reasons for the result, and also adduce dissenting votes, noted by the name of the dissenting judge. In 1956 this was introduced for the Supreme Court, in an effort to provide better guidance for the public.

A judgment will contain both a reference to the facts in the case and the law on which the judgment is based, in order to let the parties make an assessment of the possibilities for an appeal. However, the city court judge will try to reconcile the parties before the judgment, and if that is successful the parties may get an opinion advanced by the judge, but no judgment will be passed. In both cases the result can be enforced by the bailiff (Danish: *Kongens foged*).

The possibility is currently being discussed of introducing a system of small claims courts, and to an increased degree alternative dispute resolution has been seen as a method of solving a number of cases—for instance, in family law. In commercial law, arbitration is a widespread method of conflict solution.

SPECIALIZED JUDICIAL BODIES

The Danish constitution provides for a ban on special courts, those established to deal with one specific, concrete case. This ban has been enacted to bar any circumvention of the judicial system. However, some specialized bodies exist that fulfill a special function within the court system for well-defined categories of cases.

The Maritime and Commercial Court is one example. Denmark also has a special labor court, established as a result of the implementation of the worker union system in Denmark in the early twentieth century. This court hears cases concerning the legality of actions and decisions according to the collective agreements between the worker union and the employers' organization.

A special complaints court (Danish: *Den særlige Klageret*) decides on criminal cases concerning miscarriage of justice, and may decide if the case should be retried. In this it functions as a court of cassation. If parliament wishes to raise an impeachment case against a minister, that also must be tried before a special court, consisting of judges and politicians (Danish: *Rigsretten*).

THE STAFFING OF THE COURTS

Approximately twenty-six hundred people are employed at the Danish courts. About 20 percent have a law degree, while the rest are administrative staff. The office staff also carries out some paralegal functions; for example, the task of bailiff is often performed by a person having administrative abilities and on-the-job training.

Judges must have a degree in law. They are appointed by the queen upon the recommendation of an independent council (Danish: *Dommerudnævnelsesråd*). Furthermore, an applicant for a position to the Supreme Court must pass an examination by rendering an opinion before the full court in four cases. Besides their university law degree, most judges also have had a previous career, either as a deputy judge or as a civil servant in the Ministry of Justice. However, presently there is a demand that judges be recruited from a broader spectrum of the legal profession. Many judicial functions may be carried out by a deputy judge, appointed for a shorter period of time while working as a civil servant in the Ministry of Justice.

In some cases, professional judges are supplemented by lay judges and jurors. Trial by jury was introduced in the nineteenth century, inspired by Alexis de Toqueville's description of the American system. However, trial by jury is reserved for a very few serious criminal cases. Those cases are always tried in the Court of Appeals, acting as a court of first instance. The court will be staffed with three professional judges and twelve jurors that will decide on the question of guilt, while the professional judges and the jury in combination decide the penalty.

In other criminal cases, lay judges sit on the bench with professional judges. In the city court, the profes-

Legal Structure of Denmark

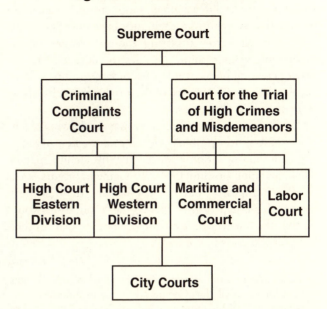

sional judge sits with two lay judges, and in the appellate court there are three lay judges and one professional.

The Maritime and Commercial Court is supplemented by experts in shipping and commerce. City courts dealing with, for instance, child custody cases and matters concerning rental of housing facilities are joined by representatives related to those fields.

Any person can dispense legal advice, however as a rule only licensed lawyers are allowed to represent others in court. As for practicing lawyers, they work as free professionals, and they are free to practice in any district they wish. In order to represent others in court, however, a lawyer must have a license, issued by the Ministry of Justice on the recommendation from the Danish Bar Association and Law Society. In order to obtain this, a law degree as well as a three-year period as a trainee in a law firm are necessary. To represent clients in the appellate courts, a lawyer must pass a test, having tried two cases at an appellate court to the satisfaction of the presiding judge. Practicing lawyers may be subject to disciplinary proceedings, exercised by a disciplinary board having lawyers, judges, and lay members.

As a rule, working in the civil service or even on administrative tribunals does not require a law degree. However, in practice there is an internal recruitment system securing a high percentage of employees with university degrees. In most cases the law provides for administrative tribunals to have as their presiding members and department heads persons qualified to be appointed city court or appellate court judges.

IMPACT OF THE LAW ON SOCIETY

Following World War II, Denmark chose the option of developing a policy-oriented approach to social welfare.

Rights and law suits have not been seen as the primary vehicles to societal development and reform. To a certain extent, that seems to be changing. Law suits and court judgments are now attracting more attention in the media, and taking public agencies to court is seen as a way of creating better conditions for large groups of people that have been deprived of their rights in the handling of their public service cases.

Legal strategies have become a way of drawing attention to a political problem as well as a method of creating new solutions. Some reasons for this change may be the focus upon on human and fundamental rights issues by the European Court of Justice and the European Court of Human Rights. Hence the implication would be that the law will have a rising impact on Danish society over the years to come.

Helle Blomquist

See also Administrative Tribunals; Adversarial System; Capital Punishment; Civil Law; Common Law; Constitutional Review; Judicial Independence; Judicial Review; Legal Realism

References and further reading
Berman, Harold. 1983. *Law and Revolution.* Cambridge: Harvard University Press.
Blomquist, Helle. 2000. *Lawyers' Ethics: The Social Construction of Lawyers' Professionalism: Danish Practicing Lawyers and Some Pre-Conditions for Their Ethics.* Copenhagen: DJØF Publishing Company.
Dahl, Børge, Torben Melchior, Lars Adam Rehof, and Ditlev Tamm, eds. 1996. *Danish Law in a European Perspective.* Copenhagen: GADJURA.
Derry, T. K. 1979. *A History of Scandinavia: Norway, Sweden, Denmark, Finland and Iceland.* London: George Allen and Unwin.
Griffith, Tony. 1991. *Scandinavia.* Kent Town, South Australia: Wakefield Press.
Jarvad, Ib Martin. 1984. *The Scandinavian Realism: A Critique. A Defence. A Restatement.* Roskilde: Institute of Economics and Planning.
Katz, Alan N., ed. 1986. *Legal Traditions and Systems: An International Handbook.* New York: Greenwood Press.
Kjærgaard, Thorkild. 1994. *The Danish Revolution 1500–1800: An Ecohistorical Interpretation.* New York: Cambridge University Press.
Pedersen, Peder J. 1994. "Post-war Growth of the Danish Economy." In *Undervisningsmateriale til Dansk Økonomisk Historie.* E. Damsgård Hansen (ed.). Århus: Århus Universitet.
Ross, Alf. 1959. *On Law and Justice.* Berkeley: University of California Press.
Zweigert, Konrad, and Heinz Kötz. 1987. *Introduction to Comparative Law.* Vols. I and II. Oxford: Clarendon Press.

DETERRENCE
See General Deterrence;
Specific (Individual) Deterrence

DISPUTE RESOLUTION UNDER REGIONAL TRADE AGREEMENTS

ASIA-PACIFIC ECONOMIC COOPERATION (APEC)

Asia-Pacific Economic Cooperation (APEC) was established in 1989 as the first intergovernmental body to discuss promotion of economic cooperation in the Asia-Pacific region. The scope of APEC activities, which have expanded to include all economic affairs, is based on three central pillars: trade and investment liberalization, trade and investment facilitation, and economic and technical cooperation (Ecotech). The Ministerial Meeting and the Informal Leaders Meeting, which are held annually, oversee APEC activities and decide its principal direction. Under the Leaders and Ministerial Meeting, many forums perform their respective duties. These include the Senior Officials Meeting, committees, working groups, expert groups, task forces, and the secretariat.

Currently APEC has twenty-one members: Australia, Brunei Darussalam, Canada, Chile, the People's Republic of China, Hong Kong China, Indonesia, Japan, the Republic of Korea, Malaysia, Mexico, New Zealand, Papua New Guinea, Peru, the Philippines, Russia, Singapore, Chinese Taipei, Thailand, the United States, and Vietnam. The combined gross domestic product (GDP) of members is equivalent to half that of the entire globe, and the amount of trade accounts for more than 40 percent of the world's total.

APEC does not have its own mechanism of dispute resolution, although it has been discussing for many years a future model for the region. Member economies have agreed so far to create a mediation mechanism, for APEC is characterized as a consultative forum on economic affairs and its agreements are not mandatory. It is also agreed that the mechanism must be supplementary to the World Trade Organization (WTO) system.

Since the mid-1990s, however, momentum to build its own body of dispute resolution seems to be waning, and member economies have been putting more emphasis on the usage of existing systems.

Mission
In 1995, APEC designated the Dispute Mediation Experts Group (DMEG) as its formal body for the discussion of dispute mediation. At their first meeting, the DMEG spelled out the following points as its goals:

- resolution of disputes between APEC member economies
- resolution of disputes between an APEC member and a private entity of another APEC member
- resolution of disputes between private entities

- the avoidance of trade disputes through increased transparency

For (a), creation of APEC's own mechanism was the main concern. The WTO Dispute Resolution Understanding (DSU) was available, but for most of the members of the region a mediation mechanism was more acceptable for sociolegal reasons. Considering the nonbinding nature of mediation, however, member economies agreed to substitute the APEC mechanism only for the consultation process of the WTO DSU and left the panel process as the primary channel for resolution.

For (b) and (c), the DMEG encouraged the use of existing international or domestic systems. The DMEG has repeatedly urged member economies to accede to international agreements such as the Convention on the Settlement of Investment Disputes Between States and Nationals of Other States (the ICSID Convention) and the Convention on the Recognition and Enforcement of Foreign Arbitral Awards (the New York Convention). In 1997, to fully utilize each economy's domestic system for dispute resolution, the DMEG published the Guide to Arbitration and Dispute Resolution in APEC Member Economies.

For (d), the DMEG reaffirmed the need to provide adequate measures to make all laws, regulations, administrative guidelines, and policies related to trade and investment publicly available. The DMEG recommended the Trade Policy Dialogue, a consultative body under the Committee on Trade and Investment (CTI) of APEC. The DMEG had pointed out that the dialogue was more appropriate for dispute prevention because of its informal, off-the-record, nonadversarial procedures. Despite this recommendation of the DMEG, it is doubtful that the dialogue is capable of becoming a core system for dispute avoidance, because it is merely a body at the working level in APEC.

History

The idea to create APEC originated with Australia, which feared being isolated from regional economic blocs. Japan, with the same concerns as Australia, collaborated in promoting the proposal. Most nations belonging to the Association of Southeast Asian Nations (ASEAN) hesitated over this proposal at the beginning. They were anxious that APEC would be dominated by the large players in the Asia-Pacific, such as Japan, China, and the United States. With assurances from Australia and Japan that the ASEAN states would be the core of the organization and that APEC would maintain a non-binding nature, ASEAN agreed to join APEC.

The United States, which was not included in the membership of the Australian proposal, saw APEC as an institution for implementing trade liberalization and in-

sisted on the necessity for stricter rules and a more formal organization to enhance the effect of member commitment to liberalization. In 1992 and 1993, under strong U.S. leadership, APEC rapidly institutionalized by establishing a permanent secretariat in Singapore and promoting the CTI to the first standing committee. The key event was the holding and regularizing of the Leaders Meeting, which would play the significant role in decision making. In this period, increasing fear that the Uruguay Round negotiations might fail to be concluded forced APEC to start liberalization in trade and investment. In order to discuss a vision for trade in the Asia Pacific region, APEC established the Eminent Persons Group (EPG) as a private advisory council.

The EPG recommended that APEC set a goal of free trade in the region and proposed a series of actions to promote and realize regional liberalization, including a mechanism for dispute settlement. In its first report, the EPG stated that an APEC dispute settlement mechanism should be modeled after the mechanism of the General Agreement on Tariffs and Trade (GATT) or the North American Free Trade Agreement (NAFTA), which is legally binding arbitration. In its second report the following year, however, it recommended creating a mediation system named the Dispute Mediation Service (DMS), since the EPG recognized that mediation with nonadversarial and peer pressure approaches was a more appropriate procedure for APEC than arbitration. This choice was a natural one for APEC, whose fundamental principle is voluntarism. In addition, binding arbitration required agreed-upon rules for compliance, which APEC did not have.

In the Bogor Declaration of 1994, APEC strengthened its nature as a body for implementing liberalization. The APEC Economic Leaders committed to a target date of 2010 for the achievement of free trade in the region for industrialized members and by 2020 for developing members. With the emergence of regional liberalization as a main objective, interest in a dispute resolution mechanism was awakened because it was generally regarded as essential to assure implementation of agreements. Leaders directed the organization to examine the possibility of creating a dispute mediation mechanism. In response to this direction, the CTI established the DMEG, which had its first meeting in June 1995 in Vancouver. The EPG had also discussed a DMS and produced a blueprint in August 1995, which precisely described the mechanism and procedure for a DMS. The Informal Leaders Meeting in Osaka of November 1995, however, did not adopt this blueprint, for it included elements that were too binding for some members.

At the Osaka meeting, the U.S. attitude toward APEC was sharply criticized by ASEAN and several Asian governments. They showed serious concern about rapid institutionalization and excessive concentration on trade liberalization and insisted on placing more importance on economic and technical cooperation. At the end of the meeting, the nonbinding and cooperative nature of APEC was reaffirmed by the members.

Such change of direction influenced the activity of the DMEG. It became clear that there was strong reluctance to form a new mechanism for dispute resolution among the member economies. While Asian members were afraid that the consultative process would be transformed into a binding one after its establishment, the United States, even though it made efforts to introduce a legal framework into APEC, was concerned about losing its bilateral leverage through the creation of a new mechanism. There was no powerful leadership in the DMEG to create a new mechanism, and gradually members shifted their arguments to the usage of the existing system.

In 1998, APEC failed to launch the Early Voluntary Sectoral Liberalization (EVSL), a new initiative for regional liberalization, because of disagreements over the measures and coverage. With suspicion growing that APEC was incapable of delivering liberalization, the DMEG was disbanded in 1999 owing to realignment of the institutional structure in APEC. Their task was taken over by the CTI, the superior body to the DMEG.

Legal Principles

APEC is unique in that every process and decision is based on the principle of voluntarism. There have been continuing discussions, however, regarding the question of how to operate APEC, because of the gap between the Western and Asian approaches reflected in the composition of its membership. The Western-style approach modeled after NAFTA is characterized as legalistic and institutional, whereas the nonbinding and nonformal Asian approach can be seen in ASEAN. Nevertheless, all the decisions of APEC to date have been based on the Asian approach, because the majority of its members support the argument that nonbinding rule making was the key element of APEC's formation from the outset.

Six standards to create an APEC dispute mediation were adopted at the 1996 DMEG meeting. The fundamental principles for the future mechanism are:

- APEC dispute mediation should be aimed at encouraging greater confidence in the Marrakesh Agreement Establishing the World Trade Organization, and should be aimed at reinforcing the integrity of the WTO procedures.
- APEC dispute mediation should be without prejudice to rights and obligations under the WTO Agreement and other international agreements, and should not duplicate or detract from WTO institutions and procedures.

- APEC dispute mediation should be voluntary and encourage nonadversarial and voluntary approaches in the mutual economic interests of the parties involved, and with due regard for the interests of other APEC members.
- Work in APEC on dispute mediation should be in keeping with the evolution of APEC's work on trade and investment liberalization and facilitation goals.
- APEC members should be encouraged to work within the framework of existing international agreements and conventions for the resolution of disputes involving private parties and to adopt appropriate domestic legislative arrangements to give effect to the aims of these agreements and conventions, including adequate enforcement of them.
- Priority should continue to be given to facilitating access to information on mediation, conciliation, and arbitration services available in member economies.

Impact

A mediation mechanism would facilitate the process of dispute settlement in APEC, because consultation is the common procedure of dispute resolution in the region. Haze pollution between Indonesia and its neighbors in 1997 and the issue of frozen over-the-counter Malaysian shares in Singapore are good examples of disputes that were resolved by consultation.

Moreover, an alternative mechanism would be useful for member economies, because the GATT-WTO settlement is limited to the area of trade, and because disputes in other areas have remained untouched. Some economies lacked financial and human resources to pursue settlements under the WTO DSU. In addition, there are APEC economies that do not belong to the GATT-WTO itself and have no access to utilization of the DSU.

APEC mediation would likewise be beneficial for the international system, for it is expected to diversify as well as to alleviate the trade disputes as a supplementary body covering a particular region, and thus to make the global system of dispute resolution function more efficiently. At present, however, many disputes are not only difficult to settle through consultation but also overwhelm the capacity of mediation, even though it would be adopted within APEC as a substitute for the DSU's consultation process while omitting arbitration. Nevertheless, APEC mediation would have a role as a mechanism for dispute resolution in the future, because both the number and the variety of disputes are expected to increase quickly as the international trade system becomes more complex and intertwined.

Akiko Yanai

See also Arbitration; Mediation; World Trade Organization
References and further reading
Asia-Pacific Economic Cooperation. 1997. *Guide to Arbitration and Dispute Resolution in APEC Member Economies.* Singapore: APEC Secretariat.
Asia-Pacific Economic Cooperation. Eminent Persons Group. 1995. *Implementing the APEC Vision: Third Report of the Eminent Persons Group.* Singapore: APEC Secretariat.
Bergsten, C. Fred, ed. 1997. *Whither APEC?: The Progress to Date and Agenda for the Future.* Washington, DC: Institute for International Economics.
Hamada, Koichi, Mitsuo Matsushita, and Chikara Komura, eds. 2000. *Dreams and Dilemmas: Economic Friction and Dispute Resolution in the Asia-Pacific.* Singapore: Institute of Southeast Asia Studies.
Kodama, Yoshi. 2000. *Asia Pacific Economic Integration and the GATT-WTO regime.* London: Kluwer Law International.
Yamazawa, Ippei, ed. 2000. *Asia Pacific Economic Cooperation (APEC): Challenges and Tasks for the Twenty-first Century.* London: Routledge.

NORTH AMERICAN FREE TRADE AGREEMENT (NAFTA)

Mission

Dispute resolution is one of the essential components of the North American Free Trade Agreement (NAFTA). In fact, one of the objectives of NAFTA is to "create effective procedures for the implementation and application of the agreement, and for its joint administration and the resolution of disputes. The purpose of having such a mechanism is to ensure that the market access commitments under the NAFTA are respected in an effort to maintain the overall balance inherent in those commitments" (Marceau 1997, 31).

Scope

Various panels deal with disputes under various chapters of NAFTA. The principle dispute settlement mechanisms of the NAFTA are found in Chapters 11, 14, 19, and 20. Under Chapter 19, a panel is discharged with the authority to review matters of antidumping (AD) and countervailing (CV) duties, so as to prevent a party from undermining any of the negotiated benefits under the free trade regime. The dispute settlement provisions can be divided into two categories: peer national review of another party's proposed legislation and panels established on an ad hoc basis to review the decisions of national courts involving final antidumping and countervailing duty determinations on final injury. For the former, a panel's authority is restricted to determining whether the national authority of the importing country was made in accordance with that country's own laws, norms, and standards. It effectively acts as a tribunal of domestic judicial review. In the latter, the panels can uphold or remand final determinations of national agencies, which must comply with the panel decisions.

Dispute resolution provisions under Chapter 20 apply to disputes concerning the interpretation or application of NAFTA, which includes disputes relating to the financial services provisions under Chapter 14, or "wherever a party considers that an actual or proposed measure of another party is or would be inconsistent with the obligations" of NAFTA or causes nullification or impairment. This discretion is fettered in disputes relating to environmental and conservation agreements, SPS (phytosanitary) measures or standards-related measures. The underlying preference is that the parties will seek agreed interpretations and "make every attempt" to reach agreed solutions. Overall, the Chapter 20 process combines the adversarial nature of dispute resolution with the political conciliatory role of international state relations.

Chapter 20 provides for the establishment of a trilateral Free Trade Commission with the authority to resolve disputes regarding interpretation and application of NAFTA. It has broad authority to resolve disputes, oversee implementation, provide further elaboration of NAFTA, supervise the work of all NAFTA committees and working groups, and consider any other matter relevant to the operation of NAFTA.

Under Chapter 14, a dispute settlement mechanism operates. NAFTA parties are required to accord national treatment and most favored nation status to investors with respect to the establishment, acquisition, expansion, management, conduct, operation, and sale or other disposition of financial institutions and investments in financial institutions in its territory. In addition, parties are prohibited from adopting any measure restricting any type of cross-border trade in financial services by cross-border financial service providers of another party.

Chapter 11 provides for dispute settlement between a host state and a private investor. It is historically based on U.S. and Canadian interests in liberalizing the investment regime in Mexico, where foreign investors were concerned about the unchecked ability of host states to expropriate foreign investments. Investors can bring a dispute against the host state for a violation of basic protections such as nondiscriminatory treatment; minimum standards for treatment of investors, including fairness, equitable treatment, and due process; no performance requirements; ability to freely transfer funds; and expropriation not in accordance with the principles of international law. Governments cannot take measures that directly or indirectly expropriate an investment or a measure that is tantamount to nationalization or expropriation unless it is done for a public purpose on a nondiscriminatory basis, in accordance with the due process of the law, and on the payment of compensation.

Legal Principles

Being a treaty, NAFTA is to be interpreted by the parties in accordance with the applicable rules of international law. Where there is an inconsistency between NAFTA and other multilateral or bilateral agreements, the provisions of the former prevail to the extent of the inconsistency unless otherwise stipulated under NAFTA. There are three multilateral environmental agreements explicitly referred to that supercede NAFTA obligations in cases of inconsistency (Convention on the International Trade in Endangered Species of Wild Fauna and Flora, or CITES; Montreal Protocol on Substances That Deplete the Ozone Layer; and the Basle Convention on the Control of Transboundary Movements of Hazardous Wastes and Their Disposal). Agreements set out in Annex 104.1 also prevail. However, where a party has a choice among equally effective and reasonably available means of complying with their obligations, the party must choose the alternative that is least inconsistent with the other NAFTA provisions.

In addition to international law, panels will apply the national laws of the various countries. For instance, under Chapter 19, panels apply the general legal principles that a court of the importing party would otherwise apply to a review of the determination of the competent investigating authority. The national law of the party provides the basis to determine if national standards have been applied, although there is no proscribed standard of review to be applied by panels when assessing national measures' compatibility with NAFTA.

The binding effect of NAFTA panel decisions is limited to what involves the parties with respect to the particular matter before the panel. Decisions serve no precedence value for future decisions.

Panel Composition and Participation

Panels under Chapter 19 are made up of five members, with two being selected by each country and the fifth agreed upon by both disputing parties. They are required to be of "good character, high standing and repute," chosen "strictly on the basis of objectivity, reliability, sound judgment and general familiarity with international trade law." The panelists must be citizens of any of the three party-countries and cannot be affiliated with or take instructions from any party.

The Free Trade Commission established under Chapter 20 is composed of cabinet-level representatives of the parties. For Chapter 20 panels, members are chosen from a permanent roster of up to thirty individuals. They are subject to a code of conduct and must have the qualities of independence, objectivity, and relevant expertise. Individual panels consist of five members. In what is known as the reverse selection process, the parties agree on a chair and then choose one or two panelists who are citizens of the other disputing party-country. Where there is no agreement, a party is chosen by lot and selects a chair within five days, although the chair cannot be a citizen of that party-country. If a party is unable to select panelists during this period, panelists are selected by lot from among the roster members, as long as they are citizens of the other party-country.

A financial services roster is to be established by the parties under Chapter 14. Its members are required to have expertise or experience in financial services law or practice, including the regulations of financial institutions; to be chosen strictly on the basis of objectivity, reliability and sound judgment; and to meet other qualifications stipulated under Chapter 20.

Under the Chapter 11 dispute settlement process, the state and the investor chooses one arbitrator while the third member of the panel is then either negotiated or chosen from a list of arbitrators with international trade and investment law experience. The place of arbitration is selected, where the parties are party to the New York Convention, in accordance with the rules of either the International Centre for the Settlement of Investment Disputes (ICSID) or the United Nations Commission on International Trade Law (UNCITRAL).

Procedure

A Chapter 19 panel conducts its review in accordance with prescribed procedures under Annex 19. They are conducted in conformity with judicial rules of appellate procedure. A party cannot request a review of another party's measure under Chapter 19 unless the party has received a request from a person who would otherwise be entitled, under the law of the importing party, to commence domestic procedures for judicial review of the final determination. The panel process involves two exchanges of written submissions and a hearing of the panel. Persons who would otherwise have a right to appear and be represented at a domestic judicial review proceeding concerning the determination of the competent investigation authority have a right to appear and be represented by counsel before the panel. The panel includes the competent investigating authority that issued the impugned final determination. Final decisions of a panel are released within 315 days from the date on which the request for a panel is made.

As an alternative to an appeal, the extraordinary challenge procedure is available following Chapter 19 panel decisions, although only in limited circumstances. They include situations in which a party alleges that a member of the panel was guilty of gross misconduct, bias, or a serious conflict of interest or otherwise materially violated the rules of conduct; the panel seriously departed from a fundamental rule of procedure; or the panel manifestly exceeded its powers, authority, or jurisdiction. These have been interpreted narrowly by Extraordinary Challenge Committees (ECC) established for particular disputes. The procedure allows a party to appeal a panel's decision to a committee made up of three judges or former judges. The ECC examines the legal and factual analysis underlying the findings and conclusions of the panel's decision and then issues a binding decision regarding the validity of the allegations.

Where a party alleges that the another party has prevented the establishment of a panel, prevented a panel from rendering a final decision, prevented the implementation of the panel's decision, or denied it binding force and effect, the party can request consultations with the other party regarding the allegations. If the matter has not been resolved within forty-five days of the request for consultations or another period agreed to by the parties, the complaining party can request the establishment of a Special Committee made up of three former or sitting judges. After the committee makes an affirmative finding, the complaining party and the party complained against are to begin consultations and seek to achieve a mutually satisfactory solution.

Under Chapter 20, a party can request consultations regarding an actual or proposed measure that it alleges might affect the operation of NAFTA. Where the parties cannot resolve the dispute through consultations within the prescribed thirty-day period, a party can request a meeting of the Tri-Lateral Commission to resolve the dispute. The commission can use technical advisers; create expert working groups; employ good offices, conciliation, mediation, or other dispute resolution procedures; and make recommendations to the consulting parties. All decisions are made by consensus, unless agreed to by the commission itself. If the matter remains unresolved after consultations and a referral to the commission, either party can request a nonbinding panel. The commission is required to establish the panel upon the delivery of the written request, irrespective of a lack of consensus of all the NAFTA parties. A third party that considers it has a substantial interest in the matter can join as a complaining party, upon notice to the other parties, within seven days of the request for the establishment of the panel. Upon satisfying the procedural requirements, a third party can attend all hearings, make written and oral submissions to the panel, and receive written submissions of the parties. Where the third party does not join as a complainant, it is still entitled to attend the hearings, make written and oral submissions, and receive written submissions of the disputing parties.

Chapter 20 panels can request the establishment scientific review boards, the members of which are selected by a panel in consultation with the disputing party, to provide a written report on any factual issue concerning environmental, health, safety, or other scientific matters.

The parties are subsequently given an opportunity to comment on the proposed factual issues referred to the board and then a further another opportunity to provide comments on the board's report to the panel. The panel can also seek expert information or advice from any appropriate source.

A disputing party is guaranteed at least one hearing before the panel and an opportunity to present initial and rebuttal submissions. All proceedings before the panel are confidential except the final report. Advisers and private lawyers are entitled to attend hearings, unless they have a financial or personal interest in the proceeding, but they cannot address the panel. The panel can pose questions to the parties, but the parties cannot direct questions to each other. A panel can make findings, determinations, and recommendations after examining the matter "in the light of the relevant provisions of the NAFTA." Before a final decision is issued, the panel presents an initial report to the disputing parties, which includes factual findings, legal determinations concerning a violation or other determinations requested in the terms of reference, and recommendations for resolution of the dispute.

In turn, the parties can submit written comments to the panel. It can request further comments by any participating party, reconsider its report, and make any further examination it considers to be appropriate. Within thirty days of presenting the initial report, the panel releases the final report to the disputing parties, including separate opinions on matters not unanimously agreed upon. After the adoption of the report, the parties are encouraged to negotiate the settlement of the dispute. Any agreement must conform to the panel's recommendations, and it must be conveyed to the NAFTA Secretariat. Where no agreement is reached and there is no voluntary implementation of the decision, the successful party can unilaterally suspend equivalent benefits to the nonconforming party. The temporary suspension must apply to benefits in the same sector that is affected by the nonconforming measure. Benefits in other sectors can be suspended only where a suspension in the same sector is neither practicable nor effective. A disputing party can request a panel to determine whether the level of benefits that is suspended is manifestly excessive. The panel's recommendations are not strictly binding, but the parties are prohibited from providing for an appeal mechanism from panel decisions in their domestic courts.

Disputes under Chapter 14 are governed by the same procedure, with a few exceptions, as applies to panels under Chapter 20. Where a measure is inconsistent with Chapter 14, a party can suspend benefits in the financial sector, if the measure affects only the financial sector. Where the measure affects another sector and any other sector, the complaining party may suspend benefits in the financial services sector that have an effect equivalent to the effect of the measure in the party's financial services sector. Investors also have recourse under Chapter 14 through a Chapter 11 claim. If an investor submits a claim and the disputing party invokes Article 1410, the matter is referred to the Financial Services Committee. The committee then determines whether Article 1410, regarding stipulated exceptions, applies. Its decision is then transmitted to the Chapter 11 tribunal, which is bound by the decision. Where the committee has not decided within sixty days of the referral, an arbitration panel under Article 2008 can be requested. In turn, the panel submits its final binding decision to the Chapter 11 panel.

Where there has been a violation of Section A of Chapter 11, an investor can submit a claim that there has been a breach and the investor has incurred losses or damages as a result. A claim must be initiated with three years of the breach and must waive any rights under domestic procedures. The parties choose between three arbitration mechanisms: ICSID Convention, ICSID's Additional Facility Rules, or UNCITRAL Rules. The disputing parties hold proceedings entirely in camera, with no provision of information available to the public without special agreement.

Arbitration under Chapter 11 is binding exclusively on the parties; the rulings establish no precedent. Each NAFTA party is required to comply with the award and provide for its enforcement in its territory. A failure to comply can lead to the establishment of an arbitration panel by the NAFTA Free Trade Commission upon the successful investor's request. Noncompliance with the declaration by this panel can authorize a NAFTA party to suspend benefits against the noncompliant party under Chapter 20. A final award can comprise costs, damages, and interest. Restitution of property can be ordered, or the award can provide that the disputing party must pay monetary damages in lieu of restitution. Punitive damages are not available, but where damages are awarded with interest, the award must state that it is without prejudice to any right of any person for relief under applicable domestic law. An investor can seek enforcement of the award under the ICSID Convention, New York Convention, or the Inter-American Convention on International Commercial Arbitration. There is no route of appeal against a panel's decision under Chapter 11, although there have been two cases in which the case has been appealed in the jurisdiction where the arbitration took place.

Caseload

More than sixty cases have been brought under the core dispute settlement provisions in Chapters 19 and 20, with twenty-eight final decisions from Chapter 19 panels. There is one extraordinary challenge procedure that has not received a final determination, although there were three completed cases under the Canada-U.S. Free Trade Agreement. Under Chapter 11, seventeen cases have been initiated, but only five disputes featured a final determination.

Impact

Although there is a great deal of controversy surrounding the fledgling NAFTA regime, one of its offsetting strengths is the presence of sophisticated dispute settlement mechanisms. The employment of peaceful means to resolve trade disputes that go to the heart of national sovereignty elevates the role of dispute settlement in international economic law. The fairness between the parties marks the cornerstone of twenty-first-century international trade diplomacy. One need only look back to the era of gunboat diplomacy and colonialism to see how far this progression spans.

Chapter 11 disputes are the most discussed NAFTA dispute settlement mechanism. It is unprecedented in international law because it gives the private sector access to a state-based multilateral dispute settlement mechanism, but it is consistent with a new trend of a privatizing international trade law. In some ways, a foreign investor retains even greater rights than domestic investors, who would not have access to Chapter 11. Its provisions were designed to provide investors with security against unwarranted and arbitrary expropriation of their property. However, use of dispute settlement has taken the purpose of Chapter 11 beyond its original meaning as intended by the parties. Various pieces of legislation relating to environmental protection and public health have been challenged, creating a chilling effect on governments. Although nongovernmental organizations have been given the authorization to submit amicus briefs, their contribution is undermined by its nonparty status. Of the sixteen Chapter 11 disputes, eight of these cases have revolved around environmental protection or natural resource management issues.

Kevin R. Gray

The author would like to thank Gabrielle Marceau for her helpful comments after reviewing a draft of this entry.

See also Arbitration; Canada; International Law; United States—Federal System

References and further reading

Eastman, Z. M. 1999. "NAFTA's Chapter 11: For Whose Benefit?" *Journal of International Arbitration* 16, no. 3: 105–118.

Esty, D. C., Gary Clyde Hufbauer, D. Orejas, L. Rubio, and Jeffrey J. Schott. 2000. *NAFTA and the Environment: Seven Years Later.* Washington, DC: Institute for International Economics.

Huntington, David S. 1993. "Settling Disputes under the North American Free Trade Agreement." *Harvard International Law Journal* 34, no. 2: 407–443.

Marceau, Gabrielle. 1997. "NAFTA and WTO Dispute Settlement Rules: A Thematic Comparison." *Journal of World Trade* 31, no. 2: 25–81.

Nolan, M., and Douglas Lippoldt. 1998. "Obscure NAFTA Clause Empowers Private Parties: Investor Protection Clause Lets Companies Haul Signatories into Arbitration For Violation of Pact." *National Law Journal* 20: 32.

Rugman, Alan, John Kirton, and Julie Soloway. 1999. "Environmental Regulation and Corporate Strategy: A NAFTA Perspective." New York: Oxford University Press.

Sardrino, G. L. 1994. "The NAFTA Investment Chapter and Foreign Direct Investment in Mexico: A Third World Perspective." *Vanderbilt Journal of Transnational Law* 24: 259–327.

Von Moltke, Konrad, and Howard Mann. 2001. "Misappropriation of Institutions: Some Lessons from the Environmental Dimension of the NAFTA Investor-State Dispute Settlement Process." *Journal of International Environmental Agreements: Politics, Law and Economics* 1: 103.

Winham, Gilbert R. 1998. "NAFTA Chapter 19 and the Development of International Administrative Law: Applications in Antidumping and Competition Law." *Journal of World Trade* 32, no. 1: 65–84.

MERCADO COMÚN DEL SUR (MERCOSUR)

Mission

Following the conclusion of the 1928 Paris Pact (the "Kellog-Briand Pact"), a customary international law obligation arose that outlawed the waging of aggressive wars. Later, the Charter of the United Nations in its Article 2(4) explicitly prohibited the use of force against the "territorial integrity" and "political independence" of states—a rule that has generally been considered being one of *jus cogens,* or peremptory norm of international law, according to Article 53 of the 1969 Vienna Convention on the Law of Treaties.

As a necessary corollary to the prohibition on the use of force in the context of international relations, there is a general obligation of states with regard to attempting to settle peacefully their international disputes. In this sense, Articles 2 and 33 of the UN Charter contain the rules that develop such an obligation, and emphasize the link between the nonuse of force and peaceful settlement of disputes.

On the other hand, there has been a dramatic growth in the number of integration processes within the international community, most notably those relating to international economic affairs. From the 1952 European Coal and Steel Community to the 1957 Treaty of Rome, which established the European Economic Community (EEC), we can see a trend toward the consolidation of accords that reflect the belief in the benefits of trade between nations.

In the context of the continent of America there are significant examples of this trend: the North-American Free Trade Agreement (or NAFTA, which comprises Canada, the United States, and Mexico); the Andean Community (containing Venezuela, Colombia, Ecuador, Bolivia, and Peru); and the Mercado Común del Sur (or Mercosur, composed of Brazil, Argentina, Uruguay, and Paraguay).

In the specific context of dispute settlement in integration agreements, it is important to underline that there is not yet a permanent system for dispute settlement in Mercosur. Nevertheless, there is a provisional system to this effect contained in the Protocolo de Brasilia para la Solución de Controversias (Brasilia Protocol for Dispute Settlement, hereinafter referred to as the Brasilia Protocol), which should be amended or improved in the forthcoming years by the countries party to Mercosur. We can summarize the mission of the current system as basically enabling the settlement of disputes that arise as a result of the application of, interpretation of, or compliance with the Tratado de Asunción (Asuncion Treaty), which in 1991 established the creation of the Mercosur Common Market.

The current Mercosur dispute settlement provisions cover disputes that can arise between the following parties:

1. The member states of Mercosur
2. Private persons and member states of Mercosur
3. Private parties in the context of Mercosur

History

Following the integrationist trend we have described, by the mid-1980s there was serious progress in the consolidation of the diplomatic, political, and economical ties between the governments of Argentina and Brazil. This consolidation led to the signature of a significant number of bilateral agreements between those two countries covering diverse aspects of their relations. Given the growing importance for the south of the continent of these accords, Brazil, Argentina, Paraguay, and Uruguay concluded an agreement in Asunción, Paraguay, on March 26, 1991, that established the Mercado Común del Sur (Common Market of the South), Mercosur.

From its origin, the Asuncion Treaty provided for the creation of a common system of rules of origin; a system of safeguard clauses; the coordination of policies tending toward protection against dumping or other unfair trading practices; and finally, the creation of a common system for dispute settlement (Article 3 and Annex III of the Asuncion Treaty).

This system was instituted on a provisional basis, and it remained in effect until the moment when a more complete dispute settlement regime came into being: the Brasilia Protocol of December 17, 1991. Among the main novelties introduced by this protocol is the inclusion of an arbitral procedure with judicial characteristics, in which independent arbiters judge on the merits of a complaint and decide on the basis of the ipso facto recognition of the binding nature of the jurisdiction of the Arbitral Tribunal.

One final adjustment was made to the institutional structure of Mercosur by the Protocolo de Ouro Preto (Ouro Preto Protocol, hereinafter referred to as OPP). This protocol created the Mercosur Commerce Commission. This body is responsible for considering complaints referred to it within the terms of Article 21 of that instrument (also related to Directive 6/96, which implements the "Consultation Mechanism before the Mercosur Trade Commission").

Legal Principles

According to Article 41 of the OPP, the sources of the law in the Mercosur system are the following:

1. The Asuncion Treaty, with all its protocols and additional instruments
2. All agreements celebrated under the Asuncion Treaty framework and its protocols
3. The decisions taken by the Common Market Council, the resolutions adopted by the Common Market Group, and the directives adopted by the Mercosur Trade Commission

Additionally, the Brasilia Protocol mentions that the Arbitral Tribunal shall also be bound by those principles of international law that are applicable in the context of the dispute. Furthermore, and if the parties so wish, the tribunal can also adjudicate on an *ex aequo et bono* basis.

It is important to note, however, that the adjudicated decisions reached by the Arbitral Tribunal are binding in nature, and do not provide for an appeal. Furthermore, the judgment rendered by the tribunal has the effect of *res judicata* with regard to the dispute at hand. In the event that the decision of the tribunal is not implemented by the defeated party within thirty days of its notification, the other parties to the dispute can impose temporary compensatory measures (such as the suspension of concessions, and so forth) tending toward the full compliance of the arbitral ruling.

Membership and Participation

In the Mercosur dispute settlement system as it stands, the main participants are the member states. Among the principal institutions that belong to the system (or are otherwise subject to its proceedings) we can mention the following:

1. *Arbitral Tribunals.* Conformed on an ad hoc basis, they are considered the most important achievement of the Brasilia Protocol, and are probably the cornerstone of the Mercosur dispute settlement system. These tribunals have obligation of settling a dispute when direct negotiations or the mediation of the Common Group Market have failed.

2. *Common Market Group.* This group is the executive organ of the Mercosur Common Market. Coordinated by the foreign ministries of the member countries, it is an intergovernmental entity that is empowered to oversee the compliance with the Asuncion Treaty, its protocols, and those agreements concluded within the Asuncion framework. In the context of dispute settlement, this group may make advisory (that is, nonbinding) recommendations to the parties to a dispute tending toward a nonarbitral settlement.

3. *Mercosur Trade Commission.* Yet another intergovernmental entity closely related to the Common Market Group, this commission may consider the claims presented to it by the national sections of the Mercosur Trade Commission. These claims can arise from those submitted by the member states or by private persons or entities. The review of such claims shall not imply the renunciation of alternative action under the Brasilia Protocol.

4. *Private parties.* The participation of private persons or entities is contemplated in the operation of the dispute settlement system of Mercosur, as indicated in Chapter V of the Brasilia Protocol. This chapter provides that private parties (whether physical persons or juridical entities) can use the procedures contained therewith. These procedures apply in the event that any member state sanctions or applies any legal or administrative measure that has a restrictive, discriminatory, or unfairly competitive effect that is in violation of the Asuncion Treaty or any of its protocols or agreements celebrated in that framework (it also applies to the decisions of the Common Market Council and the resolutions of the Common Market Group).

In the Mercosur dispute settlement system, there is no express mention of the participation of nongovernmental organizations in the dispute proceedings. It is possible, however, that these could act within the provisions designed for the participation of private parties, or that they could be called upon to render expert advice in a procedural stage that would make possible such participation.

Procedure

The Mercosur dispute settlement system is still under construction, given that there is not yet a system with a

Mercosur's Relation to Other Legal Systems

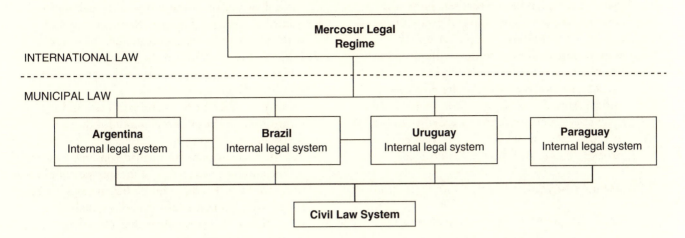

permanent character. Nonetheless, we can sum up the current procedure under the Asuncion Treaty and the Brasilia and Ouro Preto protocols as follows:

(a) Dispute settlement under the Asuncion Treaty and Annex III.

The dispute settlement procedures provided for in this treaty were extremely limited, pending the drafting of a more complete set of procedures. They implemented, on a temporary basis, a nonjudicial process limited to only those disputes arising between member states out of the application of the Asuncion Treaty. The main stages under this treaty are:

(i) Direct negotiation between the states. This stage does not mandate a time limit.
(ii) In the event that the direct negotiations fail, the parties shall then submit their dispute to the Common Market Group. This group would then formulate the necessary recommendations within a sixty-day time limit. This group is entitled to request expert advice, if necessary.
(iii) If the recommendations of the Common Market Group are not accepted by the affected party, the dispute will then be placed under the review of the Common Market Council. The council shall then also issue its recommendations. It is important to note that neither the recommendations made by the group nor those made by the council are obligatory.

Under this scheme, there are no legal consequences if the parties to the dispute do not comply with the aforesaid recommendations. Given that there are no further instances in the process, it ends here,

but without a guarantee that the dispute is any closer to having been settled.

(b) Dispute settlement under the Brasilia Protocol.

Following the expiration of the terms laid out in the Asuncion Treaty, the member countries of Mercosur in 1991 adopted the Brasilia Protocol, which improved Mercosur's dispute settlement procedures. Among the most outstanding aspects of the process in this protocol, we can list the following:

(i) *State v. state proceedings.* In the event of a dispute between states, the Brasilia Protocol left virtually untouched the procedures contained in Annex III of the Asuncion Treaty. In other words, there are slight changes to the negotiation phase and to the submitting of the dispute to the Common Market Group. (Some changes were introduced regarding the time limits for each stage, as provided in Articles 2 and 3(2) of the Brasilia Protocol.) The most outstanding difference is the establishment of an arbitral procedure as an additional and judicial stage that shall secure the settlement of the dispute and the compliance with its decisions.
(ii) *Participation of private parties in the dispute settlement process.* The Brasilia Protocol regulates the way in which a private party can participate in a dispute settlement proceeding, either against another private party or against a member state in the context of Mercosur. In general terms, should a private party wish to initiate a dispute settlement process, it shall have to address its complaint to the National

Section of the Common Market Group in the place where it has its habitual residence or conducts business. The National Section of the Common Market Group then has the administrative privilege to deal with or reject the complaint. It is notable, however, that private parties have not been granted the privilege to initiate arbitral processes on their own initiative, for that is a prerogative that is exclusive to the member states, as can be seen in Chapter V, Articles 25 et seq. of the Brasilia Protocol.

(c) Dispute settlement under the Ouro Preto Protocol.

The OPP gave Mercosur a new institutional organization. Generally speaking, the OPP did not modify the procedures contained in the Brasilia Protocol, although it introduced new attributions relative to the review of claims by the Trade Commission of Mercosur. Article 21 of the OPP mandates the review by the commission of those claims presented by its National Sections, in which the claimant is a member state or private party. These claims should refer exclusively to commercial policy (a topic that falls within the competence of the commission), and are thus limited *ratione materiae*. The OPP contains an annex that regulates in detail the process of these claims.

Staffing

Given the nature of the system, and especially that the only truly judicial stage works on an ad hoc basis, it would probably not be very technical to talk about "staffing." Nonetheless, and in the context of the arbitration procedures we have mentioned, it was agreed that the arbiters should be jurists of an acknowledged competence in the subject matters of the dispute.

These arbiters shall be selected from a list of ten, which is presented by each member state and recorded by the Administrative Secretariat of Mercosur.

Impact

In spite of the fact that the countries member to Mercosur have not initiated many dispute processes and have preferred to settle their differences through diplomatic channels, it is undeniable that the dispute settlement system is widely regarded as being of utter importance for the success of interstate integration. At the eighth meeting of the Common Market Council, held at Buenos Aires in June 2000, several recommendations were made in an attempt to perfect, at a future date, the dispute settlement system of the Brasilia Protocol.

Among the recommendations made by the CMC we find the following:

1. There is a need to perfect the stage following the arbitral award. In this regard, further elaboration is needed on the compliance with the awards and with the extent of the compensatory measures.
2. Furthermore, a review on the elaboration of lists of arbiters is required, as well as on the nature and stability of their tenure.
3. Further consideration is required to establish means for a uniform interpretation of the Mercosur legal regime.
4. Finally, an analysis has to be made on how to speed up the current process and on the implementation of summary proceedings for particular cases. There is a growing awareness of the need to establish an institution with a permanent character (that is, a permanent arbitral tribunal or a regional arbitral chamber) that will guarantee stability to the system and uniformity in its interpretation of the law, while enhancing the access of the general public to the proceedings.

Alejandro Villegas-Jaramillo

See also Alternative Dispute Resolution; Arbitration; Argentina; Brazil; Criminal Sanctions, Purposes of; International Arbitration; International Law; Law and Economics; Paraguay; Uruguay

References and further reading

García, Ricardo Alonso. 1997. "La solución de controversias en el Mercosur." Pp. 57–87 in *Tratado de libre comercio, Mercosur y Comunidad Europea: Solución de controversias e interpretación uniforme.* Madrid: Monografía Ciencias Jurídicas McGraw-Hill.

Guerrero, Juan P. 2000. *Dispute Settlement for Breaches of State Environmental Obligations in Regional Integration Processes: A Comparative Analysis of the EU, Mercosur and Nafta.* Geneva: Institut des Hautes Etudes Internationales.

Mercosur.com. "Protocolo de Brasilia para la solución de-controversias." http://www.mercosur.com/es/info/tratados_protocolo_brasilia.jsp (accessed March 2, 2001).

Mercosur.com. "Protocolo de Ouro Preto." http://www.mercosur.com/es/info/protocolo_de_ouro_preto.jsp (accessed March 2, 2001).

Mercosur.com. "Tratado de Asunción." http://www.mercosur.com/es/info/tratadosde_asuncion.jsp (accessed March 2, 2001).

Mercosur.org. "Reglamento del Protocolo de Brasilia para la solución de controversias." http://www.mercosur.org.uy/espanol/snor/normativa/decisiones/1998/9817.htm (accessed March 2, 2001).

Mercosur.org. "Relanzamiento del Mercosur: Perfeccionamiento del sistema de solución de sontroversias del Protocolo de Brasilia." http://www.mercosur.org.uy/paginabienvenida.htm (accessed March 2, 2001).

Organization of American States. "Inventory of Dispute Settlement Mechanisms, Procedures and Legal Texts Established in Existing Trade and Integration Agreements, Treaties and Arrangements in the Hemisphere and in the WTO." http://www.sice.oas.org/cp_disp/English/Mer.asp (accessed October 30, 2000).

Pérez-Otermín, J. 1995. *El Mercado común del sur: Desde Asunción a Ouro Preto: Aspectos jurídico institucionales.* Montevideo: Ed. Fundación de Cultura Universitaria.

DISTRICT OF COLUMBIA

GENERAL INFORMATION

The city of Washington, which is coextensive with the District of Columbia, is situated at the mouth of the Potomac River between Maryland to the northeast and Virginia to the southwest. The site was selected in 1790 by President George Washington to become the nation's capital, and Major Pierre Charles L'Enfant was commissioned to create a design for the city, thus making it one of the few cities in the world that was expressly planned as a national capital. L'Enfant's design, a grid with intersecting diagonals emanating from the White House and Capitol, with large areas reserved as public park and memorial space, give the city today its distinctive landscape. The original 10-mile-square district was carved from Maryland and Virginia, and in addition to Washington, consisted of several other separately administered townships, such as Georgetown (on the Maryland side) and Alexandria (on the Virginia side). In 1847 the land south of the Potomac was returned to the state of Virginia, thus reducing the district's size by about one-third. Self-governing bodies within the district existed until 1895, when Georgetown was annexed by Washington.

In 1850, the population of Washington was 40,001, and the total population of the district was 51,687. The U.S. Congress banned the slave trade within the federal district in the 1840s and in 1862 ended slavery altogether there. By 1870, the total district population was 131,700, including an African American population of 43,422. Over the course of the next century, the population steadily increased, reaching a high point in 1960 of 763,956, 55 percent of which was African American. The 1990 census shows a decline to 606,900, and in 1994 about 570, 000 people called the district home (29.6 percent white, 65.8 percent black, 4.6 percent other). By 1999, the population had further dropped to about 519,000.

Nine colleges and universities are located in Washington, including Georgetown University, the area's oldest, Howard University, opened in the 1860s as a university for blacks, George Washington University, and American University. Two major economic webs provide virtually all the employment and income to the city and its residents. Government (federal and municipal) and related activities are by far the largest source in the metropolitan area. Indeed, there are more headquarters of national trade and professional organizations and associations in Washington (about 300) than in any other area of the country. Moreover, the presence of ambassadorial residences and offices, as well as international organizations such as the World Bank and the International Monetary Fund, has increased Washington's importance as one of the principal centers on the international level.

Tourism, which includes its retail trade and related services, is also significant, as millions of people from the United States and abroad visit the capital city each year. Manufacturing and other commercial activities occupy only a minor place in the economic structure.

EVOLUTION AND HISTORY

The nation's founders believed that the seat of government should not be contained in a state but rather should be a separate entity under the federal government's control. Because of intense interstate competition, they feared that if the capital were under the jurisdiction of any one state, it would become the source of unending conflict. As a result, the framers of the U.S. Constitution provided for congressional control of the federal city in Article I, section 8, paragraph 17: "The Congress shall have power . . . to exercise exclusive legislation in all cases whatsoever over such district (not exceeding ten miles square) as may, by cession of particular States, and the acceptance of Congress, become the seat of the Government of the United States."

The actual location was a matter of some debate and was put off until later. During George Washington's first presidential term, however, Thomas Jefferson (secretary of state), Alexander Hamilton (secretary of the treasury), and two Virginia congressmen were able to work out a compromise producing the Residence Act of 1790, which authorized the president to select a location for the capital along the Potomac River on land ceded by Maryland and Virginia. Once Washington picked out a parcel of land, he named three commissioners to purchase it and to plan and build the new capital city.

Congress took residence in the capital in 1800, and, under a law passed in 1801, the federal government officially assumed control over the federal district. In addition, Congress established a circuit court staffed by a chief justice and two associates, which held four sessions per year and followed the procedures of the state (Virginia or Maryland) in which the land had been located. The judges were to be assisted by marshals and justices of the peace as needed, all to be appointed by the president.

In 1802, Congress approved a charter to establish a government for the city of Washington. Slow economic development, in addition to the fact that citizens had no vote in congressional or presidential elections, stimulated immediate debate among district residents about the pros and cons of retrocession. In 1846, the residents of Alexandria City, who were also worried about congressional moves to end slavery in the federal area, successfully won their fight to be reunited with Virginia, thus leaving the district its current size.

From 1800 to 1869, the courts of the District of Columbia were part of the federal court system, combining local and federal functions. By the late 1960s, the system consisted of the Court of General Sessions, which heard minor offenses, and the U.S. District Court for Washington, D.C., which heard major felonies. Appeals originating from the Court of General Sessions would be heard by the D.C. Court of Appeals, and appeals originating from the U.S. District Court were routed to the U.S. Court of Appeals. To address the confusing and inefficient structure, Congress passed the District of Columbia Court Reform and Procedure Act of 1970, separating federal from local courts. Under this reform, Washington's local courts attained powers comparable to those of the states. All original jurisdiction was vested in the D.C. Superior Court, and appeals would be heard by the D.C. Court of Appeals.

At long last, the Twenty-third Amendment was passed in 1961, allowing the residents of Washington to vote in presidential elections. Residents still do not have formal representation in Congress, although they do elect a delegate to a nonvoting seat in the House of Representatives. And, although the district has been granted a degree of self-governance, it remains a federal city operating under the auspices of the U.S. Congress.

CURRENT STRUCTURE

The Home Rule Act of 1973 went into effect January 2, 1975. Though not the first experiment with governing autonomy, the act provides the most far-reaching grant of self-determination since the nation's founding. The general structure of the government resembles the federal model of three separate branches—executive, legislative, and judicial. It gave the city a strong mayor, elected for four-year terms, and left the court system as it had been established by the 1970 reforms.

LEGAL PROFESSION AND LEGAL TRAINING

As the federal seat of government, a whirl of legal activities occur within the district, sweeping across all three branches and two levels of government, as well as the private sector, represented by the many administrative offices of national and international organizations located there. It is not surprising, then, that the D.C. Bar Association is one of the largest in the United States, with more than 70,000 members. The city also hosts several of the nation's largest and most prestigious law firms. A number of major law school programs, including those at Howard University, Georgetown University, George Washington University, American University, and Catholic University, feed into a robust and growing legal population.

LEGAL AID SERVICES

The primary method of providing legal aid to residents of limited financial means is offered through the D.C. Bar Pro Bono Program. Its mission is to encourage private attorneys to assist in making legal advice and representation fully available to low-income persons in the District of Columbia. Additionally, this program provides information to the public about other sources of legal help, including not-for-profit organizations, law school clinics, and governmental agencies.

The Hispanic Bar Association of D.C. also recruits lawyers to represent low-income Latino residents in pro bono cases. Given the increasing size of the Hispanic population, there is an ongoing need for Spanish-speaking lawyers in the district and surrounding areas, and members of the Hispanic bar have committed themselves to addressing this need. Finally, district law schools provide free legal assistance to low-income D.C. residents through their law clinics, assisting with such matters as battered women's protection, family law, and landlord-tenant cases. In criminal cases, the accused will be provided with a defense counsel if he or she cannot afford an attorney, usually through the D.C. public defender's office.

ADMINISTRATIVE HEARINGS

In the event of a dispute with any city executive agency, an administrative hearing can be arranged within the agency where the conflict arose. The district does not provide a central agency for administrative appeals, but in some cases the mayor has the authority to intervene to suggest a resolution. If a party is not satisfied with the decision by an agency or the mayor, an appeal may be taken to the D.C. Court of Appeals, where the court can either mandate a rehearing by the appropriate agency or issue a ruling.

JUDICIAL SYSTEM

The D.C. judicial system currently is composed of superior courts, and the D.C. Court of Appeals, in a simple two-tiered arrangement (see figure). The Superior Court has trial jurisdiction over any civil action or other matter (at law or in equity) brought in the district and over any criminal prosecution under any law applicable exclusively to the district. The Superior Court has no jurisdiction, however, in civil or criminal matters over which a U.S. court has exclusive jurisdiction pursuant to federal legislation. Currently, the Superior Court caseload is partitioned into five divisions—criminal, civil, family, tax, and probate—which are divided further into branches with narrower jurisdictions. For example, domestic relations and juvenile branches hear the bulk of cases in the Family Division; the Civil Division separates into landlord-tenant, small claims, and general civil branches.

The D.C. Court of Appeals hears appeals from the Superior Court and can review orders and decisions of the

Legal Structure of District of Columbia Courts

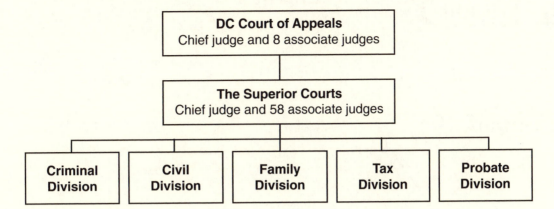

mayor, the council, or any agency of the district. Ordinarily, the Court of Appeals operates with panels of three judges; however, in unusually important cases, on order of the full court, an appeal may be heard en banc.

STAFFING

The Home Rule Act of 1973 authorizes the president to appoint judges from a list of three names submitted to him by a nominating commission (the District of Columbia Judicial Nominating Commission) that includes local representation. The U.S. Congress authorizes a budget for the court system, and the mayor and city council must grant whatever amount is requested. All judges of the District of Columbia courts are appointed by the president from among the names submitted by the nominating commission, are confirmed by the Senate, and serve renewable fifteen-year terms. The Court of Appeals consists of nine members, and at the Superior Court level, Congress has currently set the number of seats at fifty-nine. Chief judges for both the superior and appeals courts are designated by the commission from among the current court membership and serve for a term of four years, with the possibility of additional terms. In addition, both courts are assisted by retired judges who hold senior status, and there are fifteen hearing commissioners who are appointed to assist the Superior Court in conducting pretrial proceedings and disposing of minor cases.

Two offices have jurisdiction to legally prosecute in the District of Columbia, the U.S. Attorney's Office and the Office of the Corporation Counsel. The first is a federal department, and the latter is a city agency. All felony charges (cases in which the potential penalty is in excess of one year in prison) are prosecuted by the U.S. Attorney's Office. The Corporation Counsel's Office acts as the local prosecutor in the District of Columbia and has concurrent jurisdiction with the U.S. attorney to prosecute misdemeanors (less than one year imprisonment).

The Corporation Counsel's Office also prosecutes juvenile cases and all traffic charges and conducts all law business for the district, including representing the city in civil actions filed for and against the government.

Wayne V. McIntosh

See also Appellate Courts; Federalism; Trial Courts; United States—Federal System

References and further reading
Diner, Steven J. 1987. *Democracy, Federalism and the Governance of the Nation's Capital, 1790–1974.* Washington, DC: Center for Applied Research and Urban Policy.
District of Columbia City Government, http://www.dc.gov (cited October 25, 2000).
District of Columbia Home Rule Act (amended through November 19, 1997) Public Law 93–198; 87 Stat. 777; D.C. Code § 1–201 passim (approved December 24, 1973).
Green, Constance McLaughlin. 1962. *Washington, Village and Capital: 1800–1878.* Princeton: Princeton University Press.
———. 1963. *Washington, Capital City: 1879–1950.* Princeton: Princeton University Press.
Harris, Charles Wesley. 1995. *Congress and the Governance of the Nation's Capital: The Conflict of Federal and Local Interests.* Washington, DC: Georgetown University Press.

DJIBOUTI

COUNTRY INFORMATION

The Republic of Djibouti (République de Djibouti) is situated at the intersection of Eritrea, Ethiopia, and Somalia, merely 25 kilometers across the Red Sea from Yemen. The country consists of 23,200 square kilometers and is populated by 500,000 inhabitants, more than 90 percent of which are Sunni Muslims. The official languages of Djibouti are French and Arabic, although most of the population are of African descent, with ethnic and linguistic ties to Somalia (the Issas) and Ethiopia (the Afars). Literacy is very low even by African standards, only about 20 percent, especially among women.

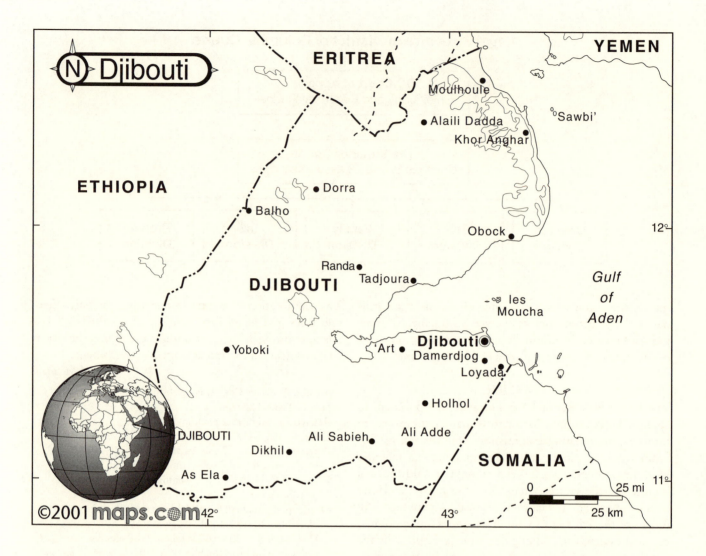

HISTORY

France acquired control of what is today Djibouti from the local sultans in the second half of the nineteenth century, and the territory attained independence, after serious unrest and a referendum, relatively recently, on June 27, 1977. Djibouti is far from being politically stable, ethnic hostilities being an important factor. Djibouti cultivates close links with France; a sizeable number of French troops remain stationed in the territory, undoubtedly constituting a stabilizing element.

LEGAL CONCEPTS

Djibouti adopted its present constitution by a referendum in September 1992, introducing, inter alia, a multiparty political system. The Preamble of the constitution affirms the country's adherence to the principles of pluralist democracy, although Article 6 of the constitution forbids political parties based on race, ethnicity, sex, religion, language, or region. In reality, the political life is totally dominated by the RPP (Rassemblement populaire pour le progrès), which has been in power for the last twenty-one years. The present government consists, since

the 1997 elections, of a coalition between the RPP and FRUD (Front for the Restoration of Unity and Democracy). FRUD was originally founded by Afar rebels, but seems now to be an appendage of the RPP. There are two legal political parties in opposition, but they have not succeeded in obtaining a single seat in the National Assembly. Djibouti is a republic of a presidential type (see below) and President Guelleh, elected in 1999, pursues policies of privatization and market economy.

The Preamble of the constitution affirms, furthermore, the determination to establish a system of rule of law (*état de droit*). Although the Preamble declares Islam to be the state religion, Article 11 of the constitution guarantees freedom of religion and conscience. Other Articles provide for, inter alia, freedom of expression (art. 15) and the right to property (which may be disturbed only in the case of public necessity and for just and immediate compensation, art. 12). Of central legal interest is Article 10, forbidding retroactive criminal legislation and stipulating the presumption of innocence and the right to defense by a legal counsel freely chosen. The same article states, furthermore, that no one may be deprived of liberty except on the basis of a judicial order. The standard list of civil rights and freedoms is complemented by the Preamble, which declares the Universal Declaration of Human Rights and the African Charter of Human Rights to be integral parts of the constitution; this goes beyond merely making these international instruments integral parts of the national legal system.

Article 7 of the constitution introduces the division of powers between the executive, legislative, and judicial institutions (it is worth noticing that the executive is mentioned first). The executive power is pursuant to Articles 21–22 vested in the president of the republic, who is both head of state and head of the government, although there is a separate prime minister. The president is elected directly by the people for a period of six years and can be reelected only once (art. 23). His position is very strong: pursuant to Article 30 it is the president who both determines and leads the policy of the country (*la politique de la nation*) and he has broad regulatory power (*pouvoir réglementaire*). The role of the government (cabinet), including the prime minister, is mainly to assist and advise the president, who appoints all ministers and to whom all ministers are responsible (art. 41).

The legislative power is vested in the National Assembly (Assemblée nationale), which is a unicameral Parliament elected for five years by direct and secret ballot. Article 57 of the constitution enumerates the areas of legislation that are reserved for the National Assembly, such as budgetary laws and certain central parts of public and private law. The remaining issues are subject to the regulatory power of the president of the republic (see above). An interesting provision is Article 69, providing that legislative proposals that, if adopted, would increase public spending without decreasing other expenditures or creating corresponding new incomes, must not even be subjected to a serious debate on their merits (*sont irrecevables*). If interpreted and applied literally, Article 69 means that the state cannot use public spending in order to stimulate the economy in times of a recession.

The judiciary is regulated summarily in Articles 71–74 of the constitution, stipulating such general principles as the independence of judges who are subject only to the law (art. 72).

The first Constitutional Act of Djibouti, dated June 27, 1977, provided in Article 5 that all preindependence statutes remained in force to the extent they were not abrogated or amended. A similar provision, preserving the principle of continued validity of existing law, is found in Article 92 of the present Constitution of 1992. This means that French law, as it was in 1977, continues to constitute the backbone of the Djibouti legal system, albeit complemented and modified by subsequent domestic legislation. Some of the principal works of French legislation, in particular the civil code (except the parts concerning family

law and successions as far as the Muslim majority is concerned), the commercial code, and the code of civil procedure, continue to be applied in Djibouti with amendments that are so minor that these codes are more Napoleonic there than contemporary French law, which has since 1977 undergone more substantial changes. On the other hand, the French penal code and the code of criminal procedure were replaced in 1995 by new, Djiboutian codes, although almost all of the new provisions can be traced back to the corresponding present French codes. The new code of criminal procedure was badly needed, since the French law used in Djibouti before 1995 was not the present French Code de procédure pénale of 1958 (which had never been promulgated there) but rather the previous, obsolete Code d'instruction criminelle dating from Napoleonic times (1808). The main purpose of the 1995 code was thus to approximate the law of penal procedure in Djibouti to the rules currently used in France. As far as the new penal code is concerned, it must be noted that it contains practically no elements of Islamic law; even this code has brought Djiboutian law closer to the present law in France. Djibouti has abolished the death penalty and belongs even in other respects to the minority of African countries with relatively moderate criminal law.

The Djiboutian system of sources of law remains also fundamentally French. The main—and officially the only—source of law in areas other than those governed by Islamic or customary law is legislation. New statutes are published in the *Journal Officiel de la République de Djibouti*. As in France, precedents and legal writings are not referred to in judgments, but they are invoked and submitted by advocates in their pleadings and appear to carry considerable persuasive authority with the judges. French decisions and writings are frequently used in this manner, while local sources of these types play a limited role due to the fact that there is no local legal writing and the decisions of Djibouti's own courts remain unpublished (although they are available in the court archives).

Current Djiboutian legislative projects include a relatively advanced labor code and a family code, which is expected to modernize the present family law following the model of Tunisian legislation. At present, family and successions law for the Muslim population is not codified at all and the religious courts of the *qadis* (see below) apply Islamic law as such. The *qadis* (*qazis*) participate in the preparation of the new family code, but it appears that they are ready to defy the state if the code at the end of the day turns out to be incompatible with Islam as they understand and interpret it. It can be mentioned that about 20 percent of Djiboutian men have more than one wife. The same minister is responsible for both justice and religion, the name of the Ministry being Ministère de la justice, des affaires penitentiaires et musulmanes.

An additional source of Djiboutian law, separate from

both the French-inspired legislation and Islamic rules, is custom, which is, however, observed in some very limited fields only, such as in matters pertaining to leases of immovable property.

CURRENT COURT SYSTEM STRUCTURE

The present court system of Djibouti is headed by the Supreme Court (Cour suprême), which is similar to the French cassation court in that it deals exclusively with points of law, but differs from the French cassation court by rendering final decisions without having to remand the cases back to a lower court. It consists of five professional judges, at present three women and two men, and always sits *in pleno*. It is formally divided into five chambers (civil, penal, social, administrative, and an Islamic and customary one), but the same judges adjudicate all cases. In disputes involving Islamic or customary law, the Supreme Court consists also of additional expert assessors, who are nonprofessional judges appointed by the president of the republic (there are different assessors for Islamic law and for customary law).

Under the Supreme Court, there is the Court of Appeals (Cour d'appel) with five professional judges (presently two women and three men), adjudicating with three judges sitting at a time. The Court of Appeals deals mainly with appeals from the decisions of the Tribunal de première instance, which is a general court of first instance, one for the whole country. The last-mentioned court is staffed by seven professional judges, including the *juges d'instruction,* and four of the judges are women. It sits with one sole judge. Despite its name, this court even functions as an appellate instance in relation to decisions made by the ten or so district courts (*tribunaux d'arrondissement*), which are courts for petty matters governed by customary law, staffed by magistrates without any formal legal (or other higher) education.

As in France, there are state attorneys (*procureurs*) attached to the court of first instance as well as to the Court of Appeals. There is no court corresponding exactly to the French Cour d'assises, but a criminal chamber at the Court of Appeals deals with serious crimes in a similar fashion, using both professional judges and lay assessors. There are no commercial tribunals and commercial disputes are adjudicated by the general courts, with the Civil Chamber of the Supreme Court as the highest instance. The official language of all proceedings in the general courts is French.

The religious courts of the *qadis* (*qazis*), financed by the state, take care of family law disputes and disputes concerning successions. There are two levels of *qadi* courts and an appeal from the decisions of the *qadi* appellate court can be lodged to the Supreme Court. This gives rise to some anomalies, since all *qadis* must, pursuant to Islamic law, be male although three of the five

Legal Structure of Djibouti Courts

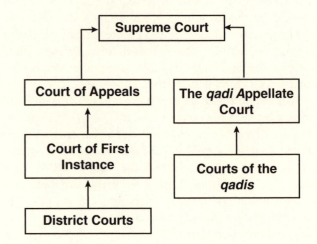

professional judges at the instance of last resort at present are female (they do not, however, constitute the majority due to the presence of male Islamic expert assessors). Most of the *qadis* have studied Islamic law in Egypt, Saudi Arabia or other Muslim countries. There are six *qadis* of first instance in Djibouti city, and four work in the four scarcely populated districts beyond the capital. They are all appointed by the president of the republic upon proposals from the minister of Justice. All paperwork in the *qadi* courts is done in Arabic, but oral proceedings usually take place in the language of the parties, most often in Somali or Afar.

STAFFING

Djibouti did not, on Independence Day, have a single Djiboutian judge, and there was not a single Djiboutian practicing lawyer. The new Republic decided, therefore, to let the French cassation court continue to function as the highest court of the land even after independence, until Djibouti created a similar court of its own, which happened in 1979. Today, the judiciary of Djibouti is staffed exclusively by local citizens, although all of them (except the *qadis*) have obtained their law degrees abroad, mostly in France but sometimes in other countries such as Morocco, since there is no institution of higher education in the country. The same applies to other members of the legal profession: there are about ten bailiffs (*huissiers de justice*), ten advocates (two of them French), and three notaries public (*notaires*) in the country. The government and foreign donors provide scholarships for young Djiboutians wishing to pursue university education abroad, mainly in France. Article 73 of the constitution provides for a Conseil supérieur de la magistrature, chaired by the president of the republic and having advisory and disciplinary powers in matters regarding judges.

SPECIALIZED JUDICIAL BODIES

Judicial review of constitutionality of laws is not in the hands of general courts, but rather a matter for the Constitutional Council (Conseil constitutionnel; arts. 75–82), consisting of six members appointed for eight years by the president, the speaker of the National Assembly and the above-mentioned Conseil supérieur de la magistrature (each appoints two). Former presidents are *ex lege* members of the Constitutional Council. Cases are brought to the council in various ways, for example by the president if he hesitates to promulgate a new act of Parliament because he finds it unconstitutional, or by a court of law hesitant to apply a statutory rule due to the same reason. If the council decides that a law is unconstitutional, the law in question ceases to be applicable even beyond the actual case.

International commercial arbitration is carried out in Djibouti pursuant to an Act (Code) of International Arbitration of February 13, 1984, modeled pursuant to international standards.

IMPACT

The legal system of Djibouti suffers from a serious lack of resources. The Palais de Justice is far from being a palace, salaries of judges are paid with substantial delays, and so on. However, Djibouti appears to have had some success in obtaining foreign aid in the legal field. Quite a few of the court offices are equipped with computers, and modern foreign (French) literature is available. The law seems to play a real role; the courthouse in Djibouti is bustling with life, with crowds in the corridors and queues at the doors of the *greffiers*.

Michael Bogdan

With the kind permission of Kluwer Law International, the original copyright holder, this entry is based on the author's article "Legal Pluralism in the Comoros and Djibouti," published in *Nordic Journal of International Law* 69:195–208 (2000).

See also Civil Law; Customary Law; Islamic Law; Legal Pluralism; Qadi (Qazi) Courts
References and further reading
There is practically no modern literature in English about the legal system of Djibouti.

DOMINICA

COUNTRY INFORMATION

Dominica, which is aptly referred to as the nature island of the Caribbean, is 29 miles from north to south and 16 miles across at its widest point. It covers 305 square miles and has a population of approximately 84,000 people. It lies between the French islands of Martinique and Guadeloupe. Dominica is a volcanic rather than a coral island, giving it a rocky coastline that is interspersed by beaches. These beaches are mostly found in the northwestern part of the island and are outstanding for being quiet, peaceful, and largely deserted. The Atlantic Ocean on Dominica's east coast generates large, exciting, and regular waves and is a natural area for surfing.

The island has the highest mountain in the eastern Caribbean—Morne Diablotin—which rises 4,747 feet. It also boasts of woodlands and virgin territory of dense mountain rain forests. Much of Dominica's interior is yet to be conquered, due to the wild and inaccessible nature of its seemingly impenetrable forests. The island is blessed with 365 rivers, and it can lay claim to being one of the very few countries in the world where it is still safe to drink the river waters. Many of these rocky rivers are highlighted by spectacular, cascading waterfalls. Dominica can also boast of freshwater lakes, a boiling lake, and numerous sulphur springs. Morne Trois Piton, which is the island's second-highest mountain, rises to a height of 4,600 feet and is located in the center of the island. It has three wonderful peaks, and the area was recently declared to be a World Heritage Site.

The official language is English, but Creole (or Patois) is extensively spoken; Creole is a French-based language that contains a smattering of English and African words. The island offers a pollution-free environment in which an abundance of food is grown on fertile land. The temperature rarely exceeds 85°F/29°C or drops below 75°F/24°C. Dominica is in the Atlantic time zone, one hour ahead of eastern standard time and four hours behind Greenwich meridian time.

HISTORY

The first inhabitants of Dominica were the Arawaks. Another wave of people, known as the Caribs, arrived later. These travelers were similar in many ways to the Arawaks but were moving through the Caribbean Islands, conquering and subduing each island as they went. The Caribs raided the Arawak settlements, killing the menfolk and taking the women as their wives.

The island was discovered by Christopher Columbus on Sunday, November 3, 1493, and was named Dominica after that day. The Caribs continued to be a thorn in the side of both the British and the French colonists who had, by the middle of the seventeenth century, largely supplanted the Spaniards in that part of the world; in 1686, British and French officials signed a treaty in America that provided, in part, that Dominica would remain a neutral island belonging only to the Caribs.

Between 1756 and 1763, Dominica became caught in what subsequently became known as the Six-Years War between the French and the British. That war also encompassed other islands of the Caribbean, and by the

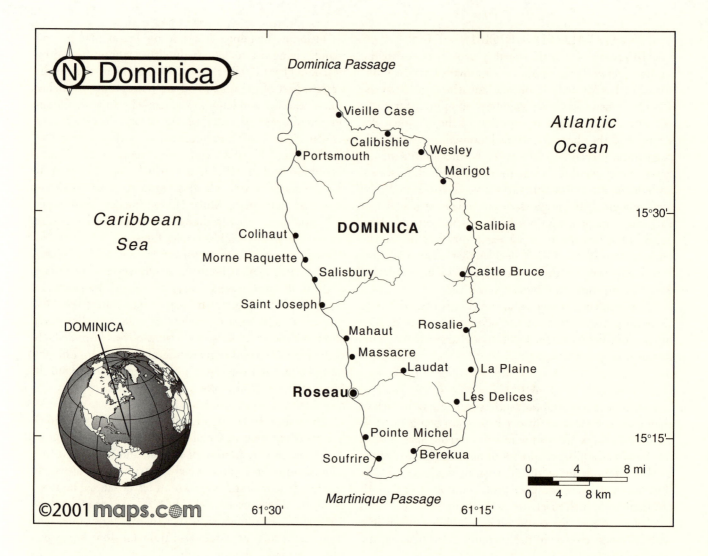

Treaty of Paris, which officially marked the end of the war, Dominica and the islands of Tobago, St. Vincent, Grenada, and the Grenadines were transferred to Great Britain. Those islands were governed together until 1770, when Dominica became a separate colony of Britain and was ruled by a governor and a council.

When the British took over the island, one of their main tasks was the redistribution, sale, and setting aside of land, and the Caribs were assigned a 232-acre plot of land in the area that they occupied. This came to be known—and continues as subsequently expanded to be referred to—as the Carib Reserve.

The second half of the nineteenth century was a period of political and social reorganization. The slave trade had been abolished by Britain in 1807, and the slaves were finally emancipated on August 1, 1834. In the other islands, the white population had entirely dominated the social life, but in Dominica, two high societies existed side by side: the mainly French mulatto families and the white attorneys who represented the absent plantation owners. These two groups continued to dominate business and government in the island well into the twentieth century.

As a consequence of a bill passed in 1832, three colored members were elected to the Dominica's legislature, and by 1838, there was a colored majority. These members immediately began to press for legislation to promote the welfare of the newly liberated citizens of the island. This Mulatto group of colored families kept control of the legislature until the introduction of Crown colony rule two generations later.

In 1862, a bill was introduced into the legislature to replace the two-house system with a single chamber. The new body of 1863 consisted of nine members appointed by the Crown and nineteen representatives. The name-calling and the accusations made by members of this overcrowded single chamber made any organized business impossible, and it was soon realized that the numbers would have to be drastically reduced. In 1865, a bill to make Dominica a Crown colony was introduced but was subsequently withdrawn after a compromise that had been proposed by the elected members was accepted. The new legislature was to comprise an equal number of elected and nominated members. In the same year, this legislature settled down under its new constitution.

Dominica was made part of the federal colony of the Leeward Islands in 1871. The other members of this federation were Antigua, Barbuda, Anguilla, St. Kitts, Nevis, and the British Virgin Islands. The seat of government was in Antigua, and Dominica became a presidency of the federation and sent representatives to the assembly in Antigua. To the elected members of the new legislature in Dominica, this was an intolerable situation, and resolutions were soon being passed in Dominica calling for a fully responsible elected government as had existed before 1863. The British government refused to accede to that request; the only concession offered was to make Dominica a Crown colony in its own right, with six official and six nominated members. This was achieved in 1898. Elected government had been dealt a final blow, and the imperial government took full control and responsibility for the affairs of the island.

Reports from Dominica on the political dissatisfaction and social unrest in the area prompted the British government to appoint a commission in 1893 to inquire into the state of affairs existing on the island. As a result of this inquiry, a number of cosmetic changes were made, including the enhancement of the status of the head of the government to that of administrator. This meant, in effect, that the adminstrator could communicate directly with the British authorities in England rather than having to go through the governor in Antigua. The island still remained, however, part of the federation of the Leeward Islands.

The withdrawal of the right to vote had been a great blow to politically conscious Dominicans, and its finality was never accepted. Resentment against the new system of government grew steadily, and a movement was soon established to bring about a change in Crown colony rule. Eventually, in 1924, a new constitution was promulgated that provided for an assembly comprising four elected and two nominated members to replace the former six members, who had all been nominated since 1898.

A new constitution was granted to Dominica in 1936. The Legislative Council was to consist of the governor, three ex officio members, four members nominated by the governor, and seven elected members. Another constitution, granted in 1951, made two fundamental changes to the 1936 Constitution. First, universal adult suffrage was introduced, which meant that every Dominican over the age of twenty-one had the right to vote, and the property qualification for voting was abolished. Second, an elected majority was created in the legislature. On March 1, 1967, a new constitution went into effect. Under that constitution, Dominica became a self-governing state in association with Great Britain. Thenceforth, the island would be responsible for its internal affairs, with only the powers relating to defense and foreign affairs being reserved to the imperial government.

The Independence Constitution took effect on November 3, 1978, and the country moved immediately to full republican status with a president as head of state. To avoid complications and confusion with the Dominican Republic, the newly independent nation was formally named the Commonwealth of Dominica.

During the first three years of independence, the country went through the most turbulent and traumatic period of its history. On May 29, 1979, the House of Assembly passed two controversial laws against which there had been vociferous and sustained protests. The Industrial Relations (Amendment) Act sought to put an end to a series of strikes by public officers, and the Libel and Slander (Amendment) Act made provisions for each newspaper publisher to deposit a sum of money from which any damages assessed against it for libel could be paid. A very large crowd had assembled outside the Parliament building. The Defence Force had been called to assist the Police Force, and in the general confusion that followed, one man was killed and several persons were injured. The Defence Force, which had been formed in 1975 as a special paramilitary group, was originally intended to assist in preserving and maintaining law and order, but until that day, it had been mainly involved in the eradication of marijuana cultivations.

Public officers went on a general strike, and it appeared that further trouble was imminent. The president unceremoniously left the country without properly designating a successor, and two attempts by the prime minister to appoint someone to act failed because of the antagonism encountered from hostile crowds. A broad-based committee, styled the Committee for National Salvation (CNS), emerged as the de facto government of the country. A civilian coup had taken place. Several members of the House of Assembly resigned, and continuous discussions involving the various factions were held until a breakthrough finally came on Tuesday, June 19. An acting president was constitutionally elected, and the thirteen members who attended the meeting of the House of Assembly that day unanimously pledged their support for a new prime minister. The CNS and the new prime minister then agreed on the nine persons who were to be appointed senators and the eight members of the cabinet. An uneasy calm prevailed.

This calm was shaken when hurricane David devastated the island on August 29 of that year, leaving almost 60 percent of the population homeless. All efforts were thenceforth concentrated on relieving the human suffering that prevailed. Earlier that year, a fire of unknown origin had completely destroyed the Registry of the Supreme Court, and many valuable records were lost.

General elections were held in July 1980, and the Dominica Labour Party, which had been successfully returned at the polls in 1961, 1966, 1970, and 1975, now found itself out of office. The new government promptly declared its intention to disband the Defence Force. This move led to an unsuccessful attempt by some disgruntled members of the force to storm their way into the police armory. They were repelled, and the Defence Force was abolished by an act of Parliament in 1981.

LEGAL CONCEPTS

According to the reception of law doctrine, when Dominica finally became a British possession the laws of the conquering country applied in the newly acquired state. This doctrine varied between territories that had been settled or occupied by the conqueror, on the one hand, and those that had been conquered or ceded, on the other. In the first case, the law of the conquering country applied in the conquered state from the date of the settlement or occupation; in the latter instance, the prevailing local laws remained in force until they were altered by the conqueror, except when they were contrary to the laws of God or when they were acts that, by their very nature, were wrong. Judging from the history of the island, one would have expected the second situation to have prevailed in respect to Dominica, but the British refused to accept or even to entertain the notion that during Dominica's periods of occupation by the French, the laws of France would have been applied in the territory. For the purpose of the origin of its laws, therefore, Dominica has been treated as a settled or occupied territory. The result is that the laws of England that were in force in that country prior to October 7, 1763, have been deemed to have been in force in the territory from that date.

The Commonwealth of Dominica is a sovereign democratic republic that nevertheless acknowledges the queen of Great Britain as the head of the commonwealth. The constitution is the supreme law of the state, and its provisions prevail over that of any other law if the other law is inconsistent with the constitution, unless the constitution itself provides to the contrary. The constitution contains provisions for the protection of the basic fundamental rights and freedoms, including the right to life and personal liberty; freedom of conscience, expression, movement, and assembly and association; and protection from slavery and forced labor, inhumane treatment, deprivation of property, and arbitrary search or entry. It also provides protection from discrimination on the grounds of sex, race, place of origin, political opinions, color, or creed. No specific guarantee of the right to work is provided by the constitution.

The rights guaranteed by the constitution are enforceable in the High Court, which has original jurisdiction to adjudicate if any person alleges that one or more of his or her fundamental rights has been, is being, or is likely to be infringed. A right of appeal is provided from a decision of the High Court to the Court of Appeal and finally to the Judicial Committee of the Privy Council in England.

Parliament consists of the president and the House of Assembly. The president is elected by the house and may hold office for a maximum of two five-year terms. Although the executive authority of the state is vested in the president, he or she has no right of veto over the acts of the House of Assembly. The president must exercise his or her functions in accordance with the advice of the cabinet or a minister acting under the general authority of the cabinet, except where the president is required by the constitution or any other law to act in accordance with the advice of or after consultation with any other person or authority. In a limited number of instances, the constitution provides that the president may act on his or her own deliberate judgment.

If the prime minister and the leader of the opposition agree on the nomination of a suitable candidate as president, that person is declared to have been duly elected. If there is no agreement on a joint nomination, an election is held, and the successful candidate must receive the votes of a majority of all the members of the house. Any question as to whether a person is qualified to be nominated for election as president or has been duly elected as such is to be decided by the Court of Appeal.

The House of Assembly consists of twenty-one elected members, each representing a constituency, and nine senators—five of whom are appointed on the advice of the prime minister and four on the advice of the leader of the opposition. If a person who is elected speaker is not a member of the house and if the office of attorney general is held by a public officer, those two individuals also automatically become members of the house.

SUPREME COURT STRUCTURE

The court system comprises the Judicial Committee of the Privy Council at its apex, followed by the Eastern Caribbean Supreme Court (which consists of the Court of Appeal and the High Court) and the Magistrates' Courts. The Judicial Committee of the Privy Council sits in London, and the membership of this court is equivalent to that of the House of Lords, which is the highest judicial body for the United Kingdom. The Eastern Caribbean Supreme Court serves the six independent countries of Antigua, Dominica, Grenada, St. Kitts, St. Lucia, and St. Vincent. It also serves the British dependent territories of Anguilla, Montserrat, and the British Virgin Islands. The Supreme Court is divided into the Court of Appeal, which is constituted by three judges and moves from country to country, and the High Court with original jurisdiction, which is manned by a single judge who is a resident in a particular country. Some islands have two High Court judges.

The Magistrates' Courts are on the bottom rung of the

judicial ladder. Dominica is divided into three magisterial districts, and a magistrate may preside over the court in one or more districts. Like the judges of the Supreme Court, all magistrates handle both civil and criminal matters, but their jurisdiction is limited to the less important cases; for example, they have no jurisdiction in matters pertaining to the ownership of land (although in special instances, Parliament has increased this jurisdiction). In regard to drug offenses, however, the jurisdiction of the magistrate is unlimited. This became necessary as a result of the number of accused persons who were acquitted when such cases were determined by a judge and jury. The decisions of the magistrates and the High Court judges can be appealed to the Court of Appeal and thence to the Judicial Committee of the Privy Council.

The chief justice of the Eastern Caribbean Supreme Court is appointed by the heads of the governments of all the states. All other appointments of judges are made by the Judicial and Legal Services Commission, which comprises the chief justice, a serving judge, a retired judge, and two chairs of the Public Service Commissions of the six independent countries. Magistrates are appointed by the Public Service Commission after consultation with the Judicial and Legal Services Commission, and they may be dismissed by the latter commission after consultation with the Public Service Commission. However, the dismissal of all judges, including the chief justice, is subject to an elaborate procedure that has the effect of guaranteeing security of tenure. The chief justice and judges of the Court of Appeal hold office until they attain the age of sixty-five, and the judges of the High Court serve until they are sixty-two.

All judges may, however, be permitted to continue in office for a further maximum period of three years. They can be removed from office only for inability to discharge the functions of their office or for misbehavior. When it becomes necessary to remove a judge, a three-member tribunal is appointed to inquire into the matter and make recommendations. During the period of the inquiry, the judge may be suspended from carrying out the functions of the office.

The Judicial Committee of the Privy Council in England is the final court for Dominica. The Privy Council started life as an administrative arm of the English government and was transformed into a body to which appeals from British overseas possessions were submitted. It was formally constituted into a court in 1833, and thereafter, appeals were heard by its judicial arm, the Judicial Committee, which is now completely independent from the council itself. It is composed of the members of the higher judiciary in England as well as senior judges and former judges of other countries of the Commonwealth. Since the early part of 1970, debate has raged in the Caribbean over the question of setting up a local appellate court to replace the Judicial Committee of the Privy Council. Practical initiatives have now been taken to establish such a court, which, in addition to its appellate jurisdiction, would be the forum for the resolution of trade disputes among member states of the Caribbean Community. These instruments were recently signed in Barbados by most Caribbean countries. Dominica was not a signatory.

There is no constitutional court for Dominica; cases involving breaches of the constitution are determined by the High Court. Judicial disputes concerning elections are also determined by the High Court, but administrative matters relating to elections are supervised by two independent commissions. The tenure of their members is secured by the constitution. The constitution has established both a Constituency Boundaries Commission and an Electoral Commission. The Constituency Boundaries Commission must, at intervals of between two and five years, review the number and boundaries of the constituencies into which the state is divided and report to the president whether or not it recommends any change in either regard. The Electoral Commission administers the law that regulates the voting process in the elections of members of the House of Assembly, as well as the procedure to be followed in those elections.

The constitution also provides for two commissions that are empowered to appoint, promote, discipline, or remove public and police officers. Each commission consists of seven members, who are appointed by the president on the advice of the prime minister; they serve for a period of three years. People are not eligible for appointment to either commission if they are members of the House of Assembly or have been members during the previous five years or if they have been a public (or police) officer or a judge during the year previous to the appointment. A member of either commission may not be appointed to or serve in any public office or the police service within three years of the date on which he or she was last a member of the commission. Members of commissions may be removed from office for the reasons and in the manner generally provided for High Court judges.

OTHER PROTECTED OFFICES

The Public Service Board of Appeal has been established by the constitution to hear appeals from decisions of the Public and Police Service Commissions. The board consists of three members appointed by the president: a chair who is appointed in the president's own deliberate judgment, one member appointed on the advice of the prime minister, and one member appointed on the advice of the body representing public servants. No member of the House of Assembly is eligible for appointment to this board. Like the Public and Police Service Commissions, the board may act despite vacancies in its membership, but decisions of all three bodies require the concurrence

Legal Structure of Dominica Courts

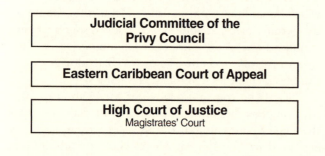

Judicial Committee of the Privy Council

Eastern Caribbean Court of Appeal

High Court of Justice
Magistrates' Court

of a majority of all their members. Members may be removed from office by a process similar to that which applies to judges. Decisions of the board can be appealed to the Court of Appeal.

The attorney general is the principal legal adviser to the government. He or she may be either a public officer or an elected or nominated member of the House of Assembly. If the attorney general is a public officer by virtue of holding the office, he or she is automatically a member of the cabinet and the House of Assembly and may also hold the office of director of public prosecutions. Prior to the attainment of independence, the office was held by a public officer, but shortly thereafter, Parliament provided that the office should thenceforth be that of a minister. That situation was reversed when a new administration assumed office after the general elections held in 1995. In 2000 there was another change, and the office of the attorney general is once again a ministerial position.

The constitution provides that the office of director of public prosecutions must always be held by a public officer. This officer is empowered to institute and undertake criminal proceedings, to take over all criminal proceedings that have been instituted by any person, and to discontinue any proceedings before judgment is delivered. The director of public prosecutions may delegate those functions to other officers. He or she is independent of the executive, and the constitution provides that in the exercise of his or her functions, the director of public prosecutions is not subject to the direction or control of any person or authority; however, if he or she decides to discontinue any criminal proceedings, he or she is subject to any general or specific instructions that the attorney general may give on the matter. Further, the director of public prosecutions may not discontinue proceedings by a person who is appealing against a criminal conviction. The director of public prosecutions is appointed by the president, acting in accordance with the advice of the Public Service Commission, which must itself consult the prime minister before tendering its advice to the president. The director's salary may not be altered to his or her disadvantage after appointment. The director's office be-

comes vacant after he or she has attained the prescribed age (now sixty-five years), and he or she can only be removed from office by a procedure that is similar to that which applies to judges.

The constitution also created the post of parliamentary commissioner (or ombudsman), but this office has never been filled. The commissioner is to be appointed by the president after consultation with the prime minister and the leader of the opposition. The commissioner is not allowed to hold any other office, whether public or private, nor can he or she engage in any other occupation for reward. The provisions for the removal from office of the commissioner are similar to those for a judge of the Supreme Court. The parliamentary commissioner is independent of the executive, and his or her principal function is to investigate actions taken by government departments in the exercise of their administrative functions. Although the commissioner's rulings are only a report to Parliament, the expectation is that the government will act on the commissioner's recommendations. He or she may be removed from office by a process that is similar to that provided for in the case of a judge.

OTHER LEGAL PROVISIONS

The Arbitration Act provides machinery for the settlement of disputes in civil and commercial matters between parties without recourse to the courts. However, although the backlog of cases in the courts is very long, this means of dispute settlement is seldom used.

Treaties are an extremely important source of domestic law in that they regulate the conduct of relations between one state and another. The making of treaties, including their signing and their later ratification, is not provided for in the constitution or the general laws of the state. But based on the common law procedure that obtains in Dominica, once a treaty has been signed and ratified, it forms part of the law of the signatory state, if only because it places international obligations on that state. Dominica is a signatory to many such treaties, including the International Convention on Economic, Social and Cultural Rights; the International Convention on Civil and Political Rights; the Convention on the Rights of the Child; the Convention on the Elimination of All Forms of Discrimination against Women; the Convention Relating to the Status of Refugees; the Convention against Illicit Traffic on Narcotic Drugs and Psychotropic Substances; the UN Convention on the Law of the Sea; and the Convention on the Prohibition of Anti-Personnel Land Mines.

The legal profession is the body from which judicial officers are chosen. To qualify for appointment as a High Court judge, the legal practitioner must have actually practiced before a court for at least ten years; for a chief justice or a member of the Court of Appeal, the period is fifteen years. Aspiring Dominican legal practitioners usually obtain their qualifications from the University of the West Indies, which has campuses in Barbados, Jamaica, and Trinidad and Tobago, and one of three professional law schools located in the Bahamas, Jamaica, and Trinidad and Tobago. The university degree consists of a three-year course of study, after which a further two years are spent at one of the law schools. No specific length of postqualification service is required for appointment to the position of magistrate. In fact, a nonlawyer can assume this position, and in the past, several experienced Dominicans with no legal qualifications have served with distinction as magistrates.

The strength of the practicing bar is currently about twenty, which is considered high for a population of between 70,000 and 80,000 inhabitants. Despite this fact, the legal and magisterial services consistently have trouble filling their posts. Lawyers can now be disciplined only by the High Court after formal legal proceedings have been instituted and investigations into the alleged misdeeds are conducted. A law has, however, been recently introduced into Parliament to establish a disciplinary committee, which will include laypersons, to act on such complaints. There is no system of continuing legal education on Dominica.

LEGAL AID
No universal system of legal aid for the poor exists in Dominica, and there is no widely available means for such individuals to obtain legal advice and assistance. Yet there are many disputes that should be litigated, foremost among them being allegations that individuals' constitutional rights have been breached. In a small island state, practicing attorneys invariably have a good idea that certain clients lack the means to pay for legal fees, and Dominica's lawyers have been known to act for such parties on a pro bono basis. The law provides that in cases of treason and murder, the state must meet the expenses associated with the defense of the accused. This scheme could be usefully extended to enable a wider variety of cases to be subject to legal representation at the state's expense.

IMPACT OF LAW
In 1998, the chief justice commissioned a report to carry out a review of civil procedure in the member states of the Eastern Caribbean Supreme Court. The shortcomings pinpointed in the report are as applicable to Dominica as they are to the other member states. It was found, inter alia, that delays in the system were rampant, that the infrastructure of the court system was inadequate to meet the demands placed on it, and that efficient use was not being made of the services of the registrars and magistrates. A general unwillingness to enforce judgments against private litigants and an inability to enforce them against the state were also noted.

The report recommended the adoption of new rules of court that would address some of the problems identified, as well as the creation of the post of master of the Supreme Court (assistant judge) and the establishment of a dedicated court registry by removing from the present registry matters pertaining to the registration of companies, lands, births, deaths, marriages, trademarks, patents, and other noncourt matters. The new Civil Procedure Code has been promulgated, and with the assistance of the U.S. Agency for International Development and the Canadian International Development Agency, it is hoped that many of the problems that have plagued the courts will be solved.

Nicholas J. O. Liverpool

See also Administrative Law; Administrative Tribunals; Adversarial System; Alternative Dispute Resolution; Common Law; Constitutional Law; Privy Council

References and further reading
Anderson, Winston A. 1998. "Treaty Making in the Caribbean—Law and Practice." *Caribbean Law Review* 8, no. 1 (June): 75 ff.
Cracknell, Basil E. 1973. *Dominica*. Harrisburg, PA: Stackpole Books.
Deutsch, Andre. 1989. *Dominica—"Nature Island of the Caribbean."* London: Hansib.
Greenslade, Dick. 1998. The Eastern Caribbean Supreme Court, Report on Rules of Civil Procedure A. Prepared for the Eastern Caribbean Supreme Court, Castries, St. Lucia.
Honychurch, Lennox. 1984. *The Dominica Story—A History of the Island.* Roseau, Dominica: The Dominica Institute.
Liverpool, Nicholas J. O. 1980. A Study in Peaceful Extra-Constitutional Change in the Caribbean Island of Dominica—An Application of the Doctrine of Necessity. Unpublished paper. Institute of International Relations, University of the West Indies, St. Augustine, Trinidad.
Williams, Eric. 1971. *From Columbus to Castro: The History of the Caribbean, 1492–1969.* London: Andre Deutsch.

THE DOMINICAN REPUBLIC

COUNTRY INFORMATION
Situated in the Caribbean between Jamaica (to the west) and Puerto Rico (to the east), the Dominican Republic is the largest island after Cuba, and shares the island of Hispaniola with Haiti. Its geographic position is ideal as the island is situated on important air and navigation routes, which permits the country to benefit economically and socially from its geographic proximity to major markets.

The national territory covers an area of 48,432 square kilometers with a population of approximately 8 million inhabitants, a majority of whom are of mulatto descent. Approximately 3.1 million of the total population live in Santo Domingo, capital of the Dominican Republic. Spanish is the official language, however English is also

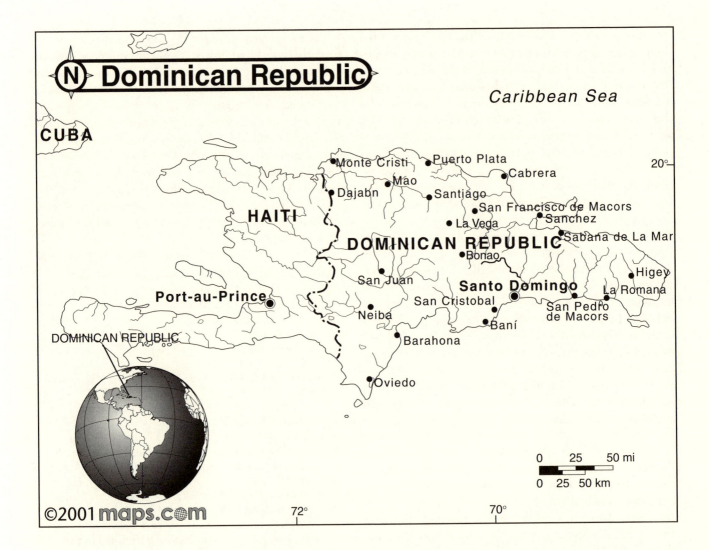

Map labels: Caribbean Sea, Dominican Republic, N, CUBA, Monte Cristi, Puerto Plata, Cabrera, Mao, Dajabn, Santiago, San Francisco de Macors, HAITI, La Vega, Sanchez, DOMINICAN REPUBLIC, Sabana de La Mar, Bonao, San Juan, Higey, Santo Domingo, La Romana, Port-au-Prince, San Cristobal, San Pedro de Macors, Neiba, Baní, DOMINICAN REPUBLIC, Barahona, Oviedo, ©2001 maps.com, 20°, 72°, 70°, 0 25 50 mi, 0 25 50 km

widely spoken. The great majority of the population profess to Roman Catholicism.

The Dominican Republic has a varied terrain, ranging from extensive beaches to large mountains with abundant tropical vegetation and native forests. The Central Mountain Range is where the highest elevations in the whole Caribbean are to be found, with the Pico Duarte reaching 3,715 meters in height. On the other hand, Lake Enriquillo, 144 meters below sea level, is the lowest point in the Caribbean. The subsoil is rich in bauxite, nickel, gold, and silver. There are also a number of areas under exploration for oil.

Traditionally, the Dominican Republic has been a large exporter of sugar, coffee, cocoa, tobacco, and nickel. However, over the last decade the island has been successful in opening new markets for a variety of products including fruit and vegetables, fertilizers, textiles, and various manufactured products. In addition, the establishment and rapid development of Industrial Tax-Free Zones (Zonas Francas Industriales) has allowed the island to develop a competitive edge vis-à-vis other islands in the region. The country is a beneficiary of the Caribbean Basin Initiative (CBI-II), which has allowed the country to become the leading commercial trading partner of the United States in the region, in both imports and exports. The Dominican Republic has become the leading tourist destination in the Caribbean and its tourism industry has experienced spectacular growth over the last five years, making it the single most important source of revenue for the government at present.

The Dominican Republic has a semitropical climate, tempered by the prevailing easterly winds. Temperatures of more than 23° C (more than 74° F) are registered in the lowlands throughout the year. During the summer months, temperatures range between 27° and 35° C (80° and 95° F) in these regions. The highlands are considerably cooler. Annual precipitation averages about 1,500 millimeters (about 60 inches). The wet season is from June to November. Tropical hurricanes occur occasionally. Hurricane Georges, which struck in 1998, caused great damage.

HISTORY

In 1492 Christopher Columbus discovered the island and claimed it for the Spanish Crown, calling his new discovery Hispaniola. As the seat of the original capital of the Spanish New World, the Dominican Republic claims a host of American firsts: the first permanent European settlement, the first university, the first church and cathedral, and the first royal court, among others.

The aboriginal inhabitants of Hispaniola were Arawak people, engaged principally in farming and fishing. Their population was decimated by disease and harsh exploitation by Spanish colonists. Black slaves were later imported as their substitutes. In time the Spanish migrated from Hispaniola to South America, and for about a century the island was sparsely populated. In 1697, by the Peace of Ryswick, the portion of Hispaniola that had been occupied by French adventurers was formally ceded to France and became known as Saint-Domingue, currently known as Haiti. The remaining Spanish section, what is now the Dominican Republic, was called Santo Domingo. The French in their part developed a flourishing plantation economy and a lively trade, while the Spanish area, bypassed by commerce and shown little interest by the administrative authorities, declined. Spain finally ceded Santo Domingo to France in 1795.

During the years that followed, the country was caught up in the convulsions of neighboring nascent Haiti, fought over by the French, Spanish, and English, as well as indigenous mixed-race and Black people. When Haiti ousted the French in 1804, Santo Domingo remained under French occupation for another five years. Then the French were expelled and nominal Spanish rule restored. After 1814, however, the Spanish administration became increasingly tyrannical, and in 1821 the Dominicans rose in revolt, proclaiming their independence. It was short-lived. The following year Haitian president Jean Pierre Boyer led his troops into the country and annexed it to Haiti, thus bringing the entire island under his control.

During French and Haitian rule, however, the Dominican Republic was influenced by legal and social developments occurring in Europe. Human rights were acknowledged following the French Declaration of the Human Rights in 1789. The French Napoleonic Codes were implemented as the official law of the island, and the French judicial system was adopted.

In 1844 Santo Domingo again declared its independence, forming the Dominican Republic. The first Dominican president was Pedro Santana, who served for three terms between 1844 and 1861. Both his administrations and the subsequent ones were characterized by popular unrest and frequent boundary disputes with Haiti. The internal strife was most clearly discernible in the two political groups that took root within the republic: One faction advocated return to Spanish rule and the other annexation to the United States. For a brief period, from 1861 to 1863, the country, led by former president

Santana, did return to Spanish rule, but a popular revolt between 1863 and 1864 and subsequent military reversals and U.S. intervention forced the Spanish government to withdraw its forces and to annul the annexation. The second Dominican Republic was proclaimed in February 1865. Political turmoil continued, however, through the rest of the nineteenth century. From 1865 until 1916 there were a total of thirty-six presidents, and thirty-two constitutions were proclaimed in a period marked by dictatorships and political instability.

Throughout the first years of the republic, the Dominican legal system was reduced. Misery, lack of population, internal and political unrest, and struggles against Haiti and Spain hampered the development of an organized legal and judicial system. Dominican legal codes and court decisions were written in French, creating a language barrier for their interpretation and implementation. The lack of an appeals court and general skepticism toward the law itself produced a vacuum of legal decisions.

Because of Dominican indebtedness to a number of European nations, some of which threatened intervention, the Dominican government signed a fifty-year treaty with the United States in 1906, turning over to the United States the administration and control of its customs department. In exchange the United States undertook to adjust the foreign financial obligations of the Dominican government. Internal disorders during the ensuing decade finally culminated in the establishment of a military government by the U.S. Marines, who began their occupation of the country on November 29, 1916. American intervention influenced the Dominican legal system with substantial law enactments as, for example, the current property registry system and the nonprofit organization regimes. Control of the country was, however, gradually restored to the people, and by March 1924 a constitutional government had assumed power. Later that year the American occupation ended.

The outstanding political development of the subsequent period was the dictatorship established by General Rafael Leonidas Trujillo Molina. Elected to the presidency in 1930, Trujillo forcibly eliminated all opposition, thereby acquiring absolute control of the nation. For the next thirty-one years, Trujillo presided over one of the tightest dictatorships in the world. With the military as the basis of his power, he and his family directed practically every aspect of the nation's life, from the courts down to the pettiest bureaucrat. The national economy, although greatly expanded and modernized, was run as the dictator's personal corporation, and the political process was completely dominated by his Dominican Party. Backed at first by the United States, Trujillo used this support to his own advantage in shoring up his power. Discontent and criticism, widespread especially after World War II, were met with terror and self-serving propaganda.

During Trujillo's rise to power, however, considerable material progress was made. Many new hospitals and housing projects were finished, a pension plan was established, and public health facilities, harbors, and roads were improved. A boundary dispute with neighboring Haiti, going back to 1844, was settled in 1935, and in 1941 the U.S. government terminated the administration of the Dominican customs. It subsequently became a charter member of the United Nations. Most of the current laws were enacted, a majority of which are still applicable. Fundamental judicial reforms were made. However, external pressures were coupled with growing internal resistance to the regime. The Trujillo era ended with the dictator's assassination on May 26, 1961.

After Trujillo's assassination, the country began a difficult democratic recovery in the post-Trujillo era, which culminated in another U.S. intervention in 1965 during a civil war. During the summer of 1965, the Organization of American States (OAS) tried to arrange a settlement between the loyalists and the rebels (who called themselves *constitutionalists* to indicate their desire to restore the constitutionally elected government of Juan Bosch). In the end, the two factions agreed to establish a provisional government and reform the constitution. In 1966, a new constitution was enacted and general elections were held. Joaquin Balaguer, a conservative, won with the majority of the votes.

Starting in 1966 a new democratic era started. Under Balaguer's administration, relative stability was restored to the country. The economy showed strength, aided by high sugar prices, foreign investment, and increased tourism. Nevertheless, some have criticized the government for circumventing legal and constitutional guarantees.

In the mid-1970s a sharp decline in world sugar prices adversely affected the Dominican economy, and Balaguer's support began to dwindle. In the 1978 elections he was turned out of office, defeated by the Dominican Revolutionary Party (PRD) candidate, Antonio Guzmán. The economy remained troubled by low sugar prices and was further damaged by two hurricanes in 1979 that left more than 200,000 people homeless and caused $1 billion in damages.

To rescue the country from its deepening economic crisis, President Jorge Blanco (elected in the 1982 elections) turned to the International Monetary Fund (IMF), which demanded austerity measures in exchange for a three-year loan package. These measures coupled with judicial and legal uncertainties, led to protest riots throughout the nation in 1984 and 1985. Balaguer returned as president in 1986. In 1988, Jorge Blanco was tried in absentia and found guilty of corruption during his presidential years. Balaguer was reelected in 1990 and governed until 1996.

In 1996, the PLD party (founded by Juan Bosch),

headed by Dr. Leonel Fernández Reyna governed one four-year term. In August of the year 2000, a new PRD administration, headed by Hipólito Mejía, assumed power.

The constant crisis of the Dominican legal system produced a breakdown of judicial institutionalism creating distrust in the state of law. These circumstances, combined with political and external pressures, called for constitutional reforms. These cries were met in 1994, when the Dominican Republic underwent major reforms as means to improve and strengthen the political, judicial, and legal systems of the Dominican Republic.

At present, the country has a strengthened and stable political, judicial, and legal system, as well as social peace, although much improvement is still needed.

LEGAL CONCEPTS

The Dominican Republic is divided politically into twenty-nine provinces and a National District. Its laws are based on the Constitution of the Republic, last amended in 1994. The government is democratically elected and is based on three main powers: the executive branch, the legislative branch, and the judicial branch. Its legal system in its majority is based on French civil codes; however, the concept of separation of powers and the system of checks and balances—core elements for the functioning of the nation—are clearly influenced by the United States. The Constitution of the Republic is considered to be the supreme law of the land.

With over thirty constitutional amendments since its independence in 1844, the Dominican Republic has always acknowledged basic political rights, including freedom of speech, religion, press, movement, and assembly. There is general recognition of proprietary rights; however, the state has discretionary power to expropriate private land with an appropriate indemnification.

Dominican constitutions, including the 1994 amendments, have increasingly recognized the mechanism for protesting against the violation of constitutional rights through a writ of habeas corpus. Other principles currently acknowledged are the due process of law, influenced by the United States, and the universal principle *non bis in idem*—one cannot be tried twice for the same cause.

Contrary to French law, the Dominican Republic grants constitutional status to the principle that laws enacted are not retroactive. Laws cannot be applied to past states of affairs.

The Dominican Republic will apply foreign law, as long as it is not contrary to the public order of their country and does not constitute fraud under its law. Judgments issued by foreign courts are only enforceable in the Dominican Republic when they are so declared by a Dominican court, without prejudice to the contrary provisions that may be contained in political laws or in international treaties. Subsequently, international treaties are incorporated as ordinary law, subsequent to ratification by Congress.

Since 1994, after political unrest, the Dominican Republic has undergone substantial constitutional reform, specifically in regards to judicial staffing and procedures. These reforms have included a more bona fide recognition of an autonomous judicial system, economically independent from the other branches of government; the creation of the judicial career, as means to shape and train future judges; the creation of the National Magistrates Council, invested with the powers to designate the Supreme Court judges (who will in turn appoint the rest of the judicial staff); the immobility of the Supreme Court justices; and the separation of presidential and congressional elections.

CURRENT JUDICIAL STRUCTURE

Since 1994 the Dominican judicial legal system has undergone substantial reforms, and more are underway. Currently, courts are grouped into two fundamental categories: common law courts (*tribunals de derecho común*), which are courts of the first instance and appeals courts, and the courts of exception, which are justices of the peace, the land courts, the confiscation courts, the labor courts, and so on. Common law courts have competence to consider all the matters that are not attributed to the courts of exception.

A general principle is that the parties have the right to appeal a decision handed down by any court, taking their suits and arguments to a higher court, which is known as the principle of double jurisdiction.

The Dominican Supreme Court of Justice is charged with naming the judges in the entire judicial system, overseeing the proper functioning of the courts and exercising the highest disciplinary action. On the other hand, it has the function of a court of cassation. In this function, the Supreme Court of Justice is not a third level of jurisdiction. Its sole aim is to decide if lower courts have properly or improperly applied the law. Via its decisions, it establishes and maintains the unity of national jurisprudence.

In the Dominican judicial system, the common law courts, that is, the courts of first instance and the courts of appeal at the second level, are competent on the matters that are of a civil, commercial, or penal nature. They have what is called *unity of jurisdiction*. But in those instances where the jurisdiction may be broader, the jurisdiction falls to two chambers, the civil and commercial chamber and the penal chamber. These in turn are divided into circumscriptions, depending on the corresponding territorial jurisdiction.

SPECIALIZED JUDICIAL BODIES

In the Dominican Republic there are also specialized judicial bodies, for example, the military courts, arbitration courts, and juvenile courts. Contrary to other countries, military courts exercise the highest disciplinary action solely vis-à-vis military officials in the Dominican Republic. Only in exceptional cases may military personnel be judged and convicted before a common law court.

Law No. 50–87 of June 15, 1987, establishes the Chamber of Commerce and Production (Cámara de Comercio y Producción–CCP) of the Dominican Republic, which has an Arbitration and Reconciliation Council (ARC). The ARC acts as a referee or arbiter on differences that may arise between one or more of its members or between a member and an individual or corporation that does not belong to the CCP. The arbitration court is composed of two to five persons elected by the parties from among the list of the members of the ARC and nominated by its Board of Directors.

Law 14–94 of April 22, 1994, established the Dominican Code for the Protection of Children and Adolescents (Código para la Protección de Niñas, Niños y Adolescentes), which creates juvenile courts (Tribunales para Ninos, Ninas y Adolescentes) in the country. These juvenile courts, categorized into the courts of first instance and the courts of appeal at the second level, are competent on matters that concern juvenile delinquent actions, as well as other issues such as child support and child abuse allegations. Like common law courts, they also have unity of jurisdiction. They are divided into circumscriptions, depending on the corresponding territorial jurisdiction. Judges, contrary to common law courts or courts of exception, are directly appointed by the Dominican Senate.

One of the most recent innovations in the Dominican Republic is the creation of the General Secretariat for Women. Although some do not consider it to be judicial protection as such, Law no. 86–99 dated July 21, 1999, establishes the General Secretariat for Women as a governmental institution responsible for regulating and coordinating the implementation of general politics, plans, and programs at a municipal and intergovernmental level, focused on achieving equity between the sexes and the improvement of women's rights in the country.

The Dominican Republic counts with other specialized judicial bodies that resolve conflicts that arise from the public administration (Tribunal Contencioso Administrativo) and tax-related issues (Tribunal Contencioso Tributario). Currently, the Tribunal Contencioso Tributario is in heavy demand following the 2000 tax reforms implemented by the current government.

STAFFING

As a result of the 1994 constitutional amendments, the Dominican Republic drastically changed the judicial staffing procedures eliminating congressional appointment of judges, and, further, creating the National Mag-

Legal Structure of the Dominican Republic

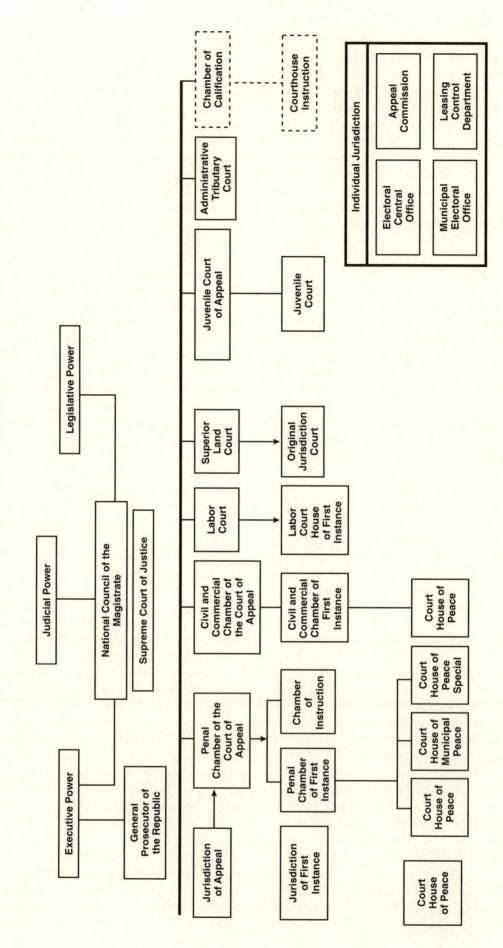

istrates Council. The National Magistrates Council is invested with the powers to designate the Supreme Court judges who will in turn appoint the rest of the judicial staff. The attorney general and key figures of the Public Ministry are still appointed by the president.

In practical terms, although during the past five years the Supreme Court has organized and supervised—to the best of its abilities—the functioning of the courts, the ratio of cases per judges is approximately fifty to one, and increasing. There are roughly one hundred judges, divided into approximately the same number of courts of first instance. Unfortunately, these numbers do not meet the heavy judicial demand. More judges and better infrastructure are still needed.

Regarding the private bar, admission to legal practice requires an executive decree and mandatory membership in the Dominican Bar Association. There are no written or verbal examinations, except those required by the law school attended. As means to implement these legal requirements, Dominican courts generally request litigating attorneys to present their identification card before taking the stand. The presiding judge has discretionary powers to deny counsel in case an attorney is not properly identified. However, no direct supervision is made to lawyers who do not litigate. Malpractice lawsuits are not common in the Dominican legal system, as opposed to other jurisdictions.

IMPACT

Unquestionably the Dominican legal system has been greatly influenced by political and social developments throughout the years. The combination of Spanish and French control, military interventions, civil wars, and internal political hostilities has traditionally made the Dominican legal system inefficient, inaccessible, and questionable. Judges have been accused of being biased and politically oriented. Court proceedings are slow and elongated.

Following the 1994 Constitution amendments, new developments are underway. A more secure and strengthened judicial and legal system is envisioned. Judicial autonomy has been comparatively acknowledged, and court decisions have attained higher social recognition. However, much is still needed.

At present, the Dominican Republic is on the verge of another constitutional reform. Questions arise as to its purpose and outcome, but only time will tell if it will bring significant results to the Dominican legal and judicial system.

Georges Santoni-Recio

See also Alternative Dispute Resolution; Appellate Courts; Arbitration; Civil Law; Constitutional Review; Government Legal Departments; Habeas Corpus, Writ of; Human Rights Law; Judicial Review; Judicial Selection, Methods of; Juvenile Justice; Legal Education; Military Justice (Law and Courts)

References and further reading
Acosta, V. E. Mariclaire. 1999. *Derechos Humanos y Deberes en la Reforma Constitucional.* Santo Domingo, Dominican Republic: Editora Nuevo Diario, S.A.
Álvarez Valdez, Francisco. 2001. *La incidencia de la Sociedad Civil en el Proceso de Reforma Judicial y en la Selección de Jueces de la Suprema Corte de Justicia.* Lecture given at the Interamerican Bar Association XXXVII Conference. June 22. Santo Domingo, Dominican Republic.
Blanco, Salvador. 1995. *Introducción al Derecho Dominicano.* Santo Domingo, Dominican Republic: Ediciones Capel Dominicana, S.A.
Brea, Ramonina. 1994. *Propuestas para la Reforma Constitucional en la República Dominicana.* Santo Domingo, Dominican Republic: Editora de Colores, S.A.
Jorge Prats, Eduardo Jorge. 1999. *La Justicia en la Reforma Constitucional.* Santo Domingo, Dominican Republic: Editora Nuevo Diario, S.A.
Pellerano Gómez, Juan Manuel. 1998. "Acción Directa en Declaratoria de Inconstitucionalidad." *Gaceta Oficial* (November 5–19).
Rodríguez Huerta, Olivo. 1999. *Los Principios Constitucionales en la Reforma Constitucional.* Santo Domingo, Dominican Republic: Editora Nuevo Diario, S.A.
Sosa Pérez, Rosalía. 1998. "El Habeas Corpus bajo Suspensión de Garantías." *Gaceta Oficial* (November 5–19).
Suárez Brea, José Darío. 1999. *La Función Legislativa en la Reforma Constitucional.* Santo Domingo, Dominican Republic: Editora Nuevo Diario, S.A.
Subero Isa, Dr. Jorge A. 2000. *Los Frutos de una Reforma, Rendición de Cuentas.* Santo Domingo, Dominican Republic: Editora Taina, S.A.
Valera Montero, Miguel. 1999. *El Control Concentrado de la Constitucionalidad en la República Dominicana.* Santo Domingo, Dominican Republic: Editorial Capel Dominicana, S.A.
Vega, Wenceslao. 1992. *Historia del Derecho Dominicano.* Santo Domingo, Dominican Republic: Instituto Tecnológico de Santo Domingo.